Archaeological
Method and Theory

GARLAND REFERENCE LIBRARY OF THE HUMANITIES (VOL. 1707)

Archaeological Method and Theory: *An Encyclopedia*

Editor
Linda Ellis

Department of Classics and Classical Archaeology
and Museum Studies Program
San Francisco State University
San Francisco, California

GARLAND PUBLISHING, INC.
A MEMBER OF THE TAYLOR & FRANCIS GROUP
New York & London
2000

Published in 2000 by
Garland Publishing, Inc.
A Member of the Taylor & Francis Group
19 Union Square West
New York, NY 10003

10 9 8 7 6 5 4 3 2 1

Library of Congress Cataloging-in-Publication Data

Archaeological method and theory / editor, Linda Ellis.
        p.   cm. — (Garland reference library of the humanities ; vol. 1707)
    Includes bibliographical references and index.
    ISBN (invalid) 0-8153-1305-1 (alk. paper)
    1. Archaeology—Methodology Encyclopedias.   2. Archaeology-Philosophy Encyclopedias.   I. Ellis, Linda.   II. Series.
CC75.A654   1999
930.1—dc21   99-39140
                                                        CIP

Printed on acid-free, 250-year-life paper
Manufactured in the United States of America

Contents

Contributors

Martin J. Aitken
Emeritus Professor of Archaeometry
Oxford University
Oxford, England

M.G.L. Baillie
Palaeoecology Centre
Queen's University
Belfast, Northern Ireland

J.N. Barrandon
Centre Ernest Babelon
Centre National de la Recherche Scientifique
Orléans, France

Joseph J. Basile
Maryland Institute, College of Art
Baltimore, Maryland
and Erikson Biographical Institute
Providence, Rhode Island

George F. Bass
Department of Anthropology
Texas A&M University
College Station, Texas

Curt W. Beck
Research Professor of Chemistry
Amber Research Laboratory
Vassar College
Poughkeepsie, New York

Robert H. Bewley
Royal Commission on the Historical
  Monuments of England
National Monuments Record Centre
Swindon, Wiltshire, England

Vaughn M. Bryant, Jr.
Department of Anthropology
Texas A&M University
College Station, Texas

Paul C. Buckland
Department of Archaeology and Prehistory
University of Sheffield
Sheffield, England

John Chapman
Department of Archaeology
University of Durham
Durham, England

Cheryl Claassen
Department of Anthropology
Appalachian State University
Boone, North Carolina

Charles E. Cook, Jr.
Wellcome/CRC Institute
Cambridge University
Cambridge, England

Graeme E. Coote
Institute of Geological and Nuclear Sciences,
  Ltd.
Lower Hutt, New Zealand

Michel Dabas
Centre de Recherches Geophysiques
Centre National de la Recherche Scientifique
Garchy, France

Ross W.A. Dallas
Architectural Photogrammetry Consultant
York, England

Jack L. Davis
Department of Classics
University of Cincinnati
Cincinnati, Ohio

J. Philip Dering
Department of Anthropology
Texas A&M University
College Station, Texas

Helen Danzeiser Dockall
United States Army Central Identification
    Laboratory
Hickam Air Force Base
Hawaii

Ronald I. Dorn
Department of Geography
Arizona State University
Tempe, Arizona

Lysbeth Drewett
Institute of Archaeology
University College London
London, England

Peter L. Drewett
Institute of Archaeology
University College London
London, England

Robert C. Dunnell
Emeritus Professor of Anthropology
University of Washington
Seattle, Washington

Linda Ellis
Department of Classics and Classical
    Archaeology
and Museum Studies Program
San Francisco State University
San Francisco, California

Tore Ericsson
Department of Physics
Uppsala University
Uppsala, Sweden

Donald A. Frey
Sualti Arkeolojisi Enstitüsü
Bodrum, Turkey

Irving Friedman
United States Geological Survey
Branch of Isotope Geology
Denver, Colorado

Angela Gernaey-Child
Fossil Fuels and Environmental Geochemistry
University of Newcastle
Newcastle-upon-Tyne, England

Robert D. Gillard
School of Chemistry and Applied Chemistry
University of Wales, College of Cardiff
Cardiff, Wales

Robert B. Gordon
Department of Geology and Geophysics
and Council on Archaeological Studies
Yale University
New Haven, Connecticut

Richard A. Gould
Department of Anthropology
Brown University
Providence, Rhode Island

Neil R. Goulty
Department of Geological Sciences
University of Durham
Durham, England

David W. Grattan
Conservation Processes Research
Canadian Conservation Institute
Ottawa, Canada

Alan Green
Institute of Geophysics
Swiss Federal Institute of Technology
Zürich, Switzerland

Rainer Grün
Quaternary Dating Research Centre
Australian National University
Canberra, Australia

Susan Hardman
School of History and Archaeology
University of Wales, College of Cardiff
Cardiff, Wales

Kelley Ann Hays-Gilpin
Department of Antrhopology
Northern Arizona University
Flagstaff, Arizona

Norman Herz
Emeritus Professor of Geology
Center for Archaeological Sciences
University of Georgia
Athens, Georgia

Albert Hesse
Centre de Recherches Geophysiques
Centre National de la Recherche Scientifique
Garchy, France

Frederick Hocker
Centre for Maritime Archaeology
National Museum of Denmark
Roskilde, Denmark

Caroline M. Jackson
Department of Archaeology and Prehistory
University of Sheffield
Sheffield, England

Michael A. Jochim
Department of Anthropology
University of California, Santa Barbara
Santa Barbara, California

Kenneth Kvamme
Department of Anthropology and Center
  for Advanced Spatial Technology
University of Arkansas
Fayetteville, Arkansas

Janet Lang
Department of Scientific Research
The British Museum
London, England

Jürg Leckebusch
Kantonsarchäologie
Zürich, Switzerland
and Institute of Geophysics
Swiss Federal Institute of Technology
Zürich, Switzerland

Daniel Lieberman
Department of Anthropology
George Washington University
Washington, D. C.

Lawrence L. Loendorf
Department of Anthropology
University of Arizona
Tucson, Arizona

Edward Luby
P.A. Hearst Museum of Anthropology
University of California
Berkeley, California

Randall H. McGuire
Department of Anthropology
Binghamton University
Binghamton, New York

Barbara McLauchlin
Department of Classics and Classical
  Archaeology
San Francisco State University
San Francisco, California

Francis P. McManamon
Archeological Assistance Division
National Park Service
Department of the Interior
Washington, D. C.

Richard H. Meadow
Zooarchaeology Laboratory
Peabody Museum of Archaeology and
  Ethnology
Harvard University
Cambridge, Massachusetts

Paul T. Nicholson
School of History and Archaeology
University of Wales, College of Cardiff
Cardiff, Wales

George H. Odell
Department of Anthropology
University of Tulsa
Tulsa, Oklahoma

Clive Orton
Institute of Archaeology
University College London
London, England

Gwil J. Owen
Photography Unit
Faculty of Archaeology and Anthropology
Cambridge University
Cambridge, England

Elizabeth E. Peacock
Institute of Archaeology and Cultural History
Norwegian University of Science and
  Technology
Trondheim, Norway

Deborah Pearsall
Department of Anthropology
American Archaeology Division
University of Missouri, Columbia
Columbia, Missouri

Clifford Price
Institute of Archaeology
University College London
London, England

Margaret Purser
Department of Anthropology
Sonoma State University
Rohnert Park, California

Elizabeth Pye
Institute of Archaeology
University College London
London, England

George R. Rapp, Jr.
Archaeometry Laboratory
College of Science and Engineering
University of Minnesota
Duluth, Minnesota

Karl Reinhard
Department of Anthropology
University of Nebraska
Lincoln, Nebraska

Glen Eugene Rice
Office of Cultural Resource Management
Department of Anthropology
Arizona State University
Tempe, Arizona

David R.K. Robertson
Fossil Fuels and Environmental Geochemistry
University of Newcastle
Newcastle-upon-Tyne, England

Jonathan P. Sadler
School of Geography
University of Birmingham
Birmingham, England

Merrilee H. Salmon
Department of History and Philosophy of
  Science
University of Pittsburgh
Pittsburgh, Pennsylvania

Edward M. Schortman
Department of Anthropology and Sociology
Kenyon College
Gambier, Ohio

Henry P. Schwarcz
Department of Geology
McMaster University
Hamilton, Ontario, Canada

David Scott
Museum Services
The Getty Conservation Institute
Marina del Rey, California

Catherine Sease
Division of Conservation
Field Museum of Natural History
Chicago, Illinois

Kent Severson
Senior Field Conservator
New York University
Expedition to Aphrodìsìas
Turkey

John Shaw
Geomagnetism Laboratory
Department of Earth Sciences
University of Liverpool
Liverpool, England

James M. Skibo
Anthropology Program
Illinois State University
Normal, Illinois

Edward Staski
Department of Sociology and Anthropology
New Mexico State University
Las Cruces, New Mexico

Zofia Anna Stos-Gale
Isotrace Laboratory
Research Laboratory of Archaeology and
    History of Art
Oxford University
Oxford, England

Lawrence G. Straus
Department of Anthropology
University of New Mexico
Albuquerque, New Mexico

Alan P. Sullivan III
Department of Anthropology
University of Cincinnati
Cincinnati, Ohio

Alain Tabbagh
Centre de Recherches Geophysiques
Centre National de la Recherche Scientifique
Garchy, France

Christopher Tilley
Department of Anthropology
and Institute of Archaeology
University College London
London, England

Michael. S. Tite
Research Laboratory for Archaeology and the
    History of Art
Oxford University
Oxford, England

Fred Trembour
United States Geological Survey
Branch of Isotope Geology
Denver, Colorado

Adrian P. Tribe
Institute of Archaeology
University College London
London, England

Patricia A. Urban
Department of Anthropology and Sociology
Kenyon College
Gambier, Ohio

Wim Van Neer
IUAP 28 Interdisciplinary Archaeology
Royal Museum of Central Africa
Tervuren, Belgium

Günther Wagner
Forschungsstelle Archäometrie
Max-Planck-Institut für Kernphysik
Heidelberg, Germany

William H. Walker
Department of Anthropology
New Mexico State University
Las Cruces, New Mexico

J. Nicholas Walsh
Department of Geology
University of London
Egham, Surrey, England

Mark C. Whiting
Emeritus Professor of Organic Chemistry
University of Bristol
Bristol, England

Olwen Williams-Thorpe
Department of Earth Sciences
The Open University
Milton Keynes, England

Acknowledgments

This encyclopedia could not have been produced without the active participation of all advisory board members who provided lists of colleagues as potential authors, reviewed manuscripts, refined the list of articles, and who even undertook the writing of a significant number of articles. Vaughn M. Bryant, Jr., Francis P. McManamon, George R. Rapp, Jr., Michael B. Schiffer, Alain Tabbagh, and Michael S. Tite all gave an incalculable amount of their time, and their valuable expertise significantly improved the content of this volume. Drs. McManamon, Rapp, and Tite cordially wrote their articles on very short notice.

All authors generously gave of their time and expertise in the writing of their articles and demonstrated a notable degree of patience during the production of this volume. Martin J. Aitken, Robert H. Bewley, Vaughn M. Bryant, Jr., John Chapman, Cheryl Claassen, Peter L. Drewett, Robert C. Dunnell, Angela Gernaey-Child, Susan Hardman, Richard H. Meadow, Clifford Price, Karl Reinhard, Glen Eugene Rice, James M. Skibo, and Lawrence G. Straus provided valuable advice on content, recommended potential authors, and/or suggested biographical entries. The professional advice given by Vaughn M. Bryant, Jr., was very much an asset during the arduous process of putting this volume together. Robert C. Dunnell showed exceptional collegiality in writing many articles on short notice. Joseph J. Basile undertook the herculean task of writing most of the biographies in this volume, with the cooperation of the Erikson Biographical Institute.

Stuart Fleming kindly provided time and expertise on topics concerning dating methods. Irwin Scollar, Diego Angelucci, and Victor Sorokin, although not directly associated with this volume, provided information necessary to the completion of several articles.

We also gratefully acknowledge the following institutions and organizations for gratis use of photographs: Royal Commission on the Historical Monuments of England (Figures 1 and 2) for the article, "Aerial Photography for Archaeology" by Robert H. Bewley; and the Tell es Sa'idiyeh Project (Figures 4 and 6), the Cambridge University Museum of Archaeology and Anthropology (Figures 9, 11, and 13), and the Egypt Exploration Society (Figures 7, 8, 10, and 14) for the article, "Photography, Archaeological," by Gwil J. Owen.

Introduction

Archaeology: A Discipline and a Profession

As a *discipline,* archaeology is the study of past human behavioral systems within the social, religious, economic, political, biological, geological, and geographic contexts. To accomplish such studies, archaeology has developed philosophical and methodological ties to many academic fields, including anthropology, history, classical studies, linguistics, art and architecture, natural history, physical sciences, biological sciences, computer and mathematical sciences, and other specialized fields that combine to assist the documentation and understanding of the human past. As a *profession,* archaeology is an occupation that must be practiced in accordance with accepted methodological practices and ethical standards of conduct that have evolved over the course of the long history of the discipline and within relevant local, national, and international legislative frameworks.

For the purposes of this volume, *method,* or how archaeological research is conducted, and *theory,* how results of archaeological research are interpreted, are broadly constructed to be inclusive rather then exclusive and comprise even some topics and issues that may not always find their way into a treatise on method or theory but that do affect the practice of archaeology as a profession as well as an academic field of inquiry. This volume covers archaeological methodology from the processes of archaeological site formation, site discovery, site excavation, site and object documentation, on-site conservation and packaging of finds, to post-excavation analysis. Archaeological theory building comprises the interpretation of archaeological research (from the initiation of site discovery to the results of laboratory analyses), theoretical models for the interpretation of finds and the understanding of human behavior, and the evolution of archaeological theory itself. Also covered for their potential in theory development are a number of disciplinary specializations arising from the application of archaeological method beyond the domain of prehistory to classical and more recent historic periods. Articles on the management and protection of archaeological resources are included, since legislative frameworks have a significant role in where and how archaeology is (or will be) conducted and, therefore, affect what and how data are collected and ultimately interpreted. Biographical entries comprise individuals who were nominated by board members and authors to this volume for their contributions to the development of archaeological method and/or theory, as well as those researchers from the fields of natural and physical sciences whose work has influenced how archaeological data are analyzed and interpreted.

This introduction places many of the articles (in CAPITAL letters) in a broader context of the discipline and practice of archaeology. However, not all articles can be referred to here. The discipline of archaeology has seen a development of specialized subject areas, some of which focus on the practice of archaeology of specific chronological periods, as well as a substantial number of subjects focusing on human behavioral and theoretical area studies. Because of the interrelatedness of methodological and theoretical topics in archaeology, the nature of many subject areas could not be easily subdivided. Therefore, the reader is encouraged to use the Subject Guide, which follows, as well as to consult the Index to locate subjects that may be referred to in articles with more comprehensive discussions.

A pedagogical feature of the sections on methodology in this encyclopedia, which students should find useful, is the organization of subjects into tiers of graduated complexity. For the sections on Site Formation, Exploration and Examination and Post-excavation Analysis of Finds in the Subject Guide, the articles were developed in a hierarchy of subject complexity—from those that were designed to be introductory in nature to those that are specific and advanced. This gradation in levels of discussion was dictated by the nature of the subjects under these sections. As stated above, archaeology has produced intellectual ties to the physical and biological sciences in order to solve specific problems concerning the documentation and interpretation of the human past. Therefore, rather than just list the analytical methods that are available, it was felt that students of archaeology should have some understanding of the geophysical and materials analytical methods that have allowed archaeologists to locate, date, and analyze excavated material remains for the maximum amount of retrievable information. A basic understanding of underlying principles will enable students to direct their archaeological inquiries to the correct method, to select the most appropriate samples and materials for analysis, to work more effectively with specialists in the analytical sciences, and to interpret the results with clarity. Students are, therefore, encouraged to read the introductory articles first for a basic understanding of the broader topic, from which they are then referred to more specialized subjects. Each section of the Outline is discussed below together with an indication as to the hierarchy of difficulty of articles in the relevant sections.

Site Formation, Exploration and Examination

Even before a surveying program can begin or an archaeological site can be excavated, archaeologists have come to realize that equally important is an understanding and analysis of how archaeological deposits form in terms of geological, biological, and human behavioral processes. A practical and theoretical comprehension of site development is critical for understanding how the larger archaeological landscape is (literally) seen and eventually surveyed (*see* ARCHAEOLOGICAL SITES, FORMATION PROCESSES). What happens to archaeological deposits over time once they become buried (*see* TAPHONOMY) is a related issue in site formation that has repercussions for the selection of appropriate methods of physico-chemical analysis in the post-excavation phase of research and the resulting quality and interpretation of the results.

In discovery, estimation, exploration, and examination of archaeological sites, theoretical discussion (*see* SURVEY DESIGN, THEORY) again is important for understanding the appearance of archaeological phenomena, the underlying assumptions about the landscape, and the resulting influences of landscape features on the conduct of archaeological surveys. Surveying may be conducted over one field season or over multiple years and traverse over extensive tracts of terrain that requires significant research, planning, and resources (*see* SURVEYS, MULTISTAGE AND LARGE-SCALE). Surveying may be conducted manually (*see* SURVEYING and SITE EXAMINATION, MANUAL METHODS) or with the assistance of an appropriate technology, adopted from the geophysical- and geographical-exploration sciences. Geophysical prospection methods are noninvasive to the surface and its underlying contents and often allow an archaeological program to save money, labor, and time (*see* AERIAL PHOTOGRAPHY FOR ARCHAEOLOGY; ELECTRICAL AND ELECTROMAGNETIC PROSPECTING; GEORADAR; MAGNETIC PROSPECTING; REMOTELY OPERATED VEHICLES; SEISMIC REFRACTION SURVEYING; SONAR; THERMAL PROSPECTING). In this section, students are advised to read the introductory article, ARCHAEOLOGICAL PROSPECTION, before consulting the more advanced articles on specific geophysical methods of exploration.

Excavation, Documentation, and Conservation of Archaeological Sites and Finds

Under the section Excavation in the Subject Guide, many of the most commonly used field techniques in excavation (e.g., GRID EXCAVATION; HALF-SECTIONING, OPEN-AREA EXCAVATION; QUARTERING; STEP-TRENCHING; STRIPPING; TRENCH EXCAVATION) and retrieval (*see* FLOTATION; SIEVING) of archaeological remains are presented. To understand how decisions are made in excavation, as well as many of the logistical issues under more specific circumstances, the reader is referred to a series of articles on excavation techniques for major categories of sites (*see* CAVES AND ROCKSHELTERS; EXCAVATION; MORTUARY SITES, EXCAVATION AND ANALYSIS; ROCK-ART SITES, RECORDING AND ANALYSIS; SETTLEMENTS, EXCAVATION; SHELL MIDDENS, EXCAVATION; UNDERWATER ARCHAEOLOGY).

Since the excavation of sites is, by its very definition, destructive, careful excavation is accompanied by thorough documentation of standing architecture (*see* PHOTOGRAMMETRY), of surfaces before and during excavation (*see* SITE MAPPING), of the interrelationships among exposed strata (*see* HARRIS MATRIX), and of the finds themselves—both in situ and after cleaning (*see* ILLUSTRATION, ARCHAEOLOGICAL; PHOTOGRAPHY, ARCHAEOLOGICAL).

Once excavation is underway, some system of handling excavated biological and cultural materials must be established to ensure preservation for future generations and to maximize the amount of data that can be later retrieved and analyzed from subsequent dating and characterization studies. During excavation and after the on-site documentation of excavated materials, careful consideration must be given to cleaning, stabilizing, and packing of archaeological remains.

The most obvious type of on-site conservation is that of standing architecture, architectural artwork, or other immobile features that require not only chemical stabilization from environmental degradation but also protection from vandalism (*see* IN SITU CONSERVATION; MOSAICS, ON-SITE CONSERVATION; WALL PAINTINGS, CONSERVATION). Excavated objects also need proper cleaning and stabilization as soon as possible after excavation (*see* CERAMICS, ON-SITE CONSERVATION; CONSERVATION OF ARCHAEOLOGICAL MATERIALS; FIBROUS MATERIALS, ON-SITE CONSERVATION; GLASS, ON-SITE CONSERVATION; LEATHER, ON-SITE CONSERVATION; METALS, ON-SITE CONSERVATION; STONE, ON-SITE CONSERVATION; WOOD (WATERLOGGED), CONSERVATION). Once objects and archaeological features become buried for a substantial period of time in soil, sand, ice, or under other geological conditions, or submerged in salt or fresh water, their depositional environment usually becomes stabilized. If excavated, objects and features are exposed to a totally new environment of temperature, humidity, and chemical conditions, which will accelerate deterioration. Proper handling procedures, cleaning, and stabilization of objects will minimize further degradation of materials. Furthermore, immediate stabilization as well as conservation-safe packaging (*see* PACKAGING OF ARCHAEOLOGICAL OBJECTS) will ensure a longer survival rate for objects when they eventually go into storage and will also assist later conservation efforts by museums to maximize survivability of the remains for museum exhibits and public education.

The success of physico-chemical methods of analysis, and any conclusions or theories on human behavior derived therefrom, is particularly dependent upon how materials are handled when they are removed from the stabilized environment of the ground or under water. One should always keep in mind that laboratory techniques are constantly being refined, and new analytical methods may yet be developed in future research. Archaeological collections that have been excavated in prior decades can greatly benefit from current and future physico-chemical analysis to yield new information and generate new interpretations on human history and human adaptation. An on-site conservation program will produce more reliable results when archaeological materials are submitted for dating or chemical analysis and, more significantly, may allow more precise analyses in the future as new analytical technologies are developed. Therefore, an on-site conservation program for excavated archaeological materials is absolutely critical.

Post-excavation Analysis

Articles under Post-excavation Analysis of Finds, focus on dating, provenance of raw materials for finished objects, methods of manufacturing, assessment of human diet and health, and reconstruction of the physical and biological environment. Archaeological research in practice has become interdisciplinary in that it has had to incorporate methods from the physical, biological, and earth sciences in order to retrieve as much information as possible about past human behavior from archaeological sites. Since the mid-1940s, archaeology has also become multidisciplinary, and this trend has resulted in the development of a vast number of specializations in archaeology. Many archaeologists themselves have undertaken serious studies in other disciplines to understand and interpret research results and to effect more meaningful collaborative research with colleagues outside of archaeology.

In the absence of accurate historical records, archaeological dating is critical to the establishment and maintenance of a chronological framework. Dating methods are divided between those that provide relative dating (which produce an ordered sequence) and those that provide absolute dating (which allow the assignment of a date) (*see* DATING, METHOD AND THEORY). Relative dating can be accomplished by analysis of variation in artifacts (*see* SERIATION; TYPE-VARIETY SYSTEM) within local or regional sequences of excavated strata. Rates of chemical reaction can also be used to provide an ordered sequence for relative dating (*see* FLUORINE-URANIUM-NITROGEN DATING). Absolute-dating techniques are based on the counting of naturally occurring annual structures (*see* DENDROCHRONOLOGY; VARVE ANALYSIS), the decay of radioactive isotopes (*see* RADIOCARBON DATING; URANIUM-SERIES DATING), the exposure of materials to radiation (*see* ELECTRON SPIN RESONANCE (ESR) DATING; FISSION-TRACK DATING; OPTICAL DATING; THERMOLUMINESCENCE DATING), or rates of chemical reaction (*see* AMINO ACID RACEMIZATION/EPIMERIZATION DATING; OBSIDIAN HYDRATION DATING).

Articles on definition, analysis, and interpretation of finds are subdivided into six sections, based on the kinds of questions asked and the nature of the interdisciplinary research required. Pure or composite materials modified or used in the manufacturing of other products or materials are grouped together, since their analysis often requires methods from the field of materials science. Four sections—on plant remains, animal remains, human remains, and geological materials—are so divided based on the natural science disciplines required for understanding and analysis of these remains. Obviously, much cross-linking can and does occur among these various categories in the analysis of archaeological finds. The broad groupings presented in the Outline facilitate general comprehension of this vast repertoire of materials. These articles are written in a hierarchy of complexity, beginning with broad discussions of materials and disciplines, with references to the more advanced studies included in the section on materials analytical methods.

Treatment of the identification and analysis of artifactual remains—including manufacture, deterioration, provenance, contextual associations, and interpretation—consists of an introductory set of articles that define the major types of pure or composite inorganic and organic materials, along with the relevant methods of analysis (*see* AMBER, CHARACTERIZATION; BONE, CHARACTERIZATION; CLAYS AND CERAMICS, CHARACTERIZATION; DYES, CHARACTERIZATION; FAIENCE, CHARACTERIZATION; GLASS, CHARACTERIZATION; MARBLE, CHARACTERIZATION; METALS, CHARACTERIZATION; ROCKS AND MINERALS, CHARACTERIZATION). These articles give readers a clear presentation of the nature of specific inorganic and organic remains used in the manufacture of objects or materials and allow better understanding of the terminology as used in archaeology.

The study of plant and animal remains from archaeological sites is undertaken for the purposes of species identification, understanding past human uses of plants and animals (e.g., for diet and secondary products), and reconstruction of the natural environment. The study of plants may involve the analysis of the surviving parts of plants and their uses (*see* PALEOETHNOBOTANY), the pollen remains (*see* PALYNOLOGY), or plant silica bodies (*see* PHYTOLITH ANALYSIS). Similarly, the study of animal remains consists of identification of species, analysis of human uses, and environmental reconstruction (*see* ANIMAL REMAINS, IDENTIFICATION AND ANALYSIS: FISH; ANIMAL REMAINS, IDENTIFICATION AND ANALYSIS: INSECTS; ANIMAL REMAINS, IDENTIFICATION AND ANALYSIS: MAMMALS; ANIMAL REMAINS, IDENTIFICATION AND ANALYSIS: MOLLUSCS; ZOOARCHAEOLOGY). Analysis of animal remains can also reveal the season of animal death—information that can be used to understand patterns in human resource exploitation and site habitation (*see* GROWTH-RING ANALYSIS AND SEASONALITY STUDIES; GROWTH STUDIES: FISH OTOLITHS; GROWTH STUDIES: MAMMAL TEETH).

The analysis of archaeological human remains is conducted to reconstruct health (*see* PALEOPATHOLOGY, HUMAN), diet (*see* PALEONUTRITION), and mortality (*see* PALEODEMOGRAPHY) in order to understand human behavior, demographic patterns over time, and the conditions of human existence within the broader environment. The biological and medical study of human remains can be conducted on bone (*see* BONE AND OTHER ORGANIC MATERIALS: ANCIENT DNA; BONE; TRACE-ELEMENT ANALYSIS), residues (*see* PALEOIMMUNOLOGY; PALEOSEROLOGY), or excrement (*see* COPROLITE ANALYSIS). Along with human remains, nonhuman animal remains and plant remains are also analyzed for direct information on, respectively, the contraction of diseases in humans (*see* ARCHAEOPARASITOLOGY) and ancient medicinal practices to prolong human health (*see* PALEOPHARMACOLOGY).

The earth sciences provide the archaeologist with a wealth of information for environmental reconstruction (*see* GEOARCHAEOLOGY; SOIL AND SEDIMENT ANALYSIS). Significant areas of interest for archaeology include landscape reconstruction, paleoclimatic and paleoenvironmental reconstructions, paleoecology and environmental changes, chronology and stratigraphic relationships, availability of mineral and potable water resources, raw materials for economic exploitation and their provenance, impact of major geological events on human history, and analysis of human influences on the environment.

For more than fifty years, analytical methods from the physical and biological sciences have found increased use in archaeology (*see* ARCHAEOMETRY), both in frequency and types of applications for both inorganic and organic materials. Ultimately, the most effective use of analytical methods in archaeology depends on the clear statement of archaeological research questions, as well as the understanding of the material and type of information desired, before any decision on appropriate methods of physical examination is made. The group of articles that deal with materials analysis are technical discussions of the underlying principles and applications to archaeological remains. Most of these articles are written at a more advanced level and are cross-referenced accordingly from articles listed under Materials Characterization in the Subject Guide, to which the reader is referred for an initial understanding on the nature of materials.

Analytical methods may be conceptualized according to the types of information they yield. Microscopy provides information on manufacturing, surface conditions and modifications, tool use, microstructure, inclusion identification, deterioration patterns, to mention just a few topics of interest (*see* METALLOGRAPHY; PETROGRAPHY; USE-WEAR ANALYSIS). Many techniques allow determination of chemical composition at the elemental level (*see* ATOMIC ABSORPTION [AA] SPECTROSCOPY; ELECTRON-PROBE MICROANALYSIS; INDUCTIVELY COUPLED PLASMA—ATOMIC EMISSION SPECTROMETRY; NUCLEAR METHODS OF ANALYSIS; X-RAY FLUORESCENCE [XRF] ANALYSIS), the isotopic level (*see* ISOTOPES, STABLE (C, N, O, H): BONE AND PALEODIET STUDIES; ISOTOPES, STABLE [Pb, Sr]: RAW MATERIALS AND PROVENANCE STUDIES), and at the molecular or crystalline structural level (*see* FOURIER TRANSFORM–INFRARED (FT-IR) MICROSCOPY; INFRARED [IR] SPECTROSCOPY; X-RAY DIFFRACTION [XRD] ANALYSIS). All articles on materials analysis discuss archaeological materials appropriate for analysis, the quality of information retrieved, and examples of archaeological applications.

Some methods of analysis are totally non-destructive to the object or require extraction of such small amounts of material as to have an almost negligible effect. Other methods are partly destructive, in that a small sample is taken, leaving the object relatively intact for other uses. Some methods of analysis require that most of the object or sample be destroyed through various laboratory techniques. In the latter instance, the archaeologist needs to ascertain the value of the object or samples versus the need for information that cannot be obtained without destruction to the object. As with surveying and excavation, sampling procedures are involved in any post-excavation analytical program. Not all archaeological materials or objects can be subjected to physico-chemical methods due to the costs and time involved. Therefore, some sample-selection process is developed that must be taken into consideration when drawing conclusions on human behavior derived from such analyses.

Quantitative Methods and Data Management

Since all phases of archaeological research—surveying, excavation, and analysis—have the propensity to generate vast bodies of information, or data, archaeologists have utilized or adapted methods from mathematics, statistics, and computer science for the storage, analysis, presentation, and management of such data (*see* QUANTITATIVE METHODS IN ARCHAEOLOGY). Sample selection—whether it be for sites to survey, portions of a single site to excavate, or objects to analyze or date—must be undertaken due to the costs of survey, excavation, or analysis and to ensure a certain level of quality in the data collected (*see* SAMPLING).

Numerous statistical methods for the manipulation, analysis, and presentation of data are at the disposal of the archaeologist. These methods may be applied before or after the archaeological data are collected depending on the theoretical orientation of the archaeologist (deductive versus inductive reasoning) and the nature of the research problem. Many archaeologists use statistical techniques for the purposes of description and comparison to classify and order data sets (*see* STATISTICAL METHODS IN ARCHAEOLOGY). These data may range from results of scientific analyses, to individual artifacts, and assemblages of artifacts, and archaeological sites. The study of spatial distributions of archaeological remains or objects and spatial distributions of sites within a defined region requires a different set of statistical techniques (*see* SPATIAL ANALYSIS) than those used in description and classification.

The rapid developments in computer science since the 1970s have provided archaeologists with accessible and affordable technology for the capture, storage, retrieval, manipulation, analysis, and presentation of archaeological data (*see* COMPUTER DATABANKS IN ARCHAEOLOGY; COMPUTER SIMULATION; COMPUTERS IN ARCHAEOLOGY; GEOGRAPHIC INFORMATION SYSTEMS). Major applications of computers in archaeology include statistical analysis, spreadsheets, word processing, desktop publishing, data processing, graphical presentatons, hyper- and multimedia techniques, solid modeling, simulation, education, and computer-network communications.

Archaeological Disciplinary Theory and Temporal-Geographic Area Studies

As archaeology has developed since the mid-nineteenth century, a vast body of theory as well as specializations within the discipline, which focus on specific historic periods and/or site locations, have evolved. Most of the articles in this section are longer, necessitated by the expository requirements of these topics. The temporal-geographic area studies are included here for their contributions to method and theory and/or for their pancontinental archaeohistorical databases and potential for theoretical development in understanding past human behavior.

Most archaeological investigations from the nineteenth century to the 1950s were involved in exploration, excavation, cultural-historical description of objects, and definition of archaeological cultures. With the exception of those areas of the world where written records provided some background for ancient history, much of the world's prehistory was unknown until archaeological excavations were conducted. But even when historical accounts were available, such as in the Mediterranean region, the Near East, or China, verification of events and chronologies through archaeology was inevitably necessary. This cultural-historical approach to archaeology had few theoretical paradigms, being primarily concerned with the documentation and description of a previously unknown, or partly known, but continuously expanding database. In the absence of documentary evidence, the traditional approach to archaeology often employed the concept of diffusion to describe the origins of features in the archaeological record—that is, to find and date the first appearance of a particular object or technology (e.g., beginnings of agriculture, invention of pottery or metal working) and then to trace the spread or distribution of this object or phenomenon geographically and temporally.

Since the 1940s, many archaeologists sought to explore new areas of research beyond the historical particularism of description of artifacts and archaeological cultures to the reconstruction of how people lived, in terms of both the social and the physical environment. Much archaeological research has focused on the identification, description, and explanation of past social units, social structure, and cultural change from the archaeological context, which may range from the individual grave, household, or settlement, extending to the landscape (*see* SOCIAL ARCHAEOLOGY). Issues as diverse as trade and exchange systems, power relationships, and social inequality are among those explored to reveal the variety of human social, economic, and political interaction (*see* CORE AND PERIPHERY SYSTEMS; EXCHANGE SYSTEMS, THEORY). Units of investigation have also broadened: from focusing on complete excavation of individual sites to the appearance of more studies examining settlement systems and archaeological landscapes (*see* SETTLEMENT ARCHAEOLOGY, THEORY).

The analysis of plant and animal remains has been a tradition in archaeology since the nineteenth century, especially in connection with the history of agriculture. The application of ecological theory in archaeology expanded research by focusing interest on the interrelationships between human development and the physical environment, especially those questions on the origins, causation, and consequences of cultural and demographic phenomena that had ecological impact (e.g., subsistence economy, settled life, development of dense population centers, and population movements). In turn, refinements in archaeological methodology in the retrieval and analysis of data for environmental reconstruction (e.g., flotation, sieving, dating, physicochemical analytical methods) have provided the archaeologist with finer levels of detail on the interrelationships among social, economic, and environmental changes (*see* ECOLOGICAL THEORY IN ARCHAEOLOGY).

New Archaeology, which developed during the 1960s, was a movement in archaeology to use scientific methods to investigate and explain past human behavioral patterns and the cultural processes that produced the archaeological record (*see* NEW/PROCESSUAL ARCHAEOLOGY). Specifically, New Archaeology advocated the use of the hypothetico-deductive model of scientific reasoning, which requires that archaeologists formulate hypotheses prior to collection of data through archaeological surveying and excavation, to test those hypotheses against the data and to develop laws on the basis of those tests. The ideas of the New Archaeologists diverged significantly from the traditional inductive approach in archaeology, by which generalizations or conclusions are formed on the basis of known data. In practice, archaeology must use both deductive and inductive reasoning, since new, previously unobservable data have the power both to confirm or negate hypotheses and to generate new hypotheses that can be tested later. New Archaeologists among themselves have generated philosophical differences of opinion, including the nature of the scientific method, how it should be applied, the definition of laws, and whether they are required for archaeological explanation.

Perhaps equally important to the philosophical and methodological growth of archaeology is the legacy that New Archaeology has left with respect to setting new standards for conducting archaeological research. Archaeologists promoting the New Archaeology considered themselves behavioral and social scientists, in that they sought to answer anthropological questions with archaeological data. In contrast to the traditional cultural-historical approach, which often emphasized the documentation and description of temporal-geographic frameworks and the classification of material culture (upon which we still rely!), New Archaeology changed the types of questions relating to human behavioral patterns, which had never been asked before: not only *what* and *when*, but also *how* and *why*. New Archaeology, in fact, has long since been referred to as *processual archaeology* because of its emphasis on identification and explanation of cultural processes that produced the archaeological materials and their patterns in space and time. Their reorientation of the discipline introduced significant changes in the practice of archaeology, as well as in the patterns of archaeological reasoning.

Interestingly, the term *processual archaeology* also serves to distinguish the growing movement of *postprocessual* archaeology, which developed during the early 1980s. Postprocessualists are less unified than their predecessors and, therefore, difficult to characterize but can be distinguished both by their divergent views of archaeology as a profession and discipline and by their opposition to New/Processual Archaeology. Postprocessual archaeology has prompted serious reevaluation and expansion of *what* archaeologists study by proposing the important question: "Whose archaeologies?" The bailiwick of postprocessual research includes the analysis of how Western, class-based society has affected *what* archaeologists study and, more revealing perhaps, *who* was studied. Some topics of postprocessual research have included studies of gender in archaeology and the archaeology of gender, the representation of indigenous pasts, the influence of imperialism and Western capitalism on society, and the analysis of the political context in which archaeology itself has been conducted (*see* GENDER ARCHAEOLOGY; MARXIST ARCHAEOLOGY; POSTPROCESSUAL ARCHAEOLOGY).

Archaeologists have always been interested in exploring different ways to derive meaning from archaeological data. How to derive such meaning and enhance understanding of human behavior and the social environment from archaeological data have generated methodological and theoretical specializations within the discipline.

Since the basis for archaeology is the retrieval and understanding of material remains, one of the fundamental questions asked is how artifacts, features, or architecture were produced and used and, ultimately, how they were impacted by the depositional or meteorological environment after discard or disuse. Both ethnoarchaeology and experimental archaeology have significant contributions in this particular avenue of research. For EXPERIMENTAL ARCHAEOLOGY, as the name implies, experiments are performed by the archaeologist to answer specifically the above question. Replication of prehistoric stone tools was the first of such experiments during the nineteenth century. Since that time, almost every conceivable prehistoric and historic material or activity has been subject to replication or experimentation—from pyrotechnologies, textile industries, agriculture and food processing, modes of transportation, and monument construction, to building and actually living in a Neolithic village. Not only how artifacts and structures were made, but also how they were used is critical in understanding both technology and human behavior. Stone tools, for example, have been subjected to microscopic analysis of traces of wear or edge damage to determine for which materials or activities they were used (*see* USE-WEAR ANALYSIS). The understanding of taphonomic and site-formation processes has also driven experimentation to see how artifacts and archaeological sites survive, erode, or deteriorate under various meteorological and surface conditions (precipitation, freezing and thawing, wind, water erosion, fire, human trampling, and cultivation), as well as in the depositional environment (e.g., effects of soil chemistry, burrowing animals, bacteria).

The study of contemporary human behavior as a model for describing the manufacture and use of objects, as well as for understanding the patterning of artifact associations (*see* ETHNOARCHAEOLOGY), has been invaluable to archaeologists since the nineteenth century. The direct observation of activities surrounding the production, use, consumption, destruction, or discard of the material cultural record is a constant reminder of the variety of behavioral patterns that are ultimately responsible for what becomes the archaeological record. However, archaeologists have found that trying to estblish a link from the past to the present, a direct historical approach, is not without its theoretical and methodological limitations, since past behavior patterns cannot be assumed to have continued to more recent or historic periods, even if the societies under consideration exist(ed) under similar ecological conditions. Furthermore, if using ethnographic analogy to understand the patterning of archaeological objects and their associations, archaeologists must take into consideration the effect of postdepositional forces (if necessary) that may have disturbed or otherwise transformed the archaeological record. Ethnographic analogy has proven especially effective when applied indirectly to archaeological data, especially with respect to examining the *variety* of cultural behavior for societies living under *similar* ecological and economic circumstances.

Since the beginning of the discipline, archaeologists have also sought to understand the nonmaterial aspects of behavioral systems, such as religion, ideology, ritual, art and iconography, or symbolism (*see* SYMBOLIC ARCHAEOLOGY). Subject matter may involve, but not be limited to, analysis of cave paintings, mortuary practices, architecture, and writing systems. Symbolic archaeology is a terminological rubric for such studies, which use structural, contextual, cognitive, neuropsychological, ethnoarchaeological, and ethnohistoric analyses for the interpretation of meaning. Symbolic archaeology is defined from its subject matter, the kinds of questons asked, and the methods of research appropriate to its domain. However, symbolic archaeology itself has evolved into a broader study of past ways of thought, or cognitive archaeology, which is more concerned with the development and roles of symbolic systems in society than with specific meanings.

The analysis of human behavior from the material cultural record, at *any* time or *any* place, has been the bailiwick of BEHAVIORAL ARCHAEOLOGY. This comprehensive field, which developed during the 1970s, combines traditional archaeological methodology of surveying and excavation with experimental archaeology and ethnographic research on Western as well as non-Western societies. Behavioral archaeology has defined as its domain the understanding of artifacts—from their creation/use/disuse/reuse cycles to final disposition in the archaeological record—with the goal of explaining the behavioral interactions of people with objects throughout the "lives" of those objects. This interrelationship of artifacts and behavior can be analyzed and interpreted in both past and present cultures. The lack of temporal and geographic boundaries in behavioral archaeology provides a limitless research landscape that includes such diverse settings as Palaeolithic caves, Classical temples, historic plantations, twentieth-century garbage landfills, and nuclear-waste sites.

Since artifacts can be anything that has been altered by human activity, most human behavior involves artifacts in some way. In behavioral archaeology, the function of artifacts is not qualified in any way, such as utilitarian or nonutilitarian, but is inclusive of all material remains as a result of all human behavior, be it economic, social, or ritual. Behavioral research on the uses of artifacts, therefore, can be conducted for analysis of technoeconomic activities, sociopolitical power, ritual life, and symbolic systems.

The aim of behavioral research on artifactual data is to reconstruct both behavior and the social processes surrounding behavioral patterns. Behavioral archaeologists, however, are mindful to take into account the changes that take place as an object goes from the systemic context (use/reuse cycle) to the archaeological context (final discard). Archaeologists are also careful in their interpretation of the depositional context of objects, whose four dimensions of space and time could have changed significantly from its formation to excavation and data retrieval.

Temporal-Geographic Area Studies

As archaeology has permeated, to a greater or lesser extent, all continents with human habitation, as well as many of their navigable waters, the application of archaeological research itself has broadened in both space and time. With the ever-expanding database, many archaeologists have focused their efforts into the development of areas of specialization other than in regional prehistoric sequences (the latter of which are covered by the relevant geographic volumes in this series). The area studies presented in this volume have a geographic focus that is broad, even intercontinental, or may be based on specific time periods later than the prehistoric past, or are, in most cases, a combination of both. In all of these areas of specialization, both archaeological methodology and analysis of written sources are applied to solve issues relating to human endeavor and behavior from ancient to more recent historical periods. The theoretical frameworks of some of these area studies are varied in their disciplinary development, some offering extensive research into human behavior in historical periods, others presenting significant and prospective avenues of theoretical inquiry for many future archaeologists.

The Mediterranean region has one of the longest records of archaeological research as a result of the plethora of architectural remains at or near the ground surface, together with a rich classical literary tradition (*see* CLASSICAL ARCHAEOLOGY). Geographically, classical archaeology encompasses not only Mediterranean cultures, but also those areas colonized by, or engaged in commerce or military action with, the Greco-Roman world. In the Mediterranean region, classical archaeology also encompasses those prehistoric periods antecedent to the rise of Greece and Rome, as well as subsequent to the collapse of Rome, usually when chronological connections with the classical period can be made. Classical archaeology has a well-established tradition of undertaking large-scale surveying programs and multi- and interdisciplinary research. Theoretical research on past human behavior is a developing area of investigation in classical archaeology, and future archaeologists can take advantage of an enormous and underutilized database.

Archaeological research has also been extended into the medieval period in Europe, North Africa, and the Middle East, specific dates considered as *medieval* depending on the locally relevant events and culture history (*see* MEDIEVAL ARCHAEOLOGY). As with research on the classical period, medieval archaeology has been more event oriented, with much work focusing on verification of historically recorded events, ethnolinguistic groups, and named individuals. But this discipline has confronted the methodological challenges of conducting excavations in major urban centers and also shows vast potential and promise for theoretical approaches such as those developed in behavioral archaeology.

The application of archaeological research to the past 500 years of human history—the archaeology of the modern era—has seen rapid development in North America, Europe, and Australia (*see* HISTORICAL ARCHAEOLOGY). The well-recognized fact that written historical records provide only a fragmentary and selected view of past events and past lives was the initial driving force behind the early development of historical archaeology. Information on peoples for whom no historical records exist, especially those of the lower economic classes, is often retrievable only through archaeological methodology. The reconstruction of the lives of those peoples left out of the historical record and the disenfranchised has also become fertile ground for much postprocessual research. European colonization throughout the world, demographic expansion from other continents (e.g., Chinese diaspora), and the impact of colonization on other peoples—both indigenous and those transported involuntarily from Europe or Africa—have been the primary areas of research in historical archaeology. This archaeological exploration of colonialism and colonization has also been referred to as the archaeology of the development and spread of capitalism.

Archaeologists have also developed specialized area studies based on the type of site excavated. INDUSTRIAL ARCHAEOLOGY focuses on the excavation and analysis of places of work outside of the domestic and agricultural spheres of production, including, but not limited to, industrial installations, mills, mines, factories, workshops, ships, and harbors. Industrial archaeologists also reconstruct technological and industrial processes and the manufacture of products of technology, thereby encompassing both historical archaeology and experimental archaeology. The examination and understanding of peoples' lives and behaviors within the industrial sphere are no less important. Having begun in the 1950s in Great Britain, industrial archaeology has seen rapid development across Europe and North America.

Technological advancements in underwater exploration have allowed more extensive and safer excavation of submerged or waterlogged sites, as well as the retrieval and conservation of archaeological finds. Worldwide interest in the human use of waterways has encouraged the development of NAUTICAL ARCHAEOLOGY, which includes excavation (both terrestrial and underwater) of not only ships and boats, but also harbors, port cities, bridges, locks, weirs, and the like, which relate to water transportation, commerce, warfare, technology, and human ways of life during prehistoric, classical, medieval, and historic times.

Management and Protective Legislation of Archaeological Resources

As we approach the twenty-first century and a new millennium, archaeology as a profession and a discipline is facing many critical issues, two of which have demanded, and will continue to require, serious attention worldwide: the legislative and legal framework within which archaeological work is conducted and the rise in destruction of archaeological and historic sites. National and international legislation has attempted to provide for preservation of terrestial and underwater archaeological and historic sites but has also demonstrated serious limitations in the protection of both movable and immovable cultural property. Together with the destruction of the archaeological heritage, archaeological work itself, as well as the data from current and prior excavations, may also be subject to cultural repatriation legislation. While the vast topic of cultural protection is a separate volume in this series, the management of archaeological resources and the relevant legislative framework are included in this volume, since these issues will determine the available archaeological database and limit what archaeologists can do and what we can know about the human past.

The clandestine excavation of the world's cultural heritage and the commercial exploitation of archaeological and historical artifacts appear to be forever on the rise. Lack of public education about the local cultural heritage and/or rural poverty are the tragic underpinnings in the looting of antiquities, and their effect on archaeology is incalculable. The loss of an irreplaceable, and very limited, archaeological database, as well as the destruction of the archaeological context, will also be a loss to the understanding of past human behavior and cultural systems. An increasing number of nations have enacted, are considering enactment, or are constantly revising national legislation for the protection of historical and archaeological sites and the cultural and biological materials buried in, or located at the surface of, the land or submerged under water within territorial jurisdictions. Protective legislation, while admirable and a necessary first step, can mete out punishment only after theft has occurred and its perpetrators are apprehended and cannot realistically provide for effective prevention or law enforcement over vast national landscapes and continents, as has been demonstrated by almost a century of national and state legislation in the United States (*see* ABANDONED SHIPWRECK ACT [ASA]; ANTIQUITIES ACT OF 1906; ARCHEOLOGICAL RESOURCES PROTECTION ACT [ARPA]; IN SITU CONSERVATION).

On a more positive note, preservation legislation in the United States has also encouraged archaeological excavation (*see* ARCHEOLOGICAL AND HISTORIC PRESERVATION ACT [AHPA]; NATIONAL HISTORIC PRESERVATION ACT [NHPA]). Urban and suburban development, as well as public engineering projects, have the ability to destroy not only individual archaeological sites, but also entire landscapes. National legislation designed to make sure that archaeological resources are excavated before construction or engineering projects are undertaken has provided mitigation of loss of archaeological sites and the permanent destruction of the archaeological database, expanded the areas available for archaeological excavation, and provided for the training and employment of archaeologists (*see* CULTURAL RESOURCE MANAGEMENT [CRM]; SALVAGE/RESCUE ARCHAEOLOGY; WPA ARCHAEOLOGY).

Cultural protection legislation may impose certain restrictions on the area surveyed and excavated by archaeologists or require permission from local- or national-heritage authorities or from the indigenous peoples on whose land the surveying will take place. Likewise, excavation itself may be affected by local religious or other cultural traditions that are not included in secular legislation. Excavation particularly of human burials or cultural levels important to religious groups may experience restrictions at various levels, depending on specific circumstances throughout the world. Under other circumstances, there may simply be limitations on excavation by requiring permission and presence of indigenous peoples or affected religious authorities when sites are excavated on their lands or within their religious domain.

Under cultural protection and repatriation legislation, American museums and universities that have received federal funding are required to return objects of cultural or religious importance and human remains from prior excavations to culturally affiliated peoples (*see* NATIVE AMERICAN GRAVES PROTECTION AND REPATRIATION ACT [NAGPRA]). Future excavations and accidental discoveries, as well as the final disposition of retrieved remains, are also controlled by NAGPRA. In some instances, cultural groups have developed agreements to allow the museum or research institution to have access to repatriated collections or to maintain collections on behalf of the respective community. Any subsequent research involving analysis of archaeological collections subject to NAGPRA may be limited to researchers who have received prior permission for access from the relevant cultural leaders, or access may be eliminated in the case of reburied human remains (*see* REBURIAL, INTERNATIONAL PERSPECTIVES). Repatriation legislation worldwide will restrict the database available to archaeologists and thus affect any subsequent interpretation of human behavior. It is for this reason that a considerable effort has been made to include in this encyclopedia a number of detailed articles on methods of physico-chemical analysis—topics that are not usually so extensively discussed under the rubric of archaeological method and theory. Analytical techniques are being refined constantly to the point where compositional information can be rapidly retrieved, with minimal or, in some cases, no intervention with the integrity of the specimen or object. Current and future archaeologists may need to be more aware of available efficient, analytical technology as museum collections and newly excavated materials become subject to repatriation legislation and for which permission has been granted to conduct tests prior to return and reburial.

However, even within the confines and limitations of legislation, archaeology will continue to evolve as both a profession and a discipline as new methods and strategies are developed to retrieve the maximum amount of information in an economic and time-efficient way, as new areas of archaeological research are explored, as public education *about* and *in* archaeology is expanded, and as more local and culturally related communities are brought into the processes of archaeological investigation.

Subject Guide

Definition, Analysis, and Interpretation of Archaeological Materials and Related Disciplinary Area Studies

Materials Characterization
  Amber, Characterization
  Bone, Characterization
  Clays and Ceramics, Characterization
  Dyes, Characterization
  Faience, Characterization
  Glass, Characterization
  Marble, Characterization
  Metals, Characterization
  Rocks and Minerals, Characterization

Plant Remains: Disciplinary and Analytical Studies
  Paleoethnobotany
  Palynology
  Phytolith Analysis

Animal Remains: Disciplinary and Analytical Studies
  Animal Remains, Identification and Analysis: Fish
  Animal Remains, Identification and Analysis: Insects
  Animal Remains, Identification and Analysis: Mammals
  Animal Remains, Identification and Analysis: Molluscs
  Animal Remains, Quantification
  Growth-Ring Analysis and Seasonality Studies
  Growth Studies: Fish Otoliths
  Growth Studies: Mammal Teeth
  Zooarchaeology

Human Remains: Disciplinary and Analytical Studies
  Archaeoparasitology
  Bone and Other Organic Materials: Ancient DNA
  Bone, Trace-Element Analysis
  Coprolite Analysis
  Paleodemography
  Paleoimmunology
  Paleonutrition
  Paleopathology, Human
  Paleopharmacology
  Paleoserology

Geological Materials: Disciplinary and Analytical Studies
  Geoarchaeology
  Grain-Size Analysis
  Soil and Sediment Analysis

Materials Analytical Methods
  Archaeometry
  Atomic Absorption Spectrometry
  Electron-Probe Microanalysis
  Electrophoresis
  Fourier Transform–Infrared (FT-IR) Microscopy
  Inductively Coupled Plasma—Atomic Emission Spectrometry
  Infrared (IR) Spectroscopy
  Isotopes, Stable (C, N, O, H): Bone and Paleodiet Studies

Isotopes, Stable (Pb, Sr): Raw Materials and Provenance Studies
Metallography
Mössbauer Spectroscopy
Nuclear Magnetic (NMR) Resonance Spectroscopy
Nuclear Methods of Analysis
Petrography
Radiography in Archaeology
Use-Wear Analysis
X-ray Diffraction (XRD) Analysis
X-ray Fluorescence (XRF) Analysis

Quantitative Methods and Data Management
Computer Databanks in Archaeology
Computer Simulation
Computers in Archaeology
Geographic Information Systems
Quantitative Methods in Archaeology
Sampling
Spatial Analysis
Statistical Methods in Archaeology

Archaeological Disciplinary Theory and Area Studies
Behavioral and Theoretical Area Studies
Behavioral Archaeology
Core and Periphery Systems
Dating, Method and Theory
Ecological Theory in Archaeology
Ethnoarchaeology
Evolution, Cultural
Evolution, Scientific
Exchange Systems, Theory
Experimental Archaeology
Gender Archaeology
Marxist Archaeology
New/Processual Archaeology
Postprocessual Archaeology
Settlement Archaeology, Theory
Social Archaeology
Survey Design, Theory
Symbolic Archaeology

Temporal-Geographic Area Studies
Classical Archaeology
Historical Archaeology
Industrial Archaeology
Medieval Archaeology
Nautical Archaeology

Management and Protective Legislation of Archaeological Resources
Abandoned Shipwreck Act (ASA)
Antiquities Act of 1906
Archeological and Historic Preservation Act (AHPA)

Archeological Resources Protection Act (ARPA)
Cultural Resource Management (CRM)
National Historic Preservation Act (NHPA)
Native American Graves Protection and Repatriation Act (NAGPRA)
Reburial, International Perspectives
Salvage/Rescue Archaeology
WPA Archaeology

Biographies

Adams, Robert McCormick (1926–)
Aitken, Martin J. (1922–)
Bada, Jeffrey L. (1942–)
Baillie, Michael G.L. (1944–)
Bass, George Fletcher (1932–)
Binford, Lewis R. (1930–)
Bordes, François (1919–1981)
Breuil, Henri (1877–1961)
Butzer, Karl W. (1934–)
Caton-Thompson, Gertrude (1889–1985)
Childe, Vere Gordon (1892–1957)
Clark, John Desmond (1916–)
Clark, John Grahame Douglas (1907–1995)
Clarke, David L. (1937–1976)
Conkey, Margaret Wright (1944–)
Crawford, Osbert G.S. (1886–1957)
Deetz, James S. Fanto (1930–)
Dunnell, Robert C. (1942–)
Evans, Sir John (1823–1908)
Fagan, Brian Murray (1936–)
Flannery, Kent Vaughn (1934–)
Ford, James Alfred (1911–1968)
Garrod, Dorothy Annie Elizabeth (1892–1968)
Gould, Richard Allan (1939–)
Hassan, Fekri A. (1943–)
Hodder, Ian (1949–)
Holmes, William Henry (1846–1933)
Howell, Francis Clark (1925–)
Kenyon, Dame Kathleen Mary (1906–1978)
Klein, Richard G. (1941–)
Klejn, Leo S. (1927–)
Leone, Mark Paul (1940–)
Lerici, Carlo M. (1890–1978)
Leroi-Gourhan, Andre (1911–1986)
Libby, Willard Frank (1908–1980)
Longacre, William A. (1937–)
McKern, William Carleton (1892–1988)
Petrie, Sir William Matthew Flinders (1853–1942)
Pitt-Rivers, General Augustus Henry (1827–1900)
Plog, Fred T. (1944–1992)
Rathje, William Laurens (1945–)
Redman, Charles L. (1945–)
Renfrew, Andrew Colin (1937–)
Rouse, Irving Benjamin (1913–)
Schiffer, Michael Brian (1947–)

Scollar, Irwin (1928–)
Semenov, Sergei Aristarkhovich (1898–1978)
Shepard, Anna Osler (1903–1973)
Spaulding, Albert Clanton (1914–1990)
St. Joseph, J. Kenneth S. (1912–1993)
Struever, Stuart McKee (1931–)
Suess, Hans Eduard (1909–1993)
Thomas, David Hurst (1945–)
Thomsen, Christian Jürgensen (1788–1865)
Trigger, Bruce Graham (1937–)
Tylecote, Ronald Frank (1916–1990)
Watson, Patty Jo (1932–)
Wheeler, Sir Robert Eric Mortimer (1890–1976)
Willey, Gordon Randolph (1913–)
Zeuner, Frederick Everard (1905–1963)

List of Articles by Contributor

Nuclear Magnetic Resonance (NMR)
  Spectroscopy

R. Bewley
Aerial Photography for Archaeology
Crawford, Osbert G.S. (1886–1957)
St. Joseph, J. Kenneth S. (1912–1993)

V. Bryant
Flotation
Paleoethnobotany (with J. Philip Dering)
Palynology

P. Buckland
Animal Remains, Identification and Analysis:
  Insects (with Jonathan P. Sadler)

J. Chapman
Hodder, Ian (1949–)
Postprocessual Archaeology
Settlement Archaeology, Theory
Social Archaeology

C. Claassen
Animal Remains, Identification and Analysis:
  Molluscs
Growth-Ring Analysis and Seasonality
  Studies
Shell Middens, Excavation

C. Cook
Bone and Other Organic Materials: Ancient
  DNA

G. Coote
Fluorine-Uranium-Nitrogen Dating

M. Dabas
Electrical and Electromagnetic Prospecting
  (with Albert Hesse and Alain Tabbagh)
Magnetic Prospecting (with Alain Tabbagh)
Thermal Prospecting (with Alain Tabbagh)

R. Dallas
Photogrammetry

J. Davis
Surveys, Multistage and Large-Scale (with
  Alan P. Sullivan III)

J. Dering
Paleoethnobotany (with Vaughn M. Bryant, Jr.)

H. Dockall
Paleodemography

Paleopathology, Human

R. Dorn
Rock-Art Dating

L. Drewett
Illustration, Archaeological

P. Drewett
Base Line
Grid Excavation
Half-Sectioning
Leveling
Offsetting
Open-Area Excavation
Quartering
Sieving
Site Mapping
Step Trenching
Stripping
Theodolite
Trench Excavation
Unit-Level Method

R. Dunnell
Archaeometry
Dating, Method and Theory
Evolution, Cultural
Evolution, Scientific
Holmes, William Henry (1846–1933)
Midwestern Taxonomic System
Rouse, Irving Benjamin (1913–)
Seriation
Type-Variety System

L. Ellis
Clays and Ceramics, Characterization
Petrography

T. Ericsson
Mössbauer Spectroscopy

D. Frey
Sonar (with George F. Bass)

I. Friedman
Obsidian Hydration Dating (with Fred
  Trembour)

A. Gernaey-Child
Bone, Characterization
Electrophoresis (with David R.K. Robertson)
Paleoimmunology
Paleoserology
Taphonomy

R. Gillard
Amino Acid Racemization/Epimerization
    Dating
Fourier Transform–Infrared (FT-IR)
    Microscopy (with Susan Hardman)

R. Gordon
Industrial Archaeology

R. Gould
Ethnoarchaeology
Remotely Operated Vehicles

N.R. Goulty
Seismic Refraction Surveying

D. Grattan
Wood (Waterlogged), Conservation

A. Green
Georadar (with Jürg Leckebusch)

R. Grün
Electron Spin Resonance (ESR) Dating
Uranium-Series Dating

S. Hardman
Fourier Transform–Infrared (FT-IR)
    Microscopy (with Robert D. Gillard)

K. Hays-Gilpin
Symbolic Archaeology

N. Herz
Marble, Characterization

A.Hesse
Archaeological Prospection
Electrical and Electromagnetic Prospecting
    (with Michel Dabas and Alain Tabbagh)

F. Hocker
Medieval Archaeology
Nautical Archaeology
Underwater Archaeology

C. Jackson
Glass, Characterization (with Paul T.
    Nicholson)

M. Jochim
Ecological Theory in Archaeology

K. Kvamme
Geographic Information Systems

J. Lang
Radiography in Archaeology

J. Leckebusch
Georadar (with Alan Green)

D. Lieberman
Growth Studies: Mammal Teeth

L. Loendorf
Rock-Art Sites, Recording and Analysis

E. Luby
Metrical Stratigraphy
Mortuary Sites, Excavation and Analysis
Natural Stratigraphy
Reverse Stratigraphy
Stratification
Stratigraphy
Triangulation

R. McGuire
Core and Periphery Systems
Historical Archaeology

B. McLauchlin
Classical Archaeology

F. McManamon
Abandoned Shipwreck Act (ASA)
Antiquities Act of 1906
Archeological and Historic Preservation Act
    (AHPA)
Archeological Resources Protection Act
    (ARPA)
Cultural Resource Management (CRM)
National Historic Preservation Act (NHPA)
Native American Graves Protection and
    Repatriation Act (NAGPRA)
Surveying and Site Examination, Manual
    Methods

R. Meadow
Animal Remains, Identification and Analysis:
    Mammals
Animal Remains, Quantification
Zooarchaeology

P. Nicholson
Faience, Characterization
Glass, Characterization (with Caroline M.
    Jackson)

G. Odell
Use-Wear Analysis

C. Orton
Computer Databanks in Archaeology
Computer Simulation
Computers in Archaeology
Harris Matrix
Quantitative Methods in Archaeology
Sampling
Spatial Analysis
Statistical Methods in Archaeology

G. Owen
Photography, Archaeological

E. Peacock
Fibrous Materials, On-Site Conservation
Leather, On-Site Conservation

D. Pearsall
Phytolith Analysis

C. Price
In Situ Conservation

M. Purser
Gender Archaeology

E. Pye
Ceramics, On-Site Conservation
Glass, On-Site Conservation
Wall Paintings, Conservation

G. Rapp
Atomic Absorption (AA) spectrometry
Geoarchaeology
Grain-Size Analysis
Metals, Characterization
Rocks and Minerals, Characterization
Soil and Sediment Analysis
Tephrochronology
Varve Analysis

K. Reinhard
Archaeoparasitology
Coprolite Analysis
Paleonutrition
Paleopharmacology
Reburial, International Perspectives

G. Rice
Dunnell, Robert C. (1942–)
Redman, Charles L. (1945–)
Salvage/Rescue Archaeology
Settlements, Excavation
WPA Archaeology

D. Robertson
Electrophoresis (with Angela Gernaey-Child)

J. Sadler
Animal Remains, Identification and Analysis:
    Insects (with Paul C. Buckland)

M. Salmon
New/Processual Archaeology

E. Schortman
Exchange Systems, Theory (with Patricia A.
    Urban)

H. Schwarcz
Bone, Trace-Element Analysis
Isotopes, Stable (C, N, O, H): Bone and
    Paleodiet Studies

D. Scott
Metallography

C. Sease
Conservation of Archaeological Materials
Metals, On-Site Conservation

K. Severson
Mosaics, On-Site Conservation
Stone, On-Site Conservation

J. Shaw
Archaeomagnetic Dating

J. Skibo
Experimental Archaeology

E. Staski
Archaeological Sites, Formation Processes

Z. Stos-Gale
Isotopes, Stable (Pb, Sr): Raw Materials and
    Provenance Studies

L. Straus
Adams, Robert McCormick (1926–)
Bordes, François (1919–1981)
Breuil, Henri (1877–1961)
Butzer, Karl W. (1934–)
Caves and Rockshelters, Excavation
Leroi-Gourhan, Andre (1911–1986)

A. Sullivan
Survey Design, Theory
Surveys, Multistage and Large-Scale (with
    Jack L. Davis)

A. Tabbagh
Electrical and Electromagnetic Prospecting
    (with Michel Dabas and Albert Hesse)
Magnetic Prospecting (with Michel Dabas)
Thermal Prospecting (with Michel Dabas)

C. Tilley
Marxist Archaeology

M. Tite
X-ray Diffraction (XRD) Analysis
X-ray Fluorescence (XRF) Analysis

F. Trembour
Obsidian Hydration Dating (with Irving
    Friedman)

A. Tribe
Packaging of Archaeological Objects

P. Urban
Exchange Systems, Theory (with Edward M.
    Schortman)

W. Van Neer
Animal Remains, Identification and Analysis:
    Fish
Growth Studies: Fish Otoliths

G. Wagner
Fission-Track Dating

W. Walker
Behavioral Archaeology

N. Walsh
Inductively Coupled Plasma–Atomic
    Emission Spectroscopy

M. Whiting
Dyes, Characterization

O. Williams-Thorpe
Electron-Probe Microanalysis

A

Abandoned Shipwreck Act (ASA)

The national law establishing how historic shipwrecks are to be managed by federal and state agencies. This statute (43 U.S. Code 2101–2106; Public Law 100–298) was enacted to provide a consistent national approach for the management of historic shipwrecks in the United States. The statute reflects a compromise worked out over nearly a decade between archaeologists and historic preservationists and those who want to exploit shipwrecks for commercial gain. The need for a national law became apparent to archaeologists and historic preservationists concerned about the protection of historic shipwrecks when several legal decisions nullified the rights of state governments that had enacted state laws protecting historic shipwrecks to control access to, and use of, these resources. The basis of these federal-court decisions was that federal admiralty law held supremacy over state laws. These decisions raised severe problems for those who wanted to protect and preserve historic shipwrecks. Admiralty law provided for means of establishing the rights of individuals to salvage shipwrecks and had been used for many years by salvors to protect their claims to specific shipwrecks. Without any federal law addressing the preservation or management of historic shipwrecks directly, treatment of shipwrecks as salvageable resources under admiralty law was the only alternative (National Trust for Historic Preservation 1988).

The statute was signed by President Ronald Reagan on April 29, 1987. It is introduced by a finding in Section 2 that asserts that state governments have a responsibility for the management of a broad range of resources in state waters and submerged lands, including abandoned shipwrecks. Abandoned shipwrecks under this statute are those that have been deserted and to which owners have relinquished ownership rights with no retention (Sec. 2[b]). Part I of the guidelines published in 1990 to implement the statute provides a more detailed definition of the term:

> Abandoned shipwreck means any shipwreck to which title voluntarily has been given up by the owner with the intent of never claiming a right or interest in the future and without vesting ownership in any other person. By not taking any action after a wreck incident either to mark and subsequently remove the wrecked vessel or its cargo or to provide legal notice of abandonment . . . an owner shows intent to give up title. Such shipwrecks ordinarily are treated as being abandoned after the expiration of 30 days from sinking (National Park Service 1990:50120).

There are two important distinctions regarding shipwreck abandonment described in the guidelines:

> (a) when the owner of a sunken vessel is paid the full value of the vessel, such as receiving payment from an insurance underwriter, the shipwreck is not considered to be abandoned. In such cases, title to the wrecked vessel is passed to the party who paid the owner; [and]
> (b) although a sunken warship or other vessel entitled to sovereign immunity often appears to have been abandoned by the flag nation, it remains the property of

the nation to which it belonged at the time of sinking unless the nation has taken formal action to abandon it or to transfer title to another party. . . . Shipwrecks [and generally their cargo] entitled to sovereign immunity are wrecks of warships and other vessels . . . used only on government non-commercial service at the time of sinking (National Park Service 1990:50120–50121).

Management and protection by state governments is a key aspect of the statute because Section 6(c) of the law, after asserting federal ownership to any abandoned shipwreck on or embedded in the submerged lands of any state, transfers title to the states in which the abandoned shipwrecks are located. Section 6(d) reserves ownership of abandoned shipwrecks on public lands for the federal government and those on Indian lands for the Indian tribe that owns the land.

The statute does not provide specific requirements to the states on how abandoned shipwrecks are to be managed; however, it directed the National Park Service to prepare guidelines that would "encourage the development of underwater parks and the administrative cooperation necessary for the comprehensive management of underwater resources related to historic shipwrecks" (Section 5[a]).

The guidelines were published in the *Federal Register* (National Park Service 1990:50116–50145) on December 4, 1990. The directions given to the Park Service for the preparation of the guidelines reflect the wide range of interests that the statute and guidelines try to satisfy and illustrate the compromise nature of the statute. The guidelines are supposed to:

(1) maximize the enhancement of cultural resources;
(2) foster a partnership among sport divers, fishermen, archeologists, salvors, and other interests to manage shipwreck resources of the States and the United States;
(3) facilitate access and utilization by recreational interests; [and]
(4) recognize the interests of individuals and groups engaged in shipwreck discovery and salvage (Section 5[a][1]–[4]).

The guidelines, which are advisory rather than regulatory, address ten areas of concern related to abandoned shipwrecks. These are: the establishment of state shipwreck-management programs, the establishment of federal shipwreck-management programs, the funding of shipwreck programs and projects, the methods and means of discovering and locating shipwrecks, the methods and means of documenting and evaluating shipwrecks, the establishment of means to allow for both private and public recovery of shipwrecks, the means of providing public access to shipwrecks, the interpretation of shipwrecks, the interpretation of shipwreck sites, volunteer programs related to shipwrecks, and the creation and operation of underwater parks containing shipwrecks.

The appropriate uses and management of historic shipwrecks continue to be subjects of debate among archaeologists, historic preservationists, salvors, artifact dealers, and sport divers. State programs exist in a number of states, including Florida, Michigan, and Texas, for the management of historic shipwrecks.

Francis P. McManamon

See also ANTIQUITIES ACT OF 1906; ARCHEOLOGICAL RESOURCES PROTECTION ACT (ARPA); CULTURAL RESOURCE MANAGEMENT (CRM); NATIONAL HISTORIC PRESERVATION ACT (NHPA); NAUTICAL ARCHAEOLOGY; REMOTELY OPERATED VEHICLES; UNDERWATER ARCHAEOLOGY

Further Readings

Johnston, P.F. (1993) Treasure salvage, archaeological ethics, and maritime museums. International Journal of Nautical Archaeology 22(1):53–60.

National Park Service (1990) Abandoned Shipwreck Act: Final guidelines. Federal Register (December 4, 1990) 55(233): 50116–50145.

National Trust for Historic Preservation (1988) The Abandoned Shipwreck Act of 1987. PLR Advance, Preservation Law Reporter (May 2, 1988).

Vrana, K.J., and Halsey, J.R. (1992) Shipwreck allocation and management in Michigan: A review of theory and practice. Historical Archaeology 6(4):81–96.

Adams, Robert McCormick (1926–)

American archaeologist and scholar of ancient civilizations. Adams received his entire university education at the University of Chicago, where he earned his doctorate in 1956 and was a member of the faculty of the Department of Anthropology and the Oriental Institute (1955 to 1984). Adams served at various times as dean of the social sciences, director of the Oriental Institute, and provost of the University of Chicago. He has been secretary of the Smithsonian Institution in Washington, D.C. (1984 to 1994) and is a member of the United States National Academy of Sciences. In the 1960s, Adams conducted among the first large-scale archaeological surveys in Mesopotamia and pioneered the modern *comparative* study of the development of complex societies, having also worked in southern Mexico. His principal books—*City Invincible* (with C.H. Kraeling), *Land Behind Baghdad, The Evolution of Urban Society, The Uruk Countryside* (with Hans J. Nissen), and *Heartland of Cities*—are landmarks in the study of the role of the development of cities as central places within their geographical surroundings, especially in the context of intensive irrigation agriculture. Adams has also been concerned with the role of the development of technology in the economic and social histories of early civilizations. As secretary of the Smithsonian, he played a significant role in redefining the relationship between museums of anthropology and Native American groups.

Lawrence G. Straus

Further Readings

Adams, R.McC. (1965) Land behind Baghdad: A History of Settlement on the Diyala Plains. Chicago: University of Chicago Press.

Adams, R.McC. (1966) The Evolution of Urban Society: Early Mesopotamia and Prehispanic Mexico. Chicago: Aldine.

Adams, R.McC. (1981) Heartland of Cities: Surveys of Ancient Settlement and Land Use on the Central Floodplain of the Euphrates. Chicago: University of Chicago Press.

Adams, R.McC. (1996) Paths of Fire: An Anthropologist's Inquiry into Western Technology. Princeton: Princeton University Press.

Kraeling, C.H., and Adams, R.McC. (1958) City Invincible. Chicago: University of Chicago Press.

Aerial Photography for Archaeology

An airborne method of archaeological survey for discovering new sites and monitoring the condition of known sites and landscapes. Aerial photography is a nondestructive technique that has been used in Britain and Europe since the early twentieth century. Aerial photographs can provide information on early prehistoric sites up to the most recent past, including recent industrial archaeological sites.

Development of Aerial Photography

The history of archaeological aerial photography has been covered extensively by a number of authors, especially Leo Deuel's *Flights into Yesterday* and David R. Wilson's *Air Photo Interpretation for Archaeologists*. The earliest aerial photographs were taken from balloons. Not surprisingly, one of the first-ever aerial photographs for archaeology was of Stonehenge, England, taken from a balloon in 1906. The development of flying, aircraft, and photography during and after the First World War (1914–1918) provided the platform from which aerial survey for archaeology could be launched. Without the foresight and understanding of one man, Osbert G.S. Crawford, the subject would not have developed so successfully. His early papers paved the way for the seminal work *Wessex from the Air,* which he coauthored with Alexander Keiller in 1928, and his professional papers *Air Survey and Archaeology* and *Air Photography for Archaeologists* are standard texts.

Perhaps the first use of aerial photographs (for military purposes) was in the American Civil War when, in 1862, the Union Army used photographs to delineate woods, swamps, and rivers. For peaceful purposes, the first useful aerial photographs were taken in 1913 by the Italians of Benghazi town and its surrounding landscape in Libya. With the beginning of the First World War, cameras and airplanes speeded up the development of aerial photography and the skills required for interpreting them. Between the two World Wars, the use of aerial photography spanned the world. In 1920, articles in the journal *Nature* drew attention to the potential of aerial photography for archaeology, botany, geography, geology, and meteorology.

Two outstanding early archaeological contributions were made by Anton Poidebard and Jean Baradez. Poidebard, a Jesuit priest, surveyed and photographed in the Middle East in the 1920s and 1930s, with superb results in helping understand the Roman occupation of what is now Syria. Jean Lucien Baradez worked in North Africa in the 1940s, also tracing the Romans and finding the southern extent of their empire.

In the years leading up to the Second World War (1939–1945), Crawford and a number of colleagues developed the technique of aerial photography and combined it with fieldwork. The results of this work were published in the archaeological quarterly *Antiquity,* whose founder and editor was Crawford himself. Despite the worldwide spread and simultaneous development of the techniques of aerial photography, it was only in Britain (and later mainland Europe) that the archaeological potential was realized. This is due partly to the nature of the landscape and its archaeology and the ability of the soils to produce excellent cropmarks, and partly to availability of aircraft, relatively free airspace, and a military establishment that encouraged archaeological discoveries. Crawford was an observer in the Royal Flying Corps (later the Royal Air Force) before taking up his post as archaeological officer with the Ordnance Survey in 1920.

During the Second World War, a number of leading scientists (archaeologists, geologists, and geographers) were employed in air-photograph interpretation, and this undoubtedly helped the postwar development of aerial photography.

In 1949, the Cambridge University Committee for Aerial Photography (CUCAP) began aerial surveys in Britain and Europe for a variety of purposes, one of which was archaeology. Cropmarked landscapes were recorded in the gravel areas of Britain by J. Kenneth S. St. Joseph and a number of individual pilot-photographers (Derrick Riley, Arnold Baker, and Jim Pickering). The massive rebuilding program and urban expansion in the late 1940s through the 1950s threatened to remove many of the archaeological sites whose existence had become known by aerial photography. The publication in 1960 of *A Matter of Time* (by the Royal Commis-

sion on the Historical Monuments of England) made the very extensive threat of gravel extraction to buried archaeological sites explicit and showed the potential of aerial photography for discovering more sites.

Apart from discovering new cropmarked sites, aerial photography was also instrumental in helping the beginnings of the new discipline of medieval archaeology. Through aerial photography, large areas of earthwork (ridge-and-furrow) field systems and medieval villages were recorded.

After the Second World War, the development of aerial photography for archaeology (in England) to the present day can be divided into three parts:

First, the Cambridge University Committee for Aerial Photography (CUCAP) was created in 1949, a year after the curatorship in aerial photography had been established; some reconnaissance had taken place since 1945 from Cambridge. The committee is still active in aerial survey, especially vertical surveys, and holds a collection of more than 400,000 prints.

Second, the Air Photographs Unit within the Royal Commission on the Historical Monuments of England (RCHME) was established in 1965. The RCHME started the Air Photographs Unit to build a comprehensive record of field monuments throughout England. Initially, this was a collection of the regional and locally based aerial photographers' work but soon came to include the results of the RCHME's own work; this collection holds ca. 750,000 prints. It also holds the collection of vertical photographs that resulted from the postwar survey by the Royal Air Force (RAF) and collections from commercial companies. The Royal Commissions for Scotland and Wales also carry out their own programs of aerial reconnaissance and maintain their own libraries of aerial photographs in the National Monuments Record for Scotland (NMRS) and the NMR for Wales (RCAHMW).

Third, the regional-based aerial photographers, often referred to as the *regional flyers,* received government funds for the first time in 1975. By 1993–1994, the funding had increased in England to £25,000, in Scotland to ca. £4,500, and in Wales to £14,000. Until 1975, all of the costs of flying were borne by the flyers themselves; the dry summers of 1975 and 1976 ushered in a new era after the Council for British Archaeology (CBA) formed an Aerial Archaeology Research Committee, which pressed for government funds to be made available for aerial photography.

From this very brief historical sketch, the current organization of aerial photography in Britain can be seen as a result of piecemeal development. Elsewhere in Europe, there are similar stories of a few pioneers (in Italy, John Bradford; in France, Roger Agache; and in Germany, Otto Braasch) whose work has led to closer integration of aerial photography and other archaeological techniques.

Aerial Photographic Process
There are three major elements of aerial photography for archaeology, sometimes known as aerial archaeology, which have to be understood:

1. Archaeological survey using cameras and an airplane is often referred to as *aerial reconnaissance*. This involves not only taking photographs, but also surveying areas from the air on a regular basis, looking for new sites. It includes photographing historic buildings and monitoring known archaeological sites for new information, as well as inspecting their condition.
2. Cataloging and maintaining libraries of negatives and prints is essential for their long-term curation and ease of retrieval. Computerized retrieval systems are becoming the standard method for swift access in locating vertical and oblique photographs.
3. Interpretation and mapping from aerial photographs, which can be at a variety of scales from distribution maps through manual transcription at 1:10,000 scale to detailed computer-aided mapping at 1:2,500 or larger scales. This is imperative if the information on the photography is to be understood for preservation purposes, as well as research into the history of the landscape.

Crop and Soil Marks
One common misconception is that aerial photography for archaeology is synonymous with crop and soil marks; although these play an important role in any archaeological study, they are only one part. Photographing earthworks, industrial archaeological sites, and buildings is equally important.

The formation of crop and soil marks can be briefly explained. Whenever the subsoil or bedrock has been cut into, there is the possibility of crop or soil marks being formed. For example, a ditch cut into bedrock will fill up with material that has different characteristics from the surrounding bedrock. This difference can manifest itself when the land above the ditch has been ploughed and sown with a crop; the ditch is likely to retain more water and more nutrients than the bedrock through which it has been cut. In dryer years, the crops above the ditch grow taller because their roots can obtain more water and nutrients for stronger growth. As they are growing longer and taller, they ripen later than the surrounding crop and are darker for longer. This color (and height) difference is clearly visible from the air, especially in the summer months (Figure 1). With soil marks, the main difference is one of color; soil marks are normally seen during the autumn, winter, and spring months and show the level of destruction by the plough. When the fields are being ploughed, the difference in color between that which has been filled up with organic matter and the bare soil is clearly visible. A full explanation of the formation of crop marks and soil marks, as well as the pitfalls of interpreting these marks, is well covered in Wilson's *Air Photo Interpretation for Archaeologists*. The crop and soil marks that reveal sites are not visible every year; their visibility depends on the nature of the crop, the temperature and weather conditions, and the time of year of the photographic surveys.

Shadow Sites
Many sites are visible as humps and bumps in fields but are not readily recognizable as a coherent pattern, perhaps revealing an ancient settlement of prehistoric or medieval date or the spoil heaps of industry. Aerial photographs taken at the right time of the day (and year) with a low light can highlight these features in relief and make their pattern recognizable. In the winter in Britain, the sun is sufficiently low, even at midday, to provide very good results (Figure 2). The advantage of winter flying is that the vegetation is also low. Evening photography in spring, summer, and autumn can also produce good results in grassland and moorland areas.

A

Figure 1. Aerial photograph taken July 3, 1990, at Standlake, Oxfordshire, England. A good range of archaeological subjects can be seen in this photograph, with the village at the top and the earthworks remains of medieval and later features below the village and to the right. The cropmarks are probably showing the remains of prehistoric and Romano-British settlements (middle). At the bottom of the picture the gravel extraction can be clearly seen, and it is the threat of this quarrying that is destroying much of Europe's archaeological resources. Royal Commission on the Historical Monuments of England, by permission.

Techniques

There are two basic types of aerial photography, vertical and oblique.

Vertical photographs are used by practitioners in a variety of disciplines, including archaeologists, geographers, soil scientists, planners, and engineers. Taking vertical photographs is, however, a highly specialized and relatively expensive technique carried out by military institutions or commercial companies, utilizing purpose-built cameras and specially adapted aircraft. Vertical photographs are generally taken in rows to allow them to be viewed stereoscopically. Viewing the photographs through a stereoscope allows the images to take on a three-dimensional effect that aids interpretation and can allow measurements of length and height to be made.

Oblique photography is usually done using hand-held cameras, from high-wing aircraft, such as a Cessna 150/152 (two-seater) or 172 (four-seater) and is much more accessible to the archaeologist. This type of photography, taken through an open window with medium-format cameras (using 120, 220, or 70 mm films) or 35 mm SLR cameras, accounts for the majority of oblique photography for archaeology. Some photographs have

Figure 2. Aerial photograph taken January 16, 1991, at Penhill, North Yorkshire, England. The black curvilinear lines are the stone walls of a prehistoric settlement. The smaller circles are the stone walls of the hut circles within the larger enclosures. A light covering of snow has helped highlight the walls. Royal Commission on the Historical Monuments of England, by permission.

been taken as stereoscopic pairs, which allows for more confident interpretations of crop and soil marks. Traditionally, photography has been on black-and-white film (using Ilford FP4 and FP3 [70 mm], Kodak Pan-X, TMAX, and Technopan), but more color photography (using slide film, as well as some color-print films) is now being taken. A small amount of false-color infrared film is used, but the difficulties in handling this sort of film outweigh the information gained. Oblique photography forms part of annual aerial archaeological surveys throughout the United Kingdom (and indeed much of Europe). More than 500 hours of flying are carried out in Britain alone each year. On average, this can yield ca. 1500–2,000 new archaeological sites or additional information on known sites each year.

Undertaking Archaeological Aerial Surveys

Before embarking on any aerial survey, there are a number of legal and practical points that have to be observed. The legality of using a particular aircraft and pilot has to be established. This will vary from country to country, and proper permissions must be obtained before surveys can begin.

Preparation for a flight or a series of flights is essential. Apart from making sure the conditions are right for a particular sortie, it is necessary to have correct in-flight maps marked with the targets and areas to be surveyed. In Britain, the most useful maps in the air is the Ordnance Survey 1:50,000-scale series (available for the whole country). Global positioning systems (GPS) are within the price range of most pilots and are proving immensely useful for locating sites and planning flights. A GPS instrument records the exact location of the aircraft by receiving signals from at least four satellites, and it can record continuously the path of a flight. This reduces the in-flight workload, and the instrument can also be used to plan the route of the flight from target to target.

Having the correct equipment is also essential. Although one person can use only one camera at a time, it is recommended that there should always be at least three cameras in the aircraft: one for color films, one for panchromatic films, and one spare. The size and type of camera depends on the budget of the survey, but it is a minimum requirement to use the best 35 mm SLR cameras with shutter priority facility. This will enable photographs to be taken at 1/500th of a second to minimize camera shake. Yellow filters to reduce haze on panchromatic film and UV filters for color film are used as a standard. Medium-format cameras are often used and, where possible, should be part of the standard equipment. The use of 70 mm film helps in the air as each magazine can take up to 100 frames, and this reduces the number of film changes in the air; 70 mm film is, however, harder to process.

Communicating in the air with the pilot and between the operators of the cameras (if there is more than one) is also very important. Headsets with microphones help in this way and reduce the noise from the aircraft's engine.

Aerial Photographic Libraries

There are three main sources of aerial photographs for archaeology in Britain: (1) national (specialist) collections, which are primarily the libraries held by the three national organizations for England (RCHME), Scotland (RCAHMS), and Wales (RCAHMW), and the Cambridge University Collection (CUCAP); (2) local or regional collections, which include counties and commercial companies; and (3) private collections which contain a variety of color slides and prints and black-and-white prints. Access to private collections and the quality of the photography are variable.

The National Association of Aerial Photographic Libraries has produced a directory of more than 360 libraries or sources of aerial photographs; the contact address is listed below. Coordination of collections and knowing which photographs are available is important if the full potential of archaeological air-photograph interpretation is to be realized.

Throughout the world, there are many different organizations that either take aerial photographs or maintain libraries of these photographs. Depending on the sensitivity of the area and the attitude of the different governments and military organizations, aerial photographs are available in many countries. In Europe, especially in the former Eastern-bloc countries, aerial photography is becoming a valuable aid to archaeological survey. In the United States, the use of vertical photography and satellite images has been greater than specialist oblique aerial photography; the potential for the latter could be explored more in the American continent.

The Purpose of Aerial Survey

Taking and curating aerial photographs are only part of the process of aerial survey. As part of archaeological survey, the benefits of aerial surveying include its extensive coverage, its cost effectiveness, and its landscape approach to the study of archaeological sites. Its main contribution to archaeology has been the discovery of sites and landscapes. It is being used more and more for recording the condition of sites and buildings. Without an analytical phase in the process of aerial archaeology, the information would remain in libraries; the analytical phase is the interpretation and mapping from the photographs.

Interpretation and Mapping

It is important to understand that there has to be an interpretative process by which the information from an aerial photograph is made into an archaeological record.

In all mapping and photogrammetry, the skill is not just in the technical mapping but in the archaeological knowledge required to interpret the features seen on the aerial photographs. This knowledge has certain fundamental principles, but the detailed knowledge required will vary from country to country.

The techniques of mapping fall into two categories, manual and computer aided, and all can be categorized as *photogrammetry* (the art of surveying from photographs), which is a separate subject in itself. The manual methods are less accurate, especially when using oblique photographs, but they are useful in understanding how the process of correcting the distortion of the photograph is achieved. The principal manual methods are paper strip, radial line, and Mobius network; all fulfill the same function in transforming the oblique image to a plan view.

Computer-aided methods are more accurate and can be more efficient. The cost of obtaining the necessary hardware and software is within the budgets of most survey teams.

Satellite Imagery

The use of satellite imagery is now part of archaeological research, and, as the images become more available and cheaper, their particular advantages—they are multispectral and are taken all year round—may assist in discovering and monitoring sites. The trials that have been undertaken so far (as of 1998) show that satellite images can detect larger archaeological features (e.g., the Car Dyke, a Roman canal in eastern England). Parts of the canal, which were not visible by conventional aerial photography, were just visible using enhanced satellite images. In the United States, satellite imagery has been used more extensively than elsewhere. The contribution from satellite images and other multispectral images has been to complement the information from archaeological photographs by revealing the nature of the underlying geology and soils.

Limitations

Aerial photography has its limitations; despite providing information about the location, shape, and form of sites, the information it produces needs further investigation. Through aerial photography alone, sites cannot be dated (except by comparison with similar or identical sites, as in the case of Roman military sites). As a technique within archaeological survey, it is only one tool, albeit a powerful one. The integration of information on computers from a number of sources, including aerial photography, is becoming possible with the development of geographical information systems (GIS). As these systems develop, the mapped information can be viewed alongside the information from other surveys and excavations in one single computerized development, rather than having to collate all of the paper maps and photographs for each survey. Being able to combine textual records with images (the original photograph and the map) will improve the archaeologist's ability to communicate the history of the landscape.

Contact Addresses

AARG. Aerial Archaeology Research Group. This group meets annually to discuss the techniques, discoveries, and all matters concerning aerial photography for archaeology. It has no permanent address as its officers rotate; for further information, write to the author at the RCHME address below.

APS. Air Photo Services, 21 Gunhild Way, Cambridge, CB1 4QZ. These are independent aerial archaeologists who undertake aerial survey and mapping projects.

CUCAP. The Mond Building, Free School Lane, Cambridge, CB2 3RF. The collection may be visited by members of the public during normal office hours. Photographs cannot be borrowed, but prints can be purchased; orders ordinarily take about a month.

Library of Congress, Washington D.C. The library holds numerous aerial photographs, including shots taken in the Second World War by the German Luftwaffe in England and Europe and by the United States Air Force in China and other countries.

NAPLIB. National Association of Aerial Photographic Libraries. (c/o National Monuments Record Centre, Swindon)

NMRAP. National Monuments Record Air Photographs. RCHME, NMRC, Kemble Drive, Swindon, SN2 2GZ. This is a branch of the National Monuments Record for England. Photographs can be consulted by prior arrangement. An express service can be provided for urgent requests.

RCAHMS. The Royal Commission on the Ancient and Historical Monuments of Scotland. John Sinclair House, 16 Bernard Terrace, Edinburgh, EH8 9NX. This is the national body of survey and record for Scotland.

RCAHMW. The Royal Commission on the Ancient and Historical Monuments of Wales. Crown Buildings, Plas Crug, Aberystwyth, Dyfed, SY23 2HP. This is the national body of survey and record for Wales.

RCHME. The Royal Commission on the Historical Monuments of England. RCHME, NMRC, Kemble Drive, Swindon, SN2 2GZ. This is the national body for survey and record in England to be amalgamated with English Heritage in 1999/2000.

United States Department of Commerce, National Technical Information Service, 5285 Port Royal Road, Springfield, VA 22161. Information about publications relating to remote sensing can be obtained from this service.

Robert H. Bewley

See also CRAWFORD, OSBERT G.S.; GEOGRAPHIC INFORMATION SYSTEMS; PHOTOGRAMMETRY; PHOTOGRAPHY, ARCHEOLOGICAL; ST. JOSEPH, J. KENNETH S.

Further Readings

Avery, T.E., and Lyons, T.R. (1981) Remote Sensing: Aerial and Terrestrial Photography for Archeologists. Washington, D.C.: Cultural Resources Management Division, National Park Service.

Baradez, J.L. (1949) Vue-aérienne de l'organisation romaine dans le Sud-Algérien: Fossatum Africae. Paris: Arts et métier graphiques.

Beresford, M., and St. Joseph, J.K.S. (1977) Medieval England. An Aerial Survey. Cambridge: Cambridge University Press.

Bradford, J.S.P (1957) Ancient Landscapes. London: Bell.

Crawford, O.G.S. (1928) Air Survey and Archaeology. Gt. Brit. Ordnance Survey. Professional Papers. New Series no. 7, 2nd ed. Southampton: Ordnance Survey.

Crawford, O.G.S., and Keiller, A. (1928) Wessex from the Air. Oxford: Clarendon.

Deuel, L. (1971) Flights into Yesterday: The Story of Aerial Archaeology. London: Macdonald.

Ebert, J.I. et al. (1980) Remote sensing in large scale cultural resources survey: a case study from the Arctic. In T.R. Lyons and F.J. Mathien (eds): Cultural Resources Remote Sensing, 7–54. Washington, D.C.: Cultural Resources Management Division, National Park Service.

Hampton, J.N. and Palmer, R. (1977) Implications of aerial photography for archaeology. Archaeological Journal 134: 157–193.

Maxwell, G.S., ed. (1983) The Impact of Aerial Reconnaissance on Archaeology (CBA Research Report 49). London: Council for British Archaeology.

St. Joseph, J.K.S. (1966) Uses of Air Photography. London.

Wilson, D.R. (1982) Air Photo Interpretation for Archaeologists. London: Batsford.

Aitken, Martin J. (1922–)

British physicist. Born on March 11, 1922, at Stamford (Lincolnshire), Aitken was educated at Oxford University, where he received his master's and doctorate in physics. After serving as a radar officer with the Royal Air Force (RAF) from 1942 to 1946, he returned to England to do research in nuclear physics at Clarendon Laboratories. From 1957 onward, he did scientific work with archaeological materials in his capacity as deputy director of the Research Laboratory for Archaeology and the History of Art at Oxford, where, in 1958, he was a founding editor of the journal *Archaeometry*. In 1983, he was elected a Fellow of the Royal Society of London, one of Britain's highest scholarly honors. Aitken became professor of archaeometry in 1985, and, although he retired from active laboratory work in 1991, he maintains close links with dating researchers throughout the world. In 1992, Aitken received the Gemant Award from the American Institute of Physics for pioneering the application of physics to archaeology and art history, especially for the development of the use of thermoluminescence and remanent magnetism for dating. In 1997, the Archaeological Institute of America awarded Aitken the Pomerance Science Medal for his scientific contributions to archaeology.

Aitken is known as a leader in the field of archaeometry, which uses scientific techniques from the field of physics to analyze archaeological materials, particularly in regard to dating (chronology). He helped make the term current with the journal *Archaeometry,* now the leading forum for research into physical-scientific methods in archaeology. Aitken's *Physics in Archaeology* became a standard textbook outlining the uses of archaeometric methods. In *Thermoluminescence Dating,* Aitken outlined advances and applications of the thermoluminescence-dating technique, which he had pioneered in the 1960s at his Oxford laboratory parallel with research into the use, for dating, of the weak magnetization acquired at firing by pottery kilns and ceramics. Earlier, he had developed the now widely used magnetic technique for detection of buried archaeological remains. Subsequently, his main research focus was in the newer luminescence technique of optical dating. Concurrent with his active research, he maintained a general interest in other chronological techniques, culminating in 1990 with the publication of *Science-Based Dating in Archaeology.*

Joseph J. Basile

See also LUMINESCENCE DATING; OPTICAL DATING; THERMOLUMINESCENCE DATING

Further Readings

Aitken, M.J. (1974) Physics and Archaeology, 2nd ed. Oxford: Clarendon Press.

Aitken, M.J. (1985) Thermoluminescence Dating. London/Orlando: Academic.

Aitken, M.J. (1990) Science-based Dating in Archaeology. London/New York: Longman.

Aitken, M.J. (1998) Introduction to Optical Dating. Oxford: Oxford University Press.

Taylor, R.E. and Aitken, M.J., eds. (1997) Chronometric Dating in Archaeology. New York: Plenum.

Amber, Characterization

Specifically, the common name of the fossil resin succinite, which originated in the Early Tertiary and is found only in northern Europe, but broadly used to mean any fossil resin of any age and geographical origin. Amber has fascinated the human mind since early prehistoric times by its extraordinary combination of properties. The puzzling fact that it is a "stone" that burns gave rise to the common names Brennstein, Bernstein, and Bärnsten in the Germanic languages. Because of its golden yellow radiance, the ancient Greeks held it sacred to the sun god Apollo. And its astonishing ability, after it has been rubbed, to attract light objects caused Thales of Miletus (ca. 600 B.C.) to imbue it, as well as the magnet stone, with a soul. This phenomenon is now understood as static electricity, a word derived from the Greek name *elektron* for amber.

As a material of beauty and mystery, amber was highly prized, especially in countries where it does not occur naturally. In the first century of our era, the Roman writer Pliny the Elder complained that the price of a small amber statuette equaled that of a live slave. Although amber deposits in Sicily had been known for centuries, the amber of the north of Europe so dominated the thinking of archaeologists well into the nineteenth century that all finds of fossil resins made in archaeological contexts in southern Europe were universally and uncritically accepted as evidence of importation from the north. There were extensive studies of the "amber trade" along the "amber routes," in which finds of "amber" in Mediterranean countries were matched by finds in northern Europe of bronze objects, coins, and ceramics of southern manufacture to document a prehistoric exchange system.

In the course of the nineteenth century, geologists and mineralogists discovered numerous fossil resins in virtually every European (as well as many non-European) countries. These were named as "ambers" of their place of origin in addition to being given mineralogical names (in parentheses): Romanian amber (rumänite or roumanite), Moravian amber (walchowite or valchovite), Austrian amber (schraufite and jaulingite), Swiss amber (allingite and plaffeïïte), Burmese amber (burmite or birmite), and many more. By 1875, nearly 100 distinct fossil resins had been named. The original amber of northern Europe had to be distinguished from these new resins by calling it Baltic amber, although its range of natural occurrence is much broader than that name suggests, because geological events during and after the Ice Ages had spread it across much of northern Europe from the east coast of England, the eastern part of Holland, northern Germany, all of Poland, and much of European Russia. Nevertheless, there remained a categorical distinction between the "true" amber of the north and the other European fossil resins. Inevitably, a southern European, the Italian mineralogist Giovanni Capellini, raised the issue that prehistoric "amber" finds in southern Europe may not invariably have been imports from the north but may have been fashioned from locally available raw materials. Not surprisingly, this notion was strongly opposed by Scandinavian and German archaeologists. It is to his credit that Heinrich Schliemann, on finding thousands of "amber" beads in 1876 of Mycenae, open-mindedly allowed that these might either be northern imports or derive from a more proximate source, such as Sicily.

The problem of amber provenance was taken up during the last quarter of the nineteenth century by the Danzig apothecary Otto Helm. His work constitutes one of the early and important chapters in archaeometry but is instructive more for its failures than for its successes. Helm used the long-established presence of from 3 to 8 percent succinic acid in Baltic amber as a criterion for its identification. To weigh the acid liberated by dry distillation, he had to destroy as much as a gram of amber. When he found that several non-Baltic ambers also produced comparable amounts of succinic acid, he fell back upon subjective criteria of appearance to maintain the validity of his method of distinguishing Baltic from non-Baltic amber and to conclude that Schliemann's amber finds from Mycenae are of Baltic succinite. Some of Helm's identifications are correct, but the method itself is unreliable. Its application was further limited by the large sample requirement that consumed much, or even all, of an artifact.

The provenance determination of archaeological amber artifacts lay fallow until modern methods of instrumental analysis permitted the rapid testing of large numbers of very small samples. In the early 1960s, it was found that infrared (IR) spectroscopy can be used to produce spectra from one to two milligrams of a fossil resin that yield significant structural information but can also be used purely empirically as "fingerprints" to distinguish the various types of ambers. Baltic amber produces a highly characteristic spectrum, the most salient feature of which is a single absorption near $1,160$ cm^{-1} that is preceded by a broad range of constant absorption, often called the *Baltic shoulder;* a second characteristic band lies at 890 cm^{-1}. The latter, which can be assigned to carbon-carbon double bonds attached to a cyclic structure, gave the first evidence that a long-held view according to which Baltic amber was formed by pine trees ca. twenty-five to forty million years ago cannot be correct: The presence of this band decisively eliminates the genus *Pinus* and points to the related but distinct genera *Araucaria* and *Agathis*. The Baltic shoulder is the key to the distinction between Baltic and non-Baltic amber: It is found in all reference samples of Baltic amber but not in any of more than 1,000 reference samples of non-Baltic European ambers (its presence in some North American ambers is palaeobotanically interesting but archaeologically irrelevant). If the depositional history of an amber artifact has permitted access of atmospheric oxygen, as in the megalithic passage graves of northern Europe or in the Etruscan chamber tombs of Italy, the ideally perfectly horizontal shoulder of Baltic amber assumes an increasingly negative slope, and the exocyclic double-bond absorption decreases in intensity, but the spectrum still permits the unequivocal identification of Baltic amber in all but a very few finds that are weathered beyond recognition. The classification of the spectra can be carried out rapidly and objectively by a computer program using pattern-recognition techniques.

Provenance analysis by infrared spectroscopy has been applied to well more than 5,000 archaeological amber artifacts. The vast majority of these, including almost all of the amber finds from Bronze Age Greece and Hungary and from Bronze and Iron Age Italy and Switzerland, have been identified as Baltic amber. Importation of Baltic amber as early as the Neolithic has been documented at Charavines (Isère) in France and even in the Late Palaeolithic at Moosbühl (Bern) in Switzerland. On the other hand, some presumed "amber" artifacts from the Palaeolithic finds in the Cave of Aurensan in the Pyrenees, long thought of as imports, are, in fact, of local origin. A pendant from a protoimperial grave (ca. 2500–2400 B.C.) at Eshnunna (Tell Asmar), Iraq, is neither of amber nor of any other fossil resin but of geologically recent copal from East Africa, while a fragmentary ring bead from Tepe Marlik, Iran, of ca. 900 B.C., is, indeed, of imported Baltic amber. Magdalenian "amber" finds of the Grotte Gazel (Aude) in France are actually inorganic apatite, possibly derived from mineralized bone. The use of Sicilian amber in early Mediterranean cultures is attested in the Eneolithic necropolis of Laterza in southern Italy and in a Mycenaean *tholos* near Pylos on the Peloponnese in Greece.

Other instrumental methods of analysis have been used not only to source archaeological amber artifacts empirically, but also to address more fundamental and related questions about the chemical structure and botanical origin of fossil resins. Mass spectroscopy is attractive because of its very small sample requirement. Mass spectra of whole fossil resins do yield "fingerprints" that distinguish between some geographical sources, but, because these spectra are a superimposition of hundreds of fragments from each of more than a hundred components of the sample, their structural interpretation is very difficult and requires great caution. Gas chromatography (GC) has the advantage of separating the components for individual identification but is, by its nature, limited to soluble components, which rarely account for more than 20 percent of the whole resin. The combination of gas chromatography with mass spectrometry (GC=MS) has proved particularly useful because it first separates the individual components and then produces separate mass spectra for each of them, allowing more reliable identification of the components. This technique has played a decisive role in confirming the nonpinaceous botanical origin of Baltic amber. Pyrolysis gas chromatography (Py-GC) and pyrolysis gas chromatography–mass spectrometry (Py-GC-MS) have made important contributions. Their principal advantage is that they can furnish structural information about the major, polymeric constituents of a fossil resin. By exposure to high temperatures, these insoluble and nonvolatile macromolecules are broken down into smaller and, hence, volatile compounds, which are then separated by gas chromatography and lastly identified by either their retention times (Py-GC) or their mass spectra (Py-GC-MS). While both techniques destroy the sample studied, the sample requirements, in the order of a fraction of a milligram, are negligible. Pyrolysis methods have been applied to problems of provenance and structure of a variety fossil, semifossil, and recent resins and have also been effectively used to identify amber imitations and forgeries.

The important contribution of solid-state carbon-13 nuclear magnetic resonance (NMR) spectrometry to the study of amber is discussed in the entry on NMR. As a means of ascertaining the provenance of amber artifacts, NMR has the disadvantage over the other analytical methods mentioned of requiring a rather large sample of 30–100 mg of powdered resin; however, the sample is not chemically altered or destroyed and remains available for other work. Ultraviolet reflectance spectroscopy, differential thermal analysis (DTA), and thermogravimetric analysis (TGA) all have been used to characterize fossil as well as recent resins. Nondestructive approaches such as photothermal beam deflection (PBD) spectroscopy, and measurements of physical properties such as acoustical absorption, dielectric loss, internal friction, and mechanical damping, have also been explored. Some methods may give misleading results. Thus, the soluble portions of Iron Age amber finds from Slovenia yielded thin-layer chromatograms (TLC) so different from those of Baltic amber that the artifacts were thought to be geologically recent local pine rosin. However, the infrared spectra of the same artifacts showed them to be of imported Baltic amber sufficiently weathered to contain many more soluble components than the unweathered reference samples and, therefore, giving many more spots on the TLC. Similarly, quantitative analyses for trace metals by optical emission spectroscopy (OES) and by neutron activation analysis (NAA) have shown differences between geographically distinct amber deposits. This is not likely to be useful for the provenance analysis of amber artifacts because metal ions are readily exchanged between amber and the surrounding matrix, and the trace-metal profile will reflect the soil composition of its most recent burial rather than of its geographic origin.

Curt W. Beck

See also INFRARED (IR) SPECTROSCOPY; NUCLEAR MAGNETIC RESONANCE (NMR) SPECTROSCOPY

Further Readings

Beck, C.W. (1986) Spectroscopic investigations of amber. Applied Spectroscopy Reviews 22(1):57–110.

Beck, C.W., and Shennan, S.J. (1991) Amber in Prehistoric Britain. Oxford: Oxbow.

Fraquet, H. (1987) Amber. London: Butterworths.

Mills, J.S., White, R., and Gough, L.J. (1984–1985) The chemical composition of Baltic amber. Chemical Geology 47:15–39.

Price, P.C. (1980) Amber: The Golden Gem of the Ages. New York: Van Nostrand.

Amino Acid Racemization/Epimerization Dating

A dating method for archaeological and geological material that uses the rate of conversion of an amino acid to its mirror image as an estimate of the passing of time. Since amino acids are the building blocks of proteins, the method can be applied only to archaeological materials that still contain indigenous proteins.

Principles

Residual protein is common in many excavated parts, such as tooth, bone, or shell, and in similar fossilized material. Its changes with time are consequently useful. Proteins are polymers of natural amino acids. The amino acid residues are linked together through peptide bonds, as in Figure 1.

With time, all of the protein originally in the live creature degrades in one way or

A

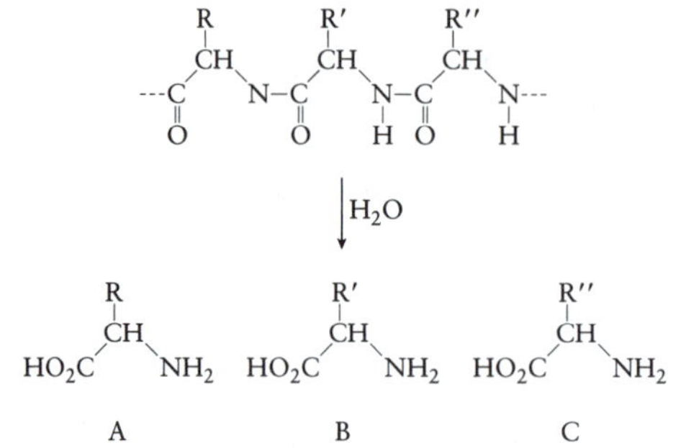

Figure 1. Protein degradation through hydrolysis. Figure by Robert D. Gillard.

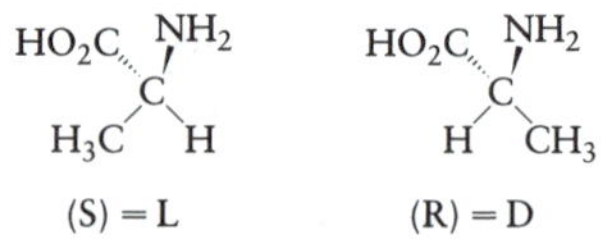

Figure 2b. Enantiomers of alanine. Figure by Robert D. Gillard.

another (e.g., by chemical or microbial action), but chief is its reaction with water. This hydrolysis cleaves the peptide bonds, giving smaller fragments of proteins and, eventually, amino acids. In archaeological time scales, such hydrolysis (and other degradation mechanisms) is quite commonly slow enough to leave residual intact protein, which is the source for dating work. The properties of the constituent amino acids are used in that work, and the first requirement is to hydrolyze the protein (as in Figure 1, but under controlled laboratory conditions).

The feature of the natural amino acids most readily used stems from their molecular shapes. In Figure 1, the letters R, R′, R″ denote simple groups such as methyl (CH_3). For example, if R is hydrogen, then the amino acid A in Figure 1 would be glycine, a common constituent of proteins. Its shape is shown in Figure 2a. Notice that the drawing of A (in Figure 1) has been reoriented.

The substituted natural amino acids may be represented as in Figure 2b, where R = CH_3.

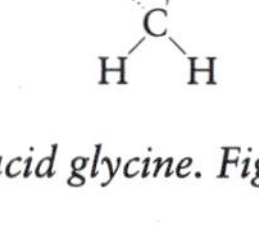

Figure 2a. Amino acid glycine. Figure by Robert D. Gillard.

This is alanine. There are two forms of alanine, as shown. In one, keeping the NH_2 group forward, the methyl group is to the left. In the other, the methyl group is to the right. These are like an object and its mirror image, so are called *enantiomers* (or optical isomers). Enantiomers are distinguished from each other by the prefix R or S. These newer terms have generally superseded the older D and L notation.

In living systems, with very rare exceptions, only one enantiomer—the S type—is found, and living cells have evolved elaborate mechanisms for keeping the "wrong" enantiomer out of protein. After death, the process of equalization to the 50:50 mixture of right- and left-handed molecules proceeds unhindered. This conversion of the pure optical isomer to the RS mixture is called *racemization*. The rate of this process follows first-order kinetics, as does the decay of any radionuclide (such as carbon-14). As with ^{14}C, racemization has a defined half-life, but, unlike ^{14}C, the half-life of amino acid racemization depends on temperature, pH, and other variable environmental factors.

Racemization, like any chemical reaction, involves the redistribution of external electrons around the unchanging nuclei of atoms. The electrons are influenced by their total surroundings; any change in their environment will have a direct effect on the rate and mechanism of the reaction. As a result, the half-life of a protein amino acid can be accurately defined only under fixed conditions (constant temperature, unchanged pH, absence of catalysis by metal ions). This is the essential difference between amino acid racemization and the well-established dating methods that depend upon events within the nuclei of atoms (radioactive decay). Fortunately, this constancy for chemical half-lives does occur for many archaeological purposes.

Each amino acid (each different R group of Figure 1) has its own half-life of racemization. Different amino acids will, therefore, be more suited to dating certain periods. Aspartic acid (R = CH_2CO_2H) is the commonly used amino acid as its racemization half-life (5,000–20,000 years, depending on temperature) is most suited to archaeological time spans. In contrast, S-isoleucine/D-alloisoleucine has been used to date geological samples. It has a half-life of 100,000 years, which is effective for dating 10^5–10^6 years ago. This is important as it fills the gap between radiocarbon dating (ending at 7×10^4 years) and potassium-argon dating, which begins at 5×10^5 years ago.

Methods

A typical process is described here. In detail, most of the steps beg questions.

Cleaned excavated material (teeth, bones, and the like) is demineralized, usually using cold acid (HCl) to leave a residue of organic matter that is then deliberately hydrolyzed in acid at raised temperatures for a particular time. With teeth, hydrochloric acid (6M) at 100°C for a few hours works quite well. After removing the acid, the individual amino acids in the product of hydrolysis must be separated. The methodology of amino acid analysis is well developed and most commonly uses ion-exchange chromatography.

The ratio of enantiomers (S/R) is required. Clearly, after one half-life of racemization, this ratio is 1. After one-tenth of a half-life, one twentieth (5 percent) has racemized, so the ratio is 19.

The distinction between S and R amino acids like aspartic acid must rely on an interaction able to pick left from right. On a social scale, we do this by holding hands (a right-left pairing) quite distinct from shaking hands (a right-right pairing in most cultures). In molecular terms, R interacting with S to give RS product is quite different in energy from R interacting with R to give RR product. So, any one-handed molecule will react with an R amino acid to give a product distinct from that with the S amino acid.

A typical discriminating reagent is R-leucine-N-carboxyanhydride (coded as R-leu-NCA here). This reacts quickly (in a few minutes) with aspartic acid at pH 10, to form the RR or the RS dipeptides, as in equations (1) and (2).

R-leu-NCA + R-aspartic acid →
$$\text{R-leu-R-aspartic acid} \qquad (1)$$
R-leu-NCA + S-aspartic acid →
$$\text{R-leu-S-aspartic acid} \qquad (2)$$

The dipeptide of (1) and of (2) have different properties, as do human pairs formed by shaking hands and holding hands. They may very readily be separated by straightforward chromatography (HPLC). Typical retention times for the RR dipeptide from (1) are

about eight minutes and for its RS isomer, the product of (2), about fifteen minutes.

The measurement of the amount of R-aspartic acid from racemization is, consequently, not difficult.

Archaeological Applications

The archaeological applications have been widespread and range from the determination of the age of a mummy from Alaska (where the finding was related to the more familiar morphological conclusions) to the evaluation of postmortem age of preserved mineralized collagen (i.e., tooth and bone) or mollusc shell. These latter applications give a date for the archaeological site.

In the past, most applications related to archaeological bone, simply because it is the most readily available biogenic material in most sites. Since the 1980s, however, racemization studies have concentrated on tooth and shell. The survival of essentially unchanged protein in excavated tooth and shell has been proven repeatedly.

It seems appropriate, while recognizing the many successful applications of aspartic acid racemization to archaeological samples of a wide range, to draw attention to the well-known problems in the method. First, the protein studied should be original. In theory, amino acids with long half-lives (e.g., isoleucine/alloisoleucine) can be used to date samples millions of years old. In practice, however, the technique is limited because, with degradation, there is little primary material left, and the likelihood of contamination is increased.

Biological factors must also be considered. It has been known since the late nineteenth century that exhumed bone manifests diagenetic tunnels. These probably originate from microbial action. It is becoming increasingly clear that many microorganisms are capable of degrading the mineralized protein in dead bone. The protein of bone is *collagen,* and the hydrolysis of its central helical part is promoted by the enzyme *collagenase.* Collagenase is present in a large range of soil and fecal bacteria even at 10°C. Microbiological degradation of this kind will increase the rate of change of archaeological collagen, increasing the rate of production of R-aspartic acid, and so giving an apparently greater postmortem age than the true age. A study by Childs and colleagues (1993) of the R-aspartic acid levels in modern, first premolar teeth gave a calibration curve that differed considerably from that for similar teeth from the Spitalfields excavation in London. The teeth from Spitalfields contained more racemized aspartic acid in the younger samples and less in the older ones. This is almost certainly due to microbial activity postmortem.

Other environmental features leading to increased reactivity of amino acids, including racemization, include the catalytic effect of metal ions. Unfortunately, copper salts are particularly effective in this regard, and for some excavations this is a common contaminant of the soil because of degradation of bronze and similar artifacts in proximity to the biogenic material.

Amino Acid Epimerization for Dating

Until now, the role of aspartic acid has been dominant because of its convenient and useful half-lives of racemization in archaeological contexts. The major cause of variance is almost certainly temperature, and the assumption that temperatures of excavated materials have been relatively constant may need validation. The use of other amino acids will give a much wider range of time scales than is available from aspartic acid, which is at the fast (young) end of the scale.

As a final example, consider the successful application of the change from the natural original L-isoleucine to the unnatural but more stable R-alloisoleucine, as shown in Figure 3.

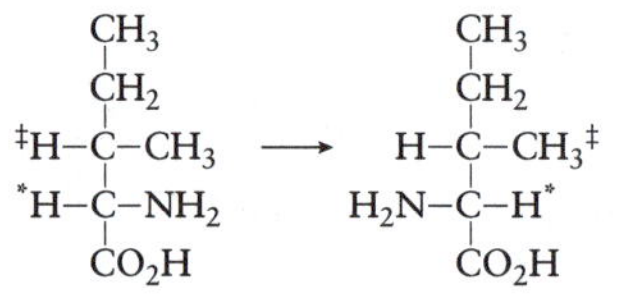

total inversion: the alloisoleucine product is chemically distinct from its isoleucine precursor. The half-life of reaction at burial temperatures (Figure 3) is much longer, so that this change at only one-handed carbon center where others are present (called *epimerization* rather than *racemization*) is chiefly used geochemically. The chief experimental material has been fossil molluscs, but the methodology is essentially as outlined here. The rate of reaction (Figure 3) seems particularly sensitive to temperature. For example, in the freshwater mollusc *Lymnaea peregra,* a rise of 4°C causes the rate of epimerization (Figure 3) to double. The potential utility in archaeology of measurements for amino acids other than aspartic acid is clear, and it is perhaps a pity that studies in that direction have not been well funded.

Among the many underlying questions of a chemical nature that will arise in future extensions of this method is the importance of the differing rates of racemization/epimerization for a particular amino acid in a given protein, depending on its actual detailed position. Here, further model laboratory studies are needed, since the early work in this direction has shown that there is, indeed, considerable variation in half-life.

The method has given excellent results in a variety of contexts, ranging from the forensic to the geological. The archaeological value has been twofold: first, some examples of age at death have been achieved, and, second, sites have been dated by R/S amino acid ratios in excavated bone.

Robert D. Gillard

See also BONE, CHARACTERIZATION; TAPHONOMY

Figure 3. Racemization of isoleucine. Figure by Robert D. Gillard.

Here, the reaction is closely akin to racemization. The α-carbon atom (marked *) bearing the amino and acid groups changes its stereochemical configuration ("handedness") from S to R. However, this particular amino acid has a second carbon atom, marked ‡, like those at * or those in Figure 2b in having four distinct chemical groups attached to it. This atom ‡ is unaffected. Consequently, this is not

Further Readings

Ambrose, S.H. (1990) Effects of diet, climate, and physiology on nitrogen isotope abundances in terrestrial foodwebs. Journal of Archaeological Science 17:431–451.

Bada, J. (1991) Amino acid cosmogeochemistry. Philosophical Transactions of the Royal Society of London B333:349–358.

Child, A.M., Gillard, R.D., and Pollard, A.M. (1993) Microbially induced racemization in archaeological bone: Isolation of the organisms and detection of their enzymes. Journal of Archaeological Science 20:159–168.

Gillard, R.D., Pollard, A.M., Sutton, P.A., and Whittaker, D.K. (1990) An improved method for age at death determination from the measurement of D-aspartic acid in dental collagen. Archaeometry 32:61–70.

Goodfriend, G. (1992) Rapid racemization of aspartic acid in mollusc shells and potential for dating over recent centuries. Nature 357:399.

Hedges, R.E.M., and Wallace, C.J.A. (1980) The survival of protein in bone. In P.E. Hare, T.C. Hoering and K. King (eds.): Biogeochemistry of the Amino Acids, pp. 35–40. New York: Wiley.

Masters, P.M., and Bada, J.L. (1978) Amino acid racemization dating of bone and shell. In G.F. Carter (ed.): Archaeological Chemistry II, pp. 117–138. (Advances in Chemistry Series 171). Washington, D.C.: American Chemical Society.

Masters, P.M., and Zimmerman, M.R. (1978) Age determination of an Alaskan mummy, morphological and biochemical correlation. Science 201:811–812.

Shimoyama, A., and Harada, K. (1984) An age determination of an ancient burial mound by apparent racemization reaction of aspartic acid in tooth dentine. Chemistry Letters 10:1661–1664.

Sykes, G.A. (1988) Amino acids on ice. Chemistry in Britain 24:235–240.

Animal Remains, Identification and Analysis: Fish

The taxonomic identification of fish remains from archaeological sites for the purposes of reconstruction of paleoecology, paleoeconomy, and paleonutrition.

Retrieval and Sampling

The small average size of fish bones makes them likely to be lost during excavations if only hand-collecting is practiced. The inadequacy of crude sampling methods is one of the factors explaining the relatively late development of fish-bone studies when compared to mammal-bone research. Sieving through a fine mesh is necessary to assure the effective recovery of fish remains. A mesh size of 1–2 mm is generally recommended; however, this depends on the type of sediment and the preservation of the bones. The systematic sieving of all the sediment from large-scale excavations can be both practically and financially impossible; in these cases, small samples can be taken within the grid system. This is done in such a way as to obtain a random sample; additional probes can always be taken at special features or structures of the site. The volume of sediment necessary to obtain a representative bone sample depends on the density of the fish bones and their state of preservation. Ineffectively sampled material can be recognized by the high percentage of identifiable bone, the large average size of the remains, and the preponderance of certain skeletal elements, usually belonging to only a few species. The reputed, almost exclusive, dependence of Mesolithic populations in Denmark on pike, as described in the literature of the 1950s, stems from such inadequate sampling. Similarly, the almost exclusive presence of gadids (cod and haddock) at many medieval sites in Europe, is a result of hand-collecting. Other economically important species, such as the herring, with its fragile and often minute bones, were not recovered from those medieval sites.

Identification and Comparative Material

Fish remains are identified according to skeletal element and taxon (family, genus or species). Ideally, the identification also comprises a reconstruction of the body size for the individuals from which each bone originated. The majority of the identifications are carried out by comparisons with modern reference collections. Since dry, disarticulated fish skeletons are rare in museums, many fish-bone workers built up their own collections. Preparation of such reference material usually starts with one specimen of the economically most important species of a given region; however, the collections should ideally comprise the total spectrum of the ichthyofauna. Several specimens of different sizes should be kept for each species, thereby permitting reliable size reconstructions. After procurement of a complete fish and before preparation of its skeleton, the fish has to be correctly identified to species, and measurements should be taken. Classical measurements are the total length, standard length, fork length (distance from tip of snout to the notch of the caudal fin), total weight, and gutted weight. Sex and reproductive state can also be noted. Many techniques of skeletal preparation are known, but, at present, the most favored ones are:

A

maceration, which is a natural process of rotting, achieved by bacterial action and accelerated by elevated temperatures not exceeding 60–70°C; the use of enzymes, such as neutrase, which decompose the flesh; or cooking followed by picking the bones out from the flesh. Dermestid beetles can be useful for obtaining articulated skeletons. Material prepared in such a way is particularly helpful for determining the skeletal position of less diagnostic bones.

Osteological treatises or atlases that depict differences between the bones of certain families or closely related species for individual bones are rare; these publications, in any case, should be used in combination with modern, comparative material. Frontal X-radiographs of vertebrae are often diagnostic for species. However, ordinarily these are only used when the discriminatory power of the general, external morphology of the vertebrae is low or when only small fragments of vertebral centra are available. This technique has been successfully applied to distinguish salmonid species, in cases in which the vertebrae were too heavily fragmented to permit alternative methods of identification.

Size Reconstructions

The reconstructed size of fishes gives valuable information for taphonomical, paleoecological, and paleoeconomic interpretations (see below). The reconstruction of fish size is based on the relationship between the dimensions of an isolated bone and the length of the complete fish. The easiest and quickest of all of the methods described in the literature is that of direct comparison (either visually or by measuring) of the archaeological specimens with skeletal material originating from modern specimens of known size. This procedure can be made more accurate as greater numbers of contemporary specimens, of different lengths, become available. Size classes of 5, 10, or more cm can be defined, depending on the maximum size that a given species can reach during life. Consequently, the number of archaeological specimens falling in each length category can be established. Diagrams that plot individual bone measurements against fish length have been published for a number of skeletal elements of certain species. Regression equations describing this relationship are available for some of these data sets.

The method used for size reconstruction will depend on the numbers of each type of bone available in the studied sample. In small archaeological samples, it is useful to reconstruct body sizes from all well-preserved bones. However, in very large collections, a choice of bones can be made for each species. In the latter case, the most frequently preserved bone of a given species can be measured, and the plotted raw measurements can give good indications of the size groups and, hence, age groups; this can be achieved even without conversion of the data into fish length.

The estimation of fish weight cannot be made with the same accuracy as the reconstruction of fish length. This is due to the fact that fishes with identical lengths may have different weights, depending on the condition of the animal and the development of its gonads.

Taphonomical Processes

These are all the events that take place between the death of an animal and the recovery of its remains as a fossil. In the case of fish, numerous agents can be responsible for the death and initial deposit of an individual. At archaeological sites, humans will usually have been the main cause of death and the principal accumulator, but other piscivorous species may also contribute. Several species of mammals and birds (such as otter, gulls, cormorants) eat fish, and their droppings or regurgitated stomach contents may be deposited at an archaeological site. Comparison with the contents of modern excrements and pellets, as well as analyses of the natural "background counts" of bone fragments found in a small area outside the site, can help recognize such intrusive material or at least help quantify the possible bias this material has on the archaeological results. Natural death of fish in isolated stretches of water that seasonally dry out, or skeletal remains washed ashore, can also contribute to a sample.

Fish that have been captured by humans and selected for consumption can be subjected to many destructive processes that result from processing, preparation of meals, gnawing, and digestion. Discarded food remains will disintegrate further through chemical and physical weathering at the ground surface and as a result of trampling. The remains may completely disappear because of their ingestion or removal by other inhabitants of the site, such as dogs, cats, pigs, rats, or birds.

Therefore, the sooner any fish remains are buried, the better are their chances for preservation. However, destruction can still continue in the sediment by the action of bacteria and fungi and by chemical attack.

Species Diversity

The diversity of species represented at a site gives valuable information on the nature of the exploited waters. The habitat requirements of the representative species can be used to reconstruct the geographical and ecological characters of these waters, including defining the water quality. Although, in many cases, the ancient fish fauna perfectly reflects the modern one near the site, it is possible that differences exist that can be related to either climatic or anthropic (human-induced) influences.

The distribution of fishes changes with climate, a phenomenon that is well illustrated in present-day arid regions such as the Sahara. The global climate was more humid during the first half of the Holocene than at present; this produced dramatically different hydrographic networks compared to those of today. Excavations in the present-day desert in Africa have revealed the presence of broad rivers and extensive lakes, harboring an aquatic fauna with crocodiles, freshwater turtles, hippopotamuses, and fish. The presence of fish in such remote places, far from any permanent water today, has important paleohydrological implications. Fish do not disperse from one body of water to another by means of eggs or larvae attached to birds (e.g., stuck to birds' feet). Therefore, their colonization of new areas must require a water connection with a stretch of permanent water that acted as a refugium during the preceding arid period. Defining these ancient water connections is a matter of geomorphological and cartographic work; however, the composition of the fish fauna may, theoretically, also indicate the refuge area.

Human impact on the aquatic environment (pollution, overfishing, introduction of species) can sometimes be indicated by the fish remains. The archaeological fish faunas often contain species that are no longer present in the waters around the site. Most local extinctions that have occurred in the industrial world since the end of the nineteenth century were probably the result of pollution, construction of channel systems, and drainage works. The gradual disappearance of these species cannot be followed archaeologically because almost no such recent sites have been investigated. However, it is clear that the decline of certain species had started earlier. This is the case for the sturgeon in Western Europe, which had already been heavily overfished in the early Middle Ages, making it a very rare and expensive fish in the following centuries. Evidence of pollution and overfishing at urban sites in late medieval Europe is available both from written sources and from fish remains. It is indicated by the scarcity of remains from freshwater species, their small size, and the massive importation of marine fish. The introduction of domestic carp to western Europe since the thirteenth century was probably in order to compensate for the decline of the native freshwater stock. All other introductions have taken place since the nineteenth century and have not been archaeologically attested.

Fish-Catching Methods

Fish-catching methods can be inferred from fishing gear if such equipment is preserved at a site. Net weights, fishing hooks, and harpoons are the most commonly found fishing gear. However, fishing tools are absent or very rare at most sites, and those that are found undoubtedly represent only a fraction of the techniques used. This is a result of the poor chances of preservation of fishing gear made from perishable plant material (e.g., nets, baskets, traps, weirs). Ethnographic works illustrate the wide range of possible methods of fish capture, as well as the low chances of recovering archaeological evidence for many of them. Nevertheless, the analyses of fish remains themselves can sometimes reveal changes that occur, through time, in fishing technology. These analyses should be based on material from a large number of sites in a given region. The species diversity and the size distribution for the species offer possibilities for detecting such technological changes. A low number of species usually results from an exploitation that is limited in time and space. During the Palaeolithic, people depended heavily on spawning salmonids in the North Atlantic region and on spawning clariid catfish in Northern Africa. Marginal, shallow waters were exploited in both cases. It was only later that there was a drastic increase in the number of species represented in the fish remains. This is related to the development of better fishing equipment and, above all, of rafts or small boats. Subsequently, it was also possible to fish in deeper waters, far from the shore. The development of nets also contributed to the increased number of species caught.

Seasonality

The exploitation of fish is often a seasonal event related to the migrations and spawning behavior of the animals. Therefore, fish remains can be particularly useful for establishing whether a site was permanently or seasonally occupied and for reconstructing the resource scheduling of its inhabitants. Seasonality can be inferred from ecological information on the species occurring at a site, as well as from the analysis of fish growth.

The presence at an inland site of anadromous fish (species living in the sea that enter fresh water to spawn) has been widely used as an indicator of seasonality. Sturgeon and salmonid species are typical examples of fish undertaking long-distance spawning runs during a certain period of the year. When this kind of information is combined with evidence from other animal groups (e.g., presence of migrating birds or of juvenile mammals for which the birth season is well established), the seasonal or permanent nature of a site's occupation can be established. Fish species living permanently in fresh water can sometimes also demonstrate seasonal fishing activities. Indications for such practices are given by the size distribution of the fish. Histograms of reconstructed lengths will show more or less distinct size groups (corresponding to age groups) if fishing is practiced only during a limited season within the year. However, when fishing is conducted over a longer period of the year, such age groups cannot be distinguished within the size distribution.

The different average sizes of specimens of the same species of fish collected from closely related sites (e.g., several neighboring locations within a single, larger area) sometimes indicate different seasons of exploitation. Fishing can be concentrated on the larger, spawning fish during one season and on the smaller, juvenile fish of the same species a few months later. The initial growth of these small fish takes place in shallow, marginal waters at a time when the larger adults have already migrated back to deeper waters.

Variations in temperature and food supply throughout the year can cause growth rings to form in the skeleton of fish. Studies on these seasonal rings in scales, otoliths, vertebrae, and fin spines have a traditional role in the analytical techniques of fisheries and fish culture; they are used to assess fish growth and the age structure of populations. Archaeologically speaking, the age of an individual animal is less important than the season of its death, which corresponds to the moment of capture. Theoretically, the season of death of a fish can be established by the thickness of the last growth zone. Such analyses have been carried out on archaeological specimens relatively infrequently. Scales are usually not suitable because of their fragile nature; their edges, which are essential to the establishment of the season of death, break off easily. Vertebrae have been used most frequently because their growth rings can be analyzed without prior preparation. Fin spines (usually coming from catfishes) need sectioning before observations can be made. This is also the case for otoliths (small calcareous concretions found in the internal ear of fishes). Analysis of growth in vertebrae and fin spines has the disadvantage that there is an error margin of two to three months; this is due to the fact that skeletal growth reacts relatively late to changes in the ambient environment of the fish (i.e., fluctuations in temperature and food supply). Otoliths react instantaneously to external stimuli and, therefore, are better suited to seasonality studies. Season of death can be inferred either from the width of the last growth zone of the otoliths or from their daily ring counts.

Processing of Fish and Trade

Fishing is often a seasonal activity, practiced during periods of great abundance; therefore, preservation for future consumption may be necessary. Sun-drying, salting, smoking, or a combination of these methods can be used, depending on the climate. Archaeological evidence is sometimes found for such practices (e.g., in the form of postholes corresponding to smoking or drying racks, or salting installations for the production of fish sauce). Evidence is also sometimes available from the fish bones, either in the form of cut marks on the bones or from the distribution of the skeletal elements. Data of the latter type should be used with great caution, as has been demonstrated by certain wrong assumptions made in the past. The presence of only vertebrae, and no head bones, from salmonids in European

Palaeolithic sites was initially explained by a scenario involving decapitation of salmons, followed by transport of the more edible parts to the sites. It is now clear that the absence of head bones is due to their low chances of survival, resulting from calcium resorption in the head skeleton during the spawning run of salmon. Similarly, the preponderance of the robust head bones of certain catfishes at African archaeological sites was initially interpreted as the result of decapitation and subsequent removal of the fishes' bodies. In fact, the high ratio of head bones compared to vertebrae is due to the different robustness, hence survival chances, of the respective skeletal elements. Indications of processing of herring in late medieval Europe are available from the skeletal distribution. At several sites, dating from the fifteenth century onward, elements of the pectoral girdle of herring are heavily underrepresented or totally absent, whereas other, more fragile bones occur in large quantities. This phenomenon can be explained as a result of the technique of gutting, involving removal of the gills, stomach, and pectoral girdle with a sharp knife, prior to salting the fish in barrels.

Cut marks are relatively seldom seen on fish bones and occur mainly when metal tools have been used to process large fish. Traces are usually found on bones of the pectoral girdle and on vertebrae and are related to decapitation, splitting, or slicing of the fish.

Processed fish are suitable for long preservation and, hence, can be transported and traded. Salted cod and herring were renowned goods in medieval times in Europe, as was *garum* in classical times. This fish sauce, obtained by fermentation of fatty species, was initially a typical product of the Mediterranean classical world. The Romans exported *garum* to the occupied territories of northwestern Europe. Eventually, this trade became less regular and was replaced by local production along the northern Atlantic coast. Indications for long-distance transport of fish also exist for a few prehistoric sites.

Wim Van Neer

See also ANIMAL REMAINS, QUANTIFICATION; GROWTH STUDIES: FISH OTOLITHS; TAPHONOMY

Further Readings

Brinkhuizen, D.C., and Clason, A.T., eds. (1986) Fish and Archaeology. (BAR International Series 294). Oxford: British Archaeological Reports.
Casteel, R.W. (1976) Fish Remains in Archaeology and Paleo-Environmental Studies. London: Academic.
Colley, S.M. (1990) The analysis and interpretation of archaeological fish remains. In M. B. Schiffer (ed.): Advances in Archaeological Method and Theory, Vol. 2, pp. 207–253. New York: Academic.
Desse-Berset, N., ed. (1984) 2nd Fish Osteoarchaeology Meeting. (Notes et Monographies Techniques 16). Paris: CRA/CNRS.
Rojo, A.L. (1991) Dictionary of Evolutionary Fish Osteology. Boca Raton: CRC.
Van Neer, W., ed. (1994) Fish Exploitation in the Past. Proceedings of the Seventh Meeting of the ICAZ Fish Remains Working Group. (Annales du Musée Royal de l'Afrique Centrale, Sciences Zoologiques 274). Tervuren, Belgium: Musée Royal de l'Afrique Centrale.
Wheeler, A., and Jones, A.K.G. (1989) Fishes. Cambridge: Cambridge University Press.

Animal Remains, Identification and Analysis: Insects

The use of insect remains for reconstructing past environments. Insects may be the most frequently identifiable invertebrate fossils in anaerobic, usually waterlogged, permanently frozen, and wholly arid terrestrial sediments, as well as deposits laid down in aquatic situations. The closely constrained habitat requirements of many species make them an ideal group for the reconstruction of immediate and regional environments.

The term insects encompasses many familiar groups, including the true flies (Diptera), fleas (Siphonaptera), lice (Anoplura), beetles (= American bugs) (Coleoptera), true bugs (Hemiptera), ants and wasps (Hymenoptera), moths and butterflies (Lepidoptera), and caddis flies (Trichoptera), as well as several less familiar groups. All are characterized by a chitinous exoskeleton, of varying potential for survival as a fossil, and six legs in the adult form. All go through varying degrees of metamorphosis between eggs and adult, and, in some groups, it is the larval stage that provides the most useful fossils. The arachnids, the spiders and mites, characterized by having eight legs, are found in the same samples as insects and may be recovered and studied by the same methods.

In nonmarine aquatic situations, other groups of Arthropoda (to which both Insecta and Arachnida belong), Cladocera (water fleas) and Ostracoda (mussel shrimp), may also provide useful evidence as to the nature of the paleoenvironment.

Retrieval and Identification of Insect Remains
Methods of concentration and recovery of insect fossils vary as to the groups being studied and to the nature of the preservation. In the purely archaeological situation, a minimum of 3 liters of each suitable context is normally necessary, although this may vary as to the nature of the sediment. Natural and man-made pitfall situations, such as wells, may contain many thousand identifiable fragments per liter, while coarse-grained waterlogged sediments may contain thinly dispersed specimens. A useful rule of thumb is that, if insect remains are noticed during the normal processes of excavation, then that deposit is likely to yield many individuals when processed in the laboratory. Where the actual archaeological excavation fails to provide suitable anaerobic contexts, contemporary environmental data may be available within the catchment of the site, in peats, lakes, caves, or pack-rat middens, and such should be sought in any integrated archaeological program.

Samples are taken immediately upon exposure of the context to avoid contamination and sealed in polythene bags before shipment back to the laboratory for processing. Where preservation is by charring, (e.g., in burnt-grain deposits), the normal methods of recovery of charred seeds are likely to be damaging to insect remains, and separate sampling will be necessary, although seeds will require examination for evidence of insect attack. All stored produce preserved either by drying or charring is likely to provide evidence of insect infestation, ranging from lice on Peruvian and Inuit mummies, through flies and bacon beetles (Dermestidae) in Egyptian mummies, to bean (Bruchidae) and grain weevils (Curculionidae) in tomb offerings and charred residues. Each sample obtained requires careful disaggregation and sorting before identification can be achieved.

The standard technique for dealing with all samples for the larger remains from peats, organic silts, and archaeological deposits consists of breaking the sample down in a bucket, using hot water and gentle pressure. More compacted sediments may require treatment with sodium carbonate, usually cheap commercial washing soda, to expedite the process, but high concentrations may damage insect cuticle if left for any length of time, and samples are best broken down in frequent changes of soda and hot water. Samples are washed out over a 300 μm sieve, taking care to remove any large items, stones, wood, and artifacts that may damage the insect fossils. In aquatic samples, such a mesh size leads to the loss of identifiable fragments, usually the larval head capsules of aquatic midges (Chironomidae, Ceratopogonidae), black fly (Simuliidae), and mosquitoes (Culicidae), and subsamples of 3–5ml of sediment may be taken for these groups; such a small volume of material may provide up to 1,000 identifiable fragments.

After the large sample has been completely disaggregated and washed of its fine sediment and humic content, it is drained of surplus water on the sieve and returned to the bucket, where kerosene (English paraffin) is added and stirred in sufficiently to wet all of the plant and animal material that has been retained by the sieve. The kerosene adsorbs onto the waxy surface of the insect cuticle, and, when cold water is added gently to the sample, these float, providing a separation of varying quality from the other, largely plant remains. Too much air in the water supply, and much of the plant debris may also float; for the unlucky ones, particularly those faced with *Sphagnum*-rich peats, most of the sample may float, and many hours may be necessary to sort out the insect remains. The flotation is usually repeated three times to recover the bulk of the insect fossils, and it is advisable to sort at least a subsample of the material from the bottom of the bucket to check the efficacy of the flotation process. The float has to be carefully poured off from the bucket onto the 300 μm sieve and washed with liquid soap and hot water and, finally, with ethanol before storing in ethanol.

The concentrate obtained by kerosene (paraffin) flotation will vary considerably both in volume and in frequency of insect remains, and their further selection requires careful sorting under a low-power binocular microscope with fine forceps. Small amounts of float material are put into a petri dish with some ethanol, and sorting is carried out using a cold light source, which helps avoid excess evaporation.

Insect fossils often retain their structural colors, which may be lost upon drying, and some groups, particularly the dung beetles (Scarabaeidae, Aphodiinae) often break up completely on drying out. In most samples, the most abundant readily identifiable fossils are the disarticulated individual sclerites of Coleoptera (beetles/bugs) and larval Diptera (fly maggots), the latter represented by the heavily sclerotized last instar larva, the puparium, containing the pupa in which the maggot metamorphoses into the fly. House floors, wells, and middens may contain many thousands of preserved insect fossils, and an effective sampling strategy will tax the ingenuity of even the most paleoecologically conscious site director. Where there are many suitable contexts, it is often better to await the results of the archaeological assessment of each context before decisions are made as to which shall be processed, although, in many cases, where only the deeper features are waterlogged, differential decay has already made the decisions necessary. Priority should be given to samples in which there are clear archaeological questions to which the insect remains might provide answers. Processing and sorting can be very time-intensive activities requiring a considerable level of skill, and identification of the fragments, often to the species level, requires not only expertise, but also access to extensive reference collections for the area where the research is being carried out. In many parts of the world, knowledge of the insect fauna is, at best, fragmentary, and the paleoentomologist may also need to be a competent field naturalist, collecting from comparative habitats, noting the apparent requirements of particular species, and identifying modern specimens from often inadequate keys. In some groups, particularly the Diptera and the Hymenoptera, the larval stages and pupae have yet to be described, and there remain many taxonomic nightmares throughout the Insecta, which, with more than a million described species, constitutes the world's most abundant animal group, ranging from mountaintop to the intertidal zone.

Insects and Paleoenvironmental Reconstruction

It is the great diversity of insects that makes them some of the most invaluable fossils. Because there is little evidence of evolutionary morphological or physiological change in insects over the duration of the Quaternary, the last 2.4 million years, knowledge of their modern habitat requirements enables a detailed picture of past environments to be constructed. In addition, many species show a close correlation with climate and, because of their often high dispersal ability, respond rapidly to climatic change. Twenty years before the precipitate nature of the end of the last glaciation Wisconsinan/Weichselian/Würm/Devensian) became evident in the Greenland ice-core data, fossil beetle faunas from the British Isles were already indicating that ca. 10,000 years ago the climate suddenly switched from a High Arctic to a warm temperate regime.

Parasitism

The precision with which insects may select their habitat is indicated by a group that are not infrequent fossils on archaeological sites, the lice. *Homo sapiens* has three species/subspecies of lice not shared with other animals: head, body, and pubic (crab) lice, largely confined to their respective areas of the body and dying rapidly when removed from their host. Other mammals may have similar suites of ectoparasites, and, in acid sediments, where bone does not survive, they may be the only trace after domestic stock. The wingless fly, the ked, ectoparasitic on sheep, is particularly well sclerotized and may survive in deposits where there is little other preservation. The reconstruction of a past environment using insect remains, however, rarely relies upon a single taxon, and as many elements in the assemblage as possible should be identified and their habitat requirements ascertained before a model is proposed. In addition, integration with other lines of evidence, from plant macrofossils and pollen to the purely archaeological data, is essential.

Agriculture and Population Movements

The level of detail available from an integrated study of samples from a series of archaeological sites is evidenced by the work of Thomas H. McGovern's team in the Western Settlement of Norse Greenland, settled ca. A.D. 1000 and abandoned by ca. 1350. The fly puparia, in particular, highlight the squalid living conditions inside the farmhouses, where the cold dictated that the door would rarely be opened. In addition, the absence of an outdoor carrion and marrow fly fauna underlines

A

the marginal nature of existence, with every last drop of fat being consumed by the occupants and their animals, a point further emphasized by the bone-fragmentation data and contrasting with the plethora of unutilized fat in excavated Inuit middens. The beetles, largely introduced with the European farmers, also provide evidence of the nature of exploitation of the landscape, dominated by species associated with the decay of stored hay, without which the farms would have been unable to overwinter their stock. Other resource exploitation is evident from the presence of larval water beetles (Coleoptera, Dytiscidae) and larval caddis flies (Trichoptera), which must have been brought in with peat for use as both human and animal litter; this should also be seen as a cautionary tale to anyone tempted to try bulk organic material for dating archaeological sites. Farmers and sheep were also afflicted with a range of ectoparasites, including the so-called human flea, whose origins appear to lie in Central America. There are some indications of climatic cooling into the Little Ice Age (ca. A.D. 1310–1700) in the insect faunas from the Greenland farms, and the species intimately associated with the European farming system were doomed to local extinction with their unwitting Norse hosts. Elsewhere, these stowaway species were more successful, and several of them form part of a cosmopolitan assemblage that can be used to track European farming expansion on the world stage. The grain weevil moves from rodent stores of wild grass seeds to the grain of the first farmers in the Middle East and, by the Middle Bronze Age, is distributed across the eastern Mediterranean, extracting a tithe of all production in storage, which anyone attempting estimates of crop production and population in prehistory should be aware of. The need for large-scale provisioning of armies took the weevil and other storage pests across the Alps and, eventually, to the frontiers of the Roman Empire in Britain and Germany. By the eleventh century, it had reached Iceland, but not Greenland, where the European connection was too slender. Renewed expansion in the sixteenth century ensured its arrival in North America, along with a range of other European species. In the reverse direction, an American bean weevil had reached one of the more remote corners of the Old World, a Dutch whaler's hut on Svalbard, by the seventeenth century. A

similar story of the insect tramps and stowaways of the Pacific has yet to be told.

Landscape Studies
The immediate detail that the fossil insect faunas from archaeological sites provide is matched on the regional scale by assemblages from natural situations, although, often, the picture is less clearly regional than that provided by the pollen. Phytophages (plant-feeding species) among the beetle and bug faunas in particular, however, may indicate plants that are poor pollen producers, just as, in the archaeological context, they may imply plants that were utilized before coming into flower. In Europe, one beetle, the elm bark beetle (*Scolytus scolytus*), has been implicated in the widespread decline in elm pollen during the Neolithic, the time of the earliest archaeological evidence for the expansion of agriculture. The beetle infects the trees with a fungus, called Dutch elm disease, to render its wood palatable to its developing larvae, and this may lead to the death of the host tree. The fossil record, however, consists of two individuals from one site, at a horizon where the remainder of the fauna clearly indicates an opening up of the forest by human activity, with increasing numbers of dung beetles and a rise in the general deadwood fauna. The case remains not proven. In the European context, the present interglacial has seen a major curtailment of the deadwood fauna, with several species becoming extinct in Britain, restricted to small surviving areas of old forest on the mainland. The European insect fauna has evolved in a landscape of virtually continuous forest during the Tertiary, and woodland species often have a low dispersal potential, with deadwood having always been available. In contrast, much of the open-ground fauna is able to disperse widely, being adapted to a habitat once patchy but now continuous. In terms of archaeological assemblages, this means that adjacent forest is less easily detected than nearby open ground; unlike pollen, it is, therefore, less easy to quantify habitats local to any site from fossil insect faunas, and the two methods should always be used in tandem.

Human-Induced Paleoenvironmental Changes
While the subtleties of climate change through the Middle and Late Holocene (ca. 3000 B.C.–present) are still being worked out, with some evidence from fossil insect faunas from Europe implying that the Little Ice Age has

been the coldest period for the last 10,000 years, it is evident that human impact upon the biota has been largely responsible for losses and contractions in range. Population pressure upon timber reserves in North America, until the late nineteenth century, was less intense than in Europe, and changes that in the Old World began in prehistory are a mark of immigrant impact in the New. This contrast is evident as much in the aquatic fauna as in other elements. As soils were eroded off the farmlands into the rivers, the increased silt load spelled the end for many species adapted to clean-water conditions, and many are now restricted to remote locations. Riffle beetles (Coleoptera, Elminthidae) and caddis fly (Trichoptera) larvae provide particularly clear evidence of changing silt loads in rivers, apparently declining from the Roman period onward in Europe and from the mid-nineteenth century on the American prairies. The processes leading to eutrophication (increased nutrient loading resulting from human activities) in Lake Ontario have been closely indexed by changes in the Chironomid (nonbiting aquatic midge) faunas, and similar techniques have been employed in the study of acidification in Scandinavia; a control on modern industrially induced change is provided by study of the more remote past.

Status of Research

In contrast with palynology, there are few practitioners of archaeological entomology. Research in Europe is more advanced than elsewhere, although even there, where sites have been examined since the early 1970s, coverage is patchy. The most extensive has been the work of Harry Kenward in Roman and medieval (ca. A.D. 1000) York, with similar, less intensive studies in a few other urban centers, including Durham, London, Dublin, Oslo, and Nuess in the Rhineland. Other than the studies of Norse and later farms in Iceland and Greenland, few rural occupation sites have been examined, although the Holocene landscape is better served. The late Maureen Girling provided several detailed analyses and synthetic studies of prehistoric (ca. 3000 B.C.–A.D. 0) trackways in the Somerset Levels in England, as well as a study of a pond within the Iron Age (ca. 400 B.C.–A.D. 50) hillfort of the Breiddin in the Welsh Borders, where, despite extensive archaeological evidence for structures, the insect evidence implies limited occupation. In southeast England, Mark Robinson provides a series of studies of sites along the River Thames, as well as the Bronze Age (ca. 2000 B.C.) settlement at Flag Fen. Sites around the Humber estuary have been the subject of several studies by the group based at the University of Sheffield, and Peter Osborne and Russell Coope, formerly at the University of Birmingham, have worked in the Severn Basin, although their greatest contribution has undoubtedly been the elucidation of interglacial and glacial environments, unfortunately not directly associated with human activity. The size of the faunal assemblages, limited taxonomic knowledge, and the paucity of suitable sites has perhaps limited work in the Mediterranean, but the more restricted faunas of stored products have been examined in Israel and Egypt, as well as the Bronze Age entrepôt of Santorini in the Aegean, which has also produced the earliest evidence for the manufacture of another insect product, wild silk. In North America, Alan Ashworth at North Dakota State University, Fargo, and Alan and Ann Morgan at the University of Waterloo have founded research schools that have largely concentrated upon natural environments, although Ashworth, as well as examining Late Glacial sites in Chile, has extended his expertise to one early archaeological site in that region. Scott Elias, now at the University of Colorado, Boulder, produced in 1994 a basic text for Quaternary entomology, which includes discussion of archaeological assemblages; he has also studied a number of Holocene sites in Colorado. The pack-rat middens of the dry deserts of the American Southwest are a useful source of paleoenvironmental data in a region where there are few other opportunities for the preservation of organic materials. Aside from Ashworth's work, little has been done in the Southern Hemisphere, although termite mounds, a trace fossil after insects, have provided some paleoecological data in southern Africa.

Insect remains in archaeological contexts continue to be an underexploited resource, to the extent that the implications of the climate curve derived from the fossils, with its precipate shifts from warm to cold and back again through the Late Quaternary, has yet to be assimilated by archaeologists in both the Old and the New World. For example, what impact did the expansion and then rapid curtailment of the "mammoth steppe," with its

A

characteristic beetle fauna, which once extended from Britain through Europe to Siberia and on to Alaska, have upon Middle and Late Palaeolithic (ca. 23,000–8000 B.C.) hunters? On their own, insects are a powerful tool in paleoenvironmental interpretation; integrated with other lines of evidence, they should be a core area of research, though as yet one rarely exploited by archaeologists.

Paul C. Buckland
Jonathan P. Sadler

See also ARCHAEOPARASITOLOGY

Further Readings

Buckland, P.C. (1981) The early dispersal of insect pests of stored products as indicated by archaeological records. Journal of Stored Product Research 17:1–12.

Coope, G.R. (1994) The response of insect faunas to glacial-interglacial climatic fluctuations. Philosophical Transactions of the Royal Society of London B344:19–26.

Elias, S.A. (1994) Quaternary Insects and Their Environments. Washington, D.C.: Smithsonian Institution Press.

Hall, W.E., van Devender, T.R., and Olson, C.A. (1990) Late Quaternary and modern arthropods from the Puerto Blanco Mountains, Organ Pipe Cactus National Monument, Southwestern Arizona. In J.L. Betancourt, T.R. van Devender, and P.S. Martin (eds.): Packrat Middens: The Last 40,000 Years of Biotic Change. Tucson: University of Arizona Press.

Kenward, H., and Allison, E. (1994) Rural origins of the urban insect fauna. In A.R. Hall and H.K. Kenward (eds.): Urban-Rural Connections: Perspectives from Environmental Archaeology, pp. 55–78. (Oxbow Monograph 47). Oxford: Oxbow.

McGovern, T.H., Buckland, P.C., Savory, D., Sveinbjarnardottir, G., Andreasen, C., and Skidmore, P. (1983) A study of the faunal and floral remains from two Norse farms in the Western Settlement of Greenland. Arctic Anthropology 20:93–120.

Sadler, J. (1990) Beetles, boats, and biogeography. Acta Archaeologia 61:199–211.

Warwick, W.F. (1981) *Chironomidae* (*Diptera*) responses to 2,800 years of cultural influences: Paleolimnological study with special reference to sedimentation, eutrophication, and contamination process. Canadian Entomologist 112:1193–1238.

Animal Remains, Identification and Analysis: Mammals

The placing of the remains of mammals into previously established taxonomic classes by deductive procedures. Identification is different from classification, which is the ordering of an assemblage of remains by inductive procedures. In other words, when faunal analysts place bones into different groups based on similarities and differences, they are carrying out a classification of those remains. When analysts determine that particular bones come from a taxon on the basis of morphological traits that are exclusively found in that taxon and in no other taxon of the same level of specificity, they are completing an identification. And for an analyst to identify a specimen to the taxonomic level of the order or below, it is almost always necessary to be able to identify the element in hand (i.e., the anatomically complete skeletal portion from which the specimen comes or the part of the element if the piece is a fragment).

Many faunal analysts choose not to spend the inordinate amount of time it takes to identify every fragment in an assemblage. Instead, they leave a portion unidentified. Some will classify this fraction by sorting the pieces into categories that they may label, for example, large, medium, and small mammal. This procedure is not truly identification, and there is often a good deal of subjectivity involved in the process. It is more like archaeological typology, in which it is possible to change the defining characteristics of the type as necessary and appropriate.

The previously established taxonomic classes used by faunal analysts are those defined by zoologists and paleontologists. These are ranked from the broadest—kingdom—through phylum, class, order, family group (superfamily, family, subfamily, tribe, subtribe), and genus group (genus or subgenus), to the species group (species or subspecies). The basic taxonomic unit is the species, which can be defined as a reproductively isolated interbreeding population. Species are designated by both a generic and a specific name, the application of which is governed by the *International Code of Zoological Nomen-*

clature (ICZN) according to rules of priority. Both the generic and the specific name must be printed in italics or underlined or otherwise differentiated from the surrounding text (e.g., *Canis lupus,* the wolf). The same is true of the subspecies name, which follows the species name as appropriate (e.g., *Canis lupus pallipes,* the South Asian wolf), although it is only rarely possible to identify faunal remains to the subspecific level based on objective morphological criteria. The species and subspecies names never have initial capital letters; the genus name always has an initial capital. Following the species name, there may appear the name of the person or persons who first defined the species followed by the year of publication of the definition, the two separated by a comma (e.g., *Canis lupus* Linnaeus, 1758). If the person who first defined the species originally placed it in a different genus than that which is being used by the writer, the authority name and date are placed in parentheses *Vulpes vulpes* (Linnaeus, 1758) since Linnaeus originally placed the red fox in the genus *Canis.* Use of the authority name and date are not mandatory, according to the ICZN.

Most zooarchaeologists deal with essentially modern faunas that have been classified by zoologists who are able to use both behavioral and morphological information. Paleontologists do not have the luxury of being able to tell if one form was reproductively isolated from another, although they can suppose so based on temporal, geographic, and morphological criteria. They depend upon morphological features to define their species, which are, thus, not "natural" taxa and, like types, are subject to change. The rules of nomenclature, however, remain the same, and each new morphospecies has to have a type specimen that is carefully described with discussion of its likely taxonomic relations with predecessor, contemporary, and successor forms. Zooarchaeologists who work with paleontological material often identify only to a family-group or genus-group level and, within a family group, sometimes classify material according to the size of animal from which it came. This is partly because species have usually been defined on the basis of dental or other cranial criteria, and the analyst is interested in working with remains from throughout the skeleton, not just the skull. In some cases, there is only one fossil species that has been identified within a genus or even within a family for the region and time period under consideration. In this case, the species name is sometimes used, although the careful analyst will explain why such usage is justified.

What might be termed probabilistic identifications are common in faunal studies. As Jonathan Driver has pointed out, if a faunal analyst is asked out of the blue to identify a specimen, he or she will usually ask two questions: Where does it come from? and How old is it? Answers to these queries greatly restrict the universe of taxa that have to be considered to make the determination. And in so restricting the universe, it is sometimes possible to make identifications to the species level based on characters that, if they had to be evaluated on a worldwide basis, would not be diagnostic to that taxonomic level. The careful zooarchaeologist, in reporting faunal data, will provide a list of the universe of animals that were considered in evaluating the collection and will state what comparative collections were used, what published guides were consulted, and what metrical methods were employed to make the determinations. For the Holocene, good sources of information on animals likely to be encountered in an area and its surroundings are field guides, taxonomic reviews, and monographs on regional faunas. From these, the analyst can develop a checklist and begin to assemble the comparative material, literature, and personal observations necessary to effect identifications. Such sources also may provide information on the behavior and habitat preferences of the different animals, which can be useful when interpreting the faunal assemblage, but they usually do not include information on the domestic animals that make up significant portions of Holocene assemblages in the Old World and historic-period assemblages in the New World.

Key to making identifications is the comparative collection. Only with a comparative collection that has a wide range of ages, both sexes, and different regional populations represented is it possible to get a good idea of the morphological variability that one may encounter in a faunal assemblage. Collections that meet these criteria are rare, although there are increasing numbers of regional centers in different parts of the world that continue to accumulate skeletal material of known species. In some instances, analysts

A

have used previously studied archaeofaunal collections to assist in making identifications. Such a practice is valid as long as the specimens in that collection are accurately identified, but this is sometimes not the case, with the result that gross errors are perpetuated through generations of analyses.

Different parts of the world have different problems as far as identification of species and even genera within certain mammal families is concerned. Sub-Saharan Africa is particularly intractable. For highly fragmented archaeofaunal assemblages, element size is often of primary importance for securing an identification, and Africa has an almost continuous range of bovids from very large to very small. Problems with like-size and osteologically similar taxa occur nearly everywhere, however, and it is only through patient and painstaking comparative osteology that it is sometimes possible to distinguish different taxa consistently and reliably. For European investigators, defining differences between domestic sheep and goat has been a particularly important research priority, and there is a long history of efforts to accomplish this. Even thirty years after the exemplary 1963 study of Joachim Boessneck and his associates that identified a large number of distinguishing characters, however, more continued to be found. Some of the features that have been defined seem to "work" for some collections of modern and archaeological material but not for others. From this there is an important lesson to be learned—namely, that different populations within the same species may manifest distinctive morphological characters somewhat differently. Since differences are often a matter of degree and not of kind, it is essential that multiple characters be used whenever possible to effect a secure identification.

In addition to identifying skeletal part and taxon, the zooarchaeologist is often interested in identifying attributes of symmetry (right or left side or median), age, sex (male, female, or castrate), and, for some animals, state of domestication. Identification of symmetry is straightforward. Accurate identification of age at death for individual animals is sometimes possible to determine through examination of incremental structures in the dentine and cementum of teeth. Approximate ages or determinations of age older than or younger than a certain number of months are commonly assessed by documenting tooth eruption and wear or by recording the state of fusion of the epiphyseal ends of the bones and of skull sutures. Identification of sex depends on the existence of sexually dimorphic characters in the taxon, such as the large canines of male pigs and the antlers of male deer. In uniparous animals (those, like humans, that normally give birth to one offspring per pregnancy), there are differences in the pelvis that sometimes can be used to distinguish between males and females. These morphological differences relate to the need for the female to have a relatively large birth canal. Human-induced conditions such as castration, however, can create intermediate morphologies, and differences are generally less clear in young animals than they are in older ones.

Another sexually dimorphic character is body size, but it is almost never possible to identify all measurable fragments as to sex using bone dimensions because of size overlap between males and females. It is sometimes possible, however, to identify a bimodal distribution in bone dimensions, with one peak representing females and the other males. Here, the analyst is not focusing on the characteristics of the individual specimen so much as on the overall picture produced by the whole assemblage. This is characterization as opposed to identification. A similar approach is taken by zooarchaeologists who study animal domestication. They are occasionally able to identify individual specimens as coming from domestic or wild stock, but more usually they focus on looking at overall changes in animal size and proportions through time, since size diminution is recognized as a characteristic feature of the initial domestication of some taxa (particularly sheep, goats, cattle, and pigs).

With the development of new chemical, isotopic, and genetic means of analyzing ancient remains, it may become possible to effect species identifications even on extremely fragmentary material. However, the expense of using these techniques is high, and it seems unlikely that they can employed in a cost-effective manner except in cases where there is an overriding need to make a secure identification. Thus, zooarchaeologists will continue to assemble comparative collections and carry out comparative morphological studies in order to be able to better identify and characterize a larger fraction of the archaeofaunas that they study.

Richard H. Meadow

See also ANIMAL REMAINS, QUANTIFICATION; GROWTH-RING ANALYSIS AND SEASONALITY STUDIES; GROWTH STUDIES; MAMMAL TEETH; ZOOARCHAEOLOGY

Further Readings

Boessneck, J., Müller, H.H., and Teichert, M. (1963) Osteologische Unterschei-dungsmerkmale zwischen Schaf (*Ovis aries* Linné) und Ziege (*Capra hircus* Linné). Kühn-Archiv 78:1–129.

Driver, J.C. (1992) Identification, classification, and zooarchaeology. Circaea 9(1):35–47.

Gilbert, B.M. (1990) Mammalian Osteology. Columbia: Missouri Archaeological Society.

Hillson, S. (1992) Mammal Bones and Teeth. London: Institute of Archaeology, University College London.

International Commission on Zoological Nomenclature (1985) International Code of Zoological Nomenclature, 3rd ed. London: International Trust for Zoological Nomenclature/British Museum (Natural History).

Mayr, E., and Ashlock, P.D. (1991) Principles of Systematic Zoology, 2nd ed. New York: McGraw Hill.

Schmid, E. (1972) Atlas of Animal Bones/Knochenatlas. Amsterdam: Elsevier.

Wilson, B., Grigson, C., and Payne, S. (1982) Ageing and Sexing Animal Bones from Archaeological Sites. (BAR British Series 109). Oxford: British Archaeological Reports.

Animal Remains, Identification and Analysis: Molluscs

Invertebrate animals, most with a calcium carbonate exoskeleton called *shell*. Molluscs have served humans in numerous ways and continue to do so. Many gastropods and some bivalve species have been modified as ornaments, many as tools, some as money. Shells appear in archaeological sites as debris left from the use of the flesh for human food; as bait for fish, crabs, lobsters, and birds; and in the search for pearls. The shells have been used as fill, architectural walls, burial layers, mounds, and lanterns; treated to extract their color; cut up to use in inlay, cameos, buttons, beads, trinkets, and pearl nuclei; and crushed for pottery temper, poultry feed, medicine, and fertilizer. Through the analysis of shells, archaeologists have found it possible to determine when the shells were harvested (using the growth lines or the height in short-lived species), where they originated, the environment in which they grew, changes in aquatic environments, past cataclysmic environmental events, the contribution of shellfish to the diet, and human competition with other predators.

Four classes of molluscs have external shells: chitons, gastropods (snails), tusks, and bivalves. Chitons are made up of eight plates on a girdle. Tusks are long, tapering tubes open at both ends. Most gastropods have a spiral growth pattern that forms as either a long tube or a disc. The central column around which gastropod shell spirals is known as the *columella,* which can be either solid or hollow. The largest shell whorl ends in an aperture through which the animal's foot and head are extended. In many species, the foot has attached to it a horny plate, the *operculum,* which closes the aperture when the animal withdraws. Bivalves have symmetrical or asymmetrical paired shells or valves. They are joined at the upper end by a ligament and articulating shelly teeth whose shape is an important taxonomic feature. The edge of the valve is called the *margin;* the apex or beak is called the *umbo* (plural, *umbones*).

Reproduction is quite complicated among the molluscs. Many species are hermaphroditic, with both sexes simultaneously combined in one animal or with alternating glandular expression in one animal. Many bivalved species shed sperm and eggs into the water with fertilization left to chance. Most naiad (freshwater bivalve) species have larvae (glochidia) that are parasitic on fish gills and are, consequently, transported beyond their parent population. Larvae settle where they will, and, if substrate (bottom of a water body) and hydraulic conditions are suitable in that place, a shelled animal will grow. To attribute the lack of shell in a riverine site to human overexploitation of a nearby molluscan population is erroneous since only the absence of fish or unsuitable environmental conditions can explain the lack of larval longevity in a specific area. The same can be said of marine gastropods and bivalves since the larvae are dispersed by tides and currents.

Recruitment is independent of the presence of a parent population. Environmental parameters that govern reproduction and recruitment are the type of substrate, the habitual quantity of dissolved oxygen, salinity, and water temperature.

Analysis of Molluscs

Sorting fragmented shell into species is usually performed on material no smaller than that which catches in a one-fourth-inch mesh screen. Quantification is usually in grams but occasionally is given as minimum numbers of individuals based on counts of columella or umbones. Leaching of the calcium by ground water (diagenesis) reduces shell weight, which greatly complicates the comparison of shell weights to vertebrate fauna weights. Shell is ca. 40 percent calcium; deviations from that percentage could be indicating diagenesis or burning. Useful measurements are the height of the shell, measured from lower margin to umbo in bivalves or end to end in gastropods, the length of the shell (the distance from side to side), and umbo height. Skeletal mass allometry (correlation of skeletal measurements with body mass) has proven useful for estimating meat weights. Attention should also be paid to evidence of boring organisms, bryozoa, sponges, and the presence of other parasitic or commensual species.

It is useful to divide molluscs into categories that reflect environmental conditions. For instance, there are marine species habituated to deep water and a hard substrate (e.g., rock) called *epifauna,* and species adapted to a soft substrate (e.g., mud) known as *infauna.* There are marine bivalves that burrow into the substrate, and other bivalves that attach to rocks and wood by means of threads. There are marine species that are exposed by low tide and those that are always under water, those that live in cold water and those that live in warm water. Among freshwater bivalved molluscs (naiads), there are those species that are habituated to deep or shallow water, to slow or fast water, to riffles or mud, and there are generalists. Terrestrial snails should be separated from aquatic snails.

Molluscan species ecology provides a picture of the aquatic or terrestrial paleoenvironment. Molluscs have tolerance ranges for many ecological factors, and there are differing environmental parameters for maintaining life, for reproducing, and for larval recruitment, complicating environmental reconstructions. For the naiads, generally speaking, the more stream habitat studies consulted, the greater the recorded diversity in response to water depth, substrate, and current speed. For many species, ecological parameters are poorly known.

Much is known about the ecology of those aquatic molluscs of commercial interest and land snails. It is difficult to use the ecological information associated with the land snails, however, because they overwinter by burrowing. In a site with a highly porous matrix, such as a shell-bearing midden, land-snail analysis can provide a list of species present and their associated habitats, but correlation with strata are typically impossible.

Much literature on naiads correlates specific features of shell morphology, such as thickness or arc, to particular aspects of the environment, such as water alkalinity and current rate. However, these correlations are compromised by sexual dimorphism, ontogeny, and growth compensation. Changes in one shell dimension are often accompanied by changes in others. There is little doubt that long-term and even short-term environmental changes affect shell growth and species ratios in detectable ways, but these relationships are still being explored.

Chemical analyses of shell have utilized $^{18}O/^{16}O$, strontium, calcium, iron, magnesium, manganese, and radioactive carbon. Ratios of oxygen-18 to oxygen-16 isotopes have been used to identify the water body of origin (trade), the season of death, and the annual influx of freshwater in an estuary. There have been numerous studies of the factors that influence the relationship between shell composition and water composition. Many authors report correlations between strontium, magnesium (the two most thoroughly studied), and calcium, and stream flow, salinity, water temperature, age of shell, and so forth. The archaeologist should be wary of an uncritical adoption of these chemical/environmental correlations, for not one species has been adequately described chemically, and chemical variations within populations and between populations are little studied.

Taphonomy

Taphonomy is the study of how the fossil record is formed. Research by taphonomists has indicated that shell does not preserve as well as archaeologists often assume. Boring organisms, solution, and abrasion of shell are the most active processes in the formation of fossil shell deposits, and the latter two are the most active in archaeological settings. With respect to abrasion, the reworking of different sediment types, varying shell architecture, different degrees of abrasion associated with different mean grain diameters, and sorting of the abrasive agent are the most relevant variables in preservation of shell.

Experiments and observations by archaeologists further emphasize the vulnerability of shell. Water and wind can fragment and remove shells. Inundation can add shells. Trampling rather quickly causes fragmentation, as well as the downward movement of shell particles. The distance between pairable shells at the time of excavation may not be indicative of deposit disturbance. Highly fragmented deposits are probably the result of activities on or in the shells after their discard.

Nutrition

There is a tremendous amount of intertaxonomic and intrataxonomic variation in all nutrients in a mollusc. Six assays of the meat of the bivalve *Mercenaria mercenaria,* from the same collection point, taken six months apart, indicated a range in calories from 54 to 95, in protein from 9.7 percent to 16.8 percent, in fat from 0.79 percent to 1.86 percent, and in carbohydrates from 1.95 g to 3.31 g. When published nutritional information on a number of shellfish species is brought together, it is evident that caloric values range from 48 to 234 calories per 100 g of wet flesh. Protein ranges from 37 percent to 68 percent of the tissue, or 0.1 g to 68 g, and carbohydrates from 0 g to 8.9 g. Many western Atlantic species rival the protein value of most fishes. Given this variation, one can argue either that shellfish are poor sources of nutrition or that they are adequate sources merely by choosing an appropriate species to illustrate the point. Consequently, specific figures are necessary when discussing molluscan nutritional value. In the past, archaeologists converting shell data to nutrition have assumed that all shellfish were equivalent in nutritive value, that all people present consumed shellfish, and that all people consumed the same quantity of shellfish. Today, many archaeologists are no longer willing to make those assumptions and forgo dietary interpretations of molluscs.

Cheryl Claassen

See also AMINO ACID RACEMIZATION/ EPIMERIZATION DATING; ANIMAL REMAINS, QUANTIFICATION; GROWTH-RING ANALYSIS AND SEASONALITY STUDIES; ISOTOPES, STABLE (C, N, O, H): BONE AND PALEODIET STUDIES; PALEONUTRITION; SHELL MIDDENS, EXCAVATION; TAPHONOMY

Further Readings

Bobrowsky, P.T. (1984) The history and sciences of gastropods in archaeology. American Antiquity 49:77–93.

Claassen, C. (1994) Washboards, pigtoes, and muckets: Historic musseling in the Mississippi watershed. Historic Archaeology 28(2):1–145.

Vermeij, G.J. (1993) A Natural History of Shells. Princeton, NJ: Princeton University Press.

Animal Remains, Quantification

In zooarchaeology and related fields, the means of numerically or visually summarizing, interpreting, and presenting data recorded during the analysis of faunal assemblages, including the use of statistical procedures, both descriptive and inferential. The basic unit in faunal analysis is the specimen. This can be a complete element or group of joined elements or skeletal parts (e.g., an unbroken metatarsal or a fully articulated cranium), or it can be a piece or fragment of the same. In some cases, it is possible to join fragments that were broken in antiquity either before deposition or while in the ground. In such an instance, the analyst must decide whether the refitted piece is to be counted as one specimen or multiple specimens and justify the decision when reporting on the material. Faunal remains are also broken during excavation and handling. A piece refitted following modern breakage is usually counted as a single specimen because the analyst is concerned with past, and not present, cultural activity. Zooarchaeology has spawned a remarkable number of quantitative units and accompanying terms, not all of which are used in the same fashion by all investigators. Here only the most commonly encountered units are discussed.

NISP is the number of identified specimens per taxon. It is a primary quantitative unit in the sense that it is a first-level abstraction from the specimens themselves. In faunal analysis, specimens can be divided into those identified to taxonomic unit (subspecies through class) and those not so identified. In theory, no specimen is "unidentifiable"; in practice, the analyst may choose not to identify a specimen beyond a particular level of specificity. But what is not identified by one analyst may be identified by another with more experience or with different questions in mind. Therefore, the terms *not identified* or *unidentified* are preferred to *not identifiable* or *unidentifiable*. And, in all cases, the analyst must define how NISP is being calculated and used. As a measure of taxonomic abundance, NISP suffers from the problem that more than one specimen may have come from any given animal. Experiments and simulations, however, have shown that proportions based on NISP are better estimators of relative abundance than those based on any other quantitative unit, particularly if the analyst is careful to compare only assemblages that have been formed in like fashion. It makes little methodological or interpretative sense to lump together a complete dog burial with fauna from surrounding midden deposits and compare the result with another assemblage. If, however, the dog burial was missed in excavation, comparison of the two assemblages using NISP would show a particularly high proportion of dog in the one. This should lead the analyst to examine the skeletal-part distributions and then to reexamine the original collection and, in so doing, identify the dog burial for what it was.

MNI is the minimum number of individuals or least number of individual animals that must have existed to produce the NISP. This is a secondary quantitative unit because it is an abstraction from the primary quantitative unit. MNI is derived in different ways by different analysts. Some merely array the counts of identified skeletal parts per taxon for each excavation unit or group of units, divide each of those counts by the number of times the particular skeletal part occurs in the living animal, and take the highest result as the MNI. For example, if there are fourteen distal tibiae and twenty-four first phalanges of deer, one would divide the number of tibiae by two (each deer has two) and the number of first phalanges by eight (each deer has eight), with a resulting MNI of seven based on the tibiae. This is what can be called a *minimal MNI*. Other analysts lay all the bones of a taxon from an excavation unit out on a table, try to match them up according to sex, age, size, and other morphological features, and then determine the least number of animals that could have produced that collection of specimens. In the above example, the investigator might ascertain that the tibiae came from at least ten animals and the phalanges from at least twelve. In this case, the MNI would be twelve based on the phalanges. This is what can be called a *maximal MNI*. Since there are many different points on the continuum between maximal and minimal, MNIs in different reports cannot be compared directly unless it is clear that they have been derived in exactly the same fashion. Because of this and other problems with MNI, more and more analysts are no longer using this measure of taxonomic abundance except for very limited purposes. Instead, they use NISP counts directly to calculate the relative contribution of each taxon to the faunal assemblage.

MNE is the minimum number of elements or least number of skeletal parts that must have existed to have produced the specimens that are identified as being from a particular element or skeletal part of a particular taxon. An element is an anatomically complete skeletal portion of an animal. It may be a complete long bone, it may be tooth, it may be a whole mandible including teeth, it may be a whole cranium, or it may be a discrete anatomical unit of the cranium such as the nasal or zygomatic. A skeletal part is a portion of the skeleton that has analytical validity for the investigator. Thus, long bones are often divided into three parts—proximal end, shaft, and distal end—each tabulated separately in order to examine differential preservation of the element. For both element and skeletal part, the investigator should specify how the term is being used.

Like MNI, MNE is a secondary quantitative unit, and it suffers from the same shortcomings, being calculated in different ways by different investigators. This has led to a great deal of cross talk in the zooarchaeological literature. One approach taken by individuals who work with highly fragmented collections is to define easily recognizable diagnostic zones and to count only those specimens on which the diagnostic zone is manifest. Another approach is to focus only on articular ends and assume that any fragment of an articular end represents a separate skeletal part unless it can be shown otherwise. A third approach is to estimate what percentage of a skeletal part is represented by each specimen and sum the results. And there are other approaches as well, none of which is intrinsically any better or worse than any other. What is important is that we understand what is being counted and why, and what method is being used. The analyst must also be consistent in using terms and quantitative units.

MAU (also MNU) is the minimum number of animal units and is calculated by dividing MNE by the number of elements or skeletal parts that occur in a complete skeleton of the taxon under consideration. Thus, if one is interested in the MAU for cervical vertebrae, one would divide the MNE for that element by seven; for distal femora, one would divide by two unless one differentiates rights and lefts, in which case the larger of the two values would be chosen (= MNI for distal femora); for first phalanges, one would divide by eight for bovids or by four for equids if one did not separate forelimb from hindlimb elements or right side from left side. Once again, it is essential that the analyst describe the precise method of calculation for each skeletal part or element. To compare assemblages, the MAU is then scaled by dividing the value for each element or skeletal part by the largest MAU value and multiplying by 100 (= percent MAU). As MAU is derived from MNE by further numerical manipulation, it can be considered a tertiary quantitative unit.

GUI and MGUI are general utility index and modified general utility index, respectively. Lewis R. Binford created these indices to reflect the contribution of meat, marrow, and grease accompanying each skeletal part. The MGUI alters the GUI for some skeletal parts to reflect the fact that a low GUI part may stay attached to a high GUI part after butchery, thereby raising its utility index or chance of being incorporated into the assemblage. The GUI and the MGUI are usually scaled in a manner similar to the MAU. The purpose of these indices is to help explain why skeletal parts are present in faunal assemblages in the proportions in which they are found. By plotting percent MGUI against percent MAU, the analyst hopes to be able to define strategies employed in the use or transport of animal carcasses.

Zooarchaeologists use descriptive statistics much more commonly than they do inferential statistics. Percentages (parts per 100) are especially widely used, with measures of central tendency and variation being employed for metrical data. Tables, histograms, bar charts, pie charts, and scatter plots are the usual methods of presenting quantified data. The use of inferential statistics in zooarchaeology is problematic because it is rarely possible to meet conditions of randomness, normalcy of distribution, and independence of observations. Some investigators have made attempts to employ exploratory multivariate methods such as factor analysis and principal-components analysis, but they often seem to overinterpret the results, which is a common problem in archaeology.

Richard H. Meadow

See also QUANTITATIVE METHODS IN ARCHAEOLOGY; SAMPLING; STATISTICAL METHODS IN ARCHAEOLOGY; ZOOARCHAEOLOGY

Further Readings

Binford, L.R. (1978) Nunamiut Ethnoarchaeology. New York: Academic.

Casteel, R.W., and Grayson, D.K. (1977) Terminological problems in quantitative faunal analysis. World Archaeology 9:235–242.

Grayson, D.K. (1984) Quantitative Zooarchaeology: Topics in the Analysis of Archaeological Faunas. Orlando: Academic.

Lyman, R.L. (1994a) Quantitative units and terminology in zooarchaeology. American Antiquity 59:36–71.

Lyman, R.L. (1994b) Vertebrate Taphonomy. Cambridge: Cambridge University Press.

Ringrose, T.J. (1993) Bone counts and statistics: A critique. Journal of Archaeological Science 20:121–157.

Antiquities Act of 1906

The first national legal protection for archaeological sites in the United States. The Antiquities Act (16 U.S. Code 431–433) was the first U.S. law to provide general protection for any general kind of cultural or natural resource. It established the first national historic-preservation policy for the United States. Section 2 of the statute gives the president the authority to set aside for protection "historic landmarks, historic and prehistoric structures, and other objects of historic or scientific interest that are situated upon the lands owned or controlled by the Government of the United States." These protected areas were then designated as "national monuments," and the federal agencies assigned to oversee them were required to afford proper care and management of the resources. This section of the statute provided an additional tool for Progressive politicians and their supporters to determine the uses of public lands and resources in the rational, conservation-oriented manner they favored (see Rothman 1989:52–71). Prior to the Antiquities Act, specific areas had been set aside as national parks or reserves, such as Yellowstone National Park (1872) and Casa Grande Ruin in Arizona (1892). However, each of these parks or reserves required an act of Congress as well as presidential approval. The authority vested in the president by Section 2 of the Antiquities Act made the creation of a national monument, which afforded the resources within the boundary of the monument special protection, an administrative action that could be taken by the president without congressional approval, a relatively quick and easy procedure, at least in the early decades of its application (see Rothman 1989 for a thorough description of this aspect of the Antiquities Act).

Section 3 of the Antiquities Act required that "the examination of ruins, the excavation of archaeological sites, or the gathering of objects of antiquity" on lands administered by the Departments of Interior, Agriculture, or War be carried out only after a permit to do so had been issued by the secretary of the department responsible for the land in question. The permits were to be issued only to institutions "properly qualified to conduct such examinations, excavations, or gatherings." Furthermore, these permitted activities were to be "for the benefit of reputable museums, universities, colleges, or other recognized scientific or educational institutions, with a view to increasing the knowledge of such objects." Finally, Section 3 required that the collections of materials from these investigations be placed in public museums for preservation and public benefit.

Enactment of the Antiquities Act required twenty-five years of work by individuals and organizations concerned about the preservation of American archaeological sites. Interest in the archaeological remains of the United States grew throughout the nineteenth century. As the final quarter of the 1800s began, much of the interest in American archaeological sites was focused on the Southwest. Some of the interested parties were those who plundered the prehistoric ruins for ancient artifacts and other materials, including building stone and roof beams, to put to modern uses. Others, such as investigators from museums and other archaeological organizations, wanted to examine and study the ruins, as well as make collections for their institutions and the public they served. Investigators who began to visit and report on the condition of prominent ruins noted the destruction that was occurring. Their descriptions moved the early advocates of government action to protect the archaeological sites. One notable success along the path to the Antiquities Act was the setting aside of Casa Grande Ruin as the first national archaeological reservation in 1892. During the 1890s, major public exhibitions, the World's Columbian Exposition in Chicago and the Louisiana Purchase Exposition in St. Louis, exposed more of the American public to U.S. antiquities. Municipal and university museums in large cities throughout the country featured American Indian antiquities in their displays, and investigators of the Southwestern ruins and of archaeological sites in other parts of the country and hemisphere published popular accounts of the sites and their exploits. The growing popular appeal of American archaeology was accompanied by a commercial demand for authentic prehistoric antiquities, which lead to a substantial rise in the looting of archaeological sites, especially in the increasingly accessible Southwest. Efforts to protect specific archaeological sites, such as Mesa Verde in Colorado and Chaco Canyon in New Mexico, became more frequent and widespread. Finally, these efforts culminated in President Theodore Roosevelt signing the Antiquities Act into law on June 8, 1906.

The Antiquities Act is important for many reasons, both specific and general.

Specifically, it asserted wide and general public interest in, and control over, archaeological resources on federal and Indian lands. This assertion of public interest and concern continues to the present and is the basis for the federal government's efforts to protect archaeological sites from looting and vandalism. The act also permitted the protection and preservation of specific areas important for their archaeological, historical, and scientific resources. It stands as an important achievement in the progress of conservation and preservation efforts in the United States. Its passage involved

a whole generation of dedicated effort by scholars, citizens, and members of Congress. . . . More important, this generation, through its explorations, publications, exhibits, and other activities, awakened the American people to a lasting consciousness of the value of American antiquities, prehistoric and historic. This public understanding, achieved only after persistent effort in the face of much ignorance, vandalism, and indifference, was a necessary foundation for many subsequent conservation achievements. Among them were several of great importance to the future National Park Service, including the establishment of many national monuments, development of a substantial educational program for visitors, and eventually the execution of a far-reaching nationwide program to salvage irreplaceable archaeological objects threatened with inundation or destruction by dams and other public works and their preservation for the American people (Lee 1970:86).

Although the Antiquities Act proved to be a means of overseeing and coordinating educational and scientific archaeological investigations on federal and Indian lands, it did not effectively prevent or deter deliberate, criminal looting of archaeological sites on those lands. Problematic for many years, this situation became critical in the 1970s when several attempts by federal land-managing agencies and prosecutors in the Southwest to convict looters, using the Antiquities Act, resulted in disastrous court decisions. In two cases, judges ruled that the terms of the act were unconstitutionally vague and, therefore, unenforceable (Collins and Michel 1985). This situation led to a concerted effort by archaeologists and preservationists, their allies in the law enforcement community, and several essential supporters in Congress to strengthen the legal protection of archaeological resources. The eventual outcome was a new statute, the Archeological Resources Protection Act of 1979, rather than an amendment of the Antiquities Act.

Francis P. McManamon

See also ARCHEOLOGICAL RESOURCES PROTECTION ACT (ARPA); CULTURAL RESOURCE MANAGEMENT (CRM)

Further Readings

Collins, R.B. and Michel, M.P. (1985) Preserving the past: Origins of the Archaeological Resources Protection Act of 1979. American Archeology 5(2):84–89.
Lee, R.F. (1970) The Antiquities Act of 1906. Washington, D.C.: National Park Service, Department of the Interior.
Rothman, H. (1989) Preserving Different Pasts: The American National Monuments. Urbana and Chicago: University of Illinois Press.

Archaeological Prospection

The recognition, description, and interpretation of traces of the past, either apparent on the surface or detectable from the surface. Although similar to excavation in its search for historical information, prospection is differentiated from excavation essentially by its nondestructive character and its ability to cover areas of land too large to excavate. Consequently, prospection offers less detailed information, often less dramatic from a materialistic point of view (museum objects), but complementary and indispensable: Without the plans, boundaries, and environmental descriptions all produced by prospection, no excavation could be managed rationally nor interpreted. Largely due to its nondestructive and predictive character, archaeological prospection is an important tool for the management and preservation of the buried heritage threatened by the industrialization, urbanization, agricultural development, and civil-engineering projects of the modern world.

Archaeological prospection can be defined simply by the scale on which it occurs:

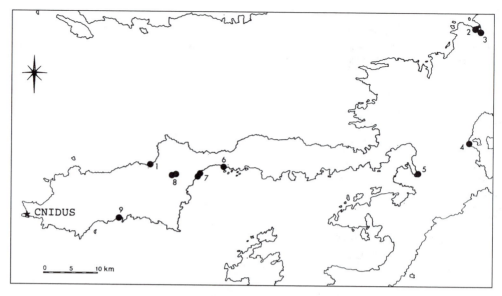

Figure 1. Amphorae-production workshops on the Cnidus and Loryma (Turkey) peninsulas. The map is the result of systematic prospection of the area and shows the preferential distribution of the sites near the sea front for logistical reasons (amphorae transport by sea). Note the important and exceptional site of Resadiye (8) at the center of the peninsula. Subsequent detailed investigation on some of the sites with geophysical prospection (electromagnetic and magnetic methods) has located many ovens and dumps. From Empereur, J.Y. and M.Picon, A la recherche de fours d'amphores, Bulletin de Correspondance Hellénique, *suppl. 13:103–126, by permission.*

On the regional scale, it will strive to detect the existence of *sites,* meaning areas of particularly concentrated and significant traces of the past. However, the boundaries between sites and *nonsites* may not be well defined if one includes the considerations of geomorphology and environment—factors that, when integrated, allow the interpretation of the totality of the ancient landscape.

For the remainder of the operations, the surveyor cannot be satisfied with a mere qualitative identification of an ancient occupation. Practically, he or she will have to face several much more constraining problems, such as the distinction, localization, and identification of the various structures according to their chronological, technical, cultural, and material aspects: settlements, workshops, cemeteries, places of worship, and so on. On larger sites, the length and diversity of occupation can present several superimposed or overlapping structures.

Ideally, site inventories and maps of archaeological traces are produced. The amount of scientific interest generated by these maps depends generally on the original motivation of the prospection: substantial in the case of a specific archaeological/historical question (Figure 1), less if the prospection is the consequence of destruction threats in a region arbitrarily defined by civil-engineering planning (dams, roads, and the like).

In reality, the distinction is less dramatic, and, since the mid-1970s, there has been a considerable increase in large-scale field-research programs and significant publications concerning both kinds of motivation (history and regional planning). Using prospection, researchers aim to reconstruct the history and prehistory of geographical regions, the evolution of artisanal or artistic productions and of food production, the exploitation of natural resources, and economic transactions, among other things. They are now in the position to present more synthetic descriptions than the straightforward archaeological-excavation report and better representative of the past than previous studies carried out over large areas.

The final level at which prospection operates (local prospection) is on a smaller scale, but with improved definition. A number of specific prospection tools will play a role, if necessary, as auxiliary to the excavation, with the aim of conducting more rigorous and more economical operations, respectful of the long-term resource of the site investigated. This careful approach should enable further studies by future generations.

The measures used at this stage are, in general, able to define the boundaries of sites and to identify their main features, such as cemeteries, buildings, and road systems. Each method, applied at its own scale, highlights one or more specific details, whose understanding needs coding, plotting, representation, and specific interpretive reading. This scalar hierarchy, as well as the need for the global perception of large areas, leads to the creation of synthetic documents comprising two-dimensional representations of the space under investigation. This results in the fact that the plans become privileged supports of the prospector's work. For the overall interpretation, all of the results of the observations will be reduced to a common scale.

The tools available to the prospector are diverse:

Archives (e.g., manuscripts, ancient maps and drawings, travelers' writings, administrative documents, land registers, photographic air surveys). Depending on the period under consideration, they make up an almost inexhaustible mine of information, allowing the identification of concealed or even disappeared archaeological sites. Essentially, this research takes place at the host institution; however, it nearly always requires verification in the field to validate the data collected and the interpretative hypothesis.

In the example shown in Figure 2, the cadastral archives of the beginning of the nineteenth century (1890, commune of Saint Romain en Gal, France) give information on the distribution of cultivated areas between the vineyards and other crops: The division of space defined in this way corresponds, respectively, to occupied or nonoccupied zones in the Gallo-Roman period.

Similarly, toponyms, whether the inventory has been collated from maps or in the field, are valuable auxiliaries for the discovery of sites whose presence is still recorded, though changed, in local topographic names.

Site Examination. Whether it occurs on the ground or from the air, direct observation helps to recognize a large number of sites or remains from often very tenuous traces revealing themselves only to the experienced and careful observer, often through choice of the most favorable timing. Depending on the season, vegetation can reduce the legibility of the landscape. Depending on the hour, the lighting can facilitate the discovery of rock inscriptions or reliefs.

Airplanes are used preferentially for regional studies looking at whole sites in their geographical environment. A number of indicators are relied upon, such as shadows produced by raking light, the different growth patterns of cereals, topographical and pedological factors, markers of humidity, color, or temperature. Photography (if necessary, using sensitive infrared film) can improve the legibility and methodical interpretation of observations. Corrections and later treatments of the pictures then allow a finer analysis of the recorded document going beyond the simple qualitative plotting of an archaeological site on the map.

On the ground, even more discrete remains can be detected: ruins, random material, topographical irregularities, and so on are the prospector's main interest in the course of field-walking operations, in conjunction with the geological and geomorphological situation. Verbal inquiry with the contemporary inhabitants of the site or area under investigation may lead rapidly to the discovery of remains until then unexpected. The perspicacity of the prospector will drive him or her just as systematically to examine the ditches, quarry fronts, riverbanks, or seafront slopes, natural or artificial sections likely to reveal hidden structures or waste deposits of domestic or industrial activities (e.g., consumed shells, metallurgical slag). Often, beyond the identification of their individual characteristics (e.g., nature, dating), the only way to understand the coherence, complementarity, organization, and, more generally, all of the relationships existing between these remains is to map them.

Systematic Ground Surveys. These surveys call for a number of other parameters spread in a continuous way on the ground that must be mapped for a more detailed site study.

The topographic survey of soil height can reveal microreliefs of underlying structures as contours almost completely leveled by ploughing. Geochemistry informs on the past distribution of industrial, domestic, or even cultural activities. The present or past distribution of

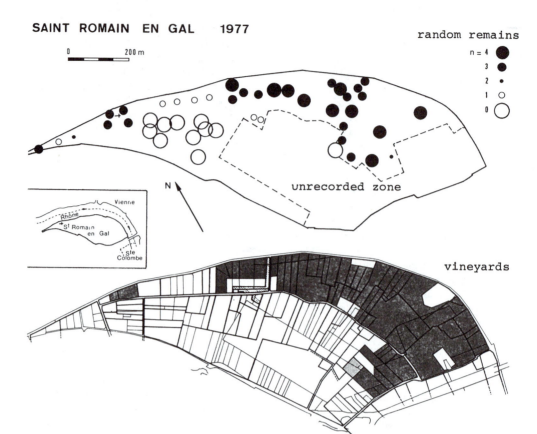

Figure 2. Maps demonstrating the integration of four kinds of data (archival data, artifacts, topography, and electrical resistivity) to establish the location of Gallo-Roman occupation. At the site of Saint Romain en Gal (France), it was possible to reconstruct the location of the vineyards at the beginning of the nineteenth century, using cadastral archives (bottom map). They correspond exactly to the location of areas of construction in the Gallo-Roman period as revealed by the plots rich in archaeological surface material. The scale in the top map (black dots = sherds, bricks, and building stones) reflects the concentration of remains from absence (0) to abundance (4). The same exceptional coincidence can be observed with high electrical resistivities and raised areas not susceptible to flooding. Historical vineyard location, surface surveys, topography and electrical resistivity lead to the same consistent zoning and their integration establishes unequivocally the location of Gallo-Roman occupation in the area under investigation. From A. Hesse et al. (1978) Succés de l'archéologie prospective à Saint Romain en Gal, Archéologia 122:7–17.

vegetable species (Figure 2) may correspond to a spatial organization very significant of an ancient situation; it can also reflect interesting elements for the botanical history of the landscape in which sites are inscribed.

Surface Distributions. Among random remains, potsherds and flints are often very abundant and can be analyzed in a much finer and rigorous way than simply recording their presence. They can inform on the nature, culture, and the date of civilizations that abandoned them. Their distribution on the ground can also be processed rigorously from samples

taken in precise locations. Those samples, which must not exhaust the totality of the visible material, are distributed at the knots of a geometric network whose stitch is chosen according to the fineness of the distribution maps that we wish to obtain: Large and often irregular for regional archaeological studies (one or several samples per site), it will become more regular and will shrink to a few meters for the detailed study of a single site. The material is then catalogued, sorted, and counted, and distribution maps of the various types of material are produced and compared. Statistical methods then constitute a valuable aid for the analysis of ground-surface distributions. The geostatistical variogram tests the sampling validity; factorial analysis compares the samples' composition and the distribution of object types in each group.

Therefore, certain limits and major structures of the different occupation zones can be identified, their chronological relations with the collected material can be compared, and specific habitation, burial, or workshops zones can be defined, avoiding the pitfalls of the sedimentary and geomorphological history of the site. Zones in which the material is more abundant on the surface are not necessarily the richest and the most archaeologically significant.

It is not possible to give a complete list of the various parameters that can be collected on the surface or at the bottom of the sea, where one faces the same problems, but with a greater technical specificity. Each site and region, depending on its specific character, can give rise to a particularly revealing investigation of signs from the past. All of this depends on what must be considered as the *external examination,* for which the prospector's imagination, controlled scientifically, must be constantly invoked. It does not aim to provide the actual detection of remains hidden in the ground (*internal examination*) which is generally the achievement of geophysical methods (e.g., magnetic prospection, electrical and electromagnetic prospection, thermal surveying, georadar). Indeed, these ensure fine and specific detections that go as far as characterizing individual structures (e.g., dispersed tombs, isolated kilns) or even objects (e.g., metallic deposits, monoliths). However, one must not attribute to these methods an almost divinatory role of prediction of the subsoil content: the collected information is not only a more or less deformed representation of the underlying reality, but it also constitutes an archaeological reality of its own. Their variations, essentially consecutive to the historical events or to the past natural phenomena, structure space in a significant manner for their reconstruction. External and internal examination work toward deciphering and interpreting them in a specific integral approach. This does not differ at all from the interpretation of a ground level such as revealed by excavation and leads one to consider the surface as level 0 of the stratigraphy. It must, therefore, be scientifically considered

as such (i.e., as rigorously as the remaining layers of the earth).

Albert Hesse, translated by Carl Heron, Bradford, U.K.

See also AERIAL PHOTOGRAPHY FOR ARCHAEOLOGY; ELECTRICAL AND ELECTROMAGNETIC PROSPECTING; GEORADAR; SONAR; MAGNETIC PROSPECTING; REMOTELY OPERATED VEHICLES; SEISMIC REFRACTION SURVEYING; SITE MAPPING; SURVEYING AND SITE EXAMINATION, MANUAL METHODS; SURVEYS, MULTISTAGE AND LARGE-SCALE; THERMAL PROSPECTING

Further Readings

Barba, L. (1990) Radiografia de un sitio arqueologico. Mexico City: Universidad Nacional Autonoma de Mexico.

Ferdière, A., and Zadora-Rio, A.E., eds. (1986) La prospection archéologique: Paysage et peuplement. Table Ronde Paris 14–15 mai 1982. Paris: Editions de la Maison des Sciences de l'Homme. Documents d'Archéologie Française 3.

Flannery, K.V., ed. (1976) The Early Mesoamerican Village. New York: Academic.

Hesse, A. (1994) La prospection archéologique: Des mesures extensives sur deux dimensions de l'espace. Histroie & Mesure 9(3/4):213–229.

——— (1981) La reconnaissance des sites archéologiques à partir de l'échantillonnage des vestiges de surface: Problèm de méthode et exemples, pp. 513–521. (Coll. Internat. du CNRS 598, Lyon 10–14 juin 1980). Paris: CNRS.

Hodder, I., and Orton, C. (1976) Spatial Analysis in Archaeology. Cambridge: Cambridge University Press.

Scollar, I. (1990) Archaeological Prospecting and Remote Sensing. Cambridge: Cambridge University Press.

Archaeological Sites, Formation Processes

Factors responsible for creating the many spatial clusterings of archaeological materials that account for so much of the archaeological record. Numerous formation processes result from human behavior. Cultural formation processes are those that result from human behavior. Environmental formation processes are those that result from the conditions and forces of nature.

Formation processes often work together or in sequence in complex ways. Some, though not all, result in materials entering archaeological context (no longer within a human behavioral system). Others can move materials from archaeological context back into systemic context (participating within a human behavioral system). Still others serve to alter (and sometimes prolong) the participation of materials in either archaeological or systemic contexts. As a result, materials can move repeatedly in and out of both archaeological and systemic contexts, while the condition and location of materials can also change while they are within these contexts. The history of objects and artifacts, from the time of initial acquisition to the time of archaeological recovery, is often long and complicated.

Archaeologists have always understood that the archaeological record is an incomplete and distorted reflection of the past. Until recently, however, this understanding has been implicit and incomplete, and strategies to interpret the record have been unsystematic and inadequate. The profound impacts formation processes have on the creation of the archaeological record, and the great variety of these processes and their impacts, have not been fully appreciated.

This unfortunate situation has been changing since the mid-1970s, primarily due to the contributions of Michael B. Schiffer. More than any other archaeologist, Schiffer has argued convincingly that formation processes are ubiquitous, very influential, and extraordinarily complex. He has also argued, however, that they can be recognized and accounted for; indeed, they must be if proper archaeological interpretation is to be achieved.

Cultural Formation Processes: Deposition
Deposition includes a number of formation processes that result in materials moving from systemic context into archaeological context. Traditionally, it has been the most widely recognized of the various types of formation processes resulting from human behavior.

Discard is the intentional throwing away of items no longer considered useful or usefully reused (*reuse* is discussed below). This process is not simple and can involve a series of intermediate events or steps, including temporary periods of storage and transport.

Discard is initiated in a number of different ways, depending on the nature of an item's intended functions. Many items lose their technological functions by breakage, use-wear, or other forms of deterioration. Other items might continue to perform well technically, while losing their ideological or sociological functions by going out of style or by no longer symbolizing the social positions of the users. A relatively small number of additional items are also discarded because they are perceived as disposable regardless of their condition or because they are the resulting waste products of production activities.

Once discard is initiated, items travel complex pathways before reaching their final resting places in the archaeological record. Of greatest importance to the archaeologist is the fact that very few items are ultimately discarded at the locations where they were used. When this does happen, which is rare, resulting deposits are called *primary refuse*. Much more common is the ultimate discard of items away from use locations, resulting in deposits called *secondary refuse*.

Loss happens when objects are misplaced and not recovered. Rates of loss are determined by the probability that an item will be misplaced in the first place and the probability that it will not be found.

Both probabilities vary inversely with the size of an item; the smaller an object, the greater the chance that it will be misplaced and not retrieved. An item's color, texture, and other formal properties can also influence rates of loss, particularly in relation to environmental characteristics that might mask the presence of an item to varying degrees. Environmental conditions are also important independent of an item's properties. The nature of the surface and the subsurface where items are being used is particularly influential.

Finally, how an item is used and perceived can influence rates of loss. Objects that were moved about considerably while in systemic context tend to be lost more often. Objects that are considered valuable, in contrast, are subject to greater retrieval efforts after they are initially misplaced.

Caching (the creation of caches) is the purposeful burying of items so that they can be recovered at a later time. There are numerous reasons why this process occurs, ranging from secular economic strategies to ritual mandates. In addition, the rates and nature of caching vary in complex ways in relation to the social positions of the participants and the technological complexity of the society in which it occurs. For these reasons, caches are difficult to identify precisely. Indeed, they are often confused with completely different types of deposition, such as discard and loss. Generally, though not always, caches are discrete deposits containing items that (apparently) retain their usefulness.

Burial is a particular type of deposition that involves placing the remains of the dead into the archaeological record. Archaeologists have always recognized that burials are fruitful sources for diverse, important information, and all of the various interpretations regarding human burial practices cannot be described adequately here.

Abandonment results in a place entering archaeological context, not necessarily any particular item or group of items. Some abandoned places are as small as individual limited-activity areas and isolated households. Other abandoned places cover entire settlements and even entire regions. The causes of abandonment also range widely and include the depletion of resources, the deterioration of materials, the emergence of diverse social pressures, and environmental changes. Of course, certain people (a number of gatherer-hunters and pastoralists, for example) abandon places on a regular, though often temporary, basis as part of a normal pattern of migration.

A somewhat common and significant outcome of abandonment is the creation of *de facto refuse*, items that are often still useful but that nevertheless enter archaeological context because they are left at the abandoned place. Items that are not left behind are subject to *curate behavior*, the removal of materials during the process of abandonment for continued use elsewhere. Numerous factors influence the nature of de facto refuse formation and curate behavior at any particular place, including the rate of abandonment, the means of available transport, the distance to the next settlement, the formal characteristics of the items involved, the perceived value of the items, and more. Archaeologists have yet to decipher the precise degrees of impact these variables have under different circumstances.

Cultural Formation Processes: Reclamation
A number of formation processes result in materials moving from archaeological context back into systemic context. These are called *reclamation.*

Scavenging is the retrieval of a settlement's archaeological materials by residents of the same settlement. A wide variety of deposited items and other material remains are deemed valuable enough to reclaim in this manner, and the greater the value, the greater the effort; degree of availability of these archaeological materials also plays a role.

General rates of scavenging are primarily determined by the relative availability of necessary or desired items within systemic context, however. People with limited economic or political power tend to scavenge more than those who can easily obtain material goods. Also, people living in marginal environments (often the same people with limited power) more often find it necessary to scavenge than do those living in more resource-rich surroundings.

Collecting occurs when residents of one settlement take archaeological materials from the surface of another. As with scavenging, the value and the availability of items influence the amount of collecting and the effort extended. Unlike scavenging, however, collecting entails the transport of items from one place to another (see salvage, below). Thus, the available means of transport is a significant factor influencing what is collected and how much is collected. Generally, large and heavy objects are ignored unless the energy to move them in a reasonable manner is available.

Collecting also differs form scavenging in that more powerful people tend to collect more often than less powerful people. Indeed, those with more economic and political wherewithal often collect from the places of those with less. This phenomenon (along with *treasure hunting*) is most obvious in the modern world, with powerful industrial nations collecting valuable items from the Third World.

Treasure hunting, in contrast to collecting, occurs when residents of one settlement take archaeological materials from the subsurface of another. Factors and conditions influencing the nature of each are similar, except that treasure hunting requires excavation. Ease of removing items from the ground is thus an important variable. Generally, among treasure hunters of equal technological level, the deeper and more firmly embedded the object, the less likely it will be subject to

A

removal. As technological sophistication increases—as the amount of available energy for excavation rises—the likelihood and the amount of treasure hunting are apt to increase as well.

Salvage is the reclamation of materials from a place previously occupied and then abandoned by either the same people or other people. Unlike scavenging, there is no continuous occupation or other use of the place from the time of the earlier activities to the time of the salvaging event. Unlike collecting and treasure hunting, there is no need to transport the material from one place to another. In other respects, it appears that many of the influences of salvage patterns are similar to those responsible for these other reclamation processes. The precise role of relative economic and political power remains unclear, however.

Archaeological excavation and other forms of archaeological recovery are, of course, the best recognized examples of reclamation, though they are clearly not the most important as measured by impacts on the archaeological record. Many aspects of archaeological excavation are treated thoroughly throughout this volume.

Cultural Formation Processes: Disturbance

Various human behaviors cause changes in either the condition or the location of materials that nevertheless remain in archaeological context. These changes are called *disturbance*. Innumerable behaviors can cause disturbance, though some cause more than others. These have been the foci of investigations by a number of archaeologists.

Trampling involves walking across the ground surface, by humans and animals, and disturbs materials on and immediately below the surface. Resulting disturbances include the vertical movement of objects into and out of the subsurface, horizontal movement of objects across the surface (lateral displacement), and breakage or other damage to objects.

More traffic will, of course, create greater trampling. Traffic tends to be greatest in areas containing few surface artifacts, however. Conversely, those places with dense surface deposits tend to be scenes of little traffic.

Ground surfaces exhibit varying degrees of penetrability. Some are hard and resist the penetration of objects, while others are soft and easily penetrated. The size, shape, and material composition of the surface materials will also have an influence. One well-documented effect involves the size-sorting of materials by depth, with larger objects more often moved upward toward the surface, and small objects more often moved downward away from the surface. The result is that surface assemblages often contain an overrepresentation of relatively large items.

These same variables have impacts on horizontal displacement, as do the slope of the land, the nature and the amount of vegetation present, and the nature of any nearby obstacles.

Plowing is the churning of soil brought about by agricultural activities, usually mechanical, though sometimes resulting from the use of animals. It disturbs materials on and below the surface to a depth of a few inches or even, more rarely, a few feet. Similar to trampling, plowing results in both the vertical and the horizontal displacement of objects, as well as their deterioration. Vertical size-sorting of materials is likely, and lateral displacement tends to be in the direction of plowing activities. The deterioration of objects can be extreme.

The major factor influencing the nature of plowing disturbances is the intensity of field preparation. Generally, the more intensive the plowing, the greater the impact.

Major construction projects are an additional source of disturbance processes. These are numerous and varied and often extensive.

Cultural Formation Processes: Reuse

Reuse consists of a variety of formation processes that prolong the time materials remain in systemic context. They do this by changing the user of an item, the use of an item, or the form of an item, or some combination of these characteristics.

Lateral cycling is a change in an object's user, without any change in the use or form of the material. It appears that lateral cycling is common in many societies, through the mechanisms of gift giving, inheritance, and theft. Yet, it remains difficult to document archaeologically, since no changes in formal attributes are involved. Indirect measures of lateral cycling might be reflected in changes in the frequency and the spatial dimensions of artifacts.

Recycling is a profound change in a object's use and form. It occurs when the item is remanufactured into a different item, after its original usefulness has been lost (assuming it had an original usefulness—waste products are also subject to recycling). Like lateral cycling, recycling is fairly common in many societies. Unlike lateral cycling (and fortunately for archaeologists), recycling is relatively easy to recognize in the archaeological record due to the physical traces it often creates on artifacts.

Secondary use is a change in use without any profound change in form. Unlike recycling, secondary use can often be observed archaeologically because the change in use commonly results in a change in use-wear patterns. When an object exhibits wear that is not considered the result of initial use, secondary use is the probable explanation. In addition, changes in the frequency and the spatial dimensions of artifacts might be indirect reflections of secondary use.

Conservation is a special form of secondary use, involving a conscious attempt to preserve an item owing to its perceived value or importance. The best-recognized conservation processes are those that result in creating a large part of the historical record, including both documents and materials. These processes are more prevalent in complex societies where the necessary institutional support is present (e.g., archives and museums).

Environmental Formation Processes

Certain environmental formation processes can move materials from systemic context to archaeological context and are, thus, analogous to deposition. Others can alter the condition and the location of materials while they remain in archaeological context and are, thus, analogous to disturbance. The important distinction in both cases is that the environmental processes do no involve a human agent.

No environmental formation process is analogous to reclamation, though some can increase the probability that reclamation will occur, while others can decrease this probability. Likewise, no environmental process is analogous to reuse, though certain environmental factors have impacts on materials that nevertheless remain in systemic context.

A large number of environmental formation processes can be related to disturbances of soils and sediments. These result in disturbances to related portions of the archaeological record. Together, these processes are called *pedoturbation*.

Aeroturbation includes all soil and sediment disturbances that are created by the action of air. Best known is soil deflation and the creation of desert pavement. *Argilliturbation* involves swelling and shrinking of clay, caused by changing amounts of moisture in the subsurface. *Cryoturbation* includes those impacts on the archaeological record that result from freezing and thawing of the subsurface. *Graviturbation,* in turn, consists of all of those impacts that are the direct and exclusive result of gravity.

Faunalturbation includes all of the various impacts nonhuman animals can have on the archaeological record. The most profound result, brought about by the actions of numerous burrowing animals, is the vertical mixing of soils and sediments. Less profound, though generally still important, is the lateral displacement of artifacts that results from animals on the surface.

Floralturbation, in contrast, consists of the impacts plant life has on the archaeological record. Root growth is the most widespread and significant of these, though the soil disturbance caused when trees fall can also be profound at times. Vegetation also results in soil formation, not just soil disturbance. The nature of surface vegetation has numerous and important impacts on site visibility and, while not a formation process per se, is nevertheless an important influence on survey and excavation sampling strategies.

Other environmental formation processes occur across entire regions, though they still have dramatic impacts on individual sites. Water and wind have extraordinary impacts on the surface of the landscape. Both have their greatest impacts under ordinary conditions over sufficient periods of time.

Dramatic, even cataclysmic, events of regional scale occur rarely, though their impacts on sites can be profound as well. Hurricanes, earthquakes, and volcanic eruptions sometimes result in the complete destruction of entire archaeological sites.

Discussion

Clearly, a great number of cultural and environmental formation processes have impacts on the creation of the archaeological record. At any archaeological site, chances are good that numerous formation processes acted

A

together or in sequence in a complex fashion.

Cultural formation processes are directly related to human behavior patterns and, as a result, are more difficult to decipher. Human behavior patterns are knowable only through proper archaeological interpretation, which itself is possible only when the impacts of formation processes are accurately and precisely understood. Yet, how can these processes be known without a knowledge of the behaviors responsible for them? Recognizing the importance of formation processes apparently presents archaeologists with the impossible requirement of knowing what is unknown in order to ever have a chance of knowing it.

The way around this seemingly impossible task is found in ethnoarchaeology, experimental archaeology, historical archaeology, and other sources of useful analogs. Now that archaeologists have come to better appreciate the great influence and complexity of formation processes, it is time to better understand their precise nature through the proper development and testing of relevant analogies.

Edward Staski

See also ETHNOARCHAEOLOGY; EXPERIMENTAL ARCHAEOLOGY; HISTORICAL ARCHAEOLOGY; MORTUARY SITES, EXCAVATION AND ANALYSIS; SCHIFFER, MICHAEL BRIAN

Further Readings

Goldberg, P., Nash, D.T., and Petraglia, M.D., eds. (1994) Formation Processes in Archaeological Context. Madison, WI: Prehistory Press.

Miksicek, C.H. (1987) Formation processes of the archaeobotanical record. In M.B. Schiffer (ed): Advances in Archaeological Method and Theory, vol. 10, pp. 211–247. New York: Academic.

Nash, D.T., and Petraglia, M.D., eds. (1987) Natural Formation Processes and the Archaeological Record. (BAR International Series 352). Oxford: British Archaeological Reports.

Schiffer, M.B. (1976) Behavioral Archaeology. New York: Academic.

Schiffer, M.B. (1987) Formation Processes of the Archaeological Record. Albuquerque: University of New Mexico Press.

Staski, E., and Sutro, L.D., eds. (1991) The Ethnoarchaeology of Refuse Disposal.
(Anthropological Research Papers 42). Tempe: Arizona State University.

Wood, W.R., and Johnson, D.L. (1978) A survey of disturbance processes in archaeological site formation. In M.B. Schiffer (ed): Advances in Archaeological Method and Theory, vol. 1, pp. 315–381. New York: Academic.

Archaeomagnetic Dating

Relative dating technique that uses the magnetic record of known changes in the Earth's magnetic field to date fired artifacts or contemporary sediments/rocks.

The Earth's magnetic field is continually changing in shape and strength. The general shape is that of a dipole field (like the field of a bar magnet) statistically aligned along the rotation axis. However, the best-fitting dipole at any one time can be tilted as much as 20° from the rotation axis and can change in strength by 50 percent. As well as the dipole field, there is also a nondipole component that can grow and decay and move and can change the strength of the field locally by 20 percent or more. Magnetic anomalies due to the nondipole field are large (1,000–2,000 km wide) and are thought to sometimes move westward at ca. 0.13°/year. The combination of changing dipole and nondipole fields means that the magnetic field at one place will change in both direction and strength with time but that the changes in one locality will not necessarily be the same as the changes at every locality.

Another feature of the Earth's magnetic field is its ability to completely reverse direction (or polarity). A field reversal occurs when the field strength collapses and the north magnetic pole moves to the south geographic pole. Field reversals have frequently occurred over the past 100 million years; the field has been normal (north magnetic pole near north geographic pole) for about half the time and reversed (north magnetic pole near south geographic pole) for the other half. The most recent field reversal occurred 740,000 years ago.

Many materials record the Earth's magnetic field at the time they are formed or heated. Sediments usually contain magnetic minerals, and the magnetization of these minerals can become statistically aligned with the Earth's field as the sediment is formed. There is often a secondary magnetization that is formed shortly after formation of the sediment as new magnetic minerals are chemically formed. The resulting bulk magnetization of the sediment is in the direction of the Earth's field at (or nearly at) the time of formation of the sediment. Heating a material containing magnetic minerals will allow the magnetization of the material to be remagnetized in the direction of the Earth's field at the time it was last cooled. Fired ceramics, fireplaces, kilns, and igneous rocks all become magnetized when they cool, and the strength of their magnetization is proportional to the strength of the magnetic field at the time they cooled. The magnetic record contained in sediments and fired material is often very stable and will remain intact for millions of years.

The magnetization carried in archaeological material is generally very weak but can be measured using sensitive laboratory magnetometers. Because the archaeological material may have had a complex history, the magnetization of the sample is usually examined by stepwise demagnetization to check that all of the magnetization has the same characteristics. Demagnetization is usually by progressive heating and cooling in zero magnetic field or progressive magnetic cleaning using an alternating magnetic field.

There are basically three ways in which one can use changes in the Earth's magnetic field for archaeomagnetic dating.

Archaeomagnetic Field Strength Dating

This technique is usually applied only to fired material since it uses the fact that the magnetization is proportional to the field strength, and this is valid only for material that has been heated and cooled. Since the determination of the archaeomagnetic field strength does not require the sample to be spatially oriented (i.e., remaining in situ after firing), it can be used on broken potsherds. Archaeomagnetic field strength dating can be carried out only if there is a *master curve* of how the field strength has varied *at the locality where the undated sample was last fired*.

The archaeointensity master curve (Figure 1) is constructed from data from northern

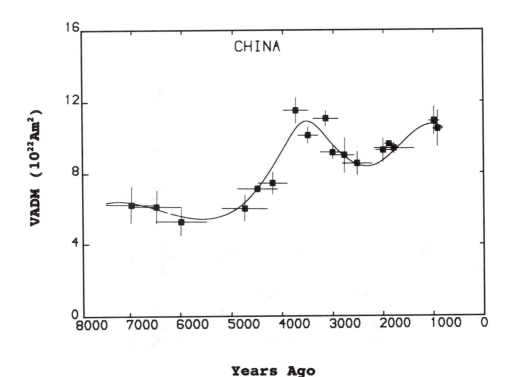

Figure 1. Archaeointensity master curve for northern central China. From Yang, S., Shaw, J., and Wei, Q.Y. (1993) Tracking a non-dipole geomagnetic anomaly using new archaeointensity results from Northeast China, Geophysical Journal International, 115:1189–1196. Blackwell Science Ltd. by permission.

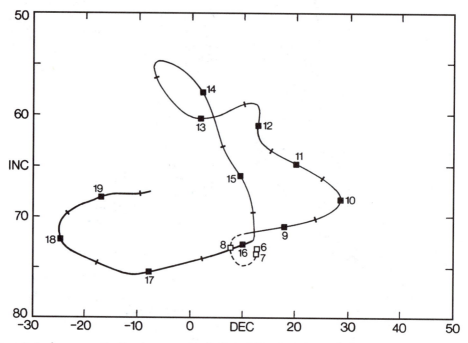

Figure 2. Archaeomagnetic direction curve for the United Kingdom. From Clark, A.J., Tarling, D.H. and Noel, M., Developments in archaeomagnetic dating in Britain, Journal of Archaeological Science *(1988)* 15:645–557, *by permission.*

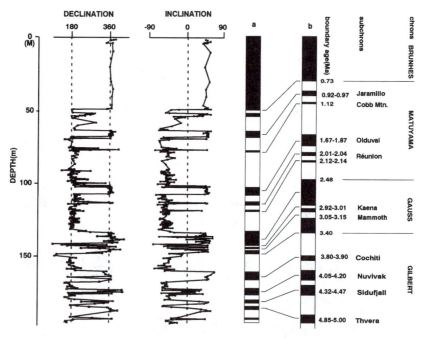

Figure 3. Magnetostratigraphy of the Lantian Homo erectus *site, China. Illustration by J. Shaw, after Zheng Hongbo, An Zisheng and Shaw, J., New contributions to Chinese Plio-Pleistocene magnetostratigraphy,* Physics of the Earth and Planetary Interiors *(1992) 70:146–153.*

central China covering the past 8,000 years. The data are expressed as VADM (Virtual Axial Dipole Moment) values (i.e., the equivalent axial dipole moment that would produce the field strength observed at the site). The present-day VADM is $8 \times 10^{22} \text{Am}^2$ (Am^2 is a unit of magnetic moment; a current of 1 amp flowing around a single loop of wire containing an area of 1 m^2 produces a magnetic moment of 1 Am^2), so the field was as strong as the present-day value at 2,500 and 4,000 years ago. This highlights one of the difficulties with archaeomagnetic field strength dating: There are often several periods in time when the field is the same value. Matching a field-strength value of unknown age to a master curve can give several possible dates, and it is frequently necessary to have additional information (contextual or other dates) to narrow the choice. The controversial Glozel archaeological site in northern France was one of the first sites to be dated in 1976 using this technique. Both thermoluminescence dating and archaeomagnetic field strength dating agreed that the site, which some people believed to be Neolithic, was only 2,000 years old.

Archaeomagnetic Field Direction Dating

The direction of the Earth's magnetic field is usually represented as two angles, declination and inclination. Declination (D) is the angle the horizontal component of the field makes with geographic north, and inclination (I) is the angle that the field makes with the horizontal. Individual directions (D,I pairs) are often plotted on a two-dimensional plot.

Measurements of kilns, fireplaces, and sedimentary sequences can provide D,I data and, like field-strength dating, local master curves are needed. Ambiguity is again a problem as it is possible to have the same D,I pair at different times. In Figure 2, we can see that the sixteenth-century and the eighth-century directions for Britain are very similar. Combining direction and intensity dates can often give a unique date.

Field Reversal Dating (Magnetostratigraphy)

This dating technique is usually applied to sedimentary sequences containing artifacts. The date refers to the sediment, and the artifact is dated by its relationship to the sediment. It is normal to make many magnetic measurements down the sedimentary sequence in order to determine the magnetic-polarity stratigraphy. The polarity stratigraphy is then matched to the well-established polarity time scale. Since field reversals are global the polarity time scale has global application, and local master curves are not necessary.

For archaeological purposes, the most recent three polarity intervals (chrons) are the most useful (Brunhes normal, Matuyama reversed, and Gauss normal chron). Within the main chrons, there are well-dated subchrons (short polarity intervals), so, over the past five million years, there are twenty-four well-dated polarity boundaries. Short sedimentary sequences cannot be easily matched to the polarity time scale, so additional information is often required to allow identification of the matching polarity boundary. If the sedimentary sequence is sufficiently long, then the correlation is unambiguous and a firm date can be given. The data in Figure 3 are from Lantian, near Xian, China. The cranium of Lantian *Homo erectus* was situated just below the record of the Cobb Mountain geomagnetic event, which is dated at 1.12 million years. A date of 1.13 million years is assigned to the cranium, making it one of the oldest early human sites in China.

John Shaw

Further Readings

Aitken, M.J. (1974) Physics and Archaeology, 2nd ed. Oxford: Clarendon.

Clark, A.J., Tarling, D.H., and Noel, M. (1988) Developments in archaeomagnetic dating in Britain. Journal of Archaeological Science 15:645–557.

Shaw, J. (1985) Recent advances in archaeomagnetism. Journal of Geomagnetism and Geoelectricity 37:119–127.

Archaeometry

The application of the physical sciences to archaeological problems and issues.

Although early formulations of the field included the natural as well as physical sciences, most contemporary usages are restricted to applications of physics and chemistry. The principal journal in the field, *Archaeometry*, published in Oxford, England, follows this convention for the most part. Natural science applications have come into their own in archaeology as geoarchaeology, zooarchaeology, and paleoethnobotany. Because European archaeology is tied to natural rather than social science historically, archaeometry developed first and remains most important and best integrated with archaeology in Europe. In the United States and areas academically influenced by American archaeology, archaeometry still tends to be regarded as an optional specialty rather than an essential component.

Archaeometry is usually divided into a number of subfields: *prospecting; provenance studies; dating methods;* and *material science* applications. Because dating is covered elsewhere in depth, the focus here is on the other three areas.

Prospecting

Traditionally grouped here are a number of dissimilar methods that share only their use in the field: initially, to find places to dig but, more recently, to generate data about archaeological phenomena that supplement those acquired by traditional means. Aerial photography is the oldest and most widely used method; serious applications date from the First World War in the Near East. The identification of hilltop enclosures of Neolithic and later ages, field systems, roads, and other structures began systematically in Britain under the initial direction of Osbert G.S. Crawford in the 1920s and continues today. Archaeological applications in the United States were later, more sporadic, and initially largely limited to providing pictorial coverage of known sites.

Engineers divide the use of aerial photographs into two components: *remote sensing,* the identification and characterization of objects at a distance; and *photogrammetry,* the quantification of photographs (emulsion-based) and images (electronic). Remote sensing depends upon interaction between a target (subject) and some part of the electromagnetic-radiation spectrum that can be detected by a sensor. Methods are usually described as passive (using ambient radiation) or active (some probative radiation is employed).

Most archaeological usages are unsophisticated and limited to remote sensing. European archaeological photography was done typically with simple equipment and at oblique angles to the surface. Such photographs could not be converted into maps or otherwise quantified efficiently until the advent of cheap computing in the 1980s. Americans, on the other hand, made extensive use of vertical-mapping photography in the public domain and developed their own special photography on that model. Consequently, occasional photogrammetric applications, some of spectacular proportions such as Rene Millon's 1973 Teotihuacan mapping project, have been carried out by U.S. archaeologists. A major effort to promote the use of aerial photography was made in the 1970s by the National Park Service through the Chaco Center, New Mexico, but application of aerial photography remains an occasional rather than a routine part of fieldwork in the United States. In large part, archaeologists have lagged decades behind other field scientists in using remote sensing and photogrammetry because the services of photogrammetrists usually are required (i.e., archaeologists cannot usually do it themselves), and archaeologists have not done the basic research to link aerial signatures with archaeological phenomena though the means to do so exist (Dunnell 1993). Historical aerial photography is also of enormous value in documenting areas since destroyed by agriculture and urbanization. While public-domain photography is mostly panchromatic (some color and color infrared [IR]), archaeologically flown missions have tended to use color infrared as the general-purpose film because of the sensitivity of IR to moisture and its ability to detect small differences in plant growth and vigor.

Satellite imagery and shuttle-based photography and imagery have not yet proved to be of much value, although long wave radar (23 cm) has detected buried channels in arid areas in Africa (which have led to archaeological discoveries) and have proved effective in detecting large-scale agricultural features in Mesoamerican jungles. Technical innovation has been driven by military application. Better sensors than are available to the public exist; their declassification may lead to an expansion of satellite-based imagery in archaeology.

Global positioning systems (GPS) are such an innovation. In GPS, a system of satellites broadcasts locational information, providing a system of known points that allows small receivers with an on-board computer to calculate the receiver location quite closely. With two receivers and corrections for the intentionally introduced inaccuracies that are designed to prevent hostile use, submeter accuracies are possible. Geographic information systems (GIS), software programs that permit large numbers of parameters to be integrated using geographic location, are becoming increasingly user friendly and will become the vehicle that will allow the integration of GPS and these small-scale remote-sensing techniques in a seamless analytic fabric. [In any case, the greater accuracy, cost effectiveness, and range of sensitivities of aerial-based remote sensing and photogrammetry will sooner or later overcome archaeological resistance and become standard parts of archaeological field work.]

While engineers do not consider near-surface technology remote sensing, archaeologists call many methods that are ground based, even with sensors in contact with the ground, remote sensing. Included here are magnetometry, resistivity, and ground-penetrating-radar (GPR) surveys.

Magnetometry is probably still the most widely employed method. Its archaeological application was initially developed at Oxford University by physicist Martin J. Aitken in the 1950s. The large, crude, first-generation machines have been replaced by highly portable one-person machines whose accuracies are at least two orders of magnitude better than the initial configurations. In magnetometry, the strength of the local magnetic field is the phenomenon measured, and archaeological applications typically involve detecting spatial anomalies in the magnetic field. Thus, magnetometry is a passive method. The generation of archaeologically significant signatures is usually linked to one or both of two unrelated phenomena. Heating causes naturally magnetic iron particles in sediments to align north-south, reinforcing the local field; pottery, bricks, and similar materials have the same effect. Second, the conversion of non-magnetic compounds, such as hematite, to magnetic ones, such as magmehematite, is enhanced by the presence of organic material, a common anthropogenic addition, making things like pits and ditches detectable.

Magnetic-field strength at any given point varies over time; consequently, raw magnetic measurements are not useful. Two solutions are employed. One is to generate a baseline of time-dependent variations by periodically remeasuring the same spot, either by returning the instrument to a control location or by stationing a second instrument at that location. Baseline data then must be subtracted from the raw readings. The other solution is to employ a gradiometer, in essence, two magnetometers held in fixed relation to each other so that only the difference between the two sensors is recorded, not the total magnetic flux. Since both magnetometers are equally affected by time-dependent fluctuations, the different measurements do not require correction. Not surprisingly, some of the best applications are in southern England, where the substrate is a rather magnetically uniform chalk, and archaeological anomalies stand out in stark contrast. Indeed, the utility of magnetometry is very much dependent upon a geologically appropriate background. Urban areas, with their multitude of magnetic fields, are inappropriate. The greatest liability of magnetometry is the relatively poor ability to differentiate depth from size and shape of anomalies. Measurement of magnetic susceptibility is a related active method in which a current is passed through the ground or sample, and the strength of the magnetic field so generated is measured.

Resistivity was also first developed in the 1950s as an archaeological tool by Aitken at Oxford. It is an active method that requires passing a small alternating (so as to be detectable against natural direct currents) current through the ground. A variety of different arrays of input and measurement probes have been, and to a limited extent still are, used; however, they all operate on the same basic principle: Different sediment compositions will display distinct resistivity (or conductivity, the inverse of resistivity) signatures. In practice, this usually means measuring pore space and, thus, moisture. Since water is a good insulator, what is typically measured is dissolved salts. Consequently, resistivity surveys are time and environment dependent to a degree not true of magnetometry (e.g., maps have to made under uniform moisture conditions). However, the volume of sediment sampled is directly dependent upon the spacing of the probes; thus, by varying probe spacing, anomaly depth can be fixed much more reliably than with magnetometry. And since different phenomena are measured (amount of organic matter, particle size, and other parameters that affect moisture levels) by resistivity, if both magnetometry and resistivity are applicable they will yield complementary information on deposit structure.

Ground-penetrating radar has seen less use because the equipment is still comparatively crude and the output is less readily interpretable without a substantial physical background. Radar is an active method. A pulse is directed at the ground, and the pulse is differentially absorbed or reflected by sediments, with water content (and dissolved salts) and particle size playing dominant roles in structuring the returning signal. An antenna/transmitter is towed across the target real estate, generating continuous transect data rather than discrete point data as in the other methods. As a ranging method, however, GPR delivers precise depth information on detectable strata and anomalies. Because the phenomena being sensed are similar, GPR has restrictions akin to those of resistivity. Particle size also plays a large role in determining the depth to which radar can penetrate—dry, coarse sediments allow the deepest penetration.

A few other geophysical exploration techniques (e.g., seismic, thermal) have been tested in archaeological contexts. None has broad potential with current equipment, though seismic surveys have been quite effective in detecting Etruscan tombs and similar structures.

Provenance Studies

Laboratory archaeometry (as opposed to field archaeometry) probably has its origins in the archaeological practice, dating to the nineteenth century, of calling upon analytic chemists to identify materials rendered enigmatic by the passage of time. Blood-residue analysis and the analysis of materials adhering to, or embedded in, ceramics continue in this tradition.

Composition studies lead rather naturally to identifying sources of raw materials, as well as their performance and technological properties. Provenance determination (sometimes called *sourcing* by Americans) is the empirical basis for studies of exchange and trade and is crucial to the estimation of technological costs in evolutionary studies. The first serious studies employed geological-petrographic techniques to identify tempering (aplastic inclusions) materials in ceramics to local and nonlocal sources. Petrographic techniques allow particular minerals to be identified.

There is a shift in modern studies to identify the elemental composition largely because of advances in instrumentation for elemental characterizations. A great number of methods are available. X-ray fluorescence (XRF) was an early method especially effective with obsidian, although the precision of these results has been called into question. Proton-induced X-ray emission (PIXE), instrumental neutron activation analysis (INAA), and inductively coupled plasma (ICP) spectrometry are important methods seeing wide use but differing in sample preparation, cost, elements that can be measured, and limits of detection. ICP-MS (ICP–mass spectrometry) combines simple sample preparation with low dectability limits and broad range of elements and promises to become the dominant method of elemental analysis in spite of high instrument cost. Gross composition can be coupled with sample visualization in wavelength dispersive spectrometry (WDS) and energy dispersive spectrometry (EDS), in which probe interaction with a sample in a scanning electron microscope (SEM) generates not only an image, but also data on composition. WDS can detect elements in trace amounts one at a time, whereas EDS generates data on a large suite of elements all at once but only major and minor constituents.

Because elemental-composition is not as distinctive as minerals or other compounds, analytic approaches tend to be inductive analyses of ad hoc (whatever are detected by the particular technique) sets of elements. Cluster analysis or principal-components analysis are usually employed to detect clusters of specimens that share the same elemental compositions on the assumption that such clusters represent distinct sources. More sophisticated approaches involve sampling geologic sources as well as archaeological specimens, and then clusters and sources are matched, hopefully, usually using discriminant-function analysis. These approaches have been applied broadly to ceramics of all sorts, lithics, and metals. Stable isotopes (lead) and thermoluminescence (TL) characteristics (obsidian) have been used in provenance determination, but neither is a general method applicable to a broad range of materials.

The primary limitation of use of such methods is the cost of the instrumentation and instrument time. But other problems are involved as well. Geological bedrock occurrences may not be archaeological sources; indeed, secondary deposits far from bedrock outcrops were widely used in antiquity. Further, prehistoric artisans were almost always selective, choosing particular varieties at the source, not random sampling the source. Thus, even a large, representative sample of a source may not be easily matched to artifacts from the source. Inductive approaches are entirely sample dependent, turning such problems into major obstacles. Some manufacturing processes also obscure matches by altering the composition of the archaeological material.

Provenance studies have been an archaeometric success story, but they remain relatively crude conceptually. Recent advances have been strongly linked to developments in instrumentation; the next wave of advances in provenance determination will almost certainly come not from new equipment but in how elemental composition is used to determine provenance.

Materials Science

Materials science, the newest of the archaeometric subfields, yields hard evidence on artifact function and performance by determining the physical and mechanical properties of materials and objects. In traditional archaeology, object function was largely a matter of analogic speculation or replicative "experiment." As it has become important to *know* what work objects did to explain their occurrence, mechanical testing has come to play an increasingly prominent role.

The earliest studies used fracture mechanics to explain how lithic chipping technologies worked—initially, percussion flaking but, more recently, the full range of techniques. Mechanical testing has been applied extensively in the study of ceramics to show how different potteries react to heating and mechanical trauma, leading to explanations for why one kind of ceramic replaces another. Such studies have also elucidated the role that different elements (e.g., temper, surface finishes) play in ceramic performance. Another major field lies in heat-treated lithics, a phenomenon just beginning to be understood as a consequence of mechanical testing under rigorous experimental conditions. The potential of mechanical testing, particularly strength testing, is beginning to be tapped in archaeological studies, and, because instrumentation is often relatively simple and inexpensive, it should see wide use. The greatest danger is the tendency among some workers to mix, or even mistake, the traditional replicative "ex-periment" for archaeometry just because some physical testing, often with ad hoc equipment, has been employed.

Mechanical testing aimed at determining performance properties has increased interest in technology, how artifacts are made, enormously. Archaeological specimens are usually broken and discarded as useless before they enter the archaeological record. Then they are subjected to diagenesis (chemical and physical transformations as a result of burial). Consequently, mechanical testing is not reasonably carried out on archaeological specimens but rather on replicates. To construct such replicates, one needs to know how, though not necessarily in a reconstructive fashion, artifacts were made. Here again, the physical properties of the objects themselves provide the empirical basis for uncovering the original technology. In ceramic technology, for example, firing temperature can be determined, in part, by the presence of minerals that form at specific temperatures, the breakdown of clay minerals and other constituents (e.g., temper, inclusions) at specific temperatures, and the oxidation state of included iron. TL and electron spin resonance (ESR) have also proved helpful in some cases. Similarly, the temperatures used in heat-treating lithic raw materials have been identified using differential thermal analysis (DTA) and thermogravimetric (TG) analysis coupled with changes in physical properties such as surface luster, the oxidation state of iron compounds, and the presence of heat-sensitive constituents (e.g., organic matter, calcite). Ancient metallurgical technologies have also been the subject of extensive investigation. Because metallurgy is of great importance in the modern world, reconstructing its technological history has attracted considerable interest from physical scientists, and a great variety of analytic tools are available. In high-temperature technologies, those that involve smelting of ores rather than simple annealing, if the initial ores are identifiable, composition of the final product can often imply a single technology or a small number of alternative technologies. Strictly metallographic methods (e.g., determination of crystal structure and size) can narrow possibilities even further and, when supplemented by remains (e.g., molds, furnaces) provide rather secure understanding of these ancient technologies.

Robert C. Dunnell

See also AERIAL PHOTOGRAPHY FOR ARCHAE-
OLOGY; ARCHAEOLOGICAL PROSPECTION; DAT-
ING, METHOD AND THEORY; ELECTRICAL AND
ELECTROMAGNETIC PROSPECTING; ELECTRON-
PROBE MICROANALYSIS; ELECTRON SPIN RESO-
NANCE (ESR) DATING; GEOGRAPHIC INFORMA-
TION SYSTEMS; GEORADAR; INDUCTIVELY
COUPLED PLASMA–ATOMIC EMISSION SPEC-
TROMETRY; INFRARED (IR) ABSORPTION SPEC-
TROSCOPY; ISOTOPES, STABLE (C, N, O, H):
BONE AND PALEODIET STUDIES; ISOTOPES,
STABLE (PB, SR): RAW MATERIALS AND PROVE-
NANCE STUDIES; MAGNETIC PROSPECTING;
METALLOGRAPHY; NUCLEAR METHODS OF
ANALYSIS; PETROGRAPHY; SEISMIC REFRACTION
SURVEYING; SONAR; THERMAL PROSPECTING;
THERMOLUMINESCENCE DATING; X-RAY DIF-
FRACTION (XRD) ANALYSIS; X-RAY FLUORES-
CENCE (XRF) ANALYSIS

Further Readings

Aitken, M.J. (1974) Physics and Archaeology,
    2nd ed. Oxford: Clarendon.
Bronitsky, G. (1986) The use of materials sci-
    ence techniques in the study of pottery
    construction and use. Advances in Ar-
    chaeological Method and Theory
    9:209–276.
Crawford, O.G.S. (1928) Air Survey and Ar-
    chaeology. Gt. Brit. Ordnance Survey
    Professional Papers. New Series no. 7,
    2nd ed. Southampton: Ordnance Survey.
Dunnell, R.C. (1993) Chemical origins of ar-
    chaeological aerial signatures. In A.J.
    Lewis (ed.): Looking into the Future with
    an Eye to the Past, vol. 2, pp. 66–75.
    (ASPRS Technical Papers, Remote Sens-
    ing). Bethesda, MD: American Society
    for Photogrammetry and Remote
    Sensing.
Dunnell, R.C., Ikeya, M., McCutcheon, P.T.,
    and Toyoda, S. (1994) Heat treatment of
    Mill Creek and Dover cherts on the
    Malden Plain. Journal of Archaeological
    Science 21:70–89.
Leute, U. (1987) Archaeometry: An Introduc-
    tion to Physical Methods in Archaeology
    and the History of Art. Weinheim: VCH
    Verlagsgesellschaft.
Lillesand, T.M., and Kiefer, R.W. (1994) Re-
    mote Sensing and Image Interpretation.
    New York: Wiley.
Millon, R., ed. (1973) Urbanization at Teoti-
    huacan, Mexico, vol. 1: The Teotihuacan
    Map. Austin: University of Texas Press.

Weymouth, J.W. (1986) Geophysical methods
    of archaeological site surveying. Ad-
    vances in Archaeological Method and
    Theory 9:311–395.

Archaeoparasitology

The field devoted to the identification of
parasite remains in the archaeological record
and the reconstruction of past human-
parasite interactions. Parasitic disease has
always been a major problem. Recent summaries of the prevalence of parasitic diseases
in the world today show that there are 4.5
billion infections with all species of parasitic
worm, 1 billion infections with giant intestinal roundworm (*Ascaris lumbricoides*),
750,000,000 infections with whipworms
(*Trichuris trichiura*), 900,000,000 infections
with hookworm (*Ancylostoma duodenale*
and *Necator americanus*), 657,000,000 infections with filarial worms, 200,000,000
with blood flukes (schistosome species), and
489,000,000 infections with malaria. These
infections cause between 1,590,000 to
3,130,000 million deaths per year (Roberts
and Janovy 1996:2). One can see from these
statistics that any contribution to understanding human parasitism will contribute
to reducing the parasite problem. The archaeological record provides the necessary
time depth to document the origins of
human parasitism. Modern archaeology is
sufficiently refined to identify the behavioral
and ecological conditions that led to the
emergence of parasitism as a threat to
human well-being. Therefore, archaeology is
a field of important basic research that can
be used to address the rise of parasitism in
addition to issues of purely archaeological
significance.

What Is a Parasite?

Parasitology is a broad field of study. It is not
defined by organisms with shared morphological traits. Instead, parasitology is defined
by the subsistence strategy of certain organisms in evolutionary context with host organisms that house and feed them. Parasites are
organisms that have evolved with host organisms such that the host organism provides
food and shelter to the parasite. All organisms that have this evolutionary relationship
with a host are termed *parasites* whether they
are worms, arthropods (insects, crustaceans),

or protozoa (single-celled animals). There are two main categories of parasite: endoparasites and ectoparasites. *Endoparasites,* such as intestinal worms, live within the tissues of the host organism. *Ectoparasites* such as lice and fleas, live on the surface of the host organism.

Parasitic protozoa are single-celled organisms. They include flagellates, amoebas, ciliates, and coccidians. These are differentiated by several features, the most obvious of which is the manner of locomotion. *Flagellates* propel themselves with a whiplike structure called a *flagellum. Amoebas* move by shifting cytoplasm through pseudodopod appendages. *Ciliates* move by the beating of the cilia, or hairlike structures that cover their surface. *Coccidians* are passive and move with the flow of whatever medium they are in (e.g., blood, chyme). *Helminths* are parasitic worms. They include two groups of flatworms, the flukes (*trematodes*) and the tapeworms (*cestodes*). Two other groups of helminths are the roundworms (*nematodes*), and the thorny-headed worms (*acanthocephalans*). *Arthropod parasites* of humans are ectoparasites and include fleas, lice, and mites.

All of these types of parasites can be found in one way or another in the archaeological record. Some are depicted in art (Figure 1), and a few are documented in written records. K.Y. Mumcuoglu and J. Zias found evidence of parasites on artifacts that were used to remove them in prehistory. The find of a lice comb from ancient Israel bears testimony to not only the presence of arthropod parasites, but also the development of technological innovations to get rid of the parasites.

Most parasite remains are not associated with artifacts. The analysis of soil samples, coprolites, skeletons, and mummies provides direct evidence of parasitism. Different types of archaeological remains present different spectra of parasites due to preservation factors. Soil samples often contain eggs of helminths that live in the digestive tract. The study of latrines and soils from cultural deposits has long been an important source of archaeoparasite data. Andrew Jones and Bernd Herrmann have been the most active researchers in Europe, and Karl Reinhard developed similar studies in North America. Such study is becoming increasingly interesting to historical archaeologists. Latrine sites provide suitable conditions for preservation of

A

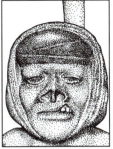

Figure 1. *The destruction of the nose and mouth by the protozoan* Leishmania brasiliensis *as depicted by ancient Moche potters in Peru. This series of ceramic depictions illustrates the levels of destruction caused by the disease from initial lesions of the nose, to destruction of the nose and lips, to exposure of bone and teeth. This disease, espundia, is endemic to the western slopes of the Andes. Humans become infected with the Leishmania flagellate protozoa through sandfly bites. Drawn by Jonathan Ham. Courtesy of the artist; source: Urtega-Ballon 1991.*

more durable eggs, but fragile eggs are susceptible to decomposition in latrine environments. European researchers have done the most extensive work with latrine deposits, especially of medieval sites. The comparative parasite ecology of medieval cities has been defined through this work, which has elucidated the role of urbanization in the rise of parasitic disease.

Coprolites contain the eggs and larvae of helminths, the cysts of protozoa, and the exoskeletons of ectoparasites (it was a common ancient custom to eat lice groomed from the hair). Reinhard in North America and Luiz Ferreira and Adauto Araújo in South America have used coprolites as their main focus of research. Although coprolite analysis was initially designed to recover dietary data, techniques were quickly devised for parasitological study. Caves offer excellent

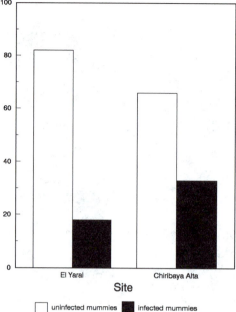

Figure 2. *The distribution of head lice between two villages in southern Peru. Chiribaya Alta is a coastal site with a high prevalence of louse infection. El Yaral is located several miles inland and at a higher elevation. Clearly, the ecological conditions at Chiribaya Alta allowed the proliferation of head lice. Drawn by Karl Reinhard.*

preservation conditions for the retrieval of helminth eggs, helminth larvae, and protozoan cysts in coprolites. Coprolites from open sites are less well preserved, and parasite eggs within such coprolites can be partly decomposed. Mummies can contain the cysts of protozoa plus the eggs, larvae, and adult forms of helminths that live in the digestive system or disperse eggs and larvae via the digestive system. Importantly, parasites that invade other organs can be recovered. Also, soft-tissue pathology caused by protozoa infection can be identified, which provides indirect evidence of parasitism. Louse nits can be identified in the hair, and infestations can be quantified for paleoepidemiological comparisons (Figure 2). Skeletons sometimes contain the calcified cysts of tapeworms (Figure 3) or exhibit bone pathology typical of other parasite infections.

What Can Parasite Remains Tell Us about Past Cultures?

The role of parasites in archaeological interpretation was summarized by Reinhard in 1992.

Here are some of the more important roles parasites have in archaeological reconstruction.

Diet is reflected by parasite remains both by the find of actual parasitic organisms and by evidence of what is called *false parasitism*. *Cryptocotyl lingua* (fluke) from St. Lawrence Island, Alaska, provides evidence of Yuit fish consumption. *Diphyllobothrium pacificum* (tapeworm) from the Pacific coast of Chile and Peru documents fish consumption among preagricultural peoples. Hymenolepidid worms (tapeworms) provide evidence of use of grain stores by Colorado Plateau agriculturalists. Acanthocephalans (thorny-headed worms) provide evidence of insect consumption among Great Basin foragers. *Taenia solium* (pork tapeworm) cysts and eggs in an Egyptian mummy demonstrate the consumption of pork. *Taenia* spp. eggs in a Jerusalem

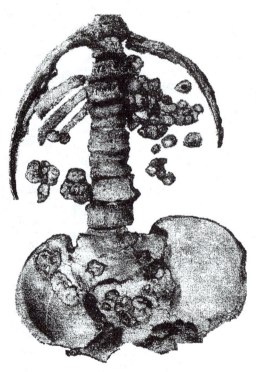

Figure 3. *Drawing of hydatid cysts found in the abdominal cavity of a medieval Danish burial. Hydatid disease is caused by two tapeworm species in the genus* Echinococcus. *In this case,* Echinococcus granulosis *caused the disease. The cysts are caused by larval stages of the worm that encyst in the visceral cavity. The larvae divide within the cyst, producing thousands of additional larvae. The proliferation of the larvae causes the cysts to enlarge. In this case, the cysts are the size of almonds. Drawn by Karl Reinhard.*

latrine dating to 486 B.C. indicate that pork or beef was consumed by the priestly class in Palestine. *Fasciola hepatica* (sheep-liver fluke) discovered in several medieval German latrines results from the consumption of unwashed greens collected from moist areas. Therefore, consumption of greens is indicated by the presence of the parasites. The presence of domestic animals is implicated by the finds, since animal domestication often is associated with human infection.

Transhumance (seasonal movements of people) and trade are indicated by the find of parasite remains in archaeological sites outside of the normal range of the parasite. *T. trichiura* (whipworm) eggs in latrine soils at the prehistoric site of Elden Pueblo near Flagstaff, Arizona, demonstrate seasonal movement from the Colorado Plateau to the Verde River Valley. *D. pacificum* finds from the site of Tiliviche (4110–1950 B.C.) in northern Chile 40 km from the Pacific coast at an altitude 950 m indicate that fish were traded inland or that coastal fisherfolk migrated seasonally inland.

Because certain parasites are specific to restricted ecological conditions, the parasite evidence provides general data regarding the environments in which the human population lives. They also reflect ecological change between modern and prehistoric times. *Strongyloides* spp. from Antelope House in Arizona and Clyde's Cavern in Utah indicate that the prehistoric conditions were more moist than at present, at least in the environments frequented by prehistoric peoples. Fluke remains from Egypt from early agricultural times suggest that utilization of irrigation resulted in modifications of local environments that were suitable for the proliferation of moisture-dependent parasites and their intermediate hosts, such as snails. Warm temperatures and moist conditions are prerequisites for hookworm infection. Hookworm eggs and adults have been found in coprolites and mummies in Brazil and Peru, indicating that the peoples represented by these mummies and coprolites lived at least occasionally in moist, warm conditions.

Hygienic conditions are reflected by parasite remains. *Enterobius vermicularis* (pinworm) prevalence in coprolite samples from Anasazi cave sites is extremely high, indicating that these early "apartment dwellers" lived in conditions of crowding and poor sanitation. The ubiquitous find of eggs from fecal-borne parasites in urban sites in Europe, the Near East, and Colonial North America shows that sanitation was poor through most of urban history. Recent archival research by Karl Reinhard (1994) combined with archaeoparasitology shows that North American cities actually resisted upgraded sanitation through the 1930s.

Sometimes the absence of certain parasites indicates sanitation precautions that lessened the health impact of parasites. For example, north European medieval latrines contain eggs of several nematode (roundworm), trematode (fluke), and cestode (tapeworm) species, but there is a near absence of *Taenia* eggs, the genus of the pork and beef tapeworms. It is probable that meat inspectors of the time were especially efficient, or that animal-rearing conditions were especially clean, or that meat-preparation techniques resulted in the killing of the tapeworm cysts by cooking. In any case, behavior mitigated parasitism with this genus.

Health and disease states are signaled by parasites. Hookworm causes severe anemia. Species of hookworm have been discovered in North and South America and may be responsible for the skeletal lesions of *cribra orbitalia* and *porotic hyperostosis* in certain regions. *D. pacificum* is another helminth that is responsible for anemia. This was a major health threat for Archaic Peruvians and Chileans who ate uncooked fish. In prehistoric Nubia, Egypt, and Persia, *Schistosoma* spp. (blood flukes) caused anemia. *Dracunculus medinensis* (guinea worm, or medina worm) is a dangerous parasite that has been identified in an Egyptian mummy. Hydatid-cyst disease (*Echinococcus* spp.) and trichinosis (*Trichinella spiralis*) are two of the most notorious diseases caused in humans by helminth parasites. Hydatid-cyst disease is documented from the Dakotas, the Aleutian Islands, Britain, and medieval Denmark. Only 2 percent of hydatid-cyst cases show osseous involvement. Therefore, the find of a single skeleton with cysts probably indicates that many others in the population were also infected. Possible *Trichinella* cysts have been found in muscle from an Inuit mummy from the north coast of Alaska, suggesting that this population may have suffered from some debilitation and fatality due to trichinosis. Other species of disease-causing parasites from archaeological contexts include acanthocephalans and *Strongyloides stercoralis.*

Site-formation processes can be inferred from parasite finds. One of the most direct applications of parasitological data to archaeology is its use in determining the nature of archaeological soils. This development has come primarily from examination by Andrew Jones of archaeological deposits in England. Jones used the concentration of eggs (number of parasite eggs per ml. of soil) to distinguish fecal from nonfecal deposits in medieval and Bronze Age sites. This approach is useful even when the majority of organic remains are leached from the soil. An obvious application of this work is in the identification of soil strata conducive to dietary study. Since parasite eggs are deposited with feces, dietary remains in the form of seeds and pollen found in soils containing high numbers of eggs also are probably of dietary origin. Since parasite eggs in low frequency are typical of urban fauna, the identification of parasite eggs in strata from an urban context indicates that those strata probably are associated with human occupation. Thus, occupational horizons may be identifiable through soil analysis for parasite eggs.

Domestic-animal presence is signaled by certain types of parasite eggs. *Toxascaris* spp. eggs in Anasazi sites and *Toxocara canis* eggs in medieval Netherlands are indicative of human-dog association. *Oxyuris equi* eggs in Roman, medieval, and historic sites are indicative of horses. Medieval Paris latrines contain the eggs of poultry, cat, and dog parasites.

Human-Parasite Ecology

The most valuable contribution of archaeoparasitology is to the understanding of the ecology of human parasitism. Within the ecological context, the role of human behavior can be defined and its impact on parasitism assessed. With the analysis of material from carefully controlled excavations, the parasite ecology can be reconstructed.

Human behaviors that affect parasitism include aspects of hygiene, sedentism, urbanism, food preferences, food storage, and other practices. Archaeoparasitological research in the Southwest United States focuses on these aspects of human ecology and parasite ecology (Reinhard 1988). Parasite data were fit into an archaeological framework with the goal of demonstrating the impact of changing behavior concurrent with agriculture on the

parasitology of Anasazi horticulturists in contrast to earlier Archaic hunter-gatherers on a general level (Figures 4 and 5). Behavioral factors that defined hunter-gatherer parasitism were: (1) low band size limited infection; (2) diffuse overall population distribution limited the introduction and establishment of parasites; (3) possible consumption of anthelmintics may have limited roundworm parasitism; and (4) eating uncooked insects resulted in acanthocephalan parasitism. Behavioral factors that defined horticultural parasitism were: (1) larger, sedentary villages resulted in exposure to feces, so fecal-borne parasites became established (whipworm and giant intestinal roundworm); (2) large village populations promoted infection; (3) trade with other villages resulted in the introduction of parasites into the region; (4) grain storage resulted in infection with hymenolepid tapeworms encysted in grain beetles; (5) irrigation allowed for the proliferation of mesic-adapted species such as *Strongyloides* ssp.

Detailed examination of Southwestern horticultural villages shows that the parasite ecology of each village was unique (Figures 6 and 7). A comparative analysis of the Anasazi sites of Salmon Ruin in New Mexico and Antelope House in Arizona on the Colorado Plateau found that the local environmental conditions, time frame, and village populations were roughly equivalent. The site of Antelope House was built in a cave in a canyon bottom. Analysis of parasites from cave sites shows a statistically higher prevalence of pinworm. This was probably due to the stagnant air in caves, which allows airborne particles, including pinworm eggs, to remain in the air column for long periods of time. The canyon walls were a natural barrier to foraging outside of the moist canyon. In addition, fecal disposal was haphazard, with many independent fecal deposits located throughout the village. In contrast, the site of Salmon Ruin was built on an open floodplain. However, its inhabitants preferred to forage for food in the xeric (dry) pinyon-juniper habitat, which was too arid for parasite egg survival. The Salmon Ruin inhabitants set aside certain deep rooms for use as latrines and, therefore, limited fecal exposure. These factors of human behavior altered the parasite ecology of the villages and resulted in profoundly different patterns of parasite infection.

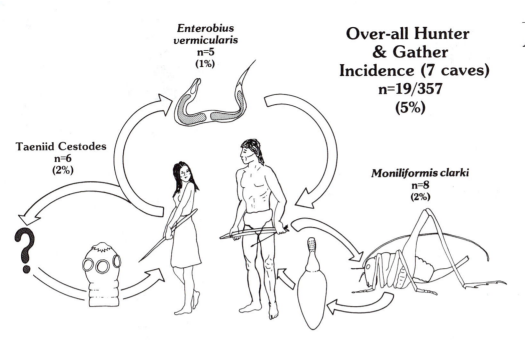

Figure 4. *The parasite ecology of hunter-gatherers and horticulturalists in the southwestern United States resulted in different patterns of parasitism between the two. As shown here, hunter-gatherers had an overall low level of parasitism. Drawn by Debra K. Meier. Courtesy of the artist.*

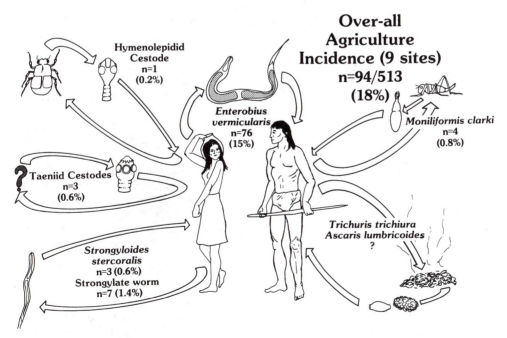

Figure 5. *In comparison to hunter-gatherers, horticulturalists had more common parasite infections with a larger number of parasite species. Drawn by Debra K. Meier. Courtesy of the artist.*

Through Jane E. Buikstra's excavations (in 1990–1991) of sites and mummies in southern Peru, the parasite ecology of the Chiribaya culture of ca. A.D. 1000 has been defined (Reinhard 1998). Chiribaya housing was based around an inner-wall construction of reeds. Such housing is good for the kissing bug, which transmits South American sleeping sickness, also called Chagas disease. This disease is caused by the flagellate protozoan, *Trypanosoma cruzi*. The presence of Chagas disease is evident in the soft-tissue pathology of some Chiribaya mummies, which exhibit enlarged intestinal organs. Thus, the ecological interaction of human-preferred house structure, the habitat preference of the kissing bug, and the presence of endemic Chagas disease resulted in human infection. Another protozoal disease that has already been mentioned is espundia, caused by a flagellate protozoan *Leishmania brasiliensis*. This disease is transmitted by the sandfly. The sandfly does not fly well and requires still air in order to do so. It also requires humid microenvironments, such as burrows, to survive. A probable case of espundia was found among the mummies, suggesting that at least some villagers came into association with an environment, perhaps in a local estuary, where the sandfly could survive. It is also possible that this environment was created in the village vicinity through the disposal of moist vegetation. The head-lice prevalence mentioned above and graphed in Figure 2 illustrates that the parasite ecologies of Chiribaya villages was different. Since head lice are more commonly spread in crowded human populations, the population of Chiribaya Alta was probably larger and more concentrated than that of El Yaral. Thus, aspects of human behavior and village conditions defined Chiribaya parasitism.

Through the analysis of a limited number of mummies, the general parasite ecology of ancient Egypt is beginning to be defined. Several parasitic worms have been found, including the guinea worm, the pork tapeworm, *T. spiralis,* and *Strongyloides* ssp. Infection with guinea worm occurs when water that contains tiny crustacea known as copopods is drunk. The larval worms encyst in copopods and emerge once consumed. Both pork tapeworm and *T. spiralis* infections occur when incompletely cooked meat is consumed. Both tapeworm eggs in the in-

Figure 6. *The comparsion of two Southwestern horticultural villages shows that the parasite ecology of each village was altered by minor variations in human behavior. The parasitism of Salmon Ruin was limited by developed hygienic practices and subsistence practices that focused on dry farming and foraging in desert environments. Drawn by Jonathan Ham. Courtesy of the artist.*

testine and tapeworm larvae in the soft tissue have been found. Since the larva of the pork tapeworm, not the beef tapeworm, can encyst in humans, the pork tapeworm is implicated. Pork can also carry *T. spiralis*, although this is uncommon in Mediterranean regions. Therefore, poorly cooked pork could be the source for both infections. *Strongyloides* larvae live freely in soil and burrow through the skin to establish infection. Their presence indicates that Egyptians were in contact with moist soils. It is interesting that fecal-borne intestinal worms are uncommon in Egypt. This may be due to the unique ecology of the area in which the Nile flooded annually. The flooding has long been recognized as the source of nutrients for Egyptian agriculture. Perhaps it also flushed away accumulated feces and reduced the potential of fecal-borne disease. So few parasitological exminations have been con-

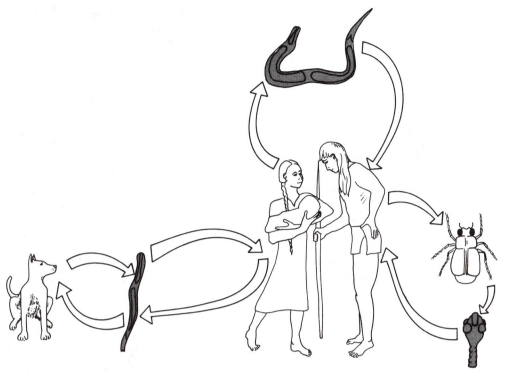

Figure 7. In contrast with Salmon Ruin, poor sanitation at Antelope House, coupled with subsistence practices carried out in moist areas, resulted in more parasitism. Drawn by Jonathan Ham. Courtesy of the artist.

ducted in Egypt that a definitive statement about Egyptian parasite ecology must await more years of study.

On a worldwide basis, archaeoparasitological data provide unique insight into the relationship between urbanization and the proliferation and spread of density-dependent and fecal-borne disease. Prior to the advent of archaeoparasitological research, it was thought that irrigation was the main reason behind the proliferation of human parasitism. Research has shown that, although irrigation increased the number of parasites that resided in human populations, it did not strongly affect the number of people infected. Urbanism, which resulted in crowded conditions and poor sanitation, is clearly associated with the spread of fecal-borne parasitism. By medieval times, fecal-borne parasitism is nearly universal for European poplulations, as demontrated by Jones and Herrmann. With European colonization of the New World, fecal-borne parasitism became commonplace in the Americas. The modern parasite prevalence, summarized

at the beginning of this entry, has an ecological origin in the beginnings of urbanized life as seen in the archaeological record.

Karl Reinhard

See also COPROLITE ANALYSIS; MEDIEVAL ARCHAEOLOGY; PALEOPHARMACOLOGY

Further Readings

Ferreira, L.F., Araújo, A.J.G., and Confalonieri, U.E.C. (1980) The finding of eggs and larvae of parasitic helminths in archaeological material from Unai, Minas Gerais, Brazil. Transactions of the Royal Society of Tropical Medicine and Hygiene 74:798–800.

Ferreira, L.F., Araújo, A.J.G., and Confalonieri, U.E.C. (1983) The finding of helminth eggs in a Brazilian mummy. Transactions of the Royal Society of Tropical Medicine and Hygiene 77:65–67.

Jones, A.K.G. (1982) Human parasite remains: Prospects for a quantitative approach. In A.R. Hall and H.K. Kenward (eds.): Environmental Archaeology in the Urban Context, pp. 66–70. (Research Report 1). London: Council for British Archaeology.

Herrmann, B. (1986) Parasitologische Untersuchung Mittelalterlicher Kloaken. In B. Herrmann (ed.): Mensch und Umwelt im Mittelalter, pp. 161–169. Stuttgart: Deutsche Verlags-Anstalt.

Mumcuoglu, K.Y., and Zias, J. (1989) How the ancients de-loused themselves. Biblical Archaeology Review 15:66–69.

Reinhard, K.J. (1988) Cultural ecology of prehistoric parasitism on the Colorado Plateau as evidenced by coprology. American Journal of Physical Anthropology 77:355–366.

Reinhard, K.J. (1990) Archaeoparasitology in North America. American Journal of Physical Anthropology 82:145–163.

Reinhard, K.J. (1992) Parasitology as an interpretive tool in archaeology. American Antiquity 57:231–245.

Reinhard, K.J. (1994) Sanitation and parasitism at Harpers Ferry, West Virginia. Historical Archaeology 28:62–67.

Reinhard, K.J. (1998) Mummy studies and archaeoparasitology. In A. Cockburn, Cockburn, E. and Reyman, T.A. (eds.): Mummies, Disease and Ancient Cultures, 2nd ed., pp. 377–380. London: Cambridge University Press.

Roberts, L.S., and Janovy, J. (1996) Foundations of Parasitology, 5th ed. Dubuque, IA: Wm. C. Brown.

Urtega-Ballon, O. (1991) Medical ceramic representation of nasal leishmaniasis and surgical amputation in ancient Peruvian civilization. In A.C. Aufderheide and D. Ortner (eds.): Human Paleopathology: Current Syntheses and Future Options, pp. 95–101. Washington, D.C.: Smithsonian Institution Press.

Archeological and Historic Preservation Act (AHPA)

The national law that specified that federal agencies were responsible for mitigating damage their actions caused to important archaeological sites. This statute also is known as the Archeological Recovery Act and the Moss-Bennett bill, the latter referring to the primary sponsors of the bills in the Senate and the House of Representatives that led to the act. Its legislative and legal titles are: Public Law 93–291 and 16 U.S. Code 469–469(c). Passed and signed into law in 1974, this act amended and expanded the Reservoir Salvage Act of 1960. The AHPA required that Federal agencies provide for "the preservation of historical and archeological data (including relics and specimens) which might otherwise be irreparably lost or destroyed as the result of . . . any alteration of the terrain caused as a result of any Federal construction project or federally licensed activity or program" (Sec. 1). This greatly expanded the number and range of federal agencies that had to take archaeological resources into account when executing, funding, or licensing projects. The Reservoir Salvage Act had required such attention only of federal agencies, mainly the Corps of Engineers and the Bureau of Reclamation, that constructed reservoirs and related structures.

The AHPA built upon the national policy, set out in the Historic Sites Act of 1935, "to provide for the preservation of historic American sites, buildings, objects, and antiquities of national significance." The AHPA expanded the policy by focusing attention on significant resources and data but did not require that they be shown to be of national significance. The connection between the 1935 statute and the AHPA is mentioned explicitly in the first section of the latter statute.

The statute is in the tradition of *salvage archaeology* as developed extensively in the Inter-agency Archaeological Salvage Program from the late 1940s onward. The impetus for the AHPA was the destruction of archaeological sites throughout the country, frequently by actions funded or otherwise supported by federal agencies, that were not covered by the Reservoir Salvage Act, which required archaeological salvage as part of dam projects (Davis 1972). The chief archaeological instigators of the statute were Carl Chapman of the University of Missouri and Charles R. McGimsey of the Arkansas Archeological Survey. The aim of the proponents of the act was to require all agencies of the federal government to undertake archaeology as part of their actions that would result in the destruction of archaeological sites.

The drafters of the act, however, did not explicitly relate this legislation with the then-developing approach to archaeological preservation as part of the wider historic-preservation movement. This latter approach, based upon the implementation of the National

Historic Preservation Act of 1966 (NHPA), eventually came to emphasize the use of planning, the importance of the National Register of Historic Places for site protection, project review under Section 106 of the NHPA, and the preservation of sites in situ when possible and feasible. It took several years of intense discussion and experimentation to develop regulations and procedures that completely integrated AHPA into the statutory framework yielding the present effective overall archaeology and historic-preservation program. The most important contribution of the AHPA is that it made it clear that all federal agencies were authorized to fund archaeological investigations, reports, and other kinds of activities to mitigate the impacts of their projects on important archaeological sites. A second important accomplishment was the pressure brought upon federal-agency managers during the process of lobbying for passage of the bill to meet their archaeological responsibilities. Finally, the extensive lobbying efforts by individual archaeologists and archaeological organizations between 1969, when the bill was first drafted, and its passage in 1974 alerted much of the archaeological professional and avocational community in the United States to the impact that government actions were having on archaeological resources and the importance of keeping alert to public statutes and regulations, government programs, and new legislation.

The statute assigns the secretary of the Interior substantial authority to act for the preservation of historical and archaeological data and remains. Section 3 allows for the secretary to assist other federal agencies and even private organizations or individuals in meeting the historical and archaeological preservation requirements under this statute if the project is expected to result in the loss or destruction of significant scientific, historical, or archaeological data. Section 4 authorizes the secretary, upon notification that significant historical or archaeological data may be irrevocably lost or destroyed, to undertake necessary studies independent of, although with some consultation with, the federal agency responsible for undertaking, funding, or licensing the project. This aspect of the statute is carried out for the secretary by the departmental consulting archeologist through "unanticipated discovery procedures" that can be initiated by agency staff or others when archaeological resources are discovered unex-

pectedly during a federal undertaking following the completion of Section 106 (of the NHPA) procedures. The procedures are designed to reach a means of avoiding unnecessary damage to significant archaeological resources by modification of project design or timely and effective data recovery of threatened remains. Typically, a consensus is sought among the agency archaeologist or consultant, agency or project proponents, the state historic-preservation officer, the Advisory Council for Historic Preservation staff, and the Department of the Interior staff. Agencies that do not wish to use this set of procedures have the alternative of following those set up as part of the Advisory Council's procedures (36 CFR 800.11).

Section 5 assigns the secretary several roles in coordinating historical or archaeological activities authorized by this statute, including consultation about the ownership and appropriate repositories for artifacts and other remains recovered by investigations conducted under the statute. This is one of the statutory authorities for the government-wide regulations for the curation and care of federal archaeological collections and associated records (36 CFR 79). Section 5 also calls for the secretary to compile a report for Congress on archaeological survey and recovery activities authorized under this statute. This particular requirement is one of the bases for the Secretary of the Interior's Report to Congress on Federal Archeological Activities and Programs (e.g., Keel et al. 1989; McManamon et al. 1993). The departmental consulting archeologist for the National Park Service carries out this reporting requirement for the secretary.

Section 7 of the statute authorizes federal agencies responsible for projects to transfer to the secretary of the Interior, funds to assist them in meeting their responsibilities, up to 1 percent of the total amount authorized for the project. Differing interpretations of this section have lead to a general understanding that it also limited agencies to expenditures for archaeological data recovery of 1 percent of a project's authorized total funding amount. In 1980, Section 208 of Public Law 96–515 provided a means by which agencies could obtain a waiver of the 1 percent limit with the concurrence of the secretary of the Interior and the notification of Congress. The departmental consulting archeologist for the National Park

Service is delegated to carry out the review and concurrence with any 1 percent waiver requests for the secretary. Section 7 also authorized specific funding amounts for the use of the secretary of the Interior to carry out investigations allowed under Sections 3 and 4 of the statute. However, these amounts were not often appropriated, and the last year for which they were authorized was Fiscal Year 1983.

Francis P. McManamon

See also CULTURAL RESOURCE MANAGEMENT (CRM); NATIONAL HISTORIC PRESERVATION ACT (NHPA)

Further Readings

Davis, H. (1972) The crisis in American archeology. Science 175:267–272.

Keel, B.C., McManamon, F.P., and Smith, G.S. (1989) Federal Archeology: The Current Program. Washington, D.C.: National Park Service, Department of the Interior,

McGimsey, C.R. (1985) "This, too, will pass": Moss-Bennett in perspective. American Antiquity 50(2):326–331.

McManamon, F.P., Knoll, P.C., Knudson, R., Smith, G.S., and Waldbauer, R.C. (1993) Federal Archeological Programs and Activities: The Secretary of the Interior's Report to Congress. Washington, D.C.: National Park Service, Department of the Interior.

Archeological Resources Protection Act (ARPA)

The national law that protects archaeological resources on public land and from illegal uses. This statute (16 U.S. Code 470aa–470mm; Public Law 96–95 and amendments to it) was enacted in 1979

> to secure, for the present and future benefit of the American people, the protection of archaeological resources and sites which are on public lands and Indian lands, and to foster increased cooperation and exchange of information between governmental authorities, the professional archaeological community, and private individuals (Sec. 2[4][b]).

The reasons behind enactment include recognition that archaeological resources are an irreplaceable part of America's heritage and that they were endangered increasingly because of the escalating commercial value of a small portion of the contents of archaeological sites.

In the statute (Sec. 3[1]) and the regulations implementing it, a definition of *archaeological resource* is provided. For the purposes of ARPA, archaeological resources include any material remains of human life or activities that are at least 100 years old and of archaeological interest. The brief definition in the statute is expanded upon in the regulations, which also include long lists giving examples of what is meant by both *material remains* and *archaeological interest*. In summary, material remains are said to be "of archaeological interest" if they are "capable of providing scientific or humanistic understandings of past human behavior . . . through the application of scientific or scholarly techniques." Material remains are considered to be "physical evidence of human habitation, occupation, use, or activity, including the site, location, or context in which such evidence is situated." The latter definition is followed by nearly a column of text in small print listing examples of material remains.

The regulations implementing ARPA are uniform among the Departments of Agriculture, Defense, and Interior, and also for the Tennessee Valley Authority (TVA). This means that in the *Code of Federal Regulations* (CFR) that pertain to each department, the text of the regulations is the same and the numbering similar. As an illustration, the section of the ARPA regulations containing the definition of material remains for the Interior Department is numbered 43 CFR 7.3(2); the same section for Agriculture is numbered 36 CFR 296.3(2); for Defense, 32 CFR 229.3(2); and for the TVA, 18 CFR 1312.3(2). Section 4 of the statute describes the requirements that must be met before federal authorities can issue a permit to excavate or remove any archaeological resource on federal or Indian lands. The curation requirements of artifacts, other materials excavated or removed, and the records related to the artifacts and materials are described in Section 5 of the act. This section also authorizes the secretary of the Interior to issue regulations describing in more detail the requirements regarding these collections. These regulations, which affect all federally owned or administered archaeological collections, were issued in 1990 as 36 CFR 79.

The primary impetus behind ARPA was the need to provide more effective law enforcement to protect public archaeological sites. Two improvements over the Antiquities Act of 1906, which was the statute designed to provide this protection prior to ARPA's enactment, were more detailed descriptions of the prohibited activities and larger financial and incarceration penalties for convicted violators. Section 6 of the statute describes the range of prohibited actions, including damage or defacement in addition to unpermitted excavation or removal. Also prohibited are selling, purchasing, and other trafficking activities whether within the United States or internationally. Section 6(c) prohibits interstate or international sale, purchase, or transport of any archaeological resource excavated or removed in violation of a state or local law, ordinance, or regulation.

ARPA substantially increased the penalties that can be levied against convicted violators. For a felony offense, first-time offenders can be fined up to $20,000 and imprisoned for up to one year. Second-time felony offenders can be fined up to $100,000 and imprisoned for up to five years. These criminal penalties were substantial increases from those set in the Antiquities Act of $500 and ninety days' imprisonment. In addition, Section 7 of ARPA enables federal or Indian authorities to prosecute violators using civil fines, either in conjunction with, or independent of, any criminal prosecution. Section 8(b) of the statute allows the court or civil authority to use forfeiture of vehicles and equipment used in the violation of the statute as another means of punishment against convicted violators.

The main focus of ARPA is on regulation of legitimate archaeological investigation on public lands and the enforcement of penalties against those who loot or vandalize archaeological resources. However, both the original statute and, especially, the amendments to it in 1988 provided authority to federal officials to better manage archaeological sites on public land. Section 9 requires that managers responsible for the protection of archaeological resources hold information about the locations and the nature of these resources confidential unless providing the information would further the purposes of the statute and not create a risk of harm for the resources.

The statute also authorizes the secretary of the Interior to cooperate with avocational and professional archaeologists and organizations in exchanging information about archaeological resources and improving the knowledge about the United States' archaeological record (Sec. 11).

The 1988 amendments to ARPA focused more attention on management actions that must be taken to improve the protection of archaeological resources. Section 10(c) was added requiring each federal land manager to "establish a program to increase public awareness of the significance of the archaeological resources located on public lands and Indian lands and the need to protect such resources." The object of this addition was to reach visitors using public lands with a message that archaeological resources are valuable to all but must be properly investigated and cared for and that they are protected legally on public lands. Anecdotal evidence from federal officials in field units indicates that such public education and outreach is effective and that casual or unknowing destruction and vandalism has been reduced substantially.

Section 14 also was added by the 1988 amendments. It requires the major land-managing federal departments (Interior, Agriculture, Defense, and the Tennessee Valley Authority) to plan and schedule archaeological surveys of the lands under their control. The aim of this new section was to emphasize the need for better knowledge of the locations and nature of archaeological resources so that they can be better protected.

ARPA was drafted, debated, and enacted relatively quickly in the late 1970s when difficulties enforcing the Antiquities Act and weaknesses in the penalties provided by the Antiquities Act became critical. Provisions for effective law enforcement and careful, detailed definitions, the two most apparent weaknesses of the Antiquities Act, were the aspects of ARPA that received the most attention in its enactment and early years of enforcement. However, several sections, including those added by the 1988 amendments, make ARPA an important part of the overall statutory basis for effective archaeological-resource management in the United States. ARPA provides a very strong basis for archaeological protection on public and

Indian lands. Its antitrafficking provision also makes it an effective tool for discouraging illegal excavation or removal of archaeological resources from state, local, or private lands throughout the United States.

Francis P. McManamon

See also ANTIQUITIES ACT OF 1906; CULTURAL RESOURCE MANAGEMENT (CRM); NATIONAL HISTORIC PRESERVATION ACT (NHPA)

Further Readings

Friedman, J.L., ed. (1985) A history of the Archaeological Resources Protection Act: Laws and regulations. American Archeology 5(2):82–119.

McManamon, F.P. (1991) The federal government's recent response to archaeological looting. In G.S. Smith and J.E. Ehrenhard (eds.): Protecting the Past, pp. 261–269. Boca Raton, FL: CRC.

Atomic Absorption (AA) Spectrometry

An analytic method for the determination of chemical elements based on the absorption of radiation by free atoms of the elements in the sample. It is virtually a universal method for determining most metallic elements in trace and major concentrations. This analytical method has been the workhorse in geology and biology for the last few decades because of its reliability, scope of applications, low limits of detection, ease of operation, suitability for automation, and lower cost of the instrumentation relative to most competing techniques. Atomic absorption techniques can analyze for more than sixty elements. Many can be detected well below 1 part per million in solution. The major disadvantage of AA is that only a single element can be measured at a time. This can be a problem if many elements are to be determined. Atomic absorption is particularly suitable when a large number of solutions must be analyzed for a single element. A second disadvantage, compared to instrumental neutron activation (INAA) methods, is that most standard methods require that the sample be put into solution. This adds to the possibility of contamination, and some materials are difficult to dissolve.

The concentration range of AA is from a part per billion for many cations in solution to tens of a percent for metals in the solid state. AA can determine elements in any matrix and from micro samples. Archaeological applications for analysis of lithics, inorganic pigments, soils, bone, and ceramics closely parallel those of geology. Determinations of trace and major concentrations of metals in organic matrices are among the easiest analyses to carry out by atomic absorption. Organic pigment, textile, and plant-material analyses are amenable to this technique.

Perhaps the most common application of AA analysis in archaeology has been in the reconstruction of paleodiets and paleopathologies. Paleodiet studies using AA have been predicated on the fact that the elements strontium (Sr), magnesium (Mg), and potassium (K) are more abundant in plant foods, while iron (Fe), copper (Cu), sodium (Na), and zinc (Zn) are found in higher concentrations in meat and seafood. Barium (Ba) concentrations in seawater are low relative to strontium when compared to the terrestrial environment. Both Ba/Sr and Ba/Ca ratios differentiate marine and terrestrial foods. Barium, strontium, and calcium (Ca) are well suited for rapid and accurate analyses by atomic absorption.

In paleopathology, a good example is found in lead toxicity. Bone has a great affinity for lead, which is not released in physiological processes. Unfortunately, bone also can scavenge lead from the soil after burial. Arthur Aufderheide and his colleagues have shown that, in the Colonial United States, lead concentration was considerably higher among landholding (pewter-using) family members than in slaves or indentured servants who did not use pewter. Analytical results using AA from this same laboratory have indicated that the Romans may, indeed, have had endemic lead poisoning.

Although not considered as desirable as INAA (but not everyone has a nuclear reactor), AA has proven to be useful in characterizing the elemental composition of pottery clays and determining their source areas. Optimum results were obtained only after removing the temper. Problems in using atomic absorption techniques in ceramic studies lie almost exclusively in sample preparation. AA is valuable in ceramic analyses because it can accurately measure the major, as well as the trace, elements.

In some geologic areas, obsidian artifacts can be traced to their volcanic sources by bulk-element analyses, making AA a highly competitive technique. Research by Joseph W. Michels presents the results of experiments evaluating bulk composition versus trace-element composition in obsidian sources. Most obsidian sourcing has used the INAA and the XRF (X-ray fluorescence) techniques.

George R. Rapp Jr.

See also X-RAY FLUORESCENCE (XRF) ANALYSIS

Further Readings

Angino, E., and Billings, G. (1972) Atomic Absorption Spectrometry in Geology, 2nd ed. Amsterdam: Elsevier.

Aufderheide, A., Neiman, F., Wittmers, L., and Rapp, G. (1981) Skeletal lead content as an indicator of lifetime lead ingestion and the social correlates in an archaeological population. American Journal of Physical Anthropology 55:285–291.

Aufderheide, A., Rapp, G., Wittmers, L., Wallgren, J., Macchiarelli, R., Fornaciari, G., Mallegni, F., and Corrucini, R. (1992) Lead exposure in Italy: 800 B.C.–A.D. 700. International Journal of Anthropology 7:9–15.

Michels, J. (1982) Bulk element composition versus trace element composition in the reconstruction of an obsidian source system. Journal of Archaeological Science 9:113–123.

Price, T.D., ed. (1989) The Chemistry of Prehistoric Bone. Cambridge: Cambridge University Press.

Price, W.J. (1983) Spectrochemical Analysis by Atomic Absorption. New York: Wiley.

Shingleton, K., Odell, G., and Harris, T. (1994) Atomic absorption spectrophotometry analysis of ceramic artefacts from a protohistoric site in Oklahoma. Journal of Archaeological Science 21:343–358.

A

B

Bada, Jeffrey L. (1942–)

American geochemist and marine chemist. Born on September 10, 1942, Bada was educated at San Diego State University, where he received his bachelor's in 1965, and at the University of California, San Diego, where he received his doctorate in chemistry in 1968. After a year at the Hoffman Labs of the Department of Geological Sciences at Harvard University, Bada returned to the University of California–San Diego as assistant professor of oceanography (1970–1974) and associate professor of oceanography (1974 to 1980). He is presently professor of marine chemistry at the Scripps Institution of Oceanography at the university. A recipient of numerous awards and prizes, Bada was an Alfred P. Sloan Fellow (1975–1979) and has been honored with grants from the National Science Foundation.

A specialist in marine organic chemistry, Bada is known to social scientists for his work in geochronology. In the 1970s and 1980s, he pioneered the development of marine-sediment dating through the measurement of the racemization rates of amino acids. While at Harvard, Bada studied oceanic core samples and measured the racemization rate of the amino-acid compound isoleucine, and et al. discovered that he could date the sediments from the bottom of the core to 1.23 million years B.P. (Bada 1970). The implications of this study were important not only for marine geology, but for anthropology and archaeology as well, because fossil and skeletal remains may contain surviving indigenous amino acids that will be subject to racemization. In studies conducted in the early 1970s on fossil remains, Bada and his collaborators demonstrated that the measurement of the racemization rates have the potential of providing a valuable chronological tool to paleoanthropologists.

Joseph J. Basile

See also AMINO ACID RACEMIZATION/ EPIMERIZATION DATING; BONE, CHARACTERIZATION

Further Readings

Bada, J.L. (1972) The dating of fossil bones using the racemization of isoleucine. Earth and Planetary Science Letters 15:223–231.

Bada, J.L. and Deems, L. (1975) Accuracy of dates beyond the C-14 dating limit using the aspartic acid racemization technique. Nature 255:218–219.

Bada, J.L. and Kvenvolden, K.A., and Peterson, E. (1973) Racemization of amino acids in bones. Nature 245:308–310.

Bada, J.L., Luyendyk, B.P. and Maynard, J.B. (1970) Marine sediments: Dating by the racemization of amino acids. Science 170:730–732.

Bada, J.L., Schroeder, R.A. and Carter, G.F. (1974) New evidence for the antiquity of man in North America deduced from aspartic acid racemization. Science 184:791–793.

King, K. and Bada, J.L. (1979) Effect of in situ leaching on amino acid racemization rates in fossil bone. Nature 281:135–137.

Baillie, Michael G.L. (1944–)

Irish paleoecologist, archaeologist, and natural scientist. Born on November 15, 1944, Baillie was educated at Queen's University in Belfast, where he received his doctorate in 1973. Baillie has remained at Queen's in the Centre for Palaeoecology, making that institution a leader in the study of ancient ecology and dating methods. He has received numerous awards and honors, including the Archaeological Institute of America's Pomerance Medal for Scientific Contributions to Archaeology (1993).

Baillie is a pioneer in the study of paleoecology and, in particular, dendrochronological dating methods. Following work done in the United States and in Europe, he began to explore the uses of dendrochronology in the 1970s and in 1982 published his *Tree-Ring Dating and Archaeology,* a standard reference in the field. Along with Jon Pilcher and Bernd Becker, Baillie was instrumental in establishing a tree-ring chronology, based on living and archaeological samples of the European oak, that spans more than 10,000 years from the modern era to the Mesolithic in western and northern Europe (the North European Oak Chronology). This chronology has been used to establish absolute dates at European sites and, of equal importance, to check radiocarbon dates. The utility of dendrochronology in this regard had already been realized, and even trumpeted by Colin Renfrew in his *Before Civilization* as "the second radiocarbon revolution," but the tree-ring chronologies that had been previously used, based on the bristlecone pine of the western United States, had proved unreliable. The European oak created a much more reliable chronology, and the recalibration of the radiocarbon technique was achieved.

Joseph J. Basile

See also DENDROCHRONOLOGY; RADIOCARBON DATING; RENFREW, ANDREW COLIN

Further Readings:

Baillie, M.G.L. (1982) Tree-ring Dating and Archaeology. Chicago: University of Chicago Press/London: Croom Helm.
Baillie, M.G.L. (1995) A Slice through Time: Dendrochronology and Precision Dating. London: Batsford.

Base Line

Any arbitrary line on the ground from which all further measurements are taken, either directly or through the construction of offsets or triangles. Ultimately, all measurements taken should relate to the base line. Some North American archaeologists use the term *base line* to indicate an east-west line at right angles to an imaginary north-south datum line. This limited use of the term should be avoided.

In land surveying, the base line should ideally be located through the center of the site being surveyed. This minimizes the length of all measurements taken from the base line. In tape surveys, the shorter the measurement taken, the more accurate it is likely to be. A base line used for recording an excavation area is, however, generally located to one side of the excavation so as not to be disturbed by the excavation.

Peter L. Drewett

See also SITE MAPPING

Further Readings

Barker, P. (1993) Techniques of Archaeological Excavation, 3rd ed. London: Batsford.
Drewett, P.L. (1999) Field Archaeology: An Introduction. London: University College London Press.

Bass, George Fletcher (1932–)

American underwater archaeologist. Born on December 9, 1932, in Columbia, South Carolina, Bass attended Johns Hopkins University, receiving his master's degree there in 1955. He went on to the University of Pennsylvania, where he was awarded a doctorate in 1964. Bass taught archaeology at the University of Pennsylvania (1964–1980), rising from assistant to full professor, and since 1980 he has been a full professor at Texas A&M University, where he established the Institute of Nautical Archaeology in 1972. Bass is currently Distinguished Professor and holds the George T. and Gladys H. Abell Chair in Nautical Archaeology. He has received the Woodrow Wilson Fellowship (1965) and the Gold Medal of the Archaeological Institute of America (1986). Bass is a member of the American Philosophical Society and President of the Institute of Nautical Archaeology.

Bass is noted as a pioneer in scientific, underwater archaeology. Although shipwreck salvage is not a new phenomenon, and attempts at maritime "archaeology" can be seen as early as the work of Leon Battista Alberti (who tried to refloat two Roman galleys from the bottom of Lake Nemi, Italy, in 1446), it was not until the work of Bass that a viable methodology for scientific archaeology underwater. While at Pennsylvania, Bass and a team of divers, including other notables in the field such as Peter Throckmorton and Joan du Plat Taylor, excavated a Bronze Age shipwreck near Cape Gelidonya off the Mediterranean coast of Turkey. The result of these excavations, aside from the material recovered from the ship itself, was the development of a scientific methodology for the investigation of submerged archaeological sites. Bass and his colleagues developed a grid system, mapping and photographic procedures, sampling techniques, and analytical paradigms that have been applied to dozens of underwater sites since the Gelidonya project began in 1960. In addition, Bass's findings have revolutionized the way archaeologists look at ancient seafaring and sea trade. His *Archaeology Underwater* and *Archaeology Beneath the Sea,* as well as the Gelidonya reports published in *Transactions of the American Philosophical Society,* remain standard works in the field.

Joseph J. Basile

See also NAUTICAL ARCHAEOLOGY; REMOTELY OPERATED VEHICLES; SONAR; UNDERWATER ARCHAEOLOGY

Further Readings

Bass, G.F. (1966) Archaeology Under Water. New York: Praeger/London: Thames and Hudson.
Bass, G.F. (1967) Cape Gelidonya: A Bronze Age Shipwreck. (Transactions of the American Philosophical Society 57, pt. 8.) Philadelphia: American Philosophical Society.
Bass, G.F. (1975) Archaeology Beneath the Sea. New York: Walker.

Behavioral Archaeology

The study of the relationship between behavior and artifacts in all times and places. Behavioralists do not prioritize the analysis of the past or archaeological deposits in terms of time or place. Instead, these heterodox scholars embrace, with equal enthusiasm, artifacts one might encounter in a Philippine farming village, a contemporary American landfill, or a desiccated prehistoric cave. They believe that understanding the uniquely human world of artifacts requires archaeological theorists to look for answers beyond the boundaries of the archaeological record. Peoples' interactions with objects, wherever and whenever they occur, are important processes that archaeologists should endeavor to explain.

In the early 1970s, three archaeologists at the University of Arizona—William L. Rathje, J. Jefferson Reid, and Michael B. Schiffer—called for the expansion of the boundaries of archaeological research (Reid et al. 1974). Labeled *behavioral archaeology,* this expansion combined traditional archaeological strategies of survey and excavation with experimental laboratory studies and ethnographic research on Western and non-Western societies.

Behavioral archaeologists posit that the most precise exploration of cultures, past or present, requires approaches that highlight behavioral evidence. The definition of an artifact as anything altered or impacted by human activity implies that almost all human behaviors involve artifacts. Behavioralists realize that this relationship between behaviors and artifacts is what makes archaeological interpretation possible. Building upon this fundamental axiom, they have constructed an approach that emphasizes artifacts. Accompanying the development of this approach are new terms—a data language, if you will—to describe in detail the behavioral interactions of people and objects.

Behavioralists classify the measurements one can make of artifacts into four *dimensions* of artifact variability. All artifacts, whether found in use, at a Tucson, Arizona, flea market, or decaying in an ancient tomb, can be measured in terms of (1) physical properties (e.g., color, material, size); (2) frequency of occurrence; (3) relation or association with other artifacts; or (4) the place they occupy in space.

Valuable objects, for example, such as finely woven Inca woolen textiles, occur in low frequencies relative to other artifacts (e.g., chipped stone, ceramic cooking pots, ground-stone metates). They are composed of laboriously manufactured raw materials. These textiles had restricted circulation patterns among the Inca elite and were also associated with similarly valuable objects. These associations were carried over into the archaeological record of Inca tombs.

In a behavioral perspective, every artifact possesses a unique life history that begins with the acquisition of raw materials and continues through its manufacture and primary uses. These are often followed by various reuses, some of which require the artifact to be redesigned. This chain of events ends when someone disposes of or loses the object, and it enters the archaeological record. The particular events in an object's life history distinguish it from all other artifacts. Nonetheless, that certain processes recur in different artifact life histories allows behavioral archaeologists to group them into classes for the purposes of analysis.

The patterned processes or interactions between people and artifacts that underlie these classes are called *correlates*. Correlates are also known as *laws of human behavior* because, like other scientific laws, they describe processes that recur under specific material conditions. Correlates allow behavioralists to identify comparable life-history events in different time periods, often in historically unrelated cultures. The identification of such correlates stands at the heart of behavioral archaeology because correlates also allow archaeologists to infer past human activities when only the objects remain.

Garbologists, a brave group of behavioralists, use data excavated from American landfills to develop general correlates for interpreting archaeological trash as well as to identify current misconceptions about modern American society (Rathje and Murphy 1992). Rathje's Projet du Garbage (Garbage Project) has also collected and interpreted Tucson household refuse before it reaches the landfill. In both activities, the behavioralists have developed material measures of human activities that should appeal to any archaeologist. These garbage data are especially satisfying because they reflect behavior-artifact patterns that are not biased by informant memories, fears, or other perceptions that can affect the results of survey questionnaires.

In its passage from unshaped raw materials to an object deposited in the archaeological record, an artifact's interactions with people and other objects create traces in the four dimensions of variability (Sullivan 1978). Behavioralists measure these traces to infer previous events in the life histories of objects. For example, behavioralists have developed a correlate that describes the special care associated with the disposal of ceremonial objects. The remains of ritual objects are often deposited in contexts different from those of nonritual objects. The ritual interactions encountered by such objects during their life histories have predisposed them to specialized discard contexts such as caches or burials, rather than trash dumps.

Market analysts seldom follow a product throughout its entire life history. Their task usually ends at the time of purchase. Schiffer, however, has identified the benefits of a behaviorally based life-history approach through his studies of electric cars and portable radios in American life. Documenting the entire life history of a shirt-pocket radio or an ancient obsidian knife blade identifies a rich set of human groups and activities that might otherwise go unrecognized. Such data can be used to reconstruct the prehistory of a site or, in the case of contemporary radios, to reevaluate an economist's interpretation of the competition between foreign and domestic radio manufacturers.

Although behavioral archaeologists have sought archaeological lessons in the present, they have by no means abandoned the past. The University of Arizona's Archaeological Field School under the direction of Reid trained two generations of fieldworkers emphasizing the behavioralist perspective. Some of these archaeologists remain in the U.S. Southwest, while others have moved to different areas of the United States and abroad, applying behavioral principles in both historical-period and prehistoric contexts.

To infer the past life histories of artifacts from the archaeological record, behavioralists have developed a series of conceptual tools to help them envision objects flowing through societies into the archaeological record. Artifacts still in use in a culture that have not yet entered the archaeological record are described as participating within a *systemic context*. Systemic context is shorthand for *cultural-system context*. In contrast, those artifacts no longer participating in cultural systems are said to be in an *archaeological context*.

Some of the earliest work conducted by behavioral archaeologists demonstrated the methodological importance of keeping these two contexts separate. In the late 1960s, New Archaeologists wanted to infer social processes, such as kinship relations, from archaeological deposits. Although skeptics asserted that such analyses were beyond the reach of artifact-based data, New Archaeologists William A. Longacre, James Hill, and others attempted to identify marital-residence patterns through the analysis of ceramic artifacts. Behavioralists, while agreeing that archaeologists should attempt to reconstruct social processes using objects, argued that these initial analyses did not fully take into account the complex life histories of the ceramics, particularly their transitions from systemic to archaeological contexts.

Frequently, the places where artifacts were used differed from their find spots. One complete Iroquois pot in systemic context, for example, could become many pieces by the time it was deposited—perhaps in several places—in archaeological context. Often, the four dimensions of artifact variability change dramatically between the two contexts; thus, archaeologists developing social interpretations of excavated artifacts have to take such change into account.

To explore these complexities in more detail, Schiffer defined a specific set of correlates, called *c-transforms,* to explain the movement of artifacts out of systemic contexts and into archaeological contexts. People deposit artifacts into archaeological context through various disposal, loss, and abandonment behaviors. These processes as a group were named *cultural formation processes* because they instrumentally contribute to the creation of archaeological sites. Behavioral archaeologists have found both ethnohistorical and ethnoarchaeological research critical for defining and exploring these processes.

In addition to the effects of human behavior, natural processes such as wind, rain, and burrowing animals can dramatically shape and alter the four dimensions of artifact variability. These nonhuman agents are called *noncultural* or *environmental formation processes.* When the cultural formation processes have been played out, it is ultimately these natural processes that determine which artifacts will be preserved for the archaeologist to find.

Theory and Behavioral Archaeology

In the 1970s and 1980s, favoring the neo-evolutionary theory of Leslie A. White, Marvin Harris, and others, behavioral archaeologists characterized human behavior within an adaptationist framework. Harris's effort to expose the behavioral world of people and objects in *The Nature of Cultural Things* particularly inspired Schiffer. Within these perspectives, it was assumed that cultures adapted to their environments through changes in their technologies, social organization, and ideology. The behavioralists argued that technological innovations, including economic strategies, were the first parts of a culture to change. These changes then resulted in modifications to social organization and the elaboration of belief systems. These new social relations (e.g., systems of kinship or labor management) and religious beliefs (clan totems, ancestral deities, ruling gods) would reinforce new subsistence practices.

A shift to irrigation agriculture from dry farming, for example, requires the cooperation of large numbers of people. To facilitate such a change, systems of kinship might expand to classify new laborers as distant, but related, clan members. Groups defined for religious activities might also serve as ready-made task groups. Modified creation myths, folktales, and symbols would ease these cultural changes by creating the illusion that the new technologies, and the often unequal social relations that obtained as a result, were divinely sanctioned.

To operationalize such social theory, archaeologists linked the attributes of artifacts to their functions within these cultural subsystems. Artifact functions were categorized as *technofunctional, sociofunctional,* and *ideofunctional.* These functions depend upon particular interactions in an object's life history, and behavioralists recognize that every artifact has variable interactions that can encompass all three different functional types (Schiffer 1992).

The technofunctions of ceramics, chipped stone, and ground stone have been a source of long-term experimentation at the University of Arizona's Laboratory of Traditional Technology, directed by Schiffer. Pottery experiments, for example, have focused on the complex relationship among the formal properties of the ceramic pots, the technical choices made by the potter, and the performance of these artifacts in particular activities.

Like many other processual archaeologists, behavioralists have found that technological functions are more easily isolated than social or ideological functions. A Star of David amulet, for example, is an artifact shape that has esoteric meaning in Judaism, but it also symbolizes a group of people that share ritual activities, and—since 1948—a country (Israel). Recognizing this difficulty, behavioralists lumped the social and ideological functions of artifacts within the general category of style, to distinguish them from technological or utilitarian functions.

In the 1990s, a new behavioral archaeology (Walker et al. 1995) has begun to question the adaptationist perspective that underlies the distinction between the utilitarian and the stylistic functions of artifacts. New Behavioralists still seek a materialist approach to human relations founded on general laws of human behavior. They believe, however, that White's and other adaptationist visions of culture actually mask important regularities in the life histories of artifacts.

Adaptationist studies emphasize cultural accommodations to the natural environment and downplay aggressive and violent behaviors among individuals and groups. Such conflicts, however, clearly create an environment that also requires accommodation, especially because such social conflicts can cause or aggravate cultural changes. Ian Hodder, Mark Leone, Randall H. McGuire, and other critics of adaptationist theory believe that too little importance has been paid to ideological systems. They suggest that considering individual desires, fears, and beliefs would redress the lack of attention paid to social conflict, individual actors, and ritual activities in adaptationist theory. New behavioral archaeologists argue just the opposite.

Ritual, although often equated with the beliefs and symbols that accompany it, *is* a behavior. Archaeologists already ask what ritual objects mean; they rarely attempt to explain how they were made, used, and discarded. Because some aspects of group behavior are not well understood, they have also been relegated to the field of symbolic analysis. Stylistic attributes are defined as unneccesary for use (nonutilitarian) and, therefore, assumed to function in a symbolic, rather than a behavioral, realm.

This dichotomy between style and function results from the treatment of some attributes of artifacts as symbolic and some as behavioral. Returning to the roots of behavioral archaeology, New Behavioralists suggest that all interactions between people and objects that create patterns in the four dimensions of artifact variability should be treated as behaviors. New behavioral archaeologists, therefore, no longer use terms such as style, utilitarian, technofunction, sociofunction, or ideofunction.

Any interaction with an object is a behavior and, therefore, involves the use of an object. Within this perspective, nonutilitarian artifacts are not symbolic artifacts. Instead, they are objects possessing life histories whose behavioral regularities remain to be discovered. This new materialism has reinvigorated behavioral research and allowed behavioralists to expand their life-history approach to prehistoric studies of social power and ritual behavior, as well as to research on other subjects, including communication theory, and the history of electrical technologies.

Behavioral archaeology past and present strives to construct a unique social science that emphasizes artifacts. Because almost all behaviors entail the use of artifacts, the study of behavior through objects is a powerful tool for archaeologists, historians, and ethnographers. Behavioral archaeologists combine all three of these sources of information, as well as experimental studies of artifact-performance characteristics. The result is an exciting and still growing field of study.

William H. Walker

See also ARCHAEOLOGICAL SITES, FORMATION PROCESSES; ETHNOARCHAEOLOGY; EXPERIMENTAL ARCHAEOLOGY; SCHIFFER, MICHAEL BRIAN

Further Readings

Harris, M. (1964) The Nature of Cultural Things. New York: Random House.

Rathje, W.L., and Murphy, C. (1992) Rubbish! The Archaeology of Garbage. New York: HarperCollins.

Reid, J.J., Rathje, W.L., and Schiffer, M.B. (1974) Expanding archaeology. American Antquity 39:125–126.

Schiffer, M.B. (1975) Archaeology as a behavioral science. American Anthropologist 77:836–848.

Schiffer, M.B. (1976) Behavioral Archeology. New York: Academic.

Schiffer, M.B. (1987) Formation Processes of the Archaeological Record. Albuquerque: University of New Mexico Press (reprinted by the University of Utah Press, Salt Lake City, 1996).

Schiffer, M.B. (1991) The Portable Radio in American Life. Tucson: University of Arizona Press.

Schiffer, M.B. (1992) Technological Perspectives on Behavioral Change. Tucson: University of Arizona Press.

Schiffer, M.B. (1994) Taking Charge: The Electric Automobile in America. Washington, D.C.: Smithsonian Institution.

Sullivan, A.P. (1978) Inference and evidence: A discussion of the conceptual problems. In M.B. Schiffer (ed.): Advances in Archaeological Method and Theory, vol. 1, pp. 182–222. New York: Academic.

Walker, W.H., Skibo, J., and Nielsen, A.E. (1995) Introduction. In J.Skibo, W.H. Walker, and A. Nielsen (eds.): Expanding Archaeology, pp. 1–12. Salt Lake City: University of Utah Press.

Binford, Lewis R. (1930–)

American anthropologist and archaeologist. Born on November 21, 1930, in Norfolk, Virginia, Binford received his bachelor's degree from the University of North Carolina in 1957, his master's degree from the University of Michigan in 1958, and his doctorate from Michigan in 1964. He served as assistant professor of anthropology at the University of Chicago (1961–1965). Binford then taught in the University of California system first at Santa Barbara (1965–1966) and then as associate professor of anthropology at Los Angeles (1966–1968). Binford then taught in the Anthropology Department at the University of New Mexico as associate professor (1968–1972), full professor (1972–1984), and Distinguished Leslie Spier Professor of Anthropology (1984–1991). From 1991, he has been University Distinguished Professor in the Anthropology Department at Southern Methodist University, Texas.

Binford was a key figure in the development of *New Archaeology* in the United States during the 1960s and 1970s. A specialist in North American prehistory, he and several other New World archaeologists, dissat-

isfied with the descriptive archaeology that was prevalent in the first half of the twentieth century, began to turn toward new methodologies being developed in anthropology and other social sciences. The New Archaeology, also known sometimes as *anthropological* or *processual archaeology,* hoped not merely to describe but also to explain cultural processes through the interpretation of archaeological remains and to make relevant contributions to the study of human culture. His classic article "Archaeology as Anthropology" became a standard work, as did the influential *New Perspectives in Archaeology,* a collection of articles defining processual archaeology that was edited by him and his wife, Sally Binford, and his well-known *An Archaeological Perspective.* In the name of processualism, Binford brought many new techniques to the practice of archaeology, including the use of ethnoarchaeology to illuminate ancient lifeways, as well as experimental techniques in the study of site formation. The New Archaeology was roundly criticized when it first arrived on the scene, particularly by European archaeologists. It can be argued, however, that processual archaeology as championed by Binford had already made an important contribution, in that it challenged many of the assumptions of descriptive archaeology and breathed new energy into the discipline.

Joseph J. Basile

See also ETHNOARCHAEOLOGY; NEW/ PROCESSUAL ARCHAEOLOGY

Further Readings
Binford, L.R. (1962) Archaeology as anthropology. American Antiquity 28:217–225.

Binford, L.R. (1972) An Archaeological Perspective. New York: Seminar.

Binford, L.R., ed. (1977) For Theory Building in Archaeology: Essays on Faunal Remains, Aquatic Resources, Spatial Analysis, and Systemic Modeling. New York: Academic.

Binford, L.R. (1983a) In Pursuit of the Past: Decoding the Archaeological Record. New York: Thames and Hudson.

Binford, L.R. (1983b) Working at Archaeology. New York: Academic.

Binford, L.R. (1989) Debating Archaeology. San Diego: Academic.

B

Binford, S.R. and Binford, L.R., eds. (1968) New Perspectives in Archaeology. Chicago: Aldine.

Sabloff, P.L.W. (1998) Conversations with Lew Binford: Drafting the New Archaeology. Norman: University of Oklahoma Press.

Bone, Characterization

The most common material of vertebrate origin to survive in the archaeological record. Provided that it is well preserved, it may still contain indigenous organic macromolecules that can be used to provide information on the age of the bone, the diet of the animal, the health and disease of the individual or population, genetic relationships between individuals or populations, and taphonomic changes. Recent advances in the fields of immunology, protein chemistry, and DNA (deoxyribonucleic acid) amplification have begun to show that macromolecular preservation exists sufficient to yield this information.

Bone Composition

Bone is a structural tissue that in life performs a number of functions (e.g., support for the soft tissues; a reservoir for the storage of essential elements). Bone matrix is a highly specialized composite material combining both an organic (chiefly the protein, collagen) and an inorganic (chiefly the mineral, calcium hydroxyapatite [HAP]) phase. Ca. 90 percent by weight of the organic fraction of bone is collagen; lipids, carbohydrates, the noncollagenous proteins (NCP) and DNA make up the remainder. Collagen is a triple helix formed from three protein chains twisted tightly together. It is characterized by a repeating amino-acid sequence that features glycine at every third residue. This small amino acid enables the helix to coil tightly with the glycine residues all aligned inward, toward the middle. Collagen is an unusual vertebrate protein, as it contains many proline and hydroxyproline residues. Once the collagen has been laid down, the mineral is deposited around it; the collagen is then said to be mineralized.

The bone mineral is calcium hydroxyapatite $Ca_{10}(PO_4)_6(OH)_2$. The Ca/P ratio is not exactly 10:6, so the apatite requires, in addition to the calcium, phosphorus and hydroxyl ions, substantial quantities of carbonate ions, pyrophosphates, magnesium, sodium, and potassium. The mineral is, therefore, able to interact with a range of other chemical species; this phenomenon is used in trace-element analyses of archaeological bone. There is much discussion concerning the exact crystal size of the mineral phase and its interaction with the organic component, but it is agreed that they are in intimate association. A water molecule is able to penetrate dried bone, but even a slightly larger molecule like ethanol cannot; this demonstrates the close association of mineral with collagen.

Bone also contains a cellular component that is never infiltrated by the mineral phase; these cells are *osteoblasts* (which synthesize the bone proteins), *osteocytes* (which maintain the bone matrix) and *osteoclasts* (which resorb the bone matrix when required). In most cases, these unmineralized cells will disappear rapidly via autolytic and/or microbial pathways following the death of the individual and cannot be demonstrated in archaeological bone. What does remain can be used as described below. It must be remembered that the degree of survival of bone components will vary in different environments, depending upon the rate of taphonomic change.

Bone as an Archaeological Resource

Archaeological bone is a valuable resource for solving clearly defined problems, but the techniques described below are useful only when specific questions have been asked. Any scientific investigation has to be justified; this is particularly important when using these methods, as they are both expensive and destructive. The effects of taphonomic change must also be considered, and the extracted information interpreted in light of that change. It is not the intention here to list and describe the methods applied to archaeological bone, but rather to discuss their application. For a detailed explanation of the methods, the reader is referred to the relevant sections herein.

Dating

There have been several methods applied for the dating of bone from archaeological deposits. These are: radiocarbon, uranium-series, electron spin resonance (ESR), amino acid racemization, and fluorine-uranium-nitrogen (FUN) dating. With the exception of radiocarbon dating, all of the methods present significant problems when applied to archaeological bone. The problems are associated with the structure, chemistry, and diagenesis of bone and are not inherent in the methods themselves.

Radiocarbon Dating

For the radiocarbon dating of bone, the collagen fraction is extracted, which destroys the bone. The carbonate fraction gives erroneous results due to the difficulty of removing secondary carbonates that have washed in from the soil and so is discarded. Problems arise due to contamination by extraneous carbon sources that are (usually but not always) more modern than the bone sample under investigation. Soil humates, soil microorganisms, plants, and insects are sources of contaminating carbon. Needless to say, the cleanup methods that remove these extraneous carbon contaminants are thorough. Generally, collagen molecules that are still intact (i.e., have high molecular weights) will give more reliable dates than those that have been modified during deposition.

A reliable method of extracting only bone-collagen carbon has been developed. The bone mineral is removed and discarded, and the collagen is treated with a bacterial collagenase to produce many small sections of peptides. The most common peptides are gly-pro-hyp and gly-pro-ala, which are isolated using a separation technique and dated. Using this method, the authors obtained radiocarbon dates for each site closer to the expected dates than those obtained by conventional sample preparation. For highly altered bone, this method may not be appropriate, since ancient collagen is not always susceptible to collagenase action. The collagen may be so highly degraded that the enzyme cannot recognize the active sites and no short-characteristic peptides are produced, or the collagen helix may be so highly cross-linked that, even if the enzyme does cleave the protein chains, no peptides are released. Both taphonomic changes would affect this sample preparation.

Uranium (Thorium)-Series Dating

The uranium concentration in living bone is less than 0.1 parts per million, but in fossil bone the concentration can be as high as 1,000 ppm. The uranium complexes with the mineral phase of the bone. It is assumed that uranium is taken up from the groundwater rapidly after burial, but thorium is not, because it is not water soluble. Uranium radioactively decays to thorium in the bone; when the ratio of these two is measured, dates can be calibrated. Calibration requires that the rate of uptake of uranium be known; uptake depends upon burial environment; hence, there must be a calibration scale for the site. A complication of this method is that there will have been periods when uranium could have leached out of the bone again, since the porous structure of bone permits the flow of water through it. Reliable dates are not the general rule for this method when applied to archaeological bone.

Electron Spin Resonance (ESR) Spectroscopy

Crystals are made up of a regular lattice of positive and negative ions. Defects in this regular lattice occur if the crystal has been cooled too rapidly, if there are impurities present, or if, once formed, the crystal is subjected to nuclear radiation. ESR spectroscopy is a method to measure the number of defects in a lattice, as is thermoluminescence (TL). ESR is applicable where TL is not, because TL involves heating the sample; heating will denature the proteins present in bone, giving an erroneous result. ESR measures defects in the mineral lattice, and time zero is the time of formation of the crystals. Eviction of the electrons does not occur in ESR dating (as it does in TL); therefore, the measurements can be made repeatedly on the same sample. Unusually for an archaeometric method, the ESR signal is not destroyed by its measurement. Recrystallization of the mineral will set the ESR clock back to zero. HAP is sparingly soluble in pure water but increasingly soluble in acidic groundwaters. The buffering effect of both the collagen and the dissolved mineral will promote re-precipitation of the HAP, nullifying any ESR signal present. This method is, therefore, not suggested for bone. However, tooth enamel at 80 percent mineral is more highly mineralized than bone (70 percent) and less susceptible to recrystallization, so can be used for ESR measurements.

Amino Acid Racemization (AAR) Dating

Amino acids are the building blocks of proteins and they exist in two mirror forms (D and L). In life, all, except glycine which does not change, exist in the L form. After death, there is a slow conversion (racemization) to D at a fixed rate until equilibrium (50:50 D:L) is reached; this racemization rate is governed primarily by temperature. The amino acid of choice for archaeological work has been aspartic acid, as the rate of racemization affords dates between 50,000–100,000 years ago. Problems with the method have been noticed, however, so that the measurement of the D/L_{asp} ratio has traditionally been used for relative dates within a single site.

In archaeological bone collagen, the aspartic acid racemization signal comes from the combined responses of aspartic acid (Asp) and asparagine (Asn), which decomposes to Asp after acid hydrolysis. This combined response is usually denoted as Asx. Collins et al (1999) have described a simplified mathematical model which includes this decomposition, and also the peptide bound racemization mechanism of the formation of a cyclic succinimide (Asu), to predict racemization kinetics at high temperatures. The model fails to predict the racemization kinetics in dentine at low temperatures, because Asu formation is highly conformationally dependent, occurring only slowly at 37°C in helical collagen. The model excludes the biological component, which is thought to be too variable to model. This is mediated by enzymatic degradation of helical collagen, producing chain cleavage and a varied amino acid composition both C- and N- terminally. The ratio of D/L_{Asx} in archaeological bone will reflect the relative amounts of helical to non-helical collagen and will also be strongly affected by the degree of leaching of the soluble peptide fraction. These factors, combined with the unpredictability of the biological effect, make any dates derived from the D/L_{Asx} ratios of archaeological bone unreliable.

Does this theoretical unreliability appear true in archaeological bone samples dated using AAR? Wide ranges in D/L_{asp} values have been measured in a series of bone samples of assumed similar age associated with a suite of ^{14}C determinations in a Late Holocene site. The major differences in D/L_{asp} ratios correlated with variability in the condition of the collagen (certain amino acid ratios and overall nitrogen content), demonstrating the importance of helical for D/L_{asp} measurements. For measurements over geological time spans, the enantiomers chosen are isoleucine/alloisoleucine. These are hydrophobic amino acids, therefore are less likely to be susceptible to hydrolysis. Hydrophobic amino acids are less likely to be present in certain soils, and therefore less likely to contaminate the bone samples. Dates for bones measured by isoleucine/alloisoleucine are taken as more reliable.

Fluorine-Uranium-Nitrogen (FUN) Dating
The fluorine and uranium contents of buried bone will increase because these elements will interact with the HAP; concomitantly, nitrogen will decrease due to the disappearance of collagen. There is a strong relationship with the burial environment, but these ratios have been used to give relative dates for samples from the same site. The most famous use of the measurement of these elements was in the detection of the Piltdown Man forgery of purportedly pre-*Homo sapiens* fossils and associated finds "discovered" in Sussex, England, in 1912. Analyses of fluorine, uranium, and nitrogen by Joseph Weiner and Kenneth Oakley in 1953 finally exposed this hoax as a pastiche of human and orangutan bones.

Paleodiet
There are two photosynthetic pathways that plants use to make energy: the C_3 pathway and the C_4 pathway. The C_3 pathway operates in higher plants (i.e., wheat, rice, fruits), while plants such as maize and sorghum use the C_4 pathway. Surprisingly, the two pathways result in a very different fractionation of stable carbon isotope ^{13}C, giving characteristic ratios of $^{13}C/^{12}C$. The ratio is called ^{13}C and is expressed as parts per thousand compared against a standard called PDB (Pee Dee Formation *Belemnitella* fossil). In C_3 plants, the ratio is −12.5 parts per thousand, while in C_4, it is much lower at −26.5 parts per thousand.

The characteristic ^{13}C values of the two plant groups are passed along the food chain so that the carbon isotopes present in the bones of an animal will reflect what that animal has eaten. Dietary carbon is deposited in both the collagen and the mineral, but there is a fractionation between proteins and other food sources. It is thought that dietary proteins are routed to collagen, while all nutrient biochemical fractions are scrambled and integrated into bone carbonate. Hence, the carbon-isotope ratios between whole plants and their biochemical fractions must be considered.

The ^{13}C values of C_3 plants are highly sensitive to microenvironmental variations, but C_4 plants are relatively insensitive to this. Carbon-13 marine food webs are highly varied but tend to be intermediate between C_3 and C_4 terrestrial values. Where terrestrial diets contain both C_3 and C_4 plants and marine foodstuffs, the estimation of the contribution of marine depends upon additional elements (i.e., nitrogen, carbon, and strontium isotopes). There are problems with the measurement of elements in bone; it has been shown that elemental contamination of bone may increase drastically with time in a fashion that is influenced strongly by the postmortem environment.

The conclusions that can be drawn from dietary studies include comments on the spatial and temporal differences in access to food resources (whether ancient humans moved between inland riverine and coastal waters), and intra- and interregional dietary differences can be addressed. Whether there is a difference in the diets between the ages and the sexes can also be examined (provided that skeletal morphology permits such distinctions).

Paleopathology

Paleopathology is the study of disease in ancient populations. Since soft tissue survives only in rare conditions, paleopathology is the study of disease in bone. Very few diseases produce diagnostic (characteristic) changes in bone because bone material can react in only a very few ways to disease processes. In medical science, confirmation of the type of disease by means other than deformation (gross change) is almost always required, and the diagnosis is made by examination of the soft tissue also. Paleopathologists do not have the extravagance of soft tissue and rely upon macroscopic and microscopic characterization of the bone. Few infectious diseases change the gross morphology of bone, but those that do include syphilis (causative organism *Treponema pallidum*), yaws (causative organism *Treponema pertenue*), and tuberculosis (causative organism *Mycobacterium tuberculosis*).

Paleohistology

The study of archaeological bone at the microscopic level (paleohistology) has become an important adjunct to paleopathology. For paleohistological examination, further deterioration and/or distortion is prevented by the application of chemicals; the bone is cut into sections either before or after demineralization and treated with a variety of stains for examination under several light-microscope sources (e.g., brightfield, darkfield, phase con-

trast, and fluorescent). Electron-microscopy studies can also be done on both gross and sectioned bone following suitable preparation. Once prepared, bone samples can be kept for repeated examination by either light or electron microscopy. There are two areas where paleohistology can be applied to archaeological bone. It can be used to speciate bone (i.e., to decide whether the sample is, for example, bovine or human) and to describe and define further the changes seen in bone, so that distinctions between pathological changes during life and postmortem taphonomic changes can be made.

Bones from a crypt in Northamptonshire in Britain showed a number of changes, but it was uncertain whether these were pathological or due to taphonomy. A histological study (Garland et al. 1988) revealed that the changes had developed postmortem. Fungal elements were also seen inside the bone.

Microbial Biomarkers

Increasingly, molecular biology has played a role in the diagnosis of ancient disease. Reliable diagnosis of tubercular disease in ancient human populations is important for paleopathological research, particularly as the historic records for disease due to *M. tuberculosis* (MTB) are incomplete over most time periods. Without modern diagnostic techniques, the disease can easily be confused with neoplasms or other infections, and, therefore, the possibility of misdiagnoses in the historic records cannot be ruled out. The true prevalence of TB in ancient human populations compared with current records would provide interesting data for medical history and would help answer some important questions concerning current treatments. Do vaccination protocols work? Is there evidence for increased or reduced resistance? Is there evidence of a change in the bacterial populations following antibiotic treatments? Studies show that TB DNA can be repeatedly extracted from bones showing characteristic tubercular lesions, and species-speficic MTB lipids have been demonstrated in ancient individuals with no gross bone change (Gernaey et al. 1998).

Paleoimmunology

The origin and spread of infectious disease in the ancient world is a probable source of information on the movement of people in the ancient world. Was syphilis spread to the Americas by Columbus's ships? There are treponemal lesions on Inca bones dated to 3000 B.P. These lesions may either be syphilitic or due to yaws (a disease endemic in that area that is nonsexually transmitted and common in children). Immunochemical studies have been done that demonstrate that there is a treponemal antigen present, but distinction between yaws (*T. pertenue*) and syphilis (*T. pallidum*) is not possible by these techniques. The original question remains then; it is unlikely that DNA studies will resolve the problem.

Genetic Relationships

DNA can be extracted from almost all of the body cells. Although the cellular component in bone does not usually survive, DNA can still be extracted from the acellular remains. This is a paradox, as the chemical stability of DNA is limited. In life, the molecule is subject to depurination, oxidation, and nonenzymic methylation. These changes are counteracted by specific DNA-repair processes. After death, these processes continue unchecked. This might argue against the recovery of ancient DNA from bone, but, as with other biomolecules, the close association of the mineral HAP with DNA is thought to promote its stability and survival.

DNA can be extracted from ancient bone and amplified by the polymerase chain reaction (PCR) technique or hybridized with a known complementary chain that has been labeled. There are two mechanisms of taphonomic loss that must be considered when DNA is being extracted: dilution by the addition of other (e.g., microbial) DNAs and loss due to chemical, physical, and biological degradation. As with the indigenous DNA, the contaminating microbial DNA is protected from degradation by the close association of the HAP, even though many soil bacteria and fungi have enzymes capable of digesting DNA (DNases).

Studies

The major uses of ancient human DNA in archaeology are the study of migration of populations, including the peopling of various regions, and phylogenetic relationships between individuals and the evolutionary pathways.

Mitochondrial deoxyribonucleic acid (mtDNA) is present as a multiple copy gene which is evolving more rapidly than the single copy nuclear genes. Because it is present as a multiple copy, it is more likely to survive in ancient bones than single copy genes simply because there is more of it. It is passed down from mother to offspring (both males and females). Because it is evolving more rapidly than nuclear genes, it can be used to study evolutionary relationships among ethnic groups. Such studies show that there is a high correlation between mtDNA types and ethnic origins. The distribution of mtDNA sequences within populations over time will yield information on the migration of people demonstrated by the transposition of a sequence to a new region.

Conclusions

The techniques mentioned above are useful tools in archaeology, but, as with all scientific investigations, their suitability to a question must always be considered. A further consideration must be the loss of the specimen; apart from ESR studies and gross pathological examination, all other techniques will destroy bone samples. Even histological examination, which can be done repeatedly on prepared specimens, will destroy gross morphology.

Throughout the entry, the effects of taphonomy on these investigations has been stressed. The degree to which bone has been altered is significant when considering the extracted information. Notwithstanding these factors, the information that can be retrieved from archaeological bone is diverse and spectacular. The date of the site, the diet of the population (or individual), their genetic relationships and some of the diseases that were prevalent in their society are all facts that can be derived from the correct examination of archaeological bone.

Angela Gernaey-Child

See also AMINO ACID RACEMIZATION/ EPIMERIZATION DATING; BONE AND OTHER ORGANIC MATERIALS: ANCIENT DNA; BONE, TRACE-ELEMENT ANALYSIS; ELECTRON SPIN RESONANCE (ESR) DATING; ELECTROPHORESIS; FLUORINE-URANIUM-NITROGEN DATING; ISOTOPES, STABLE (C, N, O, H): BONE AND PALEODIET STUDIES; PALEODEMOGRAPHY; PALEOIMMUNOLOGY; PALEOPATHOLOGY; PALEOSEROLOGY; RADIOCARBON DATING; URANIUM-SERIES DATING

Further Readings

Aitken, M.J. (1990) Science-Based Dating in Archaeology. Harlow: Longman.

Collins, M.J., Waite, E.R., and van Duin, A.C.T. (1998) Predicting protein decomposition: The case of aspartic acid racemization kinetics. Philosophical Transactions of the Royal Society, Series B, 354:51–64.

Garland, A.N., Janaway, R. and Roberts, C.A. (1988) A study of the decay processes of human remains from the Parish Church of the Holy Trinity, Rothwell, Northamptonshire. Oxford Journal of Archaeology 7:235–252.

Gernaey, A.M., et al. (1998) Detecting ancient tuberculosis. http://www.interarch.ac.uk/journal/issues/gernaey_index.html

Grupe, G., and Garland, A.N., eds. (1993) Histology of Ancient Human Bone: Methods and Diagnosis. Berlin: Springer.

Hedges, R.E.M., and van Klinken, G., eds. (1995) Proceedings of the Oxford Bone Diagenesis Workshop. Journal of Archaeological Science 22:145–340.

Lambert, J.B., and Grupe, G., eds. (1993) Prehistoric Human Bone: Archaeology at the Molecular Level. Berlin: Springer.

Lindahl, T. (1993) Instability and decay of the primary structure of DNA. Nature 362:709–715.

Pollard, A.M., ed. (1993) New Developments in Archaeological Science: A Joint Symposium of the Royal Society and the British Academy. Oxford: Oxford University Press.

Taylor, R.E., Ennis, P.J., Slota, P.J., Payen, J.R., and Payen, L.A. (1989) Non-age related variations in aspartic acid racemization in bone from a radiocarbon-dated late Holocene archaeological site. Radiocarbon 31(3):1048–1056.

Van Klinken, G., Bowles, A.D., and Hedges, R.E.M. (1994) Radiocarbon dating of peptides isolated from contaminated fossil bone collagen by collagenase digestion and reversed-phase chromatography. Geochimica et Cosmochimica Acta 58(11):2453–2551.

Bone and Other Organic Materials: Ancient DNA

Genetic material surviving in preserved ancient biological remains. "Ancient" in the context of DNA (deoxyribonucleic acid) ranges from museum specimens less than 100 years old to permafrost-preserved specimens tens of thousands of years old, and includes amber-entombed animals and plants more than 100 million years old. DNA from preserved organic remains contains valuable information that may aid in understanding historical events. Archaeologists use this information to determine how modern humans are related to prehistoric peoples, to reconstruct prehistoric migration events, to understand past cultural practices, and to gain insight into the history of animal and plant domestication. Evolutionary biologists and ecologists use ancient DNA to aid in understanding the relationships between extinct and modern taxa. Ancient DNA analysis is thus a valuable tool for students of prehistory. However, most biological remains do not have preserved DNA, and the extraction and analysis of the DNA that does exist is difficult and time consuming, so studies of ancient DNA augment, but do not replace, traditional methods in physical anthropology and archaeology.

Background

Almost every cell contains a copy of all of the genetic material (the *genome*) of an individual. This genetic material, DNA, is a ladderlike polymer consisting of paired chains of subunits called *nucleotides*. The four nucleotides—*guanine, adenine, thymine,* and *cytosine*—form the rungs of the DNA polymer. The genome of a single individual consists of billions of nucleotides, and the sequence of these nucleotides contains the biochemical blueprint for each individual. The genome of every individual is unique, but closely related individuals and members of the same species differ in only a small fraction of their nucleotide sequences, whereas members of different species, genera, or higher taxa will have an increasingly large number of genetic differences. Comparisons of genetic differences between individuals and populations lead to conclusions about the evolutionary history of a species and, on a local scale, can lead to an understanding of the relationships between two or more populations or between individuals in a single population.

Paleontological and archaeological sites yield bones, or in rare instances preserved soft tissues, but until recently the only way to assess genetic differences among the individuals represented at a site was to measure and compare phenotypic traits such as bone morphology, hair color, and, in very well preserved specimens, enzyme types. With the exception of enzyme typing such methods only indirectly measure genetic difference, but recent advances in molecular biology, and the demonstration that DNA may survive in bone and other tissue long after cell death, now allow direct measurement of genetic differences from archaeological organic materials.

Two of these advances, *cloning* and the *polymerase chain reaction* (PCR), have been the keys to unlocking the secrets of genetic diversity in a wide variety of modern organisms, and these same tools have been used to examine genetic diversity in preserved biological material. Molecular cloning, developed in the 1970s, refers to the insertion of a small piece of DNA into bacterial cells. This DNA is replicated as the bacteria grow in a culture, and the millions of copies that are produced may then be sequenced or analyzed by other means. Cloning was an important advance for genetic research, but it requires a relatively large amount of high quality DNA as a starting material, and it is therefore difficult to clone DNA directly from ancient samples.

PCR, developed in the mid-1980s, is an in vitro amplification process that uses a DNA polymerase (an enzyme that makes DNA) to make millions of copies from one or a few target DNA sequences. The original DNA used as the starting template for the process does not have to consist of very long (many millions of bases) unbroken chains of nucleotides. It can be degraded or chopped up into much shorter pieces; it is only necessary for a few of those pieces to contain the DNA segment that is the target of the PCR reaction in order for the amplification to occur. Since PCR reactions are carried out in small (0.5 ml or smaller) tubes, and tens or hundreds of reactions can be performed in one day, the technique has made possible large-scale comparative studies that were not possible in the past.

Ancient DNA Studies

Until the 1980s, it was widely assumed that DNA rapidly degraded after the death of any organism. However, in 1984 a short segment of DNA from the 140-year-old skin of an extinct equid, the quagga, was extracted, cloned, and sequenced. Shortly thereafter, DNA from the tissue of a 2,400-year-old Egyptian mummy was cloned and sequenced. These two studies were widely publicized because they demonstrated the existence of DNA in very old organic remains. Both reports also demonstrated that only a small fraction of the original DNA remained in the tissue. Furthermore, the DNA that remained was very degraded; DNA extracted from fresh material is typically tens of thousands of nucleotides long, but DNA extracted from the ancient samples is broken into fragments only 100 or 200 hundred nucleotides in length, and such fragments are particularly difficult to clone. For these reasons, studies of ancient DNA still remained rare.

The advent of PCR in 1987 and the demonstration of DNA in bone in 1989 led to a rapid expansion in ancient DNA studies. PCR is sensitive enough to amplify even the very few remaining molecules of DNA from an ancient sample, and the length of the degraded DNA from these samples is less important than for cloning, since it is possible to amplify short pieces of DNA by PCR. The discovery of DNA in bone was particularly important because most biological remains from archaeological sites are bone.

In general, ancient DNA studies can be classified into two categories: those using DNA as a tool to analyze samples (usually human or domestic animals and plants) from specific archaeological sites, and those comparing DNA sequences (usually animal) from ancient and modern samples to determine the phylogenetic relationships between the ancient samples and their modern relatives.

Much ancient DNA work focuses on answering questions of animal and plant taxonomy. Many studies take advantage of the biological collections in natural-history museums around the world, and usually the samples, which may be the dried or preserved soft tissues—leaves, feathers, or skin—of animals or plants are less than 200 years old. Other work uses older samples, usually preserved bone, excavated from archaeological sites. These archaeological materials are used not only to examine taxonomic questions, but also to aid in understanding the history of animal and plant domestication.

A very elegant use of ancient DNA was the comparison of DNA sequences from humans and a Neandertal. The sequence comparison suggested that Neandertals and modern humans diverged about four times as long ago as modern humans diverged from each other, and also suggested that Neandertals did not contribute any of their genes to modern human populations.

Elephant biologists have long debated the relationships between the two living elephant species (African and Asian) and the extinct mammoth. Analysis of sequences from mammoth and the elephants strongly supports a group including mammoths and African elephants, with Asian elephants more distantly related.

Perhaps the most well known ancient DNA studies have been those involving attempts to extract DNA from insects entombed in amber. The initial studies examined insects that were a few million years old. In 1993 DNA sequences from weevils entombed at least 125 million years ago were reported. Such studies reported very short—100–300-nucleotide—DNA sequences from the insects. The sequences were compared to the sequences of modern relatives of the trapped insect in order to place the extinct insect on a phylogenetic tree with its modern relatives. However, many scientists have been skeptical that DNA can be preserved over such a long period of time, and in 1997 a group of scientists attempted, and failed, to reproducibly extract and amplify DNA from amber-preserved specimens. The preservation of multi-million-year-old DNA must remain an open issue.

The extraction of DNA from the dinosaur meals of bloodsucking amber-preserved insects is, of course, the fundamental concept behind the movie *Jurassic Park,* and, although it is very unlikely, it is possible that dinosaur DNA may one day be discovered and analyzed from within such samples. However amber-preserved DNA, if it exists at all, would be fragmented into pieces with lengths of, at most, a few hundred bases. There is absolutely no possibility that the entire genome of a dinosaur—billions of nucleotides in length—could be reconstructed from an insect bloodmeal; hence *Jurassic Park* will always remain fiction.

Methodological Issues

Most of the DNA in every cell is contained in the cell's nucleus. However, extranuclear organelles known as *mitochondria* also contain a very small quantity of their own DNA. Each of the thousands of mitochondria in every cell contains its own complete copy of the mitochondrial genome, so there are thousands of copies of the mitochondrial DNA for each single copy of the nuclear DNA per cell. The mitochondrial DNA degrades at the same rate as the nuclear DNA, so there will always be thousands of times as many copies of a mitochondrial sequence as of a nuclear DNA sequence and, thus, a correspondingly greater likelihood of successfully recovering usable information from a given ancient DNA sample. For this reason, most studies of ancient DNA to date (1998) have analyzed mitochondrial sequences.

Organic molecules such as DNA are quite fragile and do not, in general, survive long after death. DNA is quickly consumed by bacterial and fungal enzymes, degraded by acids and bases, and is very sensitive to ultraviolet light; hence, DNA is found in only a very small percentage of archaeological remains. The initial problem for an investigator who is considering any ancient DNA work is whether the samples even contain DNA. In general, if there are any soft tissues left—if the remains are mummified or otherwise preserved—the chances of recovering some DNA are high. Bone samples are more problematic; poorly preserved (crumbly or obviously decayed) bones will usually not contain DNA, but even well-preserved, solid bones may yield no DNA.

Once it has been determined that samples may contain DNA, there are still three major technical problems to be overcome: the difficulty of extracting DNA from the samples, inhibition of PCR by other substances in the DNA extracts, and contamination of ancient samples with modern DNA.

DNA is extracted from ancient samples using techniques similar to those used for modern samples. However, because there is so little DNA in ancient samples, it is necessary to optimize the extraction procedure to maximize the amount of DNA recovered. In general, the samples are minced or ground to a powder. The DNA is separated from contaminants (i.e., everything else) in a series of extractions using organic solvents. The DNA remains in an aqueous solution and is then concentrated. In another widely used method, DNA is bound to silica (fine sand), the contaminants are washed away, then the DNA is released from the silica. Whatever method is chosen, the investigator must always use extreme care to ensure maximum DNA yield from the sample.

DNA extracted from ancient samples contains a host of other organic substances. Some of these substances inhibit the amplification of the DNA in the PCR reaction, and such inhibition is extremely common. There are a number of different techniques for eliminating the inhibitors from the samples or preventing them from affecting the PCR reaction, but it is time consuming to test each method on every problem sample.

The greatest bugbear for ancient DNA work is contamination from modern DNA. Contamination may occur at any time during or after excavation. The amount of modern DNA in skin secretions, sloughed skin cells, or a sneeze may be greater than that remaining in the ancient sample, so anyone who handles the bones must be extremely careful not to contaminate them. In addition, the products from a PCR amplification contain millions or billions of copies of the target DNA segment, so contamination of a DNA sample by amplified DNA is an ever-present danger in any laboratory. These problems are greatest for those working with human remains, since it may not be possible to distinguish between the genetic types of the ancient samples and the modern laboratory workers. Together, these technical problems mean that analysis of ancient DNA is now, and will be for the foreseeable future, a slow and time-consuming process. Nevertheless, the information gleaned from such work is worth the time invested to obtain it.

Archaeologists and paleontologists who might wish to use ancient DNA should ideally involve the molecular biologists who will be doing the laboratory analysis in the excavation process. Together, they should first determine whether the materials at a given site are likely to have DNA in them. If they are, a few simple precautions taken while excavating will greatly decrease the chances of contaminating the samples with modern DNA. These include handling samples only while wearing gloves and transferring samples to sealed bags or containers as rapidly as possible.

Charles E. Cook Jr.

See also BONE, CHARACTERIZATION

Further Readings

Audic, S, and BeraudColomb, E. (1997) Ancient DNA is thirteen years old. Nature Biotechnology 15(9):855–858.

Cano, R.J., Poinar, H.N., Pieniazek, N.J., Acra, A., and Poinar, G.O. (1993) Amplification and sequencing of DNA from a 120–135-million-year-old weevil. Nature 363:536–538.

Cooper, A., and Wayne, R. (1998) New uses for old DNA. Current Opinion in Biotechnology 9(1):49–53.

Hermann, B., and Hummel, S., eds. (1994) Ancient DNA. New York: Springer-Verlag.

Higuchi, R., Bowman, B., Freiberger, M., Ryder, O.A., and Wilson, A.C. (1984) DNA sequences from the quagga, an extinct member of the horse family. Nature 312:282–284.

Krings, M., Stone, A., Schmitz, R.W., Krainitzki, H., Stoneking, M. and Pääbo, S. (1997) Neandertal DNA sequences and the origin of modern humans. Cell 90(1):19–30.

Noro, M., Masuda, R., Dubrovo, I.S., Yoshida, M.C., and Kato, M. (1998) Molecular phylogenetic inference of the woolly mammoth *Mammuthus primigenius,* based on complete sequences of mitochondrial Cytochrome b and 12S ribosomal RNA genes. Journal of Molecular Evolution 46(3):314–326.

Pääbo, S. 1985. Molecular cloning of an ancient Egyptian mummy DNA. Nature 314:644–645.

Pääbo, S. (1993) Ancient DNA. Scientific American 269(5):60–66.

Bone, Trace-Element Analysis

The use of certain chemical elements in bones and teeth of humans as tracers of the source of foods. Bones and teeth consist of crystals of calcium phosphate (apatite) intimately intergrown with an organic matrix, largely composed of protein (collagen and minor amounts of noncollagenous protein). The mineral component has a well-defined chemical composition, made up of calcium (the chemical symbol for which is Ca), phosphate (PO_4), hydroxyl (OH), and carbonate (CO_3). In addition, variable amounts of several trace elements can substitute for these major constituents. The amounts of these trace elements in fossil bone depend, in part, on diet and have been used to reconstruct paleodiet. Many of these trace elements, such as strontium (Sr), barium (Ba) and lead (Pb), do not appear to be essential to the diet, but rather enter the body passively and can be trapped at atomic sites in the bone mineral that are normally occupied by Ca. The elements Sr and Ba resemble calcium in their chemical behavior and are grouped together with Ca in the periodic table as alkaline earth elements. Therefore, they have a particularly high affinity for bone mineral. Usually, levels of trace elements in bones are reported as the ratio of the concentration of the element to that of Ca (e.g., the Sr/Ca ratio).

Analyses of bone can be carried out on whole bone or bone powder using the nondestructive analytical method of X-ray fluorescence (XRF) or, destructively, by neutron activation analysis (NAA), atomic absorption (AA), or inductively coupled plasma (ICP) spectrometry. These methods are widely available in Departments of Geology where geochemical studies are done and, to a lesser extent, in anthropology research laboratories. Concentrations of trace elements are generally given in units of parts per million (ppm) (1 ppm = 0.0001 percent).

All animal and human bodies tend to reject nonessential elements during assimilation of nutrients. Therefore, the relative concentration of these elements is less in the consumer than in the food consumed. For example, the Sr/Ca ratio in an animal is about half of that in the food it consumes. This process of exclusion of nonessential trace elements is referred to as *biopurification*. The lowered interelement ratios are reflected in the composition of bone. In principle, this phenomenon can be utilized in the study of the *trophic level* of an individual—that is, where it lies on the gradient from herbivores (lowest trophic level) to pure carnivores (highest). At each successively higher trophic level, a consumer's body (including its bones and teeth) should exhibit a lower Sr/Ca or Ba/Ca ratio than that of its foods. There are a number of assumptions and interfering effects that must be considered, however.

First, the Sr/Ca level in any organism in a given region is determined by the average Sr/Ca ratio in the local environment, which can vary considerably as a function of the local rock and soil types. Therefore, the Sr/Ca trophic gradient at a site should always be referred to values for known herbivores and carnivores for that locality. It is unsafe to assume an average, "standard" Sr/Ca ratio for a site, since this ratio can vary by as much as a factor of 10, even over short distances. On the other hand, values can be regionally uniform to within a few percent, as in Britain, where Sr/Ca ratios do not deviate by more than 25 percent from a regional value of 3×10^{-4} (molar ratio). Equally important, the Sr/Ca ratio in a particular consumer depends on the average Sr/Ca ratio of the specific mixture of foods consumed. Two species at the same trophic level living in the same environment can, therefore, have different Sr/Ca ratios.

Another problem that affects all studies of trace elements in bone, is *diagenesis*. During their period of burial in archaeological sites, bones do not remain inert. Except in desert or permafrost areas where liquid water is absent, bones undergo continuous chemical transformations, the extent and character of which critically depend on their burial environment. The major and minor chemical constituents of the bone mineral can change as a result of chemical interaction with soil water, which is a dilute solution containing Sr, Ca, and many other elements at significant levels. As a result, the Sr/Ca ratio of a fossil bone can become quite different from that which was present at the time of death. New crystals of phosphate mineral are formed during diagenesis, locking in the new trace-element constituents so that the contamination cannot be easily removed. Certain elements such as silicon, iron, manganese, and aluminum are enriched in sediments but normally absent in living bone. The levels of these elements can be used as indicators of the degree of diagenesis.

Various strategies have been attempted to counteract the effects of diagenesis. Andrew Sillen has shown that one can partly dissolve (leach) the bone with successive portions of dilute acid and observe gradual changes in the Sr/Ca ratio in successive leachates. This ratio generally starts at some high (contaminated) value and gradually drops to a constant "plateau" that is believed to be the initial value for the living bone. This seems to yield satisfactory data in some cases but has also given anomalous results. Another approach has been to analyze tooth enamel. This material is less porous, denser, and contains less organic matter than bone. It is believed to be more resistant to diagenesis and has also been preferred for some stable-isotopic analyses. Most dental enamel (except for the third molar) is, however, formed very early in the life of the animal or human, and its composition is not representative of average lifetime diet. Other workers have suggested the selective use of the interior part of cortical bone, noting that compositional gradients can be detected for some elements such as uranium, with higher concentrations occurring near the outer surface of the cortex.

Another possible interfering effect is the variation in trace element content between different skeletal elements of the same individual. Limited studies of some living and ancient populations have shown significant intraskeletal differences. These may be partly a result of changes in diet through the lifetime of the individual, coupled with bone remodeling, which affects different skeletal elements to varying degrees. Likewise, intraskeletal variations seen in fossil or ancient bones may be due to differential degrees of diagenesis as a result of variation in initial bone density.

Sr/Ca has been used as a trophic-level indicator to evaluate the diet of early hominids (Boaz and Hampel, 1978), as well as to study later hunter-gatherers, pastoralists, and farming communities. Problems of diagenesis have generally discouraged its use, although the leachate method shows some promise.

Barium (Ba), which is also chemically similar to calcium, is also potentially useful for characterization of paleodiet, through the principle of biopurification. In fact, the largest differences in Ba concentrations between populations are found where there is a contrast between terrestrial and marine (coastal) populations. Barium is extremely insoluble in solutions containing sulfate (SO_4), such as seawater. The Ba/Sr ratio of seawater and foods that grow in it is much lower than that of terrestrial waters and foods. James Burton and Theron Douglas Price (1990) showed that even fossil bones preserved this great difference in Ba/Sr between coastal and terrestrial populations, although the actual values gave only general estimates of the percentage of terrestrial foods in the diet.

Many other trace elements can be easily analyzed in bone using AA, ICP, and NAA, and concentrations of many of these have been studied in the hope of obtaining further information about the diet of the individuals. In particular, certain foods, such as shellfish and nuts, are notably enriched in certain trace elements (vanadium, copper, zinc, manganese), and concentrations of these elements in bone were believed to be indicators of the level of consumption of certain foods. Studies of these elements in fossil bones (as well as other tissues, where preserved, such as hair and skin) have made use of various statistical procedures, including factor analysis, to search for key variables or combinations of variables that could be used to characterize populations.

Recently, however, systematic feeding studies (Lambert and Weydert-Homer 1993) have shown that concentrations of many trace elements in bone bear no relation to the content of these elements in diet. Indeed, the presence of various organic constituents, such as indigestible fiber, in the diet seems to have a larger effect on the concentration of these elements in bone than does their concentration in the diet. On further reflection, this is not surprising, since all animals tend to control their internal chemical state (homeostasis), and this control might be expected to extend to the concentrations of trace elements.

We can distinguish among three types of chemical elements with respect to their behavior in the body. Elements such as copper and vanadium, which are biologically inactive and are chemically dissimilar to Ca, are assimilated from the gut at very low levels and, therefore, are greatly depleted in the blood and tissues with respect to their concentration in foods. On the other hand, calcium, strontium, and barium resemble one another chemically, and the body is, therefore, less effective at excluding these minor elements from bone mineral. Their concentration in bone is proportional to their content in the diet. Finally, some trace elements are biologically active, and their concentration is maintained at a constant level by biochemical systems in the body; these include cobalt, zinc, and iron. Within certain broad limits, concentrations of these elements in bone should not depend on the level in diet. Extreme depletion of these elements in the diet can lead to pathologic effects that might be coupled with abnormally low levels of these elements in bone. Organic constituents of certain foods are able to form stable complexes (chelates) with some essential trace elements. For example, phytate, which is found in some grains, forms a stable complex with zinc and can prevent absorption of this element by the gut. Excessive consumption of some grains may lead to dietary deficiency in elements that have been chelated in this way.

The bone concentrations of two other elements, lead (Pb) and uranium (U), have been studied extensively. Although chemically dissimilar to the alkaline earth elements, the mineral phase of bones and teeth has a strong affinity for both. Living organisms take up lead in their bones in direct response to its concentration in the environment. Lead serves no known biological function. Rather, it is a highly toxic metal that can produce neurological disorders and general morbidity. Numerous studies have followed the variation of Pb content in ancient bones and shown that higher concentrations of Pb are found in members of complex societies in which metal production is used, while individuals from agricultural or hunter-gatherer societies have low levels of lead.

Unlike lead, the uranium content of living bone is generally almost undetectable (less than 0.01 ppm), whereas ancient bone typically contains from 1 to 100 ppm of U. The higher concentration of U in older, buried bone is due to diagenesis and the uptake of U from groundwater. Bone has a particularly high affinity for this element (some uranium-ore deposits are concentrated in bone-rich sedimentary layers). Early studies showed that it was possible to obtain crude estimates of the age of buried bone from the U content. More precise ages are obtainable by measurement of the radioactive decay of uranium to its daughter isotope, thorium-230. Uranium/thorium ages determined on bones or teeth have to take into account the gradual uptake of U by the bone and the possibility of periods of U loss as well as uptake.

Henry P. Schwarcz

See also ATOMIC ABSORPTION (AA) SPECTROSCOPY; BONE, CHARACTERIZATION; FLUORINE-URANIUM-NITROGEN DATING; GROWTH STUDIES: MAMMAL TEETH; INDUCTIVELY COUPLED PLASMA–ATOMIC EMISSION SPECTROMETRY; ISOTOPES, STABLE (C, N, O, H): BONE AND PALEODIET STUDIES; NUCLEAR METHODS OF ANALYSIS; PALEONUTRITION; X-RAY FLUORESCENCE (XRF); SPECTROSCOPY

Further Readings

Boaz, N.T., and Hampel, J. (1978) Strontium content of fossil tooth enamel and diets of early hominids. Journal of Paleontology 52:928–933.

Buikstra, J., Frankenberg, S., Lambert, J., and Xue, L. (1989) Multiple elements: Multiple expectations. In T.D. Price (ed.): The Chemistry of Prehistoric Human Bone, pp. 155–210. Cambridge: Cambridge University Press.

Burton, J., and Price, T.D. (1990) The ratio of barium to strontium as a paleodietary indicator of consumption of marine resources. Journal of Archaeological Science 17:547–557.

Lambert, J.B., and Weydert-Homer, J.M. (1993) The fundamental relationship between ancient diet and the inorganic constituents of bone as derived from feeding experiments. Archaeometry 35:279–294.

Price, T.D. (1989) Multi-element studies of diagenesis in prehistoric bone. In T.D. Price (ed.): The Chemistry of Prehistoric Human Bone, pp. 126–154. Cambridge: Cambridge University Press.

Sillen, A., and Kavanagh, M. (1982) Strontium and paleodietary research: A review. Yearbook of Physical Anthropology 25:67–90.

Sillen, A., Sealy, J.C., and van der Merwe, N.J. (1989) Chemistry and paleodietary research: No more easy answers. American Antiquity 54:504–512.

Bordes, François (1919–1981)

French prehistoric archaeologist and Quaternary geologist. Educated at the University of Bordeaux, Bordes received his doctorate in natural sciences in 1951 from the University of Paris after participation in the French Resistance movement. Although his dissertation was on the Quaternary loess deposits of the Seine basin, he became well known for his development of a systematic lithic-artifact typology for the Lower and Middle Palaeolithic (*Typologie du Paleolithique Ancien et Moyen*); for his extensive, lifelong replication of stone knapping methods (notably, reconstruction of the Levallois technique); and (first with Maurice Bourgon and later alone) for his exhaustive studies of the Mousterian industries of southwestern France. Bordes discovered and defined nontemporally patterning Mousterian variants *(facies)* and engaged in a major debate with Lewis R. Binford and Paul Mellars concerning the possible explanation of interassemblage variability (personally favoring the factor of ethnicity) that had lasting implications beyond the strict limits of the French Middle Palaeolithic. Bordes excavated numerous Palaeolithic sites in France, notably Combe Grenal and Pech de l'Azé (*A Tale of Two Caves*), and, based on his broad knowledge of the Stone Age worldwide (having excavated in Spain and Australia and studied collections in the Near East and North America) he published the influential survey textbook *The Old Stone Age*. Bordes founded the Quaternary Institute at the University of Bordeaux, where he was professor and regional director of antiquities. He pioneered the modern interdisciplinary approach to the study of early humans, stressing the importance of stratigraphy and typology.

Lawrence G. Straus

See also BINFORD, LEWIS R.; EXPERIMENTAL ARCHAEOLOGY

Further Readings

Bordes, F. (1961) Typologie du Paleolithique Ancien et Moyen. Bordeaux: Delmas

Bordes, F. (1968) The Old Stone Age. Trans. J.E. Anderson. New York: McGraw-Hill.

Bordes, F. (1972) A Tale of Two Caves. New York: Harper & Row.

Bordes, F. (1979) Typologie du Paleolithique, 3rd ed. Paris: Editions du Centre national de lar recherche scientifique.

Bordes, F. (1983) Leçons sur le Paleolithique. Paris: Editions du Centre national de la recherche scientifique.

Breuil, Henri (1877–1961)

French Palaeolithic prehistorian, specialist in cave art, and priest. Educated in seminaries and trained in archaeology by influential early French prehistorians (notably, Edouard Piette, Emile Rivière, and Emile Cartailhac), Breuil began his long professional career with the excavation of the Abri Dufaure in 1900, participation in the validation (and graphic documentation) of the parietal art of Altamira (Spain) in 1902, and, in a series of seminal articles in the years 1902–1912, development of the still generally accepted chronocultural framework for subdividing the Upper Palaeolithic of western Europe. Working with Hugo Obermaier and others, Breuil was responsible for discovering, describing, and systematizing the Palaeolithic prehistory of Spain (notably, cave art at El Castillo and other sites in the Cantabrian region, as well as at sites throughout Andalusia). Based on this work and his critical participation in the study of numerous French cave-art locations (especially the caves of the Ariège and Dordogne regions), Breuil provided the first grand synthesis of the general phenomenon of Upper Palaeolithic rock art in southwestern Europe (*Four Hundred Centuries of Cave Art*), emphasizing a supposedly chronological evolutionary scheme, elements of which survive today despite considerable criticism. Breuil generally accepted magicoreligious explanations for cave art and was personally responsible for copying the art of numerous French, Spanish, and South African sites, using his talents as a watercolorist. His numerous monographic tomes remain, in many cases, the definitive descriptions of several of the most important cave art sites. Breuil also made major contributions to the archaeological study of the Early Palaeolithic materials of the Somme Valley, Portugal, China, and South Africa. He was (with Obermaier and Marcellin Boule) a founding professor of the Institut de Paléontologie Humaine in Paris (under the patronage of Prince Albert of Monaco) and held the first chair in prehistory at the College de France. His influence is reflected in the significance of some of his disciples, including Dorothy Garrod and Pierre Teilhard de Chardin.

Lawrence G. Straus

See also GARROD, DOROTHY ANNIE ELIZABETH; ROCK-ART DATING; ROCK-ART SITES, RECORDING AND ANALYSIS

Further Reading

Brodrick, A. (1963) Father of Prehistory; the Abbe Henri Breuil: His Life and Times. New York: Morrow.

Boule, M., Breuil, H., Licent, E., and Teilhard, P. (1928) Le Paleolithique de la Chine. Paris: Masson.

Breuil, H. (1936) Ouvres d'art magdaleniennes de Laugerie basse (Dordogne). Paris: Hermann & Cie.

Breuil, H. (1957–1966) The Rock Paintings of Southern Africa. London/Paris: Trianon.

Breuil, H. (1979) Four Hundred Centuries of Cave Art. Reprinted, Hacker, New York. Originally published 1952, Montignac, France: Centre l'études et de documentation préhistoriques.

Breuil, H. and Burkitt, M.C. (1929) Rock Paintings of Southern Andalusia: A Description of a Neolithic and Copper Age Art Group. Oxford: Clarendon.

Breuil, H. and Lantier, R. (1965) The Men of the Old Stone Age (Palaeolithic and Mesolithic). London: Harrap/New York: St Martin's Press.

Breuil, H. and Obermaier, H. (1935) The Cave of Altamira at Santillana del Mar, Spain. Madrid: Junta de las Cuevas de Altamira/Hispanic Society of America/Academia de la Historia.

Butzer, Karl W. (1934–)

German-American prehistoric cultural geographer, geoarchaeologist, and cultural ecologist. Born in Germany, Butzer emigrated to Canada as a child, was educated at McGill University, and returned to Germany, where he received his doctorate in natural sciences at the University of Bonn in 1957, specializing in physical geography and ancient history. Butzer returned to North America and taught first at the University of Wisconsin at Madison and then at the University of Chicago (1966–1980). After a brief tenure at the Swiss Federal Institute of Technology in Zürich, he moved to the University of Texas at Austin, where, as at Chicago, he holds joint appointments in anthropology and geography. Butzer pioneered the cultural-ecological and geoarchaeological approaches to archaeology, as outlined in the two editions (1964, 1971) of his seminal work, *Environment and Archaeology*, and his synthetic textbook *Archaeology as Human Ecology*. In dozens of field projects in Europe, northern and southern Africa, and North America, and in hundreds of publications, Butzer has investigated the nature of past environments and of human-land relationships from remote periods such as the Oldowan, the Acheulean, and the Mousterian, to ancient Egyptian civilization on the Nile, to Mediterranean agropastoralism as practiced in Iberia and as transported to Spanish colonial Mexico. His eclectic, interdisciplinary approach to the study of past human adaptations draws on the methods and data of geology, paleobotany, geochronology, paleontology, archaeology, and, where relevant, historiography. While stressing rigorous scientific methodology, Butzer has taken a broadly comparative approach to prehistory.

Lawrence G. Straus

See also ECOLOGICAL THEORY IN ARCHAEOLOGY; GEOARCHAEOLOGY

Further Readings

Butzer, K.W. and Hansen, C.L. (1968) Desert and River in Nubia: Geomorphology and Prehistoric Environments at the Aswan Reservoir. Madison: University of Wisconsin Press.

Butzer, K.W. (1971) Environment and Archeology: An Ecological Approach to Prehistory, 2nd ed. Chicago: Aldine-Atherton.

Butzer, K.W. (1976) Early Hydraulic Civilization in Egypt: A Study in Cultural Ecology. Chicago: University of Chicago Press.

Butzer, K.W. (1982) Archaeology as Human Ecology: Method and Theory for a Contextual Approach. Cambridge/New York: Cambridge University Press.

C

Caton-Thompson, Gertrude (1889–1985)

British explorer, Egyptologist, and archaeologist. Born on February 1, 1889, in London, Gertrude Caton-Thompson was a pioneer Egyptologist in a field and a time dominated by men and by Victorian and Edwardian sensibilities. Despite the obstacles, Caton-Thompson traveled to Egypt, where she led excavations and specialized in the then poorly understood Neolithic predecessors of dynastic Egyptian civilization. From 1924 to 1928, she explored Neolithic sites in the important Fayum depression, perhaps most remarkably, with another woman, E.W. Gardner. Also in the later 1920s, Caton-Thompson teamed with Egyptologist Guy Brunton to excavate the Neolithic settlement at Hemamieh, near the modern town of Badari. The results of this excavation, published in the classic *The Badarian Civilization and the Predynastic Remains near Badari,* were revolutionary: Along with the work of Egyptian Neolithic pioneers, Caton-Thompson and Brunton's finds helped define the predynastic sequence in Egypt, establishing the Badarian and the earlier Tasian Neolithic cultures as the predecessors of pharaonic Egyptian civilization. The work of trailblazers like Caton-Thompson helped break down gender barriers and made possible later generations of women in Near Eastern archaeology. She later received an honorary bachelor's and doctorate degrees from Cambridge University. Caton-Thompson died on April 18, 1985, at the age of ninety-six.

Joseph J. Basile

Further Readings

Brunton, G. and Caton-Thompson, G. (1928) The Badarian Civilisation and Predynastic Remains near Badari. London: British School of Archaeology in Egypt.
Caton-Thompson, G. (1971) The Zimbabwe Culture: Ruins and Reactions, 2nd ed. London: Cass.
Caton-Thompson, G. (1983) Mixed Memoirs. Gateshead, Tyne & Ware: Paradigm.
Caton-Thompson, G. and Gardner, E.W. (1952) Kharga Oasis in Prehistory. London: University of London.

Caves and Rockshelters, Excavation

Carefully controlled stratigraphic dissection of a major class of archaeological sites for the study of early human environments and lifeways. Caves and rockshelters are among the most important kinds of archaeological and paleontological find spots because of their frequent use by hominids and because of their nature as excellent sediment traps. However, these significant paleoanthropological resources are also often characterized by unusually complex histories of deposition, erosion, and postdepositional sedimentary alteration. Such processes may be of geological, animal, and/or anthropogenic nature, requiring extraordinary care and interdisciplinary collaboration in the stratigraphic excavation and interpretation of cave and rockshelter infillings.

Many of the world's most important prehistoric sites, from Klasies River Mouth in South Africa to Zhoukoudian in China, from Altamira in Spain to Lascaux in France, from Tabun in Israel to Meadowcroft in the United States, are caves or rockshelters. In some, such as the avens of the Transvaal, the Sima de los

Huesos in Atapuerca, Spain, or the Neolithic and Chalcolithic ossuary caves of Europe, hominid remains came to be entombed by accident or by design. In many others, humans, beginning with *Homo erectus* and Neanderthal, lived and left behind often large amounts of residential debris. In some caves, particularly in southwest Europe, Upper Palaeolithic people created great works of art, while other karstic cavities, such as those of the U.S. Eastern Woodlands, were exploited by prehistoric miners. While the latter uses of caves are the focus of specialists in early art and paleospeleology, the emphasis here is on the dissection and analysis of archaeological deposits in rockshelters and (usually) in the entrances of caves.

Sedimentary Infilling

True (karstic) caves are the products of the dissolution of limestone by groundwater, whereas rockshelters can form as a result of the weathering of limestone or other bedrock along valley sides or bluff lines—or they can be simply overhangs at the base of huge boulders or rock outcrops. In the cases of cave entrances or deep rockshelters, there exist cavities that are normally enclosed on two or three sides, respectively, and covered by a substantial rock overhang. In many cases, the primary component of the sedimentary infilling is rock spalled from the walls and ceiling—caused by thermoclastic (heating) and cryoclastic (freezing and thawing) processes, seismic activity, and gravity. Caves and rockshelters are also traps for other sediments (from cobble to clay mineral size) that are blown in by the wind or washed in by runoff from above the mouth; by flooding from high river, lake, or sea levels; or by rejuvenation of the karstic system. Sediments can also be introduced, along with organic matter of all types, by animals or, accidentally or deliberately, by humans. Organic deposits can include wood, brush, ferns, straw and other vegetal material, bones, shells and other animal matter, and fecal waste. Bones can be introduced by natural animal deaths in caves (including noncave-dwelling species that nonetheless often seek shelter in winter or during storms), by terrestrial and avian predators and scavengers (notably, hyenas, canids, bears, felids, mustelids such as badgers, porcupines, owls, and other raptors that often dwell in caves). Humans too—whether as scavengers, hunters, or herders—introduce large amounts of animal remains. Because caves and rockshelters are generally very confined spaces, deposits can build up rapidly and can amount to very deep stratigraphies and long, relatively well-preserved records of human use, and, hence, culture history.

Rockfall, which can be massive, creates natural walls within cavities, differentially protecting some deposits from erosion and making it often difficult to correlate levels between one side of the blocks and the other. Interstices among *éboulis* (the French word for rockfall, spall, or scree that is commonly used in geological description of cave and rockshelters deposits) are prone to being washed by running water that can easily transport artifacts, bones, charcoal, and other remains downward.

Unless a cave mouth or a rockshelter is completely scoured by erosion from within a karst or from the exterior (e.g., by high-velocity river flooding), the cavity is likely to preserve at least much of its sedimentary infilling for a substantial amount of time—in some cases, hundreds of thousands or even millions of years. However many processes contribute to the disturbance, reworking, and alteration of cave and rockshelter deposits, making their excavation particularly painstaking and at times difficult.

Agencies of cave-infilling disturbance can be classified as geological, animal, and anthropogenic. Geological processes include rockfall and overburden compaction, slump into lower cave chambers, waterflow and solifluction from chimneys and crevices in the roof, slope creep and catastrophic flow on interior talus cones, cryoturbation (frost heaving), and gullying. Postdepositional alteration, dependent on temperature, humidity, pH, presence of vegetation and other organic matter, and other factors, includes calcium-carbonate precipitation, leaching, pedogenesis (soil formation), and diagenesis (weathering).

All of these processes can be spatially highly variable even within relatively small cavities. There can be major differences in disturbance and alteration between the front and the rear and between the center and the sides of a cave entrance (the area most usually inhabited by humans) or rockshelter. The effects of sunlight, temperature changes (diurnal, seasonal, and secular), precipitation, and vegetation are all far greater at the front, with much greater geomorphological (including rockfall from the rim of the overhang) and pedological activity than farther toward the rear. There is considerable percolation of water (hence, sediments, including faunal and archaeological remains) along the walls. These factors lead to *considerable natural lateral variation* in granulometry, bedding, chemistry, and preservation.

Since caves and rockshelters are attractive as shelters for a wide variety of mammals and birds, animals not only contribute deposits, but also alter the infillings, both passively (i.e., chemically) through their wastes and, especially in the case of animals that burrow or dig, actively through displacement of sediments. Such disturbances can run the gamut from tunneling by badgers and other mustelids to the excavation of massive hibernation craters by cave bears (*Ursus spelaeus*, a common and huge European species that went extinct at the end of the Last Glacial). Less obvious, but frequent churners of cave and rockshelter deposits (hence, homogenizers of levels) include rodents, worms, and molluscs.

Finally, there is a subset of animal disturbers and alterants that is particularly significant in caves and rockshelters: *Homo*. For the same reasons of good shelter, some cavities have been selected frequently by humans for short- or long-term use, including residence. Human wastes and fires alter the chemistry of the sediments and speed up diagenesis. Materials are not only introduced, but are also removed and rearranged by trampling, leveling, digging of all sorts of pits (including burials), building of structures, and other activities. On the other hand, if humans built walls or hung skins across a cavity mouth, this could alter natural processes of deposition, erosion, and alteration. Because many caves and rockshelters are so often reused, the amount of anthropogenic disturbance can be significant. Merely the fact of frequent reuse means that some of the deposits in these types of sites are massive palimpsests, the blurred residues of many episodes of occupation and activity.

In sum, caves and rockshelters have been used frequently by hominids and a wide variety of other animals for short- and long-term shelter. This fact, combined with the natural tendency for these cavities to preserve sediments, artifacts, and, in many cases, organic materials, makes them extraordinary resources for the containment of normally stratified, often lengthy records of Earth and hominid history. Because of their eminent feature as shelter from precipitation, wind, and extremes of temperature, the archaeological record from caves tends to emphasize *residential* loci; because of their unusual attribute as sediment containers, this bias is probably inevitable, especially for the Palaeolithic. Under many geomorphological circumstances (surface erosion *and* deep burial), open-air sites are underrepresented in the archaeological record. This fact must be recognized. While archaeologists must try to mitigate it by intensive surface survey and remote sensing, they must make the most of the record from caves and rockshelters by dealing with the complexity of this class of sites through appropriate and meticulous methods of excavation and analysis.

Stratigraphic Control

The fundamental key to all archaeological excavation—but especially in cave and rockshelter deposits—is *stratigraphic control*. Without it, one cannot accurately determine chronological relationships or be certain which finds were really associated with which other finds or contextual data.

Caves and rockshelters must be carefully mapped and gridded before excavation begins. Basic units of no more than 1 m × 1 m are recommended, and often these squares are subdivided into four or even nine numbered subsquares, with the fill of each separately screened and finds separately provenanced. A vertical datum point should be established at a convenient fixed point (normally on the cavity wall) above the surface of the stratigraphic deposit. Secondary datum points must be fixed near every excavation area and frequently re-checked for accuracy. For areas that are not or are only partly sunlit, adequate lighting must be provided, usually by use of electrical generators and either fluorescent or incandescent bulbs, although short-term excavations may make use of gas lamps. Lighting is critical, as subtle differences therein can make major changes in what can be seen and how it can be seen, notably in regard to stratigraphy and features. One should frequently experiment with different types and angles of lighting to enhance visibility.

To the greatest extent possible, excavation should follow natural statigraphic levels, which in cave mouths and rockshelters can often be very tilted or convoluted. However, all but the thinnest visible levels should be subdivided for practical reasons into *spits* (more or less arbitrary levels, generally 5–8 cm thick) that nonetheless also should follow the local stratigraphy's orientations. This means that even small objects found in the screen can be assigned to a small volume (sub-square and spit) and used in spatial analysis, and that, if mistakes are made (almost inevitably) and hard-to-distinguish levels become mixed in excavation, the damage can be limited.

Obviously, in a heretofore untested cave, one or a few relatively small test pit(s) must be dug to initially ascertain stratigraphy. While digging "blind" in such *sondages,* arbitrary levels (preferably thin) may have to be used. In many caves, the unfortunately frequent existence of trenches from clandestine looters (or from earlier generations of archaeologists) can serve as a guide to new, controlled excavations, without having to sacrifice some detail in test pits. Modern excavations should take advantage of old pits by cleaning and recording their stratigraphic sections and then digging back from them following the lay of the land outward. If such earlier excavations do not exist, *sondages* are usually essential, since, without a vertical view, it is extremely easy to simultaneously dig in two or more levels or lenses. An ideal situation is one in which excavators can refer to both sagittal (lengthwise) and transversal (crosswise) sections not far from their unit, since levels in caves and rockshelters can and often do have both "strike and dip," and since gullies, pits, lenses, and lateral variations in strata are extremely common. Continuous trenches are much preferable to isolated pits in cave and rockshelter excavations. It is imperative to be able to follow strata physically across the widest possible area of these depositionally complex sites. Even the smallest gap in a section can cause miscorrelation of levels. Sometimes gaps are inevitable (due to the presence of large blocks or of earlier trenches), and these frequently lead to inaccurate readings of profiles and, hence, to the incorrect analytical association of finds in reality belonging to different levels.

Dissecting Sites

Because downward percolation *and* upward movement may both result from geological and biological processes, extreme precaution must be followed in the selection and interpretation of radiocarbon and other dating samples. Large, individual bone or charcoal samples should be preferred when available and accelerator mass spectrometry (AMS) dating chosen when feasible, to avoid dates that may be more likely the result of vertical migration or mixing of items of different ages—frequent in cave and rockshelter contexts.

While most modern excavations are concerned with dissecting sites to reveal residues of activity areas, this cannot usually be done reliably in caves or rockshelters by simultaneously opening broad expanses of individual levels or living floors. This does not mean, however, that surfaces and their artifact distributions cannot sometimes be reconstructed within cave and rockshelter deposits. Even if one is forced to dig back into standing sections by narrow strips (perhaps no wider than 1 m at a time) (the well-known method of the late French prehistoric archaelogist François Bordes), if finds are systematically mapped and/or piece plotted and sediments fine screened, then three-dimensional distributions and surfaces can be reconstructed (especially by computer).

With a frequency far more common and to an extent generally much greater than in many open-air sites, the archaeological deposits in caves and rockshelters are palimpsests, requiring meticulous dissection. But even the most painstaking methods of piece plotting, recording of the orientation and inclination of elongated objects, analysis of object weight and size classes, and lithic, faunal, and ceramic refitting, can often not compensate for the palimpsest effect and cannot reveal living floors that are the results of individual occupations or "moments in time." Some experienced cave and rockshelter archaeologists have despaired of meaningfully defining occupation surfaces and have been content to excavate and to analyze assemblages merely by geological strata. In some cases, the nature of the sediments and of their disturbance may be such that one has no option but to approach the excavation and interpretation from such a purely vertical, stratigraphic standpoint. However, many recent excavations have shown that, with the right kinds of deposits and proper techniques, such surfaces with their features can be detected and dissected. In fact, the very confining nature of cave mouths and rockshelters can turn the existence of behavioral residue compounding factors in the formation of palimpsests into an interpretive advantage.

Human Activity Areas

If a series of human visits to or occupations of a cavity are redundant in basic function, length and season of stay, or group composition, then the walls and areas of rockfall, together with the extent and slope of any fronting terrace and talus, may condition the use of space at the site in repetitively structured ways. Because short occupations may, in some cases, result in the discard or loss of few objects each time (leading to low or nil archaeological visibility or resolution), the spatially compounding effect of the physical features and limits of caves and rockshelters may reinforce our ability to discern and interpret structured activity areas. When human use of a cavity underwent a fundamental change (e.g., from short-term, special-purpose hunting location to long-term, multipurpose residential camp or from burial site to shell-midden dump) and/or when the physical form of a cavity changed (e.g., due to rockfall, dripline recession, flooding, gullying, alteration of the exterior talus by deposition or solifluction, or increase in the height of sedimentary infilling), the structured deposition of behavioral residues in space would change in such a redundant fashion as to be likely observable archaeologically. In most cave mouths and rockshelters, humans do not have the liberty to spread their activities out and to choose new venues for given activities each time such a site is revisited. Certain sectors of a cave or a rockshelter would often be more appropriate for different types of activities—each with its more or less characteristic debris (e.g., areas near the rear walls may be used for sleeping and cooking in bad weather; sunlit areas near the front of the sheltered area may be used for maintenance and manufacturing activities; the terrace or talus in front of the overhang may be used for processing activities, such as carcass butchering, that require broad spaces free of interference with other activities).

The detection of such activity areas obviously requires careful, systematic piece plotting, since many distributions are what the late French prehistorian and ethnologist Andre Leroi-Gourhan called *latent structures*—structures that can be discovered only after excavation by retromapping and spatial analysis. However, discovery of structure can also be facilitated by excavation techniques that are especially sensitive to subtle textural and color differences; the "feel" of sediments, as well as their shade, is important—hence, there is an art to cave and rockshelter excavation that can be acquired only by lengthy, diverse experience in the excavation of these kinds of sites. Part of the art does involve the frequent creation of small, ad hoc sections and careful observation of the orientation of objects. It is essential to use *situationally appropriate* excavation tools (including soft brushes, small flexible trowels, knives or spatulas, bent screwdrivers, hand picks, or entrenching shovels, depending on the sediments and circumstances—rock and flowstone breaking can require use of sledgehammers, chisels, jackhammers, and even low-level explosives).

Documentation

As in all scientific excavations, thorough documentation must be assured. This should include plans, spit top and bottom depths, find lists, data on screen size, and observations (including hunches) on sediments, stratigraphy, and finds on standardized forms for each square and spit. It should also include standardized coding forms for piece-plotted finds, with spaces for x, y, and z coordinates, orientation, inclination, weight, and analytical attributes. In addition, there must be ample photographs (requiring use of a variety of film types and speeds) and, especially, stratigraphic-section drawings. These must be detailed and accurate. To aid in their production, leveled lines and even grids should be strung onto the profiles. The drawing of sections during or at the end of the excavation of each site sector is a major and time-consuming responsibility, the importance of which cannot be minimized. Section drawings, together with the retro-plotting of artifacts, provide the basis for understanding the critical temporal (hence, behavioral) relationships within a site. Notes, coding forms with their piece-plotted finds, plans, section drawings, and photographs must be coordinated. If properly done, they can permit reconstruction of sites on paper and in computer databases.

Ecofact Data

In addition to the traditional recovery of artifacts and recording of features, cave and rockshelter excavation involves a particularly significant component of ecofact observation and collection. Cave and rockshelter stratigraphies can be ideal platforms for gathering longitudinal data on paleoenvironmental change, as well as samples for radiometric dating. It is imperative that an experienced cave and rockshelter sedimentologist describe and sample the stratigraphy at as many parts of the site as are open, usually by making repeat visits during the course of excavation. Analysis of sediment samples should include both traditional granulometric and pedological studies and innovative micromorphological methods that may require the collection of columns of plastered samples in situ. The latter can provide critical information on site formation and disturbance processes.

Some limestone cave and rockshelter contexts have proven to preserve moderate amounts of pollen, but with significant lateral variation due to air currents within cavities and with differential degrees of preservation among strata. Pollen samples must be taken as complete columns in several parts of the excavation area, taking care that individual samples not crosscut visibly distinct levels or lenses. These columns must be carefully documented, with photos, notation of stratigraphic units and depths below datum, and indication of weather and vegetation conditions, taking care to carefully clean sections before sampling and to avoid windy days and local pollination seasons. Results from samples of the same stratigraphic units in different site areas should be compared.

Caves and rockshelter stratigraphies should also be systematically sampled for microfauna (terrestrial molluscs, rodents, insectivores) particularly sensitive to microenvironmental changes and useful as time markers, due, in some cases, to rapid evolutionary turnover. Such sampling can involve the removal of complete columns of sediments from the base to the top of profiles, as well as selective picking from dry- or wet-screened sediments processed during the course of regular excavation. In all cases, the excavation director (usually an archaeologist) must coordinate sample collection with a variety of specialists. All must be aware of the needs and schedules of excavation and sampling protocols. In the ideal case, preliminary natural-science analyses can be made available rapidly enough to provide guidance for ongoing excavation (to help determine methods and areas to dig).

The full-scale excavation of a cave or a rockshelter is a complex affair, necessitating major investments in time, money, and infrastructure, painstaking work, and a genuine commitment to interdisciplinary research. The rewards are often rich details on the environments, remains, and adaptations of humans across long stretches of time at favored places on the ancient landscape.

Lawrence G. Straus

See also BORDES, FRANÇOIS; BREUIL, HENRI; LEROI-GOURHAN, ANDRE; ROCK-ART DATING; ROCK-ART SITES, RECORDING AND ANALYSIS

Further Readings

Bordes, F. (1972) A Tale of Two Caves. New York: Harper and Row.

Farrand, W. (1985) Rockshelter and cave sediments. In J. Stein and W. Farrand (eds.): Archaeological Sediments in Context, pp. 21–39. Orono: University of Maine Press.

Laville, H., Rigaud, J.-P., and Sackett, J. (1980) Rockshelters of the Perigord. New York: Academic.

Straus, L. (1990) Underground archaeology: Perspectives on caves and rockshelters. In M.B. Schiffer (ed.): Archaeological Method and Theory, vol. 2, pp. 255–304. Tucson: University of Arizona Press.

Straus, L., and Clark, G. (1986) La Riera Cave. (Anthropological Research Papers 36). Tempe: Arizona State University.

Ceramics, On-Site Conservation

Emergency treatment and care of ceramics on site. The goals of on-site conservation are to minimize the deterioration of objects during excavation and to ensure that as much as possible of the evidence contained in the objects is available for further study and analysis. First-aid measures are employed to prevent rapid changes taking place to fragile ceramics when they are first exposed; most ceramics are processed on site, but those of special interest are given full assessment and treatment in a conservation laboratory that may be at some distance from the site.

Ceramics occur commonly on archaeological sites in the form of domestic and industrial objects such as pots, loom weights and crucibles, and building materials such as roof and floor tiles. They are relatively durable, survive in large quantities, and present comparatively few problems in terms of on-site conservation. They are made of clay that has been shaped and heated (fired) so that the clay particles fuse, and an inert, water-resistant material results. Their properties are affected by the nature of the clay and by the firing temperature. Earthenware and terracotta are both low-fired clay products and are soft and porous; stoneware and porcelain are fired at high temperatures and are hard and almost nonporous. Their properties are also affected by the filler mixed with the clay before firing (e.g., sand, plant material, crushed shell) and by the surface finish (e.g., burnish, slip [a fine clay coating], or glaze [a glassy coating]).

The form and fabric of a ceramic are frequently used as evidence of date and function. The ceramic can provide evidence of how it was made (clay, filler, shape, surface finish, and decoration) and of how it was used (e.g., traces of contents such as foodstuffs). Accidental evidence may also be present in the form of impressions left in the ceramic before firing (e.g., seeds, textile).

Aims of On-Site Conservation

Conservation aims to preserve evidence. On-site conservation is essentially first-aid treatment, which is followed by further assessment and treatment in the conservation laboratory. The practice of conservation rests on five central principles: (1) preservation of the integrity of the object; (2) use of the least-invasive treatments; (3) use of reversible treatments (though it is now accepted that there are limits on reversibility); (4) preventive care; and (5) documentation of object and treatment.

The integrity of the ceramic must be preserved because this preserves the information within it, not all of which may be immediately recognizable (e.g., foodstuffs). Choosing the least-invasive treatments means that the ceramic (and the information) are changed as little as possible and are available for future study and analysis; choosing reversible treatments means that first-aid treatments (e.g., a temporary adhesive) can be removed in the conservation laboratory and replaced by suitable long-term treatments. If these treatments are followed by continuous and well-monitored preventive care (good storage), then any further change is minimized. Documentation of the object and its treatment provides the information on which present and future analysis and conservation of the ceramic is based.

On-site conservation is influenced by the long-term provision for the ceramics. On many sites, large amounts of ceramic are found, much of it in good condition, so the museum conservator will see only a very small portion of the total. Material of special interest may reach the conservation laboratory; otherwise the ceramic will remain in storage, its primary function being to serve as part of the study archive for the site.

Factors Affecting the Condition of Ceramics

The extent to which ceramics deteriorate during burial depends on their nature, particularly their porosity, the way they were used, and the burial conditions. A well-fired ceramic made of carefully prepared clay will probably survive better than a crude and low-fired example (low-fired material can be significantly softened and distorted in damp conditions). Decoration may be more or less durable, depending on how it was applied (paint applied after firing is likely to be less well preserved than a decoration fired onto the ceramic). Slips and glazes can themselves deteriorate and become detached.

Highly porous ceramics are characterized by a very open structure in which materials such as foodstuffs can be deposited during use, or salts and staining materials during burial; conversely, ceramics with low porosity may be unaffected. Porous ceramics are often sealed by a slip or a glaze that is protective as long as it remains undamaged. If ceramics are cracked or broken, the exposed edges of the sherds offer a route for extraneous materials into the body.

Burial conditions are significant. In areas of low rainfall, high temperatures, and rapid evaporation, quantities of salts such as chlorides and carbonates accumulate in the soil and are deposited in or on the ceramic body; seawater is also a source of salts. While the ceramic remains buried, the salts may have little effect, but exposure to drying conditions encourages soluble salts to crystallize. As crystals form, pressure builds up in the pores of the ceramic and may be strong enough to cause blistering and disintegration of the surface. This can happen very rapidly if ceramics with a high salt content are allowed to dry. In waterlogged and oxygen-starved conditions, organic matter accumulates, and heavy staining affects all buried objects. Where burial is shallow, frost damage may occur, and roots of plants can erode softened ceramic, leaving channels in the surface. Acid burial conditions may attack and soften fillers such as calcite or shell, weakening the ceramic fabric.

One of the archaeological conservator's difficulties is that excavation sets off a series of changes. Uncovering material on an excavation inevitably exposes it to a different combination of environmental factors (e.g., oxygen, light, heat, air currents). It is removed from the soil and so loses the physical support of the burial deposit; it is handled, examined, and even cleaned. All of these activities may bring about changes in the ceramic—some may be damaging and result in loss of information; some may take place rapidly, such as crystallization of salts.

Conservation Processes

On some sites, archaeologist and conservator face the practical problem of dealing with exceptionally large quantities of sherds. Production-line approaches to processing on site are required, and, inevitably, some ceramics will be selected for more attention than others. This selection will be based on both archaeological significance and condition.

The conservator's initial assessment will embrace the soil conditions, the way the ceramic is deposited, and the condition of the ceramic itself. Thus, different conservation problems will be presented by a ceramic burial urn and by a scatter of sherds discarded in a rubbish pit, as the condition of the ceramic, the local environment, and the associated evidence will vary in each case.

Any ceramic that is required for analysis is identified at an early stage, before any on-site treatment, wrapped (together with immediately surrounding soil) in aluminum foil, kept cool, and sent to the relevant laboratory as soon as possible.

Excavation

The condition of the ceramic controls the choice of excavation technique. Much ceramic is relatively strong, though it is often cracked or broken into sherds. It can be excavated by clearing the soil away with care and gently lifting from the ground, fully supported in both hands if necessary.

Strengthening

When a ceramic is so soft that excavation may damage it or cause it to crumble when moved, the conservator must consider ways of strengthening it. The aim is normally to provide just enough additional strength to allow it to be moved rather than to strengthen it permanently.

There are three main options: to allow it to dry slowly and gain strength, to provide external support, and to apply a consolidant (a diluted adhesive). The first two are preferable to the third since they do not involve introducing any material into the ceramic itself.

The conservator will test the least-invasive treatment (drying) first and decide whether it is effective. A ceramic with a soft or a weak body may be much stronger after it has dried, but, unfortunately, there is a tendency for salts or other accretions to harden and shrink, which can damage the ceramic and make cleaning more difficult. Testing will allow the conservator to assess the advantages and disadvantages of this approach; it may be safer to keep the ceramic damp.

There are several techniques for providing support that are described in field-conservation textbooks and can be adapted to suit the particular situation. These involve retaining soil around the ceramic, using bandage to hold the soil in place or a consolidant to strengthen the soil, or applying external support after exposing the object in stages. External support may be bandaging wound around the object, or it may be a jacket of plaster of paris or polyurethane foam. In each case, the ceramic is given a protective covering (e.g., aluminum foil) before application of the support.

A particular problem may arise when the surface of the ceramic is powdering or covered with weakly adhering paint. The powdery surface may adhere better to the surrounding soil than to the ceramic, and be left behind in the soil unless special care is taken during excavation. In this situation, the conservator will retain as much soil as possible in contact with the surface, leaving consolidation and cleaning to be done in the laboratory.

Consolidants are normally dilute solutions of adhesive materials (synthetic polymers). They are applied to very weak ceramics, with the aim that they harden in the pores and strengthen the ceramic body. They are useful but carry their own dangers and are used with increasing caution by conservators, especially in site conditions. They must be chosen from a range with known and suitable conservation properties, otherwise they may prove to be unstable or totally nonreversible; they may fail to penetrate sufficiently and leave a plastic skin over the still weak ceramic body, they may darken the ceramic, particularly the low-fired terra-cottas and earthenwares; they will certainly change the ceramic irreversibly because it is impossible to remove all of a consolidant from a porous substrate. Polymers and their solvents also carry health and safety risks, and conservators must take appropriate precautions when using these materials, even in the open air.

Any ceramic given special support or consolidation will be taken to a conservation laboratory for further treatment.

On-Site Cleaning

On-site cleaning of the bulk of excavated ceramic is usually considered a routine aspect of the archaeological process, but it has conservation implications since poor cleaning can do damage. The aim is to make identification possible rather than to scrub completely clean. Undercleaning is always preferable to overcleaning because of the dangers of cleaning removing information.

Sometimes it is possible simply to brush loose soil away from the surface, but ceramics are more often washed in water. This is effective provided that ceramics are carefully sorted first and that any that would be damaged by washing are removed (including low-fired or crumbly material and objects with poorly attached paint or decaying glaze). Both washing and drying must be carefully regulated to prevent damage.

Dealing with Salts

Water-soluble salts are not generally removed on site because of the need for laboratory equipment to monitor the process, but a portion will be removed during on-site washing of ceramics. On marine sites, the high levels of salts mean that ceramics must be stored wet, initially in a mixture of sea and fresh water, then in regular changes of fresh water.

Some ceramics are covered with spots or crusts of insoluble salts that are not affected by washing. The traditional method for removing them was to use an acid bath on site. Acid removes many encrustations but may also damage fillers and surface finishes, leaving a scoured and weakened object. A further problem is that soluble salts are formed in the process, which may cause additional damage. It is better to reserve treatments for all salts for the controlled conditions of the conservation laboratory.

Routine Reconstruction

On-site conservation of ceramics usually focuses on preliminary cleaning and on basic reconstruction to a level that allows identification and recording of ceramic types.

The two main requirements for this reconstruction are a conservation-approved stable, reversible adhesive and some way of supporting the sherds during the process (e.g., clean sand in a deep tray). Adhesive tape is used only with caution since it may damage the surface of the ceramic.

Preventive Care

The temptation is to treat ceramics as if they are very robust, but some are not and are handled as little as possible. It is helpful to use a padded box or tray in which to support fragments or complete objects.

Traditionally, ceramic sherds have been packed in bags; good-quality polythene bags have replaced the old cloth or paper sherd bags, but they must be perforated to prevent condensation of moisture on the ceramics. Fragile material is packed in boxes with suitable padding around and between objects or layers of sherds. All containers are clearly labeled indicating the contents.

Good packaging is an important aspect of the long-term care of ceramics, since many are likely simply to go into storage. Resources (staff as well as money) seldom allow complete repackaging; thus, the packaging undertaken on the site should take account of long-term-storage conditions. Packaging must, of course, be adequate for the journey to storage, or to the conservation laboratory if further treatment is necessary.

Ceramics are a valuable resource for the archaeologist. With efficient on-site care and conservation, as much as possible of the material excavated is made available for further study.

Elizabeth Pye

Further Readings

Cronyn, J.M., (1990) The Elements of Archaeological Conservation. London: Routledge.

Hodges, H.W.M., ed. (1987) In Situ Archaeological Conservation. Mexico City: Instituto Nacional de Antropologia e Historia Century City, CA: J. Paul Getty Trust.

Sease, C. (1987) A Conservation Manual for the Field Archaeologist. Los Angeles: Institute of Archaeology, UCLA.

Watkinson, D., Neal, V., and Swain, H. (1998) First Aid for Finds, 3rd edition. London: Rescue—The British Archaeological Trust and Archaeology Section of the UK Institute for Conservation, with the Museum of London.

Childe, Vere Gordon (1892–1957)

British (b. Australia) prehistorian. Born on April 14, 1892, in Sydney, Childe received his bachelor's degree in his native city and continued his schooling in Britain, receiving a doctorate from Oxford University in 1916. After some years as a researcher and a librarian, he was appointed full professor and holder of the Abercromby Chair of Prehistoric Archaeology at Edinburgh in 1927. He moved on to the University of London in 1946, where he was director of the Institute of Archaeology for ten years, as well as professor of European archaeology. Childe was named emeritus professor in 1956 and received an honorary degree from Edinburgh in 1956. He died in his native Australia on October 19, 1957, at the age of sixty-five.

Childe, an expert in the Neolithic and Bronze periods of Europe and the Near East, is best remembered for his works of scholarly synthesis, which attempted broad outlines of Old World prehistory and discussed in depth such concepts as the rise of agriculture and urbanism. His writings radically changed the study of prehistory, which previously had been characterized by a limited scope and lack of emphasis on grand themes. Childe's first book, *The Dawn of European Civilization,* was published in 1925, while he was an assistant librarian at the Royal Anthropological Institute in London, and was an important early attempt to study European prehistory as a distinct phenomenon. *The Dawn of European Civilization* would set the tone for later work, including his next book, *The Danube in Prehistory.* Other specialist volumes include *The Bronze Age, The Prehistory of Scotland, The Prehistoric Communities of the British Isles, Scotland before the Scots,* and *Prehistoric Migrations in Europe.*

Of importance equal to Childe's advanced scholarship were his popular works, which include some of the most important syntheses ever written. The methodology expressed in these works set Childe in the camp of the diffusionists, who argued that important advances such as agriculture and urbanism were invented once, and only once (at least for the Old World), in the Fertile Crescent and spread into Europe, Africa, and Asia. Childe was influenced by the work of Oscar Montelius and the diffusionistic ideas of the so-called Manchester School. He tempered this approach, however, by asserting that Near Eastern ideas were modified in each of the areas to which they were diffused. This is clearly seen in his influential trilogy *Man Makes Himself, What Happened in History,* and *Social Evolution,* which were meant to be a popular introduction to the origins of human culture. Glyn Daniel, in his foreword to the fourth edition of *Man Makes Himself,* said that these three volumes " . . . are, taken together, one of the most important works of prehistoric synthesis so far attempted this century." Daniel's statement continues to have validity: Childe's works still number among the most important pieces of archaeological literature extant.

Joseph J. Basile

See also MARXIST ARCHAEOLOGY; SOCIAL ARCHAEOLOGY

Further Readings

Childe, V.G. (1929) The Danube in Prehistory. Oxford: Clarendon.

Childe, V.G. (1930) The Bronze Age. Cambridge, UK: University Press/New York: Macmillan.

Childe, V.G. (1935) The Prehistory of Scotland. London: K. Paul, Trench, Trubner.

Childe, V.G. (1944) Archaeological Ages as Technological States. London: Royal Anthropological Institute.

Childe, V.G. (1949) Prehistoric Communities of the British Isles, 3rd ed. London: Chambers.

Childe, V.G. (1950) Prehistoric Migrations in Europe. Cambridge, MA: Harvard University Press.

Childe, V.G. (1951) Social Evolution. London: Watts/New York: H. Schuman.

Childe, V.G. (1954) What Happened in History, revised ed. New York: Penguin.

Childe, V.G. (1957) The Dawn of European Civilization, 6th ed. London: Routledge & Paul/New York: Knopf.

Childe, V.G. (1965) Man Makes Himself, 4th ed. London: Watts.

Green, S. (1981) Prehistorian: A Biography of V. Gordon Childe. Bradford-on-Avon: Moonraker.

Harris, D.R., ed. (1994) The Archaeology of V. Gordon Childe: Contemporary Perspectives. London: University College London Press.

Trigger, B.G. (1980) Gordon Childe: Revolutions in Archaeology. London: Thames and Hudson.

Clark, John Desmond (1916–)

British paleoanthropologist and archaeologist. Born on October 14, 1916, in London, Clark was educated at Cambridge University, where he received his bachelor's degree in 1937 and his master's in 1942. A curator of the Rhodes-Livingstone Museum in Northern Rhodesia (now Zambia) as early as 1938, Clark served with British forces in northeast Africa, remarkably carrying out archaeological fieldwork in Ethiopia and Somalia in his "spare time." After the conclusion of the Second World War, Clark used his findings to complete his doctoral dissertation, and was awarded a doctorate from Cambridge in 1950. He also returned to the Rhodes-Livingstone until 1961, when he left his beloved East Africa to accept an appointment as professor of anthropology at the University of California at Berkeley. He retired as emeritus professor in 1986. The recipient of numerous honors and prizes, Clark was awarded honorary degrees from the Universities of Witwatersrand and Cape Town, a Guggenheim fellowship (1971), and the Gold Medal of the Archaeological Institute of America (1989).

Clark is a significant figure in the study of early humans and human culture, a pioneer in the investigation of ecological factors as they relate to the development of human behaviors, and long a proponent of the use of interdisciplinary and scientific methodologies in archaeological fieldwork. He has excavated in Ethiopia in the Awash Valley, where he discovered important remains of *Homo erectus* along the route that many paleoanthropologists suppose this hominid species took on its journeys out of Africa. He is probably most well known, however, for his excavations at Kalambo Falls at the southern end of Lake Tanganyika. There, in the late 1960s and early 1970s, Clark investigated a site inhabited from the Middle Stone Age to the Iron Age, a remarkable document illustrating human activity in eastern Africa over the course of 200,000 years. Clark's publications, which include *The Stone Age Cultures of Northern Rhodesia, The Prehistoric Cultures of the Horn of Africa,* and *The Prehistory of Africa,* have become standards in the field of African archaeology and paleoanthropology.

Joseph J. Basile

Further Readings

Clark, J.D. (1950) The Stone Age Cultures of Northern Rhodesia. Claremont, Capetown: South African Archaeological Society.

Clark, J.D. (1954) The Prehistoric Cultures of the Horn of Africa. Cambridge, UK: University Press.

Clark, J.D. (1969) Kalambo Falls Prehistoric Site. London: Cambridge University Press.

Clark, J.D. (1970) The Prehistory of Africa. London: Thames & Hudson/New York: Praeger.

Clark, J.D. (1976) Epi-Palaeolithic Aggregates from Greboun Wadi, Air, and Adrar Bous, North-Western Tenere, Republic of Niger. Addis Ababa: Panafrican Congress of Prehistory and Quarternary Studies.

Clark, J.D. (1983) New Men, Strange Faces, Other Minds: An Archaeologist's Perspective on Recent Discoveries Relating to the Origin and Spread of Modern Man. London: Oxford University Press.

Daniel, G. (1989) The Pastmasters. New York: Thames and Hudson.

Clark, John Grahame Douglas (1907–1995)

British prehistorian. Born on July 28, 1907, Clark received his bachelor's degree in 1930, a master's, and his doctorate in 1933, all from Cambridge University. He served before the Second World War as a researcher, then as a Fellow, and then as a faculty assistant lecturer in archaeology at Peterhouse, Cambridge; from 1939 to 1945, he was a member of the

Photographic Interpretation Unit of the Royal Air Force (RAF) in Europe. After the war, Clark was a university lecturer in archaeology at Cambridge and later (1952–1974) held the prestigious Disney Chair of Archaeology at that institution. Clark was head of the Department of Archaeology and Anthropology at Cambridge twice (1956–1961 and 1968–1971) and Master of Peterhouse (1973–1995).

Clark is a significant figure in British prehistory, perhaps one of the most significant since V. Gordon Childe. Clark's work, which focused on the Mesolithic in Europe, is important in three ways. First, Clark helped define the Mesolithic as a distinct period of transition from the Palaeolithic to the Neolithic, principally by recognizing changes in the prehistoric economy. Although many scholars today reject the idea of a formal Mesolithic period, Clark helped establish an economic, rather than a technological, viewpoint in the study of prehistory. Books such as *The Mesolithic Age in Britain* (1932) and *The Mesolithic Age in Northern Europe* (1936) helped set the stage for Clark's second important contribution: his work in world prehistory. Based on his study of the Mesolithic and the work of Osbert G.S. Crawford and Cyril Fox, Clark began to formulate a view of world prehistory centered upon ecological and economic aspects as opposed to the technological divisions of the standard Three Age/Four Age/Five Age paradigm. This approach can be seen in *Prehistory in Europe: The Economic Basis* (1952) and in his classic *World Prehistory*. Finally, Clark is known as a pioneer in interdisciplinary archaeology. His excavations at Star Carr, a Mesolithic site in Yorkshire that he began excavating in 1949, were a model for later prehistoric excavations. Acknowledging that his ecological/economic approach to prehistory required extensive investigation into the ancient environment, Clark included in his Star Carr project paleobiologists, paleobotanists, and a host of other specialists, who helped reconstruct the ecology of Mesolithic Yorkshire. The Star Carr project remains a landmark of scientific archaeology.

Joseph J. Basile

See also CHILDE, VERE GORDON; CRAWFORD, OSBERT G. S.

Further Readings

Clark, J.G.D. (1932) The Mesolithic Age in Britain. Cambridge: Cambridge University Press.

Clark, J.G.D. (1936) The Mesolithic Settlement of Northern Europe: A Study of the Food-Gathering Peoples of Northern Europe during the Early Post-Glacial Period. Cambridge, Cambridge University Press.

Clark, J.G.D. (1952) Prehistoric Europe: The Economic Basis. London: Methuen.

Clark, J.G.D. (1954) Excavations at Star Carr: An Early Mesolithic Site at Seamer near Scarborough, Yorkshire. Cambridge: Cambridge University Press.

Clark, J.G.D. (1977) World Prehistory in New Perspective, 3rd ed. Cambridge/New York: Cambridge University Press.

Clark, J.G.D. (1980) Mesolithic Prelude: The Paleolithic-Neolithic Transition in Old World Prehistory. Edinburgh: Edinburgh University Press.

Clark, J.G.D. (1989) Economic Prehistory: Papers on Archaeology. Cambridge/New York: Cambridge University Press.

Clark, J.G.D. (1990) Space, Time, and Man: A Prehistorian's View. Cambridge/New York: Cambridge University Press.

Clarke, David L. (1937–1976)

British anthropologist and archaeologist. Born on November 3, 1937, Clarke began his academic career at Peterhouse, Cambridge University, in 1957 after a stint in Germany with the Royal Signal Corps. He received his bachelor's degree in 1960 and immediately began graduate studies at Peterhouse under British prehistorian Grahame Clark, then Disney Professor of Archaeology, receiving his doctorate in 1964. He was named Fellow of Peterhouse College in 1966 and was elected to the Society of Antiquaries in 1970. He became assistant lecturer in archaeology in 1975 but fell ill a year later. On June 27, 1976, he died at the age of thirty-eight. Although he was still a young scholar and had never served at Cambridge in a prestigious post, his death was a shock to the discipline. In the biographical sketch for *Analytical Archaeologist: Collected Papers of David L. Clarke*, Norman Hammond writes: "He spent his entire academic life in Cambridge, in one of its smallest colleges and without a university post until he was nearly 36 years old, yet was one of a very few British prehistorians whose work was known across the world."

Clarke was an innovator long before he received his doctorate. As a graduate student working on the Beaker pottery of Britain, he rejected earlier classification schemes (mostly based on shape) and proved that through matrix analysis—a mathematical/statistical process previously unfamiliar to most scholars in the humanities and the social sciences—more complex and complete arrangements of the Beaker pottery were possible. Clarke's willingness to utilize scientific techniques and methodologies from disciplines outside of archaeology has often been credited with shaking the complacency of British scholars, as Lewis R. Binford and the New Archaeologists were doing in America.

In 1968, Clarke published *Analytical Archaeology,* one of the most influential pieces on archaeological theory and methodology to come out of Europe since the days of V. Gordon Childe and Mortimer Wheeler. Clarke had been working for a long time on a study of archaeology as a discipline and discovered that a unified "discipline" didn't really exist—there was no explicit, central body of theory or paradigm. Looking to other disciplines, particularly in the sciences, Clarke demonstrated how unified archaeological theory might be constructed. The book was received coolly at first by the British establishment but was wildly popular in America, where the New Archaeology was in full swing. Soon, however, its important place in archaeological literature was assured. Clarke's early death robbed the discipline of one of its great thinkers, but his influence, through *Analytical Archaeology* and other writings, continues today.

Joseph J. Basile

See also BINFORD, LEWIS R.; NEW PROCESSUAL ARCHAEOLOGY

Further Readings

Clarke, D.L. (1968) Analytical Archaeology. London: Methuen.
Clarke, D.L. (1970) Beaker Pottery of Great Britain and Ireland. Cambridge, UK: University Press.
Clarke, D.L., ed. (1972) Models in Archaeology. London: Methuen.
Clarke, D.L., ed. (1977) Spatial Archaeology. London/New York: Academic
Clarke, D.L. (1979) Analytical Archaeologist: Collected Papers of David L. Clarke. London/New York: Academic.

Classical Archaeology

The excavation and study of the material remains of ancient Mediterranean cultures. The boundaries of the discipline are not firmly fixed in time and space. While the historical cultures of the Greco-Roman world remain the primary focus, cultures now studied by classical archaeologists range from the prehistoric Bronze Age to the early medieval period.

History of the Discipline

Awareness of the importance of the visible remains of classical antiquity and of the need to record them began as early as the fifteenth century A.D. An Italian merchant, Cyriac of Ancona (1391–1455), who traveled widely in the Mediterranean on business, recorded Greek and Latin inscriptions and sketched building remains and sculpture. In Rome itself during the fifteenth and sixteenth centuries, an interest in studying and collecting the remains of the past often led to wholesale destruction of ancient buildings. In their search for ancient sculpture, powerful Roman families, such as the Farnese, conducted excavations that were little more than treasure hunts.

Antiquarian interest in the physical monuments of Greek and Roman lands grew in the seventeenth and eighteenth centuries, as more travelers and explorers set out to survey, record, and describe ancient sites. In 1733, a group of English gentlemen formed the Society of Dilettanti, whose goal was to foster antiquarian interest at home by sending expeditions to Greece and Asia Minor to observe and record ancient monuments. The eighteenth century in Italy also witnessed the beginning of large-scale archaeological excavation, first at Herculaneum, then at Pompeii. The potential richness of both sites was discovered by accident (by digging a well at the former and a canal at the latter). Subsequent excavation was a random process, the purpose of which was the acquisition of objects from antiquity, rather than a systematic attempt to understand the nature of these sites. The publications of early travelers and explorers, especially their often meticulous sketches and drawings, along with the private acquisition, through purchase and plunder, of objects such as vases and statues from Greco-Roman antiquity, provided a substantial corpus of material for scholarly investigation. In 1764, Johann Joachim Winckelmann (1717–1768) published his monumental *History of Ancient Art* in which he identified phases of classical art based on stylistic analysis and distinguished Roman copies of original Greek sculpture. Many scholars today consider Winckelmann to be the founder not only of art history, but also of classical archaeology. Certainly, the traditional close connection between these two fields of study is, in large part, a result of Winckelmann's influential work.

The increase of public interest in ancient material remains is reflected in the growth of private (usually royal) and public museums throughout Europe during the eighteenth century. Museums acquired choice objects for display through purchase from individual collectors and through sponsorship of excavations. It was from the British ambassador Lord Elgin, for example, that the British Museum (founded in 1759) bought the Parthenon sculptures and other material in the early nineteenth century. Lord Elgin is vilified today for the irreparable damage done to the Athenian Acropolis in general and to the Parthenon in particular during the four years it took to dismantle its sculpture. Also in the early nineteenth century, European museums began sending out representatives to excavate and bring home antiquities, especially from Asia Minor (western Turkey). Excavations to recover material for museum collections were seldom systematic, although some excavators, such as Charles Thomas Newton (1816–1894), who worked at the mausoleum at Halicarnassus on behalf of the British Museum, were scrupulous in recording all aspects of their excavations, including plans and sections.

A general movement among some classical archaeologists toward a more careful procedure in excavating, recording, and publishing took place in the mid-nineteenth century, at the same time that large-scale excavations were first being planned. In Greece, this movement was encouraged by the founding of the Greek Archaeological Society in 1837. For-

eign schools or societies for archaeological research also established permanent bases in Athens, including the French in 1846, the Germans in 1874, the Americans in 1882, and the British in 1885. Major excavation projects in the mid-to-late nineteenth and early twentieth centuries had as their goal a more holistic recovery and understanding of ancient sites, usually sanctuaries (such as Olympia and Delphi in Greece) or abandoned ancient cities (such as Pergamon and Ephesos in western Turkey).

Until the second half of the nineteenth century, the focus of classical archaeology was the recovery of Greco-Roman antiquity, usually with special emphasis on its architectural remains. There was little interest in, or understanding of, preclassical-period monuments. In 1870, Heinrich Schliemann (1822–1890) began excavating at Hissarlik in northwestern Turkey, which he believed to be the site of Homer's Troy, based on his reading of Homer's epic poems. Ignoring the visible remains of the Greco-Roman past scattered over the mound, Schliemann sunk an enormous trench into its depths, finding at the bottom, among walls and destruction debris, the now infamous "Priam's Treasure" (which was subsequently found to predate the city of Troy in Homer's *Iliad*). Although his methods are justly criticized and his conclusions about the dates of his discoveries have been proved wrong, Schliemann did initiate a new phase in classical archaeology by uncovering a rich preclassical culture. Even traditional classical archaeologists became interested. When Schliemann returned to Troy in 1882, Wilhelm Dorpfeld (1853–1940) accompanied him. Dorpfeld, who had participated in the large-scale German excavations at Olympia, was one of the earliest classical archaeologists to appreciate the value of stratigraphic analysis. The working relationship between classical and preclassical archaeology was thus established, and the contributions of each to the other have since advanced the development of both fields.

Although many excavations continued to concentrate on Greco-Roman remains, in the first half of the twentieth century there was an increasing concern for earlier phases of activity, from the Archaic back to the prehistoric (even Neolithic). In some places, this interest was the natural result of having fully exploited the historic levels. But a growing number of classical archaeologists also recognized the potential value of stratigraphic analysis through the life span of a site, as opposed to simple horizontal exposure of Greco-Roman remains. Continuing excavations, such as those of the American School of Classical Studies at Athens in the Athenian Agora (begun in the 1930s) and of the German Archaeological Institute at Olympia (begun in the 1870s) have successfully combined both approaches.

During the course of the twentieth century, the cultural remains of the Aegean Bronze Age have attracted widespread interest. The potential importance of this period, first suggested by Schliemann at Troy and Mycenae and by Sir Arthur Evans (1851–1941) at Knossos on Crete, was confirmed by the work of many archaeologists during the first half of the century (e.g., Carl Blegen [1887–1971] at Pylos and Troy and by Spyridon Marinatos [1901–1974] at Akrotiri on Thera). The wealth and complexity of the Aegean Bronze Age have given rise to a special field within the general boundaries of classical archaeology.

The mid-to-late twentieth century has witnessed a decline in large-scale excavations throughout the Greco-Roman world. At the same time, there has been a marked increase in multidisciplinary regional-survey projects. The pioneering project in this type of fieldwork was the University of Minnesota Expedition in Messenia (Greece), conducted during the 1960s, with a subsequent excavation at Nichoria to test survey observations. Similar regional surveys, on a smaller scale, have followed in many areas of the Mediterranean. The projects reflect the changes that have taken place in the goals defined within the field of classical archaeology.

Methodologies

Classical archaeology, as a discipline, has emerged in the mid-to-late twentieth century from a long tradition of antiquarianism. Its purpose no longer rests on the acquisition of choice objects for public and private display or on the maximum exposure of physical remains at a given site. Rather, classical archaeology seeks to understand the total cultural and historical record of a site and the relationship of that site to its physical environment and to other sites in the region. The methods of classical archaeology are both traditional, arising from the antiquarian interests of the

past, and scientific, resulting from a desire to obtain a variety of information from an artifact or from a site. Most archaeological projects today are multidisciplinary ventures.

Within the general field of classical archaeology are traditional subdisciplines. These include such specialty areas as *epigraphy,* the study of inscriptions, and *numismatics,* the study of coins. Publications of major excavations at Greco-Roman sites, such as the Agora in Athens, include individual studies of inscriptions and coins. The methods of art-historical analysis also continue to play an important interpretative role in understanding the physical remains of classical antiquity. Again, the publications of large-scale excavations, such as those at Corinth and Olympia in Greece, often include separate volumes devoted to stone sculpture, pottery, bronzes, and the like.

Applied science has greatly enhanced traditional methods and influenced new avenues of research. One of the most fundamental problems encountered in the field is to determine the age of an artifact and its related context. To the traditional methods of stylistic analysis, science has added such techniques as radiocarbon dating of organic remains, thermoluminesence dating of fired clay, and dendrochronological analysis when wood is preserved. In addition to providing information about the age of an object, science also assists in determining the origins of its material (e.g., by examining mineral or chemical composition of marble or bronze). Biological and physical sciences, too, have become important components in archaeological projects. The recovery and study of floral and faunal remains are as crucial to understanding a site as the excavation of artifacts. Geoarchaeological methods, such as augur coring, provide evidence for local and regional environmental conditions through time. The influence of methods used in investigating preclassical sites is evident in the scientific techniques applied with increasing frequency to Greco-Roman sites.

Economic development in many Mediterranean regions has led to a new demand in field archaeology, the rescue or salvage excavation. In response to an immediate threat posed by a major construction project, such as a coastal holiday village, a dam, or a subway system in Athens, archaeologists work quickly to recover the maximum amount of information before the site is destroyed. Usually, excavations of this kind are limited endeavors, but sometimes they can involve major international cooperation. An excellent example is the enormous international effort expended in salvage excavations along the Upper Tigris and Euphrates regions in southeastern Turkey prior to the flooding of those areas by the construction of dams in the 1980s and 1990s.

Economic pressures of a different kind, namely, the increasingly high cost of supporting large-scale excavations and the concurrent dwindling of university or government funds for such activities, have encouraged a more cost-effective field method, the local or regional surface survey. The growing popularity and importance of this method of data gathering are also the result of changes in the kinds of questions classical archaeology now seeks to answer. Although survey methods differ from project to project, depending on their intensive or extensive goals, most involve the careful visual examination and recording of the kinds and quantity of material found on the surface of a predetermined tract of ground. Major survey projects continue throughout the Mediterranean region, and even traditional large-scale excavations often incorporate regional surveys as part of their research activities.

Theory

Classical archaeology traditionally has been text and event oriented. The enormous body of literature surviving from Greco-Roman antiquity and the historical events described therein have exerted a tremendous influence on the goals of classical archaeology. In the late twentieth century, the traditional literary and historical foundation for the goals of classical archaeology is being scrutinized and questioned, especially in the wake of the New Archaeology. This new school or approach to archaeology, mainly evident in anthropology-based archaeology (as opposed to text- or event-based archaeology), stresses the importance of developing universal explanatory models for human activity and of using material remains to test these models. The New Archaeology also underscores the necessity of collaboration among archaeologists, physical scientists, and social scientists.

Throughout most of its history as a humanistic discipline, classical archaeology has attempted to interpret the material remains revealed through excavation in light of what ancient writers have to say about a place and time. Often, the goal of a particular excavation has been to illuminate the historical or literary record (e.g., by uncovering a specific building or discovering material evidence for a specific event, such as a battle). Even when an excavation's goals are not necessarily text or event based, the literary record is called upon to identify and explain prominent features in the archaeological record, as if their very prominence presupposes certain mention of them in the ancient texts.

Criticism of classical archaeology as a discipline rests on the apparent absence of a universal and informing theory within the field. In the past, the goals and results of excavation and subsequent interpretation have been descriptive rather than explanatory, particularistic rather than general or comparative. Yet the well-published corpus of material remains from excavated sites, descriptive and particular, facilitate the development of universal, explanatory models.

In the late twentieth century, classical archaeology has become less concerned with specific moments in time and more aware of the importance of long-term processes in cultural, social, historical, even ecological systems. Gender relations, urbanization and rural-urban sociology, ritual behavior and the ritual landscape, collapse theory, and core-periphery (frontier) studies are just a few of the research topics that have been presented at the international conferences on "Theoretical Roman Archaeology." These kinds of questions now being asked of the material record can seldom be answered by single-site excavation or by examination of individual artifacts. Classical archaeology has become a discipline that depends not only on its traditional association with texts and events, but also increasingly on the theory and method of the social and physical sciences. Interdisciplinary theoretical models for explaining human activity in the past are being tested in the context of interdisciplinary regional surveys.

Barbara McLauchlin

See also DENDROCHRONOLOGY; GEOARCHAEOLOGY; MARBLE, CHARACTERIZATION; NEW/PROCESSUAL ARCHAEOLOGY; RADIOCARBON DATING; SURVEYS, MULTISTAGE AND LARGE-SCALE; THERMOLUMINESCENCE DATING; UNDERWATER ARCHAEOLOGY

Further Readings

Courbin, P. (1988) What Is Archaeology? An Essay on the Nature of Archaeological Research. Trans. P. Bahn. Chicago: University of Chicago Press.

Daniel, G. (1967) The Origin and Growth of Archaeology. Harmondsworth: Penguin.

Dyson, S. (1993) From New to New Age archaeology: Archaeological theory and classical archaeology—a 1990s perspective. American Journal of Archaeology 97:195–206.

Hodder, I. (1987) The contribution of the long term. In I. Hodder (ed.): Archaeology as Long-Term History, pp. 1–8. Cambridge: Cambridge University Press.

McDonald, W.A., and Rapp, G.R. (1972) The Minnesota Messenia Expedition: Reconstructing a Bronze Age Regional Environment. Minneapolis: University of Minnesoty Press.

Renfrew, C. (1980) The Great Tradition versus the Great Divide: Archaeology as anthropology? American Journal of Archaeology 84:287–298.

Rush, P., ed. (1995) Theoretical Roman Archaeology: Second Conference Proceedings. Aldershot: Avebury.

Scott, E., ed. (1993) Theoretical Roman Archaeology: First Conference Proceedings. Aldershot: Avebury.

Snodgrass, A. (1985) The new archaeology and the classical archaeologist. American Journal of Archaeology 89:31–37.

Snodgrass, A. (1987) An Archaeology of Greece: The Present State and Future Scope of a Discipline. Berkeley and Los Angeles: University of California Press.

Whitley, J. (1987) Art history, archaeology, and idealism: The German tradition. In: I. Hodder (ed.): Archaeology as Long-Term History, pp. 9–15. Cambridge: Cambridge University Press.

Clays and Ceramics, Characterization

Respectively, a group of widely dispersed silicate minerals and a class of products defined by their manufacture from clays.

Clays have been used for a variety of utilitarian and nonutilitarian purposes in ancient times, not only for their most obvious use as an important material for manufacturing containers (e.g., pots, bowls, cups, jugs, storage vessels), but also for the fabrication of statuary, domestic and public architecture, decorative architectural elements, heating installations (e.g., hypocausts, hearths, ovens, kilns, furnaces), surface finishes or surface protectants, cosmetics, pigments, toys and gaming pieces, loom weights and spindle whorls, and as a necessary material utilized in other technologies (e.g., material for cores and molds in metal casting).

It would be rare to find a group of people, past or present, who would not find some use for clay, even if they did not produce pottery. While impossible to date the first exploitation of clay, some of the earliest surviving evidence of the use of clay comes from the Upper Paleolithic of Europe in the form of fired clay female figurines found at Dolní Věstonice in the Czech Republic (ca. 30,000 B.C.) and in the application of wet clay as an artistic medium in several caves in France. The earliest fired clay pottery dates to the ninth millennium B.C. in Anatolia and, if dating is resolved, possibly earlier for the Jōmon Culture of Japan.

Structures, features, objects, and other products made of clay survive well under most environmental conditions of burial, and, on archaeological sites where they are found, ceramics often comprise the most ubiquitous type of material. This good preservation, together with the abundance of material, allows both relative and absolute dating, as well as chemical and geological characterization by a considerable variety of analytical methods. Research on ceramic products and the clays from which they are made has provided archaeologists with a wealth of information on a vast number of subjects, including, but certainly not limited to, regional trading patterns and international commerce; individual, household, and community behavioral patterns; chronological frameworks for both individual sites and larger geographic zones; artistic development and the identification of local and regional styles; advancements in the history of technology; patterns in human demography; food consumption and dietary patterns; modes of living and residence patterns; and burial ritual and other aspects of belief systems.

Definition of Clays

Clay is a generic term that is used in the earth sciences, materials science, and the arts. Clays may be defined or classified based on their chemistry, particle size, mechanical or firing be-havior, or method of geological formation. Clays are differentiated from related pedological materials (such as soils, silt, and sand) by extremely small particle sizes, less than 0.002 mm in diameter, which accounts for much of the observed behavior of clays when water is added (i.e., plasticity and colloidal suspension).

From the geological perspective, *clay* is a term used to refer to a sedimentary rock group that consists of a variety of specific minerals. Clays are formed from the products of erosion of other rocks, predominantly feldspars, but also granite, micas, other silicates, or volcanic deposits, and may be divided into *primary clays* and *secondary clays.* Primary (also called *residual*) clays are formed at or near the parent rock from which the weathered particles derived. Secondary (or *transported*) clays are those that formed into deposits at various distances from the source rock, whose products of erosion were transported by meteorological systems, water flow, or glacial movement. The raw weathered products of primary and secondary deposits undergo both mechanical and chemical alterations that result in the formation of clay minerals. As part of the depositional process, clays also have natural inclusions that derive from the geological history of the clay deposit. These inclusions often consist of fragments of minerals that remain from the parent rock(s) or microfossils in clays formed on seabeds and subsequently exposed through plate tectonics, as well as a variety of other organic and inorganic detrital material. Clays are widely deposited on the surface of the Earth, on every continent, as well as underneath bodies of fresh and salt water.

Clay chemistry is complex, such that discussions on the definition, chemistry, and classification of what actually constitutes a clay are ongoing in the geochemical sciences. But for the majority of opinion, clay minerals have been classified as phyllosilicates (from the Greek *phyllon,* meaning leaf) based on their platy structure, one prominent cleavage, elasticity of cleavage lamellae, and softness. Some of the more commonly encountered clay minerals are kaolinite, the smectites (e.g., montmorillonite, bentonite, nontronite), the illites (illite and glauconite), and the hydrous-magnesian clays (attapulgite, palygorskite, sepiolite).

Minerals, by definition, are naturally occurring substances with a known chemical composition whose atoms are arranged in a regular geometric array *(crystallinity).* The chemical composition (atomic arrangement) of clay minerals is based on a unit of SiO_4— one silicon atom surrounded by four oxygen atoms arranged in a tetrahedral pattern (four triangular sides). Characteristic of most clay minerals is that many silica tetrahedra are joined together in a network, by sharing corner oxygen atoms, to form extensive sheets. These silicate sheets are then intercalated with layers of aluminum atoms and hydroxyl (OH) groups (i.e., chemically combined water). This sheet network structure produces clay particles in the form of hexagonal platelets that measure approximately half a micron or less. Many clay minerals are often classified as hydrous aluminum silicates. However, this basic composition can vary considerably to include magnesium, potassium, sodium, calcium, iron, and other elements, in place of, or together with, aluminum. This variable elemental composition derives from the chemistry of the weathered source rocks, mineralogical and biological contaminants, the composition of percolating waters, and other biochemical changes in the postdepositional environment. It is these contaminants that largely determine the color of the clay—if clay were a pure substance of just silicon, oxygen, and aluminum, it would most likely be white, as with the famous kaolin clays of China. Most clays, however, are contaminated with iron oxides to highly variable degrees. Ultimately, the nature of the mineralogical contaminants in the clay will determine the range of colors in the fired clay product (see below).

Definition of Ceramics

The term *ceramic* (from the Greek *keramos/keramikos,* "pottery" or "burned material") is usually applied to those objects or features made of clay and subsequently heat treated so that the final product is durable and retains its shape when exposed to water. For *clay* to become *ceramic,* heating has to be sufficient, in terms of both duration and intensity, to alter the crystallinity, or arrangement of the atoms, of the clay minerals. Once a certain temperature level has been reached during firing, the perimeters of the hexagonal clay platelets begin to melt to form a glass phase (which can be observed to any degree of clarity only with a scanning electron microscope). This means that many atoms have dissociated themselves from the orderly arrangement that defines specific minerals—in this case, clays—and are now in an unpredictable, noncrystalline pattern. This disordered phase of material is technically referred to as a *liquid,* which manifests itself as a gradual development of glass during firing. The function of this glass formation is to cement clay particles together (*sintering,* in ceramic terminology). As heating continues, the glass phase is extended *(vitrification),* with the end result being a densification and shrinkage of the clay into a permanent, irreversible shape (e.g., the fired pot). If the heating process were to continue unabated, and at sufficient temperatures, the melting of the clay platelets would be brought to completion, and the end product would be a glassy substance that would be deformed, via gravity, from the formation of too much liquid phase (usually referred to as *slumping*). So, for practical purposes, a ceramic is a transitional material on a continuum between clay mineral (solid) and glass (liquid), retaining many of the visual and tactile characteristics of clay combined with the rigidity of glass. Not all objects, features, structures, or materials made from clays should be classified as ceramic, however. Usually, clay products that have been sun dried (e.g., adobe, sun-dried brick), while quite durable in an arid environment and thus usable for a variety of purposes, are insufficiently heated to cause a change in crystallinity and thus are technically still clay and not ceramic.

The Manufacturing Process

Clay Preparation

Regardless of what type of products are being manufactured from clay, a certain series of steps need to be taken in the preparation of the raw material, object formation, surface decoration (if any), and firing. All of the production steps are dependent on, or take advantage of, the chemical and structural nature of clays as described above. Pottery production is explained in detail here, since a full range of technological processes is involved. For the production of other objects or structures or the use of clay in any other context, one or more of the following processes will most likely be employed.

After raw clay is collected, it will usually need to be sorted and cleaned to a certain de-gree, such as removal of vegetal and animal matter or other unwanted geological debris, depending on the extent of impurities that result from the history of clay deposition and subsequent geomorphological conditions. Usually, raw clay has to be pulverized to provide a more even consistency and to allow rapid and even absorption of water. If the finished product requires a certain fineness (small particle-size range), the clay may have to be refined by mixing it into a water suspension in a settling tank or basin, or even a series of settling basins, for a few days to several weeks, in order to scoop or otherwise separate the finer fractions of clay particulates.

Once the clay is cleaned and refined to the potter's satisfaction, it is prepared for working. Different clays have vastly different mechanical behaviors (e.g. workability, absorption capability, shrinkage, firing characteristics) based on the chemistry and the crystallinity of each clay mineral. Ancient potters could recognize these characteristics based on empirical evidence, repeated observations, and the accumulated knowledge of preceding generations. For this reason, potters often mix clays of varying properties, based on availability, to achieve the characteristics most favorable to their desired end product.

When water is added to clay, it becomes plastic as a result of the clay platelets being lubricated to slide over one another and to interlock at various angles among themselves. As more water is added, the distances between particles become greater, as do the sizes of pore spaces. The amount of water used by the potter depends entirely on the level of workability desired and the chemical-physical nature of the particular clay mineral(s). However, as much as clays will absorb water, so, too, they will lose water to evaporation, and the final product will shrink during the drying and firing phases. A minor amount of shrinkage is tolerable, but shrinkage beyond a certain point will result in structural weakness and possibly cracking. It is to prevent such excessive shrinkage and the propagation of microcracks that potters add *temper* to the refined clay at the beginning of the working process. Temper may consist of any particulate material that can withstand the temperatures of firing; ideally it is nonplastic and not hygroscopic, (water absorbing) in order to offset clay shrinkage. However, since prehistoric times potters have experimented with an enormous variety of materials for use as temper—some less than desirable from a technological or medical point of view—including, but not limited to, sand, crushed shell, crushed rock, crushed recycled ceramics (*sherd temper* or *grog*), crushed bone, straw, grain, asbestos, river gravels, and volcanic glass (obsidian). Moreover, the natural inclusions in the clay, which may or may not be visible to the potter, can also serve the same purposes as temper, if they are present in sufficient quantities, such as some illitic clays, which can have a very high volume percent of micaceous grains.

Object Formation

In preindustrial societies, clay objects were produced completely by hand, with the assistance of rotary motion, with molds, or with any combination thereof. Handmade clay vessels can be formed by the *pinch-pot* method (pinching and sculpting the clay into the desired form), the *coil* method (alignment of successive snake-shaped tubes of clay, with each coil smoothed and joined to the one above and below), the *paddle-and-anvil* method (beating the exterior clay surface with a paddle while holding an anvil on the interior surface, both usually made of wood), or any combination of these techniques together with the sculptural deftness of the human hand. Clay vessels were also produced with the assistance of rotary motion from a simple platen on a pivot, which is turned by hand, to a more complicated fast-wheel (sometimes referred to as a *kick-wheel*). The fast-wheel consists of a circular turntable for the working of the clay, at waist level of a seated potter, who is able to use the feet to kick (i.e., spin) a lower, horizontal wheel—both turntable and wheel being connected by a rod of wood (or, later, iron). There are several variations on the design of rotary motion methods that have been used in antiquity. Ceramic vessels can also be made with the use of molds, into which wet clay can be pressed, then allowed to dry and shrink away from the mold to allow easy removal. All of these production methods can be combined in various ways not only for vessel formation, but also for addition of appendages and decoration, as well as for the manufacture of products other than containers. Both rotary motion and molds allowed the mass production of ceramics, as exemplified by Greco-Roman ceramics that entered into international trade, although more for their contents of wine and olive oil than for the vessels themselves.

Prefire Decoration

Once the form of the clay vessel or other object is completed, the potter may decorate the clay surface, usually while 'leather-hard'. Decorative treatment before firing takes advantage of the plasticity and absorptive properties of clay, as well as the behavior of the clay platelets to surround and lock in grains of mineral pigments. A tremendous variety of decorative techniques have been used in the past, including modifying the clay surface by incising, excising (gouging of clay to produce an inverse sculptural relief effect), impressing (e.g., using shells, cord-wrapped stick, fingernails), clay appliqué, or inlay work (e. g., filling incisions/excisions with powdered mineral colorants, such as calcium carbonate or hematite).

The unfired ceramic piece may also be covered by a *slip,* which is a suspension of clay in water, the thickness of which depends on the desired visual effect. A slip is not a *glaze* (the latter is glass, see below), and occasionally these two terms are used incorrectly in the archaeological literature. The clay chosen for the slip may be the same kind of clay, thereby serving as a coating, or may be a different color, thus able to serve as a decoration. Additional colorants, such as finely powdered iron-, manganese-, or calcium-based minerals, may be added to this clay–water suspension, which can yield vibrant and durable colors under the right firing conditions (see below). If a slip is used to coat or decorate the clay object, it is usual practice to rub the surface of the slip *(burnishing)* with a smooth tool (e.g., polished bone or stone) or a piece of leather. Burnishing has the effect of aligning the clay platelets in the slip, which increases the clay's durability and enhances surface reflectivity. Burnishing itself may be a decorative process *(pattern burnishing),* since unburnished and burnished surfaces will distinguish themselves visually as a matte versus glossy effect, respectively. Other kinds of pigment decoration, such as graphite and organic carbonaceous materials, have also been applied to clay surfaces. Any of the above decorative techniques can, and have been, used in combination.

Firing

When the clay objects have been allowed to dry thoroughly (the timing depends on the nature of the clay[s] used, the season of the year, the ambient weather conditions, and the availability of fuel), they can be fired. Firing of clay not only irreversibly changes the fundamental chemistry and crystallinity of clay, as explained above, but also may change the color of the final product. There are a variety of firing procedures that have been used in the past and continue into the present—from simple pits dug into the ground to the construction of single-, double-, or multichambered kilns, which themselves may be constructed of compacted clay or brick. In pit firings and single-chamber kilns, the fuel and the objects to be fired (the *charge*) are placed together for the combustion process. In double- or multi-chambered kilns, the fuel may be segregated into its own chamber *(fire box)*, the heat from which travels updraft or downdraft, depending on the design of the kiln, to fire the objects in another chamber.

An important concept in pyrotechnology is that of *atmosphere,* (i.e., the nature and mix of gases surrounding the clay objects during firing). The success of a firing and the quality of the finished products are judged by how well the potter achieved and controlled the temperature of the fire, as well as the surrounding gases. Combustion produces a mixture of gases, usually including oxygen, carbon monoxide, and carbon dioxide (and other products such as sulfur compounds and water vapor). However, depending on how the charge and the fuel are arranged in the pit firing or how the kiln is designed, a knowledgeable potter tries to control the content and flow of the gases, since these will determine the color of the fired clay. As stated above, most clays have biological and mineralogical contaminants; the former will burn off, while the iron oxides will leave a permanent color to the fired product. If the potter desires a ceramic in the orange/pink/red range, the surrounding gases will have to be oxygen rich *(oxidation atmosphere),* (i.e., with a good circulation of oxygen during firing). If the potter wants a brown/black/gray ceramic body, the gases must be controlled to produce a *reduction atmosphere,* which is rich in carbon monoxide. Any errors in the firing process can result in the serious marring of decorated ceramic surfaces.

Postfire Treatment

A ceramic can be decorated after firing, but at that point any decoration has to be bonded in some way to the surface, since clay particles have now lost their original properties. The fired surface may also be treated in some way, such as the application of tars, resins, gums, or other organic materials. Examples of postfire decoration include the application of glazes, the use of the fresco process, or the attachment of colorants or appliqué by means of protein substances or other types of adhesives.

The best-known type of postfire decoration is the use of glazes, which are commonly formulations of finely powdered recycled glass, quartz sand, or quartz-bearing rock, with or without added metal oxides as colorants or opacifiers, mixed with water and applied on the ceramic surface. The object is then fired a second time to melt quartz-bearing substances or remelt the powdered glass, which forms the final glazed surface. Glazes may be made from other materials (e.g., salt, which reacts with the clay surface to form a thin, glassy layer); the surface of the ceramic may be painted and then overglazed; or there may be several types of glazes simultaneously or sequentially applied and fired, provided that the last glaze melts at a temperature lower than the previous application. For a glaze to bond well, the ceramic and the glaze must have similar coefficients of expansion. Glazing and its chemistry can be quite complicated, and glazing recipes are very much a protected domain by their practitioners and rightly considered an aspect of glass technology.

Some Archaeological Research Questions

Ceramic materials and the clays from which they derive have been the focus of general archaeological study for the documentation and analysis of artistic styles of ceramic form and decoration; the statistical analysis of occurrence and location of specific ceramic types; analyses of ceramic use, reuse, and disposal; reconstruction of technology and production systems; reconstruction of economic systems; relative and absolute dating; and the sourcing of raw materials.

Much early ceramic analysis in archaeology was focused on the description of ceramic form and decorative styles and organization of the production process with the view of identifying stratigraphic time markers and establishing local and regional relative chronologies. Design-structure analysis has developed further as a field of inquiry to answer questions not only of chronology, but also of social interaction within a community and to detect patterns of transmission of knowledge in ceramic production.

Archaeologists have reconstructed ancient ceramic technologies by using experimental archaeology to reproduce the technology of specific types of wares and to reconstruct the firing conditions. Ethnoarchaeology has also been used to observe living ceramic traditions in order to understand the variety of both materials and behavioral aspects of pottery production, such as the organization of ceramic-manufacturing activities. Through both experimental archaeology and ethnoarchaeology, archaeologists have also reproduced the applications of clays for purposes other than pottery, including the use of clay in the construction of domestic and public architecture and heating installations.

Methods of analysis from the geological and materials sciences have also been applied to the study of ceramic materials for insight into technological processes. Petrography allows the archaeologist to identify and distinguish visually natural geological and biological inclusions versus temper added by the potter, as well as to understand working techniques and firing conditions. Physicochemical analytical methods also provide information on the identification of raw materials (clays, inclusions, additives, pigment, and glaze chemistry) to ascertain the level of knowledge in ancient pyrotechnologies.

The sourcing of ceramics to their raw materials can be conducted using physicochemical methods of analysis (e.g., neutron activation analysis, X-ray fluorescence analysis, inductively coupled plasma–atomic emission spectrometry) that produce a chemical "fingerprint" to match clays used in ceramics with prospective geological sources of clays. Information on the chemistry of materials used in ceramic production has provided researchers in both Old World and New World archaeology with information on patterns of geological-resource exploitation and documentation of local and long-distance exchange systems, which, in turn, can supply direct evidence of culture contact.

The uses of ceramic vessels and associated information on food consumption, food storage, and dietary patterns can be ascertained through biochemical analysis of soil and residue contents of vesssels, provided the ceramics have not been cleaned at the excavation. Not only production and utilization, but also the disposal of ceramic objects as grave gifts can elucidate any patterning in mortuary behavior through analysis of burials and quantification of their inventories.

With the development of thermoluminescence (TL) dating, ceramics have proved to be a valuable material for direct and absolute dating where other datable materials are lacking and an independent check on radiocarbon dates. Among art and archaeological museums, TL dating of ceramics and of the fired clay cores of cast bronze sculptures has also been particularly successful in the dating and authentication of pieces prior to museum acquisition.

Linda Ellis

See also CERAMICS, ON-SITE CONSERVATION; ETHOARCHAEOLOGY; EXPERIMENTAL ARCHAEOLOGY; INDUCTIVELY COUPLED PLASMA—ATOMIC EMISSION SPECTROMETRY; NUCLEAR METHODS OF ANALYSIS; PETROGRAPHY; SERIATION; SHEPARD, ANNA OSLER; THERMOLUMINESCENCE DATING; TYPE-VARIETY SYSTEM; X-RAY FLUORESCENCE (XRF) ANALYSIS

Further Readings

Olin, J.S., and Franklin, A.D., eds. (1982) Archaeological Ceramics. Washington, D.C.: Smithsonian Institution Press.

Orton, C., Tyers, P., and Vince, A., (1993) Pottery in Archaeology. Cambridge: Cambridge University Press.

Rice, P.M., ed. (1984) Pots and Potters: Current Approaches in Ceramic Archaeology. (Monograph 24). Los Angeles: Institute of Archaeology, UCLA.

Rice, P.M., (1987) Pottery Analysis: A Sourcebook. Chicago: University of Chicago Press.

Rye, O.S. (1981) Pottery Technology: Principles and Reconstruction. (Manuals on Archaeology 4). Washington, D.C.: Taraxacum.

Shepard, A.O. (1956) Ceramics for the Archaeologist. Washington, D.C.: Carnegie Institution of Washington.

Computer Databanks in Archaeology

Bodies of related data stored in computer files in such a way that archaeologists can easily retrieve them or extract information from them. Many use this term synonymously with *databases,* a slightly more recent term that seems to have come into use with the introduction of commercial database-management software (DBMS) in the 1980s. The erstwhile distinction between databases, which use such software, and databanks, which do not necessarily do so, is largely redundant, as the use of specialized database software (whether commercial or not) is now ubiquitous. Databanks exist at a wide range of scales, from small personal ones to large national ones, in a wide variety of structures, from simple *flat-file* formats to complicated *relational* structures (see below), and for a wide range of purposes. Some archaeologists now use the term *database* to mean any extensive collection of data on a particular topic, whether or not it is stored on a computer.

History

The construction and use of databanks in archaeology followed the introduction of quantitative methods in a second wave of applications in the 1970s. Archaeologists began to appreciate the benefits of storing an entire body of related data (e.g., from an excavation) together and extracting information from it for analysis as they needed it, rather than entering specific subsets of their data for specific analyses. Initially, they worked on large, sometimes remote, mainframe computers (often run by a university or government computer center) and had to work within a framework whose main uses were elsewhere (e.g., in payroll or staff records).

The situation changed dramatically around 1980 when archaeologists and museums began to use personal computers on a large scale. At first, archaeologists tended to write their own software because of the dearth of commercially available packages. This threatened to lead to a state of data anarchy, as the various systems were usually incompatible with one another so that archaeologists could not readily exchange data. Attempts at standardization failed, partly because of rapid developments in both hardware and software. The advent of commercial DBMS in the 1980s overcame some of the problems, in that archaeologists stopped reinventing the database wheel and were able to exchange data in standardized formats. This also marked the beginning of a large-scale switch from paper to computer media for the storage of archaeological data, which prevented or at least delayed a crisis due to an inability to cope with ever-increasing flows of archaeological data from excavations and surveys. However, this, in turn, highlighted a deeper problem: the lack of compatibility of definitions and terminology between different archaeological organizations and, indeed sometimes, within an archaeological organization. In some topic areas, such as site inventories (see below), the development of thesauri of agreed terms proved to be a useful solution; in other areas, such as pottery studies, the difficulty of agreeing to common definitions has held back potential study (e.g., of intersite comparisons).

By the late 1980s, the use of the relational model of data, usually implemented through commercial packages, especially the dBase family, was well established. Some archaeologists began to chafe at the limitations of such structures, in particular at (1) the restrictions on the types of data that were allowed; (2) the problem of handling graphical material (e.g., maps, site plans, finds drawings, photographs) within a database structure; and (3) the handling of missing data. Various commercial developments—such as object-oriented databases, the inclusion of BLOBS (binary large objects; e.g., scanned images) in database structures, improved data storage using optical methods, and geographical information systems (GIS)—have pointed a way forward for some of these areas. Archaeologists are experimenting with integrating all of the various aspects of, for example, excavation records, but as yet no common standard is emerging. There is a risk of repeating the anarchy of the 1970s.

An issue that has come to the fore in the 1990s is that of access to information stored in archaeological databanks. Paper records are, in principle, available to anyone who has access to a library or archive. Computer database records, while in some ways more accessible, (e.g., by remote access over computer networks), are in other ways less accessible, since their use is restricted to those who have the necessary hardware and software and achieve a right of access. This may discriminate against certain classes of potential

C

users. Even the ease of access (given the necessary facilities) has its own problems, since, if one can access data, one can copy them and perhaps even change them, leading to legal problems of intellectual property rights. A related problem is that of proper recognition of the intellectual effort that goes into the design and creation of a successful database, which is often not acknowledged in current systems of publication and peer review.

Related issues that have grown in importance with the passage of time and the accumulation of databases are data standards and the preservation and re-use of digital data. Data standards are needed to ensure comparability between related datasets prepared by different organizations, but they can have the unfortunate effect of fossilizing knowledge at a particular point in time. One answer is the use of *metadata* (data about data) to explain data to potential users. Another obstacle to the re-use of hard-won data is technological obsolescence—both hardware and software can rapidly become out-of-date and data therefore inaccessible. Simply maintaining databases through technical upgrades is a major task.

Methods

The simplest structure for a databank is the flat file—a table in which, conventionally, rows represent records of objects (e. g., sites, finds, publications) and columns represent attributes (variables) of those objects. These mimic the card-index systems that were the favorite of a previous generation of archaeologists and operate in much the same way (but much faster). They can sort the records into different orders, depending on the values of one or more variable(s), extract records that satisfy certain conditions, and calculate totals and subtotals. These abilities can be useful for catalogs or lists of objects of a single category (e.g., coins) but run into great difficulties with more complicated catalogs. For example, a table including both pottery and metalwork would contain many variables that were not applicable to one or the other. The inclusion of further information, such as the context of each find, could lead to much unnecessary repetition if there were more than one find from each context, which there usually is.

A more elaborate structure is, therefore, necessary. Various models are possible, such

as the hierarchical model and the network model, but the relational model has been the most successful in matching the complexities of archaeological data. This model breaks the data down into the smallest possible tables. For example, it would break down a catalog of excavated pottery sherds, in which the ceramic variables are fabric and form (shape), into one table of context descriptions, one of fabric descriptions, one of form descriptions, and one describing the relationships among them (i.e., the occurrences of different fabric/form combinations in different contexts). Pairs of tables link to each other through a common variable (or field)—context description and occurrence link through context number; fabric description and occurrence link through fabric code; and so on. It is thus possible to link any table with any other, either directly or through intermediate table(s). This enables the archaeologist to examine any relationship of interest, such as between different types of contexts (e.g., pits, floors) and different shapes of pottery vessels (e.g., jars, bowls, plates), making it an extremely useful tool. The use of a common high-level language known as SQL (search, and/or structured, query language) ensures some sort of compatibility between different packages, though not, of course, between different archaeologists.

It is clearly desirable to add a graphical capability to such databases. An archaeologist may wish, say, to plot on a site plan the occurrences of a particular pottery fabric or to find a pottery shape that matches a certain specimen. Geographic Information Systems (GIS) have begun to provide the former, but the latter is more difficult: Retrieval of the shape of a specified type is, in principle, straightforward, but to match a specimen against a database of shapes is much more difficult—what, for example, constitutes a match? How exact must it be? What if part is missing? These and similar questions provoke continued research into database structures. For example, the advantages and disadvantages of Object-Oriented (OO) databases are under discussion. Also, archaeology has data structures and types that are not thought to exist in areas of commercial interest. An example are the latticelike structures of Harris matrices, although these may, in fact, logically relate to PERT (Project Evaluation and Review Techniques) charts. Archaeologists have, therefore, thought it necessary to devise their own ways of handling such structures.

Uses

The uses of databanks in archaeology are as wide and diverse as archaeology itself. At one extreme, many archaeologists maintain small personal databanks for a variety of purposes. Perhaps the most common type is the bibliography, which they can search to find publications on a particular topic, or by a particular author, and can extract from it to create reference sections to their own publications, without the need for extensive retyping. Also common are catalogs of artifacts of a type of especial interest to the archaeologist, which may one day form the basis of the publication of a corpus of that class of artifact. In universities, teachers often maintain teaching databanks to give students practice in database manipulation and/or statistical analysis.

Moving up in scale, a modern archaeological field unit (which may vary in size from one individual to more than 100) is likely to maintain a databank of several databases relating to its activities. Each excavation will have its own database, with information about the site, its contexts, features, and finds, and it should be able to relate to those of other excavations through a common terminology and data structure. Specialist reports and the results of scientific analyses can relate to the main database as additional tables. The results of field surveys (fieldwalking and scientific prospecting) may require a more extensive approach, with emphasis on the geography, geology, and topography of an area—data well suited to the use of GIS packages. Such organizations may well have to provide, probably on a regular basis, information for feeding into databanks held more centrally (see below). The ability to produce the required data in the required format can save much effort.

Finally, there are the large central organizations that maintain large databanks, partly for their own use and partly as a service to the public and the archaeological profession. For some, the archaeological aspects may be coincidental to their main activity, while for others it will be their *raison d'être*. Their use is being encouraged by the creation of "gateway" organizations, such as the Archaeology Data Service (ADS) in the UK, which seek to provide a common and integrated means of access to such databanks, as well as themselves archiving 'orphan' databases. In many countries, there are regional registers of archaeological sites and monuments (in Britain, Sites and Monuments Records, or SMRs). Although their main function is to provide information for administrative purposes, such as planning control, they can also serve as resources for archaeological research. Such bodies often provide data to, and receive data from, national organizations, such as the National Archaeological Record (NAR) in England. These fulfill a variety of functions, providing information on demand to individuals, museums, archaeological, educational, and commercial organizations. They provide access to their databases by a variety of means, including public-access computer terminals, online services via public computer networks, and computer printouts ordered and delivered by postal service. There are also more specialized organizations that provide information that is likely to be useful only to archaeologists, such as bibliographic information (e.g., the British and Irish Archaeological Bibliography) and databanks of radiocarbon dates.

Clive Orton

See also COMPUTER SIMULATION; COMPUTERS IN ARCHAEOLOGY; GEOGRAPHIC INFORMATION SYSTEMS

Further Readings

Cleere, H., ed. (1989) Archaeological Heritage Management in the Modern World. London: Unwin Hyman.

Cooper, M., Firth, A., Carman, J., and Wheatley, D., eds. (1995) Managing Archaeology. London: Routledge.

Gaines, S.W., ed. (1981) Data Bank Applications in Archaeology. Tucson: University of Arizona Press.

Larsen, C.U., ed. (1992) Sites and Monuments. National Archaeological Records. Copenhagen: National Museum of Denmark.

Martlew, R., ed. (1984) Information Systems in Archaeology. Gloucester: Alan Sutton.

Reilly, R., and Rahtz, S.P.Q., eds. (1992) Archaeology and the Information Age: A Global Perspective. London: Routledge.

Voorrips, A., ed. (1990) Mathematics and Information Sciences in Archaeology: A Flexible Framework. Bonn: Holos.

Computer Simulation

The imitation of a process, undertaken to expand understanding of that process. Although the imitation usually takes place on a computer, other media (e.g., board games) can function in the same way. This entry deals only with computer simulations, the main advantage of which, compared to other media, is their vastly greater speed, so that they now dominate the field. There are three broad categories: *graphical simulation, statistical simulation* and *system simulation.*

The first consists of two- and three-dimensional graphical techniques that seek to enhance understanding by giving a visual impression of data or of a process. They are closely allied to data-visualization techniques and may take the form of computer games that imitate an archaeological activity (e.g., the excavation simulation game Sygraf). The development of virtual-reality computer technology may open up new possibilities of much closer approximations to reality, but, at present (1998), the costs seem prohibitive.

The second category, statistical simulation, imitates observations that derive from a statistical process, such as a frequency distribution of a variable, to answer an archaeological question. In problems involving the study of frequency distributions (e.g., in comparing dates from radiocarbon determinations), it is best to use an analytical solution (i.e., one that can be calculated directly) if at all possible. However, a frequency distribution may be so complicated that this is not possible, as in the case of calibrated radiocarbon dates; it is then necessary to build up a frequency distribution by creating many artificial observations (using a computer's facility for generating random numbers) and observing the pattern that they create. Statisticians refer to such techniques as *Monte Carlo* methods.

The third category, system simulation, is the one that archaeologists usually think of as computer simulation. The archaeologist creates a model of a system of interest (see below) and runs the model to observe its behavior and outcomes. There is usually a built-in *stochastic* (chance) element, so that the outcomes are not identical but create a pattern of possible outcomes. The archaeologist can vary the parameters of the model to see what effect they have on the outcome, hoping to find which affect the outcome seriously and which relatively little and whether there are limiting values that have to be respected for a successful outcome (e.g., survival). In principle, such results can yield valuable insights into the operation of past ways of life that cannot be directly observed (e.g., Mesolithic foraging). At the very least, the intellectual effort and discipline needed to create the model and put it into operation can be a valuable educational process, even if the apparent results are meager.

The use of computer simulation in archaeology started in the 1960s, following its successful use in other disciplines (e.g., in studying the spread of epidemics or the mechanics of bird navigation). It was strongly advocated and practiced in the 1970s and was closely related to the systems theory and processual approaches to archaeology. In general, it has not lived up to its early promise, although recently there have been some useful studies (Boismier 1997). Small, well-defined, and specific projects have fared much better than large ambitious ones. Archaeologists have at times wasted resources by resorting to computer simulation when it was not necessary or have floundered in a sea of computer printout, since the need to carry out many runs at each chosen combination of the parameters leads to vast numbers of results. It has also been found that the simple imitation of a process may not tell very much about that process. Other techniques, such as *expert systems* and *artificial intelligence,* have encroached on computer simulation's territory, though whether they have been any more successful is open to debate. Finally, the shift from *processual* to *postprocessual* archaeology in the 1980s has removed much of the driving force behind the approach. This may, in fact, be for the good of simulation, as it is now likely to be used only when really appropriate, rather than as a fashionable tool.

Methodology

There are five stages in computer simulation: *hypothesis conceptualization, model construction, computer implementation, hypothesis validation,* and *publication.*

The first task is to express mathematically the archaeological question that one is asking. Just as any model is a simplification of the real world, so any simulation (which is really just a model in action) is also a simplification. The best advice is to keep it simple and to add complexity only if and when it is absolutely necessary.

To construct a model, archaeologists must decide which variables to include and which to omit, how much to allow each to vary, how many different values of each to consider, how the variables relate to each other, and whether there should be any feedback mechanisms. They must avoid the temptation to try every possible combination of different values of variables just to see what happens. The number of such combinations rapidly escalates, and, although a computer may be able to cope, the archaeologist probably cannot. There is a great danger of not being able to see the forest for the trees because of the sheer volume of computer output.

The writing of the simulation program itself is a relatively straightforward part of the task. Specialized computer languages are available (e.g., Lisp), but the programs can be written in general-purpose languages such as C, FORTRAN, or PASCAL. It is more important in many programs to make sure that the code is as efficient (i.e., runs as fast) as possible. The program will be performing the same calculations hundreds, if not thousands, of times, and time wasted on one particular operation will swiftly multiply. The program needs to use a *random-number generator* to create the necessary variation among the runs of the simulation. Strictly speaking, such generators create *pseudorandom numbers,* which repeat themselves in a very long cycle. Often this does not matter, but, because a simulation program requires very many random numbers, an inadequate generator may create strange or unreliable results. Archaeologists may well need to seek expert advice. Before starting, they should try to estimate the number of runs they will need to achieve an appropriate level of precision in the estimates of parameters. Shortcut techniques are sometimes available to help reduce this number.

The greatest danger in the validation of hypotheses is probably complacency. If the data that have been created by running a simulation program match those observed in the archaeological record (e.g., as checked by a *goodness-of-fit test*), that does not mean that the model underlying the simulation is true. It is perfectly possible that other models could have given rise to similar results. Statisticians sometimes call this problem *equifinality*—the same answers deriving from different starting points.

Finally, it is important to publish enough information to enable a reader to replicate the experiment (because that is what a simulation is) exactly. Otherwise, there is no way of telling that the results are genuine and not a product of a computer error or even the archaeologist's imagination. Simulation is an experiment and, therefore, should be both repeatable (i.e., by the same person) and reproducible (i.e., by someone else). This implies publishing either the name or the algorithm of the random-number generator and also its starting point, or *seed.*

Case Study

An example of a modern computer simulation is Steven Mithen's program MESO-SIM, with which he simulates Mesolithic foraging to produce hypothetical assemblages of animal bones to compare with excavated assemblages. In his model, a group of hunters forages from one site for a fixed number of days and for a fixed number of visits to the site. Each day, the foragers hunt individually, using the *encounter* method. They make decisions as to whether to stalk a particular species on a probabilistic basis (e.g., if such a stalk was unsuccessful yesterday, the forager is less likely to stalk it if encountered today). The encounter with a species is based on chance, with the chance varying according to the number of that species present at the start and how much they become depleted. There are twelve parameters: four relate to the size of the group (including number of days per trip); three relate to the environment (including its initial richness and how quickly the game is scared away); four relate to the process of retaining and sharing information; and one relates to the hunting goals of the forager.

Criticisms focus on the lack of cultural or personal preferences for a particular prey or for a particular locality. For example, the decision in the simulation to stay at a locality is based solely on the availability of food, leading to the criticism that environmental determinism has too strong an influence on the model. Nevertheless, from the simulation, Mithen concluded that some assemblages show a risk-reducing strategy by some foragers, and (as of 1998) work continued.

Clive Orton

See also COMPUTER DATABANKS IN ARCHAEOLOGY; COMPUTERS IN ARCHAEOLOGY; STATISTICAL METHODS IN ARCHAEOLOGY

Further Readings

Boismier, W.A. (1997) Modelling the Effects of Tillage Processes on Artefact Distributions in the Ploughzone. (BAR British Series 259). Oxford: British Archaeological Reports.

Doran, J.E. (1970) Systems theory, computer simulations, and archaeology. World Archaeology 1:289–298.

Freeman, P. (1988) How to simulate if you must. In C.L.N. Ruggles and S.P.Q. Rahtz (eds.): Computer Applications and Quantitative Methods in Archaeology 1987, (BAR International Series 393). pp. 139–146. Oxford: British Archaeological Reports.

Hodder, I.R., ed. (1978) Simulation Studies in Archaeology. Cambridge: Cambridge University Press.

Mithen, S.J. (1988) Simulation as a methodological tool: Inferring hunting goals from faunal assemblages. In C.L.N. Ruggles and S.P.Q. Rahtz (eds.): Computer and Quantitative Methods in Archaeology, 1987, (BAR International Series 393) pp. 119–137. Oxford: British Archaeological Reports.

Mithen, S.J. (1990) Thoughtful Foragers: A Study of Prehistoric Decision Making. Cambridge/New York: Cambridge University Press.

Sabloff, J.A., ed. (1981) Simulations in Archaeology. Albuquerque: University of New Mexico Press.

Wheatley, D. (1991) Sygraf: Resource-based teaching with graphics. In K. Lockyear and S.P.Q. Rahtz (eds.): Computer Applications and Quantitative Methods in Archaeology 1990, (BAR International Series 565). Oxford: British Archaeological Reports.

Computers in Archaeology

Covers an expanding range of ways in which archaeologists use computers for a wide variety of archaeological purposes. The uses include numerical and statistical analysis, word and data processing, storage and manipulation of graphical data, and hyper- and multimedia techniques; the capture, storage, retrieval, analysis, publication, and other means of dissemination of data collected from many sources, including results of scientific analyses and methods of prospection, catalogs and descriptions of artifacts, and records of excavations and field surveys. Other uses include, communications, education, and the reconstruction of buildings and monuments. The main outlet for publication is the annual series of proceedings of the conference Computer Applications in Archaeology (1974 onward); also, there are (or have been) specialist newsletters; including the *Newsletter for Computer Archaeology* (1965–1979), *Advances in Computer Archaeology* (1983–1987), and *Archaeological Computing Newsletter* (1984–), and, more recently, the journal *Archaeologia e Calcolatori* (1990–). Many mainstream archaeological journals (e.g., *American Antiquity, Archaeometry, Journal of Archaeological Science, Journal of Field Archaeology*) publish relevant papers, and the use of computers in archaeology is now so widespread that few archaeological reports, if any, do not have a computer involved somewhere in their production.

History

The introduction and spread of the use of computers in archaeology has followed a pattern of four waves, each reflecting different and growing perceptions of the role of computers. They are: *mathematical and statistical analysis* (number crunching), *text handling* (word processing and databases), *graphical applications,* and *integrative approaches* (multi-media). Successive waves have not replaced earlier ones but have added to them and enhanced them.

The earliest use of computers in archaeology appears to date to the late 1950s and to have been concerned with the analysis of scientific data. The 1960s were a period of experimentation, which often built on techniques that existed before the introduction of computers. In line with general trends, archaeologists saw computers as high-speed calculators, performing complex or tedious mathematical tasks and making many of them (e.g., multivariate statistical analysis) accessible to them for the first time. It was common at that time to store data on external media, such as paper tape or punched cards, and feed them into a computer for analysis.

Improvements in the technology for storing data on computers (magnetic tape, floppy disks, and hard disks) throughout the 1970s and into the 1980s led to increasing interest in the use of computers to store, sort, and retrieve data. The metaphor for the computer shifted from the calculator to the intelligent filing cabinet or card-index system, bringing in a wider range of users.

It was the advent of the personal computer (PC) in the early 1980s that transformed the computer from a narrow specialization to a working tool for archaeologists. They quickly appreciated the benefits of word processing for writing reports and of database programs for storing and retrieving information, although sometimes initially in a rather disjointed way.

Experimentation in the graphical potential of computers for archaeology (the third wave) began in the 1970s but remained small scale for some time because of the computer power and storage that it required and the difficulty of use of the early software. Since archaeology is a very visual subject, there was a clear need for ways of handling visual data at a variety of scales—distribution maps, site plans and diagrams, drawings of finds, magnified images of, for example, pottery thin-sections and traces of use-wear on flint. Early uses included the rectification of oblique aerial photographs. It took the greatly increased power and storage capabilities of computers in the late 1980s, combined with affordable specialist software, to make computer graphics a practical tool for archaeologists. The software was of types known as (1) computer-aided design (CAD), used by engineers and architects and used in archaeology particularly for site and finds drawing (see below), and as (2) geographic information systems (GIS), used by government bodies and utilities and used in archaeology for regional information and studies such as settlement patterns (see below). Further developments, such as solid modeling, also appeared to have archaeological potential (see below).

The ever-widening roles of computers in archaeology, together with the growing range of software used to fulfill these roles, exposed inefficiencies in the way archaeologists deal with the many aspects that go to make up their reports. At about the same time came the realization that the computer need not mimic the typewriter in producing linear text, intended to be read from beginning to end. Instead, the text could take a more flexible structure, with opportunities for readers to branch off (or not) into areas of special interest, to repeat areas of difficulty, and to gener-

ally choose their own way of accessing archaeological data and discussion, rather than follow a unique path laid down by the author. This is the *hypertext* approach; combined with its ability to include graphical as well as textual information, it is revolutionizing the way in which archaeologists perceive and present their information. It enables them to integrate the many aspects of their work, so that, for example, the entire record of an excavation—structures, stratigraphy, finds catalogs and drawings—can be browsed in many different exploratory ways, according to the needs of the reader. It is even possible to include sound and clips of video (true multimedia). This is a rapidly developing field in which practice is varied and standards, as yet, are few.

Uses Today

The most common use today is undoubtedly word processing, followed by spreadsheet and database applications. Spreadsheets are a valuable tool for storing and analyzing tables of data, especially if most of the data are numerical. Spreadsheets have a wide use when the full relational power of a database is not needed, and they can offer a simple introduction to statistical analysis and graphical presentation. Next come graphical applications, such as CAD and GIS, and statistical analysis. Finally, there is a range of more specialized techniques, such as expert systems, image analysis, solid modeling, and educational uses. Even word processing has evolved from the straightforward production of typescripts by a process of vertical integration into areas that were formerly part of publishing. Desktop publishing (DTP) software has enabled archaeologists to design reports in a form suitable for reproduction, including graphics as well as text, and, in many cases, to publish them themselves. While potentially reducing costs, this has demanded additional skills (e.g., in graphic design) that not all archaeologists possess, leading to variable results. It has also led to a proliferation of short-run monographs and series, making it more difficult for archaeologists to maintain an overview of the literature and for libraries to offer comprehensive coverage. To some extent, the parallel development of bibliographic services has redressed the balance.

The next step is to dispense with paper ("hard copy") altogether and distribute information via computer networks such as the

Internet. Archaeologists already make extensive use of such systems for routine correspondence and administrative matters such as arranging meetings and symposia and announcing conferences, using e-mail. A logical development is the electronic journal (such as *Internet Archaeology),* which distributes entire papers and reports in this way. This is faster than conventional journal publication, and readers can access those reports that appear to be of interest to them (the serious readership of any one paper in a journal may be very low compared to the journal's circulation). The difficulties of intellectual property rights, such as copyright, plagiarism and misrepresentation, and issues of quality control (such as refereeing), may be serious obstacles to this development.

CAD

Although it originated in fields far removed from archaeology, archaeologists quickly recognized the relevance of computer-aided design for their work. The revolution in excavation recording techniques that followed the adoption of the Harris matrix as a model for site structure meant that it was, in principle, possible to re-create an excavated site in three dimensions, including the construction of plans and sections in any location that was relevant for interpretation or exposition, rather than imposed by the initial excavation strategy. CAD provided the necessary technology, and packages such as Autocad became an essential tool for the archaeological draughtsperson. Such techniques are equally suitable for the study of ruins and standing buildings. They can bring together plans and elevations into coordinated three-dimensional drawings, which the archaeologist can observe from different angles to discover the best view for analysis or presentation. Another area in which CAD can make a valuable contribution is the analysis of very large sites (e.g., towns) where excavations have taken place over many years or under the auspices of different organizations. Provided that archaeologists can locate "old" excavations on the ground, they can integrate those old results with their own to create an overall picture of the site. Having produced a three-dimensional record of a site or a building, the next step is to reconstruct the missing parts. Again, CAD can be very useful, allowing the archaeologist to extrapolate partial features, populate postholes with posts, and experiment with height and roofing. Links with engineering packages could check on the feasibility of such reconstructions.

Solid Modeling

As CAD techniques developed, it became possible to render surfaces, (i.e., to give them color, texture, and shading). This enabled archaeologists (those with access to the expensive hardware and software) to produce reconstructions of buildings that looked more or less like buildings rather than architects' drawings. Increasing computer power permitted walk throughs of such buildings to be made, with the long-term aim (not yet achieved) of their being both photorealistic and interactive (i.e., the user rather than the designer should choose the route through the building and even the ambient conditions (e.g., lighting effects). Archaeologists cannot expect to be at the forefront of such developments, but they can expect to benefit from them, especially as the cost of computing power continues to decrease.

Education

Archaeologists have begun to appreciate the value of modern computer techniques such as simulation, solid modeling, hypertext, and multimedia methods for education, both of students in university courses and of the general public in museums and visitor centers. Simulation games such as Sygraf can teach the principles of excavation management without damage to real sites, while graphical techniques can make rare or fragile material available to far more students than would be possible if teachers had to rely on museum visits, and, again, without risk of damage. Hypertext allows students to explore evidence in an open-ended way and to develop their own strategies for learning, in contrast to more formal methods. However, serious evaluation of the benefits has yet to take place in archaeology.

Communication

The computer is rapidly becoming a standard means of communication, both within and between archaeological organizations, as well as between archaeologists and remote databases and other sources of information, such as can be found via the World Wide Web (WWW). Trends in integrating computer technology with those of mobile telephones and Global Positioning Systems (GPS) are likely to lead to the use of small portable devices for recording data in the field and transmitting them to base.

Applications for Future Development

Expert Systems

Expert systems are an attempt to use computers to organize knowledge (in contrast to simply data) to make it accessible to, and usable by, nonspecialists. It is closely related to *artificial intelligence* (AI), which seeks to imitate human reasoning and improve on its practical imperfections. Archaeological interest in these areas started early (in the 1970s, under the influence of James E. Doran) but, despite much work in the 1980s, there has been little progress, at least in comparison to other disciplines (e.g., medical diagnosis). Because of the shortage of specialists in certain closely defined areas (e.g., the study of some classes of fine and highly decorated pottery such as samian ware) and the consequent problem of bottlenecks in the production of reports, viable expert systems in such areas would be extremely valuable. So far, however, this approach has not lived up to its early promise.

Image Analysis

Image Analysis is similar to spatial analysis but is carried out on a smaller, often microscopic, scale. A typical problem is the characterization of the traces of wear caused on a flint tool by different sorts of activities (e.g., scraping hides, chopping wood). Archaeologists can replicate such activities experimentally, examine the resulting wear microscopically, and characterize the traces mathematically. The resulting descriptions can be matched against archaeological examples to suggest the purpose(s) for which their makers may have used them. This is a great improvement on the previous very subjective and unreproducible descriptions of the visual characteristics of wear-induced damage.

Another example is the characterization of the texture of ceramic fabrics in order to match material with specimens of known sources. It is very difficult for a ceramic specialist to say which characteristics determine a particularly distinctive texture and even harder to convey this to another archaeologist. The extraction of objective parameters of texture is, therefore, useful.

Archaeologists have relied on techniques developed for other subjects, such as the analysis of satellite images (itself a subject of growing archaeological interest), for both the enhancement and the analysis of their images. Fractal geometry has also shown promise as a way of characterizing texture, but its computing needs are very high.

Conclusions

The uses described above show that to study archaeology today without the use of computers is almost unthinkable and that, in the future, they can make an even bigger contribution. There are perhaps related drawbacks: Archaeologists may become so absorbed in computer representations *(virtual archaeology)* that they lose contact with the physical reality of their subject—real objects, soils, human activity, and the like. Another risk is the marginalization of archaeologists who, for whatever reason, cannot gain access to the latest technology or to information networks.

A major problem that archaeology shares with all other disciplines is that of the maintenance of its computer-based material, both data and software. Many archaeological data are held on media (floppy disks and magnetic tape) that are becoming progressively harder to read as hardware is upgraded to new standards: It is rare for archival material to be upgraded to be compatible with new hardware. Eventually, it will be impossible to access this material. Archaeologists encountered a similar problem when they upgraded from punched cards and/or paper tape to magnetic media. In general, the data were transferred while equipment to read the old media was still available, but the quantities of data then were very small in comparison to those in archives today. Software, too, must be maintained and upgraded as hardware is upgraded, or it will not be possible to use it. It will be necessary to devote a growing proportion of the total resources available to computer archaeology to these two problems in the future.

Clive Orton

See also COMPUTER DATABANKS IN ARCHAE-
OLOGY; COMPUTER SIMULATION; GEO-
GRAPHIC INFORMATION SYSTEMS; SPATIAL
ANALYSIS; STATISTICAL METHODS IN
ARCHAEOLOGY

Further Readings

Doran, J.E. and Hodson, F.R. (1975) Mathematics and Computers in Archaeology.
Edinburgh: Edinburgh University Press.

Johnson, I., ed. (1994) Method in the Mountains. Sydney University Archaeological
Methods Series, 2.

Moscati, P. (1987) Archeologia e calcolatori.
Firenze: Giunti.

Reilly, P. (1988) Data Visualisation: Recent
Advances in the Application of Graphic
Systems to Archaeology. Winchester:
IBM UK Scientific Centre.

Reilly, R., and Rahtz, S.P.Q., eds. (1992) Archaeology and the Information Age: A
Global Perspective. London: Routledge.

Richards, J.D., ed. (1986) Computer Usage in
British Archaeology. (Occasional Paper
1) Birmingham: Institute of Field
Archaeologists.

Richards, J.D., and Ryan, N.S. (1985) Data
Processing in Archaeology. Cambridge:
Cambridge University Press.

Ryan, N.S. (1988) Bibliography of computer applications and quantitative
methods. In S.P.Q. Rahtz (ed.): Computer and Quantitative Methods in Archaeology 1988, (BAR International Series 446). Oxford: British
Archaeological Reports.

Scollar, I. (1982) Thirty years of computer archaeology and the future. In S. Laflin
(ed.): Computer Applications in Archaeology 1982, pp. 189–198. Birmingham:
Centre for Computing and Computer
Science, University of Birmingham.

Conkey, Margaret Wright (1944–)

American archaeologist and anthropologist.
Born in 1944, Conkey received her doctorate
from the University of Chicago and is a professor of anthropology at the University of
California at Berkeley. A specialist in prehistoric archaeology, Conkey is well known for
her studies of the Upper Palaeolithic in Europe and the meaning of cave art. She has examined the problem of painted caves as the
meeting sites of hunter-gatherer groups and
has joined the growing number of scholars
who see the diversity of Upper Palaeolithic
cave art as evidence of a broad cultural meaning and economic function, as opposed to primarily aesthetic and stylistic analyses of art
historians. Her anthropological approach to
prehistoric art has also put her in the forefront of the movement in anthropological archaeology to redefine and reexamine the role
of stylistic studies of material culture, suggesting, counter to traditional notions, that
style tells us not about cultures or groups but
about the production processes and behaviors, through which we can reconstruct the
contexts by which group phenomena are mo-
bilized *(The Uses of Style in Archaeology)*.
Conkey is most noted, however, for her work
in feminist anthropology and archaeological
theory and her attempts, along with other
prominent female scholars, to better understand the roles of women in prehistoric societies, roles that had, for the most part, been
ignored by male scholars over the 150-year
course of prehistoric archaeology. Her volume with Joan Gero, *Engendering Archaeology: Women and Prehistory,* has become a
standard introduction to feminist theory as it
pertains to human prehistory.

Joseph J. Basile

See also GENDER ARCHAEOLOGY

Further Readings

Conkey, M.W. and Hastorf, C.A. (1990) The
Uses of Style in Archaeology. Cam-
bridge/New York: Cambridge University
Press.

Gero, J.M. and Conkey, M.W., eds. (1991)
Engendering Archaeology: Women and
Prehistory. Oxford/Cambridge, Mass.:
Blackwell.

Conservation of Archaeological Materials

The subdiscipline of conservation that provides skilled, knowledgeable, and ethical care
for the material products of past cultures. As
the tangible remnants of past societies reflecting the ideas, beliefs, and activities of those
societies, archaeological collections provide a
unique record of past human behavior and
can be regarded as primary documents of
human behavior. As such, they are valuable
sources of information, and the approach to
their conservation treatment will, of necessity,

differ from more traditional approaches. Preservation, or stabilization, rather than restoration should be the primary and ethical aim of archaeological conservation. Intervention should be kept to a minimum, and, whenever possible, nonintrusive procedures should be employed, since intervention can lessen the research potential of these objects. In treating archaeological materials, it must be kept in mind that each subsequent treatment moves the artifact further away from its original state.

Archaeological materials are collected through modern excavation techniques. Photographs and written records document their methodical retrieval and associations. Together with this documentation, the objects form a valuable systematic research collection in which the material as a whole takes on a significance far beyond the importance of a single object within the collection. The potential research and information value of the collection becomes of paramount importance. Thus, archaeological collections differ from other collections in that it is not what the objects are that sets them apart, but rather the manner in which they are collected and used.

The philosophy and practice of archaeological conservation must reflect this fundamental difference of archaeological collections and be compatible with the nature and use of the collections. At all times, the integrity and research potential of the object and the collection must be kept in mind. The goal of conservation should be to stabilize and preserve the collection without destroying any valuable data embodied in the objects. Preservation of the artifact is not necessarily restricted to just the appearance of the object or the original material of which it is made. The technological information embodied in the object, (e.g., repairs or modifications made during use in antiquity) is part of the total information that can be obtained from the study of artifacts and must be preserved.

Conservation is concerned with the overall preservation of artifacts. It consists of two main functions: *preservation* and *restoration*. The goal of preservation is to stabilize, or arrest, damage to, and deterioration of, artifacts. It usually involves controlling the immediate environment around objects and the conditions of their use but can also involve treatment when done to stabilize an object. In contrast, the purpose of restoration, a term frequently used interchangeably with conservation, is to return an object to its original or previous appearance. Restoration involves the carefully considered modification of the material and structure of an object. While generally done for exhibition or educational purposes to aid the interpretive process, restoration can also be used to stabilize an artifact.

Conservators specializing in archaeological conservation share a common background with conservators in other subdisciplines. In many countries, the work of conservators is governed by established codes of ethics. For any conservator, the underlying precept that guides all conservation work is respect for the integrity of the object, aesthetic, historic, and physical. For archaeological materials, historic and physical integrity are perhaps of greater concern than the aesthetic. The history of an artifact should be preserved and not sacrificed in order to return the object to its original condition or to restore it solely for monetary reasons. For example, if a pot was repaired with rivets during use in antiquity, such modifications should not be removed today, no matter how unsightly they may be. Respect for the integrity of an object also involves not imposing upon the artifact the conservator's own cultural values by making assumptions on how it should look, a point discussed more fully below.

Conservation procedures involve examination, analysis of materials used to make artifacts, active treatment involving stabilization and restoration, passive treatment involving environmental controls, and documentation. Three basic principles govern the work of an archaeological conservator: *reversibility, minimum intervention,* and *documentation*.

Traditionally, *reversibility* was regarded as an important principle governing any conservation treatment. Reversibility means that any treatment applied to an object must be reversible (i.e., capable of being reversed or removed at a later date with no resulting damage or change to the object). The idea of reversibility of treatment developed out of a recognition that conservation knowledge is constantly expanding. Conservators are aware that treatments thought to be the best today may be improved upon tomorrow or be found to be deleterious. Also, tomorrow's analytical methods will far surpass those available today, enabling us to extract new information from artifacts as long as they have not been compromised today by conservation treatment.

Archaeologists realize now that some treatments, by their very nature, are not reversible. For example, if an object has lost so much of its cohesiveness that it cannot be lifted out of the ground safely, it may be necessary to strengthen it with a consolidant even though this process is known to be not fully reversible. While reversibility can no longer be regarded as a principle, it remains a goal of conservation treatment and, as such, has a direct bearing on conservation practice. The concept of reversibility is of particular importance to on-site conservation because one is often forced to carry out procedures under less than ideal conditions. What is done in the field, more often than not, has to be redone in the laboratory before further treatment can be undertaken.

The concept of reversibility ensures that the conservator's choice of materials to be added to artifacts is made carefully. Only certain materials are considered acceptable for conservation use. These materials are of good quality and have withstood the test of time and reversibility. Whenever possible, conservators choose pure materials over their proprietary equivalents, which almost certainly contain additives to extend the shelf life of the substance or modify its properties. These additives are usually trade secrets that the manufacturer will not divulge. Conservators like to know exactly what it is they are adding to an object, since it could be significant, adversely affecting not only the preservation of the object, but its research potential as well.

Minimal intervention, a corollary of reversibility, is a more realistic concept for guiding conservation work. The treatment undertaken should not be more extensive than absolutely necessary. Thus, often the best treatment is the least treatment, leaving the artifact as close as possible to its original condition. If an object appears to be sound and has a good chance of survival without having anything done to it, then nothing at all should be done. While at times it may be difficult to refrain from undertaking treatment, generally restoration, for the sake of treatment, this urge must always be resisted.

When treatment is necessary, the conservation materials applied to an artifact should be used to the least possible extent so as to alter the artifact as little as possible. Only the smallest quantities needed to ensure the preservation of the object should be used. Minimal intervention is particularly important when treatment could alter or destroy technological information or analytical results.

Documentation is a vital part of any conservation treatment. Careful written and photographic records should clearly document all technological information learned about an object during treatment. They must also fully and accurately describe the materials and methods involved in treatment. These records then become an integral part of the archaeological collection and, along with all other records, must be made permanently available to future researchers and conservators.

Minimal intervention and full documentation take on particular importance when treating objects that may be used for analysis. It must always be kept in mind that any treatment an object receives, including mere cleaning, can contaminate it and invalidate any subsequent analysis, whether it be for dating purposes or elemental analysis. While conservators aspire to reversibility, they recognize that no treatment is fully reversible. Most of the added material can be removed so that the treatment may no longer be visible, but traces will always remain in the artifact, compromising it for later analysis. For this reason, it is best not to treat artifacts that will be used for analysis. At the very least, part of the artifact should be left untreated or samples taken before treatment.

The addition of foreign materials to an artifact is not the only way in which conservation treatment can invalidate the research potential of an object. Frequently, valuable information is embodied in the dirt or encrustations on the surface of an object. Thus, the removal of any material from the surface of an object can be just as damaging as adding material. Even handling can compromise future analytical work, as is the case, for example, with samples taken for carbon-14 dating.

Since the 1980s, the emphasis of conservation efforts for all kinds of collections, not just archaeological ones, has moved away from the active treatment of objects. Passive conservation techniques, referred to as *preventive conservation,* are now widely used. The concept underlying this approach is that

deterioration can be reduced by controlling its causes. Thus, through proper handling, collection maintenance, and controlling the environment in which collections are stored, studied, and exhibited, it is possible to stabilize large assemblages of objects. By preventing deterioration from taking place, the need for active treatment is considerably reduced.

Preventive conservation is in keeping with the overall approach to archaeological conservation discussed above. The collection as a whole, rather than the treatment of any individual artifact within it, becomes the emphasis of preservation. Passive techniques provide the only practical means of doing this, particularly in museums with large, diverse archaeological collections.

While most of the active treatment in archaeological conservation should be done by a trained conservator, preventive-conservation techniques can be undertaken by the archaeologist. In fact, archaeologists, especially when on site, can do the most for the preservation of their assemblages by using passive techniques. By instituting proper handling procedures, needless breakage and damage can be prevented. The natural deterioration processes of materials can be avoided or reduced by ensuring that artifacts are properly packed with appropriate materials.

Examination is just as important an aspect of archaeological conservation as stabilization and restoration. This investigative work enables archaeological conservators to develop an understanding of the technology involved in fabricating an artifact. The goal of such examination is to extract as much information as possible from artifacts to assist the archaeologist with important research questions concerning technology, provenance, and authenticity. A background in materials science, along with extensive experience in looking at a wide variety of materials and artifacts from different periods and locations, gives conservators the knowledge and skills to recognize materials and determine the components of artifacts. Their familiarity with materials analysis provides them with the means of performing simple tests to verify these identifications. While they cannot undertake sophisticated analytical tests, they understand the capabilities of different analytical techniques and can act as liaisons between archaeologists and appropriate analytical specialists.

Most archaeological conservators are knowledgeable about ancient technological procedures and are interested in how artifacts are made. With their specialized training, they are in a unique position to reveal information about objects that might otherwise be missed. For example, evidence of organic materials is frequently preserved by, or in, corrosion products on metal artifacts. In cleaning these artifacts, an experienced conservator can recognize this evidence, document, and preserve it. Chemical treatment on such an artifact by a nonconservator could destroy this information without its presence ever having been noted.

While examination is an important part of archaeological conservation, interpretation of observations should not be the central focus of the conservator. Certainly, conservators can bring an important perspective to this process and should participate in it, but the final interpretation should rest with the archaeologist.

While *restoration* is generally not an important aspect of archaeological conservation, there are times when it is appropriate. For example, by restoring the missing parts of an artifact, its educational, or interpretive, value can be increased by enabling the general public to relate to it better. The approach to restoration, when done, must be in keeping with the principles of treatment discussed above. Restoration should be done as clearly and honestly as possible and be fully documented with photographs and written reports. A clear demarcation should be made between what is original and what is added by the conservator. No attempts should be made to make repairs or restorations invisible or to make the object appear to be in better condition than it actually is. Restorations do not have to be obtrusive when viewed from a distance of 10 feet (3m) or so, but they should be readily apparent on close examination. This is quite easy to do with the plaster restorations on pots by painting them a solid color that blends in with the overall surface of the vessel. Restorations on other materials, however, may be more difficult to differentiate. Replacement silver plaques on a Precolumbian bag, for example, may look just like the originals. In this instance, an engraved date on the back of each restored piece will give a clear indication that it is not original to the object.

In restoring objects, conservators must be very careful not to impose their own aesthetics, cultural values, or interpretation on them. In the past, restoration has been dictated at times by fashion. In the early decades of the twentieth century, it was the vogue to paint archaeological bronzes green to simulate the corrosion products of copper, even after the real corrosion products had been removed.

Missing elements, such as handles, should not be added unless there is clear evidence of what the shape should be and where it should be placed. As well, decoration should not be guessed at. Even though decoration may be repetitive and symmetrical, clear evidence must be present before large sections of it should be restored. If decoration or elements are asymmetrical, then no evidence is present to support restoration. Even if the artifact is one of a group, one cannot assume that it is just like the others. Restoration is a conservation procedure that requires the conservator to work very closely with the archaeologist to determine what can ethically be done with a restoration.

The conservation process is an integral part of archaeology and must be a collaborative exercise. The conservator must never work in a vacuum, but rather work closely with the archaeologist to develop efficient and meaningful strategies for preserving archaeological collections.

Catherine Sease

See also CERAMICS, ON-SITE CONSERVATION; FIBROUS MATERIALS, ON-SITE CONSERVATION; GLASS, ON-SITE CONSERVATION; IN SITU CONSERVATION; LEATHER, ON-SITE CONSERVATION; METALS, ON-SITE CONSERVATION; MOSAICS, ON-SITE CONSERVATION; STONE, ON-SITE CONSERVATION; WALL PAINTINGS, CONSERVATION; WOOD (WATERLOGGED), CONSERVATION

Further Readings

Cronyn, J.M. (1990) The Elements of Archaeological Conservation. London: Routledge.

Foley, K. (1995) The role of the objects conservator in field archaeology. In N.P. Stanley Price (ed.): Conservation on Archaeological Excavations, 2nd ed., pp. 11–20. Rome: International Center for the Study of the Preservation and Restoration of Cultural Property.

Pye, E., and Cronyn, J.M. (1987) The archaeological conservator reexamined: A personal view. In J. Black (ed.): Recent Advances in the Conservation and Analysis of Artifacts, pp. 355–357. London: Summer Schools Press.

Sease, C. (1994) A Conservation Manual for the Field Archaeologist, 4th ed. (Archaeological Research Tools 4). Los Angeles: Institute of Archaeology, UCLA.

Seeley, N.J. (1987) Archaeological conservation: The development of a discipline. Institute of Archaeology Bulletin 24:161–175.

Coprolite Analysis

The analysis of ancient human feces for dietary data. Although archaeological fieldwork is hot and dirty, the most "earthy" side of the discipline is the laboratory analysis of coprolites. Each coprolite contains the remains of one to several actual meals eaten in prehistory, and analysis of many coprolites provides a picture of ancient diet that is unique in accuracy.

What Is a Coprolite?

The term *coprolite* originally referred to fossilized feces in paleontological context. In archaeology, the term broadened to refer to any formed fecal mass, including mineralized, desiccated, or frozen feces and even the intestinal contents of mummies. Coprolites contain the remains of animals (parasites) that lived in the humans, the foods that humans ate, and the remains of animals that lived in the feces after defecation. The majority of recognizable remains consist of undigested or partly digested food residue. With the naked eye, one can identify plant cuticle, bark, seeds, fruit coats, fibers, animal bone, feathers, lizard and fish scales, mollusc shell, crustacean fragments, fish otoliths, insects, and other food items. Microscopic remains include parasites, pollen grains, phytoliths, other small plant structures, animal hair, fungal spores, diatoms, mites, and starch granules. In short, anything indigestible that people swallowed can be found. Beyond visual identification, chemical components of coprolites include proteins, lipids, steroids, carbon and nitrogen isotopes, and many major and trace elements.

Coprolites are most common in arid areas in the Americas. In North America, coprolites are most commonly found in the Mojave Desert, the Colorado Plateau, the Great Basin, and the Chihuahuan Desert of the western and southern portion of the continent. Central Mexican sites also contain coprolites. These have been studied from the Rio Zape Valley in Durango, Mexico, and from the Tehuacan Valley of Mexico. In South America, coprolites are most commonly found in the Atacama Desert of Chile and Peru, but finds have been made in Brazil. Coprolites have also been found at York, England, and Israel. Thus, coprolites are preserved in arid areas and, on occasion, in moist regions.

How Are Coprolites Studied?

Vaughn M. Bryant, Jr., Kristin Sobolik, and Karl Reinhard are the only full-time coprolite analysts at this time. They have built their work on that of the late Eric Callen, who was the first coprolite analyst and whose contributions are summarized by Bryant. It is these four individuals who have developed the techniques of analysis. Coprolites are first photographed, described, and then rehydrated. To answer a question that most people ask, coprolites do not usually smell. After rehydration, the coprolites are disaggregated and rinsed through a fine mesh to separate macroscopic from microscopic residues. The macroscopic remains are dried and separated into component parts visually or with a dissecting microscope. Different types of microscopic remains are separated by heavy-density flotation. Light materials, such as pollen and parasite eggs, float, and heavier components, such as phytoliths and larger plant fragments, sink. After examination for parasite eggs and other items of interest, the pollen is isolated from the light remains through chemical digestion in acetolysis solution. The heavier remains are collected and examined. Phytoliths are isolated through chemical digestion in hydrogen peroxide and potassium dichromate. The end results from processing any given coprolite are many vials containing different types of remains.

Informational Potential of Constituents

Macroscopic remains tell much about the species of plants eaten. Plant cuticle is essentially the epidermal layer of plant leaves and stems (Figure 1). The cell patterns of cuticles are sometimes distinctive to specific plants. It is possible to identify the major succulent plants in the Southwestern United States based on the cuticle. In other cases, plant cuticle is less informative and can be used to iden-

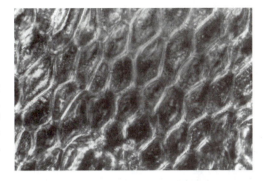

C

Figure 1. *Plant cuticle from Agave showing distinctive cell outlines. Photograph by Karl Reinhard.*

tify only plant families. Bark is outer plant tissue from woody species. It is especially difficult to identify because so few traits of bark are distinctive.

Seed coats pass through the digestive tract and are recognizable (Figure 2). The seeds are identifiable because the outer layer, called the *testa,* is very resilient, and almost every coprolite analysis reveals the consumption of seeds. Seeds, then, become an important source of comparative data. Seeds reveal different patterns of diet. In some cases, the seeds signal the consumption of fruits. For example, when whole prickly-pear seeds are found, it is usually from eating prickly-pear fruit. In other cases, the seeds represent selective harvesting of cultivated or wild species when the seeds are collected, winnowed, and make up the major portion of a meal. Seeds are often cooked, ground, or otherwise modified before consumption. Careful study of the seeds by Kate A. Rylander using scanning electron microscopy revealed the kinds of tools used to grind the seeds. Chemical analysis of the seeds also reveals how the seeds were boiled, parched, or cooked in some other way. Sometimes, the seeds are derived from fruits that are collected, dried, and mashed into a pulp (Figure 2). Again, scanning electron microscopy discloses these aspects of preparation. Seeds were such an important prehistoric food source that some cultures carried out "second harvests." This refers to the practice of sifting seeds out of old feces for consumption in times of famine. Fleshy fruits are also evident by the fruit coat called *pericarp,* or outer layer. Sometimes, the pericarp is distinctive enough for identification. Chili pericarp, for example, is identifiable in coprolites. However, the pericarp of

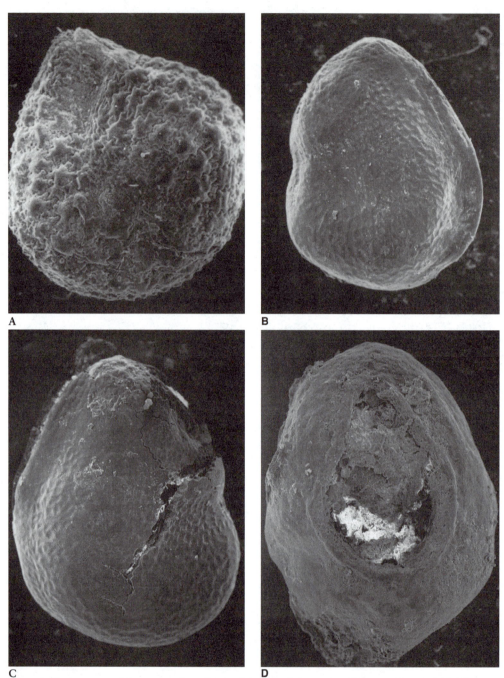

Figure 2. Seeds recovered from coprolites. (A) purslain (Portulaca spp.) seed from an Anasazi coprolite showing excellent preservation potential of unmodified seeds; (B) well-preserved saguaro cactus (Carnegia gigantea) seed from a Hohokam coprolite; (C) partly fragmented saguaro seed damaged by crushing; (D) hilum of saguaro seed damaged by crushing. Such severe damage to seeds was done by processing seeds separated from the fruit into a saguaro flour or by mashing preserved fruits into a prehistoric fruit peel. Photograph by Karl Reinhard.

other fruits is not distinctive. In these cases, examination of seeds in the same coprolite that contains pericarp may provide significant clues to the source of the fruit.

Fibers are difficult to identify, yet are common in coprolites. Fiber refers specifically to the stringlike strands of plant vascular tissue (Figure 3). Some fibers are distinctive—the fibers of mesquite (*Prospis glandulosa* and *P. pubescens*) are easily identifiable—but most are not. There are clues to the source of fiber from other plant components. Often, the plant cuticle or phytoliths found in a coprolite can be used to infer the origin of the fiber.

It is of interest that small fragments of charcoal can be found in coprolites. Even if the fragments are too tiny to allow identification of the source species, charcoal provides evidence of cooking practices. In Archaic times, for example, food was often cooked on parching trays in which food was swirled around with burning coals. This action results in the consumption of charcoal particles.

Small animals were commonly eaten by prehistoric peoples. Consequently, every coprolite study reveals animal remains such as bone, feather, shell, and exoskeleton. Bone has received the most attention, as summarized by Reinhard in 1992. The analysis of bone provides significant cultural information. In general, hunter-gatherers ate small animals more frequently than did horticulturalists. Different hunting strategies can also be analyzed by examining bone from coprolites. The diversity of animal remains, indicates the degree of specialization in hunting practices (Figure 4). The bone can also show which parts of the animals were most commonly eaten (Figure 5). Bone sometimes reflects processing of small animals; for example, fish bone in coprolites from southern Peru is typically ground but not burned. This indicates that ancient Peruvians ate fish paste that was made of raw fish, perhaps spiced or augmented with plant foods. These sorts of observations provide information on prehistoric food preferences and cuisine. Some bone is digested and absorbed and, therefore, may have been an important source of calcium for prehistoric peoples. Beyond bone, animal dermal derivatives (feathers and scales) are found in coprolites. The quills of feathers are obvious in macroscopic analysis. Microscopically, the fine details of feather fragments can be analyzed to determine the

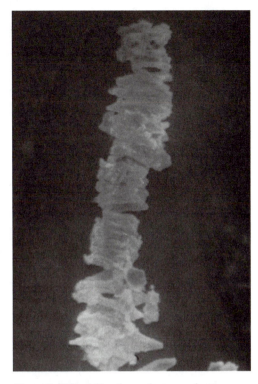

C

Figure 3. *Helical fiber from plant vascular tissue recovered from a Hohokam coprolite. Photograph by Karl Reinhard.*

taxon of bird eaten. Scales from fish or reptiles can sometimes be identified to genus or species (Figure 6).

Coprolites also contain invertebrate remains, the most common of which are insects. Insects from coprolites fall into two categories: insects that were eaten as food and insects that were eating the feces. Grasshoppers were the most common prehistoric dietary insect. Spider beetles and flies commonly infested feces and are evident in analysis. Other arthropods that occur less frequently are freshwater and saltwater crustacea such as crayfish and shrimp. Millipede remains have been found in coprolites from the lower Pecos area of Texas. Ethnocentrically, this is an unappealing food item, but millipedes may have looked good to ancient hunter-gatherers. Along coastal environments, mollusc-shell fragments are found in coprolites. Both snails and clam fragments were ingested. In the ancient Chilean Chinchorro culture, the consumption of small snails is evident in a substantial portion of coprolites from mummies (4000 B.C.). These fragments were probably accidentally ingested as the snail was

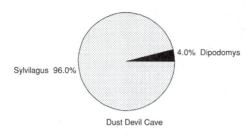

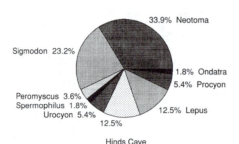

Figure 4. Comparison of animal-bone diversity from Archaic coprolites excavated from Dust Devil Cave, Utah, and Hinds Cave, Texas. The bones show that the Dust Devil Cave inhabitants specialized in rabbit hunting. In contrast, the Hinds Cave inhabitants had a broad-spectrum hunting strategy. By Karl Reinhard.

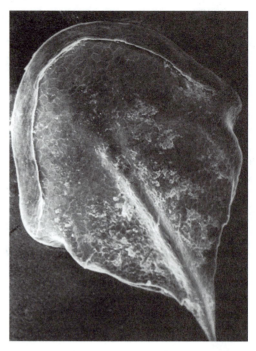

Figure 6. A scale from the giant fence lizard from an Anasazi coprolite. These are commonly recovered from human coprolites. Photograph by Karl Reinhard.

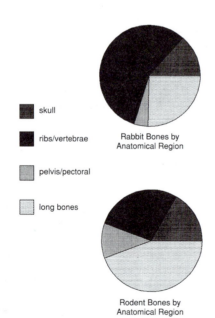

Figure 5. Comparison of rabbit and rodent bone from Dust Devil Cave coprolites by skeletal element. The inhabitants of Dust Devil Cave sectioned and ate entire rabbits but preferred to eat primarily the legs of rodents. By Karl Reinhard.

sucked or pried from its shell. Later mummies from Peru (A.D. 1000) contain finely ground shell that was intentionally consumed.

A wide variety of microscopic remains can be found in coprolites. Parasite remains are some of the most significant microscopic components. Other animal remains that are visible microscopically are mites that infested the feces after deposition.

Pollen grains can be extremely abundant in coprolites. Pollen is introduced into the intestinal tract through drinking, mucosal contamination through inhalation, and eating materials that are contaminated with airborne pollen. When the ambient airborne pollen is consumed accidentally in these ways, the amount of pollen in the digestive system is small. People intentionally ate a wide variety of foods that contained pollen. In some cases, pollen from certain plants, such as cattail and horsetail, was collected and eaten as complete meals (Figure 7). In North America, flowers of certain plants, such as squash, were eaten, and flowering parts of plants were apparently made into teas. For some fruits, such as that of the saguaro, the residual flower is attached to the fruits, and eating the fruits introduced pollen into the digestive tract. In contrast, the floral elements fall off of prickly-pear fruit. Therefore, eating saguaro fruit introduces pollen into the digestive tract but eating prickly-pear fruit does not. The seeds of certain species have pollen adhering to their surfaces. For example, eating the seeds of amaranth (*Amaranthus* spp.) also results in the consumption of pollen. By understanding which seeds or fruits carry pollen and which do not, the coprolite analyst can determine what plant foods were originally eaten.

Phytoliths are tiny crystals of calcium or silica compounds that form in plant cells (Figure 8). These are most common in the vegetative portions of plants (leaves and stems). Since humans consumed large quantities of vegetative tissue rich in phytoliths, the phytolith content of coprolites can be remarkably high. Although these microscopic remains had been identified in coprolites in the 1970s (see review by Reinhard and Bryant 1992), it was not until 1990–1993 that the full information potential of phytoliths in coprolites was explored by Dennis Danielson and Timothy Meade. This evaluation produced several important discoveries. Phytoliths can make up to 10 percent of the volume of Archaic coprolites. Because phytoliths are harder than tooth enamel, chewing them caused tooth wear and tooth loss. Phytoliths are most abundantly derived from the vegetative portions of plants and also legume pods. Therefore, phytoliths provide dietary information unavailable through other analyses. For example, beans are often completely digested except for their phytoliths. The major task ahead for phytolith analysis is the development of regional identification keys for phytoliths. Once this is accomplished, phytolith analysis will become a highly significant aspect of coprolite study.

Starch granules may prove to be important in future coprolite research. With many root crops, none of the techniques summarized above is useful in identifying the plant species that were consumed. This is a special problem in the South American Andean region, where root crops such as potatoes and manioc were commonly eaten. As of the late 1990s, researchers were exploring the potential of using starch crystals to identify plant species.

A variety of microscopic remains result from processing plants. Seed-coat fragments, for example, result from grinding seeds into

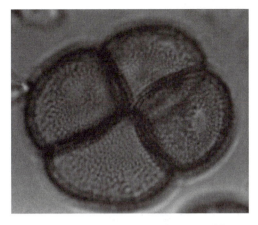

Figure 7. *Pollen grain from cattail recovered from a coprolite. In this case, the coprolite was composed almost entirely of cattail pollen grains. Photograph by Karl Reinhard.*

Figure 8. *Calcium-oxalate phytolith from prickly-pear epidermis extracted from an Archaic Utah coprolite from Dust Devil Cave. The consumption of prickly-pear pads introduced large numbers of these crystals into the coprolite. Photograph by Karl Reinhard.*

flour. The microscopic fragments of ground seed testae add to food-preparation information. Other small plant fragments also occur in coprolites. These include fragments of vascular bundles, cuticle, and silicified structures. The information potential of these other remains has not been fully investigated.

Algal and fungal remains are sometimes present in coprolites. Fungal spores provide some dietary information. Corn smut (genus

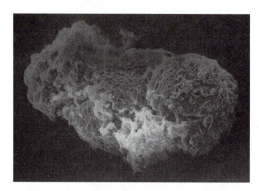

Figure 9. Spores of the fungus Endogane *ssp. from coprolites. Photograph by Karl Reinhard.*

Ustilago) was used among historic Native American tribes as a spice. Among Anasazi coprolites, the spores of corn smut are especially common and indicate that it was used prehistorically. Species of another fungus genus, *Endogane,* have been found in Archaic coprolites from Dust Devil Cave (Figure 9). The fungus grows on the roots of grasses. To disseminate its spores, the fungus produces a button-size structure, called a *sporocarp,* which is eaten by rabbits. The spores are then liberated in the rabbits' feces. The fact that the spores were in human coprolites indicates that the viscera of rabbits were eaten. On rare occasion, silica diatoms (algae) are found in microscopic examination. The distinctive morphologies of diatom species makes them readily identifiable, and, because different diatoms are found in different habitats, the diatoms indicate with which ecological zones humans have had contact.

Chemical analyses can expand even further the information potential of coprolites. Visual analysis of coprolites can reveal much about the consumption of small animals by prehistoric peoples but little about the consumption of large animals. That is because large-animal bone was not often swallowed. The development of a technique for analyzing residual animal protein (Newman et al. 1993), since applied to coprolites by Mark Q. Sutton, has solved that problem: The technique identifies the protein residue of large and small animals. Therefore, one can now assess the relative consumption of all sizes of animals through coprolite study

Another question that is important in coprolite analysis is whether men and women are equally represented in coprolites. One

might expect that coprolites were associated more with women than men, since women are more often present at a home base camp. Steroid analysis was successfully tried with nonhuman coprolites by Arden B. Bercovitz in 1989. It focuses on identifying estrogen and testosterone in coprolites and reveals whether coprolites came from females or males. This technique may be applied in the future to human coprolites.

Another class of molecules that preserve in feces are lipids. Although it has been known since the 1970s that lipids preserve in coprolites and can be extracted, the interpretive potential of lipid analysis has not been explored.

Elemental chemistry and stable carbon and nitrogen isotopic chemistry of coprolites are being evaluated. The isotopic analysis of coprolites provides insight into which plants produce what isotopic signals. Also, the defecated coprolite signals, when compared to the signals from bone, provide a good idea of the original nature of diet and of how much food material from different isotopic categories is absorbed in the body and how much is defecated. Many major and trace elements are present in coprolites. These have been used in the past to assess health of prehistoric peoples relative to excreted-element values for modern, normal human populations (Fry 1977).

These are some of the types of information and interpretive potentials in coprolite analysis. One major point that is clear from this overview is that coprolite analysts must be generalists. They must be familiar, at least on a basic level, with many fields in anthropology and biology and should have university degrees in both areas.

How Are Coprolite Data Interpreted?

Coprolite analysis presents very specific data regarding prehistoric use of particular plant, animal, and fungal species. Coprolites also provide an idea of the relative amounts of these species that were consumed (precise quantification must await further experimental research). However, they provide a picture of diet only during the few hours before defecation. Therefore, their value in long-term dietary reconstruction can be limited. Because of this, coprolite interpretation must be made with respect to the season of site occupation. If it can be demonstrated that a site was occupied year-round, then coprolites from that site provide a picture of year-long diet. However, if the site was used for a brief period of time, then the year-long dietary picture is incomplete. For example, analysis of Hogup and Danger caves in Utah shows that the caves were occupied briefly in the fall (Fry 1977). Analysis of other hunter-gatherer sites indicates that they were usually occupied temporarily, during either the warm or cold seasons. Some horticultural sites were occupied year-round, and coprolites from these sites provide data regarding the complete use of plants and animals at those sites.

Coprolite data must also be interpreted with perspective to the ancient climates. For some arid areas, the climate has stayed relatively stable, but pronounced change is true for other areas. The Archaic occupation of Dust Devil Cave in Utah predates a major climatic change event called the Altithermal. Before that time, the climate was more temperate than it is today. This affected the ecological life zones on Navajo Mountain, where the cave is located, such that the zones were lower and more accessible. Therefore, interpretation of the coprolite data in context of the ancient environment provides a more accurate idea of distances between the cave and food resources.

Recent Contributions and the Future of Coprolite Studies

The Colorado Plateau has been the research area for refinement of coprolite studies. Several recent studies and syntheses of coprolite data have led to significant conclusions about ancient diet on health. Paul E. Minnis analyzed coprolite data from Anasazi sites on the Colorado Plateau and showed that different regions of the Plateau exhibited distinct dietary patterns and that this regional differentiation was stable throughout Anasazi prehistory. Therefore, beyond distinctions in pottery styles or architectural styles, the different subgroups of the Anasazi can be distinguished by dietary traditions.

Reinhard compared hunter-gatherer diet and parasitism to that of horticultural peoples. His study showed that diet had little effect on the pathological state of Southwestern peoples in comparison to parasitism, which is a reversal of previous notions (El-Najjar and Robertson 1976). One counterintuitive revelation of the study was that hunter-gatherers had a less diverse wild-plant-food base than horticulturalists. Five alternative hypotheses were presented to account for this difference: (1) horticulturalists supplemented a diet of maize with a diversity of collected plants to augment the nutritional value of their maize; (2) horticultural diets reflect year-round use of plants, which results in apparent greater plant diversity; (3) horticulture broadened the range of available food plants through encouragement of weedy plants; (4) horticultural peoples exploited more plants to spice a relatively bland maize diet; and (5) population growth associated with horticulture stressed the subsistence base, with resultant utilization of a broad range of gathered plants.

Sutton and Reinhard (1995) applied cluster analysis to Colorado Plateau coprolite data to evaluate these hypotheses. Sutton originally adapted cluster analysis to coprolite data from California and discovered associations of plants and animals that were seasonally specific. The clustering of these associations at different sites revealed seasonal use of the sites. With the Colorado Plateau coprolites, Sutton discovered three different categories of food-component associations that provided insight into Anasazi cuisine: a fresh-maize category, a ground-maize category, and a maize-absent category. The first category included a series of plants and animals that were associated with fresh maize. The plant foods in this cluster, other than maize, are harvestable in the spring and indicate the range of spring diets. Some of the foods, such as beans and rabbit, were associated only with maize and indicate what dietary supplements and spices were eaten with maize. Fewer plants were associated with ground maize, and these were storable. Therefore, the ground-maize category reflects winter diet. The plants that were not associated with maize reflect either binging on seasonably abundant foods (pinyon nuts and prickly-pear fruits) or starvation foods (yucca leaves).

This detailed analysis addressed the hypotheses for horticultural wild-plant use presented by Reinhard. The first hypothesis is viable since it appears that wild foods were used to supplement and spice a maize diet. The second hypothesis is less valid because dietary diversity peaks in the summer and fall months, and, therefore, prolonged occupation would not enhance diversity. The third hypothesis is viable since some of the common wild-plant foods are disturbance annuals. The fourth hypothesis is viable, and it appears that the Anasazi used a variety of wild plants to

C

spice several maize-based recipes. The fifth hypothesis is not viable since very few coprolites contained strictly nonmaize foods. Therefore, the application of cluster analysis to Antelope House coprolite data (Sutton and Reinhard 1995) indicates that several factors resulted in increased use of wild plants among horticulturalists.

This series of studies defines the future of coprolite research. The analytical techniques developed by Callen, Bryant, and Reinhard, combined with the statistical techniques of Minnis and Sutton, have proven to be particularly powerful for reconstruction of ancient cuisine, diet, and health. The future of coprolite research will see more such statistical evaluation of coprolite information.

Karl Reinhard

See also ARCHAEOPARASITOLOGY; PALEONUTRITION; PALEOPHARMACOLOGY; PALYNOLOGY; PHYTOLITH ANALYSIS

Further Readings

Bryant, V.M., Jr. (1994) Callen's legacy. In K.D. Sobolik (ed.): Paleonutrition: The Diet and Health of Prehistoric Americans, pp. 151–160. (Occasional Paper 22). Carbondale: Center for Archaeological Investigations, Southern Illinois University.

Bercovitz, A.B., and Degraff, S.L. (1989) Paleoendocrine evaluation of sex steroid hormones in coprolites from Shasta ground sloths. American Journal of Physical Anthropolgy 78:192.

Danielson, D.R., and Reinhard, K.J. (1999) Human dental microwear caused by calcium oxalate phytoliths in the prehistoric diet of the lower Pecos Region, Texas. American Journal of Physical Anthropology 107:297–304.

El-Najjar, M.Y., and Robertson, A.L., Jr. (1976) Spongy bones in prehistoric America. Science 193:141–143.

Fry, G.F. (1977) Analysis of Prehistoric Coprolites from Utah. (Anthropological Papers 97). Salt Lake City: University of Utah Press.

Minnis, P.E. (1989) Prehistoric diet in the northern Southwest: Macroplant remains from Four Corners feces. American Antiquity 54:543–563.

Newman, M.E., Yohe R.M., II, Ceri, H., and Sutton, M.Q. (1993) Immunological protein analysis of non-lithic archaeological materials. Journal of Archaeological Science 20:93–100.

Reinhard, K.J. (1992) The impact of diet and parasitism on anemia in the prehistoric West. In P. Stuart-MacAdam and S. Kent (eds.): Diet, Demography, and Disease: Changing Perspectives on Anemia, pp. 219–258. New York: Aldine deGruyter.

Reinhard, K.J. and Bryant, V.M., Jr., (1992) Coprolite analysis: A biological perspective on prehistory. In M.B. Schiffer (ed.): Archaeological Method and Theory, vol. 4, pp. 245–288. Tucson: University of Arizona Press.

Rylander, K.A. (1994) Corn preparation among Basketmaker Anasazi: A scanning electron microscope study of *Zea mays* remains from coprolites. In K.D. Sobolik (ed.): Paleonutrition: The Diet and Health of Prehistoric Americans, pp. 115–133. (Occasional Paper 22). Carbondale: Center for Archaeological Investigations, Southern Illinois University.

Sutton, M.Q. (1992) Midden and coprolite derived subsistence evidence: An analysis of data from the La Quinta Site, Salton Basin, California. Journal of Ethnobiology 13:1–15.

Sutton, M.Q., and Reinhard, K.J. (1995) Cluster analysis of coprolites from Antelope House: Implications for Anasazi diet and cuisine. Journal of Archaeological Science 22:741–750.

Core and Periphery Systems

Regional systems that exhibit uneven development. Archaeologists have long known that development in the prehistoric and ancient world was uneven. They have spoken of key and dependent areas, cores and buffers, and heartlands and hinterlands. More recently, they have adopted the terms *core* and *periphery* from world-systems theory. Uneven development manifests itself in the distribution of features and artifacts in the archaeological record. Core areas are those regions in which features, artifacts, styles, or practices occur the earliest and/or with the greatest frequency and development. In contrast, peripheries are the regions in which these things occur later, in smaller quantities, and underdeveloped. The implication is that the core is somehow the source of the distribution, while the periphery is the recipient. The relationship of core and periphery implies a historical and hierarchical relationship whereby developments in the core spread out to alter or create the periphery.

A basic research problem for archaeology is how to account for these uneven distributions. The research problem raises three key questions:

1. Which regions are core and which are peripheral? In many ways, this is an empirical question related to the spatial and temporal distribution of archaeological materials. However, the choice of materials to be examined and the evaluation of what is more or less developed raise important theoretical issues. Despite these theoretical concerns, archaeologists have generally been able to come to broad consensus about what are core and peripheral regions at different times and places in the world.

2. What are the processes that create the distribution? This is the essential theoretical question. Theorists differ in what they think the behaviors and aspects of social organization that created the distributions were. They also differ in their interpretations of the social relations entailed in these behaviors and organizations.

3. What was the relative importance of core and periphery to cultural change? Generally, by saying that one area was core and another peripheral, an archaeologist implies that the core area somehow directed and/or shaped cultural change in the peripheral region. Archaeological theories differ, however, in how strong, how direct, or how interactive they make this relationship.

Core and periphery models are historical alternatives to evolutionary theories. Generally, historically oriented archaeologists focus on the study of interaction to account for uneven development. They find the source for the unevenness in the particular histories of cultural groups and in how they interact with others. Evolutionary theorists usually seek explanations for uneven development in universal generalizations or processes that account for the trajectory of single cultures. Nineteenth-century evolutionists assumed that cultures progressed through a universal set of stages. Uneven development resulted from the fact that some cultures remained frozen at an earlier stage, while others had advanced further along the ladder of progress.

Archaeological Theories of Core and Periphery

In the first half of the twentieth century, scholars studied uneven development in terms of a diffusionary theory as the center point of archaeological research. Following the Second World War, emphasis shifted first to a cultural ecology that accounted for cultural change in terms of local adaptation, and then to an evolutionary-processual archaeology.

Diffusionists assumed that cultural innovations and traits originated in a core area and diffused out to peripheral areas. The core was the center of invention or innovation, and, through the process of diffusion, it shaped cultural change in the periphery. Some diffusionists argued that the core became a center through chance, while others maintained a racist explanation for how a core became central. The German prehistorian Gustaf Kossina (1858–1931) claimed that, from the Mesolithic onward, northern Germany had been the center of cultural development in Europe and Africa. The British archaeologist V. Gordon Childe (1892–1957) countered Kossina's claims with careful chronological reconstructions that showed Europe to be the periphery of a Middle Eastern core.

The American cultural-historical school of archaeology defined large cultural areas that consisted of an environmentally demarcated region that contained cultures sharing a host of traits. Most or all of these traits originated from a cultural core and then diffused out to the peripheries of the area. These archaeologists plotted out the spatial and temporal distribution of artifacts, features, and styles to identify the cores from which they had originated.

Cultural ecology elaborated the environmental aspects of the cultural-historical approach. Rather than stressing how the environment set boundaries on cultural variation and change, the cultural ecologists argued that a culture's adaptation to the environment decided cultural variation and change. This perspective stressed adaptive functions within cultures rather than interactions between cultures. The adaptive focus lead to many more studies of peripheral sites and areas, such as Gordon R. Willey's work at the Mayan site of Barton Ramie in the 1960s. Interpretations of cultural interactions often stressed how these interactions helped cultures adapt by bringing in resources from different environmental zones. This idea of symbiosis tended to downplay hierarchical relations between cultural groups.

The *processual archaeologists* of the 1960s reintroduced evolutionary theory to archaeology. They defined the differences between cores and peripheries in terms of complexity, with cores being more culturally complex than peripheries. They sought to account for these differences by reference to universal processes or laws that caused cultures to become more complex. The key question for processual archaeologists was: How did a culture move from one evolutionary state to another? Most of their discussions focused on the specific issue of how a culture became a state. Thus, the progress of Western Europe to its dominant world position resulted from a conjunction of general processes. Other societies, the peripheries, were not so fortunate and had been left stranded at lower levels of development.

Immanuel Wallerstein's World Systems Theory

The study of cores and peripheries became important again in archaeology with the introduction of Immanuel Wallerstein's (1930–) world systems theory in the late 1970s. Wallerstein's theory led archaeologists to examine how the development of cores derives from the creation of peripheries, shifting the focus of research from diffusion or adaptation to interaction and dependencies. *World systems* refer to large-scale systems that encompass the known world of the participants. It is only in the last 500 years that such a system has encompassed the entire globe. Wallerstein assumes an interregional division of labor in which peripheral areas supply cores with raw materials. In this system, the core areas are economically, politically, and culturally dominant. The functional position of each region shapes the development of that region, so that, over time, functionally equivalent regions become more alike. Thus, the creation of complex and highly developed core areas depends upon the creation of less complex and underdeveloped peripheries. This idea

that development creates underdevelopment repudiates the evolutionary position that peripheries simply lag behind cores in their development. Wallerstein originally presented his ideas as a historical theory to account for the rise of capitalism, not as a general theory of world history.

Wallerstein identifies three modes of production, or types of world systems: *reciprocal minisystems, redistributive empires,* and a *capitalist world economy.* In reciprocal minisystems, all able-bodied individuals have direct access to the tools and resources necessary for the production of day-to-day necessities. Exchange in minisystems is based on a mutual and balanced trade. World empires have a centralized political system that allows elites to extract goods and services from peripheral areas through tribute. Tribute involves the threat and use of force to compel peripheral areas to turn over goods and services. In a capitalist world economy, core areas use market processes to dominate peripheral areas. The peripheries sell the core raw materials, which the core manufactures into finished goods that it sells to the peripheries. Both world empires and world economies entail functional and geographic divisions of labor, but world economies lack a centralized government, the empire, that controls the system. Wallerstein argues that world empires dominated ancient history, in contrast to world economies, which were inherently unstable and short-lived entities. Only with the technology to move bulk commodities large distances did capitalism arise as a world economy lasting, so far, for almost 500 years.

World systems theory has advanced the study of prehistory and the ancient world in many ways. It allows archaeologists to look at regional relationships instead of focusing on adaptations to a single river valley or basin. Cultures become dynamic entities that are defined and transformed by unequal relations in a larger system. Core areas dominate this system and establish the relationships that create diverse peripheries.

A major problem in applying world-systems theory to archaeological cases lay in Wallerstein's emphasis on the movement of bulk commodities as a precondition for stable world economies. Jane Schneider has argued that Wallerstein underestimated the importance of trade in exotic and precious commodities in noncapitalist systems.

Following Schneider's insight, archaeologists have applied world systems theory to account for uneven development in many times and places. It provides them with a tool to link culture change across culture areas and to talk about prehistory on a grand scale. In North America, Barbara Bender (1985) used world systems theory to account for the emergence of prehistoric tribal groups in the midcontinent. In Mexico and Central America, Richard E. Blanton and Gary Feinman argued that the Mesoamerican cultural area was a world system, with multiple and shifting cores. In addition, archaeologists have applied world systems theory in Africa, Europe, and Asia. These archaeologists have concentrated on the growth of long-distance interactions and the capacity of such interactions to create cultural change, on how these interactions link economic cycles across regions, and on how peripheries become cores by challenging existing power centers.

Some archaeologists have made contributions to the theory of world systems. Philip Kohl suggests that the world systems of antiquity would have differed greatly from the modern one. Such systems were far less developed and more loosely integrated than the modern world economy because of differences in the technology of transportation. He contends that cores and peripheries were less stable than in the modern system and that military force may have played a larger role in their existence. He also notes that Wallerstein's idea that world empires were more stable than world systems is an erroneous one based on an overdependence on the Roman, Persian, and Chinese empires as models for ancient history. Kohl argues that, in Southwest Asia, empires tended to be unstable and short lived and that, for most of ancient history, world economies dominated the area.

Critiques of World Systems Theory

Wallerstein's approach emphasizes how cores subjugate peripheries, but it does not adequately deal with unique cultural developments in the peripheries or how peripheries affect cores. Archaeologists identify regional interaction as important to uneven development, but accounting for how particular sequences arise from this interaction is another matter. Archaeologists need to be able to interpret the cultural variation in societies that are not cores. Simply identifying all such societies as peripheries obscures both the variability between these societies and the role of these societies in shaping cultural developments.

World systems theory also suggests that changes in core and periphery development are best understood at the highest scale of analysis. Whereas evolutionary theory studied the trajectory followed by a single culture, the world systems model identifies a vast system of social relations that generates its own patterns of change. The question must be, however, how large? In prehistory, different systems of various sizes can be identified at different scales of analysis. World systems theory suggests that it is the highest-level system that determines the workings of the others.

A more important problem with the core-periphery contrast is that it assumes that all groups and relations can be ranked. This is a questionable assumption. A great number of contrasts can be made between social groups based on linguistics, culture, adaptation, religion, and a host of other parameters. These distinctions may be rankable, or they may not.

Alternative Theories of Core and Periphery

Many archaeologists have turned to the world systems concept of the sociologist Christopher Chase-Dunn, in part because he has read extensively in the archaeological and anthropological literature and has analyzed archaeological cases. Chase-Dunn begins with Wallerstein's theory but substantially improves on it as a general theory of human history. He defines a world system as an intersocietal network in which interaction is an important condition for the reproduction of the internal structures of the composite units and in which interaction significantly affects the changes that occur in these local structures. He does not assume that all intersocietal systems will have core-periphery hierarchies and argues instead that archaeologists have to prove the existence of exploitation, domination, and unequal exchange.

Chase-Dunn retains the key notion that these intersocietal networks are systems. If these networks are systems, then they must consist of regular interacting or interdependent societies that form a unified whole. The functioning of the system is not reducible to any of the individual societies that make it up; however, the system can be broken down into unique entities and subsystems. Chase-Dunn identifies three issues as key to understanding world systems: (1) How do we define the boundaries of the system? (2) How do we define the subunits that make up the system? (3) How do we typologize world systems? This systems logic works best when economics are being discussed. Although Chase-Dunn clearly recognizes that economics are not the only, or necessarily the primary, relations structuring a world system, he consistently structures his discussions of the nature of core-periphery relations and systems logic around economic relations.

A number of European archaeologists have proposed the model of peer-polity interaction as an alternative to a core-periphery approach. The peer-polity model emphasizes an intermediate scale of analysis between the local and the interregional. These archaeologists stress interactions within a region, and they assume that these internal interactions are more important to cultural change than external links to the region. There are dangers, however, in framing an either/or choice between a peer-polity and a core-periphery model. The idea of peer-polity interaction is not really a theory but an argument for analysis at a certain scale and against a priori assumptions of economically and politically defined cores and peripheries. It is every bit as problematic to assume that the polities one is dealing with in a given case were peers as it is to a priori assume cores and peripheries. Many of the case studies of peer-polity interaction have been Iron Age societies in northern Europe. The assumption of peer interaction ignores the fact that these societies were peripheries of the Roman Empire.

A general limitation of world systems theory is its attempt to account for the totality of social reality with a single theory. This reduces the rich variation of history to a handful of categories, a few processes, and a high-order scale. World systems theory takes a systemic view that stresses the units (cores, peripheries, and semiperipheries) that are linked in such a system rather than the relations that create the units. Classificatory terms such as core and periphery unite areas in terms of a specified set of similarities, but, in doing so, they mask or hide important variation between regions placed in the same category. The theory identifies inequalities in the processes of economic exchange and development as the driving forces for change in history. In Wallerstein's theory, a social group becomes core because of its functional position in the international division of labor. A social group may, however, be central because of its position in a web of religious, social, economic, or political relations. One group may be the center for one set of relations (e.g., religion), while a different group is the center for another set of relations (e.g., economic). Finally, this theory derives all social change from processes that occur at the highest scale. The processes that occur at different scales are linked, but they are not reducible, one to another.

World systems theory points to an important aspect of social relations, unevenness in development, and to the contradictions that occur from this unevenness. Some archaeologists take this notion of unevenness and examine it as a much more multidimensional phenomenon than the world systems theory allows. They do not use a priori functionally related categories such a core and periphery and do not assume that processes of social change are best understood at a single scale. Instead, they examine the unevenness of cultural development in terms of multiple dimensions and at multiple scales.

William Marquardt and Carole Crumley speak of the "effective scale" of research, that being "any scale at which pattern may be recognized or meaning inferred" (Marquardt and Crumley 1987:609). As the effective scale of analysis changes, different webs of relations are framed. The unevenness in these relations disappears at a different scale as a new pattern of unevenness appears. Social groups live and act in a world of varying scale, and their position vis-à-vis others changes as their scale of reference changes. The choice of an effective scale, therefore, brackets an area for study allowing archaeologists to view a particular set of social relations while denying them access to sets visible at other scales. Also, they find that some theoretical models are more informative at one scale, and others at a different scale, so that the choice of models, in part, also depends on the scale of analysis. The prehistoric world that archaeologists wish to understand was a complex product of the intersection of all of these scales. As archaeologists change scales, the cores and peripheries that they see at one level become fuzzy and disappear to be replaced by new patterns of uneven development. Uneven development begets social groups that have different interests within a social order, and, as they act to meet these interests, they create conflicts that drive social change. In this perspective, it is the conflicts and contradictions between cores and peripheries that become the driving force for cultural change.

Randall H. McGuire

See also EXCHANGE SYSTEMS, THEORY

Further Readings

Bender, B. (1995) Emergent tribal formations in the American Midcontinent. American Antiquity (50)1:52–62.

Blanton, R.E., and Feinman, G. (1984) The Mesoamerican world system. American Anthropologist 86:673–682.

Champion, T.C., ed. (1989) Centre and Periphery: Comparative Studies in Archaeology. London: Unwin Hyman.

Chase-Dunn, C. and Hall, T.D., eds. (1991) Core/Periphery Relations in Precapitalist Worlds. Boulder, CO: Westview.

Kohl, P. (1987) The use and abuse of world systems theory. In M.B. Schiffer (ed.): Advances in Archaeological Method and Theory, vol. 11, pp. 1–35. New York: Academic.

Marquardt, W. and Crumley, C.L. (1987) Regional Dynamics: Burgundian Landscapes in Historical Perspective Orlando: Academic.

Renfrew, C. and Cherry, J.F. (1986) Peer Polity Interaction and Socio-Political Change. Cambridge: Cambridge University Press.

Rowlands, M.J., Larsen, M.T., and Kristiansen, K., eds. (1987) Core and Periphery Relations in the Ancient World. Cambridge: Cambridge University Press.

Schneider, J. (1977) Was there a pre-capitalist world system? Peasant Studies 6(1):20–29.

Shortman, E.M., and Urban, P.A., eds. (1992) Resources, Power, and Interregional Interaction. New York: Plenum.

Wallerstein, I. (1974) The Modern World-System, vol. 1 New York: Academic.

Willey, G.R., Bullard, V.R., Glass, J.S., and Gifford, J.C. (1965) Prehistoric Maya Settlements in the Belize Valley. Peabody Museum Papers 54. Cambridge, Mass.: Peabody Museum.

Crawford, Osbert G.S. (1886–1957)

Crawford, born on October 28, 1886, in India, has been referred to as the father of aerial photography for archaeology, and it is difficult to find anyone else who saw the worldwide potential of the technique. It is surprising that the subject developed in the way it did, concentrating on the taking of photographs in the early years after Crawford's work. Crawford's early career revolved around maps (especially in the First World War, 1914–1918). It was during the war that he became an observer with the Royal Flying Corps (later the Royal Air Force, RAF), and the skills of map reading, navigation, and observing archaeology provided the perfect training for the world's first archaeological airborne surveyor. In his autobiography, *Said and Done,* he recalls using Roman roads as means of navigating in France and Belgium during the war.

His first archaeological post was as archaeology officer to the Ordnance Survey in 1920; this link with maps featured strongly in his work, with immense effort going into the production of the first-ever map of Roman Britain. The idea of period-specific maps was one that the Ordnance Survey, under Crawford's guidance, continued. He also set up an international committee to produce a map of the Roman Empire.

His publications provided a foundation for the study of aerial photography, and *Wessex from the Air,* which he produced with Alexander Keiller, is perhaps the best known of these. His early works were published as Professional Papers by the Ordnance Survey; they provided a format for future studies, using a combination of aerial photographs, distribution maps, and plans as never before.

Between the wars, Crawford was able to convince the RAF to let him look after some of the negatives of photos it took of Britain and foreign parts. He was able to travel in the Middle East and take aerial photographs in Iraq, Jordan, and Egypt and to convince the British Museum to archive the negatives.

Above all, Crawford was an archaeologist who used aerial photography as one of many techniques for discovering new sites, as his book *Archaeology in the Field* attests. He will also be remembered for founding the quarterly journal *Antiquity.* As the editor of this journal, he wanted the new discoveries of archaeology, anywhere in the world, to be accessible to a wide audience. His connections with the Royal Geographical Society show that he was interested in the landscape, the impact of human activity on the natural environment, and how to map it. This society awarded him the Victoria Gold Medal (1940).

Robert H. Bewley

See also AERIAL PHOTOGRAPHY FOR ARCHAEOLOGY; PHOTOGRAPHY, ARCHAEOLOGICAL

Further Readings

Crawford, O.G.S. (1929) Air-Photography for Archaeologists. London: His Majesty's Stationery Office.

Crawford, O.G.S. (1953) Archaeology in the Field. New York: Praeger.

Crawford, O.G.S. (1955) Said and Done: The Autobiography of an Archaeologist. London: Phoenix House.

Crawford, O.G.S. and Keiller, A. (1928) Wessex from the Air. Oxford: Clarendon.

Cultural Resource Management (CRM)

The contemporary approach to the preservation, protection, and management of archaeological resources and other kinds of historic properties.

Historical Background

The term *cultural resource management* (CRM) developed within the discipline of archaeology in the United States during the early 1970s. Don D. Fowler (1982:1) attributes the first use of the term *cultural resources* to specialists within the National Park Service in 1971 or 1972. The word *management* was linked with cultural resources by the 1974 Cultural Resource Management Conference held in Denver (Lipe and Lindsay 1974). This conference was attended by many of the individuals working actively on the problems associated with preservation of archaeological sites in the United States.

Early proponents and developers of CRM recognized that, conceptually, it was concerned with a wide range of resource types

> including not only archeological sites but historic buildings and districts, social institutions, folkways, arts, crafts, architecture, belief systems, the integrity of social

groups, the ambiance of neighborhoods, and so on . . . all constitute aspects of the National Environmental Policy Act, the historic preservation laws pertain directly to only some of them, and archeologists are typically concerned with or knowledgeable about an even smaller subset (McGimsey and Davis 1977:27).

Despite this early recognition of the properly broad nature of CRM and the continuing adherence to this wide definition by some (e.g., Knudson 1986:401), the term frequently has been, and still is, used as a synonym for archaeology done in conjunction with public agencies' actions or projects. Imprecise use and the absence of rigorously adhered to definitions are common among a range of terms related to CRM, such as *historic preservation, archaeological resource management,* and *heritage management.* This situation ought not to be too worrisome; the existence of all of these terms is relatively new, and, in time, their definitions and relationships will become more precise. However, to avoid misunderstanding, contemporary workers in these various fields must define the terms explicitly as they use them in their own work. In this entry, the term is used mainly in reference to the development of the archaeological aspects of CRM; however, a summary of CRM issues related to nonarchaeological topics is also provided.

In the early 1970s in the United States, CRM developed from two related archaeological concerns. First, there was a continuing concern about the destruction of archaeological sites due to modern development, including road construction, large-scale agriculture, and housing. Much of this development was sponsored, endorsed, or funded by the federal government (Davis 1972). This concern was an extension of earlier concerns about large-scale federal construction projects, most notably the river-basin reservoir construction program of the Corps of Engineers and the Bureau of Reclamation that developed in the late 1940s and early 1950s. The earlier concern had led to a reaction by archaeologists, termed *salvage archaeology* by those who viewed it as second-rate work or, more positively, *rescue archaeology* or *emergency archaeology* by those who argued that it was necessary and generally successful at saving some of the archaeological data from sites that would otherwise be destroyed without any recording (e.g., Brew 1961; Jennings 1985). Emergency archaeology focused on saving archaeological data and remains through rapid excavation of sites prior to their destruction by modern construction projects.

The second concern that led to CRM was dissatisfaction with the emergency archaeology approach itself. Although emergency archaeology resulted in the excavation of sites and the preservation of some data and remains, critics justifiably pointed out that, frequently, the excavations were not followed by thorough description, analysis, and synthesis of the investigation results. We know now that the collections and records from many salvage projects were poorly cared for after the investigation ended, and, along with the lack of attention to curation associated with more recent work, these failings have contributed to the contemporary problems of archaeological curation and collections management. Perhaps most problematic about the emergency archaeology approach was the fundamental failure to modify development projects so that sites could be conserved and protected rather than destroyed, even though the destruction was preceded by scientific excavation.

CRM: A New Approach to Preserving Archaeological Resources

One result of the heightened concern about environmental issues during the late 1960s and the 1970s was the enactment of laws to protect important aspects of the cultural and natural environment. Prominent among these laws were the National Historic Preservation Act of 1966 (NHPA) and the National Environmental Policy Act of 1969 (NEPA). Both had important effects on the development of CRM in the United States. They required that federal agencies take cultural resources, defined broadly and including archaeological sites, into effect as they planned, reviewed, or undertook projects or activities. These laws, plus Executive Order 11593, signed in 1971, also required federal agencies to identify, evaluate, and protect cultural resources on land for which they had jurisdiction or control. These new requirements and government activity had two immediate effects on the development of CRM: (1) the employment of professional archaeologists in public agencies and private firms to do the archaeological work required by the new laws and regulations; and (2) the attention devoted to archaeological resources as part of the planning of public-agency operations and projects.

A National Network of Public Agency Archaeologists

During the 1970s, federal agencies began to employ professional archaeologists in numbers never before seen and to place them in offices throughout their organizations. This was especially so among land-managing agencies, such as the Bureau of Land Management and the Forest Service. Prior to this period, the relatively few professional archaeologists employed in federal service were located in the National Park Service and the Smithsonian Institution in Washington, D.C. Agencies such as the Federal Highway Administration and the Environmental Protection Agency that did not manage land but provided funding or licensing for development projects, such as highways, waste-water-treatment facilities, and energy plants, tended not to employ many archaeologists on their staffs. More frequently, these agencies met their CRM responsibilities by requiring them of the state agencies or private firms that carried out the development projects. This pattern eventually lead to the hiring of professional archaeologists by state agencies and private firms that found themselves required by federal agencies to carry out necessary cultural resource studies. By the end of the 1970s, federal and state agencies had developed a network that included hundreds of professional archaeologists filling positions in headquarters, regional, and local offices undertaking a variety of activities to implement CRM laws, policy regulations, and guidelines. At the state-government level, State Historic Preservation Offices established by the NHPA and its implementing regulations required that each state office have a professionally qualified archaeologist on its staff. This, in particular, helped in the establishment of a national network of professionally qualified archaeologists in the public sector.

In addition to the growth of professional archaeologists in the public sector, a similar growth of professional employment occurred in private firms. Such firms ranged in size from large national or international consulting firms that needed to comply with NHPA and NEPA requirements for many of the public projects they bid on to small, newly organized firms set up to undertake specific CRM investigations needed by public agencies.

These rapid, substantial changes within the archaeological community in the proportions of professional employment, duties, and responsibilities resulted in discussions, debates, and disagreements regarding the benefits of CRM and the quality of archaeological work done as part of it. Not all of the issues raised in the professional turmoil over CRM have been resolved. However, in general, the debates and disagreements have moderated from vitriolic to collegial. Much of the contemporary archaeological field work done in the United States is tied to CRM. Many, perhaps most, professional archaeologists support a conservation approach to treatment of the archaeological record that has as one major goal the management of resources for long-term preservation. There is general agreement that the archaeological network among public agencies and the statutes, policies, regulations, and guidelines that protect archaeological resources are important to maintain and perhaps strengthen.

Considering Archaeological Resources During the Planning Stages of Programs and Projects

Both the NHPA and the NEPA require that federal agencies take account of cultural resources in planning their own programs or projects that they are undertaking with state or local agencies or with private firms. The term *cultural resources* is not used in either statute. The NHPA uses the term *historic property* to cover a wide range of cultural-resource types, explicitly referring to archaeological resources; the NEPA uses the term *human environment,* which has been interpreted to include archaeological resources but does not explicitly use the latter term. Both laws are important because they establish a national policy of considering the effect of public actions on the natural and historic environment during the planning stages of public projects. This consideration requires the identification, evaluation, and determination of impacts to archaeological resources prior to decision making about proceeding on projects that will result in harm occurring to significant resources. The

approach to planning required by the NHPA and the NEPA has moved archaeologists into the planning process. Although emergency situations requiring archaeological investigations during the construction phase of projects, immediately in front of the bulldozers, still occur, they are much less common than during the days of salvage archaeology.

The Essential Aspects of the CRM Approach

There are three general aspects to CRM when considering archaeological resources: (1) identification and evaluation of resources; (2) treatment of the resource; and (3) long-term management of the resource.

Identification and Evaluation

Identification and evaluation of cultural resources is an essential aspect of CRM, and one that is particularly challenging for some kinds of archaeological resources. Discovery of archaeological resources that are unobtrusive and in areas where visibility is poor usually is difficult. For example, many archaeological resources do not contain architectural remains that help to signal their existence and location. Frequently, archaeological sites are buried below the surface, or, if they are on the surface, they are hidden by thick vegetation. Relatively costly, labor-intensive investigations often are necessary for the discovery of archaeological resources, much more so than for other kinds of cultural resources, such as historic structures.

The evaluation of archaeological sites involves the determination of the importance or significance of each site or of a group of sites. Most often, such significance is based upon what can be learned about the past from the resource being evaluated. However, archaeological resources also may be important because they are associated with important individuals, events, or historical patterns or illustrate important aspects of architecture or design. In most cases, the information needed for archaeological evaluations to be made also requires labor-intensive investigations—in these cases, at the site level.

In U. S. CRM law and regulations, archaeological resources must be determined to be significant enough to be listed on, or eligible for listing on, the National Register of Historic Places to be considered for preservation in the context of federal undertakings or programs.

On federal lands, archaeological resources also are protected from deliberate damage by the provisions of the Archaeological Resources Protection Act (ARPA). This requires that the removal or excavation of archaeological resources be undertaken only as part of a scientifically based investigation, unless these resources have been determined to be no longer of archaeological interest. Land managers may make a determination that resources have lost their significance under procedures established in the regulations implementing ARPA only after careful consideration of the facts of a case.

Treatment

After archaeological resources have been identified and evaluated as being important enough for some kind of further treatment, the exact kind of treatment must be decided upon. There are two possible treatments: excavation and data recovery prior to site destruction or in situ preservation of the site. Frequently, of course, sites are not destroyed totally by construction projects, and a portion of the area of a site might be saved in situ while another is excavated prior to destruction. At present, archaeological resources discovered and evaluated as significant that are within the impact area of a public construction project most frequently are excavated and their data recovered as an agreed upon means of mitigating the impact of the federal undertaking. There are moves afoot to use site avoidance and preservation more frequently in such situations, but the general pattern remains to condone data recovery as an acceptable means of impact mitigation. For archaeological resources on federal land that are not threatened with destruction by modern construction or agency operations, in situ preservation is the more common general treatment.

When in situ preservation is the selected treatment, the agency responsible for management of the resource must also decide if further intervention to stabilize or protect the resource is necessary and whether the agency wants to interpret the site actively. If any of these more detailed kinds of treatments are chosen or necessary, agency personnel must take further steps to implement them. A site, for example, might be threatened by erosion by fluctuating lake levels and need shoreline stabilization to protect its deposits. In other situations, an agency office might decide that a site's location near to a visitor center or public reception area

provides an opportunity for public interpretation of the site. In either case, the agency will need to take additional steps to accomplish the treatment decisions that it makes regarding the in situ preservation of the resource.

Long-Term Management

The long-term management of archaeological resources is a requirement placed upon each federal agency by the Antiquities Act of 1906, the ARPA, and Section 110 of the NHPA. For land-managing agencies, management focuses on three main duties: (1) carrying out programs to identify and evaluate archaeological resources on the lands for which they are responsible; (2) executing the treatments decided upon for in situ archaeological sites on agency lands; and (3) caring for the archaeological collections, reports, and records related to the sites that were once on agency lands. For public agencies that do not manage land, the first two aspects of long-term management may not apply or may apply in only a few instances. However, the third aspect of long-term responsibilities will apply for these agencies to the extent that their projects and programs have resulted in the excavation of archaeological sites.

Goals and Prospects of Contemporary CRM

The focus of this entry has been how CRM developed and the nature of contemporary CRM as it relates to archaeological resources. However, CRM also can be used to refer to ways of managing a range of cultural-resource types in addition to archaeological resources. Historic structures, cultural landscapes, museum collections, and other kinds of cultural resources present challenges similar to those presented by archaeological resources in the areas of identification and evaluation, treatment, and long-term management.

There are additional kinds of cultural resources that require special considerations. One of these has come to be referred to as *traditional cultural properties* (TCPs). These are places that have special, strong traditional importance for a particular ethnic, social, or cultural group. The significance of this kind of cultural resource is not linked to its archaeological, historical, or architectural value, as is the case with other kinds of cultural resources. Some also have proposed that traditional behaviors, such as special building skills, crafts, folk arts, and the like, be considered cultural resources.

Francis P. McManamon

See also ANTIQUITIES ACT OF 1906; ARCHEOLOGICAL RESOURCES PROTECTION ACT (ARPA); ARCHEOLOGICAL AND HISTORIC PRESERVATION ACT (AHPA); NATIONAL HISTORIC PRESERVATION ACT (NHPA); SALVAGE/RESCUE ARCHAEOLOGY

Further Readings

Anyon R. and Ferguson, T.J. (1995) Cultural resource management at the Pueblo of Zuni, New Mexico, USA. Antiquity 69:913–930.

Brew, J.O. (1961) Emergency archaeology: Salvage in advance of technological progress. Proceedings of the American Philosophical Society 105(1):1–10.

Davis, H. (1972) The crisis in American archaeology. Science 176:267–272.

Fowler, D.D. (1982) Cultural resource management. In M.B. Schiffer (ed.): Advances in Archaeological Method and Theory, pp. 1–50. New York: Academic.

Green, W. and Doershuk, J.F. (1998) Cultural resource management and American archaeology. Journal of Archaeological Research 6(2):121–168.

Jennings, J.D. (1985) Riverbasin surveys: Origins, operations, and results, 1945–1969. American Antiquity 50:281–296.

King, T.F., Hickman, P. P., and Berg, G. (1977) Anthropology in Historic Preservation: Caring for Culture's Clutter. New York: Academic.

Knudson, R. (1986) Contemporary cultural resource management. In D.J. Meltzer, D.D. Fowler, and J.A. Sabloff (eds.): American Archaeology: Past and Future, pp. 395–413. Washington, D.C.: Smithsonian Institution Press.

Lipe, W.D., and Lindsay, A.J. eds. (1974) Proceedings of the 1974 Conference, Federal Center, Denver, Colorado. Technical Series 14). Flagstaff: Museum of Northern Arizona,

McGimsey, C. R.and Davis, H.A., eds. (1977) The Management of Archeological Resources: The Airlie House Report. (Special Publication). Washington, D.C.: Society for American Archaeology.

McManamon F.P. (1992) Managing America's archaeological resources. In L. Wandsnider (ed.): Quandaries and Quests: Visions of Archaeology's Future, pp. 25–40. (Occasional Paper 20). Carbondale, IL: Center for Archaeological Investigations, Southern Illinois University.

Schiffer, M.B., and Gummerman, G.J. eds. (1977) Conservation Archaeology: A Guide for Cultural Resource Management Studies. New York: Academic.

D

Dating, Method and Theory

The process of assigning a value to an event on a temporal scale. Dating is, thus, relevant only to the historical sciences, even though most of the methods used in the process are derived from the physical sciences. Indeed, dating is the methodological core of historical science, for, without it, even simple historical description is impossible. Consequently, there has been a proliferation of dating methods; Development of new methods and refinement of existing ones continue to be active areas of research.

Despite its ubiquity, time is an elusive quality. Scientists distinguish two concepts. *Newtonian time,* the time of physics and chemistry, is an elapsed quantity measured on an interval scale (e.g., 10 minutes, 100 years, or 6 nanoseconds). Thus, physical science is ahistorical. Many of the familiar properties of the physical sciences stem from this view of time. Prediction, for example, often considered a hallmark of science, is possible only because Newtonian time does not have a past or a future. *Historical time,* on the other hand, is the time of the natural sciences, such as geology, paleontology, and archaeology. Here time is treated not only as an elapsed quantity, but also as historically unique; hence, it is measured on a ratio scale (e.g., 23 B.C., 157 years ago, 11,000 B.P.). When, as well as how long, is significant.

A date is an *estimate* based on a measurement or, more usually, a series of measurements. Like all such estimates, dates involve error. Careful work and redundant measurement eliminate *blunders,* large-magnitude errors such as misreading an instrument or switching sample numbers. *Measurement error* or random error is unavoidable error that arises from the process of measurement itself. Such error lacks a consistent magnitude and direction or sign (i.e., + or −). This is the error, for example, one finds expressed as a ± after a radiocarbon date (actually, it is usually the error term for beta ray counts per unit of time and, thus, is only indirectly and partly relevant to the date per se). Measurement error is largely a function of the instruments of measurement and the sample size. Consequently, there is a constant effort to improve equipment to reduce measurement error. *Systematic error* or bias is error that has a constant magnitude and sign and, therefore, is not randomly distributed. Whereas measurement error degrades dating *precision,* systematic error degrades dating *accuracy.* In dating, systematic error mostly arises in faulty method and research design. To understand these issues more thoroughly, we need a closer look at dating per se.

Contrary to popular belief and a lot of language used by archaeologists themselves, it is not possible to date objects or sites. The age of an object is obviously "now," or the sample would not exist; "site" as an archaeological construction referring to contemporaneous phenomena is even more removed. What is actually dated is what can be called an *event,* the time at which a set of attributes comes together as a set. How the set is aggregated is key, because what is dated, what constitutes the event, is a function of this decision. Further, the kind of measurement made may vary. We might measure the *mean age* of the set (i.e., the average time at which attributes were added to the set), or we might date the *median age* (i.e., the midpoint between the addition of the first and last members of the attribute set) or the *modal age* (i.e., the time at which most attributes were added). Archaeologists have not generally appreciated the differences that can arise from differences in measures used, compromising correlation and comparison when more than one method is involved.

Theory determines the choice of attributes to be included in an event and, thus, what gets dated. For example, if we were to constitute an event from attributes that a projectile point acquired at the time of manufacture (as opposed to those acquired through use, recycling, or deposition), then the event dated would be that of manufacture (and not use, recycling, or deposition). Archaeologists have not usually paid close attention to exactly what attribute sets are actually dated, contributing much error to archaeological chronologies.

Not all events thus defined can be dated. In fact, most archaeological events of interest are not strictly datable because most dating methods are not founded in archaeological theory. Rather, most methods depend on theory drawn from a physical science for their rationale. Chemical theory generates only methods to date chemical events; geological theory generates dating methods limited to geological events. One must, therefore, distinguish between the event dated and the archaeological event for which an age is being sought. Only when the dating method is founded in archaeological theory can the archaeological event of interest be strictly synonymous with the dated event. In *all* other cases, a bridging argument must be made to link the dated set of attributes to the archaeological event. The strength of the bridging argument and the quantifiability of the difference between dated event and archaeological target event is often ignored in archaeological practice and contributes much error. Regardless, one must distinguish between the precision and accuracy of a date and the precision and accuracy of an archaeological chronology.

Dating methods of high precision and accuracy do not unfailingly produce the best chronologies. Radiocarbon dating, for example, is more precise (small measurement error) and, over the time in which it has been calibrated by dendrochronology, more accurate than many other methods. Yet, because of the event it dates—the isolation of a sample's carbon from the atmospheric carbon reservoir—a ^{14}C date is often difficult to relate to an archaeological event. The archaeological event of interest is almost never the event effecting the separation of sample and atmosphere. In wood and wood charcoal, which are common samples dated by ^{14}C dating, the death of particular xylem cells is the reservoir-separation event, and it is a function of seasonal growth patterns. Growth of the outermost cells stops when the tree dies, but cells in inner rings died when growth stopped in previous years. The archaeologist may acquire a sample as charcoal from a hearth or a rafter in a building. Interest may be in when the fire burned or the house was built, archaeological events that are different from those being dated by ^{14}C dating. First, the wood sample represents not a single year, but a number of years, only the *last* of which *might* approximate the age of the fire or the construction of the house. This produces a systematic error, always overestimating the age of the archaeological event, thus degrading accuracy. The amount of overestimation is a function of how many annual rings are involved in the sample and whether the outermost ring is included. This kind of error can produce discrepancies of centuries with long-lived species. Error from this source can be obviated by using annual plants or annual structures (seeds, nuts) from perennial plants or minimized by using wood from twigs instead of trunks. The problems do not end here, however. The death of the tree may not, and therefore cannot be assumed to, have been caused by the archaeological event. The wood may have been long dead before it was used as firewood—it may have first been used to make another artifact and only after the original artifact's useful life was over was it used as firewood. House timbers may have been salvaged from earlier buildings one or more times before being used in the building in which they are found or turned into firewood. Further, the wood may have been found as deadwood/driftwood in the first place. Using multiple samples from the same archaeological event but representing different reservoir-separation events is one way to evaluate this source of error. This approach assumes that a coincidence between reservoir separations is best explained by a close linkage to the archaeological event. Yet, archaeologists have not always reported and evaluated the effect of the species/size of wood samples on ^{14}C age estimates or dated multiple samples (an obvious excuse is cost).

The net result of bridging arguments of variable reliability is that many dating methods of lower inherent precision, but in which the event dated is identical or easily linked with the archaeological event of interest, can yield chronologies of much higher precision than methods of higher intrinsic precision. Thermoluminescence (TL) dating is a case in point. Because many different quantities, each with its own error term, must be measured to calculate a TL date, this method is inherently less precise than the simpler ^{14}C dating; however, when applied to a piece of pottery, the event dated—the last time it was heated above ca. 500°C (its manufacture)—is archaeologically relevant. There is, therefore, no loss in precision or accuracy when converted to an archaeological date.

Kinds of Dating

Archaeologists frequently distinquish relative and absolute dating. This distinction refers to the kind of scale used to estimate age. *Relative dating* uses an ordinal scale (order); *absolute dating* uses either an interval or a ratio scale (magnitudes). While such a distinction is useful in an application context, it is not useful for understanding how dating methods work. For that, one needs to look to the generating theory. The Table printed here summarizes the methods commonly applicable to archaeological research.

Absolute methods are all nonarchaeological; they can be divided into four families based on the kind of "clock" employed: enumeration of annular structures (dendrochronology and varve analysis); radioactive-decay methods (radiocarbon dating [^{14}C], uranium/thorium dating [U/Th], and potassium/argon dating [K/Ar]); radioactivity dosimeters (electron spin resonance [ESR], thermoluminescence [TL], optically stimulated luminescence [OSL], and fission-track dating); and chemical-reaction rates (amino acid racemization and obsidian [glass] hydration dating).

Enumerative methods are the most reliable methods available, but they are limited in applicability to annular growth structures that can be associated with archaeological events. *Dendrochronology* is the best-known method in which simple counting of annular structures can be used for dating. Many trees in many environments have distinct quiescent and active growth phases linked to annual fluctuations in temperature and/or moisture. The growth phase, however, is variable from year to year, providing a historically unique component that allows a master sequence to be built from overlapping records taken from different trees and samples to be matched against the sequence. This method has played a major role in the American Southwest, where well-preserved archaeological wood is common, and a long master sequence has been constructed. *Varve analysis* is similar. In winter, lakes adjacent to glaciers receive little sedimentation; in summer, sedimentation increases, thus producing a distinct annular pattern in sedimentation not unlike growth rings in trees. The amount of sediment

D

TABLE I

Dating Methods Used in Archaeology

	Kind	*Clock*	*Examples*
Absolute			
	Enumerative	Annular structures	Dendrochronology, varves
	Radiometric	Isotopic decay	^{14}C, U/Th, K/Ar
	Dosimetiric	Exposure to radiation	TL, OSL, IRSL, ESR, fission track
	Chemical	Rates of reaction	Amino acid racemization, obsidian (glass) hydration
Relative			
	Chemical	Rates of reaction	Amino acid racemization, obsidian (glass) hydration, fluorine
	Geological	Sedimentary deposition	Superposition
	Archaeological	Distribution of neutral variation	Seriation

deposited, however, varies with the temperature and duration of each summer, producing the historically unique variation that allows different deposits to be correlated to form a master sequence and to date particular deposits. Obviously limited in areal extent, varve analysis has played a crucial role in some areas, notably Scandinavia.

Decay methods all use the half-life (the amount of time required for a sample to lose one half of its radioactivity) of a particular unstable (radioactive) isotope to tell time. The choice of isotope depends upon the composition of the sample—the isotope must be present in the sample—and its age. As shown in the figure, since measurement error is more or less fixed by the technique of measurement, it is the rate of change, fixed by the half-life, that determines dating error. Thus, an isotope with a short half-life like ^{14}C (half-life of 5,730 years) will exhibit large changes in radioactivity in the last few tens of thousands of years, whereas a longer-lived isotope like ^{40}K (half-life of 1.28×10^9 years) will have exhibited much less change over the same period and, thus, is much less suitable for dating in this range. After 50,000 years or so, there is so little ^{14}C left that the change in the amount of ^{14}C per unit of time is so small that it cannot be detected, but ^{40}K

is still sufficiently abundant to provide a good dating tool.

K/Ar and ^{14}C dating are similar in that the event dated is the separation of the sample reservoir from the atmospheric reservoir. Radioactive decay of the unstable isotopes in the sample, where they cannot be replenished, leads to a deficiency of the unstable isotope that is the quantity measured. U/Th dating is more complex in that it depends upon the differential solubility of uranium compounds (high) and those of thorium (low). The most common technique measures the disequilibrium between ^{230}Th and ^{234}U (^{230}Th deficiency technique), but other daughter products can be used.

As just noted, there are usually multiple techniques for effecting any particular method. In ^{14}C dating, for example, the most common techniques used to estimate the amount of ^{14}C in a sample is to count the beta-ray emissions when a ^{14}C atom disintegrates into a ^{14}N atom. Since only a tiny fraction of the ^{14}C atoms disintegrate over the course of a few days or weeks, relatively large samples are required, and old samples (more than 30,000 years) become problematic. The new AMS (atomic mass spectrometry) technique separates C atoms of different isotopes by their weights. By counting all of the ^{14}C atoms, much smaller samples can be mea-

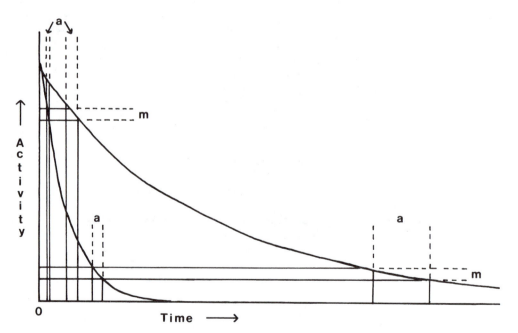

Relation of measurement error to estimates of age error using radioactive decay. Graph by Robert C. Dunnell.

sured, and the effective range of the method is extended by nearly a third. K/Ar dating supplies a different kind of example. The clock is the decay of ^{40}K into ^{40}Ar. In traditional K/Ar dating, K was measured by flame photometry and Ar by mass spectrometry. This required a large sample to be split into two. An undetermined error enters because samples are not strictly homogeneous. But bombardment of ^{40}K by fast neutrons in a reactor converts ^{40}K into ^{39}Ar, both of which can be measured simultaneously by mass spectrometry.

Dosimetric methods are ones in which the sample acts as a dosimeter, measuring the amount of radiation to which the sample has been exposed. If the annual dose rate can be estimated from contemporaneous measurements, and the susceptibility of samples to radiation determined similarly, then knowing the total amount of radiation received by a sample can be used to estimate its age. TL, OSL, and ESR all measure the same general phenomenon: Ionizing radiation dislodges electrons from atoms. While most electrons return to their ground states, some will be trapped at defects in the crystal structure. The longer a sample has been exposed to radiation, the more trapped electrons will accumulate until all of the defects are filled (saturation) setting the maximum age for a particular mineral. Commonly used minerals are quartz, calcite, feldspars, and hydroxyapatite. In OSL, IRSL (infrared stimulated luminescence), and TL, the addition of energy in the laboratory, visible light (usually green or yellow) in OSL, infrared light in IRSL, and heat in TL, will allow the trapped electrons to escape their defects and either return to the ground state or recombine with luminescence centers, emitting a photon of a particular energy associated with that luminescence center. This light is the phenomenon measured by both OSL and TL. Because it can be measured quite precisely, accurate estimates of total dose can be made. The greatest sources of error arise in determining the annual dose, because this involves estimating the amount of radiation the sample receives from its own constituents and its environment, both of which may change over time. Removing the outer 2 mm of samples eliminates alpha and beta contributions from the environment (alpha and beta rays do not travel far in solids) so that only gamma and cosmic contributions

need be figured. Water attenuates radiation effects, so the moisture history of a sample, often unknown, also contributes to errors in estimating the annual dose. In ESR, microwave bombardment of a sample in a magnetic field produces characteristic peaks that allow the direct estimation of the number of trapped electrons. While the precision of TL and OSL measurements are nearly an order of magnitude more precise, ESR has the distinct advantage of not dislodging the electrons in the measurement process, so it is essentially nondestructive and can be remeasured on the same sample over and over. The event being dated is either the growth of the crystalline structure (as in bone or travertine) or the last time it was exposed to energies high enough to empty all of the traps (as in ceramics and materials accidentally exposed to temperatures above about 500°C). The great strength of these methods is common coincidence of the event dated and the archaeological target event.

TL is widely used in Europe for ceramic dating. In the United States its potential is still largely untapped. While most applications are with ceramics, any crystalline material that has been heated to ≥500°C is potentially datable, including hearth stones and heated lithic artifacts. OSL has been primarily used to date aeolian deposits; the event being dated is exposure of silt-size particles to UV in transport, but efforts are being made to extend it to alluvial sediments as well. ESR has been used more sporadically, mainly on bone and enamel for Pleistocene-age materials, where the relatively large measurement error is not a major disadvantage.

Fission-track dating, while still dosimetric, operates rather differently. When a ^{238}U atom fissions, the nucleus breaks into two parts that are violently repelled and create damage paths (fission tracks) in glasses and crystalline minerals. Because ^{238}U fissions at a constant rate, if one knows the amount of uranium in a sample, counting the frequency of fission tracks allows one to calculate the age of the material. Because of the low rate of fission of ^{238}U and the low amounts in which it is found in many materials, fission-track dating usually carries too large an error term to be used for samples younger than 100,000 years to be dated. The event dated, the formation of crystal or glass, usually means that a geological event is dated.

Chemical dating methods all use the rate of a particular reaction or group of reactions. A reaction whose rate is entirely dependent upon time would be ideal. In reality, all reactions depend on a series of variables—rate = f(time, temperature, pressure, moisture, pH . . .)—so the best for which one can hope is a reaction in which nontemporal factors are either minor or can be measured independently. Since all reactions do have a temporal component, there is always some correlation with time, a feature that has led not a few investigators to make absolute-dating claims prematurely. This appears to be the case with the current state of amino acid racemization, a method that utilizes protein decomposition in bone.

Obsidian hydration is less problematic. Amorphous silica (glass) hydrates (OH radicals are incorporated) from the surface upon exposure to the environment. Because such materials are often highly prized by artisans for making stone tools, the event dated, the creation of a new surface, is often an archaeologically relevant event. Even recycling, if separated by a significant amount of time, could be dated independently of manufacture. The thickness of the weathered zone is directly measured under high magnification, and, if one knows the rate of hydration, an age for creation of the surface can be calculated. Hydration rates, however, are dependent upon composition, temperature, moisture, and pressure; only composition can be securely quantified from modern data.

Obsidian hydration and other chemical methods are actually more powerful in a relative-dating role. Obsidian hydration, for example, can be used to separate mixed assemblages into their constituent temporal components because, in coming from the same environment, all pieces share the same history and the environmental variables can be held constant.

Fluorine dating of bone is another case in point. Fluorine is taken up from the environment by hydroxyapatite, replacing calcium. The resulting fluoroapatite is more stable than the original material so the reaction is irreversible. Thus, in general, the greater the amount of fluorine, the greater the age. But because the amount of fluorine in the environment and the rate at which the reaction proceeds is so variable, it cannot be used to make interval age estimates. It can, however, be used to determine if bones from the same setting differ in age. This can be important. The Piltdown hoax, which consisted of human, simian, and other fauna that were claimed as pre-*Homo sapiens,* was finally exposed by fluorine-uranium-nitrogen dating in 1953, forty years after initial "discovery" in Sussex, England.

Historically more important have been two relative methods, one from geology, *superposition* or, as it is more loosely known, *stratigraphy,* and the other purely archaeological, *seriation.* Indeed, these two methods probably still see the greatest use of all dating methods in archaeology.

Superposition depends upon a law of sedimentary deposits, first enunciated in the eighteenth century, that, in a sequence of sedimentary layers, the order of the layers from top to bottom is from youngest to oldest. The event dated is the formation of the layers not, as archaeologists have often erroneously assumed, the particles making up the layer. While layers are sometimes archaeologically significant events, more often than not superposition has been used to make arguments about artifacts found in layers. A bridging argument is required to link artifact manufacture to layer deposition. Such arguments are almost always omitted, leading to occasional errors of major magnitude (e.g., reversed stratigraphy) and erroneous methods (e.g., metrical or arbitrary stratigraphy), yet the coincidence of the two distinct events is often close enough that superposition has proved to be a central chronological tool.

Seriation is one of archaeology's major methodological achievements. It was probably invented independently at least three times, each in slightly different form. Historically, the method depends upon an empirical generalization that, if artifacts are described in a certain way, a way that came to be called *stylistic,* then their distribution through time (initially supplied by stratigraphy) was continuous if recorded as present/absent, or monotonic (unimodal) if recorded as frequency of occurrence. It was quickly realized that, if one arranged undated assemblages, appropriately described, to conform with this generalization, they were arranged in chronological order. The event being dated can vary from application to application, but, commonly, it is the mean time of deposition of an assemblage. Because archaeologists simply used the generalization rather than try to figure out why it worked, errors, occasionally of large magnitude, occur. Today, the phenomenon exploited by seriation is better understood, and error can be practically eliminated. The stylistic attributes of earlier generations are understood as neutral variants (i.e., variants that do not affect fitness and which, therefore, reflect only the probabilistic transmission process. Although spatial variation may mimic temporal variation, tests have been developed to identify its effects in seriations. There are at least six families of techniques for applying the method: deterministic (the solution must meet the model) or probabilistic (the solution is taken to be the closest approximation to the model) solutions; occurrence (present or absent) or frequency descriptions; and similarity (the relation between assemblages is represented by a single number) or full descriptions. The requirement of large, representative samples remains the most serious limitation of the method.

Correlation

A major role of absolute methods, typically expensive, has been to correlate and/or calibrate relative chronologies built by seriation or stratigraphy. This is accomplished by correlating the interval-scale measurements usually obtained from such methods with our own calendar. The calendric dates serve to integrate originally disparate chronologies. Calendric correlations may be simple (as when converting a TL before-present date to B.C./A.D. date) or quite complex. In ^{14}C dating, for example, variable production rates for ^{14}C in the atmosphere mean that the amount of ^{14}C remaining in a sample is a function of two variables: age and rate of production; thus, ^{14}C dates must be corrected. Dendrochronology is used for the last several millennia; U/Th dating and/or TL dating have to be used beyond the range of dendrochronology.

Correlation is often elevated to the role of method when some historical sequence dated by one of the methods already discussed can be related to otherwise undated archaeological events. Early examples of this approach involved environmental variables. Once vegetation sequences have been worked out and dated (usually by ^{14}C), it may be possible to date archaeological deposits by matching their pollen frequencies with the sequence. Archaeomagnetic dating is of this general kind. The location of the magnetic poles varies over time. Once the apparent variation in magnetic north has been worked out for an area, it is possible to use the location of magnetic north, preserved in the alignment of iron in fixed features (e.g., hearths) by heating above the Curie point, to date fixed features.

The potential for such dating techniques is almost limitless. For example, the change in pottery-wall thickness can be carefully documented over time using ^{14}C dating. Because the change is monotonic and variability at any given point in time is low, it is possible to use mean vessel-wall thickness to date ceramic assemblages over a significant area in the midwestern United States. Unfortunately, this correlation method was erroneously called seriation.

Archaeologists often construct arguments to link undated assemblages with dated ones. This is usually called *typological dating*. The general argument is that similar assemblages are likely of similar age. Most such efforts do not distinguish analogous (by virtue of external constraints), homologous (by virtue of shared ancestry), and chance similarities. To the extent that analogous and chance similarities play a role in the assessment of similarity, the results will be erroneous. The use of homologous similarities does produce coarse-grained alignments because it amounts to poorly controlled, nonquantitative seriation.

Summary

Dating in archaeology is a complex mosaic of disparate methods. Not surprisingly, reliability varies widely. To a large extent, it is the lack of theoretical sophistication on the part of archaeologists that lies at the root of most problems. Improvements on this account and the development of new methods in the physical sciences make the possibility of better chronologies a realistic prospect.

Robert C. Dunnell

See also AMINO ACID RACEMIZATION/ EPIMERIZATION DATING; ARCHAEOMMAGNETIC DATING; DENDROCHRONOLOGY; ELECTRON SPIN RESONANCE (ESR) DATING; FISSION TRACK DATING; FLUORINE-URANIUM-NITROGEN DATING; LUMINESCENCE DATING; METRICAL STRATIGRAPHY; MIDWESTERN TAXONOMIC

D

SYSTEM; NATURAL STRATIGRAPHY; OBSIDIAN HYDRATION DATING; OPTICAL DATING; RADIO-CARBON DATING; ROCK-ART DATING; SERIATION; STRATIFICATION; STRATIGRAPHY; TEPHROCHRONOLOGY; THERMOLUMINESCENCE DATING; TYPE-VARIETY SYSTEM; URANIUM-SERIES DATING; VARVE ANALYSIS

Further Readings

Aitken, M.J. (1990) Science-Based Dating in Archaeology. London: Longman.

Dean, J.S. (1978) Independent dating in archaeological analysis. In M.B. Schiffer (ed.): Advances in Archaeological Method and Theory, vol. 1, pp. 223–255. New York: Academic.

Dunnell, R.C. and Readhead, M.L. (1988) The relation of dating and chronology: Comments on Chatters and Hoover (1986) and Butler and Stein (1988). Quaternary Research 39:232–233.

Rosholt, J.N., Colman, S.M., Stuiver, M., Damon, P.E., Naeser, C.H., Naeser, N.D., Szabo, B.J., Muhs, D.R., Liddicoat, J.C., Forman, S.L., Machette, M.N., and Pierce, K.L. (1991) Dating methods applicable to the Quaternary. In R.B. Morrison (ed.): Quaternary Nonglacial Geology: Coterminus U.S., pp. 45–74. Boulder, CO: Geological Society of America.

Deetz, James J. Fanto (1930–)

American anthropologist, archaeologist, and museum administrator. Born on February 8, 1930, in Cumberland, Maryland, Deetz was educated at Harvard University, where he received his bachelor's in 1957, his master's in 1959, and his doctorate in 1960. Deetz began his career at the University of California at Santa Barbara (1960–1967), where he first as instructor of anthropology and eventually as full professor. He returned to the East Coast as full professor of anthropology at Brown University. Deetz is currently Professor Emeritus of Anthropology at the University of California, Berkeley, and Harrison Professor of Historical Archaeology at the University of Virginia. In 1997, he received the Harrington Medal of the Society for Historical Archaeology. Since 1995, Deetz has conducted fieldwork at Plimoth Plantation in Plymouth, Massachusetts.

Deetz is a leading American archaeologist, an important figure in New World historical archaeology, and a pioneer in the New Archae-ology movement. *The Dynamics of Stylistic Change in Arikara Ceramics* (1965), based on his doctoral dissertation, is an important study that demonstrates the potential of archaeology to show changes in social structure. Knowing that the ethnohistorical data suggested that the Arikara Indians of the Plains region were originally a matrilocal society and that women made pottery, Deetz studied the cluster of pottery styles at Arikara sites and demonstrated that the material record reflected these kinship and residence patterns through concentrations of distinct pottery styles in specific habitation areas. He also showed that, as the matrilocal system breaks down (as evidenced by decreasing house size), distribution of pottery styles becomes random. This approach was highly influential and can be seen in later studies, such as the famous study of the Broken K Pueblo site, Arizona, by James Hill and William A. Longacre. Deetz is also known for his work with Edwin Dethelfsen on Colonial mortuary art, in particular their classic examination of New England grave stones and changes in the principal decorative motifs of death's head, cherub, and urn and willow which provided a useful check for seriation and its application to historical archaeology. His book *In Small Things Forgotten* is an elegant introduction to Colonial archaeology.

Joseph J. Basile

See also ETHNOARCHAEOLOGY; HISTORICAL ARCHAEOLOGY; NEW/PROCESSUAL ARCHAEOLOGY

Further Readings

Deetz, J. (1965) The Dynamics of Stylistic Change in Arikara Ceramics. Urbana, IL: University of Illinois Press.

Deetz, J. (1993) Flowerdew Hundred: The Archaeology of a Virginia Plantation, 1619–1864. Charlottesville: University Press of Virginia.

Deetz, J. (1996) In Small Things Forgotten: An Archaeology of Early American Life, revised and expanded ed. New York: Anchor Books/Doubleday.

Dendrochronology

Dating method exploiting growth-ring patterns in trees. *Dendrochronology* is an all-embracing term for the various types of dating information derived from the study of tree-ring patterns; the term was coined by Andrew E. Douglass, the pioneer of the tree-ring dating method in the early twentieth century.

The principle of the method is universal: Trees of a single species growing over the same span of years, within a coherent climatic area, tend to produce recognizably similar patterns of wide and narrow growth rings.

Most trees, outside the tropics, tend to produce a single layer of new growth cells each year; these growth layers can be viewed in any transverse section of the trunk of the tree. Tree-ring patterns can be studied by observing the transverse section of felled trees or by extracting cores from living trees using a variety of hollow metal borers. Due to changing environmental conditions, the growth layers are rarely of the same thickness in consecutive years; thus, during the lifetime of a tree, a sequence of wide and narrow rings is built up that forms the ring pattern of that tree. Trees of the same species growing over the same period of time, under similar conditions, in a coherent climatic region, tend to exhibit recognizably similar ring patterns. Trees of different species vary greatly in duration of growth so that ring patterns vary in length from a few decades, in the case of hazel (*Corylus*), to centuries, in the case of oak (*Quercus*) and most temperate pines (*Pinus*), up to millennia, in the case of giant redwoods (*Sequoia*) and bristlecone pine (*Pinus aristata*). Redwoods can live for 3,000 years, while the oldest individual specimen of bristlecone is reputed to have lived for 4,900 years.

Dendrochronology involves the construction of regional and species-specific master chronologies for trees of known felling or sampling dates. The concept of a master or reference chronology is critical in tree-ring studies and involves the *exact* synchronization of the ring patterns of a number, usually a minimum of 10 but often as many as 100, ring patterns of the same species from the same coherent climatic area. This procedure, of cross-matching many replicate ring patterns, allows the ironing out of any problems, such as missing, duplicate, or doubtful rings in individual ring patterns, and allows the establishment of an exact calendrical record of tree growth for that area and that species back to the age limits of available replicate specimens.

It has been widely observed that replicated master chronologies can be extended far back in time, beyond the limits of living trees, by overlapping the ring patterns from living trees to those from ancient specimens. Depending on locality, the ancient timbers can be obtained from buildings, from archaeological sites, from many lake, bog, and river deposits, and from desiccated contexts as well as charcoal. Continuous, year-by-year master chronologies have been constructed back to 6200 B.C. for bristlecone pines in the United States and back to 8480 B.C. for oaks in Europe.

The availability of replicated, species-specific, regional master chronologies allows the dating of new specimens by comparison of the ring pattern of the sample, at every position of overlap, against the master chronology. In most areas where tree rings have been studied intensively, it is observed that long sample ring patterns will show high-correlation matching with the master chronology at only one position; such high-correlation cross-matching positions occur when the sample and the master represent the same span of calendar years. When a unique, high-correlation dating position is found, the exact calendar years of the sample are defined. Most dendrochronological study is aimed at the establishment of the calendar date of the last year of growth of the sample (i.e., the date of the last existing growth ring).

So exact is dendrochronology that, when the sample is complete to the underbark surface, the date of the last year of growth represents the death date, normally referred to as the *felling date,* of the tree. In practice, dendrochronology is such an exact procedure that workers have to take account of the following fact. Because temperate trees tend to grow in the summer months and remain dormant over the winter, a dated ring pattern that ends in, say, 1546 could have been felled either late in 1546 or early in 1547. Thus, the date of the last year of growth in a strict sense need not be the felling date, which could have been early in the following year. However, the corollary of this is that samples that end with a partly formed final ring can be specified as having been felled in the summer of their last year. In the case of oak trees, this means that some specimens felling can be specified to within about two months. Obviously, the most useful dating information in the case of archaeological or building timbers is the felling date, while in the dating of geomorphologic processes, such as floods or landslides, workers are interested in the dates when trees died or were damaged.

The ability to date specimens by dendrochronology has caused a revolution in chronological precision in those areas of the world where long chronologies have been developed. Precise calendar dates can be provided for prehistoric archaeological remains in Europe and America and for studies of bog, lake, and river-valley history in many parts of the world, outside the tropics. Evidence of environmental change observable within the tree-ring chronologies themselves allows the dating of environmental events at a time resolution comparable with tree-ring-dated archaeological activity and, when available, historical information.

Applications

Chronologies have been constructed for numerous reasons, including astronomical (to look for sunspot cycles), geophysical (to establish the dates of natural events, such as landslips, earthquakes, volcanic eruptions, river-valley developments, water-level changes, and glacial advances), climatological (the field of dendroclimatology aims to reconstruct past climate parameters), art-historical (to date such artifacts as paintings on wooden boards and furniture), and geochemical (to look at past isotopic records at annual resolution and at trace-element evidence for pollution). To this list could be added studies aimed at ascertaining the age structure and management practices associated with ancient woodlands, as well as extensive fire histories of both natural and human origin.

Replication

Perhaps the most important aspect of dendrochronology is its absolute nature. In classic dendrochronological work, the master chronologies are both internally replicated and replicated between independent workers—so-called *tertiary* replication. An American example would be the independent replication of the last 5,200 years of the lower-forest-border Bristlecone Pine Chronology by Valmore C. LaMarche, Jr., and Thomas P. Harlan's upper-treeline chronology of the same species. In Europe, the Göttingen Oak Chronology independently replicates the Irish 7,400-year Oak Chronology. Thus, the master chronologies against which new samples are dated are

deemed absolutely correct—to exact calendar years.

In the same way, classic dendrochronological dating aims to provide exact calendar-date ranges for samples whose ring patterns are successfully cross-dated against appropriate master chronologies. However, not all samples can be definitively dated, and the most severe limitation of the method is the fact that samples that do not definitively date remain undated; there is no middle ground. There can be many reasons why samples do not cross-date successfully, and these mostly center on short ring patterns, problem rings, and imports in the broadest sense (i.e., timbers from an area incompatible with available master chronologies).

The major strength of successful dendrochronological work is that all classic dendrochronological datings, for sites or artifacts, can be compared directly. Similarly, environmental deductions from classic master chronologies can be compared directly in real time irrespective of their geographical location. Thus, over a period of time, a major new database of precisely compatible environmental and archaeological information will become available.

From an archaeological viewpoint, dendrochronology has assisted with chronological refinement in three principal ways. First, it has allowed the precise dating of some archaeological sites and structures from all periods back to Neolithic times. It is also clear that the corpus of sites dated by dendrochronology will continue to grow as more timbers are retrieved from archaeological contexts. Second, the long tree-ring chronologies have provided precisely dated samples of wood for the calibration of the radiocarbon time scale back to 8300 B.C. Thus, archaeologists and other workers can convert their radiocarbon determinations into estimates of real calendar age. Moreover, the availability of wood samples of precisely known age has allowed radiocarbon laboratories to make more realistic assessments of their own accuracy than was normal in the past. Thus, there is a greater awareness of the limitations associated with radiocarbon chronology, and interlaboratory comparisons are an accepted norm.

Archaeological Applications

The ability to provide intrinsic, absolute dating for some archaeological structures and objects has opened up a new window on the past. Chronological coverage, in terms of available reference or master chronologies, is inevitably best for the last one to two millennia. Thus, in northern Europe, oak dendrochronology is effectively available as a routine dating method for medieval sites of the last two millennia. Master chronologies for this period exist across a broad swath from Ireland to the eastern Baltic. Buildings, from humble vernacular dwellings to major castles and cathedrals, have provided samples for dating. Because of the high success rate in dating long-lived medieval oak samples, new archaeological dating information can come as easily from the waterlogged foundation of a bridge pier in a wet moat as from the roof timbers of a standing chateau. Thus, the list of dated medieval objects includes millraces, coffins, well linings, river revetments, fishweirs, wainscot boards, furniture, painted panels, and musical instruments, among others. This means that dendrochronology, with its chronological refinement, is intruding into the mundane activities of the past just as much as into high-prestige buildings. Moreover, the very act of dating a wide range of structures is beginning to provide evidence for the main periods of human constructional activity within and between areas; conversely, some widespread building pauses are being documented. Ernst Hollstein observed an essential absence of building in Germany between A.D. 1348 and 1440, while Peter I. Kuniholm and Cecil L. Striker, dating in Greece, found fourteen buildings with timber end dates in the first half of the fourteenth century, compared with only four in the second half of the century. Given the significant mid-fourteenth-century forest regeneration observed in Britain and Ireland, this widespread package of precisely dated information shows the effects of the Black Death almost as clearly as historical documentation. This, in turn, implies that, as better chronological coverage is provided for earlier periods, and more dates become available, other examples of widespread growth or decline may prove reconstructable.

Another example of the power of accumulated dating is provided by the timbers from Pueblo ruins in the American Southwest. Dendrochronological analysis has continued in the region since Douglass's time, so that a recent dendrochronological corpus from that area contains more than 1,300 dated sites composed of more than 27,000 individual dates (Robinson and Cameron 1991). With such a corpus, major patterns of building activity can be traced through time. For example, from a trickle of dates in the first few centuries A.D., the number of sites expands rapidly from the mid-sixth century with subsequent pauses in the eighth and tenth centuries, when the number of sites drop by 60 percent and 50 percent, respectively (interestingly, the sixth century expansion in the number of tree-ring dated sites is mirrored exactly in Europe, implying some macroscale influence, see below). On a more localized scale, superbly detailed reconstructions of within-site developments have been possible within individual Pueblo complexes with what amounts to historical reconstructions of the site histories.

Prehistoric Dating

While for the American Southwest the bulk of prehistoric dating is confined to the present era, in central and northern Europe, where the long oak chronologies were still under development during the 1970s and 1980s, the numbers of dated prehistoric sites are beginning to accumulate. Timbers from Swiss lake dwellings, from Bronze Age coffins and Iron Age sites in Germany, and from bog roadways and wetland sites in Britain and Ireland are starting to provide an absolute chronological framework for the pre-Roman period. The ultimate precision of dendrochronology is well exemplified in the observation that the oak timbers used in the Neolithic Sweet Track in southwest England last grew in 3807 B.C. and were felled either late in that year or early in 3806. It is hard to believe that any other dating method will ever be able to improve on such resolution.

Archaeological dating in Europe is not restricted to oak. In southeastern Europe, Kuniholm is currently working with a floating 1503 year Juniper Chronology that spans 2259 +/- 37 B.C. to 757 +/- 37 B.C. on detailed radiocarbon evidence. This chronology, which already links timbers from key sites such as the Midas Mound Tumulus at Gordion and Shaft Grave V at Mycenae, will eventually be absolutely dated and will resolve many of the long-standing questions of Mediterranean Bronze Age and Neolithic chronology. When that time arrives, direct chronological comparisons will be possible from northern to southern Europe. There seems no good reason why this chronological network will not spread to eventually include Egypt and China.

Trade
The widespread availability of local chronologies within a greater regional area opens up the possibility of tracing some nonlocal timbers back to their source area, thereby allowing archaeologists to establish physical evidence for trade or movement in the past. There are a growing number of examples of timber movement in the past, including eastern Baltic timbers brought to England and Flanders by Hansa merchants—Hans Holbein painted in England on Baltic boards—while one of the famous 1,000-year-old longboats from Roskilde, Denmark, has proven to be constructed from Irish oak from the Dublin area. This is an area of study that is bound to expand and that may prove most important in the nautical sphere, in which tree-ring evidence is likely to prove a better guide to where a ship was constructed than analysis of its contents.

Paleoenvironmental Information
It has always been apparent that tree-ring patterns in a region cross-date because the trees have shared responses to controlling environmental factors. Thus, similar ring patterns in trees within a region imply that the trees are storing environmental information—Douglass recognized at an early stage that his pines from the Southwest were exhibiting a common response to drought conditions and that the long tree-ring master chronologies were effectively proxy records of past moisture availability. Dendroclimatologists have been building on this ever since, so that there is a widespread thrust toward climate reconstruction from tree-ring patterns.

Precisely dated environmental information is becoming available from the analysis of long chronologies in both the New and Old Worlds. While, in many cases, the environmental information is coming from the same chronologies constructed for, and used in, archaeological dating, in others it is coming from chronologies from areas remote from substantial human activity (e.g., in the Sierra Nevada and Fennoscandia). With the precise time control offered by den-

drochronology, environmental effects can be studied across the Northern Hemisphere, and an understanding of the environmental context in which human activity took place in the past is gradually being developed, in real time. The fact that new long chronologies are being produced in Chile, Tasmania, and New Zealand means that information from the Southern Hemisphere will increasingly be available for the reconstruction of aspects of the past global climate.

One hypothesis concerning the possible effects of widespread climatic downturns has centered on the environmental effects of large volcanic eruptions. Hemispheric cooling, due to the stratospheric loading produced by some explosive eruptions, appears to lead to short-term climatic alterations that could easily have had severe effects on agricultural populations. Plausible evidence supports the suggestion that in at least one instance, following the dry fog of A.D. 536, widespread famines were followed by the spread of plague with apparently devastating consequences. This scenario, of widespread environmental effects following A.D. 536, is supported by an observed reduction in tree growth in many tree-ring chronologies from America and Europe. The close relationship between this environmental event and the increase in dated sites in the mid-sixth century, mentioned above, has not been explained (as of 1998) but seems likely to be causal. The example serves to show that the study of the human past is firmly linked to the study of chronology and the study of environmental change. Thus, dendroclimatology and dendroecology are destined to become as important to archaeologists as conventional dendrochronological dating for any real understanding of the archaeological record.

M.G.L. Baillie

See also DATING, METHOD AND THEORY

Further Readings
Baillie, M.G.L. (1982) Tree-ring Dating and Archaeology. London: Croom Helm.
Baillie, M.G.L. (1995) A Slice through Time. London: Routledge.
Bartholin, T.S., Berglund, B.E., Eckstein, D., and Schweingruber, F.H., eds. (1992) Tree-rings and Environment. (Proceedings of the International Dendrochrono-

logical Symposium, Ystad, South Sweden, September 3–9, 1990), Lundqua 34.

Cook, E.R., and Kairiukstis, L.A., eds. (1990) Methods of Dendrochronology: Applications in the Environmental Sciences. Dordrecht: Kluwer.

Hollstein, E. (1980) Mitteleuropäische Eichenchronologie. Mainz am Rhein: Phillip Von Zabern.

Kuniholm, P.I., and Striker, C.L. (1987) Dendrochronological investigations in the Aegean and neighbouring regions, 1983–1986. Journal of Field Archaeology 14:385–398.

LaMarche, V.C. and Harlan, T.P. (1973) Accuracy of tree-ring dating of bristlecone pine for calibration of the radiocarbon time scale. Journal of Geophysical Research 78:8849–8858.

Robinson, W.R., and Cameron, C.M. (1991) A Directory of Tree-Ring Dated Prehistoric Sites in the American Southwest. Tucson: University of Arizona Press.

Schweingruber, F.H. (1989) Tree-rings: Basics and Applications of Dendrochronology. Dordrecht: Kluwer.

Dunnell, Robert C. (1942–)

American anthropologist and archaeologist. Born in Wheeling, West Virginia, Dunnell received his bachelor's degree from the University of Kentucky in 1964 and his doctorate from Yale University, where he was a student of Irving Rouse, in 1967. He joined the Anthropology Department at the University of Washington in 1967, was department chair (1972–1985), and has been a full professor since 1974. He is a Woodrow Wilson Fellow, a recipient of National Science Foundation and Wenner-Gren Foundation grants, and has been awarded numerous contracts with federal and state agencies for the conduct of cultural-resource-management projects in Washington state. He has served on the editorial boards of the *Journal of Field Archaeology, Advances in Archaeological Method and Theory,* and the *West Virginia Archaeologist* and has been the general editor of the *SAA Papers* for the Society for American Archaeology. From 1983 to 1985, he served as vice president and subsequently president of the Association for Field Archaeology, and he has been active on committees in the Society for American

Archaeology and the American Society for Conservation Archaeology.

Dunnell is well known for his writings on both systematics (the principles of unit formation) and explanatory theory (the principles used to explain variation in those units). His *Systematics in Prehistory* presents a conceptual framework for discussing and operationalizing the scientific formation of units in archaeology and easily remains the most thorough treatment of the matter in archaeology. Much of the ambiguity in the past practice of archaeological systematics, Dunnell argues, stems from a poor articulation of the problems to be addressed by classifications and, frequently, from a confusion of description for definition. A proper understanding of systematics and classification makes it possible to scientifically evaluate archaeological systematics as practiced by archaeologists. Examples of the use of systematics to address specific archaeological problems are found in Dunnell's articles "Seriation Method and Its Evaluation" and "Archaeological Potential of Anthropological and Scientific Models of Function," the latter in a festschrift honoring Rouse.

Dunnell advocates the development of an evolutionary theory for archaeology similar to that of the biological disciplines and as something different from the cultural evolution espoused by Leslie White and other anthropologists. Archaeologists deal with the cultural transmission of human behaviors, as opposed to genetic transmission of biological traits; as in biology, selection is the primary mechanism that affects the outcome of the transmission process. For complex societies, the relevant unit of selection may not be so much the individual organism as it is the society within which the individual human organisms operate. Dunnell eschews anthropological archaeology as an approach to the development of explanatory theory, arguing that the data of archaeology are artifacts, not ethnographic units inferred or reconstructed from those artifacts. Archaeologists need to formulate theories to account for directly observable phenomena, such as changes in the spatial distribution of settlements or differences in wear patterns on artifacts, because observations based on those phenomena can be used directly to falsify implications of the theory. For anthropological archaeologists, however, the subjects of

D

explanations are social or behavioral units that are inferred from the archaeological material but that cannot be directly observed by the archaeologist; a hypothesis regarding such inferred units is incapable of being falsified, since negative results imply either that the explanatory model is incorrect or that the procedure used to infer the behavioral unit is incorrect.

Dunnell has also contributed significantly to the reformulation of the theoretical constructs that guide an understanding of what constitutes archaeological data. He argues that the archaeological record is most productively viewed as a continuous distribution of material across the landscape, and, for that reason, he and his students have focused on the refinement of survey and surface collection as methods to be used in the collection of primary archaeological data (rather than as techniques for the discovery of sites or for finding locations in which to excavate). His commitment to data analyses is reflected in the laboratories he has established at the University of Washington, which he and his students use for thermoluminescent dating, the electron spin resonance (ESR) analysis of lithics, other physical and chemical characterization of artifacts, and the analysis of archaeological sediments. Dunnell continues to both challenge and advance the practice of theory and method in American archaeology.

Glen Eugene Rice

See also EVOLUTION, CULTURAL; EVOLUTION, SCIENTIFIC

Further Readings

Dunnell, R.C. (1970) Seriation method and its evaluation. American Antiquity 35:305–319.

Dunnell, R.C. (1971) Systematics in Prehistory. New York: Free Press.

Dunnell, R.C. (1978) Archaeological potential of anthropological and scientific models of function. In R.C. Dunnell and E. Hall (eds.): Archaeological Essays in Honor of Irving B. Rouse, pp. 41–73. The Hague/New York: Mouton.

Dunnell, R.C. (1980) Evolutionary theory in archaeology. In M.B. Schiffer (ed.): Advances in Archaeological Method and Theory, vol. 3, pp. 35–99. New York: Academic.

Dyes, Characterization

The analysis and identification of natural substances, deriving from plant and animal species, used in the permanent coloration of textiles.

Textiles were far more important, relative to most other human artifacts, than is commonly realized, and our knowledge of how they were made relies all too often on technical descriptions inadequately understood because of linguistic problems. Many languages that can be read are nevertheless obscure when technical terms are involved. For example, even in eighteenth-century English, we do not necessarily understand *grain*. It could mean *cochineal*, but perhaps *lac* as well. It is important that we can confirm written evidence of ancient practice by analyzing surviving examples of early textiles.

After the inevitable failure of attempts to use substances that are not dyes (e.g., particulate pigments or colored compounds without means of fixing themselves to fibers) the two main methods of dyeing were probably discovered in very remote antiquity. Dyes are compounds that are absorbed by textiles to color them in a way that resists washing and may have been discovered in about the eighth millennium B.C. The evidence is the discovery of painted patterns on walls at the Neolithic site of Çatal Hüyük in Turkey, interpreted by James Mellaart as *kelims,* flat-woven wool textiles that are still made as carpets or hangings. The two general methods of dyeing are vat dyeing, which, in practice, means dyeing with indigo, and mordant dyeing, especially with plants of the family *Rubiaceae* for red and purple shades or with most other plants for yellows. *Vat dyeing* involves dissolving the (otherwise very insoluble) indigo by (chemical) reduction, traditionally by fermentation in an alkaline solution, giving a yellow solution into which the textile is dipped; on exposure to air, the indigo is regenerated, intimately associated with the fiber. *Mordant dyeing* involves soaking the textile in a salt of (usually) aluminum or iron, then in the suspension of the dye. In favorable circumstances, dyes of both types are known to survive for more than 2,000 years.

As the color of textiles is important, all textiles excavated should, if possible, be treated in ways that permit subsequent dye analysis. This means mild washing and mechanically careful manipulation and precludes, for example, fixing in a transparent resin matrix or washing with hydrochloric acid. Many excavated textile fragments later shown to retain identifiable dye residues are colored dark brown or black by earth, wood, or body fluids; they should nevertheless be analyzed for dyes if possible. A textile that is almost pure white, however, cannot have been dyed; the human eye is a sensitive probe of color. Cellulose (plant origin) fibers, cotton and linen, seem to have been dyed less often than protein (animal origin) fibers such as wool and silk.

Vat Dyes

Identification of dyes requires the removal of the dye from the fiber; for vat dyes, this can be done with a strong polar organic solvent miscible with water, such as pyridine or dimethylformamide. In favorable cases, analysis is possible on less than 1 mg of fiber, and 10–20 mg is normally a maximum sample. While a 1:1 mixture of water and pyridine removes indigo efficiently, Tyrian Purple (see below) requires nearly pure pyridine. Dilution with water gives a solution from which dichloromethane extracts the dye (other solvents, such as ether, can also be used). A visible blue color can be seen if indigo was present, and this can be confirmed by agitating the organic layer with sodium-hydroxide solution, then dilute sulfuric acid, when the blue color of indigo remains in the organic layer, while colored materials derived from soil are removed.

Final proof of identity can be obtained by examining the solution in a spectrophotometer. Light, of a single wavelength that can be varied, is passed through the solution, and the extent to which it is absorbed is measured electronically and the spectrum recorded. Indigo shows a maximum at ca. 600 nanometers (varies with solvent) due to indigotin and a shoulder at ca. 520 nm due to indorubin (Figure 1). These are the two components of indigo, which (however early the sample) is made by a chemical process from the precursors present in the plant. The plant (several species of diverse botanical types have been used in different areas of the Old and New Worlds) cannot be inferred from the ratio of these components, nor can natural indigo be distinguished from synthetic indigo.

Tyrian Purple, obtained from various shellfish, is essentially dibromoindigo and is much less soluble. It tends to precipitate as a bronze solid, and good solvents are needed to

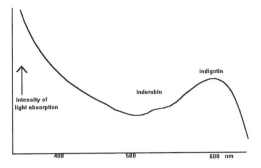

D

Figure 1. *Absorption spectrum of indigo using a spectrophotometer. Y-axis* = intensity of light absorption; X-axis = wavelength of light. Indigo, which has two components, shows a maximum at ca. 600 nm (varies with solvent) due to the indigotin, and a shoulder at ca. 520 nm due to indorubin. Graph by Mark C. Whiting.

keep it in solution, when it can be identified by its absorption maximum at ca. 590 nm. Both indigo and dibromoindigo can also be identified by mass spectrometry, and the latter by its X-ray fluorescence, due to the presence of the element bromine. It was seldom, if ever, used after ca. A.D. 700.

As a practical point, it is unwise to rely on the exact wavelength of the absorption maxima given by the instrument used, because of possible instrumental errors and because exact wavelengths of absorption maxima vary with the solvent composition. It is best to compare with an identified specimen using the same solvent.

Mordant Dyes

Mordant dyes, normally fixed to fiber with salts of aluminum, iron, or tin (other metals have been used more recently, especially chromium) may be grouped into: (1) the dyes of madder and other rubiaceous plants; (2) the dyes of cochineal, kermes, and similar insects; (3) the flavonoid dyes, present in most plants, which give a variety of yellow shades; (4) the gallotannins, used with iron mordants to give black; and (5) the dyewoods, giving blues, bluish reds, and blacks. They can be removed from the textile fiber by treatment with a mineral acid (typically, 10 percent sulfuric acid) and an organic solvent (typically, methanol).

Group 1

Madder (*Rubia tinctorum* L; the root is used) is, with indigo, one of the two dyes most often encountered in Old World textiles. It can give

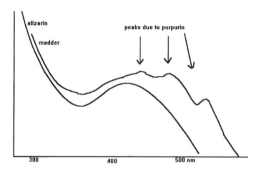

Figure 2. Absorption spectra of two red dyes, synthetic alizarin and natural madder (comprising both alizarin and purpurin). Y-axis = intensity of light absorption; X-axis = wavelength of light. Graph by Mark C. Whiting.

a range of colors, from bright red through various browns and purples to violet, as the mordant is varied from pure alumina to iron. Species of the genus *Relbunium,* used in South America, have similar dye components, mainly the anthraquinones alizarin and purpurin. In India, the related *Rubia cordifolia* L *(munjeet)* and *Oldelandia umbellata* L *(chay)* were also used; in Japan, *Akane (Rubia akane* L) had similar applications. The organic components of all of these dyes are extracted from water with ether, and the spectrum of the mixture is easily recognized, though it varies with the alizarin/purpurin ratio. Madder has been used for so long and over so wide an area that its presence, like that of indigo, seldom provides evidence of the time or place of manufacture.

The identification of a dye within this group is easy by either chromatography or spectrometry, and it is not hard to verify the presence of both alizarin and purpurin. *Akane* contains no alizarin, and *chay* is said not to contain purpurin; however, the quantitative separation of components needed for firm identification of individual plant species or varieties within this group has not yet been reported. Alizarin was made synthetically in the last quarter of the nineteenth century and gave results very similar to madder. It can easily be distinguished from madder by its absorption spectrum (Figure 2).

Group 2

The insect dyes include cochineal (*Dactylopius coccus* Costa), used from the remote past

in the New World and in other regions progressively from A.D.1530 in Spain to ca. 1800 in Persia. Similar insect dyes that were displaced by cochineal were kermes (*Kermes vermilio* Planchon) in western Europe, Polish cochineal (*Porphyrophora polonica* L) in eastern Europe and western Asia, and lac (*Kerria lacca* Kerr) from Anatolia eastward. There is shadowy evidence for other insect dyes, especially *Armenian cochineal,* sometimes called *kirmiz* and identified with *Porphyrophora hameli* Brandt. Linguistically, this area is a minefield, with names related to the Semitic root *krms,* crimson in English, being used variously with wide or narrow applications, while scientific nomenclature has its own problems. Chemically, things are easier. Cochineal and Armenian cochineal are almost pure carminic acid; kermes is almost pure kermesic acid; Polish cochineal is a mixture of the two, ratio ca. 10:1; and lac is a mixture of the laccaic acids, therefore somewhat variable in its properties, like madder. All of these dyes are visually equivalent, giving a bluer, richer shade of red than madder.

As they were used in different areas at different times, many conclusions about provenance are possible, so their identification is often informative. This can be done by thin-layer chromatography, but the writer prefers methods based on solvent extraction. Kermesic acid is extracted almost completely from acidic aqueous solutions by ether: When the solution obtained from the textile, and aqueous methanolic acid is shaken with ether, the dyestuff (and, therefore, the color) passes into the upper ether layer. It can easily be distinguished from madder by its color (orange rather than yellow) or, better, its electronic spectrum. Carminic acid from cochineal is very water soluble and is hardly extracted by ether. When its solution is shaken with the organic solvent pentan-3-one, the dyestuff does pass partly into the pentanone layer. The ratio of the concentration (constant for a given chemical constituent but variable for different constituents) in the upper to the lower layer is easily measured with a spectrophotometer. For carminic acid, it is ca. 0.85, whereas the mixture of laccaic acids from lac gives values of 1.7–3. In pentan–3–one, the electronic spectra of carminic acid and of the laccaic acids are (just) distinguishable, but not in water.

Group 3

With flavonoid dyes, the approximate methods normally successful for the red dyes described above usually fail, and it is necessary to separate the components of the mixture of flavonoids present and then identify them. The separation can be done by thin-layer chromatography, but the subsequent tests on scraped-off spots are difficult. Much better is high-pressure chromatography, which involves a stream of solvent being percolated through a tube filled with a powder on which an organic liquid is supported. The components emerge separately, and the process is best followed by a diode-array detector, which rapidly and repeatedly scans the spectrum of the liquid that comes through the column. If this is unavailable, detection at 300 or 350 nm, wavelengths at which all flavones and flavonols absorb, allows them to be observed and isolated. If their spectra are examined before and after salts of aluminum or zirconium are added, partial chemical structures for the individual flavonoids can be deduced and their identities guessed. Co-chromatography with authentic samples for comparison may then allow firm identification. Quite often, sugar molecules are attached to the flavonoid, either at oxygen, in which case hydrolysis with dilute acid removes them, or at carbon, in which case they are not removable. Such dyes are water soluble and elute rapidly from the usual chromatographic columns.

Yellow dyes are numerous, as most plants contain flavonoids, often useful amounts. Traditional dyeing methods were likely to use for yellow shades locally available plants, especially food residues (e.g., vine leaves, onion skins), rather than specially grown or imported exotic dyes, and the identification of a yellow dye is the most hopeful way of deciding where a textile was made. It is less likely to help with dating, as traditions are long lived. However, the botanical identification of a chemically known dye mixture is often difficult, and much research remains to be done. Particularly important yellow dyes include dyer's greenwood (*Genista tinctoria* L), mainly genistein, an isoflavone; weld (*Luteola tinctoria* L), mainly the flavone luteolin; isparuk (*Delphinium semibarbatum* Blemert), comprising the flavonols quercitin, kaempferol, and isorhamnetin; and Persian berries, from various *Rhamnus* species, containing the flavonols quercetin, rhamnetin, and rhamnazin. Dyes based on flavonols are less fast to light than flavones, and isoflavone dyes are paler in shade than the more golden flavones and flavonols. All yellow dyes are usually mordanted with alumina.

Group 4

The so-called tannins are a complex group of natural products, the structures of which are still emerging. With an iron mordant, they give most of the black dyes traditionally used. Unfortunately, wool or silk so dyed is weakened by light, and a combination of light and mechanical wear erodes it, so that black areas are often low or even missing; they are often replaced in restoration. Little progress has been made in identifying the organic components of tannins used in dyes, but ellagic acid can often be found in what remains of the dyed wool.

Group 5

The dyewoods are an important category, to judge from the literature. Examination of a large number of archaeological specimens has not given the writer much experience of the group, perhaps because they easily fade in light (and are, therefore, destroyed) while in use and are not resistant to degradation when buried. They are mordant dyes, brazilwood (*Caesalpinia brasiliensis* L; producing red with alumina) and logwood (*Haemotoxylon campechianum* L; producing black with iron) being the most frequently encountered. The insoluble dyewoods (camwood, barwood, and the like) are larger molecules and easier to extract; they are little known in dye-analysis work.

Other Dyes

In the residual category are several dyes of some importance. Lichens give rise to two quite different types. In one, the lichen is heated with the (protein) fiber, and the compounds called *depsides* (complex derivatives of salicaldehyde) present in the lichen undergo a chemical reaction with side chains of the fiber protein to give brown pigments covalently attached to the fiber (i.e., they become part of the actual molecules of the fiber). These substantive dyes represent the ultimate in fastness, to the extent that the dye analyst can say little about them; in no way can they be removed. The other type of lichen contains different constituents that react with

D

ammonia, or in traditional practice urea from urine, to give brightly colored compounds not originally present in the lichen. They are direct dyes for protein fibers, meaning that they fix themselves (not always very firmly) to the fiber without need for a mordant, and they can be brilliant; litmus is the most familiar and has the well-known property of changing color with acidity, which is, of course, undesirable. Dyes of this type are also notoriously liable to fade in light. The lichen dyes of the litmus/lackmuss/cudbear/orseille/roccella group are complex mixtures, made by various recipes, and the lichens from which they were made are also varied. A classical dye described by the Roman scholar Pliny the Elder as *fucus* may well be a lichen-derived dye rather than a seaweed product.

Safflower (*Carthamus tinctorius* L; the active component is called *carthamine*) has only recently had its structure determined, and wrong formulae are still being cited. It is a sharp pink in color. A direct dye, it fades rapidly to yellow in light and was used mainly for silk textiles meant to be seen in candlelight. It is easily removed from the fiber and can be identified by its absorption maximum at 510 nm. It is so water soluble that the solvents mentioned above, and even butanol, which is still more powerful, fail to remove it from water. This fact, and the limited acidity range over which its characteristic color persists, allows its identification.

Saffron (*Crocus sativus* L) contains the carotenoid compound crocetin, easily identified but almost unknown as a textile dye. Turmeric (*Curcuma longa* L) also gives a fugitive yellow. Both are well-known food colors. Saffron, in particular, is often said to be used on textiles but virtually never is (or was).

In traditional dyeing, a wide range of colors is often obtained with a very limited range of dyestuffs. Greens are always mixtures of yellows, usually flavonoid, and indigo, needing two independent dyeing operations. Orange and golden shades are usually obtained from a mixture of red and yellow mordant dyes, applied in one operation. Purple can be (but seldom is) obtained by separately dyeing with madder or an insect dye, then with indigo, but the use of madder with an iron mordant alone is far more common (Coptic textiles may have the madder/indigo mixture, or even Tyrian Purple). Reports of saffron, Tyrian Purple, or kermes should be believed only after reliable laboratory identification. These dyes are rare indeed.

Indigodisulphonic acid, a direct dye derived from natural indigo and sulfuric acid, was first reported in 1740 and is found in late-eighteenth-century samplers, for example. Other synthetic dyes become common after ca. 1860. Any identification of a natural dye in what is believed to be an old textile should be made with the possibility of a synthetic dye (of which many thousands exist) in mind; it may be a reproduction or even a forgery.

Mark C. Whiting

Further Readings

Saltzman, M. (1978) The identification of dyes in archaeological and ethnographic textiles. In G.F. Carter (ed.): Archaeological Chemistry II, pp. 172–185 (Advances in Chemistry Series 171). Washington, D.C.: American Chemical Society.

Saltzman, M. (1986) Analysis of dyes in museum textiles, or, you can't tell a dye by its color. In C. McLean and P. Connell (eds.): Textile Conservation Symposium, pp. 27–39. Los Angeles: Los Angeles County Museum of Art.

Scheppe, H., and Roosen-Runge, H. (1986) Carmine: Cochineal carmine and kermes carmine. In R.L. Feller (ed.): Artists' Pigments: A Handbook of Their History and Characteristics, pp. 255–283. Cambridge: Cambridge University Press/Washington, D.C.: National Gallery of Art.

Yamaoka, R., et al. (1989) The identification of dyes of Greco-Roman period fabric in Egypt using liquid chromatography/mass spectrometry. Mass Spectroscopy 37(4):249–253.

E

Ecological Theory in Archaeology

The application of ecological theory to the understanding of human behavior in past societies. *Ecology* is the study of the interactions between organisms and their environment, with an emphasis on how these interactions affect the behavior of the organisms. Biologists have carried out an enormous amount of ecological research, focusing on such topics as mating strategies, diet choice, grouping behavior, territoriality, predator-prey relationships, and colonization. In all cases, these aspects of behavior have been viewed, in part, as the product of particular environmental circumstances, and, as a result, a considerable body of theory about how the environment shapes behavior has been developed. The foundation for all such ecological theory is evolution, with the assumption that behavior has been shaped by natural selection to be adaptive in particular environments.

Since the 1960s, anthropologists have turned to this emerging body of theory to assist their understanding of human behavior. In part, this has been driven by the assumption that humans, like other organisms, have been subject to natural selection. At least as important, however, has been the observation that there exist clear, cross-cultural patterns of similarities and differences in behavior and organization and that these patterns are related to environmental similarities and differences. Hunter-gatherers in tropical forests of Africa, South America, and Southeast Asia, for example, all show surprising similarities in such features as economic activities, patterns of settlement and land use, and social organization. It is an easy inference that these similarities derive from the shared problems of adapting to tropical-forest environments.

Although a number of anthropologists began to explore the role of ecological relationships in influencing cultural patterns, two stand out for their impact on the discipline and, in particular, on archaeological interpretations. Leslie White's strong views on culture as a uniquely human means of adaptation were immensely influential, promoting the understanding of cultural behavior as ultimately utilitarian, serving the function of promoting that culture's "fit" with its environment. Julian Steward, through meticulous ethnographic studies in South America and the Great Basin, provided concrete examples of how particular groups adapted to their environments by various means and concluded that a *cultural core* of behaviors, especially technology, subsistence, settlement patterns, and social organization, were most important in accomplishing this adaptation.

Archaeologists, for a variety of reasons, were quick to embrace ecological approaches to understanding human behavior. Growing dissatisfaction with what was perceived as the overly descriptive nature of archaeological scholarship led, in the 1960s, to an explicit call for greater emphasis on scientific explanation of the past. The job of archaeology was seen as not only documenting what happened in 3000 B.C. along the Nile, for example, but also why it happened then and there. Explanation required a foundation of theories of human behavior, and ecological theory provided one coherent option. Moreover, because archaeologists deal with material remains, most prominently representing food and technology, prehistoric subsistence and technology have always seemed more visible than ideology or social relations. Consequently, a materialist theory emphasizing precisely these core elements of behavior was most attractive.

The adoption of ecological approaches in archaeology has profoundly shaped research. At the most general level, it has determined the dominant research questions addressed: those events or processes that dramatically altered the relationships between humans and the environment. These include questions about origins (of settled life, of agriculture, and of complex states), about collapses (of the Maya civilization, of Pueblo society in much of the American Southwest), and about population movements (into the New World, throughout the Pacific). Furthermore, these approaches suggested the nature of causation: alteration in the ecological circumstances of the groups involved, through such processes as environmental change or population growth.

Ecological Interpretations

Ecological research has had clear working assumptions underlying approaches to questions about the past: (1) prehistoric cultural similarities derive from environmental similarities, at least in general features; (2) cultural differences reflect, to a large extent, different environmental circumstances; and (3) culture change represents a response to changing ecological relationships. A few examples may illustrate the types of explanations such assumptions generate.

Agriculture appears to have been developed in several parts of the world independently. Most archaeological interpretations of this process have emphasized the causal importance of changes in the relationship between people and their food resources. Such changes could have taken many forms: (1) overall food shortage due to such factors as increased drought or population growth; (2) a decrease in certain foods, such as big game, because of either environmental change or overhunting; (3) a decrease in land available to provide wild foods because of rising sea level or population growth and competition; (4) an increase in the uncertainty of food gathering due to environmental fluctuations; or (5) an increase in the seasonality of food availability, with longer lean seasons arising from environmental changes. Despite the specific differences in these interpretations, they

all share an emphasis on changes in the ecological relationships of prehistoric hunter-gatherers, reflected by changing costs and/or risks of wild foods. The development of agriculture, then, is seen as adaptive to this stressful situation by providing a new, more manageable food source.

The origins of sociopolitical complexity, in the form of complex chiefdoms and states, is another topic that has been investigated in an ecological framework. Again, despite cross-cultural differences in specific factors involved, many interpretations have focused on a few, general approaches. In one view, complex organization, with the emergence of an elite ruling group, has been seen as adaptive for the society as a whole because the new elite can perform necessary functions more efficiently than can individuals or households working independently. Such functions might include management of irrigation canals, co-ordination of redistribution among different economic sectors, administration of long-distance trade, or conduct of warfare. The need for these managerial functions, in turn, arose from particular ecological circumstances, such as population growth in environments that are arid, vegetationally diverse, lacking in critical resources, or circumscribed by other groups.

Another approach to the emergence of a ruling elite does not emphasize the adaptive benefits to the entire society, but rather examines the potential for an emerging elite to control critical resources, thereby gaining authority over others. This approach is still ecological, however, in focusing on whether particular environments lend themselves to such control. Critical resources might include well-watered plots in otherwise arid environments, the richest soils in a diverse area, or important, but limited, occurrences of stone or metal ores. Environments in which all key resources are abundant and widespread make it difficult for any group to obtain control of others through the control of goods.

Relationship to Other Developments

The prominence of ecological theory in archaeology has complemented, and no doubt encouraged, other developments in the field. Theories of cultural evolution, which included schemes of different evolutionary stages through which societies pass, were embraced by ecologically oriented scholars. Each stage (e.g., band, tribe, chiefdom, state) represented a tightly correlated set of economic and sociopolitical institutions. Such correlations would be expected if economy and sociopolitical organization are both adaptations to environmental situations. Even though overly generalized scenarios of evolution through stages are not as popular as they once were, many scholars still use the stages as convenient ways to classify and discuss prehistoric societies. Although the focus of research in the 1990s appears to be on specific differences among societies, at a general level the patterns underlying these general stages remain impressive. Exceptions to the patterns have become hot topics precisely because they are exceptions: prehistoric hunting-and-gathering societies on the Northwest Coast of North America were more sociopolitically complex than expected from their economy; the Maya were too complex for their presumed economic base of slash-and-burn farming. Much of the research into these exceptions has also been ecological, trying to demonstrate unique environmental features (such as abundant, predictable, and controllable salmon resources on the Northwest Coast) or misconceptions about prehistoric economies (with Mayan agriculture being much more intensive and complex than previously thought).

Ecological approaches have also benefited from, and created a demand for, impressive methodological refinements in archaeology. Given the importance accorded the environment, interdisciplinary research is common. Major advances have been made in the study of prehistoric sediments, tree rings, pollen, phytoliths, insects, rodent bones, and even pack-rat middens.

As the most obvious arena of human interaction with the environment, subsistence economies have also received considerable attention. Recovery of animal remains commonly includes fine-mesh screening during excavation, and analyses typically go beyond listing identifiable species to details of prey age, sex, body parts, and butchering marks, all in order to extract as much information as possible about the organization of the economy. Knowledge of the role of prehistoric plant use has been greatly enhanced by the development of flotation techniques and by studies of food residues in pots. Investigations of farming techniques regularly include attention to remains of weed communities, as well as crops, for the information they provide on land rotation and harvesting techniques. Newly developed techniques of isotopic analysis of human skeletal remains provide additional information about prehistoric nutrition and food stress.

Techniques for studying prehistoric technology have also proliferated. Microscopic use-wear analysis of stone tools has revolutionized lithic analysis and allowed archaeologists to reconstruct much more completely prehistoric activities occurring at sites. Technological studies of ceramics allow researchers to correlate form with function more reliably, and various chemical analyses permit the determination of clay sources.

In tandem with these developments has been the emergence of a regional framework in field research. Because people exploit their environment in different ways and distribute their activities across the landscape, no one site is likely to provide sufficient information on prehistoric economies. As a result, regional surveys have become a primary tool of research, used to collect information about the distribution of sites and activities throughout an area. Often, these surveys are stratified by environmental zone, in the explicit expectation that there will be a correlation between habitat and activities.

New dating techniques—radiocarbon, thermoluminescence, tree-ring dating—have also been critical to ecological research. Testing of interpretations about causation requires precise control of the timing of events. Environmental changes supposedly involved in cultural transformations, for example, must be found to precede their presumed effects. Refined chronologies have improved immensely the ability to recognize sequences in the archaeological record.

Problems, Criticisms, and New Developments

Despite the generally positive effects of ecological theory on archaeological practice and understanding of the past, there have been a number of problems in its application and a growing dissatisfaction with the constraints it may impose. One of the main criticisms is that a central concept—*adaptation*—remains poorly defined and difficult to measure. In biology, adaptation is grounded in the concept of relative reproductive fitness, the success of organisms in surviving and reproducing relative to other organisms. In archaeological usage, however, adaptation is rarely linked directly to reproductive success and only indirectly to survival. Traditionally, whatever behaviors persisted were often assumed to be adaptive, leading to circular explanations of their persistence by virtue of their adaptedness. More recently, various behaviors have been evaluated in terms of proxy measures, such as efficiency of energy or time use, with the assumption that efficient behavior promotes fitness by providing relatively more time or energy to food getting, defense, or infant care. Much of ecological research, then, consists of cost-benefit analyses of different behaviors, with the most efficient in given circumstances assumed to be the most adaptive. In addition to requiring an intellectual leap, this approach poses particular problems in archaeology, where certain activities, such as mammoth hunting or mound building cannot be observed or timed. Ethnographic observation and experiments by archaeologists are among the few ways of trying to overcome this problem.

Another criticism of ecological approaches in archaeology is that the level of analysis has been inappropriate. The adaptation under study has usually been that of a group—a culture, a society, or a population. Although the issue of group selection has been much debated, it is commonly recognized that the primary level at which natural selection operates is that of the individual. To conclude that a society adapts to changes is to mislabel the aggregate effects of all of the individual adaptive responses. And because societies are not homogeneous groups of identical individuals, there should be considerable variation in these responses. Unfortunately, archaeology has great difficulty in reconstructing individual behavior. However, increasing attention is being given to different segments of past societies (men and women, commoners and elite, urban and rural groups), each with possibly differing goals and constraints, in an attempt to deal more adequately with the diversity inherent in all societies.

Related to this criticism is the assumption underlying many analyses that societies or cultures are tightly integrated wholes. Ecological archaeologists commonly draw models from systems theory to organize their views of past societies. In such models, every facet of society, every institution, every activity is connected to every other. A change in one realm (e.g., economic activities) very likely causes a change in others (e.g., political organization). Changing adaptations, in this view, will entail a coherent set of changes across most aspects of society. Yet, societies are not so well integrated. Some aspects of behavior, such as settlement patterns, may change much more rapidly and readily than others, such as religious ideology. The loose articulation of different societal parts means that archaeologists must expect lags in adaptive responses, with the accompanying inefficiencies and internal tensions that characterize modern societies.

Furthermore, ecological models often implicitly assume that societies are in equilibrium with their environments until some triggering event—an environmental change or the crossing of some population threshhold—upsets the balance and requires change. If, however, societies are neither homogeneous in terms of individual behavior nor tightly integrated systems, then any apparent equilibrium is likely to be extremely dynamic, with considerable variation in most factors such as crop yields, population distribution, and social relations. When this variation is coupled with environmental fluctuations (e.g., in rainfall, storm frequency), which characterize every environment to some extent, then one must assume that change in ecological relations is continual. Even apparently dramatic cultural transformations, such as the rise of states, can potentially have their roots in this internal dynamic, and the search for clear, external "triggers" may be fruitless.

Many ecological approaches in archaeology also assume that societies (or individuals) are driven by natural selection to the optimal adaptation in a particular environment. Models of optimal (most efficient) food choices or optimal (least-cost) administrative settlement patterns are frequently developed to explain the past. Such models are extremely useful as a baseline, a yardstick for measuring the effectiveness of real behavior as reconstructed from the archaeological record. Their danger lies in their tendency to promote expectations that prehistoric people really did behave this way and to bias reconstructions accordingly. Natural selection does not produce the best conceivable adaptations; it simply promotes the best of those available. Similarly, individuals do not necessarily respond to changes or stresses in any optimal manner. They carry a history of cultural tradition, social networks, and individual experience, and their behavior may be severely constrained. Archaeologists still need to devote considerable attention to the effects of such constraints on subsequent behavior.

Ecological approaches continue to be prominent in archaeological research, but they have changed considerably. Many of the changes are responses to the inadequacies of previous, oversimplified interpretations, which were founded on models of homogeneous, highly integrated cultural systems moving from one equilibrium state to another. Many of these changes pose new challenges to archaeological field and laboratory techniques, as they demand new levels of detail about internal societal differences and fine-scale economic and environmental changes. Despite these methodological problems, ecological research is certain to continue its importance. All people, past and present, are bound by a network of relationships to their environments. The cross-cultural patterns created by these relationships are still present. Understanding these varied and changing relationships is essential to understanding the past.

Michael A. Jochim

See also BUTZER, KARL W.; EVOLUTION, CULTURAL; EVOLUTION, SCIENTIFIC

Further Readings

Bettinger, R. (1991) Hunter-Gatherers: Archaeological and Evolutionary Theory. New York: Plenum.

Butzer, K. (1982) Archaeology as Human Ecology. Cambridge: Cambridge University Press.

Jochim, M. (1984) The ecosystem concept in archaeology. In E.Moran (ed.): The Ecosystem Concept in Anthropology, pp. 87–102. Boulder, CO: Westview.

Johnson, A., and Earle, T. (1987) The Evolution of Human Societies. Stanford: Stanford University Press.

Kirch, P. (1980) The archaeological study of adaptation: Theoretical and methodological issues. In M.B. Schiffer (ed.): Advances in Archaeological Method and Theory, vol. 3, pp. 101–156. New York: Academic.

Trigger, B. (1989) A History of Archaeological Thought. Cambridge: Cambridge University Press.

Electrical and Electromagnetic Prospecting

A collection of prospecting methods aimed at describing the subsurface structure of the ground by utilizing its electrical and magnetic properties. In *electrical prospecting,* an electrical voltage is applied to the ground, and, based on the nature of the material(s) or feature(s) present and the water content, the resistivity to the flow of electricity is measured. Since archaeological features (e.g., walls, kilns, ditches) and their surrounding matrix (e.g. soil, sand, clay) will absorb water differently, their different electrical resistance will assist in their identification. In *electromagnetic prospecting,* both electrical conductivity and magnetic properties are measured. These prospecting methods depend principally on the granularity of the soil, and results differ in sandy, rocky, or clayey soils. If the electric field is constant or changes only slowly with time, one speaks of the *d.c. electrical method,* and if the variation of the field with time has to be taken into consideration, reference is made to the *electromagnetic method.* But the boundary between the two domains depends on the properties of the terrain and the geometric scale.

Basic Principles

When an electric field is applied to a soil, it can produce free displacement of charges—in this case, ions—thus, an electric current or a limited displacement of charges and, thus, a polarization of the milieu. The first effect is characterized by the electric conductivity (or its inverse, the resistivity); the second, by the relative dielectric permittivity. We have

$$i = \sigma E \text{ and } D = \varepsilon_r \varepsilon_o E$$

where i is the current density, σ is the conductivity (expressed in Siemens by meter, S/m, in the international system of units, the resistivity ρ being expressed in Ohm. meter, Ω.m), E is the electric field, D is the electric induction, ε_o is the dielectric permittivity of the vacuum (in Farad per meter, F/m), and ε_r is the relative permittivity of the milieu (no units).

The ions present in the soil that are responsible for electrical conductivity can be found in two states: They may circulate freely in the volume of interstitial water, in which case one speaks of *volumic conduction,* or they may be found adsorbed on the surface of the solid grains, in which case one speaks of *surface conduction.* In the second case, there is a double-layer phenomenon, with the anions in direct contact with the crystalline structure of the grains and immobile, and the cations external to these and mobile. Cations can "slide" along the surface of the grains.

The total conductivity is the sum of the two types of conduction. The first is directly linked to the water content of the soil; the second, to its specific surface (i.e., the total surface of the grains per unit volume). In coarse-grained soil, the specific surface is limited to several dm^2 per cm^3, while in clays, it can be very large and exceed 50 m^2 per cm^3. When the water is not salty, surface conduction is dominant for fine-grained soils. Clay soils are conductive, whereas humid, sandy soils are resistive. In all of these cases, the mobility of the ions is favored at higher temperatures, and this change is of the order of 2 percent per degree centigrade. The range of variation of the resistivity of soils and rocks is the greatest of all of the properties used in prospection. The Table shows some of the resistivity values (Ohm. m) of materials that may be encountered in archaeological prospecting.

The dielectric permittivity varies with frequency. At frequencies higher than 50 MHz, it is characterized by the opposition that exists between water, for which $\varepsilon_r = 81$, and that of the other constituents, which are less than 5. It is, therefore, a good indicator of the quantity of free water present, and this original property is due to the fact that the water molecules are polar and, thus, orient easily in the direction of the field. This property is difficult to measure at frequencies below several hundred kHz, and it has not been used yet (as of 1998) in archaeological prospecting outside the high-frequency radar range.

d.c. Electrical Prospection

The injection of an electrical current in the ground can be achieved by direct conduction via electrodes inserted into the ground or electrostatically by means of poles in air near the ground surface (see below) (Figure 1). It is necessary to use at least four poles: two, named A and B, are used for current injection; the measurement of the difference of potential requires two additional electrodes, M and N. The transfer impedance of the quadripole is, therefore:

$$\frac{\Delta V}{I} = \frac{\rho}{2\pi} \left\{ \frac{1}{MA} - \frac{1}{MB} - \frac{1}{NA} + \frac{1}{NB} \right\}$$

where V is the voltage, I is the current, ρ is the resistivity. For homogenous soil, this is directly proportional to the resistivity. This measure is dependent on the geometry of the poles and the distribution of the electrical resistivities in the ground.

There are nearly an infinite variety of ways to place electrodes on a surface. The question of the best arrangement is eternally debated. However, for essentially practical reasons, the preference of archaeological prospectors has fallen on the following configurations or arrays (Figure 1): The Wenner configuration, in which the electrodes are equidistant with a separation a; the pole-pole (or bipole or twin), in which only two electrodes are moved, and the other two are kept at a distance; and the square configuration.

Table of Resistivity Values

MATERIAL	RESISTIVITY VALUE
Salted soils	1–10 Ω.m
Clay and clayed soils	3–30 Ω.m
Silt and silty soils	15–70 Ω.m
Arable layer (sedimentary context)	30–100 Ω.m
Arable layer (crystalline context)	100–1,000 Ω.m
Limestone stones	300–1,000 Ω.m
Crystalline stones	2,000–1,0000 Ω.m

The first of these electrode configurations permits a succession of measurements along a line by displacing a single electrode and switching. This allows using either the normal Wenner or the Wenner Dipole-Dipole arrangement. The second configuration permits moving only two electrodes if one takes the precaution of separating B and N from the pair M and A while maintaining a considerable distance between B and N. Its use is well adapted to small areas in which the movement of the cables poses no problems. The third, square configuration is best for mechanized continuous measurement. The quadripole is compact, and, by simple switching of the electrodes B and M, one can change the direction of the line of injection. As the anomaly shapes on a resistivity map depend on the current direction, this phenomenon is called *apparent anisotropy effect.* Such a change can provide a corrected resistivity map in clear agreement with the exact shape of the present features.

Regardless of the type of quadripole arrangement used, the method is traditionally utilized in two ways: either in the *profiling,* in which an arrangement of fixed dimensions is moved to reveal lateral variations of resistivity and, thus, map the subsurface structures, or as a *sounding,* in which the center of the arrangement remains fixed, and its size is varied in a systematic fashion so as to take into account an increasing depth of terrain. By interpreting such soundings, one can reconstruct the variation of resistivity versus depth and thus determine the depth of subsurface horizons.

A prospecting campaign carried out on a medieval farm near Montbaron (Indre, France) by Georges Ducomet constitutes a good example of automatic prospecting with a 1 meter square array to detect remains of stone walling on a medieval settlement (Figure 2). In a totally different context, the soundings carried out at the site of Susa in Iran clearly show the top and the thickness of the platform on which various buildings of an Achemenid palace were constructed (Figure 3). A sounding also permits checking the depth of investigation (i.e., the thickness of the terrain, which is taken into account by the measurements). For a Wenner arrangement, this is of the order of $3a/4$; for the pole-pole, ca. $1.5a$; and for the square array, a; in all three cases a is the distance between A and M electrodes.

The profiling and the sounding are complementary, and good prospection does both.

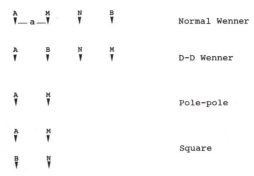

Figure 1. *Electrode array commonly used in archaeological prospecting. Figure by Michel Dabas.*

Recent developments of systems of multiple electrodes that are capable of realizing both functions simultaneously are the logical result of this complementarity.

The *electrostatic method,* in which the poles are in air without galvanic contact with the ground, is the most efficient solution among various ones proposed for the problem of dealing with the limitations of the contact between electrodes and the ground. A pair of poles carries two opposite electrostatic charges that generate in their vicinity an electrical potential depending on the electrical properties of the different existing media. By measuring the difference of potential between two other poles, one can determine these properties. For terrestrial soils, it allows determination of the apparent resistivity, and if the height of the poles is small, the transfer impedance is the same as defined above for d.c. electrical prospecting. The electrostatic method is, thus, a generalization of the electric method, and it offers the same possibilities for sounding, profiling, and multiple arrangements. The most recent measuring devices permit use of either electrostatic poles or electrodes. An example of the use of electrostatic measurement (Figure 4) is shown by a study done in the interior of the cathedral at Chartres in France. As is common, the remains of a former building exist beneath the present one. The apparent resistivity map obtained from electrostatic measurements revealed under the limestone floor older substructures, probably corresponding to the remains of the Roman cathedral built by Saint Fulbert of Chartres before A.D. 1070 and destroyed a century later by fire.

Low Frequency Electromagnetic Prospecting
Electromagnetic prospecting differs from the

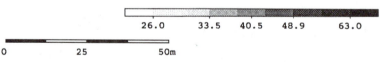

Figure 2. Mapping of the apparent resistivity (in Ω.m) at Montbaron (Indre, France) with a towed, square array (measuring 1 m each side) and automatic recording of the data (this system is named by the French acronym RATEAU). The higher resistivity values (dark areas) correspond to medieval stone walls enclosing zones of different functions: settlement, pasture, and the largest enclosure indicating the border of cultivation. These features overlay a former rectangular system of field limits (possibly dating to the Iron Age). Figure by Alain Tabbagh.

previously described methods in that a great variety of sources, waveshapes, and measurable or measured parameters are available, but all measure the ground conductivity (σ).

One may classify the methods according to the kind of variations of the source with time. If the variation is sinusoidal, one speaks of the *frequency domain*. If it is an impulse, one uses the term *time-domain* electromag-netic methods (TDEM). It is also possible to consider the geometry of the source that determines the type of primary field distribution. But a major factor is the initially unexpected influence of the magnetic properties of the soil that may mask those of electrical conductivity. In TDEM, the decay of the response generated by conductivity differs from that generated by magnetic viscosity, but their separation necessitates complex signal processing; in practice, these instruments can be used as metal detectors. For archaeological applications, only one type of frequency-domain instrument is in use: the *Slingram* type, which comprises two small coils—one transmitter and one receiver—rigidly assembled. By choosing a sufficiently low frequency (less than 40 kHz), it is possible to measure simultaneously the electrical conductivity and the magnetic susceptibility of the soil. This double measurement makes this technique particularly interesting.

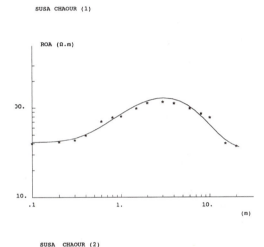

SUSA CHAOUR (1)

ROA (Ω.m)

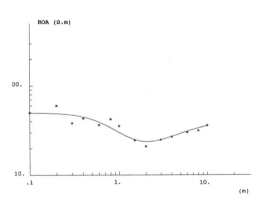

SUSA CHAOUR (2)

ROA (Ω.m)

Figure 3. Sounding curves at an Achemenid palace (Susa, Iran), showing the apparent resistivity variations versus the distance between A and M in a Wenner array. (1) Resistivity survey reveals the stony platform for the construction of the palace: One can observe, under a 0.5-m thick layer of 50 Ω.m resistivity, a resistive second layer of 230 Ω.m resistivity and 2.5 m in thickness. (2) Without the stone platform, one observes a conductive, water-saturated and fine-grained second layer of 19 Ω.m resistivity and 2 m in thickness. Figure by Michel Dabas and Albert Hesse.

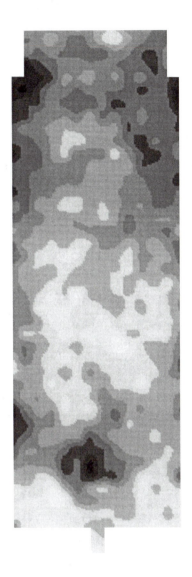

450   595   734   906   1200   Ohm.m

0   2   4m

Figure 4. Apparent resistivity map of the floor of the Chartres cathedral (electrostatic quadripole, 1.2 m each side). The resistivity is high between 500 and 1,200 Ω.m, which corresponds to a coarse subsoil. In the eastern part (top of the figure) the higher values correspond to ancient excavations. On the western part appears the limit of the former tenth–eleventh century edifice. Figure by Michel Dabas.

If only the conductivity is measured, the concept of using several receiving coils simultaneously to gain information about vertical and horizontal variations may be applied as in electrical prospecting. Nevertheless, comparison of the two methods emphasizes the following: With the Slingram instrument, the measurement is proportional to conductivity, whereas in electrical prospection it is proportional to the resistivity. The first is more interesting for highly conductive terrain, while the second is useful for highly resistive terrain. Furthermore, the Slingram technique is sensitive to the presence of metallic objects, which permits it to be used as a metal detector but limits its use considerably in urban settings.

Michel Dabas
Albert Hesse
Alain Tabbagh

See also MAGNETIC PROSPECTING

Further Readings

Clark, A.J. (1990) Seeing Beneath the Soil. London: Batsford.

Dabas, M., Stegeman, C., Hesse, A., Jolivet, A., Mounir, A., and Casas, A. (1993) Prospection géophysique dans la cathédrale de Chartres. Bulletin de la Société Archéologique d'Eure-et-Loir 36:5–24.

Heimmer, D.H., and De Vore, S.L. (1995) Near Surface, High Resolution Geophysical Methods for Cultural Resource Management and Archaeological Investigation. Washington, D.C.: National Park Service, Department of the Interior.

Scollar, I., ed. (1990) Archaeological Prospecting and Remote Sensing. Cambridge: Cambridge University Press.

Electron Probe Microanalysis

Method of chemical analysis of small areas of solid materials, typically 2–20 μm in diameter, now widely used in archaeology. A beam of electrons (accelerated to 15–30 kV) is focused onto a sample and stimulates the emission of characteristic fluorescence X-rays, from which the concentrations of major and minor elements, and the presence of trace elements, in the sample may be determined. The ability of the technique to analyze very small sample areas and to scan across sections or surfaces has been exploited in archaeology, particularly in the study of pottery clays, inclusions, glazes, and paints. Since the 1970s, the method has also been used both qualitatively and quantitatively in technological and provenancing studies of glass, metals and slags, paintings, obsidian, and other stone artifacts. Microprobe analysis of artifacts is essentially destructive, because it generally requires the removal of a sample that then must be mounted and polished. However, sample sizes can be as small as a single mineral grain, a considerable advantage for archaeological work.

Sample Preparation and Basic Principles

The accompanying Figure shows a simplified diagram of an electron microprobe (from Potts 1992). The specimen is prepared as a highly polished thin (30 μm) section mounted on a glass slide or as a block, producing the flat surface required for quantitative analysis (in contrast to the three-dimensional surface normally imaged by related scanning electron microscopy [SEM] techniques). Nonconducting materials are coated under vacuum with a thin (ca. 25nm) layer of carbon. Electrons are produced within the electron gun from an incandescent tungsten-wire filament and accelerated through a potential of typically 15–30 kV. The diverging electron beam is focused and demagnified within the electron column (which is held, like the whole instrument, under high vacuum) by two to three electromagnetic lenses consisting of cylinders of copper windings (turns of copper wire) surrounded by an iron cladding. These produce magnetic fields that radially deflect the electrons as they pass through, resulting in a beam spot size that can be focused on the sample down to a minimum diameter of ca. 0.01 μm. Electron scattering within the sample increases the smallest analyzed volume surface to a diameter of 0.5–3 μm (depending on the mean atomic number of the sample). In practice, the beam may be defocused to a diameter of up to 20 μm to avoid decomposition of some minerals due to thermal effects. The carbon coating is necessary to ensure that the charge deposited by the electron beam is conducted uniformly to Earth.

The sample may be moved within the specimen chamber by a series of gears, to allow analysis of different areas of the surface. In most instruments, additional magnetic deflection coils within the column assembly allow systematic deflection of the electron

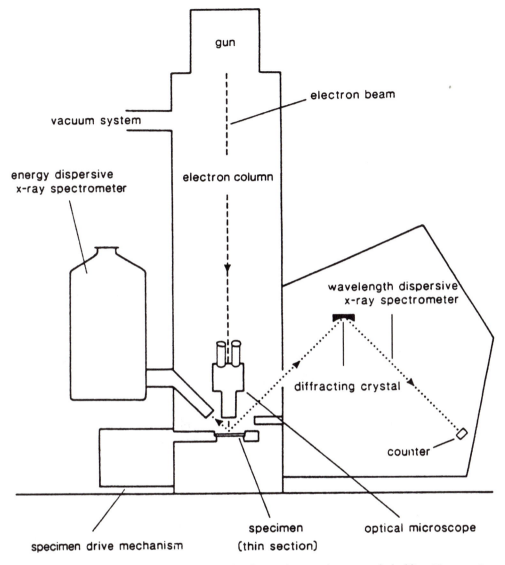

Schematic diagram of an electron microprobe. The electron beam is shown as a dashed line, X-rays emit-ted from the sample, as dotted lines. From Potts, P.J. (1992) A Handbook of Silicate Rock Analysis, *p. 328. Glasgow and London: Blackie, with permission.*

beam across the sample in a raster pattern, so that the sample can be imaged from a back-scattered (or secondary) electron micrograph.

Interactions between the electron beam and the sample include the generation of X-rays, produced when an incoming primary beam electron collides with a sample atom and causes ionization. Based on a simple elec-tron orbital model of the atom, the vacancy caused by ionization of an inner shell electron is almost immediately filled by an electron transition from a shell that is notionally far-ther from the nucleus. Energy is lost during this transition by the emission of a character-istic fluorescence X-ray photon. X-rays emit-ted following electron transitions to the K-(innermost) shell from the outer L- and M-shells are commonly denoted $K\alpha$ and $K\beta$ lines, respectively, while those resulting from transi-tions to the L-shell are denoted $L\alpha$, $L\beta$ and so on. Each X-ray has an energy characteristic of the element from which it was emitted, and the number (i.e., intensity) of characteristic X-rays is indirectly proportional to the atomic concentration of the element present in the sample. X-rays utilized in microprobe work normally lie in the 0–10 keV energy range (sometimes up to ca. 15 keV) and are emitted from a sample depth of 0 to ca. 6 μm, depending on the electron beam accelerating potential used, sample composition, and X-ray energy.

The fluorescent X-rays may be detected using either wavelength-dispersive or energy-dispersive X-ray spectrometry. In wavelength-dispersive spectrometers, X-rays are diffracted according to their wavelength (inversely related to photon energy) by one of a range of crystals made of either natural or synthetic materials, whose lattice spacing is of the same order as the magnitude of the wavelength of the fluorescence X-ray. Diffraction takes place according to Bragg's Law, represented by the equation:

$$n\lambda = 2d \sin \theta$$

where λ is the wavelength of the incident X-ray beam, d is the lattice spacing between layers of atoms in the diffracting crystal, θ is the angle between the crystal lattice layer and incident X-ray beam, and n is an integer describing the difference in path lengths of X-ray beams diffracted, respectively, from successive layers of atoms within the crystal. The diffracted X-rays are detected by a gas-proportional counter. To satisfy the Bragg equation, different X-ray lines may be selected by rotating the diffracting crystal to vary θ. Simultaneously, the proportional counter must be rotated through an angle of 2θ to maintain the correct geometric relationship. Proportional counters are normally filled with an argon/methane mixture as counter gas. X-rays penetrating into the counter cause ionization of the gas. The free electrons formed by ionization are accelerated through a potential gradient applied across the counter. The resulting electronic charge is proportional to the energy of the detected X-ray photon. The high count-rate capability and the good spectral resolution of wavelength dispersive spectrometers means that they are commonly used in quantitative microprobe work.

In the alternative, energy dispersive spectrometers, X-rays are detected by a liquid nitrogen-cooled crystal of lithium-drifted silicon (Si[Li]). X-rays cause ionization of this semiconductor crystal, and the resultant electronic charge is proportional to X-ray energy. Energy-dispersive systems have an advantage of rapid qualitative analysis since the full X-ray spectrum is detected simultaneously and can normally be viewed during spectrum acquisition. The position of the detector near the sample permits a larger solid angle of detection, allowing reduction of the probe current and avoiding decomposition effects in the sample. However, the spectral resolution of energy-dispersive systems is inferior to wavelength-dispersive spectrometers (particularly for X-rays of below 10 keV, the analytical energy range in microprobe work), so that spectrum overlap interferences are more severe. Taken in conjunction with the relatively low maximum count rate detection capability, detection limits using energy-dispersive spectrometers are typically ten times higher than those for wavelength-dispersive systems.

For quantitative analysis, instrument response is usually calibrated using a number of reference minerals of known composition. Unknown samples are then essentially compared with this calibration. However, corrections to X-ray intensities must be applied to account for sample and matrix effects, which include the absorption of a proportion of fluorescence X-rays within the sample, electron beam interactions in the sample, and secondary fluorescence effects. All of these factors depend on sample composition. Spectra recorded by energy-dispersive methods require careful computer deconvolution of overlapping X-ray peaks to compensate for their inferior energy resolution.

While electron probe microanalysis can detect most elements in the periodic table (down to boron), in practice the relatively high background radiation continuum generated by the electron beam reduces the detection limits of the method such that quantitative analysis is generally undertaken only for major and minor elements. Precision and accuracy of wavelength dispersive microprobe analyses (quoted for major and minor elements in silicate rock) are typically better than 2 percent relative standard deviation for elements present at abundances of greater than 1 percent.

Archaeological Applications

In terms of archaeological work, the microprobe technique must be regarded primarily as a surface-analysis technique, and sample orientations chosen accordingly. Bulk analysis of specimens can be achieved by crushing and homogenizing the sample in the form, for example, of a fused glass bead (in the case of rocks). While this negates the main advantage of the microprobe in terms of analysis of small areas, it does allow analysis of very small sample masses (down to 10–20 mg, assuming this is representative of the sample composition) and can, thus, reduce damage caused to artifacts by minimizing the mass required for analysis.

Microprobe analysis is a fairly rapid technique; once the thin section has been prepared and the instrument calibrated (the latter may take one–two hours and is normally done at the beginning of each analytical session), a single analysis for, say, ten elements in a silicate rock mineral will take ten–fifteen minutes.

Related microbeam techniques that have been used in archaeology include the scanning electron microscope and the transmission electron microscope, and ion probe and proton-induced X-ray emission (PIXE) techniques in which samples are excited by beams of, respectively, heavy ions and, typically, protons. Ion probe analysis and PIXE have been used in obsidian and pottery characterization.

Electron probe microanalysis instrumentation became widely available in the 1960s, and archaeologists were quick to see the potential of the technique, with articles in early issues of the journal *Archaeometry* pointing out possible applications. Since then, it has been applied extensively, especially in ceramic and metal studies, in which the ability to analyze selected parts of surface materials, such as slips and glazes, is an advantage. In general, wavelength dispersive techniques are used for quantitative analysis.

An interesting early application was carried out by James A. Charles of Cambridge University in 1968, scanning across the copper-silver interface of a Minoan dagger. He suggested that the Minoans were using a diffusion technique to bond the two metals, a technique not re-recorded until the last 200 years. More recently, microprobe work has been used to study very early (fourth–third millennia B.C.) copper and bronze artifacts and slags in the Near East.

Microprobe work on ceramics has been widespread, and the potential and applications within this area were summarized by Ian C. Freestone in 1982, noting its use for a range of technological, provenancing, and characterization studies. Applications range from compositional and microstructure study of Chinese porcelain to the provenancing and characterization of Egyptian and Mesopotamian ceramics. Diverse studies of pottery glaze and paint have been used, for example, to show local manufacture of early (fifth–fourth millennia B.C.) ceramics in Iran and to reveal manufacturing techniques of medieval Islamic pottery made in Afghanistan. Microprobe analysis has also been used to study wall paints, such as the investigation of chemical reactions taking place in Egyptian tomb murals.

Artificial glasses have been studied by the microprobe technique to determine compositional groupings and technological processes, such as sources of colorants or alkali components. Julian Henderson (1988) reported on categories of European prehistoric and Roman glasses while noting the analytical uncertainty caused by the mobility of sodium during electron excitation, common to microprobe work on alkali glasses.

Provenancing of artifacts of natural glass (obsidian) can be undertaken successfully by microprobe in some cases. The lack of trace-element data means that the method is most suitable where the range of potential sources is limited, such as in Kenya, where it was used by Harry V. Merrick and Francis H. Brown. As with artificial glasses, problems of vitreous sample decomposition required some defocusing of the electron beam. Microprobe has also been used in combination with other techniques for Anatolian obsidian characterization.

Applications to other rock types are fewer, but Richard Newman laid the groundwork for provenancing Indian (Gandharan, ca. second century B.C. to mid-first millennium A.D.) sculptures of schist and phyllite, and David P.S. Peacock and colleagues have successfully used microprobe to provenance Roman granitoid columns on the basis of mineral analyses.

Electron probe microanalysis has become one of the standard techniques available to the archaeologist, its main advantage lying in the capability of quantitative analysis of small areas and the relevance of this to artifact surface and interface investigations. Microprobe techniques complement the well-used bulk-analysis techniques, such as X-ray fluorescence and neutron activation analysis, which form the basis of many characterization and provenancing studies. Microprobe analysis has further potential for stone artifact provenancing by mineral characterization, a potential that has only begun to be realized.

Olwen Williams-Thorpe

See also X-RAY DIFFRACTION (XRD) ANALYSIS; X-RAY FLUORESCENCE (XRF) ANALYSIS

Further Readings

Charles, J.A. (1968) The first Sheffield Plate. Antiquity 42:278–285.

Freestone, I.C. (1982) Applications and potential of electron probe micro-analysis in technological and provenance investigations of ancient ceramics. Archaeometry 24:99–16.

Henderson, J. (1988) Electron probe micro-analysis of mixed-alkali glasses. Archaeometry 30:77–91.

Merrick, H.V., and Brown, F.H. (1984) Rapid chemical characterization of obsidian by electron microprobe analysis. Archaeometry 26:230–236.

Newman, R. (1992) Applications of petrography and electron microprobe analysis to the study of Indian stone sculpture. Archaeometry 34:163–174.

Peacock, D.P.S., Williams-Thorpe, O., Thorpe, R.S., and Tindle, A.G. (1994) Mons Claudianus and the problem of the *granito del foro*: A geological and geochemical approach. Antiquity 68:209–230.

Potts, P.J. (1992) A Handbook of Silicate Rock Analysis. Glasgow and London: Blackie.

Reed, S.J.B. (1993) Electron Microprobe Analysis, 2nd rev. ed. Cambridge: Cambridge University Press.

Electron Spin Resonance (ESR) Dating

A dating method that was introduced to archaeology in the 1970s. Although ESR dating is still in a rapid phase of development, it has demonstrated its value by providing new chronological evidence about the evolution of modern humans. ESR dating in archaeology has been applied to tooth enamel, speleothems, spring-deposited travertines, shells, and burnt flint. The principal dating range lies between a few thousand to ca. 500,000 years. In exceptional circumstances, samples older than one million years can successfully be analyzed.

Basic Principles

ESR may be grouped together with thermoluminescence (TL) and optically stimulated luminescence (OSL) as trapped-charge dating

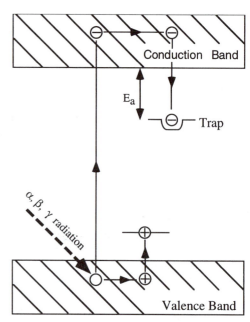

Figure 1. Trapping of electrons, the basis for ESR dating. An insulating mineral has two energy levels at which electrons may occur. The lower energy level (valence band) is separated from the higher energy level (conduction band) by a so-called forbidden zone. When a mineral is formed or reset, all electrons are in the ground state. Ionizing radiation (left) ejects negatively charged electrons from atoms. The electrons are transferred to the conduction band and positively charged holes (⊕) are left behind near the valence band. After a short time of diffusion most of the electrons recombine with these holes. Some electrons can be trapped by impurities (electron traps) in the crystal lattice. These electrons can be directly measured by electron spin resonance spectroscopy (see Figure 2). E_a is the activation energy, or trap depth, which controls the thermal stability of the trapped electrons. Figure by Rainer Grün.

methods. Figure 1 shows the basic principle for ESR dating: Radioactive rays eject negatively charged electrons from atoms in the ground state *(valence band)*. The electrons are transferred to a higher energy state *(conduction band),* leaving positively charged holes near the valence band. After a short time of diffusion, most electrons recombine with holes, and the mineral is unchanged. However, all natural minerals contain defects that can trap electrons when they fall back from the conduction band. These trapped electrons can be measured by an ESR spectrometer, giving rise to characteristic ESR lines (Figure 2). The intensity of the ESR line is proportional to the number of trapped electrons; the number of

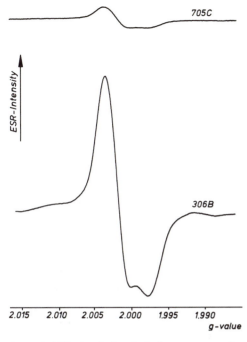

Figure 2. ESR signal of a relatively young enamel sample from the site of Le Moustier (top) and ESR signal of an old enamel sample from Sterkfontein (bottom). Figure by Rainer Grün.

trapped electrons, in turn, results from three parameters: (1) the strength of the radioactivity *(dose rate)*; (2) the number of traps *(sensitivity)*; and (3) the duration of radiation exposure *(age)*. ESR age estimates are calculated according to the following formula:

Age = Accumulated dose/Dose rate

Figure 3 shows how these parameters are connected. At the time of formation, the sample does not contain any ESR signals. The ESR signal measured in archaeological samples, the *natural ESR intensity*, is the product of age and dose rate (= dose). Laboratory irradiation is used to increase the ESR intensity; and the plot of ESR intensity versus laboratory dose is called the *dose-response curve*. This is used to estimate the dose of radiation the sample has received during its archaeological history, by fitting the data points with an exponential function and extrapolating this fit to zero ESR intensity. The uncertainty in the dose estimation that arises from the scatter of the data points around the fitted line is in the range of 2–7 percent.

The measurement of the accumulated dose is the actual ESR part of the dating procedure. An ESR signal used for dating should

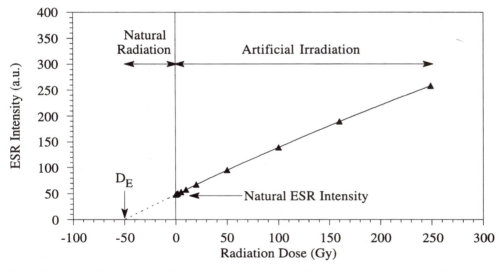

Figure 3. Relationship among signal intensity, time, dose rate, and dose. At the event to be dated, the sample has no ESR intensity. Trapped electrons are created by natural radiation and their number is dependent on the product of time and dose rate (= dose). When the sample is collected and measured, the ESR signal intensity is equivalent to the number of trapped electrons. Defined laboratory irradiation creates increased ESR signals. The plot of ESR intensity versus laboratory dose is called the "dose response curve." The accumulated dose (D_E) value results from fitting the data points of the dose response with an exponential function and extrapolating the fit to zero ESR intensity. Figure by Rainer Grün.

Table 1. Typical Dose Rates

Dose Rate	Alpha	Beta	Gamma	
1 ppm ^{238}U + ^{235}U	2,780	146	113	μGy/a
1 ppm ^{232}Th	732	27	48	μGy/a
1 % K		728	243	μGy/a

have the following properties:
1. The ESR signal is zero when the sample is formed or reset (this assumption may not be correct for some materials, such as calcretes or spring deposited travertines).
2. The signal intensity grows in proportion to the dose received.
3. The signals must have a stability that is a least one order of magnitude higher than the age of the sample.
4. The number of traps is constant or changes in a predictable manner; recrystallization, crystal growth, or phase transitions must not have occurred.
5. The signals should not show anomalous fading.
6. The ESR signal should not be influenced by preparation (grinding, exposure to laboratory light).

ESR dating is limited by two processes: (1) *Saturation:* When all traps are filled, any additional radiation cannot result in a further increase in the number of trapped electrons; and (2) *Thermal stability:* Electrons have only a limited probability of staying in the traps.

After a certain period of time, the *thermal mean life* (τ), 63 percent of an original population of trapped electrons will have left the traps and will have recombined with holes *(fading)*. Only if the mean life is at least ten times larger than the age of the sample can the effect of recombination or fading be neglected. Because the mean life is dependent on the nature of the trap, there is no general upper dating limit for ESR dating, and each case has to be evaluated individually.

The total dose rate is determined by the quantitative analysis of radioactive elements in the sample and its surroundings, plus a component of cosmic rays. In ESR studies, only the uranium (U) and thorium (Th)

decay chains and potassium-40 (^{40}K) decay are of relevance. There are three different rays that are emitted from the radioactive elements: (1) *alpha rays,* which have only a very short range of ca. 20 μm because of their large size. Alpha particles are not as efficient in producing ESR intensity as beta and gamma rays; therefore, an alpha efficiency, or k value (which is usually in the range of 0.05–0.3), has to be determined; (2) *beta rays* which have a range of ca. 2 mm; and (3) *gamma rays,* which have a range of ca. 30 cm.

The concentrations of radioactive elements in the sample and its surroundings are usually very different. Therefore, it is necessary to determine the *internal dose rate* separately from the *external dose rate.* Table 1 shows the typical dose rates for the U and Th decay chains and K.

Additionally, the effect of cosmic rays has to be considered. The cosmic dose rate is dependent on the geographic latitude, the altitude, and the thickness of the covering sediments. The cosmic dose rate is ca. 300 μGy/a (unit of dose is the gray, = Gy) at sea level and decreases with depth below ground.

Dose rate calculations become more complicated when disequilibrium in the U-decay chains or attenuation factors have to be considered. Typical errors in the estimation of the total dose rate are in the range of 4–7 percent. The overall analytical error of ESR age estimations is in the range of 5–10 percent.

Archaeological Applications
Most ESR dating applications in archaeological contexts have been carried out on tooth enamel. Organic materials such as bones and teeth show a postdepositional uptake of uranium, and this effect further complicates the dose rate determination for tooth enamel. The

process of uranium uptake cannot normally be determined exactly. For teeth, two models have been suggested: (1) early U-uptake (EU): a U-accumulation shortly after burial of the tooth; and (2) linear U-uptake (LU): a continuous U-accumulation.

As long as the uranium concentrations in the components of a tooth are low (less than 2 ppm in dentine), the discrepancy between EU and LU ages is less than 10 percent. However, with increasing uranium concentrations, this intrinsic uncertainty rises very rapidly. In the extreme, the LU model age is twice the EU age estimate. There are numerous archaeological sites where the EU model age seems closer to independent age estimates, and some uranium-series studies seem to support this model. In other cases, the linear model seems to yield more accurate age estimates. If there are no specific indications to justify a particular U-uptake model, only age estimates can be given for both models. The most probable age is somewhere between the two estimates. *It is important to note that the EU age estimate is the minimum possible age.* Most teeth older than the last interglaciation (at ca. 116,000–130,000 years), which was widely accompanied by a wetter climate, have accumulated considerable amounts of uranium, and, therefore, most ESR age estimates of such teeth are associated with large uncertainties (greater than 25 percent). An overall precision of less than 7 percent can be obtained for teeth with low uranium concentrations. A combination of ESR and U-series dating alleviates the uncertainty created by the unknown U-uptake history.

The upper range of ESR dating of tooth enamel is mainly controlled by thermal stability of the paramagnetic centers; complete saturation has not yet (as of 1998) been observed. Preliminary annealing experiments suggested a mean life in the range of 10–100 million years. Teeth from Sterkfontein, South Africa, showed no particular trend of underestimation in an age range of 1.6–2.4 million years, which corresponds more or less to the expected age. Therefore, the effect of retrapping seems negligible for the dating of Middle and Late Pleistocene samples. The lower dating range is determined by the sensitivity of the ESR spectrometer. It is possible to detect a signal that is generated by ca. 1 Gy. This signal may correspond to a few thousand years in a low-dose-rate environment or a few tens of years in a high-dose-rate environment.

Bones have been analyzed in numerous ESR studies, but it has not yet been possible to obtain reliable ESR age estimates. A published compilation lists accumulated dose values of bones from many archaeological and paleoanthropological sites, such as Sangiran (Java), Mauer (Germany), Zhoukoudian (China), and Caune de l'Arago (France) (Ikeya 1993). However, in most cases no independent ESR dating was carried out. Other studies came to the conclusion that bones are not datable with ESR. This view results from the following observations: (1) bones usually absorb more uranium than teeth; and (2) the mineral phase in bones is only somewhere in the region of 40–60 percent, and, along with the alteration of the organic constituents in bone during fossilization, the mineralogical compounds change (formation of new minerals, disintegration of the mineral phase, conversion of the amorphous phase into hydroxyapatite, and growth of the crystal size of hydroxyapatite). Formation of the new mineral phase (with new traps) with time leads to age underestimations regardless of the uranium-uptake model applied.

ESR dating studies have been carried out on numerous European, Israeli, and South African paleoanthropological sites. Neanderthal sites in Europe, such as Le Moustier or La-Chapelle-aux-Saints, have yielded ages in the expected range of 40,000–60,000 years. ESR has contributed to the changed perception that anatomically modern humans already occurred in the Levant ca. 100,000 years ago at sites such as Skhul and Qafzeh (Israel) and that they shared the same geographical region with Neanderthals, who have been dated to between 60,000 years (Kebara) and ca. 120,000 years (Tabun). A combined ESR–U-series study has shown that the uranium accumulation of most samples is close to the EU model. ESR results on South African sites such as Border Cave or Klasies River Mouth Cave have confirmed that fully modern humans occurred in southern Africa much earlier than in Europe.

Rainer Grün

See also BONE, CHARACTERIZATION; LUMINESCENCE DATING; OPTICAL DATING; THERMOLUMINESCENCE DATING; URANIUM—SERIES DATING

Further Readings

Grün, R. (1989) Electron spin resonance dating. Quaternary International 1:65–109.

Grün, R., and Stringer, C.B. (1991) ESR dating and the evolution of modern humans. Archaeometry 33:153–199.

Ikeya, M. (1993) New Applications of Electron Spin Resonance: Dating, Dosimetry, and Microscopy. London; World Scientific.

McDermott, F., Grün, R., Stringer, C.B., and Hawkesworth, C.J. (1993) Mass-spectrometric U-series dates for Israeli Neanderthal/early modern hominid sites. Nature 363:252–255.

Electrophoresis

The movement or migration of charged particles through a solution under the influence of an electric field. Different particles will move at different rates, depending upon their charge and the resistance of the medium used. Therefore, electrophoresis can be used to separate different but similar materials (e.g., proteins).

Introduction

Organic residues comprise carbohydrates, nucleic acids, proteins, and lipids. Electrophoresis in archaeology is used principally to examine remains of animal origin, and all of these classes of molecule can be present in archaeological remains of animal origin. This review focuses on proteins, although other biomolecules are discussed. Proteins are large molecules that contain nitrogen: they are made up of amino acids. Proteins may be either globular or helical and have a variety of biochemical roles. Generally, *globular proteins* regulate metabolic activities and immunological functions, while *helical proteins* have a structural function.

Few original organic residues survive in archaeological materials. Generally, they do so when enclosed in a mineral matrix such as is present in bones, shells, and teeth, although they have been demonstrated in nonmineralized materials (e.g., mummified materials). Electrophoresis is an ideal method of separating (and characterizing) some of the organic macromolecules extracted from mineralized materials.

Theory

Large molecules such as proteins and nucleic acids have distinctive shapes and will be *charged*. That means that they will contain positive or negative (usually both) charges as part of their structure. The degree of charge in the material, whether the material is denatured or not, the acidity or alkalinity of the solid medium used to separate the materials, and the electric charge used all control the degree of separation achieved.

The sample is applied to a solid support, an electric current is applied, and the molecules within the sample move toward the positive or negative poles of the support, depending upon their own net charge. Positively charged molecules will move to the negative pole, and negatively charged molecules will move to the positive pole. The primary function of the solid support is to prevent disturbances of the sample molecules, but, in the case of polyacrylamide-gel, it may also serve as a molecular sieve (to add the extra dimension of separating by size) or a stabilizing medium for pH gradients (for separating by acidity). There are two types of polyacrylamide-gel electrophoresis (PAGE): continuous and discontinuous. *Discontinuous conditions* use different gel concentrations, different pH values, or different buffers within the same gel; these gels result in very sharply defined separations from a mixture of highly similar substances. *Continuous electrophoresis* uses homogeneous gels, but applications of this in archaeology materials are rare.

Separations may also be improved by adding chemicals to the gel that disrupt the structure of the sample molecule. Sodium dodecyl sulfate (SDS), a detergent, binds to most proteins where it interferes with the bonds that maintain the three-dimensional shape of the protein. The final effect of SDS is to unwrap the proteins, producing single chains and short chains of amino acids *(denaturation)*. The combination of SDS with PAGE (called SDS-PAGE) is the most commonly used type of electrophoresis (Figure).

After separation, the proteins and nucleic acids will not be visible on the gels, so they are located by staining with specific stains (e.g., silver is used to locate proteins and complex sugars, whereas Coomassie Blue will stain only proteins). If the gels were run under nondenaturing conditions, the molecules in the samples may be recovered from the gels and purified.

Another detection system for the presence of a range of molecules (but usually proteins) is the *immunoblot method*. The gel is

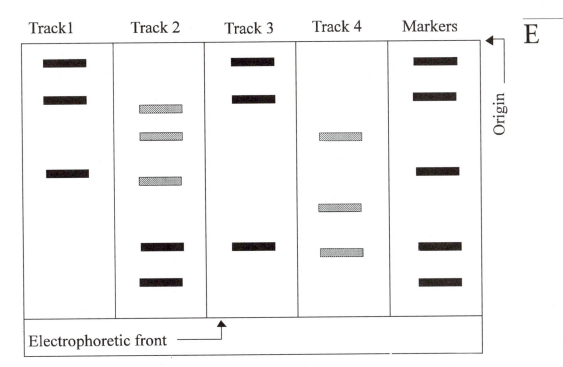

Electrophoretic front

In electrophoresis, compounds migrate from the origin, becoming separated on the basis of molecular mass. The smaller the fragment, the farther it will migrate. As can be seen, some compounds, indicated in black, match up with compounds of known molecular mass in the markers column. Others, indicated in gray, do not. An estimate of molecular mass may still be made for these unknowns. Figure by David R.K. Robertson.

placed in close proximity to a specially prepared membrane to which protein molecules will stick. The proteins in the bands are transferred to the membrane (blotted), and their presence can then be detected using immunochemical means. This detection system uses antibodies as the detector and has the added nicety that, as well as providing information about the molecular weight of the material by electrophoresis, the immunochemical reaction also gives information on its antigenicity.

The theory of electrophoresis is simple, but many problems can arise during its practice, and the number of factors that affect the separation are considerable. It is precisely because of these factors, however, that separations of closely similar molecules can be made. The following discussion reviews the application of this technique to ancient biomolecules. It is not meant to be exhaustive; electrophoresis is used for a range of other applications within archaeological science.

Applications

The ancient biomolecules that survive over archaeological time do so in a variety of envi-

ronments. Desiccation, tanning, and freezing are preservation methods well understood in modern society, and conditions in the burial environment sometimes result in proteins being preserved by these mechanisms. Archaeological (and geochemical) interest in ancient biomolecules concentrates on their carbon skeleton (radiocarbon dating), the isotopic signatures of their nitrogen and carbon (paleodiet), genetic relationships (DNA studies) and their composition, and the alteration of these and other signals by taphonomy. The ancient biomolecules for which SDS-PAGE is commonly used are the bone and tooth proteins (e.g., collagen and osteocalcin) and deoxyribonucleic acid (DNA).

Collagen

Collagen (type 1) makes up ca. 90 percent of the protein fraction of bone. It shows very little change between species or across time and is, therefore, said to be conserved, since there are few differences in the bone collagens of all mammals. It has a variety of uses to the archaeological scientist but is not really useful for phylogenetic studies because of the small differences between species. The carbon fraction can be used for radiocarbon dating, and the isotopic nitrogen/carbon ratio yields information on diet. This information can be useful only if the collagen extracted from the excavated bone has not been significantly changed by taphonomic processes. The degree of integrity of the collagen molecule cannot be assessed by such methods as amino-acid content, since this does not appear to change until a significant proportion (up to 97 percent) of the original collagen has been lost. Further, microscopic examination of the bone microstructure also fails to give reliable data on the integrity of the collagen. Electrophoresis of the extracted collagen molecule will yield information on both its purity and its integrity.

Bone and tooth collagen (type I collagen) is made up of three chains, called α-chains. Two of the three are identical, and one is different. These three chains are twisted together in a triple helix. Collagen survives in archaeological bones and teeth because of its close association with the mineral hydroxyapatite, because of its triple-helical structure, and because of the high proportion of the amino acids proline and hydroxyproline, which inhibit the action of proteases (enzymes that cleave globular proteins). In an electrophoretic separation of native, undegraded type I collagen, only two bands would be seen in the gel: one corresponding to the two identical chains, and one to the other chain. If more bands are seen, then conclusions about the integrity and the purity of the collagen fraction from a particular archaeological bone may be made. In practice, this is difficult since ancient samples tend to smear rather than separate, but some success has been achieved.

Osteocalcin

The bone protein *osteocalcin* (OC) has been claimed to survive for long periods of archaeological time, even when collagen (the major bone protein) has gone. The presence of the mineral, and its interaction with OC, has been suggested as the most probable cause of the longevity of the protein. OC is a small (49 residue) bone and tooth protein, containing an unusual amino acid, γ-carboxyglutamic acid, which is high in acidic functional groups. In the presence of Ca^{2+}, the OC molecule forms an α-helix that align these γ-carboxyglutamic acid residues with the plane of the bone mineral $(Ca_{10}(PO_4)_6(OH)_2-$ calcium hydroxyapatite) surface. This alignment promotes the interaction of the acidic (positively charged) amino acids in the OC molecule with the negatively charged areas of the mineral surface. Detection of OC from archaeological bone is usually by immunochemical means, but immunoblotting (using electrophoresis followed by immunochemical detection) can also be done.

DNA

The genome of an organism is composed of DNA, the genetic material that codes for all of the characteristics of an individual, be it animal, plant, or microbe. Under certain conditions, the DNA from some organisms has been shown to be preserved. These conditions include the presence of high concentrations of mineral (i.e., bone), and desiccated or burnt wheat seeds.

To recover and sequence DNA, the electrophoretic conditions for DNA must be different from those for proteins. Agarose (a linear polymer of the polysaccharides, D- and L galactopyranose) is the gel of choice for separations of DNA in preparation for sequencing, since DNA can be extracted directly from (low-melting) agarose gels after liquification of the gel at 65°C. To detect DNA bands in the gel, *autoradiography* is used. Radioactive phosphorus (^{32}P) is introduced to the 5'-terminus of the DNA (or RNA) fragments prior to electrophoresis. After electrophoresis, the gel is placed in close contact with an X-ray film (as with blotting), and the bands that contain ^{32}P will be revealed after the X-ray film has been developed.

Simple extraction procedures of both skin and bones from mummified human material have yielded DNA, which proved to be a mixture of the native DNA and DNA of microbial (and other) origin. Using human-specific probes, the DNA of human origin in the sample was demonstrated, extracted, and amplified. This was achieved by using specific nucleic-acid modifying enzymes on the extracted material and assessing the degree of change induced in the DNA by electrophoresis. In this way, the effects of ribonucleic acid (RNA) can be excluded, as can those of contaminating microbial DNA. Once the DNA is purified, genetic studies on archaeological populations are possible. These studies would not be conceivable without the confirmation attained by electrophoresis.

The *polymerase chain reaction* (PCR) is the method used to produce many copies of the section of ancient genome under study. Once several copies of the same part of the genome are produced, electrophoresis is used as a check of purity. More than one band would mean that more than one section of DNA had been processed, and contamination with other DNAs would lead to erroneous conclusions being made. Again, electrophoresis is an essential tool to check the validity of obtained results.

Conclusions

Electrophoresis is the movement or migration of charged particles through a solution under the influence of an electric field. Various modifications can be made to the solution to allow for separation by size or the degree of acidity. Detection systems are varied but include specific methods for proteins and DNA, more general methods for groups of biomolecules, and specific stains for detecting immunologically reactive materials.

The separation of ancient biomolecules by electrophoresis has led to a clearer understanding of the processes of taphonomy, improved extraction procedures for paleodietary studies, and the possibility of understanding the relationship between individuals and populations in archaeological deposits by studying their nucleic acids.

Angela Gernaey-Child
David R.K. Robertson

See also BONE, CHARACTERIZATION; BONE, DNA EXTRACTION; PALEOIMMUNOLOGY

Further Readings

Andrews, A.T. (1986) Electrophoresis: Theory, Techniques, and Biochemical and Clinical Applications. Oxford: Clarendon.

Engel, M.H., and Macko, S.A. (1993) Organic Geochemistry: Principles and Applications. New York: Plenum.

Hare, P.E., Hoering, T.C., and King, K. (1980) Biogeochemistry of the Amino Acids. New York: Wiley.

Ethnoarchaeology

The study of contemporary, ethnographic human behavior as a basis for explaining patterning and variability in archaeological associations. Ethnoarchaeology began in the nineteenth century as a relatively unstructured use of ethnographic observations of traditional contemporary societies to explain cultural materials in the archaeological record. The earliest efforts at ethnoarchaeology were directed primarily toward validating the historicity of oral traditions, especially in the Middle East, Scandinavia, and the Pacific. The term *ethnoarchaeology* was first coined by Jesse W. Fewkes in 1900 as a result of his archaeological work at the Tusayan Pueblo, Arizona, in the American Southwest. Prominent among studies of this kind in the region was the discovery of prehistoric materials at the top of Enchanted Mesa, New Mexico, by Frederick Webb Hodge in 1897. This find was prompted by oral traditions at the nearby modern pueblo of Acoma that described the existence of an ancient, destroyed settlement at this relatively inaccessible location. Hodge's discovery seemed to confirm the historical accuracy of this oral tradition. Such approaches, whether by Heinrich Schliemann at Troy or by Hodge and Fewkes in the American Southwest, shared the common feature of seeking confirmation of present-day information about traditional cultures in the archaeologically recorded past.

Another feature common to these initial efforts at ethnoarchaeology was the uncontrolled use of ethnographic analogues to identify and explain the manufacture and use of prehistoric artifacts and structures, as well as occasional attempts to explain cultural patterning on a larger, regional scale. The *direct historical approach* advocated by Julian Steward during the 1940s in the Great Basin of North America and extended by Robert Heizer into California attempted a direct extension from historically known hunter-gatherer cultures to the prehistoric cultural sequence of those areas. Information about material culture and subsistence behavior of ethnographically known groups, such as the Paiute and Shoshone Indians of the Great Basin, was applied continuously back through time for as much as 10,000–11,000 years to explain archaeological assemblages at sites such as Danger Cave in Utah, excavated by Jesse D. Jennings in the early 1950s. Unlike earlier studies, these efforts were directed explicitly toward understanding prehistoric ecological and technological adaptations instead of attempting to validate myths or other elements of expressive behavior in prehistory. As the direct historical approach evolved in the Great Basin, it increased an awareness among archaeologists for the need to identify and control for ecological variables, and it encouraged a search for linkages between ethnoarchaeology and research into hunter-gatherer modes of adaptation.

With the emergence of this interest in human ecology there followed attempts to formulate coherent theories about the role of ethnoarchaeology. One of the earliest efforts of this kind was Robert Ascher's concept of the *new analogy* in 1961. He argued that, by applying ecological controls, archaeologists could draw useful analogies between past and present cultures that had adapted to similar environments in similar ways. Historically, Ascher's concept was important for the way it connected already emergent interests by archaeologists in ecology to a theory that addressed structural and systemic relationships in culture instead of relying upon anecdotal resemblances between ethnographic and prehistoric cultures. Although much criticized, Ascher's study initiated the modern critical approach to the archaeological use of ethnographic information and led directly to continuing debates about the role of ethnoarchaeology.

Analogues as Hypotheses

Perhaps the most conservative position in these debates is that adopted by Patty Jo Watson, whose theoretical perspective is based on field experience derived from ethnoarchaeological studies in Iran and from archaeological excavations in the eastern United States. She argues for the role of ethnographic analogues as a source of hypotheses for archaeological testing. Watson's approach makes no a priori assumptions about the outcome of the testing process. Unlike studies by earlier ethnoarchaeologists, Watson's analogues as hypotheses do not depend upon confirmation or closeness-of-fit to an anticipated pattern in the archaeological record. This position has been challenged by claims that one cannot use the archaeological record to test ethnographically derived hypotheses despite the fact that convincing cases of such testing abound in the literature. The principal difficulty that arises in using

this approach is that it cannot always account effectively for cases in which ethnographically derived hypotheses fail to match the anticipated results. This difficulty is due, at least in part, to reliance upon analogues based on contemporary ethnographic models in situations in which past human behavior may no longer be represented by any modern or historic counterparts.

When such counterparts do occur in the ethnographic present, they can offer potent opportunities for analysis and explanation of past human behavior along the lines suggested by Watson. The 1969 analysis of prehistoric Aboriginal remains from western Arnhem Land in Australia by Carmel White and Nicolas Peterson provides an example of the ethnoarchaeological utility of analogues as hypotheses. Archaeological studies by White and Peterson indicated differences between material assemblages from prehistoric sites on the coastal and riverine plains and on the Arnhem Land plateau. During the wet season in Arnhem Land, conditions favor hunter-gatherer settlement in small, but fairly stable localities, in well-drained areas along the shore and streams. Fishing, shellfish collecting, and the capture of sea mammals and aquatic birds were important subsistence activities for the ethnographic Aborigines during this time of year. In the dry season, however, it became easier for nomadic hunter-gatherers to move about the plateaus, where hunting of terrestrial game and collection of local plant foods assumed greater importance for subsistence. To what extent would such seasonal differences in subsistence be recognizable archaeologically? And what alternative explanations might apply?

White and Peterson turned to an ethnographic study published in 1939 by anthropologist Donald Thomson of the Wik Munkan Aborigines of the Cape York Peninsula of northeastern Australia for their analogues as hypotheses. Thomson had shown how the Wik Munkan people followed a seasonally transhumant pattern of nomadic movement based upon seasonal differences in basic resources. Their wet-season camps along the shore required technologies that were markedly different from their dry-season foraging in the interior. Implements such as fishing nets and spears were present in their coastal assemblages, while throwing sticks, spearthrowers, and other terrestrial hunting-

and-gathering items characterized their dry-season activities. Thomson concluded from these observations that an archaeologist might be tempted to identify these seasonal assemblages as representing different tribes or subcultures—something that archaeologists had often done before when attempting to equate material assemblages with particular sociopolitical groupings—when, in fact, they represented seasonally different subsistence activities by the same sociopolitical group.

Although Thomson presented his findings as a caution for archaeologists, White and Peterson found it useful to apply these same alternative hypotheses to their Arnhem Land data. They determined that the seasonally transhumant pattern observed among the Wik Munkan offered a more parsimonious explanation of variability in the prehistoric assemblages from their excavated sites than the idea that these differing assemblages represented different subcultures. Like Watson's views, their study echoes Ascher's ideas about the new analogy, since it assumes that, given similarly seasonal tropical environments in Arnhem Land and in Cape York, the prehistoric Aborigines of Arnhem Land adapted in similar ways to the ethnographic Wik Munkan.

Middle-Range Theory

Lewis R. Binford has also sought to establish convincing linkages between present-day behavior in ethnographic societies and the prehistoric past. He invoked the concept of *middle-range theory* to identify cultural analogues that transcend particular cases but still depend on defined domains of human behavior (such as hunter-gatherer mobility or social status as reflected by mortuary assemblages). Binford's 1978 ethnoarchaeological study of the Nunamiut Eskimo represents an effort to identify behavioral and environmental factors that structured the use and discard of caribou meat and bone products. Binford paid particularly close attention to a wide array of circumstantial and situational microfactors that could account for variability in the bone assemblages, such as time of year, weather, ground conditions (such as snow and subsurface freezing), size and composition of the task group, and relevant technologies. He concluded that situational factors like these were more important than cultural factors in structuring the variability in faunal residues

left by the Nunamiut especially since all of the observed variability was the product of the same culture (a cautionary conclusion remarkably similar to Thomson's regarding Wik Munkan transhumance). This example of middle-range theory was intended to provide explicitly scientific explanations for the patterning of faunal remains in the archaeological record, without reference to categories of thought and symbolic meaning unique to any particular culture.

Difficulties arise in connection with this approach, especially in the requirement to link middle-range theory to a body of general theory about human behavior that, in fact, does not exist as a consensus within archaeology. But Binford's call for more explicit use of scientific reasoning in applying ethnographic results to the explanation of archaeological evidence has been widely, though not universally, adopted.

Perhaps the most serious difficulty arising with Binford's ethnoarchaeological results has been pervasive assumptions about archaeological remains as fossilized human behavior. Such a view tends to accept the patterning of material residues resulting from different human activities as leading directly to the material associations encountered in the archaeological record. Such assumptions do not always take into account the postdepositional effects of natural processes, such as weathering and erosion, or the equally intrusive reworking of archaeological deposits through later, often unrelated, human activities. Many natural and cultural factors can intervene between the cultural system that originally produced these residues and the physical associations that occur in the archaeological record. Archaeologists like Michael B. Schiffer argue that these *transformational processes* must be recognized and controlled for before ethnoarchaeological explanations for the patterning of cultural materials in archaeological deposits are attempted. Schiffer's views reflect a growing interest in taphonomic processes generally and show a greater awareness of the complexities of the archaeological record than direct inferences based upon assumptions of fossilized human behavior. One implication of such an awareness is the recognition that ethnoarchaeology works best if it is applied indirectly to the explanation of archaeological patterning. Direct approaches, such as ideas about the direct-historical approach and fossilized human behavior, have not fared well because they attempted to extrapolate contemporary human behavior into the past without any basis for assuming that it had to be that way in the past or any recognition of possible alternative modes of past human behavior that lack any modern counterpart. Michael B. Stanislawski, an ethnoarchaeologist who has studied the material culture of Southwestern Pueblo Indians of the United States, refers to this assumption as the *fallacy of affirming the consequent*: Ethnoarchaeologists always risk assuming the very thing they should be trying to find out by limiting their explanations of past human behavior to "presentist" models based upon known ethnographic and historic cases.

Stanislawski's Puebloan research provides a well-developed example of the way ethnoarchaeology can serve as a test for the behavioral realities that structure the archaeological record. In one study, he observed what happens to pieces of broken pottery. Archaeologists, he noted, had tended to regard potsherds as pieces of broken pots instead of as artifacts in their own right with histories of use and discard of their own, independent of the pot from which they were originally derived. Too often, archaeologists simply assumed that potsherds were aimlessly discarded, often in the context of a generalized midden deposit of some kind. But Stanislawski's findings indicated that potsherds were frequently reshaped and/or reused in a variety of ways, all of which had archaeological implications. Sometimes they were inserted into the adobe used in wall construction in the pueblos; in other cases, they were used as scrapers to shape and smooth pottery during the process of manufacture. In an especially interesting use, some decorated pieces performed an archival function when they were saved and stored, usually in another pot. Potters referred to these pieces whenever they needed to check design elements used on earlier vessels.

This study shows the importance of tracking the flow of material items through the cultural system, and this approach has become increasingly important within ethnoarchaeology. Ethnoarchaeological studies of ceramics among the Kalinga of the Philippines by William A. Longacre employed a system of tagging, similar to the way ornithologists tag birds, to follow the movements of individual

pots through households, from where they were made to their final locus of discard. Among the highly nomadic Ngatatjara Aborigines of Australia's Western Desert, Richard A. Gould constructed a flow model to observe and measure the reduction of lithic materials from their original source to their final disposal, with special attention to the amounts of stone used up at different stages in the process. It was especially revealing to find that the same individual Aborigines who produced usable artifacts by extremely wasteful methods when lithic materials were locally abundant were capable of production methods that used lithic materials efficiently when confronted by situations in which such materials were relatively scarce in the local environment. It was as if the same person were performing an Oldowan-level of "block-on-block" lithic reduction in one situation and a Mousterian-level of prepared-core lithic reduction in another. Since these individuals all belonged to the same cultural tradition, one can appreciate the importance of situational contexts in the manner proposed by Binford among the Nunamiut in structuring these outcomes. And, along the lines first suggested by Thomson, one can see, too, that such differences in technology cannot always be assumed to reflect different subcultures.

Stanislawski's Puebloan studies also included an examination of the social context of pottery production, indicating another direction taken by ethnoarchaeologists. In this case, Stanislawski was testing the assumption made by several Southwestern prehistorians during the 1960s that, in the ancient Puebloan cultures, mothers taught their daughters how to make and decorate pottery. This assumption led to elaborate analytical studies of spatial distribution of ceramics within prehistoric Puebloan structures, particularly at the Broken K Pueblo and Carter Ranch sites in Arizona. Stanislawski found, however, that women in the modern pueblos actually taught their daughters-in-law how to make pottery, thereby bringing the ethnographic analogy originally used by archaeologists into question and suggesting an alternative set of spatial relations for ceramic discards. In addition, he pointed out that contemporary traditions of painted pottery in the modern pueblos are not the direct historical descendants of the ancient, prehistoric traditions. There was a significant hiatus in the history of painted-pottery production in the Southwestern pueblos during the European colonial period. The practice was initially revived by Nampeyo, a Hopi Indian woman who received her inspiration from painted potsherds collected by an archaeological expedition at Sikyatki Pueblo, Arizona, in the early 1900s. This revival was increasingly directed at sales to American tourists and collectors rather than at domestic consumption within the pueblos, so it could not be regarded as a direct-historical analogue to the ancient Pueblo painted-pottery tradition. Stanislawski's studies represent a good example of what ethnoarchaeologist John E. Yellen has called the *spoiler effect* that has always been an important component of ethnoarchaeological practice and that can also be regarded as part of the hypothesis-testing process advocated by Watson in relation to her analogues as hypotheses. In this manner, ethnoarchaeology has successfully challenged facile assumptions by archaeologists about human behavior in the past and replaced them with better approximations of the behavioral realities of ancient cultures.

Cultural Transformations and Symbolic Ethnoarchaeology

A different kind of transformational theory is favored by Ian Hodder, an ethnoarchaeologist who adheres to the direct historical approach to identify changes in material culture based upon transformations from preexisting, culturally constructed patterns. Hodder's approach emphasizes continuities in specific culture-historical traditions and is less concerned with taphonomic or other postdepositional transforms of the sort addressed by Schiffer.

Hodder's approach to ethnoarchaeology drew heavily upon his field experience among traditional African societies. One of his studies, among the Njemps and the Tugen people near Lake Baringo in north-central Kenya, revealed filtering effects that occurred at the boundaries or edges where two different cultural traditions were in contact. His study focused on the selection processes that determined which kinds of material-culture items either stopped at or crossed these boundaries and how both their uses and their symbolic associations were patterned by such transfers. In a sense, his study examined the same issue alluded to earlier concerning the degree to which variability in material assemblages in archaeology accurately reflects differences between sociopolitical or ethnic groups, but with more attention to details of stylistic and expressive behavior than in the studies mentioned earlier.

Hodder found that certain material items correlated fairly closely with the boundaries between the Njemps and the Tugen, especially pottery, carved wooden stools, and the positioning of hearths within dwelling huts. These appeared to be sensitive indicators of ethnicity, although their relative exclusivity was not always equally uniform on both sides. For example, the Njemps adhered to fairly rigid rules in positioning their hearths to the right of the hut entrances, while the Tugen placed theirs on either side. Regarding pottery, the Njemps and the Tugen each obtained theirs from different preferred sources and markets, and different pottery types were regarded as symbolic markers of group identity and formed identifiable spatial patterns within the Lake Baringo district. The spatial distribution of a particular type of wooden stool, agreed by both Njemps and non-Njemps to be Njemps stools, also proved to be a potent symbol of ethnicity and produced patterns reflective of tribal boundaries.

Hodder also noted factors other than ethnicity that structured variability in material-culture items within and between the different groups. Spears and certain types of decorated calabashes cut across subcultural groupings. Differences in these classes of implements were presented as symbolic expressions of nonethnic factors such as age differences among young men. Hodder noted that spear types were similar over broad areas encompassing different tribes because all of the young men in those tribes copied spear types associated with male prowess and readiness for elderhood. While spear symbolism was related to age differences, decorated calabashes varied in a more localized manner than objects associated with differences at the level of tribes or subcultures. In this case, calabash designs were copied among women who were in regular contact at the local community level. Hodder also saw calabash decoration as one of the few domains of material culture in which women could exercise their autonomy with reference to the limitations and constraints imposed by men. Tugen and Njemps men did not demand the same conformity in the style of decorated calabashes that they otherwise expected in matters of female dress and pottery. The result of this expressive freedom was an array of complex design variations within tribal areas.

Hodder's results reinforced earlier cautions about the dangers of directly equating different material-culture assemblages in the archaeological record with different subcultures. But Hodder abandoned the ecological perspective of human culture as an adaptive mechanism in favor of a search for culturally constructed systems of meaning within each particular society. In contrast to Binford's emphasis on situational context to account for variability in material behavior, Hodder stressed the importance of cultural contexts, with all that this implied about social and symbolic factors, to explain such variability.

Difficulties can arise, however, in applying culturally constructed patterns of symbolic associations in particular societies to patterning in the archaeological record. Hodder's interpretations work better as cautionary arguments against simplistic assignments of cultural meaning to archaeological patterning than as positive assignments of past meaning in extinct cultures. They also work better for historical archaeologists who have written documents to provide a detailed level of cultural context not readily available to prehistorians. The arbitrary and complex construction of symbolic meanings in each human culture makes it difficult to know what was meant by specific symbols in specific cases. Hodder attempted to overcome this difficulty by referring historically or ethnographically known systems of meaning to earlier, preexisting systems of meaning in the same culture-historical tradition—in other words, the direct historical approach. Hodder claimed such direct historical transformations for changes in the decorations of Njemps calabashes, although here, too, documentary historical information was available to provide a level of cultural context not always present in prehistory. Even in relation to culturally assigned meaning, it is difficult for ethnoarchaeologists to produce convincing explanations for symbols in prehistoric cases that have no modern, ethnographic counterpart.

Contrastive Ethnoarchaeology

In an effort to overcome the fallacy of affirming the consequent when using ethnoarchaeology to draw conclusions about the prehistoric past, Gould and Yellen have offered what is perhaps the most radical approach to ethnoarchaeological interpretation, namely *contrastive ethnoarchaeology*. They observed marked differences in their data on household spacing among the Ngatatjara Aborigines of Australia's Western Desert and the !Kung San of the Kalahari Desert. In a departure from Ascher's concept of the new analogy, Gould and Yellen attempted to explain cultural patterning in the archaeological record based on the ethnographic study of similar kinds of cultures that manipulated comparable environments in measurably different ways. Such contrastive efforts are intended to generate hypotheses based on comparative differences between known ethnographic societies in which cultural and ecological variables can be controlled in detail. These hypotheses can be applied wherever such variables are observed in the archaeological record.

In this case, it was discovered that the Aborigines spaced their household camps much farther apart than the San, on an order of magnitude roughly ten times that of the San. What factors could account for such extreme differences in the behavior of two otherwise comparable groups of traditional hunter-gatherers? Factors relating to duration of occupation, group size and composition, interaction based on food sharing, and other variables were examined and eliminated. Only one factor remained as potentially decisive in accounting for this contrast: predation pressure by large-bodied carnivores. Such predators are common in the Kalahari Desert but have been absent in the Australian desert since at least the beginning of the Holocene. What made this comparison possible was the unique biogeographical character of Australia, which presented cultures that were similar in their technologies and general mode of adaptation to others in the world, yet had adaptive opportunities and constraints unlike those in other world environments. The Australian desert represented the only place in the world where ethnoarchaeologists could observe and measure the effects of an absence of predation pressure on a traditional society of mobile hunter-gatherers.

The results of this contrastive study can be applied to the archaeological record if one treats this as a hypothesis for testing. Unlike Watson's analogues as hypotheses, this approach does not depend upon a particular cultural analogue but upon a posited set of general relationships that can be expected to hold true given certain conditions. It is questionable whether one should even refer to hypotheses of these kinds as analogues, since they have more of the property of scientific laws. Contrastive ethnoarchaeology of the kind proposed by Gould and Yellen encourages archaeologists to develop models that will account for prehistoric cultural assemblages under a wider range of imaginable conditions than has so far been attempted, however improbable those conditions may appear in relation to historic and extant cultures. Controlled contrastive ethnoarchaeology is intended as a first step in the process of constructing convincing inferences about past human cultures represented in the archaeological record that have no modern counterpart.

As indicated by the different approaches embodied in current debates, ethnoarchaeology embraces a broad range of theoretical positions. It also has come to include a full range of traditional and modern societies, such as pastoral nomads, farming communities (including those embedded in complex, modern nation-states), and maritime cultures. Despite this increasing breadth of scope, the principal challenge for ethnoarchaeology remains that of presenting convincing explanations of material patterning in the archaeological record on the basis of ethnographic observations and analysis.

Richard A. Gould

See also BINFORD, LEWIS R.; GOULD, RICHARD ALLAN; HODDER, IAN; LONGACRE, WILLIAM A.; SCHIFFER, MICHAEL BRIAN; WATSON, PATTY JO

Further Readings

Ascher, R. (1961) Analogy in archaeological interpretation. Southwestern Journal of Anthropology 17:317–325.

Binford, L.R. (1978) Nunamiut Ethnoarchaeology. New York: Academic.

Gould, R.A. (1980) Living Archaeology. New York: Cambridge University Press.

Gould, R.A., and Yellen, J.E. (1987) Man the hunted: Determinants of household spacing in desert and tropical foraging societies. Journal of Anthropological Archaeology 6: 77–103.

Hodder, I. (1982) Symbols in Action: Ethnoarchaeological Studies of Material Culture. New York: Cambridge University Press.

Stanislawski, M.B. (1969) What good is a broken pot? An experiment in Hopi-Tewa ethno-archaeology. Southwestern Lore 35:11–18.

Watson, P.J. (1979) The idea of ethnoarchaeology. In C.Kramer (ed.): Ethnoarchaeology, pp. 277–287. New York: Columbia University Press.

White, C., and Peterson, N. (1969) Ethnographic interpretations of the prehistory of western Arnhem Land. Southwestern Journal of Anthropology 25: 45–67.

Yellen, J.E. (1977) Archaeological Approaches to the Present. New York: Academic.

Evans, Sir John (1823–1908)

British antiquarian, archaeologist, and numismatist. Born on November 17, 1823, at Britwell Court, Evans was originally a businessman, employed by the firm of John Dickinson and Company, prominent paper manufacturers. Educated at private schools, he soon became fascinated by numismatics, particularly the study of Roman coins, and by the Roman and pre-Roman archaeology of his native Britain. His successes in these fields earned him many honors; in his lifetime, Evans was a trustee of the British Museum, treasurer of the Royal Society of London (1878–1898), president of the Royal Numismatic Society (from 1874), president of the Egypt Exploration Fund (1899–1906), and president of the Society of Antiquaries. He was knighted in 1892. He is also known as the father of archaeologist Sir Arthur Evans, excavator of the Bronze Age palace at Knossos on Crete and discoverer of the Minoan civilization. Sir John Evans died on May 31, 1908.

Evans's contributions to archaeological methodology came in two fields. First, he was a pioneer in the study of Roman coins discovered in Great Britain and was among the first to use the coins archaeologically to cross-date Romano-British sites. He also studied native imitations of Roman coinage. Evans's 1864 work *The Coins of the Ancient Britons* was extremely influential and a standard numismatic work through the second half of the nineteenth century.

The most significant contributions of this important British antiquarian were, however, in the fields of prehistory and the study of pre-Roman Britain. Evans was among those early archaeologists who worked to prove the extreme antiquity of human existence and the fact that, before the use of iron, tools were made first of stone and then of bronze. Evans examined and published numerous stone and bronze implements from the British Isles and was among the first to systematically study pre-Roman Britain. His article "On the Occurrence of Flint Implements in Undisturbed Beds of Gravel, Sand, and Clay" in *Archaeologia* 38 (1860), helped confirm that the Stone Age discoveries of Jacques Boucher de Perthes at Abbeville in France were not a hoax and that, indeed, the existence of a Stone Age in Europe was fact. His *The Ancient Stone Implements of Great Britain* and *The Ancient Bronze Implements of Great Britain and Ireland* did much for the establishment of the Stone and Bronze Ages as legitimate chronological markers in the study of the prehistory of the British Isles. Evans also supported pre-Roman archaeology on the continent, excavating at the Celtic cemetery at Hallstatt in 1866 with an international team that included such luminaries as Sir John Lubbock and Louis Lartet.

Joseph J. Basile

See also CLASSICAL ARCHAEOLOGY

Further Readings

Evans, J. (1864–1890) The Coins of the Ancient Britons. London: B. Quaritch.

Evans, J. (1872) Ancient Stone Implements, Weapons, and Ornaments of Great Britain. New York: D. Appleton.

Evans, J. (1881) Ancient Bronze Implements, Weapons, and Ornaments of Great Britain and Ireland. New York: D. Appleton.

Evolution, Cultural

A vitalistic theory of cultural development in which history is driven by progress, variously defined.

Evolution is a term used widely in archaeology and anthropology, but it denotes a number of disparate concepts, as well as simply being a synonym for the term *development*. Its most common usage is, however, that identified here as *cultural evolution*. To make matters worse, cultural evolution is often used itself to mean the evolution (in any of the senses of the term) of culture or cultural phenomena, as well as the specific group of theories treated here. Consequently, one needs to ascertain the meaning of particular uses of evolution and cultural evolution from the context of usage.

Cultural evolution, as a particular theory or set of related theories of human development, is distinguished by its vitalistic structure (i.e., it calls upon some innate property of the subject matter to supply cause), and its use of a notion of progress (i.e., some particular sequence of forms or relations between forms) as an organizing principle. Biologists and other scientists sometimes talk about *progressive* trends (e.g., an increase in brain size in some particular lineage); however, such characterizations are always post hoc generalizations about the course that history has taken, about what has happened (i.e., a description), and *never* explanations or causes of that history. Indeed, failure to make this subtle distinction may be an important source of confusion in the anthropological use of evolution. Cultural evolution is also, though not inherently, an essentialist theory. It is conceptualized as a series of distinct types, stages, or states that succeed one another in an orderly fashion, the orderly fashion being the particular theory's concept of progress. Consequently, cultural evolution is not a theory of change but a theory of difference (between states). Hence, it is often characterized as a transformational theory. Methodologically, research focuses on when, how, and why one stage is transformed into another (e.g., the Mesolithic to the Neolithic); not surprisingly, *change* is typically seen as *revolutionary*.

The first expression of cultural evolution as an academic theory is usually attributed to Herbert Spencer and the enormous impact he had on the development of the social sciences in the nineteenth century. However, anthropologists such as Edward B. Tyler and Lewis Henry Morgan played important roles in popularizing this kind of theory and in shaping its use in archaeology and anthropology. Strictly archaeological theories, such as Christian Thomsen and Jens Worsaae's *Three Age System* and Sir John Lubbock's slightly later Palaeolithic-Neolithic scheme, share the main features of the anthropological constructs: stages and a progressive sequence. These resemblances are partly rooted in the notion of progress that characterized Western culture generally rather than in specific borrowings; or, at the least, the former facilitated the latter. In any case, a set of progressive stages implies a unilinear sequence; indeed, these early versions of cultural evolution are often called *unilinear evolution* for that very reason.

The failure of such simplistic sequences to be realized in empirical studies in the Old World, along with a general rejection of historical explanation, lead to the general abandonment of all but the most general and didactic uses of cultural-evolutionary schemes by the early years of the twentieth century. British archaeologist V. Gordon Childe kept a modified, Marxist, version of cultural evolution alive in Europe, where it became strongly linked with the so-called Neolithic revolution and the rise of complex society, an association that continues to characterize the use of cultural evolution to the present.

Cultural-evolutionary explanations never played an important role in nineteenth-century American archaeology. Long stratigraphic sequences that showed major technological changes, which had provided the link between cultural-evolution theory and archaeology, simply did not occur in the New World. Furthermore, the technological sequence of Europe was not repeated in North America (e.g., copper tools are found in otherwise Palaeolithic assemblages). Consequently, even though American scholars typically took their lead from their European colleagues in academic matters, and American anthropologists had played a key role in the development of cultural evolution as a theory, the dominant archaeological theory of nineteenth-century Europe had almost no impact in American archaeology.

Cultural evolution saw a revitalization in the 1940s and 1950s in the United States, largely in the hands of Leslie White and other University of Michigan anthropologists and students. Key to the rejuvenation of the theory was giving *progress* some specific a priori interpretation so that its application was no longer circular. For White and his followers, the currency was energy, and progress was increasing control/capture of energy. Subsequent formulations stressed organizational complexity rather than energy control. Again, this led to a series of stages or grades of culture (e.g., band, tribe, chiefdom, state). In an effort to link anthropological cultural evolution to scientific evolution as developed in biology, these later workers distinguished the evolution of culture (*general evolution*) from the evolution of cultures (*specific* or *adaptive evolution*), the latter accounting for diversity and being the link to biological evolution as anthropologists understood it. Missing the historicity of the biological concept, however, workers still tried to discern unilinear trends or tendencies in adaptation (e.g., increasing efficiency of energy capture). Julian H. Steward's *multilinear* (as opposed to Leslie White's *unilinear*) evolution was a short-lived alternative in the late 1950s and early 1960s that combined properties of both specific and general evolution in an effort to accommodate the scientific notion of evolution and provide stronger empirical support for cultural evolution.

Since the 1970s, there has been a proliferation of other variants of the cultural-evolutionary type, though they are not often recognized as such. Marxist approaches, when applied on regional or global scales, are of this general sort though, modern Marxist approaches owe more to French anthropology after the Second World War than they do to Childe's lead. In archaeology, their impact has been limited to explanation of complex society. More important archaeologically have been theories that treat population growth as an independent variable, as a motor, that drives human development—most traceable, directly or indirectly, to economist Ester Boserup's agricultural-intensification thesis. But population growth is clearly a dependent, not an independent, variable—people can and do starve to death—and explanations that treat it otherwise end up being ad hoc functional arguments that are just as circular as those of the nineteenth-century scholars.

Cultural evolution remains an important interpretive algorithm for traditional archaeologists of a humanistic persuasion, especially those concerned with the origins of complex society. Because of its structure, however, cultural evolution is unable to generate explanations that are empirically testable. Thus, its popularity tends to wax and wane with the archaeological commitment to science. The underlying optimism of cultural evolution—progress—assures it of a continuing role in popular archaeology.

Robert C. Dunnell

See also CHILDE, VERE GORDON; EVOLUTION, SCIENTIFIC; THOMSEN, CHRISTIAN JÜRGENSEN

Further Readings

Boserup, E. (1966) Conditions of Agricultural Growth: The Economics of Agrarian Change under Population Pressure. Chicago: Aldine.

Childe, V.G. (1944) Progress and Archaeology. London: Watts.

Childe, V.G. (1951) Man Makes Himself. New York: New American Library.

Dunnell, R.C. (1980) Evolutionary theory and archaeology. In M.B. Schiffer (ed.): Advances in Archaeological Method and Theory, vol. 3, pp. 35–99. New York: Academic.

Dunnell, R.C. (1988) The concept of progress in cultural evolution. In M.H. Nitecki (ed.): Evolutionary Progress? pp. 169–194. Chicago: University of Chicago Press.

Morgan, L.H. (1877) Ancient Society; or, Researches in the Lines of Human Progress from Savagery, Through Barbarism to Civilization. New York: Holt.

Sahlins, M.D., and Service, E.R. (1960) Evolution and Culture. Ann Arbor: University of Michigan Press.

Spencer, H. (1884) Principles of Sociology. New York: Appleton.

Steward, J.H. (1955) A Theory of Cultural Change: The Methodology of Multilinear Evolution. Urbana: University of Illinois Press.

White, L.B. (1959) The Evolution of Culture: The Development of Civilization to the Fall of Rome. New York: McGraw-Hill.

Evolution, Scientific

A theory in which the form and diversity of life is explained by a set of mechanisms operating on the transmission of variability between individuals.

The term *evolution* is widely used in anthropology and archaeology as a synonym for *development,* as well as for a number of disparate specific concepts. Here scientific evolution designates the scientific theory that was first enunciated by Charles Darwin in biology and that revolutionized scientific thought in the mid-nineteenth century. As a theory, it answers "why does it exist?" and the more standard scientific "how does it work?" questions.

It is hard to overestimate the departure from orthodox science and Western common sense that evolutionary theory represents. Instead of modeling reality as a set of fixed relations (laws) among a finite set of entities (classes like those of the periodic table), an ontological position termed *essentialism,* evolution sees reality as constantly in a state of becoming (classes are analytic tools without claim to empirical reality), a position termed *materialism.* While universally accepted as the theoretical underpinning of biology, many, if not most, biologists have but modest control of the theory. Popular understanding of evolution is usually wide the mark, replacing *selection* with *adaptation* as the principal mechanism of change.

Evolutionary theory is limited to explaining the history of living things because it addresses transmission. Furthermore, it requires variability. Organisms transmit traits from individual to individual, and individuals differ from one another. In evolutionary theory, there are two sets of processes: those that generate variability and those that act upon its transmission. Two variants of scientific evolution are recognized: *Lamarckian evolution,* in which the generation of variation is linked to conditions that act upon its transmission (e.g., long necks arise in giraffes *because* tree leaves exist to be eaten); and *Darwinian evolution,* in which the generation of variation is independent (often incorrectly called *random*) of the transmission conditions (e.g., if long necks arise in giraffes, these variants will be preserved in environments with trees [i.e., trees do not *cause* the appearance of long necks]). Darwinian evolution has completely dominated biological thought since the mid-nineteenth century because no mechanisms exist that link generation of variation to conditions of selection (i.e., the future is never known). It is often assumed, however, that evolution of cultural phenomena must be Lamarckian because that is the way change is viewed in Western common sense (we "solve problems"). In this view, the mechanism assumed to link generation of variation to the conditions of transmission is taken to be the human intellect. This, of course, conflates folk explanation with scientific explanation since humans do not know the future better than any other organism.

Darwin's most famous contribution is the principle mechanism responsible for differential transmission of traits, *natural selection.* For selection to be operative, (1) there must be variability in traits (e.g., differences in coat color); (2) some of those differences have to be transmitted (e.g., not all differences in coat color are caused by diet); and (3) some of those differences are of functional importance (e.g., predators can see color differences), said to affect the organism's fitness. If these conditions are met, then selection takes place (i.e., the frequency of different variants will change directionally [as opposed to randomly]). Since the conditions of selection (3) and the pool of variants (1) change more or less continuously, there is no single sequence or goal to selection.

Because natural selection is the most important mechanism responsible for differential transmission and because its mechanical nature contrasts so strongly with the vitalistic tack of cultural evolution, scientific evolution is often called *selectionist.* While identifying an important contrast, this name is unfortunate because selection is not the only mechanism that affects transmission in scientific evolution—some mechanisms are stochastic (a random, in a statistical sense, process that operates on historically constrained variants), such as drift. In the case of drift, population size and/or structure interacts with variant frequency to fix some variants at the expense of others unlinked to differences in fitness (e.g., a small founding population migrating to an island consisting of only a few individuals contains only two coat variants out of, say, twenty variants in the parent population).

As a transmission process, evolutionary change is continuous; however, the speed with which change occurs is variable. Darwin believed that change was slow, and that, while much change may be slow, evolutionary change can be rapid, as other workers recognized almost as soon as *On the Origin of Species* was published in 1859. Many things determine the rate: (1) magnitude of difference in fitness between variants; (2) rapidity in change of selective conditions; (3) trait architecture (e.g., some changes, such as in a growth hormone, have manifold consequences, while others, such as a change in an eye-color gene, do not). Furthermore, a new trait can spread in distribution in two fundamentally different ways: *sympatrically,* in which a change takes place more or less at the same rate throughout all or most of the populations of a species; and *allopatrically,* in which a subpopulation with a new trait expands at the expense of other populations. The so-called *punctuated-equilibrium model* (periods of stasis separated by periods of rapid change) was first offered as an epistemological model consistent with allopatric speciation (i.e., if speciation is allopatric, then small samples (such as constituted by the fossil record) of the empirical record will appear discontinuous. Punctuated equilibrium in this sense is sound. Later, it was advanced as an ontological model in which change is seen as driven by new, stochastic processes. While attracting much attention at the time, punctuated equilibrium in this second sense has largely been rejected in biology for want of an application (i.e., while everyone appreciates that large shifts can and do occur unmediated by selection, they are rare events, and the punctuated character of the record is due to sampling allopatric distributions).

Evolutionists distinguish between the codes or instructions for constructing an individual, the things that are transmitted and commonly called the *genotype,* from the realization of those instructions in an organism as mitigated by the conditions it faces, the *phenotype.* Before modern field studies in biology, the phenotype was largely conceived in morphometric terms; today, it is universally acknowledged to have both morphometric and behavioral components.

The mechanism(s) responsible for trait transmission was not known in Darwin's day. Linking evolution and genetics in the 1930s, the so-called *New Synthesis* is one of the triumphs of modern science and the breakthrough that assured evolutionary theory of its dominant explanatory role. The success of the New Synthesis was so great that genetics and evolution were, and still are in some quarters, virtually equated—hence, such terms as *genotype* that imply only a single mechanism for code transmission.

Since the 1980s, it has become clear that a second mechanism, usually called *culture,* exists for trait transmission, a second kind of mechanism for inheritance, in which traits, such as language, are learned (e.g., imprinting, teaching) by one individual from another. While culture was regarded not too long ago as the exclusive property of human beings, again modern field studies have demonstrated that all higher animals, to variable degree, transmit some of the information necessary to

E

generate a complete phenotype culturally. People are unique only in the degree to which this mechanism is employed.

Clearly, evolutionary theory is applicable to people and to cultural phenomena, yet its actual use has been quite modest. Much resistance to its application to people and, thus, to archaeology lies in the vested interests humans have in alternative explanations of human behavior. In large measure, this resistance is a resistance to scientific explanation of human affairs and has little to do with anything specifically evolutionary. Further, the confusion between cultural evolution and scientific evolution has often led to the mistaken rejection of the latter for faults of the former.

There have been three main attempts to apply scientific evolution to cultural phenomena: (1) the direct application of evolution as developed in biology (i.e., genetics) to people, often called *sociobiology;* (2) the construction of a *separate but equal* theory of cultural evolution that is analogous to, not part of or identical with, biological evolution; and (3) the generalization of the biological theory beyond its nonhuman biological history.

The sociobiological approach, pursued primarily by biologists, is closely linked to the work of Edward O. Wilson in the 1960s and followed upon the demonstration that altruism, a seemingly non-Darwinian phenomenon, could be accounted for by the action of natural selection. Sociobiologists took genetics to be the only transmission mechanism; culture was, therefore, reduced to part of the selective environment. Demonstrations that complex social behavior and cultural institutions could be explained as the effects of selection excited considerable scientific interest in the 1960s and 1970s. Resistance from social scientists, however, was strong, since their disciplines were apparently marginalized by this development. While such "turf" arguments were the loudest, the ultimate rejection of sociobiology lay with its failure to see culture as a transmission mechanism, compelling it to argue that all behavior is genetically determined at some level, an empirically indefensible position.

Anthropologists interested in a scientific approach, on the other hand, recognized culture as a transmission mechanism functionally equivalent to genetics. Being just as conservative as the sociobiologists, they took this observation as a warrant for the construction of an entire series of mechanisms (e.g., natural/cultural selection; drift/cultural drift). While culture in the role of transmission mechanism does introduce new complexities (e.g., transmission is more or less continuous rather than discrete), no compelling arguments for such phenomena as cultural selection have ever been advanced on either empirical or theoretical grounds. Rather, the role of such "mechanisms" seems to be to preserve the separation of people from other animals and has its roots in the conflation of folk explanation with scientific explanation. For this reason, this approach has proved to have limited appeal.

The final alternative is an effort to generalize the biological theory by removing the constraints it acquired accidentally by virtue of its particular history of development in nonhuman biology. This has included the recognition of culture as a transmission mechanism but also the retention of natural selection, drift, and other concepts from biology where warranted. While much progress has been made, this process is far from complete simply because the effort is in its infancy and there is strong resistance to scientific explanation of human behavior. Nonetheless, since evolution is the only scientific theory that explains change, and since the explanation of change remains at the core of archaeology, the fate of scientific evolution in archaeology would seem to rest on the degree to which archaeology continues to construe itself as science.

Robert C. Dunnell

See also EVOLUTION, CULTURAL

Further Readings

Boyd, R., and Richerson, P.J. (1985) Culture and Evolutionary Process. Chicago: University of Chicago Press.

Darwin, C. (1859) On the Origin of Species. London: John Murray.

Dunnell, R.C. (1980) Evolutionary theory and archaeology. In M.B. Schiffer (ed.): Advances in Archaeological Method and Theory, vol. 3, pp. 35–99. New York: Academic.

Dunnell, R.C. (1989) Aspects of the application of evolutionary theory in archaeology. In C.C. Lamberg-Karlovsky (ed.): Archaeological Thought in America, pp. 35–49. Cambridge: Cambridge University Press.

Gould, S.J. (1977) Ever Since Darwin: Reflections in Natural History. New York: Norton.

Gould, S.J. (1986) Evolution and the triumph of homology; or, why history matters. American Scientist 74:60–69.

Mayr, E. (1991) One Long Argument: Charles Darwin and the Genesis of Modern Evolutionary Thought. Cambridge, MA: Harvard University Press.

Mayr, E., and Provine, W.B., eds. (1980) The Evolutionary Synthesis: Perspectives on the Unification of Biology. Cambridge, MA: Harvard University Press.

O'Brien, M.J., ed. (1996) Evolutionary Archaeology: Theory and Application. Salt Lake City: University of Utah Press.

Teltser, P.A., ed. (1995) Evolutionary Archaeology: Methodological Issues. Tucson: University of Arizona Press.

Wilson, E.O. (1975) Sociobiology: A New Synthesis. Cambridge, MA: Harvard University Press.

Exchange Systems, Theory

Recognition and interpretation of intersocietal contact. Writing this entry poses certain challenges, the most significant of which is the absence of any coherent body of thought that might be labeled an archaeological theory of exchange. The reasons for this are complex and rooted in archaeology's history and present theoretical structure. Part of the problem is definitional, *exchange* being an omnibus term referring to anything from occasional gift transfers to high-volume, currency-based market transactions. It is hard to imagine a single theory that could account for the behavioral significance of such a wide range of activities. A more fundamental obstacle to the creation of exchange theory is the profound disagreement evident in the literature about the significance of this process, however it is defined, in interpretations of the past. Exchange is a process perceived differently by people subscribing to varied conceptual schemes.

This entry, therefore, examines how exchange has been used in archaeological interpretations. Exchange has frequently been equated with trade and defined as the peaceful, reciprocal movement of goods among members of different societies. Tribute and raiding, two other significant processes by which items are obtained from beyond social borders, are thereby excluded from consideration. Unfortunately, not much else is. Developing a vocabulary sensitive to nuances in intersocietal exchange mechanisms is a high priority if only because it would reduce confusion as to what sorts of cross-border relations are being discussed in any instance labeled exchange. The general definition given above, however, is at least a starting point and true to archaeological uses of the term.

Despite differing views, researchers generally agree that exchange studies should concentrate on specifying the structure of the networks through which goods moved; the manner in which exchange articulated with economic and political formations within component societies, especially exchange's effects on production, consumption, and distribution processes; and the conditions under which these systemic relations varied, yielding particular economic and political consequences within individual societies and the network as a whole. The following discussion provides a brief overview of exchange studies organized around these central issues.

History of Exchange Theory

Archaeological interest in intersocietal exchange reflects an enduring concern with the impact of extralocal forces on long-term cultural processes. During most of the early twentieth century, American anthropology and archaeology operated on the assumption that the diffusion of ideas and goods among societies determined local culture histories. *Diffusion* (including trade) and, to some extent, *migration* were widely used to account for culture change and underlay the temporal and geographic classifications of archaeological remains. The intellectual climate in which diffusion flourished was characterized by an emphasis on the uniqueness of individual cultures and the impossibility of employing generalizing, scientific approaches to the study of human behavior. Intersocietal contacts were seen as unpredictable events that played central roles in creating cultural differences. Diffusion, therefore, was closely linked with a particularizing approach to culture.

Much early work on diffusion was naive, assuming rather than establishing the operation of intersocietal connections and their behavioral effects. Efforts underway by the mid-twentieth century to develop a better understanding of diffusion's operation and systemic impacts reflect contemporary awareness of the problems (Willey and Lathrap 1956). Nevertheless, the above measures had little immediate influence on archaeological theory because interest in all manner of intersocietal relations waned during the 1950s and early 1960s. This shift is a direct result of the ascendancy of explicitly generalizing materialist paradigms, especially *cultural ecology*, in archaeological thought.

Cultural ecology and its successors sought to identify and explain cross-cultural regularities in human behavior. These commonalities were the result of predictable relations among technological and physical environmental variables that together created a balanced ecosystem and promoted adaptation. Cultures were modeled as systems of interrelated parts, whose forms were explained by their functional linkages to the physical environment. Archaeologists, therefore, focused attention on individual societies and their ecological settings at the expense of examining links among these units. Intersocietal relations, inextricably wedded with historical processes fortuitously generating cultural diversity, had no place in the new science of archaeology.

The critical point is that intersocietal interaction was excluded from a central place in archaeological theory for historical rather than empirical reasons. Its insignificance was assumed rather than proved. Fledgling efforts to develop a scientific, generalizing approach to intersocietal contacts, including goods exchange, were cut short by changes in the intellectual climate at mid-century. Attempts to resurrect this goal are still hampered by a historical legacy that links cross-border contacts with cultural divergence and particularism. Exchange remains marginal to, presumably, more causally significant adaptive or political processes.

Contemporary Exchange Theory

Archaeologists reintroduced intersocietal contacts into interpretations of the past during the late 1960s as it became increasingly obvious that no society exists in isolation. In keeping with the reigning paradigms, however, intersocietal interaction was no longer the omnipresent creator of unique histories. Instead, such contacts were to be carefully identified empirically and systemically integrated with other cultural subsystems (e.g., economy, society, politics, religion). The term *diffusion*, freighted with unscientific connotations, was replaced by *trade* as the most common way of referring to intersocietal interaction. Trade seemed less vague and more susceptible to empirical verification than diffusion.

The proliferation of articles and books prominently featuring the word *trade* in their titles between 1968 and 1977 strongly suggests release of a pent-up urge to investigate interaction processes. Much of this work, continuing today, was directed to describing trade network structures (i.e., sources of exchanged items, distribution mechanisms, and patterns of production and consumption related to trade). Origins of exchanged goods have been addressed through sophisticated chemical and mineralogical assays by which objects such as ceramics, metals, obsidian, jade, and turquoise can be linked to particular resource zones. Reconstructing trade volume (including rates of trade-good consumption), duration, and mechanisms has proved more difficult than source identification. Among the problems encountered are: (1) having to infer the above features based on samples, recovered from different portions of a putative network, whose contemporaneity and comparability are hard to establish; (2) accounting for the transfer of perishable commodities; and (3) the difficulty experienced in distinguishing different trade mechanisms from surviving distributional patterns. Exacerbating these dilemmas is the growing recognition that the intensity and behavioral significance of intersocietal linkages may not directly correlate with extant evidence of goods exchange. Important relations among populations possibly involved very little movement of material, or at least of material likely to be preserved in archaeological collections. Allowance has, therefore, been made for the importance of contacts reflected by evidence other than trade, primarily the spread of styles in media ranging from ceramics to architecture. Charting *style distributions* was a mainstay of diffusion studies, though then, as now, the significance of these linkages remains a point of contention. As difficult as the aforementioned obstacles to network reconstruction are, their very recognition and attempts to overcome them mark major advances over earlier diffusion research.

Concurrent with these descriptive efforts have been attempts to incorporate intersocietal contacts in general, and trade in particular, within archaeological theory. Explicitly or implicitly, all researchers attempt to model the systemic articulation of trade with processes of production, consumption, and distribution operating on varying spatial scales and with diverse economic, political, and social consequences. This concern owes a considerable debt to Karl Polanyi's famous caution, enunciated in the mid-twentieth century, that all economic processes in noncapitalist societies, including trade, are parts of larger sociopolitical formations and derive their significance from the roles they play in those structures. This *substantivist* position was developed in contrast to a *formalist* perspective that equated all trade with market exchanges operating on supply-and-demand principles largely free of sociopolitical constraints and contexts. There is little doubt that stressing trade's institutional setting greatly contributed to understanding goods exchange as social action. It may have also had the deleterious effect of reinforcing a tendency in archaeological thought to model exchange as an adjunct of other, presumably more basic, sociopolitical and ecological processes and structures.

Despite general agreement that ancient trade had sociopolitical as well as economic implications, archaeologists differ profoundly on the place of goods exchanges within ecological and cultural formations. These diverse views are grouped here into two broad categories, the ecological and the political, based on how the interrelations are conceived.

Ecological models envision exchange as an adaptive mechanism promoting a group's survival under conditions of significant and recurrent subsistence shortfalls within complex environmental mosaics. Extrasocietal contacts form networks through which information on resource availability and goods, especially subsistence staples, flows among societies occupying complementary environments. Such contacts encourage production of moderate surpluses for trade, thereby ensuring adequate supplies for all interactors even during times of localized environmental stress. Lux-

ury goods, objects with more social (e.g., as status markers) than economic significance, also move through the system and function as stores of value that can be exchanged in times of need for basic staples. Alternatively, these connections may adjust demographic and environmental imbalances by moving people to resources. Ecological constructs are attempts to incorporate intersocietal interaction within an adaptationist-materialist paradigm. They are most commonly applied in cases of relatively short-distance transactions in which the transfer of bulky staples is feasible (especially under primitive transportation conditions) and to egalitarian societies lacking hereditary leaders. Most important in distinguishing this perspective is the role of trade as an equilibrium-maintaining device, serving to balance production and consumption through intersocietal distribution. Trade here is one of many cultural practices functioning to *preserve* the structure of individual social systems. The organization of the overall trade network is as egalitarian as its components, no one society deriving singular advantage from these ties.

Political models operate from the opposite premise that goods exchange disrupts extant relations among production, consumption, and distribution, resulting in greatly changed sociopolitical structures. These theories can be further distinguished by the scale of trade's unsettling influence: the individual society or the network as a whole. Whatever their differences, all of these perspectives share basic assumptions derived to greater or lesser degrees from Marxist thought. Societies are not equilibrium-seeking, adaptive systems but structures by which power is distributed. These structures provide a framework, flexible but not infinitely malleable, within which people maneuver to enhance their own welfare and that of their factions. What is at issue here is control over power, the ability to direct effectively and regularly the actions of others. Power, in turn, is desired because of its use in harnessing the labor of the many to the meet the desires of the few. Within egalitarian social formations, attempts by any one bloc to centralize control over power and labor are checked by the actions of other comparable units. Stability is not a consequence of adaptive behavior but a stalemate among competing interest groups. This situation changes when one faction gains privileged access to a

E

resource or resources valued and needed by all others. That asset can assume any of a number of forms, from localized basic resources, such as water and arable land, to foreign items secured through trade.

Exchange theories that focus on individual societies posit that one faction's exclusive control over the local distribution of foreign items contributes mightily to the triumph of that bloc in power contests *(prestige good theory)*. Goods acquired from afar can be used by the monopolists to ensnare clients in dependency relations whereby those outside the charmed circle surrender labor and its fruits (e.g., food surpluses) in return for access to valuables available only from the interactors. Inequality is masked by reciprocal exchanges that consistently redound to the benefit of those with external contacts. Goods transfers, as suggested by Marcel Mauss and students of Big Man societies, are charged with political and social significance. Formation of dependency relations requires that large portions of the population need the imported goods; otherwise, there is no need to turn to the monopolists for the items in question. Exotics may function in daily maintenance tasks (e.g., stone or metals for implement manufacture) or figure in important social transactions, such as exchanges related to marriage or paying fines. Exclusive possession of imports might also distinguish the status of emergent elites, symbolizing rights to rule and control labor. Foreign items could enhance the charisma of interactors when the goods themselves are perceived to be charged with a power derived from their distant origin points. In any and all of these cases, intersocietal exchanges are a source of goods whose local rarity facilitates centralized control over regional distribution and whose high value (economically, socially, and/or ideologically) gives that exclusive control political significance.

Exchange monopolies encourage pivotal changes in local production and consumption patterns. At the very least, subsistence surpluses are increased as subordinates try to meet the demands of newly emergent elites. Specialized craft production may be stimulated as well, encouraged and supported by leaders who use its products in extrasocietal trade and/or as gifts by which to extract further surpluses from clients. Goods distribution, of exotics as well as local items, takes on

a hierarchical structure replacing the horizontal exchanges among more or less social equals in egalitarian formations. Consumption, always fraught with social and political significance, is also hierarchically organized. Whereas the quantity and nature of objects (including food) used by different social units were roughly equivalent in egalitarian systems, now consumption patterns vary meaningfully between monopolists and clients. The former have exclusive control over certain goods only they can use (e.g., status markers) while enjoying privileged access to surpluses generated by client labor. The appearance of towns and cities may also be fostered as leaders seek to increase their labor pool by attracting ever larger numbers of dependents, and clients attempt to enhance access to elite-controlled goods. If the local environment and available technology are capable of yielding ever greater surpluses and sustaining demographic increase, then trade, production, consumption, and regional distribution processes will be linked into a positive feedback system advancing political centralization, hierarchy building, and socioeconomic differentiation.

These interlinkages presume that the dominant faction can maintain its exclusive control over valued imports. Should subordinates be able to break that monopoly, obtaining goods from outside elite-controlled channels, then dependency relations and consumption distinctions crucial to the system's operation will be undercut and processes of decentralization initiated. One factor repeatedly advanced to account for systems collapse is the intrusion of market economies based on exchanges for profit that introduce some standard of value, such as currency, into elite-controlled distribution networks. Market traders, in seeking revenue, break down barriers that previously separated distinct exchange spheres. Goods that had been solely under elite control may now appear for sale in open markets, available to all of those with enough funds. Standards of value also weaken distinct exchange pathways, since they greatly facilitate establishing a uniform system of pricing and evaluation applicable to all objects. Elites can move to counter this threat (e.g., by developing coercive means to systematically impoverish clients, thereby denying them the wherewithal to acquire politically potent valuables, or through the enforcement of sumptuary laws to preserve centralized command over politically important items). Nevertheless, markets threaten power based on trade monopolies and have existed in tense relationships with centralized distribution systems within states as diverse as those of Mesopotamia in the third–second millennium B.C. and the Aztecs of central Mexico in the fourteenth–fifteenth centuries.

Prestige good theory, as opposed to ecological models, generally deals with transactions through which high-value, low-bulk social valuables *(luxuries)* were moved over long distances among elite *partners.* This perspective is most often employed to explain rapid increases in sociopolitical complexity occurring among societies in contact with larger, hierarchically structured states (e.g., Iron Age Mediterranean polities in their interactions with "barbarian" Europe and the impact of colonial regimes on varied indigenous societies during the sixteenth–eighteenth centuries). Trade has, therefore, become one way of modeling secondary state formation.

Some researchers have argued that exchanges, operating as outlined above, have an important role to play in encouraging primary state development as well. Such a position has been most consistently advanced within the *peer polity* framework. In this view, cooperative and competitive interactions among neighboring, equivalently organized societies are hypothesized to spur intensified surplus production controlled by emergent rulers in all parts of the network. Elite power, enshrined and preserved in new institutions developed along similar lines in all member societies, depends on paramount abilities to control and encourage escalating contacts and surplus production. *Peer polity models* help account for the sudden and synchronous appearance in some regions (such as southern Mesopotamia in the fifth–fourth millennia B.C.) of complexly structured societies, sharing similar material styles and organizational schemes, with no one polity taking the developmental lead. Intense intersocietal contacts, peer polity adherents argue, can incite political centralization, hierarchy, and social differentiation in the absence of established states.

Extending processes of exploitation and competition from individual societies to entire interaction networks is another theme within the general class of political-trade theories. In this context, the effect of exchanges on local sociopolitical developments is strongly conditioned by a society's structural position within an interregional exchange system. Much of the research conducted in this area involves various reworkings of Immanuel Wallerstein's *world systems theory,* originally developed to account for the spread and development of European-based capitalism beginning in the fifteenth century. World systems theorists generally conceive of intersocietal transactions as occurring within a matrix of unequal economic and political relations. Powerful cores, large, complexly organized polities, systematically exploit smaller, less centralized peripheral societies. The latter function as sources of raw materials acquired on favorable terms by core agents and used to fuel processing and manufacturing industries in the core(s). Peripheries are doubly exploited in that they not only lose raw materials, but also end up buying back those resources transformed by core artisans into finished goods. While some factions in peripheral societies may initially benefit from their favored relations with core representatives, as outlined above, they eventually find themselves presiding over polities whose specialized positions within interaction networks result in their impoverishment. Peripheral underdevelopment is assured as assets needed to sustain local political and economic expansion are siphoned off to support those processes in cores, further exacerbating inequalities within the interaction system. A society's role in such a network, as core or periphery, determines processes of production, consumption, and distribution within it.

Efforts to apply Wallerstein's model to noncapitalist exchange systems have required modification of the original scheme. There is much discussion but as yet (the late 1990s) little consensus as to how the basic assumptions and concepts of world systems theory can be profitably reworked to illuminate the realities of ancient interactions. Most of the debate centers on the roles of social valuables *(luxuries)* in creating and maintaining interregional exchange networks and the appropriateness of *underdevelopment* as a process within most prehistoric interaction systems.

Wallerstein downplays the importance of anything but basic staples trade in the forging of intersocietal ties. Bulky goods, such as subsistence products, rarely figure in the long-distance interactions archaeologists usually study, while social valuables occupy a much

E

more central position. Given the political significance of the latter class of goods, many researchers have argued that enduring competitive relations among societies can and have been based on transactions involving so-called luxuries. The very existence of systematic interregional exploitation has, however, been questioned. Unequal interregional relations seen in modern capitalist structures seem to depend on the ability of core elites to exercise monopolies over goods needed throughout the network, transportation technologies required to move those items in quantity, and military threats, and/or the ease with which core agents can insinuate themselves into local relations of production and distribution. Where such monopolies are lacking and peripheries retain control over their own political and economic systems, core agents are unable to dictate the terms of intersocietal exchange to their own advantage. Exchange, under these circumstances, may well stimulate complex sociopolitical developments and economic growth (increase in the volume and diversity of production and consumption) throughout the network and not just in cores. External demands for local products, subsistence staples, and/or social valuables would encourage intensification and broadening of surplus production everywhere in the net. Centralized distribution within societies of items acquired in return for these surpluses might then serve to further political processes, as specified earlier. This debate, and research carried out on the questions it raises, promises to yield important insights into the nature of intersocietal interaction, including trade, and the conditions favoring the development of different kinds of networks characterized by varying degrees of inequality and exploitation.

Future Exchange Theory

Intersocietal goods exchange seems to be a member of a class of processes that have been used by archaeologists as explanatory mechanisms in a variety of conceptual frameworks (migration is another component of this category). The significance of exchange in understanding human behavior varies with the theoretical scheme in which it is employed. Ecological approaches view exchange as an adaptive mechanism functioning to balance production and consumption within a number of linked societies. Political models, in contrast, look to exchange as an important stimu-

lant to change, providing scheming entrepreneurs with the extrasocietal means to enslave their compatriots. Intersocietal transactions, in turn, create dynamic relations among production, consumption, and distribution on regional and interregional scales, yielding networks whose varying structures have significant impacts on local developments. There can be no unified exchange theory in archaeology under these conditions, no coherent view of the long-term impact of exchange on human behavior. Instead, one runs the risk of being mired in fruitless arguments about whether intersocietal transactions are stabilizing or disruptive, more economically or politically significant.

Development of an archaeological exchange theory requires that attention be paid to several issues. The theory would need to address the varying conditions under which goods exchange has certain, specifiable impacts on local processes of production, consumption, and distribution. The differing approaches to trade outlined above, for example, may be complementary. Ecological models have possibly identified regularities in trade's behavioral impact operating within and among small-scale, egalitarian societies living in environments subject to persistent but unpredictable fluctuations in subsistence resources. Similarly, political exchange theories could point to commonalities applicable among societies undergoing rapid processes of political centralization, hierarchy building, and social differentiation. Though the above examples are simplistic, they suggest that exchange is not a monolithic process whose effects are always the same.

Equally important is defining units appropriate to the study of ancient interaction. Much work on the topic operates with the assumption that temporally and spatially distinct societies are the basic units of change and stability, exchange being a means to link these entities. Application of world systems theory to the study of past interaction systems has the salutary effect of reminding us that important structures and processes operate at the intersocietal level and strongly influence local developments throughout the network. Interaction systems are more than the sums of their individual societies. Complex interrelations among societal and intersocietal developments need to be studied in much greater detail over a much broader range of time periods and world areas than has been the case to date. Such work requires considerable rethinking of extant conceptual tools, creating, in some cases, new analytical units suitable to the task.

On an empirical level, more effort must be devoted to increasing the reliability of archaeological reconstructions of ancient consumption, distribution, and production patterns operating at societal and intersocietal scales. All exchange models posit specific relations among the above variables; the more securely archaeologists can reconstruct these processes, the better they can evaluate claims concerning the role(s) of exchange in encouraging stability or change. Prosaic concerns of contemporaneity, sampling, sourcing, and the like are the bases from which further advances in theory will be made. This is especially the case when dealing with prehistoric exchange systems in which there are no ethnohistoric documents to guide interpretations.

The behavioral importance ascribed over the years to intersocietal exchange by adherents of a wide range of theoretical perspectives in archaeology strongly hints at the significance of this process. Exchange studies will not make their full, independent contribution to investigations of culture change and stability until intersocietal exchanges are seen as diverse processes deserving attention in their own rights. This remains a challenge and a stimulus to future exchange research.

Edward M. Schortman
Patricia A. Urban

Further Readings

Adams, R. (1974) Anthropological perspectives on ancient trade. Current Anthropology 15:239–258.

Braun, D., and Plog, S. (1982) Evolution of "tribal" social networks: Theory and prehistoric North American evidence. American Antiquity 47:504–525.

Kohl, P. (1987) The use and abuse of world systems theory: The case of the "pristine" west Asian state. In M.B. Schiffer (ed.): Advances in Archaeological Method and Theory, vol. 11, pp. 1–35. New York: Academic.

Mauss, M. (1967) The Gift: Forms and Functions of Exchanges in Archaic Societies. New York: Norton (originally published in 1925).

Polanyi, K., Arensberg, C., and Pearson, H., eds. (1971) Trade and Market in the Early Empires. Chicago: Henry Regnery (originally published in 1957).

Renfrew, C., and Cherry, J., eds. (1986) Peer Polity Interaction and Sociopolitical Change. Cambridge: Cambridge University Press.

Rowlands, M., Larsen, M., and Kristiansen, K., eds. (1987) Centre and Periphery in the Ancient World. Cambridge: Cambridge University Press.

Schortman, E., and Urban, P., eds. (1992) Resources, Power, and Interregional Interaction. New York: Plenum.

Wallerstein, I. (1974) The Modern World System, vol. 1. New York: Academic.

Willey, G., and Lathrap, D. (1956) An archaeological classification of culture contact situations. In R. Wauchope (ed.): Seminars in Archaeology 1955, pp. 3–30. Salt Lake City: Society for American Archaeology.

Experimental Archaeology

Creation of an artificial system to explore archaeological material or processes. As the word *experimental* suggests, this subfield of archaeology performs tests to observe the relationship between human behavior and material culture (artifacts) throughout its life history. Experiments are performed to determine first how artifacts were produced, used, modified, and discarded and then to understand the processes that impact the material while in a depositional environment. Similar theoretically to ethnoarchaeology, experimental archaeology seeks to understand the past by exploring present-day material culture and behavior.

History

Experimentation with prehistoric material is as old as archaeology itself. By the late nineteenth century, the great antiquity of humans was finally realized, and modern archaeology was born. Immediately, experiments began with stone artifacts recovered from ancient geological strata. Most of the first experiments focused on stone tools because, unlike ceramics or metallurgy, the making of tools from chert, obsidian, or flint is a dead technology. No one currently made stone tools, so experiments were necessary to answer even the most basic questions. With replicas or even with the actual artifacts, these early experimenters were able to determine how stone tools were made and used. Since these first attempts at experimentation, every type of prehistoric and historical material and process has been subject to the tortures of the experimenter. These have ranged from making metal tools, butchering animals with stone tools, and replicating ceramic technology to erecting stone monuments (megaliths), replicating and sailing ancient boats, and even creating and inhabiting a small Neolithic community. But the ultimate experiment may have been performed by the American flintknapper Don Crabtree, an expert in replicating stone tools. He successfully underwent open-heart surgery with stone tools he himself had made. Although this is a dramatic demonstration, it changed forever the impression that stone tools were less effective than their modern metal counterparts.

Many of these early experimental findings have had a profound effect on archaeology and serve as the foundation for archaeologists' knowledge about prehistoric technology. It is experiments that have demonstrated how stone tools were made and used, how pots were constructed and fired, how the pyramids were built, and what happens to a wooden structure and its artifacts in a fire. A number of experiments have even shaped the direction of archaeological research by demonstrating the possibilities of human behavior. For example, to celebrate the World's Fair of 1893 and the 400th anniversary of the discovery of America by Columbus, a group of Norwegians made a 24-foot-long (ca. 8 m) replica of a Viking boat and successfully sailed from Norway to New York in twenty-seven days. This timely experiment suggested that Columbus may not have been the first European to reach North America, well before there was any archaeological evidence to support this idea. The Norwegian experiment opened minds to the possibility of Precolumbian Viking contact, and today we have conclusive archaeological evidence of Viking occupation of the northeastern shores of North America.

The mound-builder controversy captivated American scientists and lay people alike during the latter half of the nineteenth century, and experiments helped to resolve it. Often found among the massive earthen mounds located throughout the eastern United States were copper artifacts, a technology that was presumed to be beyond the capabilities of Native Americans. But in the late nineteenth century Frank Hamilton Cushing demonstrated experimentally that he could replicate all of the copper artifacts, including the sheet-copper figures made by the Hopewell mound builders, with the technology possessed by precontact Native Americans. Most researchers at the time believed that a vanished people (probably European) built the mounds, but this experiment provided key evidence that prehistoric Native Americans were the mound builders.

Experimental archaeology even has a martyr; Robert Ball burst a blood vessel and died while trying to produce a musical note on an Irish bronze horn. Ball was convinced that a side-blow horn was used to produce musical notes similar to the end-blow variety. His convictions, however, proved fatal in an experiment in the late nineteenth century.

Experimental Archaeology Today

Archaeological experiments, both then and now, usually start with a question. Is this a tool made by humans or is it a stone modified by nature? How was this tool made? How was it used? Why was this ceramic pot made with this shape? In the absence of direct informants or a time machine, prehistorians often turn to experimentation to answer their questions.

How Was the Artifact Made?

Although experiments have been done with all prehistoric technologies, there are two reasons why most experiments to date (i.e., 1998) have been performed with stone tools. First, stone tools were such an important technology. Chipped stone is the oldest tool (that survives) and the most prevalent archaeological artifact for much of the first three million years of human history. Second, stone-tool making was basically a dead technology by the time researchers developed an interest. Although in some parts of the world traditional stone-tool manufacture was observed and gun-flint makers kept the technology alive for some time, flintknapping of chopping and cutting tools was, for the most part, a skill that had to be rediscovered. Compare stone-tool making with pottery manufacture, a technology that never died. Forming a pot on a wheel is a technique developed in prehistory, but the skills have not been lost; new potters are trained every year. Because chipped-stone technology lacks this type of intergenerational transmission of knowledge, archaeologists must turn to flintknapping experiments to address even the most basic questions.

There are a number of archaeologists and flintknapping hobbyists who are keeping this technology alive. They have successfully replicated all prehistoric projectile points and tools simply by trial and error. One of the best examples of this form of replication are the experiments by Crabtree, who has mastered some of the most difficult flintknapping skills. In one series of experiments, Crabtree successfully replicated Mesoamerican prismatic blades by a special form of pressure flaking (a technique of removing flakes by exerting pressure, not by striking a blow). These long thin blades were made by specialists in prehistoric Mesoamerica, and, until Crabtree's experiments, the method of manufacture had eluded archaeologists. Although this form of replication experiment can never determine conclusively how a stone tool was made, they provide key insights into the prehistoric technology and generally leave the experimenter impressed with the high level of skill possessed by the prehistoric craftsperson.

Replication experiments have also been performed with many other materials as archaeologists became curious how, for example, a certain type of color was attained on pottery, how holes could be drilled through stone, or how monuments were constructed. The latter can even be used to infer the level of social complexity. Some experimenters have organized the construction of mounds and temples to estimate how much labor was required for their construction with traditional technology. Experiments have also been instrumental in understanding the development of metallurgy. Melting copper or making bronze tools requires temperatures beyond what can be reached with open fires, generally more than 1,000°C. Consequently, many of the experiments with metallurgy have involved reconstructing traditional furnaces and then creating various types of metal implements or ornaments with simple tools.

How Were the Artifacts Used?
A key to understanding prehistoric behavior is specific information on how tools were used.

Assumptions about artifact use are at the core of many inferences, such as attempts at reconstructing diet, demography, and population. If an archaeologist wishes to infer population of a household from the number of vessels, it is imperative that precise information about vessel use be devised. One accurate method to estimate household population is to determine the volume of everyday cooking pots, which assumes that these vessels can be discriminated from those used for water storage, dry storage, serving, or for cooking during larger household gatherings. The shape, size, and other attributes can provide general information about vessel function (e.g., cooking, water storage, serving), but use-alteration traces (e.g., carbon deposits, attrition, organic residues as a result of use) can provide more specific information about vessel use. Experiments, along with ethnoarchaeological data, have provided the links between these traces and specific uses.

Experimental data have also been critical to understanding the relationship between pottery manufacture and use. It has been determined experimentally that pottery temper (any nonclay material that must be added to ceramics to reduce shrinkage and avoid cracking) was altered by prehistoric potters to change vessel performance. For example, shell temper, common during the late prehistoric period in the midwestern United States, was found to increase the workability of excessively plastic montmorillonite clays and to improve a vessel's thermal shock resistance, an attribute that would be beneficial in many forms of cooking. Similarly, experiments have shown that organic temper, which burns out during firing, leaving pores, can significantly improve clay workability by removing moisture. This would permit people to make a vessel in one sitting. Certainly, mobile hunter-gatherers, who probably made pottery only occasionally, would have found this attribute an advantage.

Use-wear analysis of stone tools has also provided more specific information about tool function. A formal analysis of stone-tool attributes can create general categories of use, but experiments have shown that use-wear analysis can provide specific information about which material was cut, scraped, or pierced by the tool. These experiments have shown that tool use can leave traces in the form of polishes or microchips that can be linked to specific materials and processes. With use-wear analysis, one can infer, for example, that a knife was used to cut wood, meat, or vegetal material. When these types of more specific inferences about tool function are possible, they clearly provide an advantage to the archaeologist who is trying to reconstruct prehistoric diet or determine how the material was processed.

There have also been a number of experiments with stone tools that have left the laboratory and performed the tests under more realistic conditions. Animals have been butchered with replicated tools to assess their efficiency and to document use-wear patterns, and modern elephants (already deceased) have been jabbed with replicated Clovis points (made prehistorically by North American big-game hunters during the last Ice Age). The latter experiments illustrated how well Clovis points attached to thrusting spears could penetrate; they also documented conditions in which the points break, since broken points are commonly found prehistorically. Equipped only with thrusting spears and spear throwers, the Clovis people specialized in hunting the now extinct mammoth. Because both the game and the hunting techniques (i.e., hunting big-game with spears) were never witnessed ethnographically, experimental data provide one of the only means to develop prehistoric inferences.

Formation Processes

A final general category of archaeological experimentation is *formation processes*. Because archaeologists reconstruct human behavior from artifact patterns, it is important to understand the processes that both create and disturb the archaeological record. These experiments explore first the processes whereby artifacts enter the archaeological record, and second the many forces of nature that can alter artifacts after they are deposited. One of the most ambitious projects of this type to date is at Overton Down, Wiltshire, England. The project began in 1960 to study the changes that take place in an artificial site. The Overton Down project members dug a ditch and created a small mound (barrow), then recorded morphological changes (e.g., filling of the ditch and the erosion of the mound) through regular excavations. The experimenters also buried artifacts and recorded their conditions after burial and recovery.

Similar experiments on formation processes have studied the effects of various natural processes, such as wind, water, and freezing and thawing, on the distribution or breakdown of artifacts. Moving water has been shown not only to displace and abrade cultural materials, but also to provide the means to chip stone in a way that mimics artifacts. Rocks striking one another in rapidly moving water can flake and create *geofacts* (fractured rocks created by the forces of nature, not by humans).

In the Arctic, time-lapse experiments have demonstrated how frost action can displace lithic flakes up to 20 cm a year and alter significantly any prehistoric patterning of artifacts. In addition, experiments have been employed to assess how conditions of the depositional environment, such as soil chemistry, may alter the trace elements of pottery. These experiments are critical because these trace elements, often identified by neutron activation, are then used to reconstruct pottery-exchange networks and various distribution patterns. Certainly, it is first necessary to rule out the possibility that the depositional environment is not adding or deleting material before proceeding with any form of chemical analysis of archaeological materials.

The effect of humans on the distribution of artifacts while in the depositional environment has also been studied. Human trampling has been shown to disperse vertically deposited materials, to alter individual artifacts significantly, and to cause microwear on stone tools. Clearly, lithic-use-wear analysts must understand this process and incorporate it into their study. The disturbance and movement of artifacts as a result of tillage has also been investigated. Many archaeological sites worldwide occur within agricultural fields, so it is important to understand how modern cultivation disturbs an archaeological deposit.

Place Within the Discipline

Experimental archaeology, like ethnoarchaeology, attempts to understand the past by looking at modern material culture. Although both subfields of archaeology share a common objective, which is the understanding of the relationship between human behavior and material culture, they each typically employ different types of information. Ethnoarchaeology consists of an archaeologist studying a group of people and their material culture, and the strength of this approach lies on the behavioral side of the equation. The ethnoarchaeologist, for example, can observe people making, distributing, using, breaking, and depositing their pottery, as well as interview the participants involved. The latter technique is especially resourceful because the researcher can inquire why people make pottery in a certain way or why they collect their clay in this spot and not another. Such inquiries are essential for understanding the social or symbolic factors that would be part of the manufacture, distribution, and use of material culture.

Experimental archaeology, on the other hand, is best equipped to reconstruct the utilitarian function of artifacts. Again using the example of pottery, the experimental archaeologist can best look at the relationship between how a vessel was made and used. For example, in the late prehistoric period in the midwestern United States, a change occurred from grit- to shell-tempered pottery. Experiments that replicated the vessels assessed how this change affects thermal shock resistance, which is an important performance characteristic for all cooking pots (Schiffer et al. 1994). This experiment, performed in a tightly controlled situation (e.g., replicated pots were identical in all things except temper) demonstrated that shell temper would create a vessel with greater thermal-shock resistance. Would this imply necessarily that the prehistoric potters of the Midwest switched to shell temper because they wanted to increase thermal-shock resistance? Not necessarily. This limitation of experimental archaeology underscores that care must be taken when using experimental findings in archaeological inference.

Low-level principles generated in tightly controlled experimental situations of the type described above cannot stand alone. This type of experimental data, when used in archaeological inference, must be contextualized. If one is interested in the transition from sand to shell temper in the midwestern United States, the next step would be to perform more experiments under less-controlled conditions. One might attempt to replicate the sand- and shell-tempered vessels with the types of clays used prehistorically and to replicate the shape and form of the vessels of interest. Moreover, pottery-use-alteration information should be employed to reconstruct what was cooked and the activities of cooking events (e.g., suspended over a fire, placed within the fire, con-

tents stirred). As one continues to relax the controls on experiments, eventually one would be re-creating the vessels, simulating cooking on traditional hearths, and then making the evaluations about thermal-shock resistance under the least-controlled environment. Ideally, one could also perform ethnoarchaeology—a situation in which the archaeologist simply observes and has virtually no control over the variables of interest.

The most effective approach may be to explore any one topic of prehistoric technology at various levels of control. This would permit the archaeologist to explore the embedded functions of traditional technology. Certainly, all tools are designed to be used—perform some utilitarian function—and experiments are best equipped to make this determination. But all artifacts can possess, potentially, important social or symbolic functions as well. Because experimentation alone cannot be used to infer directly important symbolic functions of artifacts, ethnoarchaeology, along with the prehistoric contextual information should also be employed. The best strategy may be to first understand an artifact's utilitarian function with the help of controlled experiments, and then proceed with less-controlled experiments and ethnoarchaeology to explore the various functions of the artifact in past society. Successful reconstructions to date (i.e., 1998) have combined these sources of information.

Experimental Traditions

Most experiments to date have been isolated studies: A prehistorian or a historical archaeologist encounters a problem and then designs an experiment to address that specific problem. Although such experiments have provided invaluable information about how a tool could have made or used, such studies are inherently limited. The experimental findings that have had broader applicability are those that are part of long-term programs. Such experimental traditions have a commitment to a single problem or type of material and can generally yield information that is more readily usable in discussions about technological change. As any experimenter has discovered, all technology is complex, and to ferret out the factors important in the manufacture and use of even traditional technologies requires more than a weekend experiment. An experimental program generally requires the creation of new technology for testing and the means to pass the acquired information to the next generation of experimenters. Flintknappers often have summer field schools to train a new generation of experimenters, and lithic-use-wear analysts, a specialty that is difficult to master, typically train students in the laboratory and share their accumulated experience. American Karen D.Vitelli, who is both a potter and a prehistorian, teaches students to make pottery because she believes that experimentation provides the key to understanding pottery technology and to unlocking the causes of technological change.

Experimental archaeology, though part of archaeology since the beginning of the discipline, is just now beginning to demonstrate its possibilities. As archaeologists increasingly ask more probing questions about technological and societal change, experimental data will become more useful. The experiments that will have the most impact and inferential potential will be those that are part of experimental programs and/or are combined with ethnoarchaeological research.

Most of the important discoveries of the twentieth century have been made as archaeologists have found new sites or lost cities or have described previously unknown prehistoric cultures. The basic outline of world prehistory is known, and museums are filled to the ceilings with materials from around the globe. The significant archaeological finds of the twenty-first century will be made experimentally. Museums hold the untapped resource for experimental archaeology and for important archaeological discoveries for years to come.

James M. Skibo

See also ETHNOARCHAEOLOGY; USE-WEAR ANALYSIS

Further Readings

Coles, J. (1979) Experimental Archaeology. New York: Academic.

Crabtree, D. (1968) Mesoamerican polyhedral cores and prismatic blades. American Antiquity 33(4):446–478.

Johnson, L.L. (1978) A history of flint-knapping experimentation. Current Anthropology 19:337–372.

Schiffer, M.B., Skibo, J.M., Boelke, T.C., Neupert, M.A., and Aronson, M. (1994) New perspectives on experimental archaeology: Surface treatments and thermal response of the clay cooking pot. American Antiquity 59:197–218.

F

Fagan, Brian Murray (1936–)

British-born American anthropologist and archaeologist. Born on August 1, 1936, in Birmingham, England, Fagan was educated at Pembroke College, Cambridge, where he received his bachelor's in 1959, master's in 1962, and doctorate in 1963. After several years as keeper of prehistory at the Rhodes-Livingstone Museum in Livingstone, Northern Rhodesia (now Zambia), and a year at the British Institute of History and Archaeology in Nairobi, Kenya, he was named associate professor of anthropology at the University of California at Santa Barbara and eventually became a naturalized citizen of the United States. In 1969, Fagan was promoted to full professor. He has received numerous awards and honors, including a Guggenheim Fellowship (1972).

Fagan has worked on prehistoric and Iron Age sites in Africa but is most well known for the contributions he has made to one of the most important aspects of the discipline of archaeology: the bringing of information and advances to the general public. Beginning with the important *Introductory Readings in Archaeology* and its successor, *Corridors in Time,* Fagan has done more to make archaeology accessible to nonspecialists than any previous scholar. General works such as *Quest for the Past* and *The Adventure of Archaeology* have served as invitations to countless numbers of readers, while the now-classic *In the Beginning* and *Archaeology: A Brief Introduction* are used as basic archaeology textbooks in secondary schools and universities throughout the English-speaking world. Fagan has also made important contributions to the study of the history of archaeology, particularly the early development and history of Egyptian archaeology *(The Rape of the Nile),* Mesopotamian archaeology *(Return to Babylon),* and archaeological exploration in the New World *(Elusive Treasure).* His *People of the Earth* is a standard textbook for the study of world prehistory, while books like *Clash of Culture* and *The Great Journey* present the complex problems of migration, culture contact, and change in a format suitable for the general reader. His works are immensely popular and often run through several editions, thus presenting up-to-date information to the public. Fagan continues the all-important task of making archaeology accessible and relevant through frequent contributions to such popular journals as *Archaeology,* while continuing his work as a specialist.

Joseph J. Basile

Further Readings

Fagan, B.M., ed. (1974) Corridors in Time: A Reader in Introductory Archaeology. Boston: Little, Brown.

Fagan, B.M. (1977) Elusive Treasure: The Story of Early Archaeologists in the Americas. New York: Scribners.

Fagan, B.M. (1979) Return to Babylon: Travelers, Archaeologists, and Monuments in Mesopotamia. Boston: Little, Brown.

Fagan, B.M. (1985) The Adventure of Archaeology. Washington, D.C.: National Geographic Society.

Fagan, B.M. (1987) The Great Journey: The Peopling of Ancient America. New York: Thames and Hudson.

Fagan, B.M. (1992) The Rape of the Nile: Tomb Robbers, Tourists, and Archaeologists in Egypt. Wakefield, RI: Moyer Bell.

Fagan, B.M. (1994a) Archaeology: A Brief Introduction, 5th ed. New York: HarperCollins.

Fagan, B.M. (1994b) In the Beginning: An Introduction to Archaeology, 8th ed. New York: HarperCollins.

Fagan, B.M. (1994c) Quest for the Past: Great Discoveries in Archaeology, 2nd ed. Prospect Heights, IL: Waveland.

Fagan, B.M. (1995a) People of the Earth: An Introduction to World Prehistory, 8th ed. New York: HarperCollins.

Fagan, B.M. (1995b) Time Detectives: How Archaeologists Use Technology to Recapture the Past. New York: Simon & Schuster.

Fagan, B.M. (1998) Clash of Cultures, 2nd ed. Walnut Creek, CA: AltaMira.

Faience, Characterization

A non-clay ceramic comprising a mixture of crushed quartz (or quartz sand) with small amounts of lime and an alkali (soda) in the form of natron (hydrous sodium carbonate), or plant ashes. It is glazed, frequently in blue or green.

Faience is one of the most misunderstood terms in archaeology and is more correctly referred to as *Egyptian faience*. Even the term Egyptian faience is, strictly speaking, a misnomer for this material. The name was applied to it by European archaeologists working in Egypt because its bright colors reminded them of those on tin-glazed earthenware pottery of a type originally made at Faenze in northern Italy. Faenze became corrupted to faience and was long used in Europe for all similar pottery, although most archaeologists working on such late medieval European pottery now prefer the term *majolica*. Occasionally the terms *frit, glazed composition,* and even *porcelain* have been used as alternatives for Egyptian faience. Use of these terms should be avoided since faience is now well established in the literature, and attempts to change it are prone to lead to confusion.

Faience was widely used in the ancient Near East and Egypt from at least the fifth millennium and continued in use through early Islamic into modern times. Its origins are probably to be found in the process of glazing steatite and quartz objects. It has been suggested that more elaborate shapes could be achieved by modeling ground-up quartz and then glazing it, while still retaining the bright shiny appearance of solid quartz. It might be expected that the glazing of stones or ground quartz would lead to the early appearance of glazed pottery. However, this is not so, since the iron contained in most clays led to a poor and dull glaze. Similarly, the use of glaze on its own, as glass in its own right, was also slow to emerge, not appearing until the second millennium B.C.

Like faience, glasses may also consist of quartz, lime, and soda, so it is important to understand how faience differs from them. The essential difference is that the quartz forms a body material, rather as clay would form the body for a glazed pottery vessel. Pamela Vandiver has determined the typical composition of faience to be 92–99 percent SiO_2, 1–5 percent CaO and 0.5–3 percent Na_2O with minor quantities of CuO, Al_2O_3, TiO_2, MgO, and K_2O. The mixture is *thixotropic,* thick at first but flowing as it begins to be deformed. If deformation is too rapid or firm, the mixture will begin to crack. This makes it much more difficult to work than clay so that its shaping combines techniques common to pyrotechnical industries such as metal- and glass-working, as well as to stonework.

The body material may be roughly modeled by hand and then ground into its final shape, or it may be pressed into a mold or formed on a core. From the Egyptian New Kingdom (1550–1070 B.C.), it also seems to have been wheel thrown, as for pottery. However, this latter forming technique would have been particularly difficult, and never achieved the elegance of thrown pottery. Several shaping techniques might be employed on a single piece to achieve the final form.

The glazing of faience is also a matter of some variation. For many years, it was assumed that the glaze was applied to the quartz-based body in the same way as a glaze would be applied to pottery (i.e., the glaze constituents—a soda-lime-silica—would be painted onto the object as a slurry or powder, or the object would be dipped into the slurry. The glaze would then form during firing. There is little interstitial glass, and the glaze is often quite thick. Brush marks or flow lines are common, as are bare areas deliberately left to prevent objects sticking to one another or to kiln furniture during the firing. Scientific examination of faience, using the scanning electron microscope, has confirmed that this process was used but by no means as frequently as originally believed. Instead, two other glazing methods have been identified.

The first of these alternatives is *efflorescence,* a self-glazing process. Water-soluble alkali salts, such as carbonates, sulfates, and chlorides of sodium or potassium, in the form of natron or plant ash are mixed with the quartz of the core. The mixture is then shaped into the form of the object, and, as it dries, the salts migrate to the surface of the piece, where they form an effloresced layer. This surface becomes fused during firing to form the glaze. Typical of this method are areas of thin glaze where contact with another surface has led to incomplete efflorescence. Similarly, the thickest glaze is found where the drying rate has been greatest. Under the scanning electron microscope, interstitial glass can be seen in the core.

The second alternative technique, known as *cementation,* also involves self-glazing. Here, however, the dry faience object is buried in a glazing powder that reacts with the surface of the object during heating and so glazes it. That part of the powder not in contact with the object remains unfused and can be crumbled away from the finished object after it has been removed from the kiln. The powder comprises lime, ash, silica, charcoal, and a colorant. The technique is sometimes known as the *Qom technique* after a village in Iran where it was first recognized by American scholars in the 1960s. The glaze tends to be quite uniform, often thin, and lacks the drying or firing marks seen in the other techniques. There is little interstitial glass, and the interface between the core and the glaze is usually well defined.

Much of the strength of a faience object derives from the glaze, since the quartz would not become fused at temperatures as low as those used in firing faience. The temperatures used in all of these techniques vary and are the subject of some debate, but a range of 800–1,000°C is generally accepted.

As discussed above, faience can profitably be examined using the scanning electron microscope to examine the relationship between the glaze and the quartz core, most notably the amount of interstitial glass. However, many examples are not as clearly defined as one might wish, and it seems likely that, in some instances, more than one glazing technique was employed on a single artifact.

Paul T. Nicholson

See also GLASS, CHARACTERIZATION

Further Readings

Kaczmarczyk, A., and Hedges, R.E.M. (1983) Ancient Egyptian Faience. Warminster: Aris and Phillips.

Nicholson, P.T. (1993) Egyptian Faience and Glass. Aylesbury: Shire.

Vandiver, P., and Kingery, W.D. (1987) Egyptian faience: The first high-tech ceramic. In W.D. Kingery (ed.): Ceramics and Civilization, vol. 3. Columbus, OH: American Ceramic Society.

Fibrous Materials, Archaeological: On-Site Conservation

Basic measures undertaken to minimize the rate of damage to archaeological artifacts made of fiber materials (i.e., textiles, basketry, papyrus, bark cloth, paper) once they have been unearthed from archaeological contexts and until they reach a conservation laboratory. On-site conservation is the most important stage in the survival of textile materials. Inadequate or inappropriate measures taken on site can cause irreversible damage to the physical artifact and can contaminate or destroy associated archaeological information. A comprehensive on-site preventive conservation program consists of guidelines for the recovery, recording, packing, temporary storage, and transportation of archaeological textiles, which can be carried out competently by untrained personnel. All other conservation treatments must be carried out by a professional archaeological conservator.

Archaeological textiles are interpreted here as archaeological threads and fabrics made of flexible animal and vegetal fibers. This includes fabrics formed with threads that are twisted or spun from fibers in operations such as weaving, knitting, sprang, *nålbinding,* and knotted netting. These fabrics are in the form of cloth, braid, flexible basketry, and cordage. Fabrics formed directly from fibers include bark cloth, woolen felt, papyrus, and paper.

Archaeological contexts are rarely sympathetic to the survival of textile materials, yet desiccated, frozen, and waterlogged (i.e. terrestrially wet, submerged marine and freshwater) burial environments possess microclimates that often lead to the remarkable preservation of this material. Textile materials can be found in association with metal artifacts where fabric or fibers have been preserved by, or partly to completely replaced by, metal-corrosion products. Pseudomorphic replaced fragments of textile in association with metal artifacts should be conserved on site as for metals. Textiles can also be found as impressions on pottery sherds and should be treated as for ceramics.

Recovery

When first exposed and during recovery, textiles should be kept covered to protect from sunlight and to prevent drying out. Once cleaned of the surrounding nonadhering soil matrix, special finds should be documented in situ with drawings or photographs prior to lifting. Investigative cleaning must not be attempted either before or following recovery.

The state and recovery of fibrous materials will vary, depending on the conditions—dry, wet, or frozen—under which they are found.

Dry

Many fibrous materials can be found preserved in dry, arid climates, but they are invariably stiff and brittle. Handling causes powdering of fibers and breaking of threads. Papyrus is usually found either rolled up or badly crumpled. Prior to recovery, the surrounding soil can be carefully removed with soft brushes to delineate the features of the artifact. Metal tools damage the surface and fibers and should not be used, and any tightly adhering lumps should be left in place. Never use water or moisture to assist recovery. If it is decided to remove the dirt inside a basket, remove only that which shifts easily and fill out the interior with crumpled acid-free tissue. When the object is loosened, it can be picked up while supporting it from underneath with either two hands or a flexible horizontal support such as mylar (polyethylene terephthalate). Once the material is excavated, no attempt should be made to clean, unfold, or spread out. Items that are fragmentary or fragile can be recovered by supported lifting. Removal techniques involving directly adhered backing or consolidation (i.e., applying a consolidant directly onto an artifact) of the surface should not be attempted with dry textile materials because their fibrous nature make removal at a later stage difficult.

Human or animal remains found in desiccated environments are often clothed in textiles. These textiles should not be disturbed, and the mummy should be recovered as for archaeological leather.

Wet

Many fibrous materials, such as baskets, bark cloth, cordage, and wool and silk fabrics, survive in wet archaeological contexts. These materials often appear sound but generally are weakened because structural elements no longer support the fabric. Very deteriorated woven fabrics of wool may have a mushy consistency. Wet fibrous artifacts must be handled as little as possible because they will crumble or fragment. They must be kept wet from the moment they are exposed. This can be accomplished by spraying with water and covering with wet polyether foam sheeting, wet moss, or mud followed by polyethylene sheeting. Wet textile finds can be lifted by cleaning away some of the surrounding mud, undercutting, and lifting together with adhering mud. Do not remove the soil inside baskets. Lifting can be assisted by sliding a piece of mylar or polyethylene foam board under the textile-mud complex. Cordage can be gradually wrapped with either a stretch bandage or a bandage made of perforated polyvinylidene chloride film (plastic kitchen wrap) as it is undercut.

Never clean the surface, as there may be remains of stitching or decoration. Consolidation of badly deteriorated or fragmentary textiles with adhesives or polyethylene glycols prior to lifting should be avoided, since these materials will be difficult to remove later and will interfere with chemical analysis. Alternatively, CO_2 gas or dry ice can be used to consolidate an isolated wet object in situ by freezing and then lifting as a block.

Human remains preserved in a bog environment often are clothed in textiles. The body can be cleaned for recovery as described above, taking care to not disturb the textile material, and then blocklifted.

Fibrous materials from marine and freshwater sites are excavated using techniques employed in marine archaeological recovery. As much extraneous sediment as possible is removed from the object. Flat finds can be sandwiched in a well created between two sheets of perforated polyethylene or polypropylene board. Cordage can be lifted by gently rolling into perforated plastic drain piping, filling in with silt, and wrapping in a gauze bandage.

Frozen

A wide range of fibrous materials, including paper and linen fabric, can be found preserved in Arctic environments not only because of the cold climate, but also because many sites are relatively young. Materials frozen in permafrost are most safely removed by warming the soil-artifact matrix with either warm circulating air or warm water. Warm water can be poured gently or injected by use of a syringe around the artifact until it is loosened. Excess water is removed with sponges. The exposed surface of partly excavated artifacts must be kept wet, and this can be accomplished by spraying with water or covering the object with wet moss and then with plastic sheeting. Removal should not be attempted until the material is completely thawed. When thawed, the material can be removed as for wet artifacts. Over larger areas, this method is too time consuming, but natural thawing can be speeded up by laying out dark plastic garbage bags, which absorb the heat from the sun but prevent evaporation.

Supported Lifting

Small fragile artifacts can be lifted by isolating in a block of soil. The soil around an object is carefully removed to leave it sitting on a platform of soil, with enough soil around the object to adequately support it. The artifact is covered with polyvinylidene chloride film (plastic kitchen wrap) with or without an outer layer of aluminum foil. Bandages of paraffin wax or plaster are wrapped around and over the artifact and block, and a rigid support is slid underneath to undercut the block. Plaster bandages are not recommended for use with wet artifacts, as they deteriorate upon storage. Less flat or fragmentary artifacts can be isolated in a block that is undercut more extensively to form a pedestal. The surface of the item is isolated with a layer of plastic kitchen wrap or aluminum foil, and strips of plaster or wax bandages are laid over to hold the object in place. Consolidation of the surface prior to covering with an isolating

layer should not be attempted. When isolating the surface of wet objects, the surface should be thoroughly wetted and can be covered with water-soaked polyether foam sheeting or wet moss. The object-pedestal unit is then wrapped in bandages and undercut.

These techniques will not provide support necessary to lift larger fibrous composites. For these objects, a rigid (e.g., wood, polyethylene board, Plexiglas) vertical frame of generous size is placed around the object that has already been isolated on a pedestal of soil. For blocklifting wet finds, the rigid support must either be waterproof or lined with polyethylene sheeting. A barrier layer of plastic wrap followed by a layer of aluminum foil is pressed down gently following the surface contours of the object. The object and surrounding well are filled with expandable polyurethane foam, wet moss, or plaster. Liquid polyurethane foam is poured into the well in small quantities. For larger blocks, polystyrene foam (Styrofoam) chips can be used as filler in the liquid foam to reduce the amount of foam necessary. When cured, the top of the frame is covered, and the box is excavated by undercutting the pedestal with a rigid support, inverted, and sealed by fastening a lid in place.

Polyurethane foam is toxic and caustic. It must be used only in a well-ventilated area, and rubber gloves, goggles, and a fume mask must be worn. Alternatively, plaster of paris filled out with vermiculite or polystyrene chips can be used as the setting material. Its major disadvantages are its weight, messiness, incomplete setting in cold or wet environments, and difficulty of later removal if not carefully applied.

Packing

Dry

Robust, flat artifacts can be packed flat in perforated heavy-gauge polyethylene bags with resealable tops, or bags made from polyethylene tubing or sheets with the aid of a heat sealer with a heat-sealed or stainless-steel-stapled folded end. Items can be supported within the bag with mylar or cardboard covered with acid-free tissue. Small or fragile items should be packed in rigid containers, preferably clear polystyrene, padded with and supported by crumpled acid-free tissue. Larger items, such as papyrus or basketry, should be packed in a suitable rigid container well padded with sheet and crumpled tissue. As the fibers of cotton wool snag on textile materials, it should not be used as a packing material.

Wet

Only waterproof materials are to be used for packing wet artifacts. Wet fibrous materials are too weak to be packed immersed in water, and this may cause further water degradation of finds that are not truly waterlogged. Finds, along with adhering mud, should be triple-bagged immediately in polyethylene bags and damp (water saturated for waterlogged textiles) polyether foam sheeting and supported on mylar or polyethylene foam board. An outer layer of aluminum foil can help reduce moisture loss and exposure to light and oxygen. Larger or fragile finds can be packed in sturdy polyethylene freezer containers with tight-fitting snap-on lids or containers made to size from polyethylene board. The inside can be padded with wet polyethylene foam sheeting, moss, or seaweed.

Labeling

All packed finds (bags and containers) should be labeled inside and out. Never mark directly on fibrous objects (e.g., basketry). Labels and tags should be placed inside the bag or container. Plastic or stainless steel Dymo-type labels or spun-bonded polyethylene paper tags are recommended. Outside, information can be written either on masking tape or directly on the polyethylene bag. Use indelible markers at all times. Use of tacks and paper clips should be avoided; staples should be of stainless steel.

On-Site Storage

Dry

Dry fibrous materials should be kept at as constant a relative humidity as possible, in the range of 45–60 percent, and away from light and heat.

Wet

Fibrous materials from submerged sites should not be stored immersed in water because the fabric will begin to disintegrate. The use of biocides with freshly excavated archaeological textile materials should be avoided where possible, and attempts should be made to limit microbiological growth by controlling tem-

perature, light, and oxygen. Biocides are toxic toward the person applying them and those who later work on the treated materials. They can interfere with chemical analyses of residual dyestuffs and carbon-14 dating.

Wet and frozen fibrous materials should be stored at as low a temperature as possible. Frozen storage is recommended, with refrigerated storage a second choice. In Arctic field situations, advantage can be taken of the cool climate to create cold storage using coolers, ice packs, pits dug in the permafrost, snowbanks, and meltwater. Small amounts of wet materials can be packed with the addition of isopropanol, ethanol, or sphagnum moss to prevent mold growth. The alcohols are nontoxic to humans and evaporate upon exposure to the atmosphere, leaving no residue in the object. Sphagnum and other mosses are readily found at excavation sites in the Arctic. Sphagnum has antiseptic qualities that are attributed to the presence of polyphenols and nonionized organic acids. Although analysis has revealed the presence of only a few harmless organisms, outbreaks of sporotrichosis have been traced to handling dry sphagnum moss contaminated with the fungus *Sporothrix schenckii*; therefore, only fresh moss should be employed. Conservators have reported unusual swelling of the hands following concentrated periods of handling wet sphagnum.

Documentation

Any conservation treatment carried out on an artifact on site must be recorded, and the record must accompany the treated find or be readily accessible at all times. Field-treatment records are brief and include a description of the deposit, the object, the material(s) of construction, the condition, and the field treatment, including materials used. Treatment notes should describe cleaning, lifting, and packing. Groups of similar finds treated in a similar manner can be recorded collectively.

Transportation

Whether dry or wet, archaeological fibrous artifacts should be packed for transportation with plenty of shock-absorbent packing material.

Dry

Small dry items in perforated polyethylene bags can be packed together in small containers. Items are isolated from one another with crumpled acid-free tissue, shredded polyethylene foam sheeting, or bubble pack. Flat items must be packed flat. Several small containers of objects can be packed in sturdy boxes or crates padded with polystyrene sheeting or polyethylene sheeting. Each box must be isolated from the container and from other boxes using lightweight materials such as crumpled paper, shredded polyethylene foam, or polystyrene chips.

Wet

Wet fibrous materials in bags can be packed in polyethylene containers lined with damp polyethylene foam sheeting or bubble pack, and bags can be isolated from one another with bubble pack, damp polyethylene ether foam sheeting, or wet moss. Containers can then be packed in crates lined with polystyrene or polyethylene foam sheeting.

Health Hazards

Fibrous materials recovered from wet terrestrial environments may present health hazards in handling. Particular caution should be taken with artifacts impregnated with tar (e.g., cordage or rags used to apply tar to boats or timber buildings). The use of disposable plastic gloves at all times is recommended, and the items should be sealed in plastic food wrap and aluminum foil as soon as possible. When handling this material, either use a dual-cartridge respirator (fitted with organic vapor cartridge) or work in a well-ventilated area. Conservators have reported skin irritation when handling textile materials recovered from some sites in the Middle East. The use of gloves when handling these materials is recommended.

Elizabeth E. Peacock

See also CERAMICS, ON-SITE CONSERVATION; FOURIER TRANSFORM–INFRARED (FT-IR) MICROSCOPY; LEATHER, ON-SITE CONSERVATION; METALS, ON-SITE CONSERVATION; WOOD (WATERLOGGED), CONSERVATION

Further Readings

Cross, S., Hett, C., and Bertulli, M. (1989) Conservation Manual for Northern Archaeologists. (Archaeology Report 6). Yellowknife: Prince of Wales Northern Heritage Center.

Payton, R., ed. (1992) Retrieval of Objects from Archaeological Sites. London: Archetype.

Sease, C. (1987) A Conservation Manual for the Field Archaeologist. (Archaeological Research Tools 4). Los Angeles: Institute of Archaeology, UCLA.

Watkinson, D., ed. (1998) First Aid for Finds. London: Rescue/UKIC Archaeology Section.

Fission-Track Dating

Radiometric dating method for rocks and artifacts with applications in geology and archaeology. It is based on the accumulation of etchable tracks from uranium fission in minerals and glasses. Fission-track (FT) ages are for the formation or last heating of these materials. The FT method covers a broad age range from 10^2 to 10^9 years. Its age precision is typically between 5 and 10 percent.

Principles

Fission tracks are channels of radiation damage left by the heavy fragments of uranium fission in dielectric solids. By chemical etching, they are enlarged to a size at which they are visible under an optical microscope (see photo on page 212). One has to distinguish between *spontaneous* (also called *fossil*) and *induced* fission tracks. The former are produced by the spontaneous fission of uranium-238. This type of natural radioactive decay of ^{238}U occurs at a much lower rate (half-life 8.2×10^{15} years) compared to the α-decay (half-life 4.5×10^9 years) of the same nuclide. However, the rate is still fast enough to accumulate in uranium-bearing materials a measurable number of spontaneous-fission tracks during archaeological time. Thus, the number of spontaneous-fission tracks is a measure for the elapsed time (i.e., for the age of the material). Since the number of stored tracks depends not only on the duration, but also on the uranium content, it is necessary to determine the latter as well. This is achieved by counting induced fission tracks. These tracks are artificially produced by bombarding the sample with thermal neutrons in a nuclear reactor, whereby uranium-235 undergoes induced fission. Since in natural uranium the two isotopes ^{235}U and ^{238}U have a constant abundance ratio, the number of induced fission tracks is proportional to the ^{238}U content. For the archaeological age range (less than a few million years), the equation for

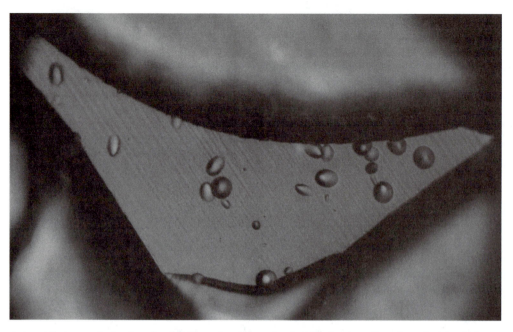

Induced fission tracks in glass shard (160 μm long) from Banks Island tephra, Canada, etched for 110 seconds at 23°C in 24 percent hydrofluoric acid. Photograph courtesy of John Westgate.

the calculation of the FT age t (in years "a") can be simplified and written as

$$t = \rho_s/\rho_i \times \phi \times 5 \times 10^{-8}$$

where ρ_s (tracks/cm^2) is the areal density of spontaneous fission tracks, ρ_i (tracks/cm^2) is the areal density of induced fission tracks, and ϕ (neutrons/cm^2) is the thermal neutron fluence. The constant factor takes into account the values for the spontaneous fission half-life, the isotopic abundance ratio, and the induced fission cross-section.

Dating Procedure

Although, in principle, many minerals and glasses contain fossil fission tracks, only few of them—mainly zircon, apatite, sphene, and various glasses—are commonly used for dating applications. There are reasons for this limitation: (1) The etched fission tracks must be clearly distinguishable in the presence of other etch pits that might be mistaken for genuine tracks; (2) the uranium content has to be high enough to produce a sufficient number of fission tracks; and (3) the fission tracks must be retained over the geological/archaeological period to be determined.

The above-mentioned mineral and glass phases of the crushed rock samples are concentrated by standard mineral-separation techniques. Usually, the grain sizes of the sep-

arated fragments range from 100 to 300 μm. After grinding and polishing, internal faces of the grains are etched. The kind and concentration as well as the temperature and duration of the etching agent vary with the material and its chemical composition. The tracks are counted under a petrographic microscope at high magnification. Image analysis techniques facilitate the counting, especially when the size of the tracks also needs to be recorded. Fully automated track analysis has not yet (as of 1998) been practiced due to the disturbing presence of spurious etch pits.

After the spontaneous fission tracks are counted, the sample is sent to a reactor with a thermal neutron irradiation facility. There are two techniques for counting the induced fission tracks: The induced tracks are recorded in the irradiated sample itself and counted there after repolishing and etching, or they are recorded by an external track detector, a plastic foil that is kept adjacent to the sample surface during irradiation and etched and counted afterward. The age determination according to the first technique follows the above age equation and requires knowledge of the *neutron fluence* (i.e., neutrons per area). The second technique includes standards of known age and, thus, is independent of uncertainties in the dose of neutrons and the fission-decay constant. It is used when dating single grains.

Formation Age and Firing Age

One requirement for the FT clock is the stability of all fossil fission tracks. However, this is often not the case because the unetched fission track represents an intense, but ultimately unstable, zone of radiation damage within a regularly built solid. The original lattice structure of the solid that was disordered by the passage of a fission fragment becomes gradually restored with time. This phenomenon is known as *fading*. Elevated temperatures rapidly accelerate the fading process according to reaction kinetics. Fading causes the reduction of the etchable length and/or the etching rate. The resulting loss of fission tracks tends to lower the apparent FT age.

The track retention properties vary with the material. For instance, fission tracks in zircon are more stable than in apatite; in the case of glass, the track stability increases generally with the silica content. Partial track fading is commonly observed in older geological materials. But even in Pleistocene samples, in particular volcanic glasses, ambient surface temperatures may have already caused some track fading. The fading is recognized by comparing the sizes of etched fossil and induced fission tracks. It is absent if both types of tracks have equal sizes; in such cases, the FT age can be interpreted as the formation age of the sample. Therefore, FT dating requires not only the counting of tracks, but also their size measurement. Since the degree of track fading can be established by track-size studies, it is possible to correct the lowered FT ages. For glasses, there exist two correction procedures—the track-size technique and the plateau technique, and only the corrected FT ages date the glass formation. The general validity of these correction techniques for volcanic glasses has been demonstrated in numerous case studies.

The high thermal sensitivity of fission tracks also enables the dating of secondary heating events, such as volcanic eruptions or the activities of ancient people. If the heating temperature was sufficiently high (say, 400°C for one hour) to anneal all former fission tracks in glass or apatite, the FT clock is reset and the subsequently accumulated fission tracks date this event. To establish whether the fission-track clock in an obsidian artifact was partly or completely reset by heat treatment, one has to study the track sizes. Partial track fading in glass results typically, but not necessarily, in a bimodal size distribution. However, after complete removal of fission tracks by a strong heating event, the newly forming fission tracks again have the same sizes as the induced ones.

Archaeological Samples

FT dating is used mostly on samples of archaeological materials from Neolithic and Palaeolithic sites, but in rare cases objects as young as 100 years can be dated. A well-suited material for the archaeological application of the FT method is glass, either as naturally formed obsidian and other volcanic glasses or as artificial glass. The FT age determines the formation or the last heating of the glass objects. Minerals in archaeological samples are usually tiny, and, therefore, only those of high uranium content are of interest, such as zircon, monazite, sphene, and, to a lesser degree, epidote and apatite. They occur as accessories in ceramics and burnt stones, and FT dating allows the determination of the date of the last firing. Although attempts have been undertaken to date apatite-bearing teeth and bones, these biogenic materials proved to be unsuitable for FT dating due to very small crystal sizes. So far, calcite crystals extracted from marrow cavities of bones have turned out to be free of fossil fission tracks. Apart from dating, FT analysis is also used for provenancing raw materials by characterizing them in terms of uranium content as well as age.

The applicability of FT dating to archaeological materials is limited by the low number of fission tracks that have accumulated during the relatively short presence of humans on Earth compared to the large half-life of spontaneous fission. To obtain sufficient age precision at least 100, and preferably several hundred, fission tracks are required. Therefore, samples of large size and/or high uranium content are desirable. The counting of low track densities (e.g., a few tracks per cm^2) is tedious and time consuming. A further obstacle that may prevent FT dating is the presence of a background of spurious tracks. Such etch pits, which resemble fission tracks, can develop along dislocations, fluid and gas inclusions, and microlites.

F

Man-Made Glass

Owing to their low uranium contents (few μg/g) and ages (up to a few thousand years), most man-made glasses bear only a few fossil fission tracks; thus, the precision of FT ages generally is low. For this reason, only a few such samples have been dated. Nevertheless, man-made glasses can be dated, provided the archaeological relevance of the age justifies the many hours that are required for track counting. Examples of successful dating include Roman glass shards and Iranian glass vessels. The time-consuming task of scanning large areas may be circumvented by automatic track-counting devices if the glass samples do not contain tiny bubbles; only the experienced human eye can distinguish such bubbles from genuine tracks. Uranium glasses, to which ca. 1 percent of uranium oxide was added to produce fluorescent yellowish green colors and that were first manufactured in Bohemia ca. 1840, are, in spite of their young age, well suited for FT dating. The authenticity of ancient glass objects can be established by the presence of a few fossil fission tracks whereby the damage to the glass could be kept minimal when etching a surface. Also, glassy metallurgical slags may be dated by fission tracks, provided they have sufficient uranium and a low background of mineral inclusions.

Obsidian

Uranium in obsidian amounts usually to a few, but may reach up to 20, μg/g. With such uranium contents, FT ages as low as a few thousand years can be measured without too much difficulty. Because of the restricted geographical occurrence of obsidian raw material, it, as well as obsidian artifacts, were widely traded. During production and use of the artifacts, the material, for some unknown reason, was occasionally subjected to heat treatment that resulted in track annealing. FT analysis may give answers to both the questions of geographic provenance of the material and the age of manufacture. The geological FT age of unheated artifacts and their uranium content may be specific for a certain source area, and by matching these parameters of artifacts with those of potential source areas, one may establish ancient trade routes. On the other hand, if the artifacts were sufficiently heated by prehistoric people, the FT age dates the moment of the artifact's manufacture or use. Complete removal of fission tracks in obsidian requires temperatures of 300–400°C. To distinguish whether the FT clock in an obsidian artifact was completely or only partly reset by the heat treatment, one uses the diameter of fission tracks. Some fading of fission tracks in natural glasses may occur already at ambient surface temperatures. This effect results in reduced FT ages and can be corrected for. There are numerous examples of successful age determinations of heated obsidian artifacts, especially from precolumbian South America and Neolithic sites in the Mediterranean and in Japan. Provenance studies of the obsidian source material have also been carried out using the uranium content and geological FT age—often after correcting for some track fading.

Fired Stones and Baked Soils

Mineral inclusions in heated rocks, baked soils, fired bricks, and ceramics can be used for FT dating of the heating event. To reset the FT clock completely and to remove all previously stored tracks, the heating temperatures have to exceed those of track retention. Their explicit values depend on the type of mineral and the duration of heating but are generally above 500°C for a one-hour firing duration. Attainment of complete track annealing in antiquity can be established by the measurement of the track length analogous to the track diameter in glass. So far, this potential of the FT technique has not been fully exploited. The main obstacle is to find enough spontaneous-fission tracks for an age determination with acceptable precision. Since the inclusions typically have a size of 100 μm, at least several hundred grains are required. The method is of particular interest for the Palaeolithic. By using several hundred zircon grains separated from large samples (ca. 10 kg) of baked soils and pottery, various Neolithic localities in Japan and Iran have been dated. Another example of FT dating is the age determination of *Homo erectus pekinensis* at Zhoukoudian near Beijing. Several hundred sphene grains between 50 and 300 μm size were collected from fire ashes with track-length criteria used to select only grains whose FT systems had been completely reset by the fire.

Palaeolithic Marker Horizons

A most important FT application in archaeology and paleoanthropology is the dating of artifact- and hominid-bearing stratigraphic sequences that contain datable tuffaceous marker horizons. Since tephra layers are instantaneously formed and extend over wide areas, they can be stratigraphically related to the over- and underlying sediments with their fossil and cultural remains. Numeric time markers of these horizons yield age brackets for fossil- and artifact-bearing sediments in between. For FT dating of tephra layers, either the glassy phases (pumice, glass shards, obsidian) or uranium-rich minerals, such as zircon, sphene, and apatite, can be used. It is of great advantage that the FT technique is grain-discrete. This allows the researcher to account for contaminating grains mixed into the tephra layer due to secondary processes, such as redeposition by water or wind, creeping, slumping, cryoturbation, and bioturbation. Besides potassium-argon (K/Ar) dating, the FT method has become the most frequently used dating technique in tephrochronologic studies.

Because glass—a common constituent of tephra—can be dated with fission tracks, glass shards (usually between 100 and 200 μm) are the most preferred material in tephrochronologic FT applications. Of special importance is the FT dating of hydrated glass shards from distal tephra occurrences that are otherwise hardly datable. If substantial fading of the fossil tracks is detected from their reduced size (when compared to induced tracks), the apparent FT ages are too low, and appropriate correction procedures need to be applied. There are many applications of FT dating to glass fragments from tephra layers in Pleistocene sedimentary sequences in various parts of the world, mainly in Japan, New Zealand, the Mediterranean, North America, and East Africa, among them pumice from Bed I at Olduvai Gorge in Tanzania.

Zircon is the other tephra constituent that is frequently used for FT dating. It does not occur in all tephra, therefore the silicic tephra are more favorable for dating than the basic ones. Zircon is generally richer in uranium than glass, facilitating single-grain age determinations. Zircon FT ages do not require correction due to full track stability at ambient temperatures. However, this apparent advantage of zircon over glass cannot often be exploited because of the absence of sufficiently large zircon grains (greater than 75 μm) in widespread distal tephra beds. Several zircon populations are commonly observed in volcanic ash layers. Apart from the FT age, morphological and optical properties of the single grains can also be used as criteria for the primary volcanic component. Important contributions to the tephrochronologies of various areas adjacent to Plio-Pleistocene volcanism have been achieved by zircon FT studies, especially for the sedimentary deposits in East Africa with remains of early hominids. There, the KBS Tuff at Lake Turkana in Kenya, the Hadar Formation in Ethiopia, the Cindery Tuff of the Middle Awash in Ethiopia, and tuffs from the Buluk Member of the Bakate Formation in Kenya have been dated. In all of these cases, the zircon FT ages supplement the potassium-argon dates of the tephra.

Günther A. Wagner

See also OBSIDIAN HYDRATION DATING; TEPHROCHRONOLOGY

Further Readings

Fleischer, R.L., Price, P.B., and Walker, R.M. (1975) Nuclear Tracks in Solids: Principles and Applications. Berkeley: University of California Press.

Gleadow, A.J.W. (1980) Fission track age of the KBS Tuff. Nature 284:225–230.

Wagner, G.A., and Van den Haute, P. (1992) Fission-Track Dating. Stuttgart: Enke.

Flannery, Kent Vaughn (1934–)

American anthropologist and archaeologist. Born on August 30, 1934, in Philadelphia, Flannery was educated at the University of Chicago, where he received his bachelor's in 1954, his master's in 1961, and his doctorate in anthropology in 1964. He served as an assistant curator at the Smithsonian Institution in Washington, D.C. (1964–1967), and was subsequently appointed assistant professor of anthropology at the University of Michigan and curator of its Kelsey Museum of Archaeology. Flannery is professor of anthropology at Ann Arbor and has received numerous honors, including membership in the American Association for the Advancement of Science, fellowship in the American Anthropological Association, election to the National Academy of Sciences (1978), and a Guggenheim Fellowship (1981).

Flannery, an archaeologist specializing primarily in the early cultures of Mesoamerica, is most well known for his theoretical work dealing with the rise of agriculture, the state, and complex societies. As a student at Chicago in the 1960s, Flannery was exposed to the ideas of scholars such as Lewis R. Binford and brought the methodologies of New Archaeology to his search for the origins of civilization. In his early work, Flannery used the systems approach to theorize that positive feedback in genetic changes in Mesoamerican food plants resulted in an increased gathering of these plants and a move toward agriculture and more complex societal development. Using the Oaxaca Valley as a model, Flannery explored evolutionary mechanisms of culture change, arguing that types of systemic changes must be identified before increases in complexity could be understood and that this was more valuable than an approach that concentrated on discovering the conditions thought to bring about change. He has also examined Mesopotamian evidence in a search for parallels between development of complex societies there and in the New World. Eventually, however, he joined other New Archaeologists in rejecting general (unilinear) evolutionary models because they did not adequately explain the extreme cultural diversity to be seen in prehistoric societies in (*The Cloud People,* 1983). He is also critical of the extreme methodological bent of processual archaeology.

Joseph J. Basile

See also BINFORD, LEWIS R.; NEW/PROCESSUAL ARCHAEOLOGY

Further Readings

Coe, M.D., and Flannery, K.V. (1967) Early Cultures and Human Ecology in South Coastal Guatemala. Washington, D.C.: Smithsonian Institution Press.

Flannery, K.V., ed. (1976) The Early Mesoamerican Village. New York: Academic.

Flannery, K.V., general editor (1973–1994) Prehistory and Human Ecology of the Valley of Oaxaca. Ann Arbor, MI: Museum of Anthropology, University of Michigan.

Flannery, K.V., ed. (1986) Guila Naquitz: Archaic Foraging and Early Agriculture in Oaxaca, Mexico. Orlando: Academic.

Flannery, K.V. and Marcus, J., eds. (1983) The Cloud People: Divergent Evolution of the Zapotec and Mixtec Civilizations. New York: Academic.

Flannery, K.V., Marcus, J. and Reynolds, R.G. (1989) The Flocks of the Wamani: A Study of Llama Herders on the Punas of Ayacucho, Peru. San Diego: Academic.

Marcus, J. and Flannery, K.V. (1996) Zapotec Civilization: How Urban Society Evolved in Mexico's Oaxaca Valley. New York: Thames and Hudson.

Flotation

A method of recovering organic remains, mostly botanical, from the sediments of archaeological sites using water as the primary separating agent. Some archaeologists rely on manual techniques carried out in flowing water (i.e., streams, lakes, oceans); others use fixed containers (i.e., tubs, metal drums, troughs) that rely on water pumped from wells or water carried to sites.

One of the earliest uses of flotation was during the 1860s when an Austrian botanist named Unger placed adobe bricks from Egyptian sites in tubs of water to loosen seeds, leaves, and plant stems in the adobe. During the 1930s, George Hendry and Michael Bellue used flotation to recover plant materials trapped in adobe recovered from the ruins of pueblos in the American Southwest. A decade later, during the 1940s, Hugh Cutler increased his recovery of botanical remains from a number of Southwestern U.S. sites by putting excavated sediments in tubs of water and collecting the floating materials. It was Stuart Struever, however, who first alerted most archaeologists to the potentials of flotation when he published his Apple Creek flotation technique in 1968.

Flotation Techniques

Struever developed his Apple Creek flotation method for use at sites located near sources of running water. The equipment he used was simple. He removed the bottoms of small wash tubs and attached a fine-mesh screen to the bottom of each tub. Sediments from the site were then placed in the tubs. Workers, standing in the stream, agitated the partly submerged tubs up and down until the passing water currents carried away most silt and sands. The remaining material in each tub was then taken to a lab, where it was separated again using chemical flotation. Each sample was placed in a large bucket containing water and zinc chloride mixed to a specific gravity of 1.62. Light organic materials (e.g., seeds, wood, charcoal, leaves) rose to the surface and were scooped off, while the heavier debris (e.g., gravel, bone, sherds, lithics) remained at the bottom.

Patty Jo Watson, working in the mid-1970s with sediments from Salts Cave in Kentucky, was one of the first to use large fifty-five-gallon oil drums as flotation devices. She found that, in areas where water is scarce, an oil drum opened at one end can be filled with water and used for flotation. As with the Apple Creek method, the bottom of a bucket is replaced with 1/16-inch (1–2 mm) window screen. Sediment samples from the site are placed in the half-submerged bucket and gently agitated. This allows silt and sand to pass freely through the screen and settle in the bottom of the drum while the light organic materials float on the surface. Scoops made from tea-strainers and lined with cheesecloth skim the floating materials off of the surface. This surface material is called the *light fraction*. When using the oil-drum method, investigators generally collect two processed samples from each original soil sample: one light fraction from the surface, and one *heavy fraction* consisting of the items remaining in the bottom of the bucket. Since Watson's use of this technique, there have been a number of modifications. Nevertheless, all rely on the same principle of using a stationary container full of water and a secondary smaller, collector-type container in which soils are placed for separation. A later modification in the early 1980s by Gail Wagner replaced the metal drum with a wooden trough and the metal bucket with screen-lined wooden boxes that float partly submerged. This innovation achieved the same degree of recovery; it could process materials faster; and it reduced the needed flotation personnel from two to one.

One of the earliest mechanized flotation devices was built by David French in the early 1970s for use at the Turkish site of Can Hasan III. His mechanized device, called the Ankara machine, differed from the drum method in several ways. A constant flow of water was pumped into the device from a nearby source, and sediment samples were floated in two separate steps. The samples were placed into a tray with a screen bottom that was suspended in a larger tank of water. Additional water was then pumped into an elevated holding tank and allowed to flow by gravity into an outlet nozzle underneath the tray. This created upwelling that agitated the soil sample and permitted silt and sand to pass through the screen and collect at the bottom of the primary tank. Light organic materials, carried to the surface by the upwelling, floated over the edge of the tray and into a second screen with openings of 1 mm. Silt and sand that collected in the primary tank was easily removed through a drain.

A number of other mechanical flotation devices have been developed, but most are based on variations of the original Ankara device. One of the more successful is called the SMAP (Shell Mound Archaeological Project) machine developed in the United States by William Robertson. The SMAP machine differs from other models in several ways. It consists of a large oil drum with a screen-bottomed bucket insert attached to the inside at the top. Sediment samples placed in the bucket are agitated by upwelling water pumped into nozzles located underneath the bucket. Water carries the floating material down a sluiceway and into a second container. Both the light and the heavy fraction for each sample are bagged separately. An added advantage of the SMAP machine is that the water pressure and the amount of upwelling can be adjusted for different types of sediments.

Processing rates are fairly consistent for most devices, even though the number of samples floated each hour will depend upon the skill of the personnel, the condition of the equipment, and the type of soil being processed. As a general rule, manual flotation systems can process ca. 0.05–0.08 m^3 of soil per day. Mechanical systems, such as the SMAP machine, can process about ten times as much (0.5–0.8m^3) per day.

Flotation Procedures

Before using flotation at an archaeological site, a number of precautionary measures should be considered. Prior to site excavation, a flotation-recovery plan should be determined. This plan should indicate the type of flotation system, the estimated cost of running the device, the salary of the personnel, how much soil will be floated, where the float samples will be collected at the site, the sources of available water, and knowledge of the soil type at the site. Next, the equipment should be checked and the personnel trained in operating the flotation device. Personnel conducting flotation must know how their machine works, what steps will ensure the best and fastest recovery rate, how to maintain adequate records, and how to prevent contamination of samples during recovery and the subsequent storage of samples. Glenna Dean has shown that a standard sample size from each excavated level in a site may not be adequate. She found that 1 liter per level may be adequate from some strata, while as much as 16 liters may be needed from others to obtain a representative sample. The amount of sediment needed per sample can be determined by discovering how often an additional sample, from the same location, will increase the number of plant taxa recovered. Finally, Deborah Pearsall and others have noted that flotation recovery rates can drop by as much as 50 percent when unskilled personnel are used, when personnel become careless due to fatigue, or when samples are not agitated adequately.

Recovery rates can be determined using exotic tracers. In the early 1980s Wagner developed the *poppy seed test* to monitor the recovery efficiency during flotation. She uses nonnative poppy seeds (*Papaver somniferum*) and chars them at 500°F (260°C). Next, she adds a known number of charred seeds to each sample before it is floated. Later, during analysis, she determines the flotation efficiency by comparing the ratio of recovered to added poppy seeds.

Many types of botanical materials recovered during flotation, especially seeds and tiny pieces of charcoal, will crack and break into tiny fragments if they are dried too quickly. This can be prevented by drying floated samples slowly in shaded areas or in direct sunlight if the samples are covered with wetted newspapers. Once dried, recovered samples should not be rewetted. In a controlled experiment in the early 1970s, Harold Jarman discovered that 4 percent of charred seeds are destroyed during one flotation cycle, and an additional 56 percent are destroyed during a second cycle.

Finally, the condition of the sediments at a site affect flotation efficiency. Deposits in dry caves and in some arid regions may be very rich in organic remains. In such cases, fine-screening may be more efficient than flotation. Also, flotation is an ineffective technique when sediments are waterlogged. Finally, some clayey sediments form hard clumps that do not dissolve easily. This can be offset by changing the ion exchange rate, thus encouraging dispersion of the sediment particles. Connie Bodner and Denise Steele found that effective deflocculating agents for clayey sediments include sodium hexametaphosphate, sodium bicarbonate, and hydrogen peroxide.

Vaughn M. Bryant Jr.

See also PALEOETHNOBOTANY; PALYNOLOGY

Further Readings

Bodner, C.C., and Rowlett, R.M. (1980) Separation of bone, charcoal, and seeds by chemical flotation. American Antiquity 45:110–116.

French, D. (1971) An experiment in water-sieving. Anatolian Studies 21:59–64.

Pearsall, D. (1989) Paleoethnobotany: A Handbook of Procedures. New York: Academic.

Renfrew, J. (1973) Paleoethnobotany: The Prehistoric Food Plants of the Near East and Europe. New York: Columbia University Press.

Steward, R., and Robertson, W. (1973) Application of the flotation technique in arid areas. Economic Botany 27:114–116.

Struever, S. (1968) Flotation techniques for the recovery of small-scale archaeological remains. American Antiquity 33:353–362.

Watson, P. (1976) In pursuit of prehistoric subsistence: A comparative account of some contemporary flotation techniques. Mid-Continental Journal of Archaeology 1:77–100.

Fluorine-Uranium-Nitrogen Dating

The chemical determination of the mean concentrations of fluorine (F), uranium (U), and nitrogen (N) in a bone in an attempt to provide a reliable date. This was only an interim method for the dating of bone in the 1950s and 1960s, and some of the estimated dates may have been quite wrong. New dating methods have become available following the invention of instruments or techniques that can reveal the distribution of minor or trace elements in a specimen. However, FUN has proven useful as a relative dating method and especially as a way of ascertaining whether bones from the same site or same stratigraphic unit differ in age—one cannot assume that materials found together were deposited simultaneously. This application of FUN dating was particularly important in exposing the Piltdown fraud perpetrated on the British Museum of Natural History and the anthropological community beginning in 1912 and is well summarized by anthropologist Frank Spencer (1990). Kenneth Oakley had discovered a long neglected paper published in 1892 by the French mineralogist, Adolphe Carnot, on the absorption of fluorine by fossil bones as a function of age. From 1948 to 1955, fluorine, nitrogen, and uranium tests were conducted on what proved to be a human-simian pastiche as well as on other "associated" faunal remains, all of which not only dated to vastly different time periods but also derived from different continents.

A promising, though largely untested, approach is to use one of the several types of microprobe to measure the radial distributions of fluorine or uranium in a bone or tooth, deduce how the element entered from the surroundings over a long period, and, from this improved understanding, attempt to date the specimen. The proton microprobe is especially effective for determining the radial distribution of F, which is held firmly once it is built into the apatite of bone or dentine, so may provide valuable information for the archaeologist. Uranium, on the other hand, can also diffuse into bone but is not firmly held to the mineral; under some conditions, it may be leached out again, so it is unlikely to provide a reliable date. However, once it had diffused into the dentine of a tooth (via the pulp cavity), it would be well isolated by tooth enamel and cementum so should remain there. Since moisture is needed to mobilize F and U, neither will provide a dating method in a completely arid site. The loss of nitrogen from bone over time has not provided a reliable dating method, so the determination of nitrogen content is most useful as an adjunct to radiocarbon dating.

Fluorine

The mineral fraction in bones and teeth is an impure form of calcium hydroxyapatite $Ca_5(PO_4)_3OH$, commonly referred to as HAP. Fluoride (F^-) ions may replace some or all of the OH^- ions, giving an F content in the range 0-3.77 percent by weight and forming the mineral fluorapatite. The stability of the crystal increases with F content. The structure of the mineral, defined by the Ca, P, and O ions, has a remarkable and important feature: The OH^- and F^- ions lie in channels along the c-axis that pass through equilateral triangles of Ca^+ ions; the fit in these channels is critical, and no other ions can fit in them.

Theoretical studies have shown that F^- ions cannot diffuse into an existing crystal of apatite. This implies that an increase in the F^- content of a bone or a tooth must have involved dissolution of some of the minute apatite crystals and the growth of new crystals with a higher ratio of F^- to OH^-. Even if the F^- concentration in groundwater is only 1–2 ppm, the F^- concentration at the outer surface of a bone may be 0.5 percent or more. In volcanic regions with high fluoride levels, such as the Olduvai Gorge in Tanzania, a fossil bone will have a F^- content close to 3.8 percent.

Microprobe studies of archaeological bones show that F^- will not diffuse into a bone if the soil is always dry or if the bone had been strongly heated before burial; the F distribution will remain as it was at death. If climatic conditions alternate between wet and dry periods, diffusion will cease in the dry periods.

It has been known since 1809 that a buried bone will absorb F^- ions from groundwater so that the average F content will slowly increase with time. A piece of bone was ground to powder and its F^- content determined by chemical methods, which were sensitive and accurate but did not show how it was distributed in the bone. It was probably assumed that the distribution was uniform throughout the bone, so that analysis of any piece of it would give the same average result for fluoride/apatite. However, microprobe measurements on bones have shown that F^- ions diffuse inward from any surface exposed to groundwater, so the distribution is far from uniform unless the bone has been buried for 100,000 years or more. The result of a chemical determination would, therefore, depend critically on which piece of the bone was chosen, and, even for a complete section of a hollow bone, it would depend on the inner and outer radii.

Comparison of results from different bones could have been most misleading, especially if they were of different thickness or came from different sites, since the fluoride concentration at the surface depends on soil conditions; the distribution is not uniform; and inward diffusion occurs only when moisture is present. For these reasons, bones from different sites or even the same site could have been quite different in age even if their mean fluoride content was similar. The average fluoride content in a piece of bone tells us nothing about its age. The real information is in the shape of the fluoride distribution, measured from the outer surface to the center along a radius; this is commonly called the *fluoride profile*.

The distribution of F in a bone or a tooth may be measured with at least three types of instrument, all using different principles: the electron microprobe, the sputter ion mass spectrometer (SIMS) instrument, and the proton microprobe. The electron microprobe employs a focused beam of electrons to excite characteristic X-rays from the elements present; it is not very sensitive for F since the X-rays have low energy and are easily absorbed in the specimen. In a SIMS instrument, a focused beam of heavy ions vaporizes a small quantity of material, which is directed into a mass spectrometer for analysis. To date, most studies of F in bones and teeth have been performed with the proton microprobe.

In a proton microprobe, a beam of energetic protons from a particle accelerator is focused on a small area of the specimen, with a diameter of 10 μm or less. As the protons pass into the specimen, they suffer many collisions and excite characteristic X-rays (by displacing electrons from the atomic shells) and gamma rays (by inducing nuclear reactions in nuclei of some of the lighter elements). Nuclear reactions with ^{19}F, the only stable isotope of fluorine, result in the emission of gamma rays, which are easy to detect with a suitable scintillation or semiconductor detector. (Details can be found in Coote 1992.)

The proton microprobe has made it possible to measure distributions of many elements, with high spatial resolution and a much higher sensitivity than the electron microprobe. The proton beam is steered along a line or in a two-dimensional array by magnetic or electric fields controlled by a microcomputer. The specimen is in an evacuated target chamber, into which pass the X-ray and gamma-ray detectors. This instrument is particularly useful for studies of bones and teeth, since the profiles of F and Ca (from its X-rays) can be determined simultaneously in a few

minutes. A complete cross-section of the specimen is not necessary, though there must be enough to allow a complete scan along at least one radius. One of its surfaces must be polished flat and smooth, but the method is non-destructive, and scans can be repeated if needed. The only sign of the passage of the proton beam across bone or dentine is a narrow dark line of carbonized protein on the surface, which is a useful record of the scan position but can be removed by polishing.

The Ca scan reveals the outer edges of the specimen, the enamel-dentine junction in a tooth, and any variations in the ratio of mineral to protein. A 200-point scan of F and Ca can be completed in ca. ten minutes. The true concentrations in mass units are established by comparing the specimen with apatite containing a known concentration of F^- and making small corrections for the effect of matrix composition on the proton penetration depth and on X-ray generation and absorption.

Some representative scans are illustrated in Figures 1–3; the maximum length of scan was 5 mm, so, for some graphs, two scans were combined. The development of the F profile with length of burial shows clearly. Bones of moa (several extinct species of flightless birds) are commonly excavated in New Zealand, and two radiocarbon-dated specimens are shown; they had been exposed to groundwater only on the outer surface. The much older *equus* bone from the Olduvai Gorge (Figure 2) had been exposed on both inner and outer surfaces, and most of the mineral had been converted to fluorapatite.

Scans of sectioned archaeological teeth show that enamel, cementum, and dentine behave differently with regard to fluoride uptake. In Figure 3, two scans of a human tooth (in the ground for 200 years) are compared with similar scans of a modern human tooth. Enamel is so resistant to recrystallization that no uptake can be detected. The thin layer of cementum over the root of the tooth had formed an effective seal; though it had absorbed a significant amount of F^-, this had diffused slowly and had not reached the dentine. Dentine, with its more porous structure and smaller crystallite size, behaves quite differently: If part of the cementum or the enamel had been lost, the F^- ions were able to enter the exposed dentine and diffuse inward, as if in bone. The most prominent feature is the inner profile in the dentine, which was

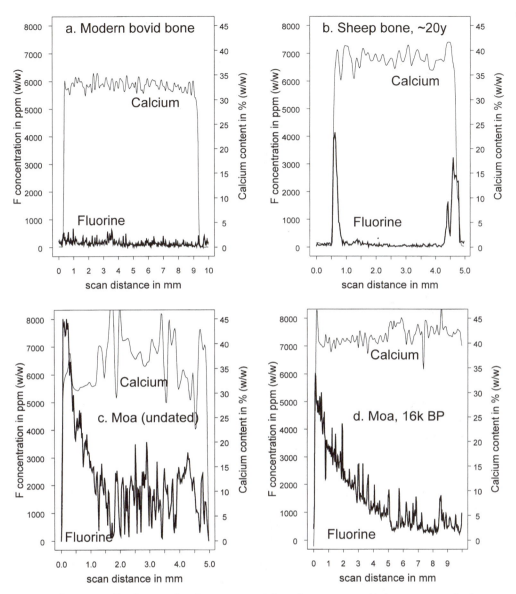

Figure 1. Fluorine profiles from modern bovine (upper left) and twenty-year-old sheep (upper right) bones compared with archaeological moa bones (lower left and lower right) excavated in New Zealand. Note that only the outer surface of the moa bones has been exposed to fluorine in groundwater. Figure by Graeme E. Coote.

formed by F^- ions diffusing in the opposite direction. They had entered the pulp cavity in groundwater, precipitated on the inside surface of the dentine, then diffused outward toward the enamel or the cementum. Other evidence indicates that this process does not occur significantly while the person is alive, since it was not found in teeth from wooden coffins that were stacked in a crypt, so the teeth would have dried out quickly.

Since dentine, unlike bone, does not have canals, these inner fluorine profiles are much smoother than the profiles in bone, so the theoretical curves can be fitted more precisely and might prove useful for relative dating of burials in a cemetery. Two-dimensional scans of excavated premolar teeth showed that the outward-moving fluoride ions diffuse more rapidly toward the front and rear of the tooth than they do to the sides, so profiles in each

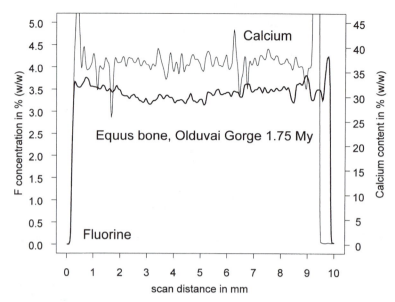

Figure 2. Fluorine profile of bone of equus from Olduvai Gorge, dating 1.75 million years. Note that this bone has been exposed to fluorine on both the inner and the outer surfaces and most of the mineral has been converted to fluorapatite. Figure by Graeme E. Coote.

tooth to be compared should be measured along the same axis.

Computer programs have been written that employ numerical integration to solve the differential equation for fluorine diffusion in three different geometries: (1) *solid bone*—diffusion inward from the outer surface, with no hole in the center of the bone; (2) *hollow bone*—diffusion into a bone from both the outer and the inner surfaces, though the surface concentration at the inner surface is usually found to be lower than that at the outer surface and may be zero; and (3) *tooth*—in which diffusion occurs outward from the pulp cavity (which has a small radius) into the dentine, with an impermeable barrier at the inner surface of the enamel.

From the mathematics of the diffusion process, the profile is calculated for two parameters that have no physical dimensions: the *scaled radius* (r/a), where a is the average radius of the bone section, and r is the distance from the center; and the *scaled time* $T = (Dt/a^2)$, where D is the diffusion constant, and t is the time that diffusion has continued. The equilibrium concentrations at exposed surfaces are taken as constant, though it is possible to alter them at any intermediate stage and follow the subsequent changes in the profile. Figure 4 shows the development of each of the three types of profile in terms of these dimensionless parameters.

The comparison of a measured fluorine profile with theoretical profiles has been done in the following way: The experimental profile is displayed on a monitor screen, and the profiles are calculated for a range of T values and overlaid on it; the calculations are continued until one particular value of T is judged by the eye to give the best fit; from T, since the radius a is known, the product Dt can be calculated. In a given site in which D could be assumed constant, relative dates are given by Dt alone; to derive t, the diffusion constant D would have to be estimated. The only way to do this is to fit the profiles of bones whose age has been established by some other method, such as radiocarbon. Variations in D between different sites have not yet been investigated. It is important to note that, although bones from a range of sites are likely to have different fluoride concentrations at the surface, this does not invalidate the fluoride profile as a possible dating method. This is because the essential property of a diffusion profile is its shape, not its height, which is always scaled to match the surface concentration. This does mean, however, that the measured profile must include the original surface of the bone.

So far, the fluorine-profile method has been tested only on bones from two Pacific islands. A collection of finger bones from one island showed that many people died during a

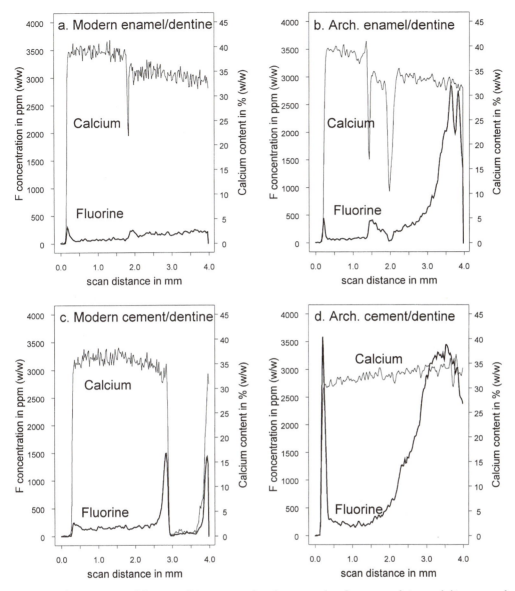

Figure 3. Fluorine scans of the enamel/dentine interface from a modern human tooth (upper left) compared with a similar scan of a human tooth buried 200 years (upper right). Fluorine scans of cementum/dentine interface from a modern human tooth (lower left) compared with a similar scan of a human tooth buried 200 years (lower right). Figure by Graeme E. Coote.

short period early in the twentieth century, supporting a tradition of a fatal epidemic on the island. In contrast, a collection of bones from a cemetery in the Marquesas Archipelago showed a wide range of ages, up to several thousand years.

To measure a fluorine profile, a section of bone is required; it does not have to be complete (a small segment would be sufficient), but it must include at least a portion of the original outer surface. The part-section could be cut from an important bone by using a small saw with a circular blade that can cut in any direction. Once the profile had been measured, the segment could be glued back in place with a gap-filling glue.

Fluorine distributions in bones might be useful in the following ways: as a dating or

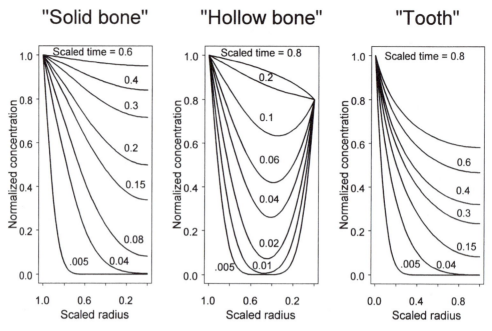

"Solid bone" **"Hollow bone"** **"Tooth"**

Figure 4. Three types of profile for fluorine diffusion: solid bone, hollow bone, and tooth. Figure by Graeme E. Coote.

relative-dating technique, with a wide range but rather low precision; for a survey of a site to guide further excavation or to select the most appropriate bones for radiocarbon dating; for investigations of recent burials, since the profiles change rapidly in the first decades after burial; or for sorting a mixture of bones from different sites according to their surface concentrations. The smooth internal profiles in dentine may prove useful for relative dating of burials, the profiles calculated from diffusion theory can be adjusted to fit them very closely.

Now that the proton microprobe can provide detailed profiles of F in bones and teeth, archaeologists and paleontologists might well take a new look at the possible applications in their disciplines. Systematic, multidisciplinary approaches might lead to important advances.

Uranium

Almost all of U exists as the two isotopes ^{238}U (99.28 percent) and ^{235}U (0.72 percent). Uranium-238 is the parent of the natural uranium series, whose members are used in uranium-series dating. Uranium-235 is the parent of the actinium series, which is not used in dating but is important because the best methods for determining uranium and its distribu-

tions employ the nuclear fission of ^{235}U, induced by thermal neutrons in a research reactor.

Fresh bones contain less than 0.1 ppm U; hence, the higher concentrations found in fossil bones (1–2,000 ppm) must have come from groundwater; it is believed that the bivalent uranyl ion UO_2^{2+} precipitates on the surfaces of the apatite crystals. Studies of the accumulation process have been concerned with determining the distribution of U in bones and teeth, the time scale during which accumulation occurs, and the stability of the adsorbed uranium and of its daughter products. The variety of answers from different sites has shown that the behavior of U depends on local conditions and their changes through time.

The distribution of U in a polished section of a bone or a tooth can be determined by using a fission-track detector—a special plastic foil 10 μm thick. With the foil clamped to the polished surface, the section is exposed to thermal neutrons in a research reactor. Nuclei of ^{235}U undergo fission near the surface and emit fission products (medium-weight ions with high energies) that pass through the foil, damaging its structure sufficiently to form latent tracks; these are developed into holes of ca. 5 μm diameter by etching the foil with an alkaline solution. An image of the distribution of holes, which can be compared with a radiograph of the section, is formed on aluminized polyester film by a device that generates high-voltage sparks. The method is sensitive down to 1 ppm U.

The U content of small samples can be reliably measured by detecting a gamma ray from thorium-234 or by the *delayed-neutron method*, which exploits another property of the fission of ^{235}U. The specimen is exposed briefly to neutrons in a nuclear reactor, then moved to a counting area. The number of neutrons emitted in a fixed period is proportional to the uranium content.

Studies have established the following: Uptake of uranium into bones is very slow and will depend on local concentrations and groundwater movement, with the process of reaching equilibrium with groundwater expected to take 10^4 to 10^6 years. Uranium is reversibly attached to the crystal surfaces and is not built into the crystal structure; hence, fluctuations in hydrology will cause changes in the pattern of uptake, which may cease or even reverse as leaching occurs. It has been suggested that uranium is precipitated in the reducing environment of the decaying organic matter; after this has decomposed, the uranium can be reoxidized and leached out by the groundwater. Studies of bone sections have revealed a variety of distributions: uniform throughout, with higher concentrations toward a surface exposed to groundwater, with higher levels in the more porous inner bone, with reduced concentration near a surface as a consequence of leaching.

A study of uranium distributions in teeth from a number of species showed that the concentration in enamel was very low, with a minimum near the outer layer and a maximum near the dentine; in the cementum layer it was higher than in enamel, while in dentine it was higher still and rather uniform. This evidence suggests that U is taken up in teeth in a similar way to F: It cannot enter enamel but can diffuse into cementum to a limited extent. Deposited from groundwater that entered through the nerve canal, it accumulates on the surface of the pulp cavity, then diffuses outward through the dentine until it is blocked at the enamel/dentine junction.

The distribution of uranium in a bone is dependent on many properties of the soil, which are likely to change with time and will differ from one site to another. Fluctuations in hydrology can cause the pattern to change and may result in leaching of the element already deposited. For these reasons, attempts at relative dating should be based on measurements of the radial distribution rather than average content, which could be misleading, but even then an accurate date seems unlikely.

Since the distribution of uranium can now be measured in small specimens, the dating of teeth should be more reliable than the dating of bones. The transport of U into a tooth appears to be similar to that of F, though much slower. In a moist environment, U can pass through the pulp cavity into the dentine, where it is protected from leaching by the impervious enamel and cementum layers. The distribution should change with time, as predicted by diffusion theory, unless the surroundings become arid or an impervious layer forms and blocks the entry of moisture. Measurement of the profiles of fluorine and uranium in the same tooth would be of great interest.

Nitrogen

Proteins, largely collagen, form the matrix for the mineral matter in bones, antlers, and dentine. The nitrogen in this protein forms ca. 4.5 percent of a fresh bone by weight and can be quickly and cheaply determined in a small sample by the *Kjeldahl method* (in which the nitrogen is converted into ammonia, which is titrated). In a bone exposed to soil bacteria, the collagen breaks down into its constituent amino acids, which are then leached out of the bone. The amount of nitrogen in the bone, therefore, decreases with time, in approximately an exponential manner, making it tempting to use the nitrogen content of a bone to determine its age.

Unfortunately, the rate of decomposition of collagen is dependent on conditions in the soil (especially temperature, moisture, pH, and porosity), which controls the supply of air to support bacterial life. These may change over short distances in a single site and may differ greatly between sites. Relative dates derived in this way may be wrong and are rarely used. However, the nitrogen content can be used to calculate the percentage of carbon in the bone and, therefore, ascertain the sample weight needed for a radiocarbon date.

Graeme E. Coote

See also BONE, CHARACTERIZATION

Further Readings

Beevers, C.A., and McIntyre, D.B. (1946) The atomic structure of fluorapatite and its relation to that of bone. Mineral Magazine 27:254–257.

Breese, M.B.H., Grime, G.W., and Watt, F. (1992) The nuclear microprobe. Annual Review of Nuclear and Particle Science 42:1–38.

Coote, G.E. (1992) Ion beam analysis of fluorine: Its principles and applications. Nuclear Instruments and Methods B66:191–204.

Coote, G.E., and Vickridge, I.C. (1988) Application of a nuclear microprobe to the study of calcified tissues. Nuclear Instruments and Methods B30:393–397.

Crank, J. (1975) The Mathematics of Diffusion, 2nd ed. Oxford: Oxford University Press.

First International Workshop on Fossil Bone (1989) Applied Geochemistry 4(3):211–343.

Geyh, M.A., and Schleicher, H. (1990) Absolute Age Determination. Berlin: Springer-Verlag.

Oxford Workshop on Bone Diagenesis (1995) Journal of Archaeological Science 22(2):145–327.

Spencer, F. (1990) Piltdown: A Scientific Forgery. London: Natural History Museum Publications; Oxford/New York: Oxford University Press.

Ford, James Alfred (1911–1968)

American anthropologist and archaeologist. Born on February 12, 1911, in Water Valley, Mississippi, Ford developed in his youth an interest in the native cultures of the American southeast. He was educated at Louisiana State University, where he received his bachelor's in 1936; the University of Michigan, where he earned his master's in 1938; and at Columbia University, where he received his doctorate in 1948. From 1946, he was a curator at the American Museum of Natural History; from this base, he produced some of his most important research. He died on February 5, 1968, working on the cultures of the New World Formative period at the Florida State Museum in Gainesville.

Ford's early work was on the Native Americans of the southeastern United States, at locations such as the Greenhouse and Crooks sites in Louisiana and the Menard site in Arkansas. His interests soon broadened however, and Ford began to look for patterns in the material cultures of the New World. He and Gordon R. Willey developed a five-stage chronology and overall synthesis of native cultures in eastern North America. Borrowing the diffusionistic models of European scholars such as V. Gordon Childe, Willey and Ford saw the cultural influences that were stimuli for important change as originating in the south (generally, from Mesoamerica) and spreading up the Mississippi Valley. Ford pioneered the use of seriation and cross-cultural dating in his attempts to create a synthesis of New World Formative cultures, as seen in his important *Measurements of Some Prehistoric Design Developments in the Southeastern States.* His systematic use of material remains and seriation techniques to identify the patterns of an overall American Formative culture culminated in *A Comparison of Formative Cultures in the Americas,* published posthumously in 1969 and called by Betty Meggers and Clifford Evans in their "Introduction" "one of the milestones of New World archaeology."

Joseph J. Basile

See also SERIATION; WILLEY, GORDON RANDOLPH

Further Readings

Ford, J.A. (1940) Crooks Site: A Marksville Period Burial Mound in the La Salle Parish, Louisiana. New Orleans: Department of Conservation, Louisiana Geological Survey.

Ford, J.A. (1951) Greenhouse: A Troyville-Coles Creek Period Site in Avoyeles Parish, Louisiana. (Anthropological Papers of the American Museum of Natural History 44, pt. 1). New York: American Museum of Natural History.

Ford, J.A. (1952) Measurements of Some Prehistoric Design Developments in the Southeastern States. (Anthropological Papers of the American Museum of Natural History 44, pt. 3). New York: American Museum of Natural History.

Ford, J.A. (1961) Menard Site: The Quapaw Village of Osotouy on the Arkansas River. (Anthropological Papers of the

American Museum of Natural History 48, pt. 2). New York: American Museum of Natural History.

Ford, J.A. (1969) A Comparison of Formative Cultures in the Americas: Diffusion or the Psychic Unity of Man. Washington, D.C.: Smithsonian Institution Press.

Phillips, P., Ford, J.A. and Griffin, J.B. (1951) Archaeological Survey in the Lower Mississippi Alluvial Valley, 1940–1947. (Papers of the Peabody Museum of Archaeology and Ethnology 25). Cambridge, MA: Peabody Museum, Harvard University.

Fourier Transform–Infrared (FT-IR) Microscopy

Analytical technique based on the theory that vibrations within molecules cause characteristic absorption bands in the infrared (IR) region of the electromagnetic spectrum (12,800 cm^{-1}–10 cm^{-1}). IR spectra provide valuable information about molecular structure, symmetry, and, of particular note, in the analysis of chemical groups present. The technique is widely used to identify unknown compounds.

The interfacing of a microscope to the IR spectrometer permits samples as small as 10 μm × 10 μm to be analyzed, significantly extending the range of analytical applications.

There are two types of spectrometers, *dispersive* and *Fourier transform*. Dispersive instruments measure the absorption at each frequency in the IR spectrum. Depending on the sample, a typical scan of the mid-IR spectrum (4,000 cm^{-1}–400 cm^{-1}) usually takes twelve–fifteen minutes. The machines are simple, dependable, and relatively inexpensive. Fourier transform infrared (FT-IR) spectroscopy was developed in the 1970s. It revolutionized the technique by reducing the total scan time to less than two seconds *(Jacquinot advantage)*.

Basic Principles

Although the theoretical and mathematical concepts are complex, the basic principle of FT-IR is quite simple. Infrared radiation is directed onto a beam splitter, whereupon half of the energy is reflected onto a fixed mirror and half transmitted onto a moving mirror (Figure 1). Both mirrors reflect the beam back to the beam splitter, where they recombine

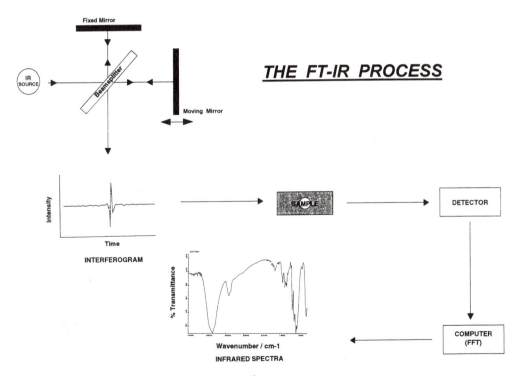

Figure 1. The FT-IR Process. Figure by Susan Hardman.

either constructively or destructively to form a new modulated wave called an *interferogram*. The new wave passes through the sample and onto a detector that monitors changes in intensity and frequency. A computer then uses fast Fourier transform (FFT) to convert the results back into infrared frequencies. The absorption over all wavelengths is recorded simultaneously. Since a single scan is so quick, multiple scans can be recorded and an average taken *(Fellgett advantage)*. This increases the signal-to-noise ratio, producing a quieter spectrum.

Rapid, multiple scanning has significantly increased the range of materials suitable for analysis. Reactions can be scanned as they progress (e.g., the curing of an epoxy resin), and a wide range of accessories have been developed to meet specific sampling problems. The interfacing of a microscope with FT-IR represented a significant advance for conservation and archaeological analysis.

Since infrared microscopy enables spectra from samples as small as 10 µm × 10 µm to be obtained, a single crystal or fiber can be analyzed. FT-IR microscopy can also be performed using either transmitted or reflected infrared radiation. In the transmission mode, the sample is initially selected and prepared under a low-power optical microscope (10x–30x magnification). Using a clean scalpel blade or a dissecting pin, a small sample is removed from the object and placed on a microscope slide. To prevent diffraction of the IR beam, the sample is gently flattened with a small roller. The sample is then placed on a small 13mm × 2mm sodium-chloride plate and transferred to the FT-IR microscope stage. Before the IR beam is passed through the sample, the area for analysis is visually selected using shutters. This is termed *redundant aperturing and targeting* and ensures that the spectrum produced is only that of the area of interest. The technique is fast, preparation is minimal, and the best, least-contaminated area of the sample can be analyzed.

Where samples cannot be taken from the artifact, analysis can be performed directly on the object by reflecting the beam off the object's surface. Transmission microscopy is preferred where possible, however, since the energy throughput is much greater.

Archaeological Applications

Archaeology, conservation, and forensic research are constantly restricted by the requirement that only small samples are available for study. The small sample requirements of transmission and the nondestructive nature of reflectance FT-IR microscopy ideally lend themselves to use in these disciplines. This includes identification of corrosion products on metal artifacts, drug identification, fiber analysis, and paint and varnish analysis on paintings and on cars used in crime. Results from artifact analysis have also been used in field and provenance studies. For example, the ratio of the mineral and the organic components in bone have been measured by FT-IR and used to map changes in local microenvironment conditions. Mechanistic studies of the degradation and aging of materials have been performed as well: These included the yellowing and the cross-linking of adhesives.

Reflectance microscopy has a number of specialized applications. They include the analysis of glazes on pottery to examine changes in ceramic technologies and research concerning the corrosion of glass. Waterlogged archaeological glass is particularly difficult to examine by standard analytical techniques because the water acts as a consolidant. Allowing it to dry out can result in disastrous consequences. Analytical techniques requiring glass to be absent from a wet environment for prolonged lengths of time or to be in a vacuum—as used for scanning electron microscopy (SEM) studies—are not suitable. Due to the speed of FT-IR, reflectance microscopy can be performed successfully without damage to the samples. This technique is being used to examine the effects of various storage environments for waterlogged glass to ascertain the optimum conditions for preservation.

Standard techniques used to prepare samples for IR transmission, such as potassium promide discs and mulls (a paste made by mixing an insoluble sample with an inert liquid), require the sample to be ground into a powder. This can often destroy or smear valuable information. To produce a painting, an artist will use a range of materials, including ground, binding media, varnishes, and pigments. If a sample is removed from the painting and examined under an optical microscope a number of discrete layers are observed. Grinding such a sample for a standard IR preparation would produce a complicated spectrum and make identification of the materials present a time-consuming, tedious, and rather uncertain process. By using FT-IR microscopy, each layer can be isolated (using the shutters) and analyzed individually. The information is used by art conservators to gain information on the techniques of Old Masters and identify later restorations and alterations. Using such detailed information makes it much easier to identify forgeries.

Textiles do not survive well in the burial environment except under the extremes of water content (i.e., of desiccation or waterlogging). Often only small, fragile fragments or even threads remain. Analysis must, therefore, be performed nondestructively or with minimal sample requirements. These criteria are fulfilled by FT-IR microscopy. In particular, it has been shown to be very suitable for the analysis of mineralized fibers.

Mineralization is defined as the combination and/or replacement of the organic matrix with an inorganic one. Mineralized fibers occur when a textile lies in close contact with a metal artifact (e.g., a buckle, brooch, or cloak pin). The resultant textiles are often fragmented and brittle; frequently, only a few fibers survive. Two types of mineralized fiber or *cast* can occur. *Negative casts* form where metal ions are deposited as corrosion prod-

ucts on the surface of the fiber. *Positive casts* form when the metal ions are deposited inside the fiber. Scanning electron microscopy has revealed that these casts can accurately record both the morphology of the fibers (e.g., the scales on wool fibers) and aspects of the technology of textiles (e.g., the spin of the thread). Because a three-dimensional replica of the fiber remains, positive casts are the more informative.

Visual identification of the type of fiber is not always possible, however, owing to excessive corrosion products that have formed on, near, or over the mineralized fiber. The mechanism by which positive and negative casts form has been studied by FT-IR microscopy. Results have shown that traces of the organic matrix can remain within the mineralized fibers. These quantities are sufficient to allow distinction between proteinaceous and cellulosic fibers, even in samples that would previously have been considered totally mineralized (Figure 2).

Dyed fibers have also been analyzed. Chromatography and ultraviolet/visible spectroscopy have been used successfully for dye characterization. However, these techniques are both time consuming and destructive,

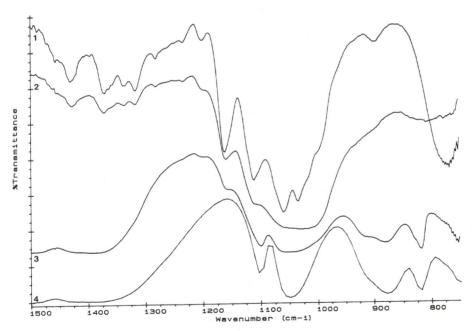

Figure 2. Infrared spectra of (1) an untreated cotton fiber, (2)–(3) two areas from a highly mineralized, seventh-century B.C. fiber; and (4) malachite ($Cu_2CO_3(OH)_2$). The archaeological sample clearly shows the presence of both a cellulose component and the copper mineral. Figure by Susan Hardman.

since the dyes must be extracted with solvent prior to analysis. Sample requirements can also be prohibitive, since relatively large amounts are needed. Remnant dyes on excavated textile fibers have been identified using FT-IR microscopy at a scale far below that which is possible by extractive techniques. An example is given in Figure 3. This spectrum was obtained from a sample taken from a sixteenth-century A.D. gentleman's tunic recovered from a coal mine. The highly degraded fibers taken from the buttonhole areas of the garment were unidentifiable using conventional microscopic techniques. FT-IR spectroscopy of the fibers not only showed them to be cellulosic but, by using a library of reference spectra, also clearly showed them to have been dyed with indigo.

To help with identification, forensic and conservation scientists have built spectroscopic libraries (databanks) of synthetic and natural materials. An unknown sample is searched against these files by computer, and the closest matching spectra found in the library are listed. The accuracy of the identification is determined by the match value. This is a measurement of how well the spectroscopic data points of the sample match those of a given library standard: A value of zero indicates a perfect match. Good library matching depends not only on the range of samples but also on the way the IR spectra are collected and prepared for the library. If the spectra are not treated in a consistent manner, spurious results are easily obtained.

There is an increasing number of microscope accessories available. These are aimed not only at extending the range of materials suitable for analysis, but also at reducing problems in sampling (e.g., interference fringes). The diamond compression cell is often used to flatten hard materials or to compress plastics and rubbers (rubbers and elastomers require constant pressure throughout analysis). Care must be taken, however, not to exert too much pressure. This can cause changes in the crystallinity of the sample and consequent alterations in the IR spectra, since crystal vibrations and imperfections modify molecular vibrational modes.

In some instances, multiple spectra may be required over the surface of the object or across a cross-section of a sample. For example, the extent of penetration of a consolidant

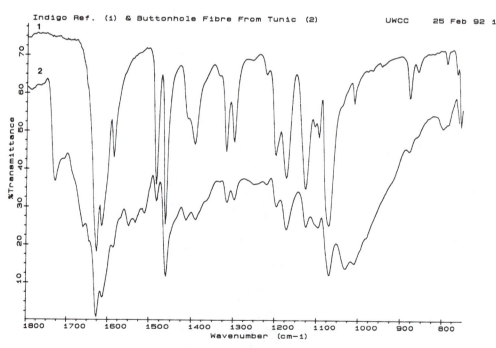

Figure 3. FT-IR spectra of (1) an indigo standard and (2) a fiber taken from the buttonhole of a sixteenth-century A.D. tunic. The spectrum clearly shows the presence of the dye in the fiber. Figure by Susan Hardman.

applied to a plaster surface can be examined by taking a series of spectra across a cross-section of the plaster. Near the plaster surface, the spectra will show peaks attributed to both the plaster and the consolidant. With increasing depth, however, the consolidant peaks will disappear. Using the vernier scale (graduated measuring instrument) on the microscope stage, the exact position of each spectrum relative to the sample surface can be recorded. This permits the penetration of the consolidant through the plaster to be mapped. Mapping is also useful for re-examining particular features at intervals (e.g., measuring the extent of pitting on glass with storage).

A correct analysis is dependent both on the skill of the operator and on the choice of sample. Careful choice of sample is essential. Erroneous data can easily result from inexperience, and practice on reliable prototypes is useful. Samples from artifacts are rarely ideal for analysis. Excavated objects can be contaminated or heavily stained with organic matter from the soil. Excessive handling can also leave (or may have left) deposits of grease on the artifact. For these reasons, it is important to be aware of the spectral characteristics of common contaminants. The small sample requirements of FT-IR microscopy significantly reduce these problems by enabling the least-contaminated area to be analyzed. With such small samples, however, care must be taken to ensure that the results are truly representative of the whole. Ideally, two or three areas should be analyzed for consistency.

Susan Hardman
Robert D. Gillard

Further Readings

Baer, N.S., and Low, M.J. D. (1977) Application of infrared Fourier transform spectroscopy to problems in conservation. I: General principles. Studies in Conservation 22:116–128.

Bartick, E.G., Montaser, A., and Tongol, M.W. (1991) Analysis of single polymer fibres by Fourier transform infrared microscopy: The results of case studies. Journal of Forensic Sciences 36:1027–1043.

Beck, C.W. (1986) Spectroscopic investigations of amber. Applied Spectroscopy Reviews 22:57–110.

Cooper, G.I., Cox, G.A., and Perutz, R.W. (1993) Infrared microspectroscopy as a complementary technique to electron-probe microanalysis for the investigation of natural corrosion on potash glass. Journal of Microscopy 170:111–118.

Earl Turner, N.J., and Watkinson, D.E. (1993) Use of FT-IR microscopy to assess the relative efficiency of various storage environments for waterlogged archaeological glass. In N.H. Tennent (ed.): Conservation Science in the U.K., pp. 77–84. London: James and James Science.

Gillard, R.D., Hardman, S.M., and Watkinson, D.E. (1993) Recent advances in textile studies using FT-IR microscopy. In N.H. Tennent (ed.): Conservation Science in the U.K., pp. 71–76. London: James and James Science.

Newton, G.H.T., Peters, D.C., and Shearer, J.C. (1983) FTIR in the service of art conservation. Analytical Chemistry 55:874A–880A.

Roush, P.B. (1987) The design, sample handling, and applications of infrared microscopes. (ASTM STP 949). Philadelphia: American Society for Testing and Materials

Weiner, S., Goldberg, P., and Bar-Yosef, O. (1993) Bone preservation in Kebara Cave, Israel, using on-site Fourier transform infrared spectrometry. Journal of Archaeological Science 20:613–627.

F

G

Garrod, Dorothy Annie Elizabeth (1892–1968)

British archaeologist and prehistorian. Born on May 5, 1892, in London, England, Garrod was a pioneer in the field of prehistory and prehistoric art. A specialist in the Upper Palaeolithic period, Garrod studied methodology, prehistoric archaeology, and art history and went on to work in the caves and rockshelters of Iraq, Palestine, and France. In 1928, Garrod made the first Palaeolithic discoveries in Iraq, at the caves of Zarzi and Hazar Merd in northern Iraq, near the headwaters of the Lower Zab River. She then went to Palestine, where she and René Neuville made a series of spectacular finds at Carmel Caves, including Lower Palaeolithic tools and a dozen burials of the Middle Palaeolithic period, among the earliest ever discovered in Israel. The fossilized skeletons were of a hominid type initially designated *Palaeoanthropus palestinensis,* showing traits of both Neanderthals and *Homo sapiens sapiens.* In 1954, Garrod and another woman, French archaeologist Suzanne de Saint-Mathurin, began a series of important excavations at the rockshelter of Angles-sur l'Anglin in the Charente region. These excavations were both models of superb specialized methodology and a means by which significant new finds were made in the area of Upper Palaeolithic art. Their discoveries included fossil and skeletal evidence of early *H. sapiens sapiens,* elegant small-scale carvings in the graceful Upper Palaeolithic style, and larger engravings on cave walls and blocks of stone. The excavations of Garrod and de Saint-Mathurin added significantly to the store of information concerning Palaeo-lithic art, which had already included the Lascaux (France) and Altamira (Spain) paintings and now includes work in other media. Also important is the groundbreaking work these two women did in opening the field of Old World prehistory to later generations of women archaeologists, anthropologists, and art historians. Garrod died on December 18, 1968, in Cambridge, England.

Joseph J. Basile

Further Readings

Roe, D.A., ed. (1983) Adlun in the Stone Age: The Excavations of D.A.E. Garrod in the Lebanon, 1958–1963. (BAR International Series 159). Oxford: British Archaeological Reports.

Ronen, A., ed. (1982) The Transition from Lower to Middle Palaeolithic and the Origin of Modern Man: International Symposium to Commemorate the 50th Anniversary of Excavations in the Mount Carmel Caves by D.A.E. Garrod. (BAR International Series 151). Oxford: British Archaeological Reports.

The Stone Age of Mount Carmel: Report of the Joint Expedition of the British School of Archaeology in Jerusalem and the American School of Prehistoric Research, 1929–1934. (1980) Reprinted, AMS Press, New York. Originally published 1937–1939, Oxford: Clarendon.

Gender Archaeology

The study of women in prehistoric and historic periods, as well as the archaeological study of sexual categories and relationships between them and of the role of gender as a fundamental structuring system in any culture.

Concepts and Historical Context

Archaeologies of gender have developed parallel to gender inquiry in a number of other anthropological subfields and related social sciences since the mid-1970s. *Gender* is a term borrowed from linguistics. In the broader contexts of ethnography and archaeology, gender has been defined in distinction to generally Western biological definitions of reproductive sexual categories. The term refers instead to the highly variable, culturally based explanations of the sexual categories themselves and, perhaps more significantly, to the varying, strategic, and manipulated relationships between them. Since the 1970s, archaeologies of gender have undergone a shift from a more remedially focused archaeology of women that addressed what was perceived as an absence, or erroneous representation, of women in the archaeological record toward a more comprehensive, process-oriented understanding of gender as one of the central structuring systems of any culture. In this regard, gender archaeology has been described as one of the emerging critiques of archaeological practice coming out of the postprocessualist work of the 1980s.

The archaeology of gender draws heavily on similar studies that have been coming out of sociocultural anthropology, or ethnography, since the late 1960s and early 1970s. Archaeologists have borrowed from this corpus of work in at least two ways, with significant consequences.

The first archaeologists to explore gender as an area of archaeological inquiry borrowed a legitimacy for pursuing the topic at all, particularly as a temporal grounding for the kinds of diversity that ethnographers were discovering in the gender constructs of contemporary cultures. Archaeology was seen as a means of describing gender diversity over time as well as cross-culturally. Above all, archaeologists argued for their ability to use the archaeological record to demonstrate that contemporary gender categories/systems were historically constructed cultural products rather than inherent, "natural" categories/systems.

Conversely, subsequent archaeological work has borrowed heavily from the ethnographic case studies themselves, usually for one of two main purposes: to support arguments about the diversity of sex/gender systems in the past and to provide alternative models for interpreting archaeological materials that either excluded mention of women and gender or assumed a noncausal, insignificant role for either women's activities or gender systems.

There have been at least two significant consequences of this strong ethnographic emphasis in the archaeological study of gender. First, the issues and facets of gender considered important have been defined ethnographically, with very powerful reference to the contemporary sociopolitics of gender equity issues, without as yet much real understanding of how to frame specifically *archaeological* approaches to gender. Second, by necessity, archaeologies of gender must engage the complex dilemma of using ethnographic analogy as an argument in archaeology. This issue has long been part of the epistemological debates in archaeology. But it has brought some of its particular difficulties to the archaeological study of gender, with particular impact on the way archaeology is being employed in current feminist debates. As universalizing, essentialist claims about women and women's lives, experiences, and general nature have collapsed under continued feminist critiques of a number of social and biological sciences, the fundamental dilemma emerges for archaeologists wishing to study the highly variable, contextualized gender systems of the past: How do you compare the present to the past? Since the mid-1980s, the direction of this inquiry has focused on turning gender from an implicit, assumed answer to an explicitly problematic question: Archaeologists exploring past gender systems are trying to understand the characteristics and the significance of those past gender systems and the varying ways that gender is integrated with other structuring elements of culture, such as ethnicity, class, status, race, economy, and ecology. These archaeologists argue for the general utility of gender studies to the rest of archaeological interpretation and the powerful relevance of archaeological approaches to gender in contemporary life.

Archaeological Applications

In the effort to address gender in the archaeological record, one of the most useful steps was the formulation of the distinctive components of gender systems, developed by Margaret Wright Conkey and Janet Spector in 1984:

Gender role refers to the differential participation of men and women in social, economic, political, and religious institutions within a specific cultural setting. Gender roles describe what people do and what activities and behaviors are deemed appropriate for the gender category. *Gender identity* refers to an individual's own feeling of whether she or he is a woman or a man. As we know from the case of transsexuals—a gender category in our culture—this aspect of gender does not necessarily coincide with the gender category others might assign to the individual. *Gender ideology* refers to the meaning, in given social and cultural contexts, of *male, female, sex and reproduction.* The system of meaning includes prescriptions and proscriptions for males, females, or persons of any other culturally defined gender category (e.g., the *berdache*). There the emphasis is on gender, sexuality and reproduction as symbols (Conkey and Spector 1984:15).

Archaeological studies of gender can be categorized in terms of which of these components of gender they emphasize. Archaeologies of *gender roles* examine the gender activities represented at sites, with strong emphases usually placed on the organization of labor that characterizes various kinds of social and economic structures—in particular, the dynamic and strategic variability of labor organization in response to social, economic, or ecological change. Such studies often target old assumptions regarding the gender division of labor, such as the relative statuses accorded women's and men's work in the shift to a state-based society or the role of biology in shaping or limiting women's activities.

Studies of *gender identity* represent significant challenges to archaeologists, because of the inherently individual nature of the issue, but have led to studies that emphasize the diversity of gender expression in the archaeological record. For instance, much recent work uses the idea of diverse gender experiences within a given society to chart the way that gender can articulate with other cultural constructs, such as race, class, or gender: Rich women and poor ones lead very different lives. This research has also dovetailed well with emerging work on archaeologies of resistance, in that variability of gender expression can constitute a significant form of resistance to oppression in a range of venues. The area of gender identity and its material expression has also seen the initial examination of cultures with multiple (more than two) genders.

Finally, studies of *gender ideologies* include those addressing the cultural and cognitive significance of gender as a system of contextualized, and often contested, meanings. This kind of research tends to take one of two approaches. Either archaeologists concentrate on assigning relatively specific gender meanings to specific objects, representations, images, or archaeologically documented behaviors, or they emphasize the way that gender ideologies, such as the relative status of women's and men's labor in a society, or the assignment of conceptualized traits (e.g., impurity, bravery, nurturing) to specific genders can be manipulated in the broader ideological systems of societies. The latter works most often focus on moments of transition in social structure, such as the shift from foraging to food production or the emergence of the state, when existing ideological systems are overhauled to either accommodate or challenge the status quo.

The kinds of archaeological evidence used in these studies reflect the kinds of questions being asked. Research into women and men as social individuals often relies on burial data, where skeletal material can provide information on relative health and diet, occupationally related pathologies, differential mortalities, infant mortality and child-care patterns, and where grave goods may reflect the individual's activities, status, and a range of features of gender identity and expression. Debates about sex-based divisions of labor and the relative status attached to women's versus men's labor can employ data at the level of individual artifacts and their contexts, but most often it revolves around analyses of activity areas within a site. Inquiries range from explicitly technological questions about who made and used specific categories of tools and resources to broader issues of concepts of property, definitions of the household, relative economic contributions of different genders, and the role of gender systems in integrating the complex task-based labor of craft production. Some of the most powerful and controversial data involve both artifacts and features depicting representational imagery, or art: figurines, paintings, and other

G

forms of expression whose analysis and interpretation form the basis for questions about the explicit meanings of female and male imagery in a given society, and from whose perspective, as well as more far-reaching queries into the dynamics of cultural continuity and debates over the relative significance of contextualized versus universal meanings.

Broader Issues for Continuing Research

Perhaps the most crucial issue for gender archaeology on the eve of the twenty-first century is methodological. The corpus of work produced argues convincingly for the need for archaeologies that not only address the issue of gender itself, but also integrate gender analyses into the entire range of archaeological research. The questions emerging from both practitioners and critics alike revolve around how to "dig it up," in any specific sense. These debates have brought the issue of ethnographic analogy to the fore, along with the explicit feminist critique that one cannot do this kind of archaeology without changing the *way* archaeology itself is done. Fundamental assumptions about the nature of the archaeological record, the levels of generalization possible, the degree of ambiguity and variability that is tolerable in analysis, and the means by which archaeological research can or should be evaluated have all come under increasing assault. In a very general sense, the kinds of work done by archaeologists studying gender are increasingly shifting away from typologically based analyses (be they aesthetic, functional, *or* gendered) toward interpretations that emphasize connections and relationships between objects and between objects, people, and processes, events, activities, and changes over time.

In this context, a number of broader issues have been raised by archaeological research into gender and gender systems. These include:

People's Use of the Past To "Ground" the Contemporary Status Quo or To Challenge it. Either it has always been this way and is "natural," or it was different then than now, and we should (1) return to the past or (2) change "now" (which is possible because it has not always been this way). *Origin stories,* whether Adam and Eve or Darwinism, have profound cultural significance as ideologically powerful explanations of where we/life came from that are fundamental to

most societies. To the extent that gender ideologies can be among the most powerful of these "taken-for-granteds," and among the most conventionally described in origin stories, archaeologies that either confirm or challenge these assumptions take on considerable significance themselves.

Recovering Diversity in the Past. Archaeologies of gender tend to produce narratives of multiple pasts, instead of "The Past," providing historical contexts that take apart both the "Universal Woman" and the "Universal Man" in reference to whom she was constructed. This raises an interesting and potentially very problematic question: To what extent *are* there universals in the area of gender relations? This echoes the strains of postmodern critique in a number of other social sciences and which is itself yet another use of the past to present ends.

How To Articulate All of This Difference. If generalization is questionable, then what can we know from this research? To what extent is it possible to integrate several approaches to the archaeological record or interpretation? What are the appropriate means for critiquing and evaluating such disparate work?

Validity of Interpretations. With regard to the debates in archaeology, what can we ultimately know about or explore in the past? If gender cannot be "recovered" in any universal sense, and if it is nonetheless a central structuring principle in all cultures, then how valid are our archaeological interpretations?

Material Correlates and Information from Objects. It is increasingly clear that, at least in terms of gender, conventionalized attempts to "sex the artifact" are problematic at best and invariably serve to obscure the very diversity and variability that seems to characterize gendered activities and expressions in a given culture. Yet, some ability to establish inferences from artifacts and their contexts is fundamental to archaeological methodology. How will the new approaches to highly contextualized and variable factors such as gender change that methodology?

Margaret Purser

See also CONKEY, MARGARET WRIGHT; POST-PROCESSUAL ARCHAEOLOGY

Further Readings

Bacus, E.A., ed. (1993) A Gendered Past: A Critical Bibliography of Gender in Archaeology. (Technical Reports 25). Ann Arbor: Museum of Anthropology, University of Michigan.

Claassen, C., ed. (1992) Exploring Gender Through Archaeology. Madison, WI: Prehistory Press.

Conkey, M.W., and Spector, J., In M.B. Schiffer (ed): Archaeology and the study of gender, Advances in Archaeological Method and Theory, vol. 7, 1–38.

Ehrenberg, M.R. (1989) Women in Prehistory. Norman: University of Oklahoma Press.

Gero, J.M., and Conkey, M.W., eds. (1991) Engendering Archaeology: Women and Prehistory. Oxford, U.K., and Cambridge, MA: Blackwell.

Scott, E.M., ed. (1994) Those of Little Note: Gender, Race, and Class in Historical Archaeology. Tucson: University of Arizona Press.

Wall, D.d. (1994) The Archaeology of Gender: Separating the Spheres in Urban America. New York: Plenum.

Geoarchaeology

The use of geological concepts, methods, and knowledge base in the solution of archaeological problems. Geology and archaeology are both historical sciences based largely on a complex stratigraphy embracing mineral, fossil, and cultural remains in a spatial and implicitly chronological context that is used to reconstruct the succession of events that produced the sedimentary record. A union of the young science of geology with the even younger discipline of archaeology occurred in the mid-nineteenth century, growing out of the same intellectual ferment that gave birth to evolutionary biology and much of modern geology.

Historical Development

The earth sciences have always played a significant role in interpreting the archaeological record. Sir Charles Lyell, one of the founders of modern geology, in his 1863 book *The Geological Evidence for the Antiquity of Man* clearly established the role of geology in archaeological inquiry. Geology and archaeology were united in a common goal—a study of the evidence for human antiquity. The British historian of archaeology Glyn Daniel has written *(A Hundred and Fifty Years of Archaeology)* in 1975 that there could be no real archaeology before geology because geology defined the limits and set the problems of prehistoric archaeology. In North America, the interactions between geology and archaeology in the late nineteenth century involved many of the best-known American geologists: John Wesley Powell, William Henry Holmes, Henry S. Washington, Newton H. Winchell, and Thomas C. Chamberlin. Powell was responsible for the birth and initial development of both the United States Geological Survey and the Bureau of American Ethnology and became director of both.

A distinction *may* be drawn between *geoarchaeology,* in which geology is used to solve expressly archaeological problems (*geo* modifies archaeology), and *archaeological geology* (with geology as the noun), in which expressly geological investigations contribute knowledge of importance to archaeology. An example of the former would be the use of sedimentology in studying the strata in an archaeological excavation. An example of the latter would be the geological determination of Late Quaternary shoreline migration near important archaeological sites. Most of Quaternary geomorphology and geochronology can be utilized as archaeological geology. Archaeological geology also grades imperceptibly into environmental geology, depending on when the human/environment interaction took place.

The interdisciplinary combination of geology and archaeology became more formalized in 1977 with the formation of the Archaeological Geology Division of the Geological Society of America. Earlier that same year, archaeological geology was added to the list of specialties reviewed yearly in *Geotimes*. The international journal *Geoarchaeology* was founded in 1986.

Most geological concepts and methods that are applicable to studying the natural forces that shape the landscape; locating subsurface features; analyzing sediments and sedimentary strata; determining the identification, genesis, and provenance of natural materials; recording climate change; and dating events recorded in earth materials are being applied to archaeological problems. Specific geological techniques covering these

G

applications are considered in detail elsewhere in this volume.

Landscape Reconstruction

Reconstruction of the geological and ecological environments has provided an increasingly clear picture of the landscapes and habitats that sustained (and constrained) the evolution of hominids and humans. In reconstructing past environments, both the geologist and the archaeologist depend on incomplete stratigraphic records and on evidence that frequently is insufficient for an absolute chronology of events. Few areas of the Earth's land surface have witnessed long and continuous periods of deposition; on the contrary, erosion is the terrestrial norm.

Paleogeomorphical reconstructions are especially useful in areas of rapid change—along major river systems and adjacent to oceans and inland seas—because these environments have also been the loci of human settlement and activity. In coastal areas, three geological processes combine to drive topographic change. Eustatic (worldwide) and local relative sea-level changes immediately affect the coastal zone. Vertical movements of the local land mass augment or offset eustatic sea-level rise or fall. Finally, deposition or erosion of coastal sedimentary deposits may cause transgressional or regressional migration of the shoreline.

Perhaps the most important geological contribution to reconstructing past coastal landscapes is in the application of Walther's Law of Correlation of Facies. Facies represent distinct rock types that correspond broadly to environments of deposition (e.g., lagoon, beach). Walther's Law states that facies occurring in a conformable vertical sequence were formed in laterally adjacent environments and that facies in vertical contact must be the product of geographically neighboring environments. Hence, by noting the vertical sequences, one can reconstruct the changes in shoreline environments over time. Identifying the environment of deposition of sedimentary facies often relies on micropaleontology. Marine, brackish, estuarine, and lacustrine deposits often contain diagnostic assemblages of diatoms, ostracods, or foraminifera. Because different species are sensitive to salinity, temperature, the supply of nutrients, and even to specific pollutants, they can be valuable indicators of the paleoenvironment.

Using intensive core drilling of the deposits in dynamic coastal environments, archaeological geologists have been able to provide paleogeomorphical reconstructions of many archaeologically important areas and sites, such as the Delaware Bay area in the eastern United States, the ancient Anatolian sites of Troy and Ephesus, and the location of the Battle of Thermopylae between the Greeks (Spartans) and the Persians in 480 B.C. The debate concerning the geography of Homeric Troy has involved scholars for more than 2,000 years. As far back as the early 1800s, it was realized that, in Homeric times, the coast at the mouth of the Scamander and Simois rivers was well inland of its present position. The floodplain of the two rivers adjacent to Troy provided an excellent opportunity to use core drilling to reconstruct the movement of the ancient shoreline of the earlier marine embayment as sediment infill forced marine regression. This, in turn, has necessitated a reassessment of views of the coastal topography of Homeric times.

In some cases, truly fundamental disagreements arise among historians, classicists, archaeologists, geographers, and natural scientists. This occurs despite a major adoption of scientific methodologies by most archaeologists. Conflicts among historians over the 480 B.C. battle of Thermopylae, centering on the inconsistencies between ancient sources and the modern topography, provided archaeological geologists another opportunity to reconstruct the relevant paleogeography following a core-drilling program. With the core recovery and analysis from seven holes, the ancient coastal physiography for the Battle of Thermopylae was delineated.

Sedimentological and geomorphological investigations are essential for recognizing past depositional environments (rivers, lakes, dunes) no longer a part of the landscape. The greatest input into archaeology from geomorphologists has concerned sites linked to fluvial landforms. The difficulties of dating and correlating complex alluvial sequences can be overcome by a combination of detailed geomorphical mapping and sediment coring.

The floodplains of three great rivers—the Nile, the Tigris/Euphrates, and the Indus—have been birthplaces of irrigation agriculture and urban civilizations. As with all floodplains, their evolution is marked by dynamic change: erosion, as lateral channel migration impinges on floodplain settlements, and deposition, along the river course and at the river mouth (often a delta). On deltas and the shores of estuaries, settlements initially in coastal locales eventually become landlocked as sedimentation advanced the land seaward. The current Nile River has two main branches traversing its delta. In the fifth century B.C., Herodotus reported five active branches; in the second century A.D., Ptolemy recorded eight. The Tigris/Euphrates system has been depositing heavy loads for millennia. Cuneiform texts suggest that the Sumerian city of Ur—now more than 200 km from the Persian Gulf—was a port in the third millennium B.C.

In many parts of the world, lakes were nonexistent, rivers were ephemeral, and rainfall sparse. Such regions were uninhabitable unless springs were available. Springs are very local environments where groundwater emerges at the surface through natural openings in the bedrock. Spring water is available where the surface topography intersects the water table or where groundwater emerges under artesian pressure. Springs may be perennial or ephemeral, but geological conditions in many areas of high topographic relief lead to a consistent supply of water. Human groups have always used spring environments because springs provided fresh water and vegetation and also attracted animals. Like other depositional environments, spring environments, even if long extinct, can be identified in the sedimentary record.

Archaeological Sediments

The principle of *stratigraphic succession,* the core of archaeological excavation, is one of the primary constructs of geology. In excavating, archaeologists have developed expertise in resolving complex stratigraphies. However, few have expertise in sedimentology. Most often, too little is done to utilize the attributes and relationships of archaeological sediments in reconstructing the cultural components of prehistoric sites. It has become the task of geoarchaeologists to interpret the lithology, paleontology, geochemistry, pedology, and textures from the normal mix of geologic, biogenic, and anthropogenic components of archaeological sediments. This requires geoarchaeologists to deal with human and natural events on the site level of analysis. Sediments that have been formed or transformed by cultural processes are measurably different from geological sediments. Attributes such as lithology and texture are important indicators of the genesis and history of any sediment. Geological and pedological training is necessary to determine if physical and chemical attributes result from natural or cultural processes. Diagenetic, taphonomic, and related postdepositional changes can disturb the original structure and stratigraphy.

Artifacts and archaeological features are found in or on sedimentary deposits. Most archaeological data are recovered from sedimentary deposits, and artifacts can be considered as sedimentary particles in terms of formation processes. Clastic sediments are a collection of mineral or rock particles that have been weathered and eroded from their original context and redeposited mechanically elsewhere. From a geoarchaeological perspective, archaeological sediments are just a special case of geological deposit, and the same sedimentological principles apply, regardless of whether they contain artifacts or other archaeological features.

Geologists have long used *peels* for the study of unconsolidated sediments. Peels are impregnated surface samples that show sedimentary textures and structures, as well as objects such as bone, charcoal, ash, and sherds contained in the earth matrix. Peels are, therefore, both outcrop samples and replicas that can be brought into the laboratory for study. Some measurements and observations not easily made in the excavation trench walls thus can be deferred to the laboratory. Peels can be photographed and X-rayed under controlled conditions. For some reason, peels are still rarely used in archaeology.

Settlement and agricultural soils are quite different from other soils. There are three principal types of inorganic phosphate found in soils: (1) easily extractable mainly aluminum and iron phosphate, associated with growing plants, including crops; (2) more tightly bound phosphate, commonly associated with human activity; and (3) natural geologic phosphate. Based only on quantifying these types of phosphates, geoarchaeologists can identify ranching, farming, dwelling, manufacturing, burial, and refuse areas in archaeological context. The silt fraction of archaeological sediments often contains phytoliths that can indicate the paleoecology of the area, as well as be the only material remains of agricultural plants. Phytoliths are

G

opaline silica bodies that are particularly characteristic of grasses. Many dietary staples, such as rice, corn, wheat, barley, rye, and sugarcane, are grasses. Phytoliths have been recovered from a wide range of sediments, but research is still in its infancy to determine the extent to which these fossil forms can be used to reconstruct paleoenvironments and ancient agricultural practices.

The current distribution of archaeological sites is based on the environmental conditions that existed at the time of occupation and that made a particular functional activity possible and also governed the circumstances that later preserved, altered, or destroyed the artifactual evidence of human behavior. An archaeological site is a preserved locus of human activity. The remains include the sedimentary matrix, artifacts and features, ecofacts, and geofacts. Besides human activity, a variety of geological and biological processes can introduce patterns into the archaeological accumulations. Natural materials are incorporated in archaeological deposits in many ways. Local geological and geochemical processes can form new objects (e.g., concretions), move earth (in erosion and soil formation), dissolve materials (e.g., bone phosphate), and deposit materials (e.g., manganese oxide) during and after cultural deposition. Manganese oxide, which is soft and black, has often been mistaken for carbon.

Interpreting archaeological materials associated with specific depositional settings relies on evaluating what types of destructive and preservational processes prevailed. Where weathering and erosion were dominant processes, the spatial arrangement and composition of sites will have been modified. Destruction by weathering or rearrangement by erosion and redeposition will remove some or most of the patterns imposed by the systemic human behavioral context and introduce other patterns of geological and biological structuring.

Micromorphology is concerned with the study of soils and unconsolidated sediments and other materials (e.g., mud bricks) at a microscopic scale. This technique uses thin-section petrography (using the polarizing microscope) to examine the composition and fabric of soils and sediments. Such studies can reveal (1) the origin and environment of deposition of sediments; (2) land-use practices; (3) anthropogenic materials and features, such as ash, mud bricks, mortar, cremations, floors, and microartifacts; (4) whether clays are inherited from mud brick or introduced secondarily by soil-forming processes; (5) salinization problems in agriculture; (6) vegetational cover; (7) postdepositional processes, including diagenesis and soil formation; and (8) the context of burning (determining the fuel, the temperature, and possibly even the purpose).

Archaeologists often use color as a diagnostic criterion to recognize units. Unfortunately, many color variations are the result of natural geochemical processes and have no archaeological significance. Soil scientists and geochemists can use color to reflect pedological processes. On some sites, a distinct reddening of certain horizons or sections of a profile has been cited by archaeologists as evidence of an intense fire. Such interpretations should be approached with caution. The chief coloring agent in all soils is the element iron (Fe) in some combined state. Goethite, $HFeO_2$ (sometimes referred to as limonite), lends a yellow-brown color to soils or fine-grained sediments. Hematite, Fe_2O_3, is red. Goethite will transform to hematite when heated to 250–400°C, but other geochemical reactions can cause brown-red discoloration in soils and sediments.

Darker colors may reflect an accumulation of organic matter (mostly carbon) or manganese oxide but can also reflect the presence of dark-colored minerals or rock fragments. Grayish and olive-gray colors indicate reducing conditions. An overall mottled appearance in sediments can result from the migration in solution of manganese and iron ions, leading to patchy accumulations of oxides and hydroxides, and is characteristic of gley soils. Seepage of colloids, organic matter, or iron compounds may result in streaks. Mottled gray and brown may indicate impeded drainage. Mottling also occurs in soil horizons that are incompletely weathered. Anaerobic decay of biological materials in marshes and stagnant lakes is usually quite dark. Green colors in sediments can be the result of the presence of particular minerals (mostly hydrous silicates), including epidote, chlorite, and serpentine.

White or light-gray colors can indicate leaching or concentrations of calcium carbonate. Sands composed mostly of quartz are generally light colored. Reddish and yellowish colors result from oxidation, often due to good drainage and aeration. The surface layers of muds, because they may have access to dissolved air in overlying water, can remain oxidized, giving a reddish brown or yellowish color. Under this surface layer, the circulation of oxidizing solution can be restricted enough to allow reducing conditions to prevail, forming darker-colored sediments.

Soils in Geoarchaeology

An understanding of soils is vital to archaeology. Unfortunately, semantic confusion is common in archaeology because the word *soil* is used for two very different things. Incorrectly, *soil* is used loosely for surface and near-surface sediments of many descriptions. Correctly, *soil* is the portion of the Earth's surface materials that supports plant life and thereby is a chemically and biologically active medium that has been altered by the continuous chemical and biological activity. The lower limit (depth) of a soil is normally the lower limit of biological activity. Sediments can be thought of as normally biologically *dead,* whereas soils are very much *alive.* A cubic meter of agricultural soil contains more than one million living creatures. Most sediments do not have biological properties. All soils have biological properties.

Soils are related directly to rock weathering and reflect the composition of the underlying (parent) rock modified by climate, vegetation, and biological and human activity through time. Soil formation results in the development of a *soil profile* exhibiting a vertical series of horizons. A soil horizon is a layer of soil, approximately parallel to the Earth's surface, with characteristics produced by soil-forming processes. Archaeologists also deal with a series of roughly horizontal layers due to depositional phenomena. It is imperative that depositional phenomena not be confused with postdepositional alteration (*diagenetic*) phenomena such as soil formation. So the same word (*soil*) should not be used for both.

A *paleosol* is simply a soil that formed on a landscape in the past (i.e., a fossil soil). Paleosols are abundant in the geological record and are coming to be recognized in archaeological contexts. These buried soils are important as position and time markers of stable landscape environments where ecological (and sometimes human) forces dominated rather than erosion or deposition. Unfortunately, there is no simple set of criteria by which one can recognize a paleosol. To recognize a paleosol, it is necessary to identify a horizon that was developed as the result of soil-forming processes. In addition to helping clarify local archaeological stratigraphy, the identification of a paleosol can be used for stratigraphic correlation and chronological resolution.

Archaeoseismology

Archaeologists define chronological horizons by stratigraphic and/or cultural discontinuities. Stratigraphic discontinuities are sometimes defined by *destruction layers* that may or may not be accompanied by a cultural change evident in ceramic or other artifact typologies. Historic records chronicle earthquake events of tragic cultural consequences, and such catastrophic seismic disturbances should be recorded in geological and archaeological strata. From the geophysical point of view, however, one must be cautious about attributing structural damage observed in excavations to seismic violence. For example, structures built on slopes underlain by shale, unconsolidated sediments, or fill can topple or come apart as the result of uncommonly heavy rainfall that saturates new parts of the underlying ground, causing major downslope earth movements. Careful analysis of the geological and geophysical setting of the archaeological strata is necessary before any attribution to seismic events can be made.

Geological Raw Materials

The excavation of an archaeological site usually brings to light only a small portion of what once was the total material culture of a society. Because they are stable in the earth-surface environment, artifacts of rocks and minerals, as well as the debris produced during their manufacture, make up a large part of what is recovered. Most inorganic remains are derived from geological raw materials. From Early Palaeolithic tools through building materials and ceramics to sophisticated metal alloys, the source materials are rocks and minerals. Some basic definitions are in order. A *rock* is a specific aggregate of one or more minerals that occurs commonly enough to be given a name (e.g., granite, limestone); a *mineral* is a naturally occurring inorganic element or compound having a specific crystal structure and a characteristic chemical composition (e.g., quartz, mica). *Obsidian* is a *volcanic glass* that has not yet crystallized but, in all other respects, is a rock.

G

Few areas of lithic nomenclature are as confusing as the names for the fine-grained varieties of quartz (SiO_2). Quartz is important because rocks and minerals composed chiefly of quartz make up a large percentage of lithic artifacts. Quartz is one of the most stable of all minerals under sedimentary conditions and in the Earth's surface environment. *Chert*, primarily the mineral quartz, has been used as a general term for fine-grained siliceous rock of chemical, biochemical, or biogenic origin. It is comparatively very hard (quartz has a Mohs hardness of seven) compact material that fractures conchoidally when struck.

Chert occurs as bedded deposits, discontinuous lenses, and nodules usually interstratified with chalk, limestone, or dolomite. It has a microcrystalline structure composed of interlocking, often roughly equigranular, grains. Chert can be almost any color and can accommodate a wide variety of impurities that affect its workability in lithic manufacture. Throughout human prehistory, people have prospected stream gravels for lithic raw materials. People realized that the boulders surviving the rough and tumble ride down watercourses did not shatter easily. In most parts of the world, these boulders were composed largely of chert and related quartzose rocks and minerals.

Semiprecious stones (actually, they are minerals) are gemstones of lesser value than precious stones such as diamond and emerald. They normally have a hardness of seven or less on the Mohs hardness scale. The most common semiprecious stones used by ancient crafters are varieties of quartz.

Nearly all rocks and minerals that hold their color when ground to a powder (most silicates turn white) have been used as pigments. Goethite (yellow ocher), hematite (red ocher), malachite (green), azurite (blue), cinnabar (a deep red mercury sulfide), calcite and magnesite (white), and varieties of coal, manganese oxides, and graphite (for their deep black color) are among the most commonly used mineral pigments.

The primary raw materials for archaeological ceramics were local clay-rich sediments and soils for the paste and coarse sedimentary particles for the temper. Sedimentary clay deposits are of two general types: *primary deposits* formed in situ by the weathering of bedrock such as granite or shale and *secondary deposits* formed by river (fluvial) or lake (lacustrine) deposition. These are often referred to as *transported clays*. In soils, clay minerals form as part of the natural chemical weathering of the parent bedrock. Clay minerals are low-temperature hydrous minerals stable in the Earth's surface environment. They form in soils from the breakdown of minerals formed in high-temperature anhydrous environments. These primary minerals are not stable at the Earth's surface. Plant nutrients become available during this chemical weathering. The supply of potassium in a soil correlates well with the rate of clay formation.

It must be noted that the word *clay* has two meanings: as a particle size (less than 2 microns) and as the name of a group of silicate minerals that have a sheetlike structure. Because of their small size and sheet structure, clays become plastic when mixed with a limited amount of water. This allows the mixture to be shaped and to retain the new shape. Whether a clayey raw material will make good pottery depends on which clay mineral predominates, the shape and the size distribution of nonclay minerals, the organic content, the exchangeable ions present, and the size distribution in the whole mass. Good pottery clays also contain fine-grained quartz, which provides the refractory backbone during firing.

The nature of the building materials employed by any society depends primarily on the kind of materials available. It was no accident that the great tells of the Middle East formed from the disintegration of mud-brick buildings. There were neither hard rock outcrops nor trees for hundreds of kilometers. Where indurated bedrock was available, large blocks of building stone were secured through quarrying. Quarries are not easily eroded or removed from the landscape unless replaced by an even larger later quarry, so many landscapes are dotted with ancient quarries.

When considering the geological raw materials that may be found in an archaeological context, it also pays to become acquainted with objects that resemble some natural material in shape or other aspect but have a very different origin. Conspicuous among these are *concretions*. Concretions are hard, compact segregations of mineral matter found in sedimentary rocks, particularly shales and sandstones. They are formed by precipitation from aqueous solution, growing outward from a nucleus, and usually are of a composition somewhat different from the host rock. Concretions represent a concentration of some cementing material, such as iron oxide, silica, calcite, or gypsum. Most concretions are spheroidal, ellipsoidal, or discoidal, although many attain odd or fantastic shapes, sometimes mimicking turtle shells.

Provenance Studies

A frequent question concerning artifacts is where they came from. When this question refers to the source of the raw material from which the object was made, finding the answer will involve geology. The information desired by the archaeologist is for geographic provenance but is determined by geochemical (trace-element or isotopic analyses) or petrographic methods. Trace-element *fingerprinting* has been successful in determining the provenance of ceramic clays, native copper, chert, obsidian, and other lithic materials. Trace-element analysis involves determining the concentrations of fifteen or more trace elements in the parts-per-billion or low parts-per-million range. The large number of geochemical variables in a geological deposit normally provides a unique trace-element signature.

Trace-element analyses (using neutron activation analysis) has been especially successful in sourcing obsidian artifacts in many parts of the world. Neutron activation analysis has been used to show that the two larger-than-life (a combined 720 metric tons) quartzite statues on the Plain of Thebes in Egypt most likely came from the Gebel el Amar quarry more than 400 km *down* the river Nile rather than quarries *up* river and much nearer to Thebes. Because Precolumbian cultures in North America (north of the Rio Grande) neither smelted copper ores nor melted native copper to cast into implements, native-copper artifacts from this region retain the trace-element fingerprint of the original deposit. Hence, copper artifacts from the United States and Canada can be sourced using trace-element analyses.

Some rocks and smelted copper ores cannot be sourced by trace-element analyses. In the case of marble (particularly from statues and monuments in the eastern Mediterranean region), distinctive variations in the concentrations of carbon-13 and oxygen-18 isotopes allow sourcing to the ancient quarries. In the process of smelting copper ore to copper metal, some trace elements from the ore go into the metal, and some go into the slag. In addition, trace elements in the metal can come from the flux and the fuel used during smelting. Hence, determination of the provenance of the copper in bronze by trace-element analyses is fruitless. Fortunately, copper ores contain a small concentration of the element lead. Lead-isotope ratios are not altered during smelting so can be used in sourcing smelted copper (in bronze), as well as lead and silver.

One of the most important (and as yet unsolved) provenance questions in Old World archaeology is the source of ancient tin. The Bronze Age is defined by the introduction of copper alloy metallurgy. First arsenic, then (more importantly) tin was alloyed with copper to make bronze. Copper deposits are fairly common across the Earth, but tin ores are rare. Numerous prehistoric copper-mining sites have been excavated. However, the search is still on for identifying the tin sources for the Bronze Age of the Mediterranean and the Near East. The ore mineral of tin, cassiterite (SnO_2), can be sourced using neutron activation analyses, but archaeologists have not yet (i.e., as of 1998) identified cassiterite ore at any bronze-metalsmithing site.

The study of rocks and minerals by means of transmitted plane-polarized light has been an important tool for geologists since the nineteenth century. Minerals may be studied under the polarizing microscope (*petrography*), using either small grains or thin slices known as *thin sections*. In some geological terrains, the rocks are composed of minerals or assemblages of minerals that are rare enough to be diagnostic of the source locality. This feature has led to the use of petrography to determine the source of lithic artifacts and monument stone. Petrography has been adapted to the study of ceramics in thin section. Ceramic petrography is useful in determining the provenance of temper and the coarser components of the ceramic raw material, as well as the technology used in the manufacturing.

Environmental Geoarchaeology

The study of human cultures cannot be divorced from a study of their environment and the mutual interaction between human activities and environmental processes. Environmental archaeology is rooted in two sciences: earth science and ecology. An archaeological site or region must be understood in its context. The geology and the ecology of the region control the landscape, hydrology, arable

G

land, soil fertility and vegetation, and mineral and potable-water resources. The ecology also reflects the climate. Paleontology (both micro and macro), a branch of geology, provides archaeologists with much of the detail needed for paleoclimatic and paleoenvironmental reconstructions. Fossils highly sensitive to environmental change were encapsulated in the sedimentary record, along with the other products of geological processes and human activities. Human activities since the beginnings of agriculture and complex societies have had a major effect on the Earth's surface.

Changing depositional environments, geomorphical contexts, and climatological processes are valuable devices for evaluating both spatial and temporal patterns of human behavior. To a large extent, the visibility of an artifact accumulation will depend on the patterns of landscape development with which it is associated.

The influence humans have had on geomorphic features is directly connected to the types of behavior humans employed to adapt to, and function in, their environment. Agriculture, in particular, has had a major impact on landscape development because it disturbs the natural hydrological, pedogenic, and sedimentological processes that affect the landscape. The consequences of human construction activities have direct effects on the soil/sediment system primarily by modifying the drainage of water. Many of these features are still recognizable. Terraces, dams, and irrigation ditches used to increase moisture retention also cause the accumulation of sediments. Roads and paths can lead to increased erosion, and buildings concentrate runoff, increasing erosion. The construction of burial mounds, the accumulation of tell debris and middens, and mining and quarrying all affect geomorphical process well beyond their perimeters.

Patterns of Holocene erosion and deposition linked to human landscape modification are also set down in the sedimentological record of lakes. The biological, mineralogical, and chemical components of lake sediments have been used to infer human activities. Mesolithic and Neolithic landscape use during the mid-Holocene in Britain led to increases in fine-grained clastics and salt concentrations, which were associated with the decrease in forests. Pollen diagrams from lake sediments are routinely used to trace patterns of land clearance and cultivation.

Isotopic signals contained in marine sediment and ice-core sequences record the global climatic changes for the time interval associated with the archaeological record. The isotopic signals can be related to relative sea-level changes and alternating periods of colder global climate (*glacials*) and warmer climate (*interglacials*). Evidence for these alternating glacial and interglacial periods and even finer-scaled environmental/climatic intervals are also contained in the continental stratigraphic record.

The time framework of *geoarchaeology* extends from the present back through hominid evolution. The spatial scale encompasses essentially the whole range between the *atomic* of trace-element analysis and the *global* of climate change. And the range of disciplinary expertise is almost as broad as the full spectrum of the combined fields of archaeology and earth science.

George R. Rapp Jr.

See also GRAIN-SIZE ANALYSIS; HOLMES, WILLIAM HENRY; PETROGRAPHY; PHYTOLITH ANALYSIS; SOIL AND SEDIMENT ANALYSIS

Further Readings

Butzer, K.W. (1982) Archaeology as Human Ecology. Cambridge: Cambridge University Press.

Rapp, G., Jr., and Gifford, J.A., eds. (1982) Troy: The Archaeological Geology. (Troy Supplementary Monograph 4). Princeton, NJ: Princeton University Press.

Rapp, G., Jr., and Gifford, J.A., eds. (1985) Archaeological Geology. New Haven, CT: Yale University Press.

Rosen, A.M. (1986) Cities of Clay. Chicago: University of Chicago Press.

Stein, J.K., and Farrand, W.R., eds. (1985) Archaeological Sediments in Context. Orono, ME: Center for the Study of Early Man, Institute for Quaternary Studies, University of Maine.

Waters, M.R. (1992) Principles of Geoarchaeology: A North American Perspective. Tucson: University of Arizona Press.

Geographic Information Systems

Computer software for managing, analyzing, and manipulating spatially distributed information. Geographic information systems (GIS) are a collection of interrelated computer programs designed for the handling and processing of mappable data. The spatial link allows capabilities not found in other computer software, such as traditional database management systems (DBMS): A variety of social, environmental, land use, and other data sets may be compared at the same points on the ground, and the results of queries, searches, analyses, or modeling efforts can be displayed in map form, providing ready visualization of data in the spatial domain. Indeed, it is the synergism that results from the association between data and location that gives GIS their special character and that has promoted their adoption in geographically oriented disciplines. This is particularly true of archaeology, in which sites are spatially distributed within regions, and artifacts and features are located within sites.

Software and Hardware Components

The unique capabilities of GIS are derived from the interaction of four software components: (1) data-input systems for capturing spatially distributed information from maps, photographs, or remote sensors; (2) geographically organized data storage and retrieval programs that allow rapid access and display of information and provide basic editing functions; (3) data analysis and manipulation routines for transforming, overlaying, and aggregating information, for generating new data, and for providing statistical summaries and modeling capabilities; and (4) reporting systems that can display all or part of the database in the form of maps, but also as tables, charts, and graphs. It is the union of these four components that defines GIS. Other computer software, such as DBMS or computer-assisted drafting (CAD), typically lacks one or more of these elements.

GIS software has been written for every type of computer platform, from low-cost microcomputers, to workstations, to mainframes. Regardless of the computing environment, large disk capacity is necessary because complex spatial data sets from large regions can require significant space. A high-resolution color-graphics monitor is essential for displaying cartographic output, and a high-speed CPU is desirable to reduce the time it takes to process complex instructions and large data files.

Because the focus of GIS is on mappable information, specialized input and output devices are required. The most common input devices are coordinate digitizers and optical scanners, which convert map graphics into digital form. Digital map data may also be purchased from private businesses that specialize in data capture or from many government mapping agencies.

Output devices include line, dot-matrix, or laser printers for black-and-white (more accurately, gray-scale) graphics. Color ink-jet, wax or thermal printers are essential for solid-fill color rendering, while the pen-plotter remains the standard for color and black-and-white line-drawn maps.

Fundamental Concepts

There are a number of concepts fundamental to an understanding of GIS. Each map or spatial-data source can be regarded as a distinct *layer* of information in a database region. Map layers are coregistered to each other such that the spatial coordinates in one coincide with those of the other layers. Data layers can be derived from digitized paper maps, manually keyed-in information with spatial coordinates, scanned aerial photographs, or satellite imagery. *Primary layers* refer to the digital equivalences of the original thematic coverages for a region (e.g., hydrology, soils, roads, elevation contours, satellite imagery). The processing power of the computer and the flexibility of GIS software allow *secondary layers* to be derived analytically from the primary data. For example, digital elevation contours can be processed by interpolation programs to yield an elevation surface in which altitudes are estimated systematically at a regular spacing across the database region. This layer, in turn, can be used to generate a gradient surface that contains ground-steepness measurements. Distance programs can generate a distance-to-water layer from digitized lake, river, and stream locations. Such secondary information often is of more use than the original primary layers.

In cartography, map features are typically displayed using three concepts: points, lines, and areas. *Points* portray such features as a mountain peak, a surveyor's datum, or a town on a small-scale map. *Line* features represent entities such as roads, rivers, and elevation contours. The *area* concept (also referred to as *polygon*) is used to encompass regions of homogeneity, such as a forest, a lake, or a property parcel.

Vector GIS refer to systems that possess data structures and display capabilities closely

G

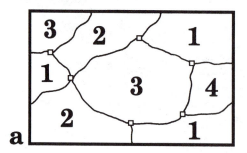 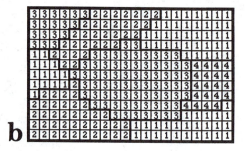

Figure 1. (a) vector and (b) raster representations of the area or polygon data type. In vector format, arcs (black lines) are represented by a sequence of spatial coordinates while nodes (hollow boxes) are the intersection points of three or more arcs. The numbers represent the attribute codes. Figure by Kenneth Kvamme.

allied to these fundamental cartographic types. The spatial x,y-coordinates representing point, line, and area features are referred to as *topology,* which are data distinct from *attributes* that describe characteristics of the features. A lake, for example, is represented by a sequence of coordinates (the topology) that denote the location of its perimeter, plus an attribute label identifying it as "lake."

Most vector GIS employ an arc-node data structure (Figure 1). *Arcs* are line segments (consisting of coordinate sequences), while *nodes* represent arc end-points or points where three or more arcs intersect. The area data type is represented by multiple arcs that completely enclose a region; a line contains one or more arcs that do not necessarily enclose an area; a point is a free-standing node. A simple relational DBMS is employed to store and retrieve these entities as needed.

Raster GIS represent a conceptually different way in which spatial information is encoded, managed, and manipulated. In these systems, a grid is superimposed over the database region, and, within each grid element, a code is stored that describes what occurs in that cell. Topology is controlled by row and column position, while the cell values are the attributes in any given layer. A soils layer will contain soils codes, elevation-layer altitude measurements, and distance-to-water layer distance values. Cell size controls spatial resolution and accuracy and influences storage requirements, which can be enormous if regions are large and cell sizes small. Storage needs are greatly reduced in spatially redundant layers (e.g., soils polygons with similar attributes codes over broad areas) through use of data compaction schemes, however. Some raster systems employ a *quadtree* data structure, which

allows more efficient retrieval of individual data elements and compact storage. This is achieved through a hierarchical organization in which a region is partitioned into quadrants, in successive stages of increasing resolution, until the detail required of a feature, or the minimum defined cell size, is reached.

Vector GIS are essential whenever great accuracy is needed in portraying spatial location, such as with property parcels, or in computing area and perimeter data. They are also ideal for regional database applications because individual arcs and nodes can be linked with data elements in a relational DBMS, allowing the instantaneous display of maps showing the results of searches and queries. The *vector* data structure is ideal for the construction of maps in a traditional line-drawn format composed of point, line, and area features, and vector systems are best suited for the analysis of travel times or flow through network structures, such as road or hydrologic systems.

Owing to their grid cell structure, raster GIS are spatially less precise, causing the display of point, line, or area entities to suffer from a jagged, or stair-step, appearance and inaccurate area and perimeter estimates. On the other hand, spatial data sets such as satellite imagery, aerial photographs, geophysical survey data, and continuous surfaces (e.g., interpolated elevation data) occur naturally within a raster structure and are best displayed as continuous-tone imagery (gray or color shading in contiguous grid cells). Raster GIS tend to be better suited for the numerical processing of spatial data and are the preferred systems for most spatial analysis and modeling applications.

Most GIS software is either vector or raster, but, typically, limited functionality is allowed in the other domain. Raster or vector

GIS may allow road or stream vectors, or archaeological site polygons, to be superimposed over a raster backdrop in the form of a shaded relief map, for example. In any case, the conversion of point, line, and area features from vector to raster formats, or vice versa, is a common capability.

Fundamental Operations

There are a series of operations that are fundamental to most GIS. One is *map reclassification*. This is a form of data generalization in which the number of class categories (unique attribute labels) in a layer is reduced. Ten soils classes might be simplified to only three, for example, denoting "poor," "moderate," and "good" soils for agriculture. *Map overlaying* shows the co-occurrence of all categories in two or more layers. If classes A, B, C, and D occur in one layer, and a, b, and c in a second, then the result will map the intersection of all possible combinations: Aa, Ab, Ac, Ba, Bb, Bc, Ca, Cb, Cc, Da, Db, Dc.

Map algebra is peculiar to raster GIS and forms the basis of most modeling operations. It refers to the application of simple algebraic rules to entire map layers on a grid cell–by–grid cell basis. The operations include the traditional algebraic definitions of addition, subtraction, multiplication, division, and exponentiation, and such functions as the square root, logarithmic, and trigonometric. To illustrate, the simple operation "newlayer = 0.3048*oldlayer," where "oldlayer" contains elevations in feet and "*" means "multiply," will create elevations scaled in meters held in "newlayer." A more complex operation might consider several layers as input, as in "newlayer = layer1 + layer2 + layer3," where the layers on the right side represent artifact counts per grid square for early, middle, and late periods, respectively, and "newlayer" contains the resultant sum or total artifact count. Map-algebra techniques also include a series of operations unique to GIS. These typically include *minimum* (each grid cell in the new layer receives the lowest value in that cell in two or more input layers), *maximum* (as above, but the largest value is assigned), *average* (the mean of the inputs), *diversity* (the number of different input values per cell), and *cover* (nonzero grid cells in one layer overwrite grid cells in a second layer).

Boolean techniques allow the application of "true-false" or Boolean logic to map layers encoded in binary form (where the numeral 1 represents true and 0 indicates false). The principal operations include *unions* (the OR operation), *intersections* (the AND operation), and *negation* (the NOT operation). To illustrate, let **W** represent the event "near water" (e.g., every location within 1 km of a water source) and **S** the event "good soil." Then the statement "newlayer = **W** will map those locations in a region near water (as 1; 0 otherwise), and "newlayer = NOT(**W**)" will map the complementary condition, locations far from water. The union of locations near water, on good soil, or both, is achieved by "newlayer = **W** OR **S**," while "newlayer = **W** AND **S**" maps the intersection that includes only locations close to water and with good soils simultaneously. Boolean methods frequently are used as a basis for spatial decision models.

Distance operations utilize a layer in which discrete entities are defined as *targets*. In raster systems, the Euclidean distance from each grid cell to the nearest target is computed, yielding a *distance surface*. In vector GIS, zones with perimeters an equidistance from the nearest target are defined, producing *distance buffers,* which are represented by the area data type. In raster systems, a simple reclassification of a distance surface into zones of fixed distance may be used to generate distance buffers. Fixed distance buffers around archaeological settlements provide an easy means for defining catchment territories.

The fundamental operations provide a set of powerful tools for the manipulation of spatial data. In a regional analysis or modeling context, a sequence of these operations typically is followed to achieve a desired result. It is through this combination of operations that the real power of GIS is realized.

Image-Processing Software

Raster GIS readily allow the manipulation of pixel-based or gridded data, such as satellite imagery, scanned photography, or geophysical-prospection data sets. As a consequence, image-processing software typically exists in raster systems for the registration of images to database coordinate systems, for contrast enhancement, and for other imaging techniques, such as filtering, smoothing, and edge detection. Moreover, supervised and unsupervised classification programs are

G

provided in order that imagery may be interpreted into mappable land cover classes.

The DEM and Its Products

The digital elevation model (DEM) is simply a layer containing ground-surface altitudes (Figure 2). They may be created through GIS by digitizing known elevation data (e.g., contour lines) and subsequently processing these data with interpolation programs, which yield estimates of altitude throughout the region in the form of a surface. In raster GIS, each grid cell contains an altitude. Vector systems employ a variable-resolution triangulated irregular network (TIN), in which the ground surface is represented by a mosaic of triangles with known elevation points located at the vertices. In landscape sciences, including archaeology, the DEM is extremely important because it provides a means to visualize the terrain form of a region, and GIS, with rotatable, three-dimensional color views, are ideal for this. Most GIS allow cross-sectioning of surfaces, providing a means to

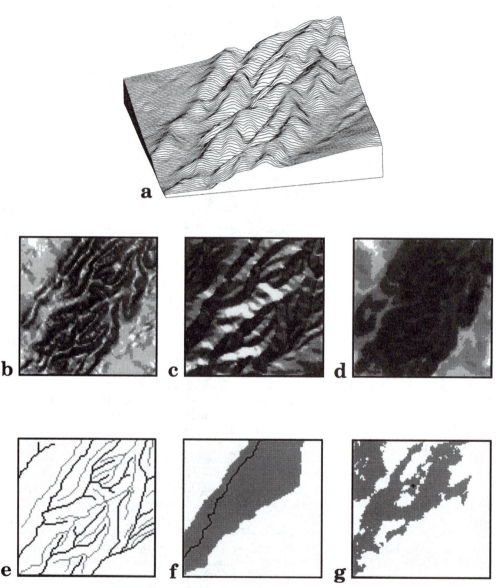

Figure 2. (a) the digital elevation model and its products: (b) slope, (c) aspect, (d) local relief, (e) ridge and drainage lines, (f) the watershed of a drainage, and (g) a viewshed from the indicated locus. Figure by Kenneth Kvamme.

generate profiles through terrain, as well as relief shading of the ground surface with variable positioning of the light source.

It is possible to derive from the DEM a variety of landform and other data types that often are of more use than the DEM itself. These secondary layers may be functions of *local neighborhoods* (making use of adjacent data values), which include slope (ground steepness), aspect (direction of sloping ground), ridge-line, and drainage-basin data. *Extended neighborhood* terrain operations (which use data from a larger region) yield more diverse forms of landscape information. With a fixed inclusion radius of large size, the range or the variance of the elevations in the neighborhood can be computed. The former yields a surface known as *relief,* which is a useful means for examining relative changes in the height of a group of hills or the depth of a canyon, for example. The latter provides a measure of terrain variability, or *texture. Watersheds* may be defined by determining all locations that drain into a specified locus. A related concept is that of a *viewshed,* which includes all locations visible from a point or points.

Archaeological Application Areas

As GIS technology has become increasingly consolidated within archaeology, certain trends have emerged. Most applications have occurred in the area of regional or national databases of sites and monuments records, and this dominance will increase in the future. This is a natural evolution from paper records and aspatial DBMS formats. GIS allow maps of archaeological sites, monuments, and find spots (e.g., regions threatened by development or destruction) to be quickly generated, greatly assisting archaeologists, managers, planners, and governmental decision makers in their tasks. Such regional databases are of great use to researchers as well, because they provide an easy means to extract what is known about the archaeology of a region.

Much interest in the analytical capabilities of GIS has also been generated by archaeologists. Viewshed analyses have been used to locate archaeological-park boundaries with respect to the visibility of ruins and monuments. More common, GIS have been employed in regional studies to examine samples of archaeological sites for patterns and associations with such environmental factors as elevation, slope, aspect, relief, soils, geology, or

distance-to-water classes. In these studies, GIS visualization tools play a large role, but so, too, do quantitative statistical approaches.

Cost surfaces, typically derived from DEM and other environmental data, have received considerable attention. They attempt to measure the cumulative cost of travel outward from a defined point or points based on the nature of terrain form and land cover, which are regarded as *frictional* effects offering variable impedance to movement. Cost-of-movement surfaces relate to land accessibility and have provided more realistic alternatives to simple circular catchments in settlement-location studies.

GIS-based predictive locational models are a major focus of archaeological activity (Figure 3). The purpose of a predictive model is to make indications in map form of the likelihood of archaeological finds in a region, generally for cultural-resource management and planning purposes. Such models can be used to guide land-disturbing activities away from, or future research toward, archaeologically sensitive localities. The methodology requires the examination of known archaeological-site samples for statistical associations with various environmental or other mappable conditions. Decision rules on any variable may then be calibrated against the known site samples and the results combined through Boolean or map-algebra techniques to yield locational models. Alternatively, multivariate discriminant functions provide a particularly robust solution that can be used to estimate the probability of site occurrence at individual locations (provided that the initial sample was gained through random sampling). GIS are necessary for procuring appropriate environmental data at a location and processing it through the model decision rule to yield a prediction for or against archaeological finds. This process is repeated location by location to produce model decision surfaces. Independent archaeological samples are then used to test and assess model performance.

The large focus by archaeologists on aspects of the physical environment has raised the criticism that GIS have a built-in bias toward this domain, but it is a simple fact that environmental maps tend to be available for a region, while data pertaining to prehistoric social landscapes often are not. Nevertheless, a number of studies have analyzed prehistoric distributions with respect to contemporary central-place villages and road networks, for example, and intersettlement-visibility studies

G

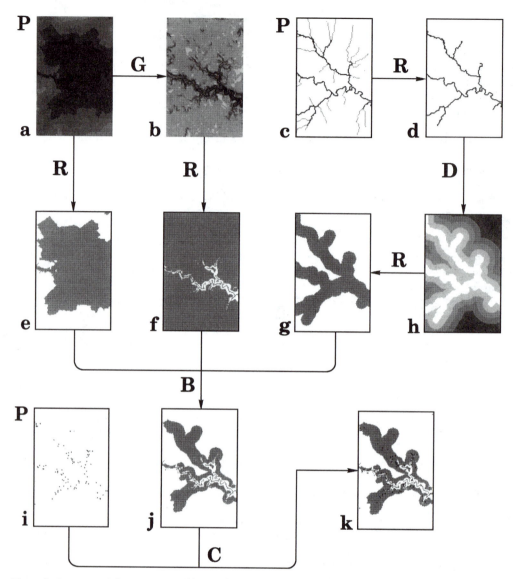

Figure 3. A sequence of operations and layers that might be used in the development of a model of archaeological-site suitability, based on the assumption that sites tend to occur at low elevation, on level ground, and close to permanent sources of water. The primary (P) layers are (a) elevation, (c) hydrology, and (i) known archaeological sites. A reclass (R) operation applied to the elevation data yields (e) a low elevation zone. A gradient (G) operation on the elevation surface yields (b) a slope layer that is reclassified to map (f) level ground. The initial hydrologic network is reclassified to indicate (d) permanent water only, which is subjected to a distance (D) operation, yielding (h) a distance-to-permanent-water surface. This layer then is reclassified to form (g) fixed-distance buffers around permanent water. The (j) archaeological location model is formed by the Boolean (B) "AND" operation applied to layers e, f, and g. Finally, the cover (C) operation is employed to superimpose (i) the known archaeological sites over the model to allow (k) an assessment of model performance or fit. Figure by Kenneth Kvamme.

have provided a means to examine this dimension of the social landscape.

There are many aspects of GIS that remain to be exploited by archaeologists, including three-dimensional GIS for investigating within-site structure, the incorporation of geophysical data sets with other forms of information (e.g., crop marks, surface artifact distributions, DEM data) for comprehensive site-exploration data sets, and the use of GIS representations of landform and land cover as a background for more realistic computer simulations at the regional level. The archaeological potential of GIS in the future, therefore, remains great.

Kenneth L. Kvamme

See also COMPUTERS IN ARCHAEOLOGY

Further Readings

Allen, K.M.S., Green, S.W., and Zubrow, E.B.W., eds. (1990) Interpreting Space: GIS and Archaeology. London: Taylor and Francis.

Andresen, J., Madsen, T., and Scollar, I., eds. (1993) Computing the Past: Computer Applications and Quantitative Methods in Archaeology, CAA92. Aarhus: Aarhus University Press.

Brandt, R., Groenewoudt, B.J., and Kvamme, K.L. (1992) An experiment in archaeological site location: Modeling in the Netherlands using GIS techniques. World Archaeology 24:268–282.

Gaffney, V., and Stancic, Z. (1991) GIS Approaches to Regional Analysis: A Case Study of the Island of Hvar. Ljubljana: Znanstveni Institut Filozofske Fakultete.

Kvamme, K.L. (1989) Geographic information systems in regional archaeological research and data management. In M.B. Schiffer (ed.): Archaeological Method and Theory, vol. 1, pp. 139–203. Tucson: University of Arizona Press.

Larsen, C.U., ed. (1992) Sites and Monuments: National Archaeological Records. Copenhagen: National Museum of Denmark.

Georadar

A geophysical method that employs relatively high-frequency electromagnetic waves to obtain images of the subsurface. The term *radar* is an acronym for **ra**dio **d**etection **a**nd **r**anging. In ground-penetrating radar (georadar, also known as GPR or electromagnetic subsurface profiling [ESP]), the antennae are moved across stationary underground targets. The method is relatively new compared to other prospecting methods, and, although the underlying theory is well understood and the basic equipment is available commercially (Figure 1), further rapid development is ongoing. Since georadar is capable of providing high-resolution information, it is a potentially powerful tool for archaeological investigations.

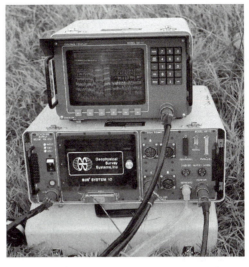

Figure 1. Digital radar equipment, known as the SIR-10. It consists of a monitor, a computer with special hardware, and the antennae. Photograph by Jürg Leckebusch.

Most geophysical prospecting methods employed in archaeology detect changes of a physical property in the subsurface. Information about the depth, shape, and thickness of archaeological features is generally possible only with time-consuming measurements and complex signal processing or modeling. In contrast, reflected radar waves can provide this information relatively directly.

History

The theoretical basis for georadar measurements has been known since 1910; with the development of new electronics in the 1960s, ground-penetrating radar became practical. In the early systems, single radar scans were displayed on cathode-ray oscilloscopes. By the 1970s, georadar profiles were recorded on paper. The application of georadar to archaeological investigations was realized early in the development of the method. However, it was only with the development of small portable computers with large digital data storage capabilities that the method could be applied generally for resolving archaeological problems.

Basic Theory

Three fundamental physical parameters appear in the electromagnetic-wave equations that describe georadar propagation: *relative magnetic permeability, relative electrical permittivity* (dielectric number or constant), and *electrical conductivity*. For nearly all practical archaeological applications, the effect of magnetic permeability can be ignored; relative permittivity and electrical conductivity control, respectively, radar-wave velocity and attenuation.

The velocity v of a georadar wave in a medium with relatively low electrical conductivity is given by:

$$v = \frac{c}{\sqrt{\varepsilon}}$$

where c is the velocity of light in a vacuum (~0.3 m/ns; 1 ns = 10^{-9} s), and ε is the relative permittivity of the medium. In dry soils, ε varies from ca. 3 to ca. 12, corresponding to a velocity range of 0.17–0.086 m/ns; in wet soils, ε may attain values exceeding 30, corresponding to velocities of less than 0.055 m/ns.

Given a georadar signal with input frequency f, the corresponding wavelength λ may be computed as follows:

$$\lambda = \frac{v}{f} = \frac{c}{f\sqrt{\varepsilon}}$$

Wavelength is a measure of the resolution that can be obtained, such that shorter-wavelength (i.e., higher-frequency) signals provide higher resolution. Simultaneously, however, depth of penetration decreases. In practice, the desired resolution must be weighed against the desired depth of penetration; as for all geophysical techniques, there is an inevitable trade-off between resolution and penetration depth.

Georadar frequencies overlap the radio frequency bands (10 kHz–10 GHz) and are close to the microwave frequency bands (4–100 GHz). For example, the center frequency and bandwidth of antennae used in commercial georadar systems vary from 12.5 MHz to ca. 2 GHz. A high center frequency of 300–500 MHz is generally used in archaeological prospecting, since the objects of interest are usually near the surface and often small. In theory, a georadar pulse with dominant wavelength λ has the potential to resolve features separated by greater than $\lambda/4$ in the vertical direction, or features separated by greater than $(\lambda z/2)^{1/2}$ in the horizontal direction, where z is the depth to the target of interest.

A simple example will help clarify some of the points described above. The wavelength of a 400-MHz georadar wave traveling through sandy soil with velocity 0.12 m/ns is 0.30 m. From the above relationships, the limit of vertical resolution for such a wave is 0.075 m, and the limit of horizontal resolution at 1-m depth is 0.38 m. This means that two objects greater than 0.075 m apart in a vertical direction, or greater than 0.38 m apart in a horizontal direction, have the potential to be distinguished from each other.

The transmission and reflection of georadar waves may be described by equations similar to those used in optics and elastic-wave theory. The reflection coefficient R is a measure of the reflected energy. A near-vertical-incident radar ray at a boundary between two low-conductivity media has a reflection coefficient given by:

$$R = \frac{\sqrt{\varepsilon_1} - \sqrt{\varepsilon_2}}{\sqrt{\varepsilon_1} + \sqrt{\varepsilon_2}}$$

where the indices 1 and 2 refer to the two media. It is clear from this relationship that the strength of a radar reflection and, therefore, the detectability of a buried object is dependent primarily on the relative-permittivity contrasts with the surrounding soils.

Perhaps the most serious limitation of the georadar method is the strong attenuation or absorption that occurs in media characterized by high electrical conductivities. Since the electrical conductivity of soils increases significantly as the clay and water content increases, it follows that the depth penetration of georadar waves may be severely restricted in regions covered by wet clays. In clay-free soils, reflections of 300–500 MHz georadar waves may be expected from depths as great as 5–10 m; in clay-rich soils, depth penetration may be limited to only a few tens of centimeters. When clay is present in the underground, it is advisable to conduct georadar surveys during relatively dry periods.

When interpreting georadar images, the three-dimensional aspects of the subsurface must be considered. Although georadar data are generally collected along two-dimensional profiles, the receiver antenna may record returned signals from a large volume distributed about a profile. With only single-profile information, energy arriving from outside of the vertical plane containing the profile may be misinterpreted as reflected energy from beneath the profile. Interpretation of single georadar profiles may, therefore, be highly ambiguous. To avoid uncertainties, the prospectors should record either a series of parallel, or a number of crossing, profiles.

Equipment and Measurement Techniques

The equipment used for georadar prospecting comprises transmitting and receiving antennae, an electronic control console that includes amplifiers and filters, a computer with appropriate data storage capacity, and a power supply (Figure 1). The commonly employed antennae have radiation angles of ca. 60°–120°. This angle can be minimized by moving the antennae directly on the surface. An antenna is composed, typically, of an electromagnetic dipole, which responds to changes in properties both below and above it. For sensitive underground studies, the antennae should be shielded against disturbances from above. The antennae are connected to the electronic control console by either shielded metallic or fiber optic cables. The latter are less sensitive to electrical disturbances, but systems connected by fiber optic cables require separate power supplies for the antennae.

There are two basic profiling techniques: *monostatic* and *bistatic*. For monostatic measurements, the coincident antennae act as both the transmitter and the receiver, so that the incident and reflected waves travel along the same path. Separate transmitter and receiver antennae are employed in bistatic profiling. It should be noted that wave propagation paths may be changed by increasing the distance between the two antennae, so that the influence of near-surface features is reduced. Since it is these features that are of interest in archaeology, the monostatic technique is generally used (Figure 2).

The quality of recorded data is dependent on the noise of the amplifiers. Signal quality can be improved by stacking or summing the records of consecutive pulses; the quality (signal-to-noise ratio) improves by a factor of

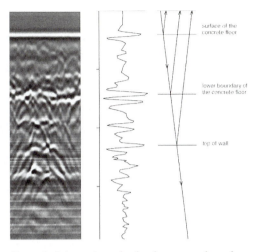

Figure 2. Schematic path of radar rays and an observed radar scan from a measurement in a church. On the right side are the archaeological structures responsible for the reflections of the radar wave. Figure by Jürg Leckebusch.

$\sqrt{n}$, where n is the number of records stacked.

When using georadar systems with limited dynamic range and storage capacity, the gain functions, time scales, and filter settings need to be established for each survey. This is best achieved by surveying areas with and without anomalies. Although this setup procedure is time consuming, it is necessary to ensure optimum results (Figure 3).

Since the actual time required for a single measurement is short, a continuous profile can be recorded relatively quickly by pulling the antennae along a line. This is often achieved by mounting the antennae on a frame connected to a vehicle. During registration, short pulses are generated, and the related responses

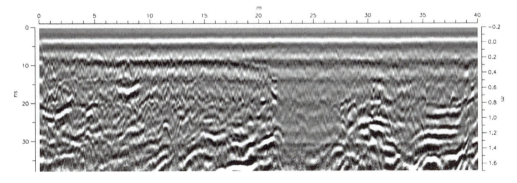

Figure 3. Ground-penetrating radar profile across an early medieval village (Unterstammheim, Ömdwiesen). The areas having low-amplitude reflections (medium gray values) represent two "Grubenhäuser" (pit houses), dug out of the surrounding gravel. The entire profile is 40 meters long. Figure by Jürg Leckebusch.

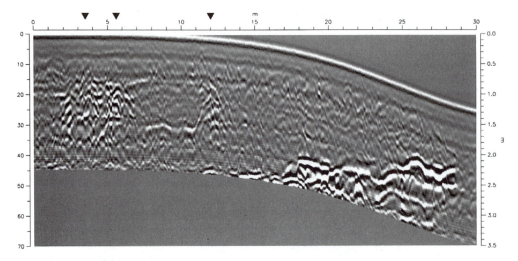

Figure 4. Ground-penetrating-radar profile across an Iron Age settlement (Rheinau, Au). Ditches marked by arrowheads appear as inhomogeneities in the soil. At the base of the figure are signals originating from a horizontal gravel layer. Figure by Jürg Leckebusch.

recorded. Generally, only single profiles are collected. However, profiles can be collected at regular intervals, so that three-dimensional subsurface images may be constructed.

Data Processing

The geometries of subsurface structures recorded by georadar equipment are affected by several different mechanisms, which must be compensated for by appropriate data-processing procedures. Many georadar processing procedures are similar to those developed by the hydrocarbon-exploration industry for processing of seismic reflection data. A typical georadar processing flow chart is shown in the accompanying Table.

Before a georadar profile can be treated, the data have to be transferred from the field recording system to the processing system, and the data format suitably transformed. Each profile should then be adjusted to have the same length scale, which, in practice, requires that each profile have the same number of scans (traces) per meter. Simple linear interpolation is usually adequate for transforming data recorded at constant time intervals to constant spatial intervals.

Amplitudes of the data are adjusted to yield uniform average signal levels over the length of the recording window, and, if required, the data are frequency filtered to remove unwanted noise and improve the signal waveform (see Table below). Corrections are

Georadar Data-Processing Scheme

1.	Transfer Data (field system to processing system)
2.	Transform Data Format (field-recording to processing-system format)
3.	Data Interpolation
4.	Amplitude Gain
5.	Frequency Filter*
6.	Static Corrections
7.	Velocity Analysis/Time-to-Depth Conversion
8.	Deconvolution*
9.	Migration*
10.	Display

Typical georadar data processing scheme. The order of the processing may be changed to suit the individual data sets. * shows optional processing procedures.

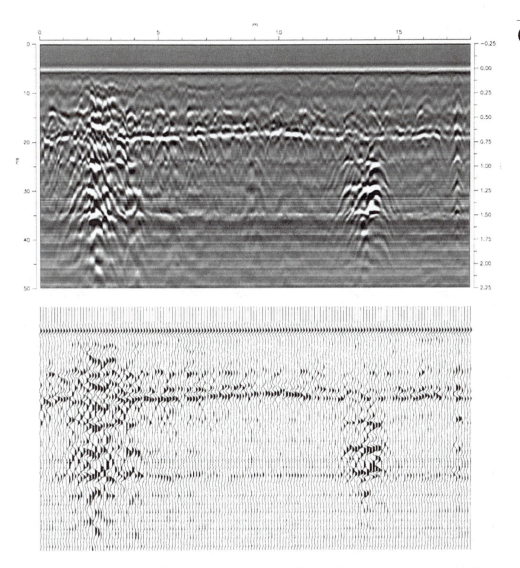

Figure 5. Representation of a profile data set, as a wiggle-variable area plot (bottom) and as a gray-scale image (top). Generally, the human eye can resolve more details in the gray-scale image. These data were recorded in a church (Predigerkirche, Zurich) that is underlain by the walls of an older church. Figure by Jürg Leckebusch.

then required to compensate for elevation variations along and between profiles. Surface topography can have a significant effect on the form of imaged structures. For example, without these *static* corrections, horizontal boundaries beneath sloping surfaces would appear as dipping reflections. A good example of a static-corrected georadar section is shown in Figure 4.

The vertical scale of a georadar section is often shown as two-way-travel time, which is the time required for a radar wave to travel from the surface to a reflecting feature and back to the surface again (Figure 2). An impor-

tant processing step involves transforming the vertical time scale in nanoseconds into an equivalent depth scale in meters. To perform this time-to-depth conversion, information on the variation of radar velocity with depth is required. Georadar velocities commonly depend on soil composition, particle size, and water content, all of which can vary significantly with depth and position along a profile. There are various methods for determining radar velocities. One straightforward approach involves comparing the times observed on georadar sections with measured depths on exposed cross-sections (e.g., in trenches) or in drill holes.

A second, more common method requires a special field procedure in which data are recorded continuously as two antennae are simultaneously moved away from a common center point. In this manner, the travel times (t) to the reflecting features increase with increasing distance (x) between the antennae. For relatively flat-flying features, the resultant t versus x curve is a hyperbola. Velocities may be estimated by either fitting hyperbolae to the t versus x data or more simply by fitting straight lines to the t^2 versus x^2 data. Other processing schemes (e.g., velocity spectra) for determining velocities are described in reflection seismology textbooks.

Processing steps eight and nine in the Table are specialized procedures that are applied infrequently to georadar data. *Deconvolution* operators are a class of filter designed to remove the effects of multiple reflections and harmonic noise and to sharpen the signal pulse. Multiple reflections occur when energy is trapped between two strongly reflecting boundaries, one of which is often the free surface. Features underlying such boundaries may be difficult to resolve in the presence of multiple reflections. *Migration* is an operation that removes various "artifacts" that are a function of the data recording geometry and size, shape and location of underground structures. Diffraction hyperbolae generated by relatively small isolated features (e.g., small metal objects) or by the edges of flat reflecting boundaries (e.g., a buried wall) are examples of artifacts that may be removed by migration.

Georadar data can be displayed in several forms. They can be plotted as simple graphs of radar reflection signal versus time (*wiggle trace representation*), or as graphs with either the positive or the negative radar reflections shaded (*wiggle-variable area plot;* Figure 4). Software packages available for georadar data processing also provide output in color, such that varying amplitudes in the signal are represented by different colors. The greater the range of colors, the more details are visible. The same applies for gray-scale representations (Figure 5).

Applications
Georadar measurements have been used for a wide variety of purposes, including civil engineering and geological/hydrological investigations, metal-drum and waste-disposal detec-

tion, and even murder inquiries. To employ the method for archaeological studies, it is necessary to have a contrast in relative permittivity between the buried objects of interest and the host soils. Archaeological features that often meet this criterion include stone walls, ditches, grave sites, wooden artifacts, and many other items that interrupt the natural soil profile. Examples of georadar data recorded across archaeological sites are represented in Figures 3–7. All examples are from the Canton of Zurich, Switzerland, and most aspects of the interpretations have been confirmed by excavation.

The first example shows the results of a georadar survey conducted over medieval pit houses (Grubenhäuser) that were built into a near-surface layer of gravel (Figure 3). Subsequently, relatively homogeneous soils filled the pit houses. As is often observed in agricultural regions, the depth of ploughing is clearly seen on the georadar image (here at ca. 8 ns). At locations 22–30 m and 32–38 m, reflections associated with the gravel layer are disrupted by the pit houses, and there is a marked decrease in reflected energy from the homogeneous fill. Depths to the base of the reflection-free zones in both houses decrease to the right, perhaps indicating entrance locations.

Former ditches may appear either more reflective or less reflective than the surrounding soils. Examples of reflective ditches, possibly containing boulders and man-made artifacts, within nonreflective homogeneous soils are marked by arrowheads in Figure 4. Georadar profiles collected along parallel lines have allowed the geometry and extent of these Iron Age constructions to be mapped. Strong horizontal reflections on the lower right of the figure are generated by a gravel layer. These reflections are truncated by an opaque zone that delineates the location of a buried river channel, which is also plainly observed on aerial photographs.

Well-shielded antennae allow measurements to be taken inside buildings. Results of measurements recorded in a city church are shown in Figure 5. Georadar waves have penetrated the existing church's concrete floor to reveal the walls of an underlying older church, one at 1.8–3.2 m (the top of this wall is at a depth of ~0.25 m) and one at 13–14.1 m (top at ~0.9 m). The base of the concrete floor, clearly visible as a coherent reflection at 20 ns, is intersected by the left wall. Radar penetra-

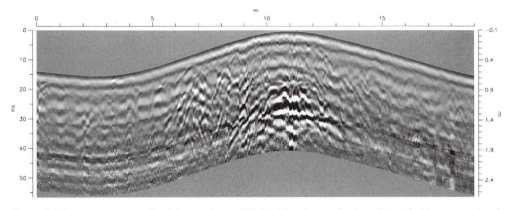

Figure 6. Measurement over a burial mound on a hill (Uetliberg) near the city of Zurich. The strong signals in the middle suggest a central burial chamber, probably dating to the Early Iron Age. Figure by Jürg Leckebusch.

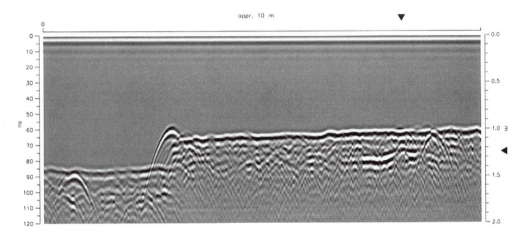

Figure 7. Tests over a Bronze Age lake settlement (Greifensee, Böschen) with a layer of archaeological significance visible as strong reflections to the right, compared to the previously excavated area to the left. The border of the excavation is marked by an iron pipe having the characteristic form of a hyperbole. At the lake floor a wooden post within the cultural layer is discernible to the right. Figure by Jürg Leckebusch.

tion through this concrete floor was possible only because it is not reinforced with metal; metallic objects are perfect reflectors that shield underlying structures. Other georadar profiles collected in the church have demonstrated the lack of an expected apse in the middle of the underlying older church but have suggested the existence of an unrecorded altar.

Burial mounds are topographic features that often entail the application of significant static corrections. Figure 6 shows a static-corrected georadar profile recorded across the center of a burial mound probably dating to the early Iron Age. Distinctive high-amplitude reflections at 10–12 m (depth ~0.8 m) are unlikely to be caused by natural features. Equiv-

alent high-amplitude reflections on a corresponding perpendicular profile extend over a greater length than those shown in Figure 6. These high-amplitude reflections are confidently interpreted to mark the position of a central burial chamber.

Georadar data may also be recorded across bodies of fresh water; floating antennae are pulled along the surface of the water. The results of a georadar test conducted across a portion of a sunken Bronze Age lake settlement are shown in Figure 7. In comparison to the deeper region of the lake, which has already been excavated (left part of the figure), layers of archaeological significance remain in the shallower regions (center and right portions of figure). On and near the floor of the deeper region are hyperbolic-shaped reflections generated by boulders and lumps of soil left by the divers involved with the excavation. Diffraction patterns are also recorded across a modern metal marker (iron pipe) at the boundary between the two depth levels and across a buried wooden post near the right side of the figure (where the two arrowheads would intersect). The wooden post cuts through the cultural layer.

Prospective Use

Since ground-penetrating-radar prospecting is a relatively new method for archaeological investigations, further development and new applications can be expected. Data quality will improve with the development of antennae with smaller radiation angles. Advances are also being made in reducing the weight and size of the control unit. Improvements in the data-processing techniques and interpretation strategies will be made as more experience with the method is acquired. Optimally, it should be possible to construct three-dimensional geo-radar images of archaeological sites either as an alternative to, or as a guide for, excavation.

Jürg Leckebusch
Alan Green

See also ELECTRICAL AND ELECTROMAGNETIC PROSPECTING; SEISMIC REFRACTION SURVEYING

Further Readings

Davies, J.L., and Annan, A.P. (1989) Ground-penetrating radar for high-resolution mapping of soil and rock stratigraphy. Geophysical Prospecting 37:531–551.

Goodman, D., and Nishimura, Y. (1993) A ground-radar view of Japanese burial mounds. Antiquity 67:349–354.

Imai, T., Sakayama, T., and Kanemori, T. (1987) Use of ground-probing radar and resistivity surveys for archaeological investigations. Geophysics 52:137–150.

Scollar, I., Tabbagh, A., Hesse, A., and Herzog, I. (1990) Archaeological Prospecting and Remote Sensing. (Topics in Remote Sensing 2). Cambridge: Cambridge University Press.

Vogel, A., and Tsokas, G.N. (1993) Geophysical Exploration of Archaeological Sites. Wiesbaden: Vieweg and Sohn Verlagsgesellschaft mbH.

Yilmaz, Ö. (1987) Seismic Data Processing. Tulsa, OK: Society of Exploration Geophysicists.

Glass, Characterization

A material consisting primarily of fused silica—together with other substances that modify visual and/or chemicomechanical properties of glass—and used in the manufacture or decoration of objects (glazes and enamels). This entry focuses on the characterization and history of manufactured glass in the archaeological record.

Glass is a highly complex material, the nature of which is not fully understood. However, as a working definition, the material may be regarded as combining "the rigidity of a crystal with the largely random molecular structure of a liquid" (Brill 1963:120). Strictly speaking, one should speak of glasses, rather than glass, since many hundreds of different compositions have been made, and no two have identical structures.

Glass has been described as a super-cooled liquid. This means that, when the crystalline raw materials are heated to a sufficiently high temperature, their crystal structures break down, and subsequent rapid cooling produces a network of randomly ordered atoms whose positions become "frozen" as the glass solidifies. In silicate glasses, this network is composed of silicate chains interspersed with sodium and calcium ions held in the matrix by negatively charged oxygen atoms. In such a glass, the silicate is described as a *network former;* the sodium and calcium ions, as *network modifiers.*

Although today it is possible to make glass from pure silica, this has a melting temperature of more than 1,700°C, too high for ancient technologies. The addition of an alkali, such as soda or potash, to the silica serves as a flux and significantly lowers the melting temperature. However, the resulting glass would not be chemically stable and would rapidly decay. The addition of lime to the mixture renders the glass chemically more stable, and it is this soda-lime-silicate glass that is the first known from the archaeological record.

Such glasses were the standard production of the early glassmakers of Mesopotamia and Egypt. The composition of a typical

Egyptian glass of the fifteenth century B.C. might have been: silica (SiO_2), 65 percent; soda (Na_2O), 20 percent; potash (K_2O), 2 percent; lime (CaO), 8 percent; and minor components, 5 percent. The minor components comprise impurities introduced with the raw materials and additional materials such as colorants and opacifiers.

Subsequently, variations on this basic glass were introduced, such as potash glass, a typical thirteenth-century A.D. composition of which might have been: silica (SiO_2), 53 percent; potash (K_2O), 17 percent; soda (Na_2O), 3 percent; lime (CaO), 12 percent; minor components, 15 percent.

Other, usually later, variants are commonly known by their principal modifier (e.g., lead glass and borax/borosilicate glass). Transparent lead-crystal glass was developed for aesthetic properties, notably its brilliance.

Raw Materials
The most common sources of the raw materials used in glassmaking are summarized below. The chemical formulae given refer to the compounds measured in analyses. The actual raw materials that yield these may vary from this composition due to impurities.

The silica (SiO_2) used for glass may have come from crushed quartz pebbles or quartz sand, while the alkali used was either soda (Na_2O) or potash (K_2O). In the case of soda, the material used would have been either the ashes of certain halophytic (salt-tolerant) plants, particularly those of the salicornia family, or mineral-soda such as natron, a sodium sesquicarbonate that occurs as a natural evaporite sediment, particularly in Egypt. Potash may also have been obtained from the ash of burnt plant material, particularly wood. Lime (CaO) can be obtained from calcareous rocks, such as crushed limestone or dolomite, from plant ashes or from calcareous sands. There is no documentary evidence that, in the most ancient glasses, lime was deliberately added; it may have been introduced as an impurity with the other materials, notably the sand.

Colorants, Decolorants, and Opacifiers
In addition to the raw materials used to form the basic body glass, various others were used to alter the color or to render the otherwise translucent glass opaque. Among the most common mineral colorants used in antiquity

were cobalt for blue or black; copper for turquoise or red, depending upon furnace conditions; and manganese for purple. In opaque glasses, yellow was produced by lead antimonate or lead stannate crystals, and opaque white by calcium antimonate or tin oxide. Opacity can also result from numerous small gas bubbles (known as *seed*) in the glass matrix.

Glass naturally has a blue-green hue resulting from the presence of iron impurities introduced with the raw materials. This tint can be removed to render the glass colorless by the addition of small amounts of antimony or manganese. If colorless glass is not required, the iron may be exploited in combination with furnace conditions to produce shades of green, brown, or blue.

Techniques of Glass Manufacture
There is relatively little documentary evidence for the techniques used to produce the earliest glass; for most areas, the production sequence described is based on archaeological evidence. However, it is known from Assyrian texts, dated to the seventh century B.C., that glass at that time was made in two stages—*fritting* and *melting*—and it has been assumed that this applies to the earliest glass also.

Fritting is a solid-state reaction between the raw materials used in glass production. It generally takes place at temperatures ca. 850°C, so that the materials react together but do not become molten. The resulting frit can be ground up and melted at temperatures below those that would be necessary for the production of a single-stage glass melt. Fritting also allows most of the gases produced by the raw materials to be liberated, so that, when the frit is eventually melted, the glass produced is relatively free of bubbles.

The next stage is to melt the frit to form a fully fused glass, which in the case of a soda-lime-silicate glass takes place at ca. 1,100°C. The glass so produced can either be cast into ingots for later working or be worked directly. Archaeologists need to distinguish between glass making from the raw materials and glass working using preprepared glass, perhaps made elsewhere, including recycled glass known as *cullet*.

Glass can be worked in a variety of ways. The earliest glasses were used to produce small items such as beads and amulets that could be formed around a rod or a wire or in molds. Prior to the first century B.C., glass vessels were core formed. In this method, a core of coarse mud, sometimes with straw or dung, was made in the shape of the interior of the vessel, and this was then coated with glass by dipping the core into the semimolten mass, by trailing the glass onto the core, or by coating it in powdered glass and subsequently reheating. Once the body had been formed in this way, the rim and the foot of the vessel would be shaped, and decorative threads of glass in other colors might be added.

Mold forming of glass vessels was also an early development. Fragments of glass of different colors might be placed in a mold and fused together to give a conglomerate glass, or canes—often multicolored—might be fused to make a mosaic glass. Sometimes details, or even whole shapes, might be made by the cold cutting of molded glass; examples include two of the headrests made for the Egyptian pharaoh Tutankhamun (1333–1323 B.C.). The inverse of molding was also used, a technique in which flat plates of glass were heated until they sagged over a raised former.

In the first century B.C., glassblowing was discovered, probably somewhere on the Syrian coast, and rapidly became established as a means of mass-producing glass in a wide range of shapes. When used in combination with a mold, glassblowing made it possible to produce vessels with elaborate scenes in relief, such as the Roman gladiator cups of the first–second centuries A.D. In this technique, a mass of molten glass, known as a *gob,* was gathered on the end of a hollow tube, called a *blowing iron,* and air was introduced into the mass by blowing. In the case of mold-blown vessels, the gob of glass was inflated within the confines of a mold, often made of stone.

The use of glass for windows developed from the first century B.C. This glass could be cast, but blown glass, known as *crown glass,* in small roundels was also used. In this technique, a bubble of glass was blown, and a metal rod, the *pontil,* was attached to the opposite side of the bubble. The blowing iron was then detached, and the pontil and glass spun until the open-ended bubble "flashed" open into a flat disc or crown. This was then cut into individual panes. The point at which the pontil was attached remained raised as a *bulls eye.* The crown-glass process remained common into modern times.

The Romans also made cylinder glass: A mass of glass was blown into a cylinder, and then slit along its length before being reheated and flattened, cooled, and cut into panes. This technique became the most common method of making window glass from around the seventh century A.D. At that time, the use of stained glass for decorative purposes, mainly in religious buildings, also developed. The glass might have been manufactured as single-colored pieces, or flashes of color might have been painted as a thin layer of colored glass on an otherwise colorless piece.

Whatever technique is used in the production of glass objects, it is necessary to cool them slowly to gradually release the internal stresses inherent in the material. In the case of core-formed vessels, the friable core mud is removed after cooling. Where the vessel is narrow necked, complete removal of the core may not be possible, adding to the opacity of the object.

Powdered glass may be fused onto a fully formed glass object to decorate it. This technique was developed as early as the fifteenth century B.C. and is sometimes referred to, somewhat confusingly, as *enameled glass* or *emaille.* When glass is fused to a metal, this is known as enameling. Two main techniques are known: *cloisonné,* in which fine wire is attached to the metal to form a cell, and *champlevé,* in which the metal is gouged out to form a hollow. Powdered glass is then placed in the cell or hollow and heated until the glass melts. After cooling, the glass is ground and polished to produce a smooth surface.

Glass may also be applied to the surface of pottery or stone in the process known as *glazing.* To be successful, the thermal expansion and shrinkage coefficients must be similar in the two materials. The glaze is usually applied as a slurry or a powder that has a melting temperature below that of the pottery body material. The glazing of faience is a related process.

History
The Roman author Pliny (A.D. 23/24–79) attributes the discovery of glass to natron traders whose campfires at the mouth of the river Belus reacted with the natron and local sand to accidentally produce glass. Though a sufficient explanation for his readers, archaeology has suggested an earlier origin for the craft.

The earliest-known glass comes from Mesopotamia, where it seems to have been discovered ca. 2500 B.C. Burial conditions in Mesopotamia are not conducive to the preservation of glass, but it appears that core-formed vessels were among the first products to be manufactured. Glass appears in Egypt shortly after 1500 B.C., perhaps being introduced by craftsmen from Mesopotamia; certainly, the earliest vessel forms are similar in the two areas. Most manufacturing evidence for glass in Egypt comes from the site of Tell el-Amarna, where the earliest indigenous industry may have been established.

At a time not long after the introduction of glass to Egypt, the craft became established in the Mycenaean world, and, by the sixth century B.C., a Mediterranean glass industry was flourishing. With the discovery of glass-blowing in the first century B.C., knowledge of glass and its production was rapidly spread throughout the Roman Empire.

With the fall of the Roman Empire in the west, glass production became less centralized and more difficult to detect archaeologically until the tenth century A.D. when *Forest glass* was introduced. Its makers used woodland plants as an alkali source rather than the soda favored by Roman and early medieval glass-makers. Forest glass persisted in northern and western Europe until as late as the seventeenth century. However, glass production in the eastern Roman Empire continued, until this Byzantine industry became merged with that of Islam. Some of this eastern glass found its way into the western sphere as a result of Viking trade with the area.

After the fall of Damascus in A.D. 1400, refugees from the city included glassmakers, who settled on the island of Murano in the lagoon of Venice in Italy. A glass industry had already been established there in the thirteenth century when the Venetian glass industry, the first significant western industry since Roman times, was transferred from the city to the island. By the mid-fifteenth century, Murano had become the major center of a southern European glass industry. Glass continued to be made by broadly the same methods until the Industrial Revolution of the nineteenth century and even later.

Methods of Analysis

As with the examination of other archaeological materials, the techniques appropriate to the study of glass are largely determined by the particular questions to be answered.

Dating

The detailed recording of stylistic forms and decorative detail, and the change in these forms and distributions through time, has lead to the development of type series for glass, as for other archaeological materials. These have provided a framework on which scientific analyses have been based. It is also possible to use chemical analyses in a way analogous to typology, since certain compositions have been found to be broadly characteristic of particular time periods (Sayre and Smith 1961). The thermoluminescence technique has been used to attempt to date glasses. However, it has been less successful than when applied to pottery, which—unlike glass—has a well-developed crystal lattice.

Provenance

Although there may be documentary evidence for the manufacture of glass in certain regions (e.g., the cuneiform tablets bearing glass recipes from Assyria), it is difficult to assign particular glasses to individual workshops or regions, particularly if they are discovered outside their supposed region of origin. In such cases, distribution studies might help lend weight to production at a particular center, and sometimes this is aided by the occurrence of the maker's name stamp on vessels, most notably "ENNION," who worked in the first century A.D.

Chemical characterization is the major technique for determining the place of manufacture, known as *provenance,* for archaeological glasses. It has been practiced with varying degrees of success because of the complex nature of glass and its raw materials. Among the most successfully used methods is lead-isotope analysis, which characterizes lead-containing glasses according to the source of the lead (which is not necessarily the same as the source of manufacture of the glass). Glasses with similar lead-isotope ratios are likely to have originated from the same source.

Methods of Manufacture

Details of the manufacturing methods employed in producing ancient glasses can be gained from the examination of materials discarded in ancient workshops, such as those at

Tell el-Amarna in Egypt, and also by the examination of the finished products themselves. A first stage in this process is the physical examination of the glass, often using a hand lens or a microscope. Higher-powered microscopes, including scanning electron microscopes, might be used for more detailed examination. Such examination may reveal information on the source of opacity, such as bubbles, crystals, or fragments of a vessel core, as well as details of decorative techniques such as engraving.

Experimental archaeology, including the reconstruction of furnaces and the production of glass from a range of raw materials, can also help in the understanding of those processes, which may not be apparent from examination of the glass alone, or help confirm conclusions reached from physical or chemical examination. The melting temperature of an archaeological glass, for example, might be ascertained by replicating the glass recipe derived from chemical examination and determining the melting point and working properties of this replicate glass.

Chemical Characterization

Various methods can be used for the chemical characterization of glasses, which can itself be used to answer questions relating to date, provenance, and technology. These include atomic absorption spectrometry (AAS), inductively coupled plasma–atomic emission spectrometry (ICP-AES), inductively coupled plasma–mass spectrometry (ICP-MS), neutron activation analysis (NAA), proton-induced X-ray emission (PIXE), X-ray fluorescence (XRF), scanning electron microscopy (SEM), and electron-probe Microanalysis (EPMA), which are used to measure a wide range of elemental compositions from minor to trace levels in glasses. All of these methods are destructive to some degree, since small samples must be taken and weathering layers removed. X-ray diffraction (XRD) has also been used to examine the crystalline components in glass raw materials.

Perhaps the most common field in which chemical analysis can supplement glass studies is the examination of raw materials and their sources. At the simplest level, the analysis of the major raw materials used to make the glass, such as the sand and alkali, can tell the archaeologist something of the basic nature of those components and how they contribute to the glass chemistry. A glass that contains high levels of potassium and low levels of soda is likely to have been made using (forest) wood ashes, while a glass that is high in sodium but low in potassium and magnesium would have been produced using a mineral evaporite alkali source such as natron. More commonly, the colorant raw materials have been examined and linked to the colorants found in ancient glasses (e.g., cobalt). Cobalt is found in only a few exploitable deposits, and each source has been shown to have a characteristic elemental *fingerprint*. This provides a higher probability of differentiating between cobalt sources used in ancient glasses, providing information that is used to infer exploitation patterns and trade between different peoples.

Conservation

Glass survives well in stable, dry, environments but will decay in damp environments, where water may remove or deposit soluble salts. Weathering is often apparent on ancient glass as an opalescent layer, which is often removed in conservation, and/or pitting of the surface. Conservation is a specialized area of glass study, but concentrates on maintaining a stable environment, both immediately after excavation and during museum display.

Significance of Glass Studies

As with many other archaeological materials, glass can be used as an indicator of socioeconomic activity, such as trade, migration, and the spread of technology. These can also be regarded as a measure of the spread of cultural diversity and ideas.

Paul T. Nicholson
Caroline M. Jackson

See also ATOMIC ABSORPTION (AA) SPECTROMETRY; ELECTRON-PROBE MICROANALYSIS; FAIENCE, CHARACTERIZATION; FOURIER TRANSFORM–INFRARED (FT-IR) MICROSCOPY; GLASS, ON-SITE CONSERVATION; INDUCTIVELY COUPLED PLASMA–ATOMIC EMISSION SPECTROMETRY; ISOTOPES, STABLE (PB, SR): RAW MATERIALS AND PROVENANCE STUDIES; NUCLEAR METHODS OF ANALYSIS; OBSIDIAN HYDRATION DATING; THERMOLUMINESCENCE DATING; X-RAY DIFFRACTION (XRD)

Further Readings

Brill, R.H. (1962) A note on the scientist's definition of glass. Journal of Glass Studies 4:127–138.

Brill, R.H. (1963) Ancient glass. Scientific American 209(5):120–130.

Freestone, I. (1991) Looking into glass. In S. Bowman (ed.): Science and the Past, pp. 37–57. London: British Museum.

Harden, D.B. (1969) Ancient glass I: Pre-Roman. Archaeological Journal 125:46–72.

Harden, D.B. (1970) Ancient glass II: Roman. Archaeological Journal 126:44–77.

Harden, D.B. (1972) Ancient glass III: Post-Roman. Archaeological Journal 128:78–117.

Henderson, J. (1989) The scientific analysis of ancient glass and its archaeological interpretation. In J. Henderson (ed.): Scientific Analysis in Archaeology, pp. 30–58. Oxford: Oxford University Committee for Archaeology.

Newton, R.G., and Davison, S. (1989) Conservation of Glass. London: Butterworths.

Oppenheim, A.L., Brill, R.H., Barag, D., and von Saldern, A. (1970) Glass and Glassmaking in Ancient Mesopotamia. Corning, Corning Museum of Glass.

Sayre, E.V., and Smith, R.W. (1961) Compositional categories of ancient glass. Science 133: 1824–1826.

Tait, H., ed. (1991) Five Thousand Years of Glass. London: British Museum.

Turner, W.E.S. (1956) Studies in ancient glasses and glassmaking processes IV: The chemical composition of ancient glasses. Journal of the Society of Glass Technology 40(193):162–186T.

Glass, On-Site Conservation

Emergency treatment and care of glass on site. The goals of archaeological conservation are to minimize the deterioration of objects during excavation and to ensure that as much as possible of the evidence contained in the objects is available for further study and analysis. First-aid measures are used to prevent rapid changes taking place when the glass is first exposed; further conservation treatment takes place in a conservation laboratory, which may be at some distance from the site.

Glass can be found in the form of vessels, window glass, and small artifacts, such as beads and imitation gemstones. It is normally transparent, though it may be translucent or opaque if it has deteriorated. Almost all early glass tends to be colored to some extent, since clear glass was difficult to achieve. Related materials include enamels applied to metals, glazes applied to ceramics, and small objects made from soft vitreous (glasslike) pastes, known as *frit* or *faience*.

Glass composition is complex, and glass from different periods and areas varies in composition and properties. The main ingredient is silica in the form of sand, flint, or quartz, which is heated with the addition of alkaline plant ashes—soda (sodium oxide) or potash (potassium oxide)—as modifiers to lower the working temperature and lime (calcium or magnesium oxide) as a stabilizer. Metal salts, either naturally present in the basic ingredients or deliberately added, provide color. Objects are shaped in various ways, including molding and blowing. The finished object may be decorated by painting, staining, gilding, or abrasion.

The deterioration of glass is also complex. It is not durable during burial and survives well only in very dry conditions (in adverse conditions, it may deteriorate completely). Composition affects its durability (e.g., soda glass tends to survive better than potash glass).

The form, color, and decoration of a glass object are all important evidence of date and of manufacturing technique. Analysis can provide information on composition, coloring agents, and deterioration characteristics.

Aims of On-Site Conservation

The aim of conservation is to preserve archaeological evidence. On-site conservation is essentially first-aid, which is followed by full assessment and further treatment in the conservation laboratory. The practice of conservation rests on five central principles: (1) preservation of the integrity of the object; (2) use of the least-invasive treatments; (3) use of reversible treatments (although there are known limits to reversibility); (4) preventive care; and (5) documentation of the object and its treatment.

The integrity of the glass object must be preserved because this preserves the information within it. Choosing the least-invasive treatments means that the glass is changed as little as possible, and the evidence within it is available for further study and analysis; choosing reversible treatments means that first-aid treatments (e.g., a temporary adhesive) can be removed in the conservation laboratory and replaced by suitable long-term treatments. If these treatments are followed by continuous and well-monitored preventive care (good storage), then any further change is minimized. Documentation of the object and its treatment provides the information on which all analysis and conservation of the glass are based.

Glass normally requires more than simple on-site treatments. Where effective arrangements have been made for prompt laboratory conservation, very little will be done to the glass on site, and it will be taken as soon as possible to the laboratory for full assessment and decisions on further treatment. This is particularly important for wet glass, which can deteriorate considerably during storage.

Factors Affecting Condition

The way the glass deteriorates (and the problems presented to the conservator) depends on composition of the glass, the state of the artifact at the time of burial, and the burial conditions.

Glass artifacts are frequently broken and fragmentary. The glass itself is sometimes in remarkably good condition, but more often it has deteriorated during burial, though this may not be immediately obvious. In mild cases, deterioration may be limited to the surface; in serious cases, the glass may be altered to a considerable depth. The deterioration most frequently seen in excavated glass happens in damp conditions, which cause the leaching of the modifiers from the structure of the glass and the formation of a silica-rich surface. This silica surface is hydrated (contains water), and, while it remains hydrated, the extent of deterioration may not be evident.

When the surface dries, the deterioration becomes obvious because the crust on the surface contracts and the glass becomes dull. Glass that is only slightly affected may acquire an attractive iridescent surface when it dries, caused by the shrinkage and separation of very thin layers of silica. When highly deteriorated, it may lose its glassy appearance completely and look opaque or granular.

The coloring salts may change within the deteriorated surface, apparently changing the color of the object (e.g., copper salts used to color glass deep red can react to form a bright green copper compound in the deteriorated surface). Enamels may become chalky and change color; they may also be covered by the corrosion products of the metal to which they are attached. Ceramic glazes can become dull, iridescent, or crazed and opaque when the glassy structure deteriorates. Frit or faience can be weak and friable.

The burial conditions are also important. Glass tends to be well preserved in very dry conditions but poorly preserved in damp or wet conditions, particularly in alkaline conditions, such as seawater. In areas of low rainfall, high temperatures, and rapid evaporation, large quantities of salts, such as chlorides and carbonates, may be present in the burial deposit and can be found in and on the surface of deteriorated glass; in waterlogged oxygen-free conditions, dark staining can be caused by iron and other salts, which can change the color of the glass.

Effects of Excavation

One of the archaeological conservator's difficulties is that excavation sets off a series of changes. Uncovering material inevitably exposes it to new combination of environmental factors (e.g., oxygen, light, heat, air currents). It is removed from the soil and so loses the physical support of the burial deposit; it is handled, examined, and even cleaned. All of these activities may bring about damaging changes in glass, resulting in loss of information, and some may take place very rapidly.

Glass must not be exposed to the sun or to drying winds on site because of the rapid changes that can take place when the hydrated surface dries. Not only can the surface layer contract and become opaque, masking the transparency of the glass, but salts in solution in the porous hydrated silica layers can crystallize on the surface and add to the opacity. There is also a tendency for any salts or other accretions on the surface to harden and toughen if they are allowed to dry and to become much more difficult to remove.

Conservation Processes

Normally, the conservator will aim to do only the very minimum to excavated glass on site, and the emphasis is put on assessment and treatment in the conservation laboratory. On-site conservation will, therefore, concentrate on removal from the ground and packaging for transport to the laboratory. Glass is usually found in manageable quantities, but an industrial site might yield large amounts, making it necessary for some preliminary sorting and conservation to take place on site. Material for future analysis is identified as early as possible and excluded from any on-site handling or treatment.

Assessment of Material
The conservator will assess the general and local soil conditions and the condition of the glass itself. Careful examination will establish whether the glass is cracked or broken, but the extent of deterioration of the glass may be difficult to establish at this stage. The way the glass is deposited is also important, since this affects the approach to conservation—different problems will be presented by a complete vessel, a string of beads in a burial, or a scatter of broken window glass.

Excavation
Some glass is strong enough to uncover and remove from the soil in the normal way, but the conservator checks the condition carefully as the glass is being exposed. If the surface is obviously deteriorated or there is paint or other decoration present, special care is taken in excavation and handling. In this situation, it is better to leave as much soil as possible in contact with the surface or lift the glass in a block of surrounding soil, leaving the consolidation and cleaning to be done in the laboratory. Wet glass is packaged immediately to keep it wet and taken to a laboratory as soon as possible.

Strengthening
Some glass may be so weak or cracked that troweling and handling may damage it. There are two main ways of providing strength: furnishing external support and applying a consolidant (usually a diluted adhesive material). The first method is preferable to the second since it does not involve introducing any material into the glass itself. In fact, the vulnerability of deteriorated glass means that conservators avoid applying any materials such as adhesives to glass on site if they possibly can.

There are several techniques for providing support that are described in field-conservation textbooks and can be adapted to suit the particular situation. These involve retaining soil around the glass, using bandage to hold the soil in place or a consolidant to strengthen the soil, or applying external support after exposing the object in stages. External support may be bandaging wound round an object or it may be a collar or a jacket of plaster of paris or polyurethane foam. In each case, a protective covering (e.g., food wrap) is applied first to prevent damage to the glass. Any material lifted in this way is taken to the laboratory for removal of the support and further conservation treatment.

Cleaning
Material that is not encased in soil or a support will be examined on site, but it is not normally cleaned because of the danger of damaging the surface of the glass. It is very important to retain the deteriorated surface crust, even if it masks the glasslike appearance and color, since it defines the original thickness and shape of the glass. If it is removed, there may be little or no glass remaining beneath, and, even under a thin crust, the newly exposed surface of the glass may be pitted and depleted. Unlike ceramics, glass cannot withstand washing, since the crust of hydrated silica on deteriorated glass can swell in water, contract on drying, and separate from the underlying glass. Brushing very loose soil away may be possible, but this method can score or dislodge the surface. The laboratory method of cleaning is to soften accretions with local applications of industrial alcohol, which does not cause swelling of the hydrated surface. This method can be used with caution on site if accretions make initial identification of the glass impossible, but it must be used with great care if there is any possibility that the glass may be decorated.

Reconstruction
Glass is difficult to reconstruct because of the way it breaks and the nature of the adhesives needed. Reconstruction is not normally undertaken on site.

Preventive Care
Glass is handled as little as possible and then only with great care. Hydrated silica layers can be dislodged by handling. It is helpful to use a padded box or tray in which to support fragments or complete objects so that they are touched as little as possible.

G

Polyethylene bags do not provide effective support for fragile material; the best solution is to pack glass fragments laid out flat in boxes with inert plastic foam sheet or plenty of good-quality (preferably acid-free) paper between each layer. The paper is folded over several times and slightly crumpled to make a resilient cushion between each layer. All containers are clearly labeled providing details of the contents. Packaging must, of course, be adequate for the journey to the laboratory.

An important aspect of preventive care is dealing with the packaging and storage of damp or wet glass. Where glass is stored in water, the leaching of the alkaline modifiers continues, and the environment around the glass becomes increasingly alkaline. Eventually, the conditions may become so alkaline and aggressive that the glass structure itself is attacked. It is important, therefore, that wet glass is treated as soon as possible.

Glass is a vulnerable material, but, with proper care on site, it will survive excavation with minimal change and can be stabilized in the conservation laboratory.

Elizabeth Pye

See also GLASS, CHARACTERIZATION

Further Readings

Cronyn, J.M. (1990) The Elements of Archaeological Conservation. London: Routledge.

Sease, C. (1994) A Conservation Manual for the Field Archaeologist, 4th ed. Los Angeles: Institute of Archaeology, UCLA.

Watkinson, D., Neal, V., and Swain, H. (1998). First Aid for Finds, 3rd edition. London: Rescue—The British Archaeological Trust and Archaeology Section of the UK Institute for Conservation, with the Museum of London.

Gould, Richard Allan (1939-)

American anthropologist and archaeologist. Born on October 22, 1939, in Newton, Massachusetts. Gould was educated at Harvard University, where he received his bachelor's cum laude in 1961, and at the University of California at Berkeley, where he earned his doctorate in anthropology in 1965. He began his career in New York City as assistant curator of North American archaeology at the American Museum of Natural History (1965–1971). He then moved to Hawaii, where he was an associate professor of anthropology at the University of Hawaii until 1976 and a full professor until 1980, returning to the East Coast as a full professor of anthropology at Brown University. He has received numerous grants from the Social Science Research Council, the American Museum of Natural History, and the National Science Foundation and is a Fellow of the American Anthropological Association and the Society for American Archaeology.

Gould is an important figure in the field of ethnoarchaeology, which uses the ethnographic study of contemporary societies to gain insight into the behavior of archaeological societies as evidenced by their material remains. In works such as *Explorations in Ethnoarchaeology, Living Archaeology* and *Recovering the Past* Gould argues for a systematic methodology in the use of ethnoarchaeology and criticizes previous uses of ethnoarchaeology (particularly that of Lewis R. Binford) as lacking an overall view of the operation of cultural systems within their total context (ecological, geographic, sociocultural). Gould has applied ethnoarchaeological principles and his expertise in underwater archaeology to a study of turn-of-the-century armaments (including the wrecks of pre-*Dreadnought* era warships) and the arms race, resulting ultimately in a model for studying the archaeology of war.

Joseph J. Basile

See also ETHNOARCHAEOLOGY; REMOTELY OPERATED VEHICLES; UNDERWATER ARCHAEOLOGY

Further Readings

Gould, R.A. (1978) Explorations in Ethnoarchaeology. Albuquerque: University of New Mexico Press.

Gould, R.A. (1980) Living Archaeology. Cambridge/New York: Cambridge University Press.

Gould, R.A. (1983) Shipwreck Anthropology. Albuquerque: University of New Mexico Press.

Gould, R.A. (1990) Recovering the Past. Albuquerque: University of New Mexico Press.

Gould, R.A., and Schiffer, M.B., eds. (1981) Modern Material Culture: The Archaeology of Us. New York: Academic.

Grain Size Analysis

The determination of the size distribution of a sediment for description, comparison, and interpretation. Grain size analysis is used frequently in archaeology to reconstruct the source of the site sedimentation matrix and has been applied to the understanding of the depositional history of caves, rockshelters, tells, middens, and alluvial sites. Perhaps the most successful use of grain size analysis in archaeology has been in the unraveling of the sedimentology, stratigraphy, and chronology of cave deposits containing the remains of human activity. Cave deposits are usually more complex than the layer-cake strata found in tells and fluvial sites.

Grain-size frequency distributions in sediments can be obtained by diverse methods. Each method defines the "size" of a particle in somewhat different ways, and each has its advantages and drawbacks. For the archaeologist, the choice of method will depend on the nature of the problem and the availability and cost effectiveness of the equipment needed.

The distribution of sizes of sedimentary (clastic) particles with diameters in the range of 1/16–16 mm (sand and fine gravel) is normally determined by sieving. Before sieving, individual particles must be separated from one another. For indurated sediments (i.e., sediments compacted and hardened by pressure, cementation, or heat) or for micromorphological studies, thin sections also can be used to measure grain sizes. These measurements can be done using a standard petrographic microscope or image-analysis instruments. Computer programs allow automated procedures for thin-section imaging and analyses. Multivariate statistical techniques are used to enhance the interpretive possibilities of grain-size data. The bibliography at the end of this entry gives references to sources that detail the standard techniques. In all such analyses, samples must be large enough to give statistically meaningful results.

Size distributions for particles less than 1/16 mm in diameter, the silt and clay fractions, are determined by sedimentation in a settling tube using pipette analysis, hydrometer methods, or an optical/electronic instrument such as a Coulter Counter. Laser-diffraction grain-size analyzers are coming into use. Although the traditional pipette analysis is time consuming, many laboratories have greater confidence in pipette methods

compared to other methods. This would also be the method of choice for most archaeological projects because the equipment is inexpensive and widely available.

Pipette analysis relies on calculations of settling velocities of different-size particles based on Stokes's Law. Although these calculations ignore the density and shape differences of particles, this technique is by far the most accepted and the most commonly used. Sedimentation methods normally require a disaggregation or dispersal pretreatment because of the tendency of clays to stick together.

Grain size analysis by sieving and settling-tube techniques conceptually replaces the natural, irregularly shaped grains with equivalent spheres. In most cases, this deviates considerably from the natural situation. To compensate, analytical techniques have been developed so that both sieving and settling-tube measurements yield distributions of the intermediate diameters of sediment grains. Differences in grain-size distributions between optical/electronic counters and pipette analyses appear to be due to the lack of complete detection of fine clay particles by the optical/electronic counters. In addition, the optical/electronic methods appear to measure the same grains as somewhat finer than the pipette method. The optical/electronic methods have demonstrated good accuracy and precision using standard latex spheres but have been less accurate in natural sediment analyses. Optical/electronic methods achieve considerable time saving because only a single analysis is needed to obtain the entire particle-size distribution.

In laser-diffraction methods, the suspension fluid must be inert. Experiments performed over periods of longer than fifteen minutes may be biased if the temperature rises, causing gas-bubble generation. Laser diffraction and other optical/electronic methods compute size distribution in volume units, whereas sieving and pipette results are in weight units. This leads to a lack of comparability if the densities of the mineral constituents vary significantly.

Once the data have been collected by one of the several laboratory methods, two choices are available to assist in interpretation. The first employs plotting some type of graph of the data for visual analysis. The second uses statistical parameters obtained from a computer analysis of the size data, without graph plotting. Graphs of particle-size data typically are presented as histograms or cumulative curves to depict the relative abundance of size fractions. In geology, interpretation of these measures of clastic sediments is used to infer the energy of the transporting agent at the point of deposition. Mean particle size is related to current velocity or to the overall energy of the environment. Coarser mean sizes in aqueous and eolian contexts are indicative of high energy, while finer mean sizes are related to lower-energy systems.

The statistical measures used to describe and interpret archaeological sediments include *mean particle size, modes, sorting,* and *skewness,* as well as *bivariate comparisons* of these attributes. The most common size fraction in a particle distribution is its mode. If there is a single mode, it is an indication that the sediment reflects a single agent of transportation and deposition. Bimodality of size frequencies generally indicates mixing of sediment from two sources.

Sorting. In well-sorted sediments, particles are of similar size, while poorly sorted deposits consist of a wide range of particle sizes. A high degree of sorting is an indication of a narrow range of energies available in transport and deposition. Eolian microdepositional environments have a high degree of sorting. Dunes typically consist of coarse to fine sand with good sorting. They can exhibit internal sorting causing cross-bedding. This is in contrast to loess deposits, which can be so well sorted that they appear massive. Sandy beaches tend to be well sorted. However, where energy levels fluctuate and sediments are not continually reworked, sediments on beaches can be less well sorted. Spring, lake, and marsh sediments commonly exhibit poor to good sorting primarily because of fluctuating energy levels. Sediments deposited by glaciers, called *till,* are poorly sorted. They typically contain very large particles in a finer matrix.

The measure of asymmetry of a grain-size distribution, termed *skewness,* also is related to selective transport of sediment-size fractions. Variations in transport energy affect the extremes of a particle-size distribution and influence skewness. Beach sediments can be negatively skewed (more coarse particles). Dune and river sands are positively skewed (more fine particles). Besides interpre-

tations based on single statistical parameters of a particle-size distribution, inferences can be made by comparing two or more attributes. Relationships such as the ratios between coarse and fine clastics are used as a means to differentiate sedimentary facies. Relations between *kurtosis* (peakedness of the distribution curve) and skewness provide an expression of sediment/energy relationships. In both archaeological and geological sediments, strongly skewed material usually indicates mixing.

A plot of two statistical measures of size distribution can be used to separate depositional environments. In deposits consisting of sand-sized particles, for example, eolian-dune, lake-beach and river sands can be distinguished by their sorting and skewness. Beach sands have been distinguished by negative skewness and good sorting. River sands can be positively skewed and less well sorted. Dune sands can have positive skewness and are somewhat finer grained than beach sands.

George R. Rapp Jr.

See also ARCHAEOLOGICAL SITES, FORMATION PROCESSES; CAVES AND ROCKSHELTERS; EXCAVATION; GEOARCHAEOLOGY; SOIL AND SEDIMENT ANALYSIS

Further Readings

Brown, A. (1985) Traditional and multivariate techniques in the interpretation of floodplain sediment grain size variations. Earth Surface Processes and Landforms 10:281–291.

Folk, R. (1980) Petrology of Sedimentary Rocks. Austin: Hemphill.

Komar, P., and Cui, B. (1984) The analysis of grain-size measurements by sieving and settling-tube techniques. Journal of Sedimentary Petrology 54:603–614.

Lewis, D. (1984) Practical Sedimentology. New York: Van Nostrand Rheinhold.

Loizeau, J.-L., Arbouille, D., Santiago, S., and Vernet, J.-P. (1994) Evaluation of a wide range laser diffraction grain size analyzer for use with sediments. Sedimentology 41:353–361.

Pareschi, M., Pompilio, M., and Innocenti, F. (1990) Automated evaluation of volumetric grain-size distribution from thin section images. Computers and Geosciences 16:1067–1084.

Grid Excavation

Method of excavating sites by digging squares separated by a regular grid of standing soil sections, or *baulks*. The technique was developed by Sir Mortimer Wheeler (1943) in Britain and spread to much of the English-speaking world. The heyday of this method was the 1930s and 1940s, with a rapid fall from favor in the early 1960s.

The aim of grid excavation was to obtain information in both the vertical and the horizontal planes (i.e. sequences and events). The basic problem was that the baulks masked much of the plan of the various phases, while they rarely provided sections where required, being arbitrarily placed in a grid prior to the start of the excavation. The system did, however, introduce real control onto archaeological sites and detailed stratigraphical recording.

Peter L. Drewett

See also STRATIGRAPHY; WHEELER, SIR ROBERT ERIC MORTIMER

Further Readings

Barker, P. (1993) Techniques of Archaeological Excavation, 3rd ed. London: Batsford.
Drewett, P.L. (1999) Field Archaeology: An Introduction. London: University College London Press.
Wheeler, R.E.M., Sir (1943) Maiden Castle, Dorset. (Reports of the Research Committee of the Society of Antiquaries of London, no. 12). Oxford: Printed at the University press for the Society of Antiquaries.

Growth-Ring Analysis and Seasonality Studies

Analysis of incremental growth structures to determine season of death or age of an animal or a tree. Numerous biological materials add daily, monthly, and seasonal increments of wood, bone, shell, cementum, and the like, such as trees; mollusc shells; turtle shells; fish scales, otoliths, spines, and vertebrae; and sea-mammal and herbivore teeth. These increments are marked visibly by changes in topography, changes in coloration and opacity, and changes in crystal structure, as well as invisibly by changes in chemistry typically measured as the ratio of stable oxygen isotopes.

History of Research

Incremental growth was recognized at least as early as the seventeenth century A.D., and aging trees, shells, and mammals by this method was common in the late nineteenth century. Growth-ring analysis by archaeologists began in 1969 with publications on death time/harvest time of sheep, based on growth lines in their teeth; and of pismo clamshells from a California site, based on the opacity of the final increment of the shells. Throughout the 1970s, many students uncritically applied the technique to archaeological materials, failing to tackle questions of sample size or annual variation. By the late 1980s, archaeologists were interpreting few archaeological samples, directing their attention instead to technical problems, such as sample preparation and which skeletal elements to use; to developing a standard terminology; and to procedural problems, such as replicability, control collections, and necessary sample sizes. While most practitioners continue to believe that growth-line analysis does produce useful information for determining harvest time, few believe that the results are infallible or even preferable to other techniques for determining time of death, such as species presence or absence or birthing schedules. The advantages to a carefully constructed study of growth rings on archaeological materials are the increased sample sizes upon which to base interpretations of site occupation or scheduling of specific activities and the inclusion of both female and male herbivores whereas other materials (antler, horn) allowed for the study of the harvest of only male animals.

Dozens of species of shellfish and fish have been examined by archaeologists. Among the mammals can be found studies of white-tailed deer, caribou, elk, bison, musk-ox, marten, fisher, dog, human, pig, goat, sheep, cattle, and fur, harp, and ring seals.

Incremental Growth

Within an annual cycle, living organisms often experience a long period with conditions conducive to growth and a shorter period with conditions detrimental to growth. The conditions of relevance are those such as food supply, salinity, reproduction, and air temperature, which are found in polar, temperate, tropical and benthic settings. The annual variation in these growth stimuli results

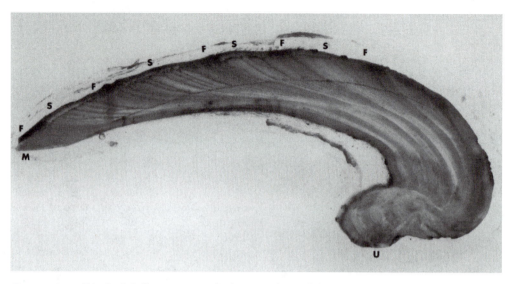

Cross-section of bivalved shell. m = margin, f = fast growth, s = slow growth, u = umbo. Photograph by Cheryl Claassen.

in chemical and crystalline changes in skeletal elements and in plant tissues. In most skeletal elements, macroscopic indications of seasonal growth variation are apparent as rings of lighter-colored material alternating with darker-colored material, each called a *growth band* (see Figure). The increment deposited during slow growth is known as the *annulus*. The annulus in bone, teeth, or shell is translucent when light is passed through it, and it is the major feature in analysis. Experimental work with many species has established that it is formed on an annual basis. Methods of analysis are many, but most attempt to establish how much growth had accrued when the animal died since the previous annulus. One must then turn to growth controls to determine how much time had passed.

A major problem with any growth-ring analysis is distinguishing between a true annulus and a false annulus caused by a long interruption in feeding due to spawning, bad weather, or unseasonable temperatures. Other problems are split and missing annuli, resorbed cementum and bone, and sample preparation that destroys or obscures growth rings.

For mammal teeth, the preferred skeletal elements are the neck of first mandibular molars or other multirooted teeth sectioned longitudinally. For shells, it is the outer edge or margin.

Growth Controls

The analysis requires a growth control—a collection of animals (their shells, teeth, or bones) that have died at known times across the calendar to observe the amount and type of growth at the time of death—and an archaeological collection of the same skeletal element (not necessarily the same species) upon which observations are made and then interpreted based on the growth control. Some practitioners are skeptical of the uniformitarian assumption that the timing of contemporary environmental growth stimuli is no different from that in the past, but others counter that the annual period of slow growth is triggered by the seasonal reduction in the amount of daylight, which was uneffected by any known past climatic changes.

Early archaeological growth-ring studies attempted to interpret archaeological specimens aided only by growth controls found in the biological literature. Biologists work to develop aging techniques for the management of commercially important animals, and they are concerned only with annual increments. Archaeologists need to subdivide the calendar year into as many increments as possible to derive time of death, which requires knowledge of how growth proceeds throughout the year, individual response to growth stimuli, and how the timing of growth stimuli varies from year to year.

The challenge in amassing a modern growth control is to utilize the variability that will be evident in the animals collected in a predictive model rather than normalizing the variability. Rarely have sample-size requirements been discussed, but requirements of at least twenty-seven shells killed monthly have been published, and the largest shell controls have utilized fifty animals killed monthly over at least three years. Growth controls are the weakest aspect of the development of this technique in archaeology.

Different parts of the skeleton differ in their response to growth stimuli. For instance, slow growth is recorded on the otolith and the spine of fish at different times, as well as in the margin and umbo (a lateral prominence above the hinge of a bivalve shell) of shells. Younger animals will be in fast growth when older animals have passed into slow growth. These observations underscore the necessity of comparing controls and archaeological samples of the same skeletal element and age range.

Techniques

Two methods are particularly useful for season-of-death predictions in shell. These are the fast/slow, or opaque/translucent, technique and the measurement of oxygen isotopes. The former technique avoids a number of methodological problems associated with measuring the increment or counting daily lines by simply recording the opacity of the final increment and referring to controls indicating the proportion of animals with opaque shell each month. This method still suffers from the problem of false annuli (i.e., when to interpret a translucent band as annual slow growth or unseasonable slow growth).

Stable oxygen isotopes are measured in tiny samples of shell or bone drilled from each growth band. The ratio of oxygen-18 to oxygen-16 is governed by water temperature and water salinity, both typically seasonal in their fluctuation. Here, too, false annuli present problems, and the cost of analysis greatly reduces the sample size available. But for species that lack a geographically relevant control collection, oxygen isotopes permit season-of-death interpretations.

Several techniques are now known to be useless for seasonality work. For shells, it has been demonstrated that size of the increments and the number of daily lines are not regular enough to be reliable indicators of the passage of time. The amount of growth varies tremendously among individual shellfish. On any day of the year, shells can be found that are in slow growth or in fast growth, 15 percent grown or 120 percent grown, with 12 new daily growth lines since the annulus or with 270. The new year's growth was initiated over a 109-day period in Rhode Island shellfish and a 65-day period in a Massachusetts study. Annulus formation began as early as mid-May or as late as mid-July in Resolute Bay ring seals. There is no zero date when all shells, mammals, or fish begin growing.

Interpretation

Basic assumptions about incremental growth influence the prediction of harvest season. The normative assumptions that all shells and mammalian teeth respond to growth stimuli identically, and that the timing of these stimuli is predictable each year, have resulted in the practice of assigning harvest time to individual shells, teeth, and bones. With large growth controls for shells, it is clear that neither assumption is true. There is marked growth variation in any population on any day in the year and from year to year. Individual shells cannot be assigned a death time using growth-ring analysis. Fortunately, the range and the mean of that variation do permit prediction of death time, although their use requires sets of archaeological shells from a single death assemblage to be interpreted. This criterion is the major stumbling block in utilizing this technique on archaeological materials but is assumed to be satisfied when the specimens come from a sealed feature or a column sample of small proportions. Archaeologists working with other skeletal elements have also lamented that, once the methodological problems are solved, interpreting archaeological samples still presents some stumbling blocks. Not least among them are the questions of necessary sample sizes, the geographical flexibility of the controls, and site formation processes that move specimens about in multicomponent sites.

Cheryl Claassen

See also ANIMAL REMAINS, IDENTIFICATION AND ANALYSIS: FISH; ANIMAL REMAINS, IDENTIFICATION AND ANALYSIS: MAMMALS; ANIMAL REMAINS, IDENTIFICATION AND ANALYSIS: MOLLUSCS; DENDROCHRONOLOGY;

G

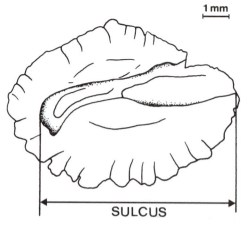

1 mm

Left otolith of a perchlike fish. Figure by Wim Van Neer.

Further Readings

Claassen, C. (1986) Shellfishing seasons in the southeastern U.S. American Antiquity 51:21–37.

Claassen, C. (1990) The shell seasonality technique in the eastern U.S. Archaeology of Eastern North America 18:75–87.

Growth Studies: Fish Otoliths

The analysis of small calcareous concretions found in the internal ear of fishes and used to determine season of death or age of an animal. In archaeozoological studies, otoliths can serve for species identification, for size and age reconstruction, and for seasonality studies at archaeological sites.

Each ear contains three otoliths: the *sagitta,* the *lapillus,* and the *asterisk.* The sagitta is the largest otolith in most fishes, but in certain families, such as the cyprinids (carp family), the asterisk is also well developed. Chemically, otoliths differ from bone in that they are made from aragonite, a calcareous substance that is less stable than the hydroxyapatite component of bone. A consequence of these physical properties is that otoliths are less likely than bones to survive in archaeological deposits. It is only in exceptional cases that otoliths are found in large numbers. They usually belong to species with very robust sagittae, such as codlike or perchlike fishes (see Figure 4). Sites that yield numerous, small otoliths are usually in arid regions.

Identification of the highly diagnostic otoliths is based on their general shape (outline) and on anatomical details such as the shape of the *sulcus* (groove). Direct comparison with adequate reference material is preferable to identification based solely on resemblance to figures in atlases. The latter can, however, be very helpful in the initial stages of the identification process.

Otoliths are frequently studied in systematic and biostratigraphic fields of paleontology. However, they have been seldom studied in archaeology, mainly because of the rarity with which they are retrieved during excavations. In most cases, the absence of otoliths is due to their inherent poor chance of preservation. Nevertheless, in cases in which the otoliths are present, they may be overlooked either as a result of poor techniques of recovery or simply because they are not correctly recognized and are confused with large particles of sediment. The conventional methods of sieving will retain otoliths on a 1-mm and a 2-mm mesh, but it is preferable to take bulk samples for finer sieving in the laboratory once the presence of otoliths has been attested at the site. Numerous methods for laboratory treatment have been described in the paleontological literature (Ward 1984).

Otoliths have been widely used in growth studies for fishery purposes. The variation throughout the year in the growth rate of a fish results from seasonal changes in temperature and food availability and is reflected in the development of the otoliths. The alternation of zones of rapid and slow growth allows the establishment of the age of fishes from a given population. However, more important in archaeological terms, is that the amount of last incremental growth allows the establishment of the season of death and, hence, the season of capture of the fish. Those increment studies of archaeological otoliths base their seasonal inferences on the width of the last external growth zone or on the number of last-deposited daily growth rings. Scales, vertebrae, and fin spines also display seasonal increments. These remains are preserved more frequently than otoliths but have the disadvantage that their incremental growth always lags behind that of otoliths by six weeks to three months.

Wim Van Neer

See also ANIMAL REMAINS, IDENTIFICATION AND ANALYSIS: FISH; GROWTH-RING ANALYSIS AND SEASONALITY STUDIES

Further Readings

Nolf, D. (1985) Otolithi Piscium. (Handbook of Paleoichthyology 10). Stuttgart and New York: G. Fischer Verlag.

Van Neer, W., Augustynen, S., and Linkowski, T. (1993) Daily growth increments on fish otoliths as seasonality indicators on archaeological sites: The tilapia from Late Palaeolithic Makhadma in Egypt. International Journal of Osteoarchaeology 3:241–248.

Ward, D.J. (1984) Collecting isolated microvertebrate fossils. Zoological Journal of the Linnaean Society 82:245–259.

Growth Studies: Mammal Teeth

Analysis of histological markers of developmentally significant life-history influences on the growth of dental tissues can be used to determine season of death or age of an animal. All mineralized skeletal tissues tend to grow in phasic cycles, thereby creating structures that preserve certain kinds of information about their development. These increments—which can be daily, weekly, monthly, seasonal, and even yearly—are especially useful to archaeologists who wish to reconstruct seasonal patterns or age profiles of animal hunting or culling, and they may also be useful for estimating the age at death of human remains. While incremental structures occur in most types of bone, increments in dental tissues are of special interest to archaeologists for four reasons. First, dental tissues, unlike bone, rarely remodel or resorb, leaving behind a fairly complete record of their growth history. Second, some dental tissues (especially cementum) accrue throughout an animal's lifetime and consequently provide life-history data on mature animals. Third, cementum can also preserve information about seasonal variations in an animal's diet and growth rate. Finally, teeth tend to survive better in the archaeological record than other parts of the skeleton, providing a plentiful source of reliable, accurate data.

Teeth consist of three distinct tissues, *enamel, dentine,* and *cementum* (see Figure), each of which grows incrementally. Since these tissues differ in their embryonic origin, mode of growth, and functional morphology, their increments develop differently and, therefore, provide different types of data. In addition, their histological contrasts require that they be prepared and analyzed in different ways.

Cementum

Cementum is the least plentiful and most poorly studied dental tissue, but it is probably the most useful for archaeologists. Cementum is essentially a type of bone that consists of ca. 60 percent calcium-phosphate mineral and 40 percent collagen; it is produced by *cementoblasts* that derive from the gum (the *periodontal ligament*), and it grows around dental roots until the tooth falls out or the animal dies. As its name implies, cementum functions to fix the tooth root to the periodontal ligament. It does so by growing and mineralizing tissue around collagen fiber bundles (*Sharpey's fibers*) that extrude from the periodontal ligament, thereby "cementing" the tooth to the soft tissue of the mandible or maxilla. Since Sharpey's fibers are produced by the periodontal ligament, they are often referred to as *extrinsic collagen fibers* to distinguish them from the *intrinsic collagen matrix* that cementoblasts produce around them, often at right angles to the Sharpey's fibers. Cementum also functions at the apical end of the tooth root to fill in space between the root and the periodontal ligament, and it may play an important role in tooth eruption.

When a tooth is sectioned (ca. 50–100 microns thick) and viewed using a microscope under transmitted polarized light, cementum increments appear as alternating translucent and opaque bands that vary in their width and optical property. For many (but not all) species, the number of cementum increments correlates well with the age at death of the animal, and the nature of the outermost band corresponds to its season of death. Opaque bands, which are more mineralized and narrower than translucent bands, usually deposit during seasons of reduced somatic growth (such as the winter and autumn in temperate climates). In contrast, translucent bands, which are less mineralized and usually wider than opaque bands, tend to deposit during seasons of increased somatic growth (such as the spring and summer). As a general rule, the number of cementum increments reflects the number of seasons an animal has lived since

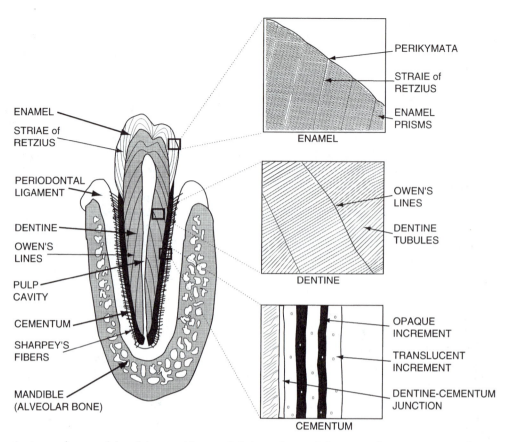

Anatomy of mammal dental tissues with expanded views of enamel, dentine, and cementum. Figure by Daniel Lieberman.

its tooth erupted. There is much histological variability in the tissue, however, both between and within animals. For example, the number of cementoblasts that become entrapped in the tissue behind the mineralizing front is largely a function of tissue growth rate. In general, cementum toward the crown end of the root tends to grow more slowly and regularly and appears in parallel bands that contain few cementoblasts (*acellular cementum*). Cementum toward the apical end of the tooth tends to grow more irregularly and rapidly, leaving behind more cementoblasts (*cellular cementum*).

Two independent processes contribute to increments in cementum. First, changes in the seasonal rate of growth of the tissue alter its degree of mineralization and, hence, its optical density. Because cementum tends to grow from a single mineralizing front along the margin of the periodontal ligament, variations in the rate of tissue growth alter the amount

of time cementoblasts remain in contact with the collagen matrix in which they deposit mineral. Consequently, in many species, the cementum increments that grow during seasons or periods of more rapid tissue growth are thicker but less mineralized than those increments that grow during seasons of diminished or arrested growth. Mechanical forces are a second potential influence on cementum histology. Since the function of cementum is to resist chewing forces, seasonal variations in the accumulated strain (deformation) that teeth experience can cause variations in Sharpey's fibers orientation in some species, particularly in acellular cementum, toward the crown of the tooth. During seasons in which animals chew more and/or harder food, their Sharpey's fibers may become aligned closer to the long axis of the tooth root. Such variations contribute to the optical phenomenon of banding in cross-polarized light because the collagen (and perhaps the mineral) of neighboring increments tends to bend light in different directions. It is possible that the density of extrinsic (Sharpey's) and/or intrinsic collagen fibers also varies seasonally because of changes in mechanical forces.

Great care is often necessary to analyze cementum increments. Archaeologists should analyze only teeth whose roots are still protected by the alveolar bone of the mandible or maxilla because cementum bands can delaminate in isolated teeth, thereby yielding incorrect estimates of age at, or season of, death. In addition, it is necessary to know something about seasonal diets and growth patterns of the animals involved, particularly for the environment in question. For this reason, evaluation of the accuracy and the reliability of seasonal estimates requires comparison with a sample of recent specimens of known age and season of death. Finally, cementum bands can have complicated histologies, particularly in diagenetically altered specimens, requiring careful preparation and analysis techniques.

Enamel

Enamel, which makes up the crown of a tooth, also grows in increments that can be useful for aging young mammals. Enamel is a highly mineralized substance (ca. 97 percent calcium phosphate) that is deposited by specialized cells, *ameloblasts,* that derive from epithelial tissue in each developing tooth germ. Ameloblasts secrete small amounts of enamel on a daily (circadian) basis, usually in bundles of crystallites known as *rods* or *prisms.* Variations in the rate of prism deposition create daily increments that are often visible at high magnifications using a scanning electron microscope. Because of interference patterns in the hormonal cycles that regulate its secretion, enamel prism growth is also interrupted on a roughly weekly basis (seven–nine days), causing brown-colored increments known as the *striae of Retzius* that are visible in sections under a transmitted-light microscope. The striae of Retzius record previous stages of the surface of the crown at various points in its development, and they sometimes extend to the surface of the tooth, creating small steps, known as *perikymata.* Since each Retzius line represents approximately seven to nine days of growth, one can count them on a sectioned tooth to estimate the amount of time it took the crown to develop. Such data, along with information about the growth of

the root, can allow estimation of the age at eruption of the dentition and, hence, an estimate of the age at death of young individuals. Striae of Retzius have been particularly useful for estimating the age of death of immature hominid fossils.

Dentine

Dentine is a somewhat bonelike tissue (ca. 70 percent mineral) that forms the majority of the tooth root. Dentine is deposited by elongated cells, *odontoblasts,* that extend from either the dentine-enamel or the dentine-cementum junction toward the center of the tooth root. Histologically, the most characteristic aspect of dentine are its long tubules in which the odontoblasts lie and which, therefore, record the direction of growth of each cell. As in other mineralized tissues, odontoblasts first secrete a collagen matrix into which they then precipitate calcium-phosphate mineral. Once the root of the tooth is fully formed, the odontoblasts remain alive and are capable of producing *secondary dentine* that can slowly fill up portions of the pulp cavity. Because the odontoblasts remain alive as an animal ages, dentine generally becomes more densely mineralized with time, particularly around each tubule. Consequently, the mineral density of the root often provides a rough means of estimating an animal's age at death. Like enamel, dentine grows in hierarchical increments because of daily, as well as longer, rhythms. *Von Ebner's lines,* which are visible at high magnifications, represent daily variations in the rate of tubule elongation; *Owen's lines,* which appear in sections as changes in the direction of tubule growth, are similar to the striae of Retzius in enamel because they record the shape of the internal surface of the developing root at various stages. To date, there is little information about the rate of formation of Owen's lines; however, variation in the isotopic content of dentine between Owen's lines can record long-term changes in animal diets.

Preparation Methods and Problems of Interpretation

Different preparation and analysis techniques are necessary for each tissue, particularly for archaeological or paleontological samples, which are often fragmented or modified by diagenetic processes that can potentially reduce the number of increments or obscure their histology. Striae of Retzius can be analyzed directly on naturally fragmented crowns or using perikymata on unworn crowns, but they are best studied with a scanning electron microscope (SEM), using sections cut through unworn crowns and then etched using a mild acid solution. Histological structures in dentine and cementum are best analyzed with a cross-polarized transmitted-light microscope using ground thin sections. For age and season-of-death estimates using cementum increments, which are often fragile and easily lost, it is especially important to analyze teeth whose roots have not been seriously damaged. To make sections, dry teeth are impregnated under a vacuum in a hard embedding medium such as epoxy or methyl-methacrylate, cut using a diamond saw, mounted on a glass slide, ground to a final thickness (usually 50–100 microns), and then polished. Computer-assisted image-analysis techniques help increase the accuracy and the objectivity of interpretations of dental increments because they can compute the number and width of increments on the basis of changes in optical density.

Estimates of seasonality and age at death from dental increments are important because they have a sound biological basis and, therefore, provide accurate, reliable, and potentially inexpensive data on life-history variables of mammals from archaeological sites. Like all archaeological data, however, they can present numerous problems of interpretation that must be integrated with information on the depositional and cultural contexts of the teeth from which they come. For example, cementum increments provide only minimum estimates for seasonal behaviors at an archaeological site, and it is important to consider them along with other types of evidence for seasonal activities. Nevertheless, cementum increments have been used successfully by archaeologists to estimate the season and age of death of animals from Pleistocene hunter-gatherer sites in Europe, the Middle East, and the New World. Cementum analysis is also used routinely by wildlife biologists to monitor wild populations of many mammal species. Enamel increments have been especially useful for estimating the age at death of fossil hominids to document changes in the rate of ontogeny in human evolution.

Daniel Lieberman

See also ANIMAL REMAINS, IDENTIFICATION AND ANALYSIS: MAMMALS; GROWTH-RING ANALYSIS AND SEASONALITY STUDIES

Further Readings

Aiello, L., and Dean, M.C. (1990) Human Evolutionary Anatomy. London: Academic.

Dean, M.C. (1987) Growth layers and incremental markings in hard tissues: A review of the literature and some preliminary observations about enamel microstructure in *Paranthropus boisei*. Journal of Human Evolution 16:157–172.

Klevezal, G.A., and Kleinenberg, S.E. (1967) Age determination of mammals by layered structure in teeth and bone. (Translation Series 1024). Quebec: Foreign Languages Division, Department of the Secretary of State of Canada, Fisheries Research Board of Canada.

Lieberman, D.E. (1993) Life history variables preserved in dental cementum microstructure. Science 261:1162–1164.

Lieberman, D.E. (1994) The biological basis for seasonal increments in dental cementum and their application to archaeological research. Journal of Archaeological Science 21:525–539.

H

Half-Sectioning

Method of obtaining vertical information through small archaeological features, such as pits, postholes, and ditches. Although half-sectioning can be applied to features of any size, larger features are more appropriately quartered or excavated in plan. Half-sectioning involves cutting a feature in half and removing half of the feature, thus temporarily leaving a vertical section through it. The position of the section must be carefully considered before any soil is removed. First, the feature must be carefully cleaned and drawn in plan. If more than one context is visible (e.g., the post stain can be differentiated from the post packing in a posthole), then the section line should cut through the various contexts. Also, the orientation of a posthole section line should be considered in relation to the structure of which the posthole is part. Postholes of a circular structure, for example, may be most appropriately sectioned in a radial pattern, as sections may show how posts were pushed out by the weight of the roof. In contrast, the location of the section line through a rubbish pit may have minimal significance. If, however, pits intersect, then the section line must be through the intersection to obtain information about their relationship and chronology (see Figure).

Half-sectioning a posthole should proceed as follows: Having cleaned the posthole in plan and decided on the orientation of the section, the archaeologist should mark the section line on the feature with a thin string and two nails. The half-section is then excavated in plan, keeping artifacts separate from the postpipe and packing material. When all material has been removed from the half-

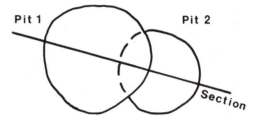

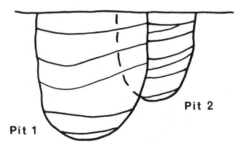

Half-sectioning intersecting pits. Figure by Peter L. Drewett.

section, the section should be cleaned and photographed. The section should then be drawn at a scale large enough to record details. Scales of 1:10 or even 1:5 may be suitable for small postholes. The section should always be drawn from a horizontal datum, usually a piece of string nailed onto the section and leveled using a spirit level. Having recorded the section, the archaeologist should remove the second half of the posthole to enable the whole posthole to be planned.

In interpreting the half-section, it may be possible to determine the size of the post, as distinct from the posthole (or postpit) and whether the post had been removed or left to rot in situ. If rotted in situ, the postpipe is likely to be clear, as fine soil particles will replace the gradually rotting wood. If removed, the void created by the removed timber will probably have filled in rapidly with collapsed packing material.

The dating of postholes, unless clearly part of a structure datable by its form or shape, is often difficult. Objects found within postholes rarely provide a reliable date, as most are residual. When the posthole was originally dug, it cut through earlier deposits. Much of this material will be returned to the posthole as packing material, thus giving a date earlier than the actual date of the posthole. The most reliable date can be obtained by establishing the date of the layer from which the post was originally dug. In deep sites this is possible, but on shallow, ploughed sites these data are often lost.

Half-sectioning of pits should proceed in a way similar to that for postholes, but the information provided from pits is different. Most pits found filled with rubbish on archaeological sites were used only secondarily as rubbish pits. Evidence for primary use as quarry pits, storage pits, cess pits, cooking pits, or ritual pits may still be visible in plan and section. The final use of the pit as a rubbish pit will, however, probably provide most information. Phases of rubbish deposition may be visible in the vertical section. This rubbish is, of course, generally secondary rubbish, indicating the range of activities taking place on the site or foods eaten but not where the activities took place.

Half-sectioning of deeper features may create a dangerous work situation. Wells can be half-sectioned but only by building up a cumulative section. This involves excavating not more than 1 m of the half-section, recording the section, and then removing the other half-section. This process can be continued to the bottom of the well. Each meter of section can then be added together to produce a complete cross-section of the well.

Peter L. Drewett

Further Readings

Barker, P. (1993) Techniques of Archaeological Excavation, 3rd ed. London: Batsford.

Drewett, P.L. (1999) Field Archaeology: An Introduction. London: University College London Press.

Harris Matrix

A formal representation of the stratigraphy of an archaeological site as a set of relationships: in mathematical terms, as a partly ordered set. The stratigraphic units that make up a site are either *deposits,* consisting of deposited material or *interfaces,* the boundaries between deposits. Both the deposition of material and its removal (e.g., the digging of a pit) create interfaces. The Harris-matrix system recognizes only three types of relationship between stratigraphic units: (1) there is no direct stratigraphic connection; (2) one unit is superimposed on the other; or (3) two units are correlated as part of a once whole deposit or interface. It then puts together these relationships to form a representation of the whole stratigraphic sequence of a site. In the usual format, boxes represent units, and lines between them the relationships; the system removes all redundant relationships (ones that can be predicted from other relationships) to create a minimal representation of the entire stratigraphic sequence.

Edward C. Harris invented the system in 1973, building on and developing the analogy between archaeological and geological stratigraphy but noting important differences. He used the term *matrix* to denote the form on which the archaeologist records the relationships; archaeologists who used his method applied the term *Harris Matrix* to the whole system of recording and, indeed, to this whole way of thinking about stratigraphy. This has caused some confusion, as the Harris matrix is essentially (though not by design) a mathematical concept, and the term *matrix* already had a mathematical meaning. However, the usage is now well established and is not likely to change.

Harris underpinned the system by developing the theory about archaeological stratigraphy, which he codified with four laws: *Original Continuity, Original Horizontality, Stratigraphical Succession,* and *Superposition.* He divided deposits into *natural strata* and *man-made layers* (e.g., floors, deliberate fills of pits) and defined a new class, *upstanding strata* (e.g., walls), which has no parallels in geology. He also divided interfaces into *layer interfaces* and *feature interfaces.* The former result from deposition or accumulation and subdivide into *horizontal layer interfaces* and *vertical layer interfaces.* The latter result from the destruction of stratification and again subdivide into the horizontal and the vertical. The introduction of vertical elements means that the system can be applied to the recording and analysis of standing buildings, as well as archaeological sites. The system has practical, as well as theoretical, implications and led very quickly to developments in the methods of excavation and recording. The most important is probably the *single-layer planning system*. As its name suggests, this system records each unit of stratification separately. Archaeologists record on a separate plan (1) site coordinates, (2) the boundary of each layer or feature, and (3) an appropriate number of elevations (i.e., spot heights). They can combine such plans to produce composite plans, as well as sections, and can use them to check recorded relationships.

The establishment of a stratigraphic sequence, although crucial, is not enough. A site sequence commonly consists of two or more separate sequences, which the archaeologist must correlate to establish the contemporaneity of various parts of different sequences. The next step is to divide the correlated sequence into phases and/or periods. To some extent, this is a stratigraphic task, but it should also bring in dating evidence from artifacts found in the units. This last step, which usually takes place after an excavation has finished, must take account of the possibility that some artifacts may not be *indigenous* (i.e., roughly contemporary with the layer in which they were found). They may be either *residual* (much earlier than the layer in which they were found) or *infiltrated* or *intrusive* (later than the layer in which they were found). Both states can cause confusion and error if not detected; testing against the sequence is one of the main means of detection.

The adoption of the Harris matrix by archaeologists has been rapid and widespread. It met the needs of archaeologists working on the large urban excavations that characterized European archaeology in the 1970s and 1980s. It also related to the growing interest at that time in site-formation processes, but its main achievement was to create a formal and logical system for the presentation and interpretation of archaeological stratigraphy. Although the basic principles are now well established, archaeologists continue to develop further refinements.

Clive Orton

See also ARCHAEOLOGICAL SITES, FORMATION PROCESSES; STRATIFICATION; STRATIGRAPHY

Further Readings

Alvey, B., and Moffett, J. (1986) Single Context Planning and the Computer: The Plan Database. (Computer Applications in Archaeology 1986). Birmingham: Birmingham University Computer Centre.

Dalland, M. (1984) A procedure for use in stratigraphic analysis. Scottish Archaeological Review 3:116–26.

Harris, E.C. (1989) Principles of Archaeological Stratigraphy, 2nd ed. London: Academic.

Harris, E.C., Brown, M.R., and Brown, G.J., eds. (1993) Practices of Archaeological Stratigraphy. London: Academic.

Hassan, Fekri A. (1943–)

Egyptian prehistorian and geoarchaeologist. Born on August 11, 1943, Hassan received his doctorate from Southern Methodist University (Dallas, Texas) in 1973. From 1975 to 1994, he taught in the geoarchaeology section of the Department of Anthropology at Washington State University at Pullman. In 1994, Hassan was appointed Petrie Professor of Egyptology at University College, London. A specialist in Near Eastern and northeast African prehistory, Hassan has been an important figure in the development of modern methods of typological and attribute analysis of lithic materials and in the application of geological principles and Quaternary geology (geoarchaeology), particularly in the study of the Nile Valley. Hassan has played a major role in the development of geoarchaeology, in his work on site formation and distribution in the Nile Valley ("Sebillian Sites from the Dishna Plain"; "Prehistoric Settlements along the Main Nile"), on paleoclimate and the origins of agriculture in Palestine, on geomorphology and depositional studies in Washington State, and on the general methodology and applications of geoarchaeology ("Sediments in Archaeology"; "Palaeoenvironments and Contemporary Archaeology: A Geoarchaeological Approach").

Joseph J. Basile

See also GEOARCHAEOLOGY

Further Readings

Hassan, F.A. (1972) Sebillian sites from the Dishna Plain. Chronique d'Egypte 47:11–16.

Hassan, F.A. (1974) The Archaeology of the Dishna Plain, Egypt: A Study of a Late Palaeolithic Settlement. Cairo: Geological Survey of Egypt.

Hassan, F.A. (1978) Sediments in archaeology. Journal of Field Archaeology 5:197–213.

Hassan, F.A. (1980) Prehistoric settlements along the main Nile. In M.A.J. Williams and H. Faure (eds.): The Sahara and the Nile: Quaternary Environments and Prehistoric Occupation in Northern Africa, pp. 421–450. Rotterdam: Balkema.

Hassan, F.A. (1981) Demographic Archaeology. New York: Academic.

Hassan, F.A. (1985) Palaeoenvironments and contemporary archaeology: A geoarchaeological approach. In G. Rapp and J.A. Gifford (eds.): Archaeological Geology, pp. 85–102. New Haven/London: Yale University Press.

Historical Archaeology

The branch of archaeology that studies the expansion of European culture throughout the world over the last 500 years and the impact of that expansion on the other peoples of the world. In essence, historical archaeology is the archaeology of the modern era or, more specifically, of the origins, growth, and spread of capitalism. In North America, the Society for Historical Archaeology promotes the study of historical archaeology and publishes the journal *Historical Archaeology*. In Great Britain, the Society for Post Medieval Archaeology publishes the journal *Post Medieval Archaeology*. In Australia, there is the Australian Society of Historical Archaeology with its *Australian Journal of Historical Archaeology*. The topics, content, methods, and theory of historical archaeology substantially overlap with underwater/nautical archaeology and industrial archaeology, although these branches of archaeology have their own special concerns, societies and journals.

History

Historical archaeology developed as a distinct branch of archaeology first in the United States and Canada. Here archaeologists draw a distinction between prehistoric archaeology, which studies the pasts of indigenous peoples, and historical archaeology, which studies European sites and indigenous sites with evidence of European contact. Scattered references exist for excavations in European sites from the eighteenth and nineteenth centuries, but it is only in the 1920s and 1930s that historical archaeology developed as a coherent field of study. This was a period of great interest in historical reconstruction. Numerous private foundations and the U.S. and Canadian governments sought to study and reconstruct important historical sites. These efforts led to the establishment of many of the major living-history museums. Historical archaeology began in places such as Jamestown, Port Royal, Plimoth Plantation, Saint Marie One, and Colonial Williamsburg. Archaeologists contributed to these efforts by supplying information on the correct placement and reconstruction of buildings, forts, roads, wells, and other features. They also provided details, such as what artifacts should be placed in the reconstructions. These reconstructions emphasized great men, first settlements, and great events.

Jean Carl Harrington's research at George Washington's Fort Necessity characterizes this early period. In 1933, the National Park Service reconstructed the rude fort that troops under George Washington had thrown up during the opening battle of the French and Indian War in 1754. Harrington's excavations in 1952–1953 revealed the reconstruction to be incorrect, and the Park Service used his findings to build a new reconstruction.

In the 1960s and 1970s, historical archaeology became a distinct branch of archaeology, partly as a reaction to the rejection of historical archaeology by prehistoric archaeologists. Prehistoric archaeologists frequently did not accept the excavation of historic sites as a legitimate part of archaeology. The Southeast Archaeology Conference's refusal to accept papers on historic sites led to the founding of the Conference on Historic Sites Archaeology in 1960. This conference met and published proceedings of its papers until 1980, after the Southeastern Archaeological Conference began accepting papers on historic sites. The Society for Historical Archaeology was founded in 1967. In 1970, Ivor

Noël Hume published *A Guide to the Artifacts of Colonial America*. This seminal work remains a guide to the identification and dating of Colonial artifacts. The field grew greatly in the 1970s, in part because the burgeoning enterprise of contract archaeology recruited many archaeologists to study historic sites.

From the late 1960s to the end of the 1970s, the core theoretical debate in historical archaeology revolved around whether the field should be history or anthropology. Some archaeologists argued that historical archaeology should be a humanistic field that contributed to our understanding of particular historical events and processes. Other archaeologists maintained that historical archaeology should join the scientific research program of the New Archaeology and seek universal generalizations to explain cultural change. Working in the latter paradigm, Stanley South proposed a series of artifact patterns that would predict the cultural and functional character of sites. Neither of these positions ever came to dominate the field, as the scientific position of the New Archaeology came to dominate in prehistoric archaeology. Because this division was never resolved, historical archaeology was one of the few parts of American archaeology in which humanistic and historical approaches flourished in the 1970s.

James J. F. Deetz's structuralist studies of changes in Puritan worldview and material culture exemplify the humanistic approach. Deetz argued that the Pilgrims brought with them a medieval worldview that was traditional, governed by nature, communal, and emphasized kin relations. He maintains that, in the mid-eighteenth century, this worldview was transformed into a Georgian worldview. The new worldview was innovative, governed by reason, and emphasized individual achievement. He found evidence for this shift in a variety of mundane activities or small things forgotten. These included shifts in household trash disposal from broadcasting it around the houseyard to burying it in small pits, changes in dishes from communal bowls to individual plates, and changes in rooms from multiple uses to single-purpose uses.

The social upheavals of the 1960s and the academic reactions to them had a more profound effect on historical archaeology than the challenges of the New Archaeology. Many historical archaeologists asserted that archaeology was a particularly good technique for studying the history of oppressed and underrepresented groups in American and Canadian history. Studies in the 1970s such as Charles Fairbanks's excavations in the cabins of enslaved Africans in Florida and Georgia and Kathleen Deagan's research on the process of Native American–to–Spanish assimilation, or mestiziation, in Saint Augustine, Florida, helped alter the focus of the field away from great men and great events. This emphasis on the archaeology of the disempowered continues to dominate the field.

In the 1980s, historical archaeology gained recognition as a legitimate part of North American archaeology, and it became a center of theoretical innovation in the larger discipline. By the 1980s, papers on historical archaeology were routinely presented at all major archaeology conferences, and articles on historical sites appeared in the major journals. The postprocessual critique of processual archaeology found fertile ground in historical archaeology, and the vast majority of early postprocessual research was on historic sites. This was because a structuralist approach existed in historical archaeology and because documents made many of the questions that the postprocessualists wished to ask easier to answer.

Mark Paul Leone and his colleagues pioneered postprocessual research in their studies of Annapolis, Maryland. Drawing on critical theory and structural Marxism, they sought to ask how history had been created in Annapolis. Rather than simply supply the Historic Annapolis foundation with details to assist in reconstructions, they asked how eighteenth-century elites had used gardens, printing type, clocks, toothbrushes, and a host of other aspects of material culture to foster the belief that their rule was just and natural. They also sought to study how subsequent elites had manipulated the historical district of Annapolis to their own ends and how modern tourists interpreted what they saw there.

Theory and Method in Historical Archaeology

Historical archaeology continues to be divided between humanists and scientists, but much of the fervor of the debate has been lost.

This reflects the fact that, since the 1970s, anthropology has become more historical, and history more anthropological. It also indicates a growing realization that good work can be done through both approaches. The core methodological question remains how to integrate artifacts and documents in the study of historic sites. Historical archaeologists promote two complementary positions that stress the value of the study of material culture.

The first position grows out of historical archaeology's original role of filling in missing information from the documentary record. It focuses on the incompleteness of the documentary record and how material culture can be used to complete historical knowledge.

Historical archaeologists recognize that not all time periods and events are equally well represented in the documentary record. In the European history of North America, the number of documents that were produced, and that survive, increases geometrically over time. This makes historical archaeology especially useful in early periods when few, and often only fragmentary, documents are available. Certain events may also not leave a rich documentary record. For example, at the Battle of the Little Big Horn, none of the Seventh Cavalry who rode with George Armstrong Custer (1839–1876) survived the battle, and the Native American victors left no written accounts of the battle. Historical archaeologists, such as Richard A. Fox, have been able to reconstruct what happened to Custer's command on that day and substantially confirm Native American oral accounts of the action.

Historical archaeologists note that the documentary record tends to focus on great people and great events. Even when common documents survive, such as diaries and letters, they tend to focus on the personal and emotional concerns of individuals. People do not generally write about the mundane and day-to-day activities that make up most of their lives. In contrast, the archaeological record is primarily made up of the remains of these day-to-day activities. Many of the great events of history (e.g., the signing of the Declaration of Independence) leave little in the way of material remains, but the day-to-day activities of life do.

Historical archaeologists stress the consistent biases to the documentary record. It is primarily the literate and the powerful who produce documents and see to their survival.

In North American history, wealthy European males tend to dominate the documentary record. The vast majority of people who have lived in North America are poorly represented in the documentary record or not represented at all. This is particularly true of groups that were disenfranchised and the oppressed, such as enslaved Africans, Native Americans, workers, and women. These people did leave physical traces of their lives that historical archaeologists can study. Through these traces, historical archaeologists can learn about the day-to-day experience, the nutrition, and the health of everybody in history.

Finally, much of the information in the documentary record is prescriptive (i.e., it tells people how they should have acted). People did not always act the way that they were told to. Indeed, if they had, we would not have so many books, articles, religious tracts, and other documents telling them what they should be doing. Many of the activities that people engaged in in the past, and that had a profound effect on history, were illegal. The archaeological record provides a check between the prescriptive literature and what people actually did. It also provides a record of a wide range of illicit and illegal activities ranging from opium smoking to smuggling.

The second line of argument begins with the position that archaeology is not simply a poor substitute for the written word. It is, instead, a unique way of studying the world that allows us to learn things we could not learn otherwise. People create material culture, and it bears the mark of that creation. From these marks, archaeologists can reconstruct technologies, costs, trade, and even aspects of the organization of work that created these objects. In these ways, material culture gives archaeologists a means to reconstruct past behaviors. Material culture is also an active agent in peoples lives. Material culture structures what people do, and it carries meaning. Thus, material culture may embody emotions, aesthetics, social relations, and beliefs, and these things affect how people will think and act. In this way, material culture becomes an active instrument that affects what people will do. Documents are valuable from this perspective because they allow the historical archaeologist greater access to meaning and belief. In this way they supplement the study of material culture, rather than the material culture just filling in what the documents lack.

The archaeological study of two nineteenth-century houses owned by the Boott Textile Mills in Lowell, Massachusetts, illustrates this second perspective. After excavating these two tenement buildings, Mary C. Beaudry and Stephen A. Mrozowski were able to show how the buildings, outbuildings, and yards structured the lives of the working-class inhabitants. They were also able to show how these inhabitants used various aspects of material culture, such as tobacco pipes, dishes, and personal items, to create a subculture of resistance in this company housing.

Issues in Historical Archaeology

Historical archaeologists tend to specialize in specific substantive issues and topics. Some of these topics reflect concerns that crosscut all of historical archaeology (e.g., the study of artifacts). Others relate to certain historical periods, such as the contact period, or specific contexts of doing archaeology, such as urban archaeology. These topics form subcommunities within historical archaeology in which researchers can share information and help one another resolve similar problems. The most successful research in these areas integrates the study of material culture with documents and, increasingly, with oral histories.

The traditional concerns of historical reconstruction and artifact studies continue to draw considerable attention in historical archaeology. Historical archaeologists still contribute information for the reconstruction of historical buildings, and most of the major living-history museums in the United States and Canada have archaeologists on their staff. Artifact research has focused on the chronology of change in form through time and the technologies of manufacture. For many years, Parks Canada, Ottawa, has been a leader in these studies, publishing detailed manuals on a host of different types of artifacts. Other research has concentrated on establishing the relative costs of artifacts, such as the Creamware index (which refers to the cheapest type of available dishes) that George L. Miller created in 1987 for nineteenth-century ceramics.

Another continuing traditional focus of historical archaeology is military archaeology, the archaeological study of war and warfare in North America and the North American military experience. Military archaeologists research both military sites, such as forts and posts, and battlefields, such as the Little Big Horn.

The colonialization process has always held a great fascination for historical archaeologists, and archaeological studies of this process have been done throughout the world. The time of initial European contact with indigenous peoples, or the contact period, holds special interest. The study of this experience unites traditional anthropological concerns with a usually incomplete, and strongly European-biased, documentary record. In the Spanish colonies, one of the primary agents of colonization were the missions, and mission archaeology focuses on this history. David Hurst Thomas has used his study of the Spanish mission of Santa Catalina de Guale in Georgia to highlight the forgotten history of Spanish missions in the southeastern United States.

Gender studies rapidly became important in historical archaeology after the first symposium on gender at the Society for Historical Archaeology meetings in 1989. These studies spring from feminist critiques of male bias in previous research. At a minimum, they identify women in contexts in which they have traditionally been ignored, such as logging camps and in the fur trade. More sophisticated studies emphasize the active role of women in important cultural and historical transitions. Diana diZerega Wall studied how middle-class women in early-nineteenth-century New York City used meals and place settings to create the home as the woman's sphere, apart from the man's sphere in the workplace.

Wall's work is not unusual in its urban context. Urban renewal in the late 1960s launched substantial archaeological projects in cities. Urban archaeology concerns itself with the problems of doing archaeology in the city and the intellectual challenge of doing an archaeology of the city. The former concern focuses on the methodological and formation processes that are unique in the urban context. An archaeology of the city investigates those social processes that characterize cities.

In the western United States, urban renewal often meant destroying the neighborhoods of overseas Chinese. Many of these dated to the nineteenth century. Archaeological research for these projects established the study of the overseas Chinese as a research area. Initially, archaeological inquiry concentrated on Chinese cultural practices, including foodways and opium smoking. Increasingly, research has focused on the contributions of the Chinese to the historical development of the western United States.

African American archaeology essentially began with Fairbanks's excavations of slave cabins, but it has grown far beyond that. Today, archaeologists concern themselves with the totality of the African American experience in U.S. history. Archaeologists have engaged in a massive search for Africanisms, (i.e., cultural practices that can be traced to Africa). Examples of these include the production of handmade earthenware ceramics called *colono-ware,* and the shotgun-house plan popular in nineteenth-century southern homes. Such practices are important because they show that Africans managed to preserve a cultural heritage despite the horrors of slavery. Cemeteries of African- and American-born slaves have also been a major focus of research, and these have yielded information about the health and nutrition of both free and enslaved Africans.

Studies of plantation archaeology frequently overlap African American archaeology. They often focus on plantation social relations among enslaved Africans, White employees, and the plantation owners. Theresa Singleton's research has shown that enslaved Africans actively contributed to the construction of southern culture and economy and resisted their enslavement in many ways. Researchers have also examined the post–Civil War transformation of the plantation system to a system of tenant farming.

The thread that ties all of these topics together is capitalism. The European conquest of the world that began in 1492 set in motion the economic, social, and cultural changes that would create capitalism. The topics that historical archaeologists have focused on are all part of this larger process. Southern plantation owners enslaved Africans to grow cotton to feed textile factories such as Boott Mills in Lowell, Massachusetts. The Seventh Cavalry was defeated in a war to clear the West of Native Americans, and Chinese workers built railroads that opened that West to capitalist development. The massive explosion in the number and forms of objects from the eighteenth to the twentieth century provides the basic data of historical archaeology.

The capitalist drive for profit propelled this explosion. The variation that archaeologists study in these objects records the transformation of machines from objects that serve workers to things that the workers must serve. Thus, many archaeologists argue that historical archaeology is the archaeology of capitalism.

Randall H. McGuire

See also DEETZ, JAMES J. FANTO; INDUSTRIAL ARCHAEOLOGY; LEONE, MARK PAUL; NAUTICAL ARCHAEOLOGY; NEW/PROCESSUAL ARCHAEOLOGY; THOMAS, DAVID HURST; UNDERWATER ARCHAEOLOGY

Further Readings

Beaudry, M.C., and Mrozowski, S.A., eds. (1989) The Boarding House System as a Way of Life. Interdisciplinary Investigations of the Boott Mills, Lowell, Massachusetts, vol. 3. (Cultural Resource Management Study 21). Boston: North Atlantic Regional Office, National Park Service.

Deetz, J.J.F. (1977) In Small Things Forgotten. Garden City: Anchor.

Feder, K.L. (1994) A Village of Outcasts: Historical Archaeology and Documentary Research at the Lighthouse Site. Mountain View, CA: Mayfield.

Fox, R.A. (1993) Archaeology, History, and Custer's Last Battle: The Little Big Horn Reexamined. Norman: University of Oklahoma Press.

Leone, M.P., and Potter, P.B., Jr. (1988) The Recovery of Meaning: Historical Archaeology in the Eastern United States. Washington, D.C.: Smithsonian Institution Press.

McGuire, R. and Paynter, R., eds. (1991) The Archaeology of Inequality. Oxford: Blackwell.

Noël Hume, I. (1970) A Guide to Artifacts of Colonial America. New York: Knopf.

Singleton, T. (1985) The Archaeology of Slavery and Plantation Life. Orlando: Academic.

Wall, D.d. (1994) The Archaeology of Gender: Separating the Spheres in Urban America. New York: Plenum.

Yentsch, A., ed. (1992) The Art and Mystery of Historical Archaeology: Essays in Honor of James Deetz. Boca Raton, FL: CRC.

Hodder, Ian (1949–)

British archaeologist. After completing a doctorate at Cambridge University, Hodder took up the post of lecturer at the University of Leeds, where he coauthored (with Clive Orton) *Spatial Analysis in Archaeology,* a key processual text for multivariate, computer-based analysis. His other main processual research can be found in his edited collection *Simulation Studies in Archaeology.* Under the influence of recent anthropological theory and his own ethnoarchaeological fieldwork, Hodder turned from processual archaeology in the early 1980s to develop key theoretical concepts found in his collection *Symbolic and Structural Archaeology.* This approach matured into postprocessual archaeology. Hodder wrote several key ethnoarchaeological texts on the significance of material culture, including *Symbols in Action, The Present Past,* and *Reading the Past.* Hodder explored the potential in long-term symbolic structures both in Europe, in *The Domestication of Europe* and elsewhere. He is director of the Southern Fenlands Archaeological Project and has recently started the reexcavation of Çatal Hüyük, a key Neolithic site in Turkey.

John Chapman

See also ETHNOARCHAEOLOGY; NEW/PROCESSUAL ARCHAEOLOGY; POSTPROCESSUAL ARCHAEOLOGY

Further Readings

Hodder, I. (1982a) The Present Past: An Introduction to Anthropology for Archaeologists. London: B.T. Batsford.

Hodder, I. (1982b) Symbols in Action: Ethnoarchaeological Studies of Material Culture. Cambridge/New York: Cambridge University Press.

Hodder, I. (1990) The domestication of Europe: Structure and Contingency in Neolithic Societies. Oxford/Cambridge, MA: Blackwell.

Hodder, I. (1991) Reading the Past: Current Approaches to Interpretation in Archaeology, 2nd ed. Cambridge/New York: Cambridge University Press.

Hodder, I. (1992) Theory and Practice in Archaeology. London/New York: Routledge.

Hodder, I., ed. (1978) Simulation Studies in Archaeology. Cambridge/New York: Cambridge University Press.

Hodder, I., ed. (1982) Symbolic and Structural Archaeology. Cambridge/New York: Cambridge University Press.

Hodder, I., ed. (1991) Archaeological Theory in Europe: The Last Three Decades. London/New York: Routledge.

Hodder, I., ed. (1987a) Archaeology as Long-Term History. Cambridge/New York: Cambridge University Press.

Hodder, I., ed. (1987b) The Archaeology of Contextual Meanings. Cambridge/New York: Cambridge University Press.

Hodder, I., ed. (1989) The Meanings of Things: Material Culture and Symbolic Expression. London/Boston: Unwin Hyman.

Hodder, I. and Orton, C. (1976) Spatial Analysis in Archaeology. Cambridge/New York: Cambridge University Press.

Hodder, I., Shanks, M., Alexandri, A., Buchli, V., Carman, J., Last, J., and Lucas, G., eds. (1995) Interpreting Archaeology: Finding Meaning in the Past. London/New York: Routledge.

Holmes, William Henry (1846–1933)

Leading American archaeologist of the late nineteenth and early twentieth centuries and distinguished artist/illustrator. Born in Cadiz, Ohio, Holmes completed his formal training in education, graduating from McNeely Normal School in Hopedale, Ohio. An 1871 trip to Washington, D.C., with the objective of training in art led to his employment by the Smithsonian Institution as a specimen illustrator. In 1872, he joined the Geological Survey of the Territories, later the United States Geological Survey (USGS), as an artist and a mapmaker. He began publishing archaeological treatises while still with the USGS; he became a Bureau of (American) Ethnology (BAE) employee in 1889. Except from 1894 to 1897, when he was a curator at the Field Museum of Natural History in Chicago and professor of anthropologic geology at the University of Chicago, he remained associated with the Smithsonian Institution, serving as curator of the United States National Museum (USNM) (1889–1894), head curator of the USNM (1897–1902); chief of the BAE (1902–1910), head of anthropology at the USNM (1910–1920), and curator of the American Gallery of Art (1910–1920). He became director of the National Gallery of Art in 1920, a position he held for the next twelve years. He died in 1933.

The intellectual character of Holmes's work set it apart from that of his contemporaries. He did not simply describe finds; he attempted to ascertain how and why artifacts had the forms and distributions they did. The driving force behind his approach was a strident advocacy of archaeology as science. Holmes wrote the first expressly theoretical papers in archaeology, making the bases of his classifications and interpretations explicit and justified. He laid the basis for modern ceramic analysis in a series of papers in the 1880s and 1890s, culminating in 1903 in his massive survey, *Aboriginal Pottery of the Eastern United States*. Much of his research was devoted to debunking the notion of an American Palaeolithic comparable to Europe. His exemplary excavations showed that key deposits were Cretaceous, not Pleistocene, that they were quarries, not occupation sites, and that the primitive tools were not tools at all but quarry blanks and rejects. A Loubat Prize (1898) and likely his election to the National Academy of Science (1905) followed from this work. The *Handbook of American Antiquities, Part 1* summarized his vast experience with lithics, their technology, variation, and distribution. Holmes regarded North Americans as recent arrivals in the New World; thus, when new material proved to be Pleistocene (barely) and interest shifted to chronology in the 1930s, much of Holmes's work lost its impact. Holmes's answers have proved mostly wrong, but many of the questions central to later archaeologists, as well as the concepts used to frame them, were first given form by Holmes.

Robert C. Dunnell

Further Readings

Holmes, W.H. (1903) Aboriginal Pottery of the Eastern United States. (Annual Report of the Bureau of American Ethnology to the Secretary of the Smithsonian Institution 20). Washington, D.C.: Government Printing Office.

Holmes, W.H. (1919) Handbook of Aboriginal American Antiquities. (Bulletin of the Bureau of American Ethnology, Smithsonian Institution 60). Washington, D.C.: Government Printing Office.

Meltzer, D.J. and Dunnell, R.C., eds. (1992) The Archaeology of William Henry Holmes. Washington, D.C.: Smithsonian Institution Press.

Howell, Francis Clark (1925–)

American paleoanthropologist and archaeologist. Born on November 27, 1925, in Kansas City, Missouri, Howell was educated at the University of Chicago, where he received his bachelor's degree in 1949, his master's in 1951, and his doctorate in 1953. He began his career as an educator in his native state, as instructor of anthropology at Washington University in 1953, but returned to Chicago two years later as assistant professor of anthropology. He was appointed associate professor in 1959 and full professor in 1962. Howell also served as the chairman of the Anthropology Department (1966–1969). He is currently emeritus professor of anthropology at the University of California at Berkeley. Howell is a member of the American Anthropological Association, the American Association of Physical Anthropologists, the American Association for the Advancement of Science, the American Antiquarian Society, the American Philosophical Society, the American Academy of Arts and Sciences, and the National Academy of Sciences and was also a recipient of the Guggenheim Fellowship (1985).

Howell is an important figure in the study of early hominids and the movement of humans from Africa into the rest of the Old World. In the Omo River Valley in southern Ethiopia, Howell and Yves Coppens of the Université de Paris excavated important australopithecine remains, as well as the remains of *Homo habilis,* including the first complete forearm bone recovered. The site, at which layers of Omo River sediment are sandwiched between layers of volcanic material datable to as early as 4 million B.P., has been hailed as one of the most significant sites illustrating human evolution in Africa. He is probably most well known, however, for his excavations at Torralba in Spain, a remote site high on the Castillian Plateau. There, he and Leslie Freeman of the University of Chicago discovered a butchering site dated to 500,000–300,000 B.P. Tools, living floors, and the skeletons of dozens of game animals—elephants, horses, rhinoceri, deer, and oxen—were recovered, giving a detailed picture of early human subsistence patterns in Europe. While Howell's interpretations of the Torralba site have been questioned, the site remains one of the most important Palaeolithic discoveries in Europe.

Joseph J. Basile

Further Readings

Coppens, Y. and Howell, F.C. (1985–1987) Les Faunes Plio-Pleistocenes de la Basse Vallee de l'Omo (Ethiopie). Cahiers de Paleontologie, Travaux de Paleontologie Est-Africaine). Paris: Editions du Centre National de la Recherche Scientifique.

Howell, F.C. and Bourliere, F., eds. (1963) African Ecology and Human Evolution. Chicago: Aldine.

Meikle, W.E., Howell, F.C. and Jablonski, N.G., eds. (1996) Contemporary Issues in Human Evolution. (Memoir, California Academy of Sciences 21). San Francisco: California Academy of Sciences.

H

I

Illustration, Archaeological

A system of recording dimensions and relevant information from excavated objects as a series of measured projections, used as data presentation in initial excavation reports and as examples in comparative/synthetic papers. Advantages over photography are that measurements can be taken directly from the drawings, and artifactual features given clarity.

The limited technique of ink drawing with line or dot, stipple, is very well suited to this selective approach. Before drawing, the quality and quantity of information recordable should be assessed. Morphology, decoration, and indications of manufacture and wear are among the primary characteristics to be recorded. Any other aspects that can easily be described in the accompanying text should be.

Archaeological drawing technique is a hybrid of technical drawing and shaded engraving. However, shading is used only to describe curved surfaces or modeling. Where it is used, the light source is always from the top left of the drawing so that any projections are described by shading around the bottom right, while depressions are described with shading at the top left.

The level of sophistication of equipment used is variable. Traditionally, all stages of drawing can be executed on the same piece of good-quality bleedproof cartridge paper. Measurements and initial drawing are completed in pencil, which can then be inked over, with the pencil marking erased later. Alternatively, a top copy may be made in ink on a transparent plastic film overlay. This procedure has two advantages over the first. Plastic film is completely bleedproof, so ink is not absorbed into the surface as on paper and, therefore, cannot spread. It stays where put, producing a sharp, clean line. Also, the next stage necessary for publication, producing a camera-ready page proof of traditionally pasted-up arrangements of drawings, can be incorporated as part of the copy taking.

The most sophisticated equipment that is easily obtainable is a computer-aided design (CAD) program into which the pencil drawing can be scanned and reproduced in any size, position, combination, or line width requested.

For manual inking up, technical pens that produce lines of controlled, consistent widths are used, as very rarely is an object drawing published at full scale. Economies of page space and the advantage of showing groups of objects on the same page lead to size reduction of drawings. Reductions of different materials are no longer standardized, but, generally, the more commonplace the type of object, the greater will be the reduction, while the rarer or most decorated objects will be least reduced, if at all. In principle, objects similar to types already illustrated and identified should not be illustrated again but referred to these examples.

It is essential to know the scale at which the drawing will be reproduced before the inking-up process, to enable the illustrator to select the most suitable line width. The finest reliably reproducible line under all traditional printing processes is ca. 0.125 mm, so, for a drawing that is to be reduced to 1.2 linear scale, a minimum penline width of 0.25 mm is required; for a drawing reduced to 1.4 linear scale, a minimum penline width of 0.5 mm is required, and so on.

On reduction, not only the width of the line narrows, but the spaces between the lines also reduce. If too much detail has been drawn, so that lines are too close together, the spaces will black in and the detail will be lost. Drawing must remain more open when reduction is involved than when the drawing is not to be reduced.

For small objects or very fine details, such as jewelry or microliths, the whole object or part of it is drawn at an enlarged scale. This allows the detail to be drawn more clearly. Such a drawing can be reproduced at the same scale or reduced. The detail will remain clearer on a reduced reproduction than if it had been drawn at a smaller scale.

On every page of illustrations, the scale of the drawings must be indicated. If the scale is definite before completion, it can be incorporated into the figure title, but, if there is any doubt, it is safer to draw a linear scale on each page.

The basic illustration system is one of plans, perpendicularly related projections, or elevations and sections. One view is selected that gives the maximum relevant information about the artifact. This view is recorded with as few further views or sections as are necessary to describe the whole object, laid out horizontally or vertically adjacent. For each new view, the object is rotated 90° through one plane so that the two views of any one feature are adjacent and can be read together. Where sections can give sufficient information, side or end views may be dispensed with.

Sections may be taken from any part of the object but must always be perpendicular to the drawn view (Figure 1). Section lines, one short line on each side of the object but not touching it, must always be drawn to indicate the point where the section was measured. The section drawing may be placed beside the section line or moved above or below the drawing to save space. The section is rotated 90° on a horizontal axis through the view already drawn so that the face drawn becomes the top of the section. Pottery sections follow a different convention (see below). To obtain the section, the width of the object as drawn is repeated horizontally beside the drawing, and the distance through the object is plotted vertically through the midpoint of the width.

A box or frame is constructed through these points. The outline of the section is drawn by eye or profile gauge so that maximum dimensions coincide with this frame. Sections of pottery and small objects are usually printed in black, but larger areas of solid black become overwhelming on the page and so are infilled with parallel diagonal lines.

There are two basic approaches to obtaining the outline or profile of an object. The first approach, which sounds the simplest, is accomplished by taking measurements and is used when the artifact is so large that it needs to be drawn at a reduced scale. A framework of baselines is built up around the object, from which perpendicular offsets are measured, but these are cumbersome and fiddly, becoming more fiddly with smaller objects. Electronic and laser equipment does exist that utilizes this method, but it is very expensive.

The second approach involves using the most useful piece of equipment for archaeological illustration, one eye trained to be used as a technical viewpoint.

The object must first be positioned correctly on the drawing surface, propped at such an angle that the required outline or profile is parallel to the drawing surface. All points of this profile must now be projected perpendicularly down onto the paper. This can be achieved, in principle, by positioning the eye as viewpoint perpendicularly above the point on the profile being drawn and the drawing point on the paper. This relationship must be retained throughout the drawing process by moving the eye as the pencil moves.

The *one eye as technical viewpoint* concept is fundamental to all archaeological illustration and must be employed at all stages of measurement. However, technical equipment can aid parts of this process. Once the object is positioned correctly, an *engineer's square,* one that stands on a flat surface with a perpendicular, rising edge, can be used to project points of the profile down onto the paper. The standing edge is brought into contact with the profile; the point where this edge also touches the paper is plotted. When a sufficient number of plots has been taken, the profile can reliably be drawn through them. A *profile gauge* can also be used for taking impressions of short lengths of profiles but is most suited to obtaining profiles from robust ceramic vessels. A profile gauge consists of a parallel row of slideable needlelike strips of steel held in a lockable girdle so that, when brought into contact with an object, the edges of the needles take up the impression of that object, which can be retained by locking.

The position of features within the profile must then be measured across a horizontal plane (i.e., parallel to the drawing surface), by eye, using dividers or with the aid of a rigid transparent surface such as perspex laid horizontally over the object. Features can actually be plotted onto this surface and then traced back off onto the drawing surface. Another method involves using graph paper as a background. Measurements are taken along a straight edge held horizontally above and linking any given graph line.

The most common materials excavated and, therefore, in need of illustrating are ceramics, sometimes as whole vessels but most often as sherds; stone implements, both flaked or chipped and often polished; metal; and organic materials, such as wood, bone, leather, and shell, that have been modified into implements or symbolically charged objects. Rarer are organic materials, spun and woven into textiles.

Different conventions have evolved, since the late nineteenth century, when archaeological illustration was first used systematically, to develop an optimum method of recording artifacts. Ceramics, flaked-stone, and textile illustration employ the more extreme separate conventions. Stone, metal, and most organic objects are grouped together and treated similarly as small finds.

Ceramics

The format of the whole-pot drawing has evolved to incorporate the maximum number of variable features within the one profile. Its convention lines, the center line and the rim line, must accurately record the height at midpoint of the vessel and the diameter of the rim, respectively. The profile records the maximum diameter of the outer pot wall through a vertical plane. This profile must be taken individually from both sides of the vessel, as, particularly in prehistoric hand-built pots, the walls are rarely symmetrical. The section or thickness of the pot wall is measured with calipers and recorded on one side only of the pot profile. Which side varies from country to country. In North America, it tends to be on the right, while in Britain and some European countries it is placed on the left. Between the section and the center line, any internal features, decoration, or manufacture marks are shown; on the other

side of the center line, external features are recorded (Figure 2).

Irregular features, such as lips or handles, can be incorporated into the same profile if this does not obscure the clarity of recording, in which case details may be shown repeated horizontally adjacent. If the wall of the vessel has irregularities that cannot be incorporated into this format, further sections may also be placed horizontally adjacent to the main section. This conventional pot format works very well for vessels that are round; other forms will need additional drawings. Vessels of other materials, such as glass or pewter, also follow this format.

All sherd drawing is an abbreviation of the whole-pot format. The sherds should follow the same orientation on the paper as they would if the whole pot had been drawn. All horizontal attributes, rim, base, wheel marks, and decoration will be drawn as lines, not arcs. As much of the whole pot as is possible is reconstructed. If enough arc of the rim or the base of a round pot survives, an estimate is made of the original diameter of either, and an appropriate-length center line can be used to reconstruct the relevant band of the pot (Figure 3A).

The original diameter is estimated by comparing, in the same plane, the remaining arc of rim or base with a printed sheet of concentric arcs of known diameters. If the pot is not round, or an estimate of the original pot diameter is not obtainable, the center line cannot be used, but a part of the rim or the base line is still drawn, linking the section to the external outline and features (Figure 3B). If no useful information can be recorded from the external view, only the section is shown with vestigial rim or base line (Figure 3C).

Body sherds are usually illustrated only for decoration or manufacturing marks. The only other information recorded is the section, but, if orientation is difficult to establish, the section is drawn as vertical. A short horizontal link line is still needed but not across the top or bottom of the views, as this would be confused either with a rim or a base line (Figure 3D).

Treatment of decoration on pots depends on the type of decoration and the shape of pot. If the decoration is a simple repeat or nondeveloping, it can be incorporated into the whole-pot format between center line and profile as a perspective drawing or an unrolled two-dimensional sample (Figure 4).

I

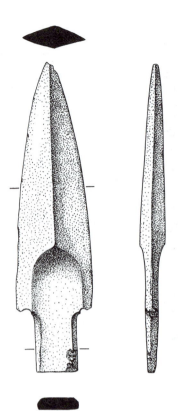

Figure 2. *Illustration convention for drawing whole ceramics, showing profile, center line, rim line, and external decoration. Drawn by Lysbeth Drewett.*

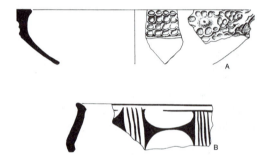

Figure 1. *Illustration of spearhead, showing conventions for frontal view, longitudinal section, and cross-sections. Drawn by Lysbeth Drewett.*

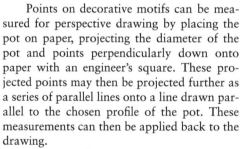

Points on decorative motifs can be measured for perspective drawing by placing the pot on paper, projecting the diameter of the pot and points perpendicularly down onto paper with an engineer's square. These projected points may then be projected further as a series of parallel lines onto a line drawn parallel to the chosen profile of the pot. These measurements can then be applied back to the drawing.

More complicated or developing decoration must be drawn as unrolled panels (Figure 4). These are positioned beyond the profile. If the decoration is around a straight or cylindrical body, this is straightforward and can be achieved using tracing paper or, if the decoration is incised and the vessel is robust enough, by taking a rubbing with soft tissue paper and graphite powder applied by finger. However, if the decoration covers an area of the pot with a convex or concave profile, it cannot be unfurled without adjustments. The best strategy in this case is to wrap and tape a band of

Figure 3. *Illustration conventions for drawing ceramic sherds. A = decorated rim sherds with enough information to include an estimate of the original diameter of the pot; B = drawing of decorated rim sherd when ceramic is not round or there is insufficient information to estimate diameter; C = section drawing of rim sherd with insufficient information to reconstruct diameter and with no surface decoration; D = drawing convention for decorated body sherds. Drawn by Lysbeth Drewett.*

tracing paper around the maximum diameter of the body of the vessel and snip into it from the top or bottom so that overlapping segments can be tailored and taped onto the curving wall. When the design has been flat-

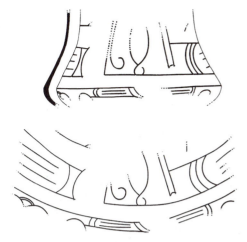

tened back onto the drawing surface, adjustments have to be made between these extended segments.

Decoration from above or below the maximum diameter of the pot most accurately becomes arched bands of decoration when flattened (Figure 4).

Figure 4. Illustrative treatment of complicated decoration on pots in an unrolled two-dimensional panel placed beyond the profile. Drawn by Lysbeth Drewett.

Stone, Flint, and Obsidian Tools

Different conventions apply to the illustration of flint, chert, and obsidian tools. These fracture conchoidally. This reaction can be used to illustrate the method and the sequence of manufacture. Conchoidal rings or ripples of percussion fan out from the point of impact over the whole fractured surface. When further fracturing occurs over a smaller surface or facet, new whole ripples cut through the previous larger ones. In good light, shade from individual ripples can be analyzed and recorded within each facet. The number of views drawn will depend on distribution of working or wear.

Generally, simple flaked tools need only one view, while points and bifaces need both faces plus side or end views. Layout and procedure follow the same principles as for small finds. Flint illustrations are not normally reduced to smaller than 1.2 linear. If necessary, separate drawings of detailed areas can be drawn at 2.1 and reduced to 1.1. These are placed alongside the same area on the whole drawing but not linked by line.

Outline and facet edges are drawn in medium-width line, while the finest line, 0.25 mm if 1.2 reduction, is reserved for ripples.

Small finds are treated in the least conventional, most straightforward way but still must conform to the system of plans, elevations, and section drawing.

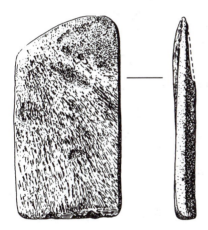

Figure 5. Illustration technique for stone objects, showing texture and surface treatment. Drawn by Lysbeth Drewett.

Stone objects other than flaked flints are treated as small finds, and a representative texture is used to describe the reaction of the type of stone to the surface treatment. This usually combines short line and stipple or dot (Figure 5). Fine stipple is used for fine grain, with areas left blank for highlighted polished areas, while a coarser arrangement of short, jagged line and stipple is used to describe pecked or worn coarse sandstone.

Other Objects

Corroded iron objects can be problematic. There is no value in drawing lumps of amorphous corrosion. Outline drawings should be

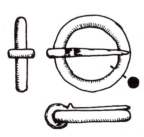

Figure 6. Illustration technique for metallic objects. Drawn by Lysbeth Drewett.

made by comparing objects with X rays. Broken, hand-drawn parallel lines are used to indicate surfaces parallel to the drawing surface (Figure 6). The surfaces of bronze objects are usually described by stipple. Artifacts made from organic material, such as wood, bone, shell, or leather, are treated differently: The grain and natural characteristics of these objects are used to describe their surfaces, lines for bone, wood, and shell and groups of stipple for leather. Often, these natural characteristics can be used to further describe the nature of any human modification, but, where this causes conflict or lack of clarity, the artifactual description must be presented most clearly at the expense of the natural.

Preserved woven textiles can be drawn realistically, but more information can be recorded by illustrating as per the textile weaver's manual with the number of warps and wefts counted over a given area and reconstructed as a diagram.

Traditionally, archaeological illustrations did not use color, due to the high cost. Color is usually described in the text, or, where it is important, as in polychrome ceramics and medieval glazes, textual legends have evolved for these specialties. Now, however, computer-aided illustration can produce individual colored drawings cheaply.

Lysbeth Drewett

Further Readings

Addington, L.R. (1986) Lithic Illustration: Drawing Flaked Stone Artifacts for Publication. (Prehistoric Archaeology and Ecology Series). Chicago: University of Chicago Press.

Adkins, L., and Adkins, R. (1989) Archaeological Illustration. (Cambridge Manuals in Archaeology.) Cambridge: Cambridge University Press.

Dillon, B.D., ed. (1981) The Student's Guide to Archaeological Illustrating. (Archaeological Research Tools 1). Los Angeles: Institute of Archaeology, UCLA.

Griffiths, N., and Jenner, A., with Wilson, C. (1990) Drawing Archaeological Finds: A Handbook. London: Archetype.

Joukowsky, M. (1980) A Complete Manual of Field Archaeology. Englewood Cliffs, NJ: Prentice-Hall.

Orton, C., Tyers, P., and Vince, A. (1993) Ceramics in Archaeology. Cambridge: Cambridge University Press.

Rice, P.M. (1987) Pottery Analysis: A Sourcebook. Chicago: University of Chicago Press.

In Situ Conservation

The means of ensuring the long-term survival of archaeological sites. The objective of conservation is to reduce the rate at which an exposed site deteriorates, in order to retain its cultural significance and to maximize its potential for scholarly study, education, and enjoyment. In situ (i.e., in original place) conservation of sites covers all archaeological sites that are no longer inhabited, whether they be standing ruins or excavated sites. The term may also be extended to cover the protection of sites that have not been excavated, and many of the same principles apply.

The long-term survival of sites is impossible unless there is a will to conserve them. Regrettably, this will is not always present. Deliberate destruction, vandalism, and looting can denude a site of its value. Many sites are lost through warfare. Neglect, though less rapid, may be equally damaging and irreversible. One of the first steps in site conservation is to assess the significance of the site and, through education, communication, and negotiation, to secure the support of all those who have an interest in the site.

It is not just local people who may have an interest in a site. Many sites have a worldwide significance, and there have been a number of attempts by international organizations to draw up guidelines for site conservation. The 1966 Venice Charter of the International Congress of Architects and Technicians of Historic Monuments was an important milestone, but one of the most helpful documents has been the Burra Charter: the Charter for the Conservation of Places of Cultural Significance drawn up by the Australian section of ICOMOS. The latter charter places a strong emphasis on cultural significance as the justification for conservation and stresses the need to consider a site in association with its surroundings. It sets out nine conservation principles, on which it bases detailed recommendations for conservation processes and practice.

Documentation

The assessment of cultural significance is only one part of the process of drawing up a management plan for a site. Close scrutiny of the material remains is also vital, followed by documentation. In many cases, it will prove impossible to arrest the deterioration of the site completely, but the records that are made at an early stage will serve to preserve the site on paper and on computer disc. Close scrutiny will also lead to an assessment of the physical condition of the site and of the factors that may cause it to deteriorate. Such a diagnosis is an essential precursor of any conservation policy.

Conservation Options

Conservation, like much in life, is subject to fashion. In much of the Western world, the current fashion is to "conserve as found"—to keep the site in a state as close as possible to that in which it was found. The principles of *minimum intervention* (doing no more than is absolutely necessary) and of *reversibility* (not doing anything that could not one day be undone) are strongly upheld, though sometimes more in word than in action. In other parts of the world, however, the function of a site may be more important than its material remains. Preserving the religious significance and function of a temple, say, may be of more importance than retaining the materials from which the temple was originally made. Equally, the extent to which restoration or reconstruction is regarded as acceptable may vary from place to place and from time to time.

In considering conservation options, it is helpful to distinguish between active and passive conservation. *Active* (or direct) *conservation* entails intervention with the fabric itself; *passive* (or indirect) *conservation* embraces all of those other activities that seek to minimize deterioration without direct contact.

Passive Conservation

Passive conservation may take many forms. At its most remote, it may consist of legislation to protect the site and its immediate surroundings. Such legislation would exert controls over further excavation or might, indeed, prevent any excavation of a known site from taking place until other conservation procedures were available. Legislation might also control development on the site or exploitation for farming or quarrying, for example. Legislation alone will seldom be sufficient protection for an excavated site, but it can form an important part of the overall protection strategy.

Visitor management is another important part of passive conservation. Visitors are to be encouraged, for the cultural heritage is the preserve not only of the professional, and visitors may provide a vital source of revenue. They present a problem, nonetheless. Car parks, toilets, shops, and refreshment facilities may detract from the atmosphere of a site. The constant tramp of feet will quickly erode earthworks and will eventually damage floors. Moisture from breathing and perspiration may initiate salt damage or promote biological growths in enclosed spaces. In extreme circumstances, it may be necessary to exclude visitors altogether or to regulate their numbers rigidly to save the site. Such measures have been taken to preserve the wall paintings in the prehistoric caves at Lascaux in France and in the Tomb of Queen Nefertari in Egypt's Valley of the Queens.

Some visitors are unable to resist the temptation to prize off a small piece for a souvenir, while others may be intent on deliberate vandalism or looting. Site security is, thus, another aspect of passive conservation. In some cases, it is necessary to mount guards for twenty-four hours a day, but this can be wholly impractical in remote sites. Here a program of education and public awareness may be appropriate, so that those who live near the site become unofficial guardians. Other approaches rely upon alarm systems and more traditional security devices, but these, too, may have severe limitations, especially where the response time is long.

Finally, we come to the topic that is most commonly associated with passive conservation: environmental control. The intention is to control the environment around the site in such a way as to minimize deterioration, and this can be achieved in many different ways. At its simplest, it may consist of nothing more than a windbreak of indigenous plants around the site to reduce wind erosion. At its most sophisticated, it may consist of a protective structure built over the site, complete with air conditioning.

Those aspects of the environment that are most commonly considered include soil water and floodwater, the amount of moisture vapor in the air (i.e., the relative humidity), rain, air pollution, and direct heating by the sun. Soil water and floodwater are matters of irrigation and land drainage. Sometimes the objective is to reduce the water table and so reduce the amount of water that rises by capillarity into the structures on the site, thereby endangering mudbrick and stone structures. The site of Mohenjodaro in Pakistan provides an example of this approach. On other occasions, the objective may be to prevent dewatering and drainage of the soil and thereby prevent the aerobic degradation of organic remains, such as timber structures. Prehistoric trackways in the Somerset Levels in England have been protected in this way.

With the other aspects of environmental control, it is normally necessary to rely upon protective roofs and shelters or to resort to the complete enclosure of sites to ensure museum-like conditions. Roofs and shelters will give a measure of protection against rain and sunlight, but they will be less effective in controlling relative humidity and will have no effect on pollution. Nonetheless, they have been used extensively, in a wide variety of forms and materials. Sometimes the form is sympathetic to the site, suggesting perhaps the outline of a previous structure. Sometimes the form is wholly intrusive. Sometimes the materials are carefully selected to ensure a desired level of vapor permeability or of impermeability to ultraviolet light, for example. Sometimes the materials consist of corrugated iron and concrete—whatever was readily available. An interesting development is the *hexashelter*—a lightweight, modular structure designed for the temporary protection of sites. It has an aluminum frame with fabric roof and side panels, and it is anchored by concrete blocks, thus minimizing its impact on archaeologically sensitive areas. It was used to protect the Orpheus mosaic at Paphos in Cyprus during conservation. The use of shelters to protect sites is an area that warrants further research. It is easy to erect a shelter, but less easy to specify exactly what function the shelter is to fulfill and then to produce a design that meets those specifications.

The building that encloses a site completely is the ultimate in environmental control, provided that the internal environment can be maintained at constant temperature and relative humidity. The building totally changes the character of the site, but it may, nonetheless, be the only means of ensuring the survival of an important site. Perhaps the largest of all such structures is the hangarlike exhibition hall, with a floor area of 16,000 m², that protects the terra-cotta warriors in the tomb of Qin Shi Huang in Xian, China. Another notable example is the proposal to enclose the standing ruins of Hamar Cathedral in Norway in an air-conditioned envelope of glass and aluminum. Sometimes the protective structure was the reason for the site's discovery in the first place: There are many instances of sites that were discovered during the construction of shops or offices, and that are now on display in the protected environment of the basement.

Perhaps the most extreme instance of environmental protection is to be found in reburial, which is in the gray area between active and passive conservation. Reburial, in principle, is the surest means of ensuring the survival of a site, even though it is lost to public view. If one can re-create the conditions that allowed the site to survive to the present day, then it should survive well into the future. In practice, this may be difficult to achieve. Reburial frequently consists of no more than backfilling with the soil that was removed during excavation. It would be naive to suppose that the original conditions could be rapidly reestablished in this manner. Even if the soil itself could be replaced in the correct sequence, it would not be possible to reproduce the original degree of compaction, permeability, water content, or oxygen content. Further deterioration of the site could well take place during the time that is necessary for the original conditions to be reestablished. Some research in this area is in progress, and further research is necessary to optimize conditions and to identify the best materials to be used for reburial.

If a site is to be reburied, it may be desirable to lay a membrane between the excavated surface and the backfill. The membrane provides some protection to underlying features during reburial; it serves as a marker to delineate the excavated horizon; and it facilitates reexcavation at some future date. Such a membrane may also be used when a site is backfilled between the seasons of a long-running excavation. Many archaeologists have used polyethylene (polyethene) sheeting for this purpose, and many still do so, but it is becoming increasingly recognized that impermeable membranes like polyethylene may do damage to a site. They prevent drainage and the natural migration of moisture and air within the soil, with the result that the soil may be unusually dry in some areas and unusually wet in others. These conditions could threaten the continuing survival of both artifacts and ecofacts. Wet conditions, for example, could attract microorganisms, earthworms, and preferential root growth, while dry conditions could cause damage by salt crystallization and would threaten organic remains that had previously survived through waterlogging. To avoid these problems, permeable membranes known as *geotextiles* are attracting increasing attention. They are made of durable plastic, with a texture and appearance resembling felt. They have high mechanical strength and good resistance to chemicals and to biological organisms. They have been available since the 1970s, although their use in archaeology is comparatively recent. While more experience of their performance is required, they offer considerable promise.

Active Conservation

Active conservation means "doing something" to the fabric of the site, and all too often it conjures up an image of an elixir that can be applied to the fabric to prevent all further deterioration. Sadly, no such elixir exists and probably never will. All manner of materials have been tried in an attempt to consolidate and protect both earthen and stone structures, and, while a measure of success has been achieved, no product has emerged that can be relied upon to prolong life for long periods without undesirable side effects. Active conservation, in practice, then, is usually a matter of traditional methods for repair and maintenance. Mudbrick structures, for example, may be capped to prevent rain from penetrating into the core. Masonry structures may require grouting or repointing, and individual stones may need replacement. Documentation is important to ensure that there is no future confusion between what is original and what is a repair; sometimes the repairs are set into a very distinctive mortar or delineated in some comparable manner. The materials that are used must be physically and chemically compatible with the original, and the skill of the craftsperson is important in ensuring a sympathetic and durable repair. Active conservation may also include restoration or reconstruction: returning the site (or a part of it) as nearly as possible to a known earlier state.

Mosaics form an important group that has been the subject of much active conservation in situ. Conservation frequently entails lifting the mosaic and relaying it on a more durable base to prevent the loss of individual tesserae. Wall paintings, too, may be removed and reinstated.

The importance of regular inspection and maintenance cannot be overemphasized. The form that maintenance takes will vary from site to site, but it may include the unblocking of drains, the filling of minor cracks, or the use of biocides to control vegetation. Prompt attention to small defects can prevent the development of major problems and thereby avoid both major expenditure and the disruption of original material.

It is unrealistic to think that any site can be made to last forever. Nonetheless, by adopting rational and responsible conservation policies, we can aim to hand on our cultural heritage to the next generation in the best possible condition. After that, it is up to them.

Clifford Price

See also MOSAICS, ON-SITE CONSERVATION; ROCK-ART SITES, RECORDING AND ANALYSIS; WALL PAINTINGS, CONSERVATION

Further Readings

Agnew, N., and Coffman, R. (1991) Development and evaluation of the hexashelter. In The Conservation of the Orpheus Mosaic at Paphos, Cyprus, pp. 36–41. Marina del Rey: Getty Conservation Institute.

Australia ICOMOS Charter for the Conservation of Places of Cultural Significance (the Burra Charter). Adopted 1979, with revisions in 1981 and 1988. International Council on Monuments and Sites.

Hodges, H.W.M., ed. (1987) In situ archaeological conservation. Mexico City: Instituto Nacional de Antropología/Century City, CA: J. Paul Getty Trust.

Preventive measures during excavation and site protection. (1986) Rome: International Centre for the Study of the Preservation and the Restoration of Cultural Property (ICCROM).

Stanley Price, N.P., ed. (1995) Conservation on Archaeological Excavations, 2nd ed. Rome: International Centre for the Study of the Preservation and the Restoration of Cultural Property (ICCROM).

Inductively Coupled Plasma—Atomic Emission Spectrometry

An analytical technique developed in the physical sciences that is used for chemical (elemental) characterization of archaeological materials such as pottery (ceramics), soils, metals, bone, and other comparable samples.

Inductively coupled plasma–atomic emission spectrometry (ICP-AES) has become an accepted and valuable technique for the chemical characterization of archaeological materials. The technique is destructive, but only very small amounts of material are needed, and a rapid and reliable chemical analysis can be prepared. A wide range of elements are measured, including many diagnostic trace elements and most major constituents. Quantitative elemental analysis is a valuable archaeological method that allows a chemical "signature" to be established. A diversity of archaeological materials can be analyzed. Many of the applications have involved ceramic (pottery) material, but metals, bones, soils, and a range of artifacts can be investigated.

Chemical analysis and characterization have been used to a limited extent in archaeological research, but increasing numbers of researchers are adopting the technique. In the past, there have been several practical difficulties to obtaining good-quality analytical data. Limited access to analytical facilities, the high costs, the large numbers of samples that must be processed to obtain representative data, and the diversity of sample matrices have all contributed to the restricted use of elemental analysis in archaeology. ICP-AES addresses many of these problems, although it is not without limitations, and it should not be seen as a universal panacea. It has become reasonably accessible: Several universities and commercial organizations have instrumentation, and commercial analytical services are well established. Costs have come down substantially, and multielement analysis (twenty–thirty elements) can be obtained on large numbers of samples at reasonable cost (ca. $10 per sample for a wide-ranging multielement analysis). Not all sample matrices can be analyzed routinely, but ceramic and metallic samples should represent no real difficulties.

There are several additional considerations that should be recognized before selecting ICP-AES as a part of an archaeological study. The technique is destructive, but it can work with very small sample weights (100 mg or less). Hence, high-quality museum specimens may not be suitable, but, in pottery studies, the large numbers of sherds found at many excavated sites can be sampled and analyzed without serious damage. The major components in a sample can be readily determined, and many trace elements are well within the attainable detection limits of the method. However, other chemical techniques (notably inductively coupled plasma–mass spectrometry and instrumented neutron activation) may achieve even lower levels of determination. This may be important for some elements. The technique does not provide information on a microscopic level; it provides data only on the bulk material sampled. A further consideration is that ICP-AES will give elemental analysis for many elements, but isotopic data cannot be obtained.

In practice, ICP-AES is a solution method of analysis, and all samples must be dissolved. This is normally a straightforward operation, but it is a limitation of the method. There are well-established methods for dissolving samples. One widely used procedure is treating the samples with a nitric acid or nitric and hydrochloric acids. This approach is suitable for many metals, bones, and leaching elements from soil samples. An alternative (and more rigorous) approach to sample dissolution is treating the sample with hydrofluoric acid in combination with nitric or perchloric acids. This will dissolve silicate-based samples, including ceramics and pottery. A further method available to the researcher is fusing the sample with an appropriate flux. Sodium hydroxide, lithium metaborate, and several other salts are used routinely as fluxes. This approach will dissolve almost any sample type, including refractory mineral phases. Fusing the sample ensures complete dissolution; it also introduces substantial quantities of flux into the solution; and this may degrade detection limits.

There are three stages in the analysis of a dissolved sample using ICP-AES. First, the sample is introduced into the inductively coupled plasma source unit. Second, the emission signal produced as the sample enters the high-temperature plasma is resolved into its separate spectral lines and their intensity measured. Finally, there is the quantification of the signals emitted for each analyte element. A detailed schematic diagram showing the operation of a typical ICP-AES configuration is shown in the accompanying Figure. There is an extensive literature on the principles and the practice of how ICP systems operate, and this should be consulted (see Thompson and Walsh, 1989).

Calibration of the ICP-AES system can be made with either natural or synthetic standards. Calibration lines are prepared for all of the elements to be measured in an analytical program. Most calibration lines are linear, even for the measurement of major elements at high levels (100–1,000 g/ml). Interferences are found for some trace elements, and these can normally be corrected with computer software. Although ICP emission spectrometry is generally free from the chemical interferences that occur in atomic absorption spectrometry, there are cases of spectral-line overlaps. This can be significant for interferences from a major element on some trace elements. However, there is now sufficient

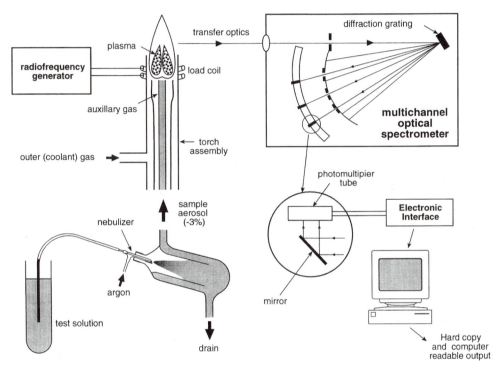

Samples for analysis are introduced into a nebulizer system as dissolved material. An aerosol of the solution to be analyzed (the analyte) is formed by the flow of high-pressure argon gas. In the spray chamber, large solution droplets are removed and go to waste via the drain; only fine aerosol particles travel up into the plasma. The plasma is sustained by inductive heating from the radio-frequency generator of argon gas as it flows through a quartz glass tube. The plasma (defined as an ionized gas that is electrically conducting) operates at a temperature between 6,000° and 10,000°C, and the analyte solution is introduced into this through a central injector tube. The high temperature of the plasma produces intense emission spectral lines and eliminates almost all chemical interferences. Elements emit emission lines at discrete wavelengths, and the combined light is focused onto the diffraction grating within the spectrometer. This resolves the emitted spectral lines into their separate wavelengths. The intensity of the lines, which should be proportional to the concentration of the element in the analyte solution, is measured by photomultiplier tubes. The electrical signal from each element photomultiplier is then compared with the signal emitted by known concentrations of the appropriate element. This allows a quantitative measurement to be made of the concentration of the element in the original solution. Providing the dilution of the sample in the solution is known, it is possible to obtain concentrations of the element in the original material. Figure by J. Nicholas Walsh.

practical experience to be able to confidently predict likely interferences in most good commercial ICP-AES instruments.

Most (but not all) ICP-AES systems are capable of measuring elements simultaneously, and it is possible to analyze one sample every minute for twenty–thirty elements. This excludes the time required to dissolve the original material. Although ICP-AES instruments are more expensive than some comparable analytical techniques (e.g., atomic absorption), the sample throughput is such that, for the analysis of many archaeological materials, the technique is very cost effective. The method will analyze for a wide range of elements. All of the major constituents—silicon (Si), aluminum (Al), iron (Fe), magnesium (Mg), calcium (Ca), sodium (Na), potassium (K), titanium (Ti), magnesium (Mn), and Phosphorus (P)—and many trace elements can be measured in ceramic materials. The technique is capable of analytical precision (reproducibility) of 2 percent or better in routine operation, and accuracy for the major constituents of ceramics has been shown to be not worse than the precision. The precision can be improved further (to less than 1 percent) by using multiple internal standards for major-element analysis. This takes advantage of the simultaneous measurement system in ICP-AES. An element that is known to be not present in the samples at significant levels is added to each solution prior to analysis. The major element to be determined is then measured to this internal standard, and any instrumental fluctuations can be reduced to a minimum. Detection limits obtainable with ICP-AES will vary for different elements and must take into account the sample dilution during dissolution, but the limit is usually 1–10 ppm (parts per million) in the original solid samples.

Chemical analysis of archaeological materials should introduce quantitative, objective data. However, interpretation of the significance of the implications of the chemical analyses will continue to be a subjective process. The analytical technique has been available since the 1980s, with modern simultaneous analytical systems in operation in numerous laboratories. Its application in archaeological research has been limited, but an increasing number of studies have been successfully completed. Many of the studies using the technique to date (i.e., 1998) have been provenance studies for ceramics; in favorable cases, the chemical signature obtained from pottery can confirm or disprove source clays. The technique can also be used to confirm or deny the validity of groupings of pottery samples. Methods for treating the chemical data have varied, but the use of simple bivariate plots for pairs of elements can be helpful. This approach allows grouping of sample types to be seen in a manner that is clear and convincing to the nonmathematically inclined researcher. More sophisticated statistical methods (cluster analysis, factor analysis) have been used, but controversy over the statistics will often detract from the archaeological credibility of the conclusions.

A study made of the extensive collections of pottery sherds excavated from Roman sites in Colchester, England, was able to confirm that some of the samian ware (*terra sigillata*) was made locally (Storey et al. 1989). The elemental analytical data provided by the ICP-AES system was used to show considerable chemical similarities among several groups of pottery fragments, which could be linked chemically to local clay samples that were collected in Colchester. This study was also able to identify some pottery fragments that were clearly distinct and different from the Colchester material; the authors suggested that these were examples of imported Sinzig pottery (Rhineland, Germany).

With the completion of other ICP-AES analytical research, the technique is likely to find increasing relevance in pottery-provenance studies. In addition, the technique can and has found applications in other aspects of archaeological investigations. The emphasis placed on environmental archaeological investigations and the use of soil analysis is an area in which ICP-AES can make a valid contribution. Chemical analytical data is especially valuable when it can be used to provide quantitative data to arbitrate between alternative hypotheses. Interpretation of chemical data is probably not yet sufficiently well developed to use the technique to suggest origins for materials without supporting archaeological evidence.

J. Nicholas Walsh

See also ATOMIC ABSORPTION (AA) SPECTROMETRY

Further Readings

Hatcher H., Tite M.S., and Walsh J.N. (1995) A comparison of inductively coupled plasma emission spectrometry and atomic absorption spectrometry on standard reference silicate materials and ceramics. Archaeometry 37:83–94.

Storey, J.M.V., Symonds, R.P., Hart, F.A., and Walsh, J.N. (1989) A chemical investigation of "Colchester" samian by means of inductively coupled plasma emission spectrometry. Journal of Roman Pottery Studies 2:33–43.

Thompson, M., and Walsh, J.N. (1989) A Handbook of ICP Spectrometry, 2nd ed. Glasgow: Blackie.

Walsh, J.N. (1992) The use of multiple internal standards for high precision analysis of geological samples. Chemical Geology 95:113–121.

Industrial Archaeology

The study of the material record of peoples' work outside the home and field. Industrial archaeologists examine tasks done in factories, mills, mines, and ships, as well as in the shops of individual artisans. Through its focus on material evidence, industrial archaeology complements the history of technology studied with the written record. Although they could apply many of their methods to any time in the past, most industrial archaeologists have interested themselves in historic times, and some would like to restrict the field to the remains of industrialization that occurred after the seventeenth century A.D.

Industrial archaeology, like other branches of archaeology, began with antiquarian curiosity. Engineers saw the material heritage of industrialization disappear with the redevelopment of old industrial sites and undertook to record it. The British, with their particularly long history of industrialization, led the way, beginning with the work of organizations such as the Newcomen Society. After the Second World War, individuals interested in particular industries began to organize groups, such as the Historical Metallurgy Society, to conduct research and publish journals. By 1955, some of them were beginning to use the term *industrial archaeology* for their work, and, in 1963, they began publishing the *Journal of Industrial Archaeology* (now the *Industrial Archaeology Review*). A group of Americans organized in 1971 to hold meetings and publish *IA, the Journal of the Society for Industrial Archeology*. When the federal government and many states began to require that historic sites be recorded before demolition or reuse, they created new professional opportunities for industrial archaeologists. Practitioners of industrial archaeology are in transition from their antiquarian heritage to a profession with academic underpinnings.

Artisans have long carried out sophisticated, technical tasks without the aid of written instructions. Most learned their skills "through their fingers," by doing tasks rather than talking about them, and they often developed a lifelong taciturnity. Some were secretive, and some deliberately deceived curious observers. Even if they were willing (and many were not), they would have found it difficult to tell what they were about to someone watching them at work. Anyone who may have wanted to record artisans' work faced formidable obstacles: It was easy to keep records of quantities of products made, of prices, tariffs, wages, and numbers of people at work but difficult to describe the tasks artisans carried out. Until recently, no one had an adequate vocabulary for techniques that involved invisible processes, such as smelting metals or dyeing cloth. Even describing the fully visible steps of operating a device such as a loom taxed written language. (Think of the assembly instructions supplied by the makers of toys and household devices.) Even where drawings of equipment or specifications for a task survive, industrial archaeologists often find that artisans altered the equipment they used, or the procedures they followed, to make their work easier or to overcome difficulties that had not been anticipated by managers or designers. Consequently, the artifacts that archaeologists learn to "read" provide a record of work with a precision that oral accounts or documents cannot match.

Methods

Industrial archaeologists learn about past work by examining artifacts, the remains of workplaces, and the geographical settings in which industries operated.

Work Sites

In examining a work site, industrial archaeologists first look for the routes used to bring in the materials and power needed and to remove the completed products. They search for evidence that artisans used specialized materials obtained from distant sources, perhaps along transportation routes that can be traced or inferred. The remains of the facilities needed to transport heavy or bulky materials often outlast other remains. Although artisans have always used hand tools, most industries supplemented the efforts of individuals with power from wind, water, or burning fuel. Proprietors in some industries considered access to a power source the single most important factor determining the location of their works. Remains of a water-power system, such as dams, raceways, and wheelpits, or the foundations of a boiler, stack, and steam engine are often enduring, easily recognized features at an industrial site.

Industrial work produces wastes. While industries recycled some directly and reworked others years later (as when the piles of *culm* at anthracite mines were salvaged after new combustion techniques made it possible to burn fine coal), they left much untouched. Consequently, waste deposits are often the most permanent and, sometimes, abundant remains at an industrial site once its aboveground structures are gone. Analysis of these wastes can reveal aspects of the processes that were carried on at the site. (In sampling waste piles, archaeologists must be alert for the possible presence of hazardous materials.)

Operators of mines and of industries that relied on water power had to locate at the natural resource they used, often an isolated or rural site, where they had to build housing for their workers. Additionally, owners of mills and factories in towns and cities sometimes built blocks of worker housing near their establishments. Some proprietors took the opportunity to build model communities that expressed their social beliefs: Samuel Collins, president of the Collins Company in Connecticut, forbade saloons in Collinsville. Industrial archaeologists often find rich evidence of living patterns in communities that served a specific industry. The physical fabric of these communities often survives long after the parent industry vanished. Even when there are no standing structures, excavations may reveal the layout of worker housing in a former mill village or mining camp. The home of an artisan practicing a craft alone is generally more difficult to locate, while, in a large city, artisans from different industries may have lived throughout the community, making it hard for an archaeologist to trace their domestic arrangements.

Workplaces

Although industrial archaeologists sometimes manage to record the work of one of the last artisans to practice an abandoned craft, or the processes used in a shop about to be closed, many obsolete industrial processes vanished before anyone recorded the techniques and knowledge that their artisans brought to the work. The owners of an abandoned workplace could sell much of their surviving equipment as scrap. Only rarely does a workplace survive with its equipment intact. Sometimes this is because it was located in such a remote place that no one found it worthwhile to salvage the equipment for scrap: When the proprietors of the last gold dredges operating in the Yukon abandoned their operations, they left their repair shops at Bear Creek with everything in place. It is now a historic site operated by Parks Canada. Some industrial equipment that had little scrap value survived long after others traces of an industry vanished: Stone blast-furnace stacks in rural locations are common remains of former ironmaking. The accidents of survival can create an unrepresentative record of the relative importance of different components of industry: Remains of smelting iron with charcoal are abundant, while almost nothing survives above ground from the equally important refining branch of the industry.

Successful industries adapted new techniques and reworked or replaced old equipment, often without keeping records of these changes. The material and documentary records of some important industries are, consequently, sparse: Throughout most of the nineteenth century, puddlers working at their individual reverberatory furnaces made the wrought iron used in railways, bridges, ships, armaments, and manufactured goods. No one recorded the layout of a puddling shop or the procedures followed by American puddlers before the last puddling works was razed. Industrial archaeologists have to study these industries by excavations and analyses of wastes and other artifacts. They face a further complication because workplaces were frequently reused; archaeologists often find evidence of a succession of different enterprises carried on at one site.

Even after its equipment has been removed, a shop or a factory may retain evidence of the work artisans carried out in it. The location of machinery and equipment is recorded in marks left on the floors, ceilings, and walls. Paths followed by workers as they went about their tasks can be found worn into floors. Archaeologists can read evidence of accidents from the traces left on the fabric of the building, such as the pock marks dug into mill walls by shuttles that escaped from looms in a weave room. However, after a multistory workplace is demolished and its equipment removed, there may be little left for an archaeologist to investigate other than the building's foundations. At the site of a single-story shop, investigators may be able to find the layout of the workplaces and equipment used there: From the excavated remains of the shop floor at Valley Forge in Pennsylvania, archaeologists reconstructed the work areas of the artisans who converted pig iron to bar iron by fining.

Artifacts

Archaeologists can learn from an object itself about the techniques used by the artisans that made the object. Examples of the products of an industry often survive long after the place where they were made has vanished. Collectors assemble and catalog artisans' tools, particularly those used in the crafts. They often work out typologies and compile data on the toolmakers that archaeologists can use. Collectors are less likely to interest themselves in large or mundane tools. In excavating an industrial site, archaeologists may find broken and discarded tools, expendable supplies (such as crucibles used for melting metals), scrap that was not worth recycling, defective parts (often thrown out the shop window by an artisan so a foreman would not see it), and slag and dross at metallurgical works. Archaeologists often find unfinished parts and waste materials a richer source of information about work processes than finished products.

Investigators can apply all of the laboratory techniques familiar in other branches of archaeology to industrial artifacts. Among these, however, dating methods are usually of limited value since they lack the resolution needed to fix the dates of most industrial artifacts. The microstructures of metal and ceramic products and their associated wastes retain evidence of the techniques used to make them. An investigator can observe these with metallographic or petrographic microscopes and use electron microprobe analyses to identify the constituents in the microstructures.

Artisans who cut and shaped wood and metal left distinctive markings on the surfaces they touched with their tools. Archaeologists can often observe these markings with a magnifying glass and use them, for example, to distinguish between hand and machine work. Often, they can identify the tools used by the artisan. Since these markings record the artisan's individual tool strokes, the investigator may be able to learn about this individual's particular style of working.

Reconstruction and Experimental Archaeology

Artisans' skills and knowledge are often lost when they stop practicing a craft or making a product no longer in demand. Unless archaeologists can rediscover this knowledge, scholars may remain inadequately informed about the extent of past artisanal knowledge and, therefore, undervalue it in comparison to formal knowledge recorded in documents. One way that industrial archaeologists learn about past artisans' skills and knowledge is by reconstructing and operating examples of the equipment that these artisans made and used. An investigator may think that he or she understands how a device works after looking at drawings or examining a surviving example. An archaeologist can test this understanding by building a replica: Constructing and operating it will reveal many of the problems that past artisans had to overcome. When industrial archaeologists at the Wilkinson Mill (part of the Slater Mill Historic Site in Pawtucket, Rhode Island) built a new waterwheel to drive their machinery, they found that their wheel, designed from study of old drawings and surviving traces of the original equipment, would not generate power. Eventually, they found that they had to add a system of valves to vent the buckets: They had rediscovered something so well known to past wheel builders that no one had thought it necessary to write it down.

Experimental archaeology can protect against the easy assumption that, because we know the principles on which an industrial process operates, we know what the artisans of the past knew. Metallurgists have known the thermodynamic principles that govern the reduction of iron ore to metal in a bloomery since the late nineteenth century. Archaeologists, guided by artisans who had participated in smelting as youths and by skilled metallurgists, have built and operated experimental bloomeries in several localities in Africa. Others in Europe and America have built instrumented bloomeries in laboratories and in the field. All of these investigators found that they could not reach the efficiencies and product qualities that past artisans routinely attained: They lacked some essential knowledge. One reason was that their metallurgical theory described bloomery operation in terms of homogeneous, equilibrium conditions that could never be attained in a operating bloomery. This was a barrier to the application of theory but not to artisanal skill.

Sometimes industrial archaeologists can support reconstructions of equipment for obsolete processes by the sale of their products, such as stone-ground flour from gristmills. However, the cost of making reconstructions or of carrying out experimental archaeology restricts these projects to small-scale work and the occasional opportunity to engage in a large project intended to commemorate a past event, such as building a replica of a ship used in a famous voyage. It would be impossibly expensive or impractical to rediscover the now-lost skills of operating a Bessemer converter or a whaling ship. In these circumstances, archaeologists can rediscover some aspects of past tasks with thought experiments: The investigator determines each step an artisan must complete, the information the artisan had available in reaching decisions on what to do, the time available to decide, and the consequences of a wrong decision. From study of the layout of the workplace and knowledge of the equipment used, the investigator can reconstruct the sizes and weights of the objects that the artisan had to handle, the space available, the amount of light on the work, and the heat and noise levels. With this information, the archaeologist can deduce aspects of the task. While thought experiments can never substitute for actually operating equipment, the investigator can test hypotheses and rule out possibilities.

Principles of Interpretation

Workplaces and industrial artifacts, like other materials studied by archaeologists, are shaped by the belief systems of the cultures that produced them. Unlike artifacts made only for the display of wealth or power, most industrial artifacts had to serve utilitarian as well as symbolic functions. An industrial archaeologist applies the principles of natural science and engineering to analyze an artifact or a workplace to discover the characteristics that enabled it to perform its utilitarian functions. While doing this, the archaeologist can draw conclusions about the skills and knowledge of past artisans. The archaeologist may also be able to discover evidence of artisans' creativity. Workers often modified the tools and machinery they used to solve problems encountered in their tasks or to adapt equipment to their particular needs. Generally, no one recorded these changes in plans and specifications, and they might well have been done without the knowledge or approval of managers. Incremental innovation by artisans has been an essential component of industrial success; archaeological study of artifacts is the principal source of evidence of artisanal participation in the development of manufacturing expertise.

Within the range of possibilities allowed by the principles of natural science and engineering, which are always applicable, and the natural resources available, there is a range of alternative ways of accomplishing an industrial task. Some of these will require less labor than others. Past artisans could have discovered the easiest way of accomplishing a given task with a given set of tools, energy sources, and raw materials. Archaeologists can apply the principles of engineering to discover these techniques, and, by comparing artifacts with them, infer how nearly their makers and users had minimized their expenditure of labor. Additionally, they may be able to study the remains of mines, quarries, forests, and water-supply and transportation systems to deduce limitations imposed on the artisans by natural resources. Deviation from the principle of least work applied within the resource constraints may imply less-developed skills, social constraints that limited the exercise of these skills, or values that a culture placed higher than minimizing labor.

Artifacts often retain evidence left by the individuals who used them, as well as those who made them. An edge tool such as an axe will have its shape changed by repeated sharpening and carry characteristic marks left by contact with the different materials cut with it. Abuse of the tools by unskillful users may show up as damage to the blade or distortion of the tool. Even if the surficial marks of use have been obliterated by corrosion, underlying distortion of the metal can be detected on specimens prepared for the optical or electron microscope.

The rapid pace of de-industrialization in the North Atlantic nations and the replacement of traditional industrial techniques by modern methods in less well developed countries are creating sites and artifacts far faster than industrial archaeologists can adequately record and interpret them. Practitioners in this field can fully occupy themselves for many decades.

Robert B. Gordon

See also EXPERIMENTAL ARCHAEOLOGY; HISTORICAL ARCHAEOLOGY

Further Readings

Bracegirdle, B. (1973) The Archaeology of the Industrial Revolution. London: Heinemann.

Gordon, R.B., and Malone, P.M. (1993) The Texture of Industry: An Archaeological View of the Industrialization of North America. New York: Oxford University Press.

Hudson, K. (1979) World Industrial Archaeology. Cambridge: Cambridge University Press.

Trinder, B. ed., (1992) The Blackwell Encyclopedia of Industrial Archaeology. Oxford: Blackwell.

Infrared (IR) Spectroscopy

A physical method of determining chemical structure and composition by the selective absorption of infrared radiation. Spectroscopy is based on the interaction of energy and matter. In absorption spectroscopy, visible light or other radiation impinges on a substance where it may be consumed to promote physical changes. Only the wavelengths of radiation whose energy corresponds exactly to the energy requirements of the material will be absorbed and, hence, will be absent in the emerging radiation. The result is a spectrum (i.e., a plot showing which wavelengths of radiation have been absorbed and which have passed through). If the radiation is in the infrared range (wavelengths of 2.5–20 microm-

eters [microns], corresponding to wavenumbers of 4,000–500 reciprocal centimeters [cm]), the energy will be used to promote the vibration of atoms within molecules or polyatomic ions, a process involving both stretching and bending of the bonds between atoms. The infrared spectrum will, therefore, show what bonds are present in the material studied, information that allows a chemist to deduce the chemical composition of the sample.

Infrared spectra may also be used purely empirically as fingerprints without attempting any structural interpretation. If an artifact gives the same infrared spectrum as a known substance, then the artifact must have been made of that substance. Both identification and fingerprinting can be applied to pure substances containing a single chemical compound and to multicomponent mixtures. In the former case, which is relatively rare in archaeology, the spectra of the unknown and of a reference sample will coincide perfectly. Most organic archaeological materials, such as oils, fats, resins, or tars, are complex combinations of many individual compounds; their spectra are actually superimpositions of the spectra of all of the individual components. Since the relative amounts of the components in a mixture are likely to vary, the spectra will not be perfectly reproducible, but they may still be used to identify structures with specific and characteristic absorptions and to classify a material empirically. Computer programs for pattern recognition have been found effective to make quite specific identifications. Most of the applications of infrared spectroscopy have been to organic substances, but minerals, pigments, and bone containing inorganic polyatomic anions also give useful spectra.

In older IR spectrophotometers, prisms or gratings disperse the infrared radiation into separate wavelengths of distinct energies, which are then sequentially directed to the sample. A detector measures the degree of absorption of successive wavelengths, producing a signal that is amplified and fed into a recording device to produce the spectrum. This approach has been almost entirely superseded by Fourier Transform–Infrared (FT-IR) instruments, which are simply interferometers using unresolved infrared light. The interferogram must then be converted to a conventional spectrum by a mathematical operation called a *Fourier transform,* a complex process that would be prohibitively time consuming by ordinary means but can be completed by a computer in less than a minute. All modern FT-IR instruments, therefore, have an integral or associated computer. FT-IR offers many advantages over the old dispersive technique, among them speed, stability of frequency calibration constant resolution, constant signal-to-noise ratio, and elimination of stray light. In addition, the computer permits the repetitive scanning of a sample by storing the individual runs in memory and then adding them up, which means that very small or weakly absorbing samples can still give useful spectra. The computer also allows the enlargement of a portion of the spectrum, the comparison of two spectra by subtraction, the printing of a list of absorption peaks, and the electronic storage of spectra on hard or floppy disks.

Sample preparation depends on the state of the material studied. Any part of a sample container that lies in the optical path must be made of a substance that does not itself absorb infrared radiation. This is usually an alkali metal salt, most commonly potassium bromide (KBr). Gases, which are very rarely encountered in archaeology, can be confined to a long-path cell with KBr windows; the path length may be further enhanced by multiple reflection. Liquids are conveniently run by squeezing a drop between two KBr plates. Liquids, as well as soluble solids, may also be studied in solutions confined to KBr cells, but provision must be made to subtract the spectrum of the solvent. Insoluble solids are ground with powdered KBr, and the mixture pressed into a transparent pellet. Of particular interest to archaeology are a variety of completely nondestructive reflectance techniques, in which the infrared light is bounced off, rather than passed through, the sample. Lastly, accessory microscopes permit the study of extremely small samples by transmitted or reflected light, again without any damage to the artifact.

Applications to Archaeology

Commercial infrared spectrophotometers became available in the early 1950s and were soon used in art conservation research to analyze the materials of paintings (e.g., drying oils, binders, varnishes, and the natural resins used in them, as well as pigments, both organic [saffron] and inorganic [verdigris]). In graphic arts conservation, infrared spectra aided the study of paper and its degradation products. This work was easily extended to older materials, such as to the beeswax and Punic wax in the Fayum portraits of Egypt and in the wall paintings of Pompeii in Italy and to organic textile dyes used in Palestine in the Roman era. More recently, the study of painting materials has been carried out by infrared microscopy and reflectance techniques. Paper, paper sizing, and ink on paper have been studied by attenuated total reflection (ATR) and by Raman spectroscopy, a technique closely related to infrared spectroscopy. Work on textile dyes has included the study of alizarin metal complexes by near-infrared spectroscopy, using radiation with wavelengths of 0.75–2.5 microns and wavenumbers of 13,300–4,000 reciprocal cm. The manufacture of royal purple from snails of the genera *Murex* and *Purpura* along the coast of ancient Phoenicia in the thirteenth century B.C. was demonstrated by diffuse reflectance spectra of the dye adhering to pottery used in its preparation and storage.

An important development in organic archaeometry is the investigation of ancient food remains and other sources of information about prehistoric diet. Infrared spectroscopy has been used in the analysis of residues in cooking and storage vessels from the South Pacific and from Celtic France. Charred grains recovered in Syria were assigned to specific cereal plants by comparing the infrared spectra of propanol extracts with corresponding extracts of modern grains. Evidence for wine has been adduced from the presence of tartaric acid in Mesopotamian pottery sherds established by means of reflectance infrared spectroscopy and from resinous deposits in Mediterranean transport amphoras.

Analysis of cosmetic or medicinal preparations include an ointment jar of Twelfth Dynasty Egypt containing myrrh and frankincense and identification of the ore and mineral components of the Near Eastern eye paint known as *kohl* as used during the Late Roman and Byzantine period. Extensively degraded waterlogged leather has been identified, while conformational changes in collagen from leather and skin have been followed by measuring the loss of infrared linear dichroism. The degradation of wood from old Indian Ocean shipwrecks has been documented by infrared spectra and quantified by measuring the lignin/cellulose ratio. Near-infrared spectra permit the species identification of wood. Both the organic collagen and the inorganic apatite components of bone are accessible to infrared. The probable age of a child skeleton was revised downward by comparing the intensities of infrared absorption of protein versus hydroxyapatite. The age of fossil bones can be assessed by the increasing crystallinity of the apatite, a calcium phosphate with a characteristic doublet absorption in the infrared that can be conveniently measured by diffuse reflection infrared Fourier transform (DRIFT) spectroscopy.

No material has been more extensively studied by infrared spectroscopy than natural resins and the tars and pitches made from them. Infrared spectroscopy has been used in determining the provenance of prehistoric amber artifacts in Europe. Geologically recent, but archaeologically ancient, resins are widely found in Mediterranean transport amphorae, where they served as waterproof linings, sealants, and preservative and flavoring additives to wine. Work on natural resins of Malaysia and their identification in archaeological artifacts has relied heavily on infrared spectra, as has the identification of resinous ceramic coatings in West Africa and of resin adhesives in Neolithic tools from Slovakia. Resins and resin-rich wood of birch, beech, and pine have been the raw material for the manufacture of tar and pitch in the oldest human pyrotechnology known. Infrared spectroscopy has traced the use of birchbark tar as a material for hafting tools and caulking vessels back to the Palaeolithic. A rapidly growing body of literature on the uses, composition, and ancient methods of manufacture of tar and pitch uses infrared spectroscopy, along with other methods of analysis. A wide assortment of other archaeological materials has benefited from infrared analysis, including humic acids, black coral, and Oriental lacquer. Genuine jet can be distinguished by infrared spectroscopy from similar materials, such as lignite, shale, and cannel coal, that have also been used to fashion ornaments.

In much of the recent research in archaeometry, infrared spectroscopy is used alongside other analytical techniques, including nuclear magnetic resonance spectrometry, gas chromatography, mass spectrometry, and microprobe analysis. But because of the unique information it can provide and its rapidity and relatively low cost, it continues to be a valuable technique in archaeological science.

Curt W. Beck

See also AMBER, CHARACTERIZATION; FOURIER TRANSFORM–INFRARED (FT-IR) MICROSCOPY

Further Readings

Griffiths, P.R., and de Haseth, J.A. (1986) Fourier Transform Infrared Spectrometry. New York: Wiley.

Olin, J.S. (1966) The use of infrared spectrophotometry in the examination of paintings and ancient artifacts. Instrument News 17(2):1, 4–5.

Isotopes, Stable (C, N, O, H): Bone and Paleodiet Studies

The study and use of stable isotopes of carbon (C), nitrogen (N), oxygen (O), and hydrogen (H) in preserved human tissue, usually bone, to determine the proportions of foods in the diet of ancient populations.

Basic Principles and Techniques

The human body is built up of the atoms that are consumed in the diet. Most of these atoms possess more than one stable isotope (i.e., atoms that are otherwise identical but differ only in their mass). For example, carbon has two stable isotopes, carbon-12 (written ^{12}C) and carbon-13 (^{13}C), which has an additional neutron in the nucleus. The difference in mass causes isotopes of light elements, such as hydrogen and carbon, to have slightly different chemical properties. As a result, the isotopes are chemically separated from one another in chemical and biological processes, leading to small variations in the relative isotopic abundances in different foods, expressed as a variation in the isotope-abundance ratio, such as $^{13}C/^{12}C$.

Variations in the abundance of stable isotopes can, thus, be used as natural labels to determine the source of dietary constituents ("you are what you eat": DeNiro and Epstein 1978). The isotopes of carbon ($^{13}C/^{12}C$) and nitrogen ($^{15}N/^{14}N$) are widely used, while isotopes of hydrogen (D/H = deuterium/hydrogen) and oxygen ($^{18}O/^{16}O$) in bone serve as indicators of provenance and climate. Stable-isotope ratios vary in nature by only a few percent. Therefore, researchers report these variations in terms of the fractional shift in the isotopic-abundance ratio with respect to that in a standard, using the δ notation (δ = delta). For example, for carbon:

$$\delta^{13}C_x = ((^{13}C/^{12}C)_x/(^{13}C/^{12}C)_{std} - 1) \times 1,000$$

x refers to an archaeological sample, and std = a standard. For $\delta^{13}C$, one uses the PDB standard (a standard for measurement, with calculated carbon and oxygen ratios, that is distributed to labs internationally). All dietary materials have a $^{13}C/^{12}C$ ratio less than that of PDB; by definition, their $\delta^{13}C$ values are negative. Similar definitions are used for $\delta^{15}N$ (std = atmospheric nitrogen), $\delta^{18}O$ (std = PDB) and δD (where D = deuterium, ^2H, the heavy isotope of hydrogen; std = SMOW = Standard Mean Ocean Water). The units of all δ values are per mil (‰). Stable-isotope ratios are determined on an isotope-ratio mass spectrometer. The samples must first be converted into a gas, either CO_2 (for $\delta^{13}C$, $\delta^{18}O$), nitrogen for $\delta^{15}N$, or hydrogen for δD. The precision of analyses of $\delta^{13}C$, $\delta^{18}O$ and $\delta^{15}N$ is typically ca. 0.1 ‰, while for δD it is 1 ‰.

The use of stable-isotope variations in paleodietary reconstruction is based on the observation that the isotopic compositions of wild and cultivated foods vary widely. The isotopic composition of all of the tissues in a body is determined by the δ values of the average diet. Therefore, one can use the δ values of preserved human tissues from ancient populations to determine the isotopic composition of past diet. The main separation in $\delta^{13}C$ is between two groups of terrestrial plants, called C3 and C4, which differ in $\delta^{13}C$ by ca. 14 ‰. Most wild plants in temperate and tropical environments are C3; C4 plants, especially grasses, tend to occur in subarid environments. Several important food plants are C4: corn (maize), sorghum, and millet. A third plant group, CAM, is isotopically intermediate to C3 and C4; CAM plants are succulents and include few food sources. Marine foods have higher $\delta^{13}C$ values than terrestrial (C3-based) plants and animals. The $\delta^{13}C$ values of the flesh of animals is approximately equal to the average $\delta^{13}C$ of the diet and is, therefore, determined by the dietary proportions of C3, C4, and marine foods. Some animal tissues are, however, enriched or depleted in ^{13}C. Body fat (lipid) of animals has $\delta^{13}C$ values ca. 3–5 ‰ lower than the diet, while bone collagen is ^{13}C enriched.

Plants vary in $\delta^{15}N$ by ca. 5 ‰; legumes have generally lower values. Animal consumers of plants are enriched in ^{15}N with respect to their intake by ca. 3 ppt; likewise, carnivores are enriched with respect to the flesh of their herbivorous prey. These isotopic variations based on the hierarchical strata of organisms in the food web (referred to as the *trophic-level effect*) are a major source of variation in $\delta^{15}N$ of human tissues. In principle, the more carnivorous an individual, the higher should be its $\delta^{15}N$. However, $\delta^{15}N$ reflects only the source of the dietary nitrogen, and predominantly herbivorous individuals or persons who habitually consumes high-carbohydrate, low-protein foods, and who obtain most of their protein from a small amount of meat, will also exhibit high $\delta^{15}N$ values.

Isotopic paleodiet measurements can be made on any tissues that have survived postmortem. The longest-surviving component of the human body is bone, which is a composite material made of crystals of carbonate bearing calcium phosphate (the mineral apatite) embedded in a matrix of protein, mainly collagen. Collagen that is biochemically similar to that in living bones can be extracted from well-preserved ancient bones after first dissolving the mineral component of the bone in weak acid (e.g., hydrochloric). In less well preserved bone, the collagen molecular structure breaks down and exhibits anomalous chemical properties. Collagen that is usable for isotopic analysis has a C/N (atomic) ratio between 2.9 and 3.2, and the total yield of collagen extracted from a sample of bone should be greater than ca. 5 percent (by weight). Bone extracts that do not satisfy these criteria are found to give anomalous isotopic results. Purified collagen extracted from bone can be analyzed for $\delta^{13}C$, $\delta^{15}N$, and δD by oxidation with copper oxide at high temperature in an evacuated glass tube. The carbon-isotopic composition of the carbonate component of bone apatite gives an additional indication of paleodiet. Its $\delta^{13}C$ value is normally higher than that of collagen by ca. 12 ‰. It can be analyzed by reacting bone with acid to liberate carbon dioxide.

Issues in Interpreting Results

The stable-isotopic composition of bone and other preserved tissues presents a record of the dietary intake of foods. Although the general relationship between these analyses and the δ values and proportions of foods in the diet is well known, some details are not altogether clear. One factor is the turnover time of atoms of C, N, O, and H in the body. Soft tissues, such as muscle, organs, skin, and hair, are totally renewed on a time scale of a few months to a year; therefore, their isotopic composition reflects only the recent diet. The lifetime of bone collagen is estimated to be ca. 10–25 years, depending on the skeletal element; therefore, isotopic analyses of collagen give a measure of long-term diet. There appear to be no intrinsic differences in δ^{13}C as a function of age or sex.

The δ^{13}C and δ^{15}N values of collagen do not directly represent those of the diet but are offset from them by more or less constant amounts, called *isotopic fractionations* (Δ values). The isotopic fractionation between collagen and diet, Δ_{c-d}, is estimated to be ca. 5 ‰ in humans, although smaller values than this are observed in experimental studies of animals. The δ^{15}N value of collagen is ca. 3 ‰ higher than that of the diet due to the trophic-level effect. By correcting for these fractionations, one can reconstruct the approximate δ^{13}C and δ^{15}N values of the average diet of an individual. This assumes, however, that any atom of C or N consumed by an individual has an equal probability of entering into the collagen molecules of the bone: this is the linear-mixing (or "scrambled") model. Based on this model, one can determine the proportions of two or three distinct food sources using one or two isotopic analyses, respectively. Experimental feeding studies on rats by Stanley H. Ambrose and Lynette Norr suggest that dietary protein is preferentially shunted to collagen; they fed mice with proteins and nonprotein components with significantly different δ^{13}C values and showed that the δ^{13}C of collagen preferentially reflected that of dietary collagen and is poorly correlated with that of whole diet. By contrast, δ^{13}C of bone carbonate represents the δ^{13}C of total diet. Julia A. Lee-Thorp and colleagues showed that the δ^{13}C spacing between collagen and carbonate is smaller for carnivores than for herbivores and can be used as an estimate of trophic level.

Collagen, like all proteins, is built of amino acids, some of which (essential) must be derived directly from other plant foods, while others (nonessential) can be synthesized by the body. The N atoms of all amino acids are scrambled in the body through transamination (oxidation-reduction reactions involving amino acids). Thus, only essential amino acids, which are of lower abundance in collagen, can "remember" the source of their nitrogen. In general, δ^{15}N values of collagen reflect only the combined effects of trophic level and the basic δ^{15}N value of the diet. In semi-arid regions, δ^{15}N of animals increases with decreasing annual amount of local rainfall. Shifts of up to 8 ‰ are observed as rainfall varies from 100 to 800 mm per year.

Applications of Stable Isotopes to Paleodiet Studies

Variations in δ^{13}C and δ^{15}N values of collagen have been widely used to study the relative degree of dependence of ancient populations on isotopically different nutrients and how this has varied through time. Principally, the emphasis has been on the two types of dietary differences mentioned above: C3 versus C4 foods and marine versus terrestrial foods. The first isotopic paleodiet studies investigated the spread of agriculture in North America, which was largely coupled with the spread in the use of the C4 plant maize. The introduction of maize ca. A.D. 700 can be recognized by a shift to higher δ^{13}C values in human bone collagen (Schwarcz et al. 1985); by A.D. 1100, ca. 55 percent of the diet in southern Ontario consisted of maize. δ^{15}N values suggested that most dietary nitrogen was obtained from fish and herbivore flesh, even after the arrival of the maize-squash-beans complex to Ontario. Similar studies have been done elsewhere in North America. In Maya populations of Yucatan and Belize, δ^{13}C data show that maize constituted up to 70 percent of total diet.

Using carbon isotopes, Brian S. Chisholm and colleagues showed that ancient coastal peoples of British Columbia obtained more than 95 percent of their diet from marine resources. Using both δ^{15}N and δ^{13}C, other researchers found that Mesolithic coastal populations in Portugal subsisted on mixtures of terrestrial and marine resources (Lubell et al. 1994), whereas Neolithic populations abandoned marine resources. In South Africa, a coastal population believed to have practiced transhumance exhibited no evidence of a mixed terrestrial/marine diet.

Nitrogen-isotopic analyses are especially useful in identifying sources of dietary protein. Care should be taken, however, to analyze reference animal tissues from the same area because the $\delta^{15}N$ of animal tissues can vary regionally. This is especially true where marine foods are present in the diet, because of the larger range of trophic levels that exist in the sea. A special case of the trophic-level effect is seen in the weaning of human infants; because a breast-fed baby is obtaining all of its nutrients from its mother, the baby is effectively one trophic level higher than the mother and exhibits correspondingly higher $\delta^{15}N$ values in all of its proteins, including bone collagen (Fogel et al. 1989). This ^{15}N enrichment can be seen in ancient skeletal remains of infants with respect to adults of the same population and disappears in postweaning children.

Isotopes of other elements have not been used extensively in studies of human diet. Hydrogen isotope (D/H) ratios in collagen and $\delta^{18}O$ values of bone mineral (phosphate) are indicative of the past climate at the site where the animal lived and, thus, can give some idea of the provenance of the bones (Luz et al. 1990).

Besides bones, other tissues are occasionally available for isotopic analysis. Burials in deserts, permanently frozen terrain, or bogs can result in preservation of soft tissues, hair, and skin. Hair is particularly useful because analyses along the length of hair strands give a record of seasonal changes in diet (White 1993).

Limitations

While isotopic analyses of ancient human tissues have great potential for revealing diet of the past, there are inevitably some limitations in the applicability of these methods. Conversion of δ values into proportions of specific foods may need to take into account the preferential tendency for some components of foods to be routed to particular tissues. Nevertheless, there seems to be a fairly good correspondence between shifts in diet and changes in $\delta^{13}C$ and $\delta^{15}N$ of collagen, where these changes can be independently controlled. Preservation of the isotopic signals in ancient, buried bones is a serious problem, as the bones are gradually fossilized. In temperate regions, the collagen content of buried bones gradually decreases with time, and the content and the quality of collagen in bones older than ca. 10,000 years are usually not ad-equate for isotopic analysis. In some regions (e.g., the Middle East and parts of North Africa), collagen has disappeared from bones within ca. 3,000 years (Weiner and Bar-Yosef 1990), although the $\delta^{13}C$ values of carbonate may survive longer in tooth enamel. A simple but effective test of the quality of collagen preservation is to demineralize a piece of bone in dilute hydrochloric acid; a gelatinous "pseudomorph" in the form of the original bone fragment should remain. Poorly preserved bones yield only a shapeless smear of dark-colored organic matter. Isotopic analyses, especially $\delta^{15}N$ values, of such samples may be grossly in error.

Henry P. Schwarcz

See also BONE, CHARACTERIZATION; BONE, TRACE-ELEMENT ANALYSIS; PALEONUTRITION

Further Readings

Ambrose, S.H., and Norr, L. (1993) Experimental evidence for the relation of the carbon isotope ratios of whole diet and dietary protein to those of collagen and carbonate. In J.B. Lambert and G. Grupe (eds.): Prehistoric Human Bone: Archaeology at the Molecular Level, pp. 1–37. Berlin: Springer.

Chisholm, B.S., Nelson, D.E., and Schwarcz, H.P. (1982) Stable carbon isotope ratios as a measure of marine versus terrestrial protein in ancient diets. Science 216:1131–1132.

DeNiro, M., and Epstein, S. (1978) Influence of the diet on the distribution of carbon isotopes in animals. Geochimica et Cosmochimica Acta 42:495–506.

Fogel, M.L., Tuross, N. and Owsley, D.W. (1989) Nitrogen isotope tracers of human lactation in modern and archaeological populations. Carnegie Institution of Washington, Yearbook 1989: 111–117.

Lee-Thorp, J.A., Sealy, J.C., and van der Merwe, N.J. (1989) Stable carbon isotope ratio differences between bone collagen and bone apatite, and their relationship to diet. Journal of Archaeological Science 16:585–599.

Lubell, D.R., Jackes, M., Schwarcz, H.P., and Knyf, M. (1994) The Mesolithic-Neolithic transition in Portugal: Isotopic and dental evidence of diet. Journal of Archaeological Science 21:201–216.

Luz, B., Cormie, A., and Schwarcz, H.P. (1990) Oxygen isotope variations in phosphate of deer bones. Geochimica et Cosmochimica Acta 54:1723–1728.

Schwarcz, H.P. (1991) Some theoretical aspects of isotope paleodiet studies. Journal of Archaeological Science 18:261–275.

Schwarcz, H.P., Melbye, J., and Katzenberg, M.A. (1985) Stable isotopes in human skeletons of southern Ontario: Reconstructing paleodiet. Journal of Archaeological Science 12:187–206.

Weiner, S., and Bar-Yosef, O. (1990) States of preservation of bones from prehistoric sites in the Near East: A survey. Journal of Archaeological Science 17:187–196.

White, C. (1993) Isotopic determination of seasonality in diet and death from Nubian mummy hair. Journal of Archaeological Science 20: 657–666.

Isotopes, Stable (Pb, Sr): Raw Materials and Provenance Studies

The discovery and significance of natural variations in the isotopic composition of the elements and the use of stable strontium (Sr) and lead (Pb) isotopes as indicators of the origin of raw materials; utilized in archaeological provenance studies.

In 1914, English physicist Sir Joseph John Thomson observed by means of his "positive ray" apparatus that neon is composed of two types of atoms of atomic weights ca. 20 and 22. Several other scientists confirmed in the following years the hypothesis that the place occupied in the periodic table by a particular element must accommodate more than one kind of atom. These different atoms of the same element, having different masses, English chemist Frederick Soddy called (1912–1920) for the first time the *isotopes*, from the Greek for "same place" in the periodic table. In the 1940s, with advances in mass spectrometry, researchers discovered that small variations that exist in the isotopic composition of many of the common elements are significant in investigating the geological, biological, and chemical histories of rocks, minerals, and organic materials.

The natural radioactive decay of parent isotopes is the major cause of variations in the isotopic composition of the particular elements lead and strontium. The rate of decay can be measured and, in conjunction, say, with the isotopic composition of one of these elements in a mineral or rock, used to calculate the time since the beginning of a process in which they have been involved. In principle, therefore, the radioactive isotopes can be used for dating materials in which they are found. Isotopes of many elements are used today in geology for dating and for tracing the history and the mode of formation of rocks and minerals.

The same isotope variations can be used for different purposes in archaeological research. The isotopic compositions of strontium and lead in rocks and minerals from different locations and environments can be treated as their characteristic "fingerprints," which can be also measured in ancient artifacts made from these materials. The methodology of isotope provenance studies relies on measuring stable (i.e., nonradioactive) isotope compositions of minerals and rocks from known locations and then comparing them with the isotope compositions of artifacts. In this way, it is possible to identify the sources of raw materials used in antiquity and their distribution, independent of the style (or lack of it) and character of the final object.

Sample Preparation and Measurements of Isotopic Ratios of Sr and Pb

At present (i.e., 1998), the most commonly used method for accurate measurements of the isotopic compositions of Sr and Pb is thermal ionization mass spectrometry (TIMS). The element analyzed by TIMS has first to be chemically extracted in a pure form from a sample taken from an ancient artifact. A comparatively new technique called ICP-MS (inductively coupled plasma mass spectrometry) allows isotope analyses from a solution of a sample without a prior extraction of elements. As of 1998, a new, state-of-the-art mass spectrometer using an ICP source is on the market (for example: VG Plasma 54, Field Proven ICP-Multicollector MS), but only a few laboratories in the world are equipped with these instruments. The more widely available ICP-MS quadruple mass spectrometers are not sufficiently accurate to be useful for wide ranging provenance studies of ancient materials based on isotopic compositions.

The element lead (Pb) is present in many archaeological materials in concentrations ranging from as little as a part per million to

100 percent. To determine its isotopic composition using TIMS, lead must be extracted in a very pure form. The most commonly used methods of lead extraction and purification are *ion-exchange chromatography* and *anodic deposition*. The amount of pure lead needed for one isotope-ratio measurement (one run) is ca. 100–200 ng (nanograms). Therefore, the amount of sample required for analysis depends chiefly on the lead concentration in the specimen. For example, a 1-mg sample of copper alloy or mineral containing 0.05 percent of lead would yield 500 ng of lead if the extraction process is 100 percent efficient. The efficiency of the extraction is usually lower, mainly due to the interference of other elements present in a sample. It is preferable to take 20–50-mg samples in the case of low-lead materials (e.g., unleaded copper-based metals) to allow for repeated extraction and analysis if necessary; in addition, such sample sizes are necessary to allow chemical analyses also to be made. Samples of archaeological metal objects are usually taken with a 1–2-mm drill, depending on the size and the thickness of the object.

The chemical separation of low-lead samples (below 1 percent Pb) is susceptible to contamination with lead from the environment (reagents, tools, air). It is not usually possible to distinguish samples that were contaminated with "foreign" lead during the sampling, storage, or preparation at any later stage of the isotope analysis. The lead-isotope ratios measured will be those of any lead that had been obtained during the extraction, which might, for example, come partly from the car fumes getting into an ordinary chemistry lab through the windows of the building. For this reason, low-lead separation should take place in a class-100 clean chemistry laboratory that is supplied and overpressured with highly filtered air. All commercial ultrapure reagents and water should be further purified in this laboratory, and lead blanks regularly checked at all stages of lead extraction. The overall procedural lead blank (i.e., the lead content going through without any sample) should be below 1 ng (10^{-9}g).

Several different procedures for lead extraction have been developed to suit best the type of samples that are analyzed. For high-lead ores and metals, samples are dissolved in pure nitric acid; the lead, converted into nitrate in solution, undergoes anodic deposition as the oxide on platinum electrodes, then is stripped using a hydrogen peroxide/nitric acid mixture (this is conducted in a high-lead laboratory). Samples of silver and copper artifacts, copper and polymetallic ores with low lead content, copper slags, glasses, and glazes are processed in the clean laboratory. Depending on the chemical composition, the procedure then includes either only anodic deposition or ion-exchange chromatography using special crown ethers followed by anodic deposition. In cases in which the bismuth (Bi) content is appreciable, final separation of Bi from Pb is conducted using an anion-exchange resin.

Extracted lead is converted into lead nitrate, diluted with ultrapure water, and a very small drop of this solution (containing ca. 100–200 ng of lead) is deposited together with a drop of silica gel and phosphoric acid on a short, flat metal strip (made of Rhenium), called a *filament*. The filament ribbon is soldered to a mount with "legs," which, in the source of the machine, are connected to a supply of electrical current. For an isotope measurement, a current of ca. 2.5 A passes through the filament, causing evaporation of the atoms of lead and thermal ionization of some of them.

A beam of lead ions is accelerated by a high voltage in the source into an electromagnetic-mass analyzer that separates the single beam emerging from the source slit into several beams of ions of different mass/charge ratio. The beam travels in a curved evacuated tube consisting of highly polished stainless steel that is placed between the pole pieces of the electromagnet. Most thermal-ionization mass spectrometers built since 1990 have multiple collector systems. In such machines, a number of Faraday collectors (usually six or seven) are spaced along the plane of focal points of the ion beams. With the appropriate settings for different masses, several ion beams are detected simultaneously. The ions collected in the Faraday cups result in a very small electric current (10^{-11}–10^{-12} A), which is amplified and measured. The isotope ratios are measured as ratios of ion currents caused by the collection of ions of different masses in the respective collectors. The multicollector system provides much better precision of measurements than the earlier single collector because the fluctuation in ion-beam intensity is averaged out very effectively.

The isotope ratios measured in a specific laboratory have to be normalized using the NBS/NIST lead isotopic standards SRM981 or SRM982. Each good isotope laboratory keeps records of sets of standard runs, which provide grounds for calculating a correction specific for a given mass spectrometer and procedures. Adherence to this protocol makes it possible always to cross-compare directly the isotope data obtained in different laboratories.

It is generally agreed that the absolute accuracy of currently measured lead-isotope ratios in good laboratories is ca. ± 0.05 percent for $^{207}Pb/^{206}Pb$ and $^{208}Pb/^{206}Pb$ and ± 0.1 percent for $^{206}Pb/^{204}Pb$ ratios. From the four lead isotopes measured, it is possible to calculate five isotope ratios, but only three of them are independent. It is quite easy to re-calculate the lead-isotope ratios into any form desired. Geochronologists conventionally use the three ratios computed with respect to ^{204}Pb. For archaeological provenance studies, it is convenient to use two ratios to ^{206}Pb and one to ^{204}Pb because the accuracy of the ratios to ^{206}Pb are better than those to ^{204}Pb. However, in practice, it seems to make little difference which sets of ratios are used, or even to use the atomic abundances. One run (a set of repeated ratio measurements obtained from the same sample in a continuous manner) consists usually of 100 separate measurements. The final isotope ratios are calculated as mean values of each set of ratios.

Strontium (Sr) is usually extracted by ion-exchange chromatography. The sample size depends on the concentration of strontium in the material, but normally 30–50 mg is sufficient for bones and rocks. Isotopic measurements are easily made on as little as 50 ng of strontium. Strontium-isotope ratios can be measured with an accuracy better than 0.001 percent; this is due to the possibility of correcting for isotope fractionation in the mass spectrometer by normalizing to the ratio $^{86}Sr/^{88}Sr = 0.11940$, which is invariant in nature.

Figure 1 shows the TIMS at the Isotrace Laboratory in Oxford, England. It is a modern, fully automated VG 38-54-30 double-focusing mass spectrometer. The multicollector system allows simultaneous measurement of up to seven isotopes, while a twenty-sample turret ion source reduces considerably the time necessary for routine measurements.

Times of analyses vary from ca. thirty minutes for lead to ca. two hours for strontium and a little longer for neodymium, uranium, and thorium. The machine can run automatically under computer control; therefore, it is possible to run samples unattended overnight.

Geochemistry of Strontium

Strontium is a member of the alkaline earths and is known to replace calcium in many minerals. Therefore, it is dispersed in all calcium-bearing minerals, its salts are dissolved in fresh and sea waters, and it is present in sedimentary and igneous rocks. Strontium compounds in the soil and water enter plants, animals, and humans through direct uptake or the food chain. Strontium has four naturally occurring isotopes: ^{88}Sr, ^{87}Sr, ^{86}Sr, and ^{84}Sr. Their isotopic abundances are ca. 82.53 percent, 7.04 percent, 9.87 percent and 0.56 percent, respectively. The isotopic abundances of ^{87}Sr are variable because this isotope is formed through the radioactive decay of naturally occurring ^{87}Rb (rubidium). For this reason, the precise isotopic composition of strontium in a rock or a mineral that contains rubidium depends on the age and Rb/Sr ratio of that rock or mineral. Usually, the characterization of a material is based on the $^{87}Sr/^{86}Sr$ composition and the ratio of Rb/Sr concentration. Concentrations of rubidium and strontium in igneous, sedimentary, and metamorphic rocks range from a few parts per million to several hundred parts per million.

Strontium in Archaeological Provenance Studies

In 1981, Noel H. Gale suggested that Sr isotopes could be used for studies of the origin of obsidian for sources that are not easy to differentiate on the basis of their trace-element composition (Gale 1981). A few years later, strontium proved successful in isotope provenance studies of gypsum used in the Minoan and Mycenaean palaces in Crete and mainland Greece (Gale et al. 1988). Deposits of gypsum are rather dispersed on Crete, but there are no deposits of gypsum near Tiryns or Mycenae or in the Cycladic islands. Apart from Crete, other principal deposits of gypsum in Greece lie in Kefallonia and Zakinthos and along the far south coast of mainland Greece. Various suggestions were made by archaeologists about the origin of gypsum found in the Late Bronze Age

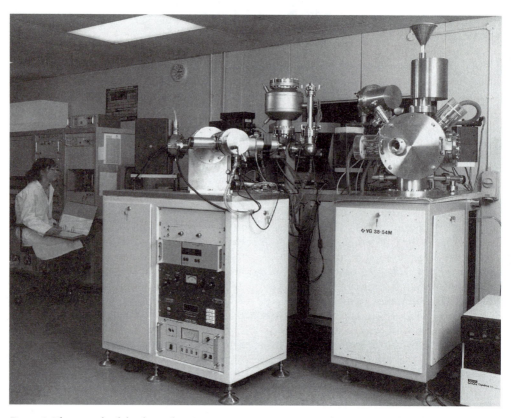

Figure 1. Photograph of the thermal-ionization mass spectrometer at the Isotrace Laboratory, Oxford. Oxford University, Isotrace Laboratory, by permission.

buildings outside Crete, but traditional archaeological methods could not take the question any further, since gypsum is a material without any straightforward discriminative criteria such as physical appearance or mineralogical composition. Strontium-isotope analyses of gypsum from the geological deposits in Greece and on Crete, when compared with samples of gypsum from the Bronze Age buildings, proved unequivocally that the Cretan gypsum quarries supplied this material not only for the Cretan palaces, but also for the architectural details in the palace of Mycenae and houses on the island of Santorini. In contrast, the benches in Tiryns were made of gypsum from a quite different source, possibly the Ionian islands of Kefallonia or Zakinthos. In the same study, the isotopic composition of sulfur was measured in the gypsum samples for comparison with the conclusions obtained on the basis of Sr-isotope ratios. Both isotopic studies are in full agreement.

Another successful application of strontium isotopes (combined this time with carbon- and nitrogen-isotope analyses) is in the determination of the source area of elephant ivory (van der Merve et al. 1990; Vogel et al. 1990). These studies were undertaken in isotope laboratories in South Africa and at Harvard University, primarily in connection with the international efforts to preserve the African elephant and to halt the trade in ivory. The isotopic analyses allow the determination of the specific area in southern Africa from which individual tusks were derived; therefore, sources of modern ivory traded illegally can be identified. So far, this research has not been extended to archaeology in the strict sense, and, because of the similarities of the geology in various parts of the world, it might not be possible to distinguish between the ivory from India and Africa, for example. Much work would be needed to establish the necessary database of Sr-isotope data to decide if such distinctions are possible. On the other hand, the isotopic composition of strontium in the oceans appears to be everywhere the same and is characterized by an $^{87}Sr/^{86}Sr$

ratio of 0.70906 based on the average of hundreds of analyses performed in different laboratories. This composition should be broadly reflected in the bones and tusks of sea mammals such as the walrus. This should allow the easy distinction of walrus "ivory" from the land-animal bone and ivory, for which all of the strontium-isotope ratios measured so far are higher than 0.710; preliminary measurements at Oxford University suggest that this distinction is, in fact, possible.

Geochemistry of Lead

Terrestrial lead consists of four stable isotopes. One of them, ^{204}Pb, is nonradiogenic in origin (it was incorporated in the Earth when it was formed from the proto solar system). Lead isotopes 206, 207, and 208 are daughters of radioactive ^{238}U, ^{235}U, and ^{232}Th, respectively. The half-lives of radioactive uranium and thorium isotopes, from which the radiogenic lead isotopes are formed, are very long: An original amount of ^{235}U is reduced by half, due to its decay to ^{207}Pb, in 704 million years, while ^{238}U decays to ^{206}Pb with a half-life of 4,468 million years. The half-life of ^{232}Th decaying to ^{208}Pb is 14,010 million years.

In the last 4.57 billion years (the age of the Earth), lead present in rocks and minerals underwent various geochemical processes: At first, uranium, thorium, and lead were uniformly mixed together in the hot, liquid Earth. When the Earth started to cool, the relative concentrations of these elements differentiated from place to place. During those millions of years, uranium (U) and thorium (Th) were continuously producing more and more of lead 206, 207, and 208 but in slightly different amounts, depending on their relative concentrations. An important stage of differentiation of the amounts of the isotopes came with the process of ore formation. Common lead occurs in minerals, such as galena, whose U/Pb and Th/Pb ratios are so low that its isotopic composition does not change appreciably with time since it was laid down in a mineral deposit. Due to their chemistry, U and Th largely separate from Pb during geochemical processes, such as the formation of ore deposits. Therefore, no more lead isotopes are added to lead after ore formation. On the other hand, later on, other geological and geochemical processes might disturb the isotope composition of already formed ore. Therefore, the lead-isotope composition of each of the mineral deposits depends not only on the time of their formation, but also on the amount of uranium and thorium present and the subsequent geochemical history of the ore.

In principle, therefore, minerals of different geographical origin have a high probability of displaying different lead-isotope compositions. In 1965, this principle was used for the first time by Robert Brill and John Wampler, and independently by a group of German scientists (Grogler et al. 1966), to identify the origin of some ancient lead objects. Since 1970, lead-isotope provenance studies have broadened to include analysis of glass, silver coins, copper metal, iron, and artists' pigments.

The accuracy of measurements of lead-isotope ratios in the early days of mass spectrometry was not very high (ca. 1 percent), and there was no interlaboratory standardization. For these reasons, nearly all lead-isotope work reported before 1974 should not be used for comparisons with later, more accurate, measurements. In archaeological provenance studies, different ore sources must be very accurately defined isotopically. The whole range of lead-isotope compositions found in ore deposits is only about 8 percent, while most fall in a region covering a range of only ca. 1.7 percent. To be able to discriminate effectively between the lead-isotope compositions of ore sources, it is necessary to determine lead-isotope ratios with accuracy of better than, or equal to, ± 0.1 percent.

Lead Isotopes in Archaeological Provenance Studies

Finding the origin of lead in ancient materials (glasses, glazes, metals, pigments) using their isotopic compositions is very simple in principle: It is enough to make accurate measurements of lead-isotope compositions of artifacts and ore deposits and to compare them with each other. This simple principle requires considerable research into possible sources of pigments and metals in antiquity, followed by extensive geological and archaeometallurgical fieldwork to characterize the ore deposits and to collect samples of minerals for lead-isotope characterization of the sources.

To a major degree, the lead-isotope composition of a particular ore body is related directly to the age of the mineral formation and, as such, can include only a very limited range of different lead-isotope compositions, correlated with the geological history of the formation. Each lead isotope composition gives three parameters of a point in three-dimensional space: the three lead isotope ratios (those most often used are $^{208}Pb/^{206}Pb$, $^{207}Pb/^{206}Pb$, and $^{206}Pb/^{204}Pb$). Many data points form the lead isotope "fingerprint" of an ore deposit, which has a form of an irregular globule in three-dimensional space, usually not extending in size beyond 0.2–0.5 percent of all three lead isotope ratios. A succession of isotopically well characterized ore deposits form a set of such globules in isotope ratio coordinate space. The presentation and interpretation of lead isotope data is most conveniently done by using two mirror-image lead isotope diagrams representing the pattern of the data projected on two planes (Figure 2). To obtain a properly representative lead isotope characterization of an ore deposit, it is necessary to analyze a number of ore samples collected from various parts and depths and from different minerals present in the deposit. The comparisons of the lead isotope "fingerprints" of ores with artifacts can be then achieved by plotting the artifact lead isotope ratios on the same diagram as those of the ores. In the earlier stages of lead isotope studies, probability ellipses were often used to determine the characteristic range of lead isotope ratios when the number of ores analyzed was not sufficient. However, since 1995, the Isotrace Laboratory (Oxford) has been publishing in the journal *Archaeometry* lead isotope databases of ore deposits; having many hundreds of ore data available, it is possible now to make "point-to-point" comparisons which give far more reliable answers.

Some ore deposits might have a complicated geological history and may consist of minerals formed at different times and under different conditions. In such cases one geographical area can have a large number of different fingerprints for different ore bodies within the area. For example, the data plotted on Figure 2 demonstrates that various mining regions of Cyprus have very different isotopic fingerprints. However, since the provenance method is based on direct comparisons, the correct interpretation depends chiefly on the correct isotope characterization of each ore deposit used for comparison. Another typical example of such complicated isotope geology

are the ore deposits on Sardinia, which range in geological age from Tertiary (66.4–1.6 million years ago) to Cambrian (540–505 million years ago). This is reflected in a range of lead isotope compositions of more than 2 percent between the ore deposits of different ages, so that there is no one characteristic "Sardinian" lead isotope composition but a number of them characteristic of the individual mines or small regions (Stos–Gale et al. 1995). Other complicated ore occurrences include the British and the North American lead deposits and the relatively rare ores with a wide range of lead-isotope compositions due to the presence of uranium in the ore. Also, some ore deposits from different geographical regions can have similar (partly overlapping) lead-isotope compositions. In all cases, it is necessary to have in mind the geochemistry and the mineralogy of the deposits (e.g., one can compare copper metal only with lead-isotope compositions of minerals from copper mines). Other important discriminating factors are the ore type (deep or surface), size, and antiquity of mining in any given region.

The fact that a lead-isotope composition does not change during the pyrotechnological processes is vital for provenance studies. It means that the ore, pigment, slag, and metal produced from a given ore deposit have the same, unchanged, lead-isotope composition. Providing that a single source of mineral is used throughout the process of production of pigment or metal, application of lead isotope analyses allows the researcher to identify a deposit from which the mineral was extracted and to trace the further distribution of the final product. Simple remelting of one object, or several originating from the same ore, will preserve, in the new metal, the original lead-isotope "fingerprint." Only if a new object was made from several artifacts containing lead of different origins, will a mixed fingerprint emerge. The interpretation of lead-isotope data of ancient artifacts must always take into account the possibility of a mixed origin of the metal. For example, if a copper artifact made of copper from the main group of Cypriot mines (Solea, Larnaca, Limassol, and Limni) was melted together with an object made of copper from Lavrion (see Figure 2), then the newly made metal would have a lead isotope composition falling somewhere along the straight line drawn between the group of Lavrion and these particular Cypriot

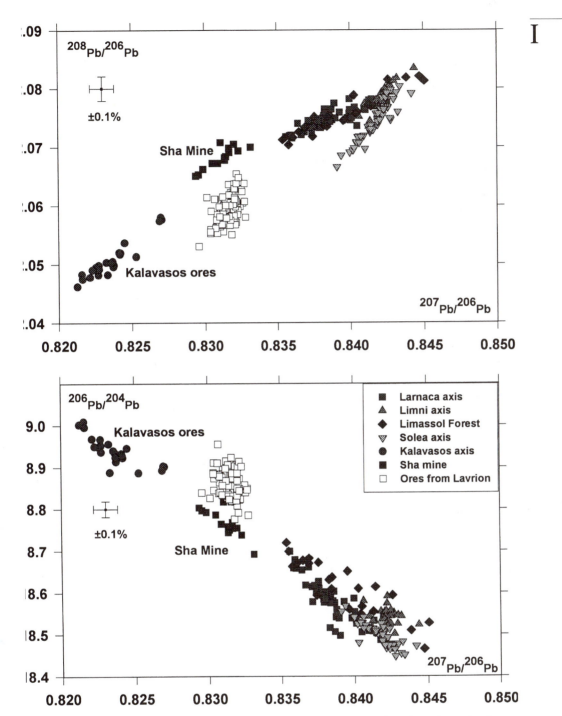

Figure 2. Lead-isotope composition of lead ores from the Aegean islands (number of samples analyzed appears in parentheses): Antiparos (11)—open circles; Euboea, Kallianou (4)—open circle with a dot; Siphnos (25)—S; Syros (24)—filled triangle down; Thasos (24)—filled square; Kea (54)—open square; Seriphos (40)—star; Kythnos (10)—filled circle; Thera (19)—open triangle up. Figure by Zofia Anna Stos-Gale.

ores on both diagrams of Figure 2. The exact position along this line of the point representing such a mixture depends on the amount of lead introduced with each of the copper pieces melted together. Most likely each artifact made of a combination of metals would fall on a different part of this straight line depending on the relative amounts of lead in the metals used. Therefore, a group of artifacts from one archaeological site and/or period would form a scatter of points falling in and between the groups of ore samples.

With the sufficient numbers of ores analyzed, the visual comparison of lead isotope data of ores and ancient artifacts is sufficient to assess the origin of an archaeological object. A few years ago, the use of statistical methods for the interpretation of lead isotope studies was widely discussed, in particular Stepwise Discriminant Analysis. This method helps to discriminate between overlapping groups of the lead isotope data measured for ores from known occurrences and to find a numerical probability of the origin of a given archaeological sample from each of the bodies under discussion. However, the statistical approach is only possible if a sufficient number of ores from one deposit have been analyzed. The practice of having large numbers of lead isotope analyses of ores and artifacts shows that, in fact, the visual comparison is more informative than the statistical treatment and there is no particular advantage in using the statistical approach.

Reconstructing the Economy of Prehistoric Societies

Since 1980, considerable effort has been spent on lead-isotope and archaeometallurgical investigations of Mediterranean and Anatolian ore deposits in an attempt to reconstruct the beginnings of metallurgy and Bronze Age trade routes in southern Europe.

Thousands of lead-isotope analyses of Bronze Age metals from southern Europe show that, in fact, at any given time, only certain sources of metals were used, relatively few in number. Some ore deposits well known in modern times were never exploited in antiquity, for reasons of inaccessibility of ores or unsuitability of their mineralogical composition. For example, in spite of many occurrences of lead ore in the Aegean, the isotope analyses of many hundreds of lead artifacts from Bronze Age Greece show uniformly only two sources of origin: Siphnos and Lavrion in the Early Bronze Age and chiefly Lavrion in later periods. This result might be connected with the fact that lead was probably made

mainly as a by-product of silver extraction. As long as the supply of rich silver ore lasted, there was no need to search for another, less satisfactory, source. Lavrion in that part of the Aegean was certainly the richest and largest lead/silver (and also copper) deposit. Once the production and distribution were organized, the system seems to have persisted there for centuries (or even millennia). In a parallel way, the copper sources identified by lead isotopes are not always those that are traditionally mentioned in the archaeological literature. For example, the research conducted by a group of scientists from Heidelberg/Mainz in Germany suggests that the ancient mine of Rudna Glava in Serbia did not provide the main bulk of copper for the earliest artifacts made in that region (Pernicka et al. 1993). The results of long studies of the Bronze Age trade in metals in the Mediterranean conducted at Oxford indicate that, contrary to a widely accepted opinion, Cypriot copper was most likely not the main reason for the appearance of the Minoan and Mycenaean pottery on Cyprus. On the other hand, the lead-isotope data indicate that the copper metal from Cyprus was widely traded in the Late Bronze Age in the form of oxhide ingots (Gale 1991; Stos-Gale et al. 1997), while, at the same time copper, lead and silver from other sources were also coming to Cyprus (Stos-Gale and Gale 1994).

Zofia Anna Stos-Gale

Further Readings

Brill, R.H., and Wampler, J.M. (1965) Isotope studies of ancient lead. American Journal of Archaeology 69:165–166.

Gale, N.H. (1981) Mediterranean obsidian source characterisation by strontium isotope analysis. Archaeometry 23(1):41–52.

Gale, N.H. (1991) Copper oxhide ingots: Their origin and their place in the Bronze Age metals trade in the Mediterranean. In N.H. Gale (ed): Bronze Age Trade in the Mediterranean, pp. 197–239. (Studies in Mediterranean Archaeology 90). Jonsered, Sweden: Paul Åströms Förlag.

Gale, N.H., Einfalt, H.C., Hubberten, H.W., and Jones, R.E. (1988) The sources of Mycenaean gypsum. Journal of Archaeological Science 15:57–72.

Gale, N.H., Stos-Gale, Z.A., Maliotis, G., and Annetts, N. (1997) Lead isotope data from the Isotrace Laboratory, Oxford,

Archaeometry Database 4, ores from Cyprus. Archaeometry 39(1):237–246.

Grogler, N., Geiss, J., Grunenfelder, M., and Houtermans, F.G. (1966) Isotopenuntersuchungen zur Bestimmung der Herkunft römischer Bleirohre und Bleibarren. Zeitschrift für Naturforschung 21:1167–1172.

Pernicka, E., Begemann, F., Schmitt-Strecker, S., and Wagner, G.A. (1993) Eneolithic and Early Bronze Age copper artefacts from the Balkans and their relation to Serbian copper ores. Praehistorische Zeitschrift 68(1): 1–54.

Rohl, B.M. (1996) Lead isotope data from the Isotrace Laboratory, Oxford, Archaeometry Database 2, ores from Britain and Ireland. Archaeometry 38(1):165–180.

Stos-Gale, Z.A., and Gale N.H. (1994). The origin of metals excavated on Cyprus. In B. Knapp and J. Cherry (eds.): Provenance Studies and Bronze Age Cyprus: Production Exchange and Politico-Economic Change, pp. 92–122, 210–216. Chap. 3. Madison, WI: Prehistory Press.

Stos-Gale, Z.A., Gale, N.H., and Annetts, N. (1996) Lead isotope analyses of ores from the Aegean. Archaeometry 38(2):381–390.

Stos-Gale, Z.A., Gale, N.H., Annetts, N. Todorov, T., Lilov, P., Raduncheva, A., and Panayotov, I. (1998) Lead isotope data from the Isotrace Laboratory, Oxford: Archaeometry Database 5, ores from Bulgaria. Archaeometry 40(1):217–226.

Stos-Gale, Z.A., Gale, N.H., Houghton, J., and Speakman, R. (1995) Lead isotope analyses of ores from the Western Mediterranean. Archaeometry 37(2):407–415.

Stos-Gale, Z.A., Maliotis, G., Gale, N.H., and Annetts, N. (1997) Lead isotope characteristics of the Cyprus copper ore deposits applied to provenance studies of copper oxhide ingots. Archaeometry 39(1):83–124.

van der Merwe, N.J., Lee-Thorp, J.A., Thackeray, J.F., Hall-Martin, A., Kruger, F.J., Coetzee, H., Bell, R.H.V., and Lindeque, M. (1990) Source-area determination of elephant ivory by isotopic analysis. Nature 346:744–746.

Vogel, J.C., Eglington, B., and Auret, J.M. (1990) Isotope fingerprints in elephant bone and ivory. Nature 346:747–749.

I

K

Kenyon, Dame Kathleen Mary (1906–1978)

British archaeologist. Born on January 5, 1906, in London, Kathleen Kenyon was educated at St. Paul's and Somerville College, Oxford. She began her career as an excavator and educator at the University of London, where she was secretary of the Institute of Archaeology (1935–1948 and acting director throughout much of the Second World War). Kenyon was a lecturer in Palestinian Archaeology at the institute (1948–1962) and was the director of the British School of Archaeology in Jerusalem (1951–1966). She was also principal of St. Hugh's College, Oxford (1962–1973). The recipient of many awards and prizes, Kenyon was given honorary degrees by Exon and Tübingen Universities, named a trustee of the British Museum, and received the title Dame of the British Empire (1973). She died on August 24, 1978.

Kenyon, a specialist in Syro-Palestinian archaeology, is most well known for her excavations at Jericho. Though widely traveled, with excavation experience in Rhodesia and Great Britain, Kenyon began excavating at Jericho in 1952, and it became the better part of her life's work. Throughout the 1950s, Kenyon made a series of startling discoveries at the site, a Neolithic and Bronze Age farming community known from the Old Testament. Among the most remarkable finds were the fortification walls and the tower from Jericho's earliest aceramic Neolithic levels. Monumental defensive works were long considered hallmarks of urbanization, and Kenyon and her supporters soon came to claim Jericho as "the world's oldest city." Jericho's urban status is still an area of debate, but Kenyon's work served to shake up conventional notions of the Neolithic in the Near East. A series of plastered skulls from the site also attacks notions of Neolithic simplicity; to some, these skulls are evidence of complex religious beliefs, including ancestor worship; to others, they point to advanced artistic and aesthetic development. Jericho ranks as one of the most important finds for the study of world prehistory.

Also not to be overlooked are Kenyon's contributions to field methodology in Palestinian archaeology. A student of Sir Mortimer Wheeler, Kenyon brought rigid, scientific British archaeology to the Jericho excavations. As director of the British School of Archaeology in Jerusalem, Kenyon was responsible for educating a generation of British, Palestinian, and Israeli archaeologists in Wheeler's methods and for helping make rigidly scientific excavation the norm in the Holy Land.

Joseph J. Basile

See also WHEELER, SIR ERIC ROBERT MORTIMER

Further Readings

Kenyon, K.M. (1957) Digging up Jericho: The Results of the Jericho Excavations, 1952–1956. London: E. Benn/New York: Praeger.

Kenyon, K.M. (1960–1983) Excavations at Jericho. London: British School of Archaeology in Jerusalem.

Kenyon, K.M. (1967) Jerusalem: Excavating 3000 years of History. London: Thames and Hudson/New York: McGraw-Hill.

Kenyon, K.M. (1978) The Bible and Recent Archaeology. London: British Museum.

Kenyon, K.M. (1979) Archaeology in the Holy Land, 4th ed. London: E. Benn/New York: W.W. Norton

Klein, Richard G. (1941–)

American archaeologist and paleoanthropologist. Born on April 11, 1941, in Chicago, Illinois, Klein was an undergraduate at the University of Michigan, where he received his bachelor's degree in 1962. He then began graduate study at the University of Chicago, earning his master's degree in 1964 and his doctorate in 1966. Klein was appointed assistant professor of anthropology at the University of Wisconsin in 1966 and at Northwestern University in 1967. He became associate professor of anthropology at the University of Washington in 1969 but returned to the University of Chicago in 1973, first as associate professor and then as professor of anthropology. He is currently professor of anthropology at Stanford University. Klein is a member of the American Association of Physical Anthropologists and the American Academy of Arts and Sciences.

Klein is a specialist in the Palaeolithic period and in the appearance of modern humans in the Old World. His earliest works contributed to the study of human cultural variability in the Late Pleistocene *(Man and Culture in the Late Pleistocene)* and he has been among only a small group of Western anthropologists permitted to excavate in the former Soviet Union in the 1960s and 1970s *(Ice Age Hunters of the Ukraine).* He is probably most well known, however, for his studies of faunal remains from Late Pleistocene sites and his analyses of human hunting techniques and subsistence patterns during this period. His synthesis of Palaeolithic sites in South Africa demonstrated that, based on evidence from this region, a picture of hunting advances in Africa develops, from a period when hominids produced little meat by hunting, to the Late Stone Age when modern *Homo sapiens sapiens* proved a deadly predator, driving many game animals to extinction. Klein has examined faunal assemblages from sites such as Torralba in Spain, excavated by American archaeologist F. Clark Howell, and has suggested that caution needs to be exercised when interpreting such finds, since post-

depositional disturbance and destruction probably affect bone and fossil assemblages from nearly *all* prehistoric sites. His *Analysis of Animal Bones from Archaeological Sites,* written with Kathryn Cruz-Uribe, is a useful guide to the analysis of faunal remains.

Joseph J. Basile

See also HOWELL, FRANCIS CLARK; TAPHONOMY

Further Readings

Klein, R.G. (1969) Man and Culture in the late Pleistocene: A Case Study. San Francisco: Chandler.

Klein, R.G. (1973) Ice-Age Hunters of the Ukraine. Chicago: University of Chicago Press.

Klein, R.G. (1982) Patterns of Ungulate Mortality and Ungulate Mortality Profiles from Langebaanweg (Early Pliocene) and Elandsfontein (Middle Pleistocene), South-Western Cape Province, South Africa. (Annals of the South African Museum 90, pt. 2). Cape Town: South African Museum.

Klein, R.G., ed. (1984) Southern African Prehistory and Paleoenvironments. Rotterdam/Boston: Balkema.

Klein, R.G. (1989) The Human Career: Human Biological and Cultural Origins. Chicago: University of Chicago Press.

Klein, R.G. and Cruz-Uribe, K. (1984) The Analysis of Animal Bones from Archaeological Sites. Chicago: University of Chicago Press.

Martin, P.S. and Klein, R.G., eds. (1984) Quaternary Extinctions: A Prehistoric Revolution. Tucson, AZ: University of Arizona Press.

Klejn, Leo S. (1927–)

Russian anthropologist and archaeologist. Born on January 7, 1927, in the former Soviet Union, Klejn was a professor of the historical faculty and chair of the Archaeology Department of the University of Leningrad (now St. Petersburg). A specialist in Scythian archaeology and the archaeology of the Pontic steppes, the Ukraine, and the Balkans, Klejn is also known as an important theorist of the Soviet Marxist archaeology movement and an archaeological historian. He has proposed a model for defining the archaeological cultures of the vast and complex Russian landscape *(Archaeological Typology)* and has been a critic of Soviet archaeology, its lack of a coherent methodological base, and its apparent inability to construct a complete chronology that would allow comparison of cultures and a systematic study of culture change. Acknowledging that archaeological material constitutes a unique body of evidence and that Marxist theory does not necessarily provide a framework for the interpretation of archaeological material in order to describe the past, Klejn and other Soviet archaeologists of the 1960s and 1970s have argued that archaeological material must be studied independently before it can be applied to problems of past human behavior. As a historian of archaeology, Klejn sees the development of archaeological thought as a result of regional "schools" with differing methodological views ("A Panorama of Theoretical Archaeology"). In addition, his English and German publications from the 1970s onward provide an important window into the complex world of Soviet and Marxist archaeology.

Joseph J. Basile

See also MARXIST ARCHAEOLOGY

Further Reading

Klejn, L.S. (1969) Characteristic methods in the current critique of Marxism in archeology. Soviet Anthropology and Archeology 7(4):41–53.

Klejn, L.S. (1973) On major aspects of the interrelationship of archaeology and ethnology. Current Anthropology 14: 311–320.

Klejn, L.S. (1977) A panorama of theoretical archaeology. Current Anthropology 18:1–42.

Klejn, L.S. (1982) Archaeological Typology. (BAR International Series, 153). Oxford: British Archaeological Reports.

K

L

Leather, On-Site Conservation

Basic measures undertaken to minimize the rate of damage to archaeological artifacts made of skin materials once they have been unearthed from archaeological contexts and until they reach a conservation laboratory. On-site conservation is the most important stage in the survival of artifacts made of skin. Inadequate or inappropriate measures taken on site can cause irreversible damage to the physical artifact and can contaminate or destroy associated archaeological information. A comprehensive on-site preventive conservation program consists of guidelines for the recovery, recording, packing, temporary storage, and transportation of archaeological skin artifacts that can be carried out competently by untrained personnel. All other conservation treatments must be carried out by a professional archaeological conservator.

Archaeological leather is interpreted here in the broad sense of archaeological artifacts made of animal skin and gut. In addition to leather, which is fully tanned skin, these materials include: rawhide, parchment and vellum, semitanned skin, gut, sinew, and fur. Naturally and artificially mummified bodies, both human and animal, are also considered here.

Archaeological contexts are rarely sympathetic to the survival of skin materials, yet desiccated, frozen, and waterlogged (i.e., terrestrially wet and submerged marine and freshwater) burial environments possess microclimates that often lead to the remarkable preservation of this material. Skin materials, including fur, can be found in association with metal artifacts where organic material has been preserved by, or partly to completely replaced by, metal corrosion prod-

ucts. Pseudomorphic replaced fragments of skin or fur in association with metal artifacts should be conserved on site as for metals. Decayed skin materials, specifically leather, can also be found as stains in an archaeological soil context. These finds should be treated as for horizontal soil sections.

Recovery

When first exposed and during recovery, skin artifacts should be kept covered to protect from sunlight and to prevent drying out. Once cleaned of the surrounding, nonadhering, soil matrix, special finds should be documented in situ with drawings or photographs prior to lifting. Investigative cleaning must not be attempted either before or following recovery. Archaeological skin materials can be decorated with, for example, paint, gilding, or stitching, all of which, as well as the grain surface, can be damaged with unskilled cleaning.

Dry

Most skin materials can be found preserved in dry, arid climates, but they are generally rigid and brittle and may be delaminating. Prior to recovery, the surrounding soil can be carefully removed with soft brushes to delineate the features of the artifact. Metal tools should not be used, nor should water or moisture to assist recovery, and any tightly adhering lumps should be left in place. When the object is loosened, it can be picked up while supporting it from underneath with either two hands or a rigid horizontal support. Once the leather is excavated, no attempt should be made to clean, flatten, consolidate, or join broken pieces. Items that are fragmentary or fragile are more safely recovered by supported lifting.

Removal techniques involving directly adhered backing or consolidation (i.e., applying a consolidant directly onto an artifact) either of the surface or of the entire object should not be used with skin materials because their fibrous nature makes removal at a later stage difficult. Never attempt consolidation using CO_2 gas or dry ice. If the surface of a skin object is decorated with gilding or paint that is flaking, expert advice should be sought before lifting.

Human or animal remains should be cleaned of surrounding dirt by brushing. Small, compact bodies can be removed by undercutting and lifting with one or more pairs of hands while a rigid support is slid underneath. It is recommended that larger, extended, or more fragile bodies be lifted in a block together with the surrounding soil. In situations in which it is not possible to carry out block lifting, the body can be gradually wrapped with cloth or stretch bandage as it is undercut.

Wet

Only skin artifacts that are fully tanned survive in wet archaeological contexts. Wet leather often appears sound but generally is weakened and may be mushy or delaminating. It should be kept wet from the moment it is exposed. This can be accomplished by spraying with water and covering with wet polyether foam sheeting, wet moss, or mud followed by polyethylene sheeting. Wet leather objects can be lifted by cleaning away some of the surrounding mud, undercutting, and lifting together with adhering mud. Lifting can be assisted by sliding a support under the leather-mud complex. Consolidation of wet leather that is badly deteriorated or fragmentary with adhesives or polyethylene glycols prior to lifting should be avoided, as these materials may be difficult to remove later. Alternatively, CO_2 gas or dry ice can be used to consolidate an isolated wet object in situ by freezing it and then lifting it as a block. There may be remnants of stitching or decoration, so cleaning of wet leather should not be attempted.

Human and animal remains can be preserved in a bog environment. These bodies can be cleaned for recovery as described above followed by block lifting.

Leather from submerged marine and freshwater sites is excavated using techniques employed in marine archaeological recovery. Robust finds are placed in sealed perforated polyethylene bags or containers, and fragile flat items can be sandwiched between two sheets of perforated polyethylene or polypropylene board prior to being brought to the surface. Groups of bags can be collected in perforated containers.

Frozen

A wide range of skin artifacts (e.g., parchment, semitanned skin) can be found preserved in Arctic environments not only because of the cold climate, but also because many of the sites are relatively young. Many skin artifacts frozen in permafrost are most safely removed by warming the soil-artifact matrix with either warm circulating air or warm water. Warm water can be poured gently, sprayed, or injected by use of a syringe around the object until it is loosened. Excess water is removed with sponges. The exposed surface of partly excavated artifacts must be kept wet, which can be accomplished by spraying with water or covering the object with wet moss and then covering with plastic sheeting. Removal should not be attempted until the material is completely thawed. Over larger areas, this method is too time consuming; but natural thawing can be speeded up by laying out dark plastic garbage bags, which absorb the heat from the sun but prevent evaporation.

Supported Lifting

Small fragile artifacts of skin can be lifted by isolating them in a block of soil. The soil around an object is carefully removed to leave it sitting on a platform of soil, though the archaeologist must pay attention to leave enough soil around the object to adequately support it. The artifact is covered with polyvinylidene chloride film (plastic kitchen wrap) with or without an outer layer of aluminum foil. Bandages of paraffin wax or plaster are wrapped around and over the artifact and block, and a rigid support is slid underneath to undercut the block. Plaster bandages are not recommended for use with wet artifacts, as they can deteriorate upon storage. Less flat or fragmentary artifacts can be isolated in a block that is more extensively undercut to form a pedestal. Consolidation of the surface prior to covering with an isolating layer should not be attempted. When isolating the surface of wet skin objects, the surface should be thoroughly wetted and can be covered with water-soaked polyether foam sheeting or wet moss. The object-pedestal unit is then wrapped in bandages and undercut.

These techniques will not provide support necessary to lift larger objects, such as human remains. For these objects, a rigid (e.g., wood, polyethylene board, or Plexiglas) vertical frame of generous size is placed around the object that has already been isolated on a pedestal of soil. For block lifting wet finds, the rigid support must either be waterproof or lined with polyethylene sheeting. A barrier layer of plastic wrap followed by a layer of aluminum foil is pressed down gently following the surface contours of the object. The object and the surrounding well are filled with expandable polyurethane foam, plaster, or moss. Liquid polyurethane foam is poured into the well in small quantities. For larger blocks, polystyrene foam (Styrofoam) chips can be used as filler in the liquid foam to reduce the amount of foam necessary. When cured, the top of the frame is covered, and the box is excavated by undercutting the pedestal with a rigid support, inverted, and sealed by fastening a lid in place.

Polyurethane foam is toxic and caustic. It must be used only in a well-ventilated area, and rubber gloves, goggles, and a fume mask must be worn. Alternatively, plaster of paris filled out with vermiculite or polystyrene chips can be used as the setting material. Its major disadvantages are its weight, messiness, incomplete setting in cold or wet environments, and difficulty of later removal if not carefully applied. When block lifting bog bodies, turf and moss can be used to fill the well and cover the body.

Packing

Dry

Robust items of dry skin can be packed flat in perforated heavy-gauge polyethylene bags with resealable tops or in bags made from polyethylene tubing or sheets with the aid of a heat sealer with a heat-sealed or stainless-steel-stapled folded end. Items can be supported within the bag with cardboard covered with acid-free tissue. Small or fragile items should be packed in rigid containers, preferably clear polystyrene, padded with and supported by crumpled acid-free tissue. Cotton wool snags on skin materials. Larger items, including human and animal remains, should be packed in a suitable rigid container well padded with sheet and crumpled tissue. If necessary, padding can be accomplished with plain white or unbleached kitchen toweling or toilet tissue; but the artifact must be isolated from these materials with acid-free tissue.

Wet

Only waterproof materials are to be used for packing wet artifacts. Wet and frozen skin artifacts that are not truly waterlogged should not be packed with immersion in water, as this may cause further water degradation. These finds should be triple-bagged immediately in polyethylene bags along with adhering mud and damp polyether foam sheeting. An outer layer of aluminum foil can help reduce moisture loss and exposure to light and oxygen. Larger or fragile finds can be packed in sturdy polyethylene freezer containers with tight-fitting snap-on lids or containers made to size from polyethylene board. The inside can be padded with damp polyethylene foam sheeting, moss, or seaweed.

Truly waterlogged finds should be packed immersed in water. This can be accomplished by packing in perforated polyethylene bags and placing in containers lined with polyethylene foam sheeting and filled with water.

Labeling

All packed finds (bags and containers) should be labeled inside and out. Never mark directly on skin artifacts. Labels and tags should be placed inside the bag or container. Plastic or stainless-steel Dymo-type labels or spunbonded polyethylene paper tags are recommended. Outside, information can be written either on masking tape or directly on the polyethylene bag. Use indelible markers at all times. Use of tacks and paper clips should be avoided; if staples are used, they must be stainless steel. With containers holding groups of artifacts, each item should be listed on the outside.

On-Site Storage

Dry

Dry skin materials should be keep at as constant a relative humidity as possible, in the range of 45–60 percent, and away from light and heat.

Wet

The use of biocides with freshly excavated archaeological skin materials should be avoided where possible, and attempts should be made to limit microbiological growth by controlling temperature, light, and oxygen. Biocides are toxic toward the person applying them and those who later work on the treated materials. They can cause detanning and alter skin color of artifacts, and they can interfere with chemical analyses of residual dyestuffs, tanning agents, and pathological analysis that might be carried out on human and animal remains.

Wet and frozen skin materials should be stored at as low a temperature as possible. Frozen storage is recommended, with refrigerated storage a second choice. In Arctic field situations, advantage can be taken of the cool climate to create cold storage using coolers, ice packs, pits dug in the permafrost, snowbanks, and meltwater. Small amounts of wet skin materials can be packed with the addition of isopropanol, ethanol, or sphagnum moss to prevent mold growth. The alcohols are nontoxic to humans and evaporate upon exposure to the atmosphere, leaving no residue in the object. Sphagnum and other mosses are readily found at excavation sites in the Arctic. Sphagnum has antiseptic qualities that are attributed to the presence of polyphenols and nonionized organic acids. Although analysis has revealed the presence of only a few harmless organisms, outbreaks of sporotrichosis have been traced to handling dry sphagnum moss contaminated with the fungus *Sporothrix schenckii;* therefore, only fresh moss should be employed. Conservators have reported unusual swelling of their hands following concentrated periods of handling wet sphagnum.

Attempts must be made to store frozen skin materials that are not tanned (e.g., parchment) frozen and not wet, as damp or wet storage will lead to hydrolysis of the collagen, rendering the material gelatinous.

Small finds from submerged sites should be packed in sealed perforated polyethylene bags or nylon netting (although the latter can leave imprints on soft materials) and stored in holding tanks in which the water is either circulating or changed at regular intervals. It is recommended that skin materials not be stored together with other wet materials. Alternatively, they can be packed in multiple polyethylene bags or padded containers to which water has been added and air excluded prior to sealing.

Documentation

Any conservation treatment carried out on an artifact on site must be recorded, and the record must accompany the treated find or be readily accessible at all times. Field-treatment records are brief and include a description of the deposit, the object, the material(s) of construction, the condition, and the field treatment, including materials used. Treatment should describe cleaning, lifting, and packing. Groups of similar finds treated in a similar manner can be recorded collectively.

Transportation

Whether dry or wet, archaeological skin artifacts should be packed for transportation with plenty of shock-absorbent packing material.

Dry

Small dry items in perforated polyethylene bags can be packed together in small containers. Items are isolated from one another with crumpled acid-free tissue, shredded polyethylene foam sheeting, or bubble-pack. Several small containers of objects can be packed in sturdy boxes or crates padded with polystyrene or polyethylene sheeting. Each box must be isolated from the container and from other boxes, using lightweight materials such as crumpled paper, shredded polyethylene foam, or polystyrene foam chips.

Wet

Truly waterlogged leather finds in perforated bags can be packed in groups in polyethylene containers that are lined with wet polyethylene foam sheeting or bubble pack, and bags can be isolated from one another with bubble pack, water-soaked polyethylene ether foam sheeting, or wet moss. Bagged wet leather can also be packed in this manner, but with damp packing materials (e.g., moss). Containers can then be packed in crates lined with polystyrene or polyethylene foam sheeting.

Health Hazards

Skin materials recovered from wet terrestrial environments, in particular Arctic sites, may present health hazards in handling. Particular caution should be taken with human or animal remains and native skin items and artifacts impregnated with sea-mammal fat. The use of disposable plastic gloves at all times is recommended, and the items should be sealed in either food wrap or polyethylene sheeting as soon as possible. Disposable gloves and a dust mask should be worn when handling dry human or animal remains.

Elizabeth E. Peacock

Further Readings

Cross, S., Hett, C., and Bertulli, M. (1989) Conservation Manual for Northern Archaeologists. (Archaeology Report 6). Yellowknife: Prince of Wales Northern Heritage Center.

Payton, R., ed. (1992) Retrieval of Objects from Archaeological Sites. London: Archetype.

Peacock, E.E. (1987) Archaeological skin materials. In H.W. M. Hodges (ed.): In Situ Archaeological Conservation, pp. 122–131. Mexico City: Instituto Nacional de Antropología e Historia de Mexico/Century City, CA: J. Paul Getty Trust.

Peacock, E.E. (1993) Materiales arqueológicos de piel. In H.W. M. Hodges (ed.): Conservación Arqueológica In situ, pp. 128–139. Mexico City: Instituto Nacional de Antropología e Historia de Mexico and Century City, CA: J. Paul Getty Trust.

Sease, C. (1994) A Conservation Manual for the Field Archaeologist, 3rd ed. (Archaeological Research Tools 4). Los Angeles: Institute of Archaeology, UCLA.

Watkinson, D., ed. (1981) First Aid for Finds. London: Rescue/UKIC Archaeology Section.

Leone, Mark Paul (1940–)

American anthropologist and archaeologist. Born on June 2, 1940, in Waltham, Massachusetts, Leone was educated at Tufts University, where he received his bachelor's in 1963, and at the University of Arizona, where he was awarded a master's in 1965 and a doctorate in 1968, both in anthropology. After his graduate work, Leone was appointed assistant professor of anthropology at Princeton University in 1968; in 1976, he moved on to the University of Maryland at College Park as associate professor of anthropology. He was named full professor in 1990. In 1975, he was named Fellow of the National Endowment of the Humanities.

Leone is a well-known proponent of anthropological archaeology and pioneered, along with William A. Longacre and others, the use of the statistical analysis of distribution patterns of archaeological materials in answering questions about social organization and interaction. The volume *Contemporary Archaeology*, which Leone edited in 1972, became an important resource for anthropological archaeologists and included articles by such notables as Lewis R. Binford.

Leone has since shifted his emphasis to the eastern United States, particularly Colonial Maryland, but continues to use spatial analysis and the methodologies of symbolic and structural archaeology as a tool for recovering the ancient mind. His recent work includes archaeological and sociological study of Colonial garden design in order to interpret eighteenth-century ideology and the study of how living-history museums, such as the one at Colonial Williamsburg, affect the public's perceptions of the past. Leone's *The Recovery of Meaning: Historical Archaeology in the Eastern United States* illustrates his approach to historical archaeology as a means for reconstructing past mindsets.

Joseph J. Basile

See also HISTORICAL ARCHAEOLOGY; NEW/PROCESSUAL ARCHAEOLOGY

Further Readings

Leone, M.P., ed. (1972) Contemporary Archaeology: A Guide to Theory and Contributions. Carbondale, IL: Southern Illinois University Press.

Leone, M.P., (1975) Views of traditional archaeology. Reviews in Anthropology 2:191–199.

Leone, M.P., (1981) The relationship between artifacts and the public in outdoor history museums. Annals of the New York Academy of Sciences 376:301–314.

Leone, M.P., (1982) Some opinions about recovering mind. American Antiquity 47:742–760.

Leone, M.P., (1984) Interpreting ideology in historical archaeology: Using the rules of perspective in the William Paca Garden in Annapolis, Maryland. In D. Miller and C. Tilley (eds.): Ideology, Power and Prehistory, pp. 25–35. Cambridge: University Press.

Leone, M.P., (1986) Symbolic, structural, and critical archaeology. In D.J. Meltzer, D.D. Fowler, and J.A. Sabloff (eds.): American Archaeology Past and Future: A Celebration of the Society for American Archaeology 1935–1985, pp. 415–438. Washington, D.C.: Smithsonian Institution Press.

Leone, M.P. and Potter, P.B., eds. (1988) The Recovery of Meaning: Historical Archaeology in the Eastern United States. Washington, D.C.: Smithsonian Insitution Press.

Leone, M.P. and Potter, P.B. (1992) Legitimation and the classification of archaeological sites. American Antiquity 57:137–145.

Leone, M.P., Potter, P.B. and Shackel, P.A. (1987) Toward a critical archaeology. Current Anthropology 28:283–302.

Leone, M.P. and Silberman, N.A., eds. (1995) Invisible America: Unearthing Our Hidden History. New York: H. Holt.

Lerici, Carlo M. (1890–1978)

Italian civil engineer, archaeologist and specialist in remote sensing. In the 1950s, Lerici developed a periscopic camera for the investigation of phenomena such as sealed tombs and chambers without archaeological excavation. The Lerici technique circumvents the destructive nature of excavation and allows photographic documentation of archaeological materials while, at the same time, preserving them by leaving them in their depositional environment. After identification of a site, an access hole is bored through the roof of the chamber or tomb (damaging, but far less destructive than full-scale excavation), and the camera is lowered on a periscopic stalk. In 1955, Lerici founded the Fondazione Politecnico of Milan for the archaeometric study of Italian sites, and the following year he proceeded to use nondestructive, remote-sensing survey techniques and the periscopic camera he invented to locate and investigate Etruscan tombs at the necropoleis of Tarquinia and Cerveteri. The investigations were successful, and the results, published in *Prospezioni Archeologiche,* the journal of the Fondazione Politecnico, caused a stir in the archaeological community. Lerici's work, which leaves archaeological deposits preserved for future scientists, led the way in the development of ar-

chaeometry and the nondestructive exploration of important cultural remains.

Joseph J. Basile

See also ARCHAEOLOGICAL PROSPECTION

Further Readings

Lerici, C.M. (1955) Prospezioni archeologiche. Rivista di Geofisica Applicata 16:7–31.

Lerici, C.M. (1958) Le applicazioni geogisiche nella ricerca archeologica. Studi Etruschi 26:297–301.

Lerici, C.M. (1959) Prospezioni Archeologiche a Tarquinia: La Necropoli delle Tombe Dipinte. Milan: Fondazioni C.M. Lerici, Politecnico di Milano.

Lerici, C.M. (1961) I Nuovi Metodi di Prospezione Archeologica alla Scoperta delle Civiltà Sepolte. Milan: Fondazioni C.M. Lerici. Politecnico di Milano.

Lerici, C.M. (1961) Archaeological surveys with the proton magnetometer in Italy. Archaeometry 4:76–82.

Lerici, C.M. (1961) Methods used in the archaeological prospecting of Etrucscan tombs. Studies in Conservation 6(1):1–8.

Rainey, F.G. and Lerici, C.M. (1967) The Search for Sybaris, 1960–1965. Rome: Lerici Editori.

Leroi-Gourhan, Andre (1911–1986)

French prehistorian and ethnologist. Trained originally in Russian and Chinese languages, Leroi-Gourhan studied ethnology under Marcel Mauss, Paul Rivet, and others and participated in the reorganization of the Musée de l'Homme in Paris during the 1930s. After ethnographic research among the Ainu of Japan and then military service in the Second World War, he conducted a doctorate on northern Pacific archaeology and taught at the Universities of Lyon and Paris. He became professor of prehistory at the Collège de France in 1969. Leroi-Gourhan founded the vibrant French school of prehistoric ethnology, especially with his excavations of the Middle and early Upper Palaeolithic cave sites of Arcy-sur-Cure and of the open-air Magdalenian site of Pincevent (*Fouilles de Pincevent,* with Michel Brézillon), all in northern France.

Leroi-Gourhan's archaeology is a visionary attempt to reconstruct the intimate details of prehistoric life, especially within meticulously excavated, recorded, and analyzed sites. He was a pioneer of site structure and spatial analyses, informed by his rich knowledge of world ethnology. Leroi-Gourhan conducted monumental studies of Franco-Cantabrian cave art of the Upper Palaeolithic, bringing structuralist analysis to a subject that until then had been analyzed in a fragmentary fashion that emphasized chronology and speculative explanations. In contrast, he saw decorated caves as wholes, subject to detailed mapping, spatial analysis, and comparative study. Although controversial and now generally downplayed, his theory that much of cave art represents a complementary opposition between male- and femaleness is embedded in a book that has lasting value for its systematic, well-documented presentation of the corpus of the Franco-Cantabrian sites: *Préhistoire de l'Art Occidental,* translated as *Treasures of Prehistoric Art.*

Leroi-Gourhan was a genuine polymath, writing on subjects from the development of the human mind and religion, to paleobotany and archaeozoology, to lithic-artifact function; these diverse interests are represented in volumes of his collected publications: *La Geste et la Parole, Le Fils du Temps.* His broad comparative perspective is reflected in such works as *La Préhistoire* and *Les Religions de la Préhistoire.* Leroi-Gourhan's vision of prehistoric archaeology was a holistic one, integrating applications of research from the natural sciences, cultural anthropology, and the humanities.

Lawrence G. Straus

See also CAVES AND ROCKSHELTERS, EXCAVATION; ROCK-ART SITES, RECORDING AND ANALYSIS

Further Readings

André Leroi-Gourhan, ou, Les Voies de l'Homme. (1988) Paris: A. Michel.

Groenen, M. (1996) Leroi-Gourhan: Essence et Contingence dans la Destinée Humaine. Paris: De Boeck Université.

L'Homme, Hier et Aujourd'hui. Recueil d'Études en Hommage á André Leroi-Gourhan. (1973) Paris: Cujas.

Leroi-Gourhan, A. (1946) Archéologie du Pacifique-nord: Matériaux pour l'Étude des Relations entre les Peuples Riverains d'Asie et d'Amérique. Paris: Institute d'Ethnologie.

Leroi-Gourhan, A. (1982) The Dawn of European Art: An Introduction to Palaeolithic Cave Painting. Trans. S. Champion. Cambridge/New York: Cambridge University Press.

Leroi-Gourhan, A. (1983) Le Fil du Temps. Paris: Fayard.

Leroi-Gourhan, A. and Brézillon, M. (1972) Fouilles de Pincevent: Essai d'Analyse Ethnographique d'un Habitat Magdalénien. Paris: Centre National de la Recherche Scientifique.

Leroi-Gourhan, A. (1993) Gesture and Speech. Trans. A.B. Berger. Cambridge, MA: MIT Press. Originally published 1964–1965, as Le Geste et la Parole, Paris: A. Michel.

Leroi-Gourhan, A. (1968) La Préhistoire, 2nd ed. Paris: Presses Universitaires de France.

Leroi-Gourhan, A. (1971) Préhistoire de l'Art Occidental, 4th ed. Paris: L. Mazenod.

Leroi-Gourhan, A. (1983) Les Religions de la Préhistoire: Paléolithique, 4th ed. Paris: Quadrige/Presses Universitaires de France.

Leroi-Gourhan, A. (1967) Treasures of Prehistoric Art. New York: H.N. Abrams.

Leveling

A surveying technique used to establish the height of things. Leveling is usually done with simple optical equipment like the *engineer's transit* or the *level*. The three most commonly used levels are the *dumpy,* the *quick-set* and the *automatic.* Each of these instruments consists essentially of a telescope mounted on a tripod. The telescope is equipped with a minimum of one vertical and one horizontal cross hair. Most, however, also have two shorter stadia hairs parallel to the main horizontal cross hair. The horizontal cross hair is made level by making level one or more spirit levels attached to the telescope mounting.

Having made the horizontal cross hair level, it is possible to rotate the telescope so that the cross hair can be seen as a level line in the landscape being viewed. This level line may be visualized as a plane of equal height. This is known as the *plane of collimation.* To establish whether the point being measured is above or below the plane of collimation, a

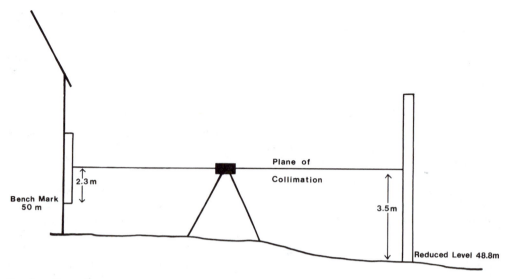

Leveling. *Figure by Peter L. Drewett.*

leveling staff is used. The staff is clearly graduated in centimeters, decimeters, and meters, alternating in red and black. Staffs vary in length but are usually between 4 m and 6 m long.

To provide information about the relative height of points within the area being leveled, all readings must be related to an agreed height. In many countries, spot heights have been established in the landscape. These are known as *bench marks* and are related to sea level. If no bench marks are available, a temporary bench mark may be established.

All leveling starts from the bench mark. The transit or level is set up as close to the site as possible, but with a clear view of the bench mark. The staff is then held on the bench mark, and the plane of collimation is read on the staff. This reading is then added to the bench-mark value. For example, if the bench mark is 50 m above sea level and the staff reading is 2.3 m, then the plane of collimation is 52.3 m. above sea level (see Figure). The plane of collimation can then be swung round into the area to be leveled by rotating the head of the level. The staff is placed on the spot to be recorded, and the plane of collimation is read against the staff. If the staff reading is now 3.5 m, then this figure may be taken away from the height of the plane of collimation to give the actual height (or reduced level) at that point (i.e. 52.3 m minus 3.5 m equals a reduced level of 48.8 m).

This process may be repeated anywhere within sight across the area being leveled. To produce contours, spot heights are usually taken on a regular grid, and the contours are interpolated between the spot heights. The smaller the grid squares, the more accurate these contours will be.

Peter L. Drewett

See also SITE MAPPING

Further Reading

Barker, P. (1993) Techniques of Archaeological Excavation, 3rd ed. London: Batsford.

Drewett, P.L. (1999) Field Archaeology: An Introduction. London: University College London Press.

Libby, Willard Frank (1908–1980)

American nuclear chemist. Born on December 17, 1908, in Colorado, Libby studied at the University of California at Berkeley, where he received his bachelor's degree in 1931 and his doctorate in 1933. He began his career as an educator at Berkeley, where he taught in the Department of Chemistry (1933–1945). After reaching the rank of associate professor, Libby left the University of California for a full professorship at the University of Chicago, where he taught (1945–1959) and did his most significant work. He returned to the University of California, this time at Los

Angeles, as a full professor beginning in 1959. Before his death in 1980, Libby won numerous honors for his work in chemistry and nuclear chemistry, including three Guggenheim fellowships (1941, 1951, 1959), the Elliot Cresson Medal (1957), the Gold Medal of the American Institute of Chemists (1970), membership in the Royal Swedish Academy of Sciences, the American Philosophical Society, the American Academy of Arts and Sciences, the National Academy of Sciences (U.S.), and the Nobel Prize in Chemistry (1960).

Libby won his Nobel Prize for the work he did on radiocarbon, culminating in 1949 with the development of the technique of radiocarbon dating, perhaps the single most significant advance in the history of the sciences in archaeology. Libby discovered that ^{14}C, also known as radiocarbon, a radioactive isotope of carbon that is present in all living matter, had a measurable half-life that he estimated at 5,568 plus or minus 30 years. The process Libby developed measures the amount of radiocarbon remaining in a sample of organic material and thus is able to determine a date. Although subsequent recalibration work, in part based upon advances in dendrochronology, has shown a more accurate half-life figure of 5,730 plus or minus 40 years, the implications of Libby's work were staggering: It revolutionized archaeology and all sciences dealing with the past.

Joseph J. Basile

See also DENDROCHRONOLOGY; RADIO-CARBON DATING

Further Readings

Berger, R. and Libby, L.M., eds. (1981) Tritium and Radiocarbon. (Willard F. Libby Collected Papers, 1). Santa Monica, CA: Geo Science Analytical.
Libby, L.M., ed. (1981) Radiochemistry, Hot Atoms and Physical Chemistry. (Willard F. Libby Collected Papers, 2). Santa Monica, CA: Geo Science Analytical/Los Angeles: University of California at Los Angeles.
Libby, W.F. (1955) Radiocardon Dating, 2nd ed. Chicago: University of Chicago Press.

Longacre, William A. (1937–)

American archaeologist and anthropologist. Born on December 16, 1937, Longacre re-ceived his doctorate from the Department of Anthropology at the University of Chicago in 1963. He has spent most of his career in the American Southwest, particularly in Arizona, where he was a full professor and chair of the Department of Anthropology at the University of Arizona. He is currently Riecker Professor of Anthropology there. A key figure in the development of scientific and systemic archaeology in the United States in the 1960s, called the New Archaeology, Longacre is most famous for the landmark Carter Ranch Pueblo Arizona study, which, along with James N. Hill's excavations at nearby Broken K Pueblo Arizona, demonstrated the precepts of New Archaeology in action. Longacre approached Carter Ranch with a series of explicitly scientific research problems, especially in regard to sociocultural organization as a means of adaptation to environmental factors. Viewing culture systemically, Longacre examined all aspects of material culture and paleoenvironment, as well as ethnographic data, in search of connections. One of the most important aspects of his work was the recognition, based on models previously established by James J.F. Deetz's work with the Arikara of North and South Dakota, of a correlation between scatters of certain types of ceramics (and ceramic decoration) and residence patterns, which Longacre knew from contemporary examples were often matrilocal in the American Southwest. Basing a series of hypotheses on the archaeological and ethnographic information, Longacre proceeded to test his assumptions in the material record at Carter Ranch. These findings, along with work at other sites, such as Grasshopper Pueblo in Arizona, were published in a series of important monographs on Pueblo Indian society and archaeology, which include *Archaeology as Anthropology: A Case Study, Reconstructing Prehistoric Pueblo Societies* (which Longacre edited), and *Multidisciplinary Research at Grasshopper Pueblo, Arizona* (which he edited with Sally Holbrook and Michael Graves). Longacre has applied his ideas of ethnographic and archaeological examination of ceramic production, spatial relationships, and sociocultural adaptations to other cultures, including the Kalinga of the Philippines (see *Ceramic Ethnoarchaeology,* and *Kalinga Ethnoarchaeology: Expanding Archaeological Method and Theory,* edited with James M. Skibo). Longacre continues to explore the usefulness of the scientific method in archaeology.

Joseph J. Basile

See also DEETZ, JAMES J. FANTO; ETHNOAR-CHAEOLOGY; NEW/PROCESSUAL ARCHAEOLOGY

Further Readings

Longacre, W.A. (1970) Archaeology as Anthropology: A Case Study. Tucson, AZ: University of Arizona Press.

Longacre, W.A., ed. (1970) Reconstructing Prehistoric Pueblo Societies. Albuquerque, NM: University of New Mexico Press.

Longacre, W.A., ed. (1991) Ceramic Ethnoarchaeology. Tucson, AZ: University of Arizona Press.

Longacre, W.A., Holbrook, S.J., and Graves, M.W., eds. (1982) Multidisciplinary Research at Grasshopper Pueblo, Arizona. Tucson, AZ: University of Arizona Press.

Longacre, W.A. and Skibo, J.M., eds. (1994) Kalinga Ethnoarchaeology: Expanding Archaeological Method and Theory. Washington, D.C.: Smithsonian Institution Press.

Luminescence Dating

A dating technique applicable to such materials as pottery and other forms of baked clay, burnt stone, burnt flint, volcanic products, stalagmitic calcite, and windblown/waterborne sediment. There are two branches: *thermoluminescence dating* (TL) and *optical dating* (OD), the latter primarily used for sediment. With the former, the dating signal consists of the luminescence emitted when, in the laboratory, an extract from the sample is heated. Various minerals emit thermoluminescence suitable for dating, principally quartz, feldspar, and calcite, but there are others also, such as zircon and volcanic glass. With optical dating, the signal is obtained by exposure to a beam of light or infrared radiation and is termed *optically stimulated luminescence* (OSL) with *infrared-stimulated luminescence* (IRSL) being used to specify the latter method of stimulation; the term *photostimulated luminescence* (PL) is also employed.

The latent dating signal is stored in the form of electrons that have been trapped away from their usual locations within the crystal lattice of the mineral grains concerned; the greater the number of trapped electrons, the stronger the luminescence. The trapping is the result of exposure to the weak flux of alpha, beta, and gamma radiation emitted by potassium, rubidium, thorium, and uranium in the sample itself and in the surrounding soil (or other burial medium); cosmic radiation also makes a contribution. The longer the duration of exposure to radiation, the greater the number of trapped electrons, and, hence, the emitted luminescence is a measure of the years that have elapsed since the number of trapped electrons was last set to zero. In the case of pottery, the setting to zero occurs upon firing of the clay by the potter; heat is the zeroing agency for other burnt materials, too. For stalagmitic calcite, the trapped-electron population is effectively zero at crystal formation. For unburnt sediment, the zeroing occurs through exposure to daylight during deposition, but, depending on circumstances, it is not always complete.

Because of dependence on trapped electrons, luminescence dating is often referred to as a branch of *trapped-electron dating* (TED), the other branch being *electron spin resonance* (ESR). A preferred term is *trapped-charge dating* (TCD) because the luminescence can equally well be produced by positive charges (positrons), but it is simpler in discussion to use "electrons."

Martin J. Aitken

See also ELECTRON SPIN RESONANCE (ESR) DATING; OPTICAL DATING; THERMOLUMINESCENCE DATING

M

Magnetic Prospecting

The prospecting technique based on mapping local variations in the Earth's magnetic field (magnetic prospecting in the restricted sense of the term) and the ensemble of methods that utilize time-dependent fields generated by the prospecting instrument itself, thus called *artificial*. These are capable of measuring the magnetic properties of soil (electromagnetic prospecting). (For a discussion of the dating method based on the permanent magnetization of archaeological structures, see the entry titled ARCHAEOMAGNETIC DATING.)

Magnetic Properties of Soils and Archaeological Structures

In the absence of any magnetic field, only a very limited number of chemical substances show magnetism; the magnetization that may exist is called *remanent* because it remains after the process that generated it. These substances are called *ferromagnetic* based on the characteristics of iron.

Generally, in the presence of a magnetic field (H), a magnetization (J) proportional to it appears. We call χ the magnetic susceptibility, the ratio J/H. This permits distinguishing between bodies that are *diamagnetic* (having susceptibilities that are weakly negative), *paramagnetic* (having weakly positive susceptibilities), and *ferromagnetic* (which have a large positive susceptibility). Soils and rocks are mixtures of various materials in which the proportions of ferromagnetic minerals are small, but nevertheless, they are the ones that determine all the magnetic properties that can be observed. Therefore, it is necessary to explain some of the characteristics of these ferromagnetic bodies.

Paramagnetic bodies have carriers of magnetism (atoms or molecules) with random orientation, at a microscopic level, due to thermal agitation. In contrast, in ferromagnetic bodies, the elementary carriers of magnetism, the atoms of the crystal lattice, have a coherent orientation, either parallel or antiparallel in small volumes (called *Weiss domains*). A solid ferromagnetic particle in a soil may contain one or several domains. If the former, it is called single or *monodomain;* if the latter, *polydomain*. When heated above a certain temperature (called the *Curie point*), the organization of the domains is destroyed, and the particle becomes paramagnetic. The size of the domains influences the totality of magnetic properties.

The magnetic minerals in soil are essentially the three oxides of iron: hematite $Fe_2O_3\alpha$, magnetite Fe_3O_4, and maghaemite $Fe_2O_3\gamma$. Only the last two are really magnetic, having the same face-centered cubic crystalline structure.

Artificially generated magnetic fields used in prospection are of limited strength in order to avoid any nonlinear or irreversible magnetic effect (as opposed to excavation, any prospecting measurement must be repeatable). These allow the measurement of two properties: the *magnetic susceptibility* and the *magnetic viscosity* (which corresponds to a delay in the acquisition or the loss of induced magnetization).

Magnetic prospection that uses the Earth's magnetic field as a primary field does not alter the milieu. It detects variations in total magnetization and, thus, detects the induced magnetization due to susceptibility, viscosity, and all forms of remanent magnetization.

Apart from soils that develop on very magnetic volcanic rocks, soils have a magnetic susceptibility that is greater than that of the rock from which they come. This effect is particularly marked in archaeological-occupation soils. One might be tempted to explain this by a loss of nonmagnetic minerals such as calcite or silicates, but this does not explain all of the cases and cannot explain cases of rapid transformation. Two explanations have been advanced. The first process involves a reduction of hematite by the heating of fires; the second, the production of magnetite by bacteria. In the first, fire of either natural or anthropogenic origin reduces the hematite to magnetite, favored by the presence of organic materials. These fires may result from the clearing of land for cultivation. On cooling, the magnetite is partly conserved and partly reoxidized to maghaemite. In both cases, the magnetic susceptibility is considerably raised. This process was verified by laboratory experiments that have also shown that, in temperate climates, the in situ conversion to magnetic oxides represents only a fraction of that which can be attained in the laboratory. The second process is observed not only in soils, but also in marine or lake sediments. Only magnetite is produced, and it has a very homogeneous grain structure. This explains perfectly the great uniformity of the ratio of magnetic viscosity to magnetic susceptibility observed in many varied types of soils. The augmented ratio corresponds to small monodomain grains (less than 0.1 µm). The above two processes are not mutually exclusive.

The importance of the phenomenon of amplification of the magnetic properties of soil makes magnetic prospection a method that is generally well adapted to detection of burned structures and filled features (ditches, pits), which may have accumulated a considerable proportion of highly magnetic surface soils, and occupation sites. Fired-clay structures (e.g., kilns, floors of dwellings) also show the phenomenon of thermoremanent magnetism. Most unfired clays contain iron-oxide grains at random orientations; during firing, these grains become thermally agitated such that their magnetic domains can become parallel to the Earth's magnetic field. Upon cooling, the clay is left with a permanent magnetic moment that is detectable during magnetic prospection.

Utilizing the Earth's Magnetic Field

The Earth's magnetic field is that of a centered magnetic dipole with an orientation approximately that of the Earth's axis of rotation. It varies considerably with latitude. The magnetic field points downward in the Northern Hemisphere; it is horizontal in the equatorial regions; and it points upward in Antarctica. At the scale of an archaeological site, it may be considered as a primary uniform field whose orientation depends on the latitude of the site. The magnetic field undergoes secular variation, which does not disturb its utilization in prospecting, but the existence of temporally variable ionic currents in the upper layers of the atmosphere induces variations of the order of minutes, hours, and days that must be corrected for or compensated. In addition, the presence of industrial installations and, above all, direct-current electrified railroads, add variations of human origin which must also be corrected. In practicality, these disturbances prevent all prospecting of this type in an urban environment.

The Earth's magnetic field is a weak field whose intensity varies between 30,000 and 60,000 nT (nano Tesla). It must be measured with a precision of the order of 0.1 nT for archaeological prospecting while eliminating the variations that may attain several hundred nT a minute.

The magnetometers utilized in archaeological prospecting use either nuclear magnetic resonance (protons) or optical pumping, both of which measure a frequency directly proportional to the modulus of the total field. Magnetometers may also be the directional fluxgate type, which are used for the measurement of the gradient of the vertical component of the Earth's magnetic field. Fluxgate gradiometers are lighter but also less sensitive than proton or optically pumped magnetometers.

Magnetic prospection of archaeological sites began at the end of the 1950s with the first proton magnetometers having a sensitivity of ca. 1 nT. The first experiments were attempts to detect the anomalies caused by pottery kilns where remanent magnetism was to be expected. Practice showed that anomalies corresponding to induced magnetization were more abundant and permitted the detection not only of burned structures, but also a large number of filled-in features (ditches, pits). Differential measurement using a mobile detector and a fixed detector was quickly recognized as being the most effective way of eliminating temporal variations of the Earth's magnetic field, whatever the origin. It later appeared logical to bring the two measuring positions close together to prospect in very disturbed areas. Placing the two detector elements on the same, vertical staff gives good rejection of temporal variation and allows the gradient measurement. When using two fluxgate detectors, they are maintained in a rigid alignment and measure the same component.

In terms of interpretation, the different arrangements of the detectors are theoretically equivalent, and the choice between different types of measurements is a matter of the sensitivity of the instruments and their ease of use. The measurement of the modulus of the total magnetic field is approximately equivalent to the measurement of the component of the magnetic anomaly parallel to the (most often oblique) primary field. If the inclination of the field is not too weak, the information gained is neither better nor worse than that gained by measurement of the vertical component. From data of one component, a linear filtering process can be applied to reconstruct the gradient. Reciprocally, from the gradient, it is possible to reconstitute the measurement of a component at a single level. These filtering operations may add noise.

The interpretation of the measurements from magnetic surveys suffers from several limitations. The first is that no anomaly is observable above a layered ground and that one does not measure the magnetic susceptibility of the soil but records only its lateral variation. Thus, the boundaries for archaeological structures are thus more evident the more they are vertical. It is not possible to dissociate the viscous from the induced magnetization. They add up and may often be of equivalent amplitude. The appearance of the observed magnetic anomalies varies completely with the inclination of the Earth's field at the point under consideration, as shown in Figure 1. This effect may be corrected by calculating what the measurements would have been if the field had been vertical. To this treatment, which improves the localization and nature of the contrasts given by a structure, one may add a downward continuation calculation that improves the visibility of its lateral extent.

All things considered, magnetic prospecting is an excellent method for mapping buried structures as seen in Figure 2, which shows

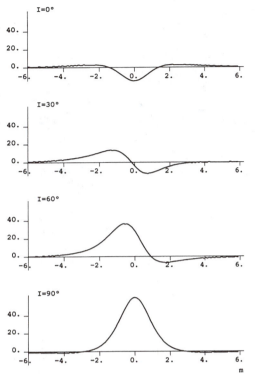

Figure 1. Variation of the magnetic anomaly (in nT) versus the distance (in m) for a spherical body bearing an induced magnetization depending on the inclination of the Earth's magnetic field. Figure by Michel Dabas and Alain Tabbagh.

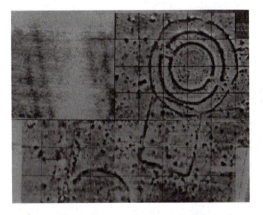

Figure 2. Magnetic anomaly map at Schmiedorf (Bavaria, Germany). The concentric enclosures date from the Middle Neolithic; the quadrangular one, the first Iron Age. Courtesy of Helmut Becker, Bayerisches Landesamt für Denkmalpflege (Munich).

pits and ditches at the site of Schmiedorf, and Figure 3, which shows the map of the Roman town of Colonia Ulpia Trajana, near Xanten

Figure 3. Magnetic anomaly map of the Roman city of Colonia Ulpia Trajana (North Rheinland, Germany). The two big ditches dating from the third century are cross-checking the former city plan of larger extension. Photograph by I. Scollar; from I. Scollar et al. (1986) Geophysics *51–53, 623–633. Courtesy of the Society of Exploration Geophysicists, by permission.*

in Germany. In the first site, archaeological structures were naturally filled with topsoil more magnetic than the loess in which they were dug. This process can also be seen in the second site, where the surrounding medium consists of alluvial gravel—but some volcanic material (tuffa) was used in a few of the larger buildings, which produced large anomalies at some parts of the site.

Utilizing Artificial Variable Fields

Artificial fields are emitted by a loop or a small coil, a *dipole,* and they produce a variation of the magnetic field with time that belongs to either the *frequency domain* (if alternating) or the *time domain* (if they result from an applied pulse of current).

In the time domain, the primary field is created using a loop, and the measurement of the secondary field is done after emission, using the same loop or another detector. For loops of less than 1 m in diameter, effectively only the viscosity is measured, the electrical-conductivity response being negligible.

In frequency domain, where the measurement of the secondary field is made at the same time as the emission of the primary field, a rigid assembly of the transmitter and the receiver coils is necessary to reduce the variations of the primary field at the receiver as far as possible. The Slingram type of instrument is used (*see* ELECTRICAL AND

ELECTROMAGNETIC PROSPECTING). The depth of investigation required for archaeological prospecting defines the distance between the two coils. The frequencies must be sufficiently low (less than 40 kHz) so that the susceptibility is measured by the in-phase secondary field. The measurement of the viscosity is possible only with a multifrequency instrument that permits one to separate the part due to the viscosity from that due to conductivity in the secondary field, which is in quadrature with the primary field.

Tests with the first instruments made during the 1960s showed an insufficient depth of investigation, which limited their application. The problem has not been taken up again since the development of the first-time domain instrument, and their use for magnetic-viscosity measurement has remained limited (but they are widely employed as metal detectors). In the frequency domain, a more profound study defined the value of coil separation needed for a depth of investigation sufficient for archaeological purposes, even though the continued use of the Earth's field remains the best solution for investigating deep structures presenting a good ratio of height to lateral extension, especially at higher latitudes.

Two other points emerge from the comparison of the utilization of the Earth's magnetic field as opposed to artificial fields. The

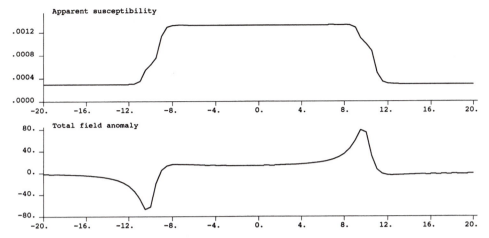

Figure 4. Theoretical anomaly for 10-m-x-10-m slab feature of 0.5 m thickness. Top, apparent susceptibility variation for a Slingram device (having perpendicular coils 1.5 m apart); bottom, magnetic anomaly. On the top, the slab corresponds to a global increase of the apparent susceptibility, whereas, on the bottom, the slab limits correspond only to anomalies. Figure by Michel Dabas and Alain Tabbagh.

first concerns the separation between the measurement of viscosity and susceptibility, which is possible only in an artificial field. This route has not been well explored, and it is hard to say whether the information given by the two properties is redundant or not. The second point is that, with the dipole-dipole type of instrument, one measures not only the variations in the susceptibility, but the susceptibility itself. An isolated reading thus has an intrinsic significance that is characteristic of the material in the soil, allowing rapid prospecting using a very sparse grid to outline areas where the magnetic susceptibility is raised. This is of general archaeological significance. The detection of lens-shaped structures is also easy, and the detection of laterally extended structures is much easier with this technique. Figure 4 shows a comparison between the theoretical response from the same structure with a Slingram instrument and one using the gradient of the Earth's magnetic field. This method is especially useful for the detection of ancient occupation zones such as pottery- and metallurgical-production areas.

The possibilities offered by automatic recording of field measurements allow one to envision a simultaneous utilization of the Earth's field and an artificial field. With this technique, there are considerable prospects for the detection of all types of structures, for an estimate of their depth, and for a simultaneous determination of the susceptibility and magnetic viscosity for the different features in situ.

Michel Dabas
Alain Tabbagh

See also ARCHAEOMAGNETIC DATING; ELECTRICAL AND ELECTROMAGNETIC PROSPECTING

Further Readings

Clark, A.J. (1990) *Seeing Beneath the Soil.* London: Batsford.

Heimmer, D.H., and De Vore, S.L. (1995) *Near Surface, High Resolution Geophysical Methods for Cultural Resource Management and Archaeological Investigation.* Washington, D.C.: National Park Service, Department of the Interior.

Scollar, I., ed. (1990) *Archaeological Prospecting and Remote Sensing.* Cambridge: Cambridge University Press.

Marble, Characterization

The use of geochemical methods to solve many vexing problems of archaeological marble, especially by analysis of petrography and mineralogy, stable-isotopic ratios, trace elements, cathodoluminescence (CL), and electron spin resonance (ESR) spectroscopy. For marble artifacts of the Mediterranean region, these problems are: (1) provenance, (2) association of broken fragments, and (3) authenticity.

Previously, esthetic criteria or *a priori* reasoning were used to assign the provenance of classical marble artifacts. *Pentelic, Hymettian, Island,* and *Parian* were used as descriptive terms for alleged Greek marbles, and *Carrara* for Italian, depending on the archaeologist. Since the criteria were subjective, with one person's Carrara being another's Pentelic, many controversies for important pieces remained unresolved.

Broken fragments of marble artifacts were also associated by subjective criteria. Inscriptions and statuary were commonly assembled ignoring the physical characteristics of the marble. Stable-isotopic analysis of carbon (C) and oxygen (O) was able to show, however, that associated fragments of some inscriptions in the Epigraphical and Agora Museums in Athens could not have been parts of the same marble slab and that some classical Greek and Roman statues also consisted of unrelated marble fragments.

Modern forgeries or ancient copies of even older artifacts can be evinced by an incorrect provenance (e.g., an archaic Greek statue cannot be made of Roman marble). In addition, the long-term weathering effects of geochemical or geobiological processes on marble surfaces are known. Comparing the weathered surface of an artifact against its fresh interior by chemical, isotopic, and mineralogic analysis can often show whether a surface patina was natural or faked by man.

Mineralogically and chemically marble is a mixture of calcite: 44 percent CO_2 and 56 percent CaO; and dolomite: 47.9 percent carbon dioxide (CO_2), 30.4 percent calcium oxide (CaO), and 21.7 percent magnesium oxide (MgO). The number and the amount of individual trace elements are highly variable from one marble quarry to another, suggesting the use of trace elements as geochemical fingerprints. However, since the variation in abundance of each trace element within a quarry is commonly as great or greater than the variation between quarries, trace elements alone cannot be used as indicators of provenance. Statistical treatment has overcome this problem to some extent. Multivariate statistical analysis, incorporating data from other types of geochemical analysis, has allowed a more positive identification of quarry sources than was possible by trace elements alone.

Because of varying geological histories, marbles in different quarries have distinctive isotopic ratios of oxygen, carbon, and strontium (Sr), all of which are abundant and can be used as signatures of provenance. Variations in isotopic composition of oxygen and carbon in carbonates are controlled by fractionation reactions that take place during sedimentation, lithification, and metamorphism and by their mode of origin (e.g., as a chemical precipitate or as organic shell hash). Variations in strontium isotopic ratios, $^{87}Sr/^{86}Sr$, are due to the composition of seawater at the time of the original carbonate deposition, the source materials, and additions by later fluids.

Two additional ancillary methods that are becoming viable are electron spin resonance (ESR) spectroscopy and cathodoluminescence (CL). As extensive ESR and CL databases are accumulated, they are providing new geochemical "fingerprints" for classical marble quarries.

Marble occurs abundantly on most of the Cycladic islands of the Aegean Sea. It was worked from at least the Early Neolithic (6000–5000 B.C.) and found as imported ornaments in Franchthi Cave in the Argolid of Greece and as anthropomorphic figures of the Middle (5000 B.C.) and Late Neolithic in the Cyclades. Marble was also used widely in the Early Bronze Age (EBA). Marble objects, including bowls and small figurines, have been found in the oldest dated settlement in the Cyclades (ca. 4800 B.C.) on the small island of Saliagos near Antiparos. Cycladic marble figurines and bowls have been found in mainland Greece, Crete, Egypt, and western Anatolia.

Detailed study of Aegean marble sources have concluded that the islands of Keros and Naxos were important sources for EBA marble, with lesser amounts coming from Paros and Ios. Clearly, trade in marble and marble artifacts around the Aegean, which started in the Late Neolithic, flourished in the EBA.

The Bronze Age civilizations of the Aegean Basin collapsed ca. the twelfth century B.C., and marble was not used again to any extent until the end of the seventh century B.C. Quarrying of marble began in the Cyclades in the seventh century B.C. and became common throughout the Aegean Basin by the sixth century. In the seventh century B.C., marble was exploited almost exclusively for sculpture and to a much lesser extent for building construction. Regular-shaped blocks were needed for sculpture, so commercial quarries came into use for the extraction of polygonal- and rectangular-shaped blocks. The first commercial marble was very coarse grained and almost certainly came from Naxos. By the sixth century B.C., quarries had become more widespread, with new ones opening up around the Aegean both on islands and in mainland Greece and Anatolia.

Coarse-grained Island marbles were traded extensively until the finer-grained, translucent lychnites marble of Paros was exploited in the early sixth century B.C. By the late sixth and early fifth centuries B.C., quarries on Mount Pentelikon near Athens were opened both for architecture—the buildings of the Acropolis—and sculpture. Parian marble was still preferred by many sculptors for important statues well into Roman times. The bluish, fine-grained marble of Mount Hymettos near Athens, quarried from the late fifth century B.C. on, was popular in Hellenistic and Roman times. Other important marble sources include Doliana, used for temples in the Peloponessus, including Tegea; Aliki on Thasos in the northern Aegean; Proconnesus in the Sea of Marmara; and sites in Asia Minor, all of which continued to be exploited in Roman and Byzantine times. Pyrenean marble was exploited, especially at Saint-Béat, France, and may have been exported as far as Constantinople. In 48 B.C. the Roman savant Pliny noted that Italian Lunense (Carrara) marble was readily available, widely used, and easily transported. The Carrara quarries were well organized, and many are still operating.

Marble had royal associations in the history of Rome and was always used exclusively in the construction of victory monuments. Octavian Augustus boasted when he became Augustus Caesar that he had found Rome a city of brick but left it one of marble. He had Agrippa, the Roman political and military commander, develop a network of imperial quarries, which continued to flourish under the control of emperors, more or less non-profit, until the late first or early second century.

Determination of Provenance

In the nineteenth century and for most of the first three-quarters of the twentieth, provenance of marble was determined by comparison of general physical characteristics, including grain size, mineralogy, and fabric of the artifact, to the quarry descriptions of G.R. Lepsius, the German geologist, published in 1890. Lepsius was the first to describe the major marble quarries of classical times petrographically. Analytical methods and databanks for determining provenance were not available, so Lepsius's descriptions remained, until quite recently, archaeological gospel.

In 1964, trace elements sodium (Na) and manganese (Mn) were analyzed by neutron activation (NAA) in an attempt to characterize Greek marbles. The variation was found to be too great, with factors of more than 100 within the same quarry, so the method was judged not satisfactory for determining the source of individual artifacts. Trace-element studies of archaeological materials require many samples and a statistical handling of the data to overcome the inherent variability in the material. To improve the discriminating powers of NAA, the results of trace-element analysis are paired with other types of analysis, with the results then handled statistically.

ESR spectra of $Mn^{2}+$ has been tried with some success. Preliminary work suggests that some quarries can be distinguished and that detailed work in establishing inter-341and intraquarry variation is needed. An adequate database of quarry samples is being compiled to make the method viable.

CL of white marble has proven to be a successful discriminating test. More than 500 white marble samples from classical quarries have been analyzed and a database of cathodomicrofacies has been compiled. Another database using CL ultraviolet (UV) spectra is also being compiled. CL shows much promise to discriminate between the many marbles that could not previously be distinguished because their other physical characteristics overlapped.

Stable-isotopic signatures are the most widely used system for determining marble provenance. Isotopic plots on a $\delta^{18}O$–$\delta^{13}C$ diagram show that many individual quarries can be distinguished. Isotopic analysis involves measuring the ratios of $^{13}C/^{12}C$ and $^{18}O/^{16}O$ in samples and expressing the results in terms of the deviation from a conventional

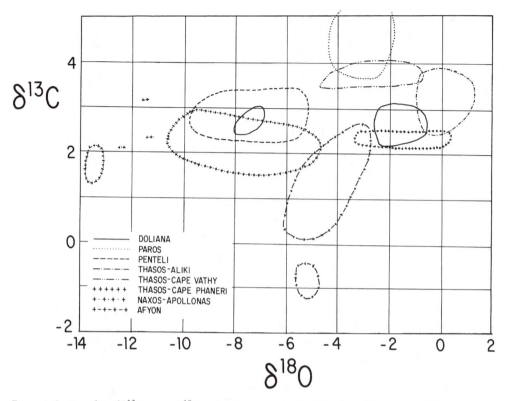

Figure 1. Scatter plot of $\delta^{13}C$ versus $\delta^{18}O$ values for some classical Greek and Roman marble quarries. Figure by Norman Herz.

standard. For archaeological marble, the standard used is the Pee Dee belemnite, a carbonate fossil from South Carolina.

Isotopic ratios of $^{13}C/^{12}C$ and $^{18}O/^{16}O$ in natural materials vary as a result of geochemical fractionation. On average, ^{16}O = 99.76 percent and ^{18}O = 0.19 percent of world oxygen; ^{12}C = 98.89 percent and ^{13}C = 1.11 percent of world carbon. Measurements of stable-isotopic ratios are carried out with a mass spectrometer, an instrument that measures proportions in very small samples of different isotopic masses of several elements. In the newer, state-of-the-art machines, less than 5 mg of sample are needed for an analysis, an amount readily acquired without causing harm to museum specimens. The precise measurement of the isotopic ratios $^{18}O/^{16}O$ and $^{13}C/^{12}C$ in marble is carried out after suitable chemical treatment has separated these elements in the form of CO_2 from the calcium carbonate. After the measurements by the mass spectrometer, the data are expressed as a deviation from the Pee Dee belemnite. This

deviation, called δ, is expressed as $\delta^{13}C$ or $\delta^{18}O$, measured in parts per thousand (ppt; or per mil, ‰), and calculated as follows:

$\delta(ppt) = [R \text{ sample}/R \text{ standard} - 1]1000$

where R = $^{13}C/^{12}C$ or $^{18}O/^{16}O$. Thus, if marble has a $\delta^{18}O$ = +10 ppt, the isotopic ratio of the oxygen is ten parts per thousand enriched in the heavy isotope ^{18}O compared to the standard. The isotopic-variability data are usually expressed as a scatter plot of $\delta^{18}O$ and $\delta^{13}C$ values (Figure 1).

In carbonate rocks, high $\delta^{13}C$ values may indicate a substantial contribution by inorganic $CaCO_3$, either detrital or as a chemical precipitate. The range in $\delta^{13}C$ values in many marbles may be largely due to a mixture of inorganic materials and organic shell fragments. Weathering, by meteoric waters or biological agencies, will also fractionate oxygen and carbon.

For a signature to be viable, it must be uniform throughout an artifact, should be relatively uniform in a quarry, and show only small variations within the limits of a mining district. Carbon and oxygen isotopes have been tested and found to meet these requirements. Uniform isotopic composition can be attained over a wide area if (1) isotopic equilibrium was attained during the formation of the limestone and its later metamorphism to marble; (2) the marble unit is thick and relatively pure (i.e., free of other mineral phases); (3) the metamorphic temperature gradient was not too steep.

Most classical quarries have been found to have relatively homogeneous isotopic signatures that can serve as valid geochemical signatures. Enough data have been accumulated to construct an isotopic database for all known principal archaeologically described marble sources of classical Greece and Rome, as well as some new ones discovered more recently. Where the isotopic data overlap between quarries, ancillary databanks based on other properties are needed for a more certain determination of provenance.

Another database being established is for $^{87}Sr/^{86}Sr$ ratios, which may provide an additional signature for the quarries whose O and C isotopic values overlap. Samples from the Thasos Aliki quarry had ratios of 0.70769 to 0.70792, Paros 0.70757, and Pentelikon 0.70830. For all of these quarries, Sr isotopic data improved the discriminating power over the use of oxygen and carbon alone.

Determining Provenance by the Marble Database

Before figuring the provenance of an artifact, a selection of probable sources is sometimes necessary, based on historical knowledge of the site, times of operation of the quarries, and known trading patterns. In a large test of the database, a study (Herz et al. 1985) of the marble statuary of the Demeter Sanctuary in Cyrene, eleven quarries were selected on the basis of historical trading patterns. All but six of sixty-one pieces could be assigned a provenance. Quarries used in the test were those that had operated during the time frame for the sanctuary (seventh to the sixth century B.C.).

The J. Paul Getty Museum of Malibu, California, owns a larger than life statue of a Greek kouros that allegedly dated from 530 B.C. Since only about a dozen complete kouroi are known worldwide, it was ranked in importance with some of the museum's most important acquisitions.

The results of isotopic analysis on the kouros showed $\delta^{18}O = -2.37$ ppt; $\delta^{13}C = +2.88$ ppt. This data, plus the fact that the piece was dolomitic, allowed a positive identification to be made: The statue was made of marble from the northeastern part of the island of Thasos.

Reconstruction of Artifacts and Determining Authenticity

Comparison of isotopic ratios in broken pieces is by far the best method for associating and reconstructing statuary and inscriptions. Isotopic tests were first applied in 1972 to broken fragments of inscriptions whose association had been debated by epigraphers. Four of eight alleged inscriptions were found to be invalid (i.e., the isotopic ratios of the individual fragments did not allow an association).

Similar tests were carried out on five fragments making up the Antonia Minor portrait in the Fogg Museum at Harvard University (Herz and Wenner 1981). Isotopic analysis showed that three pieces were Parian and two were Carrara marble. Antonia represented fragments of three different classical statues—each Parian fragment was different isotopically—patched up at some later time with local Italian marble (Figure 2).

Although copies can be made of marble statuary, it is very difficult to falsify a natural weathering patina. During the course of weathering, the marble surface will be in contact with meteoric water. Oxygen isotopes of the artifact and the water will tend to equilibrate. Meteoric water around the latitude of the Cyclades is ca. $\delta^{18}O = -32.4$ ppt indicating that any process of weathering in this area should decrease $\delta^{18}O$ in the patina of ancient artifacts.

Another expected change is due to the action of biological agents. The most significant deterioration of the marble surface is seen where encrustations of lichens were present. The organisms generate oxalic acid and chelate Mg from dolomite leaving a Ca-oxalate byproduct, whewellite. The fractionation factor for the formation of oxalate is $\delta^{13}C = -19$ ppt. Although dolomitic marbles will react and form oxalate and have strongly fractionated carbon, pure calcite marble will only be etched by the oxalic-acid solution but produce no new mineral phases. However, the same effects produced by oxalate-forming organisms over long periods of time can also be accelerated artificially and

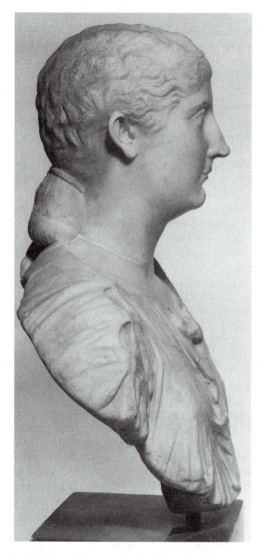

Figure 2. Marble Portrait of Antonia Minor, Fogg Art Museum, Harvard University (#1972.306). Roman sculpture, ca. 50 A.D. The portrait is made of five fragments; stable-isotopic analysis showed that none of them were related. The nose and the ponytail are of Italian Carrara marble; the rest are Greek marble from the island of Paros. (Courtesy of the Arthur M. Sackler Museum, Harvard University Art Museums. Fund in Memory of John Randolph III, Harvard Class of 1964, and the David M. Robinson Fund.)

resemble natural-appearing weathering phenomena (i.e., these effects can be faked).

Norman Herz

See also PETROGRAPHY; ROCKS AND MINERALS, CHARACTERIZATION

Further Readings

Herz, N. (1985) Isotopic analysis of marble. In G. Rapp and J.A. Gifford (eds.): Archaeological Geology, pp. 331–351. New Haven, CT: Yale University Press.

Herz, N., Kane, S.E. and Hayes, W.N. (1985) Isotopic analysis of sculpture from the Cyrene Demeter Sanctuary. In P.A. England and L. van Zelst (eds.): Application of Science in Examination of Works of Art, pp. 142–150. Boston: Museum of Fine Arts.

Herz, N., and Waelkens, M., eds. (1988) Classical Marble: Geochemistry, Technology, Trade. (NATO ASI Series E 153). Dordrecht: Kluwer.

Herz, N., and Wenner, D.B. (1981) Tracing the origins of marble. Archaeology 34(5):14–21.

Margolis, S.V. (1988) Authenticating ancient marble sculpture. Scientific American 260:104–110.

Waelkens, M., Herz, N., and Moens, L., eds. (1992) Ancient Stones: Quarrying, Trade, and Provenance. (Acta Archaeologica Lovaniensia Monographiae 4). Leuven, Belgium: Leuven University Press.

Marxist Archaeology

The influence of the ideas of Karl Marx (1818–1883) on archaeological research. The writings of Marx have had a profound impact on virtually all aspects of social and political thought throughout the twentieth century, and it would be difficult to underestimate his importance. Until the late 1980s, more than one-third of the world's population was ruled by administrations claiming to be directly inspired by Marxist thought. Since Marxism runs parallel to the birth and development of archaeology as a scientific discipline, it is not surprising that in many countries their destinies have been intertwined. Both have changed enormously since their nineteenth-century origins. Just as there is much diversity of opinion among archaeologists, there are many different strands of Marxist thought. It would be surprising if everything Marx wrote more than 100 years ago were relevant today, and much debate has concerned trying to separate out and develop living ideas from dead wood. Consequently, Marxist ideas have been combined, in one way or another, or contrasted with every other major theoretical and philosophical approach in the social and historical sciences. Many scholars today who would not like to label themselves "Marxist" are, nevertheless, directly or indirectly influenced by him.

Marx's writings are concerned with a great diversity of areas of study. He did not leave behind a fixed and static position and did not even want to call himself a Marxist. His writings are open to many different interpretations. As one commentator has put it, his words are like bats: You can see in them both birds and mice. A recurrent feature of a number of books and articles about Marxist archaeology (Spriggs 1984; McGuire 1992; Trigger 1993) has been the great difficulty in deciding which scholars are, or are not, Marxist or adopt what can be identified as a Marxist approach. It is probably best to regard Marxism as a tradition of research and scholarship that overlaps with and influences the writings of archaeologists rather than a single unified perspective, or research tradition, within the discipline.

Marxism, in its various forms, has attempted to provide: (1) a philosophy for understanding and interpreting the social world; (2) a theory of society; (3) a theory of historical change; and (4) a political program for social action. All of these areas are of concern to archaeologists. Archaeology needs a philosophical and theoretical framework to guide interpretation of the traces of the past. To understand the past, there is a need to relate artifacts to the social groups who made and used them and to understand how and why change took place. As archaeology takes place in the present, it cannot divorce itself from contemporary society and politics.

Dialectical Materialism

The Marxist philosophical understanding of the world, and method of inquiry, is founded in the notion of the *dialectic,* a philosophy of *internal relations.* It is a term used to understand a relationship between things in which the things themselves are understood as being part of each other, and affecting each other, without collapsing into each other. For example, in a standard empiricist philosophy, production and consumption would be understood as entirely different things. Boxes might be drawn around them and external links, or feedback relations, posited. From a dialectical perspective, production and consumption cannot be neatly separated out. One activity simply does not make sense without the other, yet they remain different and opposed activities, as shown in the accompanying graphic.

Understanding the world dialectically means attempting to understand it in terms of the relationships *between* things rather than in terms of the things themselves. Dialectical thinking provides a major challenge and alternative to an empiricist philosophy that has been dominant in archaeology.

Historical Materialism

A Marxist view of society and historical change is founded on what is called *historical materialism.* It is the practical, material conditions of social life, rather than ideals or values, that are given primacy in any analysis. How people think is determined by the economic circumstances in which they live out their lives. When the economy changes, so, eventually, does every other area of social life—from politics to ideologies to legal systems. Marxists strongly emphasize that societies have to be understood as *totalities.* An analysis of art, film, music, religion, political structures, or anything else cannot, therefore, be conducted independently but must be related to the generality of the material conditions of life. Marxist theories of society and social change are thus *holistic*: The sum is much greater than its component parts. In understanding the social totality and the way it changes, the actions and thoughts of individual persons are largely

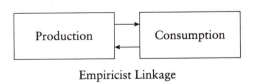

Empiricist Linkage

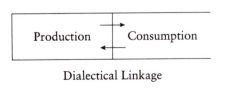

Dialectical Linkage

irrelevant since these themselves are determined by social circumstances. A "great person" view of history, stressing the uniqueness of certain individuals, is rejected. Since archaeologists primarily study artifacts, have to infer patterns of social life from material traces, and have great difficulty in identifying individuals, such a perspective has some obvious advantages.

The Social Totality

Marxist ideas about the social totality typically conceive of it in terms of a layer-cake model. Society (in Marxist terminology, the *social formation*) consists of an economic infrastructure, or base, and an ideological superstructure. The base is made up of the *forces of production* and the *social relations of production*. The forces of production include the means of production: technologies and the manner in which people take and utilize natural resources from the environment in the labor process. The forces of production differ according to the way in which labor is socially organized in the production process (e.g., what kinds of divisions of labor and forms of cooperation between persons exist). The social relations of production organize the manner in which the environment is exploited, given the available technology, and how the labor product is distributed and consumed by various classes or groups. The superstructure, or top layer of society, consists of everything else that is not part of the economic base: areas of social life grounded in systems of thought and values (e.g., ideologies, politics, legal systems, more generally what we typically refer to as "culture" [religion, philosophies, art, literature, and the like]).

Marx's own work was primarily concerned with the nature of nineteenth-century industrial capitalism and how it developed out of a feudal order. He links an analysis of economic change to class conflict, providing the stimulus for social change. Human history, for Marx, was the history of class struggle prompted by economic change. The crucial point here is a view of society as being internally conflict ridden rather than a smoothly integrated whole, the hallmark of a functionalist approach. Consequently, Marxists, unlike functionalists, have little difficulty in explaining why social change occurs. The seeds of change are embedded in the very makeup of society.

There are some serious difficulties in trying to apply such a perspective to precapitalist societies. The very attempt to do so has been regarded as ethnocentric and anachronistic by some. If there is no definite class structure, there are obvious problems; and, in relatively undifferentiated societies, precisely where the "economy" is supposed to begin or end, as opposed to, for example, kin relations or religion, may be far from clear. One solution within structural-Marxist (see below) anthropology and archaeology has been to regard differences and struggles, such as those between clans or lineages, elders and juniors, or men and women in small-scale societies, as being more or less equivalent to a notion of class in capitalist societies and to regard kinship relations as acting as the social relations of production. Consequently, it is argued, Marxist concepts can be used to understand all societies from the Palaeolithic to the present.

Social Change and Social Evolution

The source of social change is conceived as being rooted in *contradictions* in the economic base of society. From Marx's writings, these contradictions can be located either between the forces of production and the social relations of production or within the latter. In the first case, an explanation for change is grounded in an analysis of the manner in which new technologies grow out of step with the social relations of production. For example, the feudal order was based on small-scale agricultural production, with the principal classes being serfs and aristocrats who owned the land. As new technologies for production developed and trade expanded, major changes occurred in the infrastructure, leading to a new set of forces of production grounded in the large-scale mass production of commodities in cities. These new productive forces rapidly became incompatible with the feudal social relations of production, leading to conflict between the aristocrats and the new capitalist class and the revolutionary emergence of a new capitalist social order. These economic changes, in turn, led to a transformation of the political and ideological superstructure. Another interpretation of the change from feudalism to capitalism would locate it within the social relations of production: the development of a disjunction between an aristocratic ruling class and an emerging entrepreneurial mercantile class. The growing power and ascendancy of the latter promoted changes in the forces of production, ultimately leading to a transformation of both the economic base and the superstructure.

Australian-born British prehistorian V. Gordon Childe (1892–1957), until his death virtually the only Western archaeologist to explicitly label his work Marxist, used ideas of contradictions between the forces and the social relations of production to explain both the origins of agriculture and the development of civilizations, referring to a Neolithic "revolution" and an urban "revolution," respectively. Archaeology, for him, revealed the progressive extension of humanity's control over external nature by the invention and discovery of more efficient tools and processes. This provided a foundation for the whole of history, conditioning and limiting all other human activities.

Marx, in collaboration with Friedrich Engels (1820–1895), in *The German Ideology,* formulated a general series of evolutionary stages, termed *modes of production,* through which human societies had progressed: the tribal, the ancient, the feudal and the capitalist, with a predicted forthcoming socialist stage, perceived in a utopian manner. They were heavily influenced by the early anthropological work of Lewis Henry Morgan (1818–1881). The general idea of conceiving the past in terms of evolutionary lines of development from simpler to more complex societies remains a primary element in many Marxist works, firmly linking them with a more general currency of evolutionary ideas in archaeology, whether of a *unilineal* or a *multilineal* nature. General ideas of social evolution strongly influenced Childe's archaeology: He interpreted archaeological remains in terms of evolutionary pathways leading from "savagery" to "barbarism" to "civilization" (Childe 1951). They have also influenced structural-Marxist approaches to long-term change.

A major problem with much older Marxist writing, up to the 1960s, whether about society or social change, is that it easily collapsed into a simple technological and/or economic determinism; this is a strand found in most of Childe's work. Cultural (superstructural) change was simply determined by economic change, with the forces of production usually being conceived as of primary importance. Furthermore, pessimism on the part of most archaeologists with regard to the possibility of reconstructing social relations from the evidence had a predictable outcome in focusing analyses on technological change, which could be relatively easily assessed and measured. There was little need for a detailed Marxist analysis of the superstructure because its form and nature, and why it changed, could be read off from an analysis of the economic base. Religion is simply an opiate for the masses, the juridical system a means of protecting the interests of those who control the forces of production, and so forth. For many scholars working in the social and historical sciences in the 1950s, Marxist approaches increasingly appeared as an intellectual dead end. Apart from Childe's work, there was very little explicit use of a Marxist approach in archaeology outside the Soviet Union and its satellites, in which it dominated.

Structural Marxism

This situation altered dramatically with the combination of structuralist ideas with a Marxist approach to create various forms of structural-Marxist theory from the mid-1960s onward. The primary influence was the work of the French Marxist theoretician Louis Althusser, who set out to reread Marx. This led to a reconceptualization of the social formation as a complex unity of levels (or *instances*)—minimally, the economic, the ideological and the political—making up a *structure in dominance.* These instances were conceived as relatively *autonomous* from each other. In other words, there was, for example, no simple way of predicting politics from the economy or vice versa—a major break with traditional Marxist thought. Since the superstructure of society could not be read off from the economy, it required detailed analysis in its own right. The economic instance was regarded as a combination of the forces and the social relations of production in which the latter were always *dominant.* Gone, then, was any possibility of an analysis of change asserting the primacy of technological change. Althusser sought to distinguish very carefully between the concepts of *dominance* and *determination.* He maintained that the economic instance might be both dominant and determinant at any one time or that, alternatively, the political and ideological levels could dominate (i.e., have the major influence on) the social formation. Maintaining a more traditional aspect of Marxist thought, he claimed that the economy only determined the nature of the rest of society in the last resort.

This general position and modifications of it by others (Friedman and Rowlands 1977; Rowlands et al. 1987) had an enormous impact on rejuvenating Marxist theory from the mid-1960s to the mid-1980s in the social sciences, creating a fresh intellectual space for the analysis of superstructural forms such as art, literature, and religion and a rethinking of socioeconomic relations. In archaeology, a structural-Marxist approach led to a rethinking of approaches to long-term change and social evolution in terms of longer- and shorter-term cycles of change and relations between centers and peripheries, stressing the primacy of the social relations of production. The use of a structural-Marxist position in anthropology and archaeology in the study of precapitalist societies led to a position in which ideological political and economic processes were regarded as dialectically interrelated rather than as relatively independent levels or instances of the totality. So, for example, religion and the economy were held to constitute each other. Primacy was granted to the political articulation, or linkage, between the social relations and the forces of production. This work produced some of the most stimulating and exciting discussions within archaeology during the 1970s and 1980s and represented a powerful alternative to the types of approaches advocated within the New or processual Archaeology that developed in the 1960s. Insights gained from structural-Marxist approaches played a key role in the development of what has been labeled postprocessual archaeology from the 1980s onward.

The Critique of Ideology
The concept of *ideology* is crucial to Marxist thinking. The meaning of the concept has been hotly debated, and there are many different definitions. Within Marxism, the concept has a specialized meaning, differing from that in ordinary language use in which it is often used to refer to any sets of beliefs motivated by social or personal interests. Within Marxism, ideology is most generally considered to be a sectional form of power acting, in various ways, to reproduce social inequality and block social change. While the concept of *contradiction* within Marxism plays a vital role in explaining social transformation, ideology is similarly important in the explanation of why societies remain stable for long periods. A standard Marxist approach is to regard ideology as a set of beliefs arising from false consciousness. People are simply unaware of their real social conditions of existence: Exploitation is masked by a mistaken view of the world that acts so as to maintain the position and power of a select socially dominant group.

Discussions and different uses of the concept of ideology, sometimes differing quite markedly from the false-consciousness view mentioned above (Miller and Tilley 1984) have played an important role in recent archaeological works. These have investigated the manner in which material forms can be used to legitimize structures of social dominance. One effect of this research has been to reconceptualize the nature of archaeological evidence at a very basic level. Material culture does not, in any simple manner, relate to social reality by directly reflecting or mirroring it. It may equally well *invert,* disguise, or transform the nature of social power.

It is but a short step from using the concept of ideology, linked to a discussion of power, to interpret the past to turn itself—reflexively—on the practice of contemporary archaeology as a discipline and a mode of discourse within late-twentieth century capitalist societies. This is precisely what has happened in recent archaeological writings inspired by a Marxist approach (Shanks and Tilley 1987; 1992). One of the important questions raised is the following: To what extent can the work of archaeologists be regarded as promoting dominant interests and sectional values in society? An archaeology concerned with social inequality (McGuire and Paynter 1991) needs to think not just about interpreting the past, but also about its own social practices and constitution and relationship with the public. There are strong common foundations to this critical archaeology and feminist approaches concerned with the whole issue of gender relations in the past and in the present. Various analyses have been concerned with the nature of archaeological interpretations, the manner in which the past is written, hierarchies and power within the structure of archaeological organizations, and the manner in which museums represent the past in the present. This has led to much discussion with regard to the politics of the past and what role archaeology should play in the contemporary world. To paraphrase Marx: Archaeologists have only interpreted the world; the point is to change it.

Christopher Tilley

See also CHILDE, VERE GORDON; CORE AND PERIPHERY SYSTEMS; NEW/PROCESSUAL ARCHAEOLOGY; POSTPROCESSUAL ARCHAEOLOGY

Further Readings

Childe, V.G. (1951) Social Evolution. London: Watts.

Friedman, J., and Rowlands, M., eds. (1977) The Evolution of Social Systems. London: Duckworth.

McGuire, R. (1992) A Marxist Archaeology. San Diego: Academic.

McGuire, R., and Paynter, R., eds. (1991) The Archaeology of Inequality. Oxford: Blackwell.

Miller, D. and Tilley, C., eds. (1984) Ideology, Power, and Prehistory. Cambridge: Cambridge University Press.

Rowlands, M., Larsen, M., and Kristiansen, K., eds. (1987) Centre and Periphery in the Ancient World. Cambridge: Cambridge University Press.

Shanks, M., and Tilley, C. (1987) Social Theory and Archaeology. Cambridge: Polity.

Shanks, M., and Tilley, C. (1992) Re-Constructing Archaeology, 2nd ed. London: Routledge.

Spriggs, M., ed. (1984) Marxist Perspectives in Archaeology. Cambridge: Cambridge University Press.

Trigger, B. (1993) Marxism in contemporary Western archaeology. In M.B. Schiffer (ed.): Archaeological Method and Theory, vol. 5, pp. 159–200. Tucson: University of Arizona Press.

McKern, William Carleton (1892–1988)

American archaeologist, anthropologist, and museologist. Born on July 6, 1892, in Medicine Lake, Washington, McKern was educated at the University of California at Berkeley, where he received his bachelor's in 1917. He was instructor of anthropology at the University of Washington (1919–1920) but subsequently concentrated on fieldwork and museum studies. McKern did research at the B.P. Bishop Museum in Honolulu (1920–1922) and joined the Bureau of American Ethnology in 1923. In 1925, he began his long career at the Milwaukee Public Museum, first as curator, then as director from 1943. A member of the American Anthropological Association (he was president in 1933), the Society for American Archaeology (president, 1940), the American Association for the Advancement of Science, and the American Association of Museums, McKern was editor of *American Antiquity* (1934–1938) and received an honorary doctorate from Marquette University in (1956).

McKern, a specialist in the Native American archaeology of the midwestern United States, was a pioneer in the development of a typology for that region in the 1930s and 1940s. McKern utilized the Midwestern Taxonomic Method, a typological system that ordered material culture into six units of increasing specificity and was organized at a conference of midwestern specialists in 1932. The system soon came to be known as the McKern Classification, however, as McKern became its chief proponent and utilized it for the study and ordering of the anthropological collections of the Milwaukee Public Museum ("The Midwestern Taxonomic Method as an Aid to Archaeological Study"). Materials were grouped into *components,* which usually described a site or a stratum within a site, and from there into *foci, aspects, phases, patterns,* and *bases,* which describe categories of decreasing trait sharing. The McKern Classification tended to operate independently of chronological considerations, but this because of a lack of stratified sites in the Midwest in the 1930s and McKern's use of museum collections, not because of a disregard for the chronological component inherent in any ordering of archaeological material. While the creation of such overall taxonomies is no longer a focus of anthropological archaeology, McKern's use of the Midwestern Taxonomic Method ranks among the most important scientific attempts to order the past of the New World. McKern died on November 20, 1988, in Waukesa, Wisconsin.

Joseph J. Basile

See also MIDWESTERN TAXONOMIC SYSTEM

Further Readings

McKern, W.C. (1928) The Neale and Mc-Claughry Mound Groups. Milwaukee, WI: Milwaukee Public Museum.

McKern, W.C. (1930) The Kletzien and Nitschke Mound Groups. Milwaukee, WI: Milwaukee Public Museum.

McKern, W.C. (1931) A Wisconsin Variant of the Hopewell Culture. Milwaukee, WI: Milwaukee Public Museum.

McKern, W.C. (1939) The Midwestern Taxonomic Method as an aid to archaeological study. American Antiquity 4:301–313.

McKern, W.C. (1945) Preliminary Report on the Upper Mississippi Phase in Wisconsin. Milwaukee, WI: Milwaukee Public Museum.

McKern, W.C. (1963) The Clam River Focus. Milwaukee, WI: Milwaukee Public Museum.

Medieval Archaeology

The archaeological investigation of sites dating from the collapse of the western Roman Empire (fifth century A.D.) to the end of the Middle Ages (ca. the fifteenth century A.D.). There is considerable regional variation in chronological limits. The term generally refers to European sites but includes portions of the Middle East and North Africa, To confuse the issue, different terms apply in different countries: in much of northern Europe, *medieval* more commonly refers to the half-millennium from ca. A.D. 1000 to 1500, while earlier periods are defined by regional cultures, such as Anglo-Saxon, Merovingian, or Viking. In countries that lie outside the boundaries of the former Roman Empire, the collapse of the empire marks a less distinct horizon (both archaeologically and historically), and so the first millennium A.D. tends to be distinguished less decisively from the prehistoric Iron Age. In Germany especially, early medieval archaeology traditionally overlaps and mixes with the archaeology of the pre-Roman and Roman Iron Age in the broader discipline of prehistory (*Vor und Frühgeschichte*), while the archaeology of the High Middle Ages is largely the province of architectural and art historians. In a similar fashion, pre-Viking (before ca.

A.D. 800) archaeology in Scandinavia is rarely clearly distinguished from prehistory. In these countries, the dividing line in the organization of scholarship tends to fall somewhere toward the end of the eighth century, which marks both the first outburst of Viking activity and the Carolingian conquest of much of what is now western Germany. In the Mediterranean, the medieval distinction is also blurred by the inclusion of early Byzantine history and archaeology (usually up through the seventh century A.D.) in the period called Late Antiquity (French *bas empire*). Perhaps more confusingly, "Byzantine" as used by art historians and an older generation of archaeologists usually refers only to the fifth through the seventh centuries, while the later Byzantine Empire is referred to as "medieval." A clearer distinction is observed in parts of the western Mediterranean, where Roman culture was overrun by barbarian invasions in the fifth and sixth centuries, and the Visigoths were, in turn, displaced by Islamic invaders early in the eighth century. In the Arabic world, another dividing line stands at the Hegira (A.D. 622), which separates Islamic history from Arabic prehistory.

History

Medieval archaeology can be said to begin with the discovery in 1653 of the tomb of the Merovingian Frank Childeric in Tournai (now in Belgium). The richly furnished grave, dated by historical sources to A.D. 481–482, was identified by a ring bearing the king's name and portrait, and the discovery led to the investigation of several other early tombs in France. More importantly, the finds were drawn to a high standard of accuracy and published with a description only two years later. This is most fortunate, as nearly all of the finds were stolen and melted down in 1831. Other tombs found in the eighteenth century were not so carefully recorded, but Merovingian graves and cemeteries eventually became the basis of modern medieval archaeology, with the excavation, to varying standards, of thousands of early medieval graves in nineteenth-century France and western Germany. These graves, laid out in orderly rows (German *Reihengräber*), provided a wealth of artifacts to museums and collectors and formed the foundations of many of the early theories of Merovingian trade and cultural interaction. The development of typologies for common grave goods, such as ceramics, glass, weapons, and jewelry, established relative chronologies, and many scholars thought they could see in the burials evidence of the Frankish invasion and conquest of Roman Gaul. Physical anthropologists identified a "long-skulled" *(dolichocephalic)* form in the skeletal remains that was distinguishable from the "round-skulled" *(brachycephalic)* Gallo-Roman population, and changes in burial practice also testified to the arrival of newcomers, especially in northern Gaul. Later, more scientific studies of early medieval burials, as well as a more thorough understanding of late Roman Gaul and early Germanic population movements, revealed the simplistic flaws in such early theories, but much of the scholarship surrounding Merovingian culture is still based on the extensive evidence from grave fields and cemeteries.

At the same time that archaeologists were studying the Merovingians, art historians took a great interest in the sculpture and buildings of the later Middle Ages. Many of the great Gothic cathedrals of France were recorded and restored (often under the creative direction of Eugene Viollet-le-Duc), as were a large number of castles, palaces, and chateaux. In many cases, these buildings were restored to rather fanciful ideas of what medieval buildings "should" have been like or were "improved" with neo-Gothic additions. Still, the Gothic revival resulted in the surveying of a large number of the more prominent medieval monuments in Europe.

Contemporaneous developments in English and Scandinavian archaeology paralleled the French and German concentration on burials and grave goods. English archaeologists and antiquarians excavated a large number of Anglo-Saxon cemeteries, and Danish, Swedish, and Norwegian archaeologists, in some of the most careful European excavations of the nineteenth century, opened a series of Viking tombs, including the royal burial mounds of Uppsala, Sweden, and the magnificent ship burials of Gokstad (1880) and Oseberg (1903) in Norway. The Danish prehistorian Conrad Engelhardt also added much to the history of the migrations with his excavations between 1858 and 1865 of Iron Age votive deposits in the peat bogs at Nydam, Kragehul, and Vimose. In contrast,

Mediterranean excavations of the nineteenth century too often treated medieval levels of complex sites as little more than overburden, so that much of the later history of many classical and Roman sites was lost.

In the twentieth century, medieval archaeologists began to branch out from the traditional focus on burials and investigate other types of sites. In particular, medieval settlements received a great deal of emphasis. The excavation of two great early medieval emporia, Haithabu on the neck of the Danish peninsula and Dorestad on the lower Rhine, began in the 1930s, as did the excavation of the medieval harbor of Kalmar, Sweden. The interwar years also saw continued, if more careful, excavations of burials, both in Christian cemeteries and in pagan mounds and grave fields, such as the large Swedish field at Valsgärde, and, in the summer of 1939, English archaeologists were called in to investigate an Anglo-Saxon mound on the Suffolk coast. The Sutton Hoo ship burial was eventually revealed as perhaps the richest medieval grave ever discovered, and the study of its spectacular contents, which could be traced to sources in Merovingian Gaul, Byzantine Thrace, Coptic Egypt, and Vendel Sweden, as well as Anglo-Saxon England, provided new insight into the international nature of Anglo-Saxon kingship and led to new interdisciplinary studies involving archaeologists, historians, philologists, and students of Old English literature.

The Second World War, while it resulted in the destruction of a large number of medieval buildings, sites, and artifacts, also provided medieval archaeologists with a host of new opportunities. Medieval archaeology had long concentrated on burials because other types of sites, particularly the remains of medieval settlements, towns, and cities, had been buried under, or obliterated by, Renaissance and modern construction. The destruction by bombing of so many old European cities between 1939 and 1945 left large areas of historic property in need of redevelopment and gave archaeologists a chance to investigate, as part of the reconstruction effort, the medieval and Roman origins of those cities. In the case of Rotterdam in the Netherlands, a deliberate effort was made to excavate a large portion of the medieval city, and a long series of publications (*The Rotterdam Papers*) have resulted from this research program.

M

Since the war, medieval archaeology has often been concentrated in urban centers. This avenue of investigation has been particularly popular in the British Isles, with well-publicized excavations in London, Winchester, York, Southampton, and Dublin. Much of this work has been the result of the growth of governmental agencies, often at the municipal or county level, responsible for cultural resource management; the work of the Archaeological Department of the Museum of London (and its predecessors) provides an excellent example of the potential of rescue archaeology in a modern urban context. Similar agencies and projects can be found throughout Europe and around the Mediterranean. The long series of excavations at Bryggen in Bergen, Norway, have revealed a deeply stratified deposit in the heart of the medieval commercial district of this important Hanseatic town, and an even more extensive program of excavations in Novgorod, Russia (begun before the war but greatly expanded in the 1950s and 1960s), has made much of similar deep deposits with excellent preservation of organic remains, from wooden causeways and buildings to a large assemblage of documents written on bark.

Significant contributions are still being made by careful, thorough excavations of small sites, including the traditional burials. In particular, there has been a great increase in the archaeological investigation of churches, especially in England, with numerous excavations of sites from small parish churches to large cathedrals. Much of this work has been carried out in conjunction with renovation programs requiring renewal of floors, and the historic preservation movement has been helpful in encouraging the archaeological documentation of medieval structures. In addition to the excavation of structures and habitation sites, an interest in rural archaeology has led to extensive field surveys and the excavation of cultivation layers in search of information on medieval agricultural technique and productivity. Rural sites, such as Raunds in England and Wijster in the Netherlands, are also providing some of the clearest information on a range of aspects of early medieval life, including the nature of settlements in the Migrations, the degree of survival of Roman culture, and changes and continuity in family organization.

In the Mediterranean, medieval sites have received greater attention than in the past, with a renewed interest in sites such as the early Byzantine church of St. Polyeuktos in Saraçhane, Istanbul, the monastery of San Vicenzo al Volturno in Italy, and Fustat, the medieval heart of Old Cairo. At the same time, greater care has been devoted to the medieval layers overlying ancient sites; a particularly good example is the series of Byzantine shops excavated next to the ancient synagogue at Sardis, Turkey, and published in detail (Crawford 1990).

Medieval archaeology has been especially important in the Balkans in recent decades, and although it has often been caught up in regional political maneuvering, with national governments encouraging projects that could support nationalistic claims, many sites in Bulgaria and Romania have received detailed attention. The fortresses of Sucidava (Romania) and Pliska (Bulgaria) are only two of many medieval sites excavated and published since the 1950s. These excavations have been helpful not only to scholars investigating the history and the anthropology of the Balkans, but, due to the importance of the area to the Byzantine Empire, much of this material has found its way into the corpus studied by Byzantinists.

An important development in medieval archaeology has been the growth of nautical archaeology. The wrecks at Yassı Ada and Serçe Limanı, Turkey, have provided snapshots of trade and politics in the eastern Mediterranean in the seventh and eleventh centuries, respectively, and partial excavations of seventh- and ninth-century wrecks in France have helped illuminate Islamic involvement in western Mediterranean commerce. Finds such as the tenth-century coasting vessel at Graveney, England, five eleventh-century vessels at Skuldelev, Denmark, the fourteenth-century Bremen cog, and a large number of medieval wrecks in the reclaimed land of the former Zuiderzee in the Netherlands have contributed substantially to an understanding of medieval material culture, trade mechanisms, and warfare in northern Europe.

Method and Theory

The dominant theoretical viewpoint in the early medieval archaeology of northern Europe has traditionally been *historical particularism*. Beginning with the discovery of Childeric's tomb in the seventeenth century, medieval archaeologists have often been at pains to reconcile what they find in the ground with well-known historical sources and to identify the physical remains of historical events. Thus, a major concern of Anglo-Saxon archaeologists was, for many years, the identification of culturally distinct Angles, Saxons, and Jutes, since Bede had mentioned these peoples as the most important Germanic settlers of England in the Migrations. This tendency was once common to all archaeology that dealt with historical periods (witness Heinrich Schliemann's obsession with Troy and its cast of Homeric heroes) but has held on longer in medieval archaeology than in other disciplines.

Since the 1980s, the theoretical debate has paralleled that in historical archaeology, where it is not the relative value of archaeological and historical resources that is at issue, nor the proper method of integrating the two, but the nature of the questions being asked of the material. Because of the long traditions of medieval scholarship, it has been difficult to completely divorce medieval archaeology from its essential particularism; Colin Renfrew's Great Awakening and Lewis R. Binford's New Archaeology nearly passed the field by, and only in England, where medieval archaeology is most fully developed and where scholars such as Richard Hodges have succeeded in integrating historical and anthropological approaches, and France, where medieval history was affected by the semianthropological methodology of the Annales school, has the field begun to move away from hard-line particularism. In England especially, medieval archaeology has successfully merged into the mainstream of archaeological research and shares fully in theoretical discussion. In contrast, in Germany in the mid-1980s, medievalists were still "holding the line" against the the more anthropological New Archaeology that was already considered old-fashioned elsewhere. Much of the early medieval archaeology associated with structures, particularly churches and palaces, and most late medieval archaeology is more akin to traditional classical archaeology, with its close connections to art history. This separation, which dates back to the nineteenth century, has not completely healed, especially in Germany, but increasing interaction between archaeologists and art historians and the gradual development of more broad-based theoretical approaches that can encompass both anthropological concerns and traditional connoisseurship are leading to a more unified field.

In terms of field or laboratory methodology, there is little that is unique to medieval archaeology. Excavation strategies may be partly dictated by the peculiar working conditions encountered in rescue excavations in urban construction sites, but this is a problem shared with Roman specialists and historical archaeologists. One contribution to field methodology developed on medieval sites is a system for schematically representing complex stratigraphic relationships on deep habitation sites. This system, sometimes referred to as the Harris Matrix or the Harris Strat system, resulted from attempts to correlate stratigraphic levels in scattered excavation units on medieval urban sites in England, particularly at Winchester.

Frederick Hocker

See also CLASSICAL ARCHAEOLOGY; HARRIS MATRIX; HISTORICAL ARCHAEOLOGY

Further Readings

Bestemann, J.C., Bos, J.M., and Heidinga, H.A., eds. (1990) Medieval Archaeology in the Netherlands. Assen and Maastricht: van Gorem.

Biddick, K., ed. (1984) Archaeological Approaches to Medieval Europe. Kalamazoo: Western Michigan University Press.

Clark, H. (1984) The Archaeology of Medieval England. London: British Museum.

Crawford, J.S. (1990) The Byzantine Shops at Sardis. Cambridge, MA: Harvard University Press.

Fehring, G. (1991) The Archaeology of Medieval Germany: An Introduction. Trans. R. Samson. London and New York: Routledge. Originally published 1987 as Einführung in die Archäologie des Mittelalters. Darmstadt: Wissenschaftliche Buchgesellschaft.

Rahtz, P. (1984) The Nuer medieval archaeology: Comment on theory vs. history. Scottish Archaeological Review 3: 109–113.

Redman, C.L., ed. (1989) Medieval Archaeology. Binghamton: State University of New York at Binghamton.

M

Metallography

The application of microstructural studies of metals to ancient metallic materials using a polished surface or section of the object, which is examined with a reflected-light microscope. Details of morphology and microstructure are revealed by the technique, which may provide important information concerning technological, compositional, or corrosion studies of the metal artifact. Additionally, metallography of objects in the course of conservation treatment may provide essential information that can decide the course a treatment should take, depending on the extent of mineralization and the nature of the metallic corrosion and structure.

Metals are crystalline solids, and it is because of this that metallography is such a useful tool in the examination of ancient metals. Most of the metals utilized in antiquity have been the subject of detailed metallographic reports. The most important metals and alloys in this context are iron, steel, cast iron, tin bronze, arsenical copper, brass, silver and silver alloys, gold and gold alloys, lead, tin, zinc, and pewter. Archaeological metals usually have a patina or corrosion crust, and the metallographic examination of this layer and of the interface between the metallic and the corroded region of the material may be of considerable interest in studies of authenticity and of burial environment of the object.

Sample Selection, Preparation, and Analysis

To carry out a metallographic study, a sample is usually removed from the object. This specimen is mounted in synthetic resin, with the orientation of the sample carefully noted. The mounted sample is then ground on wet silicon carbide papers, usually from 240 to 600 grit in size, before polishing on synthetic napped cloth wheels using diamond powder as an abrasive. Polishing is usually carried out with six, one and one-quarter diamond paste in an oil or water suspension. Examination of the prepared section can utilize the light microscope, or the sample can be coated, if necessary, and examined by scanning electron microscopy, X-ray fluorescence analysis, or electron-probe microanalysis, all of which are invaluable in the analytical study of composition and morphology of ancient metals.

The light microscope used in the study of these metallic cross-sections must be capable of reflecting light from the lamp through the objective lens directly onto the surface of the sample. The light reflected back from the surface of the sample passes through the objective lens and to the eyepiece, monitor, or camera port. A general-purpose reflected-light microscope can be used for metallography; more specific microscopes, specially made for examination of polished sections, are called *metallographic microscopes* or *metallographs*. It is possible to polish selected areas of objects to examine the metallographic structure in situ, where it may be impossible to cut or remove a section from the object, as long as they can be held in position for reflected-light microscopy. This technique has found considerable application in studies of ancient coins when an edge can be polished without disturbance of the numismatic information. Replication of unprepared surfaces of ancient objects with silicon rubber and examination of these silicon rubber impressions may also reveal structural detail that could ordinarily be obtained only by destructive metallographic sampling of the object. Microstructural features may be selectively etched or pseudomorphically preserved on metallic surfaces, which allows this technique to reveal morphology directly. A polished section is a two-dimensional representation of a three-dimensional object. If the structure is complex, as in pattern-welded steel blades, supplementary techniques, such as X-radiography to reveal the internal pattern, should be employed.

When mounted samples are studied, the surface of the metallic specimen is examined first in the polished state and then after etching with a suitable reagent; etching selectively attacks crystals or phases at different rates and so reveals microstructural detail. The etching process may dissolve patina, corrosion products, or nonmetallic inclusions present in the sample, which is why it is important, particularly with archaeological material, to study carefully the polished section before etching. For the same reason, corrosion crusts should generally not be removed from the surface before the metallic sample is mounted: Considerable information may be preserved in these corrosion layers.

There are often severe restrictions on the quantity of metal that can be removed from an artifact for metallographic examination. On the other hand, even a very small sample, smaller than a pinhead if necessary, can be mounted and polished for examination, although great care has to be exercised at all stages of preparation. It is much easier to work with larger samples, although, by archaeological standards, samples the size of a pea are already unusually large, unless whole artifacts or substantial fragments are available for sectioning. There are a number of criteria that should be considered before any sampling is undertaken:

1. The microstructure of the samples should not be altered in the process of removal.
2. The sample should be representative of the object as a whole or of a selected feature or area of the object.
3. The orientation of the sample in its dimensional relationship to the object should be carefully recorded.
4. If it is not obvious from where the sample was taken, the position on the object concerned should be marked on a photograph or a drawing of the object.
5. The sample should be assigned a laboratory number together with sufficient documentation to enable its identity to be preserved.
6. The object should be photographed or drawn before the sample is taken. This is especially important if the dimensions of the object are fundamentally altered by the material removed.

Metallographic studies should be integrated as far as possible with archaeological data, provenance, chemical composition, and technology of manufacture to extract the maximum benefit from the removal of a small sample from the object.

The range of features that may be made visible in prepared samples is variable, depending on the type of specimen examined and how it is prepared; detail not apparent using one etchant may become visible only after another reagent has been employed. The following are some of the major microstructural features that can be examined:

1. The range and the type of grains present. Their size can be compared with an eyepiece marked with grain sizes for comparison or with American Society for Testing Materials (ASTM) standard grain-size numbers.
2. The presence of different phases in the metal or corrosion.
3. Gross heterogeneity or differences between various areas of the sample.
4. The grain sizes or surface deformation features or heat-treated zones at cutting edges and worked surfaces.
5. The distribution of inclusions, weld lines, slag particles, or porosity.
6. The presence of any surface coating or gilding. Sometimes, careful examination at high magnification is necessary to establish the presence of surface coatings, leaf gilding, amalgam gilding, and the like.
7. The distribution of any corrosion products present and the existence within corrosion layers of pseudomorphic remnants of grain structure or other microstructural features, remnant metallic grains, and layering or unusual features.
8. Indications of grain-boundary thickening or precipitation of another phase at the grain boundaries.
9. The presence of twin lines within the grains and whether the twin lines are straight or curved. In face-centered cubic metals, these features are common.
10. The presence of strain lines (or *slip lines* as they may also be called) within the grains.
11. Whether dendrites (a structure that is common in cast alloys and that may look like an intersecting snowflake pattern) show indications of coring and the approximate spacing, in microns, of the dendritic arms, if these are clearly visible.
12. The presence of intercrystalline or transcrystalline cracking in the specimen.

Crystal Structure

The properties of metallic materials are fundamentally altered by the lattice group to which they belong. *Lattice group* refers to the arrangement of atoms into one of the crystallographic systems present in nature. The principal groups are face-centered cubic (FCC) metals, such as silver, aluminum, gold, copper, nickel, and platinum; close-packed hexagonal (CPH) metals, including zinc and cadmium; and body-centered cubic (BCC) metals, such as iron. Some other metals of importance in antiquity, principally as alloying additions to copper, belong to different lattice systems. Tin is body-centered tetragonal, and arsenic and antimony are rhombohedral. Metals of the FCC group tend to be soft and easily worked; CPH metals are rather brittle; and BCC

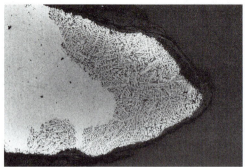

Figure 1. *Microstructure of a Bronze Age arrowhead from the Palestine site of Tell Ajjul, dated to about the XVIII Dynasty. The etched structure, shown here at a magnification of 40x, shows the cast, dendritic structure. The arrowhead was, therefore, cast directly into a mold with no further working. The composition about 9.9 percent tin, 1.5 percent lead, 3.9 percent arsenic, 0.85 percent zinc, and the remainder copper. Etched in lead thiosulphate complex solution. Photograph by David Scott.*

Figure 2. *Unetched view of a Bronze Age arrowhead, the same as shown Figure 1, taken from one of the three fins of the arrow. Corrosion has outlined the microstructure, on the as-polished surface, showing the dendritic structure preferentially revealed by corrosion of the interdendritic, tin-rich eutectoid phase. Magnification 20x. Photograph by David Scott.*

metals (the only common example in antiquity is iron) have a good combination of ductility and toughness. (For further details of structure and lattice effects, see Bailey 1984; Samans 1963).

Melting and Casting

Metallic materials can be deformed by hammering and can be molten and cast into shape. The temperatures attainable with a charcoal fire or a wood fire and forced draught are generally high enough to melt most of the metals and alloys used in antiquity with the exception of wrought iron and platinum, neither of which were used from the molten state.

In ancient metals, there is often *segregation,* or compositional separation, of different alloy components of the melt from the cast state. *Dendritic segregation,* in which small fernlike growths develop in the solid and grow toward each other until the liquid metal is consumed and solidified, is the most common form of segregation on casting; an example is shown in Figure 1. The section is taken across a small bronze arrowhead from Palestine and illustrates many of the features to be found in ancient bronze castings. There is substantial dendritic segregation, visible in Figure 1 as orientated patches of fernlike growth, with a second phase, the alpha + delta phase, of the bronze system occupying the interdendritic spaces in the cast solid. The ar-

rowhead has been cast to shape in a mold, without any further working. Figure 2 is of part of the same Bronze Age arrowhead, in the polished condition, showing that natural corrosion processes in burial have resulted in selective dissolution of the arrowhead, clearly revealing the microstructure. Etching the polished surface is still necessary to examine all of the detail that can be revealed by this process. Inverse segregation may occur in ancient metals, particularly in copper alloys—tin sweat in copper-tin bronzes may force tin-rich liquid to the exterior surface of the mold. Long columnar grains of relatively pure metals, such as copper, may be observed in cast ingots, but these are uncommon.

Hammering and Annealing

When metals are hammered at room temperature, or *cold-worked,* the hardness and the strength of the metals are increased, but they also become brittle. *Annealing* (reheating) the worked metal restores malleability, or ductility, and the object may go through many cycles of working and annealing before the required shape is attained. The two processes, working and annealing, may be combined into one operation by *hot-working.* Hot-working allows plastic movement of the metal to be attained so that the shape is altered and, when cooled, retains the new deformation. Some metals, such as iron and gold, can be welded when hot to produce objects of different shape and size, although with most metals the presence of an

Figure 3. Photomicrograph of part of an Early Bronze Age palstave from County Carlow, Ireland, dated to ca. 2700 B.C. The microstructure shows that this axe, cast in an open mold, was worked and annealed to shape quite extensively after casting. The twinned crystals of the bronze can be seen together with dark regions, which are areas of corrosion. Corrosion along slip planes where the palstave has been heavily cold worked occurs close to the surface where the axe would have been decorated. The axe is made in a tin bronze composed of 91.7 percent copper, 7.5 percent tin, 0.02 percent lead, 0.2 percent arsenic, 0.3 percent antimony, 0.04 percent nickel, 0.002 percent bismuth, 0.03 percent iron, 0.01 percent zinc, and 0.2 percent silver. Etched in alcoholic ferric chloride. Magnification 65x. Photograph by David Scott.

Figure 4. Photomicrograph of part of the structure of the Bronze Age palstave shown in Figure 3. The twinned grains can now be clearly seen. The twin lines are straight, showing that annealing was the final fabrication step. Selective corrosion along slip planes can be seen as dark crosshatching in some of the grains. Etched in alcoholic ferric chloride. Magnification 125x. Photograph by David Scott.

oxide film makes it difficult to combine smaller pieces of metal without recourse to melting them together into a new cast ingot or joining them with the use of a solder.

The ability to cold-work and deform metals is related to the imperfections in the lattice structure of the crystal (i.e., the arrangement of the atoms), which are called *dislocations*. These dislocations may be of two principal types: *edge* and *screw*. When metals are worked, dislocations get entangled, and the metal must be annealed to restore malleability. In face-centered cubic metals, this working and annealing operation results in a microstructure of recrystallized and twinned grains, in which the twin lines are quite straight. *Twins* mark a region of re-formation in the solid, a mirror plane, that produces the most favorable energy requirement for recrystallization in face-centered cubic metals.

An example of twinned structures found in copper alloys that have been cast, cold-worked and annealed is shown in Figure 3. The section is taken from an Early Bronze Age palstave dated to ca. 2700 B.C. Although the

axe is cast in an open mold and might be expected to show a cast, dendritic structure, these open-mold Bronze Age axes were often finished by working and annealing of the cast form to shape the final product. The cutting edge could be work-hardened by selective cold-working in this area, increasing substantially the hardness of these bronze tools. Both corrosion and some porosity are present in this microstructure, but the essentially worked and annealed nature of the axe can be seen in the twinned-grain structure shown in Figure 3.

When an annealed object with twinned grains is cold-worked, the twin lines become deformed and will no longer appear straight: This is indicative that the final stage of manufacture was cold-working. Additional features such as *strain lines* may be visible in the metal after etching, especially if the material has been heavily cold-worked. Strain lines, visible in Figure 4, occur as a result of the slip of crystal planes over one another in the bronze. This photomicrograph is an enlarged view of the structure shown in Figure 3, in which selective corrosion is just starting to occur along the strain lines. Etching reveals these structural lines, which sometimes cross one another at oblique angles in copper alloys and which may be subject to preferential corrosion during burial.

Coring, the remains of the original dendritic segregation from the cast solid, may be present even after many cycles of working and annealing, and cored structures are frequently observed in ancient copper alloys. The structure shown in Figure 5 illustrates coring in the alpha solid solution of the bronze, revealed as subtle differences in shading of the polished and the etched surfaces, as well as microstructural features due to corrosion during burial, in which large twinned crystals of redeposited copper occur in areas formerly occupied by the alpha + delta eutectoid (a structure formed by the decomposition from one solid phase into two finely dispersed solid phases).

Alloying

When two or more pure metals are mixed together, the resulting alloy system can be examined using phase diagrams for specific alloys. The details of the phases (variations in composition of an alloy) that may be present can be examined by means of these diagrams, which are charts of temperature against composition, the different areas on the resulting phase diagram showing boundaries between equilibrium phases. Phase diagrams must be interpreted with caution, as ancient materials may be far removed in microstructure from an idealized equilibrium state. A description of how phase diagrams are derived from melting-point data and of how to interpret the diagrams can be found in many standard metallographic textbooks (e.g., Brick et al. 1965).

Alloys do not have a particular melting point: They soften and pass through a pasty stage between temperature zones shown on the phase diagram as *solidus* and *liquidus* curves. The solidus is the line in the phase diagram that separates the pasty stage of the alloy, usually a mixture of solid and liquid, from the completely solid alloy below the temperature of the solidus line. The liquidus is the line on a phase diagram that shows the temperature at which solidification begins on cooling from the melt. The boundary region between these lines can be narrow or broad. In some alloys of importance in antiquity, such as copper-tin or gold-copper-silver, there is considerable separation between liquidus and solidus curves, which exacerbates the difficulties of attaining equilibrium cooling conditions from the melt and enhances the segregation (compositional separation) effects that can be observed in these alloys. The deliberate retention of high-temperature phases by *quenching* (rapid cooling) the alloy during manufacture may be revealed by metallographic studies.

Figure 5. *Photomicrograph of redeposited copper in a Luristan ceremonial axe fragment from Iran, dated to ca. the eighth century* B.C. *The grains of the bronze are twinned, while the redeposited copper, which occupies a region where the eutectoid phase has corroded, is lighter in color and has a long, curved, twinned-grain structure of a single crystal radiating from a point, quite unlike the usual twinned grains seen in worked and annealed copper. Etched in lead thiosulphate complex solution. Magnification 150x. Photograph by David Scott.*

Bronze

An example of the microscopic effects of quenching is shown in Figure 6, part of a high-tin-bronze bowl from the site of Ban Don Ta Phet in Thailand, dated to ca. A.D. 100 and of composition 22.7 percent tin and 76.2 percent copper. Examination of the etched section shows the presence of some alpha-phase copper-rich islands, sometimes jagged and which occur in areas with specific orientation as well as random scatter. In the background matrix of this bronze is a banded martensite, a variety of the beta phase that proves that the bowl must have been quenched from the region of 520–586°C during manufacture. This is slightly lower than the usual quenching temperature for these bronzes, which is generally in the 650–750°C range. The bowls were fabricated in this way to prevent the very brittle alpha + delta eutectoid phase—the usual equilibrium constituent under normal cooling which would have made the bowls unworkable—from forming. This working procedure, on an empirical basis, formed a solution to the problem of being able to shape these alloys effectively. The beta phase is hard, but the bowls can be turned on a lath after hot-working and quenching to smooth and polish the surfaces. The metastable beta phase has remained unchanged, even after thousands of years, as the

Figure 6. Fragment from the rim of a bronze vessel from the Thailand site of Ban Don Ta Phet, dated to ca. A.D. 100. The bronze contains about 22.7 percent tin, and the structure consists of a banded martensite with islands of alpha phase, which shows that the bronze was quenched from about 580° C, preserving some of the high-temperature beta material. Etched in alcohol ferric chloride. Magnification 280x. Photograph by David Scott.

metallography of these quenched high-tin alloys shows.

Gold and Copper

Gold-copper alloys may have been quenched in ancient working practices, too, for the purpose of preventing any of the ordered phases of the gold-copper system to form: If slowly cooled in air, some gold-copper alloys may develop ordered phases that would prevent further working without embrittlement. Ordered phases in metallic systems may have a definite atomic arrangement and, therefore, no ductility. Their presence is usually detrimental if the alloys are expected to be worked and annealed.

Iron and Steel

Iron and steel alloys may have been produced from bloomery iron, and, consequently, they have never been molten and cast. These alloys are, therefore, subject to considerable variation in properties and microstructural composition from one region of the object to another. Segregation of different alloying elements, or

inadvertent impurities, such as nickel, copper, arsenic, or phosphorus, may be present, and these elements may produce banding or inhomogeneous regions in the grain structure of the iron.

The carbon content of steels may be variable for this reason, too. Wrought iron, steel, and cast iron were all produced in antiquity, and each has a different amount of carbon in the material. Wrought iron has negligible or very small amounts of carbon, perhaps up to ca 0.2 percent. Steels may have up to ca. 1.2 percent of carbon, but most ancient steels do not have more than 0.8 percent of carbon, which corresponds to the eutectoid composition, known as *pearlite* (a fine mixture of ferrite and cementite found in steels). *Ferrite* is the name given to pure alpha iron, and *cementite* is a hard intermetallic compound of fixed composition Fe_3C. The great variation in the microstructure of steel, depending on heat-treatment and alloying components, allows many interesting inferences to be made as a result of metallographic examination.

Figure 8. Section of a wrought-steel blade from the site of Ardingley, Sussex, from the late medieval period sixteenth–seventeenth century A.D. The unetched view of the polished section here shows the extensive corrosion of this medieval blade. Some metallic remnants are seen in the central core of the knife, surrounded by a thick accretion of iron corrosion products and the relict structure of the wrought iron preserved in corrosion. Magnification 70x. Photograph by David Scott.

Figure 7. Cross-section through part of a Wootz ingot from the Deccan region of India, dated to the eighteenth century A.D. The structure is mostly pearlite with cementite laths. Etched in nital. Magnification 380x. Photograph by David Scott.

An example of a heterogeneous steel is shown in Figure 7. It is a section through part of an Indian Wootz steel ingot from the eighteenth century A.D. Indian metalsmiths specialized in the production of high-quality steels in a crucible process. The steel could be made as a molten cake, and the cast morphology of these cakes has been verified by metallographic examination. The carbon content was usually 1–1.2 percent, and the resulting cast-steel wootz cake consists of cementite needles in a matrix of pearlite, sometimes with a little steadite as well. Figure 7 illustrates some of these features, showing long cementite needles in a matrix of pearlite. The cementite needles become fragmented when these high-carbon steels are forged. Quenching wrought iron has little effect on the working properties of the iron, but, with some carbon content, it was soon appreciated that quenching could produce a harder alloy. Carbon contents of 0.3–0.7 percent were quite sufficient to produce a much harder working edge on quenching of these low-carbon steels.

A typical wrought-iron low-carbon-steel blade edge is shown unetched in Figure 8, from

late medieval (sixteenth–seventeenth centuries A.D.) England. Extensive corrosion has occurred, with some relict features preserved as pseudomorphic structures within the corrosion crust, but the photomicrograph also exemplifies some of the difficulties that may be encountered in the metallography of ancient materials because of corrosion. An etched view of part of the same cross-section is shown in Figure 9. The etchant has revealed differences in carbon content between parts of the wrought-iron and low-carbon steel pieces that have been welded together to make the knife blade. Many iron artifacts are made by joining together a number of different pieces of iron or steel by hot-working in the forge. Figure 9 shows lighter-colored bands corresponding to the welds as a result of arsenic segregation during heating and welding, and the zones of higher carbon content appear darker after etching in Nital. The low-carbon areas consist of ferrite grains and pearlite, which can often assume a Widmanstätten morphology as a consequence of the heating and cooling regimes from the austenitic solid solution region, as the smith works the material at the forge.

Figure 10 shows a higher-carbon steel artifact: It is a cut steel bead from France of the eighteenth century A.D. In the manufacture of these beads, the high-carbon steel was forged and cut before quenching to produce a particu-

Figure 9. *Etched view of the blade illustrated in Figure 8, showing the region of a welded join where different pieces of low-carbon steel have been forged together. The lighter band, which can be seen at the junction of the welds, is due to the segregation of some arsenic. The darker etching region to the top of the photomicrograph indicates that this component has a higher carbon content, especially compared with the wedge-shaped wrought-iron component to which it has been joined. Etched in nital. Magnification 130x. Photograph by David Scott.*

Figure 10. *Part of a section through a cut and polished French steel jewelry bead of the eighteenth century A.D. The steel bead, with a carbon content ca. 1.1 percent, was first cut and then quenched and the surfaces polished. Note the plate-martensite that forms in carbon steels with more than 1 percent of carbon. Microhardness readings gave an average of 1035 HV on the Vickers scale. Etched in alkaline picral. Magnification 420x. Photograph by David Scott.*

lar form of martensite, known as *plate martensite*, which forms only in steels of high carbon content, over ca. 1 percent. The quenched bead is then polished. These steels are very hard: Measurement of a Vickers microhardness on this object gave a result of 1035HV, a normal quenched low-carbon steel having a hardness of 500–750HV. Quenched steels are often too brittle to use without danger of small fractures in the hardened edge, and tool edges were usually tempered to mitigate this effect. Tempered martensite etches darker than quenched and untempered martensite, so can be revealed by metallography.

Iron alloys with higher carbon content (2–4 percent) are called *cast irons* and have very different properties from their lower-carbon alloy counterparts: They are hard and brittle. An example is shown in the photomicrograph in Figure 11, part of a section through a cannonball of the sixteenth century A.D. from the Tower of London. The iron is predominantly a grey cast iron with free carbon in the form of graphite, although cementite laths are also to be seen. Corrosion has occurred around each of the clusters of graphite flakes, and much of the remaining uncorroded material is steadite. The cannonball was cast to shape, and the structure of the etched section is typical for such a product.

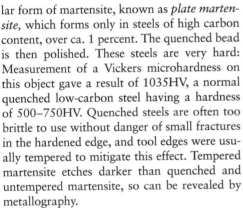

Figure 11. *Part of a section from a cast-iron cannonball from the Tower of London dating to ca. the sixteenth century A.D. The cast iron has suffered extensive corrosion, with the dark spotty regions representing graphite flakes embedded in corrosion. Much of the remaining matrix consists of steadite, the ternary eutectic (three-part alloy composition with the lowest melting point) between iron, copper and phosphorus. Long cementite needles also occur in the structure. Etched in nital. Magnification 170x. Photograph by David Scott.*

Brass

Other materials such as copper-zinc alloys and copper-silver alloys were important early products. A historical example of a cast brass (copper-zinc alloy) is shown in Figure 12: It is a section from a brass medallion from the La Perouse shipwreck, which occurred off the

Figure 12. Cross-section of a brass medallion from the La Perouse shipwreck, which occurred off the coast of the Solomon Islands around 1788. The medallion is cast, and both copper and zinc have been lost in corrosion. Unetched showing remnant dendrite structure. Magnification 75x. Photograph by David Scott.

Figure 13. Silver-coated copper nose ornament from the site of La Compañia, Los Rios Province, Ecuador, from a burial of the late Milagro phase (ca. A.D. 1000). The nose ring has a very thick silvered surface that was applied probably by dipping it into molten silver-copper alloy with a composition of ca. 65 percent copper and 35 percent silver. The silvered surface was finished with some hammering and annealing, and the outer surface is enriched in silver. Etched in alcoholic ferric chloride. Magnification 85x. Photograph by David Scott.

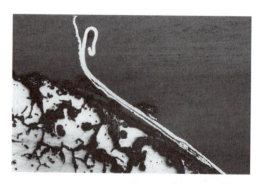

Figure 14. Photomicrograph, as polished, of a part of a gilded nose ornament from the burial at La Compañia, Los Rios Province, Ecuador, dating to the late Milagro phase (ca. A.D. 1000). The nose ornament has been gilded by application of gold foil, which is seen here lifting away from the corroded surface that is made from relatively pure copper. The leaf can be seen to be separating into two sheets due to the application of a multiple thickness of gold foil. In some areas, interdiffusion has occurred between the copper and the gold foil, showing that some heating took place. Unetched. Magnification 80x. Photograph by David Scott.

coast of the Solomon Islands in 1788–1789. The section is unetched, since corrosion has already outlined the dendritic morphology of the medallion, as well as revealing the cored nature of the dendritic growth. Often, dezincification occurs in brass alloys, but here, the loss of both copper and zinc has occurred, with the dendritic voids filled with zinc and copper corrosion products. The metallography shows the medallion to have been cast with no further working.

Surface Treatments

Patination and surface treatment were important aspects of metallic surfaces. Figure 13 illustrates a fusion silvered coating over copper taken from a small penannular nose ring from Ecuador, dating to ca. A.D. 1000. Here a silver-copper alloy has been diffusion bonded to the copper substrate by dipping the finished and cleaned copper object into a bath of molten silver-copper alloy followed by some heating, working, and annealing of the surface coating to consolidate and smooth it: all this can be deduced from the metallographic study and is an example of the importance of metallographic investigations to understanding technological processes such as this unusual fusion silvered example.

Figure 14, of the same period as the previous sample, shows the application of gold foil. Typical features of such foil applications can be seen in the photomicrograph: the use of more than one thickness of foil; one piece being overlapped with another; the peeling away from the surface beneath, in this case a copper nose-

ornament; and the folding of the foil back on itself. The gold foil is bonded to the copper by diffusion bonding rather than mechanical burnishing. Figure 15 reveals a subtle gold coating over a copper dangle from Peru that has large equiaxial (equal dimensions) twinned grains

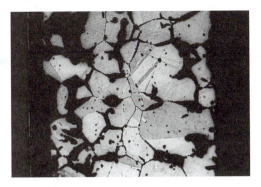

Figure 15. Microstructure of a copper dangle from the Moche culture of Peru (ca. A.D. 500). The surface of the copper dangle has been coated with gold by the electrochemical replacement plating technique. Note the very even and very thin gold coating over the corroded copper, which can be seen on the lefthand side of the photomicrograph. A twinned-grain structure can be seen in the copper grains of the dangle. Etched in alcohol ferric chloride. Magnification 110x. Photograph by David Scott.

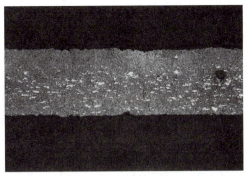

Figure 16. Cross-section through a platinum gold sintered ornament from the site of La Tolita, Esmeraldas Province, Ecuador, ca. A.D. 50. The white phases are undissolved platinum particles in a matrix of gold and some dissolved platinum. Etched in aqua regia. Magnification 65x. Photograph by David Scott.

and a very thin gold coating over one side. This coating was made using an electrochemical replacement plating technology that was developed by the Moche metalsmiths of ancient Peru. The deposited gold film may be from 0.5 microns to 2 microns thick.

Other Technological Operations

Figure 16 is an example of the first use of powder metallurgy, in the manufacture of a gold-platinum alloy, by the Ecuadorian Indians, from ca. A.D. 50. The metallographic evidence reveals a sintered product in which the platinum laths were never molten, but were mixed with gold as a matrix to form a composite material. In some alloys, platinum was used as a surface cladding over gold.

The metallography of ancient silver has revealed that alloying with small amounts of copper, in the range 1–8 percent by weight, has been practiced for thousands of years. In the process of manufacture, these silver alloys are often quenched after annealing, which prevents the copper content from precipitating out, since the mutual solubility of silver in copper or of copper in silver is very low. Over time, precipitation of copper can occur at the silver grain boundaries, a process called *discontinuous precipitation*. The small precipitates result in migration of the grain boundary; in the classic development of this type of grain

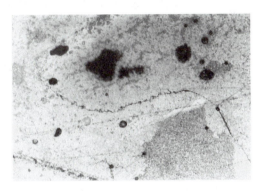

Figure 17. Section through a Middle Bronze Age gilded silver earring, from the site of Tell Farah, Jordan, Middle Bronze Age, first half of the second millennium B.C. The silver contains ca. 1.5 percent copper. In ancient silver objects, discontinuous precipitation at the grain boundaries results in displacement, with the effect illustrated here in which one grain boundary passes across the central region of the photomicrograph. This kind of meander in silver-grain boundaries is associated with natural aging over long periods of time. Etched in acidified potassium dichromate. Magnification 500x. Photograph by David Scott.

structure, a "jig-saw" effect can be produced from the meanders of the boundaries, an effect that can often be seen in ancient silver objects.

An example of one such grain boundary is shown in Figure 17, taken from an Egyptian earring dating to the first half of the second millennium B.C. The central line passing across the photomicrograph is a grain boundary that has migrated as a result of the precipitation of

Figure 18. Part of a cross-section through a silver copper alloy coin from Skandagupta, western India, dated to ca. A.D. 470. The microstructure shows that this silver coin is made in a heavily debased alloy with ca. 18 percent silver and 82 percent copper. The silver-rich phase has been elongated along the length of the coin section, and the coin has probably been hot-struck to shape the design. Etched in acidified potassium dichromate. Magnification 140x. Photograph by David Scott.

copper. The observation of this effect is limited to silver alloys with low percentages of copper: If the copper content is much higher, the equiaxial grain structure is disrupted, and, instead, a duplex structure of silver-rich and copper-rich dendritic remnants is usually present. An example is shown in Figure 18, part of a small coin from western India. It is a heavily debased silver-copper alloy with ca. 18 percent silver. The worked and annealed sheet was hot-struck to make the coin; the silver phase remains segregated and is merely strung out or flattened along the coin. After the coin was struck, the surface was pickled to remove some of the copper and improve the silvery color of the surface.

These examples taken from microstructural studies of historic and prehistoric metals are representative of the kind of information metallography can provide to those archaeologists working in the historic, medieval, classical, or prehistoric periods. It is often an indispensable tool for studying the alloying, manufacture, patination, and corrosion of metallic materials from terrestrial and underwater archaeological sites.

David Scott

See also ELECTRON-PROBE MICROANALYSIS; METALS, CHARACTERIZATION; METALS, ON-SITE CONSERVATION; X-RAY FLUORESCENCE (XRF) ANALYSIS

Further Readings

Bailey, A.R. (1984) A Textbook of Metallurgy. London: Macmillan.

Brick, R.M., Gordon, R.B. and Phillips, A. (1965) Structure and Properties of Alloys, 3rd ed. New York: McGraw-Hill.

Brown, F., et al., eds. (1977) Corrosion and Metal Artifacts. Washington: U.S. Dept. of Commerce, National Bureau of Standards.

Cottrell, A. (1975) An Introduction to Metallurgy. London: Edward Arnold.

Craddock, P., ed. (1990) 2000 Years of Zinc and Brass. London: British Museum.

Metals Handbook, 9th ed. vol. 9: Metallography and Microstructure (1985) Metals Park, OH: American Society for Metals.

Samans, C.H. (1963) Metallic Materials in Engineering. New York: Macmillan.

Scott, B. (1990) Early Irish Ironworking. Belfast: Ulster Museum.

Scott, D.A. (1991) Metallography and Microstructure of Ancient and Historic Metals. Malibu, CA: Getty Conservation Institute/Getty Museum.

Smith, C.S. (1960) A History of Metallography. Cambridge, MA: MIT Press.

Smith, C.S. (1980) A Search for Structure. Cambridge, MA: MIT Press.

Tylecote, R.F. (1974) A History of Metallurgy. London: Institute of Metals.

Tylecote, R.F. (1986) The Prehistory of Metallurgy in the British Isles. London: Institute of Metals.

Metals, Characterization

A group of inorganic, crystalline materials—naturally occurring in the metallic state or derived from the pyrotechnological processing of minerals—and the methods used in materials science, geology, and archaeology for chemical analysis, sourcing of raw materials, and identification of ore-processing and metalworking techniques.

Definitions

As crystallized materials, metals are defined by their chemical composition and their crystal structure. Chemical composition can be divided into *major elements* and *trace elements*. In archaeology, trace elements are used primarily for provenance studies. Many metals are composed of only one chemical element plus trace impurities (e.g., gold, copper, lead, aluminum). When these metals are found in the metallic state in nature (not produced from ores by smelting), the adjective *native* is applied (e.g., native copper). Other metals are *alloys*. An alloy is a compound of two or more miscible metals (e.g., bronze, an alloy of copper and tin). The discovery that the addition of a second metal to copper improved many important properties probably took place in the mid-fourth millennium in Southwest Asia. *Ores* are minerals (naturally occurring, inorganic, crystalline materials), the processing (*smelting*) of which yields products of economic value to human society—in this case, metals. Smelting is different from melting. Smelting is the process in which an ore (one or more minerals containing the metal) is heated, and the metal separated from the other chemical constituents by reducing the metal to its metallic state.

Research Issues in Ancient Metallurgy

The indigenous peoples of North America north of the Rio Grande did not smelt, melt, or cast copper. For most of the region, native copper was plentiful and could be shaped and hardened by hammering. Smelted copper was introduced with the arrival of Europeans. Using chemical characterization, it is possible to distinguish these distinct materials.

In Old World metallurgy, the transition from the use of copper to the introduction of bronze is marked by the use of coppers with a range of arsenic contents. The question arises as to whether these are deliberate alloys or the accidental consequence of the composition of the ores. Resolution of this question requires characterization of the metal objects, the slags, and the ores. Thus, our knowledge of the origins of copper-alloy metallurgy is primarily indirect, derived from analyses and interpretations of the composition and structure of available artifacts, slags, and ores.

The tin-oxide mineral cassiterite is the only ore of tin. Bronze, an alloy of copper and tin, goes back more than 6,000 years in the Near East. Because of its specific gravity of 7 g/cm^3, cassiterite is found in placer deposits, often along with gold. Cassiterite is widely distributed in small amounts, but cassiterite deposits of ore grade are rare. Perhaps the greatest unsolved problem in Old World Bronze Age metallurgy is the source(s) of the tin. The plentiful placer cassiterite from Cornwall was certainly utilized in British Isles Bronze Age metallurgy, but it is unknown how widely it was traded. By Roman times, cassiterite from Iberia and Cornwall was available throughout the Mediterranean. The resolution of tin sources for the Bronze Age awaits the fuller characterization of available tin ores and the identification by archaeologists of imported cassiterite when it occurs at a site.

A somewhat related question is: At what time in the Bronze Age in various parts of the world could craftsmen smelt sulfide copper minerals? Oxide-zone copper deposits, which undoubtedly provided the first raw material for copper smelting, are not normally as rich or as extensive as sulfide-zone copper deposits. As the Bronze Age developed, oxide-zone deposits would have become depleted, and sulfide copper would have been the only secure source of copper. Yet, sulfide-ore smelting requires a much more advanced technology than oxide-ore smelting. The author has used trace-element characterization to determine whether a copper object was derived from native copper, smelted oxide copper, or smelted sulfide copper (Rapp 1989).

Methods of Characterization and Types of Studies

The characterization needed for research on metals and alloys depends on the problems or questions at hand. Investigations may focus on such issues as manufacturing technology, provenance of metal ores, smelting technology, casting techniques, gilding, corrosion, or authentication. Each of these will require a distinct analytic approach.

Modern metal-characterization techniques can ascertain levels of achievement of ancient metalsmiths. Most of the metals used in antiquity preserve evidence of their thermal and mechanical history in their microstructures that can be easily observed with the metallographic microscope. Evidence of work-hardening and annealing are recorded in these microstructures. Metallurgists make wide use of the metallographic microscope in analyzing the structural features in metals and identifying distinct compositional phases. The metallographc microscope plus the electron microprobe can provide the structural and chemical analyses needed for most archaeometallurgic problems. These techniques require the destruction of a portion of the object. Nondestructive techniques such as X-radiography (which may give clues to the manufacturing technique) or X-ray fluorescence (for the composition of the surface of a metal) may be the only methods allowed.

A primary technique for identifying a crystalline material based on its crystal structure is X-ray diffraction (XRD). Materials with the same composition (diamond and graphite are both composed of carbon) can be distinguished by their distinct crystal structures. Although XRD instruments are expensive, all universities and most larger museum laboratories have them.

Numerous analytical techniques are available for determining the major-element chemistry of metals. Which method to use depends on availability, sensitivity to specific elements, and cost. For trace elements in metals, instrumental neutron activation analysis (INAA), inductively coupled plasma–atomic emission spectrometry (ICP-AES), and atomic absorption (AA) spectrometry are commonly used instrumental techniques. A distinction must be made between the bulk chemistry of an object and the chemistry of a small region or phase. For analyzing specific phases or regions within a metal object, an electron microprobe or a scanning electron microscope equipped with an energy dispersive X-ray spectrometer must be used.

Chemical characterization of native copper is done on the basis of trace-element concentrations. Several analytic methods are available to determine the chemical elements in the low parts per million or parts per billion range. By far the most commonly used is INAA. It must be kept in mind that, since trace elements may vary by orders of magnitude among deposits and by more than 100 percent in one nugget, absolute values are not as critical as the overall pattern of elemental concentrations.

Many of the best-known examples of chemical characterization of metals are those that have focused on the study of coins. Both destructive and nondestructive analytic methods have been used to provide thousands of analyses that now allow authentication, an understanding of the historical development of metal coinage and metals technology, a determination of practices for debasing coinage, and, in some cases, geographic sources of the metals.

Provenance studies do not address the question of where an artifact was manufactured, but only the source of the raw material(s). A very large number of chemical, physical, and biological parameters can be used to source natural materials. For example, DNA (deoxyribonucleic acid) has received wide attention in forensics, archaeology, and paleontology. Geologists use trace elements, isotopes, diagnostic minerals or assemblages, microfossils, geophysical parameters, and many other distinguishing characteristics to determine the source or origin of geologic materials.

Survival and Corrosion Products of Ancient Metals

A major problem for archaeologists is the deterioration of metals during burial and the rapid corrosion following excavation. Most metals are not stable under the conditions prevailing at or near the Earth's surface. The resulting corrosion has two important aspects: It most often leads to structural deterioration and disfigurement, but, depending on the metal or alloy, a thin layer of corrosion may form a protective film on the surface, inhibiting further deterioration.

The characteristic weathering phenomenon associated with copper and high-copper alloys such as bronze is the formation of a green patina on the surface of the metal. The patina consists of copper-hydroxide salts of sulfate, carbonate, or chloride, as well as salts of lead and tin when these have been alloying elements. In fact, more than a dozen minerals have been found as corrosion products on bronze. The rate of corrosion will depend upon environmental factors, especially the acidity due to sulfuric and carbonic acids in the atmosphere and in soils. Chemical and mineral characterization of the surface alteration is required to assess the problem and consider any remedies.

Ancient iron is not pure iron but an alloy with ca. 0.1 percent carbon, called *wrought iron*. Later, an alloy called cast iron was developed, with a carbon content of more than 2 percent. Steel is also an alloy of iron and carbon, but it is a very different material. Iron corrodes easily to a porous and inhomogeneous iron-oxide rust. Highly corroded artifacts require immediate conservation that depends on accurate characterization of the problem.

By Roman times, lead was in common use in Europe. Fresh lead has a bright, metallic, bluish-gray color. Corrosion first dulls this color, then produces a gray and, finally, a grayish-white surface. Most excavated lead is covered with this grayish-white alteration product. Because lead is so soft, the corrosion products have a higher Mohs hardness than the underlying metal. The tin-lead alloy, pewter, has a very similar dull, grayish-white corroded surface when excavated. It is imperative to characterize (identify) the metal and its alteration products before new corrosion phenomena begin in the new atmospheric environment.

George R. Rapp Jr.

See also ATOMIC ABSORPTION (AA) SPECTROMETRY; ELECTRON-PROBE MICROANALYSIS; METALLOGRAPHY; METALS, ON-SITE CONSERVATION; X-RAY DIFFRACTION (XRD) ANALYSIS; X-RAY FLUORESCENCE (XRF) ANALYSIS

Further Readings

Hancock, R., Pavlish, L., Farquhr, R., Salloum, R., Fox, W., and Wilson, G. (1991) Distinguishing European trade copper and northeastern North American native copper. Archaeometry 33:69–86.

Meyers, P. (1978) Applications of X-ray radiography in the study of archaeological objects. In G. Carter (ed.): Archaeological Chemistry, pp. 79–96. Washington D.C.: American Chemical Society.

Rapp, G., Jr. (1989) Determining the origins of sulfide smelting. Der Anschnitt (Journal of the German Mining Museum) 1989:107–110.

Tylecote, R. (1976) A History of Metallurgy. London: Metals Society.

Wertime, T. and Muhly, J., eds. (1980) The Coming of the Age of Iron. New Haven, CT: Yale University Press.

Metals, On-Site Conservation

Emergency treatment and care of metals on site. Metallic artifacts present difficult on-site conservation problems for nonconservators. Instead of attempting to treat them, efforts should be channeled toward handling and housing objects properly in order to get them safely to a conservation facility where they can be treated. If this is not possible, an experienced, trained field conservator should be part of the excavation team.

It is not always possible to determine in the field the nature and the composition of the metal and the techniques used to make the object. This information must be known before any object can receive conservation treatment. For example, silver can be difficult to recognize when excavated. If it has a high copper content, it will be covered with the green corrosion products of copper and can easily be mistaken for copper or one of its alloys. Conservation treatments appropriate for copper are not necessarily appropriate for silver.

Surface coatings present further complications. Objects frequently are coated or decorated with one metal that obscures the underlying metal. Bronze objects, for example, can be decorated with thin layers of gold, silver, or tin. Often, these layers are cracked and flake off. Silver objects, especially jewelry, can be decorated with niello, which is a silver sulfide. Any chemicals used to clean the silver will remove this decoration.

The nature of the corrosion itself is often difficult to assess. The most commonly found metals on excavations are copper alloys, iron, lead, silver, and gold. They are all subject to the same destructive agents: water, oxygen, and chlorides; however, they all corrode differently. Copper corrodes in layers, while iron corrodes unevenly, presenting a warty appearance. As iron corrosion products take up a larger volume than the metal itself, iron objects have a tendency to crack and explode apart. Excavated lead is generally covered with grayish-white corrosion products. This corrosion is accompanied by a decrease in the metal's cohesiveness, causing the surface to become powdery and the lead to lose its characteristic ductility.

In badly deteriorated objects, corrosion is frequently only a thin shell encasing what remains of the metal of the object, which can be powdery or mineralized.

For these reasons, it is best for nonconservators to not attempt to treat metal objects in the field. There are things, however, that the nonconservator can do to ensure the preservation of finds. Before doing anything, remember that it is important to record everything that is done to an object. Written, and sometimes photographic, records detailing condition and adhesives used can be invaluable to conservators later treating the object. For example, if it is necessary to back an object to get it out of the ground safely, record what adhesive was used and the conditions under which it was applied, if relevant.

Lifting

The handling of metal objects is mostly a matter of common sense. When excavating and removing metal objects from the ground, always assume that they are more fragile than they might appear. Unnecessary handling can cause considerable damage; handle the object as little as possible. Encrusted dirt can hide cracks and structural weaknesses in the metal. One does not know how much metal may remain in the object. Silver, for example, is particularly fragile, as it is most likely to be mineralized.

From the moment an object is lifted, give it as much support as possible; do not wait until it gets back to the dig house in pieces. Later on, if special or unusual objects are brought out to show visitors, pack them in a rigid box first, so that they are not directly handled.

When lifted from the ground, metal objects should be placed in paper envelopes. Plastic bags are not recommended, as they do not allow the object to dry out as envelopes do. In fact, if left in the sun, even unsealed plastic bags sweat, and the metal object will be sitting in a pool of water that can initiate or exacerbate corrosion. If plastic bags are used, be sure to remove the objects from them as soon as possible back at the dig house to allow the objects to dry out. The use of paper envelopes must be regarded as a temporary measure. It is not a suitable material for the long-term storage of metal objects.

Sometimes a metal object is shattered or so badly corroded with cracks that it needs to be backed to remove it from the ground. In this procedure, gauze or other fabric is adhered to the surface of the metal, using a 10 percent solution of a resin in a solvent. Do not use an emulsion, as the water in the emulsion could start or exacerbate corrosion.

Cleaning

Metal objects should not be cleaned by an untrained person in the field. The removal of corrosion products can be a difficult process and should be undertaken only by a trained conservator. Without knowing the composition of the metal and the nature of its corrosion, it is impossible for untrained people to determine the appropriate cleaning procedure. For example, when corrosion is only a thin shell encasing what remains of the metal, any pressure exerted to remove the corrosion will shatter the object. As well, the injudicious use of chemicals can completely dissolve the objects.

Chemicals, including acids, and other cleaning agents should never be used. Chemicals in the wrong hands can do irreparable damage to objects. For example, it is possible to deposit a layer of copper over the surface of a gold-alloy object by cleaning it with acid. This layer of copper is extremely difficult to remove and subjects the object to considerable and unnecessary further treatment. Also, if the object is likely to be used for testing or metallographic analysis, the use of chemicals may invalidate any results.

Even robust metal objects are vulnerable. Surfaces can be scratched easily by untrained hands, and surface detail and decoration can be obliterated. Lead, for example, is a soft, easily scratched metal, and its corrosion products are generally harder than the metal itself, making cleaning difficult.

Injudicious cleaning, as well, can easily damage and destroy not only surface detail, but also organic and environmental evidence preserved by or in the corrosion. Frequently, this is the only way this information is preserved.

For these reasons, no attempt should be made to clean dirt or corrosion products from metal objects. Only superficial cleaning should be undertaken in the field. Do not pry or flick off hard lumps of adhering dirt or pebbles because the pressure necessary to remove them can break the object. Loosen such lumps of dirt by touching them with a brush filled with alcohol and then scrape them off with a wooden tool or stiff brush. If the lumps do not come off easily, leave them for a conservator to remove.

If the object comes out of the ground wet, it should be allowed to dry out slowly and uniformly away from any direct sources of heat, including sunlight. Gently brush off any adhering dirt with a soft, stiff brush. Never scrape dirt off with a metal tool because it will scratch the surface of the object. If a metal object is found dry, do not wash it in water; washing can initiate the corrosion process. This is especially true in areas where the water naturally contains large amounts of salts or where the water supply has been chlorinated.

More persistent dirt can be removed with swabs dipped in distilled water or alcohol. Do not rub the surface with the swab, as this process can scratch it. Rather, gently roll the swab over the surface. As soon as a swab is dirty, discard it for a new one; a dirty swab can be very abrasive.

Other Treatment

Many metal objects, especially those made of gold and lead, are frequently found crushed, bent, or folded over. Pieces of gold foil are invariably crushed or crumpled. Although the temptation is strong to try to unbend them or push the metal back into shape, resist doing so. Chances are that intergranular corrosion has rendered the metal extremely brittle; any attempt by an inexperienced person to manipulate it will result in cracking and breaking. Sometimes even experienced conservators are not able to reshape the metal.

Do not attempt to join any broken pieces of a metal object in the field. The condition of corroded metal is never easy to determine. Although an object may seem sound, an adhesive can, in fact, be stronger than the metal. If the object is subjected to considerable handling, especially rough handling, the adhesive will hold, but the object can break in new places, usually on either side of the join. Once the mended object gets to a conservator, the adhesive must be removed before any further treatment can be carried out. This process can result in the loss of edges, making for more difficult, if not impossible, joining later on.

Packing

The archaeologist can do the most to preserve finds by assuring that they are properly packed and housed until they can be treated by a trained conservator. Metal objects should be packed individually in polystyrene boxes that are well padded with acid-free tissue or polyethylene foam. In areas where the relative humidity goes above 40 percent, silica gel should be used inside the boxes to prevent corrosion from occurring.

Silica gel is a desiccant that is indispensable in helping keep moisture-sensitive materials, such as metals, dry. It is only effective, however, when used in an airtight container, such as a plastic box with a snap lid or metal boxes. To make the boxes as airtight as possible, the crack between the halves of the box can be taped to seal it.

Silica gel should not come in direct contact with the object. If it does touch the metal, it will hold the moisture against the object rather than protect it by keeping the moisture away. To separate the silica gel, fill the bottom of the box with a layer of silica gel before padding it. Several layers of padding should separate the object from the gel. The gel can also be packed in perforated packets to ensure that it will not come in direct contact with the object. Place the gel in a sealed polyethylene bag to form a packet. The packet must be thin and flat to provide as much surface area of the gel as possible. Then perforate the packet all over with a needle or other small, sharp object. Place the object in a depression in the padding and cover it with another flat wad of tissue or foam to hold it firmly in place. Be careful, however, that no undue pressure is exerted on the object when the lid is closed or the object may break. Then tape the crack between the halves of the box to make it airtight.

Robust metal objects can be packed in polyethylene bags, but make very sure that the objects are thoroughly dry before placing them in the bags. A packet of silica gel should be placed in the bag before sealing it. If silica gel is not available, the polyethylene bags holding the objects should be perforated to allow air to circulate around them, and the bags should not be sealed. The bags of objects should be kept in a well-padded, rigid box or container.

An alternative method of packing robust metal objects is to place them in unsealed, perforated polyethylene bags, together with a packet of silica gel, and then put them into a metal or plastic container with a tight-fitting lid. A metal cookie tin or a plastic food container with a snap-on lid is ideal for this purpose. The container can be further sealed with tape. This method provides an effective means of keeping metals safe even in a damp storeroom.

Bags holding small objects such as coins or rings can be kept in order by being stapled to a file card. The card can then be filed, along with silica gel, in an airtight container.

Another excellent means of packing metal objects, especially unstable ones, is to use a glass Mason jar. Fill the bottom of the jar with 4–5 cm of silica gel. Insert into the jar a rack or other device that will not allow the metal to touch the silica gel, then place the

M

object on the rack. The plastic seal makes the jar airtight and will keep objects safe, even in a damp storeroom.

If airtight containers are not available, metal objects, with the exception of lead and pewter, can be packed in cardboard boxes. The box, however, must then be placed, along with a perforated packet of silica gel, inside a thick-gauge polyethylene bag.

Objects of lead and pewter should be packed only in acid-free tissue or plastic. The vapors given off by organic materials will attack lead; therefore, paper, cardboard, and wood—especially when freshly cut—should always be avoided.

On-Site Storage

When objects are kept on site, it is generally difficult, if not impossible, to control storage conditions. Dampness is always a problem in the winter in countries where central heating is not common. In such places, however, if packing materials are chosen carefully and proper packing procedures are used, much can be done to counter adverse circumstances.

Metals should be stored in as dry a place as possible. If metals are stored on site for some time, the silica gel must be checked at least once a year and regenerated when necessary.

The objects themselves should also be checked on a regular basis. Copper-alloy objects must be checked for the appearance of the bright green powdery spots of bronze disease. Active corrosion of iron usually takes the form of wet droplets or pustules surrounded by the orange color associated with rust. This condition, known as weeping iron, indicates extremely unstable iron. Both of these conditions require the immediate attention of a conservator. Any copper or iron in this condition should be packed in airtight containers with silica gel and taken to a conservator as soon as possible.

On-Site Conservator

If a field conservator is part of the excavation team, much can be done with metal objects. Experienced conservators are able to identify metals and make informed assessments of the nature and the extent of corrosion. They can clean and restore metal objects, facilitating the work of the rest of the team. For example, once cleaned and restored, objects can be photographed, drawn, and studied in the field. This can be an important consideration in

countries where finds cannot be exported for conservation or research. In cleaning an object, an experienced conservator can reveal detail and decoration hidden by corrosion. As well, most archaeological conservators are knowledgeable about ancient technology and can frequently provide the archaeologist with information about how an object was made.

An experienced on-site conservator can provide expertise in lifting delicate or difficult objects. Using a variety of materials and techniques, a conservator can back objects or lift them out in a block of protective dirt. The block can be lifted relatively quickly. The slow, meticulous excavating of the object can then proceed at whatever pace is necessary without holding up work at the site.

Conservators are knowledgeable in the handling, packing, and storage needs of metal artifacts and can play an important role in advising or overseeing the processing of finds.

Catherine Sease

See also METALLOGRAPHY; METALS, CHARACTERIZATION

Further Readings

Cross, S., Hett, C., and Bertulli, M. (1989) Conservation Manual for Northern Archaeologists. (Archaeology Report). Yellowknife: Prince of Wales Northern Heritage Centre.

Payton, R., ed. (1992) Retrieval of Objects from Archaeological Sites. London: Archetype.

Sease, C. (1994) A Conservation Manual for the Field Archaeologist, 3rd ed. (Archaeological Research Tools). Los Angeles: Institute of Archaeology, UCLA.

Singley, K. (1988) The Conservation of Archaeological Artifacts from Freshwater Environments. South Haven, MI: Lake Michigan Maritime Museum.

Watkinson, D.E., ed. (1998) First Aid for Finds, 3rd ed. London: Rescue/UKIC Archaeology Section.

Metrical Stratigraphy

The excavation and analysis of archaeological deposits using uniform measurements of predetermined intervals in situations in which natural strata are not clearly visible. Metrical or arbitrary stratigraphy is a method of excavation in which layers of a uniform thickness are imposed by excavators at sites that do not possess observable depositional layers. Each layer is usually fully excavated before moving to the next, and layers are removed sequentially. Arbitrary levels are particularly useful in the excavation of shell middens, which are often composed of ephemeral lenses of crushed shell, fire-cracked rock, ash, and charcoal. Nels Nelson and Alfred V. Kidder are credited with introducing arbitrary stratigraphy to American archaeology in the early 1900s, and where it is widely used today. Some archaeologists whose excavation experience is primarily with sites with highly visible layers discourage the use of arbitrary levels. However, for sites lacking clearly observable strata, imposing predetermined levels is a viable alternative. When the archaeological material recovered by arbitrary levels is analyzed, meaningful chronological and behavioral patterns can be established.

Edward Luby

See also NATURAL STRATIGRAPHY; STRATIFICATION; STRATIGRAPHY

Further Readings

Barker, P. (1993) Techniques of Archaeological Excavation, 3rd ed. London: Batsford.

Joukowsky, M. (1980) A Complete Manual of Field Archaeology. Englewood Cliffs, NJ: Prentice-Hall.

Midwestern Taxonomic System

A system for classification of artifacts used in the United States from the 1930s to the 1960s. By the 1930s, American archaeologists had come to something of an impasse about the means used to describe and discuss collections of artifact assemblages. The term *culture* was ubiquitous in this role, but it varied tremendously in scope and meaning from one application to the next. In the Southwest, Winifred and Harold S. Gladwin had proposed a hierarchic system of roots, stems, and branches. Most archaeologists, however, abjured what they saw as the genetic implications of the Gladwin system either because they disapproved of evolutionary constructions in principle or thought the data required to make such connections were lacking.

The Midwestern Taxonomic System (MTS) was created in the mid-1930s to rec-

tify this problem by providing an "objective," broadly useful means of categorizing assemblages. It is intimately associated with American archaeologist William C. McKern; it is often called the McKern system. But, as he pointed out, it was the product of a consensus reached about a proposal that was originally made by McKern but that had been subjected to broad discussion, even including polling the profession with a questionnaire, over a period of years. Thus, while McKern was the guiding light, many other leading archaeologists of the day, including James B. Griffin and William A. Ritchie, had a role in the ultimate formulation published by McKern in 1939.

In outline, the system is quite simple. The entities arranged were called *components,* assemblages that represented the occupation of a place by a people. Component was not equivalent to site unless a place had experienced only a single occupation. In practice, components were devined on the basis of trait similarity.

Traits were used to assign components to groups. Five levels of units were recognized: *focus, aspect, pattern, phase,* and *base.* Components belonging to a single focus shared most traits, and the traits were specific (e.g., particular designs); foci that shared many traits, usually more general (e.g., technique of decoration) than those used for establishing foci, were grouped as an aspect and so on until one reached base, where only a few, often inferential (e.g., agriculture) traits were held in common. Three kinds of traits were identified: *shared traits,* which were common to more than one unit; *diagnostic traits,* which were limited to a single unit; and *determinants,* traits that occurred in all members of a unit but in no other unit.

McKern's description of the method is typical methodologizing of the period. Some astute points are made in ad hoc fashion (e.g., the need to have representative collections), but he avoided most critical issues (e.g., how traits were defined [McKern did worry over some aspects of this, but subsequent users did not] or what similarity meant and how it was to be measured). Reliance upon common sense to justify such crucial decisions as these gives the MTS an intuitive aura to the modern reader.

Analysis of the system makes it clear that it is a grouping method: Its units were not classes to which assemblages were assigned;

they were aggregates of assemblages per se. McKern was also clear that the units did not have any necessary temporal or spatial meaning. Such meaning had to be acquired independently of the MTS method. In modern terms, the MTS is an application of numerical taxonomy (numerical phenetics) without recourse to actual *measurement* of similarity. Indeed, contemporary critics such as Alfred L. Kroeber were quick to point out that the failure to measure similarity quantitatively was a major flaw. The difficulties in doing so were underestimated by critics, however. Numerical phenetics would not come into its own until the 1960s and cheap computing, and then only for a couple of decades and almost exclusively in biology.

One characteristic of grouping methods is that they are expressly atheoretical: They claim to find "natural" or "real" groups without the influence of theoretical input. This claim is easily shown to be false and led to the demise of numerical taxonomy in the 1980s, but this feature made it very attractive to the atheoretic archaeology of the 1930s. Another characteristic is that grouping systems simply describe a data set; the addition of new data implies that all of the old categories have to be abandoned and the whole system of relations recalculated. In short, grouping as a method cannot be applied in the real world. But the MTS proved eminently usable. McKern's determinates cleverly circumvented this problem with extentional definition. By inspecting the components assigned to a focus or higher-level unit for traits common to all *and* limited to members of a unit, criteria for the addition of future members had been generated. Of course, the particular traits that met these conditions depended upon the components polled, and that list changed as knowledge of the archaeological record grew. Thus the price paid was that all MTS foci, aspects, and so forth were rendered historical accidents, accidents of the assemblages known at the time that determinants were derived.

The MTS was widely applied in the United States (outside of the Southwest) over the next two decades. The emergence of culture history in the 1930s was heavily predicated on stylistic descriptions. As McKern himself noted, styles dominated the lower units of focus and aspect, whereas functional traits tended to dominate in the higher levels of the MTS. Thus, it is not surprising that the focus and, to a lesser extent, the aspect were the principal units of the the MTS to find application. With few exceptions, the higher levels were largely abandoned.

Although its terminology passed from the scene in the 1960s, such units as Archaic, Woodland, and Mississippian either originated as higher-level categories in the MTS or were passed on to us through it. More important, the phase system propounded by Gordon R. Willey and Philip Phillips and that came to dominate American archaeology in the 1960s is, in many respects, just the MTS reworked by jettisoning the higher categories and modifying the focus to include explicit temporal and spatial parameters. Many "phases" are the very same constructs first proposed as foci in the MTS. This, of course, is not particularly good; it means that many of the "basic units" of prehistory are historical accidents that exist solely because particular assemblages were known when the MTS was applied in a given area. But the impact of the MTS on contemporary ideas of prehistory remains enormous if largely unremarked.

Robert C. Dunnell

See also MCKERN, WILLIAM CARLETON; TYPE-VARIETY SYSTEM; WILLEY, GORDON RANDOLPH

Mortuary Sites, Excavation and Analysis

The excavation and analysis of sites associated with human burials. All cultural groups express concern for their dead, some in more elaborate and monumental ways than others. Everything from Egyptian pyramids and Mayan tombs to California shell midden burials attest to the human need to commemorate death. The material remains of the events surrounding death are often preserved well enough that archaeologists can describe and reconstruct mortuary behavior. The archaeological analysis of these remains, which include a variety of burial structures and the objects buried with the dead, enable archaeologists to characterize the social and economic life of a society.

Mortuary site archaeology is the excavation, study, and analysis of burials. Although mortuary sites can vary widely—ranging from a few scattered burials in pots beneath house floors to a multitude of large tombs, each containing hundreds of objects—a similar set of methodological problems, ethical concerns, and theoretical issues confronts archaeologists when burials are encountered. For instance, burials are often difficult to excavate because of their stratigraphic complexities. Excavation must proceed carefully and respectfully, and, in some areas of the world, with participation from native groups. Moreover, a thorough understanding of mortuary theory in archaeology is required to offer valid reconstructions of behavior.

Many elements of modern archaeology are brought together in mortuary site archaeology. The history of archaeology is rich with references to burials; in many regions of the world, the earliest professional excavations involved mortuary sites. Major advances in the understanding of stratigraphy and chronology were accomplished with burial data. Specialized excavation and mapping techniques were developed for working with burials, and the need to organize burials and associated artifacts provided important insight into typology.

The excavation and analysis of burials also requires a consideration of law and a review of ethics. The 1990 passage of the Native American Graves Protection and Repatriation Act (NAGPRA), together with a variety of state and local ordinances, provides a legal framework for the excavation of burials from certain kinds of land in the United States. Most archaeologists would agree that these laws, together with the views of native groups, have prompted a reexamination of the ethics of excavating burials. Indeed, the entire issue of whether or not to disturb burials for research is a central focus of archaeological ethics today.

History

Burials played an important role in the historical development of archaeology. In particular, key advances in relative chronology, stratigraphy, and techniques in excavation were brought about by scholars working with mortuary data.

Until the emergence of modern archaeology in western Europe and North America in the mid-nineteenth century, the primary interest in ancient burials was in linking them to groups referred to in religious or historical texts. The Greeks and the Romans, for instance, sometimes opened a grave when they believed it was related to an important historical figure. However, a framework for identifying and analyzing prehistoric groups did not exist.

Attempts to identify and account for the archaeological remains associated with prehistoric groups began, in part, with the development of antiquarianism, a proto-archaeology that emerged in late-seventeenth-century Europe. Antiquarians were mostly interested in relics associated with European history and classical antiquity. Many of these objects were derived from the undisturbed deposits of prehistoric burials. One notable antiquarian was William Stukeley (1687–1765), who worked with English burial mounds. He noted the similarity of grave goods from barrows (earthen-covered burial mounds) and those at prehistoric megaliths and linked the two temporally. Most antiquarians, however, were unsuccessful in linking burials to prehistoric groups, despite the excavation of scores of burial sites throughout England and Scandinavia. Burials remained a secondary focus of interest, because the objects associated with them were considered more important than the burials themselves.

Antiquarianism evolved into modern archaeology with the incorporation of principles from geology and biology and the work of some important Danish scholars. The analysis of material from mortuary sites was a significant part of this process. For example, the Three Age system (Stone, Bronze, and Iron), developed by the Dane Christian J. Thomsen (1788–1865), revolutionized the concept of relative chronology in Europe. Using material collected from burials, Thomsen and other scholars realized that artifacts could be assigned to typologies. These typologies could then provide a firm basis for developing temporal frameworks for sites and, eventually, for entire regions. Another Dane, Jens Worsaae (1821–1885), worked extensively with burial mounds in Scandinavia and is often credited with introducing a basic stratigraphic tenet into archaeology, the Law of Superposition.

Many of the major advances in excavation techniques and methodology of the late nineteenth and early twentieth centuries were accomplished by archaeologists working at mortuary sites. Sir William Flinders Petrie, for example, developed a widely used relative-dating method called *seriation* by observing changes in the shape of ceramic vessels derived from Egyptian graves. Max Uhle in Peru and Alfred V. Kidder in the American Southwest also made influential contributions in stratigraphic interpretation and methodology with data derived from mortuary sites.

In the early part of the twentieth century, archaeologists were concerned with classifying artifacts and developing site and regional chronologies. The analysis of material from burials played a key role in most regional chronologies, especially before the advent of radiocarbon dating, and continues to be an important component of establishing temporal frameworks for sites and regions.

Logistical and Ethical Considerations for Excavating Burials

Burials are sometimes the last features archaeologists want to find while excavating an archaeological site. Indeed, when a burial is encountered unexpectedly, some archaeologists may view it as a nuisance for "disrupting" the strata and forcing a change in excavation plans. However, because the full range of mortuary practices is not yet known for most ancient groups, it should not be surprising that burials are detected in unforeseen locations.

Excavation of burials demands a consideration of several issues at once. First, it is necessary to determine whether burials are associated with visible architecture. The techniques for excavating a cemeterylike area with scores of individual graves dug into the ground differ from those used when burials are placed beneath the floors of structures occupied for long periods of time. In the latter case, the relationship of the burials to the architecture is critically important in how one approaches excavation.

Second, burials often pose complex stratigraphic questions that need to be resolved to build a viable temporal framework for a site. For example, while excavating burials, archaeologists are concerned with identifying the *grave cut,* or physical evidence that establishes the level from which the grave was dug. By definition, burials intrude into the soils below; if these soils are composed of archaeological deposits, earlier strata must have been removed and deposited elsewhere. The relationship of a burial to surrounding soils, and the level from which it was originally dug, should be fully investigated.

Third, to control for bias in analyses of burials, it is essential to know if they were disturbed or looted in the past. Some chronological analyses of burials assume that the contents of graves represent the original, sealed situation at the time of burial. However, in a field setting, this can be very difficult to establish. Looters do not always leave behind obvious signs of disturbance, and the indicators of looting may become obscured over time. Worse, looters may remove only certain kinds of objects, such as precious metals or items of symbolic importance, and then reseal the burials. Some graves may also contain material from much earlier time periods, but this does not necessarily mean that the burial is disturbed; individuals are sometimes buried with heirlooms, valuable objects from much earlier time periods. In addition, disturbance by natural factors, such as rodents or erosion, may result in the movement of objects. Furthermore, because of various soil characteristics in certain environments, the boundaries and the contents of graves may not preserve very well.

Finally, archaeologists must be sensitive to the views of groups who express concern over excavation activities at mortuary sites. In some parts of the world, archaeologists also need to understand legislation enacted to protect burials. The passage of NAGPRA forever altered the process of excavating burials from federal lands in the United States. Native American groups can request that no photographs of burials be taken, and they can define the extent of scientific analyses and the pace of subsequent reburial.

Excavation Techniques

Because mortuary sites vary greatly, there is no single methodological approach to excavation. The recovery of mortuary data is often just one of the goals formulated by archaeologists when excavating sites. Nevertheless, there are several techniques to consider while excavating burials to maximize the recovery of mortuary data.

Proper excavation of burials requires an extensive period of time. Complex stratigraphic questions may need to be resolved. Human skeletal remains and associated objects need to be examined and removed without being damaged. Small tools, such as dental pics and paint brushes, are used to excavate skeletons; surrounding soils require larger brushes and trowels. Since certain kinds of objects may be found only in graves, minor conservation of artifacts and bone often takes place, a practice that can also slow the pace of excavation.

The positions of objects, and skeletons in graves must be carefully recorded, along with depth measurements, soil descriptions, and architectural associations. This information is usually recorded on special burial sheets designed by the excavators. Detailed maps are also completed. Maps of skeletons, associated objects, and architecture often pose a challenge because they need to be precise and very detailed. Some archaeologists place gridded frames over the skeleton to speed up the mapping of burials; this helps the process by breaking the task into smaller parts. In addition to detailed maps, rough sketches are made, and photographs are taken of the grave if it is deemed appropriate. The accurate recording of a burial is critical for subsequent analyses. Knowing the precise position of shell beads in a grave, for example, may help determine whether they were once strung together along a now-decayed string or simply thrown atop the body.

Osteological training is essential for excavating burials carefully and efficiently. Archaeologists with backgrounds in human skeletal anatomy can sketch bones more quickly. In the field, they can also identify and label bones, take measurements on fragile remains, and concentrate their efforts on areas of the skeleton that yield the most information in skeletal analyses.

Human skeletal remains must be excavated slowly. The entire skeleton should be exposed before mapping and removal. Many archaeologists excavate skeletons by leaving them on a pedestal, a slightly raised area of soil immediately surrounding the skeleton, while they determine the boundaries of the grave and resolve stratigraphic questions. Care must be taken to conserve bone and to keep it away from direct sunlight, which degrades it rapidly. The best way to remove bones is to carefully excavate around them with dental pics until they can be gently moved; bones should never be pried or lifted with force. Upon removal, bone should be placed in thoroughly labeled storage containers appropriate for holding fragile material. Several excellent osteological guides outline the basics of nomenclature and excavation and are available for archaeologists.

Burial Characteristics and Types

When a burial is discovered, several basic features are usually noted, such as the orientation and the position of the individual. Terms such as *flexed* and *extended* are used to describe position, but archaeologists often employ their own definitions. In general, flexed refers to an individual with its arms or knees bent, while extended refers to an individual who is completely stretched out, without any bending in the joint areas. The side on which the individual is resting (left or right) is usually recorded and whether the individual is face down, face up, or sitting. Some archaeologists also determine the direction in which the skeleton is facing, such as north or south. Evidence of treatments, such as burning, coating with pigment, or wrapping the body in reeds, is also described.

Archaeologists generally recognize a few basic ways of burying people. *Inhumation* refers to the placement of individuals into the ground, with or without a burial container. A *primary burial* occurs when the interred individual is not disturbed in any subsequent mortuary activities after initial burial. *Secondary burial* refers to the burial of an already defleshed or decomposed individual; archaeologists can identify these burials because the bones are usually disarticulated or bundled together. A *multiple burial* consists of several individuals buried together, either at once or over a period of time. *Cremations* refer to burials with evidence of burning, usually to the point that only small pieces of bone remain.

Many different kinds of containers can be used to bury individuals, including ceramic pots, coffins, and small stone or brick tombs. These items may or may not have been used exclusively for burial purposes; at some sites, infants have been found buried in ordinary cooking vessels beneath the floors of houses, and at others, in specialized mortuary pots.

Archaeologists also categorize burials according to the structures with which they are associated and their general location within a site. *Barrows* are earthen-covered, artificial mounds that are sometimes called *burial mounds*. In many coastal areas, burials are found in shell middens, which are accumulations of ash, fauna, rock, and cultural material. Tombs made of stone or brick are common, and burials are often found in caves and rockshelters. Most people are

M

aware of elaborate mortuary structures, such as the Egyptian pyramids and the Royal Tombs of Mexico and Mesopotamia. Formalized disposal areas are usually referred to as *cemeteries,* which are places where many bodies are placed in the ground over time, often in a variety of containers. Individuals are also buried beneath the floors of structures, including temples, public buildings and houses, in which case they are called *intramural* burials.

Information from Burials

Information derived from the excavation of burials is central to archaeological investigation. Through analyses of changes in artifact associations, mortuary data remain important for establishing chronological control at many sites. More recently, archaeologists have explored the social and economic life of groups by analyzing grave goods and burial placement. When doing so, various sources of bias from excavated samples must be considered carefully. For example, in samples in which no infant burials are found, researchers must consider the possibility that their sample is too small or that infants were buried off the main site.

Since the 1960s, a popular research area in archaeology has been to establish the relative rank of individuals derived from a population of burials by examining the range and wealth of associated grave goods. In some societies, the rich have been differentiated from the poor, and intermediate wealth and status levels identified. Analyses of the nature of the society in question can then be offered, including a consideration of the sources of wealth and the manner in which wealth was maintained and managed. Although some problems have been identified with searching for rank, it has lead to an increased understanding of societies with formalized inequalities, such as chiefdoms and states.

In the 1980s, some archaeologists began to examine mortuary symbolism. Searching for sets of co-occurring objects or looking for patterns in burial placement or treatment forms, they made statements about the likely symbols for age, sex, and social-group membership. Some archaeologists also suggested that burial mounds in certain areas should be viewed as territorial markers. Yet others concluded that burials beneath the floors of domestic structures were indicative of continuity, ownership, or group solidarity. Although this approach has become increasingly popular, many archaeologists believe that it is untestable and too speculative.

The analysis of human skeletal remains is also useful for archaeological investigations. Age, sex, demography, and disease can often be established by analyzing properly excavated human bone. Since the 1970s, archaeologists have worked more closely with skeletal biologists to elucidate the biological and cultural factors responsible for the pathologies and disease patterns observed in excavated populations. An event such as famine, for example, can leave biological markers on bone. Because famine is often the result of interacting biological and cultural processes, such as crowded living conditions, political tensions, and changes in environmental conditions, archaeologists hope to identify some of the factors responsible for the situation by working with skeletal biologists.

The large body of techniques, methodologies, and theoretical approaches that has developed for investigating mortuary sites has yielded a wealth of information about the mortuary behavior of cultural groups. However, the late twentieth century has seen mortuary-site archaeology undergoing a critical, and somewhat painful, realignment of its approach to native peoples in some areas of the world. The framework for excavating and studying burials continues to evolve and will undoubtedly adapt to these changes. Whatever the outcome of this process, however, burials will continue to be exposed. Professionals will be needed to excavate the remains properly and to reconstruct a human behavior that is associated with all cultural groups: the treatment and burial of the dead.

Edward Luby

See also NATIVE AMERICAN GRAVES PROTECTION AND REPATRIATION ACT (NAGPRA); REBURIAL, INTERNATIONAL PERSPECTIVES

Further Readings

Brothwell, D. (1981) Digging Up Bones. Ithaca, NY: Cornell University Press.

Chapman, R., Kinnes, I., and Randsborg, K. (1981) The Archaeology of Death. New York: Cambridge University Press.

Goldstein, L., and Kintigh, K. (1990) Ethics and the reburial controversy. American Antiquity 55(3):585–591.

Joukowsky, M. (1980) A Complete Manual of Field Archaeology: Tools and Techniques of Field Work for Archaeologists. Englewood Cliffs, NJ: Prentice-Hall.

O'Shea, B. (1984) Mortuary Variability. Orlando: Academic.

Trigger, B. (1989) A History of Archaeological Thought. New York: Cambridge University Press.

Mosaics, On-Site Conservation

Techniques for protection and treatment of mosaics during and immediately after excavation. Mosaics are composite materials usually consisting of small pieces of cut stone, pebbles, ceramic, or glass, called *tesserae,* embedded in a base of mortar or adhesive. The mortar-tesserae matrix of most mosaics is essentially brittle and is subject to damage from breakage, detachment from the substrate on which it is constructed, and disassociation of tesserae from the matrix. Retention of the tesserae in position of the mortar the substrate is of primary importance to the on-site conservation of mosaics. Mosaics are most often constructed as decorative floor or wall surfaces, and so their excavation and preservation are integrally connected to the preservation of the primary structure in which they are constructed.

Methods of Construction

Typical floor-mosaic construction consists of a firm foundation of soil, subsoil, or large stones and several subsequent layers of mortar. The mortar used in most mosaics is a mixture of lime and aggregate (sand, pebbles, and/or brick particles) with increasingly fine aggregates used in layers nearer the final surface, ending with a thin layer of mortar containing only very fine aggregate particles. The preparation of walls for mosaic construction is similar to that for floor mosaics, with thinner layers of mortar and finer aggregate particles. Rarely, wall mosaics are constructed by embedding the tesserae in a layer of bitumen or natural resin-based adhesive.

Mechanisms of Deterioration of Mosaics

Settling foundations of structures in which mosaics are constructed will yield uneven and broken mosaics. Catastrophic destruction of primary structures causes breakage and fragmentation of mosaics, sometimes resulting in overturned fragments and general cracking of bedding mortar and loosening of tesserae. The fragility of the matrix is exacerbated during burial by partial leaching of the bedding mortar by groundwater and/or the decomposition of organic additives. Penetration by roots will also disrupt the integrity of mosaics.

Like other porous materials, the mosaic matrix and some materials used as tesserae (notably ceramics) are susceptible to damage from soluble salts present in groundwater. Postexcavation drying may cause water-soluble salts, spread throughout the mosaic by groundwater, to crystallize within the pores of the mortar and the tesserae, causing disruption of the matrix, disintegration of the surface (powdering, crumbling, or friability), and general weakening of the structure. Similarly, water within the mosaic matrix may repeatedly freeze and thaw, resulting in disruption and loosening of tesserae.

Precautions in Excavation

While all loose tesserae should be retained during excavation, much of their significance is lost if they are dislodged from the mosaic matrix. Once a mosaic is located, the use of heavy tools (picks or shovels) should be discontinued. Metal tools (trowels and knives) should not be used to scrape mosaic surfaces as they can easily dislodge tesserae. Initial cleaning should be accomplished only with brushes or soft wooden sticks.

Mosaics in situ are most vulnerable at broken edges where tesserae are loose and the supporting foundations are dislodged or disrupted. Disintegration at broken edges is progressive, in that dislodged tesserae and mortar fragments loosen adjacent material and create space for additional movement. The outer edges of a floor space often include important information about the dimensions of the room and the sequence of construction of both floor and wall decoration. Therefore, particular effort must be made to preserve both the constructed and the broken edges of mosaics.

Initial Stabilization

If a mosaic is located at the edge of a deeper excavation or in sloping terrain, care must be taken to prevent slumping of the substrate and, hence, the edges of the mosaic into the lower portion of the excavation until further

M

stabilization can be undertaken. Protection of edges in sloping sectors may be accomplished through the construction of temporary dry-masonry retaining walls, which are backfilled with soil, around the edges of the mosaic and substrate. At no time should mosaics be shored up with cement "edgings," as these will almost inevitably tear away, carrying some of the mosaic with them.

The weight and the movement of excavators can be extremely damaging to the mosaic matrix, causing loosening of tesserae and crushing of mortar beds, particularly in areas where there are subsurface voids. Damage can be mitigated by working from existing balks (earth left unexcavated) backward, provided sufficient depth of balk is retained and the soil is compact and stable. Otherwise, excavation must proceed on a platform suspended above the mosaic or, on well-preserved floors, from platforms resting on soft padding. At no time should general foot traffic be allowed on excavated mosaic surfaces; where limited foot traffic is necessary, soft-soled or padded shoes should be employed.

Wall mosaics are easily loosened from their supporting structures by salt efflorescence, weakening of the bedding mortar by groundwater, and disruption due to organic growth. If, during excavation, a section of mosaic is found attached to a wall surface, the excavator must assess the strength of the attachment before continuing excavation, as the fill soil may be the only thing holding the mosaic in place. Any unstable wall mosaic should be protected by gentle backfilling until a conservator can be consulted.

Partly excavated mosaics frequently require protection from rapid drying that may result in formation of salt efflorescence. Protection may consist of shading with a temporary structure and/or covering plastic sheeting or moisture-permeable synthetic mesh. Once excavated, mosaics will require further protection until their condition can be evaluated by a conservator. If an excavated mosaic is to remain in situ for any length of time (e.g., between seasons), it must be well covered by a durable structure or by backfilling. Backfilling usually includes the application of a separating layer consisting of, a stable, moisture-permeable material, such as plastic mesh or geotextile (synthetic resin mesh designed for subsoil applications). Subsequent protective layers may include sand, expanded clay, or vermiculite, followed by a layer of soil. The choice of backfilling materials and depth of covering layers should be made in consultation with a conservator and will depend on the stability of the mosaic and its substructure and the climate in which it is located.

Field Treatment

Except for physical protection, very little treatment of mosaics should be undertaken in the field without consultation with, or under the supervision of, a conservator. Materials applied to mosaics in unplanned attempts at preservation may interfere with the future cleaning, lifting, or consolidation.

In many cases, a conservator will apply a protective layer of cloth or paper, bound with synthetic or natural resin (a facing), to the surface of a mosaic to temporarily stabilize and preserve the integrity of the tesserae-mortar matrix prior further treatment. The choice of facing materials will depend on the climatic conditions and the overall plan of treatment of the mosaic.

Removal

Frequently, mosaics will be lifted from an excavation for further treatment in a laboratory, to allow for excavation beneath the mosaic, or to treat the mosaic for display in a museum environment. Lifting is a complex operation that requires careful planning and skilled execution. *The Conservation of the Orpheus Mosaic at Paphos, Cyprus* (1991) is a detailed description of one such project. Once removed from an excavation, a mosaic will require the application of a new backing to substitute for the original substrate. The choice of a backing material will depend on the ultimate destination and use of the artifact and may include honeycomb panels, new lime mortars, synthetic resins, or a combination of the above.

Treatment In Situ

Mosaics that are to remain in situ will almost always require some treatment by a conservator for long-term preservation. Treatment will likely include reinforcing the edges of a mosaic, particularly where the edges are fragmentary and not bound by walls, with mortars. Such edgings are designed to complement the existing mortar and avoid additional damage. A mosaic matrix may also be strengthened by the application of a liquid consolidant through injection or application from the surface. Consolidants consisting of thin solutions of mortarlike materials are known as *grouts*. Other consolidants include synthetic resins in organic solvents or in aqueous emulsions. The treatment of wall mosaics often includes facing, consolidation, and grout injection, often with the insertion of metal (stainless steel or copper alloy) attachments to the substrate.

Additional cleaning of mosaics, to remove accretions and stains, is likewise a highly specialized skill and should be undertaken only by a conservator. The choice of cleaning materials will depend on the type of accretion to be removed, the materials and techniques to be used in further treatment, and the aesthetic requirements for the final display of the mosaic. Secondary cleaning may involve poultices containing aqueous chemical solutions or simply mechanical cleaning with low-power magnification and stainless-steel scalpels.

Kent Severson

See also IN SITU CONSERVATION

Further Readings

The Conservation of the Orpheus Mosaic at Paphos, Cyprus. (1991) Marina del Rey, CA: Getty Conservation Institute.

Cronyn, J.N. (1990) The Elements of Archaeological Conservation. London and New York: Routledge.

Mora, P. (1995) Conservation of excavated intonaco, stucco, and mosaics, 2nd ed. In N.P. Stanley Price (ed.): Conservation on Archaeological Excavations, pp. 91–100. Rome: ICCROM.

Sease, C. (1994) A Conservation Manual for the Field Archaeologist, 3rd ed. Los Angeles: Institute of Archaeology, UCA.

Mössbauer Spectroscopy

Nuclear instrumental method, named after its discoverer, German physicist Rudolph L. Mössbauer (1929–), who won the Nobel Prize (1961). Mössbauer spectroscopy (MS) is also called *nuclear gamma resonance spectroscopy*. MS is mostly applied in chemistry and solid-state physics but has been employed in archaeology, especially as a method to establish provenance, manufacturing conditions, and age of artifacts containing iron-bearing minerals.

The Mössbauer Effect: Basic Principles

When an excited nucleus in a solid material decays by emission of a gamma ray (photon), it sometimes happens that the recoil is taken up directly by the solid material (and not by the nucleus of the atom), resulting in an extremely small recoil energy loss, which is negligible in most cases. This recoil-less fraction of the actual radiation, called the *Mössbauer f-factor,* is higher at lower temperatures, for less energetic radiation, and for a heavier atom. The *Mössbauer effect,* a resonance effect, refers to the recoil-less emission of gamma rays from excited nuclei formed in a radioactive source and their subsequent recoil-less absorption by nuclei of the same isotope in the specimen under examination. The Mössbauer effect has been demonstrated for many isotopes (ca. 100), but for most of them it occurs only at very low temperatures (less than 100 K). For a few isotopes, in particular iron-57 (^{57}Fe) and tin-119 (^{119}Sn), the nuclear transition energies are such that the effect can be observed even at room temperature and above.

In the study of iron-bearing minerals in archaeological artifacts, the radioactive cobalt isotope, ^{57}Co, provides the gamma-ray source. This isotope decays, in general, to an excited state of the stable iron isotope ^{57}Fe, which assumes its ground state by emission of a photon of 14.4 keV energy. The gamma rays are directed onto the specimen under examination, which is typically a thin disc of a few hundred milligrams in weight. The transmitted intensity of the radiation is measured using conventional detectors, such as proportional, scintillation, or semiconductor counters. The resonance condition is studied by varying the energy of the incident gamma rays over a range of ca. 10^{-6} eV as a result of the Doppler effect, by moving the source relative to the specimen at various velocities up to ca. 1 cm s^{-1}. It is, thus, possible to obtain a plot of the percentage transmission of the gamma-rays by the specimen versus gamma ray energy (i.e., velocity of the source), which is referred to as the *Mössbauer spectrum.*

In addition to measuring the Mössbauer transmission spectrum, it is also possible to detect secondary emitted conversion electrons or X-rays in a back-scatter geometry (*conversion electron Mössbauer spectroscopy* [CEMS] and *conversion X-ray Mössbauer spectroscopy* [CXMS]), making nondestructive in situ measurements possible.

As the electrons have a limited escape depth, normally ca. 0.1 mm, CEMS is a surface-sensitive method of special advantage when studying weathering processes. Using CXMS, it is possible to examine the surface to a depth of ca. 50 μm. However, CEMS and CXMS geometries normally need a longer measuring time than transmission MS to get a spectrum of high quality.

Hyperfine Interaction

Although the Mössbauer effect is of a nuclear nature, the nuclear-energy levels are influenced to a very small extent by the electrons surrounding the nucleus (*hyperfine interaction*) and also by external magnetic fields. As the properties of the surrounding electrons depend on the ligands and the type of chemical bonds, a Mössbauer spectrum can give both chemical and physical information. A special feature is the microscopic character of the method as the information is provided by individual Mössbauer atoms, emitting and absorbing photons.

The hyperfine interaction is described by the Mössbauer parameters of *isomer shift, magnetic hyperfine field,* and *quadrupole splitting.* The isomer shift is sensitive to the electron density at the Mössbauer nucleus, influenced by, for example, the valence state of the atom. The hyperfine field gives information about the magnetic state at the Mössbauer atom. The quadrupole splitting is sensitive to asymmetries in the electron cloud around the Mössbauer nucleus, being influenced by the valence state of the Mössbauer atom itself as well as of other atoms in the nearest surrounding. The intensity of the Mössbauer signal, emitted by atoms in a certain crystallographic site in the solid material, is roughly proportional to the number of Mössbauer atoms in that site and to the strength of the bonds to the ligands. Thus, besides ordinary phase identification, MS can give information on bond strengths, site occupancies, valence states, crystallographic distortions, magnetic structures, and the like.

Applications to Archaeology

In the 100 or so Mössbauer research reports of archaeological interest that have been published in scientific journals to date, only ^{57}Fe and ^{119}Sn have been used as Mössbauer isotopes. The major area for archaeological application, using ^{57}Fe, has been the study of ancient pottery, with emphasis put on provenance and the determination of firing temperature and atmospheric conditions in ancient kilns when manufacturing the wares. Iron-57 MS has also been used in studying the aging effects from weathering and natural radiation on artifacts buried in the ground. Tin-119 spectroscopy has been used in a few studies of ancient bronzes (e.g., to study the surface of ancient Chinese bronze mirrors from the Han and Tang dynasties).

Examples and Considerations

The Mössbauer parameters, especially isomer shifts and quadrupole splittings for the nonmagnetic Fe^{2+} and Fe^{3+} components, may fall within a comparatively limited range for pottery wares manufactured from clays coming from the same locality. Samples of Mycenaean and Minoan potteries from the Greek Late Bronze Age period have shown small but systematic differences in quadrupole splittings, which could be used as an indication of provenance (Kostikas et al, 1974). In another study, Mössbauer spectra of pottery samples from Qatar and Saudi Arabia were nearly identical, but different from spectra of Egyptian pottery. All samples came from the early Islamic period, ca. eighth century A.D. Infrared spectroscopy gave similar results, indicating that the Qatar and El-Medina potteries could have the same origin or at least have been manufactured from the same type of clay (Eissa et al. 1979).

Obsidian, a volcanic glass, may be used as an indicator of trade routes in prehistoric periods. In the western Mediterranean area, there were only four main geological sources of obsidian available to people during the period spanning the Neolithic to the Copper Age, namely Lipari, Pantelleria, Palmarola, and Sardinia. An MS study of obsidians from these localities both in form of geological samples and archaeological artifacts (chips, blades, and flakes) assigned the archaeological samples to these island sources on the basis of their trace-element composition as determined by neutron activation analyses. (Longworth and Warren 1979). The nonmagnetic Fe^{2+} and Fe^{3+} quadrupole splittings were compared between the geological and the archaeological obsidian samples from the same source, and the agreements were quite good. The obtained quadrupole splittings were different for the different geological sources, and obsidian samples from Sardinia and Pantelleria could be distinguished both from each other and from the other sources. The samples from Lipari and Palmarola showed some overlap in quadrupole splittings recorded at room temperature. However, comparing spectra recorded at a temperature of 77 K and at room temperature, the Lipari samples had an increase in quadrupole splittings at low temperature of 10 percent, but the Palmarola samples showed an increase of only 3 percent. Thus, it seems possible to establish the provenance of these samples using MS. Obsidian is largely amorphous glass and, thus, not easily studied by X-ray diffraction (XRD). MS is more microscopic in character than XRD, giving sharp (although somewhat broadened) spectra even of amorphous materials. The effects of weathering and hydration on the surface of the obsidian samples were studied using CXMS, and it was shown that the ferric fraction of iron was significantly higher in the surface than in the bulk.

In geological obsidian samples from the Gabellotto flow on Lipari, which took place ca. 10,000 BP, MS revealed inclusions of magnetite, not detected in geological samples of obsidian from near-by localities and not in the archaeological samples from Lipari either. However, there is a possibility that the Gabellotto geological material has been weathered and altered in its oxide composition with time, making it less reliable to transform the results directly to archaeological samples to determine their origins.

On the whole, MS is an important method in establishing the provenance for archaeological ceramic wares. However, several instrumental methods have normally been used for a reliable provenance determination, especially elemental analysis methods and XRD for crystalline materials, as there are considerable variations in the appearance of ancient pottery coming even from the same site, as a result of variation in clay composition and manufacturing techniques.

The color of a glaze is often related to environmental conditions (e.g., Fe^{3+} in hematite gives a reddish-brown color, while Fe^{2+} in magnetite and wüstite [composition close to FeO] gives a grey-to-black surface). The valence state of iron is easily determined by Mössbauer spectroscopy. Nonmagnetic, high-spin (when the electrons of an atom tend to maximize their total magnetic moment) ferrous and high-spin ferric iron give different Mössbauer parameters (see Figure). Carbon, in graphite or in soot, also often gives rise to the black color, but MS, being insensitive to carbon, may be used to investigate the Fe^{2+} influence. In a Mössbauer study of Egyptian potsherds from ca. 2000 B.C. with differently

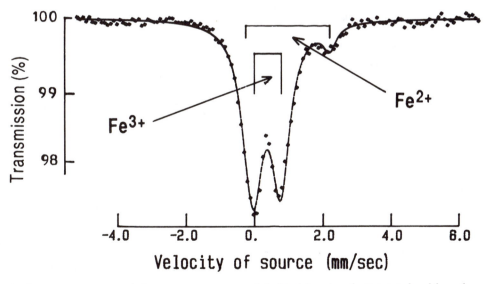

Mössbauer spectrum, recorded at room temperature, of the black interior of a Cypriote bowl from the Bronze Age. The Mössbauer profile is decomposed into two doublets, a strong, narrow peak coming from Fe^{3+} and a wide, but weaker, peak coming from Fe^{2+} (peak positions are indicated by the bar diagram). Here, the isomer shift for a site is the average value in mm/sec for the two peaks defining a doublet, and the quadrupole splitting is the span of the doublet. The full line is the fitted function, and the dots are the experimental data points. Figure by Tore Ericsson.

colored layers, it was found that the different colors (a reddish outer surface with a violet layer below, a dark grey core and a dark brown surface on the concave inside) represented different degrees of oxidation. As the clay was appearing fairly homogeneous throughout, the layered structure most probably had arisen during the firing process. In manufacturing Egyptian ceramics of this period, heat was used in a reducing atmosphere, and air was admitted into the kiln only in the final firing. MS showed a large amount of Fe^{2+} present in the core and in the dark brown face but none in the red surface layer. Probably the vessel was so positioned in the kiln that the oxidizing fumes in the final firing could not readily penetrate into the vessel (Riederer et al. 1979). An MS study of blacktopped Cypriote and Nubian potteries showed the black color to emanate from both Fe^{2+} in nonmagnetic compounds and carbon in free or organic form, as the black color was retained even after carbon was removed by combustion. The black parts of the vessels were probably achieved during the firing in a reducing atmosphere, with the vessels placed upside down in sand on a kiln floor (Makundi et al. 1989).

Besides kiln atmosphere (reducing or oxidizing environment) firing conditions (temperature and time) also influence the Mössbauer spectra in a characteristic way. Sometimes the Mössbauer parameters are determined by the maximum temperature achieved during the firing process of the pottery. In this case, the maximum temperature may be determined by repeated and increased heating of a sample from the ceramic ware, recording Mössbauer spectra (in general at room temperature) after each heat treatment. When the Mössbauer spectra change, the maximum firing temperature has been exceeded. A prerequisite is that the firing atmosphere is at least roughly the same as in the original firing. Researchers reheated the ancient Egyptian ceramics mentioned above for four hours at different temperatures and recorded Mössbauer spectra after each treatment. The nonmagnetic contribution of the oxidized outer layer remained constant for temperatures up to 750°C but decreased markedly above. Thus, the sherd had not been fired above that temperature in the ancient kiln during its final oxidizing heat treatment (Riederer et al. 1979).

Sometimes it is also possible to perform MS before and after heat treatment of the original clay, as obtained from the site of the ancient kiln. The variation of isomer shift, quadrupole splitting, and intensity of the nonmagnetic ferric components with firing temperature may then be determined. By comparing the Mössbauer parameters of the ancient sherds with the data obtained from the heat-treated clay, researchers determined the original firing temperatures of ancient unearthed wares from Xudun in China (Hsia et al. 1988).

Various particles in the pottery may disintegrate with time, depending on weathering conditions and natural radiation. Thus, the grain size of a certain component in the pottery may be used as a measure of age. Especially the presence of very fine oxide or hydroxide particles in the ancient ware may be detected using MS. Both hematite (Fe_2O_3) and goethite (FeOOH) normally show magnetic properties in MS recorded at room and lower temperatures. However, when the oxide or the hydroxide is in very small grains (less than 10 nm), the magnetic character shows up only in MS recorded at low temperatures. This transition temperature, called the *blocking temperature,* is lower for smaller grains. A study of archaeological samples from the mouth of the Amazon river found a lower blocking temperature for potteries ca. 3,000 years old than for samples ca. 1,500 years old (Danon et al. 1976). However, the differences in grain size are not easily translated into an age scale, as particle-size distribution of the original clay, firing temperature, and burial site also influence the size distribution.

In some of the Sn-119 Mössbauer studies, both CEMS and transmission MS have been used to determine the valence state of tin as a function of depth on bronze mirrors and cooking vessels from the Shang to the Tang Dynasty (ca. 1600 B.C.–A.D. 900). At the surface of bronzes, there is Sn^{4+} oxide, but, in the interior of the artifacts, Sn is normally in copper-tin-lead alloys. Special surface properties such as glare and color showing up on some artifacts did not seem to be related to the valence state of tin but could sometimes be attributed to the oxidation of copper.

Tore Ericsson

Further Readings

Cohen, R.L. (1976) Applications of Mössbauer spectroscopy. New York: Academic.

Danon, J., Enriquez, E., Mattievich, E., and Beltrao, M. (1976) Mössbauer study of aging effects in ancient pottery from the mouth of the Amazon River. Journal de Physique 37 (Colloque C6): 866–871.

Eissa, N.A., et al. (1979) Mössbauer effect study of the origin of ancient Qatari pottery. Indian Journal of Pure and Applied Physics 17:731–737.

Hsia, Y., Hu, Z; and Liu, R. (1988) Fe-57 Mössbauer effect studies of some ancient Chinese pottery from Xudun. Hyperfine Interactions 41:803–806.

Kostikas, A., Simoloulos, A., and Gangas, N.H. (1974) Mössbauer study of Mycenaean and Minoan pottery. Journal de Physique 35 (Colloque C6): 537–539.

Longworth, G. (1984) Studies of ceramics and archaeological materials. In G.J. Long (ed.): Mössbauer Spectroscopy Applied to Inorganic Chemistry, vol. 1, pp. 511–526. New York and London: Plenum.

Longworth, G. and Warren, S.E. (1979) The application of Mössbauer spectroscopy to the characterisation of western Mediterranean obsidian. Journal of Archaeological Science 6(2):179–193.

Makundi, I.N., Warn-Sperber, A., and Ericsson, T. (1989) A Mössbauer study of the black colour in early Cypriote and Nubian C-group black-topped pottery. Archaeometry 31:54–65.

Riederer, J., Wagner, U., and Wagner, F.E. (1979) Mössbauer study of firing conditions and ancient Egyptian ceramics with multicoloured layers. Radiochemical and Radioanalytical Letters 40:319–328.

Zheng, Y. and Hsia Y. (1991) Studies of archaeological problems by Mössbauer spectroscopy. Hyperfine Interactions 68:131–142.

M

N

National Historic Preservation Act (NHPA)

The national law under under which much of contemporary American archaeology is conducted for environmental review purposes. The National Historic Preservation Act (Public Law 89–665 and amendments thereto; 16 U.S. Code 470 et seq.) was enacted in 1966. It has had major amendments, primarily additions to expand the effect of the law or to clarify its implementation, in 1980 and 1992. The law contains a strong policy statement supporting historic preservation activities and programs. Section 2 of the statute calls for the federal government

> in partnership with States, local governments, Indian tribes, and private organizations and individuals to . . . use measures, including financial and technical assistance, to foster conditions under which our modern society and our prehistoric and historic resources can exist in productive harmony and fulfill the social, economic, and other requirements of present and future generations (Sec. 2 [1]).

This subsection of the statute highlights two important aspects of national historic-preservation policy in the United States. First, historic preservation, including public archaeology and archaeological preservation, is an activity that occurs at all levels of government, federal, state, and local, and that also involves private organizations and individuals. It is not the province of a single national government agency or national museum. This multitude of involved public and private parties can sometimes make a comprehensive description of archaeological and historic preservation in the United States complicated, but it also has the value of giving many organizations and individuals some responsibility for preserving archaeological and historic sites, structures, and other kinds of historic properties.

Another key aspect of U.S. preservation embodied by this subsection text is that preservation is to be considered as one aspect of modern life (i.e., contemporary development and economic activities). This can be seen as a double-edged sword. Archaeological and historic properties often must be considered when plans are made for modern development or economic activity; however, their preservation is not an assured part of the outcome of these activities.

Title I of the statute established the National Register of Historic Places as a national listing of *historic properties* (i.e., districts, sites, buildings, structures, and objects significant in American history, architecture, archaeology, engineering, and culture). The statutory language and the regulations and procedures that implement the National Register of Historic Places have been written to include historic and prehistoric archaeological sites within the definition of historic properties. This inclusive approach and broad definition have enabled those concerned with public archaeology and archaeological preservation to work within the general umbrella of the national historic preservation program.

Title I also expanded the level of federal concern to include the preservation of historic properties of local and state significance, an expansion of the concern with nationally significant resources expressed in the 1935

Historic Sites Act. This title also established state historic preservation officers (SHPO) as partners in the national historic-preservation program and describes how the SHPO function, or portions of this function, can be assumed by local governments or Indian tribes in certain circumstances.

Section 106 of the statute also is contained in Title I. Implementation of this short, one-paragraph-long section has had a major impact on the structure and functioning of archaeology and archaeological preservation in the United States. Section 106 requires that all federal agencies provide the Advisory Council on Historic Preservation, which is established in Title II of the statute, an opportunity to comment on any undertaking for which an agency has direct or indirect jurisdiction when the undertaking has an effect on a historic property listed on, or eligible for listing on, the National Register of Historic Places. In practice, this has meant that federal agencies, or state, local, and private organizations that are involved in federal undertakings, have been required to identify and assess archaeological sites that their planned actions might affect. This has required tens of thousands of archaeological investigations since the mid-1970s, when the procedures for implementing Section 106 were established in regulations (36 CFR 800). These investigations have been undertaken in a variety of ways. In some cases, federal agencies responsible for complying with the NHPA have hired archaeologists, creating their own professional staffs to meet these requirements. In other cases, federal agencies have contracted with consulting firms or with universities to undertake studies necessary to meet their requirements.

One result has been that professional archaeologists have come to be employed as frequently by public agencies or private consulting and engineering firms as by academic institutions. During this period, hundreds of millions of dollars in government funds have paid for tens of thousands of archaeological investigations, including general archaeological overviews, site discovery and evaluation studies, and extensive excavation of individual or groups of sites that would have been subject to destruction by public undertakings (e.g., McManamon et al. 1993).

The statute also envisions that all federal agencies should develop their own programs to care for historic resources under their jurisdiction or control or that are affected by their undertakings. Section 110, which was expanded and enhanced by the 1992 amendments, describes the responsibilities as including the identification, evaluation, nomination to the National Register of Historic Places, and protection of historic resources. In the past, agencies have been far more active in complying with Section 106 of the statute than with Section 110. Perhaps the newly amended text of this section will provoke greater attention to the responsibilities that it describes.

Title II of the statute established the Advisory Council on Historic Preservation, an independent federal agency composed of twenty members, including the secretaries of Interior and Agriculture and four other departments. Also on the council are elected officials and citizens appointed by the president. The council and its staff play an important role in the national historic preservation program, especially in the day-to-day implementation of Section 106, but also in providing programmatic advice to federal agencies and training in historic preservation methods, techniques, and procedures.

Title IV of the statute, newly added in the 1992 amendments, established the National Center for Preservation Technology and Training. In so doing, Congress recognized ". . . the complexity of technical problems encountered in preserving historic properties and the lack of adequate distribution of technical information to preserve such properties" (Sec. 401). The center was established to ". . . coordinate and promote research [in historic preservation], distribute information, and provide training about preservation skills and technologies . . ." (Sec. 401).

Francis P. McManamon

See also ARCHEOLOGICAL RESOURCES PROTECTION ACT (ARPA); CULTURAL RESOURCE MANAGEMENT (CRM)

Further Readings

Glass, J.A. (1990) The Beginnings of a New National Historic Preservation Program, 1957 to 1969. Nashville: American Association for State and Local History.

King, T., Parker Hickman, F.P., and Berg, G. (1977) Anthropology in Historic Preservation: Caring for Culture's Clutter. New York: Academic.

McManamon, F.P., Knoll, P.C., Knudson, R., Smith, G.S., and Waldbauer, R.C. (1993)

Federal Archeological Programs and Activities: The Secretary of the Interior's Report to Congress. Washington, D.C.: National Park Service, Department of the Interior.

Native American Graves Protection and Repatriation Act (NAGPRA)

The national law that specifies special treatment for Native American human remains, funerary objects, sacred objects, and objects of cultural patrimony. The Native American Graves Protection and Repatriation Act (Public Law 101–601; 25 U.S. Code 3001–3013), enacted in 1990, describes the rights of Native American lineal descendants, Indian tribes, and Native Hawaiian organizations with respect to the treatment, repatriation, and disposition of Native American human remains, funerary objects, sacred objects, and objects of cultural patrimony, referred to collectively in the statute as cultural items, with which they can show a relationship of lineal descent or cultural affiliation. One major purpose of this statute (Sec. 5–7) is to require that federal agencies and museums receiving federal funds inventory holdings of Native American human remains and funerary objects and provide written summaries of other cultural items. The agencies and museums must consult with Indian tribes and Native Hawaiian organizations to attempt to reach agreements on the repatriation or other disposition of these remains and objects. Once lineal descent or cultural affiliation has been established and, in some cases, the right of possession also has been demonstrated, lineal descendants, affiliated Indian tribes, or affiliated Native Hawaiian organizations normally make the final determination about the disposition of cultural items. Disposition may take many forms, from reburial to long-term curation, according to the wishes of the lineal descendent(s) or culturally affiliated tribe(s).

The second major purpose of the statute is to provide greater protection for Native American burial sites and more careful control over the removal of Native American human remains, funerary objects, sacred objects, and items of cultural patrimony on federal and tribal lands. NAGPRA requires that Indian tribes and Native Hawaiian organizations be consulted whenever archaeological investigations encounter, or are expected to

encounter, Native American cultural items or when such items are unexpectedly discovered on federal or tribal lands (Sec. 3). Excavation or removal of any such items also must be done under procedures required by the 1979 Archaeological Resources Protection Act (Sec. 3 [c][1]). This NAGPRA requirement is likely to encourage the in situ preservation of archaeological sites or at least the portions of them that contain burials or other kinds of cultural items. In many situations, it will be advantageous for federal agencies and tribes undertaking land-modifying activities on their lands to engage in careful consultations with traditional users of the land and intensive archaeological surveys to locate and then protect unmarked Native American graves, cemeteries, or other places where cultural items might be located.

NAGPRA also: (1) stipulates that illegal trafficking in human remains and cultural items may result in criminal penalties (Sec. 4); (2) authorizes the secretary of the Interior to administer a grants program to assist museums and Indian tribes in complying with certain requirements of the statute (Sec. 10); (3) requires the secretary of the Interior to establish a review committee to provide advice and assistance in carrying out key provisions of the statute (Sec. 8); (4) authorizes the secretary of the Interior to penalize museums that fail to comply with the statute (Sec. 9); and (5) directs the secretary to develop regulations in consultation with this review committee (Sec. 13).

Cultural affiliation is a key concept for implementing this statute; it is a cornerstone for repatriation requests and for asserting claims related to new discoveries on federal or tribal land. The statute defines cultural affiliation as "a relationship of shared group identity which can be reasonably traced historically or prehistorically between a present day Indian tribe or Native Hawaiian organization and an identifiable earlier group" (Sec. 2[2]). This implies that contemporary groups of Native Americans of diverse backgrounds who voluntarily associate together for some purpose or purposes are not viewed as proper claimants under the provisions of the statute.

Whether new discoveries from federal or tribal land or existing collections are being considered, it is not necessary for the agency, museum, lineal descendent, Indian tribe, or Native Hawaiian organization to establish beyond all doubt which descendent or Native American group is a proper claimant for purposes of repatriation. This is true in situations involving cultural items in collections, as well as when dealing with newly discovered materials.

The types of evidence which may be offered to show cultural affiliation may include, but are not limited to, geographical, kinship, biological, archaeological, anthropological, linguistic, oral tradition, or historical evidence or other relevant information or expert opinion. The requirement of continuity between present day Indian tribes and materials from historic or prehistoric Indian tribes is intended to ensure that the claimant has a reasonable connection with the materials. Where human remains and funerary objects are concerned, the Committee is aware that it may be extremely difficult, unfair, or even impossible in many instances for claimants to show an absolute continuity from present day Indian tribes to older, prehistoric remains without some reasonable gaps in the historic or prehistoric record. In such instances, a finding of cultural affiliation should be based upon an overall evaluation of the totality of the circumstances and evidence pertaining to the connection between the claimant and the material being claimed and should not be precluded solely because of gaps in the record (Senate 1990:9).

Executing the provisions of the Native American Graves Protection and Repatriation Act involves three primary participants: federal agencies, all museums receiving federal funds (including state, local, and private institutions), and Indian tribes and Native Hawaiian organizations. Oversight of, and directions for, the activities required of these three types of organizations are to be provided by the secretary of the Interior and the NAGPRA review committee established by the statute.

The kinds of remains and the artifacts covered by provisions of the statute are: (1) human remains and associated funerary objects; (2) unassociated funerary objects; (3) sacred objects; and (4) objects of cultural patrimony.

Human remains are not defined in the statute, and, consequently, all kinds of Native American human remains are covered. This means isolated human bones, teeth, or other kinds of bodily remains that may have been disturbed from a burial site are still subject to the provisions of this statute.

Associated funerary objects are objects reasonably believed to have been placed with human remains as part of a death rite or ceremony. The use of the adjective "associated" refers to the fact that these items retain their association with the human remains with which they were found and that these human remains can be located. It applies to all objects that are stored together, as well as objects for which adequate records exist permitting a reasonable reassociation between the funerary objects and the human remains with which they were buried.

It frequently occurs in archaeological sites that artifacts seemingly from burials were not placed with the human remains as part of a death rite, but rather were introduced into the burial later by natural processes or cultural activities unrelated to death rites or ceremonies. These latter objects would not be considered funerary objects.

Unassociated funerary objects are items that ". . . as a part of a death rite or ceremony of a culture are reasonably believed to have been placed with individual human remains either at the time of death or later . . . ," but for which the human remains are not in the possession or control of the museum or federal agency. These objects also must meet one of two further conditions. They must be identified by a preponderance of the evidence as either ". . . related to specific individuals or families or to known human remains . . ." or ". . . as having been removed from a specific burial site of an individual culturally affiliated with a particular Indian tribe" (Sec. 2[3][B]).

Sacred objects are defined in the statute as ". . . specific ceremonial objects which are needed by traditional Native American religious leaders for the practice of traditional Native American religions by their present-day adherents . . ." (Sec. 2[3][C]). Further discussion of this term is supplied by the report of the Senate Select Committee on Indian Affairs:

There has been some concern expressed that any object could be imbued with sacredness in the eyes of a Native American, from an ancient pottery sherd to an arrowhead. The Committee does not intend this result. The primary purpose of the object is that the object must be used in a Native American religious ceremony in order to fall within the protection afforded by the bill (Senate 1990:7).

Objects of cultural patrimony are defined in the statute as having ". . . ongoing historical, traditional, or cultural importance central to the Native American group or culture itself, rather than property owned by an individual Native American, and which, therefore, cannot be alienated, appropriated, or conveyed by any individual . . ." (Sec. 2[3][D]). The key provision in this definition is whether the property was of such central importance to the tribe or group that it was owned communally. The potential vagueness of this term again produced comment by the Senate committee:

> The Committee intends this term to refer to only those items that have such great importance to an Indian tribe or to the Native Hawaiian culture that they cannot be conveyed, appropriated or transferred by an individual member. Objects of Native American cultural patrimony would include items such as Zuni War Gods, the Wampum belts of the Iroquois, and other objects of a similar character and significance to the Indian tribe as a whole (Senate 1990:7–8).

Many objects in archaeological or ethnographic collections are not subject to the statute because they never had a burial, funerary, religious, or cultural-patrimonial context in the culture of which they were part. Such objects would be retained in existing repositories with appropriate treatments and care. When archaeological investigations or unanticipated discoveries on federal or tribal land result in the recovery of such items, they are to be treated and disposed of according to the requirements of the appropriate archaeological or historic preservation laws.

Francis P. McManamon

See also ARCHEOLOGICAL RESOURCES PROTECTION ACT (ARPA); CULTURAL RESOURCE MANAGEMENT (CRM); REBURIAL, INTERNATIONAL PERSPECTIVES

Further Readings

Pace, J.A., ed. (1992) Symposium: The Native American Graves Protection and Repatriation Act of 1990 and State Repatriation-Related Legislation. Arizona State Law Journal 24(1):xi–562.
United States Senate, Select Committee on Indian Affairs (1990) Senate Report 473, 101st Cong., 2nd Sess. Washington, D.C.: GPO.

Natural Stratigraphy

The excavation and analysis of readily visible depositional layers. Natural stratigraphy is a method of excavation in which clearly observable strata are slowly and usually sequentially peeled off one another. The term *natural* also implies that the depositional layers retain some of their original integrity and that the material associated with each layer is broadly contemporaneous. For instance, during the excavation of a structure containing several successively occupied and clearly identifiable floors, archaeologists are likely to excavate each floor as a natural layer. Each floor would be fully excavated, regardless of the variation in associated deposits. Interpreting behavioral patterns associated with each of the layers is assisted by their excavation as natural units, or, in this case, as floors. Many archaeologists distinguish natural stratigraphy from metrical or arbitrary stratigraphy, which is a method of excavation in which layers of uniform thickness, such as 10 or 20 cm, are imposed by excavators at sites that do not possess clearly observable depositional layers. The relative merits of natural versus arbitrary stratigraphy are the subject of debate, but most archaeologists prefer to follow visible depositional layers. Excavating visible layers is not without its difficulties, however; surfaces may slope sharply, and deep pits associated with floors usually require complete excavation.

Edward Luby

See also METRICAL STRATIGRAPHY; STRATIFICATION; STRATIGRAPHY

Further Readings

Barker, P. (1993) Techniques of Archaeological Excavation, 3rd ed. London: Batsford.
Joukowsky, M. (1980) A Complete Manual of Field Archaeology. Englewood Cliffs, NJ: Prentice-Hall.

N

Nautical Archaeology

The archaeological investigation of human use of waterways. Other, related terms that have been used include *marine archaeology, maritime archaeology,* and most recently, *hydroarchaeology,* but the field should not be confused with underwater archaeology, even though the majority of modern nautical archaeological excavations have been under water. Nautical archaeology is most commonly pursued through the excavation of ships and boats, including wrecks, derelicts, and deliberate burials, but other types of sites can be equally important. Harbor works, port cities, whaling stations, locks, bridges, and fishing weirs have all contributed valuable information to the history of seafaring, fishing, commerce, naval warfare, and technology.

History

Although old ships and boats had been found in the course of public-works excavations during the eighteenth century, if not before, the real beginnings of the discipline can be traced to 1822, when the Dutch naval architect Cornelis Glavimans directed the excavation and recording of the remains of a medieval vessel discovered near Rotterdam. Glavimans built a model of his reconstruction of the remains and published the results of his research within three years. Although the excavation predated the development of many archaeological techniques now considered standard, the recording and analysis of the hull remains themselves are of extremely high quality and are still useful to scholars studying the history of shipbuilding.

In the 1850s, Conrad Engelhardt's excavations in the Nydam peat bog (then in Denmark, now in Germany) revealed the remains of several Iron Age/Migration Period vessels buried as part of one or more votive offerings. The Nydam vessels became the first in a series of spectacular ship and boat burials excavated in Scandinavia during the second half of the nineteenth century, culminating in the Gokstad and Oseberg ships (the latter actually excavated in 1903), two Viking vessels interred as tombs for their owners. The burials stimulated popular interest in ancient ships and prompted scholarly inquiry into the history of European (especially northern European) shipping and shipbuilding. The nineteenth century also saw the beginnings of maritime ethnography in the writings of Admiral F.E. Paris, who published a study of non-European shipbuilding in 1841 and his *Souvenirs de Marine* in 1882. The years around the turn of the twentieth century also produced several finds of derelict vessels and shipwrecks, such as the Roman hulls found at the County Hall in London and in Bruges, Belgium, and the pre-Roman riverboat discovered in Ljubljana (Laibach), Slovenia. While many of these finds were poorly preserved, they offered a different perspective on the maritime past, since they were clearly working vessels rather than elite transports deliberately buried.

The period between the World Wars saw a more systematic approach to nautical archaeology, with carefully planned and executed excavations of more burials, such as the Anglian ship grave at Sutton Hoo, England, and the first thorough investigations of other types of nautical sites. The extensive excavation of the old harbor at Kalmar, Sweden, in the 1930s stands out, with detailed information recovered from more than twenty derelict vessels dating as far back as the late thirteenth century A.D. In Mussolini's Italy, Lake Nemi was partly drained, so that two enormous first-century A.D. barges, the largest wooden objects to survive from antiquity, could be hauled out of the lake and installed in a purpose-built museum. The Nemi barges provided the first clear information on how ancient ships were constructed, but the ships were destroyed during the Second World War before the study of the remains was complete. The 1930s also marked the beginnings of excavation of the medieval emporia at Dorestad in the Netherlands and Haithabu (Hedeby) on the Danish Peninsula, which provided the first archaeological indications of the role of ports in medieval maritime commerce.

While the Second World War interrupted archaeological work in most of the world, Dutch archaeologists were allowed to continue some work under the German occupation, and it is during the war that one of the great long-term programs in nautical archaeology began. In the process of planning the Zuiderzee Project, the diking off and draining of the southern arm of the North Sea that had for centuries provided a natural highway in the northern Netherlands, it was realized that the reclaimed land would probably contain the remains of early medieval villages known to have existed in the region, so some provision was made for archaeological investigations of the newly reclaimed land. In 1944, during the first of these excavations, the remains of a medieval ship were discovered and documented. The results of this excavation were published shortly thereafter by Pieter J.R. Modderman, the Dutch archaeologist, and this little cog, known as M 107 after the number of the plot in which it was found, became the first of over 400 shipwrecks and derelicts investigated in the polders (reclaimed land). After the war, a separate archaeological branch of the scientific division responsible for research in the polders was formed, and this branch, originally the Museum for Ship Archaeology, now the Netherlands Institute for Ship Archaeology (NISA), has maintained a steady program of survey, excavation, and publication since the 1950s.

Another wartime development, the invention by Jacques Cousteau and Emil Gagnan of the portable demand regulator for breathing compressed air, led to the great revolution in nautical archaeology after the war. Previous excavations had all been on land, using conventional terrestrial techniques, and, although there had been some diving on submerged sites using old-style hard-hat equipment, the heavy bronze helmet and lead shoes of the prewar diver were hardly conducive to careful, detailed work under water. In addition, the majority of hulls found on land (with the exception of the vessels excavated in the reclaimed land of the Zuiderzee) were either deliberate burials or derelicts and, as such, did not provide a complete picture of maritime trade. By making the seafloor and its wrecks of fully laden merchant vessels easily accessible to a free-swimming, lightly equipped diver, Cousteau and Gagnan's invention greatly expanded the potential reach of the archaeologist. Unfortunately, it also expanded the reach of the looter, and it was not long before hundreds of wrecks in the warm, shallow waters of the Mediterranean coast were being plundered of amphoras and other artifacts for the antiquities trade.

The archaeological potential of the aqualung was not immediately realized or was dismissed by traditional scholars as impractical or irrelevant, but the salvage by Cousteau of two Roman wrecks (originally misinterpreted as a single ship) off Grand Congloué in 1955 provided immediate evidence of the standard of preservation to be expected under water. In the late 1950s, the Danish National Museum had begun the underwater excavation of five Viking ships deliberately sunk near Skuldelev (Roskilde), but it had abandoned underwater work as impractical and had completed the excavation by building a cofferdam around the site, draining it, and employing conventional land techniques. In 1959, the journalist Peter Throckmorton, who had discovered a number of wrecks off the Turkish coast, took the decisive step of informing a major archaeological institution, the University Museum in Philadelphia, that one of the wrecks, a Late Bronze Age ship off Cape Gelidonya, was of great historical importance and should be excavated by professional archaeologists. The University of Pennsylvania agreed to participate and sent George F. Bass, a graduate student specializing in the Aegean Bronze Age, to direct a season of investigation. The site, which consisted of the tools and raw materials of an itinerant bronzesmith, was excavated during the summer of 1960 in the first controlled archaeological excavation completed under water. The results of the excavation were published in 1967 as a conventional scholarly catalog and interpretation of the finds. In the following decade, in a series of excavations off the Turkish island of Yassı Ada, Bass and his colleagues, a growing body of professional archaeologists, photographers, draftsmen, and conservators, developed many of the underwater techniques now considered standard in the field.

The 1950s and early 1960s also witnessed several grand projects, partly sponsored by national governments, to recover the remains of submerged or buried ships. In Egypt, the opening of a pit next to the Great Pyramid at Giza revealed the complete remains of a disassembled riverboat, which were conserved and reassembled to reveal a royal barge of the Old Kingdom, complete with deck cabin and sun canopy. The Skuldelev ships in Denmark were paralleled by the German excavation in 1962 in the Weser River of a nearly complete fourteenth-century cog near Bremen. This ship, sunk in a flood before construction had even finished, provided archaeologists and historians with the first clear look at the type of ship that had been the backbone of the Hanseatic fleets. By far the grandest of these projects was the raising of the Swedish warship *Wasa*, sunk in

1628 and successfully refloated in 1960. The preservation of organic matter, from hull timbers and carvings to sailcloth and butter, created a worldwide sensation and clearly demonstrated the potential of underwater archaeology to the public.

Concurrently, archaeologists began to explore the possibilities of underwater excavation in bodies of water as diverse as the Caribbean Sea and the fast-flowing rivers along the U.S.-Canadian border. In this period, much of the emphasis in research was on field technique, as archaeologists attempted to develop the most effective methods of finding sites, mapping, removing overburden, and conserving waterlogged artifacts. The rapid development of field technique was exemplified by Michael Katzev's excavation of a Hellenistic merchantman off Kyrenia, Cyprus, in the late 1960s and the conservation and reassembly of the well-preserved hull remains by Richard Steffy in the early 1970s. By the 1970s, with improvements in field methodology and increasing academic acceptance of the discipline as a valid avenue of archaeological research, research goals began to shift to more traditional concerns of site interpretation. In 1972, a dedicated journal, the *International Journal of Nautical Archaeology and Underwater Exploration* (*IJNA*) was launched, and, by 1976, the first graduate program with a specific emphasis on nautical archaeology was established by Bass at Texas A&M University. This was followed by programs in North Carolina, Scotland, Australia, Sweden, Israel, and the Netherlands.

By the 1980s, nautical archaeology had successfully merged with the archaeological mainstream in many areas. State archaeologists' offices in many coastal states included a staff underwater or nautical archaeologist (the first was appointed in Texas in the early 1970s); many states had enacted legislation to bring the protection of submerged cultural resources into line with existing cultural resource management programs; contract archaeology firms included underwater divisions; and archaeologists specializing in nautical subjects began to appear on the faculties of conventional anthropology departments. National legislation to protect historic wrecks was not enacted in the United States until 1987 (the Abandoned Shipwreck Act), but other countries had begun protecting historic underwater sites in the 1970s.

Theory

Nautical archaeology has no specific body of theory as such, although Richard A. Gould and others have tried to formulate a theoretical background; a recent (Gale 1993) article in the *International Journal of Nautical Archaeology* has proposed a new name for the field (*hydroarchaeology*) with a theoretical and methodological structure to justify the term on the basis of the integration of topics of research, location of research, and field methods. After the early, formative years of the discipline, in which the emphasis was on field methodology, nautical archaeologists have engaged in the theoretical debates specific to their area of research. Scholars working on ancient and medieval shipwrecks in the Mediterranean have tended to retain the historical particularism common to the terrestrial archaeology of their periods, while those working on Colonial American ports and ships have debated the relative merits of historical versus anthropological approaches. Nautical archaeologists in England in the 1970s were much influenced by the New Archaeology, while continental specialists have often been preoccupied with the problems of taxonomy and classification popular in Europe.

One of the factors that set nautical sites apart from much terrestrial archaeology, and the theoretical structure associated with it, is the closed, catastrophic nature of most shipwreck sites, which lends itself to a more particularistic research design. Rather than a long period of habitation, a typical shipwreck represents an instant in which everything found is exactly contemporaneous. As such, ships provide snapshots of the cultures that produced them, with direct and indirect clues to prevailing economic, political, social, and technological conditions, in addition to the more obvious information on shipbuilding, material culture, and seafaring technology, but broad trends cannot be deduced from a single site. Compounding the problem is the relatively small number of sites so far investigated. The theoretical underpinnings of modern terrestrial archaeology are based on a large body of data accumulated over more than a century of careful excavation in many areas. In comparison, the number of shipwrecks excavated for any particular region or culture is normally not yet large enough to permit the development of broad, anthropological conclusions about human behavior at sea. Possible exceptions to this limitation are the Roman Mediterranean and the Zuiderzee, where a sufficient number of sites (a statistically significant sample) have been excavated that it is possible to draw some conclusions about what is typical for a particular period and to identify broad trends.

Research goals in nautical archaeology have tended to focus on a few general areas. Most notable of these are the history of ship construction and its related technologies (e.g., anchor design, tool use) and the structures and commodities of maritime commerce. Since the mid-1980s, there has been an increasing effort to relate the findings of ship excavations to cultural trends outside the strictly maritime. Shipwrecks can provide types of evidence uncommon on land sites; for example, the Ulu Burun shipwreck, excavated between 1984 and 1994 by Bass and Cemal Pulak off the southern coast of Turkey, has produced some of the clearest evidence for the composition and form of important Bronze Age raw materials, such as aromatic resins, glass, copper, and tin. As the field continues to develop, it will be less concerned with the minutiae of ships and cargoes and more with how seafaring reflects and influences broader social, political, economic, and environmental trends in parent cultures.

Methodology

Excavation strategies for most ship sites differ somewhat from those employed on typical terrestrial sites, or even on submerged coastal habitation sites, where random sampling and partial excavation are tied to area survey and environmental reconstruction. Shipwrecks are generally small, closed sites in an alien environment and are often characterized by an extreme degree of compartmentalization. Random sampling and partial excavation run the very great risk of producing a badly distorted picture of the site and the culture that produced it by missing key areas of structure, cargo, or living space. In addition, partial excavation necessitates leaving the hull remains largely imbedded in the matrix, which prevents any kind of detailed examination of the structure. A complete understanding of the site can be achieved only by full excavation followed by recovery and study of the hull remains. This is not always practical, especially with ships with much more than 15 m of preserved hull structure, but it is the ultimate goal of many long-term projects. Even where the hull will not be raised, it is common to uncover it completely or at least down one entire side so that the maximum amount of information can be collected. Where partial excavation is practiced, it is normally part of a preliminary survey, and it has been determined that a primary test trench should be dug across the center of the remains, with secondary pits or trenches at the ends. The central trench will provide immediate information on cargo types and basic hull structure, if it survives, and living spaces are normally located at the ends of the hull.

There are few field techniques specific to nautical sites per se; the appropriate terrestrial or underwater techniques are applied as needed. There are some variations of conventional techniques necessitated or encouraged by the problems of working with hull structures. Where the structure is well preserved and not broken up into pieces lying at odd angles, it has been found that aligning the grid to the centerline of the hull allows the excavation to proceed more efficiently. The regular, rectilinear layout of the frames in most ships is a ready-made grid that divides the interior into a series of equal-size bays that can be used effectively to locate artifacts and orient excavators. The process of documenting the hull structure itself has benefited from centuries of naval practice at recording the shape of captured or purchased ships, so that conventional naval architectural methods of taking offsets are preferred for recording hull cross-sections.

Frederick Hocker

See also ABANDONED SHIPWRECK ACT (ASA); UNDERWATER ARCHAEOLOGY

Further Readings

Basch, L. (1972) Ancient wrecks and the archaeology of ships. International Journal of Nautical Archaeology 1:1–48.

Bass, G.F. (1967) Cape Gelidonya: A Bronze Age Shipwreck (Transactions of the American Philosophical Society, new series, v. 57, pt. 8). Philadelphia: American Philosophical Society.

Gale, A. (1993) Hydroarchaeology: A subject framework. International Journal of Nautical Archaeology 22:209–217.

Gould, R., ed. (1983) Shipwreck Anthropology. Albuquerque: University of New Mexico Press.

Greenhill, B. (1976) Archaeology of the Boat: A New Introductory Study. London and Middletown: Wesleyan University Press.

Muckelroy, K. (1978) Maritime Archaeology. Cambridge: Cambridge University Press.

New/Processual Archaeology

Distinguished from the "old" cultural-history approach to archaeology by its use of scientific methods to discover the processes that produce and modify archaeological materials. Although Walter Taylor's *A Study of Archeology* (1948) prefigures views associated with the New Archaeology, the label specifically applies to the approach taken in the 1960s by Sally and Lewis R. Binford (1968) and David L. Clarke (1968). New Archaeologists tried to reorient the discipline from spatial and temporal classifications of archaeological materials to scientific investigations of prehistoric cultural development and behavior. Their program demands changes in both the form and the substance of archaeological reasoning. Using the latest technological resources and methods of quantitative analysis, New Archaeology proposes new ways to collect data and to reason about them. It also suggests and tries to confirm novel theoretical principles and to use them in scientific explanations.

Matters of Form

Drawing on the philosophy of science, especially Carl G. Hempel's work on confirmation and explanation, for their account of the scientific method, Patty J. Watson, Steven A. LeBlanc, and Charles L. Redman (1971) urged their colleagues to follow the hypothetico-deductive (H-D) model of confirmation and the deductive-nomological (D-N) model of explanation. They argued that, by structuring research in this way, archaeologists could substitute well-founded scientific explanations of cultural change for mere imaginative reconstructions of past lifeways. Conforming to these models of confirmation and explanation requires archaeologists (1) to formulate explicit hypotheses prior to collecting data; (2) to test hypotheses by deriving predictions from them and checking those predictions against the data; and (3) to estab-

lish *laws* on the basis of such tests. With *laws* in hand, archaeologists can explain the phenomena by showing that they follow deductively from the laws together with appropriate initial (or boundary) conditions.

New Archaeologists rejected the simplistic inductive generalizations and appeals to authority that they found in works of some of their predecessors. Such criticism, along with the commitment to H-D confirmation and D-N explanation, resulted in the movement's being called *deductive archaeology*. This label is misleading because archaeology, as any discipline that seeks knowledge of unobservable portions of the world, must depend on inductive reasoning. Properly understood, *induction* refers not only to framing generalizations on the basis of a few instances, but also to any inference with a conclusion that goes beyond merely recombining information contained in the premises. The H-D method of confirming hypotheses, despite its name, is an inductive method because, whereas predictions can be *deduced* from a particular hypothesis (plus auxiliary assumptions about underlying theories and the observational setup), that hypothesis is only inductively supported by the truth of the predictions. This is because the same true predictions may be derivable from other, incompatible hypothesis as well. For example, assume that methods of dating bone are reliable. Finding 30,000-year-old bone artifacts in Beringia provides only inductive support for human presence at that time. Bones heaved from the permafrost after lying there for 18,000 years and worked by humans who arrived only 12,000 years ago would account for the same observation. Scientists who evaluate hypotheses must consider not only their predictive success, but also the initial plausibility of the hypotheses, their conformity with accepted scientific theories, and the status of competing hypotheses.

Matters of Substance

Philosophical models of confirmation and explanation, such as the H-D and D-N models, focus on formal or logical requirements of scientific method instead of on the substantive content of scientific laws or explanatory principles. The only substantive feature of Hempel's D-N model, for example, is the requirement that the explanatory premises be true. The philosophical model of explanation is indifferent to the content of the explanatory principles, which is a matter left to those with appropriate knowledge of the field of study. An explanation fits the D-N pattern if it can be construed as an argument in which the fact to be explained follows deductively from the explanatory premises, which must include at least one universal law. Thus, rival models of explanation with respect to their substance or content, such as a diffusionist model of the spread of agriculture and an opposing systems model, could both be framed in the same logical D-N pattern.

New Archaeologists appropriately attend to the substantive features of archaeological explanations as well as their formal features. Thus, they reject some hypotheses as unsuitable for testing and worthless as explanatory principles. In the early days of New Archaeology, for example, they rejected most explanatory hypotheses that referred to beliefs and desires of people known only through their archaeological remains. On scientific grounds, they preferred hypotheses that referred to environmental constraints and to patterned distribution of archaeological materials. That is to say, New Archaeologists argued that the materials and relationships that form the archaeological record could support reliable inferences concerning such matters as the subsistence economy and gross features of social organization. For example, in light of ethnohistoric and ethnographic support for the assumption that females make pottery for domestic use, James J.F. Deetz and William A. Longacre argued that patterned distribution in the design elements of household pottery could support inferences about postmarital residence patterns. Nevertheless, Deetz and Longacre did not attempt to reconstruct prehistoric belief systems on the basis of those design elements.

In the 1960s and early 1970s, explanations offered by New Archaeologists focused on functional and social aspects of human behavior, ignoring, for the most part, its ideological and symbolic components, on the grounds that paleopsychology was not a scientific activity. Acutely cognizant of cultural variation, New Archaeologists doubted that they could find laws concerning beliefs, desires, symbolic meanings, or ritual behavior of humans. They were reluctant to speculate, therefore, about the *meaning* that pottery-design elements had for the people who produced them.

New Archaeology's concern with environmental and evolutionary principles of culture formation reflects the heritage of Leslie White and Julian Steward. New Archaeologists who embrace *systems explanations* of the archaeological record adopt many evolutionary hypotheses. Unlike diffusionist explanations that account for cultural change and innovation by looking for an external source and tracing its spread (diffusion) to other cultures, systemic explanations focus on the following internal features: (1) multiple interacting causes that can reinforce or counterbalance one another; (2) negative-feedback mechanisms that promote stability in the face of pressures for change; and (3) positive-feedback mechanisms that amplify some factors, allowing for change from within the system.

Systems explanations resemble the structural-functionalist explanations of Alfred R. Radcliffe-Brown in some respects. Both emphasize the contributions of interacting components to the maintenance of a system. Both also emphasize the similarities between biological organisms and social structures. The older functional explanations and the new systems explanations differ, however, in their ability to explain changes in a system. Radcliffe-Brown essentially ignored the issue of changes in prehistoric cultures—which he thought could not be documented or explained without historical documents—and focused on mechanisms that enable systems to preserve their structural stability. In line with philosophical and scientific views of his time, such as those of Ernst Mach, he believed that one could find (noncausal) *laws* by investigating functional relationships among components of systems. Structural-functionalist explanations have long been criticized for their failure to account for obvious changes in social systems, not all of which result in the system's disintegration. Because of archaeologists' concern with explaining change over time, structural-functionalist explanations are inadequate. Contemporary systems explanations differ in several ways. First, they treat the archaeological record on a par with historical documents as a source of evidence; second, they provide a mechanism—positive feedback—to explain changes. Whereas structural-functionalist explanations recognized negative-feedback mechanisms, such as joking relationships, that maintained stability, they could not account for nondisintegrative changes in systems. Third, systems explanations emphasize the significance of humans' physical environment, as well as their social environment. A central tenet of the New Archaeology is that societies cannot be considered in isolation from the physical surroundings that both shape and are shaped by them. In contemporary terms, social structures are never closed systems. By supplementing negative-feedback mechanisms with positive feedback, by broadening the notion of a system to include the physical environment of a society, and by analyzing the archaeological record for appropriate evidence, systems explanations offer a satisfactory theoretical framework for organizing and extending archaeological knowledge.

Because of Radcliffe-Brown's pessimistic views concerning prehistory in the absence of documentary evidence, the older, cultural-historical archaeologists employed diffusionist models of explanation rather than structural-functional models. That is to say, they tried to explain the presence of some feature in the archeological record by trying to find and date the first instance of the feature and then to trace the path by which the idea for the feature traveled to the place where it was found. Systems explanations thus differ from both diffusionist and structural-functional explanations. Since different data are needed to support diffusionist and systematic explanations of stability and change in the archaeological record, research strategies and problems for diffusionists and New Archaeologists differ. For example, instead of looking for the source of the first cultivars and the paths by which they traveled, Kent V. Flannery, a proponent of the systems approach, employs both negative and positive feedback to explain how, over thousands of years, an agricultural food-procurement system gradually developed from a hunter-gatherer subsistence system in prehistoric Mexico.

Archaeology as a Social Science

New Archaeologists explicitly identify themselves as anthropologists (i.e., as behavioral and social scientists). This is hardly surprising since most of the New Archaeologists are educated in the United States, where most receive their training in departments of anthropology. New Archaeologists typically see themselves as using archaeological data to answer anthropological questions. Breaking explicitly with the art-historical and museum-collection orientation of much traditional archaeology, these archaeologist affirm their commitment to the goals and methods of (social) science. They do not limit their scientific horizons to the data, methods, and theories of anthropology, however. They embrace the methods of statistics, along with relevant work in geology, ecology, paleontology, paleobotany, history, and economics to try to answer archaeological questions. They marshal the whole gamut of new technological devices—from computers and high-powered microscopes to fine flotation screens and backhoes—to aid their scientific understanding of prehistoric cultural change.

Criticisms and Responses

New Archaeology was never a homogeneous movement. While all who work under its banner share a commitment to the aims and practices of science, they sometimes disagree about the nature of the scientific method and how it should be applied. Their disputes have a large philosophical component, which accounts for the interest of philosophers of science in the details of the New Archaeology. The issues of how to distinguish *laws* from mere empirical generalizations, how to understand various scientific models of confirmation and explanation, and whether these models suit archaeology evoke critical discussion from philosophers, as well as New Archaeologists. Whether archaeological explanations require *laws* is a particularly divisive issue, with some insisting both on the necessity of laws and the possibility of finding them (Michael B. Schiffer), and others calling attention to the trivial character of proposed archaeological laws (Flannery). Bruce Trigger, a historian of archaeology, cites Schiffer's work as an example of the antithesis between the historical concerns of traditional archaeology, with its emphasis on particular events and their position in a spatiotemporal framework, and the New Archaeology. Jeremy Sabloff, another historian of the discipline, as well as a practitioner of New Archaeology, denies that the different approaches of traditional archaeologists and New Archaeologists conflict. Instead, he see traditionalist's concern with particular details and the laws or generalizations sought by New Archaeologists as mutually reinforcing.

Some archaeologists share New Archaeology's commitment to scientific archaeology but disassociate themselves from New Archaeologists. Robert C. Dunnell, for example, rejects the identification of archaeology with anthropology. In his view, evolutionary biology provides the appropriate scientific model for archaeology. Accordingly, he has tried to work out an evolutionary account of the archaeological record, adapting such concepts as *species* and *selection* for archaeological use.

Analogical reasoning, also rejected by Dunnell, has been another point of disagreement among New Archaeologists as well. The premises of arguments from analogy refer to observed similarities among various things, while their conclusions state that the things resemble one another also in some other, unobserved respect. Every archaeologist is familiar with analogical arguments that infer similarity in (unobserved) function from similarity in (observed) form. That is to say, when archaeologists find materials that are similar in form to ethnographically known items, and they observe the function of the latter in the ethnographic context, they infer that the archaeological materials were used in the same way. One need only to reflect on how many terms for archaeological objects attribute some function to them (e.g., bowl, scraper, ax, ball court, and so forth) to realize the persuasiveness of such inferences. Lewis Binford and other New Archaeologists acknowledge analogy's role in *suggesting* hypotheses for testing but insist that analogy lacks probative value. Nevertheless, some analogical arguments support their conclusions with evidence that goes far beyond merely establishing the plausibility of a hypothesis. As in other inductive forms of reasoning, the strength of analogical arguments varies, depending in large part on the *relevance* of the features mentioned in the premises to the feature inferred by analogy in the conclusion. Historical continuity between the makers of the archaeological objects and the makers of ethnographically known materials, structural and causal features (such as edge wear on tools), as well as the existence of a limited range of physical possibilities for accomplishing certain utilitarian tasks, are some relevant considerations for assessing the strength of analogical arguments.

Despite the preceding emphasis on the philosophical issues that distinguish New Ar-

chaeologists from their predecessors, it would be a mistake to think that the writings of New Archaeologists focus mainly on these matters. Only a small portion of the output of New Archaeology is self-consciously philosophical. Far more important than its philosophical pronouncements are the standards New Archaeologists set for themselves in conducting archaeological research, in broadening the scope of questions that can be asked of archaeological materials, and in stimulating new ways of thinking about archaeological problems.

New Archaeologists have clarified many issues in prehistory. A brief selection includes: the impact of environmental degradation on societies, the change from hunter-gatherer to agricultural economy that occurred in many parts of the New World, and the decline of major urban centers, such as the cities of the Maya. New techniques for using archaeological materials to supplement and correct information from historical documents have enriched our knowledge of Colonial society in North and South America. William L. Rathje's archaeological studies of household garbage in contemporary society have thrown light on both traditional archaeological knowledge and contemporary social life. Some of the initial resistance of New Archaeologists to inferring beliefs and desires of humans known only through their archaeological remains has dissipated. As a result, some New Archaeologists are presenting carefully argued systemic analyses of art and iconography. Gordon R. Willey and Sabloff (1993) present brief descriptions of significant work done under the auspices of New Archaeology, along with many references.

No Longer New

In the 1960s and early 1970s, the proponents of New Archaeology defined themselves in contrast to "old" cultural-historical approaches. New Archaeologists criticized cultural historians more for their scientific naivete than for any specific opposition to scientific aims and methods. New Archaeologists share with other reformers a tendency to exaggerate the differences between their predecessors' work and their own. A survey of the archaeological literature of the early twentieth century, however, shows that many cultural historians admonished their colleagues to follow standard scientific practices in gathering data and to try to *prove* archaeological claims instead of merely guessing how things might have been. At the same time, many studies done in the latter part of the twentieth century under the aegis of New Archaeology would be indistinguishable—perhaps barring some opening remarks about methodology—from work done by culture historians.

Seeing the truth of this claim requires putting aside a great deal of rhetorical flourish that accompanies any introduction of a new or reformed way of conceiving a discipline. Flamboyant rhetoric notwithstanding, the New Archaeology can be seen as a development of the best of the old, aided by improved technology and increased attention to details of scientific method, rather than a revolutionary rejection of all earlier archaeological work. In fact, the New Archaeologists continue to rely heavily on their predecessors for chronologies and classifications, as well as other information. It is also fair to say that, although many archaeologists who are not in the group that first called themselves New Archaeologists disdain the philosophical pronouncements of the New Archaeology, they adhere to the standards of rigor and the techniques New Archaeologists promoted. These features have been, for the most part, absorbed into mainstream archaeology in many parts of the world.

The New Archaeology is no longer so "new" and is now usually called *processual archaeology*. The name is descriptively appropriate because it accurately reflects a feature that unites those who might disagree about the nature of explanation, the role of analogy, and other philosophical matters. New/processual archaeologists all focus on processes that produced the (static) materials that they study, and they believe that a proper analysis of the archaeological record will reveal information about those processes. The name is also appropriate because, since the mid-1980s, the movement has increasingly defined itself in contrast to its postprocessual critics.

Postprocessualism is both less unified than the New Archaeology and more concerned to mark its differences from its predecessor. Some postprocessualists reject the processualists' caution about what archaeological evidence shows, such as the type of inferences that stylistic features of pottery support. Others object to the political conservatism of New Archaeology. Still others

take up issues, such as the archaeological visibility of women, that were not part of New Archaeology's original agenda but are by no means incompatible with it.

One of the most serious postprocessual challenges to New Archaeology is whether the goal of a science of archaeology is desirable or even possible. New Archaeologists themselves first questioned overblown claims about the archaeological "science" that was to result from adopting "deductive methods." As they have worked to establish their scientific credentials, they have continued to debate about how to conduct archaeological research. Not surprisingly, Thomas Kuhn's *The Structure of Scientific Revolutions* exercises considerable influence on archaeological thinking about these matters. Kuhn analyzes revolutionary replacements of one scientific theory by another. These episodes—in which what is "known" by the best science of the day is superseded by a new theory that renders its predecessor not only false but barely comprehensible—have both rational and nonrational aspects. Kuhn argues that theories shape even the so-called facts in such a way that understanding the "factual" claims of the old science is difficult after such revolutions. In "Understanding the Archaeological Record," Sabloff and colleagues apply some of these lessons when they discuss how archaeologists' training and theoretical knowledge determine what they "see" in the archaeological record. Thus, interpretation occurs even at the level of observation. Recognizing the interplay between fact and theory, however, need not undermine scientific objectivity and may enhance it by raising one's sensitivity to sources of bias in dealing with archaeological remains. Alison Wylie and Peter Kosso, among others, have given careful attention to the possibility of achieving objective knowledge of past human behavior, even though interpretations can never be totally free from the biases of a contemporary perspective.

Postprocessualist critics of scientific archaeology take different lessons from Kuhn, emphasizing those strains of cognitive relativism that occur in his text. When New Archaeologists consider the nonrational aspects of science and the difficulty of separating theory from fact, they try to find a reasonable sense of objectivity that will not do violence to traditional standards of scientific knowledge. Postprocessualists, such as Michael Shanks, Christopher Tilley, and, to a lesser extent, Ian Hodder, do not share that concern, allying themselves instead with strong-program relativists of the Edinburgh school, critical theorists, and others who see objectivity as a phantom, scientific knowledge as socially constructed, and social science as a manipulative tool of the elite establishment. With varying degrees of fervor, they portray New Archaeologists as naive positivists who are unaware of the barriers to objective knowledge and insensitive to social influences on interpretation of archaeological materials. At the same time, postprocessual archaeologists do not recommend abandoning the all of the methods and techniques used by New Archaeologists. In *The Archaeology of Contextual Meanings,* Hodder finds symbolic meanings in archaeological materials by statistically analyzing similarities and differences with respect to spatial and temporal features. Then he interprets patterns of similarity and difference in terms of general anthropological principles, such as the distinction between nature and culture or between raw and cooked. These interpretive principles, however, are *lawlike* statements (i.e., they formally resemble laws, though their truth status may be questioned). Thus, far from abandoning the nomological approach of the New Archaeologists, Hodder adopts it—though the "laws" he wants to use may be too vague and lacking in empirical support to satisfy New Archaeologists.

Future Prospects

One aim of scientific research is to make the results accessible to other scientists. The results of archaeological research of New Archaeologists in North America have encouraged many archaeologists working in Latin America, Australia, Europe, Asia, and Africa to adopt some of the same methods. This has eased communication between formerly disparate groups, encouraged the exchange of information, and promoted the growth of knowledge. As new information about archaeological sites in many parts of the world becomes available, the prospects for integrating and extending archaeological knowledge are enhanced in no small part by New Archaeologists' insistence on scientific standards for their discipline.

Merrilee H. Salmon

See also BINFORD, LEWIS R.; CLARKE, DAVID L.; DEETZ, JAMES J. FANTO; DUNNELL, ROBERT C.; FLANNERY, KENT VAUGHN; HODDER, IAN; LONGACRE, WILLIAM A., POSTPROCESSUAL ARCHAEOLOGY; RATHJE, WILLIAM LAURENS; REDMAN, CHARLES L.; SCHIFFER, MICHAEL BRIAN; STRUEVER, STUART MCKEE; TRIGGER, BRUCE GRAHAM; WATSON, PATTY JO

Further Readings

Binford, S. and Binford, L., eds. (1968) New Perspectives in Archaeology. Chicago: Aldine.

Clarke, D. (1968) Analytical Archaeology. London: Methuen.

Dunnell, R.C. (1980) Evolutionary theory and archeology. In M.B. Schiffer (ed.): Advances in Archaeological Method and Theory, vol. 3, pp. 35–99. New York: Academic.

Hempel, C.G. and Oppenheim, P. (1948) Studies in the logic of explanation. Philosophy of Science 15: 135–175.

Hempel, C.G. (1965) Aspects of Scientific Explanation. New York: Free Press.

Hodder, I., ed. (1987) The Archaeology of Contextual Meanings. Cambridge/New York: Cambridge University Press.

Kuhn, T.S. (1970) The Structure of Scientific Revolutions, 2nd ed. Chicago: University of Chicago Press.

Sabloff, J., Binford, L., and McAnany, P. (1987) Understanding the archaeological record. Antiquity 61:327–332.

Taylor, W.W. (1948) A Study of Archeology. (Memoir Series of the American Anthropological Association, 69). Menasha, WI: American Anthropological Association.

Trigger, B.G. (1989) A History of Archaeological Thought. Cambridge/New York: Cambridge University Press.

Watson, P., LeBlanc, S., and Redman, C. (1971) Archeological Explanation. New York: Columbia University Press.

Willey, G. and Sabloff, J. (1993) A History of American Archaeology, 3rd ed. New York: W.H. Freeman.

Nuclear Magnetic Resonance (NMR) Spectroscopy

A physical method to determine chemical structure, based on the selective absorption of low-energy radiation by certain atomic nuclei that have been placed in a strong magnetic field. Some atomic nuclei with odd mass numbers have magnetic properties. The most important of these, and the only ones as yet used in archaeological science, are ordinary hydrogen, ^1H, and the stable carbon isotope, ^{13}C. They are often referred to as *proton magnetic resonance* (PMR) and *carbon magnetic resonance* (CMR). When such nuclei are placed in an external magnetic field, they may exist in two different energy states: aligned or opposed to that field. The energy required to promote nuclei from alignment to opposition can be provided by radiofrequency radiation, which is thus absorbed. In a molecule, the electron cloud shields the nuclei of atoms from the external field to varying degrees, depending on the other atoms to which it is bonded. Identical atoms in different molecular environments will absorb at different wavelengths, while identical atoms in identical environments will absorb at the same wavelength but will absorb more energy and give a more intense signal. Thus, the NMR spectrum will show as many signals for each kind of atom as there are different environments, and the area or integral of each signal will be a measure of the number of atoms in any given environment.

The counting of atoms is further aided by the splitting of each signal into a number of subpeaks, that number being one greater than the number of neighboring atoms with magnetic properties. Splitting can also be a disadvantage, as in CMR, in which the splitting of the carbon signals by the adjacent hydrogen atoms produces a profusion of overlapping signals. It is possible to suppress this unwanted splitting by irradiating nuclei selectively with radiofrequencies of the wavelength required to keep them in the higher-energy state. The programming of this irradiation, called *partial decoupling,* can furnish highly specific structural information. For a pure compound, the combination of PMR and CMR spectra is usually enough to determine the molecular structure completely, including the very subtle spatial details of configuration and even conformation. For complex mixtures, NMR spectra can provide valuable information about structural categories, such as unsaturation, aromaticity, acid content, and the presence of specific functional groups (e.g., methoxy groups in lignin and carbomethoxy groups in tar and pitch). This is made possible by the easy and immediate quantitative analysis of NMR spectra, a fea-

ture not offered by other spectroscopic methods. Current instruments use Fourier-transform technology, analogous to that described for infrared spectroscopy. One of its advantages—the storage and addition of a large number of individual runs in a computer—is essential to CMR, since the ^{13}C isotope comprises only 1.1 percent of natural carbon, and a single scan would, therefore, give only a very weak signal.

Applications to Archaeology
The first applications of PMR to archaeological science dealt with the identification of olive oil in a sixth-century B.C. glass bottle from Syria, of fatty acids characteristic of tallow in a third-century pilgrim flask from the German Rhineland, and the quantitative analysis of oil of amber. Both PMR and CMR have more recently been used to identify fats and waxes in food vessels of Celtic France. PMR has shown hydration patterns in ancient parchment, leather, and wool. PMR and CMR have allowed the sourcing of asphalt found at Babylon and other Iraqi sites. CMR has given evidence of pure beeswax in medieval, and beeswax and rosin in early-nineteenth-century British, Royal document seals, suggesting the possibility of dating seals by their composition. Both PMR and CMR have been essential in the study of tar and pitch, including the identification of birchbark tar on Hallstatt ceramics, of pine tar in English Tudor and ancient Etruscan shipwrecks, and of pine and spruce tars in historical shipwrecks from western Australia. By measuring the loss of acid groups, CMR can determine the operating temperature of prehistoric and early historic manufacturing techniques of tar and pitch.

Because solids give only broad, unstructured resonance patterns, standard NMR practice requires a liquid sample. This limitation can, however, be overcome by highly sophisticated techniques whose very names show that they are too technical to be discussed here: high-power decoupling, cross-polarization (CP), and magic angle spinning (MAS). Although it requires a rather large sample of 0.2–0.3, CP-MAS-CMR gives very serviceable spectra of insoluble materials, such as Chinese and Japanese Oriental lacquer and jet (black lignite) from England and Spain. It has been extensively applied to fossil resins (or amber), where it has allowed the relative dating of Dominican amber, the determination of the botanical sources of Dominican, Mexican, and North American amber and of fossil kauri from New Zealand and Australia, the provenance analysis of European amber, and the identification of the fossil resin beckerite as a succinite contaminated by insect frass (excrement).

A well-established technique in medicine, magnetic resonance imaging (MRI), is a modification of computerized axial tomography (CAT) and takes proton spectra of very thin slices of a three-dimensional object that a computer then recombines into a representation of the whole. It is sensitive to variations in the concentration of water and, thus, furnishes anatomical detail inaccessible to X-ray methods. MRI is the method of choice for the study of major human remains and has been used on an Egyptian mummy of ca. 1000 B.C. and on an Iron Age bog body of a man in Cheshire, England, whose last meal was bread rather than hot porridge, according to the completely noninvasive MRI analysis of his stomach contents. The potential for other materials is indicated by work on waterlogged archaeological wood, for which it can provide structural information toward the identification of genera. There is no doubt that this and all other NMR techniques will find increasing use in archaeology in the future.

Curt W. Beck

Further Readings

Abraham, R.J., Fisher, J., and Loftus, P. (1988) Introduction to NMR Spectroscopy. New York: Wiley.

Ghisalberti, E.L., and Godfrey, I.M. (in press) Application of nuclear magnetic resonance spectroscopy to the analysis of organic archaeological materials. In I. Davidson and N. Cook, (eds.): Proceedings of the Fifth Australasian Archaeometry Conference, Armidale, New South Wales, Australia, February 2–4, 1994.

Robins, G.V., Pendlebury, D., Fletton, R.A., and Elliott, J. (1985) The application of carbon-13 Fourier transform nuclear magnetic resonance spectroscopy to the analysis of art objects and archaeological artifacts. In P.A. England and L. van Zelst (eds.): Application of Science in Examination of Works of Art: Proceedings of the

Seminar September 7–9, 1983. Boston: Museum of Fine Arts.

Nuclear Methods of Analysis

A group of related and sensitive analytical techniques used to determine trace element impurities in a wide variety of materials through irradiation. Nuclear analytical methods were used for the first time in 1936 and have since seen rapid development and application throughout the sciences. The application of nuclear methods in archaeometry was no exception, and the first papers on their use in the characterization of archaeomaterials were published in the 1950s.

This entry discusses two types of techniques: the activation techniques and the excitation techniques. In *activation techniques,* irradiation produces radioactive isotopes through several types of nuclear reaction. Subsequent to the completion of the irradiation, the radioactivity emitted by these radioisotopes is measured. In *excitation techniques,* irradiation from a small accelerator results in the excitation of the constitutent atoms. During the irradiation, the characteristic X rays emitted by the excited atoms are detected; this technique is referred to as PIXE (particle-induced X-ray emission).

Activation Analysis

When a sample is bombarded by particles (e.g., neutrons, ions, or protons) of adequate energy, the natural stable isotopes produce radioactive isotopes. The measurement of the radioactivity emitted by these radioisotopes allows one to make qualitative and quantitative analyses. *Qualitative analysis* refers to the identification of the radioisotopes produced by bombardment, which then can be traced back to the original stable isotopes, allowing identification of the elements in the sample being analyzed. A *quantitative analysis* is made by the measurement of the radioactivity and comparison to a known chemical standard that was irradiated under the same conditions, thus allowing measurement of the quantity of each element present. There are several methods of activation analysis, each identified according to the type of bombarding particles used to produce the radioisotopes in the samples to be analyzed. The most frequently used methods in the field of archaeology are: neutron activation analysis (NAA), fast neutron activation analysis (FNAA), and proton activation analysis (PAA).

Neutron Activation Analysis

In the case of NAA, the sample, which usually weighs a few milligrams to a fraction of a gram, is irradiated in a research nuclear reactor. The elements present in the sample capture neutrons and often become radioactive isotopes. The irradiation time varies from a few minutes to several hours, depending on the type of sample and the nature of the elements to be determined.

At the end of irradiation, the samples are removed from the reactor and gamma-ray spectroscopy is used to measure the radioactive emissions that accompany the disintegration of the radioisotopes. The measurement of radioactivity after irradiation depends on the half-life of the radioisotope under study: The shorter the half-life, the smaller the lapse of time between the end of the irradiation and the beginning of measurement. On the other hand, the measurement of longer half-lives will be done under better conditions after the appropriate lapse of time, sometimes a few weeks. A semiconductor detector of a Ge (Li) or Ge (hyperpure) type is used, as it has very good resolution. The signal is amplified and analyzed via an associated microcomputer. Several software programs are used by the microcomputer to treat the spectrum and to evaluate the concentration of the different elements present in the irradiated sample.

There are advantages and disadvantages of activation analysis using neutrons. The advantages are that there is good sensitivity: A large number of elements can be determined, with detection limits at the ppb (parts per billion, or 10^{-9} g/g) level. In NAA, the intensity of the radioactivity varies linearly with the concentrations of the associated elements over all concentration ranges. Furthermore, there are no matrix effects, no chemical effects, and no contamination. The major disadvantages of NAA are that it can be conducted only in a nuclear reactor facility, and it is quite expensive. Only a few hundred samples can be analyzed per year, which may be an important restriction when studying certain archaeological problems.

Three archaeological areas of interest have mainly used this analytical method: the provenance of ceramics and of obsidian and the study of the variation of the fineness of gold coins using microsampling.

The main application of NAA has been for the characterization of siliceous materials, mainly ceramics and both manufactured and natural glasses (e.g., obsidian). The main constituents of these archaeomaterials—oxygen (O), silicon (Si), aluminum (Al), magnesium (Mg), calcium (Ca), and titanium (Ti)—produce, by nuclear activation with thermal neutrons, either radioisotopes of very short half-life (less than ten minutes) or radioisotopes that are not gamma-ray emitters (Figure 1). After a decay time of a few hours, one can, by simple gamma spectroscopy and without chemical separation, determine a large number of minor and trace elements. More than twenty elements may be identified, including rare earth elements that are of great importance to geochemistry.

The precision of identification is, depending on the element, ca. 5–10 percent. Figure 2 gives the results obtained on Roman period terra sigillata ceramics from Arezzo, Italy, and from the Lyon region of France. This example clearly shows the achievements of the NAA technique, which allows very good "fingerprinting," to solve one of the most important archaeological problems requiring characterization: the provenance of archaeological materials and the identification of commercial trade routes in ancient times. The results obtained by NAA for the composition of terra sigillata ceramics allow the differentiation of the Gallic workshop from that of Arezzo. Figure 3 shows the concentration of cesium (Cs) versus chromium (Cr) in ppm; the analysis clearly divides the different production workshops into four groups and allows the study of this pottery circulation, which was an important industry in antiquity.

Obsidian artifacts from Central America have also been analyzed with NAA. The main obsidian sources of the Mayan period come from the volcanic deposits in Guatemala: El Chayal from the Uramacinta and Sarstoon basins and Ixtepeque from the Motagua River. Archaeologists have questioned the origin of the obsidians from the island of Moho Cay, Belize. The analysis of both reference samples and obsidian artifacts from the site demonstrated definitively that El Chayal was the source of the raw material (Figure 4).

Fast Neutron Activation Analysis

The FNAA technique uses fast neutrons of several MeV, which are produced by nuclear

Element	Nuclide	Half-life	γ-radiation
Oxygen	^{19}O	27 s	0.2 and 1.36 MeV
Silicon	^{31}Si	2.62 h	no γ
Aluminum	^{28}Al	2.3 m	1.78 MeV
Magnesium	^{27}Mg	9.46 m	0.84 and 1.01 MeV
Titanium	^{51}Ti	5.8 m	0.32 and 0.93 MeV
Calcium	^{47}Ca-^{47}Sc	4.54 and 3.34 d	0.158 and 1.297 MeV

Figure 1. Half-lives of radioisotopes of elements found in ceramics and glasses and produced by neutron activation analysis. (s = seconds; m = minutes; h = hours; d = days). Figure by J.N. Barrandon.

Group	Arezzo	La Muette	Loyasse
Quantity of sherds	23	4	5
Al(%)	9.23 ± 0.55	6.41 ± 0.23	5.37 ± 0.38
Ca(%)	9.5 ± 1.3	18.2 ± 2.4	12.7 ± 1.2
Dy	5.39 ± 0.21	4.58 ± 0.31	4.04 ± 0.44
Mn	1117 ± 41	905 ± 53	774 ± 89
Na(%)	0.606 ± 0.027	0.454 ± 0.014	0.507 ± 0.037
U	2.70 ± 0.09	2.61 ± 0.22	2.33 ± 0.33
Sm	6.56 ± 0.20	5.04 ± 0.05	4.69 ± 0.28
La	39.4 ± 1.1	29.7 ± 0.5	27.4 ± 1.7
Ti(%)	0.477 ± 0.024	0.270 ± 0.020	0.287 ± 0.015
Ta	1.241 ± 0.039	0.772 ± 0.018	0.785 ± 0.048
Co	22.55 ± 0.86	12.87 ± 0.19	10.27 ± 0.82
Sc	19.06 ± 0.59	11.07 ± 0.33	9.80 ± 0.69
Fe(%)	5.24 ± 0.19	3.71 ± 0.06	2.96 + 0.09
Yb	2.79 ± 0.08	2.25 ± 0.05	2.19 ± 0.11
Hf	3.95 ± 0.12	3.06 ± 0.13	4.12 ± 0.47
Cs	6.98 ± 1.10	3.68 ± 0.61	5.30 ± 0.95
Cr	182 ± 6	79 ± 7	73 ± 6
Th	13.44 ± 0.47	10.48 ± 0.13	9.70 ± 0.62
Eu	1.465 ± 0.054	1.122 ± 0.018	1.017 ± 0.059
Rb	132 ± 16	82 ± 21	92 ± 19

Figure 2. Results of neutron activation analysis of ceramics from Arezzo, Italy, and from the Lyon region of France (La Muette and Loyasse). Notice that the chemical "fingerprint" of ceramics from Lyon can be easily differentiated from that of ceramics from Arezzo. Values are given in ppm, unless indicated by percent. Figure by J.N. Barrandon.

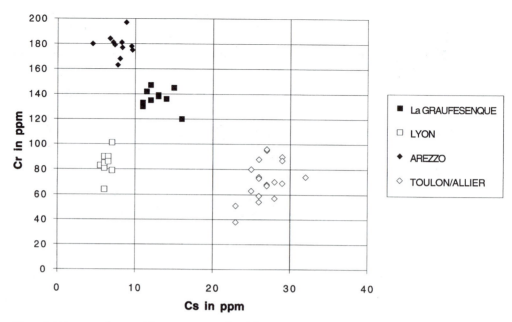

Figure 3. Diagram of cesium/chromium ratios for different ceramic production centers in France and Italy during the Roman period. Figure by J.N. Barrandon.

Catalog number	Dy (ppm)	Mn (ppm)	Na (%)	K (%)	Ba (ppm)	Source
37/193-1-53	2.73 ± 0.11	656 ± 13	3.28 ± 0.07	3.44 ± 0.18	912 ± 44	El Chayal
37/193-1-113	2.66 ± 0.12	660 ± 13	3.26 ± 0.07	3.74 ± 0.18	973 ± 43	El Chayal
El Chayal reference	2.66 ± 0.11	649 ± 13	3.15 ± 0.06	3.46 + 0.25	915 ± 35	
Ixtepeque reference	2.30 ± 0.11	449 ± 9	3.05 ± 0.05	3.61 ± 0.26	1030 ± 27	

Figure 4. Table of trace elements in archaeological obsidian artifacts (37/193–1–53 and 37–193–1–113) from the island of Moho Cay, Belize, in comparison to reference samples. NAA was able to trace the source of obsidian to El Chayal in Guatemala. Figure by J.N. Barrandon.

reactions of light particles (protons, deuterium, tritium, and helium) impinging on a light element, usually beryllium. These light particles either come from an isotopic source or are accelerated by an electrostatic accelerator or by a cyclotron. The use of a cyclotron produces neutron fluxes with higher intensities and with a large variety of mean energies, which translates into a better sensitivity of analysis.

The significant increase in the energy of the neutrons has two consequences from the analytical point of view: Because many nuclear reactions, other than the neutron, gamma-ray reaction, can occur, a wide range of radioisotopes is produced. Interferences occur between the radioactivity resulting from these radioisotopes, and, therefore, the sensitivity for detecting individual elements can be worse than for NAA. The choice of the neutron energy will, therefore, be of great importance in maintaining sensitivity.

Samples to be analyzed by FNAA are more transparent to the neutron flux. This characteristic of the FNAA technique has been demonstrated by the analysis of obsidian artifacts of the same origin but with different weight and shapes. The results obtained clearly show the compositions to be similar regardless of the size or shape of the artifacts themselves. The possibility of performing a global elemental analysis of entire objects having quite different sizes has two important archaeological applications. The first concerns the characterization of natural glass (obsidian) and manufactured glass objects without sampling. In the case of glass, thirty-two elements may be determined, including the major constituents introduced by the flux and the source of silica, the main additives for glass manufacture (e.g., colorants, opacifying agents), and a certain number of trace elements from different origins. A good understanding of glass composition enables the study of two types of problematic archaeological issues: the evolution of manufacturing technology and the origin of raw materials or of the glass itself. With respect to obsidian, the main application of the FNAA technique is the analysis of tools from archaeological sites located far away from the production deposit. At these distant sites, very few obsidian tools are found, and it is impossible to destroy them to perform analysis using other techniques, such as activation in a nuclear reactor.

Copper and copper-alloy coins and objects also may be analyzed by FNAA. Unfortunately, many copper-alloy objects have a surface corrosion layer, or patina, that has a very different chemical composition from the remaining metal below. This patina inhibits the use of analytical techniques, such as X-ray fluorescence (XRF) or particle-induced X-ray emission (PIXE), which provide elemental composition at the surface only. The FNAA technique, however, allows a nondestructive bulk analysis of the entire object for the main constituents of copper and copper-alloy (e.g., bronze, brass, and ancient orichalcum) coinages for the study of manufacturing technologies.

Proton Activation Analysis
The PAA technique was developed during the 1970s. Researchers demonstrated that a judicious choice of the energy of protons (11 MeV) permitted, for the first time, a multielement activation analysis such as NAA. If the energy of the protons is limited to 11 MeV, only (proton, neutron) nuclear reactions are produced, which means that interferences are not observed. This

activation technique obviously needs a variable energy cyclotron on a tandem electrostatic accelerator or 12 MeV. This equipment is heavy and not in general use.

When the charged particles (protons) bombard the sample, they slow down over a certain range (i.e., the distance traveled by the proton until it attains zero energy), depending on the nature of the material. The thickness of the layer analyzed by PAA will be smaller than that for the neutron activation techniques (NAA and FNAA) but larger than the layer penetrated by XRF or PIXE. With the exception of the slowing down of the protons, PAA is an activation technique with the same characteristics as NAA: good sensitivity from the ppb to the ppm level, an absence of contamination, and good selectivity.

This activation technique immediately had a large number of applications in the sciences and, since 1973, has found archaeological applications for the nondestructive analysis of gold, silver, and gold-silver-alloy objects.

Silver has two isotopes (^{107}Ag and ^{109}Ag) that, through PAA, lead to two radioisotopes of cadmium (^{109}Cd and ^{107}Cd). The first isotope does not emit gamma rays, and the second has a short half-life of 6.49 hours. If one waits for its decay (ca. three days), one can perform direct gamma spectrometry and then determine the impurities present in silver.

Gold, which is a monoisotropic element, yields, through PAA, two isomers of mercury-197. These two isomers have different half-lives (23.8 and 64.1 hours, respectively), and they both emit gamma rays of low energies (all lower than 300 keV). This common characteristic allows, subject to the use of a radioactivity measuring device, the analysis by gamma spectrometry directly on the gold object or sample. However, a lead sheet, which absorbs most of the gamma rays of low energy emitted by the interfering mercury isomers, must be placed between the sample and the detector. This allows detection of the trace elements in gold immediately at the end of irradiation.

The main applications of PAA are in the numismatic area. This activation method enables good characterization of ancient gold and silver coinages, as well as the study of various research questions asked by numismatists and economic historians. Among the different problems that have been studied using

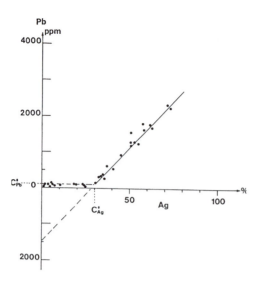

Figure 5. Graph of the variations of lead (Pb) content of Byzantine coins (A.D. 491–1081). When silver (Ag) is present in native gold, the lead content remains constant (C°$_{Pb}$) regardless of the percentage of silver. When silver is deliberately added to gold, the lead content increases in correlation with the percentage of silver added. Figure by J.N. Barrandon.

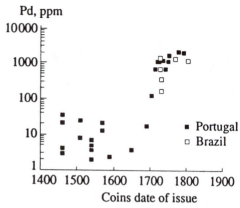

Figure 6. Log-scale graph of the palladium (Pd) content in coins struck in Portugal and Brazil. The arrival date of Brazilian gold in Portugal is ca. A.D. 1700. Figure by J.N. Barrandon.

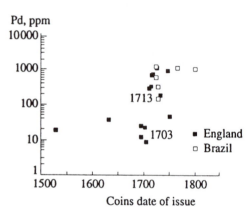

Figure 7. Log-scale graph of the palladium (Pd) content in coins struck in Britain. The arrival date of Brazilian gold is between A.D. 1703 and 1713. Figure by J.N. Barrandon.

PAA, two show clearly the possibilities of the method: the study of the debasement of Byzantine coinages and the impact of Brazilian gold on the European economy. The study of the variation of lead (Pb) and silver in Byzantine coinage struck in Constantinople from the fifth to the eleventh centuries differentiates coinage made of nonrefined native gold (in which the Pb content remains constant) from coinage with the deliberate addition of silver (in which the Pb content grows with the increase in silver concentration for debasement). Two phases of gold-coinage debasement were shown: the first relating to the addition of native gold, and the second corresponding to the remelting and reuse of silver coins (Figure 5). The evolution of palladium (Pd) content in gold (high palladium in gold derived from Brazilian mines) allowed the determination of the date of arrival of Brazilian gold to Portugal, England, and France (Figures 6 and 7).

Particle-Induced X-Ray Emission

This nuclear method was developed and refined during the late 1960s and 1970s for quantitative, nondestructive analysis of a wide range of materials and has applications to both art history and archaeology. The sample is bombarded with protons to produce a spectrum of X rays identifying the constituent elements. PIXE can be used to detect elements from sodium (Na) to uranium (U). Compared with X-ray fluorescence, the main advantages of PIXE are that PIXE has a greater sensitivity for detection of trace elements; point-by-point analyses can be accomplished using a microprobe; and PIXE is preferable for analysis of very thin samples, surface layers, and small sample sizes.

J.N. Barrandon

See also ARCHAEOMETRY; CLAYS AND CERAMICS, CHARACTERIZATION; ELECTRON-PROBE MICROANALYSIS; GLASS, CHARACTERIZATION;

INDUCTIVELY COUPLED PLASMA—ATOMIC
EMISSION SPECTROMETRY; METALS, CHARAC-
TERIZATION; X-RAY FLUORESCENCE (XRF)
ANALYSIS

Further Readings

Barrandon, J.N. (1994) The nuclear analytical method in historical sciences: The care of precious metals from the New World. Journal of Analytical Chemistry 49(1):89–93.

Bird, J.R., Duerden, P., and Wilson, D.J. (1983) Ion beam techniques in archaeology and the arts. Nuclear Science Applications 1:357–516. Chur, Switzerland: Harwood Academic.

Furlan, G., Cassola Guida, P., and Tuniz, C., eds. (1986) New Paths in the Use of Nuclear Techniques for Art and Archaeology. Singapore: World Scientific.

Goffer, Z. (1980) Archaeological Chemistry. New York: Wiley.

Healy, P.F., McKillop, H.I., and Walsh, B. (1984) Analysis of obsidian from Moho Cay, Belize: New evidence on classic Maya trade routes. Science 225:414.

International Workshop on Ion Beam Analysis in the Arts and Archaeology (1986). Proceedings of the International Workshop on Ion Beam Analysis in the Arts and Archaeology, Pont-a-Mousson, France. (Nuclear Instruments and Methods in Physics Research B14, no. 1). Amsterdam: North Holland.

La vie mystérieuse des chefs-d'oeuvre: La science au service de l'art (1980) Paris: Edition de la Réunion des musées nationaux.

Leute, U. (1987) Archaeometry: An Introduction to Physical Methods in Archaeology and the History of Art. Weinheim and New York: VCH.

Sayre, E.V. (1972) Activation analysis applications in art and archaeology. Advances in Activation Analysis 2:155–184.

Wideman, F., Picon, M., Asaro, F., Michel, H.V., and Perlman, I. (1975) A Lyons branch of the pottery-making firm of Ateius of Arezzo. Archaeometry 17(1):45–59.

N

Obsidian Hydration Dating

Dating of obsidian artifacts based on diffusion of atmospheric or soil moisture into obsidian. Obsidian is a natural glass that forms when rhyolite (acidic) lavas cool rapidly on the Earth's surface. It is a hard glass, easily worked, and was used by ancient peoples for making sharp tools and weapons. For examples, see the percussion-chipped artifacts of obsidian illustrated in Figure 1, which are similar to those found in many volcanic areas of the globe, including the western part of the Americas, the Pacific Rim, and the periphery of the Mediterranean Sea. In the late 1950s, geochemists Irving Friedman and Robert L. Smith discovered that obsidian acquired a slowly growing hydration surface layer by absorption of molecular water from the environment. The formation of this macroscopically unnoticeable adherent layer begins with the first exposure to the air of a new surface, and, in time, the layer becomes measurable under the microscope (Figure 2). Its thickness increases with age, and, with this discovery, a new dating method for prehistoric studies was born. Measurable hydration can form in as little as a few hundred years and continues to increase in thickness for a million or more years, after which the hydrated layer spalls off and a new layer begins to form.

Interest in the application of obsidian hydration is strongest in the western United States and Mesoamerica. The establishment in 1989 of the International Association for Obsidian Studies testifies to the rapid expansion of the use of this dating tool (see Meighan and Scalise 1988; Skinner and Tremaine 1993 for extensive bibliographies). Since the 1980s, obsidian studies have expanded to include tracing the artifact material to its geologic source. This has two uses (Figure 3): facilitating the determination of the artifact's intrinsic hydration rate and discovering ancient trade routes for obsidian.

Laboratory Procedures

Obtaining the basic measurement—the depth of the hydration layer—calls for the accessories usually found in a geology laboratory, including a microscope equipped for examination under polarized light and materials used for preparing thin sections of rocks for microscopic examination. Only two items of special equipment are required. The first is a thin (~0.5 mm thick) saw blade that has a continuous rim containing fine (less than 400 mesh) diamond powder attached to the rim of the blade. This continuous-rim construction and the very fine diamond powder are necessary to prevent the loss of the hydrated layer by chipping resulting from the use of the usual saw blade in which coarse grit-size diamonds are contained in discrete slots along the rim of the blade. The second special item is a microscope eyepiece that will allow the measurement of the size of objects.

To remove a small specimen from the obsidian object, two parallel saw cuts ca. 1 mm apart and 5 mm deep are made at right angles to a selected edge or facet of the artifact, and the isolated specimen is broken away. The specimen is then cemented to a glass microscope slide, ground, using fine abrasive (less than 10 microns in diameter, ~1,000 grit size), to ca. one-half its original thickness, removed from the slide, inverted, and recemented and ground to a final thickness of ca. 0.08–0.10 mm. The grinding must remove the edge

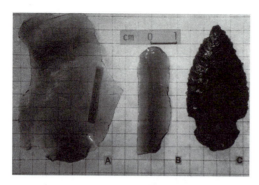

Figure 1. Obsidian artifacts of comparable thickness may be transparent, translucent, or opaque. A is a flake from Columbia, B a blade from Guatemala, and C a spear point from Mexico. Figure by Irving Friedman and Fred Trembour.

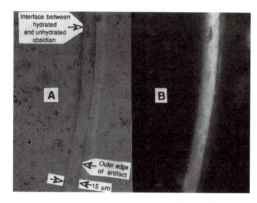

Figure 2. Photomicrographs showing a thin section of an artifact from Iraq viewed under (A) plain light and under (B) polarized light with crossed polarizers. The hydrated rim has a thickness of 15 micrometers. Photograph by Irving Friedman and Fred Trembour.

damage caused during sawing. A cover-glass is cemented in place to finish the slide. Under crossed polarizers, under transmitted light, the hydration layer appears as a bright white band against a dark background, the birefringence effect caused by mechanical strain in the hydrated layer. This serves to confirm the presence of hydration but is not recommended for measurement. With plain-light illumination, the inner edge of the hydrated layer appears as a thin dark line against a light background. This plain-light image is the preferred one for making readings.

Measurements are made using either a filar micrometer or an image-splitting eyepiece and a magnification of ca. 500x. Two features

have to be distinguished: the outer edge of the specimen and the inner boundary of the hydration front. The spacing between the two is the desired measurement; measurements are made at several points and averaged. Useful hydration rims begin at ca. 1 micron (μm) and range up to 10 or 20 μm for archaeological material and up to 100 μm for dating geological samples. The precision of the measurements is 0.1 μm under optimum conditions but 0.2 μm for most cases.

Calculation of Age

To convert the hydration-thickness readings to age requires knowledge of the hydration rate of the obsidian, which is an intrinsic property of the glass and is determined mainly by its chemical composition. On the basis of experimental hydration experiments, the following relationship was developed:

Age = k(hydration thickness)^x (Equation 1)

where k is a constant and x is 2. Based on data from stratified field sites, some archaeologists prefer using x = 1. Figure 4 illustrates graphically the difference between the two approaches. The curved solid line is a plot of Equation 1, where x = 2 in accord with laboratory findings, while the dotted and dashed straight lines are constructed using x = 1 and the "known" anchor points A and B as provided by radiocarbon dating of an archaeological stratum containing obsidian. The two types of plots are in approximate agreement only over short time spans. All published experimental studies support the squared relationship (x = 2) and not the linear one (x = 1).

For relative-dating purposes, it is not necessary to know the constant k. Obsidian from a single archaeological site will have been exposed to the same environmental histories. If these objects were all from the same geologic source (flow), which normally guarantees that they will have the same chemical composition (and hydration rates), then their ages are in the ratio of the squares of their measured hydration thicknesses (e.g., twice the thickness means four times as old).

The temperature at which hydration occurs affects the rate of hydration. The influence of temperature on the rate is given by the Arrhenius equation:

k = Ae$^{(E/RT)}$ (Equation 2)

where k is the hydration rate in μm squared per 1,000 years, A is a constant, E is the acti-

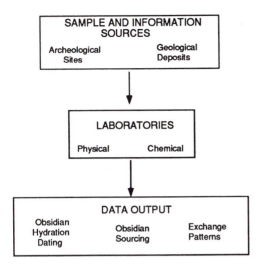

Figure 3. Information flow chart showing pathways between sample sites and the products of obsidian analysis. It demonstrates the interrelations between the different data outputs. Figure by Irving Friedman and Fred Trembour.

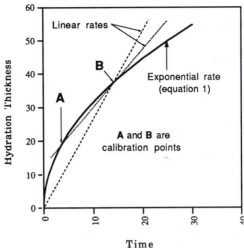

Figure 4. Plot showing the development of hydration as a function of time. The curved line is for an exponential rate (x = 2), while the dotted and dashed lines are for linear rates (x = 1). A and B are calibration points usually determined from radiocarbon ages. The dotted line is drawn from the origin to a calibration point, while the dashed line is drawn between two calibration points. This figure illustrates the extent of error introduced by the use of linear rather than exponential hydration rates. Figure by Irving Friedman and Fred Trembour.

vation energy of hydration in calories per mole, R is the gas constant in calories per degrees per mole, T is the temperature in Kelvin, and e is the base of natural logarithms.

Equation 2 shows that the hydration rate varies exponentially with temperature; experiments show that the rate approximately doubles for every 6°C rise in temperature. Obsidian found at most archaeological sites is exposed to temperatures that vary seasonally, and often daily, as well. To arrive at the hydration temperature given in Equation 2, one cannot simply average the minimum and maximum temperatures. There are two reasons for this: allowance must be made for the time intervals that each increment of temperature has acted on the obsidian, and the nonlinear response of hydration to temperature means that a rise in temperature of 1°C will speed up the hydration more than a fall of 1°C will slow it down. As a result, the concept of *effective hydration temperature* (EHT) has been developed. The EHT is a temperature that, if maintained constantly for the total time that the obsidian has hydrated, will duplicate the hydration thickness that resulted from the fluctuating temperature. Although the EHT can be calculated from long-term weather records collected adjacent to the archaeological site (if available), it is best measured using temperature-integrating

thermal-diffusion cells, developed by Walter Ambrose and by Fred Trembour and colleagues, deployed at the archaeological site for a time period of at least one, and preferably several, years. The response of these inexpensive cells to varying temperatures is similar to that of obsidian, and they give a direct measure of EHT, as found by Trembour and colleagues in 1988. The constants of Equation 2 are evaluated from data on samples hydrated in the laboratory at elevated temperatures. Using measured (or estimated) EHT for the artifact recovery site will allow the calculation of the hydration rate. The date at which the measured surface of the artifact was created is then calculated using Equation 1.

In 1976, Friedman and William Long found that the intrinsic hydration rate is controlled by the chemical composition of the obsidian and that the rate varies by as much as a factor of 20 to 1. To date, there is still some disagreement as to the individual role of the various major elements that constitute obsidian in affecting the hydration rate. Therefore, to achieve absolute dating for the differing glasses, it has been necessary to conduct accelerated laboratory tests at elevated temperatures and pressures on samples of the source obsidian.

The calibration of obsidian hydration rates can also be made if satisfactory dating by an independent method—usually radiocarbon dating—exists. The requirement with this approach is that the material dated by this independent method—associated wood or charcoal in the case of radiocarbon—must be of the same age as the flaking of the obsidian, a fact that is not always easy to confirm. The relative humidity (rH) at which hydration occurs has been recognized as a further factor that may affect the hydration rate. The higher the average rH, the faster the rate. However, due to compensating influences in nature, the practical effect of this parameter seems to be negligible. For example, solar heating of obsidian exposed on the surface of the ground may speed up hydration but, at the same time, induces drier conditions, which slows down hydration. In any case, obsidian buried more than ca. 20 cm deep in soil in the Mojave Desert of California, as well as in semiarid regions in Utah, Nevada, Colorado, and Wyoming, has been found to be exposed to a constant rH of 100 percent.

Obsidian Source Identification

The process of calibrating the hydration rate of widely differing obsidians has been simplified by the finding that all artifacts made from a given geologic source or volcanic lava flow usually have the same chemical composition and, therefore, the same inherent hydration rate. Fortunately, the identification of source by the matching of the trace-element composition of archaeological material with known volcanic sources has proven effective. The analytical methods for this purpose are X-ray fluorescence (XRF) and instrumental neutron activation analysis (INAA), both of which are nondestructive tests. The diagnostic elements measured by these procedures include, for example, the rare earths, rubidium, titanium and zirconium. The geologic source is identified by characteristic element clusters when concentrations are plotted in binary or tertiary composition diagrams.

Another means of distinguishing obsidians is by comparing physical properties, such as the optical index of refraction of the glasses. This property can be measured microscopically using a few grains of powdered material and a series of immersion liquids of known index and having high optical dispersion. As a rule, the hydration rate of obsidians decreases as the index of refraction increases.

The Dating of Other Natural Glasses

The usefulness of hydration measurements for dating glasses seems to be confined to obsidian. Research done in 1970 raised hopes of developing a similar dating method for the more basic (basalt) glasses exploited by the Polynesians in Hawaii. The weathering product of these glasses, palagonite, was thought to accumulate at a linear rate that could be calibrated for age. However, the process is not simple hydration but chemically complex and involves ion exchange with the environment, which often includes seawater. Subsequent investigations have led to contradictory interpretations of artifact age in archaeological layered sequences and have cast doubt on the validity of this dating application to Hawaiian glass.

Irving Friedman
Fred Trembour

See also NUCLEAR METHODS OF ANALYSIS; X-RAY FLUORESCENCE; (XRF) ANALYSIS

Further Readings

Aitken, M., and Taylor, R.E., eds. (1997) Chronometric Dating in Archaeology. New York: Plenum.

Friedman, I., and Long, W. (1976) Hydration rate of obsidian. Science 191:347–352.

Friedman, I., and Smith, R.L. (1960) A new dating method using obsidian, part 1: The development of the method. American Antiquity 25: 476–493.

International Association for Obsidian Studies Bulletin (1989) San Jose, CA: Department of Anthropology, San Jose State University.

Meighan, C.W., and Scalise, J.L. (1988) A compendium of the obsidian hydration determinations made at the UCLA obsidian hydration laboratory: Obsidian Dates IV, pp. 473–511 (Monograph 29). Los Angeles: Institute of Archaeology, UCLA.

Skinner, C.E., and Tremaine, K.J. (1993) Obsidian: An Interdisciplinary Bibliography, pp. 1–174. (International Association for

Obsidian Studies Occasional Paper 1).
San Jose, CA: Department of Anthropology, San Jose State University.

Taylor, R.E., ed. (1976) Advances in Obsidian Glass Studies. Park Ridge, NJ: Noyes.

Trembour, F., Smith, F.L., and Friedman, I. (1988) Cells for integrating temperature and humidity over long periods of time. In E. Sayre (ed.): Materials Issues in Art and Archaeology, pp. 245–251. (Materials Research Society Symposium Proceedings 123).

Offsetting

Measurements taken perpendicular to a base line at any point along its length. Offsetting can be used for simple land surveying or recording within an excavated area. To produce an offset line, a right angle must be constructed from the base line. This may be done with tapes, constructing a triangle with sides of the ratio 3:4:5. Alternatively, simple surveying instruments, such as the cross-head or optical square, can be used. A series of offset measurements can be used to record the shape and position of features, such as walls or banks. A single offset can be used to locate individual special finds within an excavated area.

Peter L. Drewett

See also SITE MAPPING

Further Readings

Barker, P. (1993) Techniques of Archaeological Excavation, 3rd ed. London: Batsford.

Drewett, P.L. (1999) Field Archaeology: An Introduction. London: University College Press.

Open-Area Excavation

A technique of excavation involving clearing large areas so whole archaeological deposits or features such as buildings can be excavated without the confusing presence of baulks (see Figure 1). Initially, this approach was applied mainly to fairly shallow sites of prehistoric and medieval date, especially in Denmark and Britain. During the 1970s, however, it was shown that the technique can be applied to all

Figure 1. A Bronze Age round house (ca. 1000 B.C.) excavated by the open-area method at Black Patch, Sussex, England. Photograph by Peter L. Drewett.

types of archaeological sites, including those with deep, complex stratigraphy, such as the City of London.

Open-area excavation requires as large an area of the site as possible, preferably the whole site, to be cleared of all postoccupation overburden. This is often done by machine. Each archaeological context (layer or feature, e.g. a pit, a posthole, or a wall) is defined and accurately recorded three dimensionally. Some archaeologists record all visible contexts on a single site plan, while others use the single-context recording system. This involves planning and recording each context on a separate plan. Either way, the sequence of events is reconstructed on paper after the end of the excavation.

The obvious advantage of the open-area excavation technique is that whole features can be seen in the accompanying figure see page 413. Only by seeing complete plans of buildings can any real attempt be made at their reconstruction. The formerly used grid system often revealed scatters of largely unintelligible postholes or wall fragments.

Open-area excavation does not preclude all use of standing soil sections. It does, however, enable sections to be placed where required to answer a specific problem, like a complex stratigraphical relationship, rather than having arbitrary sections imposed before the site is even vaguely understood.

Peter L. Drewett

See also STRIPPING

Further Readings

Barker, P. (1993) Techniques of Archaeological Excavation, 3rd ed. London: Batsford.

Drewett, P.L. (1999) Field Archaeology: An Introduction. London: University College London Press.

Optical Dating

A branch of luminescence dating developed primarily for windblown and waterborne sediment. As with thermoluminescence (TL), the latent dating signal is carried in the form of electrons trapped away from their normal locations in the crystal structure of the mineral grains concerned (e.g., of quartz, of feldspar, of zircon). Whereas for thermoluminescence the signal is obtained by heating, for optical dating it is obtained by shining onto the sample a beam of light or of infrared radiation. The emitted luminescence is termed *optically stimulated luminescence* (OSL), with *infrared-stimulated luminescence* (IRSL) being used to specify the latter method of stimulation; the term *photostimulated luminescence* (PL) is also employed.

During transportation and deposition, windblown and waterborne sediment grains are exposed to daylight; this releases any electrons already trapped (i.e., the clock is reset to zero). Thereafter, there is slow accumulation of trapped electrons on account of the flux of nuclear radiation from the weak natural radioactivity of the sediment (due to potassium, rubidium, thorium, and uranium); cosmic radiation also makes a contribution. When, in the laboratory, a prepared portion of the sample is exposed to a beam of light (or of infrared radiation), the electrons are released, and there is consequent emission of luminescence. This is the dating signal, and it is proportional to the years that have elapsed since deposition. Since, by its mode of stimulation, it is restricted to luminescence associated with electron traps that can easily be emptied by exposure to light, it is much more rapidly and much more effectively set to zero at deposition than the thermoluminescence dating signal; this is because the latter also includes luminescence associated with traps less easily emptied by light. This advantage allows poorly bleached deposits to be dated—particularly relevant for sediment that was deposited under water and for young samples, too. Stringent precautions need to be taken to avoid light exposure during sample extraction and laboratory processing. The optical technique can also be used for samples, such as pottery, for which the zeroing was by heat.

Development and Scope

The technique was pioneered at Simon Fraser University, British Columbia, in the mid-1980s, and, in less than a decade, it was in general use around the world. Optical dating is of particular value for Quaternary Earth-science studies, but the location of Palaeolithic remains in sediment makes it an archaeological tool, too; for example, as with TL, it has been important in dating the first arrival of humans in Australia. It is applicable at the recent end of the time scale as well—in dating silt deposited on archaeological and environmentally interesting sites. In Earth-science studies, it is useful in such widely divergent contexts as sand dunes and other features of climatic aridity, raised shoreline and fluvial deposits, and Arctic glacial-marine sediments. Above all, it is applicable to the windblown *loess* deposits that cover vast areas of the Earth's surface and in which many Palaeolithic sites are located.

Measurement

Much of the methodology is similar to thermoluminescence dating, but there is the important disadvantage that there is no intrinsic indication of signal stability as is given by the glow curve in TL dating. Instead, it is necessary to employ preheating before measurement so as to empty traps having inadequate lifetimes of electron retention (i.e., to empty traps that would give rise to thermoluminescence at a lower temperature than the plateau region). Typically, a preheat of 220°C for five minutes is used with quartz and 160°C for five hours with feldspar.

The stimulation light for quartz is usually green, and the resulting luminescence is sometimes referred to as *green-light-stimulated luminescence* (GLSL). A laser can be used to provide the beam (as in the pioneering studies) or, alternatively, a quartz halogen lamp restricted in spectral range by means of color filters. Detection by the photomultiplier of the emitted luminescence is restricted to violet and ultraviolet (also by color filters), as this gives good rejection of the stimulating light. In the case of quartz, further restriction to ultraviolet also has the advantage of isolating the emission associated with the trap that is most easily bleachable (it is the trap that gives rise to thermoluminescence at a temperature of ca. 325°C). The luminescence begins instantaneously with switch on of the light beam and then decreases rapidly as the traps are emptied. The *shine-down* curve so obtained is the dating signal. Alternatively, the *short-shine* mode may be employed in which the light beam is switched on only for a fraction of a second; this causes only slight depletion of the trapped electrons, and so repeated measurements can be made. When the shine-down mode is used, data analysis can be carried out for consecutive time intervals, and a value for the paleodose obtained for each interval. As with TL, the paleodose is evaluated as the dose of laboratory nuclear radiation needed to induce a level of luminescence equal to the *as-found* or *natural* luminescence. In this way, a plot of paleodose *versus* shine time is obtained; a constant level of paleodose is termed a *shine plateau*. As with TL, the age is obtained by dividing the paleodose by the dose rate.

For most types of feldspar, stimulation by infrared radiation is an alternative to green light. The radiation is conveniently, and cheaply, provided by an array of a dozen or so infrared-emitting diodes (with emission centered on 880 nm). One advantage over green light is that a wide wavelength range is available for measurement (the wavelengths reaching the photomultiplier must be shorter than used for stimulation), and, by means of color filters, a degree of mineral selectivity is possible. Whereas the majority of feldspar types respond to the infrared from the diodes, quartz responds only weakly, if at all; hence, absence of an infrared-stimulated signal is a convenient purity test for quartz portions prepared for measurement.

The situation regarding anomalous fading in feldspars is the same as with thermoluminescence, and the same tests have to be made, with sample rejection where appropriate. However, there are indications that, when microinclusions of feldspar are contained in quartz grains, and thereby shielded from weathering, such fading is absent or, at any rate, much reduced.

Age Range and Accuracy

The upper age limits are likely to be the same as for thermoluminescence except that, for the microinclusions just mentioned, ages of up to nearly half-a-million years have been reached—well beyond the usual limit for polymineral fine grains. At the recent end of the time scale, ages as young as a few hundred years can be obtained for well-bleached depositions and a level of radioactivity that is not too low. In other circumstances, a limit of ca. 1,000 years is to be expected. Accuracy attainable is similar to that of thermoluminescence.

Martin J. Aitken

See also LUMINESCENCE DATING; THERMOLU-MINESCENCE DATING

Further Readings

Aitken, M.J. (1994) Optical dating: A non-specialist review. Quaternary Geochronology 13:503–508.

Aitken, M.J. (1995) Introduction to Optical Dating. Oxford: Oxford University Press.

Huntley, D.J., Godfrey-Smith, D.I., and Thewalt, M.L.W. (1985) Optical dating of sediments. Nature 313:105–107.

Huntley, D.J., Hutton, J.T. and Prescott, J.R. (1993) Optical dating using inclusions within quartz grains. Geology 21:1087–1090.

P

Packaging of Archaeological Objects

The provision of support and protection for finds retrieved from excavations. The general aims in the packaging of archaeological objects are to support and protect objects weakened by deterioration processes that have occurred during burial and to prevent further deterioration, if possible, usually by control of the storage environment. The former is achieved using inert packaging materials to cushion, support, and enclose the objects; the latter, by the establishment of appropriate microclimates within enclosed packaging.

Archaeologists have a responsibility to ensure that the artifacts recovered from excavations are handled and packaged appropriately from the moment they are removed from their burial contexts until they are deposited in an institution that will take over that responsibility. Although active conservation treatments may also need to be applied to fully stabilize some items, the packaging of archaeological objects, as a passive conservation technique, is a crucial aspect of the postexcavation care of finds.

An object that survives burial will often have reached a state of equilibrium with its burial environment, in which the rate of deterioration is considerably slower than when the object first became incorporated into its archaeological context. When an object is excavated, the sudden change in environment inevitably disrupts that equilibrium and potentially accelerates deterioration until a new state of equilibrium is reached. One of the roles of correct packaging is to reduce that disruption to a minimum, thus keeping the rate of deterioration as low as possible, helping ensure the long-term survival of the object.

By the control of moisture and/or oxygen levels, the postexcavation deterioration of many objects can be reduced considerably. In practice, direct regulation of the oxygen content of the environment surrounding objects is often not practicable, so it is generally by the manipulation and control of the amount of water present that deterioration is minimized. Many objects recovered from waterlogged contexts are packaged wet prior to conservation to help reduce deterioration. Dry objects are often most stable at particular levels of humidity, according to the materials from which they are made. In air, the moisture content is measured by the amount of water vapor present in a fixed volume of air at a particular temperature relative to the maximum amount of water vapor that the air can hold, and it is expressed as percentage relative humidity (rH). Recommended rH levels for the storage environments of different materials are given later.

Archaeological objects are generally packaged individually, although bulk finds, such as iron nails, are usually packaged together by context, at least initially. When an object is recovered in fragments, these are packaged together, although care is taken to avoid damage occurring by abrasion. Discrete assemblages of finds are packaged together when excavated, preferably as blocks with surrounding soil so that the relative positions of the finds within them are preserved. Valuable information can be retrieved from such assemblages by careful examination and excavation in the conservation laboratory that could be lost if the individual objects were to be packaged separately on site.

Packaging Categories

There are basically four categories of packaging used for archaeological objects: *desiccated,* dry, damp, and wet. Damp and wet methods are used only for the storage of finds prior to conservation. The bags and boxes used to package individual objects are always selected to match the size of each object and are labeled clearly. Rot-proof spun-bonded polyethylene labels are included with each object, and all labeling is carried out using black spirit-based markers that are waterproof and light fast. Finds are padded using inert materials, with greatest support obtained by placing them in shaped recesses formed in the padding materials. Individually packaged finds are placed with other finds of the same material within larger boxes in which appropriate microclimates can be established if required.

For desiccated packaging, objects are allowed to dry out gradually, in the shade and away from direct heat, before being packaged in individual, pierced, self-seal polyethylene bags or rigid polystyrene boxes, padded to provide as much support as required. Open- or closed-cell polyethylene foams, polyethylene bubblepack, or crumpled acid-free tissue are usually used as padding materials. The packaged finds are placed together in padded, air-tight polyethylene boxes with silica-gel desiccant contained in pierced, self-seal polyethylene bags or netting bags. At least 100 g of dry silica gel are used per liter of container. An rH-indicator card is positioned inside each box so as to be visible without the lid having to be removed. When the rH is seen to rise above the recommended levels, the silica gel is regenerated by being heated in an oven to ca. 110°C for several hours before being allowed to cool and being rebagged and placed back in each box.

With dry packaging, objects are individually packaged as in the desiccated method, but the finds are then placed together in acid-free cardboxes or rigid polystyrene boxes padded with acid-free tissue, polyethylene foams, or polyethylene bubblepack. These boxes are stored in an environment with a humidity appropriate to the needs of the objects they contain. Alternatively, air-tight polyethylene boxes containing silica gel that has been conditioned to maintain the necessary rH are used.

Damp packaging involves placing objects between layers of open-cell polyethylene foam (or other rot-proof foam) that are saturated with water, contained within three unpierced self-seal polyethylene bags, or within rigid

polystyrene boxes within the three bags. These are placed in air-tight polyethylene boxes, sometimes containing yet more saturated foam, to ensure that no drying out occurs.

In the wet packaging of finds, pierced, self-seal polyethylene bags or heat-sealed polyethylene net bags are used to contain the objects, which are placed together inside air-tight polyethylene boxes filled completely with water to exclude air, padded with open-cell polyethylene foam. Alternatively, the finds are packaged within three unpierced, heat-sealed or self-seal polyethylene bags, with extra water and no air in the inner bag, and padded with saturated foam. Larger objects are packaged in purpose-made bags constructed from polyethylene sheeting or tubing that is heat sealed or stapled using stainless steel staples, or in boxes made from rigid corrugated polyethylene board.

Most objects are tolerant of a fairly wide range of temperatures, although generally a steady temperature between 10 and 25°C is advisable. In the case of objects stored wet or damp, a temperature between 2 and 4°C is recommended, as this considerably reduces deterioration rates and, in the short-term, can remove the need to use biocides. In long-term wet or damp storage, a conservator may advise the use of particular biocides prior to conservation. It must be remembered that biocides can pose a health hazard to those subsequently handling the finds, can cause problems if not thoroughly rinsed out prior to some conservation treatments, and must never be used with objects or samples that are to be submitted for radiocarbon dating.

Light levels are kept to a minimum, as some dry materials are susceptible to embrittlement or color fading when exposed to ultraviolet light; in wet or damp storage, light encourages some biological deterioration processes.

Metal Objects

Metals encountered on archaeological excavations include iron, copper, lead, tin, silver, and gold, although nonferrous objects (those made from metals other than iron) are often made from alloys of two or more nonferrous metals, such as bronze (copper and tin) or brass (copper and zinc). Most metal objects recovered from archaeological sites will have suffered some degree of corrosion. In aggressive burial environments, mineralization is usually extensive, sometimes complete, leaving a very fragile object susceptible to physical damage if not adequately supported following excavation. Under less harsh burial conditions, a considerable proportion of sound metal can be present. In such cases, the object may be quite robust although susceptible to postexcavation corrosion. As it is not always possible on an excavation to discern the extent of mineralization, it is safest to assume that some sound metal is present and that further corrosion could occur. Desiccated packaging is, therefore, used. Iron objects are stored below 15 percent rH, while other metals are kept below 35 percent rH. It must be noted that desiccated storage requires rigorous curation if it is to be maintained indefinitely.

Tin objects, although not often found, are ideally kept above 14°C, as prolonged storage below this temperature can cause a gradual change in crystal structure that may lead to some damage occurring.

As lead and lead-alloy objects are very susceptible to corrosion in the presence of organic acid vapors, paper-based products are not used in their packaging because they can act as a source of such vapors.

The packaging of metal/organic composite objects requires more careful consideration. When recovered from a waterlogged context, such an object is stored wet or damp prior to conservation. When recovered from a nonwaterlogged context, the packaging is governed by the components present, their condition and stability, and their relative importance. Each case is decided individually, although, as a general guideline, the potential damage arising from further corrosion of the metal component is weighed against the damage that could be caused to the organic component by desiccated storage. Such considerations are also important following the conservation of such finds.

Organic Objects

Organic materials sometimes encountered on archaeological excavations include wood, leather, textile, bone, antler, ivory, horn, basketry, and altered organics, such as amber (fossilized resin) and jet (black lignite). In many burial environments, objects made from wood, leather, textile, horn, and basketry do not survive. The most common situation in which these are recovered is from waterlogged contexts, although frozen or desiccated environments will also help to preserve them. Bone, antler, ivory, amber, and jet objects tend to survive under a wider range of conditions. In all cases, any surviving objects will have been weakened by physical and/or biochemical deterioration during burial, so packaging is used that gives good physical support and protection.

Small waterlogged organic objects are packaged wet or damp. Larger objects are wrapped in several layers of polyethylene sheet or metallized plastic sheet or placed inside several layers of polyethylene tubing, which are then heat sealed or folded over and stapled using stainless steel staples. Open-cell polyethylene or polyether foams, saturated with water, are used as padding and to hold moisture onto the surface of the objects. Support is provided for small waterlogged objects using padded rigid corrugated polyethylene board; for larger and heavier objects, padded marine plywood boards or padded stainless steel sheets are used.

Organic finds recovered from waterlogged frozen contexts are kept frozen prior to conservation unless allowed to thaw during excavation, in which case wet or damp packaging methods are used.

Organic objects that have survived in desiccated environments are packaged dry, with plenty of support. Brittleness is a particular problem in these cases.

Objects recovered from damp nonwaterlogged contexts are generally packaged dry. Exceptions to this are ivory, which is stored damp until conserved, and jet, which is stored wet prior to conservation.

Following conservation treatment, organic objects are packaged dry and stored at an rH of 50–55 percent, with as few fluctuations as possible.

Objects or samples made from organic materials that are to be submitted for radiocarbon dating are given special attention. Such items are kept away from any extraneous organic materials that could cause contamination, such as biocides. They are packaged in sealed polyethylene bags if waterlogged or wrapped in aluminum foil if not, and placed in rigid boxes until being transferred to the dating laboratory, which is done as soon as possible after excavation.

Inorganic Objects

Objects made from nonmetallic inorganic materials are often recovered by archaeologists, as they usually survive in a wide range of burial environments. The materials that may be found include fired clay (ceramics), unfired clay (adobe, sun-dried clay tablets), stone, plaster, glass, and semivitreous substances (e.g., frit and faience). Well-fired ceramic items and stone objects are generally very resilient and in quite robust condition when excavated, although often fragmented. Poorly fired and unfired clay objects and some stone objects, such as finds made from shale, are more vulnerable to postexcavation deterioration. Glass of a stable composition survives quite well in a range of conditions, although unstable glass, such as European medieval potash glass, deteriorates badly and is usually recovered in poor condition, weakened by chemical and physical deterioration.

Although most objects made from inorganic materials are packaged dry, there are exceptions. Wet shale objects are kept in wet or damp packaging prior to conservation to prevent them from splitting into layers. Painted wall plaster can be left with a fine layer of dirt on the surface that is very difficult to remove if it is allowed to dry before being cleaned, so it is packaged damp if surface soiling is a problem. Porous materials known to contain soluble salts are either stored wet until desalinated or in desiccated conditions to prevent damaging salt crystallization/hydration cycles from occurring. Glass recovered from waterlogged contexts is allowed to dry only after a test piece has been observed to dry without damage occurring. Otherwise, it is stored wet or damp prior to conservation.

Once conserved, most inorganic materials tolerate a wide range of storage conditions. However, it is considered best to store inorganic objects at an rH of 50–55 percent, although unstable glass may be better stored at an rH of 40 percent.

Adrian P. Tribe

See also CERAMICS, ON-SITE CONSERVATION; CONSERVATION OF ARCHAEOLOGICAL MATERIALS; FIBROUS METALS, ON-SITE CONSERVATION; GLASS, ON-SITE CONSERVATION; LEATHER, ON-SITE CONSERVATION; METALS, ON-SITE CONSERVATION; STONE, ON-SITE CONSERVATION; WOOD (WATERLOGGED), CONSERVATION

Further Readings

Cronyn, J.M. (1990) The Elements of Archaeological Conservation. London and New York: Routledge.

Sease, C. (1994) A Conservation Manual for the Field Archaeologist, 3rd ed. (Archaeological Research Tools 4). Los Angeles: Institute of Archaeology, UCLA.

Watkinson, D. and Neal, V. (1998) First Aid for Finds. Hertford, U.K.: RESCUE/and UKIC Archaeology Section.

Paleodemography

Reconstruction of population structure based on the analysis of human skeletal remains from historic and prehistoric contexts.

History

Paleodemography has been defined by Jane Buikstra and Lyle Konigsberg as "the study of vital rates, population distribution and density in extinct human populations, especially those for which there are no written records" (Buikstra and Konigsberg 1985:316). The field has its roots in traditional demography, which concentrates on three areas of population change: mortality, fertility, and migration. Anthropological demography focuses on the same areas but uses a smaller, usually nonliterate, population. Paleodemography can be viewed as a more specialized area of anthropological demography using archaeological material, particularly human skeletal remains, as its primary data set. Demographers and paleodemographers have similar goals but vastly different data sets.

Paleodemography is a relatively new research area of anthropology and, in the New World, has its foundations in Earnest A. Hooton's 1920 analysis of an Ohio prehistoric cemetery. This was followed by a paleodemographic analysis of the material recovered from Pecos Pueblo, New Mexico, and later by work done at Indian Knoll, Kentucky. However, it was not until the 1960s that paleodemographic research became more common. In part, this was due to Ester Boserup's treatise (The Conditions of Agricultural Growth, 1965) maintaining that populations are capable of driving cultural evolution. In 1969, J. Lawrence Angel wrote a seminal paper detailing the uses of paleodemography. Angel's work in the 1960s was followed by other key works such as György Acsádi and János

Nemeskéri's *History of Human Life Span and Mortality*. During the 1970s, several graduate schools developed programs focusing on this topic. Although paleodemography seemed very promising during this time period, critics of the field arose in the late 1970s and early 1980s (discussed later).

Concepts and Applications

Angel believed that paleodemography could provide basically five different types of information. Paleodemography can allow an assessment of the age and sex composition of a population. In addition, age-specific mortality can be examined, as can adult longevity of each sex. Fertility and population size can also be estimated. All of this information can be examined to understand the adaptive efficiency of a group of people to their environment. The demographic analysis of human skeletal remains strengthens information pertaining to the growth, migration, and collapse of prehistoric populations.

Paleodemographic research has been applied to various research questions in an effort to elucidate information about past peoples. Hugh Berryman noted that one early use included a study of the relationship between subsistence type and mortality pattern by comparing age- and sex-specific mortality in hunting-and-gathering versus agricultural groups. Other studies have focused on the effects of disease and cultural conditions on mortality profiles. More specifically, Douglas Owsley has used paleodemographic research to establish the presence of intertribal warfare at the Larsen site in South Dakota. However, the most common archaeological use of paleodemographic data involves the analysis of age and sex composition present at a site, as well as the study of adult longevity, in an effort to determine the amount of stress that a population was experiencing.

Paleodemographic information can be valuable to anthropologists, but, because of the nature of the data set, it can be quite controversial. Traditional demographers have access to much information that a paleodemographer does not. Paleodemography is rooted in methodologies that have not always been as accurate as possible. In addition, many assumptions are necessary for basic paleodemographic techniques to be of utility. For instance, *life tables,* one of the techniques used by paleodemographers to convert age-at-death data into statistics such as mortality and life expectancy, require two major simplifying assumptions. The first assumption is that the sample yielding data for use in the life table was stable. This refers to a condition in which the mortality, fertility, and growth rates are unchanging. The second assumption states that the sample must be stationary. A stationary population is a specific type of a stable population in which birth and death rates are assumed to be equal to each other so that no growth occurs.

Paleodemographers are also limited by the nature of their data set. The major limitations come from problems in sampling and preservation, as well as aging and sexing biases. Poorly preserved samples limit the amount of age and sex characteristics that can be assessed. In addition, infant and child remains often do not preserve well and are, therefore, frequently underenumerated. This is a particular problem in paleodemography since children are very sensitive to adaptive indicators and make the best gauge of a group's health. Another problem comes from differential burial practices in which different segments of a population are interred in varying areas. Failure to realize that this has occurred can result in falsely applying paleodemographic assumptions to a population.

Because of the nature of archaeologically recovered skeletal samples, Douglas Ubelaker has established several prerequisites that samples must meet before paleodemographic analyses can be undertaken. Foremost among these is knowledge that the sample is complete. This ensures against gaps in the sample due to differential burial practices, for example. In addition, information pertaining to the archaeological associations of the skeletons is necessary. An estimate must be obtained of the length of time the sample represents, and reliable estimates of age and sex of the individuals must be made. Lastly, paleodemographic techniques appropriate to the sample must be selected.

The accuracy of paleodemographic research relies entirely on the accurate assessment of age and sex of individuals within a sample. Therefore, these methodologies are critical to the field. Much of the advance made in paleodemography in the 1960s and 1970s was the result of osteological improvements in aging and sexing techniques.

P

Methodological Limitations

Because paleodemography is dependent upon so many different factors and assumptions, this area of research has been plagued with controversy, especially since the early 1980s. One of the most serious threats came from Jean-Pierre Bocquet-Appel and Claude Masset in an article entitled "Farewell to Paleodemography" published in 1982. The authors argued that the uses of paleodemography had been overestimated. Most of their complaints were methodological in origin and consisted of assertions that aging techniques were too inaccurate to be of use. They asserted that mortality structures could not be accurately estimated using accepted aging techniques. In addition, they contended that age structures obtained from skeletal samples too closely resembled the age structure of the population from which the technique was derived.

Bocquet-Appel and Masset's contentions relating to the field were quickly challenged by different researchers. Analysis of a Nubian skeletal sample by Dennis P. Van Gerven and George J. Armelagos demonstrated that age structures of a studied population do not follow that of the reference group. Later, Buikstra and Konigsberg challenged the ideas put forth by Bocquet-Appel and Masset and effectively silenced most of them. However, while methodologies for aging have been improved since the original criticisms against them, the accuracy of many of these techniques applied to skeletal material is still debated. In addition, Kenneth Weiss's life tables, so frequently used by paleodemographers, have been attacked because there is little agreement between information obtained from them when compared to other data. Mary Jackes suggests that the Weiss tables, which presume low infant but high adolescent mortality, exhibit this configuration because of their basis in biased archaeological samples.

A recent blow to paleodemography comes from a 1992 article by James W. Wood and colleagues entitled "The Osteological Paradox." The authors suggest that paleodemography as used to interpret prehistoric health has certain deficiencies that need to be acknowledged. They argue that the concepts of *demographic nonstationarity, selective mortality,* and *hidden heterogeneity* must be addressed. Demographic nonstationarity refers to the idea that a population is not stationary (discussed earlier). In a nonstationary population, age at death is a more responsive indicator of changes in fertility than in mortality. Therefore, the calculated age at death may better assess fertility than mortality. Selective mortality, the second necessary issue to address, relates to the idea that a certain age category recovered and identified in archaeological samples contains only those individuals who actually died at that age, not others who were at risk at that age but able to survive. The authors argue that an age category is selective of medical disorders that escalate the chance of death at that age. Therefore, the rate of lesions seen in a sample overestimates the frequency present in the population. Hidden heterogeneity describes the idea that, within a given population, people differ in their susceptibility to a disease. The fact that this heterogeneity cannot be assessed from skeletal remains makes it "virtually impossible to interpret aggregate-level age-specific mortality rates in terms of individual risks of death" (Wood et al. 1992:345). Failure to take these three ideas into consideration when making inferences can result in meaningless data. While the authors note the difficulty in determining the health of a prehistoric population, their article did not have the fatality to the field of paleodemography that has been associated with work of Bocquet-Appel and Masset. Rather, they ask for consideration of the concepts they address, as well as the development of multiple hypotheses when referring to paleodemography and health.

Paleodemographic research is an interdisciplinary area within anthropology that combines the work of forensic anthropologists, physical anthropologists, archaeologists, and traditional demographers. All play a vital role in assessing the population structure of prehistoric groups. However, this area of research remains controversial in both methodology and theory. Eric A. Roth noted, though, that in some ways controversy has helped strengthen the field.

Helen Danzeiser Dockall

See also PALEOPATHOLOGY, HUMAN

Further Readings

Angel, J.L. (1969) The bases of paleodemography. American Journal of Physical Anthropology 30:427–438.

Bocquet-Appel, J.-P. and Masset, C., (1982) Farewell to paleodemography. Journal of Human Evolution 11:321–333.

Buikstra, J.E., and Konigsberg, L.W. (1985) Paleodemography: Critiques and controversies. American Anthropologist 87:316–333.

Jackes, M. (1992) Paleodemography: Problems and techniques. In S.R. Saunders and M.A. Katzenberg (eds.): Skeletal Biology of Past Peoples: Research Methods, pp. 189–224. New York: Wiley-Liss.

Roth, E.A. (1992) Applications of demographic models to paleodemography. In S.R. Saunders and M.A. Katzenberg (eds.): Skeletal Biology of Past Peoples: Research Methods, pp. 175–188. New York: Wiley-Liss.

Van Gerven, D.P., and Armelagos, G.J. (1983) "Farewell to paleodemography?" Rumors of its death have been greatly exaggerated. Journal of Human Evolution 12:353–360.

Weiss, K.M. (1973) Demographic Models for Anthropology. (Memoirs of the Society of American Archaeology 27 [American Antiquity 38(2): Part 2]).Washington, D.C.: Society for American Archaeology.

Wood, J.W., Milner, G.R., Harpending, H.C., and Weiss, K.M. (1992) The osteological paradox: Problems of inferring prehistoric health from skeletal samples. Current Anthropology 33(4):343–370.

Paleoethnobotany

The specific discipline that trains specialists to investigate and analyze the botanical record from archaeological sites; referred to either as *archaeobotany* or *paleoethnobotany*. Although occasionally used to refer to the recovery of botanical remains from archaeological sites, the term *paleobotany* refers more specifically to the recovery of plant remains from the pre-Quaternary geologic record.

During the late 1890s, the American scientist John Harshberger was studying the dried plant remains recovered from pueblo sites in the American Southwest and was searching for a word to represent his type of research. The term *ethnobotany*, as he narrowly defined it, was the study of how primitive or aboriginal people used plants.

Later, in a classic essay, "The Nature and Status of Ethnobotany," Volney H. Jones emphasized that the study of ethnobotany "should be concerned not only with uses of plants, but with the entire range of relations between primitive man and plants" (Jones 1941:219). He suggested adopting the broadest possible definition of ethnobotany as "the study of the interrelations of primitive man and plants" (Jones 1941:220). During the first half of the twentieth century, the term *ethnobotany* did not distinguish between the study of archaeological or ethnographically observed plants.

During the late 1950s, the Danish scientist Hans Helbaek introduced a new term, *paleoethnobotany*. Helbaek first used this word to refer to the botanical research he and others were conducting in the Middle East, especially as it pertained to documentation of the earliest stages of plant domestication. For nearly two decades after Helbaek introduced the term *paleoethnobotany*, most archaeologists still referred to his type of study as ethnobotany.

By the late 1970s, American researcher Richard I. Ford introduced another new term, *archaeobotany*, which he said referred specifically to the study of that part of archaeology pertaining to "the recovery and identification of plants by specialists regardless of discipline" (Ford 1979:299). Ford explains that he introduced the new word because the term paleoethnobotany implied both the identification and the subsequent interpretation of botanical remains, while the term archaeobotany could be used to define only the techniques of recovery and identification of botanical remains.

Plants and Culture

Jones emphasized the dependence of the human species on plants: "Man is basically dependent on plants for his very existence, as plants are the ultimate source of all food and fuel" (Jones 1941:219). Throughout human history, people have utilized a wide variety of plant foods derived from all parts of the plant: fruits, seeds, nuts, flowers, pollen, nectar, leaves, wood, underground storage parts, and bark, just to name a few. These foods are prepared in a wide variety of ways that modify the plants for consumption, including grinding, grating, pounding, chewing, soaking in water, and fermentation. The addition of heat can be accomplished by boiling, steaming, parching, and baking in earth ovens. Thus, fire becomes a major contributor to the archaeobotanical record. Not only does fire produce evidence in the form of carbonized fuel wood, but the accidental burning of foods during preparation provides a durable record of charred remains.

In addition to being the only ultimate source of food and fuel, plants have provided the raw material to fulfill human needs for clothing, shelter, tools, transportation, weapons, and the fashioning of social or religious iconic expressions, such as totems, paint for pictographs, and so forth. Plants are also valuable as the main source of medicinal compounds for healing and for achieving altered states of consciousness. For example, the nicotine in tobacco and the hallucinogenic alkaloids in jimsonweed or peyote have had a profound impact on belief systems in human societies.

The botanical remains deposited at archaeological sites include a wide range of macroremains (i.e., roots, wood, leaves, bark, flowers, seeds, charcoal, and fibers), microremains (i.e., pollen, spores, diatoms, and phytoliths), and chemicals (i.e., pH, Eh, trace elements, DNA, amino acids). Collectively, the plant remains that are recovered, identified, and quantified at an archaeological site usually are referred to as the *archaeobotanical record*.

The highly modified plant parts that make up the archaeobotanical record are left in site sediments, on artifacts such as stone knives, manos and metates or in vessels, and in coprolites (preserved human feces). Coprolites are especially useful because they contain plant remains that have passed through a human digestive system. As such, they reflect foods that were eaten.

Once the botanical remains are collected and analyzed, the archaeologist can use the data to reconstruct or interpret patterns of plant utilization; environmental changes brought about by human or climatic influences; land-use patterns, including plant foraging or plant production; and trade and diet. As ideal as all of this may sound, the practical reality of recovering all of these types of botanical information is often limited by a variety of factors over which the archaeologist has little control. These include: (1) whether or not artifacts made from plant materials were lost or discarded in the precise areas of a site that are later excavated; (2)

whether or not plant debris was discarded as refuse; (3) whether or not plant remains discarded at a site are later destroyed by a variety of weathering agents; and (4) whether or not the excavation procedures specifically searched for all types of potential botanical remains.

Developmental History
Plant Macroremains

In most scientific fields, it often takes something unique, or spectacular, to attract the attention of professionals and to create widespread interest. So it was with the recovery and analysis of plant remains from archaeological sites. In the case of archaeology, it was the German scientist Conrad Kunth's report on the identification and analysis of desiccated plant remains recovered from ancient Egyptian tombs excavated during the early 1820s that first caught the interest and imagination of many archaeologists. Later, during the 1850s, more interest was generated by the work of the Danish biologist Japetus Steenstrup, who published a series of reports on the plant remains from shell middens in Denmark.

A few years later, Oswald Heer of Zurich, Switzerland, published a report on the identification of preserved plant materials found in a number of waterlogged sites once occupied by ancient Swiss lake dwellers. His report was especially important because it demonstrated that plant remains could be recovered and analyzed from sites in areas that were not dry or desertlike conditions of the Middle East.

In the Americas, the field of paleoethnobotany began in the mid-1870s when the French botanist David Saffray was asked to examine and identify the plant materials from a mummy burial found in a Peruvian dry cave. A few years later, in 1879, another French botanist, Anthony T. de Rochebrune, described the plant remains from several Peruvian cemetery sites found in the coastal Ancon region. During the 1880s, the German botanist Ludwig Wittmack reexamined the Ancon materials and analyzed additional plant remains from other Peruvian sites. However, in spite of these early botanical accomplishments in South America, the primary concerns of most North American archaeologists during the late nineteenth century focused on constructing artifact typologies and chronological controls rather than on the recovery and identification of botanical remains.

From the beginnings of North American archaeology through the end of the late 1920s, little attention was given to the recovery or analysis of plant materials recovered during archaeological excavations. As noted by Jones (1957), some of the reasons for this were caused by the perishability and intermittent occurrence of plant remains in archaeological sediments, existing excavation and recovery techniques that were not designed to maximize the recovery of plant remains, and the fact that, once the paleoethnobotanical remains were collected, few botanists were willing to examine and identify them.

During the 1930s, attitudes toward the recovery of archaeobotanical remains changed. On September 17, 1930, Carl Guthe of the University of Michigan sent a circular to most of the professional archaeologists of that day stating that Melvin R. Gilmore, an anthropologist and botanist working for the Museum of Anthropology at the University of Michigan, would be willing to examine and identify botanical remains from archaeological sites—for free. In a subsequent circular, Gilmore (1932) outlined the importance of saving botanical remains from sites and explained the free services that would be provided by the newly created Ethnobotanical Laboratory of the University of Michigan.

To say that Guthe's 1930 invitation was a success is an understatement. During the next two decades, the newly created Ethnobotanical Laboratory received more than 4,700 groups of samples from 390 different archaeological sites, and the total number of specimens numbered in the thousands.

Later, during his career as director of the Ethnobotanical Laboratory, Volney Jones would establish many of the analytical techniques and standards that are still used in the discipline. More important, Jones also trained a new generation of botanical specialists who combined academic and research training from both archaeology and botany. These graduates went on to establish their own research laboratories and academic training centers and are still training other generations of paleoethnobotanists.

Plant Microremains

Of equal importance is the developmental history of two other specialized areas of paleoethnobotany: *palynology* (pollen studies) and *phytoliths* (plant-crystal studies).

As with the study of plant macroremains, Europeans were the first to take the initiative in using pollen data from archaeological sites. The application of palynology to the field of archaeology came later and grew more slowly in North America than it did in Europe. In an article published in a 1932 issue of the *American Anthropologist,* Paul B. Sears became the first American to use fossil pollen data to interpret the archaeological record. In his initial study, he noted that fossil pollen evidence indicated that there was an environmental shift just over 1,000 years ago in the eastern United States that would have provided favorable conditions for growing maize. This climatic warming occurred during the same chronological time period as the first widespread expansion of Hopewell cultures into many new areas of eastern North America.

Sears also pioneered the early fossil pollen investigations of sediments in the Southwest, an area where much of the early focus on American archaeological work was concentrated. However, it wasn't until the early 1960s that Paul S. Martin and his graduate students at the University of Arizona began the first systematic study of fossil-pollen records in the American Southwest.

Between the early 1960s and the late 1970s, more attention was given to the pollen sampling of archaeological sites. Even so, four factors slowed this technique from becoming commonplace. First, prior to the 1970s and 1980s, the number of trained palynologists who had an understanding of archaeology and were willing to examine archaeological pollen samples was limited. Second, widespread interest in trying to use archaeological pollen data did not become popular until after the 1980s because many of the early attempts were conducted in locales where pollen preservation was marginal or nonexistent; thus, those sites produced little usable information. Third, the initial pollen extraction and analytical techniques were developed and perfected for use in the European bogs, where organic preservation is ideal and the analytical objective is to derive vegetational reconstructions. Adequate extraction and interpretive techniques for use on archaeological sediments were developed slowly over three decades of research between 1960 and 1990. Fourth, it was not until pollen data became required as part of the scope of work for most contract-type archaeological projects that many archaeologists began conducting fossil pollen studies as part of their routine studies of sites.

The recovery and study of phytoliths in archaeology is still underutilized. Even though in 1908 Schellenberg became the first researcher to recover and analyze phytoliths from an archaeological site, other scientists were slow to utilize this new recovery technique. By the late 1950s, Helbaek was reporting that he had found phytoliths present in the soils of a number of archaeological sites located in the Middle East. He recovered and identified phytoliths produced by wheat, oats, millet, and rice embedded in Neolithic pottery sherds and in the ash and midden soils of Neolithic-age sites. More recently, American scientists, such as Deborah Pearsall and Dolores Piperno, have shown how phytoliths can be used to document farming and domesticated plant use in tropical regions where other forms of prehistoric botanical evidence are missing because of harsh soil conditions.

Diatoms are microscopic forms of algae that produce outer shells of inorganic silica. Although uncommon in the soils of most archaeological sites, diatoms, when they are found, are useful indicators of nearby water sources and of certain types of paleoenvironmental conditions. Diatom species, which thrive in wet environments or survive only within a narrow range of water temperature and salinity conditions, are the most useful for paleoenvironmental indicators.

Although diatoms do not represent a known human food source, they occur in some drinking-water sources and can adhere to the roots of aquatic plants. In both ways, diatoms can be introduced into the soils of archaeological sites or into the human digestive tract and later into human fecal material.

Human Coprolites

The recovery and analysis of human coprolite remains from archaeological sites have a long history. In his now famous 1896 article, Harshberger not only introduced the new term *ethnobotany*, but he also was one of the first researchers to examine and then report on the importance of human coprolite studies. A few years later, during the early 1900s, Col. Bennett Young examined human coprolites recovered from Salts and Mammoth caves in Kentucky. From his study, Young concluded that prehistoric cultures who used those caves had eaten diets of sunflower seeds and hickory nuts.

During the next half-century, there were few additional coprolite studies, and it wasn't until 1960 that Canadians Eric Callen and Thomas Cameron introduced new processing techniques that revolutionized coprolite analysis. In their initial study of human coprolites from the Huaca Prieta site in Peru, they discovered a faster and better way to process coprolites and demonstrated how coprolite remains were effective ways to reconstruct the diets of prehistoric peoples. As Vaughn Bryant noted in an article about Callen's life, Callen went on to become the father of coprolite studies until his untimely death in 1970.

Using the new analytical techniques perfected by Callen, other researchers went on to examine human coprolites from many regions of the world. During the late 1960s, a number of coprolite reports focused on prehistoric diets in the American Southwest, while a few others concentrated on sites in the eastern part of North America. By the 1970s and 1980s, scientists were examining large numbers of human coprolites recovered from many arid regions of South America.

Formation Processes Affecting the Botanical Record

Potentially, the total botanical record consists of all the plant materials used or discarded by a given culture, at a specific location, during a specified unit of time. Depending on the research goals and the researcher, the time unit studied might be a few hours or thousands of years. Unfortunately, the total botanical record at any archaeological site is rarely, if ever, recovered. Only a small portion of the original archaeobotanical record, the portion preserved, remains at a site. Of that portion, comparatively small samples are generally collected for analysis.

The formation processes that affect the botanical record begin with the human selection and modification of the plants. They continue after the plant is discarded and begins to decompose under a variety of depositional conditions. The archaeobotanical record is further fashioned by a variety of physical and/or biological agents during both site occupation and later abandonment. Finally, the decisions made by researchers during excavation, sampling, and analysis contribute to the nature of the reported archaeobotanical record. All of these processes that affect the composition of the archaeobotanical record are referred to as *formation processes*.

Human Behavior

The length of time a site was originally used and how extensively it was occupied will influence the types of botanical information that can be recovered. Likewise, and equally important, are the subsequent changes that occur to archaeological deposits after they are formed. Groups who use a previously occupied site might alter, remove, or disassemble some of the botanical record left by earlier occupants. Later groups might also dig storage or burial pits through earlier deposits, or they might collect wood or stone from structures left by a previous culture and reuse or burn it. Commonly, hearths or earth ovens are cleaned out, and the refuse is scattered across a site. Pits originally used as hearths or storage pits often are reused as trash pits. All of these actions will alter the original context of the botanical data at an archaeological site.

Preservation

The preservation of botanical remains at any archaeological site is dependent on the interplay between destructive processes and local environmental conditions that tend to mitigate these processes. An archaeologist should be aware of specific environments that favor the survival of plant remains. Arid environments, such as dry caves or open sites in areas of extremely low precipitation, favor the survival of plant remains. Perpetually waterlogged environments, such as the lakeshore sites of Switzerland or the bogs of Denmark, are also excellent areas of preservation. The worst environments are archaeological sites in unprotected areas that are subjected to moderate or high precipitation. At these sites, only carbonized plant remains often survive.

Some plant parts tend to survive better than others, hence are continually overrepresented in the record. The most likely to survive include wood, nuts, and corn cobs. Edible seeds, especially those that are subjected to parching, are next. Least likely to survive are plant parts with higher water content such as beans, underground plant-storage organs such as tubers or bulbs, and greens.

At all archaeological sites, regardless of the quality of environmental preservation, most plant remains are subjected to processes that eventually damage them and move them around in the site. The first process is termed *reduction* or *decomposition;* the second, *turbation.*

Plant remains are reduced or decomposed by a variety of agents, both biological and physical. Uncharred fruits and seeds are immediately attacked by arthropods and small vertebrates. Mechanical reduction is further speeded by wetting-drying cycles, freeze-thaw cycles, and temperature extremes. Bacterial and fungal activities also reduce the materials. Chemical decomposition will affect the record as well. High pH tends to destroy both macroremains and pollen, while low pH tends to favor their preservation.

A number of physical and biological agents move plant remains from their original context. Physical agents include wind, flooding, shrink-swell actions of clays, and tree falls. Biological agents include all burrowing animals. The latter are especially troublesome because they often introduce rich deposits of plant materials that have nothing to do with the occupational history of a site.

All of these activities alter the original context and makeup of the botanical record. The archaeologist and the botanical analyst must cooperate closely in an effort to interpret the effects of these formation processes on the archaeobotanical record. When successful, a more nearly accurate understanding of human-plant interrelationships can be achieved.

Recovery of Botanical Remains
Sampling

General guidelines for the sampling strategies of both microremains and macroremains are similar. There is neither enough time nor sufficient funds to collect, sort, and identify the contents of most archaeological sites, and a wide range of factors affect sampling and recovery of botanical remains. Therefore, one of the most important questions that should be asked is: "How much of a sample is needed?" Decisions regarding sampling involve three main questions: (1) how many samples should be taken, (2) how large should each individual sample be, and (3) from what contexts should the samples be taken?

Due to a variety of factors, such as the amount of funding and time available, the size and history of a site, and conditions of preservation at the site, no two archaeological sites are generally sampled identically. The size, or volume, of each sample should be adjusted to fit the needs of each site. Generally, the larger the volume or weight of a sample, the more plant remains should be recovered. However, beyond a certain point, the increase in returns begins to diminish. The point of diminishing returns can be estimated by sampling a site during the testing phase and counting the numbers of plant parts and taxa against a series of increasing sample volumes. The best volume would be the point at which the curve begins to level off. For microremains, the same guidelines hold true, but if the researcher is interested in multiple studies of pollen, phytoliths, and the like, extra samples of the same material should be collected for each extraction process.

For macrobotanical recovery, larger sample sizes are often more difficult and time consuming to process. Thus, there is a trade-off between the volume of each sample and the number of samples that can be effectively processed. The larger the volume of each sample, the larger the database becomes from each sample. However, larger sample numbers often provide a more extensive list of recovered botanical remains. Once adequate sample volumes are determined, an archaeologist should try to keep the sample size as uniform as possible. This will simplify the use of statistical data needed for intra- and intersite comparisons.

The areas of the site to be sampled should be determined during the planning stages of the excavation. At the very minimum, a group of samples should be taken from the site proper and from areas just outside the site, which serve as control samples used to compare taxa recovered from the archaeological sediments with taxa from sediments that accumulated under less-anthropogenic processes. This comparison allows the analyst to compare the "natural" seed rain with the potential cultural use of plant materials found in the archaeological sediments.

On the site, a series of samples within features should be compared to a series of samples outside the features. At sites with more complex architecture, most botanical analysts also would want to sample specific archaeological features, such as hearths, roasting pits, or vessel contents. By emphasizing a particular

suite of features, activity areas within a large site can be studied more expeditiously.

Macroremains

How samples are recovered also depends on time, funding, objectives, site location, and the type of the site being excavated. At open sites, where botanical preservation is often limited to carbonized plant remains, flotation is one of the preferred techniques.

An alternative collection process is screening. There are two commonly used screening procedures: dry and wet. Dry screening is the preferred technique at sites where the sediments consist of dry, sandy, and powdery-dry silts. The mesh size used for dry screens will determine how fast silts and sands can be screened and the particle size of the botanical remains that will be captured. When dry screening is used, all excavated deposits are generally processed first through large-mesh-size (6 mm) screens. Small portions of the screened sediments, passing through the large-mesh screens, are then reprocessed through a small-mesh-size (3 mm) screen. The amount of sediment selected for fine screening will generally depend on the excavation objectives, time, and level of funding for a project.

Wet screening is a procedure in which excavated soils are washed through screens using a fine spray of water. It is often used in areas where water is plentiful or where dry screening is difficult because of a site's sediment consisting of dirt clods, large pieces of clumped silts, or waterlogged soils. Wet screening can include the use of screens with various mesh sizes, and it is a rapid method of artifact recovery.

Tests have shown that screening and flotation will not produce the same recovery rates of botanical remains. The recovery of fragile plant parts, some carbonized seeds, and other tiny organic fragments is greater during flotation than during screening. Both dry and wet screening are more abrasive to plant remains and frequently use mesh sizes that may not capture the tiniest seeds.

Microremains

Recovery of microremains from archaeological sediments is fairly standardized. These techniques, usually referred to as *extraction* procedures, are designed to concentrate microremains by screening, settling, separation using heavy liquids, and chemical-reduction methods. The extraction process can be modified, depending on whether pollen, diatom, or phytolith recovery is the primary objective.

Microfossil sampling strategies for pollen and phytolith recovery are similar. Sediment samples, generally consisting of ca. 250 g, can be collected from many locations at a site. The number of samples collected will vary, depending on the data objectives, time, and funding. Nevertheless, sampling is fairly quick; thus, it is generally wiser to collect more samples than may be needed than not to collect enough samples. Pearsall details recommendations on how and where to sample for microremains at archaeological sites.

Analysis

After botanical materials are recovered, the next phase consists of analysis and eventual interpretation of the data. The analysis strategy selected may, to some degree, influence the interpretation of the results. Therefore, selecting the best analysis strategy is often critical.

Macroremains

Sample selection and processing, either by flotation or screening, is usually conducted by the archaeological field or laboratory crew. Once the samples are floated or screened, the recovered material is sent to a botanist for analysis. Analysis takes place in three stages: *sorting, identification,* and *quantification.* Each of these three tasks should be performed by the macrobotanical analyst who will interpret the results.

Sorting. Macrobotanical samples should be sorted as completely as possible. The most expedient way to do this is to pass a sample through a series of four or five size-graded geological screens that usually range from 4-mm mesh to 0.25-mm mesh. The analyst then examines the remains from each size-graded screen through a low-power (8-10x) stereoscopic microscope and sorts the seeds, fruit fragments, and floral parts from roots, stems, and other woody or vegetative parts.

The degree to which the material is separated depends on the goals of the analyst and the goals of the project. Samples are seldom completely sorted, and some practical constraints are usually needed on the amount of material that can be sorted. Often, the wood fragments that are small enough to pass through a 2-mm mesh screen are ignored because they are too difficult to identify easily. On the other hand, seeds, fruit fragments, and other floral parts are usually examined from all mesh-size samples. Some seeds are minute. For example, tobacco seeds can pass through a 0.45-mm mesh screen, meaning that they are only one-eighth the size of the head of a straight pen. Unlike wood, even the smallest seeds are relatively easy to identify, if the analyst has an adequate seed reference collection.

Time and monetary constraints may impose limits on the degree to which the samples may be sorted. One way to speed up the process and to increase the number of samples examined is to scan the material rather than to sort it completely. Using this technique, the analyst scans each sample at low magnification, searching for a predetermined suite of macroremains, often limited to cultigens. This allows for rapid analysis of many samples, but it introduces sample biases toward overlooking smaller seeds and often neglecting carbonized wood or vegetal plant parts that can take more time to identify.

Identification. Once the samples have been sorted, the plant material must be identified. Botanical remains from archaeological sites are not easy to identify because they are usually recovered in a highly altered state. Furthermore, any part of a plant can appear in a sample: seeds, bark, fruits, flowers, inflorescence, stems, or roots, to name a few. Some of these parts are more distinctive than others, thus easier to identify. To complicate matters, plants can be modified by humans for cultural purposes or processed in a variety of ways for consumption. Both of these processes can drastically change the appearance of a plant part. For these reasons, an extensive plant reference collection from the area being studied is necessary to perform an adequate macrobotanical analysis. Many archaeologists do not recognize this need, and funds are seldom budgeted to provide for the preparation of such collections. A reference collection needs to be large enough to record variations in plant growth and to provide material for experimental modification and carbonization when needed.

Some plant identifications can be made by the unaided eye, but usually a low-powered dissecting microscope capable of magnifications of up to 45–60 power is essential. Other techniques that are sometimes needed include the microscopic examination of plant cuticle/ epidermal fragments using a light microscope at magnifications of 200–500 power. Occasionally, when the material is both well preserved and sufficiently important, an electron microscope (scanning or transmission) can be used for high-resolution studies of seeds or fruits.

Quantification. Knowing how to quantify the macrobotanical record most effectively is often a problem. For example, should plant parts be quantified by volume, by weight, or should each one be counted? Regardless of which technique is used, one often discovers that regional data comparisons are difficult because databases from other archaeological sites may have been generated using different quantification techniques.

Some of the more commonly used quantification systems in paleoethnobotany include: (1) *ranking* each taxon, or plant part, in the order of its relative abundance; (2) using a *seed-density index* that measures the number of seeds encountered per liter of sediment; (3) using a *relative-abundance* index based on the number of seeds of each taxon divided by the total number of seeds counted in all samples; and (4) using the most common method, called *ubiquity,* which measures whether or not a plant taxon is present but does not indicate its abundance.

The ubiquity technique is useful because it is quick and can indicate in how many samples a specific plant type appears. For example, if corn (maize) remains occur in 17 of 100 samples, it has a presence/absence value of 17 percent. An advantage to the ubiquity technique is that it permits a quick and easy way to compare the presence of specific botanical remains from different areas within the same site or from a number of different sites. Finally, it is important to remember that *relative abundance* uses absolute counts of taxa in a deposit, while *frequency* measures how often a taxon appears in a group of samples.

Microremains

Identifications of pollen and phytoliths should be verified by using comprehensive reference collections. Counting techniques for quantifying microremains are fairly standardized. When counting fossil pollen grains in a sample, a count of the first 200 pollen grains seen on a prepared slide is considered statistically valid for most types of samples. Usually, pollen samples from archaeological sites are scanned beyond the 200-grain limit to search for pollen grains from certain types of cultigens. Once the grains are counted, the percentages in a pollen count are expressed either as relative frequencies or as concentrations in grains per mm or g. The presence, or number, of cultigens encountered during scans is also noted.

Not all quantification techniques used in phytolith analyses are the same. Some authorities use a ubiquity technique, while others use the number of phytoliths found in a specific unit or sample (i.e., phytoliths per one drop of processed material). Still others, such as Piperno, use quantification techniques similar to those used in pollen analysis.

Interpretation

Once the botanical record has been recovered, identified, and quantified, it must be interpreted. The simplest way to interpret the data is to produce a list of identified taxa, then interpret the results. For several decades, the most commonly used method for interpreting botanical remains was limited to providing a list of taxa, combined with a potential list of how the plants may have been used.

Beginning in the 1930s, the analysis of botanical remains advanced from providing simple lists to in-depth anthropological interpretation when Gilmore and Jones began examining archaeological materials on a regular basis. Having been trained in both anthropology and botany, Gilmore and Jones were the first to utilize ethnographic analogy to interpret the uses of plant remains found at North American sites.

Most paleoethnobotanists agree that one should not attempt to interpret the probable prehistoric uses of plants without first having a broad-based understanding of how indigenous peoples utilize plants. Information on how humans use plants can come from a variety of sources: (1) journal or diary sources written by travelers, soldiers, priests, missionaries, or explorers; (2) ethnographic studies conducted by anthropologists or botanists; and (3) descriptive accounts by observers who lived with indigenous peoples, such as Indian agents, missionaries, captives, or settlers. Each of these sources can provide descriptive information useful for interpreting the plant remains recovered from archaeological sites.

Because different uses of plants can result in different types of modifications, what the analyst identifies and describes is, to a certain degree, the result of a series of human activities. Some human activities can be implied by examining the plant remains. Further, one might be able to match the interpretation with existing ethnographic/ethnohistoric accounts of how a plant was used. This is called an *ethnographic analogy*: a process by which past human behavior is modeled or described by combining two types of data: archaeobotanical interpretation and known ethnographic descriptions. Ethnographic analogy can increase interpretive accuracy and resolution but researchers also need to provide a conceptual framework that could encompass what Jones termed the "entire range of relations between . . . man and plants."

A newer type of conceptual framework is the *ecological approach*. This framework is an ideal means of integrating cultural factors—such as indigenous taxonomies, rules for behavior toward plants, and the manipulation of plants—and data gained from studies of plant systematics, chemistry, genetics, and physiology. Once synthesized, these types of data can be used to model both past and present human-plant interactions, to study the effect of human behavior on plant populations, and to study the historical impact of certain plants on human populations. This approach is also useful for a study of overall environmental changes, such as changes in the composition of plant communities brought about by human-plant interactions.

Examples of how the ecological approach is being employed in paleoethnobotany include using carbonized wood remains to document the human impact on an environment and to postulate environmental degradation caused by a combination of climatic change and human activities. Pollen remains are being used to document the effects of slash-and-burn agriculture in some tropical ecosystems. The identification of domesticated chenopod seeds using scanning electron microscopy has documented the adoption and movement of cultigens native to temperate North America. The ecological approach has also helped us realize that some indigenous groups have cleared forests, burned grasslands, and moved large quantities of earth. Thus, the archaeobotanical record plays an important role in helping us understand prehistoric land-use systems.

Researchers in the discipline are like detectives who have arrived on the scene long after events have occurred. Like detectives, paleoethnobotanists must scurry about at the place where past events occurred and search for the tiniest clues in hope of re-creating what events took place. In both cases, for detectives and paleoethnobotanists, the ability to re-create what really happened is only as good as the evidence that remains, the procedure used to collect the evidence, and the ability of the investigator to make logical sense out of the clues that still exist.

Vaughn M. Bryant, Jr.
J. Philip Dering

See also COPROLITE ANALYSIS; FLOTATION; PALYNOLOGY; PHYTOLITH ANALYSIS

Further Readings
Bryant, V. (1994) Callen's legacy. In K. Sobolik (ed.): The Diet and Health of Prehistoric Americans, pp. 151–160. (Center for Archaeological Investigations Occasional Paper 22). Carbondale: Southern Illinois University Press.
Ford, R.I. (1979) Paleoethnobotany in American archaeology. In M.B. Schiffer (ed.): Advances in Archaeological Method and Theory, vol. 2, pp. 286–336. New York: Academic.
Ford, R.I. (1985) Anthropological perspective of ethnobotany in the Greater Southwest. Economic Botany 39(4):400–415.
Gilmore, M.R. (1932) The Ethnobotanical Laboratory at the University of Michigan. (Occasional Contributions from the Museum of Anthropology of the University of Michigan 1.) Ann Arbor: University of Michigan Press.
Hastorf, C., and Popper, V.S. (1988) Current Paleoethnobotany. Chicago: University of Chicago Press.
Jones, V.H. (1941) The nature and status of ethnobotany. Chronica Botanica 6:219–221.
Jones, V.H. (1957) Botany. In W.H. Taylor (ed.): The Identification of Non-Artifactual Archaeological Materials, pp. 35–38. Washington, D.C.: National Academy of Sciences, (National Research Council Publication 565).

P

Miksicek, C.H. (1987) Formation processes of the archaeobotanical record. In M.B. Schiffer (ed.): Advances in Archaeological Method and Theory, vol. 10, pp. 211–247. New York: Academic.

Morlot, A. (1861) General views on archaeology. Annual Report of the Smithsonian Institution for 1860:284–343.

Pearsall, D. (1989) Paleoethnobotany: A Handbook of Procedures. New York: Academic.

Paleoimmunology

The application of immunochemical methods to archaeological and paleological material, with the intention of detecting indigenous organic materials. These organic materials may then be used for further studies.

Introduction

Methods of immunochemical study have been borrowed from both clinical medicine and molecular biology, and it is from these areas that improvements in the techniques come. Since the 1960s, however, there have been significant advances in the application of these techniques to molecular archaeology. Proteins have been shown to survive in fossilized remains, and DNA (deoxyribonucleic acid) has been extracted from archaeological bones, seeds, and plant residues. Improvements in paleoimmunological techniques have enabled direct comparisons between extracts made from modern and ancient animals and plants.

Theory

Unlike paleoserological methods, which detect carbohydrate markers that occur on the surface of red blood cells, paleoimmunological methods can be used to detect a range of different biomarkers. These markers are called *antigens,* which are molecules that generate an immune response (i.e., may induce *antibody* production in a competent host) and will also react with antibodies. Antibodies are Y-shaped proteins; the upper tips of the "Y" are highly variable and are composed of six peptide chains that react with the antigen.

Terminology

An explanation of some of the terms commonly used in immunology is required. Antigens are composed of several different *epitopes,* which may be either continuous or discontinuous sequences of components (i.e., amino acids or sugars). Epitopes on globular and helical antigens are usually discontinuous because of the folding (tertiary structure) of the molecule. The parts of the antibody that react with the epitopes are called *paratopes.* Most antigens are composed of several different epitopes, and, when inoculated into a competent host, they induce the production of a *polyclonal serum* (a serum containing antibodies to several different antigens) that reacts with several different epitopes. A *monoclonal serum* (which contains only one antibody) is one that reacts with only one epitope.

Unrelated antigens may contain identical epitopes, so an antibody that reacts with an unrelated antigen, or an epitope that reacts with several different paratopes, is said to cross-react. Cross-reactions will give rise to erroneous results, but, provided that epitopes are defined, the degree to which epitopes and paratopes cross-react can be used to show associations (affinity studies) between different but related antigens. These studies can only be done using polyclonal sera.

Producing Antibodies

The use of ancient materials for inducing antibody production may give rise to problems. Organic residues that have been denatured will have lost their tertiary structure to an undefined degree. In a modern molecule, the folding of the tertiary structure ensures that some parts of the molecule are never exposed, and, generally, epitopic sites occur only on the exposed parts of the molecule. The "hidden" parts of the molecule normally appear to be incapable of inducing an antibody response, but taphonomic processes, as well as chemical-extraction methods, often lead to unfolding *(denaturation)* of the antigen. This denaturation will expose uncharacteristic epitopic regions; the hydrolysis of the molecule will release antigenic short sequences, and, thus, the molecule will lose its characteristic antigenic signal. If this changed material is used to induce antibodies in a competent host, these antibodies will be undefined and uncharacteristic for the native material. The degree of cross-reactivity of these antibodies with other unrelated proteins will be unknown, and *heterocliticity* may arise. This is the binding of an antibody with a nonrelated antigen more strongly than with the antigen against which it was raised.

For immunochemical methods to be applied to archaeology, the degree of specificity of the reaction between the epitope and the paratope must be assessed as far as is practical and possible. Extremely low levels of antigen can be detected using immunochemical methods; micrograms (sometimes nanograms) may be detected; and, because of the sensitive nature of these tests, care must be taken to exclude cross-reactive or inhibitory substances.

Applications

Archaeological and paleological remains are degraded, and any epitopes they contain will have been altered to an undefined degree. Any application of immunochemical methods to these materials must be properly controlled. Nonetheless, proteins have been shown to survive in an immunologically recognizable form in archaeological remains and fossils for many hundreds of years.

An explanation of how (it is thought) epitopes survive in the burial environment is required. Generally speaking, carbohydrates, proteins, DNA, and fats are susceptible to physical, chemical, and microbial degradation, and the soil is the natural habitat for a range of different microbes (except in naturally sterile systems such as peat bogs) that have the capacity to decompose these materials. Several factors, some of which are environmental, will limit this decomposition: desiccation, low temperatures, the presence of substances inhibitory to microbes (i.e., humics), and close association with mineral. Desiccation (e.g., sun-drying), the presence of microbial inhibitors (e.g., preservatives) and low temperatures (e.g., refrigeration) are well-known methods of improving the keeping quality of foods, and these same principles apply to the preservation of archaeological remains. Less well recognized, however, is the ability of inorganic matrices to inhibit decomposition.

In bones, teeth, shells, ivory, and antlers, there are two closely associated phases: the organic and the inorganic. Indeed, the association between the protein and the mineral in bone is so close that, while the water molecule can enter the dried compact bone tissue, the slightly larger ethanol molecule cannot. It would, therefore, be unlikely that large molecules, such as proteolytic enzymes, could gain access. Provided that the mineral remained intact, bacteria and fungi would be unable to attack the organic component either, but, in this situation, the organic components are still susceptible to chemical change (principally hydrolysis, which would produce many short chains from one long one).

Paleoimmunological techniques have been applied most successfully to organic residues present in or on mineralized matrices such as bone, tooth, shell, and rock (cave art and stone tools); the antigens most commonly detected are discussed below.

Albumin

Albumin is a globular protein present in the blood and tissues of all vertebrates; there are immunological differences between the albumins of different species. The amino-acid sequences for some mammals (i.e., human and bovine) are sufficiently close to induce cross-reactive antibodies. The albumins in the members of the different groups within the vertebrates are sufficiently different so that piscine albumins, for example, will not cross-react with antibodies raised against mammalian ones.

Immunochemical techniques to demonstrate albumins from different species of mammal have been applied to stains on stone spears. The authors (Kooyman et al. 1992) claimed to be able to speciate the blood residues using these methods, but they recognized the problems of cross-reactivity and contamination. (Some of the spears examined in the study came from museums, and the results obtained had been confused by the presence of human albumins, presumably from curatorial handling of the artifacts).

Albumins have been demonstrated immunologically in ancient British human bones using monoclonal antibodies. The possibility of detecting contaminating modern albumins due to handling was eradicated by examining only the central portion of bone cores. Using these methods, extracts of bone from the English Civil War (A.D. 1644), the medieval period (A.D. 1100–1400), the Early Saxon period (A.D. 450–600), the Roman period (A.D. 100–200), the Iron Age (ca. 400 B.C.) and the Bronze Age (2200–1700 B.C.) all tested positive for albumin. The implication is that albumin, when in intimate contact with bone mineral, is able to survive in an immunologically recognizable form for up to 4,000 years.

Hemoglobin

Hemoglobin (Hb) is the globular protein that transports oxygen around the body. In its active form, it is a *metalloprotein,* comprising four multihelical peptide chains, which hold at their center ferroprotoporphyrine (hem). If the hem is lost, the molecule is termed *apohemoglobin* (ApoHb). Early attempts to detect this antigen in bone were unsuccessful; the techniques used, which worked well for modern medical applications, were unable to detect the small amounts of ApoHb that may have survived.

With the advent of the more sensitive techniques, ApoHb has been shown to survive in human femur bones from Roman Britain. Similar methods to detect ApoHb in pigments used in cave art have been less successful. Taphonomic changes are most probably the cause.

Collagen

Collagen is a long, triple-helical protein molecule with short variable globular terminal proteins. It is the structural protein present in skin and bone; generally, the helix is weakly antigenic because the molecule is highly conserved across species. This means that the amino-acid sequences of the collagen helices between different species are very similar. Therefore, a competent host, such as a rabbit, would not necessarily produce antibodies to the triple-helical portion of human collagen, since it would not be sufficiently different from its own, although the rabbit would produce antibodies to the short globular terminal proteins.

The short terminal proteins are highly antigenic, and, to a degree, they are also species specific. Studies using antibodies raised against collagens have been attempted on extracts from the frozen soft tissue of mammoths. These studies tried to demonstrate the lineage, if any, between mammoths and modern elephants and/or cows. Due to the degraded nature of the extracted collagen, it was difficult to draw any firm conclusions concerning the phylogenetic relationship. Genetic studies using extracted RNA (ribonucleic acid) species are underway to confirm the suspected associations.

Osteocalcin

Osteocalcin (OC) is a bone-specific protein that is enriched in acidic amino-acid residues. These acidic residues have a strong affinity for the mineral phase of bone, and it is this interaction that is thought to promote the survival of this protein in archaeological bone.

The percentage of collagen in bone is ca. 100 times greater than that of OC; nonetheless, using immunological methods, it has been shown that osteocalcin survives for a much greater time than does collagen. This is important; it may be possible to extract the OC from small samples of bone, concentrate it using immunological methods, and use it for radiocarbon dating of the bones in which collagen has not survived. The survival of OC for longer time periods than collagen is thought to be due to the close association of OC with the mineral phase of the bone.

Antibodies

Antibodies are present in the blood of mammals. If blood is applied to the surface of a mineral, such as a cave wall or a stone tool, and dried, antibodies may be recovered from the residue. Speciation of the blood may then be possible. The method employs an antibody that reacts with the base of the Y-shaped antibodies present within the deposits and is generally species specific, although cross-reactions will occur.

In forensic applications, this method has been successful in differentiating 16-month-old human blood deposits from other animal ones, but cross-reactions do occur with chimpanzee, mouse, rat, and eel antibodies. The method, when applied to archaeological residues, gave less successful results, probably due to the increased taphonomic alteration to which the older samples had been exposed.

Conclusions

Archaeological and paleological materials have been shown to contain immunologically recognizable organic fractions. The nature of the organic materials can, in part, be assessed by their degree of affinity to the polyclonal antibodies used to detect them. This gives information on the state of these antigens and, to a certain extent, the taphonomic processes that affect them. Antigens apparently survive better in environments in which chemical and microbial degradation are inhibited; most particularly, it is from desiccated environments (e.g., amber entombment) that there has been the most success.

There are problems with the application of immunochemical techniques within paleontology, however. Cross-reactions, nonspecific reactions, and heteroclitic reactions due to the degraded nature of the antigen can never be ruled out. Paleoimmunology is an exciting and expanding field that is yielding information of taphonomic processes and increasing the known span of survival for organic residues.

Angela Gernaey-Child

See also BONE, CHARACTERIZATION; PALEOSEROLOGY; TAPHONOMY

Further Readings

Catteano, C., Gelsthorpe, K., Philips, P., and Sokol, R.J. (1992) Reliable identification of human albumin in ancient bone using ELISA and monoclonal antibodies. American Journal of Physical Anthropology 87:365–372.

Child, A.M., and Pollard, A.M. (1992) A review of the applications of immunochemistry to archaeological bone. Journal of Archaeological Science 19:39–47.

Hare, P.E., Hoering, T.C., and King, K. (1980) Biogeochemistry of Amino Acids. New York: Wiley.

Kooyman, B., Newman, M.E., and Ceri, H. (1992) Verifying the reliability of blood residue analysis on archaeological tools. Journal of Archaeological Science 19:265–269.

Linsenmayer, T.F. (1991) Collagen. In E.D. Hay (ed.): Cell Biology of the Extracellular Matrix, 2nd ed, pp. 7–44. New York: Plenum.

Paleonutrition

The multidisciplinary study of ancient diets through synthesis of paleopathology, botany, palynology, phytolith analysis, bone chemistry, zooarchaeology, and coprolite studies. This field was first defined by Elizabeth Wing and Antoinette Brown in 1979, but the methods of paleonutrition were not defined until Robert Gilbert and James Mielke published *The Analysis of Prehistoric Diets* in 1985. In 1994, Kristin Sobolik presented an edited volume addressing the field. Paleonutrition also incorporates experimental approaches to assess the productivity of wild and domestic plants and the efficiency of animal harvesting and butchering techniques. By synthesizing various analytical approaches, the nature of traditional diets can be assessed. However, each type of analysis has its own particular bias. Therefore, interpreting the nature of prehistoric diet requires an understanding of the biases in each type of analysis. Presented below are examples of how separate fields of study can be integrated to reconstruct past diets. Following the examples are general comments regarding paleonutrition and modern health problems.

Botanical Analyses

Macrobotanical study through flotation or dry screening of archaeological sediments has long been a significant aspect of paleonutrition. Many archaeobotanists combine analysis of remains from sites with experimental work in cultivating and harvesting plant foods. The primary limitation is identification of cultural versus environmental deposits of seeds and fibers. In some regions, only charred remains are considered to be culturally significant. A second bias is in the favor of durable plant remains and against fragile plant remains. Thus, differential preservation of remains is a significant problem and hinders the estimation of the actual proportion of different plant foods in the diet. Despite these problems, excellent paleonutrition data are derived from macrobotanical studies. For example, Bruce Smith summarized several years of research into the origins of agriculture in the eastern United States and the Eastern Agricultural Complex. His 1992 presentation begins with a summary of evidence that delineates a center of domestication in eastern North America. Following this, he examines the general ecology of the region and develops an ecological-behavioral model of how domestication initiated and became fixed in the area. This is the *floodplain weed theory* of cultivation, which views the floodplain ecological zone with its annual weedy species as the focus of behavioral modification of plants through domestication. The potentiality of the cultivation of indigenous plants (pigweed, sumpweed, sunflower, gourds, squash) is evaluated. Scanning electron microscopy (SEM) is applied to seeds recovered from archaeological sites in comparison to their wild progenitors. SEM study demonstrates differences in morphology of the seeds that evolved under domestication. On a macroscopic level, the sizes of the seeds are compared, focusing on pigweed and sumpweed. It is demonstrated that the cultivated seeds have evolved larger seed sizes. Through a variety of morphologic and genetic indicators, the origins of eastern domesticated crops are traced to wild precursors. Experimentally, stands of sumpweed and goosefoot were harvested to determine the time expenditure necessary to bring in large quantities of seed. These experiments showed that the eastern crop plants produced an abundance of seed and were, therefore, economically significant.

By integrating the archaeological findings, experiment results, and ethnohistoric records of eastern tribal diets, Smith demonstrates a continuity of cultivation of wild indigenous plants from prehistory to history. Maize was eventually added to this indigenous Eastern Agricultural Complex. Although maize was introduced into the region ca. A.D. 200, the dietary reliance on maize did not occur until later. To document the period of maize reliance, Smith turns to stable carbon isotopic study of skeletons. The isotopic data indicate that maize became a dietary mainstay after A.D. 1000. From the perspective of paleonutrition, the introduction of maize, may coincide with a period of declining health, since maize is deficient in several essential amino acids, a point that was highlighted in previous (1984) work by Mark Cohen and George J. Armelagos. Therefore, after A.D. 1000, the diversified diet, which was dependent primarily on indigenous plants, was replaced by a diet primarily dependent on maize, which is of questionable nutritional diversity. Ultimately, Smith presents an overview of traditional plant diet and demonstrates the evolution and change of this diet. This demonstrates that traditional Native American diets have gone through considerable evolutionary change, a significant point that can only be revealed by paleonutrition studies.

The Hohokam: An Example of Multidisciplinary Research

Multidisciplinary dietary study is necessary for areas of poor preservation. Such an area is southern Arizona which was once home to the farming Hohokam culture. A model study for this culture was published in Volume 56 of *The Kiva* (the journal of the Arizona Archaeological and Historical Society). The articles from that volume are summarized here. The multidisciplinary study includes palynology,

paleopathology, macrobotany, zooarchaeology, ethnography, coprolite research, and spatial analysis of archaeobotanical features. Robert Gasser and Scott Kwiatkowski describe regional differences in flotation data and explain them in terms of variations in ecological availability of plants, variations in Hohokam food preferences, culture, trade, and differential preservation. Vorsila Bohrer describes five indigenous plant species that exhibit morphological change in archaeological context due to domestication. She also presents a case that at least five more indigenous species were "encouraged" by Hohokam farmers. Thus, the Hohokam domesticated indigenous plants, as well as those introduced from Mexico. Suzanne Fish and M. Donaldson present a summary of plant remains from archaeological features on an intra- and inter-site basis to demonstrate patterns of production. Christine Szuter describes the pattern of Hohokam use of animal protein. She notes that the Hohokam relied on small (mouse-size) to medium (rabbit-size) animals. Many animals were hunted in the irrigation systems that increased the productivity of the land. Some sites were located where larger animals, such as deer, could be obtained. Michael Fink and Charles Merbs look at the physiological ramifications of Hohokam diet. They find abundant evidence of nutrition-related diseases, such as dental decay, tooth wear, tooth loss, childhood disease, anemic responses, rickets, bladder stone disease, and short stature. Nutritional problems were common especially in childhood.

Jan Gish presents pollen data relating to Hohokam plant use and environment. Because of the poor preservation potential of south Arizona soils, pollen-recovery techniques had to be modified in the area. Once the techniques were altered, Hohokam-site soils revealed a wide array of pollen. Determining cultural use of plants from pollen, especially wind-pollinated plants, is difficult. To ensure proper identification of cultural use of plants, Gish emphasizes the importance of pollen clumps in interpretation. Pollen clumps result from the cultural selection of flowering portions or seeds with adherent pollen. The pollen studies have revealed the differential destruction of pollen in Hohokam site soils. For example, *Plantago* (plantain) deteriorates rapidly in site soils. Therefore, one cannot anticipate that the pollen spectrum from a soil sample represents the proportion of plants used at the site. Hohokam palynologists have spent considerable time in distinguishing the pollen morphology of economically important species. Examination of pollen rain for different plant communities and Native American gardens is done to identify plant communities and zonation, local floristic variability, and wetland agriculture weeds in Hohokam plant selection and diet. Pollen was used to differentiate between ecological communities. Garden areas can be identified based on weed indices (proportion of weedy plants represented). Examination of dietary pollen focuses on regional economic diversity, differential participation by different villages in the general subsistence spectrum, the role of subsistence items in trade networks, and subgroup preference for certain plant foods.

This multidisciplinary study demonstrates profound dietary diversity in the Hohokam regions. In the Salt-Gila River confluence, cholla cactus appears to have been cultivated. In the area between modern Tucson and Phoenix, *Agave* was cultivated. On the Salt River, cotton was cultivated, and three wild potherbs were used more than in any other region. The area of modern Tucson and west of Tucson saw extensive use of mustards. In general, pollen evidence indicates that the following spectrum of plants were used by the Hohokam: cotton *(Gossypium),* squash *(Cucurbita),* maize *(Zea mays),* cholla cactus *(Opuntia* type), *Cereus* type (probably saguaro cactus), prickly pear *(Opuntia* type), mesquite *(Prosopis),* cattail *(Typha), Agave,* dandelion-type potherb *(Ligulaflorae),* sunflower *(Helianthus* type), *Dytheria* type, some Cheno Am, probably *Chenopodium* or *Amaranthus, Plantago,* and globe mallow *(Sphaeralcea).* These plants are of significant nutritional value, especially with regard to micronutrients. Most of these plants could not have been identified from any remains other than pollen.

Paleonutrition: An Ecological Synthesis

So far, the plant components of diet have been discussed. The animal-protein component is identifiable through zooarchaeological analysis. Zooarchaeology is the study of animal remains, usually bone, recovered from archaeological sites. Biases in zooarchaeological analysis stem from depositional, postdepositional, and archaeological-recovery factors.

There is an abundance of zooarchaeolgical literature addressing these issues (see Brewer 1992). When zooarchaeological data are combined with botanical data, an accurate picture of diet emerges. If put in ecological context, a picture of the interaction between humans and their environments emerges, and the ecological pressures that form diets can be inferred.

A classic example of this integrative approach is Kent V. Flannery's 1986 study of the subsistence of Oaxaca, Mexico, through the excavation and analysis of the cave Guilá Naquitz. Flannery approaches the study from the perspective of an ecologist, considering human activity in context with the environment energetics and plant and animal components of that environment. For him, hunter-gatherers participated in the dynamics of the environment and contributed to it. For example, rather than simply harvesting wild plant foods, human activity augmented the productivity of many species through reducing intraspecific competition and dispersing seeds. Flannery studies archaeological remains in the ecological framework. For example, the sources of raw stone are traced. The functions of stone tools in subsistence are inferred by morphology and spatial distribution in the cave. The strata are evaluated with respect to seasonality, intensity of cave use, and subsistence function. Palynology was used to document changes in climate during the occupation history of the cave and to identify cultural use of wild and domestic plants. Zooarchaeological analysis revealed the types of animals eaten. Once plant and animal resources were identified, the seasonal and annual productivity was assessed in terms of density and number of edible parts. The nutritional values of the foods were obtained and calculated with regard to nutritional intake of prehistoric cave inhabitants, based on the abundances of different foods found in the caves. To identify where food processing occurred within the cave, the spatial variation of each food item was traced. This led to *episodal analysis,* which reveals the sequence of events that led to the accumulation of archaeological deposits. Once the environment was defined and the archaeology studied, the data were used to create a computer model of subsistence activities. In turn, the computer modeling led to an ecological model of the development of agriculture in the region. The development of agriculture is ultimately an outgrowth of the ecological interaction of hunter-gatherers with their environment, which ultimately led to modification of the region to optimize nutritional return for energy spent. Flannery's study demonstrates the value of an ecological approach to studying paleonutrition.

Coprolites and Chemistry: Long-Term and Short-Term Evidence

The examples presented above depict a harmonious reconstruction of diet. With the advent of bone-chemistry data, the potential for integrating this evidence of long-term diet with the species-specific, short-term evidence from coprolites became available. Surprisingly, the evidence from these two data sources conflict, even when they are derived from the same population. This has highlighted the need to address the biases in different types of paleonutrition data in order to bring about an accurate reconstruction of past diet.

The first indication of the disparity between bone chemistry and coprolite analysis occurred in the Southwest United States. In the late 1970s, the notion emerged that prehistoric inhabitants of this region were maize dependent, based on paleopathological research by Mahmaud El-Najjar. Subsequently, coprolite researchers showed that this was not the case. Southwestern agriculturalists subsisted on a mixed variety of wild and domesticated plants, as indicated by Gary Fry in 1980. Later, stable isotopic analysis of carbon from skeletons suggested again that Southwesterners had a diet that was strongly reliant on maize, reaching as high as 90 percent of the total diet, as summarized in 1992 by Ann Stodder and Debra Martin. Thus, the coprolite and isotopic studies conflict. The reason for the conflict lies in the basic fact that coprolites represent the portion of diet that was excreted, while isotopic study of bone reflects that portion of diet (protein, in the case of collagen) that was absorbed. A second factor is that many wild plants in the Southwest have a C_4 isotopic signature, which is very similar to that of maize. Plants may have one of three paths of photosynthesis, referred to as C_3, C_4, and CAM (intermediate between the other two), each of which can be identified by the ratio of the two stable carbon ($^{13}C/^{12}C$) isotopes. Of wild plants eaten by

prehistoric peoples, at least eleven have isotopic signatures similar to maize. These plants include monocot species, CAM monocot species, C_4 amaranths, and CAM cactus species. Therefore, there is a danger in interpreting a C_4 isotopic signal as solely maize derived. Similarly, the digested and absorbed portion of diet is not represented in coprolites, so there is a danger in making one-to-one inferences from the proportion of species in coprolites to the proportion of species actually eaten.

The analysis of mummies has further highlighted the problem. In these analyses, the coprolite and bone-chemistry signals are derived from the same mummies, so there is no chance that the variation between dietary reconstructions is due to sampling different populations. The first example compares coprolite data with chemical data derived from Chilean mummies of the Chincorro culture. Coprolite analysis indicates that 50 percent of the dietary components came from the marine environment, most likely as fish and sea-lion meat. Strontium analysis of bone indicates that nearly 90 percent of the diet came from the marine environment. This is a drastic difference and highlights the biases in each type of analysis. Chemical analysis overemphasizes the contribution of meat because chemical reconstruction of bone measures the digested dietary component. Coprolite analysis underrepresents meat because past coprolite analysis has been unable to detect meat that is largely digested. Therefore, the two techniques by themselves cannot be considered to reflect the proportion of marine food that was actually eaten.

These examples highlight a problem in paleonutrition research. Each type of analysis has its own inherent bias. Only by careful consideration of these biases can diet be reconstructed with some accuracy. Despite these problems, paleonutrition provides significant insight into past dietary patterns.

Relevance of Paleonutrition to Modern Health

Archaeology's strongest contribution to modern medicine is in the realm of paleonutrition. This is due to the fact that the rise in many modern diseases among Native North Americans has a base in dietary change from prehistoric time to historic times. These diseases include diabetes, coronary disease, hypertension, and some types of cancer. The changes in diet from prehistory to history include an increase in fat and cholesterol combined with a decrease in dietary fiber.

Since the 1950s, there has been an increasing prevalence of Type II noninsulin-dependent diabetes melitis (NIDDM) among Native Americans, Australian Aborigines, and South Pacific Islanders to epidemic proportions. Up to 50 percent of Native Americans suffer from the disease. It is clear that the change in diet among tribal peoples from traditional food practices to modern European-derived diets is a basal cause of the disease. However, the precise nature of the traditional diet is obscure. Berry Brenton noted in 1994 that the greatest contribution to be made to eliminating this problem comes from paleonutrition. Only through paleonutrition studies can traditional diets be defined and incorporated into medical-intervention strategies. This approach has been tried successfully with the Pima Indians of Arizona and will undoubtedly be expanded to most, if not all, Native North Americans.

Karl Reinhard

See also ATOMIC ABSORPTION (AA) SPECTROMETRY; BONE, TRACE-ELEMENT ANALYSIS; COPROLITE ANALYSIS; FLOTATION; ISOTOPES, STABLE (C, N, O, H): BONE AND PALEODIET STUDIES; PALEOPATHOLOGY, HUMAN; PALYNOLOGY; PHYTOLITH ANALYSIS; ZOOARCHAEOLOGY

Further Readings

Brenton, B.P. (1994) Paleonutrition: Implications for contemporary Native Americans. In K.D. Sobolik (ed.): Paleonutrition: The Diet and Health of Prehistoric Americans, (Occasional Paper 22) pp. 294–305. Carbondale: Center for Archaeological Investigations, Southern Illinois University.

Brewer, D.J. (1992) Zooarchaeology: Method, theory, and goals. In M.B. Schiffer (ed.): Archaeological Method and Theory, vol. 4, pp. 195–244. Tucson: University of Arizona Press.

Cohen, M.N., and Armelagos, G.J. (1984) Paleopathology at the Origins of Agriculture. Orlando: Academic.

Flannery, K.V. (1986) Guilá Naquitz: Archaic Foraging and Early Agriculture in Oaxaca, Mexico. New York: Academic.

Fry, G.F. (1980) Prehistoric diet and parasites in the desert west of North America. In D.L. Browman (ed.): Early Native Americans, pp. 325–339. The Hague: Mouton.

Gibert, R.I., Jr., and Mielke, J.H. (1985) The Analysis of Prehistoric Diets. New York: Academic.

Smith, B.D. (1992) Rivers of Change: Essays on Early Agriculture in Eastern North America. Washington, D.C.: Smithsonian Institution Press.

Sobolik, K.D., ed. (1994) Paleonutrition: The Diet and Health of Prehistoric Americans. (Occasional Paper 22). Carbondale: Center for Archaeological Investigations, Southern Illinois University.

Stodder, A.L.W., and Martin, D.L. (1992) Health and disease in the Southwest before and after contact. In J.W. Verano and D.H. Ubelaker (eds.): Disease and Demography in the Americas, pp. 55–73. Washington, D.C.: Smithsonian Institution Press.

Wing, E.S., and Brown, A.B. (1979) Paleonutrition: Method and Theory in Prehistoric Foodways. New York: Academic.

Paleopathology, Human

Study of disease as evidenced on human skeletal remains of historic and prehistoric populations.

Definition and History

While paleopathology can be broadly defined as the study of diseases and disorders of ancient peoples and animals, this entry will focus primarily on human paleopathology. The majority of paleopathological evidence comes from examining human skeletal remains, although analyses of historical paintings and prehistoric and historic pottery renderings have also yielded data useful to the discussion of ancient diseases.

The identification of paleopathology as a field of study began in 1774 with Johann Esper's report on the pathological conditions noted on a cave bear from France. Work continued throughout the nineteenth century, with a considerable amount of interest placed on human artificial cranial modification and the origin of syphilis. One of the first significant works on diseases seen at an archaeological assemblage was published in 1876 by Joseph Jones. Following this, many reports dealing with medical disorders identified in archaeological samples were published. While early work in the field of paleopathology was published, most of the analyses were sporadic and were discussed primarily as interesting phenomena written up by medical doctors, rather than studied in an anthropological context. The field itself was not defined until the early twentieth century with Marc Armand Ruffer's work on mummies. He stated that paleopathology is "the science of the disease which can be demonstrated in human and animal remains of ancient times" (Moodie 1923 from Bush and Zvelebil 1991:3).

Earnest A. Hooton's analysis and subsequent 1930 publication on *The Indians of Pecos Pueblo* is a significant work in the field. This paleopathological analysis, done on a large archaeological assemblage from the Southwestern United States, introduced the concept of a *paleoepidemiological* approach. Previous work had focused primarily on describing interesting anomalies and disorders, but early researchers did not attempt to voice their discussions using an ecological approach. Hooton, however, examined the individual skeletons for signs of arthritis, trauma, porotic hyperostosis, infectious lesions, and cranial lesions. He then discussed his findings in terms of age, sex, and time period. His analysis of changes in disease frequencies at the site over time was particularly important, as he explained his findings in terms of diet and culture changes at the pueblo. This set the foundation for the epidemiological studies of paleopathology seen now.

Concepts and Application

An examination of human paleopathology can provide data relating to many different topics. First, the identification of disorders on human skeletal remains can provide an indication of the origin and antiquity of a disease. For instance, the identification of syphilitic lesions on human skeletons has been instrumental in attempting to determine the temporal and spatial origins of that disease complex (treponematosis). The identification of syphilitic lesions on precolumbian New World human remains suggests either that the disease arose independently in both the Old and the New Worlds or that it appeared first in the New World and was taken to the Old World by sailors on Columbus's ships. In addition, the description of lesions identified as rheumatoid arthritis have confirmed the disease to be of a New World origin, appearing at least 4,000 years ago.

Second, the identification of paleopathological conditions in human skeletal remains can be used to assess the relative rank of individuals within a society. Within certain groups, it may be expected that people of a higher status would have better health than those of a lower status. For instance, a researcher could hypothesize that higher-status people would have a lower rate of infectious diseases, better dental health, and more traumatic lesions representing war wounds. In addition, cranial modification was frequently practiced solely by members of a higher status.

Third, paleopathological evidence can be used to deduce broadly defined occupations and activities. Enthesopathies (enlarged muscle-attachment areas), degenerative arthritis, and microtrauma are the primary indicators of professions. Work done by Charles Merbs on a Sadlermiut Eskimo sample extensively explores the issue of occupation-related disorders. He related vertebral compression to long hours spent sledding over rough terrain, and degenerative arthritis seen on some shoulder blades to kayaking and paddling. Facets identified at the front of the lower end of the tibia, as well as on the top of the talus (ankle bone), have been commonly associated with squatting activities.

Fourth, paleopathological evidence provides direct confirmation of aggression between groups and within a group. Projectile-point wounds, parry fractures, cranial depressions, and scalping marks all represent signs of violence that are preserved on human skeletal remains. Patrick Willey's research at the Crow Creek site, South Dakota, provides an example of how these types of medical disorders can be interpreted. Almost 500 individuals were massacred at the site, with evidence of scalping, skull fractures, and decapitations being most common. Archaeological structures at the site aided in the interpretation of events. The site was a fortified village, and the attack occurred while one fortification wall was down and another was being constructed. Most accounts of prehistoric aggression recognized through paleopathological means are not as striking as those observed at Crow Creek. The majority of examples pertaining to violent behavior are limited to one or a few individuals at a location, probably representing random attacks made by enemies while the attacked group was away from the base camp, often on a foraging excursion.

Lastly, evidence provided from paleopathology can be used to interpret the ability of a group of people to adapt to their environment. Disorders in human skeletal remains indicate growth disturbances and repair to bone and can thus be used to deduce the stressors that produced them. Skeletal lesions identified on bone provide general health and nutrition information that can be extrapolated to the health of the community as a whole. Efforts to relate paleopathology to the adaptive ability of a group often revolve around the adaptivist model recently revised by Alan Goodman and George J. Armelagos (1989). The model considers environmental constraints affecting a population and the cultural buffering systems used by the group to mitigate the environmental constraints. The buffering system introduces other cultural stressors that an individual must contend with. If individuals cannot successfully cope with the environmental and cultural stressors, then they show signs of stress, which sometimes are evident on skeletal material. Instead of stopping at the point at which the individual shows skeletal stress markers, the model adds another stage that reflects the impact of the stress on the population as a whole. These repercussions include lowered work capacity, lowered reproductive capacity, and sociocultural disruptions.

Goodman and Armelagos have divided the skeletal stress markers discussed in their model into three categories: *general cumulative indicators, general episodic indicators,* and *specific indicators.* The rate of mortality in a population is an example of a general cumulative stress indicator. Frequently examined episodic markers of stress include Harris lines (transverse lines visible in radiographs of long bones) and enamel hypoplasias (areas of deficient enamel on a tooth crown). These indicators are considered episodic because their presence is confined only to that time in which the stress occurred. In some cases, episodic markers can be used to estimate the

time at which the stress occurred. Diseases that leave a diagnostic, distinctive marker on the skeletal remains are considered to be specific stress indicators. Examples of this type of marker include signs of trauma, such as those discussed earlier with violence, as well as fractures and dislocations unrelated to aggressive activity. Degenerative disorders, such as osteoarthritis, are also placed in this category. As discussed earlier, these types of disorders may be linked to occupation and activity patterns. Dental disorders, such as caries, abscesses, and periodontal disease, are also considered specific stress indicators and can be very useful in estimating the type of subsistence practiced by a population. When attempting to determine the amount of stress to which a population had to adapt, it is best to use as many of these indicators as is possible; they may then be used to find patterns of stress in a group. For instance, questions relating to whether males or females, children or adults, or high-status or low-status people were more negatively impacted by stress can be answered.

In attempting to assess the ability of a group to adapt to its environment by analyzing stress markers left on the skeleton, an important issue must be addressed. In the past, paleopathologists have assumed a direct relationship between the frequency of skeletal lesions and the success of a group in adapting to its environment. A group that had a high frequency of disorders was believed to be poorly adapted, while a group with no, or relatively few disorders, was regarded as well adapted. However, individuals may be so severely affected by a disease process that they die prior to the formation of a skeletal lesion. Other individuals, affected by the same disease process, may survive long enough to develop a skeletal lesion, which may or may not heal. According to standard paleopathological analysis, the individuals who survived longer would be considered not well adapted (because they showed a lesion), while the individuals who were so seriously affected that they died prior to the formation of a lesion would be considered healthy. The possibility of misinterpretation must be considered in paleopathological analyses. Therefore, it is important to consider the active or inactive state of a lesion (healed lesions are probably suggestive of a better-adapted individual) and to offer many different explanations for the

P

results seen in an adaptive analysis of a group.

Paleopathology and Genetic Research

Advances in biomedical technology are having positive effects on paleopathological research. Recovery of DNA (deoxyribonucleic acid) and of proteins from human tissue obtained from an archaeological context has provided important data on disease in past populations. One of the prominent examples is Noreen Tuross's recovery of noncollagenous proteins from sites in South Dakota. The recognition that immunoglobins can be retrieved from archaeological material supports the idea that disease records exist and are maintained in human bone, even if an individual was only exposed to a disease but did not develop it. In addition to the work done with skeletal remains from the Dakota area, immunological testing of Woodland samples from the southeastern United States has confirmed the presence of a treponemal antigen prehistorically. In spite of the success offered in this type of research, some problems still exist. For instance, it is not yet clear how diagenic processes acting on bone can affect results, nor is it clear if soil contamination is a problem.

Status of the Discipline

The area of paleopathological research is highly interdisciplinary, with research being done by medical doctors, anthropologists, and paleontologists. At its inception, the field was originally dominated by medical doctors and was characterized by descriptive and classificatory research aimed primarily at documenting the rare occurrence of certain diseases and anomalies. Since that time, the field has moved beyond the descriptive phase to a more analytical phase. Instead of merely trying to identify a disorder on skeletal remains, paleopathologists attempt to understand the effect that disorder frequency had on the population as a whole in terms of lifestyle and culture changes, as well as how lifestyle and culture modifications affected disease rates. This can be most clearly seen in the interest paleopathologists have in studying the relationship between disease in the New World and the origin of agriculture, as well in the initial contact between Native Americans and European peoples.

Helen Danzeiser Dockall

See also ARCHAEOPARASITOLOGY; BONE AND OTHER ORGANIC MATERIALS: ANCIENT DNA; BONE, TRACE-ELEMENT ANALYSIS; COPROLITE ANALYSIS; PALEOIMMUNOLOGY; PALEOPHARMACOLOGY; PALEOSEROLOGY

Further Readings

Bush, H., and Zvelebil, M. (1991) Pathology and health in past societies: An introduction. In H. Bush and M. Zvelebil (eds.): Health in Past Societies: Biocultural Interpretations of Human Skeletal Remains in Archaeological Contexts, pp. 2–9. (Tempus Reparatum International Series 567). Oxford: British Archaeological Reports.

Goodman, A., and Armelagos, G.J. (1989) Infant and childhood morbidity and mortality risks in archaeological populations. World Archaeology 21(2): 225–243.

Hooton, E.A. (1930) The Indians of Pecos Pueblo: A Study of Their Skeletal Remains. (Papers of the Southwestern Expedition 4). New Haven, CT: Yale University Press.

Iscan, M.Y., and Kennedy, A.R., eds. (1989) Reconstruction of Life from the Skeleton. New York: Allan R. Liss.

Merbs, C.F. (1983) Patterns of Activity-Induced Pathology in a Canadian Inuit Population. (Paper, Archaeological Survey of Canada, 119). Ottawa: National Museum of Man.

Moodie, R.L. (1923) Paleopathology: An Introduction to the Study of Ancient Evidences of Disease. Urbana: University of Illinois Press.

Ortner, D.J., and Aufderheide, A.C., eds. (1991) Human Paleopathology: Current Syntheses and Future Options. Washington, D.C.: Smithsonian Institution Press.

Ortner, D.J., and Putschar, W.G.J. (1981) Identification of Pathological Conditions in Human Skeletal Remains. (Smithsonian Contributions to Anthropology 28). Washington, D.C.: Smithsonian Institution Press.

Tuross, H. (1991) Recovery of bone and serum proteins from human skeletal tissue: IgG, osteonectin, and albumin. In D.J. Ortner and A.C. Aufderheide (eds.): Human Paleopathology: Current Syntheses and Future Options, pp. 51–54.

Washington, D.C.: Smithsonian Institution Press.

Ubelaker, D.H. (1982) The development of American paleopathology. In F. Spencer (ed.): A History of American Physical Anthropology, 1930–1980, pp. 337–356. New York: Academic.

Verano, J.W., and Ubelaker, D.H., eds. (1992) Disease and Demography in the Americas. Washington, D.C.: Smithsonian Institution Press.

Wood, J.W., Milner, G.R., Harpending, H.C., and Weiss, K.M.(1992) The osteological paradox. Current Anthropology 33(4):343–358.

Paleopharmacology

An emerging field devoted to the exploration of the archaeological record for evidence of medicinal plants. In the future, archaeology will have a role in pharmaceutical research. In the late twentieth century, much of the world's pharmaceutical research has been based on ethnographic documentation of tribally recognized medicinal plants. Once the active chemical compounds in the plants are identified, they are either extracted or synthesized for commercial use. The American film *Medicine Man* depicts this approach. As shown in the film, such pharmacological research is threatened by declining tribal populations with loss of traditional herbal knowledge coupled with declining biodiversity. With the loss of ethnopharmacological information, the knowledge of ancient cultures can be tapped through archaeology. Every prehistoric culture had some sort of healthcare system, and a pharmacopoeia was integral in each ancient cultural system. Most medicinal compounds used were derived from plants. In theory, the archaeological record can be used to identify medicinal plants used in ancient times. In practice, new archaeological research has demonstrated the presence of anomalous plant finds that, under scrutiny, prove to have had a medicinal use. Therefore, the reserve knowledge of medicinal plants can be expanded by exploring the archaeological record for relevant botanical remains.

The paleopharmacological approach compares archaeological data with ethnographic and plant-chemistry data. Through this approach, researchers identify specific ailments treated with plant extracts and identify the physiologically active compounds in the plant. Thus, paleopharmacology employs archaeological and ethnographic investigation of the ancient use of medicinal plants in the light of what is known about plant chemistry and physiology.

The paleopharmacological record also includes textual information from ancient cultures that document medicinal plant usage. Most documentation of pharmacopoeias comes from the Old World. For example, Morris Weiss and Raoul Perrot have separately summarized aspects of Etruscan medicine and medieval medicine, respectively. In A.D. 77, Dioscorides (Greek physician and pharmacologist) wrote the *De Materia Medica*, which summarized Greco-Roman knowledge of medicinal plants. Medieval medical practitioners based their *Materia Medicalis* on this work. The Greeks and Romans were influenced by the herbal knowledge of the Egyptians. In 1989, Lise Manniche summarized the Egyptian pharmacopoeia from several Egyptian texts, including the *Papyrus Ebers,* which dates to 1550 B.C. At least three Aztec documents describe a New World pharmacopoeia that was studied by Bernard Ortiz de Montellano in 1975.

Method of Textual Study

The pharmacopoeia of the Aztecs was extensive. The Aztecs maintained botanical gardens for the main propose of supplying botanical remedies and as a source of pharmaceutical experimentation. The Spanish were impressed by Aztec medicinal knowledge and sponsored the documentation of their pharmacopoeia. Three sixteenth-century documents survived from this effort: *Primeros Memoriales, Codex Matritense,* and the larger *Florentine Codex.* Ortiz de Montellano's analysis of these documents stands as a model for text-based paleopharmacology. The analysis had three goals: identification of the described plants, analysis of the plants for physiologically active compounds, and determination of their therapeutic effectiveness for native-defined illnesses. Ortiz de Montellano identified the precise species for twenty-five plants that had a wide variety of native uses, including anthelminthics, sedatives, expectorants, digestive remedies, purgatives, and diuretics. The active chemicals in each plant were identified in twenty-one species and then were evaluated with respect to their effectiveness in native use. Of twenty-five plants, sixteen are effective in their native uses, four are possibly effective, and five are not effective. Two of the plants that are not effective for the native-described use are effective in other ways. This study demonstrates how textual paleopharmacological information can lead to the discovery of traditional plant remedies and the chemical evaluation of their effectiveness. The fact that 80 percent of these plants are effective and 85 percent have physiologically active compounds also demonstrates the accuracy of ancient peoples in identifying medicinal properties in plants.

Method of Nontextual Study

Unfortunately, for most ancient New World cultures, no written record exists of the plants utilized for medicinal purposes. However, ethnographies show that New World cultures had a rich plant pharmacopoeia. Daniel Moerman (1986) has summarized nearly 2,400 plant species that have been documented ethnographically as having medicinal value among Native Americans (Moerman 1986). Native American medicinal plants provided significant additions to the European remedies. For example, quinine, which was a South American malaria cure, is obtained from the bark of the cinchona tree *(Cinchona officinalis)*. This remedy was introduced into Europe in the seventeenth century and, by 1681, became the universally recognized antimalarial drug. Quinine was eventually synthesized in 1944. Another South American plant, coca *(Erythroxylum coca)*, is the source of medicinal cocaine. Cocaine has never been synthesized. Considering that Native Americans were ravaged by epidemics and war for 300 years before the ethnographic record was compiled, it is very likely that many more medicinal plants were part of the precolumbian Native American pharmacopoeia and wait to be found in the archaeological record.

In the absence of native textual documentation, ethnographic analysis of extant or historical Native Americans has provided the bulk of our knowledge of New World pharmacopoeia to date (i.e., 1998). However, evidence of medicinal and psychotropic plants is growing in the archaeological record. The data come from several sources: corporeal remains, coprolites, and standard plant finds.

The study of prehistoric psychotropic plants has the longest history. In 1977, Gary Fry identified dogwood *(Cornus stolonifera)* bark, which produces an opiumlike, narcotic effect, in a coprolite from Utah. The use of this plant among Archaic hunter-gatherers in Utah signals either its medicinal or ceremonial use. In the lower Pecos region of Texas and adjoining northeastern Mexico, a long tradition of psychotropic plant use dating from 10,500 to 1,000 years ago has been documented (Adovasio and Fry 1976). This tradition included three psychotropic plants that were used in succession. Texas buckeye *(Ungnadia speciosa)* was used with mescal bean *(Sophora secundiflora)* in the earliest part of this time period. Later, the use of buckeye declined as mescal bean became the preferred psychotropic. Finally, by ca. A.D. 1000, peyote *(Lophophora williamsi)* began to occur. The earliest find of peyote consists of a necklace on which peyote buttons were strung. One main trend indicated by this analysis is the sequential abandonment of more-lethal, in favor of less-lethal, plants. Buckeye is the most poisonous of the three, followed by mescal bean, and then peyote.

Many early finds went unnoticed for their pharmaceutical value. For example, Paul Martin and John Rinaldo noted the find of jimsonweed *(Datura* spp.) seeds from a pueblo in New Mexico. Jimsonweed is a strong, but dangerous, psychotropic plant. The seeds were cached with ceremonial objects in a kiva (men's ceremonial structure). The association of seeds with the objects in the kiva suggests that the Mogollon people of New Mexico used this hallucinogen in ceremonial rites. The connection between the seeds, their psychotropic potential, and the ceremonial association was not made in the original report. This suggests that surveys of previous archaeological studies hold the promise of recovering more information regarding medicinal plants.

Evidence of medicinal plants appears in some of the more than 1,000 coprolites analyzed from the Southwestern and southeastern United States. Coprolite analysis provides a means to view plants or plant parts directly consumed by humans, including evidence of medicinal plants. Macrofossils present evidence of medicinal plant use. Perhaps the longest-acknowledged pharmaceutical plant from the archaeological record is

Chenopodium spp. as an anthelminthic (Riley 1993). Decades of research demonstrate Chenopodium as an important part of several Native American pharmacopoeias. Five North American tribes, the Cherokee, Rappahannock, Houma, Koasait, and Natchez, used various species of Chenopodium to treat parasitic-worm infection. In the study of Aztec medicinal plants summarized above, Ortiz de Montellano discovered that the Aztecs also used Chenopodium species as a treatment. Coprolite studies in North America also indicate prehistoric use of the plant. The 1991 study by Karl Reinhard and colleagues presents a case that certain species of Chenopodium were used in the Southwest as anthelminthics. This study also suggests the inadvertent use of Chenopodium as a prophylaxis when it was a dietary staple among Archaic hunter-gatherers. Among agriculturalists, there is limited coprolite evidence that suggests that certain species, C. graveolens and C. botrys, were recognized and specifically used as anthelminthics. It has been pointed out that a weakness in this study is that pinworm was the parasite under research, whereas Chenopodium is a recognized remedy for hookworm genera and the giant intestinal roundworm, Ascaris lumbricoides (Riley 1993). Secondly, data from the sites of Salts and Mammoth caves in Kentucky provide evidence of both hookworm and A. lumbricoides infection. There is evidence for the use of certain Chenopodium species in ancient southeastern pharmacopeias.

One of the significant aspects of these Chenopodium studies is the depiction of the development of pharmaceuticals in prehistory. Species of Chenopodium were used by ancient hunter-gatherers and agriculturalists primarily as a food source. As knowledge of various species of Chenopodium progressed, there came the recognition that certain species had a pharmacological value. These were C. graveolens, C. botrys, and C. ambrosioides (also called C. anthelminticus). The physiologically active compound in these species is ascaridole, which induces paralysis in at least some roundworm species. By the protohistoric and historic periods, there was complete recognition of the medicinal value of these plants with their incorporation into the Native American pharmacopoeia. Eventually, this Native American knowledge was transferred to Europeans.

Pollen provides evidence of medicinal plant teas. The analysis of coprolites for their pollen content by Reinhard and colleagues revealed the presence of pollen from several plant species not particularly known for their dietary value. Ephedra (mormon tea) pollen was found in Mojave Desert, Chihuahua Desert, and Colorado Plateau hunter-gatherer coprolites. The pollen occurred in large quantities, often exceeding one million pollen grains per gram of coprolite. These large quantities demonstrate intentional consumption of the plant. Traditional uses of Ephedra species include antirheumatic, antidiarrheal, diuretic, burn-dressing, and cold-remedy uses. One active compound in at least Asian and Spanish Ephedra species is ephedrine which constricts blood vessels, raises blood pressure, dilates pupils, and relaxes the intestinal and bronchial muscles (Moerman 1986). Contemporary uses of ephedrine include reduction of nasal congestion due to colds or allergies. Ephedrine is not present in North American Ephedra species, at least not in economically significant amounts. Consequently, identification of other physiologically active compounds in North American species awaits further research.

Larrea (creosote) was consumed in the Rustler Hills of west Texas. As with the Ephedra finds, there are large numbers of creosote pollen grains in coprolites from this part of the world. This indicates intentional consumption. Since creosote is not a dietary plant, its potential as an antidiarrheal medicine was evaluated. As a hot tea, decoctions of creosote have been used as a treatment for diarrhea. In addition, it is also a Mexican folk remedy for bladder ailments and for removing calcium deposits from kidneys. Creosote contains many physiologically active compounds, but specific antidiarrheal compounds have not been identified as yet.

Salix species (willow) were used by Native Americans in ancient and historical times. The bark or foliage of the tree is used to make medicinal tea. Willow contains salicin, an analgesic. Its analgesic use has been documented ethnographically among many New World indigenous cultures by Moerman in 1986. Willow pollen was found in coprolites from three prehistoric cave sites, two in the Rustler Hills of west Texas (A.D. 200–1400), and one in the Mojave Desert of Arizona (A.D. 600–900). The presence of the pollen in great quantities suggest strongly the use of willow as a medicine. All of these finds come from hunter-gatherer sites and demonstrate that hunter-gatherers identified medicinally important plants. The plants provide evidence of the treatment of minor health problems, such as aches, colds, diarrhea, and urinary problems.

In addition, medicinal plant remains have been found in the intestinal contents of burials. The analysis of these remains provides a unique opportunity to examine the medicinal treatment of seriously ill individuals. For example, coprolites were found in the abdominal cavity of a Mimbres burial from the NAN Ranch Ruin in New Mexico (ca. A.D. 1000) and analyzed by Reinhard and colleagues. These coprolites showed that the dying man was fed very finely ground corn, probably in a soup form. The pollen analysis revealed willow and unknown mustard-family pollen. The willow was administered as an analgesic. Because pollen from the mustard family has not yet been identified as to genus or species, the specific use of this plant is unknown. Several mustard species are used to maintain movement of material through the intestinal tracts of bedridden people. This may have been the use of mustard; however, unless the plant can be definitively identified, its use and its active compounds cannot be assessed. A second series of coprolites was found with an Anasazi child mummy from Glen Canyon in Utah. The analysis of these coprolites showed that the individual was fed wild grasses before death. *Ephedra* pollen was also found in the coprolites, which suggests that this was administered to the dying individual.

Other Methodological and Theoretical Considerations

Because medicinal plants are much less often used than dietary plants, they are especially cryptic in the archaeological record. Therefore, archaeologists must be carefully attuned to searching for evidence of medicinal plants. Attention should be focused on places where medicinal plants are likely to be present. Because certain plants have ceremonial significance, evidence should be sought in ceremonial contexts. The jimsonweed noted above is an example of such a find. Mummies and burials should provide a particularly rich source of medicinal data. These individuals may have been ill at the time of death and, therefore, may have been under medicinal

treatment. The Mimbres and Anasazi burials noted above illustrate the potential of recovering medicinal plant data.

It is important to ask whether a specific population is at risk for specific diseases treated with medicinal plants. For example, prehistoric inhabitants of the Rustler Hills were environmentally predisposed to diarrhea. The Rustler Hills of Texas are composed of dolomite and lie in the center of the Great Gypsum Plain; the water contains very high levels of magnesium and sulfur and acts as a laxative. The most direct evidence that diarrhea was a common prehistoric malady is a high percentage of the diarrheal coprolites recovered from the caves. In light of these observations, the inhabitants of Rustler Hills were in need of antidiarrheal compounds, such as *Larrea* and perhaps *Ephedra*. From South America, autopsies of Peruvian and Chilean mummies indicate that pulmonary disease had a very high prehistoric prevalence. During the analysis of materials from Jane E. Buikstra's recent excavations in Peru, aromatic fruits were discovered in coprolites that produced a menthol smell. The fruits may represent medicinal use of plants for pulmonary disorders. Currently, these fruits are still under investigation by Buikstra and Reinhard to determine the genus and species of the plant that produced them and the physiologically active compounds that they contain. Dental disease was a problem for horticultural people due to high carbohydrate diet and among desert hunter-gatherers due to the highly abrasive nature of their diets. The early use of willow among hunter-gatherers and later horticulturalists may have been stimulated by toothaches. Thus, medicinal plant use in prehistory can be incorporated into the overall picture of disease ecology to arrive at an understanding of ancient health problems.

Theoretically, it is unwise to assume that plants were used to treat the same illnesses in the past as those existing today. It is also unwise to project contemporary uses of medicinal plants into the past. Ortiz de Montellano, analyzed the effectiveness of Aztec plants in treating the diseases defined by the Aztecs. This is the proper approach to paleopharmacology. In the absence of written records, defining the disease ecology allows one to infer what symptoms were most common among ancient peoples and then guess the application of medicinal plants to these symptoms.

It is possible that the medicinal plant species were used for food or beverages rather than as medicines. However, this does not negate the medicinal value of the plants. Among modern tribal peoples, up to 50 percent of the plants in the diet can have a tribally recognized medicinal role as well (Etkin and Robs 1992). This is especially true of spices that often have physiologically active compounds. The difference in a plant's value as a spice as opposed to a medicine is often determined by the quantity that is consumed. Therefore, when large amounts of plant foods are found that normally appear in small or trace amounts, medicinal use is possibly signaled.

The origin of medicinal plants has been a topic of recent discussion as reviewed by Reinhard and colleagues in 1991. In 1989, Moerman statistically identified "high use" and "low use" categories for thirty-nine plant families. He then inferred mechanisms by which people originally identified high-use plants as medicinal. Many medicinal components are secondary compounds produced in the plants to reduce browsing by animals. Plants signal the presence of these compounds by visual or olfactory signals. Moerman and Michael Logan have suggested that humans used these signals as clues to identify plants of potential pharmaceutical value. This discussion is related to the question of whether or not some medicinal plants originated as dietary foodstuffs. The suggestion has been made that goosefoot was used first as a dietary plant before the medicinal property of a limited number of its species was recognized. However, at least *C. graveolens,* an anthelminthic species, produces an intense odor and color change in the autumn. Cattle recognize these signals and avoid the plant. Perhaps prehistoric humans recognized two varieties of goosefoot, dietary and pharmaceutical, defined by smell and color. In 1988, Logan contributed another perspective to the discussion of the origin of medicinal plants—proposing a scenario in which the introduction of agriculture resulted in land disturbance with consequent growth of pioneer species, thus increasing the spectrum of plants available to human populations (cited in Reinhard et al. 1991). After experimentation, agriculturalists discovered that some of these weeds had medicinal value. Therefore, agriculture could have resulted in substantial expansion of the medicinal knowledge.

Paleopharmacology provides important time depth to the study of the origin of medicinal plants. It adds significantly to the understanding of human manipulation of plants for medicinal purposes. The understanding of the history of medicine and medical discovery is expanded by the field. Finally, paleopharmacology has the potential to add new knowledge of heretofore unrecognized medicinal plant species.

Karl Reinhard

See also ARCHAEOPARASITOLOGY; COPROLITE ANALYSIS; PALEOETHNO-BOTANY

Further Readings

Adovasio, J.M., and Fry, G.F. (1976) Prehistoric psychotropic drug use in northeastern Mexico and Trans-Pecos, Texas. Economic Botany 30:94–96.

Etkin, N.L., and Robs, P.L. (1992) Food as medicine and medicine as food: An adaptive framework for the interpretation of plant utilization among the Hausa of northern Nigeria. Social Science and Medicine 16:1559–1573.

Holloway, R.G. (1985) Diet and medicinal plant usage of a Late Archaic population from Culberson County, Texas. Bulletin of the Texas Archaeological Society 54:319–329.

Manniche, L. (1989) An Ancient Egyptian Herbal. London: British Museum.

Moerman, D.E. (1986) Medicinal Plants of Native America. (University of Michigan Technical Reports 19). Ann Arbor: Museum of Anthropology, University of Michigan.

Moerman, D.E. (1989) Poisoned apples and honeysuckles: The medicinal plants of Native America. Medical Anthropology Quarterly 3:52–61.

Ortiz de Montellano, B. (1975) Empirical Aztec medicine. Science 188:215–220.

Perrot, R. (1988) The *Materia Medicalis* in the therapy of medieval injuries. Journal of Paleopathology 1:146–156.

Reinhard, K.J., Hevly, R.H., and Hamilton, D.H. (1991) Use of pollen concentration in paleopharmacology: Coprolite evidence of medicinal plants. Journal of Ethnobiology 11:117–134.

Riley, T.J. (1993) Ascarids, American Indians, and the modern world: Parasites and the prehistoric record of a pharmacological tradition. Perspectives in Biology and Medicine 36:369–375.

Weiss, M.M. (1989) Etruscan medicine. Journal of Paleopathology 2:129–164.

Paleoserology

The demonstration of blood on ancient materials using immunochemical means—in particular, blood-grouping methods. In this way, paleoserology can be differentiated from paleoimmunology, which is defined elsewhere in this volume.

Theory

There are many different systems described that classify the nature of blood. In blood transfusion, the most important is the ABO blood group. Red blood cells have a variety of different glycoproteins and carbohydrates on their surface, called *antigens*. Modern red blood cells, with a particular antigenic surface (e.g., B), when inoculated into a competent host animal induce that animal to produce antibodies (e.g., anti-B). These antibodies appear in the blood and can be extracted, purified, and used in the laboratory to detect the antigen that gave rise to them.

Humans can be divided into four groups based on the presence of their ABO antigens: A, B, AB (both) or O (neither). The antigens of the ABO blood group are glycoproteins, and the difference between A- and B-antigens is determined by the nature of a single carbohydrate (saccharide) attached to the terminal sugar of the glycoprotein chain. Group O individuals secrete a glycoprotein (H-antigen) that is devoid of additional saccharide.

The antigens of the ABO system are widely distributed throughout the human body, being present in muscle, organs of the alimentary tract, the kidney and bladder, the myocardium, the spleen, and the lungs, to name but a few. There are many commercially available reagents for the detection of these immunochemical markers because of the importance of the ABO blood-group system in blood transfusion. When using these reagents, anthropologists should be rigorous in their screening procedures, as discussed below.

Applications

The development of reliable methods to determine blood groups in decomposed human material has been prompted by the interests of two major independent fields: legal medicine and physical anthropology. In medicolegal terms, interest derives from the need to identify human remains. In physical anthropology, however, ABO blood-group distribution was seen as a possible means of tracing human migrations and of determining the degree of relatedness between different populations.

It is not the intention here to list and describe the different methods applied to the serological diagnosis of blood type in ancient materials. Essentially, routine forensic methods were applied and modified so that only small amounts of material were needed for the testing.

The *standard-inhibition* method for antigen detection was applied to characterize the ABO antigens present in the mummified soft tissues of Chilean and Peruvian Indians. The apparent lack of O (H) antigens among these populations was the cause of many speculations as to population migration and miscegenation among ancient peoples. This lack also led to the formation of theories concerning the origins of the ABO systems within the Americas. The standard-inhibition (agglutination inhibition) method was modified in 1940 for the demonstration of ABO antigens in bone, and this enabled the technique to be applied to archaeological and historic bone samples.

The application of the standard-inhibition methods in 1976 to ancient skeletal material from Israel yielded similar information; the very low incidence of H-antigen among the population encouraged the authors to speculate about population migration. Further, 19 percent of the skeletons could not be diagnosed. The authors (Micle et al. 1976) suggested that the antigen had possibly been leached out of these tissues.

Generally, controls for these studies used postmortem material for which the ABO group had been measured antemortem. The blood/muscle tissue had been dried and held following postmortem examination. These tissues repeatedly gave results consistent with those obtained antemortem.

Problems Associated with Application to Archaeological Materials

In the medicolegal field, these methods have been applied to forensic material (both soft tissues and bone), but the percentage of incorrect results in these studies has been so high that the techniques have been regarded as unreliable. There have been suggestions that more reliable results may be obtained from forensic material by using at least two techniques in combination when the specimens are more than six months postmortem.

If the methods cannot successfully be applied to forensic material, it would seem optimistic to apply the same methods to archaeological materials. There are two problems associated with the application of ABO typing to degraded tissue: Environmental (burial) conditions may have led to a change in the ABO blood group, and various contaminating materials present in the burial environment may mimic the A, B, and H substances.

Change in the ABO Determinants

Alteration of the established ABO group by the burial environment is well recognized among forensic serologists. Water may leach out the water-soluble fraction of the blood-group substances in bone; mild acid hydrolysis of ABO blood groups does remove the carbohydrate determinants. The surrounding environment of a decomposing body may be predominantly acidic, due to the presence of decomposition products. In this case, the loss of ABO blood-group substances from buried remains as a result of acid hydrolysis may be a significant problem.

A number of microorganisms produce enzymes (glycosidases) that destroy blood-group substances by removing sugars from the glycoside component. Three genera of these microorganisms (*Clostridium*, *Pseudomonas*, and *Bacillus*) are prevalent in soils. Some members of these groups may destroy the A, B, and H specificities completely. For example, the soil bacterium *Bacillus fulminans* converts B antigens to H antigens by removing the sugars from the glycoside side chain unit.

These organisms are not restricted to the soil; some of them are present in the human body. At the beginning of putrefaction, organisms from the gut and respiratory systems migrate into local tissue, from where they invade the lymphatics and general circulation system. From there, they can invade all of the tissues of the body. Any postmortem or archaeological tissue used for ABO grouping must be suspect. There is the probability that it has been contaminated by microorganisms capable of destroying the blood-group substances.

Presence of Contaminating ABO Determinants

The ABO antigens are present in many parts of the body, not only the red cell surfaces. They are also present in many other unrelated substances; for example, the H-antigen is commercially produced from extracts of the plant *Ulex europeus*.

Some microorganisms possess membrane components with structures similar to the ABO antigens. Microorganisms present in both soil and gut have been linked with the introduction of both A and B antigens into the same forensic material. Microorganisms produce these antigens when grown on laboratory media. The bacterium *Escherichia coli* 086, common in the gut, has long been known to show high B-antigen activity.

Interpretation of Results

When grouping mummified materials, the tissues must be screened for the presence of microorganisms prior to extraction procedures. Even if no microorganisms capable of changing the ABO determinants are found, the possibility of microbial change cannot be excluded, for this may have occurred in the past. As well as testing the tissues, samples of soil must also be tested for the presence of ABO-like antigens, but even this will not completely exclude the possibility that contamination has happened. Leaching may have removed these components from the surrounding soil but not from the skeletal remains.

Assuming that all of these conditions are met, what reliance can be placed upon the results obtained for archaeological material? The answer is uncertain. These conditions have been filled in some studies, and the results obtained show a high incidence of A, AB, and B and a very low incidence of O (H) antigens. This is very different from the ABO distribution within modern populations but matches what one would expect from remains that have been contaminated by the activities of the decomposing microorganisms.

Angela Gernaey-Child

See also PALEOIMMUNOLOGY

Further Readings

Child, A.M., and Pollard, A.M. (1992) A review of the applications of immunochemistry to archaeological bone. Journal of Archaeological Science 19:39–47.

Micle, S., Kobilyansky, E., Nathan, M., Arensburg, A., and Nathan, H. (1976) ABO-typing of ancient skeletons from Israel. American Journal of Anthropology 47:89–92.

Roitt, I. (1986) Essential Immunology, 6th ed. Oxford: Blackwell.

Rowe, W.F. (1986) The ABO grouping of human remains: A review. In S. Barry, D.R. Houghton, G.C. Llewellyn, and C.E. O'Rear (eds.): Proceedings of the Sixth International Biodeterioration Symposium, pp. 134–142. Slough, UK: Commonwealth Agricultural Bureaux.

Palynology

The study of pollen and spores. In archaeology, fossil pollen can be used to validate the presence of agriculture, determine plant foods used in prehistoric diets, predict the functional use of certain types of artifacts, calculate seasonality of site occupation, reconstruct paleoenvironmental conditions, and identify a variety of cultural traits and rituals.

In technical terms, pollen is the multinucleate gametophyte generation of flowering plants. In simple terms, its most important function is to carry the sperms needed for plant reproduction. Spores are the male and female gametes of nonvascular plants such as algae, fungi, mosses, and ferns. Spores and pollen are similar in size; both are found in the sediments of archaeological sites; both can remain preserved in sediments for millions of years; and both are often produced and dispersed by the millions.

The principles that validate the use of pollen analyses in archaeology, as well as in other disciplines, are based on five observations outlined in 1916 by the Norwegian geologist Lennart von Post. First, he pointed out that many plants produce great quantities of pollen or spores, which are dispersed by wind currents. Second, he noted that pollen and spores have very durable outer walls (exine) that remain preserved for long periods of time. Third, the morphological features of pollen and spores can be used as a key to plant taxa because each species produces its own unique form of pollen or spore. Fourth, each pollen and spore-producing plant is restricted to specific habitats and is most abundant in areas that best fit the plant's optimum needs. Fifth, most windborne pollen and spores tend to fall to the Earth's surface within a small radius (ca. 50–100 km) of where they are produced and dispersed.

Palynologists working with archaeological sediments rely upon these five principles and a sixth that assumes that some patterns found in the fossil-pollen record are the result of human actions rather than those of nature.

Pollen Applications in Archaeology

In the late 1930s and early 1940s, Johannes Iversen, a Danish geologist, was the first palynologist to alert archaeologists to some of the potential ways fossil-pollen studies could be used in their discipline. During the late 1930s, Peter Glob, an archaeologist who had been excavating the Barkaer site in northern Denmark, asked Iversen for help. Like other archaeologists of that time, Glob surmised that people with a knowledge of farming and animal husbandry had migrated into Denmark from the south and had introduced these new ideas to others living in the region. Danish archaeological records indicated that, soon after the first migrant farmers arrived, cultures living in northern Europe quickly converted from foraging to agriculture and animal domestication. The problem facing Glob was how to pinpoint when, and how, this change to farming had occurred.

Today, the Barkaer site is on a low hill, but when it was first occupied more than 4,000 years ago, it was a small island. As the land around the site rose, the lake surrounding the island became shallow, filled in, and became a bog. By examining fossil pollen collected in core samples from the bog, Iversen determined how and when the local transformation from hunting and gathering to agriculture had occurred. First, Iversen noted that the record ca. 4,000 years ago showed a sudden decline in pollen from elms and other hardwood trees, indicating that the nearby forest had been cleared quickly to prepare the area for planting. Second, Iversen found numerous microscopic flecks of charcoal in the same deposits, suggesting that the fallen trees and brush had been burned. Third, the record showed that sediments deposited immediately after the forest disappeared contained fossil pollen from domestic cereal crops and pasture plants, such as clover. Together, these data provide convincing evidence that ca. 4,000–4,500 years ago the inhabitants were growing wheat and barley and raising domestic animals. Iversen dated the precise time of these events at the Barkaer site by correlating his fossil-pollen record with other pollen sequences from nearby sites where dated chronologies had already been established.

In the 1960s, James Schoenwetter of Arizona State University was one of the first to collect and analyze fossil pollen recovered from the floors of ancient pueblo dwellings. He used the fossil pollen found in floor scrapings to date the time of site occupation and infer climatic sequences. He did this by comparing the fossil-pollen spectrum, the percentages of each pollen type in a sample, in each floor sample with the known pollen chronology for that region. When the pollen spectrum of an undated floor sample matched a similar pollen sequence from the regional dated chronology, Schoenwetter assigned the same date to his sample.

In a later study, James Hill and Richard Hevly of the University of Arizona used the recovered fossil pollen from floor surfaces of the Broken K Pueblo on the Colorado Plateau to infer the functional use of rooms. They categorized the functional use of fifty-four rooms in the pueblo to one of three categories: habitation use, storage use, or ceremonial use. They made their room assignments based on the percentages of various fossil-pollen types found embedded in the floors of each room.

In a similar study in the 1970s, Vaughn M. Bryant, Jr., and Glen Weir of Texas A&M University found that fossil pollen from floor scrapings collected at Antelope House pueblo in Arizona confirmed many of the assumptions made by archaeologists while excavating the site. Bryant and Weir's pollen data revealed that, between A.D. 900 and 1250, the pueblo's residents continued to collect and eat a wide variety of wild plants and seeds, including beeweed *(Cleome)*, pigweed *(Chenopodium)*, amaranth *(Amaranthus)*, and sunflower *(Helianthus)*, even though their primary subsistence was maize, bean, and squash farming.

Long-held views that the Neanderthals did not have religious beliefs or compassion for others changed dramatically when French palynologist Arlette Leroi-Gourhan conducted fossil-pollen studies of burial soils in Shanidar Cave in Iraq in the 1960s. She found that fossil pollen in deposits located directly on top of a Neanderthal burial contained unusually high percentages of alpine flower pollen. In addition, the same soils also contained clusters of fossil pollen confirming that anthers from the same flowers were also present. Because those alpine flowers are insect pollinated, only a small fraction of their pollen would normally be carried by wind currents into the cave. Therefore, the high percentages of fossil flower pollen could only have come from a graveside ceremony in which many flowers from nearby hillsides were picked and then placed on the Neanderthal's body at the time of interment. Even today, it is the fossil-pollen evidence that remains as the most important evidence linking Neanderthals with graveside rituals and perhaps religious beliefs.

The recovery of fossil pollen from human burial sites has not been limited to Shanidar Cave. Today, archaeologists routinely collect soil samples from burials for pollen analysis. At Broken K Pueblo, unusually high amounts of mallow *(Sphaeralcea)* and pine *(Pinus)* pollen were found in the soils of an infant's burial. In addition, Antelope House pueblo burial soils revealed that handfuls of maize *(Zea)* pollen were probably dusted on Anasazi-period bodies during graveside rituals. Taken together, these data suggest that many prehistoric cultures had graveside rites and that they often used flowers and/or handfuls of pollen in some type of mortuary rite.

In England, James Greig is noted for his innovative use of fossil-pollen data recovered from ancient urban centers. His analyses have provided detailed insights about how pollen can reach urban locations and what happens to pollen once it is deposited in an urban environment. His experiments using ancient food-collecting and food-processing techniques showed that ca. 2,000 barley pollen grains become trapped in each cubic centimeter of soil in areas where it is being crushed into flour. He also found that in areas where barley, wheat, and oats are winnowed, their chaff contains thousands of pollen grains. Finally, his studies showed that currant and quince pollen should be expected in the soils of medieval-age archaeological sites because both fruits retain significant numbers of pollen grains, even after they are picked and transported.

Mud used to make the adobe bricks in Anasazi-age pueblos contains significant amounts of fossil pollen. In the 1970s, Mary Kay O'Rourke of the University of Arizona found that, by comparing the pollen spectra recovered from different adobe bricks, located in different areas of the site, she could determine which structural walls were built at the same time and which ones were constructed during later or earlier periods. This type of fossil-pollen application has promise for many regions of the world where adobe and mud have been used as building materials for thousands of years.

Pollen analyses are useful for determining the functional use of baskets, ceramic vessels, bedrock mortars, and milling stones. In the 1960s Vorsila Bohrer of the University of Arizona demonstrated that pollen is inadvertently included during the gathering and storage of many types of foods, such as maize, oats, barley, and wheat. This also occurs while collecting and storing wild foods, such as amaranth seeds *(Amaranthus)*, cattail stalks *(Typha)*, beeweed leaves *(Cleome)*, and goosefoot seeds *(Chenopodium)*.

During the collection and storage of plant foods, loose pollen from those plants will often adhere to the inside of ceramic vessels and baskets or become lodged in a basket's weave. When the fossil pollen they still contain is examined, the functional use of baskets and ceramic vessels can often be determined. However, there is little chance that archaeologists will find pollen trapped in the clay used to make most well-fired ceramic pottery. Pollen is oxidized in fire, and all attempts to recover pollen from well-fired pottery vessels have thus far failed.

In their 1970s study of pottery-vessel use, V. Bryant and Donald Morris carefully scraped the inside bottom portion of vessels recovered from abandoned rooms and burial sites at the Antelope House pueblo. Next, they analyzed each sample for fossil pollen and then compared the pollen spectrum from each scraping sample with fossil-pollen spectra recovered from other locations in the vessel's dirt matrix. Using Chi-square tests, they determined what types of food products had been stored, or prepared, in each vessel and whether or not their samples were contaminated by dirt that later filled each pot.

Studies of the surfaces of grinding stones and seed-grinding slabs recovered from rooms at the Antelope House pueblo indicated that they still contained pollen traces of the various seed types ground into flour. Experiments also revealed that, when seeds are ground on stone surfaces, pollen trapped with the seeds will often be fractured into specific types of patterns. These same types of fractured pollen are commonly found in the cracks and crevices of many prehistoric seed-grinding implements.

Like grinding stones, bedrock mortars may contain fossil pollen. Careful removal of modern dirt and debris in mortar holes, and an analysis of the fossil pollen trapped in the bottommost layers of dirt in these mortars, may indicate types of plant foods that were being ground. However, for most bedrock mortars, it may be difficult to separate possible modern pollen contaminants from ancient fossil pollen.

Archaeologists have discovered that, in arid regions of the world, fossil pollen may still be attached to the cutting edges of ancient stone tools. During the late 1970s at Hinds Cave in southwest Texas, Harry Shafer and Richard Holloway of Texas A&M University found that 6,000-year-old flint scrapers and knives still had dried plant sap cemented to their cutting edges. Microscopic examination revealed that the dried plant sap contained phytoliths, pieces of leaf tissue, and pollen grains. Although their study showed that attached fossil pollen is a rarity, this type of study has future promise.

The study of fossil pollen found in human coprolites is becoming a useful source of information on prehistoric diets and food-preparation techniques. To date, archaeological sites in arid regions have yielded the best samples of human coprolites. Pollen from human coprolites reveal that many cultures ate flowers or may have used flowers to brew medicinal teas. Studies in the late 1970s by Gerald Kelso of the National Park Service and by Glenna Williams of the University of New Mexico in the early 1980s have traced the movement of pollen through the human digestive system. Their findings reveal how different pollen types can indicate which types of foods may have been eaten together and which were most often eaten separately during prehistoric times.

Samples from the French archaeological site of Lascaux were used by Arlette Leroi-Gourhan in the 1970s to reconstruct the first pollen-based paleoenvironmental chronology for the time of the Lascaux interstadial (ca. 17,000 years ago). Her fossil-pollen studies also produced a list of plants that she believed were used as food by the cave's inhabitants. However, she noted that other fossil-pollen types deposited in the cave's soils were most probably carried there on clothing or shoes worn by the cave artists. Finally, she found that a third group of fossil-pollen types, such as sage *(Artemisia)* and grass pollen, reflect plants that may have been brought into the cave as fuel or for ritual use.

Like the early discoveries made by Iversen in Denmark, fossil-pollen records from Bonfire Shelter and the Devil's Mouth site in west Texas helped solve an archaeological mystery. Bonfire Shelter is the southernmost site in North America in which prehistoric hunters are known to have driven large herds of bison over cliffs onto the rocks below. The site contains two buried strata of bison bones that accumulated from multiple bison drives. The lower bison-bone strata dates from the Paleoindian period ca. 10,000 years ago. The upper zone dates to ca. 2,500 years ago. However, in between these two time periods the site was abandoned. What puzzled archaeologists was why the site was not in continuous use as a bison-jump location for the entire time between the lower and upper bison-bone deposits.

Fossil-pollen studies from Bonfire Shelter and other nearby archaeological sites provided the answer. During the past 12,000 years, climatic conditions in west Texas favored maximum grass cover only twice. In other words, grazing conditions were optimally suited for bison grazing only twice, and both times coincided precisely with the times both strata of bison bones were deposited at Bonfire Shelter. Also, the absence of Bonfire Shelter's continuous occupation during the intervening 7,500 years between the two bison jumps suggests two things. First, large bison herds were probably common in the Bonfire Shelter region during only two brief intervals; second, nomadic bison hunters from other regions were probably the ones who stampeded the bison to their death. The archaeological record indicates that, when the large grazing areas disappeared, both the bison and their hunters left the area and returned to more northern regions.

New ways to use archaeological pollen data continue to be developed. In the 1980s, underwater archaeologists began sampling inside the hulls of sunken wrecks for traces of fossil pollen. Like fossil pollen found in the floor surfaces of pueblos or in the bottom of pottery, fossil pollen found in containers on shipwrecks provide clues about the cargoes being shipped and the foods that were eaten by their crews. Also, the fossil-pollen spectra trapped in the bilges of sunken ships are like fingerprints that can link the ship to a specific home port.

One of the most novel examples of using archaeological pollen evidence was documented by François Damblon. While examining newly formed stalactites from Remouchamps Cave in Belgium during the mid-1970s, he found that some of their cemented layers contained high percentages of grass and hazelnut *(Corylus)* pollen. Because the stalactites were located far inside the cave, beyond the areas where outside air could have carried pollen, Damblon concluded that the pollen could only have come from the cultural activities of the prehistoric peoples who inhabited the cave more than 45,000 years ago.

Pollen Sampling in Archaeology

Many types of pollen grains and spores become airborne and eventually settle to the surface. This process is called *pollen rain*. Even in winter, when few plants are pollinating, already deposited pollen can become recycled into the atmosphere and will be deposited in new locations. Therefore, the first rule for pollen sampling is to use clean sampling implements and pollen-free containers (i.e., heavy-duty resealable bags) and collect fossil samples only from cleaned surfaces. When one is sampling from an excavated profile, cleaning the surface with a brush or a trowel immediately before sampling is mandatory.

The number of pollen samples that one should collect at an archaeological site will vary. When in doubt, remember that it is better to collect too many samples than not enough. Once areas are disturbed and removed during excavations, it is impossible to go back and collect pollen samples that "should" have been taken during the excavation. Likewise, it is also essential to collect control samples. Control samples should be collected from surface locations near archaeological sites and are essential because they provide a guide to the types and percentages of modern pollen being deposited near the site. When this information is compared with data about the contemporary vegetation, that information helps the palynologist determine which pollen types might be over- or under-represented in both the modern and the fossil record of the region.

Control samples should consist of no less than eight to twenty *pinches* (a pinch = ca. 1 cubic cm^3) of surface soils collected within a small area. All of the pinches from one collection area should then be combined into a single sample and thoroughly mixed to prevent potential overrepresentation of one pollen type from a pinch location. Generally, a control sample should be collected from an area ca. 50–100 m^2. The number of control samples one should collect will vary, depending on how extensive the fossil pollen testing will be and how many different archaeological-site locations will be tested for fossil pollen. As a general rule, one should collect at least three to five separate control samples from different areas ca. 200 m or more from the excavation area of a site. It is always better to collect too many control samples than not enough.

Correct pollen sampling was exemplified during the excavations at Antelope House pueblo by archaeologist Donald Morris. He collected ca. 1,000 fossil-pollen samples while the site was being excavated. Later, only one-third of the total number were actually examined. Nevertheless, because he collected pollen samples from every important location at the site, it was possible to search for the answer to many related questions using the fossil-pollen data.

Most pollen laboratories process 20–50 g of soil from each archaeological or control sample, but there are exceptions. Sometimes, the amount of sediment inside a sealed container or ceramic bowl may be meager. Also, pollen washes of manos and metates generally produce only a few grams of soil residue, and the scrapings from a pueblo floor surface may consist of less than 10 g of sediment. Other exceptions include small amounts of residue extracted from coprolites, soils and residues that might be adhering to the surface of stone tools, or dirt trapped between the weave of ancient matting and baskets. Whenever possible, one should try to collect approximately one large handful of soil per pollen sample. This amount will permit a palynologist to process several different samples and will leave sufficient soil to permit other types of analyses, if desired.

Archaeological sites vary in their contents and complexity. This is why no one pollen-sampling strategy will work for all sites. One of the first considerations should be the types of information one hopes to obtain from fossil-pollen data. If one is searching for possible differences in the economic use of plants or changes in the use of specific plant foods through time, then collecting pollen samples from individual strata or at fixed intervals from exposed profiles is recommended. Collecting pollen samples from features is also advisable. The only exception might be sampling from the center of ash-filled hearths. These areas sometimes do contain fossil pollen, but most often they are not ideal areas because pollen oxidizes quickly when it is exposed to an open fire. Also, hearths are filled with microscopic-size flecks of charcoal that are inert and cannot be separated easily from other organic particles, such as fossil pollen, during laboratory processing. This prevents the small amounts of fossil pollen from becoming concentrated enough to examine.

One should routinely sample soils in burials. As mentioned earlier, burials may contain evidence of graveside rituals involving pollen, flowers, or other plant parts. Burial locations that should be sampled include the soils in direct contact with the top and underside of skeletons, dirt from inside the pelvic area, areas inside the chest cavity, and the matrix dirt that was used to cover the burial.

If an ancient house or ceremonial structure, such as a pueblo or a historic building, is being excavated, samples should be collected from floor scrapings in each recognizable room and from each of the different floor levels. When collecting these types of samples, one should collect them like control samples. Small amounts of scrapings from at least six to ten different locations in a room should be collected and then combined into a single sample. As with control samples, combining multiple subsamples from one room provides a generalized record that is not influenced by the overrepresentation of pollen from a single area of the room. Likewise, samples for pollen studies should be collected from adobe used to build individual walls in a structure and from the mortar used to cement different layers of a wall together.

If fairly complete ceramic vessels are found, the dirt in direct contact with the inside bottom portion should be collected and examined for its fossil pollen. However, when broken pottery is found, sampling is discouraged because the dirt adhering to individual sherds may be too contaminated to provide reliable fossil-pollen data on functional use. Dirt trapped in the textured surfaces of grinding stones or in the weave of matting and baskets may provide excellent traces of fossil pollen useful for predicting the original functional use of those items. Finally, the dirt adhering to the cutting surfaces of lithic tools found in dry rockshelters or caves should be saved for analysis. It is possible that attached pollen might indicate the functional use of the tool.

Human coprolites have provided some of the most detailed information about prehistoric nutrition and diet. When found in the deposits of archaeological sites, each coprolite specimen should be stored in a separate sterile bag so that it does not become contaminated with modern atmospheric pollen. Later, in the laboratory, each specimen should be carefully cleaned before a small portion of it is sampled for its fossil pollen contents. Some researchers believe that a coprolite sample of 1 cm^3 is sufficient to provide reliable pollen data about diet. Other researchers believe that as much as one-half of the total bulk of each coprolite specimen must be sampled to obtain reliable dietary information. Another concern centers on how many coprolites one should examine from a single horizon or area within a site before an accurate record of the prehistoric diet emerges. Here again, there is controversy. Some believe that as few as eighteen to twenty coprolites are sufficient; others believe that two or three times that number are needed to achieve accurate dietary information.

Special types of sites require special types of pollen sampling. In underwater sites, it may be necessary to use special techniques to collect samples from sunken storage containers, from the bilges of sunken ships, or from the soils directly underneath a sunken ship. One effective way to sample underwater is to use a large 20–40-cc plastic syringe, with the front end cut off. This cut-off syringe can be placed directly in contact with sediments to be sampled and then used as a small coring device, or sediments can be drawn into the syringe as the plunger is pulled out. Once sampling is complete, the ends should be sealed and the syringe placed in a plastic bag before being carried to the surface. Once removed from the water, the samples can be frozen until they can be removed in a laboratory and examined for fossil pollen.

Regardless of location, when fossil-pollen samples are collected from wet or moist environments or if the soil is damp, steps must be taken to ensure that bacteria and fungi do not attack and destroy the remaining preserved pollen. The easiest way to prevent damage to fossil pollen is to freeze samples until they can be processed in a laboratory. Freezing will not damage fossil pollen, and it prevents the growth of microbes. If freezing is not possible, several capfuls of rubbing alcohol poured into the sample will achieve the same result.

Pollen Analyses

Before palynologists can correctly interpret the fossil-pollen data from an archaeological site, they must be certain that the collected samples are not contaminated and that they contain sufficient preserved pollen to produce statistically valid analyses. Contamination can be prevented by careful sampling and then placing samples in sterile, sealed containers. These containers should not be opened until the palynologist is ready to process the samples in a contamination-free laboratory facility.

Determining the status of pollen preservation in samples is a major concern. In some samples, trying to identify broken, folded, crumpled, and degraded pollen grains is a difficult task. Some pollen grains are so badly deteriorated that their identity is uncertain. When identification of degraded pollen is not possible, they are usually called *indeterminable*. As a general guide, when the number of indeterminable grains in a sample exceeds 50 percent of the total count, the reliability of the pollen assemblage should be sharply questioned, especially if the sample's fossil-pollen concentration also falls below 1,000 grains per g or 2,500 grains per cc of sediment.

Another key to pollen preservation is a sample's diversity. When an archaeological sample contains only a few different pollen types, mostly of ones that have very durable outer walls, one should be cautious when using those samples to reconstruct the fossil record. Likewise, when most of the recovered fossil pollen comes from degraded types having easy-to-recognize, distinctive morphological characteristics, the value of the data is questionable. When these situations exist, it generally means that large numbers of fragile pollen types have already been destroyed and that the remaining fossil record represents only a small fraction of what was once present.

Palynologists also use pollen-concentration studies to determine how well fossil pollen has been preserved. These values are calculated by adding a known quantity of *tracer* pollen or spores to a sample of known size before beginning the laboratory extraction procedure. After completing the laboratory phase, the ratio of fossil pollen to tracer grains seen during a normal pollen count of 200–300 fossil grains is used to calculate the concentration of fossil pollen per unit of a sediment. High levels of pollen concentration generally mean little fossil-pollen destruction; low concentration levels may reflect significant loss of fossil-pollen due to destructive forces.

Although the causes of pollen destruction in archaeological sites are not well understood, some factors are known. Rapid changes in atmospheric moisture levels can cause some pollen types to rupture and fragment even before they are deposited. This is most common among thin-walled pollen types, such as those of cypress *(Taxodium)*, juniper *(Juniperus)*, and cedar *(Thuja)*.

The chemical composition of a pollen grain's wall also determines if it will become preserved. During a twenty-year experimental study beginning in the 1960s, A. Havinga of the Netherlands found that the ratio of sporopollenin (a carotenoidlike compound) to cellulose in the wall of a pollen grain determined its susceptibility to destruction. Pollen and spore walls containing high amounts of sporopollenin persist longer in sediments. Having also noted that, in soils with high oxidation rates, some pollen types—composites *(Asteraceae)*, oak *(Quercus)*, pine *(Pinus)*, beech *(Fagus)*, and basswood *(Tilia)*—persist for long periods of time, while other pollen types—hazelnut *(Corylus)*, alder *(Alnus)*, elm *(Ulmus)*, poplar *(Populus)*, maple *(Acer)*, willow *(Salix)*, and ash *(Fraxinus)*—are destroyed quickly. Therefore, the types of pollen and the percentages of each pollen type found at some archaeological sites will depend mostly on what type of soil is present and how long the pollen has been buried.

Other agents that damage deposited pollen include high pH (acid/alkaline ratio), high Eh (oxidation/reduction ratio), high microbial activity, and the cultural activities of humans (land modification, fire, plowing, planting). Still other destructive factors include repeated wetting and drying, which cause the walls of pollen to crumple, fold, and crack.

The pollen recovered from archaeological-site sediments represents the sum total of the originally deposited pollen *minus* the pollen lost to the processes of deterioration. If the percentage of lost pollen is not great, then the data will probably reflect an accurate representation of the original deposited pollen. On the other hand, when too much of the originally deposited pollen is destroyed, the reliability of the remaining pollen data is questionable. The difficult task is determining at what point in an archaeological site's preservation-destruction cycle the fossil-pollen record becomes unreliable.

In summary, pollen data from archaeological sites should be suspect when they contain at least one, or all, of the following: (1) when fossil pollen is from only a few plant taxa, especially when the pollen taxa represented are from the most durable types of pollen and have very distinctive and easy-to-recognize morphological features; (2) when fossil pollen concentration levels are below 1,000 grains per g or 2,500 grains per cc of sediment; and (3) when a sample contains a high percentage of indeterminable pollen grains.

Fossil-pollen analyses are useful, but they cannot always produce answers to the questions asked by archaeologists. Sometimes, soils are barren of fossil pollen, and analyses will produce nothing more than explanations of why fossil pollen may not be present. In other cases, fossil-pollen data can provide meaningful insights about the cultural use of plants, prehistoric rituals, probable room use in pueblolike structures, the functional use of artifacts, the presence of agriculture, and, under the right conditions, insights about paleovegetational sequences that might not be obtained by any other means.

Vaughn M. Bryant, Jr.

See also FLOTATION; PALEOETHNOBOTANY; PHYTOLITH ANALYSIS

Further Readings
Bryant, V.M., Jr. and Holloway, R.G. (1983) The role of palynology in archaeology. In M.B. Schiffer (ed.): Advances in

Archaeological Method and Theory, vol.
6, pp. 191–224. New York: Academic.

Bryant, V.M., Jr., and Hall, S.H. (1993) Archaeological palynology in the United States: A critique. American Antiquity 58:416–421.

Dimbleby, G.W. (1985) The Palynology of Archaeological Sites. New York: Academic.

Faegri, K., Kaland, P., and Krzywinski, K. (1989) Textbook of Pollen Analysis. New York: Wiley.

Greig, J. (1982) The interpretation of pollen spectra from urban archaeological deposits. In A. Hall and H. Kenward (eds.): Environmental Archaeology in the Urban Context, pp. 47–65. (Council for British Archaeology Research Report 43). London: Council for British Archaeology.

Hall, S.H. (1990) Progressive deterioration of pollen grains in south-central U.S. rockshelters. Journal of Palynology (Current Perspectives in Palynological Research, Silver Jubilee Commemoration Volume 1990–1991):159–169.

Horowit, A. (1992) Palynology of Arid Lands. Amsterdam: Elsevier.

Petrie, Sir William Matthew Flinders (1853–1942)

British archaeologist and Egyptologist. The grandson of Captain Matthew Flinders, explorer of Australia, Petrie was born on June 3, 1853, and educated privately. He served as the Edwards Professor of Egyptology at the University College, London (1892–1933), then was named Emeritus Professor. His efforts in the field of archaeology were rewarded with a knighthood in 1923. Petrie's interest in the discipline began early; he wrote in his 1931 autobiography, *Seventy Years in Archaeology,* that, at the age of eight, while visiting the Isle of Wight, he saw a Roman villa being excavated and was upset that the earth was not being removed in layers, so that one could recover all of the information one could from the precious soil.

Petrie was a pioneer in the field of Egyptology and introduced scientific excavation to Egypt. Appalled by the methods being used by his Continental counterparts, Petrie adopted the strict stratigraphic excavation technique that was being used in Britain. He also adopted the seriation method, by which material from different levels at different sites could be compared statistically to establish a relative chronology. Petrie excavated at Abydos, Naucratis, Tanis, Naqada, Gurob, Kahun, and Tell el-Amarna and had triumphs at each, particularly at Amarna, where he discovered the palace of the New Kingdom Pharaoh Akhnaten and a library containing the correspondence of the Egyptian Empire. At Gurob and Kahun, Petrie discovered pre-Mycenaean and Mycenaean Greek pottery and worked out a cross-cultural dating scheme that had a profound impact on Aegean archaeology. By associating the Greek finds with datable Egyptian finds in the same stratum, Petrie could attach absolute dates to the Greek material and, thus, apply these dates to archaeological finds in Greece itself. In this way, Petrie dated the beginnings of Greek culture (what is now called Early Helladic) at ca. 2500 B.C. and Mycenaean culture from 1500 to 1000 B.C. While it has strict limitations, Petrie's cross-dating work continues to influence Aegean archaeology.

Petrie's contributions to archaeological methodology were introduced to readers in his influential *Methods and Aims in Archaeology.* Here, Petrie described his stratigraphic technique and seriation and cross-dating methods and issued a call for formal training for archaeologists. His methodologies had a profound and immediate impact on Egyptian archaeology in particular and archaeology in general and played a large part in the transition of the discipline from dilettante's hobby to scientific pursuit.

Joseph J. Basile

See also SERIATION; STRATIGRAPHY

Further Reading

Drower, M. (1985) Flinders Petrie: A Life in Archaeology. London: V. Gollancz.

Petrie, W.M.F. (1969) Seventy Years in Archaeology. Reprinted, Greenwood, New York. Originally published 1931, London: S. Low, Marston.

Petrie, W.M.F. (1972) Methods and Aims in Archaeology. Reprinted, B. Blom, New York. Originally published 1904, New York: Macmillan.

Petrie, W.M.F. (1974) Illahun, Kahun, and Gurob. Reprinted, Aris & Phillips,

Warminster, UK/J.L. Walter, Encino, CA. Originally published 1891, London: D. Nutt.

Petrie, W.M.F. (1974) Tell el Amarna. Reprinted, Aris & Phillips, Warminster, UK/J.L. Walter, Encino, CA. Originally published 1894, London: Methuen.

Petrie, W.M.F. (1976) Ten Years' Digging in Egypt, 1881–1891, 2nd ed. Reprinted, Ares, Chicago. Originally published 1893, London: Religious Tract Society/New York: F.H. Revell.

Petrie, W.M.F. (1978) Syria and Egypt: From the Tel el Amarna Letters. Reprinted, Ares, Chicago. Originally published 1898, London: Methuen.

Petrography

The application of transmitted light microscopy for analysis of prepared thin-sections of archaeological and geological materials for determination of composition, structure, and technology. *Petrography,* a long-established field of study in geology, is the description and systematic classification of rocks and minerals conducted with the assistance of a polarizing microscope. Petrography and petrology are sometimes used interchangeably in archaeological application, and, among archaeologists involved in ceramic analysis, there is a preference for the term *petrography* in the United States and *petrology* or even *ceramic petrology* in Britain. However, in geological usage, *petrology* refers to the origin, geological history, occurrence, and structure of rocks, as well as their chemical composition and classification, and is not concerned with manufactured composite materials, such as ceramics. Although the term *ceramic petrology* is published with increasing frequency, *petrographic analysis* (for microscopy of stone artifacts or architecture) or *ceramic petrography* (for microscopy of objects or features made of fired clay) are perhaps more appropriate terms.

The principles of mineral optics, sample-preparation techniques, and microscope setup have been adopted from geology for archaeological applications. There are two major differences between the use of petrography in archaeology and geology: First, the range of materials studied in archaeology is expanded to include not only rocks and minerals (both natural and altered through technology, such as stone tools), but also composite materials altered through pyrotechnology (e.g., ceramics, bricks, tiles). Second, the range of research questions is broader in archaeological application to include (but not be limited to): (1) mineralogical identification of rocks and minerals used in the manufacture of objects or construction of architecture found at archaeological sites; (2) identification of the geological outcrop from which these objects or architectural elements derive; (3) reconstruction of fragmentary objects or architecture; (4) identification of surface modifications (e.g., pigments, protectants, postdepositional accretions, residues); (5) analysis of ceramic materials (e.g., pottery, bricks, tiles, kilns, molds, statuary) for fabric characterization (identification and quantification of additives and natural inclusions in the clay and assessment of manufacturing operations); and (6) identification and assessment of damage and deterioration for determination of appropriate conservation treatment.

Samples

Sample Selection

Since petrography is invasive to the object, samples for petrographic analysis should be carefully selected only after research questions have been formulated and the need for petrography is well founded. Samples are usually chosen because of the potential value of the information contained both on the surfaces and in cross-section. For either ceramic materials or stone, the portion of the object (e.g., sherd, stone tool) that shows the least amount of weathering or other evidence of deterioration is preferred for the maximum amount of information retrievable. For composite materials, there is often an underlying assumption that the mineralogical or temper (additives) composition is uniformly distributed; however, many samples would have to be cut from different portions of the objects to document the distribution factor.

Sample Preparation

The best preserved, longitudinal cross-section of the object, that is located usually away from edges or any fractures, is marked for sawing. Using a pottery fragment *(sherd)* as an example, two parallel lines ca. 0.5 cm apart are marked off on the surface (these will be cutting lines, which can be closer together if the sherd is small but will produce a sample difficult to manipulate and increase risk of damage). The sample is then cut from the sherd using a water-lubricated rotary saw.

Both cut faces of the sample will require grinding and polishing to remove saw marks and fine powder debris from the sawing process. Depending on the thickness or thinness of the finished cut sample, the first cut surface can be roughly ground and then polished prior to the second cut, which releases the sample from the body of the sherd, for ease in handling. Grinding, to even the cut surfaces, is done on a graduated series of silicon carbide papers 120–600 grit in size. Polishing to remove fine powder is done on water-lubricated cloth surfaces with alumina abrasive.

After drying, samples are then mounted on glass slides, using either Canada balsam or epoxy resins as adhesive, depending on the friability and fragility of the specimen. Poorly fired ceramics, or specimens with large inclusions that run the risk of being "pulled out" by cutting or grinding, can be impregnated with epoxy resin under vacuum to consolidate the composite material.

Grinding and polishing of the second cut surface can be done after the first polished surface is mounted to the glass slide to facilitate handling of the specimen. This second surface is ground down and finally polished to a thickness of 30 microns. This *thin-section* allows the transmission of light through the sample, which, in turn, provides identification of minerals and other materials with the microscope.

Finally, a small glass cover slide can be mounted on top of the polished thin-section to protect it. However, as an alternative method, if the thin-section is ground to a thickness of 50 microns and left without a cover slide, specific points (such as in a pigmented slip or glaze or even individual mineral grains) on the sample can be analyzed for chemical composition with an electron microprobe.

Microscopy

The purpose of grinding and polishing a cross-section of a sample to a thickness of 30–50 microns is to allow effective transmission of light from below the microscope stage, through the sample, and to the eyepiece, as well as through a variety of available analytical lenses and optical devices (e.g., polarizer,

Bertrand lens, mica plate, quartz wedge). These *transmitted light microscopes,* also referred to as *polarizing light microscopes* or *petrographic microscopes,* allow the identification of rocks, minerals, microfossils, and additives to composite materials. Plane and crossed polarized light are particularly useful for both archaeological and geological purposes, since minerals exhibit an array of optical properties as transmitted light is bent by the unique crystalline structures of individual minerals.

Petrography is a relatively inexpensive method, the major investment being a transmitted light microscope with the necessary optical accessories, magnification capability up to 400x, and photographic attachments, as well as equipment for sawing, grinding, polishing, and slide mounting—all of which can be found in a Department of Geology at a university.

Applications to Archaeology

Thin-section microscopy has been used in the field of geology since the mid-nineteenth century. The application of petrography in archaeology appeared sporadically from the 1930s to the 1950s. Its use grew in German archaeology on ceramic materials from sites ranging in date from the Neolithic to the Middle Ages. Also during the 1930s, Anna Shepard pioneered the use of methods from both chemistry and geology to the study of ceramic technology in the United States. In particular, she developed a comprehensive program of petrographic analysis in her work on prehistoric pottery from the Southwestern United States. The application of petrography fluoresced during the 1960s and 1970s in England with the work of David Peacock and David Williams, and petrography has seen its most frequent application in Great Britain, where international conferences and multiauthor volumes are devoted to this topic. Since the 1960s, petrographic analysis has been applied to archaeological materials on every continent.

Petrography can be used to address a number of archaeological research questions for (1) geological information (e.g., the identification and sourcing of geological types of clays and the changes in the clay source utilization over time); (2) technological information (e.g., the identification of temper additives, changes in ceramic technology over

Figure 1. Thin-section of utilitarian pottery, showing a large fragment of quartzite-micaceous schist in a dark mass of clay. Fragments of this size, and in quantities up to 15 percent by volume, might be confused with temper, but, in this case, they represent natural geological inclusions. This unrefined, local clay derived from schist formations in the foothills of the eastern Carpathian Mountains. Site Petricica, Neamţ County, Romania; second—third centuries A.D. Photographed with crossed polars at 100x by Linda Ellis.

Figure 2. Thin-section of utilitarian pottery, showing oolite (rounded fragment) together with relatively large, irregularly shaped shell fragments in a mass of clay and other natural inclusions. The quantity of shell does not indicate temper additives. The oolites could be traced to clay beds deriving from massive oolitic formations with impressive quantities of shell from when the Black Sea inundated the Moldavian Platform. Site Vlădiceni, Neamţ County, Romania; second—third centuries A.D. Photographed with crossed polars at 20x by Linda Ellis.

time, the utilization of different types of clays for different types of ceramic/clay products); (3) provenance information (e.g., identification and sourcing of local vs. imported pottery, the identification and sourcing of recycled pottery used as temper); and (4) behavioral information (e.g., did potters understand the unique properties and thermal behavior of the clays available to them?).

It should be kept in mind that petrography is often used in conjunction with other physicochemical methods of analysis to resolve some research questions. When tracing pottery back to its sources of clay, for instance, it may be necessary to use neutron activation analysis, X-ray fluorescence spectroscopy, or inductively coupled plasma-atomic emission spectrometry for elemental composition of both archaeological ceramics and samples from presumed geological sources of clay. However, petrography should in many instances be the first step in an analytical program because of its low cost, for the significant amount of information which can be retrieved through microscopy in general, and to assist the focus or redirection of research questions.

Likewise for geological materials used in the manufacture of objects (e.g., Neolithic polished stone axes) or in building construction (e.g., Greco-Roman architecture), petrography can successfully identify the types of rocks and minerals used. Minerals can be pre-

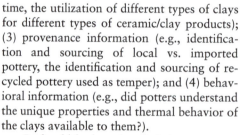

Figure 3. Thin-section of utilitarian pottery, showing complete shell surrounded by clay matrix. Petrographic analysis may require a range of magnifications from 10x to 400x in order to identify natural inclusions. This particular biological inclusion was rare and could be seen only at magnifications beginning at 200x. Site Scaloria, southeastern coast of Italy, Early Neolithic. Photographed with crossed polars at 200x by Linda Ellis.

cisely identified as to species and if multiple sources of the same mineral(s) exist in a region, then either historical or exploratory research to discover quarrying sites or chemical characterization studies can be conducted to narrow down the possible source material. Petrographic analysis can also assist the correct reconstruction of fragmentary marble inscriptions and sculpture from the Greco-Roman world, especially those pieces that lie

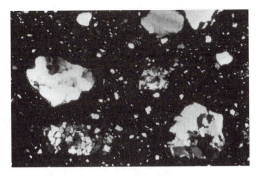

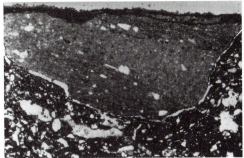

Figure 4. Thin-section of utilitarian pottery, showing both natural quartz inclusions (very small, background fragments) and added sand temper (larger grains). The contrast of what is natural to the geological history of the clay versus what has been added by the potter is clear. Site Doina Girov, Neamţ County, Romania; second—third centuries A.D. Photographed with crossed polars at 20x by Linda Ellis.

Figure 5. Thin-section of utilitarian pottery, showing a large sherd fragment (lighter shade) used as temper. The surrounding clay matrix is dark due to a reduction firing atmosphere and also contains other natural fragments in a poorly prepared clay paste that has irregular and oval-shaped spaces. The recycled pottery used as temper, however, derives from a completely different type of fine, high-fired ware from this site. The sherd fragment is lighter in color because it was red pottery originally fired in an oxidizing atmosphere. The fineness of the clay matrix and some preferred orientation of the grains indicate that it was well-prepared, wheel-made pottery. Note the characteristic white space surrounding the sherd fragment—this is caused by the shrinkage of the surrounding clay during firing. Site Bâtca Doamnei, Neamţ County, Romania; first century B.C.–first century A.D. Photographed with crossed polars at 20x by Linda Ellis.

at or near the ground surface and become disassociated from their original context.

An underutilized application of petrography is in soil and sediment analysis for an analysis of site-formation processes. During excavation, samples can be taken from living floors, burnt clay house platforms, cooking hearths, garbage pits, postholes, and trenches, as well as from sterile soil beyond the boundary of the site as a control. With petrographic documentation of soil lenses and stratification, together with the above features, a more detailed depositional history can be constructed.

Issues in Methodology and Interpretation

Despite the broad range of applications and the variety of materials available for analysis, there are a few caveats to the archaeological application of petrography that should be taken into consideration.

While the identification of geological materials used to manufacture stone objects or architecture is usually straightforward, the identification of heat-treated manufactured materials presents major challenges. Ceramics, for instance, are composite materials that contain natural geological inclusions in the clay, as well as additives (temper) introduced by the potter. Temper may consist of other geological fragments (volcanic glass, sand, gravel, crushed rock), organic materials (shell, bone, grain), or recycled ceramics. The identification of what is natural to the geolog-

ical history of the clay and what has been added, as well as the determination of whether different clay types were mixed, takes a considerable amount of experience with sedimentary geology and ceramic production, and, occasionally, some issues may not be resolved (see various examples in Figures 1–5). Similarly, ceramic materials, by their very definition, have undergone considerable heat treatment, not only during production, but possibly also in their use for cooking, as well as in any postdepositional fire. Many minerals, especially the micas and carbonates, physically and chemically transform under thermal conditions and this must be taken into consideration in mineral identification.

Quantification is particularly problematic in petrography as applied to archaeological ceramics. A number of research issues surround changes in ceramic technology through time and identification of the products of different workshops or regions. Temper identification and quantification are often used to assist resolution of these research questions.

Several systems have been developed to count and measure temper grains in the hope of detecting temporal or geographic variations. Ironically, although ceramic sherds are unquestionably the most ubiquitous type of material on archaeological sites, the time involved in sample preparation and analysis often precludes vast numbers of sherds from being submitted for petrographic analysis.

Sampling from just one ceramic piece alone involves a number of assumptions. Rarely is more than one petrographic section made from the same object, and, therefore, one always questions the representativeness of the selected location for sawing a sample, not to mention the representativeness of the few samples selected from each typological variety of ceramic, as well as the samples from different chronological horizons or geographic points. Since the archaeological record itself is incomplete and cannot be analyzed in its entirety, quantitative analyses from petrographic studies of ceramics must be used with caution and with a realization of the limitations on interpreting the results.

Although petrography is relatively inexpensive when compared to the instrumentation necessary for physicochemical analysis, it is a more time-consuming method. Mineral optics is a specialized field unto itself and requires that the archaeologist study mineralogy and optical microscopy in some depth. However, for those archaeologists who have made the necessary time investment, the rewards are, indeed, rich, and one can retrieve an understanding of geological and manufactured materials, and the human behavior that produced them, that might never have been revealed otherwise.

Linda Ellis

See also CLAYS AND CERAMICS, CHARACTERIZATION; GEOARCHAEOLOGY; MARBLE, CHARACTERIZATION; SOIL AND SEDIMENT ANALYSIS; ROCKS AND MINERALS, CHARACTERIZATION; X-RAY FLUORESCENCE (XRF) ANALYSIS

Further Readings

Kempe, D.R.C., and Harvey, A.P., eds. (1983) The Petrology of Archaeological Artefacts. New York: Oxford University Press.

Nesse, W.D. (1991) Introduction to Optical Mineralogy, 2nd ed. New York: Oxford University Press.

MacKenzie, W.S., and Adams, A.E. (1994) A Color Atlas of Rocks and Minerals in Thin Section. New York and Toronto: Wiley/Halsted.

Middleton, A. and Freestone, I., eds. (1991) Recent Developments in Ceramic Petrology. (British Museum Occasional Paper 81). London: British Museum.

Peacock, D.P.S. (1970) The scientific analysis of ancient ceramics: A review. World Archaeology 1:375–389.

Peacock, D.P.S. and Williams, D.F. (1986) Amphorae and the Roman Economy: An Introductory Guide. London and New York: Longman.

Shepard, A.O. (1956) Ceramics for the Archaeologist. Washington, D.C.: Carnegie Institution.

Stribrny, C. (1987) Die Herkunft der römischen Werksteine aus Mainz und Umgebung: Vergleichende petrographische und geochimische Untersuchungen an skulptierten Kalksteinen. Mainz: Verlag der Römisch-Germanischen Zentralmuseums/Bonn: R. Habelt.

Photogrammetry

The technique of measurement through photography. The broadest definition of photogrammetry would include any measurement from any photograph. In practice, the expression *photogrammetry* tends to be used for the most advanced processes of obtaining accurate measurements through stereophotography. This photography is usually taken with specialized metric cameras. This process will be described first, then less conventional processes, before illustrating, with a range of examples, the applications in archaeology.

The field in which photogrammetry has been most widely applied is mapping, often referred to as *aerial survey*. Most national series of topographic maps around the world today make use of photogrammetric base material. There is much application in archaeology of both the primary product (i.e., 23×23 cm) vertical aerial photograph) and maps at various scales derived from it, to that further reference will be made later.

Basic Principles

A brief description of the theory of photogrammetry is needed in order that its application can be better understood. However, it should be pointed out first that this is a complex, mathematically oriented methodology. The end user of the products normally need know little of this, but, if active involvement in data production through photogrammetry is anticipated, the complexity of the process should not be underestimated. If a deeper understanding of the photogrammetric theory is required, the American Society for Photogrammetry and Remote Sensing (ASPRS) in Bethesda, Maryland, publishes excellent textbooks on both aerial and close-range photogrammetry, as well as a monthly journal, *Photogrammetric Engineering and Remote Sensing*. Another good general textbook is Paul Wolf's *Elements of Photogrammetry*, listed in the Further Readings.

Perhaps the best way to understand stereophotogrammetry is to think of it in terms of human eyesight. When the observer looks at a scene, the brain receives not one but two images—one from the left eye and one from the right eye. The separation of the eyes provides a base distance and an angular separation, and the brain then computes the position of objects in the scene in relation to one another.

This is a very simplistic idea, but the geometrical conditions do, nevertheless, relate directly to the photogrammetric process. To replicate this human process, it is necessary to take two photographs of a scene from different viewpoints and then mathematically compute the geometry of the intersections to give three-dimensional coordinates of points in the scene. In theory, these two camera stations can be anywhere in relation to the scene. In practice, the cameras are usually lined up to give the familiar stereopair, that has a specific advantage in that it enables the human viewer to study this material stereoscopically.

Carrying out the process is, in practice, much more complex than this description. In the first place, the camera used usually has to be a metric camera, so called from its precise construction, which ensures that the geometrical characteristics of each photograph are identical. Next, dimensional-scale control must be provided. This is usually achieved by observing target points by theodolites. Then, a method of extracting accurate measurements from the stereopair of photographs is required. This is normally accomplished with an instrument known as a *photogrammetric plotter*. This instrument enables the operator to see a view of the stereopair. It is provided with a facility called the *measuring mark*, which enables dimensions to be taken off. This is achieved by the operator tracing around all of the detail to be measured. It is very important to appreciate that this is not an automatic process. While automation is entering the photogrammetric process, most work is still completed manually.

The above describes what might most appropriately be called conventional photogrammetry. Much work carried out in the field is done by just these methods, especially in aerial survey. The reader should keep in mind these basic procedures, as, to a certain extent, most other methods are derived from these principles. However, there have been many interesting and novel developments in the field in the last few years that make the process more accessible and flexible to potential archaeological users.

Rectified Photography

The stereo measurement method has been described in some detail, for it is the technique that provides the most accurate and reliable results. Before considering areas of development from stereo principles, the field of single-photograph measurement should also be considered. When applied to standing buildings, this technique is usually referred to as *rectified photography*. There has always been much interest in deriving measurement from single photographs, both within the photogrammetric community and by users such as archaeologists.

The key restricting factor on the use of single photographs concerns their geometrical characteristics. If the subject being photographed forms a perfectly flat plane, then dimensions can be quite accurately retrieved. However, few subjects, and especially not archaeological ones, fulfill this condition of flatness. Where the subject being photographed has any *depth* at all, the photographic image is subject to what are referred to as scale and displacement errors. While considerable ingenuity can be applied to reduce these errors, ultimately it is these factors that restrict the value of single-photograph measurement. For a fuller understanding of the geometry involved, consult one of the standard textbooks on photogrammetry referred to in the Further Reading.

New Tools

Before describing a range of applications in archaeology and illustrating some of these with

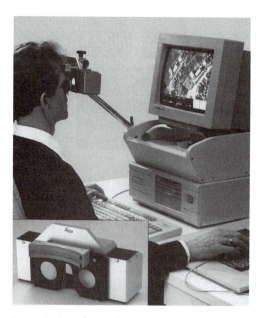

Figure 1. A modern softcopy photogrammetric system, the Leica DVP. The operator looks through the eyepieces and views the scene in stereo on a conventional PC computer monitor. The detail is traced from the stereo image using the mouse, which controls the position of the measuring mark on the screen in a similar manner to a cursor. Reproduced by permission of Leica North Europe.

examples, some discussion on the newly developed processes seems relevant. The process described above relates very much to the conventional application of photogrammetry. However, as with many scientific areas, the development of cheap PC computers has had a profound effect on the field. The traditional approach was concerned with what could be achieved with mechanical equipment. Computing power has enabled processes that were understood in theory to be applied in practice. Many of these have direct and important implications for archaeology.

Perhaps the first and most important development is the freedom from having to utilize the traditional metric camera. With the newer computer-driven analytical plotters, photography from a much wider range of camera types can be accepted. In particular, virtually standard cameras can be used for many applications. This is important for archaeological applications, where cost-effective solutions are often necessary. For the extraction of data, new types of plotting machines have become available at significantly lower cost than the traditional machines. Also, plotting systems that do not require stereo viewing have become available, and these may have particular application in archaeological work.

There are also now fully digital photogrammetric systems, grouped under the general title of *softcopy photogrammetry*. The Leica DVP (digital video plotter), developed at Laval University in Quebec, Canada, is a relatively low-cost system (Figure 1). Softcopy photogrammetry should become very important for archaeological applications as the systems become more user friendly and economically priced.

Applications in Archaeology

Why, then, might the archaeologist consider using this method, which is clearly quite complex and usually requires both specialized equipment and trained operatives? In the first place, it is perhaps because the camera captures so much information. This is a familiar concept from conventional pictorial photography, but the ability to then obtain accurate measurements from the photography is an important bonus. The noncontact nature of the measurement process can also be important, exemplified by the use of photogrammetry in recording inaccessible building facades. The speed and safety of recording may be vital (e.g., in rescue archaeology). If it is not known exactly what information will be required after the site visit, this can be important, as the photographic image will have captured the whole scene. The output of measurement data is not limited to dimensions taken only on site, for the stereopair can be remeasured to obtain extra information. This list is not definitive, and clearly the nature of the specific project will be important in deciding whether a photogrammetric approach will be of value or not.

It should also be recognized that the process may have disadvantages. Some of these have already been referred to, namely the requirement for a range of specialist equipment and the need for trained operatives. Also, the process is generally a complex one, which is susceptible to mistakes and errors at various stages. While it is certainly possible for the archaeologist to be trained in photogrammetric techniques, this is unlikely to be cost effective unless a sustained program of work is anticipated.

Photogrammetric techniques have the potential to be applied in virtually every area of archaeological endeavor, from underwater ar-

Figure 2. A section of the Romano-Celtic boat found in 1993 in Magor, Wales. One of a stereo pair imaged with a metric camera, the Leica-Wild P31, with 90 × 120 mm format. The control targets can also be seen. Figure by Ross W.A. Dallas.

chaeology to artifact measuring and drawing. Whether it will be appropriate or not to use photogrammetry requires analysis of a number of factors concerning the size of the project, the resources available, the attitude of staff to technology, and so on. To help decide and to illustrate the application of photogrammetry, examples are drawn from three areas of interest to archaeologists: the excavation of sites, the recording of standing buildings, and extensive coverage of landscape through aerial survey.

Perhaps surprisingly, the area of excavation has seen the least application of photogrammetry. This is probably because classical photogrammetry is perhaps rightly seen as too slow, too unwieldy, and too complex for application to the normal type of excavation, as discussed in Ross W.A. Dallas's chapter in *Close Range Photogrammetry*. Where photogrammetry has tended to be applied is in specialized cases in which one of the parameters referred to above, such as urgency of recording, has applied.

The following example would be typical of this philosophy. In 1993, the extensive remains of a third-century A.D. Romano-Celtic

timber boat were uncovered in Magor in the county of Gwent in Wales and excavated and preserved under the direction of Nigel Nayling of the Glamorgan-Gwent Archaeological Trust. Difficult winter weather conditions and the urgency of vacating the site led to the archaeological team looking for alternatives to conventional recording. A photogrammetric team from Atkins AMC was called in. The team recorded the site with metric stereophotography (Figure 2) and produced a plot of the site at 1:10 scale. This plot was returned to the site for archaeological interpretation, having saved the recording team many hours of laborious measurement (Figure 3).

This work was carried out in the classic vein (i.e., with metric cameras, an analytical plotter, off-site contractors, and stereo plotting). However, new photogrammetric systems utilizing computers and digitizing tablets are now available that have the potential to reorient the archaeologist's attitude to the use of photogrammetry in recording excavations. There are a number of such new systems, which may all have a role in archaeological recording. To keep up to date with this field, readers

Figure 3. The photogrammetric plot of the Magor boat. The original drawing scale was 1:10. The planks and the cross-framing timbers of the hull can be clearly seen. This drawing shows the first plot produced by Atkins AMC photogrammetric engineers, before annotation by the archaeologists from the Glamorgan-Gwent Archaeological Trust. Figure by Ross W.A. Dallas.

should consult recent copies of the journal *Photogrammetric Engineering and Remote Sensing,* published monthly by the ASPRS.

The use of photogrammetry to record standing buildings has become well established, particularly in European countries, although there are many examples from other parts of the world. This area is a multidisciplinary field, in which the survey drawings are needed not just for the archaeologist, but for all professionals involved in building conservation. In England, English Heritage makes extensive use of the technique, as described by Dallas (1993). In Germany, several of the federal states have photogrammetric equipment. The field is thoroughly reviewed through the work of the International Committee for Architectural Photogrammetry (CIPA). This specialist committee can be contacted through the Paris headquarters of the International Council on Monuments and Sites (ICOMOS). Descriptions of many detailed applications of standing-building recording can be found in *Buildings Archaeology: Applications in Practice,* edited by Jason Wood of Lancaster University in Britain.

An example of recording standing buildings in North America comes from Mexico, where a start has been made on photogrammetric recording of ancient Maya structures in Yucatan by Lawrence Desmond. In 1989, the Adivino Pyramid at Uxmal and the La Iglesia building at Chichen Itza were both recorded in a study to test the ability of archaeologists, only minimally trained in photogrammetry, to record such buildings (Figure 4). Due to the difficulties of access to the site of the Adivino Pyramid, innovative techniques were employed, such as the use of nonmetric cameras and balloons to obtain elevated camera positions. Though limited in

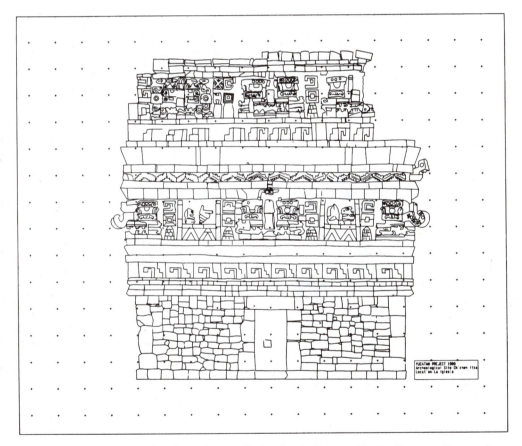

Figure 4. Photogrammetric plot of La Iglesia at Chichen Itza in Yucatan, Mexico. Lawrence Desmond's team photographed the stone structure with a 70mm-format Bronica camera. Plotting was carried out by John Garcia of American Measuring Instruments Dell Foster Division of San Antonio, Texas. Courtesy of Dr. Lawrence Desmond.

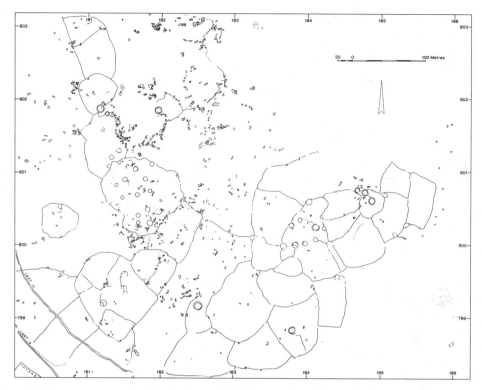

Figure 5. Photogrammetric plot of an extensive landscape on Bodmin Moor in southwest England, prepared by the Royal Commission on Historical Monuments of England in association with English Heritage and the Cornwall Archaeology Unit. Vertical aerial photographs in the 23 × 23 cm format were plotted in a Galileo Siscam Digicart stereo plotter to produce this detailed record. Figure by Ross W.A. Dallas.

scope, the results were generally successful and have helped stimulate interest in the application of photogrammetry in the United States.

The area of aerial applications is perhaps the most well established field. Most archaeologists will be familiar with vertical aerial photographs. The use of aerial photography is well exemplified by the work of the Royal Commission on Historical Monuments of England (RCHME) and described in its numerous publications. Among other tasks, this government agency is responsible for recording archaeological sites throughout England. Extensive use is made of all forms of aerial recording, from photo interpretation of oblique photographs to photogrammetric mapping from stereo photography.

The Air Photography Unit's teams of specialized air-photo interpreters devote the majority of their time to primary 1:10,000-scale mapping and documentation of archae-

ological sites. Much of this work is done using single-photograph techniques described above. The information is traced off using computerized techniques onto a base of the national map series. More specialized tasks carried out include large-scale precision photogrammetric surveys of archaeological earthworks. A typical example of this type of work would be a survey on Bodmin Moor in southwest England to record Bronze Age circular house and field patterns (Johnston and Rose 1994). For this survey, vertical aerial photographs at 1:8,000 scale were plotted on a Galileo Siscam Digicart photogrammetric plotter (Figure 5).

These examples of photogrammetric work are very selective, but they should give the reader an idea of the wide range of possible applications of photogrammetric techniques in archaeology and in situ monument conservation.

Ross W.A. Dallas

See also AERIAL PHOTOGRAPHY FOR ARCHAE-OLOGY; PHOTOGRAPHY, ARCHAEOLOGICAL

Further Readings

Dallas, R.W.A. (1981) Architectural and archaeological photogrammetry. In K.B. Atkinson (ed.): Close Range Photogrammetry. Barking, Essex: Elsevier.

Dallas, R.W.A. (1993) Architectural photogrammetry: Continuing the topographer's tradition? Photogrammetric Record (London) 14(81):391–404.

Desmond, L.G. (1994) The use of close-range photogrammetry for archaeological documentation: Chichen Itza and Uxmal 1989. In V.M. Fields (ed.): Proceedings of the Seventh Palenque Roundtable Conference, vol. 9, pp. 43–48. San Francisco: Pre-Columbian Art Research Institute.

Drager, D.L. and Lyons, T.R. (1985) Remote Sensing: Photogrammetry in Archeology: The Chaco Mapping Project. Albuquerque: Branch of Remote Sensing, National Park Service, U.S. Dept. of the Interior.

International Committee for Architectural Photogrammetry (1993). Architectural Photogrammetry: Activity and Research Area. Colombo, Sri Lanka: International Council on Monuments and Sites (ICOMOS)/International Committee for Architectural Photogrammetry (CIPA). (CIPA has also been responsible for a series of symposia publications from 1970 onward).

Johnston, N., and Rose, P. (1994) Bodmin Moor: An Archaeological Survey, vol. 1: The Human Landscape to c. 1800. (English Heritage Archaeological Report 24). London: English Heritage.

Royal Commission on Historical Monuments of England Annual Reports. (These provide information on the commission's work and publications; to 1993, London, then Swindon).

Whimster, R. (1989) The Emerging Past: Air Photography and the Buried Landscape. London: Royal Commission on Historical Monuments of England (RCHME).

Wolf, P.R. (1983) Elements of Photogrammetry, 2nd ed. Singapore: McGraw-Hill.

Wood, J., ed. (1994) Buildings Archaeology: Applications in Practice. Oxford: Oxbow/Institute of Field Archaeologists.

Photography, Archaeological

The techniques and organization of photography for archaeological recording.

Photography has been used in archaeology since its earliest days in the mid-nineteenth century. At that time, most emphasis was placed on the depiction of archaeological monuments as wonders or curiosities of the ancient world. Today, photography is directed more objectively toward the factual recording of excavations and of the varied finds deriving from them. The excellence of much early archaeological photography serves to emphasize that advanced technology is not necessary for this branch of photography. Basic photographic knowledge is needed, however, both for technical accuracy and an appreciation of how the various photographic processes can be best employed. Such knowledge underpins the two areas into which archaeological photography can be divided: *site photography* and *object photography*.

Archaeological Site Photography

Purpose

Common uses for the site photographic record include archival record, publication, research, exhibition, and lecturing. Each of these categories will demand a different style of output and, possibly, different equipment or materials. Suitable equipment and specific photographic techniques are defined, therefore, as much by the use to which the record is put as by the type of site.

Publication. This is usually in monochrome, for reasons of cost. The requirement is for a good-quality print at ca. 10×8 inches. At that size, ultrafine-grain films or lenses of ultimate quality are not necessary. Color is sometimes used for general illustration and can be taken from 35mm slides. The quality of color reproduction in this case is more dependent on accurate exposure than on film size or camera type.

Archival Record. The general site record is conventionally monochrome, backed up by color slide. The processing and storage of all films should be to archival standards. Color films, in particular, need careful storage. It is good practice for the working archive to be in print form and for the negatives to be stored in conditions of controlled temperature and humidity. Prints need not be of such a high print quality as those for publication or so large. Many projects store the record as contact

Figure 1. Photograph of an archaeological site in its environment: Montezuma's Castle in Arizona. The choice of viewpoint and the time of day are crucial in showing a site to its best advantage. Photograph courtesy by Joseph Kovacic.

sheets until specific illustrations are needed. Transparencies can be duplicated, with only those duplicates forming the working collection. The archives of a site will be the source for all other illustrative use. Much of the record may be of seemingly unnecessarily high quality to allow for later specialized needs.

Research. Site photographs should be available for later study. When it is known that site photographs will be used for subsequent analysis or measurement, extra care is needed in their execution. Large-format cameras (see below) or other specialized films and equipment may be necessary. Note, however, that measurements derived from conventional photography are rarely as accurate as those taken independently. Photography is better as an illustrative medium for results obtained by measurements in the field.

Exhibition. The provision of exhibition prints in monochrome or color needs the finest-grain films, the best-quality optics, and often larger-format cameras. Where exhibition is a known end, allowance for such uses should be made at the outset.

Lectures. Archaeology is beholden to its supporting bodies, both academic and public. A comprehensive coverage of all aspects of the work of an excavation should be made for public presentation. This can be done by color slides.

The site record. With the above uses in mind, the photographic record can be usefully divided into separate sections: excavation, environment, progress, techniques, and personnel.

Excavation. This is the main purpose of site photography: accurate and informative records of prepared sections or areas. The requirement here is for technically accurate camera work and proper presentation of the site.

Environment. All sites have a geographical and temporal relationship with their surroundings. No site can be fully understood without knowledge of its place in the landscape. Photography can show, for example, local topography and vegetation, geology, and relationships to other nearby sites (Figure 1).

Progress. Progress of an excavation is often recorded only in notebooks. A valuable addition to these notes can be regular-progress photography, taken without any formal tidying of the site. On complex projects, it may be more convenient to issue Polaroid cameras to workers in each area of activity for this purpose (Figure 2).

Techniques. Many sites modify common excavation techniques to suit local problems

Figure 2. Photograph taken to illustrate both work in progress and excavation techniques at Haddenham, Britain, a large Neolithic enclosure with later Bronze Age features. Photograph by Gwil J. Owen.

or to extract otherwise unobtainable information. It is useful to be able to present these for review later or for public interest.

Personnel. In a similar fashion to the recording of the techniques of excavation, a record of personnel is often useful. Apart from general interest and team spirit, such photography will be available much later as part of the history of archaeology.

Site photography is no different from any other archaeological activity in that it has its own aims and objectives. Formal planning of the photographic record, its scope, and purpose is essential; only then can an informed choice of equipment and techniques be made.

Equipment

Cameras. For the vast majority of site photography, 35mm equipment is satisfactory. In monochrome, prints of good publication quality can be produced, and prints for exhibition are possible using fine-grain film. Color work is commonly done in the 35mm-slide format, from which prints can be made if needed. Larger camera sizes are discussed later.

It is usual to have a system based on a single-lens reflex (SLR) camera, mainly to take advantage of the ability to change lens focal length to suit the constraints of different sites. A typical outfit consists of two camera bodies, one for monochrome and one for color. It is perfectly possible to use one body and to rewind partly used film when a change to color or monochrome is wanted. With care,

such partly used films can be reloaded, and wound past the last-used frame, to be completed in the usual way. This is obviously a potential source of confusion in record keeping, when each film is often assumed to be an unbroken sequence in the record. Additionally, a spare camera body is a common-sense precaution against failure or damage. The 35mm SLRs used for archaeology need not have a wide variety of extra facilities over and above those needed for simple control of exposure and aperture.

Traditionally, it was held that manual metering was essential for accurate exposure under the variable lighting conditions that are commonly found in archaeological activities. Modern multipatterned sensors and the clever weighting of their input have made auto-exposure more than sufficiently reliable for most archaeological photography. In any case, standard practice should be to bracket exposures, making three exposures, one nominally correct, and one on either side of it by one f stop (or by one-half of a stop in the case of reversal film). This should take care of any lack of precision in the assessed exposure and provide a substitute negative for one damaged.

Control of aperture is necessary for depth of field. Cameras with only fully automated exposure control, often called *programmed exposure,* are not suitable. Depth-of-field preview is essential, particularly for close work. Also very useful is the ability to auto-bracket exposure. This, coupled with motor drive, is a great asset. An exposure override of plus or minus two stops is essential if auto-bracketing is absent and useful when auto-bracketing is present. In many archaeological situations, the effective film speed needs to be altered to allow for areas of unusual light or shade. This is done before any exposure bracketing is brought into play.

Flash is frequently offered as built in. This is of minimal use on open sites. Sometimes, on smaller sections in bright sunlight, a small amount of fill-in flash is useful. Any flash on a camera must be controllable to one-half or one-fourth power for this function. Where the flash is to be the main, or only, light source, it is better off-camera. Any flash connections on the camera should allow for this.

SLR cameras are of two types: manual-, and auto-focus. Given that site photography is done without undue haste, preferably from a tripod, there is no need for auto-focus. Similarly, control of depth of field by automated assessment is unnecessary. Also, in close-up and macrophotography, the choice of the plane of focus is a critical factor, not always allowed for in automated systems. That is not to say that auto-focus cameras are not suitable for archaeological photography. Given a manual-focus option when needed, auto-focus is often a convenient accessory. Much of a general color-slide record can be done with ease, using zoom lenses and auto-focusing.

The final choice of camera will be made often on financial terms rather than purely technical ones. In this context, the marketplace has dictated that manual-focus cameras are either relatively unsophisticated or at the very top of a manufacturer's range. Many of these latter will be simply too expensive. A better compromise may be to come down a reputable manufacturer's range to a mid-priced, auto-focus camera to take advantage of other automated features that may be built in, which will still allow use of that manufacturer's top-class lenses.

Lenses. A set of three lenses is common, in the following focal lengths:

A 28mm wide-angle lens: Since most sites are of restricted access, wide-angle lenses are frequently needed to cover entire sections. The 28mm lens is commonly that which has the widest angle of view, consistent with accurate drawing at the edges of the frame.

Top-quality manufacturers may offer lenses of slightly wider angle of view with little distortion. Funds permitting, a 24mm focal length lens is an alternative. With the use of shorter focal lengths than this, distortions due to viewpoint become obtrusive and should be avoided.

A 50mm standard lens: Where possible, a standard focal length lens should be used. Distortion of shapes at the edges of the frame is minimized, and the perspective of the photograph overall is closer to that of the human viewpoint. Understanding and interpretation of the record is made easier.

A lens of longer focal length: such a lens, commonly of telephoto construction, is useful. Close study of otherwise inaccessible parts of the site is made possible and from distances that minimize the convergence of parallel lines due to viewpoint. This lens is most usefully a 100mm macro lens, that can then be the standard lens for artifact photography. A tele-extender can further add to the long focal length facilities of an outfit.

Zoom lenses are marketed as a first choice lens for many 35mm SLR cameras. Apart from low weight and convenience of use, they have little to offer the archaeological photographer. Except for those at the pinnacle of modern construction and, therefore, at the apex of current prices, zoom lenses do not control distortions as well as prime lenses of equal focal length. This is particularly so where accurate recording of shape is concerned. Barrel and/or pincushion distortion is usually noticeable at either end of the zoom range. The greater the zoom range, the more this is likely. Zooms with a macro facility are common, but they do not approach the standards of prime macro lenses in optical performance or close-focusing capability. Nevertheless, many photographers, given two camera bodies, will use a zoom lens as standard on the camera dedicated to color slides. Useful focal length ranges are either 35–75mm or 28–80mm. It should be noted that lenshoods normally provided with zoom lenses are designed for the widest focal length of the lens in order to avoid vignetting at the corners of the frame at wide-angle settings. They are less effective at other focal lengths.

Each lens should have its own UV (ultraviolet) absorbent filter. There is a small loss of optical performance whenever extra glass is put in front of a lens, but this is apparent only under laboratory conditions. This is less important than the physical protection that a filter gives to the front glass of the lens. Dust, water, and accidental knocks are part and parcel of archaeology. A rigid lenshood can also protect against physical damage. In any case, a lenshood is needed at all times to maximize lens performance by reducing flare.

Larger-Format Cameras. All other things being equal, the larger the film the better. More information can be carried, tonal values can be more subtly defined, and the effects of blemishes on the film, such as dust spots, are minimized. The latter is particularly useful when working in the field. Large-format cameras, also known as *view cameras, plate cameras,* or *monorail cameras,* depending on their precise construction, vary in film size from roll film (6 cm wide) to sheet film at 10 × 8 inches. The most useful sizes for the field archaeologist are 5 × 4 inch sheet film, or roll film, if individual processing of each sheet is not likely to be needed. Each size of camera will have a matching range of lenses from wide angle to long focal length. On such cameras, it is possible to change the position and the angle of the film and the lens relative to each other, a facility commonly called *movements.* It is possible in this way to correct converging parallel lines, apparent when conventional cameras are pointed up or down. More accurate measurements can be taken from the resulting photographs than from those taken by conventional 35mm or roll-film cameras. Large-format cameras are often used to record monumental structures and subjects containing much fine detail. The increased resolution that is possible is particularly useful for wall decorations and skeletons and their associated grave goods. For most archaeological work, however, the weight and cumbersome methods of use of such equipment outweigh the advantages in image quality and accuracy.

Roll-film cameras are a much more appropriate choice. Nearly all currently available are single-lens reflex in construction. They can be considered as sized-up 35mm cameras. Indeed, most of the features of 35mm equipment can be found on roll-film cameras, the notable exception being autofocus. Negative sizes vary from 6 × 4.5 cm to 6 × 8 cm, some models offering a choice by changing just the camera back. For the archaeologist, cameras with a rectangular film format tend to make the best use of the film area. The ability to rotate the back from landscape to portrait format is particularly useful when working from a tripod. Though they are as easy to use as 35mm cameras, roll-film cameras are much heavier. Factors to consider are transport to and from the site—baggage allowance by air, for example—and the need for upgraded supports, such as tripods or extension poles for elevated viewpoints on site. Nevertheless, roll-film cameras are the best compromise between quality and portability for archaeological photography. Generally speaking, prints produced from roll film are of a perceptibly better quality than those from 35mm negatives of the same film type.

An alternative outfit to the two-bodied 35mm kit already listed would be one roll-film camera, four lenses (wide angle, normal, long focal length, and macro), and two film backs. For the additional 35mm photography, one camera will suffice, with a zoom lens and possibly a long focal length macro lens.

Other Equipment. The site photographer's toolkit is not complex. A tripod is essential. Nearly all of the photography will be done at small apertures for maximum depth of field, which will necessitate longish exposure times. Cable releases are required. These can be best considered as consumable items, against certain loss or breakage. Filters have been mentioned as protectors. Other filters can be used to compensate for changes in the color balance of the light at different times of day or under different weather conditions. They are useful, too, in emphasizing small changes in soil density or color. Flash equipment is not often needed on open sites but can be used underground or in caves.

Other items reflect a pragmatic approach to work in the field. Dust- and moisture-proof cases should be obvious, as should backup sets of batteries where used. Cleaning tissues, a soft lens brush, and jeweler's screwdrivers all have a place.

Lastly, there are the tools needed to prepare the site for photography. Dustpan, brush, and trowel may duplicate those already on site, but their availability from site stocks should not be taken for granted. Likewise, scales, from ranging pole size down to a few centimeters, are part of the photographer's kit. A spirit level is also needed to set poles and scales accurately. Some sites have a requirement for a north-pointing arrow in each photograph, for which a compass is needed. Finally, no archaeological photographer would feel complete without the multipurpose Swiss army knife.

Films

There are three main types of monochrome film currently available: conventional, those with artificially generated grain shapes, and those that develop a color dye for the image. These last—chromogenic films—are not suitable for archaeological work, as they are not sufficiently archivally stable.

All archaeological photography can be done adequately with conventional monochrome films. The vast majority of the record, even in 35mm, is possible with a medium-speed film of ca. 100 ASA (= 21 DIN). For exhibition work, slower-speed films, of finer grain structure, 50 ASA or 25 ASA (= 18 DIN or 15 DIN, respectively), offer better resolution, though such films are not necessary with the larger film formats. Where photography has to be in very dull conditions, films of 400 ASA (= 27 DIN) can be used, but, at print sizes more than 10 × 8 inches, the granularity of the image on 35mm stock begins to interfere with resolution. The larger the format, the less this is a problem.

Films with artificially shaped silver halide crystals can offer distinct advantages where fine grain is required for the same film speed. Here, the crystal structure is grown to offer a more receptive surface to the image from the lens or, in some cases, to allow more efficient development for a given exposure. Set against these advantages are the relative lack of latitude in their exposure and the need for precise, controlled development. In the field, processing, particularly in hot climates, makes the use of such films particularly difficult.

Typical conventional films are Kodak PlusX (100 ASA) and TriX (400 ASA), and Ilford FP4+ (100 ASA), PanF (50 ASA), and HP5+ (400 ASA). Agfa also makes a similar range of films. Their equivalents, with modified grain structure, are the Kodak TMax series and the Ilford Delta series.

In color, there is a choice between negative and reversal (transparency) stock. Transparency film offers better accuracy of color in its initial processing than does a negative subsequently printed, due to possible variations in filtration at the printing stage. Transparency film, as 35mm slides, is more commonly used for the site record, unless it is a known requirement for everything to be in color-print form. If accurate color recording is needed, color patches can be included in the shot, along with scales and other information. It should be noted that precise, scientifically accurate color measurement is rarely possible photographically.

For all films, the less the film speed, the finer the resolution. 100 ASA color film is generally suitable for site work; indeed, many films in this category use the modified crystal types mentioned above for finer resolution. Such films are available in 400 ASA form for duller conditions, where the need for extra speed is unavoidable. Where conditions are brightest, it is rarely a good idea to use the very slowest speed color stock. As film speed falls, the inherent contrast rises. This is controllable in monochrome at the processing stage but is not so practicable in color. Under bright sunlight, the contrast range of the scene may be more than a slow-speed film can cope with. It is particularly difficult to produce prints from transparencies of high-contrast subjects rather than from negatives.

If large color prints are needed for exhibition, it will be better to use one of the slowest, fine-grain negative films, such as Kodak Ektar25.

When artificial lighting is used, tungsten light balanced film is available in several film speeds. Some filtration on the camera may be necessary to fine-tune such an arrangement. Daylight balanced film stock is used outdoors and for flash photography.

Site Preparation and Photography

To some extent, the degree of preparation of the site will depend on the end use envisaged for the photograph. Where there is any doubt as to the later use, the most careful methods should be used. This is not as onerous a task as might be thought. Much of it is common sense. Sections should be at an appropriate stage of excavation, and clean and tidy. The background of the particular shot should be scrutinized to find and remove any unnecessary items of equipment. The days when every single stone was buffed up and every blade of grass cut to length are long gone, fortunately. It is acceptable nowadays to

Figure 3. Final photograph of completed excavations at Haddenham, Britain, shows a double ditch and, in the background, a Bronze Age barrow. A high viewpoint gives a sense of scale, otherwise shown only by ranging poles. Photograph by Gwil J. Owen.

leave many of the operational activities of the site within the field of view. For example, it would be difficult and unduly time consuming, if not downright risky, to take up all of the strings and measuring stakes on a large site in the middle of an excavation just to get a cleaner picture. Planning in advance with the site director may help avoid placing spoil heaps or permanently sited items of equipment where they will be later immediately adjacent to that one vital section. When setting up a site for publication, as distinct from record photography, extra time and labor should be allowed for.

With the site clean and neat, a viewpoint can be chosen (Figure 3). The photographer should not fall into the trap of showing only the exact subject chosen and nothing else. Care should be taken to show a certain amount of the site around the immediate subject matter. This will frequently add useful information to the photograph and will certainly present it more attractively. Often, the relationship to other features can be included. To this end, the photographer should not forget the vertical component of viewpoint. Ladders, car roofs, and heavy plant can all be used to get a definitive angle of view. Needless to say, full safety precautions must be

taken if unusual supports are used. The photographer must make sure that the site insurance covers any hazardous procedures.

There is then the question of the use of scales, large or small. It is conventional to put scales into all site photographs, but this is not a hard and fast rule. Many think that, for publication purposes, scales are too obtrusive. Where other visual clues are available, scales can be left out. As noted above, precise scientific measurements from photographs are difficult to obtain and are rarely requested. Such accuracy is usually noted in plans from on-site measurement. The site photograph is most frequently used as an illustration, giving general and relative sizing, and accompanies precise textual and statistical information. Nevertheless, information on size remains essential in some form. A useful principle is to use scales always, unless their exclusion is formally required. Their use, and that of other reference labels recorded in the photograph, should be noted in the written site record.

Scales will be set to the vertical or horizontal according to the layout of the photograph. It is usual to have horizontal scales lying parallel to the film plane, though longer sections may make this impractical. Larger excavations frequently need two or more ranging poles to show vertical depth within the overall area. In such cases, it is helpful to have an assistant adjust the poles while the photographer checks the result from the camera position. In general, scales should be positioned, tidily, close to the salient features but not so as to obscure information.

Lighting for photography on open sites is most often a question of recognizing that different aspects of the site can be emphasized by the changing angles of the sun. Definitive shapes and textures will become apparent at different times of day. However, there is a danger that the contrast of such directly lit scenes will be so great that detail in shadow areas will be unclear. Where there are deeper sections, direct sunlight is frequently unsuitable. Techniques exist to diffuse the light and provide a more even illumination. In some climates, a normal overcast sky will suffice. Alternatively, photography can be done at dawn in the period just before the sun has risen. If such methods are not practical, large cloths or white boards can create shaded conditions or be used as reflectors to achieve similar effects (Figure 4).

Site Types

A short survey of the types of sites typically encountered can indicate particular photographic techniques.

Freestanding monuments vary from complete temples to short sections of wall. In many cases, there will be a requirement for photography from which reasonably accurate drawings can later be made. In such cases, a large-format camera has distinct advantages. Converging verticals can be controlled and maximum detail recorded. Where possible, a sequence of photographs can be made along a length of wall, moving the camera along parallel to the wall and giving some overlap between images. A rough rule of thumb is for 60 percent overlap. A mosaic is then made using the middle 40 percent of each photograph, this being a narrow enough angle of view to give accurate drawing (Figure 5). This and similar techniques are known as *rectified photography*.

Monuments in plan includes buildings that are evident from the remains of their

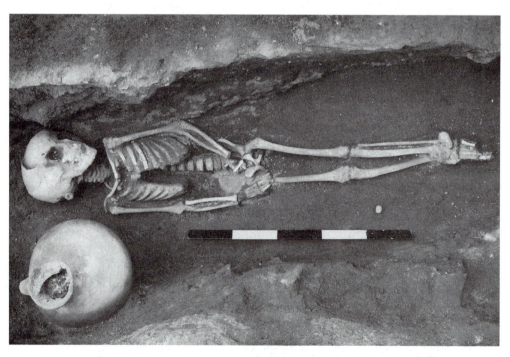

Figure 4. Photograph of flat lighting on site at Tell es Saʿidiyeh, Jordan: a skeleton of a young girl, twelfth century B.C. Flat lighting allows full detail to be recorded. Photograph by A. Hills, by permission of the Tell es Saʿidiyeh Project, courtesy of the Trustees of the British Museum.

foundations. For these, photography from a high viewpoint is needed to show the layout. For illustrative purposes, a not quite vertical viewpoint will suffice. Various items of site furniture and equipment can be used to achieve this. Mention has been made of the necessity for proper safety precautions. Greater height can be obtained using poles and remote camera controls. Elementary geometry can be used to calculate the camera angle required and the area covered. Longer poles can be cantilevered over the site to give vertical coverage, though this technique is restricted to relatively small areas at a time (Figure 6). Larger sites may need aerial photography of some kind. Where airplanes or helicopters are not permitted or too expensive, good-quality photography can be done from steerable kites or small balloons. Model airplanes can be used, but problems may occur with vibrations from the engine.

Subterranean chambers and the deeper recesses of *caves* may need extra lighting (Figure 7). Continuous lighting using a generator is best, wherever possible. Lights can be positioned and adjusted to give even coverage or to show specific features. Where one light only is available, it can, during a long exposure, be moved around and the area "painted" with light. With daylight also present, tungsten lights must be filtered to the blue of daylight color temperature when using color film.

Ease of use, portability, and a daylight color balance may make flash the only practical choice underground, but it is difficult to foresee lighting effects. Flash on or near the camera will be less effective the more depth there is to the chamber, due to fall off in the intensity of the light toward the rear of the scene. Multiple flash can be used to overcome this, each extra flash head being triggered by its own sensor. Obviously, flash heads must not appear in the field of view. They can be hidden behind protruding walls or in recesses. This technique is particularly useful when photographing long passages.

Open sites present few problems. Soil types do make some difference. Sand or loess soils, for example, may show features only when moist. Photography may be possible only at dawn in hotter climates. Alternatively, sections may be lightly sprayed with water immediately before photography. Some very subtle differences in light-colored soils can be

emphasized by filters. In monochrome, filters of one color will darken other colors. For example, blue filtration will darken a reddish stain, and red will darken green or bluish stains. Some experimentation may be necessary before a precise filtration is chosen for a specific feature. Where a stain is not of a different color, but just a slight darkening of the soil, a deep red or green filter may help emphasize this contrast. With color films, extra color saturation and contrast can be obtained using a polarizing filter.

Very dark soils present problems with exposure assessment. In such cases, exposure should be estimated for the area of main interest. Where a section is surrounded by lighter material, or when the sky is included in the photograph, compensation must be made in order to expose the darker areas accurately. This is particularly so where the darker material is itself in shade at the bottom of a pit. The use of diffuse lighting can help minimize this problem.

On the majority of sites, great technical virtuosity is not needed to produce accurate and informative photographs. More important for a successful site record are site preparation, viewpoint, and correct exposure assessment.

Archaeological Object Photography
Equipment
A 35mm camera is adequate for most object photography, particularly in the field, where portability and ease of use are powerful considerations. Roll-film format will give better results, if available. In the studio, serious consideration should be given to large-format cameras for images of pots and other objects photographed from a horizontal viewpoint. Cameras with *movements*—the facility to change the position and the angle of the lens and the film relative to each other—can avoid converging parallel lines by maintaining the film in the same plane as the object's alignment. Such distortions are more apparent in close-up. It is important to recognize that, with pots or irregularly shaped objects, there are no visual clues to indicate such distortion. Though it is true that scientifically accurate measurements are rarely possible from photographs, the true size relationship between top and bottom of objects should be maintained wherever possible.

The effects of distortions due to viewpoint can be minimized by using a longer

Figure 6. Vertical site photography. Tell es Sa'idiyeh, Jordan detail of a storeroom complex, Early Bronze Age. A vertical viewpoint can be obtained from a pole cantilevered over the site, as here, or from balloons or kites. Photograph by A. Hills, by permission of the Tell es Sa'idiyeh Project, courtesy of the Trustees of the British Museum.

Figure 5. Rectified photography at Whalley Abbey, Britain: a doorway prepared for formal recording. The fiducial marks are part of a series that will provide a reference for measurements taken later from a print or for better accuracy using computer-aided analysis. Photograph courtesy of J. Brown.

Figure 7. Lighting underground. A tomb at Tell el Amarna, Egypt. Artificial lighting is necessary to bring out architectural details. Photograph by Gwil J. Owen. Courtesy of the Egypt Exploration Society.

focal length lens than that that is standard for the film format used. In 35mm, a lens of ca. 100mm focal length is ideal; in roll film, ca. 140mm; in 5″ × 4″, ca. 210mm. These focal lengths are most conveniently to be found in a macro lens, that will then cope with all but those smallest of archaeological finds, that need microscopy.

If a specialist macro lens is not available, close-focusing capability can be achieved in two ways. Most simply, close-up lenses can be screwed onto the front of the camera lens. These can be bought as sets to give a range of magnifications up to life size. Some higher-power close-up lenses are available. A better alternative is to use extension tubes or a set of bellows placed between the camera body and the lens to increase the close-focusing capability. For magnifications of life size or greater, reversing rings can be used to turn the camera lens back to front, which will improve its performance.

As in site photography, a camera support is essential. Objects photographed in close-up require maximum depth of field. Achieving this by using the smallest aperture available (commonly f16 or f22 on a standard lens for a 35mm SLR) will lead to long exposure times. For horizontal viewing a tripod will suffice, but tripods are less suitable for vertical setups. Legs tend to intrude, either into the picture or into the light beam. Where an additional arm is used to avoid this, problems occur with the balance of the combination. In all but the smallest of operations, a copy stand should be considered essential equipment for small-find recording.

Exposure measurement is best done with a separate handheld meter. The recommended method is that of incident-light measurement, in which the meter records the intensity of light falling on the object rather than that reflected from it. This will avoid errors due to either the background or the object being unusually light or dark. Assessing the relative brightnesses of the components of a lighting system (see below) is also done more easily by this method. If camera metering has to be used, it should be through the lens metering, which will allow a specific part of the object to be assessed. A better method is to use a *gray card* of known reflectance, substituted for the object, from which to take measurements. More consistent results are possible in this way. Gray cards are commercially available.

Through the lens metering will take into account the increase in exposure necessary at very close range. With a separate meter, compensation must be calculated when the subject is photographed at a scale of 1:10 or greater. Formulae are readily available for this procedure. As with site photography, good practice is to bracket each exposure, one stop more and one stop less, or half a stop for reversal film.

Filters are rarely necessary, except for those that balance the film stock to the light source.

No problem is to be found in choice of film stock. As with site photography, a medium-speed, 100 ASA film is adequate for both monochrome and color. With controllable lighting contrast, slow, fine-grain films can be easily used. In macro work, and when exhibition prints are needed, the extra resolution and contrast are beneficial. When processing in the field, it is best to avoid films that need specialist treatment or very short development times.

A scale is essential for object photography. Unlike site photography, no visual clues to actual size are usually present. The particular scale used should be of a comparable size to the object, where that is feasible. A set of scales is usually needed, varying from one of 2 to 3 cm, marked in millimeters, to larger sizes perhaps as much as 50 cm long. These latter are more effectively marked in blocks of 5 or 10 cm. Scales are best in black and white, though black and gray, or black and blue for color work can be effective.

The precise positioning of a scale requires some care. Generally, it should be close to the object, but able to be cut out later, if measurements are to be given in textual form. The shadow of the scale should not fall onto the object. Commonly, scales are placed parallel to, and in the plane of focus, of the camera. However, where precise measurement is to be taken from the photograph, the scale should be in the plane from which the measurement is to be taken. Care is necessary in these circumstances to make sure that there exists sufficient depth of field on stopping the lens down to bring the scale into sharp focus.

Lighting
Lighting is the key to informative object photography. The simplest lighting arrangement is that which is used for copying documents or

P

other flat material. Two lights, of equal power, are placed equidistantly either side of the subject at an angle of ca. 45 degrees. The camera is vertically above the subject, usually on some sort of stand. A rough guide is that each light should be at least twice the distance from the edge of the subject as the subject is wide. This will ensure even illumination across the photograph. When combined with a shadow-free background (see below), this copying setup can be used for quick and simple recording of many small finds.

However, most archaeological objects are better photographed using one main light to show shape and detail to their best advantage. There are three stages in arranging such lighting for object photography: (1) the positioning of the main light; (2) the addition of fill-in illumination to make the lighting balance suitable for the film used; and (3) the addition of extra lighting, if needed, to achieve a pleasing overall image by selectively lighting the background or the edge of the object.

It is conventional that objects are viewed as being lit by one light source, positioned so as to reveal the main features of the object: shape, facets, material, color, and so on. This can be planned easily. An analytical assessment of the object is the first step: What is it? What are its characteristics? Then the object can be brought to a light source and manipulated until the chosen angle of view is best illuminated. This assessment and manipulation are essential but, with experience, can become a routine, almost subconscious activity, best expressed as "move the object around until it looks right." It remains then only to translate the light-to-object relationship to a position in front of the camera. For small finds, this is usually vertically below the camera; pots and other large objects are more often photographed from a roughly horizontal viewpoint.

The main light source can be varied in terms of size. The smaller the light, the sharper will appear edge details and incised marks (Figure 8). Flints and cut marks on bones are typical examples of materials that benefit from small light sources. Larger light sources, with their ability to illuminate "round the edges" of objects show better general shapes or color (Figure 9). Larger sources can be used with less precision in their positioning and are often a useful compromise in routine recording.

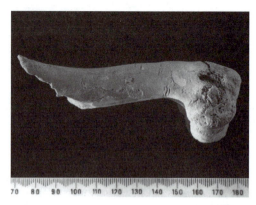

Figure 8. A small light source at an oblique angle is necessary to bring out the butchery marks on this pig bone. With the object on glass, oblique lighting emphasizes any blemishes or dust on the glass. Note also the reflections of the scale and of the inner edges of the object. All of these marks can be blacked out easily on a final print. The scale is in millimeters. Photograph by Gwil J. Owen. Courtesy of the Egypt Exploration Society.

The essential attributes of the main light—position and size—apply whether in a studio or in the field. Under optimum conditions in a studio, lights vary from fiber-optic sources of a few millimeters in diameter to light banks at more than 1 m across. A general-purpose floodlight of ca. 25 cm in diameter will suffice for most routine work. Variable light sizes can be created in field situations with a little ingenuity, if artificial lighting is not available. The smallest light source in nature is the sun; small, relatively, because of its distance. It can be made larger by diffusing it through a piece of tracing paper or a thin cloth. Illumination from a window through which there is no direct sunlight is another useful large light source. The use of natural lighting may restrict photography in the field to certain times of the day. Color balance, too, will change over a daily period, and with varying proportions of sun and blue sky. With color film, filters can be used to compensate for this.

With the object positioned and lit to best effect, it is then necessary to balance the highlights and shadows so that their different densities can be placed within the range that the film, and any subsequent printing, can cope with. This may not appear to be necessary at first sight. The human eye-brain combination has the ability to see into the shadows of a scene in a way that the camera-film combination cannot. In monochrome, the ratio be-

Figure 9. Broad lighting. A group of pottery in a more illustrative style. A large light source, here 1 m², shows the general shape of the pots and emphasizes their smoothness. The scale can be cropped off, if not required. Photograph by Gwil J. Owen, Cambridge University Museum of Archaeology and Anthropology.

tween highlight and shadow should not exceed four stops, a ratio of 16:1; in color, one stop less. The ratio chosen will depend on whether the image is to be strong and dramatic (16:1), or relatively neutral (2:1) (Figure 10). However dramatic the image, detail should be usefully visible in both highlights and shadows.

Fill-in light can be added in two ways. An additional light can be positioned as close to the lens axis as possible and its power adjusted as required. This can be done electronically or by moving the light closer to, or further from, the object. In this position, it will not cast so much of an obtrusive shadow of its own, thus avoiding the confusing appearance of two main light sources. Alternatively, this light can be replaced by one or more reflectors. For smaller objects, this is often the preferred method. White card or polystyrene is suitable. Metallized reflectors are available and are more efficient, though their angle of use must be more specific. The relative brightness of reflectors is changed by their distance from the object in relation to the distance of the main light source from the object. The farther away the main light, the more efficient a reflector will be at a given distance.

Extra lights are sometimes needed for control of background density or to show clearly the edges or other small details of an object. In particular, white backgrounds need more illumination than the object to show as pure white. On darker backgrounds, it improves the image if the object can be separated from its background by edge lighting from behind. A specifically an-

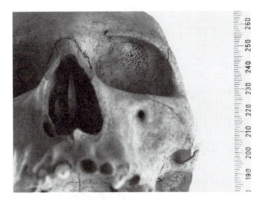

Figure 10. Balanced fill-in lighting. The eye socket of a human skull, showing the typical marks of cribra, indicating anemia. Directional lighting shows the shape of the socket, with fill-in at an almost equal intensity to avoid loss of detail in the shadows. Photograph by Gwil J. Owen. Courtesy of the Egypt Exploration Society.

gled small mirror can be used to obtain this effect.

Measurement of the relative brightness of the light sources and of the overall exposure is best done with a handheld meter. Metering from the camera position (reflected-light measurement), either through the camera or with a separate meter, is likely to be less accurate than incident-light measurement.

Backgrounds

For most small-finds photography using a vertical setup, a background is either white or black. Gray can be used, but it is difficult to achieve in a print a consistent density over a wide range of objects. If the background is

P

PHOTOGRAPHY, ARCHAEOLOGICAL 481

Figure 11. Photographic distortions due to viewpoint. (A) a medieval pot viewed from directly in front. (B) viewed from a high viewpoint. Note the change in proportions, particularly the relative diameters of the base and the neck. (C) the same viewpoint as B; here, the movements of a studio camera prevent such distortion. Photograph by Gwil J. Owen, Cambridge University Museum of Archaeology and Anthropology.

white, it is best shadow free. This effect is obtained by raising the object on glass above the background. To avoid showing the shadow of the object or the shadows of the edges of the glass plate, the size of the glass and/or its distance above the background has to be varied.

It is not sufficient to use just a sheet of white card for a white background and to rely on the object illumination only. White backgrounds must have extra illumination to appear fully white. Very dark objects on white can be an exception. The lighter the object tone, the brighter the background has to be. Background illumination can be up to twice as powerful as the main light source. Care must be taken with objects having shiny edges that they do not disappear into a white background.

Black backgrounds are the reverse of white (i.e., they must be both black and unlit). Good-quality black velvet is one of the best materials. Black card is often no better than very dark gray. Whatever the material, it must be shielded from the object illumination. Raising the object from the background is equally necessary on black as on white, but it can be problematic using glass. Under these circumstances, glass acts as a mirror and shows whatever is above the camera. Indeed, if there are two or more objects on the glass, the reflection of the camera lens itself and of the inside edges of the objects may become visible. A better solution is to balance the object on a post or similar support that is hidden under the object itself. Warning: This can be a very delicate and tricky arrangement.

For horizontal viewpoints, a background that appears seamless is preferable. This is achieved by using a curved material that extends behind the object and then curves upward out of the frame of the image. Thin cardboard or heavyweight paper is usual, though other flexible materials, such as cloth or plastic sheet, can be used. With control of the cut-off point of the object illumination, such a background can be darkened at the top for a more pleasing effect. The shadow of the object itself is usually left, though this can be eliminated if the background is made of translucent plastic and lit from below.

In the field, curved-paper backgrounds may not be feasible. It is often possible to arrange freestanding objects on a bench against a white or black wall. The more naturalistic look that this produces is not always a disadvantage.

Types of Object

Within the general considerations of lighting and equipment, certain object types need individual care. It is worthwhile listing some of these to illustrate the variety of images that can be made using relatively simple arrangements. Whatever the object, the photographer should ascertain the use to which the image is

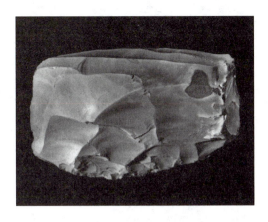

Figure 12. A flint core from Cresswell Crags, Britain, ca. 10,050 B.C. The main facets are shown by oblique lighting. Other details are picked out using mirrors or small reflectors. Length is 87 mm. Photograph by Gwil J. Owen.

to be put. For example, the requirements of illustration and those of subsequent drawing of objects are frequently incompatible. Two or more photographs from different viewpoints or with different lighting are often necessary.

Pottery, freestanding, is usually photographed on a curved background. The precise angle of view is determined by the end use for the image. A general view is from slightly above, just enough to show the curved rim (Figure 11). Bear in mind that the more downward the viewpoint, the worse any perspective distortion will be. Further research use for the photograph may dictate that the viewpoint is opposite the rim or halfway down the pot.

Pots are lit, conventionally, from top left. The precise angle will vary according to shape and/or decoration. In extreme cases, the lighting may be vertical or horizontal. Care has to be taken with fill-in lighting on pots. If another light source is used, shadows on the background are difficult to avoid. Reflectors, on the other hand, tend to leave a darker strip immediately opposite the camera. Smaller, more directional reflectors can minimize this. Pots with wide bellies and narrow bases are prone to lose detail under the overhang. White backgrounds do help avoid this, but extra reflectors may be needed. The technique mentioned above of using a translucent plastic background, lit from below, is useful here.

Potsherds are usually viewed vertically. They should be lit using the same criteria as any other object. Sherds, flatly lit by lighting

that is not oblique enough, lose all traces of curvature of body or rim. Incisions, too, need very oblique lighting. Where groups of sherds are required, the photographer has two choices. One can photograph them singly, shadow free, and plates for publication can be made from joined images. Alternatively, sherds can be photographed in groups. Large groups may make it impractical to use a glass sheet standing off the background. When sherds are put directly onto the background, it is essential to ensure that there is adequate fill-in illumination; otherwise, the edges of the sherds may be lost in shadow. Where shadows are unavoidable, plates for publication can be prepared by cutting out individual sherds and reassembling them minus the shadows. It is advantageous to arrange groups of objects, each one in its own rectangle, to facilitate subsequent editing.

Flints are perhaps the most complicated objects that appear before the archaeological photographer (Figure 12). Lighting needs to be highly specific in both direction and size. It is often better to dispense with conventional reflectors and to use one or two small mirrors to introduce other directional lighting. Great care has to be taken to ensure that each light source illuminates only one set of facets. Translucency and high polish are equally problematic when choosing strength and positioning of extra light sources. Flints are often published as line drawings: Photography can rarely show all facets adequately at one time. Techniques exist, however, to enable drawings to be made from prepared photographs. It is generally easier to consider flint photography as providing an illustrative or reference record.

Bones can be photographed, often with more generalized lighting. With the exception of cut marks, many angles of lighting will show size and shape adequately. Care is needed with light-colored bones, and with those having shiny edges, that the edges do not bleed into a white background (this is also a problem when photographing teeth). Bones are often fragile and friable. When choosing supports for objects that are easily damaged, the photographer must avoid materials that would adhere to the loose surface or remain in the cracks.

Human bones as complete skeletons are most often photographed in situ. When disarticulated bones are brought into the studio, a

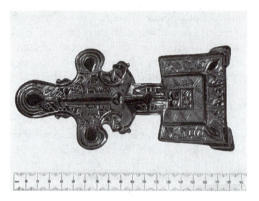

Figure 13. A gilded and incised brooch. A combination of oblique lighting to show the incisions and a broad reflector to bring out the gilding is appropriate. Photograph by Gwil J. Owen, Cambridge University Museum of Archaeology and Anthropology.

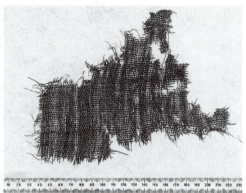

Figure 14. In dry climates, textiles are often well preserved. Specifically angled lighting is needed to show structural details. The scale is in millimeters. Photograph by Gwil J. Owen.

knowledge of anatomy helps avoid silly errors. Pairs of bones should be correctly positioned, left and right. Indeed, some form of skeletal reconstruction may be called for. For medical illustration, there are conventional viewpoints for the photography of skulls relating to the Frankfort plane, an internationally agreed upon orientation of the skull (for the purposes of measurement and illustration) based on a horizontal plane from the base of the orbital through the auditory meatus. These may necessitate purpose-built stands to achieve correct positioning. For more general purposes, skulls may be balanced at their natural angles.

Metal finds are frequently corroded and very dark in tone. Considerable extra exposure is needed to overcome this. Where metal retains polish, broad light sources may be the only way to show surface texture or decoration. Gold and silver surfaces can be shown in their true color only by direct reflection from a light source. White reflectors at appropriate angles usually suffice (Figure 13). Where there exists both gilded and incised decoration, a combination of oblique and reflected lighting can be used.

Inscriptions require oblique lighting also. Where detail is sought within the lettering, the angle of lighting can be matched to the angle of cut. Where this is not necessary, the lighting can be highly oblique to give an enhanced effect. In this case, fill-in illumination may be discarded. Coins, too, unless photographed by reflected light, need highly oblique illumination. Techniques exist to produce a ring-light effect at a very shallow angle.

Textiles are often photographed to record pattern and decoration. In this case, copy lighting can be used. Where the structure of the material is important, oblique lighting from a single source will be necessary (Figure 14). To help separate details of structure, a shadow-free background can help lighten shadows within the fabric. In a similar fashion to corroded metals, darker textiles may need abnormally high levels of illumination for correct exposure.

Wood retrieved from waterlogged sites can present problems. For one thing, it is fragile and has to be handled with great care. This often restricts the supports that can be used and, consequently, the angles at which it can be easily photographed. Wood is often darkened by the very acids that have preserved it. This, and its wetness, make lighting for photography difficult. Broad light sources are often the only way to show shape or facets; smaller sources will result in confusingly bright specular reflections (Figure 15). As with other shiny objects, the edges are easily blended into the background. Some experimentation is needed to choose the correct background density to minimize this effect. Wood conserved with waxy compounds displays similar characteristics.

Smaller finds need photography at abnormally close range. Such macrophotography brings additional technical problems. Where possible, lighting techniques should be as normal, though relative light size will inevitably

Figure 15. The shape of wet or shiny material is often best shown by reflection, as with this ca. 10-cm-diameter wooden stake from the Somerset Levels, Britain. Photograph courtesy of John Coles.

grow. Some compensation for this can be made by feathering the light source, thus using only the edge of the beam. A frequently useful light source for smaller objects is a *light tent* (Figure 16). This is a translucent hemisphere or cone, positioned over the object, with a hole for the camera lens. Lighting is from the outside: Some directionality can be introduced by varying the intensity of the lighting on one side.

Depth of field becomes minimal at extreme close-up. This is changed only by lens aperture or magnification. If magnification has to be high, the use of very small apertures introduces unsharpness due to diffraction effects around the lens diaphragm. As a rough rule of thumb, this becomes apparent at an effective aperture of ca. f64. Some trade-off between lower magnification on the negative and higher magnification at the printing stage may be possible.

The recording of archaeological objects can be considered as a logical series of activities, from object assessment, through exposure measurement, to final exposure. Individual objects can be presented to their best advantage in this way. However, many sites will have too much material for each object to be individually treated. Under such circumstances, permanent arrangements of lighting and background may be set up, that will not be ideal for every object but will offer a working compromise for a larger collection.

Gwil J. Owen

Figure 16. Charred grains of spelt wheat, photographed in a light tent, over a white-card background. The scale is in millimeters. Photograph by Gwil J. Owen.

See also AERIAL PHOTOGRAPHY FOR ARCHAEOLOGY; PHOTOGRAMMETRY

Further Readings

Dorrell, P.G. (1989) Photography in Archaeology and Conservation. Cambridge: Cambridge University Press.

Langford, M. (1986) Basic Photography, 5th ed. London and New York: Focal.

Langford, M. (1989) Advanced Photography, 5th ed. London and New York: Focal.

Phytolith Analysis

Study of plant opaline silica bodies deposited in archaeological and geological sediments.

The goals of phytolith analysis are to understand past human uses of plants and to reconstruct vegetation. Phytoliths, composed of opaline silica ($SiO_2 \cdot nH_2O$), are produced in the reproductive structures and vegetative tissues of plants in many, but not all, botanical families. Formed by the deposition of silica drawn into the plant from groundwater, in many taxonomic groups distinctively shaped bodies are formed that take on the shape of the cell in which the silica is deposited. When plant tissues decay or are burned, phytoliths are deposited in soil. Like other plant crystals, they are inorganic and so preserve well in many soil environments, including settings where pollen grains or other organic plant remains may not survive. Once recovered from the soil (by means of a chemical flotation procedure), phytoliths are identified to plant group by one-to-one comparisons with botanical reference materials and published identification aids. The specificity of the identification (species, genus, family, or higher taxonomic level) is dependent on the taxonomic group in question. Phytolith analysis, like analysis of pollen or plant macroremains (seeds, nuts, wood), aids in reconstructing what plants were used at an archaeological site or what vegetation grew around a sampling location. Phytoliths can also be recovered from the surfaces of tools (grinding stones, pottery vessels, cutting tools), from the clay used to make pottery or adobes, from calcified plaque (calculus) on teeth or embedded in tooth enamel, and from dried human or animal feces (coprolites). Phytoliths can be directly dated by radiocarbon or thermoluminescence techniques and can be chemically analyzed to yield stable-isotope ratios of carbon, hydrogen, and oxygen. Since the mid-1970s, incorporation of phytolith analysis into research on patterns of past plant use by humans and the impact of humans and natural events on past vegetation has added considerably to the understanding of issues as diverse as the antiquity of rice cultivation in the Old World tropics, the diet of an extinct ape, patterns of planting in a historic garden, and the history of land clearance for maize cultivation in the New World tropics.

As detailed by Dolores Piperno in 1988, the history of phytolith research can be divided into the discovery and exploratory stage (1835–1900), the botanical phase (1900–1936), the period of ecological research (1955–1975), and the modern period of archaeological research (1971). While phytoliths, like pollen, were discovered in the early nineteenth century, phytolith analysis lagged behind palynology as an independent paleoecological discipline. Much of the early-twentieth-century research by botanists into phytolith production and taxonomy was published in German, with the result that phytoliths went largely unnoticed by English-speaking researchers. This changed in the mid-1950s, when soil scientists in Britain, Australia, and North America became interested in applying phytolith analysis to reconstructing the environment, with many studies focused on forest-grassland transitions. Phytolith production and morphology in grasses were intensely studied, and, while some researchers investigated phytoliths of other monocotyledons (subclass of seed plants having embryos with a single leaf) and dicotyledons (subclass of seed plants having embryos with two leaves), few detailed descriptions or comparisons of phytolith shapes were made for nongrasses. This bias led to several misimpressions about phytolith production and specificity, namely, that phytoliths are produced abundantly only by grasses, that dicots do not produce diagnostic phytoliths, and that the "redundancy problem" (the fact that unrelated taxa may produce similar phytoliths) makes genus- or species-level identifications difficult. Basic research into phytolith production patterns conducted since the early 1970s, much of it by archaeological phytolith researchers, has corrected these misimpressions.

Although much research remains to be done, patterns of phytolith production are now understood for many families. It has been demonstrated that families exhibit a tendency to either silicify or not silicify their tissues, and that, in groups in which silica is deposited, phytolith morphology exhibits a strong correspondence to taxonomic group, regardless of environmental conditions. In other words, whether or not silica is deposited, and the shapes of the resulting bodies, are under genetic control. Environmental factors can influence silicification in some types of tissues; for example, in grasses, the degree of silicification of large epidermal cells may vary with moisture, with large groups of cells silicified under moist conditions. Other grass cells, such as short cells, silicify regardless of moisture. Research in the New World tropics has demonstrated that the Cyperaceae, Poaceae, Heliconiaceae, Marantaceae, Musaceae, and Arecaceae (monocotyledons), and the Acanthaceae, Annonaceae, Burseraceae, Chrysobalanaceae, Compositae, Cucurbitaceae, Dilleniaceae, Moraceae, Podostemaceae, Ulmaceae, and Urticaceae (dicotyledons) produce phytoliths identifiable at the family level or below (i.e., subfamily, genus, species). Another dozen families are characterized by common to abundant production of less-diagnostic phytolith forms. Research in North America reveals at least nine major phytolith types formed only in dicots.

Identifying phytoliths deposited in the soil to the plant of origin is not as straightforward as identifying pollen or plant macroremains. This is because some phytolith shapes are widely produced by unrelated plants. These redundant forms may occur commonly in soil samples, making scanning and counting of the identifiable, diagnostic phytoliths time consuming and causing potential confusion for the novice. With experience and careful study of comparative materials, analysts develop sums of diagnostic phytoliths tailored to specific research problems. Many one-to-one correspondences of distinctive phytolith shapes and plant genera exist, and more are discovered as comparative collections are studied. In addition, some phytoliths that are redundant within plant families can be used for genus- or species-level identifications if size and three-dimensional morphology of phytolith forms are utilized. This is the case for identifying corn (Zea mays) using the size and shape of cross-shaped phytoliths. Other identifications can be made through the application of multivariate statistical techniques. A recent example of this approach is identification of rice (Oryza sativa) glume-cell bodies, conducted by Zhijun Zhao and Deborah Pearsall in the mid-1990s.

Recovery and Identification
Most phytolith research carried out in conjunction with archaeological research projects is focused on analyzing sediments from cultural contexts, such as middens, features, and house floors. While phytolith samples taken from such contexts contribute information on background vegetation, they are better used for investigating patterns of human activities,

since cultural contexts yield a biased picture of the natural environment. Phytolith analysis for the purpose of reconstructing past vegetation requires sampling in contexts free of direct human disturbances, such as lake sediments or buried paleosols.

The key to successful phytolith sampling during excavation of a habitation site, former agricultural field, or other locus of human activity is to fit the sampling design to the questions to be answered. Since the amount of soil needed for phytolith analysis is small (100–200 g), a large number of samples can easily be taken. Selection of samples for analysis can then take place after preliminary assessment of the context and dating of the sampling loci.

Three common archaeological sampling situations—profile sampling, sampling a horizontal surface, and sampling within pit features—provide examples of sampling strategy and technique. Phytolith sampling is patterned after pollen sampling. Since phytoliths are inorganic, samples do not have to be treated to kill soil microorganisms. If soil samples are to be divided and processed for both pollen and phytoliths, then they should be dried, treated with a fungicide, or cooled to preserve the pollen; none of these procedures will harm phytoliths. Although phytoliths are not aerodynamic like many pollen grains, they will move if the soil in which they are deposited moves. Care should be taken to avoid contamination of sampling loci.

Collecting phytolith samples from vertical profiles is done for sampling midden deposits and during exploratory analysis in testing situations. After a fresh profile surface has been cut, upper and lower limits of each stratum to be sampled are identified. Sampling proceeds from the bottom of the profile toward the top (including sterile base and modern surface), so that soil dislodged during sampling falls only on previously sampled areas. Soil is removed from each stratum by cutting straight back into the profile; a plastic bag or vial labeled with provenance information holds the sample. Tools are cleaned between samples. A profile drawing, with sampling locations and soil color and texture information included on it, is helpful for the analyst. Profile samples are useful for investigating temporal trends in plant use, especially if the depositional context remains constant throughout the profile, as in a garbage midden. In testing situations, profile sampling can reveal the presence or absence of important plant taxa and allow assessment of the utility of further phytolith investigation.

Phytolith sampling from a horizontal surface, such as a house floor, is carried out once overlying soil layers or fill have been removed (and several fill samples taken for comparison). Areas to be covered by each sample are delineated by a grid. Features (hearths, pits) in the floor are sampled separately. Samples are taken unit by unit across the floor from freshly cleaned surfaces and bagged and labeled as described above. A map of the sampling area is prepared. Grid sampling a house floor to identify activity areas might lead to recovery of phytoliths from food plants (food-preparation and storage areas), bedding, floor mats, or other remains of activities involving plant use.

Subterranean-pit features are excellent loci for phytolith sampling. To distinguish pit fill (secondary use) from deposition resulting from the original use, pit features are profiled prior to phytolith sampling, then sampled as described above. All discrete episodes of deposition within the fill should be sampled; these might represent garbage dumping from different seasons or occupations. The bottom and sides of the pit are sampled separately, since silica residues of the original lining or contents may be present.

While much archaeological phytolith research focuses on discovering past uses of plants by people, the importance of phytolith analysis for reconstructing past vegetation and documenting human impact on vegetation should not be overlooked. Such studies set the stage for understanding people-plant interactions. Documenting the impact of humans on the landscape through study of vegetation change may be easier than locating early archaeological sites. All archaeological projects seeking to study subsistence should incorporate recovery of direct data on past environments into their research designs. This application of phytolith analysis requires sampling in areas free of direct human disturbance. Phytoliths preserved in lake sediments, alluvial deposits, loess deposits, and buried paleosols have been analyzed for vegetation reconstruction. A brief discussion of lake coring will illustrate how phytolith samples are recovered and analyzed for this purpose.

As lake sediments build up over time, phytoliths transported into the lake by streams or in airborne dust are incorporated into bottom sediments. Alteration of vegetation in the watershed by climatic change, fire, or human disturbance (e.g., deforestation for agriculture) is reflected in the phytolith record within lake sediments. This sequence is revealed by extracting a sediment core from bottom deposits. Dating of organic materials at intervals along the core permits reconstruction of the rate of buildup of sediments and the timing of changes in vegetation.

Methodology for lake coring for phytolith analysis is taken from palynology. Coring is done from an anchored platform near the sedimentation center of the lake. More than one core is usually taken, since this permits evaluation of variation in sedimentation and provides more material for analysis. A closed-chamber corer (e.g., Livingstone piston sampler) is pushed into the sediments, opened, rotated (side filling) or pushed (bottom filling) to fill the chamber, closed, and extracted. The sediment core is removed from the chamber, wrapped, and labeled. Before analysis, the outermost portion of the core is cut off, since contamination between samples may occur. The corer is reinserted into the bore hole as many times as necessary to obtain a complete core. Auger-type samplers or open-chamber samples are unacceptable because of the very high risk of contamination as the sampler is lowered and raised.

Extraction of phytoliths from soil and sediment samples is a chemical flotation procedure. Since phytoliths vary in specific gravity from 1.5 to 2.3, once light clay particles have been removed by sedimentation, a liquid of 2.3 specific gravity can be used to float phytoliths out of the sample matrix. Phytoliths are then precipitated by reducing the specific gravity below 1.5. A variety of extraction procedures have been developed; zinc bromide or a mixture of potassium iodide and cadmium iodide are commonly used for flotation. A fume hood must be employed when using these toxic chemicals. Sodium polytungstate and zinc iodide show promise as less-toxic alternatives. Before flotation, samples are treated chemically to remove organic matter, carbonates, and mineral oxides, all of that bond to phytoliths and impede their flotation. Extracted phytoliths are slide mounted in Permount or thinned Canada Balsam for microscopic examination. Scanning slides while mounts are still semi fluid is preferable, so that the three-dimensional structure of the phytoliths can be examined by rotating the bodies.

Identifying and quantifying phytoliths are the foundation for interpretation. Counts are either relative (to a predetermined sum, often 500) or absolute (all phytoliths from a known quantity of sediment). The phytolith sum (types included in the count) is tailored to the goal of the analysis. If the objective is to determine if maize is present, for example, a count of cross-bodies, with measurements and evaluation of three-dimensional morphologies, would be made. For determining the nature of the grass component of vegetation, a detailed count of short-cell phytoliths is done. Complete counts of all diagnostic phytoliths in lake sediments are used for vegetation reconstruction; these are tallied as absolute counts, so that the quantity of phytoliths deposited over a certain time (deposition rate) can be calculated.

Interpreting phytolith assemblages (types of phytoliths identified and their abundances) is often based on the comparative, or analog, approach. The archaeological or geological phytolith assemblage is compared to assemblages produced by known vegetation formations or depositional contexts (processing areas, living floors). A close match between the kinds and abundances of phytoliths represented in the archaeological sample and those in the known sample suggests that the archaeological sample was produced by a similar mixture of plants. Multivariate statistical techniques are usefully employed for comparing assemblages. Since there is no known direct relationship between abundance of phytoliths in a soil or sediment and abundance of plants that produced the phytoliths in the vegetation cover—due to differences in phytolith production among plant taxa—the comparative approach is a powerful interpretive tool for both vegetation reconstruction and archaeological phytolith interpretation. The presence or absence of individual plant species is evaluated by searching for phytoliths produced by that species, as determined by study of comparative plant specimens.

Applications of Phytolith Analysis

Identifying crop plants is one of the greatest challenges and greatest successes of modern phytolith research. In the New World, it is now possible to identify a suite of indigenous crops, including corn, beans *(Phaseolus)*, squash and gourd *(Cucurbita, Lagenaria)*, the tuber crops achira *(Canna)* and arrowroot *(Maranta)*, the native North American domesticates sunflower *(Helianthus)* and sumpweed *(Iva)*, and a variety of other useful plants.

Corn, domesticated in Mesoamerica and spread throughout the New World prior to European contact, is identified by distinctive cob phytoliths in North America and by large, Variant 1 crosses (both broad surfaces are cross-shaped) in Central and South America (Figure 1). Phytolith identifications of corn have been made at many sites, including Big Hidatsa in North Dakota, Cueva de los Ladrones and Aguadulce in Panama, Las Vegas and Real Alto in Ecuador, and Cardal in Peru. Cob phytoliths may prove diagnostic in the tropical American flora, but further study of indigenous grasses must be done. Corn is most difficult to identify by phytolith characteristics in Mesoamerica, where closely related teosinte species *(Zea spp.)* occur. It is impossible to separate corn and all races of teosinte by cross characteristics, for example. However, since teosinte produces diagnostic fruitcase phytoliths that are not present in corn, the *absence* of these distinctive phytoliths, combined with the *presence* of large, Variant 1 cross bodies, permits identification of corn within its homeland in some cases.

Common bean *(Phaseolus vulgaris)* can be identified in North America on the basis of distinctive silicified hairs (Figure 2). Comparative studies of wild tropical legumes must be done before beans can be identified reliably outside North America, however, since similar hairs have been observed in tropical plants. Squash and gourd produce distinctive large, spherical phytoliths in the fruit epidermis (Figure 3). Application throughout the New World seems feasible, since similar bodies have not been observed in other plants. Cucurbit bodies occur in early contexts in Ecuador at the Vegas site.

Two New World cultivated tubers, achira and arrowroot, and one widely utilized wild (tended?) root, sedge *(Cyperus/Kyllinga, Scirpus)*, can be identified through phytolith analysis (Figure 4). Presence of these plants has been documented at numerous sites and coring localities in the New World. It should also be possible to identify Old World sedge species.Unfortunately, manioc *(Manihot esculenta)* and sweet potato *(Ipomoea batata)*

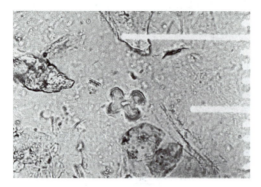

Figure 1. Phytolith from large Variant 1 cross from maize (Zea mays). Photograph by Deborah Pearsall.

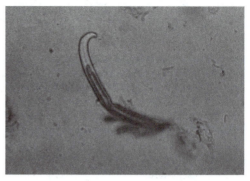

Figure 2. Hooked hair from bean (Phaseolus vulgaris). *Photograph by Deborah Pearsall.*

Figure 3. Large, segmented hair from squash (Cucurbita). Photograph by Deborah Pearsall.

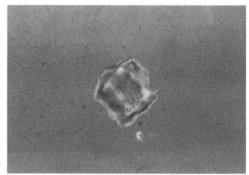

Figure 4. Seed phytolith from arrowroot (Maranta). *Photograph by Deborah Pearsall.*

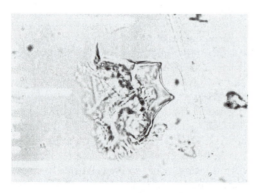

Figure 5. Two-peaked glume cell from rice (Oryza sativa). Photograph by Deborah Pearsall.

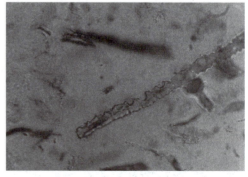

Figure 6. Trough bodies from banana (Musa). *Photograph by Deborah Pearsall.*

cannot be identified through phytolith analysis (manioc produces a distinctive hair base but in very low quantities). This is also the case for the Old World yams (Dioscorea) and all aroid tubers (Araceae).

Numerous wild plants used for food, fuel, or construction, and also useful as vegetation indicators, can be identified in archaeological sites in the New World through phytolith analysis. In the boreal forests of North America, for example, it is possible to identify species of spruce, pine, fir, and larch. Use of plants in the Compositae (aster family), that are also indicators of open habitats, can be documented. Grasses are readily identifiable at the subfamily level, which can indicate past moisture conditions at a site or collection of grasses for use. Ongoing research suggests that wild rice *(Zizania)* can be identified. Numerous tropical-forest trees and lower-story plants are identifiable by phytoliths, permitting detailed reconstruction of forest type and identification of utilized species. Research by Susan Mulholland in the Great Plains indicates that many temperate-zone woody and herbaceous dicots can be identified as well (Pearsall and Piperno 1993).

Phytolith analysis has also contributed to reconstructing past plant use at archaeological sites in the temperate and tropical regions of the Old World. Among the crops that can be identified are rice *(Oryza sativa)* (Figure 5), wheat (*Triticum* spp.), barley (*Hordeum* spp.), and banana (*Musa* spp.) (Figure 6). Efforts are underway to identify other cultivated grasses, such as sugar cane, Job's Tears, and the millets. Many other important crops, including domesticated legumes, remain to be investigated.

Wheat and barley, two major Old World cereals, can be distinguished from each other and from some common weedy grasses on the basis of husk epidermal phytoliths. During a pilot study, wheat and barley husk phytoliths were identified by Arlene Miller Rosen at Neolithic sites in the Levant. Husk and straw produce distinctive phytolith assemblages, potentially useful for distinguishing animal fodder from food residues. Multicelled phytoliths, produced more frequently in the epidermis of irrigated crops, may provide a means of identifying this farming technology in the Near East. Although further studies of wild grasses remain to be completed, combinations of distinctive phytoliths may eventually permit identification of many of the Southwest Asian and European cereals.

Cultivated Asian rice can be identified outside the range of wild rice by means of leaf bulliform cells. This method has been used in Japan to identify rice at numerous archaeological sites and to locate former rice paddy areas. Using discriminant analysis, bulliform phytoliths permit separation of the two rice subspecies in situations in which no other *Oryza* species occur. In regions of overlap with wild rice, such as South China and Southeast Asia, distinctive double-peaked glume hair cells give better separation of domesticated rice and wild species. Rice glume cells have been recovered from lake cores and archaeological sites in Thailand and China.

Bananas can be identified on the basis of distinct trough-shaped bodies produced in the leaf. These have been documented at Kuk, an early agricultural site in Papua New Guinea.

Research is ongoing into phytolith production patterns in domesticated and utilized plants and vegetation in Europe, Southwest Asia, Southeast Asia, China, and the Pacific. Much remains to be done, especially regional studies of vegetation permitting precise vegetation reconstruction and increased confidence in crop identifications, before phytolith analysis reaches the potential it has demonstrated for the New World.

An archaeological application that shows particular promise for reconstructing human diet is analysis of phytoliths from dentitions and fecal material. These unique contexts provide secure associations between recovered phytoliths and uses of plants as foods. In addition, nonsilicious plant crystals, such as calcium-oxalate crystals produced in the Cactaceae and the Agavaceae, are more easily recovered from calculus or coprolites than from soil, increasing the numbers of potentially identifiable food plants.

Applications in Paleoecology

The potential of phytolith analysis for paleoecological reconstruction has been recognized since the mid-1980s. Lake-core studies in the American tropics and analysis of loess deposits from the midcontinental United States demonstrate the utility of phytoliths for documenting sequential changes in vegetation governed by climate and for identifying the impact of humans on vegetation.

Through study of a series of deep lake cores from Panama, Piperno (Pearsall and Piperno 1993) has demonstrated that identifiable phytoliths are present in large numbers in lake sediments and that major changes in phytolith assemblages occur in synchrony with shifts in pollen occurrence, indicating that phytoliths are sensitive indicators of vegetation change. Key plant taxa not identifiable through pollen analysis (i.e., insect-pollinated taxa) are documented through phytoliths, increasing the reliability of vegetation reconstructions. For example, the Lake La Yeguada and Lake El Valle phytolith profiles document that, between 16,000 B.P. and 11,050 B.P., the vegetation of the central coast of Pacific Panama was dominated by a mix of montane-forest taxa, including *Magnolia,* highland *Chusquea,* and Ulmaceae. Pollen from these cores recorded the same vegetation profile through identification of *Quercus, Symplocos,* and *Gunnera,* among other taxa indicating montane-forest conditions. Presence of taxa not found today below 1500 m elevation during this epoch suggests a downslope movement of montane vegetation of ca. 800 m. After 11,050 B.P. the development of the lowland forest is documented in the phytolith and pollen spectra.

Phytoliths, in consort with microscopic charcoal fragments, have also proven to be sensitive indicators of human influences on vegetation. In the cores discussed above, several episodes of forest clearing are documented by a sudden rise in abundance of charcoal particles (from burning) and phytoliths from plants typical of forest openings, such as sedges and *Heliconia.* The abundance of charcoal particles and phytoliths of disturbance taxa suggests that clearing was widespread and likely represented human, rather than natural, disturbance of the environment.

Phytolith analysis (by James Donahue and Elizabeth Dinan) at the Bear Creek and (by Elizabeth Dinan and Ralph Rowlett) Shriver sites in Missouri also focused on paleoenvironmental reconstruction (in Pearsall and Piperno 1993). Although the details of vegetation changes are not documented as precisely as in the Panamanian example because of differences in the floras of the two regions, vegetation changes governed by climate were revealed. At Shriver, for example, shifts between forest and grassland were documented for the Wisconsin glaciation

(20,000–18,000 B.P.). At Bear Creek, paleoclimatic variation during the Sub-boreal episode of the Holocene (5060–2760 B.P.) was delineated though analysis of grass phytoliths, specifically, ratios of grasses indicating mesic (moderately moist) and xeric (dry) conditions.

As study of phytolith production patterns in vegetation progresses worldwide, phytoliths will contribute ever more to reconstructions of paleoenvironment, subsistence, and diet. Phytoliths are tough, versatile fossils that can be directly dated, serve as precise indicators of past vegetation, be chemically analyzed to yield stable isotopes of carbon, hydrogen, and oxygen, and provide data on functional uses of artifacts. Phytoliths recovered from archaeological sites provide information on plants grown or gathered as foods and those used to build shelters. These identifications, in combination with other paleoethnobotanical data, enhance the understanding of past human-plant interrelationships.

Deborah M. Pearsall

See also FLOTATION; PALEOETHNOBOTANY; PALYNOLOGY

Further Readings

Pearsall, D.M. (1989) Paleoethnobotany: A Handbook of Procedures. San Diego: Academic.

Pearsall, D.M., and Piperno, D.R., eds. (1993) Current Research in Phytolith Analysis: Applications in Archaeology and Paleoecology. (MASCA Research Papers in Science and Archaeology 10). Philadelphia: University Museum, University of Pennsylvania.

Piperno, D.R. (1988) Phytolith Analysis: An Archaeological and Geological Perspective. San Diego: Academic.

Piperno, D.R. (1991) The status of phytolith analysis in the American tropics. Journal of World Prehistory 5:155–191.

Rapp, G.R., Jr., and Mulholland, S., eds. (1992) Phytolith Systematics: Emerging Issues. (Advances in Archaeological and Museum Science 1). New York: Plenum.

Pitt-Rivers, General Augustus Henry (1827–1900)

British archaeologist and prehistorian; also known as A.H. Lane Fox–Pitt-Rivers. Born

Lane Fox, he changed his name to Pitt-Rivers in 1880 when he inherited the estate of his great uncle, the second Baron Rivers, at Cranborne Chase. Educated at Sandhurst, he was a standout in the military, rising to the rank of colonel in the South Lancashire Regiment. He served in Crimea and retired a lieutenant-general.

Pitt-Rivers is noted for his contributions to scientific excavation techniques and is considered by many to be the father of stratigraphic excavation. A wealthy man after his inheritance, Pitt-Rivers spent his time excavating barrows, villages, and cemeteries all over England and Wales. He developed a rigorous and exacting excavation style in his work at sites such as Wor Barrow and Bokerly Dyke, following strict stratigraphic principles and meticulously recording all objects found. His explorations, many of that were outlined in *Excavations in Cranborne Chase*, were models of scientific discipline and soon came to influence archaeology elsewhere in England and throughout Europe. Later generations of archaeologists, including such important figures as Flinders Petrie and Mortimer Wheeler, owed much to Pitt-Rivers' groundbreaking work.

The general was also a pioneer in the analysis of artifacts after excavation and the ordering and typing of artifacts. Even before he acquired his great wealth, Pitt-Rivers was an avid collector, mainly of military artifacts, and was interested in the ordering of these artifacts for display. He arranged his holdings by type and developed an evolutionary scheme for his collection of muskets, which showed the development of the weapon from its beginnings to its replacement by the rifle and other firearms in the nineteenth century. After his inheritance, he added to his collections through purchases and excavations, creating typologies and evolutionary schemes for archaeological materials. He also stressed the importance of studying *all* artifacts, not just art objects, as archaeology was properly the study of the entire range of human material culture. His collections became the basis of the Pitt-Rivers Museum at Oxford, an important center of archaeological education and research many years after the general's death. Pitt-Rivers is rightly credited with being a central figure in the transformation of archaeology from hobby to scholarly discipline.

Joseph J. Basile

See also PETRIE, SIR WILLIAM MATTHEW FLINDERS; STRATIGRAPHY; WHEELER, SIR ROBERT ERIC MORTIMER

Further Readings

Bowden, M. (1991) Pitt-Rivers: The Life and Archaeological Work of Lieutenant-General Augustus Henry Lane Fox–Pitt-Rivers. Cambridge and New York: Cambridge University Press.

Pitt-Rivers, A.H. (1887–1905) Excavations in Cranborne Chase, near Rushmore, on the Borders of Dorset and Wilts (1880–1896), 4 vols. London: [Harrison and Sons, Printers], published privately.

Thompson, M.W. (1977) General Pitt-Rivers: Evolution and Archaeology in the Nineteenth Century. Bradford-on-Avon: Moonraker.

Plog, Fred T. (1944–1992)

American anthropologist and archaeologist. Born on July 19, 1944, in Ft. Monmouth, New Jersey, Plog was educated at Northwestern University, where he received his bachelor's in 1966, and at the University of Chicago, where he earned his master's in 1968 and his doctorate in anthropology in 1969. Plog served as assistant professor of anthropology at the University of California at Los Angeles (1969–1972) and associate professor of anthropology at the State University of New York at Binghamton (1972–1976). He was also the chairman of the department at Binghamton (1974–1976), then moved on to Arizona State University (1976–1981) and thereafter became professor in the Department of Sociology and Anthropology at New Mexico State University, Las Cruces. Plog was a member of the American Anthropological Association, the Society for American Archaeology, and the American Association for the Advancement of Science.

Plog was a specialist in the prehistory of the Southwestern United States. As a proponent of the New Archaeology, Plog attempted to prove that models explaining social phenomenan can be tested through a deductive, positivist approach. In his important *The Study of Prehistoric Change,* he proposed a series of models, or *covering laws,* to explain how cultural change might occur in prehistoric societies. He used as his test case a study of sites in the American Southwest, and, with an analysis of surface

P

surveys and limited excavation, attempted to explain the transition from the Basketmaker to the Pueblo phase in Arizona. While some find his study unconvincing (see Willey and Sabloff 1974) and Plog admitted that more data was needed before change could be modeled and explained with a reasonable amount of certainty, his work illustrates the important attempts made in the New Archaeology of the 1960s and 1970s toward explaining, rather than describing, past behavior.

Joseph J. Basile

See also NEW/PROCESSUAL ARCHAEOLOGY

Further Readings

Bohannan, P. and Plog, F., eds. (1967) Beyond the Frontier: Social Process and Cultural Change. Garden City, NJ: Natural History Press.

Cordell, L.S. and Plog, F. (1979) Escaping the confines of normative thought: A reevaluation of Puebloan Prehistory. American Antiquity 44:405–429.

Doyel, D. and Plog, F., eds. (1980) Current Issues in Hohokam Prehistory: Proceedings of a Symposium. Tempe, AZ: Arizona State University.

Martin, P.S. and Plog, F. (1973) The Archaeology of Arizona: A Study of the Southwest Region. Garden City, NJ: Natural History Press.

Plog, F. (1974) The Study of Prehistoric Change. New York: Academic.

Postprocessual Archaeology

A loose group of alternatives to processual archaeology, based on insights from poststructuralism, critical theory, and long-term history. Postprocessual archaeology has evolved since the seminal Cambridge conference *Symbolic and Structural Archaeology* (Hodder 1982) yet remains a largely British form of intellectual inquiry, with some outposts in North America and in other countries. From the outset, postprocessual archaeologists were characterized by strongly divergent views as much as by opposition to the main tenets of processual archaeology. Indeed, postprocessual archaeology celebrates diversity and resists easy summary. Two principal strands can be distinguished in postprocessual theory building: symbolic and cognitive archaeology, and archaeology as a political act in the present. Both strands overlap considerably in analyses of power structures and ideologies past and present.

Diversity

An important postprocessual question is: "Whose archaeologies?" This has prompted studies of imperialism and Western capitalism, class-based archaeologies, indigenous pasts, and feminist and gender archaeologies. By their insistence on deconstructing the roots of archaeological production, postprocessualists have challenged the hegemony of White male positivist scientists in modern archaeology. If there is a single defining trend of postprocessual archaeology, it is its practitioners' insistence on the diversity of people's pasts.

The Archaeological Record as Text

The rhetoric of archaeology and its production frames a basic field for postprocessual research. A starting point is that the archaeological record resembles a text requiring an interpretation that can be variously read by different individuals. Just as an excavation may be regarded as theater, with the recovery of finds the production of a material record, so the publication of an excavation represents the dominant group's style of writing. These styles may be impersonal, scientific, neutral *or* personal, emotional, and value laden. Hence, the texts making up the archaeological record do not exist independently of the way that its interpretations are framed. In this sense, archaeology may be defined not so much as reading the signs of the past as a process in which these signs are written into the present, through the transformation of material culture into an archaeological text *about* material culture. Archaeologists are not only *interpreters*, giving meaning to the texts of the archaeological record, but also *critics* who view the text through different lenses and provide alternative readings.

Criticisms of Processual Archaeology

Postprocessual archaeologists are critical of many aspects of processual archaeology, to the extent that Colin Renfrew (1979) terms them "anti-processualists." The processualist concept of science has been attacked for its reliance on positivism, its aim of lawmaking, and its assumption of neutral, value-free facts. In their enthusiasm for criticizing traditional empirical archaeology, processualists overlooked the empiricist basis of their favored positivism. The search for lawlike generalizations ignored the fact that the concrete detail of archaeology was more important than processualist generalizations. The epistemological status of "facts" independent of prior theoretical understanding was highly questionable; this problem undermined processualist claims to practicing objective science.

Human Subjects and Objects of Study

The anonymity of classic archaeological systems theory, in which changes in the values of systemic variables created change, led to two forms of postprocessual criticism: the exclusion of individuals who practiced meaningful actions leading to past change, and the absence of cultural meaning as the primary context for stability, as well as change. Much postprocessual analysis has focused on the tension between structure and agency—the manner in which people carry out social action within a structured context of prior meanings. But an even more fundamental question for postprocessual archaeologists is the relation between knowing human subjects and their objects of study. The heart of the poststructuralist position is an attack on the individual subject as the origin of meaning. Instead of individuals being self-present, their identities are cultural and social products. Both human subjects and their objects of study can be viewed in relation to a preexisting system of meaning, into which both are ideologically incorporated. Thus, the social and cultural identities of archaeologists as authors (whether Black, female, Catholic, or Third World) are of critical significance for postprocessual archaeologists, since these identities determine the differing viewpoints that form the basis for archaeological writing.

Empathetic Understanding

A key issue facing all archaeologists is the interpretation of the mute remnants of the past. Those archaeologists seeking to interpret the symbolic domain appear to have a particular problem, since there are no bilingual texts to help prehistorians decipher the meanings of past symbols. For most postprocessualists, the source of *meaning* in the past is located in cultural *contexts,* mediated by the emphasis on material culture as meaningfully constituted. They are mindful that meaning is a product of

the past in the present rather than deriving from any abstraction in the past in itself. In the search for a methodology of meaning, the notion of *empathetic understanding* (the idea that one can understand past actions only if one can grasp the reasons for such actions) developed by Robin Collingwood has been espoused by many postprocessualists. Ian Hodder (1984) argues that, in fact, *all* archaeologists make use of a similar process to understand anything about past artifacts and structures. The process of understanding requires the asking of specific questions of the data in order to define a meaning for the action resulting in any segment of the archaeological record. The questions require careful and rigorous formulation to produce genuine understanding.

Relativism or Reason?

The very diversity of postprocessual archaeology has been attacked as its principal methodological weakness. It is argued that the only outcome of postprocessual theory building must be a disabling relativity in that all pasts are equally valid, since there are no criteria of discrimination between those written by, for example, the British archaeologist Michael Shanks or Erik von Däniken, a Swiss author of books on extraterrestrial visits to Earth. Postprocessualists deny total relativity, but their development of criteria of exclusion—the criteria used to define what is authentic knowledge and what is not—has not yet been fully developed. For postprocessualists, "good" explanation relates to the coherence of the reading of any specific material text and its ability to correspond to significant proportions of the contextual data.

Structures of Meaning

The symbolic core of postprocessual archaeology derives from poststructuralist critiques of structuralist linguistics and anthropology. The notion of formal-structural universals, created through the attribution of meaning *(the signified)* to items of material culture or words *(the signifier),* has given way to the more fluid and relativistic concept of material culture as a language. The various meanings of artifacts and buildings are negotiated by different individuals in specific cultural contexts through time. This inherent ambiguity in material culture not only prohibits the formulation of general symbolic laws, but also creates a

P

potentially unstable set of meanings that are created and re-created constantly through cultural action. In this way, power relations between individuals and groups are reflexively created through the use of material culture. The stability of long-term symbolic structures is closely dependent upon small-scale social action in the everyday contexts of life and death. An example of this is Hodder's (1984) application of Collingwood's method to two broadly similar Neolithic monument classes in Northern Europe: long houses and long mounds containing burial chambers. The first question concerned the dating of the two monument classes; since contemporary, they could be somehow related. To the question of the structural-formal relationship between the monuments, six formal similarities were found and two distributional points were noted: construction of both barrows and houses in clusters and construction of many barrows over previous domestic middens. The notion of cultural continuity was considered insufficient to explain these similarities. Instead, the idea of two identical structuring principles—monumentality and linear ordering of space—was favored to "explain" these formal similarities. Thus, daily cultural practices, such as the construction of family houses, are inscribed into much wider, long-term symbolic structures.

The Material Record

Many postprocessual archaeologists have challenged the processual dichotomy between material and ideal through the demonstration that artifacts assume an ideological, as much as a material, existence. Artifacts take on their form as much because of their meanings as their functions, both of which derive from a preexisting cultural tradition. Hodder (1984) stresses the active role of material culture in constituting a meaningful cultural world. This is opposed to the processualists' tendency to regard material culture as a reflection of social realities. Social actors make use of material culture to establish or stress their individual or group identities in opposition to the identity of others or to emphasize their individual or group status or dominance. Gender differences in the food quest led Elizabeth Brumfiel to question the androcentric Aztec ethnohistories and redefine women's weaving and cooking activities in terms not only of domestic action, but also in relation to male and female statuses

and the position of the female's household in the wider political network. Marie-Louise Stig Sorenson identifies material-culture differences between low-status, local, frequent female-associated bronze artifacts and high-status, exotic, rare male-associated bronze grave goods as an important mechanism for males to maintain gender and political dominance in the Scandinavian Bronze Age.

Ideology

Postprocessual archaeologists have developed divergent views on the key concept of ideology. Hodder accepts an almost depoliticized view of ideology as a worldview, revealing rather than masking. For Daniel Miller and Christopher Tilley, ideology relates not to all social practice, but to those questions generated by, and reproducing, conflicts of interests. Similarly, Mark Paul Leone hides and masks exploitation or rationalizes it through mystification. For John Barrett, ideology concerns all practical, taken-for-granted knowledges that social actors rework to achieve social authority. Ideology operates in all cultural contexts, but a particularly important context is the field of ritual, which is separated from other fields of discourse in order to reproduce statements about cosmological order. Postprocessual archaeologists have contributed important analyses of ritual as a form of ideological practice.

A good example of ideological reconstruction is Tilley's reading of the Scandinavian Bronze Age rock art at Nämsforsen, Sweden (Tilley 1991). Here, three grammatical principles are found to order the 234 rock carvings at the end of a fjord: (1) oppositions between land, sea, and air creatures and artifacts; (2) oppositions between subtypes of the first set of oppositions; and (3) the association of images with two clans. Analysis of the chronological development of the site indicates three phases of rock art, each representing major social change; the carvings of the last phase show close parallels with ethnohistorical cosmologies. Tilley interprets the carvings as representations of a series of fundamental ideas about social relations, which provide the foundation for legitimization of economic and social forms and systems of exchange. Just like writing, the rock-art images use spacing, differentiation, and articulation to provide the material fixation of meaning on the landscape.

Archaeology as Long-Term History

One of the main postprocessual criticisms of processualism is its neglect of history in favor of synchronic analysis by scientific means or sequential analysis of successive time frames. Important insights into long-term history are provided by the incorporation of the tripartite structure of Fernand Braudel's 'Annales' history into archaeology (Bintliff 1991). Braudel and his school argued that it was the conjunction of three different time scales—the long-term, or geographical time; the medium-term, or social time; and the history of events, or individual time—that provided the best context for historical explanation. Despite criticism of the success with which such integration is possible, the Annales school is flourishing and has been taken up by advanced processualists, such as John Bintliff, as well as by postprocessualists. A Braudelian approach to symbolic structures has been adopted by Hodder (1990) in his exploration of the origins of the European Neolithic. Hodder argues that social domestication precedes economic domestication through the social control over the wild. He identifies two principal concepts in this process: the *domus* and the *agrios*. The former signifies the home, the hearth, nurturing, tending, and caring, while the latter signifies the wildwood, the outer world, warring, trading, competition, and hunting. In a significantly structuralist position, Hodder discusses the transformations of these concepts across Europe coeval with the adoption of farming, while nonetheless stressing the existence of these structuring principles for several millennia across most of Europe.

Critical Theory

Another major influence on some postprocessual archaeologists is the Frankfurt School of sociologists, dominated by Theodore Adorno, Herbert Marcuse, and Jürgen Habermas and whose writings have crystallized in critical theory. The key claim of a critical archaeology is that less contingent archaeological knowledge can be achieved by a clarification of the relationship between archaeology and politics. Hence, deconstruction of the roots and ideological constructs of a position leads to a clearer idea of the relationship between historical knowledge and the ideological power, or hegemony, of the author and/or her or his tradition. An example from America is Leone and colleagues' work on Annapolis, Maryland, from the eighteenth through the twentieth centuries. Presentations of the city's history and its current archaeological excavations are analyzed in terms of the influence of famous visitors (George Washington), the cultural outworkings of mercantilism (spatial and artifactual differentiation), and the contributions of both Blacks and Whites to the city's past. However, other postprocessualists have, in turn, criticized critical archaeologists for not extending their self-reflexive approach to their own theories, thereby suggesting that they are using a more objective approach than others.

Time, Space, and Place

A development in postprocessual archaeology is a concern with social time and place. It is an irony of the discipline that the first century of modern archaeology (1850–1950) was concerned primarily with recapturing chronological sequences using stratigraphy and typology, while radiocarbon dating "liberated" archaeologists from such concerns for the next fifty years, without the devotion of much attention to social time. Similarly, spatial analysis has been increasing in sophistication since the 1970s, with little attention to the archaeology of place. Recent studies have characterized settlement and mortuary sequences in terms of cyclical and linear time, while the changes found at major ritual monuments may be understood in terms of ritual rather than mundane time. The most significant difference between a flat settlement and an upstanding monument is in the manner in which later generations can make use of the monumental remains, whether by ancestral linkages or claims to long-term social continuity.

Barrett has defined two contrasting temporalities for the periods 5000–2000 B.C. and 2000–1000 B.C. in British prehistory. An earlier period of *becoming,* based on a cyclical view of time, with horizontal divisions of age and religious authority linking the generalized communities of the present with the ancestral worlds of the past, is contrasted with a later period of *being,* based on linear time, with vertical divisions for inheritance of fixed land by closed households who possessed different family histories. This distinction is paralleled by two contrasting ways of occupying the land: the former with movement across the

P

surface between places each imbued with social and ritual significance; the latter with land tenure as a central concept for houses scattered across a fully utilized landscape.

Archaeology as a Political Practice

A further direction in postprocessual archaeology leads to competing definitions of the role of archaeology in contemporary politics. Shanks and Tilley have argued for a value-committed archaeology, with critical archaeologists adopting an oppositional role to contemporary society through the use of their knowledge to fight against the prevailing regime of the production of truth. If archaeology is a cultural practice, then it is also a political practice with its own basis of morality, and its aim should be to transform the present in terms of its conceived connection to the past. Russell Handsman and Leone echo this notion with a call to enfranchise people with the means to see for themselves how their history has been shaped by the present to form their own identity. Critical production of archaeological films, museum displays, stories, and videos is the weapon to be used in this struggle.

First Peoples and Their Past

A related field of inquiry is the development of indigenous pasts by First Peoples, whose own identities have so often been denied or obscured within a catchall such as "the people without history." In some cases, First Peoples have taken the initiative for re-creating their own histories from archaeologists. In other cases, they have collaborated with White Western anthropologists in finding a common language for telling. Mamami Condori rejects the legitimization that White Bolivian archaeology gives to Spanish colonialism, presenting an alternative Andean version of history in four stages. The first two are mythical, the third relates to the Inca state, and the fourth to the Spanish conquest. While both myth and history have been used in the struggle against White oppression as a potent means of keeping Bolivian identity alive and free, archaeology is now being used in the same manner. Similarly, Jo Mangi takes the view that the prehistory of Papua New Guinea, as interpreted by Western archaeologists, is a valuable resource in creating a national self-identity and unity among modern-day Papuans, provided that multiple diffusion is

challenged as the explanatory principle behind all major innovations, and due credit is given to local processes of change.

These examples differ subtly from the research of archaeologists who provide new evidence for ethnic or land claims by documenting long-term continuity of settlement from deep past to present. A good example is the demonstration of close links between the designs on medieval Sami (Norwegian Lapp) drums and the motifs that dominate northern Scandinavian rock art dating back to the mid-Holocene. Far from supporting the interpretation that Arctic shamanism was part of a set of cultural traits introduced through Norse or Christian religion, this study by Tim Yates in the late 1980s reinforces the idea of long-term Lapp cultural continuity and the possibilities of an independent and millennial past for Arctic shamanism.

The Phenomenology of the Past

Another direction in postprocessual archaeology is the exploration of the impact of personal experience on archaeological activities. A traditional approach is concerned with critical biographies, in that the personal and social experiences of scholars are dissected to forge links with the theoretical *oeuvre*. With the exception of a handful of famous archaeologists, such as V. Gordon Childe, this approach is relatively rare even in postprocessual archaeology and could, with profit, be expanded. A more archetypically postprocessual approach is the analysis of what it means to experience archaeological sites and landscapes, exhibitions, and publications. Shanks (1992) has explored this terrain, hitherto excluded by scientific archaeology, linking his childhood experiences, visits to different sites and monuments, research projects, and deconstructions of all of the media used to portray archaeological information. Tilley (1994) has explored the phenomenology of place by relating personal experiences of walking with the construction of a narrative of the past. Such studies at once make archaeologists more accessible to other people and define archaeology as a cultural product whose basic approaches to the transmission of information are heavily laden with ideological baggage.

In summary, postprocessual archaeology has created under its capacious umbrella a series of new approaches to the past, all of which reject positivist scientism and lawlike generalizations, and most of which profess a radical self-criticism and a healthy pluralism based on the deconstruction characteristic of poststructuralism and critical theory.

John Chapman

See also CHILDE, VERE GORDON; GENDER ARCHAEOLOGY; HODDER, IAN; LEONE, MARK PAUL; MARXIST ARCHAEOLOGY; NEW/ PROCESSUAL ARCHAEOLOGY; RENFREW, ANDREW COLIN; SOCIAL ARCHAEOLOGY

Further Readings
Bapty, I., and Yates, T., eds. (1990) Archaeology after Structuralism: Post-Structuralism and the Practice of Archaeology. London: Routledge.

Barrett, J. (1994) Fragments from Antiquity. Oxford: Blackwell.

Bintliff, J., ed. (1991) The Annales School and Archaeology. Leicester: Leicester University Press.

Collingwood, R. (1946) The idea of History. Oxford: Oxford University Press.

Hodder, I., ed. (1982) Symbolic and Structural Archaeology. Cambridge: Cambridge University Press.

Hodder, I. (1984) Burials, houses, men and women in the European Neolithic. In D. Miller, and Tilley, C. (eds.): Ideology, Power and Prehistory, pp. 51–68. Cambridge: Cambridge University Press.

Hodder, I., ed. (1987) Archaeology as Long-Term History. Cambridge: Cambridge University Press.

Hodder, I. (1990) The Domestication of Europe. Oxford: Blackwell.

Hodder, I. (1992) Reading the Past. Cambridge: Cambridge University Press.

Layton, R., ed. (1989) Conflict in the Archaeology of Living Tradition. London: Unwin Hyman.

Leone, M.P., Potter, P.B., and Shackel, P.A. (1987) Towards a critical archaeology. Current Anthropology 28(3):283–302.

Renfrew, C. (1979) Comments on "Archaeology into the 1990s." Norwegian Archaeological Review 22:33–41.

Shanks, M. (1992) Experiencing the Past. London: Routledge.

Shanks, M. and Tilley, C. (1987) Social Theory and Archaeology. Cambridge: Polity.

Tilley, C. (1991) Material Culture and Text: The Art of Ambiguity. London: Routledge.

Tilley, C. (1994) A Phenomenology of Place. Oxford: Berg.

P

Q

Quantitative Methods in Archaeology

Ways of treating archaeological information as *data,* by imposing a formal structure on them and subjecting them to techniques of data storage, analysis, and presentation. Although not necessarily going so far as to describe archaeology as a science, this approach is based on the belief that the scientific method is appropriate for the discussion of at least some archaeological problems. The imposition of such a structure for a particular problem, known as the process of *quantification* in the general sense of that word, is the crucial task of the quantitative approach, since an inappropriate or incorrect quantification cannot lead to useful results. The conventional quantitative approach is to create data *tables,* in which each row represents an archaeological object (in the widest possible sense; e.g., an artifact, a site, an outcome of a scientific analysis), and each column represents a *variable* (i.e., a particular characteristic of the set of objects). Archaeologists can store such tables as computer files and relate them to each other using database-management software. More elaborate data structures are possible; some archaeologists advocate them as a way of escaping from the limitations of the data-table approach. The term *quantification* also carries a more specific meaning: the process of saying "how much" archaeological material a particular collection represents (e.g. how much pottery a collection of sherds represents).

Spatial data have been an important part of archaeology since at least the nineteenth century. Their interpretation was a matter of subjective archaeological impression until spatial analysis emerged as a subdiscipline in

its own right in the 1970s. Other types of graphical information, such as site and finds drawings and photographs, have also come within the category of data, since there are now computer techniques for capturing, sorting and analyzing them.

The *quantitative idiom* in archaeology has a long history. Sir William Matthew Flinders Petrie's work on Egyptian cemeteries in the 1890s shows the approach in action, and archaeologists were publishing tables of data much earlier in the nineteenth century. After slow but steady progress throughout the first half of the twentieth century, under the influence of archaeologists like Alfred L. Kroeber, the approach received an impetus from the New Archaeology of the 1960s, although it is in no sense a product of the New Archaeology. Quantitative methods came of age with the holding of a major international conference *Mathematics in the Archaeological and Historical Sciences* in Romania in 1970. The increased use of computers since the 1970s, for database and other purposes, has increased the need for archaeologists to take a quantitative view of their work and to confront the difficult question of quantification.

A minority of archaeologists have actively opposed the quantitative approach on the ground that it is dehumanizing. Archaeology is about people, the argument runs, and quantitative methods are about numbers; to reduce people to numbers is to diminish them and intellectually impoverish the subject. The counterargument is that, although archaeologists are studying people, they do so through their material remains, which inevitably lead to data and the use of appropriate techniques of data analysis. There is, nevertheless, a place for archaeological input, and that is in the quantification of material and in the interpretation of the results of subsequent analyses. In the latter, the archaeological imagination can be given full rein, provided that it is subject to the discipline of checking against further data.

Another issue that has come to the fore is that of the relationship between a quantitative approach and archaeological theory. The question is whether the use of quantitative methods predisposes an archaeologist toward a particular theoretical viewpoint. For example, the history of computer simulation links it with a systems-theory approach, and some archaeologists have argued that the use of geographic information systems (GIS) encourages reliance on ecological or geographical determinism as a mode of explanation.

Conversely, archaeological theory influences the way in which quantitative methods are used. With the rise of interest in site-formation processes in the 1980s came greater understanding that data might not always be what they seem. Differences between two excavated assemblages, for example, may be due to differences in their postdepositional histories as much as to differences between the original assemblages from which they derive. Methods of analysis need to take account of this and to be able to disentangle, as far as is possible, the two sources of difference. How, and the extent to which this can be done, will be an important research topic in the 1990s and beyond.

Clive Orton

See also ANIMAL REMAINS, QUANTIFICATION; COMPUTER DATABANKS IN ARCHAEOLOGY; COMPUTER SIMULATION; COMPUTERS IN ARCHAEOLOGY; GEOGRAPHIC INFORMATION SYSTEMS; SPATIAL ANALYSIS; STATISTICAL METHODS IN ARCHAEOLOGY

Further Readings

Aldenderfer, M.S. (1987) Assessing the impact of quantitative thinking on archaeological research. In M.S. Aldenderfer (ed.): Quantitative Research in Archaeology, pp. 9–29. Newbury Hill, CA: Sage.

Dallas, C. (1991) Relational description, similarity, and classification of complex archaeological entities. In G. Lock and J. Moffett (eds.): Computer Applications and Quantitative Methods in Archaeol-ogy 1991, pp. 167–178. (BAR International Series 577). Oxford: British Archaeological Reports.

Hodson, F.R., Kendall, D.G., and Tautu, P. (1971) Mathematics in the Archaeological and Historical Sciences. Edinburgh: Edinburgh University Press.

Orton, C.R. (1991) Quantitative methods in the 1990s. In G. Lock and J. Moffett (eds.): Computer Applications and Quantitative Methods in Archaeology 1991, pp. 137–140. (BAR International Series 557). Oxford: British Archaeological Reports.

Quartering

An excavation technique involving cutting sites into four quadrants to obtain maximum vertical and horizontal information. It is generally applied to the excavation of small mounds. It has been widely used in Europe for the excavation of Bronze Age round barrows or burial mounds (see Figure 1).

After a detailed contour plan of the round mound is produced, a string should be pegged across the mound through its central (usually the highest) point. Another string is then set out at right angles to the first. Secondary strings are then laid parallel to these strings within any two opposed quadrants. The strings are usually ca. 1 m from the primary strings. These meter-wide strips form the standing baulks, or vertical soil sections, left across the site as the excavation proceeds. The outer limits of the excavation should be outside the maximum limit of the site (usually a surrounding ditch) but can be of any shape: circular, polygonal, or square.

Although quadrants are sometimes excavated in sequence down to the base of archaeological levels, it is better to excavate one context (discrete archaeological deposit) across all four quadrants at the same time. After the excavation of all four quadrants is completed, the standing sections are then recorded and removed to complete the area excavation under the whole of the mound site. Leaving any part of the baulks standing invariably presents the risk of missing burials or other key features.

When a burial or other feature is found partly within a quadrant and partly under a baulk, it is generally better to delay excavation until the baulk has been removed. This is

A Bronze Age round barrow (ca. 1800 B.C.) being excavated by the quadrant method at West Heath, Sussex, England. Photograph by Peter L. Drewett.

particularly important for burials, which should not be partly excavated and then left, perhaps for several weeks, until the baulk is removed. Partly excavated burials run the risk of disturbance by natural erosion, animals, or even robbers. Ideally, a single burial should be excavated, recorded, and removed within a single working day. In some parts of the world where this is not possible, guards may have to be posted.

Peter L. Drewett

Further Readings

Barker, P. (1993) Techniques of Archaeological Excavation, 3rd ed. London: Batsford.

Drewett, P.L. (1999) Field Archaeology: An Introduction. London: University College London Press.

R

Radiocarbon Dating

A widely used technique, applicable to organic remains such as wood, charcoal, seeds, and bone. Living organic matter contains a minute amount of carbon-14, the concentration being ca. one atom of carbon-14 per million million atoms of carbon-12; in contrast to the latter, carbon-14 is weakly radioactive, with a half-life of 5,730 years. From death onward the concentration of carbon-14 in a sample decreases as dictated by this half-life; thus for a 5,730-year-old sample, the concentration is one-half of that for living matter; for an 11,460-year-old sample, one-quarter; for a 17,190-year-old sample, one-eighth, and so on. Hence, measurement of the concentration can be used as a basis for dating. Because of small variations of the concentration ratio in the past, it is necessary, for accuracy, to use a calibration curve to convert ages in radiocarbon years into ages in calendar years.

Development

The idea of radiocarbon dating arose in the late 1940s in the course studies of the effects of cosmic rays on the Earth's atmosphere by Willard F. Libby and his group at the University of Chicago. These studies led to the prediction that carbon-14 should be present throughout the atmosphere and the biosphere (also in ocean carbonate), at a concentration measurable by means of the beta particles emitted in the course of radioactive decay. This proved to be the case. The further expectation that ancient wood from the Egyptian pyramids would have a lower concentration was fulfilled also: Wood from the tombs of the kings Zoser and Sneferu, who died ca. 4,600–4,700 years ago, had an appropriately lower beta activity. Further measurements of known age samples confirmed the essential validity of the technique for dating, and application to prehistoric archaeology soon followed. This was the start of the *radiocarbon revolution,* for humans' antiquity was shown to be substantially greater than had been conjectured; for example, the beginning of the Neolithic town of Jericho was pushed back by several thousand years.

With improved measurement precision during the late 1950s and the 1960s, it eventually became evident that radiocarbon ages tended to underestimate true ages, by several hundred years around 2000 B.C. and increasing further back in time. This led to the realization that, to obtain a true calendar age, a radiocarbon age needed to be corrected by means of a calibration curve; this latter was obtained by measurements on wood dated by tree-ring counting (i.e., dendrochronology), the age so obtained sometimes being referred to as *tree-ring age* or *dendro age.* Initially, bristlecone pines of California were used, but later other species, too, notably European oak. Application of calibration—the *second radiocarbon revolution*—further lengthened prehistoric time scales. In addition, it led to some fundamental reassessments; for example, the model of cultural and technological diffusion to Europe from the eastern Mediterranean and western Asia was called into question and replaced by a model in which independent invention played a strong part.

Further intensive work confirmed that results from high-altitude American trees were in agreement with trees from lowland Europe, and, in the late 1980s, a definitive high-precision calibration became available reaching back to ca. 7000 B.C., in which period the underestimation amounted to ca. 800 years. Subsequently, there was extension of the tree-ring measurements and, together with data based on the counting of annual layers (*varves*) of lake sediment, there were reliable indications of the appropriate correction to be applied back to 12,000 B.C. In the early 1990s, comparison was made with the uranium-series technique using corals; this further extended, back to ca. 30,000 years ago, the period in which radiocarbon could yield ages in calendar years.

A revolution in measurement technique began in the late 1970s when, as an alternative to measurement of beta-particle emission, *accelerator mass spectrometry* (AMS) was introduced, the so-called *atom-counting* method. One of its advantages is that, instead of several grams of sample, only a few milligrams, and even less, are required. This allows contaminated samples to be dated more securely—by extracting different organic components. It also gives access to a range of samples that otherwise would be excluded because of the destructiveness of obtaining a few grams. The dating of linen threads from the Turin Shroud, to ca. A.D. 1300, is an example.

Physical Basis

The carbon-14 concentration in living matter basically represents the equilibrium level reached between production of carbon-14 high up in the atmosphere and its loss by radioactive decay. Production is due to the transmutation of atmospheric nitrogen-14 into carbon-14 by neutrons produced by cosmic radiation. The carbon-14 rapidly forms "heavy" carbon dioxide, and this mixes in with nonradioactive carbon dioxide, predominantly that formed with carbon-12 (plus ca. 1 percent formed with carbon-13). There is rapid mixing of carbon dioxide throughout the atmosphere, and, by photosynthesis, there is entry into plant life and, hence, into animals. Atmospheric carbon dioxide also enters the oceans as dissolved carbonate, so that this, too, contains carbon-14 as do any shells and deposits formed from it. The totality of atmosphere, biosphere, and oceans is known as the *carbon-exchange reservoir*. The concentration ratio between carbon-14 atoms and nonradioactive carbon atoms is approximately the same throughout the reservoir and stays approximately constant with time.

In organic matter that is no longer exchanging its carbon with the reservoir, the carbon-14 lost by radioactive decay is not replenished. Cessation of replenishment begins at death, and this is *time zero*. Thereafter, the concentration begins to fall according to the 5,730-year half-life; this corresponds to a decrease by 1 percent every eighty-three years, so very careful measurement is required to achieve dating precision. Essentially, the age is obtained by comparing the concentration ratio (carbon-14 to carbon-12) in the sample (C) with that in living organic matter (C_o) and using the relation:

$$C = C_o \exp (-0.693 \times age/5{,}730)$$

where exp indicates the exponential function available on most hand calculators. With the conventional method of measurement, it is the radiocarbon *activity* (i.e., the emission rate of beta particles per gram of carbon) that is measured; this is proportional to the concentration ratio.

The indication just given that time-zero is synonymous with death is an oversimplification with some sample types, particularly wood; the time at which exchange with the reservoir ceases corresponds to the wood's formation rather than to the death of the tree; for the inner rings, the difference may be substantial. Hence, for precise dating, short-lived material is used. There are a number of other complicating effects, too, some of which are briefly indicated below.

Variation of Concentration Ratio in Living Matter. If cosmic radiation varied in the past, then the equilibrium level of carbon-14 will have varied also. A higher cosmic-ray intensity would have caused the starting ratio to have been higher, and, if the present-day ratio is assumed, the calculated age will be too small. Another possible cause of variation in the ratio is a change in the size of the carbon-exchange reservoir such as might result from climatic influence. It is because of these effects, of which cosmic-ray variation is the dominant one, that raw radiocarbon ages have to be corrected by means of a calibration curve to obtain ages in calendar years. In addition to the major variations having a time scale of thousands of years, there is a fine structure of smaller short-term *wiggles;* these have the unfortunate consequence that a given radiocarbon age can sometimes yield more than one calendar age. On the other hand, in the dating of large timbers, the specialized technique of *wiggle matching* can be used to obtain calendar ages with remarkably small error limits.

Cosmic-ray variations are associated with changes in the strength of the Earth's magnetic field. A weak field allows more cosmic radiation to reach the upper atmosphere, and the production of carbon-14 is consequently enhanced—causing raw radiocarbon ages to be underestimates of calendar ages. The short-term wiggles mentioned above are associated with sunspot activity.

Isotopic Fractionation. Although plants obtain their carbon from the atmosphere, the actual carbon-14 concentration ratio in them is lower by 3–4 percent. This is because, in the process of photosynthesis, carbon-14 is not taken up as readily as carbon-12; there are small variations from species to species in the degree of this isotopic fractionation. Correction for the effect can be made by measurement of the carbon-13 concentration ratio; this stable isotope, midway between carbon-12 and carbon-14, suffers fractionation to half the degree suffered by carbon-14. Sometimes this is measured for each sample that is dated; sometimes the average value for the type of material concerned is used.

Mixing Rates and Residence Times. Carbon atoms spend only a few tens of years in the atmosphere and surface ocean before reaching the deep ocean. The residence time there is of the order of 1,000 years, and, as a consequence of radioactive decay without replenishment, carbonate in the deep ocean is deficient in carbon-14 and has a substantial apparent age; the carbonate in the surface ocean is intermediate, with the result that living shells typically have an apparent age of ca. 400 years—but, in regions in which there is upwelling of ocean water, this may be substantially greater.

The Hard-Water Effect. In a limestone region, a substantial part of the dissolved carbon in groundwater and rivers is derived from the carbonate of the rocks over which the water has flowed. Since this carbonate was removed from the exchange reservoir a very long time ago, the carbon-14 that was in it initially has long since decayed. Hence, the ages obtained for aquatic plants and shells into which this carbonate has been incorporated will be erroneously too old.

The Fossil-Fuel Effect. The combustion of coal and oil releases into the atmosphere large quantities of carbon dioxide deficient in carbon-14, because, as in the hard-water effect, it was removed from the exchange reservoir millions of years ago. The amount of this "old" carbon is enough to dilute significantly the carbon-14 in the atmosphere; this is reflected in wood grown subsequent to the Industrial Revolution by an age overestimate of 100 or 200 years.

Nuclear Weapons Testing. The neutrons released during a nuclear explosion in the atmosphere cause production of carbon-14; around 1960, there was enough weapons testing for the atmospheric concentration to be substantially enhanced, increasing each year that testing continued. This has allowed year-by-year dating of whisky made during the decades concerned! More important, the excess concentration gives a valuable way of testing the integrity of sample materials. For instance, in tree rings that grew prior to the onset of weapons testing, the cellulose shows no carbon-14 enhancement, whereas for the resin extract there is enhancement for rings formed up to a dozen years earlier.

Samples and Sampling

An essential characteristic of a sample is that, over the centuries of burial, it should not have acquired any fresh carbon from the atmosphere (e.g., by fungal growth). A minute amount of modern carbon can cause the date that is determined to be substantially too recent, particularly for samples near the 40,000-year limit. Conversely, incorporation of dead carbon at formation can cause the opposite effect. Although the sample material itself may have high integrity, there may be intrusive contamination acquired during burial; the humic acids carried in percolating groundwater are an example. It follows that the extent to which a sample is reliable is bound up with the stringency of the laboratory pretreatment that can be applied. The severity that a laboratory can afford to use is dependent both on the size of the initial sample and on the amount of carbon required by the measurement facility; the severity needed depends also on the age.

For *wood*, the use of extracted cellulose avoids lignin and humic acids. For precise dating, a serious problem with wood and charcoal is estimation of the extent to which the wood's formation predated the archaeological event of interest; this is avoided if short-lived wood such as twigs are used. For *bone,* use of the extracted protein fraction (collagen, gelatin) is necessary. Unfortunately, the amount remaining decreases with age, and in some burial environments, among them western Asia, too little is left in bones from periods earlier than, say, the Neolithic. Charred bone is a good alternative.

Grain can be dated reliably, particularly if charred. With the accelerator technique, single grains can be dated, but site association is a severe problem. Among other datable sample types are *shell, peat, sediment* and *soils, ivory, paper* and *textiles, straw* in mud bricks, and traces of *charcoal* in iron objects. Because of the effort and expense involved in making a radiocarbon measurement, prior discussion with the laboratory concerned is always desirable, not least to ascertain the amount of sample required for that laboratory's installation; certainty of archaeological association is another important consideration.

Accuracy and Age Range

In early days, the error limits quoted for a date were based only on measurement precision, but it is now common practice for laboratories to make an assessment of additional experimental uncertainties, widening the quoted error limits appropriately. From a typical laboratory, one expects radiocarbon ages with error limits (at the 68 percent level of confidence) of ca. ±100 years; high-precision laboratories, such as those involved in establishment of the tree-ring calibration, can achieve ± 20 years. Unfortunately, this is not the end of the story because, after correction to calendar years, the error limits are usually wider; also, as mentioned above, there may be more than one calendar age span that corresponds to a given radiocarbon age span.

The age that can be reached is dependent on the measuring installation, the sample type, and the amount available. In an extended-range laboratory, in which a thermal-diffusion column is used to achieve isotopic enrichment before measurement, the limiting age can be pushed back to ca. 70,000 years; sample integrity and the avoidance of the slightest contamination during sample preparation are then of critical importance. For most laboratories, the limiting age is ca. 40,000–50,000 years, scrupulous attention to integrity and avoidance of contamination still being necessary. Inevitably, the achievable error limits widen for samples nearing the limiting age.

At the recent end of the time scale, there is effective limitation to ca. A.D. 1700 due to wiggles in the calibration curve; there are also periods, of which 800–400 B.C. is one of the worst, when flatness of the calibration curve dramatically widens the calendar-age error limits.

Terminology

A *raw* (i.e., uncalibrated) date in conventional radiocarbon years is quoted as "so many years B.P.," the letters standing for Before Present, with Present defined as A.D. 1950; *conventional* signifies that the so-called Libby half-life of 5,568 years was used in calculating the age rather than the more recently determined value of 5,730 years. Ages calculated using the former are less by 3 percent, but this small correction is subsumed in the overall calibration correction. A *calibrated* age is given as "cal B.P."; sometimes "cal B.C." and "cal A.D." are also used though "cal" is often omitted in these cases since B.C. and A.D. traditionally imply calendar years. The convention that lowercase letters imply an uncalibrated date or age has been used to some extent in the past. The terminology just given, B.P. and so forth, is specific to radiocarbon dating. Most other techniques yield ages directly in calendar years, and the use of B.P. is then confusing (since it implies radiocarbon years rather than calendar years); exceptions to this are amino-acid dates and obsidian dates calibrated by reference to radiocarbon.

Martin J. Aitken

See also DENDROCHRONOLOGY; LIBBY, WILLIAM FRANK; URANIUM-SERIES DATING; VARVE ANALYSIS

Further Readings

Aitken, M.J. (1990) Science-Based Dating in Archaeology. London and New York: Longman.

Bard, E., Arnold, M., Fairbanks, R.G., and Hamelin, B. (1993) ^{230}Th–^{234}U and ^{14}C ages obtained by mass spectrometry on corals. Radiocarbon 35:191–199.

Libby, W.F. (1965) Radiocarbon Dating, 2nd ed. Chicago: University of Chicago Press.

Renfrew, C. (1973) Before Civilization: The Radiocarbon Revolution and Prehistoric Europe. London: Jonathan Cape.

Stuiver, M. and Reimer, P.J. (1993) Extended C-14 data base and revised CALIB 3.0 C-14 calibration program. Radiocarbon 35:215-230.

Taylor, R.E. (1987) Radicarbon Dating: An Archaeological Perspective. Orlando: Academic.

Taylor, R.E. (1997) Radiocarbon dating. In R.E. Taylor and M.J. Aitken (eds.): Chronometric Dating in Archaeology. New York: Plenum.

Radiography in Archaeology

The production of photographs (radiographs) using radiation as a nondestructive method of examining the interior of objects. If an object is exposed to a beam of radiation, although some of the radiation is absorbed and some is scattered, the remainder passes through. If the emerging beam falls on a photographic film or a sensitive screen or plate, an image of the object is formed. Hidden differences in thickness, such as hollow cores in cast objects, or changes in density are revealed. Radiography is used in archaeology at all stages from excavation to conservation, study, and cataloging. Its value in providing information for identification and conservation without damage is considerable.

The radiation most frequently used is X rays, although gamma and beta rays are also used. Beta rays are electrons. They have little penetrating power and are used to radiograph light materials, such as paper. X rays and gamma rays are at the shorter-wavelength end of the electromagnetic spectrum and cover similar ranges of wavelength (10^{-6} cm–10^{-19} cm) but are produced in different ways. Radioisotopes such as cobalt (^{60}Co) and iridium (^{192}Ir) emit gamma rays continuously and nondirectionally in a characteristic spectrum. They are generally not suited for light materials, and their main use is in radiographing heavy sections. X rays are emitted with a range of different wavelengths when a stream of electrons impacts on matter. In practice, they are produced by an X-ray tube. The electrons are produced by heating a tungsten filament with a small current (*tube current*). The tube is under vacuum, which allows the electrons to move freely from the cathode to the target anode. A potential difference (*tube voltage*) accelerates the electrons from the cathode area that surrounds the filament to the anode. A high potential makes the electrons move faster and produces a higher proportion of shorter-wavelength X rays. These are more penetrative (*hard X rays*). A low tube potential (kVp) produces less-penetrative X rays (*soft X rays*). The stream of X rays passes out of the tube through the tube window. This is often made of beryllium, a light element.

The target anode is usually a piece of tungsten embedded in a block of copper that acts as a heat sink, as a considerable amount of heat is evolved by the impacting electrons. Anodes are either panoramic or directional. Panoramic anodes emit X rays through a 360° angle, which is useful for radiographing a hollow object without the confusion of both sides being superimposed. However, it is less versatile than the directional anode and is little used in archaeology. Directional anodes are set at an angle to the exit window to reduce the effective target area (*focal spot*). The smaller the focal spot, the less geometric unsharpness (loss of definition) occurs in the image. Industrial X ray sets have focal spots between 2.4 mm^2 and 0.8 mm^2. Microfocus tubes have very small focal spots (30–5 microns) and give high-definition images. Because the image quality is so good, it is possible to make magnified images. This is achieved by increasing the distance between the object and the film, so that an enlarged image (up to 50x) is obtained with little loss of quality. Microfocus X-ray sets have been used to examine welded and riveted links on the ninth-century A.D. Anglian helmet from Coppergate in York and to identify fish species from vertebrae excavated at a Bronze Age site at Ra's al Hadd in Oman.

The beam diameter can be restricted by a diaphragm to reduce scatter. In addition, copper or aluminum filters can be fitted in front of the exit window. Both increase the proportion of hard X rays in the beam by absorbing the less-penetrating components. The effect is to decrease the intensity at the thinner parts of the section, thus reducing scatter. The overall contrast is reduced, but a wider range of thickness can be reproduced effectively.

The intensity of the X-ray beam depends inversely on the square of the distance from the source (*Inverse Square Law*). This means that, if the object is moved away from the X ray to double the distance, for example, the exposure time must be increased four times to compensate for the reduced intensity.

R

Backscatter of softer X rays reflected from the object and anything in its vicinity fogs the film and reduces image quality. Minimizing the distance between the object and the film and using lead shielding around the object helps reduce scatter. Cylindrical medieval English iron-coin dies, for example, need to be surrounded with small bags of lead shot or barium putty to give meaningful radiographs.

Film is widely used to record the image film. It provides a permanent record and gives a high-quality image. A variety of films are available. Double-sided, high-definition, high-contrast industrial X-ray film is often used in archaeological applications. Film is usually exposed in a light-tight cassette for ease of handling. Lead screens are sometimes put behind or on both sides of the film. This cuts out scatter and also intensifies the image by electron emission from the screen supplementing an X-ray induced photochemical effect.

An imaging plate can be used instead of film. The plate is coated with a material that is sensitized to X rays. After exposure, it retains the image until it is read or developed and the image recorded. The plate is then prepared for reuse. Two systems exist. In the medical field, an energy-storage-type (photostimulable) phosphor plate on a plastic support is scanned, after exposure, using a laser beam and a photomultiplier. The analog image is converted to a digital one. This means that it can be processed, annotated, and archived immediately. The second system, *xeroradiography*, was developed in the medical field but is now used more in archaeology. In xeroradiography, an aluminium image plate coated with a photoconductor (amorphous selenium) is conditioned with an even electrostatic charge. On exposure, X rays induce conductivity, which causes the charge to leak away in proportion to the relative intensity of the charge. Once the charge has dissipated, no further change can take place in the residual image. The exposure time is also short, since the image is not being built up and scatter is reduced. The image is developed with powder that can carry a negative or a positive charge, depending on whether a positive or a negative image is wanted.

Xeroradiography has several advantages. The hard-copy xeroradiograph, usually a blue image on white plastic-coated paper is durable and easy to understand, handle, and reproduce. It copes well with a wide range of radiographic densities in one radiograph. Because there is little scatter, it is less affected by geometrical unsharpness than film, so the object-to-plate distance is not so critical. This makes it useful when the object geometry is a problem. The biggest advantage is that edges are enhanced. This happens because differences in the radiographic charge at discontinuities in the image cause steps in the charge distribution. Lines of force form loops locally at the steps. The charged powder follows the path of the loops, so that one side of the discontinuity has more powder while the other side is depleted. The net effect is to enhance the edges. Xeroradiography is especially effective in radiographing ceramics. The small discontinuities due to porosity or temper show up very clearly.

X-ray-sensitive detectors allow the image to be seen immediately by eye. The simplest is a fluorescent screen. Various arrangements of X-ray-sensitive screens or linear arrays are linked to an image enhancer to improve image quality. In a typical system, X rays coming from the object cause light emission, and the light is then converted into electrons. The electron image is focused on a second fluorescent screen and transmitted via a television camera to a monitor and an A-D converter. Real-time imaging allows a quick examination, which can be recorded either continuously as a video or as a series of stills. It is useful for looking at recently excavated assemblages to record, identify, and locate finds. Moving the object on a remotely controlled turntable during the examination gives a three-dimensional impression.

Analog-to-digital conversion allows a great range of image-processing features to be applied to elicit more information. Features can be measured. Mathematical filters can be used to sharpen or smooth the image, to enhance edges, or for contouring. An Anglo-Saxon horse bit, excavated in 1991 at Sutton Hoo, East Anglia, in Britain, was identified; gold chip carved decorative panels were revealed and enhanced although they were completely obscured by corrosion. A regular pattern, such as cloth marks, which are preserved in corrosion products, may be difficult to see and impossible to measure. The pattern, embedded in the radiograph, can be revealed and measured by applying a Fourier transform (a mathematical operation). Histogram equalization or the application of false color will often make features of interest more readily visible to the eye. Subtraction allows images of two different but apparently identical images to be compared. Three-dimensional images can be compiled from stereopairs, displayed in red and green. A vast number of routines are available. A digitized image can also be archived to disc and easily retrieved for further examination or for incorporation in a report.

Tomography, pioneered in the medical field, allows radiographic slices to be made through an object at intervals of 1 mm or more. The slices can be viewed individually or used to form a complete picture after processing. CAT (computer-assisted tomography) scans have been used to study Egyptian mummies without breaking the seals of the coffin. Information on the age, health traumas, dentition, and funerary ornaments of the mummy were obtained. Features of interest (e.g., teeth) can be called up from a total body scan by entering the right parameters and examined in detail.

Janet Lang

Further Readings

David, A.R. and Tapp, E., eds. (1993) The Mummy's Tale: The Scientific and Medical Investigation of Natsef-Amun, Priest in the Temple of Karnak.
London: Michael O'Mara/New York: St. Martin's.
Lang, J. and Middleton, A., eds. (1997) Radiography of Cultural Materials. Oxford/Boston, MA: Butterworth-Heinemann.
Meyers, P. (1978) Applications of X-ray radiography in the study of archaeological objects. In G.F. Carter (ed.): Archaeological Chemistry II, pp. 79–96. (Advances in Chemistry Series 171). Washington, D.C.: American Chemical Society.

Rathje, William Laurens (1945–)

American anthropologist and archaeologist. Born on July 1, 1945, Rathje was educated at the University of Arizona, where he received his bachelor's in 1967, and at Harvard University, where he earned his doctorate in 1971. He returned to Arizona in 1971 as an assistant professor of anthropology, was promoted to the rank of associate professor in 1975, and is currently a full professor of anthropology. A Mesoamerican archaeologist, Rathje has studied changes in archaeological material recovered from Lowland Maya burials in order to model social change. He has also proposed models for the origins of Maya culture and later studied mortuary evidence to model the general collapse of the Lowland Maya system. Rathje has become most well known, however, for his work in experimental archaeology. He gained notoriety as the head of the Tucson Garbage Project at the University of Arizona, a systematic examination of garbage and landfills in the Tucson area. The goal was to study refuse patterns, deposition information, and decay rates to observe the relationships between a contemporary society and the material culture they leave behind. The on-going project also produced valuable information on how archaeological sites are formed, how stratigraphy is created and altered, and how materials become stable or decay in the record. ("The Garbage Project"; *Rubbish!: The Archaeology of Garbage,* coauthored with Cullen Murphy). While some scholars have questioned the usefulness of such experimental methods, the Garbage Project is one of many experiments supplementing more traditional archaeological approaches.

Joseph J. Basile

See also ARCHAEOLOGICAL SITES, FORMATION PROCESSES; EXPERIMENTAL ARCHAEOLOGY

Further Readings

Rathje, W.J. (1974) The Garbage Project: A new way of looking at the problems of archaeology. Archaeology 27:236–241.
Rathje, W.J. and Murphy, C. (1992) Rubbish! The Archaeology of Garbage. New York: HarperCollins.
Rathje, W.J. and Ritenbaugh, C.K. eds. (1984) Household Refuse Analysis: Theory, Methods, and Applications in Social Science. (American Behavioral Scientist 28, no. 1). Beverly Hills, CA: Sage.
Sabloff, J.A. and Rathje, W.L., eds. (1975) Cozumel Archaeological Project: A Study of Changing Pre-Columbian Commercial Systems. (Peabody Museum Monographs 3). Cambridge, MA: Peabody Museum of Archaeology and Ethnology.

R

Wilk, R.R. and Rathje, W.L., eds. (1982) Archaeology of the Household: Building a Prehistory of Domestic Life. (American Behavioral Scientist 25, no. 6). Beverly Hills, CA: Sage.

Reburial, International Perspectives

The repatriation of excavated archaeological human remains to their closest attributable living descendants for reburial and the effects of reburial legislation on the discipline and practice of archaeology throughout the world.

The reburial movement that has swept across parts of the developed world has had a profound effect on the field of archaeology. The movement is a result of the assertion of Native Peoples over the control of their heritage. In regions most strongly affected by reburial concerns, archaeologists must alter methodological and theoretical approaches in the context of Native autonomy and perspectives. This will result in research based largely on tribal issues and concerns. There will be a spin-off effect in regions that are not subject to reburial concerns. These areas will be the training grounds where development of new methodological approaches will occur. Traditional scientific theoretical paradigms will shift to regions where archaeological research is not channeled by the concerns of indigenous people, while nontraditional, culturally sensitive paradigms will evolve in reburial-prone areas. Usually, the issue of reburial is discussed in narrow geographical contexts. This entry presents the issue in a more global perspective and, therefore, includes discussion of the status of the reburial movement in selected countries representing regions that are reburial prone and reburial free. By presenting reburial in a global perspective, it is hoped that readers will gain a deeper understanding of the movement and its impact on the international training of archaeologists.

The accompanying figure depicts the distribution of reburial sentiments. The United States, Canada, and Australia host the greatest proportion of reburial proponents. Australia has had the longest history of repatriation. There is also a fundamentalist Judaic population in Israel that advocates limited archaeological research and opposes disturbance of the dead, as addressed in 1995 by Herbert Watzman. In general, the reburial movement is a political reaction to the imposition of European scientific values on tribal peoples who have no such history of such values. It should be remembered that even Europeans struggled with the emergence of Renaissance science, which conflicted with social and spiritual values associated with the dead. In medieval times, corpses had significant spiritual value. As science fostered increased emphasis on rational study of the natural world, there was a new emphasis on corpses as being sources of scientific knowledge. After the nineteenth century, the science-versus-spirit debate concerning the dead ended in the favor of science. In the twentieth century, the scientific value of the corpse emerged in the tendency for individuals to volunteer their bodies for postmortem scientific purposes. The bodies also have a medical value as represented by the voluntary organ-donation projects. In essence, among Europeans and European-derived cultures, individuals perceive corpses and their component organs to have little spiritual value relative to scientific and medical value. Thus, the scientific ethic prevails in the determination of the value of the body. Archaeology is a field of science that specializes in the study of the dead and is, therefore, consistent with this scientific ethic. This ethic is not shared by the tribal cultures that fell under European domination in the Americas and Australia. For such peoples, the corpse and burial place had significant spiritual value. It was perhaps inevitable that ethics concerning the dead would collide and that tribal peoples would revolt against European science.

Now that the revolt is established in the reburial movement and its codification in relevant legislation, the extent to which archaeology is affected varies from country to country. Most often, students think of reburial as focused on skeletons. Various articles by Sandra Bowdler and Graeme O'Neill indicate that this is true for Australia. Australian museums have developed a policy regarding human skeletal remains. However, the heightened awareness of Aborigine concerns in Australia has resulted in consideration of native interpretations in rock art and artifacts. It is apparent from the literature that Australian archaeology, bioarchaeology, and museums cooperated with Aborigines in resolving the issue.

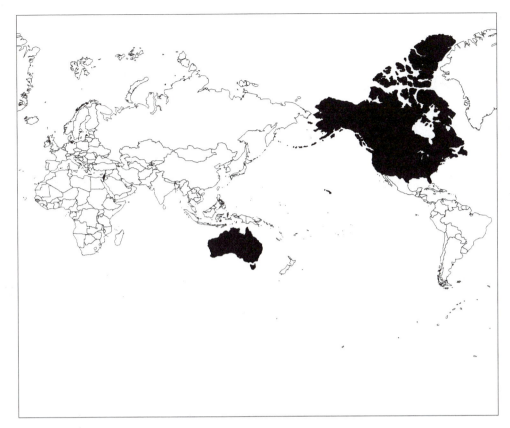

World map showing the reburial-prone regions in black. Australia, the United States, Canada, and Israel are the nations in which reburial laws have been enacted. Drawn by Karl Reinhard.

In North America, a greater variety of artifacts are subject to reburial. There seems to be no consensus among different museums concerning reburial policy. By U.S. federal law, skeletons, burial artifacts, and sacred artifacts are subject to reburial. In practice, museums sometimes go beyond the law to rebury artifacts, animal bone, botanical remains, pollen samples, and even sediment samples excavated from domestic contexts. In North America, the reburial issue has divided the three fields that should cooperate on the issue: museum studies, bioarchaeology, and archaeology.

Bioarchaeology is the study of human skeletal remains. Bioarchaeologists have long emphasized the scientific value of collections both as a source for information about the past and for biological information relating to the health status of modern Native Americans, as exemplified by Douglas H. Ubelaker and Lauryn Grant. Archaeologists disagree among themselves about the approach to the reburial issue. Anthony Klesert and Shirley Powell present the perspective that archaeologists have no unique right of access to skeletons, grave offerings, or objects of cultural heritage. They argue that archaeologists have been insensitive to the views of Native Americans, and that archaeologists must develop ethics that are harmonious with the concerns of Native Americans. Other archaeologists, such as Clement Meighan, disagree and argue that this attitude will contribute to the disappearance of North American archaeology. The latter opinion seems to be a minority opinion but is, nonetheless, valid. Thus, most archaeolgists are attempting to cooperate with Native Americans. Museum studies, as represented by Raymond Thompson, takes the position that curators and directors must look beyond the current debate and bring Native Americans into cooperative ventures in display and interpretation of indigenous cultures. Thus, the division exists between bioarchaeology and the other two fields. Bioarchaeology tends to focus on the values of Western science, while archaeology and museum studies tend to work toward compromise and reconciliation with Native American groups.

The basis of the difference among the various fields is both philosophical and pragmatic. Bioarchaeology is a biological field (i.e., a natural science) and is, therefore, grounded in the principles of Western scientific investigation. Bioarchaeologists have training in anatomy that can be applied in any geographical region. Therefore, neither by philosophical inclination nor research imperatives do bioarchaeologists need compromise to continue their research. Bioarchaeologists have adjusted to the reburial movement by changing the geographic area of research, studying nonnative skeletons, or increasing their emphases in forensic anthropology.

In contrast, archaeologists and museum curators are more often regionally or temporally focused. Therefore, to continue study in reburial-prone regions, reconciliation and compromise with tribal peoples are necessary. Also, archaeologists are more often social scientists and, therefore, have the philosophical flexibility to change research paradigms. It is important to note that, in practice, none of these fields opposes reburial. There has been local opposition by small groups of archaeologists. These small battles have been used by Native American writers such as R.C. Echo-Hawk and W.R. Echo-Hawk to unjustly characterize the whole fields of anthropology and museum studies.

There is no doubt that bioarchaeology of tribal peoples will be heavily impacted in reburial-prone countries. This is due to the destruction of skeletal collections through reburial, which undermines the basis of the field. Bioarchaeological research is dependent on curated skeletal collections. Research is done in a serial fashion, so that, as each new technique develops, it is applied to skeletal collections housed in museums. Thus, skeletal collections are constantly under study by researchers as new techniques are developed. Collections are also essential for study replication and verification, which is the basis of scientific technique. Therefore, more is learned each decade based on analysis and reanalysis of existing skeletal collections. Essentially, all

skeletal collections of Native Americans will be reburied, and access to skeletons that are excavated in the future will be limited. Some tribes have already adopted an "in field" analysis policy. Only such analysis that can be done within a few hours in the field setting is permitted. Thus, the standard approach to bioarchaeology cannot be continued in reburial-prone areas, and opportunities to study Native American and Aborigine bioarchaeology will diminish.

The loss of burial data will reduce the rigor of archaeology in the United States and Australia. Bioarchaeology has made highly significant contributions to the understanding of historic and prehistoric archaeology in Australia and North America, as exemplified by studies edited by Clark Spencer Larsen and George Milner. Issues such as demography, disease, genetic affiliations, and cultural patterns can be best approached by skeletal analysis. There can be no replacement for skeletal data in archaeological studies. Therefore, archaeologists in the future will have to adjust their approaches to research in the absence of biological information about archaeological populations.

Australian skeletons have also shed light on the essence of human evolution. Comparative research on aborigine and *Homo erectus* skeletons has provided invaluable information supporting the theory of indigenous evolution of humans in Asia. Therefore, the reburial of Palaeolithic skeletons impacts the field of paleoanthropology (the study of human evolution), as pointed out by Derek John Mulvaney.

Tied to the decline of bioarchaeology is the study of mortuary archaeology and archaeological investigations of religion. More than any other aspect of archaeology, mortuary archaeology provides significant information regarding social and political organization. The importance of this work is emphasized by Lane Beck and by Robert Chapman and colleagues. Essential in mortuary archaeology is the excavation of cemeteries and the bioarchaeological determination of age and sex of skeletons. At least in the United States, excavation of Native American cemeteries for archaeological research is prohibited. Artifact and skeletal analyses of graves that are excavated under salvage conditions are limited. Therefore, it is likely that Native American mortuary archaeology in the United

States will stop. It is probable that archaeologists will be limited in their investigations of sites that are perceived as sacred by Native Americans. This includes rock-art sites and structures that may have had ceremonial significance. Ultimately, archaeology will be unaffected only in domestic contexts.

One can imagine what archaeology will be like in North America and Australia in the twenty-first century. There are certain trends in these areas that are clear. Archaeologists will become more sensitive to Native American and Aborigine constituents. Individual tribes will decide upon study possibilities and will direct study. There will be an absence of bioarchaeology. Certain types of chemical analysis are opposed by most tribes and will continue to be opposed by some. Therefore, there will be reduced studies by stable-isotopic and trace-elemental techniques of essential cultural factors, such as diet. Theoretically, there will be increased emphasis on tying archaeological research to Native belief systems. Hypotheses will be generated from Native perceptions of the past. On a practical level, more Native Americans will be incorporated in archaeological research at all levels.

Analysis of Omaha Ancestors: Example of Cooperation

None of these developments is inherently wrong. Science, and the way science is done, has always been influenced by the cultural milieu of the day. The paradigmatic shifts in reburial-prone areas are useful in presenting the Native perspective on the past. One successful, tribal-based study has been sponsored by the Omaha tribe of Nebraska. This study has been covered by the British Broadcasting Corporation's Horizon production *Bones of Contention* and is featured by Fergus Bordewich's *Killing the White Man's Indian*.

The Omaha tribe of Nebraska has had a long history in repatriation issues. The tribe sponsored state legislation in 1985 that would have required the reburial of tribal remains, but the bill was defeated. Later, the tribe supported another bill that was signed into law in 1989. The Omaha tribe then approached the University of Nebraska and requested that studies be done of Omaha skeletons and mortuary artifacts before reburial, which occurred in 1991. The burials dated between A.D. 1780 and A.D. 1840. Working with University of Nebraska officials, the tribe defined the following study goals: (1) to provide an idea of what Omaha life was like during the eighteenth and nineteenth centuries; (2) to correct some misinterpretations of Omaha culture and history, especially past archaeological studies that suggested the Omaha were warlike; (3) to address past and modern health issues, including diet, diabetes, cancer, and other diseases; (4) to explain the science of the analysis so that young Omaha people might become interested in pursuing careers in science and technology; (5) to define the contributions of Omaha culture to Native American society as a whole and the world at large.

The breadth of the studies is too great to be summarized completely here, but certain aspects will be highlighted. Further information is available elsewhere by Karl Reinhard and colleagues published in Larsen and Milner's 1994 volume *In the Wake of Contact: Biological Responses to Conquest*.

The diabetes issue is especially important to the Omaha, who recognize that the disease is caused by lifestyle changes. The tribe requested baseline data regarding traditional diet and activity patterns. Therefore, the research emphasized analyses relevant to defining diet and activity, including chemical analysis of bones. The dietary analysis showed that the traditional Omaha diet was diverse, with low-fat and high-fiber content. This contrasts with the modern Omaha diet, which is high in fat relative to fiber. Also, analysis of arthritis, bone fractures, bone density, and bone thickness showed that the traditional Omaha activities were strenuous and that the Omaha were constantly active during their lives. Modern Omaha are much less active. The studies confirm that changes in diet and activity occurred and support the hypothesis that the high prevalence of diabetes (30 percent of Omaha adults) results from recent changes in lifestyle.

The Omaha take exception to archaeological research that suggests that a decline in Omaha population beginning at 1800 was due to warfare (O'Shea and Ludwickson 1992). The Omaha traditions state that a smallpox epidemic caused a population crash. Analysis of the skeletal remains revealed that only one of 120 skeletons had clear evidence of warfare. There was, however, an increased death rate in all age categories and in both sexes after 1800. The change in patterns of death is consistent with an epidemic and with the Omaha version of history. The depiction of the Omaha culture as prone to warfare is not valid in the light of the skeletal analysis.

The analysis also tested aspects of Omaha oral tradition regarding the tribe's famous leader, Chief Blackbird. The traditions state that Blackbird used poison to eliminate his rivals. The analysis of the bones shows that lead was absorbed into the bodies. Analysis of pigments found on the skeletons showed them to be composed of lead and mercury. The pigments were most often used when Blackbird was alive, between 1780 and 1800. Therefore, the analysis confirms that poisoning occurred during Blackbird's life. However, it cannot be confirmed that Blackbird poisoned his enemies or was even aware of the poisoning of his people. However, the correlation generally supports Omaha oral traditions.

The contributions of the Omaha tribe to the history of the Great Plains were delineated by skeletal and mortuary study. The analysis of mortuary artifacts and burial patterns had previously demonstrated that the Omaha had a three-tier social system tied to trade with European powers in the eighteenth century. The further analysis of skeletal remains in context of the artifact data showed that there were a variety of craft and role specializations as well. For example, the first documented gunsmith in the Plains was an Omaha. The oldest evidence of powwow celebrations comes from drumsticks and paraphernalia found with the skeletons. The find of healed gunshot wounds and fractures, as well as infectious lesions, shows that the Omaha in the nineteenth century were more advanced in their medical skills than contemporaneous Europeans and Euroamericans. Thus, the Omaha were one of the most complex tribes in the history of the Great Plains. Because of their dominance, it appears that their rituals, such as the powwow, were adopted by other Plains tribes. It is also clear that, technologically, they adopted certain aspects of European technology, such as weapons, while maintaining their own advanced technology in medicine. Therefore, the analysis of Omaha remains from an Omaha perspective resulted in conclusions that would have been missed by standard scientific hypothesis generation and testing methods.

This indigenous-based approach to archaeology will become the common approach in reburial-prone areas. Eventually, Native American archaeologists will replace Euroamerican archaeologists. Thus, the cooperation exhibited by researchers now is a transitional phase to a later phase in which Native Americans take full control of hypothesis generation and testing. Klesert points out that the Navajo Nation of Arizona and New Mexico has already established such a program.

Trends in Reburial-Free Countries

At a time when mortuary archaeology and bioarchaeology are most threatened in reburial-prone countries, they are building momentum in reburial-free countries. In Peru and Chile, a decidedly non reburial ethic exists, although for different reasons in each country. Luiz Jaime Castillo Butters and Elias Mujica Barreda have summarized the changing conditions in Peru and the future of archaeology in that country. There is a new emphasis on archaeological research, which coincides with other changes in the economic, social, and political structure of the country. The new trends in archaeology include bioarchaeology and mortuary archaeology. The importance of mortuary archaeology in Peru is highlighted by Walter Alva's discovery of royal Moche tombs at Sipan. The emphasis on burial excavation and interpretation shows no signs of diminishing in Peru. Culturally, the vast majority of the population is at least partly Native American, and many of the archaeologists and archaeology students have Native ancestry. Among the Peruvian population, which has strong ties to the Inca past, there is a political assertion of the intrinsic value of indigenous culture in the face of the dominant, Spanish-derived political system. Archaeology is a field in which the supporters of this indigenous movement can demonstrate the vitality of prehistoric cultures and the contributions of those cultures to the world today. The discovery of mummies in the region, including Inca sacrifices, will reinforce the development of Peruvian bioarchaeology and mortuary archaeology. Modern Peruvian bioarchaeology is developing in this environment. There is a new Association of Peruvian Bioanthropologists and a new foundation, the Centro Mallqui, which is specifically committed to the bioarchaeology of Peru.

In Chile, the Native American population has died out, and the modern population is of European descent. However, Chile has long had a strong archaeological tradition. Because of the recovery of mummies in the Atacama

Desert of Chile, mummy studies have contributed to the development of bioarchaeology in Chile. One of the most noteworthy Chilean-born bioarchaeologists is Bernardo Arriaza, who has explored the biology and culture of the ancient Chinchorro culture, the first culture in the world to practice mummification. The sponsorship of archaeology by the Chilean government is indicated by its commitment to host the 1998 Mummy Conferences in Arica, Chile.

Chile and Peru are typical of Latin American countries with regard to the reburial issue. To date, there is no large reburial movement in any Latin American country. Bioarchaeology, mortuary archaeology, and archaeology of ceremonial sites are the fields of archaeological research that are most emphasized in Latin America. Thus, Latin America will provide the opportunities to study antiquity from all archaeological perspectives in the Western Hemisphere.

The fields of bioarchaeology and mortuary archaeology are highly advanced in Europe. With regard to skeletal remains, Europeans are particularly good in methodology and technique. This is evidenced by developments in histology and DNA (deoxyribonucleic acid) technology. Mortuary archaeology theory is also well advanced in Europe. Therefore, Europe will dominate bioarchaeology and mortuary archaeology as the major region for the innovation of new techniques and the proliferation of scientific investigation of skeletons and mortuary remains. Meighan in 1992 predicted a time when "[North American] leadership in archaeological research . . . will be lost, and it will be left to other nations to make future advances in archaeological methods, techniques, and scholarly investigations into the ancient past. (Meighan 1992: 708)." Europe is in a position to take over the leadership to which Meighan refers in the immediate future; in the near future, leadership will be shared between European and Latin American researchers.

Thus, in a global perspective, the reburial movement has resulted in the development of new theoretical paradigms and new, unique approaches to archaeology, based on indigenous cultural beliefs. It has created a new cultural sensitivity among archaeologists. It will benefit those countries that are building mortuary and skeletal studies as North American

researchers move to other areas, especially Central and South America. European universities will become the training grounds for future bioarchaeologists and will house the laboratories needed for the development of new techniques. Therefore, the reburial movement will cause a regional rearrangement of the theoretical and methodological approaches to mortuary studies.

Karl Reinhard

See also BONE AND OTHER ORGANIC MATERIALS: ANCIENT DNA; BONE, TRACE-ELEMENT ANALYSIS; ISOTOPES, STABLE (C, N, O, H): BONE AND PALEODIET STUDIES; MORTUARY SITES, EXCAVATION AND ANALYSIS; NATIVE AMERICAN GRAVES PROTECTION AND REPATRIATION ACT (NAGPRA); PALEOPATHOLOGY, HUMAN

Further Readings

Alva, W. (1990) New tomb of royal splendor: The Moche of ancient Peru. National Geographic 177:2–16.

Arriaza, B. (1995) Chile's Chinchorro mummies. National Geographic 187:68–90.

Beck, L. (1995) Regional Approaches to Mortuary Analysis. New York: Plenum.

Bordewich, F. (1996) Killing the White Man's Indian. New York: Doubleday.

Bowdler, S. (1992) Unquiet slumber: The return of the Kow Swamp burials. Antiquity 66:103–106.

Castillo Butters, L.J., and Mujica Barreda, E. (1995) Peruvian archaeology: Crisis or development? Society for American Archaeology Bulletin 13 (3):25–27.

Chapman, R., Kinnes, I., and Randsborg, K. (1991) The Archaeology of Death. Cambridge: Cambridge University Press.

Echo-Hawk, R.C., and Echo-Hawk, W.R. (1994) Battlefields and Burial Grounds: The Indian Struggle to Protect Ancestral Graves in the United States. Minneapolis: Lerner.

Klesert, A.L. (1992) A view from Navajoland on the reconciliation of anthropologists and Native Americans. Human Organization 51:17–22.

Klesert, A.L., and Powell, S. (1993) A perspective on ethics and the reburial controversy. American Antiquity 58:348–354.

Larsen, C.S., and Milner, G.R. (1994) In the Wake of Contact: Biological Responses to Conquest. New York: Wiley-Liss.

Meighan, C.W. (1992) Some scholars' views on reburial. American Antiquity 57:704–710.

Mulvaney, D.J. (1991) Past regained, future lost: The Kow Swamp Pleistocene burials. Antiquity 65:12–22.

O'Neill, G. (1988) Clash over skulls mars Australia's anniversary. New Scientist 119:29.

O'Shea, J.M., and Ludwickson, J. (1992) Archaeology and Ethnohistory of the Omaha Indians: The Big Village Site. Lincoln: University of Nebraska Press.

Thompson, R.H. (1991) Looking to the future. Museum News 70:36–40.

Ubelaker, D.H., and Grant, L.G. (1988) Human skeletal remains: Preservation or reburial? Yearbook of Physical Anthropology 32:249–287.

Watzman, H.M. (1995) Israeli scholars seek new law on human remains. Chronicle of Higher Education 41:A38.

Redman, Charles L. (1945–)

American anthropologist and archaeologist. Redman received his bachelor's degree from Harvard University in 1967 and undertook graduate studies at the University of Chicago, completing his master's in 1969 and his doctorate in 1971. Redman began his career as an assistant professor at New York University in 1970, followed by two years at the Miller Institute for Research at the University of California at Berkeley. In 1974, he joined the faculty of the State University of New York at Binghamton and became a full professor in 1982; in 1983, he moved to Arizona State University, where he was the chair of the Department of Anthropology (1986–1995). He also spent a year (1982–1983) as a program officer for the National Science Foundation. In 1989, Redman was the first recipient of the American Anthropological Association's Distinguished Lecturer in Archaeology Award. Redman is active in archaeology at both the national and the state levels; he has served on various committees of the Society for American Archaeology, was the archaeology editor for *American Anthropologist* (1986–1989) and chair of the governor's Archaeological Advisory Commission for the State of Arizona (1986–1988), and has been a trustee of the Museum of Northern Arizona since 1991. Redman's research has been supported by grants from the National Science Foundation and the National Endowment for the Humanities, as well as by cultural-resources management contracts with state and federal agencies and private companies. He was also awarded a Fulbright Research Fellowship and, while a graduate student, was a Ford Foundation archaeological trainee. He continues to teach and conduct research at Arizona State University, and, as the president of the board of directors for the Southwest Center for Education and the Natural Environment, he is working toward the establishment of a new natural history museum.

Redman was one of a group of archaeologists who helped articulate the paradigm of the New Archaeology in the 1970s. He is well known as a coauthor (with Patty Jo Watson and Steven A. LeBlanc) of *Explanation in Archaeology: An Explicitly Scientific Approach,* and for promoting a more anthropological perspective of the past, as reflected in the title of his edited volume *Social Archaeology: Beyond Subsistence and Dating.* Redman defines archaeology (in *Research and Theory in Current Archaeology,*) as the study of the cultural behavior of humans conducted by analyzing the material remains of past activities. The characteristics that separate archaeology from other fields of anthropology and social sciences thus lie in the particular methods and techniques that are used to reconstruct and study human behavior. Redman is particularly interested in the processes that contribute to the development of complex societies, a topic that he explores at length in *The Rise of Civilization: From Early Farmers to Urban Society in the Ancient Near East.* The volume is important as a particularly successful and highly readable application of systems theory in archaeology. Redman uses systemic concepts and models, for instance, to map out alternate ways in which hunter-gatherers might have made the transition to sedentary village life. He shows that two different sets of processes, appropriate to different ecological conditions, are needed to account for the appearance of sedentary agricultural villages in the Middle East.

Redman's contributions to the refinement and improvement of fieldwork methods have addressed issues ranging from statistical sampling to strategies for integrating surface collection and excavation techniques into multistage programs for field research. More recently, Redman has become interested in the study of human impacts on the environment, especially as viewed in the archaeological record of preindustrial societies. His research has included a period of extensive work in a medieval city in Morocco (*Qsar es-Seghir*) and, more recently, in the American Southwest, where his *People of the Tonto Rim* has had popular appeal while also providing the profession with a synthesis of a poorly understood region. Redman continues to be an innovative researcher in the anthropological study of prehistoric societies.

Glen Eugene Rice

See also NEW/PROCESSUAL ARCHAEOLOGY; WATSON, PATTY JO

Further Readings

Redman, C.L., ed. (1973) Research and Theory in Current Archeology. New York: Wiley.

Redman, C.L. (1978a) The Rise of Civilization: From Early Farmers to Urban Society in the Ancient Near East. San Francisco: W.H. Freeman.

Redman, C.L. ed. (1978b) Social Archeology: Beyond Subsistence and Dating. New York: Academic.

Redman, C.L. (1986) Qsar es-Seghir: An Archaeological View of Medieval Life. Orlando, FL: Academic

Redman, C.L. (1993) People of Tonto Rim: Archaeological Discovery in Prehistoric Arizona. Washington, D.C.: Smithsonian Institution Press.

Watson, P.J., LeBlanc, S.A., and Redman, C.L. (1971) Explanation in Archeology: An Explicitly Scientific Approach. New York: Columbia University Press.

Watson, P.J., LeBlanc, S.A., and Redman, C.L. (1984) Archeological Explanation: The Scientific Method in Archeology. New York: Columbia University Press.

Remotely Operated Vehicles

Unmanned electronically guided vehicles capable of archaeological recording underwater at depths below which human divers can function safely or effectively. *Remotely operated vehicles* (ROVs) represent a new technology that has the potential for changing the character and direction of underwater archae-ology. Anything one says about this technology today may become obsolete tomorrow. ROVs come in many sizes and degrees of sophistication. Some of the smaller, less-expensive types fit into foot-locker-size containers, while larger, complex varieties require a fully equipped mother ship with heavy-lift cranes and monitoring devices. The simpler ROVs have limited capabilities and generally can accommodate only a television monitor and video or camera contained in a forward-facing transparent housing. More sophisticated ROVs have additional attachments for instrument arrays, and some even have manipulator arms for simple tasks.

Initially, ROVs attracted attention in underwater archaeology for their excellent-quality still photographs and video sequences of deeply submerged shipwrecks like the *Titanic* and the *Bismarck* in the North Atlantic and the *Hamilton* and the *Scourge,* wooden ships from the War of 1812, in the Great Lakes. Operated as camera platforms, ROVs were attached to long umbilical cables from the mother ship. The operator aboard the mother ship steered the ROV, aided by television images from the vehicle itself.

Since conventional SCUBA (self-contained underwater breathing apparatus) diving operations are limited, for practical and safety reasons, to a maximum depth of ca. 65 m, ROVs offer the advantage of being able to operate at any depth without regard for the limitations imposed on human divers. In the case of very deep operations, such as the photographic survey of the *Titanic* at ca. 4,000 m, it was advantageous to deploy the ROV, called "Jason," from a manned deep submersible known as "Alvin." At the present time (i.e., 1998), all operational ROVs, of whatever size and complexity, rely upon signals from a surface operator or a submersible via an umbilical cable to maneuver the vehicle. The cable is necessary because of difficulties in transmitting electronic signals through an aquatic environment. The umbilical cable presents practical difficulties when operating ROVs at great depths, mainly due to drag when strong currents are present or when bad weather occurs at the surface.

ROVs are already an established technology for underwater exploration and for industrial purposes, such as tending offshore oil-drilling platforms. But their archaeological applications are still somewhat experimental.

The archaeological effectiveness of ROVs depends upon their coordinated use with other underwater systems in the context of an organized, scientifically controlled methodology. Unlike other underwater sciences, archaeological recording demands accurate three-dimensional positioning to document the physical associations of material remains at a site good enough to draw convincing inferences. ROVs are intended to produce a level of accuracy in underwater archaeological recording comparable to techniques used on land, regardless of depth. Generalized locations on the seabed or in the water column provide insufficient control for acceptable archaeological recording, making accurate underwater positioning for the ROV a unique requirement for archaeology. The degree of precision may vary according to circumstances, but it usually involves submeter levels of accuracy.

The first step in accurate underwater positioning is to fix a precise position on the ocean surface at or near the underwater site. When operating within sight of land, relatively reliable and accurate microwave systems are available. Beyond sight of land, the most useful system is the differential global positioning system (DGPS). This system can be used near shore, as well. DGPS is an evolved version of the global positioning system (GPS), based on coordinated signals transmitted from space-based satellites. Following the Gulf War in 1991, when GPS was used extensively, the United States Department of Defense selectively degraded GPS signals to a reduced level of accuracy for security reasons. To obtain high levels of accuracy since then, special reprogramming is needed. Standard GPS is widely used as a navigational tool in aviation and at sea, where it is steadily replacing the earlier LORAN-C system. LORAN-C (long-range navigation-model C), which relies on ground-based chains of transmitters, and standard GPS are both useful for establishing the general position of an underwater site (especially when the archaeologist needs to revisit the site but does not want to mark the site and risk exposing it to treasure hunters and relic collectors). But GPS and LORAN-C lack the fine accuracy of DGPS.

Once the site's position is fixed on the surface, the fix can serve as the site datum. Then data points established on the seabed are connected to the surface datum. Microwave and other electronic signals cannot be used underwater. Subsurface positioning relies upon the propagation of acoustical signals from transponders at fixed locations. Receivers (transducers) echo-locate the transponders on the seabed. In essence, a network of transponders interrogated by a transducer creates an electronic grid over the seabed covering the area of the site. By maneuvering the ROV within this grid, the operator can determine the ROV's position accurately enough for on-site archaeological recording.

Acoustic signals underwater travel at the speed of sound, which is much slower than the speed of light for microwave and other electronic signals on the surface. So real-time positioning is easier on the surface than it is underwater, where there are delays between transmission and reception of signals. This makes the relative geometry of positioning within the underwater grid and its coordination with the position on the surface fairly complicated. Nevertheless, computer technology has been applied successfully to this problem.

The approach just described was used for the 1985 and 1987 remote-sensing surveys of the U.S.S. *Monitor* shipwreck site, ca. 24 km off Cape Hatteras, North Carolina. In 1985, the survey ship relocated the wreck using LORAN-C. A microwave system with two shore-based transmitters was used to establish and navigate along a series of parallel lanes on the surface above the sites, which lay at a depth of 75–80 m. These lanes served as controls for a remote-sensing survey involving magnetometry (which detects and measures magnetic anomalies, especially from ferrous metals), bathymetry (precise depth finding to reveal seabed contours and features), sub-bottom profiling (mainly detecting variations in silt layers underneath the seabed), and side-scan sonar. Side-scan sonar provides acoustical imaging of features on the seabed and is widely used in underwater archaeology. Five transponders were placed on the seabed around the *Monitor* wreck and positioned in relation to the surface datum and electronically established lanes. Trailing a transducer through the field covered by the transponders on the seabed, the ship determined the necessary relative geometry for the electronic grid over the site on the seabed. In 1987, this electronic grid was reactivated and used for the exact positioning of a sophisticated ROV, "Deep Drone," which took measurements and photographs, including a computerized imaging system that produced a three-dimensional map of the wreck.

The U.S.S. *Monitor* study by the National Oceanic and Atmospheric Administration (NOAA) demonstrated how to use ROVs effectively for true archaeological research. But the cost of the NOAA system was high, and the results should be viewed more as a proof-of-concept trial than as a strict guide to the future conduct of controlled archaeological recording at depths below practical SCUBA diving limits. Since 1987, more compact and cheaper underwater positioning systems have been developed, such as SHARPS (sonic high-accuracy ranging and positioning system).

Effective deep-water use of ROVs depends upon the prior establishment of controls during the initial site survey. Research designs involving the use of ROVs must address issues of sampling within the survey area and monitoring of such variables as underwater terrain and seabed conditions, currents, marine growths, and other factors affecting the post-depositional history of the site. Most scientific principles guiding systematic archaeological surveys on land also apply under-water. Unsystematic and uncontrolled discovery-mode-type searches using ROVs cannot be expected to produce convincing results in underwater archaeology, no matter how sophisticated the technology.

A relatively new development in ROV technology, autonomous ROVs, seeks to eliminate the unwieldy umbilical cable required by the current generation of ROVs. Autonomous ROVs, like *Odyssey* at the MIT Sea Grant Underwater Vehicles Laboratory and *Antonomous Benthic Explorer* operated by the Woods Hole Oceanographic Institution, are still experimental but have been undergoing trials at sea and hold promise for underwater archaeology. Autonomous ROVs employ artificial intelligence and navigate and position themselves as they move through the underwater environment. This requires a high order of artificial intelligence, and the designers regard some of their solutions as comparable to kinetic responses exhibited by many animals. Elements of autonomous intelligence systems being tested range from the use of straightforward preprogrammed navigational landmarks and underwater terrain indicators to more sophisticated feedback interaction between the vehicle's guidance system and underwater features and terrain.

The first generation of autonomous ROVs is expected to be capable of conducting controlled surveys at great depths, mainly by transporting cameras and/or basic instrument packages through assigned underwater domains. Future development may include an ability to perform tasks involving measurement, site clearance, and recording more akin to conventional archaeology. It will probably be at least a decade before autonomous ROVs become operational and can offer results comparable or superior to existing ROV technology, but the results so far are promising.

Richard A. Gould

See also NAUTICAL ARCHAEOLOGY; UNDERWATER ARCHAEOLOGY

Further Readings

Gould, R.A. (1988) The U.S. S. *Monitor* Project research design. In W.B. Cogar (ed.): Naval History: The Seventh Symposium of the U.S. Naval Academy, Wilmington: Scholarly Resource, pp. 83–88.

Holden, C. (1985) Americans and French find the *Titanic. Science* 229:1368–1369.

Stewart, W.K. (1991) Multisensor visualization for underwater archaeology. Institute of Electrical and Electronics Engineers (IEEE) Computer Graphics and Application 11(2):13–18.

Travis, J. (1993) ABE and *Odyssey:* AUVs test the waters. *Science* 259:1534–1535.

Renfrew, Andrew Colin (1937–)

British archaeologist and prehistorian. More widely known as Colin Renfrew, he was born on July 25, 1937, and educated at Saint John's College, Cambridge, where he studied archaeology under such luminaries as Glyn Daniel and Sheppard Frere. Renfrew received his bachelor's (with honors) in 1962, his master's in 1964, and his doctorate in 1965, writing his dissertation on Cycladic prehistory. After a brief period at the British School of Archaeology in Athens, Renfrew returned to Britain to teach at the University of Sheffield, where he was lecturer in archaeology and prehistory (1965–1972). He then moved on to Southampton University, where he taught until 1981, before returning to Cambridge and succeeding Glyn Daniel as the Disney Professor of Archaeology. Renfrew was named master of Jesus College, Cambridge, in 1986, and created Life Peer and Baron Renfrew of Kaimsthorn (of Hurlet in the District of Renfrew) in 1991.

Renfrew is an important British prehistorian who has, in the tradition of V. Gordon Childe and Grahame Clark, challenged conventional notions concerning Old World prehistory and archaeological methodology. As a graduate student, Renfrew was influenced by the systems-theory movement and utilized systems models in his studies of Cycladic prehistory. In the now-classic *Emergence of Civilization*, Renfrew used work he had done at Saliagos and other Cycladic islands to illustrate the usefulness of characterizing human culture as a series of interrelating systems and offered convincing models explaining prehistoric Aegean trade systems. While at Sheffield, Renfrew had an opportunity to lecture in the United States and came into contact with important figures in the American New Archaeology movement. At UCLA, he met Lewis R. Binford, and at the University of Michigan Robert Braidwood; in later years, he would continually renew his contacts with influential New World archaeologists, keeping him in the forefront of methodological developments.

Renfrew is also well known for his support of radiocarbon dating and its role in the rewriting of prehistory. Ignoring early skepticism, Renfrew espoused a new view of European prehistory in his landmark *Before Civilisation,* a view that was based upon a radiocarbon chronology, rejected the diffusionism of Childe and his followers, and treated prehistoric European culture not as a backwater but as an innovative cultural phenomenon. *Before Civilization* also revealed Renfrew's interest in discovering and studying nonmaterial aspects of human societies, what he calls *social archaeology* or *the archaeology of the mind,* not just chronologies and artifact studies. He has continued this in *The Archaeology of Cult,* in which he attempts to reconstruct cult and other complex societal phenomena based on his excavations at sites such as Phylakopi on the Aegean island of Melos, and *Archaeology and Language,* his controversial reevaluation of Indo-European studies. Renfrew continues to be a force in world prehistory.

Joseph J. Basile

See also BINFORD, LEWIS R.; CHILDE, VERE GORDON; CLARK, JOHN GRAHAME DOUGLAS; NEW/PROCESSUAL ARCHAEOLOGY; RADIOCARBON DATING; SOCIAL ARCHAEOLOGY

Further Readings

Renfrew, A.C. (1972) The Emergence of Civilisation: The Cyclades and the Aegean in the Third Millennium B.C. London: Methuen.

Renfrew, A.C. (1979a) Before Civilisation: The Radiocarbon Revolution and Prehistoric Europe, rev. ed. Cambridge, UK/New York: Cambridge University Press.

Renfrew, A.C. (1979b) Problems in European Prehistory: A Collection of 18 Papers. Edinburgh: Edinburgh University Press/New York: Cambridge University Press.

Renfrew, A.C. (1984) Approaches to Social Archaeology. Edinburgh: Edinburgh University Press/Cambridge, MA: Harvard University Press.

Renfrew, A.C. (1985) The Archaeology of Cult: The Sanctuary of Phylakopi. London: British School of Archaeology at Athens.

Renfrew, A.C. (1987) Archaeology and Language: The Puzzle of Indo-European Origins. London: J. Cape/New York: Cambridge University Press.

Renfrew, A.C. (1993) The Roots of Ethnicity, Archaeology, Genetics and the Origins of Europe. Rome: Unione Internazionale degli Istituti di Archeologia, Storia e Storia del Arte in Roma.

Renfrew, A.C. and Bahn, P. (1996) Archaeology: Theories, Methods, and Practice, 2nd. ed. London: Thames and Hudson.

Renfrew, A.C. and Cherry, J.F., eds. (1986) Peer Polity Interaction and Socio-Political Change. Cambridge, UK/New York: Cambridge University Press.

Renfrew, A.C. and Shennan, S., eds. (1982) Ranking, Resource, and Exchange: Aspects of the Archaeology of Early European Society. Cambridge, UK/New York: Cambridge University Press.

Renfrew, A.C. and Zubrow, E.B.W., eds. (1994) The Ancient Mind: Elements of Cognitive Archaeology. Cambridge, UK/New York: Cambridge University Press.

Reverse Stratigraphy

A situation in which some archaeologists consider that the order of clearly observable depositional layers at a site is reversed. A basic principle in the analysis and interpretation of strata is the *Law of Superposition,* which means that, at archaeological sites, the earliest depositional layers are found at the bottom, while the latest are found at the top. Reverse stratigraphy refers to a specific stratigraphic situation in which the usual depositional and chronological order of strata are reversed, requiring strata to be interpreted upside down. For instance, when graves are placed beneath the floors of structures or in large mounds, the soil that is removed by the original inhabitants to create a burial area is redeposited elsewhere. In the process, strata are reordered; in the redeposited soil removed from the graves, later layers are likely to be situated at the base of the soil and earlier layers at the top. The causes of reversed strata may be cultural, as the example above suggests, or natural, such as geological movement or flooding, although there is less agreement among archaeologists on the validity of the latter. Indeed, some archaeologists insist that the entire notion of reverse stratigraphy is a false one and that the real issue is the repositioning of temporally sensitive artifacts, and not entire strata, into different areas of a site.

Edward Luby

See also STRATIFICATION; STRATIGRAPHY

Further Readings

Barker, P. (1993) Techniques of Archaeological Excavation, 3rd ed. London: Batsford.

Joukowsky, M. (1980) A Complete Manual of Field Archaeology. Englewood Cliffs, NJ: Prentice-Hall.

Rock-Art Dating

Rock art can be divided into *pictographs* (rock paintings), *petroglyphs* (rock engravings), or *geoglyphs* (ground figures). This entry divides new advances on rock-art dating into the different types of age-determination techniques. Dating (or age-determination) techniques are subdivided into those that yield numerical, correlated, calibrated, or relative ages. Numerical methods provide specific interval data on ages; radiometric clocks, such as radiocarbon or K/Ar (potassium-argon), are common numerical methods; other numerical approaches include thermoluminescence and uranium-series dating. Correlated approaches depend upon an event of known age to be used as the correlation tool, such as a unique symbol in iconography or a unique volcanic ash in tephrochronology. Calibrated methods use numerical ages to calibrate a time signal; an example would be radiocarbon ages used to calibrate the thickness of obsidian hydration rinds. Relative techniques provide only an ordering from oldest to youngest. *Absolute* and *date* are now considered to be imprecise geochronological terms because they connote far more precision than most age-determination techniques are able to yield.

Relative Ages

The most common and most reliable relative-dating method is superimposition of one motif over another. When the art is not in direct physical contact, it is still possible to extract a relative age sequence for petroglyphs through differential development of rock-varnish layers. Climatic changes can alter the type of rock varnish that forms on petroglyphs, leaving behind layers (Figure 1). Younger engravings experience fewer climatic changes than older petroglyphs and, hence, have a simpler layering pattern.

The progressive darkening of a petroglyph over time, often called *repatination,* is used to infer older ages for darker engravings. The assumption is that the rock coating darkens and covers more of the petroglyph with time. Progressive weathering of an engraved rock is also thought to relate to time because frost weathering, lichen acids, fire, and various chemical weathering processes all act to give an engraving a more decayed appearance, and more time exposed to weathering increases the appearance of decay.

Although repatination and weathering are used extensively, they are influenced by microenvironmental variables other than time that are almost impossible to control from panel to panel, including potential evapotranspiration, energy balance, runoff patterns, dust deposition, proximity to different types of vegetation, proximity to different types of rock-surface organisms, the acidity of rock-surface solutions, and surface roughness.

Petroglyph PEFO-7

Backscatter image (organics black)

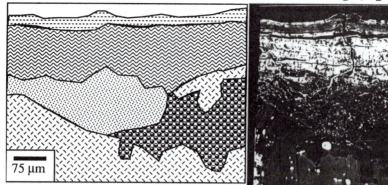

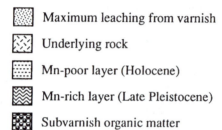

Secondary image, PEFO-7(organics bright)

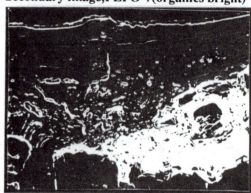

▨ Maximum leaching from varnish

▧ Underlying rock

▦ Mn-poor layer (Holocene)

〰 Mn-rich layer (Late Pleistocene)

▦ Subvarnish organic matter

Figure 1. Late Pleistocene microstratigraphy of rock varnish found on a grid petroglyph, PEFO-7, from Petrified Forest National Park in Arizona. The purpose of this figure is to illustrate the layering seen in varnishes formed on a petroglyph, as well as the context of subvarnish organic matter. Areas of cation leaching (for cation-ratio dating) are also shown. The upper row shows a backscatter electron micrograph (in which brightness is proportional to average atomic number) and a map showing an Mn-poor Holocene layer on the Mn-rich Late Pleistocene layer. The bottom row presents a matching view of PEFO-7, but imaged by secondary electrons, a technique in which topography is shown and organic matter often charges brightly. Color views of different degrees of varnish layering are shown in R.I. Dorn (1992), and the theory behind the dating of varnish layers is presented by Liu (1994). Figure by Ronald I. Dorn.

In other words, a petroglyph may appear darker or more weathered (and, hence, look older) than a nearby motif, but this could simply be from a different microenvironment.

Calibrated Ages

Cation-ratio (CR) dating is based on the observation by researchers from Russia, China, South Africa, Australia, and the United States that the ratio of $(K^+ + Ca^{2+})/Ti^{4+}$ lowers over time. The process involved in the lowering of the CR is leaching of mobile cations, such as K^+ and Ca^{2+}, from locations of capillary waterflow in rock varnish, while stable cations, such as Ti^{4+}, remain, leading to a lowering of the CR over time. When calibrated by inde-

pendent ages for landforms, cation-leaching curves (Figure 2) have yielded calibrated ages for petroglyphs in the western United States and Australia. (For a review on the method and results, see Dorn 1998). CR dating is experimental and controversial, but Lawrence L. Loendorf has subjected this method to blind tests, and it has performed well; its great advantages rest in its low cost and the fact that ages can be estimated in circumstances in which no other technique will work.

Another calibrated method is *microerosion dating*, used only by Robert Bednarik (1992). The assumption is that progressive weathering occurs on crystals originally fractured during

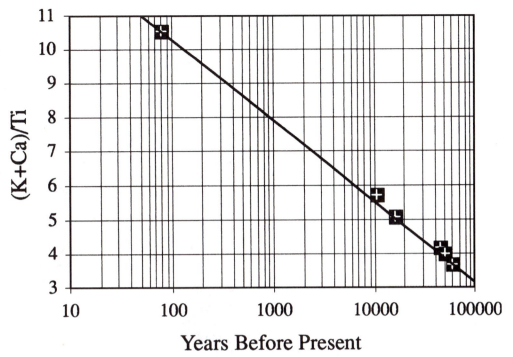

Figure 2. Cation-leaching curve for the Coso Range in eastern California, a least-squares semilog regression that compares cosmogenic and radiocarbon ages for nearby landforms (x-axis) with cation ratios (y-axis) on varnishes. Crosses show one sigma uncertainties. Petroglyph dating from this region is discussed in detail by Whitley (1998) Figure by Ronald I. Dorn.

petroglyph manufacturing, and the rate of weathering can be calibrated at sites of known age. Like any other weathering-based method discussed above in the relative-age section, microenvironmental influences remain uncontrolled. In addition, the method suffers from an inherent contradiction that makes it unworkable. A key assumption with the method is that it cannot be used where rock coatings form over petroglyphs or where the minerals in a petroglyph are eroding. Yet, rock coatings form on petroglyphs in *all* terrestrial weathering environments, except motifs that are eroding too fast for them to develop. This means that microerosion dating is applicable only in places where petroglyphs are too young (generally less than a few thousand years) for a coating to form.

Correlated Ages
Symbols in rock art have been correlated to similar motifs associated with specific time periods. In some circumstances, such as Chinese rock art, correlated ages can be quite precise because they are in writing styles of known

calendar age. In other cases, such as the geoglyphs of Peru, geoglyphs are correlated with pottery iconography. Iconographic correlations are controversial, in some cases, because motif identifications are sometimes subjective.

Some progress is being made in the correlation of rock art with tephrochronology–the identification of volcanic ash (*tephra*). Volcanic ash has been identified in rock varnishes from petroglyphs in the Coso Range and from silica-oxalate coatings from the Mono Basin, both in eastern California. It is, therefore, possible that coatings on rock art might contain identifiable volcanic ashes. If so, the rock art would predate the ash.

Numerical Ages
The development of accelerator mass spectrometry (AMS) radiocarbon (carbon-14) dating has revolutionized numerical age-determination of rock art, because milligram-quantities of material can be measured with a precision of less than 5 percent. This continues to open up new possibilities in rock art-dating.

Two basic approaches are taken to the radiocarbon dating of rock art. Pictograph dating is accomplished by AMS ^{14}C dating of milligrams of organic carbon used in making the paint pigment. In determining petroglyph and geoglyph ages, archaeologists use natural rock coatings that form over the human-modified rock surfaces.

Analyses of the pigment or overlying rock coating are considered by most researchers to be experimental because the contemporaneity of organic matter at rock surfaces is uncertain. For pictographs, the carbon in the paint may have predated the painting, because it could have been from older sources of carbon (e.g., old wood), or the carbon could have been added after the painting was made (e.g., organic molecules washed down a rock face and adsorbed by the pigment). For petroglyphs and geoglyphs, the rock coating does definitely postdate the art, but this provides only a minimum-limiting age. Also, both approaches usually suffer from the uncertainty of not knowing exactly the nature of the organic matter being dated. Despite these uncertainties, since the mid-1980s there has been an explosion of research on AMS ^{14}C dating of rock art.

Pictographs are being assigned numerical ages by AMS ^{14}C dating of charcoal, human blood, plant fibers, and beeswax found within the paint pigment. Yet, many pictographs have organic constituents that disseminated throughout the pigment and cannot be identified clearly. One of the most exciting new advances is the nondestructive *plasma-chemical selective* removal of organic carbon from pictographs—pioneered at the Department of Chemistry at Texas A&M University by Jon Russ and colleagues. This is an especially appealing approach because the type of carbon can be preselected by varying the plasma treatment; organic carbon can be separated from the carbon contained in calcium carbonate, oxalate, and magnesium carbonate or the effects of the underlying rock. Unlike any other approach being used in the late twentieth century, the plasma approach can remove organic carbon from any paint sample that contains organic matter. This is especially valuable in the very many paintings in which specific compounds cannot be identified or extracted by any other method.

Petroglyphs and geoglyphs have also been assigned ages by AMS ^{14}C dating of organic carbon encapsulated within rock coatings or under rock coatings. This approach of dating encapsulated organics has been applied to rock art from Australia, Europe, Hawaii, South America, as well as the western United States.

Research in Portugal has shown that this approach yields ambiguous ages, because the carbon system appears to be open. For example, although Alan Watchman and Ronald Dorn obtained statistically identical results in a blind test, the radiocarbon ages for these petroglyphs are not valid. This is because there is a mixture of younger and older types of carbon—making any archaeological interpretation of the radiocarbon ages ambiguous (Dorn, 1997).

The Future of Rock Art Dating

Several key trends hold great promise for the age determination of rock art. First, where specific materials (e.g., charcoal) can be mechanically extracted from paint pigment, AMS ^{14}C dating can be tested by understanding the potential for contamination in these specific materials. Second, for the many pictographs in which organic matter is disseminated throughout the pigment, the plasma-chemical selective approach offers the only hope for numerical age control. Third, for petroglyphs and geoglyphs, the layering patterns of rock varnish hold the greatest potential for assigning ages. Fourth, ongoing studies of the contemporeneity of carbon in rock-art contexts are vital to help resolve uncertainties regarding whether older or younger organic matter can contaminate a sample. As blind tests continue to assess uncertainties, the age-determination of rock art will become less experimental.

Ronald I. Dorn

See also DATING, METHOD AND THEORY; RADIOCARBON DATING; ROCK-ART SITES, RECORDING AND ANALYSIS; TEPHROCHRONOLOGY; THERMOLUMINESCENCE DATING; URANIUM-SERIES DATING

Further Readings

Bednarik, R. (1992) A new method to date petroglyphs. Archaeometry 34:279–291.

Clarkson, P. (1990) The archaeology of the Nazca Pampa: Environmental and cultural parameters. In A.F. Aveni (ed.): The Lines of Nazca, pp. 117–172. (American Philosophical Society Memoirs 183). Philadelphia: American Philosophical Society.

Clottes, J. (1993) Paint analyses from several Magdalenian caves in the Ariège region of France. Journal of Archaeological Science 20:223–235.

Dorn, R.I. (1992) Paleoenvironmental signals in rock varnish on petroglyphs. American Indian Rock Art 18:1–17.

Dorn, R.I. (1997) Constraining the age of the Cta Valley (Portugal) engravings with radiocarbon dating. Antiquity 71:105–115.

Dorn, R.I. (1998) Age determination of the Coso rock art. In E. Younkin (ed.) Coso Rock Art, pp. 69–96. Ridgecrest: Maturango.

Ilger, W., Hyman, M., Southon, J., and Rowe, M. (1995) Dating pictographs with radiocarbon. Radiocarbon 37:299–310.

Liu, T. (1994) Visual Microlaminations in Rock Varnish: A New Paleoenvironmental and Geomorphic Tool in Drylands. Ph.D. Dissertation. Tempe: Arizona State University.

Loendorf, L. (1991) Cation-ratio varnish dating and petroglyph chronology in southeastern Colorado. Antiquity 65:246–255.

Whitley, D.S. (1998) A Guide to Rock Art Sites. Southern California and Southern Nevada. Missoula, MT: Mountain Press.

Rock-Art Sites, Recording and Analysis

The mapping, illustration, photography, excavation, analysis, and interpretation of prehistoric rock-art sites. Rock-art sites are places where there are *pictographs* (paintings) or *petroglyphs* (engravings or pecked designs) on rock. Through the years, researchers recording rock art have used a variety of techniques, but archaeologists have learned that many of these techniques damage or destroy the art. Experiments have shown that techniques such as making molds for casts damage the rock varnish or patina and that rubbings introduce chemical changes in the rock's surface. One of the unfortunate consequences of these previously accepted recording techniques is that they alter the ability to use new and developing rock-art-dating methods. Because of such problems, recommended rock-art recording techniques are those that can be completed without touching the rock surface.

Basic rock-art recording is much like other archaeological-site recording. Using the best available maps, archaeologists locate the site. A datum is established on the site, usually by burying a 30-cm length of iron bar to serve as a permanent reference point. The purpose of establishing a datum is so that researchers can relocate the rock art and its mapping reference points at a future date. Researchers then make a site map showing the locations of various features on site. On large sites, low-level aerial photographs can be useful in recording the locations of outcrops of rock with rock art on them.

Rock-art sites are divided into panels of pictographs or petroglyphs. A *panel* is defined as a single image or a group of images in proximity to one another on a rock surface that is oriented, for the most part, in one direction. The division of rock art into panels is a classification procedure used to assist the archaeologist in recording the site; like many classification systems, its definition can change from site to site.

Archaeologists usually subdivide rock-art panels into elements or individual pictographs and petroglyphs. The generic term *anthropomorph* is used for humanlike figures because they may represent either supernatural beings or human beings. For a similar reason, the term *zoomorph* is used for animal figures that cannot be differentiated, like an elk from a deer.

Scale drawings and *sketches* are a frequent rock-art-recording technique. In scale drawings, the artist employs a ruler or tape measure to assist in reducing the images on the rock to a scale rendering on paper. Grids made of string or other flexible materials are sometimes placed over the rock-art panel to assist in making the scale drawing. Considerable care has to be used so as to not damage the rock art when placing the grid system over a panel.

Photography is a common way to record rock art. Because they are relatively inexpensive and have readily available interchangeable lens and filters, 35mm cameras are usually used in rock-art photography. Natural light is employed whenever possible, and archaeologists usually do a light study of the site to learn when the rock art appears best. For example, subdued light can enhance colors in some pictographs, and side light will usually make petroglyphs easier to photograph. Reflectors are useful in directing sunlight toward a rock-art panel. Artificial light is often necessary in caves and rockshelters. Extensions that allow the photographer to orient the flash from different angles, such as side-flash for petroglyphs, are also helpful.

Black-and-white and color films can each be used with success and will often show different details on the same site. Experiments with infrared films suggest that they are sometimes useful in capturing details of faded paint. Filters can be used to reduce surface glare and to improve the color in a pictograph. At least one photograph of each panel is taken directly from the front. That photo should include a scale, a directional arrow, and a data board with information such as the site number, the panel number, and the date. Other photographs are taken, without the recording paraphernalia, from the angles that most appropriately show the rock art.

Written information accompanies the sketches, scale drawings, and photographs; it includes measurements of the size of the panels and the individual petroglyphs or pictographs, the direction the panel is facing, the hardness of the rock, and the color of the rock and the rock art. It is often possible to determine whether the painting was put on the rock with the artist's finger or with a brush or to learn whether a petroglyph was made by incising or by pecking into the rock surface. This sort of information is important for comparison of the rock art between sites and regions.

Usually, after the basic recording is completed, specialists are invited to the site to obtain samples for analyzing the pigment and to obtain dates for the rock art. Since the 1980s in North America and Australia, the sampling of rock art is completed with consultation from indigenous peoples.

Periodically, an archaeologist might undertake controlled excavations at a rock-art site. These can be useful to uncover any buried parts of a panel, and, in some instances, the archaeologist can recover datable materials from deposits overlying a rock-art panel. The artifacts used in making the rock art can be recovered and can assist the archaeologist in learning how the art was completed. Specialized samples—pollen, flotation, and so on—taken during excavation may help an archaeologist identify medicinal or ceremonial plants that were used at the site.

Another important part of rock-art research is the protection and conservation of the sites. There are conservators that special-ize in the study of rock art and the methods by which sites can be protected. Frequently, rock-art sites are destroyed by people who leave graffiti, shoot at or chip away at the art, or perform other acts of vandalism. Conservators have developed methods for controlling visitors at rock-art sites. In instances in which graffiti has been put on the rocks, they use various methods to reduce or remove it.

Basic analysis of rock art follows standard archaeological procedures. Rock-art *types* are created with the same rules and procedures that are employed in developing any typology. Rock-art types are combined into *styles,* which can be defined as similar types of pictographs and petroglyphs found within established space and time boundaries.

Although typologies have been developed, few archaeologists have emphasized rock art in their research. This is especially true in North America, where traditional archaeological models have relied upon the historical sequences of cultures, because rock art has often defied placement within those sequences. Until recently, there have been few ways to date rock art, and the lack of time control has hampered the use of rock-art styles as a culturally diagnostic tool. As better control on the age of pictographs and petroglyphs is developed, rock art will play an increasingly important role in studies of migration and other movements of people from one region to another.

In the study of former societies, rock art is extremely important because it allows archaeologists an opportunity to make inferences about the ideological component of culture. This is particularly true with hunting-and-gathering cultures, in which there is much interaction between humans and the supernatural world. Rock art offers a glimpse into the ideology of these individuals and the cultures they represent.

Significant progress has been made with the interpretation of rock art. One model suggests that many basic rock-art forms are interrelated with the initial stages of an altered state of consciousness or a trance when human beings see phosphenes or little patterns of light within their eyes (called *entoptic phenomena*). Other rock-art images are related to later stages in the trance. In many parts of the world, rock-art sites are considered by Native people to be places of power where individuals went to fast, pray, and seek supernatural power. The power the supplicant receives at these sites can be used for curing or prophesy. Native American individuals who receive rattlesnake power can usually cure rattlesnake bites, and those who get prophesy power can forecast the weather. It is also apparent that some people recognize spiritual forces that inhabit the rocks. The rock art is related to communication with these spirits.

Rock-art researchers have learned that rock-art designs are frequently symbolic. Groups of pictographs that appear to represent one thing are often a metaphor for something else. In South Africa, a wounded and stumbling eland appears to represent a successful hunting expedition, but the Bushman envision the eland as a power animal. A pictograph of a dying eland is actually a symbolic metaphor that indicates a trance when a shaman visited a supernatural realm.

Although the meaning of much rock art is lost to time, some figures are still recognizable within indigenous cultures. In Australia, supernatural figures important to the Aborigines are depicted on the rocks. Other rock art, especially among groups that practice horticulture, is related to calendrical events. In these cultures, spirals and circles can be used to denote the solstices and other phases of the solar calendar. Some researchers claim to have found ancient Ogam writings from the European Celtic culture on the rocks in North America, but these interpretations are questionable and highly controversial.

Because rock art is so apparent and visible on the landscape, it is popular with the public. Throughout the world, much of the significant research at rock-art sites has been completed by artists, astronomers, and interested avocational researchers. Organizations such as the American Rock Art Research Association (ARARA) and the Australian Rock Art Association (AURA) are made up of a mix of people who have an interest in recording and preserving rock art.

Larry L. Loendorf

See also BREUIL, HENRI; CAVES AND ROCK-SHELTERS, EXCAVATION; LEROI-GOURHAN, ANDRE; ROCK-ART DATING; SYMBOLIC ARCHAEOLOGY

Further Readings

Keyser, J. (1992) Indian Rock Art of the Columbia Plateau. Seattle and London: University of Washington Press.

Lewis-Williams, J.D. (1981) Believing and Seeing: Symbolic Meaning in Southern San Rock Paintings. London: Academic.

Lewis-Williams, J.D., and Dowson, T.A. (1988) The signs of all times: Entoptic phenomena in Upper Paleolithic art. Current Anthropology 29:201–245.

Sanger, K.K., and Meighan C.W. (1990) Discovering Prehistoric Rock Art. Calabasas, CA: Wormwood.

Schaafsma, P. (1980) Indian Rock Art of the Southwest. Albuquerque: University of New Mexico Press.

Turpin, S. ed. (1994) Shamanism and Rock Art in North America. San Antonio, TX: Rock Art Foundation.

Wellman, K. (1979) A Survey of North American Indian Rock Art. Graz, Austria: Akademische Druck und Verlagsanstalt.

Whitley, D.S. (1992) Shamanism and rock art in far western North America. Cambridge Archaeological Journal 2:89–113.

Whitley, D.S. (1994) By the hunter, for the gatherer: Art, subsistence, and social relations in the prehistoric Great Basin. World Archaeology 25:356–373.

Whitley, D., and Loendorf, L., eds. (1994) New Light on Old Art: Recent Advances in Hunter-Gatherer Rock Art Research. (Monograph 36). Los Angeles, CA: Institute of Archaeology, UCLA.

Rocks and Minerals, Characterization

A class of inorganic, naturally occurring materials, and the methods used by archaeologists and geologists for identification and for technological reconstruction, the determination of tool use, and the establishment of provenance. The history of the use of rocks and minerals follows the evolution of humans themselves, in continuity to the present, and their modification constitutes perhaps the oldest surviving evidence for technology. Rocks and minerals have been used for the production of utilitarian (e.g., tools, vessels, and weapons) and ornamental (e.g., jewelry), objects, statuary, and other sculptures; as a surface for inscriptions and painted or incised artwork; in the building of structures (domestic, public, and monumental); in ancient engineering (e.g., arches, aquaducts, road-building); as materials in the service of other technologies (e.g., food preparation, pottery production, abrasives, concrete, plaster, pigments); and in the practice of religious ritual (e.g., construction of stone circles, cairns, tombs, sarcophagi). As a result, the description, analysis, and understanding of stone materials in history and prehistory have produced a considerable corpus of archaeological and geoarchaeological scholarship.

Definitions

Archaeologists use the word *lithic* (from the Greek *lithos,* meaning stone or rock) for materials made from rocks or minerals. Geological nomenclature also makes extensive use of this Greek root, in such terms as *lithification* (the compaction and cementation of an unconsolidated sediment into a coherent, solid rock), *lithology* (the description of the characteristics of a rock, such as color, mineralogy, and grain size) and *lithosphere* (the solid portion of the Earth, as contrasted with atmosphere and hydrosphere).

A *rock* is a specific aggregate of one or more minerals that occurs commonly enough to be given a name (e.g., granite, limestone); a *mineral* is a naturally occurring inorganic element or compound having a specific crystal structure and a characteristic chemical composition (e.g. quartz, mica). Obsidian is a volcanic glass that has not yet crystallized into minerals but in all other respects is a rock. The word *stone* has many meanings. Within an archaeological context, the usage should be restricted to building stone and gemstone.

Few areas of lithic nomenclature are as confusing as the names for the fine-grained varieties of quartz (SiO_2). Quartz is important because rocks and minerals composed chiefly of quartz make up a large percentage of lithic artifacts. Quartz is the most stable of all minerals under sedimentary conditions and in the Earth's surface environment. *Chert* is the general term for fine-grained quartzose rocks of chemical, biochemical, or biogenic origin. It is a very hard (quartz has a Mohs hardness of seven—see below) and compact material that fractures conchoidally when struck. Chert can be almost any color and can accommodate a wide variety of impurities that affect its workability in lithic manufacture. Grain size also has a significant effect on fracture properties. X-ray diffraction (XRD) or petrography

(using a polarizing microscope) can be used to identify and characterize lithic materials.

Semiprecious stones (actually they are minerals) are gemstones of lesser value than precious stones, such as diamond and emerald. They normally have a hardness of seven or less on the Mohs hardness scale. The most common semiprecious stones used by ancient craftsmen are varieties of quartz.

Hardness

The hardness of a mineral is defined as its resistance to scratching. Relative hardness has been employed as a useful diagnostic property since the earliest systematic mineralogy. Hardness was quantified by the Austrian mineralogist Friedrich Mohs, who proposed the following scale of relative hardness in 1822: (1) talc; (2) gypsum; (3) calcite; (4) fluorite; (5) apatite; (6) orthoclase; (7) quartz; (8) topaz; (9) corundum; (10) diamond. In practice, this means that each of the minerals lower in the scale will be scratched by those higher in the scale. It must be noted that the scale is not linear; in absolute hardness, diamond is three orders of magnitude harder than talc. However, it is a tribute to Mohs that the scale he established is still used today in unaltered form.

Hardness is an important diagnostic property for the field identification of minerals. In addition to the minerals in the scale, or any mineral for that matter, the following materials serve as handy reference for hardness: fingernail: from a little more than 2 to 2.5; copper coin: ca. 3; pocket knife: from a little more than 5 to 5.5; window glass: 5.5; steel file : 6.5.

Rocks per se, as assemblages of minerals, do not have a Mohs hardness. Some monomineralic rocks like quartzite and marble will exhibit the hardness of the constituent mineral. A rocklike granite, composed of orthoclase and quartz, would exhibit a Mohs hardness between six and seven. However, the importance of granite for building stone lies not in its hardness but in its cohesiveness and its mechanical strength.

Classification of Rocks

The major rock types are classified as *igneous* (from the Latin for fire), those that formed from molten magma; *sedimentary,* those that formed from the consolidation of deposited clastic particles or by precipitation from solution; and *metamorphic* (from the Greek for change of form), those that formed by major alteration of preexisting rocks by the action of high temperature and pressure.

Coarse-grained igneous rocks, such as granite and diorite, are fairly abundant, often mechanically tough and free of cracks, aesthetically pleasing, and capable of taking a high polish; they have been widely used in construction of large monuments. The Pharaonic Egyptians carved single large obelisks from the granite at Aswan and used diorite for large statues. Not all coarse-grained igneous rocks used in ancient Egypt and called diorite by archaeologists are actually diorites. Granite and diorite vary considerably in composition, texture, color, and durability.

Utilization of Materials and Methods of Analysis

Construction

The nature of the building materials employed by any society depends primarily on the kind of materials available. It was no accident that the great tells of the Middle East formed from the disintegration of mud-brick buildings. There were neither hard-rock outcrops nor trees for hundreds of kilometers. Except for timber, almost all building materials are minerals or based on minerals. Ancient Egypt, Greece, and Rome were responsible for great advances in the use of stone for building. By 3050 B.C., the Egyptians had learned to shape their comparatively soft Tertiary limestones into rectangular blocks. Before 2050 B.C., they had learned how shape the more difficult granite.

Numerous distinct types of hard rocks, including limestone, sandstone, granite, and gneiss, make good building stone. The necessary characteristics are: (1) structural strength (ability to carry a load without failure); (2) durability (resistance to weathering); (3) ease of quarrying and dressing; and (4) availability (the energy cost of transportation).

Areas of analytical research interest in ancient structures have focused on the provenance of the raw materials used in the construction of buildings and monuments. In any determination of provenance, geological maps of the region should always be consulted first, followed by research into the history of quarrying in the region and study of any prior archaeological or geological surveys or reports of evidence of prehistoric quarrying or incidental discoveries of abandoned prehistoric

tools. Surveys of potential geological outcrops may have to made, together with assessments of the logistics of quarrying and the feasibility of land or water transportation in antiquity. Where multiple sources of rocks or minerals were available, making identification of sources ambiguous, petrographic analysis, as well as trace-element analysis (if necessary), of multiple samples from both archaeological structures and the possible geological outcrops may have to be conducted. Significant success has been achieved in the determination of the provenance of marble used for building, sculpture, and inscriptions in the Mediterranean region through analysis of stable isotopes of carbon and oxygen, as exemplified by the work of Norman Herz.

Objects

Objects made of rocks and minerals are perhaps the oldest surviving evidence of technology in human society. The manufacture of stone tools and weapons, as well as any other products, is dependent on local geological resources. Most stone tools were manufactured through a subtractive technology (i.e., through mechanical fracture, such as percussion flaking or pressure flaking) until the desired form was achieved. Therefore, where possible, fine-grained varieties of quartz (e.g., chert, flint) or volcanic glass (obsidian) were preferred for the production of chipped-stone tools, since these materials are hard, capable of producing a sharp edge, and can be flaked easily since there are no preferential lines of fracture. Basaltic and quartzitic rocks—which, although more durable, are more difficult to work—were also used in stone-tool manufacture. Other types of rocks, either because of grain size or the method of formation, could not be utilized for flaking and, therefore, if they were useful at all, were shaped by pounding with hammers made of harder rocks or by grinding with rocks or sand and by polishing with sand impregnated in another substance (leather or tarred surface).

Areas of archaeological research on objects manufactured from rocks and minerals include, but are not limited to, documenting advancements in lithic technology, understanding the uses to which objects were put, identifying geological sources for objects of local production, and determining the provenance of imported objects with documentation of trade routes. Some of the earliest and most prolific archaeological studies of stone tools focused on the reconstruction of ancient technology and were accomplished through both microscopic examination of artifacts and the production of lithic objects by archaeologists themselves (experimental archaeology). The determination of how stone artifacts are used, especially tools for everyday tasks, has developed into a specialization *(use-wear analysis)* requiring experimental archaeology together with studies of edge use and damage, using a binocular microscope and, occasionally, a scanning electron microscope (SEM). Determining the provenance of raw materials, both local and long distance, used in the manufacture of objects requires procedures similar to the determination of the provenance of building stone (i.e., archaeological surveying, geological research, petrographic analysis of samples taken from both objects and possible rock outcrops, and, if necessary, trace-element analysis). X-ray fluorescence (XRF) analysis, neutron activation analysis, atomic absorption (AA) spectrometry, and inductively coupled plasma–atomic emission spectrometry can be used for trace-element determination on geological materials.

Survival of Stone Artifacts and Structures in the Archaeological Record

The deterioration of stone artifacts and monuments proceeds from (1) chemical attack and dissolution; (2) mechanical disintegration caused by water freezing in pores and cracks; (3) abrasion due to wind-driven particles; (4) exfoliation due to rapid heating and cooling; (5) disintegration resulting from the activities of organisms; (6) the formation of crystals on the surface; and (7) damage from ill-advised efforts at conservation or restoration.

All materials expand and contract with temperature change. These changes in dimensions are not in themselves harmful. It is the combination of dissimilar expansions or contractions where two different materials are combined that produces mechanical disintegration. For example, lime mortar has a coefficient of linear thermal expansion that is ca. 50 percent greater than that for bricks.

An important part of human culture is chiseled in stone, and these stones are slowly weathering away. Even ancient Greek and Roman writers were aware of this phenomenon. In sandstones in which the clastic particles are composed of quartz—a highly resistant mineral—the cementing agent is likely to be the vulnerable component. Calcite cement suffers from the same chemical problems as limestone and marble. If the cementing is weak, abrasion caused by particles in wind can cause rapid mechanical disintegration. Even quarrying methods can have an effect on stone deterioration. Ancient manual quarrying methods will have done less mechanical damage than modern methods using a pneumatic hammer whose vibrations cause microcracks. All worked surfaces more easily acquire adhering carbonaceous particles that are good catalysts for the hydration of atmospheric sulfur dioxide to sulfuric acid. Mineralogical and petrographic analyses, along with chemical analysis when necessary, are the methods needed to understand rocks and rock weathering. Many geologists can identify upward of 200 minerals with the aid of a hand lens. Petrographic analysis permits the determination of porosity and permeability, two important parameters in judging the susceptibility of rocks to chemical weathering.

The chemical treatments of stone undergoing conservation or restoration are beyond the scope of this entry. What the archaeologist needs to understand about stone conservation is the stability or instability of rock materials in various environments. It is largely a consequence of insufficient knowledge of rocks in given chemical environments that has resulted in a century of failures in conservation treatment of stone sculpture, monuments, and buildings.

George R. Rapp Jr.

See also ATOMIC ABSORPTION (AA) SPECTROMETRY; EXPERIMENTAL ARCHAEOLOGY; INDUCTIVELY COUPLED PLASMA–ATOMIC EMISSION SPECTROMETRY; MARBLE, CHARACTERIZATION; PETROGRAPHY; STONE, ON-SITE CONSERVATION; USE-WEAR ANALYSIS; X-RAY DIFFRACTION (XRD) ANALYSIS; X-RAY FLUORESCENCE (XRF) ANALYSIS

Further Readings

Herz, N. (1982) Geological sources of building stone. In Conservation of Historic Stone Buildings and Monuments, pp. 49–61. Washington, D.C.: National Academy Press.

Kempe, D., and Harvey, A., eds. (1983) The Petrology of Archaeological Artefacts. Oxford: Clarendon.

Luedtke, B. (1992) Archaeologist's Guide to Chert and Flint. (Archaeological Research Tools 7). Los Angeles: Institute of Archaeology, UCLA.

Winkler, E. (1982) Problems in the deterioration of stone. In Conservation of Historic Stone Buildings and Monuments, pp. 108–119. Washington, D.C.: National Academy Press.

Rouse, Irving Benjamin (1913–)

Noted theoretical archaeologist and Caribbean specialist. Rouse was born in Rochester, New York, where an exceptional high school academic record led to a fellowship to Yale University and the award of a bachelor's in 1934. He received his doctorate in anthropology, also at Yale, in 1938. Rouse spent his entire professional career at Yale (instructor, 1939–1943; assistant professor, 1943–1948; associate professor, 1948–1954; professor, 1954–1970; Charles J. McCurdy Professor of Anthropology, 1970–1984; professor emeritus, 1984–). He twice chaired the Department of Anthropology (1957–1963, 1979–1980). Rouse also was associated with the Yale Peabody Museum from his student days; after receiving his doctorate, he progressed through ranks there as well (assistant curator, 1938–1947; associate curator, 1947–1954; research associate, 1954–1962; research affiliate, 1975–1977; curator of anthropology, 1977–1984; curator emeritus, 1984–). Rouse served as editor of *American Antiquity* (1946–1950); he was also president of the Society for American Archaeology (1952–1953) and the American Anthropological Association (1967–1968). Other recognitions include the prestigious Viking Fund Medal (1959) and election to the National Academy of Science (1968).

His dissertation was based on fieldwork in Haiti, and one of the resulting publications, *Prehistory in Haiti: A Study in Method* was a crucial methodological component in the emergence of culture history as a paradigm. One of the central issues addressed is archaeological classification, an interest Rouse continued to pursue throughout his career. His classic "Classification of Artifacts in Archaeology" has been widely reprinted as well as cited. The interest in Caribbean archaeology has likewise been lifelong, and Rouse's effectiveness in this arena has been enhanced by his collaborations with Latin American scholars. Also growing out of *Prehistory in Haiti* has been an interest in migration as a mechanism to explain artifact distributions. His *Migrations in Prehistory: Inferring Population Movement from Cultural Remains* not only summarizes that work, but also provides the most modern exegesis of the culture-historical approach extant. He continues to be an active researcher in Caribbean archaeology.

While the Caribbean has always been his principal interest, he played an active role in New England archaeology from his graduate student days through the 1950s. His focus was on ceramic classification and chronology, and he made lasting contributions in these areas. His New England work was marked by close and effective interaction with amateur archaeologists.

Robert C. Dunnell

Further Readings

Rouse, I.B. (1958) The inference of migrations from anthropological evidence. In R.H. Thompson (ed.): Migrations in New World Culture History, pp. 63–68. Tucson, AZ: University of Arizona Press.

Rouse, I.B. (1960) The classification of artifacts in archaeology. American Antiquity 25:313–323.

Rouse, I.B. (1964) Prehistory in Haiti: A Study in Method. (Yale University Publications in Anthropology 21). Reprinted, Human Relations Area Files, New Haven. Originally published 1939, New Haven, CT: Yale University Press/ London: Oxford University Press.

Rouse, I.B. (1965) The place of 'peoples' in prehistoric research. Journal of the Royal Anthropological Institute 95:1–15.

Rouse, I.B. (1986) Migrations in Prehistory: Inferring Population Movement from Cultural Remains. New Haven, CT: Yale University Press.

Rouse, I.B. (1992) The Tainos: Rise and Decline of the People Who Greeted Columbus. New Haven, CT: Yale University Press.

R

S

Salvage/Rescue Archaeology

Field research, usually involving excavation, conducted at sites scheduled for destruction by some modern undertaking, such as the construction of a highway, dam, or building. In the United States, the term *salvage archaeology* is most closely associated with a set of government-funded programs that were initiated following the end of the Second World War and persisted until the advent of cultural resource management legislation in the 1960s. There is a tendency in the United States to draw a contrast between salvage archaeology and cultural resource management, and the latter term is now used almost exclusively. Rescue archaeology has a more common usage internationally and in England.

Salvage archaeology programs in the United States began with the implementation of the River Basin Surveys in 1947. This was a government-funded program established following the end of the war to deal with archaeological sites threatened by plans for the construction of reservoirs. A second initiative resulted in the passing of the Federal Aid Highway Act of 1956 and established a program to salvage archaeological sites threatened by the construction of federal highways. These kinds of programs, dealing with specific types of actions and a limited number of federal agencies, were gradually superseded in the late 1960s and early 1970s with the passage of legislation calling for the management of all cultural resources, prehistoric and historic, that were threatened by all federally funded undertakings and/or were on land administered by federal agencies.

The River Basin Surveys

The history of the River Basin Surveys begins with the formation in 1945 of the Committee for the Recovery of Archaeological Remains to present the concern of archaeologists to the federal government and to work with the federal agencies in developing a program to salvage sites that were to be inundated by the proposed construction of a series of dams throughout the country. The committee was drawn from the membership of the Society for American Archaeology, the American Anthropological Association, and the American Council of Learned Societies, and included John O. Brew (Peabody Museum), Alfred V. Kidder (Carnegie Institute of Washington), Frederick Johnson (R.S. Peabody Foundation for Archaeology) and William S. Webb (University of Kentucky).

In the years just prior to the Second World War, the Bureau of Reclamation and the United States Army Corps of Engineers had developed plans for the construction of dams on the Missouri River and its tributaries, as well as on smaller drainage systems in other parts of the country. With the end of the war, these agencies were prepared to begin, and in some cases had already begun, the construction of these dams. The directors of these agencies, aware that archaeological sites lay within the areas that were to be inundated, notified the National Park Service and the archaeological community in general about the scale and immediacy of the potential threat to archaeological sites. The scientific community responded with the formation of the Committee for the Recovery of Archaeological Remains, which was delegated to work with the government agencies in developing a course of action.

The result was the establishment of the River Basin Surveys. This federal program was initially placed under the supervision of the Smithsonian Institution, although funding from Congress was channeled through the National Park Service, which also coordinated with the Army Corps of Engineers and the Bureau of Reclamation. The most immediate problem lay in the Missouri River Valley, and in 1946 a field office for the Missouri River Basin Survey was established at the University of Nebraska.

The Smithsonian Institution eventually established three other River Basin Survey offices, in Eugene, Oregon; Austin, Texas; and Atlanta, Georgia. However, the involvement of the National Park Service continued to grow, and following 1957 it assumed direct administrative responsibility for all but the Missouri River Basin Survey. The National Park Service, through the establishment of its Interagency Archeological Salvage Program ("salvage" was later dropped from the name), increasingly assisted other agencies in the funding of archaeological programs; to this day, it maintains a major role in defining the role of federally funded archaeology. During the era of salvage programs, the National Park Service generally established cooperative agreements (rather than contracts) with local academic institutions to conduct the research, and the institutions regularly matched the funding from the Park Service, either in services or in funds, in nearly equal amounts.

Most of the effort of the River Basin Surveys focused in the Missouri River drainage, an area extending across ten states and two Canadian provinces and comparable to one-sixth of the area of the United States. In physiographic terms, the drainage encompasses most of the central Plains, and the Missouri River Basin Survey was a major force in the development of Plains archaeology. Even as early as 1945, the plans by the Bureau of Reclamation and the Army Corps of Engineers called for the construction of more than 100 dams in the Missouri watershed, creating lakes of up to 150–300 km in length and inundating long stretches of valley bottomland. The riparian areas of the local river valleys figured heavily in the prehistoric adaptations to the plains, and George C. Frison, well known for his work in Plains archaeology, estimates that nearly 80 percent of all archaeological sites in the region were ultimately submerged beneath the lakes formed behind these dams.

Archaeologists were well aware in 1946 that major portions of the nation's prehistory were threatened. The sense of urgency and the enthusiasm of the discipline in rising to the challenge are well reflected in the writings from that period. In a symposium held at the forty-fifth annual meeting (1946) of the American Anthropological Association and subsequently published in *American Antiquity* (Brew et al. 1947), the contributors describe the enormity of the potential loss and an appreciation for the organizational skills that were to be needed in implementing the program. The discussion provided by Frederick Johnson sounds particularly current. The information (rather than simply the artifacts) contained in sites was described as a national cultural resource for which archaeologists had assumed responsibility. The objective of the Committee for the Recovery of Archaeological Remains was ensuring that the information about the threatened archaeological remains was preserved, not only through excavation but also through publication. This was not to be another "make work" project, like the archaeology conducted under the Works Progress Administration (WPA) during the Depression; this time, the objective was completely scientific. The research was to be problem oriented, but, unlike past archaeological projects that had been developed around the interests of a few researchers, archaeologists were now confronted with a need to deal at one time with the full range of problems that might arise for any given region. Other participants in the symposium observed that the discipline was embarking on a new kind of archaeology, one that was scientifically oriented and was to draw on the full cooperation of the profession. To provide the necessary pool of trained archaeologists, work on other cherished projects not threatened by the construction might have to be postponed. As early as a year following the formation of the committee, a number of institutions had begun contributing the results of their own field surveys into a growing pool of information. State historical and archaeological societies, which included avocationalists, were also busy conducting surveys of threatened valleys in an effort to identify the numbers of threatened sites.

Highway Salvage Archaeology

In 1954, Fred Wendorf, an archaeologist working in New Mexico, voiced his concern about archaeological sites that were being destroyed by the construction of both state and federal highways. This led the Department of Transportation (then the Bureau of Public Roads) to institute provisions for the funding of archaeological salvage programs, and these provisions were subsequently formalized in the Federal Aid Highway Act of 1956. Passage of this act established an interesting precedent by authorizing a federal agency not directly involved with archaeology (such as the National Park Service) to expend its own funds on the excavation of archaeological remains. Now, under cultural resources management legislation, it is common for federal agencies to include funding in their annual budgets for the excavation or protection of cultural resources.

State involvement in the federal highway salvage programs was voluntary, and participation by the states varied considerably. One constraint was that the individual state governments had to match some of the funds received for archaeology from the federal government, which required both a willingness and the necessary legislation authorizing the expenditures of funds for that purpose. The most active archaeological salvage programs were in the states of New Mexico and Illinois, followed by Arizona, California, and Idaho. Twenty-one states had not participated in highway archaeological salvage programs at all in the period 1956–1969.

Criticisms of Salvage Archaeology on Substantive Grounds

The criticisms of salvage archaeology are grouped into two categories: substantive and theoretical. Substantive criticisms stem from the assumption that the urgency of the situation does not allow archaeologists sufficient time for the proper execution of the fieldwork, and this may result in the lowering of standards. With adequate planning, however, salvage and rescue excavations can be conducted long before the sites are actually destroyed, and the impending destruction of the sites does not necessarily need to be a factor constraining the research. Furthermore, all archaeological fieldwork, whether funded through a salvage program or conducted in an academic setting, is always conducted under constraints of available personnel, funding, and, by extension, the amount of time available. Academic programs frequently include the use of student assistants who are in the process of gaining field experience and constitute essentially untrained personnel. The potential for substandard work is a specter that faces research conducted in any context. The one difference may lie in visibility, since inferior research conducted in academic settings lies unreported and unnoticed even within the sponsoring institution.

A related criticism is that salvage archaeology projects may not be adequately supervised. Because archaeological fieldwork is labor intensive and frequently necessitates the use of large crews, the success of field research has very much to do with the competency and managerial skills of the supervising researchers. The management of the research can be adversely affected through poor organization, such as by an inadequate ratio of supervisors to fieldworkers, or the inabilities of a senior researcher to deal with the complexities of the decision making required during fieldwork and in the management of large numbers of field personnel. Again, such shortcomings are scarcely limited to only rescue and salvage operations. The success of archaeological fieldwork rests heavily on the strategic and tactical skills of the senior field personnel, and, while such skills can be discussed in the literature and taught in classroom settings, they are honed through application in the field. To this extent, then, the researchers who have large levels of involvement in salvage operations are likely to have greater opportunities to practice such skills than their peers who received funding for "pure" research.

Salvage archaeology is also subject to the criticism that the fieldwork cannot be checked by other archaeologists since the sites are destroyed following the fieldwork. Clearly, there is little to be gained among archaeologists in the falsification of data, but there is the possibility that the observations of the supervising archaeologists may be subconsciously biased and that they may have inadequate time to examine the deposits (especially stratigraphic profiles) under varying lighting and conditions. This is an appropriate concern. Emil Haury, the eminent Southwestern archaeologist from the University of Arizona who conducted extensive excavations at the Hohokam site of Snaketown in Arizona, reported that canals from the earliest period in the development of the site were not visible until the profiles of several exploratory trenches had been allowed to weather over several weeks. There is also considerable utility in having an opportunity to discuss the interpretation of archaeological deposits with fellow archaeologists. Again, these kinds of problems are not inherent in salvage and rescue archaeology. If there is adequate coordination, the rescue archaeology can be conducted long in advance of the project that will ultimately destroy the sites. Work performed under the aegis of cultural resources management frequently allows sufficient time for such considerations, and the federal agencies almost invariably insist that provisions be made to consult with one's peers.

This criticism that field observations conducted in salvage work may be unconsciously biased is also overstated, in that it fails to acknowledge the important role that analysis plays during and after the fieldwork. Inconsistencies or outright errors in field observations can be detected by an adequate program of analysis, and the analytical program can either rectify the biases or at least demonstrate that bias exists to such an extent as to make the data unusable. There is, therefore, little danger that archaeological interpretations will build on an increasingly more erroneous database.

Criticisms of Salvage Archaeology on Theoretical Grounds

Salvage archaeology has also been criticized as largely atheoretical, inductive, and particularistic and characterized as having fundamentally different values than academic archaeology. This criticism elevates a funding program to nearly the status of a discipline and could as easily have been applied at the time to many of the field schools being taught within academic settings. The greater scale of funding for salvage archaeology (the annual National Park Service funding of archaeology was at least double that of the National Science Foundation throughout most of the 1960s) made such projects more visible and, therefore, more likely subjects for criticism. Salvage archaeology developed within the intellectual framework of American archaeology and involved some of the most prestigious scholars in the discipline. Moreover, salvage

work conducted between the end of the Second World War and the mid-1960s was performed almost exclusively through academic departments in national universities and colleges. Salvage archaeology may have been the most visible component of field research, and perhaps the implementation of some programs merited criticism, but it was also very much a part of American archaeology.

There is no denying that much of the archaeological research conducted in the 1950s and 1960s, salvage or otherwise, lacked explicitly formulated designs. Culture history dominated archaeological thinking at the time, and the lack of major competing paradigms might account for the implicit course many archaeologists followed in the implementation of research. This did not make the culture history paradigm unscientific, though, in some cases, it may have made for sloppy science. The primary objective of culture history was, and remains, the construction of chronologies, and in this the paradigm has had some of its greatest success as a science. Culture history makes use of laws (e.g., the Law of Superposition) and mathematical principles (e.g., the Law of Monotonic Decline on which the seriation method is founded), and propositions in culture history are capable of being rejected on the basis of empirical evidence.

By the late 1960s, however, American archaeologists had expanded their interests beyond chronology and were more concerned with explaining cultural change (the recognition of which rested upon the success of chronological studies). The adoption of new goals within the discipline necessitated the modification of research, in both the field and the laboratory, but these changes did not occur immediately in salvage archaeology or in academic programs. The frustrations on the part of some archaeologists with the way that data were being collected was valid. However, the imagined threat that government agencies might limit salvage funding to only one paradigm of research, while the academic realm pursued another, did not materialize.

The growth of federal funding of rescue archaeology, from the WPA programs of the 1930s through salvage archaeology (1945–1969) to the cultural resources management projects of today (since 1969), has advanced archaeological research methods in a particularly unique way. With the progression of these programs, American archaeology has increasingly improved the body of managerial methods and strategies needed for the conduct of large-scale research. Since the funding of very large projects is rare to nonexistent within the realm of pure academic research, the development of this body of methods has lain almost completely within the sphere of salvage work. Archaeological research requires the formation and coordination of large research teams, the handling of formidable logistical issues at times, the management and tracking of complex sequences of tasks (many conducted concurrently), and, increasingly, the synthesis of data from multidisciplinary studies. WPA archaeology suffered on all of these grounds; there were too few trained personnel attempting to supervise too many untrained workers, and virtually no provisions were made for the arduous tasks of analyzing and reporting results. From its inception, salvage archaeology incorporated a more sophisticated concern for the staging of research; it recognized the need for adequate supervision and well-trained workers, and, in the area of publication of results, it was frequently more successful and timely than research conducted for strictly academic purposes. Archaeology performed in the service of cultural resources management programs has continued to keep abreast of developments within the discipline at large. Survey work is conducted well in advance of the planned construction events, which allows for a considered approach to the research and for the modification of planned construction projects in ways that help to physically preserve cultural properties. Research programs begin with the development of detailed research designs; time and funds are available for laboratory analysis and the writing of reports; and, increasingly, federal agencies are interested in the funding of programs for public interpretation.

Glen Eugene Rice

See also CULTURAL RESOURCE MANAGEMENT (CRM); WPA ARCHAEOLOGY

Further Readings

Brew, J.O., Strong, W.D., Johnson, F., Kahler, H.E., Roberts, F.H.H., Jr., Wedel, W.R., Champe, J.L., and Caldwell, J.C. (1947) Symposium on river valley archaeology. American Antiquity 12(4):209–225.
Frison, G.C. (1973) The Plains. In J.E. Fitting (ed.): The Development of North American Archaeology, pp. 151–184. Garden City, NJ: Anchor/Doubleday.
Jennings, J.D. (1963) Administration of contract emergency archaeological programs. American Antiquity 28(3):282–285.
King, T.F. (1971) A conflict of values in American archaeology. American Antiquity 36(3):255–262.
McGimsey, C.R., III (1972) Public Archaeology. New York and London: Seminar.

Sampling

The selection of a subset from a collection of objects in order to draw conclusions about the collection as a whole. The usual term for a collection is *population*; for the subset, the term is *sample*. The aim may be either to estimate parameter(s) of the population or to test a hypothesis about it. The reasons for sampling rather than examining the whole population are twofold: It may cost too much to examine the whole population, and, by examining a reduced number of objects, it may be possible to devote more time to each, thus improving the quality of the data collected.

In a sense, sampling is something that archaeologists have always done in an intuitive way. A more rigorous approach emerged in the 1970s out of the New Archaeology of the late 1960s and, after some mistakes and criticisms, settled down as a routine part of fieldwork methodology.

Today, uses of sampling are widespread in archaeology, at many scales. At the largest scale, archaeologists may select samples from a region, for field walking or other types of survey, to gain an impression of the nature of the region without having to examine all of it. Much the same applies at the level of the excavation of a site: Resources (time, money, and personnel) may not be sufficient for the total excavation of a site, or total excavation may not be needed to achieve the objectives of the excavation. During excavation, archaeologists may wish to take samples from features (e.g., soil samples from pits) for further analysis, or they may wish to sample on site from excavated groups of common "bulk" materials (e.g., building materials, such as brick or tile).

At the postexcavation stage, archaeologists may take samples for scientific or other analyses or even (though this is contentious) for retention. Surveys of the condition of museum collections often use sampling strategies to reduce the task to manageable size. Even at a microscopic level, archaeologists may use sampling methods (e.g., in the selection of inclusions in a pottery section for particle-size analysis). Finally, there is the view that, because of archaeological transforms, all archaeological materials are samples, and that sampling theory is, therefore, central to their interpretation.

In each situation, archaeologists must choose an appropriate sampling strategy; the fundamental requirement is that the sample should be representative of its population (i.e., that it should, within limitations imposed by its size, accurately reflect the parameter[s] of its population). The only way to ensure this is to use *random sampling;* other approaches (e.g., *grab sampling, judgment* or *purposive sampling*) are in use but do not permit the calculation of the precision of estimates based on them. Secondary requirements of a sampling method or strategy are that it should be efficient (i.e., it should give the required information with the minimum of effort or as much information as possible from the effort devoted to it) and practical. Various strategies can improve the efficiency of a random-sampling strategy; the two most commonly used in archaeology are *stratified sampling* and *cluster sampling,* but many others are available, including *multistage sampling* and sampling with *probability proportional to size (pps).* A new technique which could prove of great value in archaeology is *adaptive sampling,* and in particular *adaptive cluster sampling.* The baseline on which they must improve if they are to be of value is *simple random sampling.* The technique of *systematic sampling,* which is additional to, not a substitute for, any of the above techniques, can sometimes make the practical taking of samples much easier, though it is not always without risk to the accuracy of the results.

An important feature of the design of a sampling strategy is the need for a *pilot sample.* This is a preliminary sample based on a small fraction of the ultimate sample size that gives information that goes into producing an efficient sample design and identifies any practical problems that need resolution before the main program goes ahead.

Random Sampling

A sampling strategy is *random,* and samples selected by it are *random samples,* if, for each member of the population, there is a known or calculable probability that it will be selected for a sample. It is important to note that one cannot tell whether a sample is random or not simply by inspection; one must know the procedure by which it was selected. This definition implies that the archaeologist knows the population well enough to be able to list it (the technical term is to *enumerate* it). For example, in selecting artifacts from a collection for further study, there must be a list of them or at least a way of listing them. This requirement can cause problems in field survey, in which, typically, an aim is to search for and characterize sites. Unless the area is very well known, the population cannot consist of sites (since many are unknown and, therefore, not enumerable). The population consists of units of land, which are enumerable (e.g., as grid squares on a map or plot numbers in a cadastral survey), and the sites are properties or variables of the land.

The simplest random-sampling strategy is, not surprisingly, *simple random sampling.* Its definition is that all members of the population have the same probability of selection. This formulation makes the statistical theory particularly simple, so that it is easy to calculate standard deviations of estimate, giving limits within which the true values of parameters are likely to lie, at a chosen level of confidence. The selection of a sample is also relatively simple; the archaeologist gives all members a unique identifying number and selects by using a computer random-number generator or published tables of random numbers. The archaeologist should avoid less formal ways of selecting random numbers. A small point that is often overlooked is that most of the statistical theory assumes *sampling with replacement* (i.e., selected objects return to the population and are available for reselection), while practice is usually *sampling without replacement* (i.e., selected objects do not return to the population). However, the distinction is not serious unless the sampling fraction (the ratio of sample size to population size) is large.

Stratified Sampling

The term *stratified sampling* sometimes causes confusion because it has nothing whatever to do with archaeological stratification. The idea is to improve the efficiency of a sampling strategy by bringing together in groups, or *strata,* members of a population that are expected to have broadly similar values of the parameter of interest. For example, a region might consist of several topographical or ecological zones, which could form the basis for a stratification of the grid squares that make up the region. The archaeologist takes a separate sample from each stratum and calculates the results for each stratum separately, before aggregating the figures to give overall results. Sensible definition of the strata eliminates, from the overall variability between the objects, that part that is due to the variability between the strata, thus improving the efficiency of the strategy, since there is less variability left to reduce. The choice of different sampling fractions for the different strata further improves efficiency, provided that the most variable strata have the highest sampling fractions. It is essential to carry out a pilot sample to check that the definitions of strata are sensible and to ascertain which are the most variable.

Cluster Sampling

An ideal sample survey devotes as much of its resources as possible to examining the selected objects and as little as possible to the overheads of selecting and locating them. In practice, there is little scope for streamlining the selection process (but see *systematic sampling* below), but locating objects can cause severe problems. For example, in a field survey it may be time consuming to locate the chosen quadrats (cells in a grid pattern) or transects. One solution is to select small groups of contiguous units, or *clusters,* instead of individual ones. This may well be statistically less efficient, in the sense that the archaeologist has to select a larger sample (more units) to achieve the required level of precision, since there is a tendency for data values at nearby locations to be correlated with each other and, therefore, give less information than the same number of noncontiguous ones (referred to as *spatial autocorrelation*). But the savings in time and effort that result from the need to find fewer locations, since locating one member of a cluster effectively locates the whole cluster, may mean that, overall, the archaeologist can sample more units in the same time. This increase may outweigh the loss in efficiency of the individual units. Again, theory can take one only so far, and a pilot sample is necessary to make it relevant to the situation.

Adaptive Sampling

The basic idea of adaptive sampling is that the design of the sample is modified, or adapted, in light of the outcome of the early stages of sampling, according to statistical principles that are specified in advance. In adaptive cluster sampling, for example, an initial sample of quadrats is selected and examined. Further quadrats are sampled adjacent to those in which *objects* (e.g., archaeological sites) were discovered, and so on. The technique is particularly advantageous when the spatial distribution of objects being studied is itself clustered.

Systematic Sampling

Systematic sampling is a way of speeding up the selection of samples while maintaining a necessary element of randomness. Instead of choosing a fresh random number for each selection, the archaeologist chooses one random number for the first selected object, and then increases it by uniform amounts until the whole sample has been selected. For example, if one wants to select a sample of 100 from a population of 1,000 objects, one would, rather than select 100 random numbers, select one random number between 1 and 10 (the 10 is because the sampling fraction is 100/1,000, i.e., 1/10) and then add multiples of 10 to get all of the other numbers (e.g., 7, 17, 27, and so on). This is much quicker, but it can be risky, especially if the population has a spatial pattern. For example, if they are grid squares on a map, a systematic sample could consist of squares all lying toward one edge of the map or lying in a line across it. The archaeologist must check the sample to make sure this does not happen.

Other Techniques

Sampling theory contains many techniques that archaeologists rarely, if ever, use. One such is *multistage sampling:* the archaeologist first selects a sample of *first-stage units* (clusters of the units under study) and, from each selected first-stage unit, makes a selection of *second-stage units,* which the archaeologist then samples (this is *two-stage sampling,* extensible to any number of stages but, in practice, rarely beyond three). This can be a useful approach in collection-condition surveys, in which the first-stage units can be shelves, the second-stage boxes, and the third individual objects. This effectively controls the time spent locating objects and so improves efficiency. A refinement is to vary the probability of selection of first-stage units according to the number of second-stage ones they contain (*probability proportional to size,* or *pps sampling;* or *ppes, probability proportional to estimated size,* if it uses estimates of the numbers contained). This approach would also allow basic topographical features (e.g., fields) to be first-stage units in a field survey, again speeding up the processes of selection and location.

More work is needed to make a wider range of statistical theory more accessible to archaeologists.

Clive Orton

See also COMPUTER SIMULATION; NEW/ PROCESSUAL ARCHAEOLOGY; SPATIAL ANALYSIS

Further Readings

Cherry, J.F., Gamble, C., and Shennan, S., eds. (1978) Sampling in Contemporary British Archaeology. (BAR British Series 50). Oxford: British Archaeological Reports.

Hole, B. (1980) Sampling in archaeology: A critique. Annual Review of Anthropology 9:217–234.

Keene, S., and Orton, C. (1992) Measuring the condition of museum collections. In G. Lock and J. Moffett (eds.): Computer Applications and Quantitative Methods in Archaeology 1991, pp. 163–166. (BAR International Series 577). Oxford: British Archaeological Reports.

Mueller, J.W., ed. (1975) Sampling in Archaeology. Tucson: University of Arizona Press.

Shennan, S.J. (1997) Quantifying Archaeology, 2nd ed. Edinburgh: Edinburgh University Press.

Schiffer, Michael Brian (1947–)

American archaeologist and anthropologist. Born on October 4, 1947, in Winnipeg, Manitoba, Canada, Schiffer came to the United States in 1953 and was naturalized in 1962. He was awarded a bachelor's from UCLA in 1969 and took his master's and Ph.D. at the University of Arizona in 1972 and 1973, respectively. Schiffer began his professional career in Arkansas, with the Arkansas Archeological Survey, as assistant archeologist, and at the University of Arkansas at Fayetteville, as an assistant professor of anthropology (1973–1975). He returned to the American Southwest, as assistant professor of anthropology at the University of Arizona (1975–1979), associate professor 1979–1982), and then full professor. He is a Fellow of the American Anthropological Association and the American Association for the Advancement of Science and was designated a Woodrow Wilson Fellow (1969).

Schiffer's work with the Arkansas Archeological Survey culminated in a monograph, coassembled with John A. House, *The Cache River Archeological Project: An Experiment in Contract Archeology* and a book, coedited with George J. Gumerman, *Conservation Archaeology: A Guide for Cultural Resource Management Studies,* both of which had a major impact on the development of contract/conservation/CRM archaeology in the United States and elsewhere. Schiffer and colleagues demonstrated that cultural resources management (CRM) projects could and had to meet the highest standards of academic research and, moreover, could contribute to the growth of archaeological method and theory.

Schiffer became well known in the 1970s for his development of an analytical approach to the study of material culture and human behavior, which was labeled *behavioral archaeology* by a collective of scholars at the University of Arizona and which is defined in his publications "Behavioral Archaeology: Four Strategies," coauthored with J. Jefferson Reid and William L. Rathje, and *Behavioral Archeology.* A major contribution to the study of archaeological formation processes to understand past behavior patterns is Schiffer's *Formation Processes of the Archaeological Record.* In addition to his individual contributions to method and theory, Schiffer has edited three serial publications that have served as a forum for other archaeologists of every theoretical persuasion to address issues of theory and method: *Advances in Archaeological Method and Theory, Archaeological Method and Theory,* and *Journal of Archaeological Method and Theory.*

Since the mid-1980s, Schiffer's work has moved into other arenas in behavioral archaeology, particularly the study of technological and behavioral change. To facilitate the work on technology, especially in the area of experimental archaeology, Schiffer built the Laboratory of Traditional Technology (LTT) at the University of Arizona. This facility is dedicated to studying experimentally the effects of technical choices on the performance characteristics of artifacts, especially ceramic artifacts. Many publications have resulted from the work carried out by Schiffer and his students at LTT. Two of the most important experimental ceramic studies, which explicitly address issues of theory, especially the place of experimental archaeology in contributing to the growth of explanatory theory, are "Theory and Experiment in the Study of Technological Change," coauthored with James M. Skibo, and "New Perspectives on Experimental Archaeology: Surface Treatments and Thermal Response of the Clay Cooking Pot," co-authored with the collective team from LTT. Schiffer has extended his anthropological and archaeological studies of technology and behavioral change to include the recent past and present, which is reflected in three books: *The Portable Radio in American Life, Technological Perspectives on Behavioral Change,* and *Taking Charge: The Electric Automobile in America,* coauthored with Tamara Butts and Kimberly Grimm.

Joseph J. Basile

See also BEHAVIORAL ARCHAEOLOGY; EXPERIMENTAL ARCHAEOLOGY; CULTURAL RESOURCES MANAGEMENT (CRM)

Further Readings

Schiffer, M.B. (1976) Behavioral Archeology. New York: Academic.

Schiffer, M.B., ed. (1978–1987) Advances in Archaeological Method and Theory, 11 vols. New York: Academic.

Schiffer, M.B., ed. (1989–1993) Archaeological Method and Theory, 5 vols. Tucson: University of Arizona Press.

Schiffer, M.B. (1991) The Portable Radio in American Life. Tucson: University of Arizona Press.

Schiffer, M.B. (1992) Technological Perspectives on Behavioral Change. Tucson: University of Arizona Press.

Schiffer, M.B., ed. (1994–) Journal of Archaeological Method and Theory 1–. New York: Plenum.

Schiffer, M.B. (1995) Behavioral Archaeology: First Principles. Salt Lake City: University of Utah Press.

Schiffer, M.B. (1996) Formation Processes of the Archaeological Record. Reprinted, University of Utah Press, Salt Lake City. Originally published 1987, Albuquerque: University of New Mexico Press.

Schiffer, M.B., and Gumerman, G.J., eds. (1977) Conservation Archaeology: A Guide for Cultural Resource Management Studies. New York: Academic.

Schiffer, M.B., with House, J.A. (1975) The Cache River Archeological Project: An Experiment in Contract Archeology. (Research Series 8). Fayetteville: Arkansas Archeological Survey.

Schiffer, M.B., and Skibo, J.M. (1987) Theory and experiment in the study of technological change. Current Anthropology 28:595–622.

Schiffer, M.B., Butts, T., and Grimm, K. (1994) Taking Charge: The Electric Automobile in America. Washington, D.C.: Smithsonian Institution Press.

Schiffer, M.B., Reid, J.J., and Rathje, W.L. (1975) Behavioral archaeology: Four strategies. American Anthropologist 77:864–869.

Schiffer, M.B., Skibo, J.M., Boelke, T.C., Newpert, M.A., and Aronson, M. (1994) New perspectives in experimental archaeology: Surface treatments and thermal response of the clay cooking pot. American Antiquity 59:197–217.

Trigger, B. (1989) A History of Archaeological Thought. Cambridge: Cambridge University Press.

S

Scollar, Irwin (1928–)

American-born archaeologist Scollar received a bachelor's in electrical engineering from Lehigh University in 1948, a master's in classical archaeology from Columbia University in 1951, and a doctorate in prehistoric archaeology from the University of Edinburgh in 1959. He has been working in Germany since 1959 and is a specialist in aerial photography, archaeological prospection, computer methods, and remote sensing. Formerly head of the Department for Archaeological Prospecting at the Rheinisches Landesmuseum, Scollar was transferred to the Rheinisches Amt für Bodendenkmalpflege when it was separated from its parent organization in 1987. He retired in 1991. Scollar was awarded life chair for computer methods in archaeology at Cologne University in 1989. After retirement, he continued to program and distribute a collection of software tools for archaeological statistics and cartography, which has been registered by more than 400 institutions throughout the world and has been downloaded from the Internet by countless more. In 1999, he was awarded the German Archaeological Prize.

Scollar has been an important figure in the adoption and development of scientific techniques for mapping and detecting buried features in modern archaeology. He was among the first to call for a wider use of aerial photography and pioneered the exploitation of crop marks in Germany (1960–1970), even though such phenomena had been described in the 1920s in Britain and exploited actively thereafter.

He also was a leading figure in the development of accurate maps and plans based on aerial photographs, particularly through the use of computer-generated orthophotographs (the geometric transformation of oblique aerial photos into a picture with uniform scale and vertical orientation). The first large image-processing computer in a museum was installed at his laboratory at the Rheinisches Landesmuseum in 1975 for this purpose.

In the field of archaeometry, Scollar pioneered computer evaluation of resistivity methods (1959) and differential magnetometry (1966) and developed field methods and hardware for these, along with such figures as Martin J. Aitken, Albert Hesse, and Carlo M. Lerici, for the remote sensing of buried archaeological features. His work is summarized in his book *Archaeological Prospecting and Remote Sensing* (1990) which contains a full bibliography up to that date.

Joseph J. Basile

See also AERIAL PHOTOGRAPHY FOR ARCHAEOLOGY; ARCHAEOLOGICAL PROSPECTION; COMPUTERS IN ARCHAEOLOGY

Further Readings

Andresen, J., Madsen, T., and Scollar, I., eds. (1993) *Computing the Past: Computer Applications and Quantitative Methods in Archaeology: CAA92.* (20th Computer Applications in Archaeology Conference.) Aarhus, Denmark: Aarhus University Press.

Scollar, I., Tabbagh, A., Hesse, A., and Herzog, I. (1990) *Archaeological Prospecting and Remote Sensing.* Cambridge, UK/New York: Cambridge University Press.

Seismic Refraction Surveying

Prospecting method based on the detection of seismic waves generated by an artificial source. The method was developed for geological investigations of the Earth's crust. Investigation of near-surface archaeological targets is at the extreme small-scale end of the range of applications.

For small-scale surveys, the source that is commonly used to generate seismic waves is a 6-kg sledgehammer, wielded by hand to strike a rubber pad placed on the ground. Alternatively, explosive detonating caps could be fired in shallow shot holes, but the hammer may be preferred if the geophysical investigation is required to be noninvasive. The signals are detected by geophones at the ground surface. The sensor element in the geophone is a moving coil of copper wire, wound on a former, and suspended on a spring between the poles of a fixed magnet. The dimensions of a geophone are ca. 4×4 cm $\times$ 6 cm high, and each one is fitted with a spike 8 cm long to ensure good mechanical coupling to the ground. Geophones, cables, and suitable

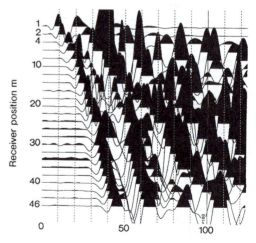

Figure 1. A set of seismograms recorded during a seismic refraction survey using a hammer as the source. The horizontal scale is in milliseconds. Figure by Neil R. Goulty.

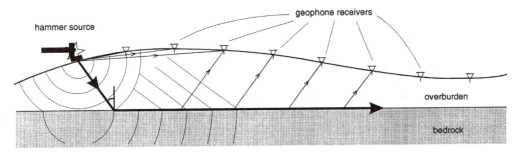

Figure 2. Seismic waves spread out from the source point and refract at the rockhead interface. The first arrival at geophones nearest the source is the direct wave, which has followed a straight-line raypath from source to geophone. At geophones farther from the source, the first arrival is the head wave, resulting from energy incident on the rockhead interface at the critical angle and refracting along the top of bedrock (raypath shown in bold). Energy leaks back up to the surface along parallel raypaths leaving the interface at the critical angle. Figure by Neil R. Goulty.

multichannel recording systems are produced commercially by several manufacturers.

Surveying is carried out along linear profiles. Typically, the recording array consists of twenty-four geophones, spaced 2 m apart. A complete set of twenty-four seismograms is recorded for hammer impacts at each end of the array (Figure 1). To extend the profile, the geophone array can be shifted along the line. Sets of seismograms are then recorded for hammer impacts at each end of the new array position. This process of moving up the geophone array may be repeated indefinitely to make a profile of any chosen length. The overlap between successive array positions must be large enough to ensure that continuous coverage is obtained.

For shallow seismic refraction investigations, the only information normally required from the seismograms are the travel times of the first impulsive seismic arrivals from the source received at each geophone. These are easy to identify as the instants on the record where the seismic traces first deviate from the ambient background noise level. For example, in Figure 1 the first arrival on the geophone located 46 m from the source is at 35 milliseconds.

The first seismic arrival recorded by the geophones closest to the source will be the direct wave that has traveled through the surficial layer. However, seismic velocity generally increases with depth; in particular, the seismic velocity in bedrock is greater than that in the unconsolidated overburden. Consequently, the first arrivals received on geophones farther from the source will be head waves, which have followed raypaths such as those shown in Figure 2. Seismic energy that is incident on

the rockhead interface at the critical angle is refracted along the top of the bedrock at a higher velocity. As it travels along the interface, energy continuously leaks up to the surface, following an upward raypath, which is also defined by the critical angle.

The most commonly used interpretation method for obtaining the depth profile to a refracting interface, such as rockhead, is the *plus-minus method* of Johan G. Hagedoorn. The reader is referred to the Further Readings for details.

There are two types of elastic wave that travel through the body of a solid: In a *compressional wave,* the particle motion is parallel to the direction of propagation; in a *shear wave,* the particle motion is perpendicular to the direction of propagation. Shear-wave velocity is always less than compressional-wave velocity in the same material, and shear waves cannot propagate through fluids. Thus, there is very little shear-wave velocity contrast across the water table in unconsolidated deposits, but a large compressional-wave velocity contrast, which readily gives rise to head waves in a seismic refraction survey.

Where both types of wave can be used successfully, compressional waves tend to yield the better data. The shear-wave data are liable to be contaminated by interference from earlier arriving compressional-wave energy, and horizontal geophones are more susceptible to wind noise. In a new survey area, it may be advisable to run test profiles with both types of wave, as the velocity contrasts in the near surface can be so different for each wave type. For compressional waves, the hammer strikes downward

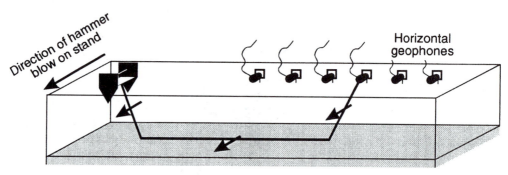

Figure 3. Seismic refraction surveying with shear waves. The hammer strikes the stand in the horizontal direction transverse to the profile. Head-wave energy follows the refracted raypath (shown for the fourth geophone) in the vertical plane, but particle motion is also in the transverse direction. Horizontal geophones must be used as receivers. Figure by Neil R. Goulty.

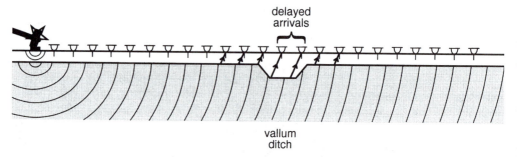

Figure 4. Diagram to illustrate how the vallum ditch was detected at Vindobala in England. The head-wave raypaths leaving the rockhead at the base of the ditch travel through a greater thickness of overburden. Since the overburden has lower seismic velocity than bedrock, the first arrivals at geophones above the ditch show anomalous delays. Figure by Neil R. Goulty.

on to the pad, and geophones are sensitive to particle motion in the vertical direction (Figure 2). For shear waves, a transverse impact may be obtained by swinging a rubber hammer to impact horizontally on a steel stand embedded in the ground surface; geophones sensitive to particle motion in the horizontal direction are used, also oriented transversely to the line of profile, as shown in Figure 3.

The seismic refraction method has been used successfully to locate the course of the vallum around the Roman fort of Vindobala, on Hadrian's Wall, Northumberland, England (Goulty et al. 1990; Goulty and Hudson 1994). The vallum is an earthwork constructed on the south side of Hadrian's Wall along its full length. It is thought not to be a defensive feature, but rather a demarcation line at the southern boundary of the Roman military zone. Its central feature is a ditch, ca. 3 m deep. Around the fort, rockhead is within 3 m of the ground surface, so the ditch was

cut down into bedrock. The site of the fort was grassed over in the mid-eighteenth century, following drastic stone robbing to construct a military road on top of the foundations of Hadrian's Wall. In its neighborhood, all traces of the vallum were obliterated by ridge-and-furrow cultivation and by the construction of a farmstead.

The site was not considered to have high priority for archaeological excavation due to cost, so it provided a good test site for the seismic refraction method where the results would potentially be of interest. Permission to carry out the survey was readily granted, thanks to its noninvasive nature.

Compressional waves gave good results where the water table was below rockhead because there was a large seismic-velocity contrast between the unsaturated glacial drift overburden and the Carboniferous sediments that made up the bedrock. Where the overburden was saturated with water, compressional head waves arose from the water-table interface, masking head-wave arrivals from the rockhead interface below. Fortunately, shear waves gave good results over this part of the survey area.

The data shown in Figure 1 are an example of compressional-wave records obtained from the Vindobala site. The first arrivals on the two geophones nearest the source point are direct waves. The first arrivals on the other geophones are head waves from the rockhead interface, and their arrival times increase approximately linearly with offset from the source. On careful inspection of the records, it may be seen that the first arrivals on the geophones at 26 m and 28 m along the profile are delayed with respect to the linear trend. These geophones correspond to the position of the vallum ditch. The extra travel time is accounted for by the longer raypath through the low-velocity overburden for the head-wave energy returning to the surface from the bottom of the ditch, as shown in Figure 4.

For archaeological applications, the seismic refraction method is a low-resolution technique because of the long wavelength of the seismic waves. Its use is likely to be limited to the investigation of large-scale earthworks, especially where ditches have been cut down into bedrock.

Neil R. Goulty

Further Readings

Goulty, N.R., and Hudson, A.L. (1994) Completion of the seismic refraction survey to locate the vallum at Vindobala, Hadrian's Wall. Archaeometry 36:327–335.

Goulty, N.R., Gibson, J.P. C., Moore, J.G., and Welfare, H. (1990) Delineation of the vallum at Vindobala, Hadrian's Wall, by a shear-wave seismic refraction survey. Archaeometry 32:71–82.

Hagedoorn, J.G. (1959) The plus-minus method of interpreting seismic refraction sections. Geophysical Prospecting 7:158–182.

Sjogren, B. (1984) Shallow Refraction Seismics. Cambridge: Cambridge University Press.

Tsokas, G.N., Papazachos, C. B., Vafidis, A., Loukoyiannakis, M.Z., Vargemezis, G., and Tzimeas, K. (1995) The detection of monumental tombs buried in tumuli by seismic refraction. Geophysics 60:1735–1742.

Semenov, Sergei Aristarkhovich (1898–1978)

Russian anthropologist and archaeologist. Born on September 25, 1898, in Vilnius, Lithuania, Semenov was chief of the Laboratory of Experimental Traseology of the Leningrad Section of the Institute of Archaeology, USSR Academy of Sciences. Semenov was employed as a worker and a teacher until the Russian Revolution of 1917. During the civil war (1917–1920), he fought in Central Asia (Azerbaijan), after which he continued his undergraduate education in social sciences at a military-pedagogical school and in history at the A.I. Hertsen State Pedagogical Institute in Petrograd-Leningrad. In 1937, he completed his thesis in historical sciences, *The Study of the Function of Tools from the Upper Palaeolithic after Traces of Their Use*. After the Second World War, he continued his research in use-wear analysis, and, in 1958, he completed his doctorate in historical sciences. He received first prize from the Presidium of the Academy of Sciences of the USSR (1957) and the State Prize of the USSR (1974). Semenov died on December 6, 1978.

Prominent in the Soviet Union in the late 1950s and 1960s, Semenov was an expert on stone tools and their manufacture and a pioneer in the study of use wear, referred to in Russian publications as *traseology*. Use-wear analysis is the study of microscopic grooves, striations, wear patterns, and other alterations of the working surfaces of stone tools caused by the use of the tool. Different uses will cause distinctive wear patterns; thus, a blade used to cut grasses will have a wear pattern different from one used to dress meat. Prior to modern advances in use-wear analysis, archaeologists and anthropologists were limited to ethnological studies of contemporary stone-tool makers and experimental use of stone tools for the reconstruction of ancient behaviors and tool uses. Semenov was a leader in the development of these modern techniques, including the method for removing samples of the working surfaces of archaeologically recovered stone tools that were small enough and thin enough to be rendered opaque for microscopic analysis. In this way, even the tiniest striations and evidence of wear can be identified. Semenov outlined this technique, as well as comparative analyses of use wear and a study of the manufacture, use, and distribution of stone and bone tools from the Soviet Union in his groundbreaking 1957 volume *Pervobytnaja Tekhnika;* this work was seen as so important when first published that it was translated into English in 1964 under the title *Prehistoric Technology: An Experimental Study of the Oldest Tools and Artefacts from Traces of Manufacture and Wear*. Semenov wrote more than 100 publications, including the books *Razvitie Tekhniki v Kamennom Veke* (The Development of Technology in the Stone Age, 1968), *Proiskhoždenie Zemledelija* (The Origins of Agriculture, 1974), and *Tekhnologija Drevnejšikh Proizvodstv: Mezolit-Eneolit* (The Technology of Ancient Production: Mesolithic to Eneolithic), published posthumously in 1983 with Galina Fedorovna Korobkova.

Joseph J. Basile

See also USE-WEAR ANALYSIS

Further Readings

Semenov, S.A. (1964) Prehistoric Technology: An Experimental Study of the Oldest Tools and Artefacts from Traces of Manufacture and Wear. Trans. M.W. Thompson. London: Cory, Adams & Mackay/New York: Barnes & Noble. [Reprinted, Adams & Dart, Bath, UK (1973); Barnes & Noble, Totowa, NJ (1985).]

Seriation

An archaeological method that uses the temporal distribution of historical classes to chronologically order archaeological events.

The term *seriation* is occasionally used as a synonym for scaling techniques, sometimes to designate any cultural (using artifacts), as opposed to chronometric, dating method, and even, on occasion, simple frequency paragons based on stratigraphy. However, as a method using historical classes to describe archaeological events so that they may be ordered chronologically, seriation has played a critical role in the development of archaeology, especially American archaeology, and remains an important dating tool, as well as the subject of continued development today.

The basic idea from which seriation developed, sometimes called Worsaae's Dictum, is that "kind tells time." This notion played a major role in the differentiation of archaeology from natural history in mid-nineteenth-century Europe, especially in the hands of the Danish scholars Christian Thomsen and Jens Worsaae. Initially, criteria for constructing sequences were technological (e.g., stone-bronze-iron) and theoretically based (a notion of "progress" provides the ordering principle), but, over time, criteria became more opportunistic and empirical (i.e., any criterion that could be shown, usually stratigraphically, to be time sensitive).

Sir Matthew Flinders Petrie is credited with inventing seriation in a 1899 paper. Working with predynastic Egyptian materials, Petrie used ceramics found in graves to develop a chronology. Petrie's break with archaeological tradition was to treat each grave lot as a sample of a continuous sequence of changing forms instead of as an exemplar of a period or a stage. Since the history of Egyptian ceramics must have followed some particular course and thus presented a unique sequence of ceramic type replacements, the *combinations* of ceramic types found in grave lots allowed him to reconstruct the history of ceramics and to arrange the grave lots in chronological order. As in all seriation, the product was just an order; one had to determine independently (usually through superposition) which end of the order was most recent.

Alfred L. Kroeber is credited with stimulating the American development. Kroeber did not cite Petrie's work; further, that the form and context of his proposal were dramatically different from Petrie's argues strongly for independence. Even more convincing is the format of his 1916 seminal *Zuni Potsherds* paper because, in it, Kroeber describes how the idea of extracting chronology from type composition occurred to him. The primitive seriation proposed by Kroeber was quickly amended by Leslie Spier, Alfred V. Kidder, and Nels C. Nelson, all of whom were conducting stratigraphic excavations in the American Southwest. They noticed that when ceramics were described in a particular way—called *stylistic* by Kidder—the temporal distribution of the types took the form of *normal curves*. Coupled with Kroeber's initial insight, it was apparent that a series of assemblages collected from the surface or otherwise undated could be arranged in chronological order by rearranging them so that all type distributions approximated normal curves simultaneously.

As powerful as seriation proved to be, these early formulations were entirely intuitive. The distributions were not normal in a statistical sense. Since knowledge of rates of change was impossible, all that one could say about the characteristic distributions were that they were unimodal (had a single peak frequency and decreased in value away from the peak in both directions; *monotonic* in modern terminology). Furthermore, there was little interest in figuring out why the characteristic distributions occurred. It was enough that they did and could be used to order assemblages. Rationalization was limited to rephrasing the frequency observations as *popularity;* an answer to the question of why stylistic types display normal distributions was that styles simply increased in popularity until they reached a peak and then declined. Such statements are, of course, just descriptions of the observed frequencies. Thus, seriation, was based on an empirical generalization about the distribution of stylistic classes through time.

By the 1930s, use of the method had spread from the Southwest to include the eastern United States and the Arctic; by the 1940s, even Peru and Amazonia had chronologies based on seriation. James A. Ford played a critical role in many of these disseminations and was the only scholar, until recently (Dunnell 1971), to take an interest in seriation as a method. Although Kroeber had been aware of potential problems derived from sample-size effects, Ford brought these considerations to the fore, albeit in an highly intuitive, unquantitative, and, ultimately, incorrect way. More important, he deduced a series of conditions under which the empirical generalization driving seriation might be expected to hold: (1) assemblages seriated must represent brief intervals of time; (2) assemblages seriated must come from the same cultural tradition; and (3) assemblages seriated must come from the same local area. Key terms, such as *brief interval, cultural tradition,* and *local area,* were left undefined.

Ford, like his predecessor, arrived at the final arrangement by eyeballing trial-and-error orderings for conformance to the unimodal-distribution model. For some workers, this was a critical failure of Ford's technique. George Brainerd (1951) and W.S. Robinson (1951) proposed an entirely new technique for arriving at the order of groups. They devised a measure of similarity, since termed the *Brainerd and Robinson Index of Agreement* or simply the *Brainerd and Robinson Coefficient,* with which pairs of assemblages could be compared in terms of type composition. Thus described, they noted that, in correct solutions, the most similar assemblages were adjacent since this order was unique, groups could be chronologically ordered simply by arranging them so that the most similar units were adjacent. Brainerd and Robinson did this by rearranging rows and columns in a square matrix (each group is compared with every other group) of similarity coefficients; in a perfect solution, the magnitude of the similarity coefficients would decrease uniformly (monotonically) away from the axis of identity (the groups compared with themselves). The bulk of the programmatic literature since then has concerned the development of computer programs to find the best solution when a perfect solution is not possible (almost always) and measuring the departure from a perfect solution (stress). Practical work, however, continues to be done much as Ford did it in the 1950s.

Almost all of the early work involved frequencies of stylistic (historical) pottery classes used as attributes of assemblages, the assemblages being groups of artifacts, usually, but not always, pottery. But as Petrie's work showed, the groups ordered might be objects (i.e., groups of attributes). Descriptions used for assemblages were frequencies of historical classes; those for objects were presence/absence tabulations. Robert C. Dunnell (1971) named these alternative forms *frequency* and *occurrence seriation,* respectively. Occurrence seriation was also often used, improperly, for assemblages in which sample sizes were inadequate for frequency seriation. The following year, George L. Cowgill developed a similarity-based approach for occurrence descriptions paralleling the techniques developed by Brainerd and Robinson for frequency descriptions.

There is one final choice. One could insist on an exact match with the unimodal model before regarding an order as chronological, a *deterministic* solution; alternatively, one could accept the "best fit" to the unimodal model as chronological, a *probabilistic* solution. Thus, with two kinds of description (frequency/occurrence), two approaches to ordering (identity/similarity), and two possible solutions (deterministic/probabilistic), there are eight different families of seriation techniques available to archaeologists (see Figure 1).

In his 1971 paper, Dunnell also evaluated Ford's criteria. He found that Ford's first two

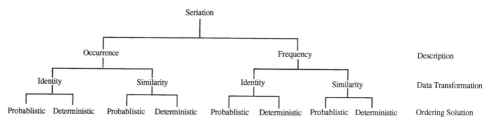

Techniques of seriation. Figure by Robert C. Dunnell.

conditions were sound, and that conditions that groups to be seriated (objects or assemblages of objects) had to meet for the generalization warranting the method were applicable. Groups did not have to be of short duration (time between the addition of the first and last element to the group) in some absolute sense as Ford supposed, but group duration did have to be comparable among the included cases. Groups did have to belong to the same tradition (ancestor-descendent relationships). While there was no way to assess whether these conditions were met a priori by a given set of assemblages, Dunnell showed, using deterministic-identity approaches, seriation could not be made to yield incorrect answers on these grounds, thus securing the chronological warrant for arrangements derived by these techniques. The other techniques are not robust in this regard, and the orders arrived by those means may or may not be chronological.

The local-area criterion proved to be another matter. Dunnell showed that this condition did not apply to the groups to be seriated, as Ford had assumed. Rather, it was a deficiency in the warranting generalization; the method was underdetermined. The generalization spoke only to temporal distributions of types, not their spatial distributions. As Ford intuitively appreciated and others showed empirically in the 1960s, frequencies of types varied in space, and that variation could be mistaken for difference in age. Ford's solution was to limit the amount of space in a seriation, but this was a jerry-rigged solution. To get rid of spatial variations would limit a seriation to a simple point in space; it would be the same thing as superposition. Using the different properties of space and time, Dunnell showed that spatial variation could be eliminated by multiple seriations of the same events using different materials (e.g., pottery types, point types,

grave types) and extracting the common order as chronological. Seriation thus became a more complicated and demanding dating method. Archaeological reaction to this was mixed. Many simply abandoned the method, relying on other methods, such as radiocarbon (^{14}C) dating, wherever possible; others simply ignored the limitations of seriation and continued in the manner of Ford.

A modern resurgence of interest has been simulated by theoretical development. Dunnell (1982) showed that evolutionary theory could explain why the empirical generalizations driving seriation were true to the extent they were and why they failed when they failed. Taking historical classes to represent neutral traits (i.e., traits not under selection because they have no functional impact), the only forces that could act on their temporal and spatial distribution are strictly stochastic (drift). This is what produced the unique, historically unrepetitive sequence of forms on which the method depended and also accounted for the unimodal distributions. Other workers (Neiman 1995; Teltser 1995) have extended this work considerably. Now that the underlying theory is understood, the liability posed by spatial variation for seriation as an empirical method promises to become a major tool for investigating spatial organization of human communities, as well as a dating method.

Robert C. Dunnell

See also DATING, METHOD AND THEORY; DUNNELL, ROBERT C.; FORD, JAMES ALFRED; PETRIE, SIR WILLIAM MATTHEW FLINDERS; THOMSEN, CHRISTIAN JÜRGENSEN

Further Readings

Brainerd, G.W. (1951) The place of chronological ordering in archaeological analysis. American Antiquity 16:301–312.

Cowgill, G.L. (1972) Models, methods, and techniques for seriation. In D.L. Clarke (ed.): Models in Archaeology, pp. 381–424. London: Methuen.

Dunnell, R.C. (1971) Seriation method and its evaluation. American Antiquity 35:305–319.

Dunnell, R.C. (1982) Science, social science, and common sense: The dilemma of modern archaeology. Journal of Anthropological Research 38:1–25.

Ford, J.A. (1949) Cultural dating of prehistoric sites in Viru Valley, Peru. In J.A. Ford and G.R. Willey (eds.): Surface Survey of Viru Valley, Peru. Anthropological Papers of the American Museum of Anthropology 43(2): 29–89.

Kroeber, A.L. (1916) Zuni Potsherds. Anthropological Papers of the American Museum of Natural History 18(1).

Neiman, F.D. (1995) Stylistic variation in evolutionary perspective: Inferences from decorative diversity and inter-assemblage distance in Illinois Woodland ceramic assemblages. American Antiquity 60:7–36.

Petrie, W.M.F. (1899) Sequences in prehistoric remains. Journal of the Royal Anthropological Institute of Great Britain and Ireland 29:295–301.

Robinson, W.S. (1951) A method for chronologically ordering archaeological deposits. American Antiquity 16:293–301.

Teltser, P.A. (1995) Culture history, evolutionary theory, and frequency seriation. In P.A. Teltser (ed.): Evolutionary Archaeology: Methodological Issues, pp. 51–68. Tucson: University of Arizona Press.

Settlement Archaeology, Theory

The study of how people lived in the past from the remains of their living sites in the landscape, as well as coeval monuments. In most cases, domestic settlements were smaller and more insignificant than public monuments, whether barrows or ceremonial centers. The discovery of such settlements and the careful excavation of their contexts and contents stimulated a range of new questions about everyday life, spatial patterning, and social organization. The comparison of many contemporary settlements allows the recovery of a settlement *pattern,* which provides information about larger-scale spatial organization across a whole landscape. The integration of settlement studies with paleoenvironmental reconstructions enables a more complete picture of the long-term structure of social networks and their short-term variations.

Origins of Settlement Archaeology

An interest in settlements began in Europe with the onset of the Industrial Revolution, when new sites were discovered in both town and country. Special types of settlement sites dominated much of nineteenth-century investigations. This began with the establishment of a Danish commission to excavate shell middens in 1848 (leading to publication of six volumes of results in the 1850s) and continued with the excavation of Swiss lake dwellings from 1854 onward and Palaeolithic cave sites in the Dordogne in southwestern France from 1860. Thanks to advances in excavation techniques in the 1870s in Britain, General Augustus Pitt-Rivers was able to recognize settlement features, such as postholes and ditches; these techniques were integrated into American archaeology from the 1910s. An expansion in settlement studies can be documented in Europe from the 1890s to the 1910s, not least in Russia, where the world's first Palaeolithic structures were excavated at Kostienki and some of the world's first total Neolithic village excavations were conducted at Tripolye sites. In this period, settlement sites were recognized as a specific type of archaeological site, which included ordinary dwelling sites, as well as caves and pile dwellings. In 1912, Albert Kiekebusch published the first textbook of settlement archaeology.

In the 1920s and 1930s, settlement sites were increasingly integrated into archaeological *cultures.* Large-scale settlement-excavation projects blossomed in the United States as a response to the Depression, in Soviet Russia as part of state identity, and in Nazi Germany as part of a search for the Aryan heritage. The new projects offered opportunities for large-scale synthesis of archaeological and ethnographic data, which led Julian Steward (in the United States) and Grahame Clark (in England) to formulate new approaches to social and economic organization among past foragers and farmers. An example of new questions that typology could not answer was the attempt by Steward and Frank Setzler, in 1937, to identify population sizes through settlement-pattern studies. These approaches were combined with the importance of *context* in Walter Taylor's *conjunctive* approach to settlements, in which the associations of artifacts and ecofacts in specific contexts became a key tool for reconstructing past lifeways. Taylor proposed in 1948 that the site, rather than the culture, become the primary unit of analysis, the functioning unit of the social group in its environment.

Regional Survey Projects

The conjunctive and the ethnoarchaeological approaches formed the background to one of the key advances in settlement-pattern archaeology: the Viru Valley project, led by Gordon R. Willey, and including Julian Steward, in 1946. This was the first project to rely on the concept of regional settlement networks and their changes over 1,500 years. Willey focused on the definition of differential site function and context within the wider hierarchy of sites in a region with a secure ceramic sequence. The integration of aerial photography, surface survey, architectural mapping, and excavation provided the basis for analysis of community patterning, including hypotheses about population sizes and sociopolitical organization. It is now recognized that the Viru Valley data contained considerably more theoretical potential than was actualized in Willey's 1953 publication. It was left to New Archaeologists to exploit themes of settlement process and the causes of settlement change more fully.

Intrasite Techniques

An equally significant advance in intrasite-settlement archaeology was made in a coeval British project developed by Grahame Clark at the site of Star Carr, an Early Mesolithic lakeside platform in northern England. Prior to this excavation, evidence for the British Mesolithic was restricted almost entirely to lithic scatters, small faunal samples, and refuse pits. Clark exploited the potential of the excellent organic preservation at this waterlogged site to characterize the site-formation processes, the local vegetation record (through pollen analysis), the subsistence economy (faunal and botanical analysis), production strategies (analysis of waste products), and the paleoenvironment of the occupants (palynology and sedimentology). Although subsequent analysis of seasonality,

reinterpretation of the faunal remains, and new excavations have changed perceptions of Star Carr, Clark's project offered new perspectives on settlement excavation and the integration of site and nonsite data.

Scales of Study

Settlement-pattern and ecological approaches began to dominate archaeological thinking in the 1950s and contributed much to the growth of the Anglo-American New Archaeology. There was a realization that settlement patterns reflected so many aspects of human lifeways that they were the fundamental first step in an awareness of communities' social structures. Early work focused on the length and seasonality of settlement occupation, using associated structural information, the context of finds, and seasonality of faunal assemblages to develop alternative hypotheses. Advances in research design led to complementary emphases on intrasite variability and function, the analysis of complete sites, and a regional framework for settlement analysis; these three spatial scales have remained the basis for settlement analysis ever since.

Processual Approaches

Settlement archaeology was ideally suited to the systems approach of the New Archaeologists for several reasons: the systems emphasis on internal change and/or homeostasis, its totalizing theoretical structure, and its emphasis on population estimates and ecological change in explaining cultural change. While Lewis R. Binford, Kent V. Flannery, and others explored internal change using settlement systems as primary data in positive- or negative-feedback models, Paul Martin, James Hill, and yet others identified population increase or environmental change as two key prime movers causing cultural change. The estimation of population size from settlement data, at both intrasite and regional levels, played a key role in such hypotheses, as did the relationships between sites and the changing form of their local environment. A striking example of a complex systemic approach is Colin Renfrew's model for the emergence of Aegean Bronze Age palace civilizations. Here, a positive-feedback model using changes in agricultural and metallurgical production and exchange systems is ultimately dependent upon cumulative and unbroken population increases on Crete and in Messenia based on regional settlement analyses. A large-scale study by Ezra Zubrow in the American Southwest, related settlement and population changes to the changing carrying capacity of semiarid and marginal environments. Both studies show how, in the 1960s, settlement studies shifted from a concern with elite centers alone to a focus on the total settlement pattern, including ordinary rural residential structures.

Site Catchment Analysis

A reaction against the zonal approach to environmental studies (the correlation of site distributions with ecological zones) stimulated Eric Higgs and Claudio Vita-Finzi to develop Site Catchment Analysis (SCA) in the early 1970s. Inspired largely by the New, or Quantitative, Geography of the 1960s, SCA provided a framework for integrating on- and off-site data through the notions of a *site exploitation territory*, within which much of the daily activities of the occupants would occur, and a *site catchment*, the extended zone incorporating all economic activities in the annual cycle. Geographical data were used to define a territory of 2-hours' (10-km) radius for more mobile hunter-gatherers and a territory of 1-hour's (5-km) radius for more settled farmers. In an early study, Vita-Finzi and Higgs explored the site exploration territories of late forager and early farming sites in the Levant, finding that contrasting territories dominated the two site classes. Early SCA work had important implications for the reevaluation of domestication in the late 1960s and early 1970s.

What Constitutes a Site?

An important spin-off from the emphasis on the distinction between on- and off-site resources, upon which SCA insisted, was the question of the definition of a *site*. The interpretation as *settlements* of dense surface lithic or sherd scatters during field survey remained unproblematic until the 1970s, when scholars such as David Hurst Thomas recognized the presence of low densities of material across entire landscapes that could not readily be interpreted as evidence of residence. The greater intensity of survey and the more careful interpretation of survey results led, first, to a dichotomy between sites and off-site remains and, later, to the concept of a continuous artifact distribution, with settlements represented by dense artifact accumulations. The application of the off-site concept to Palaeolithic re-

mains led Robert Foley to recognize that each mobile band of twenty-five–thirty people could produce more than 100,000 tools per annum, the vast proportion of which would be discarded off-site but with several different kinds of high artifact concentrations representing varying site types within an annual catchment. An even more severe interpretative challenge concerned the existence of sites on taphonomic grounds—the issue of whether animal-bone assemblages in caves documented human settlement at all. Faunal assemblages at caves such as Swartkrans in South Africa, with supposedly classic evidence of early hominids, are now believed to have been the product of carnivore rather than human activity. These theoretical developments complicated the estimation of populations from settlement remains, in turn stimulating different approaches.

Landscape Archaeology

The integration of on- and off-site archaeology led to the emergence of a distinctive tradition of landscape archaeology, with its ultimate derivation in the Enlightenment genre of landscape painting, with its distinctive ways of perceiving. The British variant had its roots in William G. Hoskins's *The Making of the English Landscape* and the fieldwork tradition of the Royal Commission on Historical Monuments of England (RCHME). The aim of the total reconstruction of the processes that made past and incomplete landscapes into the present-day cumulative palimpsest bears important implications for settlement archaeology. Since the 1980s, there has been renewed attention to often slightly upstanding monuments and flat sites, as well as the spectacular monuments with which field archaeology began in the Early Modern period (A.D. 1600–1800). The Stonehenge Environs Project, undertaken during the late 1980s, sought to relate off-site lithic and sherd scatters to sites and monuments adjoining the famous central monument, as well as to the paleoenvironmental evidence for changing forest and soil conditions: The notion of a ritual landscape was challenged on the basis of the high density of domestic debris and agrarian traces located through much of the Stonehenge environs.

State-Level Settlement Patterning

Similarly, large-scale American projects have examined the settlement evidence for the emergence of states in both Mesoamerica and South America. In the Oaxaca Project in Mexico, Flannery, Joyce Marcus, Richard Blanton, and others investigated the origins of farming and the emergence of the Zapotec state. In the Archaic period, families living at microband camps such as Guilá Naquitz engaged in broad-spectrum hunting and gathering, with the shift to food production the result of interannual variations in wild-resource availability. In the Formative period, permanent villages and hamlets of up to sixty people were established for the first time, with one central place, at San Jose Mogote, of several hundred people. In the Late Formative, a three-tier hierarchy was documented on the basis of site size, with a ceremonial center at the largest site. The foundation of Monte Alban on unoccupied, politically neutral territory indicates the fusion of village lands in a state organization with more than 10,000 people living at its central place.

Intrasite Studies: Foragers and Farmers

The continued interest in intrasite function, segregation, and differentiation has led to the refinement of analytical techniques in many different kinds of settlements. In hunter-gatherer archaeology, advances in refitting of lithic debris and the technological stages of production *(the operational chain)* have combined with precise three-dimensional excavation of finds to produce startling results. At the Magdelenian campsite of Pincevent, near Paris, France, Sylvie Ploux and colleagues have identified the presence of several individual flintknappers, including unskilled children, who worked at different places (near hearths but not in tents or cooking areas) and whose products were bilaterally exchanged, as was animal meat, among all ten structures during the six-week occupation of Level 15. The detailed evidence from tool and bone refitting complements the three-dimensional spatial recording of every find to produce a detailed picture of Palaeolithic lifeways at the microlevel of a single campsite.

David L. Clarke's 1972 reanalysis of the well-preserved Iron Age crannog (lake settlement) of Glastonbury in southwestern England is a classic of New Archaeological settlement analysis. The complex stratified deposits of timber and earth floors were interpreted as a series of horizontal and vertical divisions in site usage, including the identifica-

tion of thirteen different types of structure through a combination of artifact association and structural remains: men's houses, women's houses, ancillary huts, workshop huts, baking huts, annex huts, guard huts, courtyards, work floors, clay patches, granaries, stables, and kennels. Although the interpretation of men's houses and women's houses has been challenged, the study remains a model of originality and insight.

The Value of Place

A sine qua non of processual archaeology's perception of settlement archaeology was that settlements were places insofar as the debris of past activities characterized them as sites. This characterization of sites is deficient through its omission of any notion of *place value*: Places are as much the loci of meaning as they are the foci of activity. One of the merits of a postprocessual approach to settlement archaeology is the introduction of meaning into settlement remains, through the use of two contrasting problematics: the search for generative spatial rules and the search for symbolic structure. Both approaches begin by questioning the processual assumption that spatial patterning is no more than a reflection of social organization.

Social Space

The generation of rules from the spatial record derives from a search for spatial order in the mass of pronounced architectural variability. Roland Fletcher has used settlement remains to analyze dimensional order in the context of information theory, with the settlement structures acting as communication devices transmitting messages about the organization of space. He defines two factors contributing to dimensional order: coherence in the absolute dimensions of structures, such as houses, rooms, doors, and gates, and the consistent variation found within these dimensions. The ideological power necessary to maintain strict dimensional coherence can be used as a measure of social control and hierarchy.

A more ambitious approach to settlements is space syntax (the subset appropriate to the internal analysis of settlement spaces—*access analysis*). Defining buildings as transformations of space through objects, Bill Hillier and Julienne Hanson start from the premise that the ordering of space in buildings concerns the ordering of people. The core of access analysis is the notion that access to buildings for residents, friends, and strangers implies a series of constraints built into the structure, which can be inferred from the relative ease of movement within the building. The success of archaeological applications of access analysis depends on the availability of complete settlement plans and the clear identification of all doors and gates. However, *alpha analysis* (analysis of exterior settlement space) has not been found to be so suitable in the archaeological contexts.

Symbolic Space

A more culturally relative set of approaches to settlement structure relies on the deconstruction of symbolic order from material remains. These approaches are founded in the human propensity to classify as a means of imposing order on a (partly) unknowable world. While anthropologists have often discovered a direct reflection of cosmic or social order in tribal architecture (e.g., the Dogon village plan in Mali and the Berber Kabyle house in Algeria), there are many examples of the noncoincidence of material and symbolic structures. Thus, the starting point in symbolic analyses is that each community transforms neutral space into the places that are marked and that take on meaning in their own particular way but using common principles of classification. In this way, the culturally significant spaces in a landscape are transformed into more or less permanent markers to which accrues the place value of long-term history and experience. These monuments provided the stage for the dramatic performance of the past, the context provided by culture itself for the use of settlements and other sites for social reproduction. The symbolic order expressed in spatial practice may relate inter alia to gender constructs, ancestor principles, status divisions and/or cosmological principles.

Gendered Space

In the Anasazi occupation of the Broken Flute Cave in northern Arizona, gender differentiation is negotiated through spatial oppositions in art styles, craft products, and burials. Female figurines are associated exclusively with pit-houses and a geometric art style, which is linked to motifs on pottery, baskets, and belts, all related to female food-processing tasks. On the opposite side of the cave, male figures, often masked or in procession, are painted on the cave wall, adjoining the kiva and male burials. The importance of women's food production and textile manufacture is underlined in contrast to male domination of ritual life.

Time and Place

One of the strong contrasts noted in the settlement record of the Neolithic and Copper Age of southeast Europe is the construction of settlements as either flat sites or *tells* (mounds composed of accumulated settlement debris). While flat sites are often reoccupied, they do not dominate the landscape in the same manner as the monumental tells, with their sequence of superimposed building levels, often including houses positioned directly above previous houses. One of the implications of the tell settlement form is the creation of an ancestor ideology, within which people live where their ancestors lived and in which social power is derived from close association with long sequences of ancestral occupation. The concept of *cyclic time* is built into settlements such as tells, with their long-term sequences of building and abandonment, departure and reoccupation.

The study of Late Neolithic tombs and settlements on the archipelago of Orkney in northeastern Scotland provides an example of the overlay of cosmic principles onto the everyday. There is a fusion of time and space in the orientation of the central hearths in most houses along cardinal points relating to midsummer and midwinter sunrise and sunset, which, in turn, divide the interior of each house according to gender principles. The hearth symbolizes warmth, light, heat, and domesticity in the subarctic environment—the opposite of the largest tomb on Orkney, Maes Howe, whose passage to the funerary chamber is oriented to face midwinter sunset, the shortest and darkest day of the year. Many architectural details are shared by the houses of the dead and those of the living.

In summary, the diversification of the study of settlements and settlement patterns over more than a century of archaeological investigations has provided a wide range of insights about daily life, subsistence economies, spatial order and the built environment, the landscape context for settlement, and the creation of meaning in human communities.

John Chapman

S

Further Readings

Bailey, G.N., and Davidson, I. (1983) Site exploitation territories and topography: Two case studies from Palaeolithic Spain. Journal of Archaeological Science 10:87–115.

Chang, K-C. (1972) Settlement Patterns in Archaeology. Reading, MA: Addison-Wesley.

Clarke, D.L. (1972) A provisional model of an Iron Age society and its settlement system. In D.L. Clarke (ed.): Models in Archaeology. London: Methuen.

Clarke, D.L., ed. (1977) Spatial Archaeology. London: Academic.

Fletcher, R. (1984) Identifying spatial disorder: A case study of a Mongol fort. In H. Hietala (ed.): Intra-Site Spatial Analysis in Archaeology. Cambridge: Cambridge University Press.

Hillier, B., and Hanson, J. (1984) The Social Logic of Space. Cambridge/New York: Cambridge University Press.

Parker Pearson, M., and Richards, C., eds. (1994) Architecture and Order: Approaches to Social Space. London: Routledge.

Ucko, P.J., Dimbleby, G.W., and Tringham, R., eds. (1972) Man, Settlement, and Urbanism. London: Duckworth.

Vogt, E.Z., ed. (1983) Prehistoric Settlement Patterns: Essays in Honor of G.R. Willey. Albuquerque: University of New Mexico Press.

Willey, G.R. (1953) Prehistoric Settlement Patterns in the Viru Valley, Peru. (Bureau of American Ethnology Bulletin 155). Washington, D.C.: Smithsonian Institution.

Settlements, Excavation

The excavation, recording, and analysis of a spatially associated collection (patterned arrangement) of artifacts deposited at a single locality by the same set of people over a relatively continuous segment of time.

Settlement studies began in American archaeology with the 1953 publication of Gordon R. Willey's *Prehistoric Settlement Patterns in the Viru Valley, Peru,* based on fieldwork he conducted in 1946. This shift away from chronological studies was urged on Willey by Julian Steward, who had used a regional approach in an ethnographic study of Native American groups in the Great Basin. Settlement studies are an examination of how people organized their use of space and can pertain to a continuum of phenomena ranging from the use of space within structures, to the arrangement of structures or other features within the context of a local occupation, to the location of occupations within the broader landscape. A settlement approach formulates archaeological units at a scale beyond that of the discrete artifact; units are essentially formed that pertain to clusters, or aggregates, of discrete artifacts. Archaeological units at this scale are particularly appropriate for the study of subsistence, technology, exchange, and the various ways in which human groups organize themselves with respect to one another.

Settlements as Communities

There has been a tendency to think of settlements as the archaeological version of the ethnographic community, and, for a time, there was some suggestion that archaeological sites viewed from the perspective of social groups rather than cultures and phases represented a completely different kind of archaeology (Chang 1968). Time has resolved the issue in favor of a single archaeology, but archaeologists have continued to struggle with the ethnographic baggage that has, for historic reasons, accompanied the concept of *settlement.* Kwang-Chih Chang, in *Rethinking Archaeology,* sought to formalize the relationship by defining a settlement as an archaeological deposit containing the artifacts and features discarded by a community during its occupation of a particular location, but Chang was also quick to add that the associated community could never be more than a logical abstract, since the basic components of the community, humans and their interactions, were no longer observable. But when Chang discusses actual examples of archaeological settlements, it is in such time-hallowed archaeological terms as *components, artifacts,* and *stratigraphic units.*

There are valid reasons why archaeologists have not, in practice, sought to rigorously operationlize the definition of settlements by reference to communities. Chief among these is that an archaeological test for community—hence, settlement—requires a resort to analogy. Since arguments based on analogy cannot be disconfirmed, archaeologists could not use the settlement-as-community definition to successfully reject a unit. Constrained in this way, archaeologists would be able only to make relatively stronger or weaker cases for particular collections of artifacts as settlements, but literally any primary cultural deposit containing artifacts would be acceptable as a settlement as long as some archaeologist was willing to make an argument for it.

One can also question the wisdom of borrowing a concept that is poorly defined and much debated even by ethnographers. George P. Murdock's often-used definition of a community as "the maximal set of people involved in face-to-face interaction on a daily basis" (1949:79) might work well for villages involving several hundred people, but it scarcely characterizes large urban centers. There are numerous examples of social groupings that are of considerable interest to ethnographer and archaeologist alike but that do not satisfy the definition of a community. The O'odham people of southern Arizona traveled every June to join people from other communities in large camps to collect the fruit of the saguaro cactus fruit and drink the slightly intoxicating syrup during the performance of an important ceremony for rain. Despite the importance of these camps in both archaeological and ethnographic studies, these social groups did not constitute communities. There seems little utility in limiting the area of inquiry to only communities, when much of the way in which societies use the landscape is conducted outside of communities.

Settlements as Archaeological Units

There is considerable value, then, in disassociating archaeological settlements from ethnographic communities and in defining settlements in strictly archaeological terms.

Settlements are archaeological units formulated at the scale of aggregates of objects (Dunnell 1971). A level of subjectivity enters into the perception of an aggregate of things that does not exist in the perception of individual things. The recognition of a discrete object can be based completely on experience; when part of the object is moved, everything else that follows is the remaining complement of that object. The means of distinguishing one aggregate from another, while founded partly on observation, also has a very important conceptual component. If it were acceptable to simply claim that any collection of artifacts constituted a settlement, there would be no problem. But the goal is to define settlements as a spatially clustered set of artifacts and features, the aggregatedness of which has to do with human behavior. Where there is a collection of things, the potential exists for subdividing that collection in different ways. There is no simple empirical test for determining the boundaries of a unit that exists as an aggregate of objects. If part of the aggregate is moved, the rest of the aggregate remains where it was, and the end result has been only to destroy some of the aggregated character of the unit.

As in any science, the procedure for generating comparable and replicable units in archaeology is based on the application of a set of appropriate methods and definitions. Archaeologists, in fact, have little difficulty in implementing studies of settlements; they routinely conduct regional studies of settlement distributions and analyze patterning within individual settlements. But despite the success of such studies, the delineation of the units called *settlements* is largely intuitive. There is no unified method for identifying settlements in archaeology. This is not because archaeologists eschew the scientific method. Archaeology as a discipline has a well-established body of scientific method, especially in the area of chronology. Nor has this issue suffered from a lack of attention, since it has been addressed by a number of well-established theorists in the discipline. Rather, the lack of progress in developing a unified method is a measure of the intractability of the issue.

In the absence of a theoretical definition of settlements, archaeologists take what Robert C. Dunnell refers to as a tactical approach to the problem and delineate settlement units for the purpose of a particular problem and region. Willey, in his settlement-pattern study in the Viru Valley of Peru, used the terms *settlement* and *site* interchangeably, and, from the perspective of an entire valley, the variability in density of structures was sufficient for his purpose in studying the prehistoric use of the landscape. In other contexts, however, a site could easily be argued to consist of multiple settlements.

There is fairly good consensus among archaeologists on what the definition of a settlement must accomplish. Settlements should have some of the general character of communities in the sense of constituting an association of people involved in the use of a particular location in space, but settlements must be based completely on properties of material culture observable in the archaeological record. Dunnell's definition of an *occupation,* which can serve equally well for a settlement, covers these general objectives and sums up what archaeologists tend to do (rather than say) when using units at the scale of settlements. An occupation/settlement is a spatially associated collection of artifacts deposited at a single locality by the same set of people over a relatively continuous segment of time "comparable to other such units in the same study" (Dunnell 1971:151). Chang, in *Rethinking Archaeology,* applies many of these criteria when discussing the actual procedures he uses to distinguish one settlement from another.

Much of the subjectivity in defining settlements or occupations stems from the need to differentiate a given settlement from settlements that both preceded and followed it in time. Human societies are continually changing, and frequently the differences are noticeable (in the sense of being relevant to an explanation) only after a number of small increments of change have accumulated over time to make a big difference. How the temporal continuum is sliced in such situations is a relatively arbitrary process. To retain comparability, the archaeologist needs to apply a consistent procedure for distinguishing settlements within the context of a single study. Similarly, multiple studies within a single region can attain a level of comparability to one another only by adhering to the same tactics in identifying settlements. What is not possible, however, is to define settlements in completely theoretical terms.

How Settlements Are Formed

Use of a tactical approach in defining settlements leaves open the possibility that units labeled as settlements need not be comparable, and, in practice, that has been very much the case. There is, nonetheless, a partial solution to this dilemma. It turns out that there is a high level of consistency in how archaeological deposits are formed because there are only a relatively limited number of ways for humans to discard or abandon items of material culture

(consisting of *artifacts* and *features*), and these processes affect the morphology of archaeological deposits in exactly the same way that processes of erosion (e.g., wind, water) are responsible for the formation of geological strata.

Archaeological deposits are collections of artifacts. Artifacts (objects with one or more properties attributable to human behavior) include discrete objects and features; the latter occur at the scale of objects but do not remain discrete when moved and can be adequately documented only at the location in which they are found. Features are either pits created by the removal of deposits or facilities ranging in complexity and size from an arrangement of rocks around a hearth to a massive building containing other features within it. In usage, the term *artifact* is frequently restricted to whole objects, allowing archaeologists to draw a contrast between whole objects and features.

To become part of the archaeological record, artifacts and features have to have been abandoned. There are essentially three ways in which this can be done. An artifact may be discarded as refuse at the location in which it was produced; an artifact may be collected as refuse from one location and redeposited in another; and, finally, an artifact may be cached or stored in a location from which it might be retrieved if needed on future occasions. Features are essentially abandoned at the location in which they were produced, but their function at the time of abandonment may differ considerably from the initial uses for which they were intended. Michael B. Schiffer, in his book *Behavioral Archaeology,* refers to the deposits that result from these depositional processes as *primary, secondary* and *de facto* refuse. The processes all lead to the creation of deposits, or refuse, although in the third case the items that were cached become refuse only by virtue of the fact that they were never retrieved.

One of the intriguing properties of a social group composed of humans is that, within such a group, depositional activities are highly patterned and differentiated in space. If each individual in the group abandoned artifacts in a random fashion, the resulting deposit would be homogenous, but this turns out to be far from the case in many situations. Both contemporary and archaeological settlements can be broken down into different zones based on differences in depositional processes.

Lewis R. Binford, in a 1978 study of an Eskimo hunting blind, found that such zonation of deposits arose even when the social group was as ephemeral as that of a group of Eskimo men sitting around a fire behind a large boulder while they awaited the arrival of suitable game. Small, unobtrusive artifacts, such as the shavings generated while carving a piece of wood, were allowed to drop in a zone around the fire where the men sat to keep warm. Relatively large or messy artifacts, such as pieces of chicken bone that remained after a snack, were thrown away from the fire so they would not be underfoot in the area used for sitting. Valuable objects, such as binoculars, were cached on suitable ledges or crevices in a nearby boulder. The hunting blind was organized into drop zones (containing what Schiffer would call primary refuse), toss zones (secondary refuse), and caches (de facto refuse). Martha Graham found that larger settlements can also have a maintained activity area or zone, which is essentially a drop zone that is cleaned on a regular basis. Large items of waste generated by activities conducted in the maintained zone are collected and removed to a refuse zone similar in character to the toss zone of Binford's hunting blind.

Archaeological settlements are also capable of being divided into three kinds of zones, as illustrated by the small part of the prehistoric Hohokam site of La Ciudad, Arizona, shown in Figure 1. The area can be divided into three kinds of zones: a central zone, called the yard, around which the houses are located, an outer zone that lies behind the houses and circles the inner yard, and the space contained within the structures. The houses, made of wood frames interwoven with brush and plastered on the exterior with a coating of mud, were built on floors recessed into shallow pits. The locations of the entrances into the structures are marked by short ramps that led down to the level of the house floor.

The central zone, or yard, was a maintained (i.e., cleaned) activity area. The artifact deposit of this central zone had the following properties: Sherds occurred in low densities, lithic artifacts tended to be small (less than 2 cm in size), and tertiary flakes were by far the most common kind of lithic. The process of sweeping and cleaning this zone had removed large flakes and broken vessels, leaving behind small tertiary flakes, many probably produced by the soft-hammer-percussion technique,

that were trampled into the surface by the heavy traffic in the area.

The artifact deposit in the outer zone was quite different. It had a high density of sherds and lithics; the lithic assemblage included many large items; and secondary flakes and pieces of shatter were the most common category of lithic artifact. This zone contained the refuse that had been collected in other parts of the site (the centrally located, maintained activity zone and the interiors of the houses) and carried to this area to be dumped. Some activities that produced quantities of undesired waste products were also performed in this outer zone. Large thermal pits were located in this zone because they were regularly emptied of the rocks that were used to retain heat while the ovens were in use. The outer zone was also apparently used for hard-hammer flaking because it contained large quantities of shatter. Like tertiary flakes, shatter pieces tend to be very small and are not likely to be collected during the process of cleaning an area. They tend, therefore, to remain in the deposit where they were generated, and their presence in the outer zone indicates that they were produced there rather than in the interior yard. Had activities producing shattered flakes been conducted in the central yard, the pieces of shatter would have remained in that area rather than occur in the outer zone.

The central zone also included small areas of heavily used flakes and hammer stones. These were deposits of primary refuse that were used during some activity, and the area had not yet been cleaned (or had been missed by cleaning) at the time the occupation ended.

As houses fell into disrepair, they were replaced by new structures that were also built along the boundary between the inner and the outer zones. The structure of the settlement was, thus, more rigidly defined by the location of the yard than by the locations of the buildings themselves. The single location shown in Figure 1 was used for the duration of nearly a century with little alteration in the location of the yard, although structures were abandoned and new ones built on a regular basis. More remarkable is that this pattern—of an inner maintained zone ringed by houses and the whole encircled by an outer ring of midden deposits—is repeated throughout the site of La Ciudad with considerable consistency. This pattern is, essentially, the basic

La Ciudad, Moreland Locus North
950 - 1040 A.D.

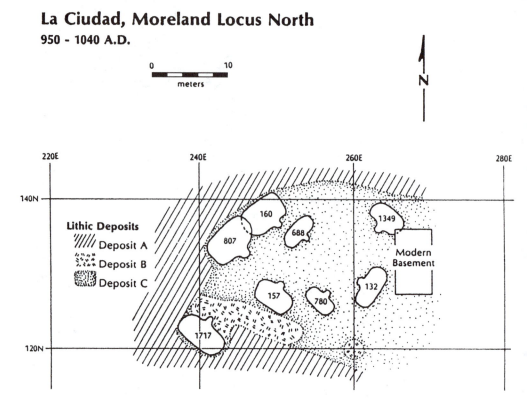

Figure 1. *The maintained (swept) zone, refuse zone, and locations of structures in a portion of the Hohokam settlement of La Ciudad. Deposit C is a swept area of primary refuse constituting the central yard area. Deposit B is a nonswept portion of the yard containing heavily used flakes. Deposit A is an area of secondary refuse, or midden, containing artifacts dumped in a zone around the periphery of the houses. Figure by Glen Eugene Rice.*

building block for a settlement covering several hectares.

It is tempting to refer to such basic units as *households,* and to a collection of such units as a *community,* and there is little doubt that they represent the operation of some such social units. But doing so gains little and is scarcely necessary; these units are archaeological arrangements of deposits and can be compared to one another in strictly archaeological terms. This method of depositional analysis can be applied to the study of modern settlements in exactly the same way as prehistoric settlements, as is evident in the examples that have been used to illustrate this discussion. Archaeologists should, in fact, be alarmed if their methods did not work when applied to the study of ongoing occupations.

A Method for the Investigation of Settlements
Archaeological settlements can be investigated using a variety of techniques, including surface collections, remote sensing, and mapping of visible architecture or soil marks, in addition to excavation. Although this discussion refers regularly to excavation, these other techniques might be far more productive than excavation when the size of an actual settlement and the availability of time and resources for a particular project are taken into consideration.

A method to investigate settlements as patterned arrangements of depositional zones must take the following into consideration. To map the extent and boundaries of different depositional zones, the method must lead to the recovery of artifactual data in considerably smaller spatial units than covered by the depositional zones. These units are subsequently used to map the extent of the spatially more inclusive depositional zones. The method must ensure that small as well as large objects are recovered, since variability in artifact size is an important means of distinguishing between various depositional processes.

The method must establish the nature of the total settlement, so that the data collected by time-consuming techniques such as excavation can be evaluated. The method for the study of depositional zones must also incorporate means of establishing chronological control. The method of stratigraphic analysis, for instance, becomes part of the method for the excavation of settlements.

The goal is to recover data in a way that makes possible the mapping of different depositional zones constituting a settlement. This is a particularly important concern if the settlement area cannot be excavated in its entirety and needs to be sampled. Since the spatial extent of each zone is not known at the outset of the investigation, it is necessary to artificially divide the site into sampling units that are spatially much smaller than that expected for the zones, obtain artifact samples from each of these arbitrary units, and then, through analysis, fit the many overdifferentiated spatial blocks back into the larger depositional zones. Conversely, it is not possible to find spatial patterns that are smaller than the spacing between sample units. The extramural areas at La Ciudad were sampled by dividing the surface area into 5 × 5 m squares and then excavating a test unit (usually 1 × 1 m, but sometimes larger to deal with areas of low artifact density) within each arbitrary 25 m² block. The artifact content of each such unit was then examined, and the boundaries between the inner and the outer zones were extrapolated on the basis of that information. Obviously, the boundary between zones cannot be determined with any greater precision than 5 m, given that that is the minimum spacing between test units.

House interiors at La Ciudad were excavated in squares that measured 1 m on each side. When a test unit extended beyond the edges of the structure, only the portion of the unit within the house was excavated. Many large objects found resting on the floors were left in place, and their provenance was measured exactly. Smaller flakes and pieces of shatter, however, were frequently found only after they had been moved by the trowel or as the excavated material was screened. The provenance of those objects, therefore, is known only to the closest meter. The zones of different deposits within the structure were determined by analytically recombining the 1 × 1 m squares into large spatial zones of

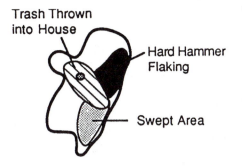

Feature 1105:
Trash thown into house from door area; Previous flaking and cleaning events along back of house.

Figure 2. An example of an abandoned house at La Ciudad that had been reused as a trash dump. The trash deposit extends from the door of the structure toward the rear wall. The maintained (or swept) area in the lower half of the map is a deposit that developed during the time the structure was being used as a residence. Figure by Glen Eugene Rice.

similar artifact deposits. A map of one of the structures at La Ciudad (Figure 2) shows several different artifact zones within the house. A zone of refuse extends from the area of the door past the hearth toward the rear of the house. To one side of the structure is a maintained zone containing small tertiary flakes and pieces of shatter. Apparently, the house floor had at one time been swept and maintained, but the structure was subsequently abandoned and used as a trash dumping area. Not too surprisingly, this refuse accumulated in the center of the structure, which was most easily reached from the doorway. This information about the final use of the structure would not have been possible if the area within had been excavated in larger units. The practice of dividing house spaces into quarters and excavating and recording provenance in such units greatly lessen the ability to study the zonation within rooms, while the excavation of a house floor as a single provenance unit completely eliminates any such potential.

A method for the study of settlements also needs to take into account the different categories of information that need to be collected and analyzed. The distinctions among maintained zones, drop zones, and refuse zones rest, to a great extent, on differences in the sizes of artifacts. The excavation method must ensure that small as well as large objects are collected; screening of the deposits with a fine mesh is an important requirement of the method. Soil samples can also be taken and examined microscopically for flakes and shatter, to better pinpoint the locations in which lithic production was performed and to distinguish between maintained and nonmaintained areas.

The method must also delineate populations of features, rather than locate only individual instances. If available early in the investigation, such information is useful in the selection of the sample of features to be excavated; it is needed eventually as a basis for evaluating the significance of what was excavated. *Remote sensing* and *mechanical trenching* are frequently used to map the distributions of features, and mechanical trenching is particularly valuable in providing data from which the total numbers of different kinds of features can be estimated. In settlements that contain adobe or masonry walls, the wall alignments can be exposed using relatively limited excavation effort over large areas, thereby providing accurate counts and maps of the population of room features at the site.

Excavation with a horizontal emphasis, when possible, provides the most secure data on features, since all features within the excavated area are encountered. The use of such an approach can, of course, be sped up if the purpose of the excavation is narrowed to a search for features alone and the concern for the recovery of artifacts from nonfeature space is handled in other ways. That makes it possible to excavate the horizontal exposure without screening or even with the use of mechanical equipment, such as a grader or a backhoe. As features are encountered, they are mapped and documented, and some or all can be excavated, depending on the requirement of the research design.

Of considerable importance, however, is the need to recognize that the use of expedient techniques to achieve a horizontal exposure is possible only when the archaeologist has already collected all of the necessary samples of artifacts from nonfeature contexts and has exhausted any other uses of the overlying deposits. The expedient excavation of large areas for the purpose of mapping the distribu-tions of features must, of necessity, come late in the investigation of the settlement, after the excavation needed to delineate depositional zones and conduct stratigraphic studies has been successfully concluded.

Finally, excavation must also incorporate other methods and techniques that are needed to differentiate chronologically distinct settlements from one another. Clearly, an important tool in such studies is excavation with a vertical emphasis, which makes it possible to draw maps (called *stratigraphic profiles*) of the vertical relationships of deposits. Balks might be left in a grid pattern across the site, forming a continuous record of the stratigraphy. Other techniques might also prove useful in chronological studies. A collection of surface materials (the antithesis of the archaeologically renowned *strata cut*) might help separate early from late portions of the settlements that are only partly overlapping in area.

This method for the excavation of settlements is based on the definition of a settlement as a systemically related set of depositional zones. It places an equal emphasis on both artifacts (as objects) and features, and it provides a comprehensive basis for comparing very different kinds of settlements to one another, such as those with and without structures or settlements of considerably different size, by focusing on the size and spatial organization of the depositional zones. To investigate a settlement in this manner, however, requires a considerable amount of excavation effort. Frequently, a far lower level of excavation effort will provide more than adequate data for chronological studies, subsistence studies, and even many classes of intersettlement investigation (such as those focusing on long-distance exchange). Such objectives are accomplished with different methods than those required for the investigation of a settlement. It is fully acceptable, of course, to set other goals for an investigation and to employ the methods appropriate for those goals. What is unfortunate, however, is to invest effort in the investigation of a settlement while using methods that will fail to produce the data needed to delineate the settlement units.

Glen Eugene Rice

See also SETTLEMENT ARCHAEOLOGY, THEORY; SPATIAL ANALYSIS

Further Readings

Binford, L.R. (1978) Dimensional analysis of behavior and site structure: Learning from an Eskimo hunting stand. American Antiquity 43(3):330–361.

Chang, K.-C. (1967) Rethinking Archaeology. New York: Random House.

Chang, K.-C., ed. (1968) Settlement Archaeology. Palo Alto, CA: National Press Books.

Dunnell, R.C. (1971) Systematics in Prehistory. New York: Free Press.

Murdock, G.P. (1949) Social Structure. New York: Macmillan.

Rice, G. (1987) La Ciudad: A perspective on Hohokam community systems. In D. Doyel (ed.): The Hohokam Village: Site Structure and Organization, pp. 127–156. Glenwood Springs, CO: Southwestern and Rock Mountain Division of the American Association for the Advancement of Science.

Schiffer, M.B. (1976) Behavioral Archaeology. New York: Academic.

Willey, G.R. (1953) Prehistoric Settlement Patterns in the Viru Valley, Peru. (Bureau of American Ethnology Bulletin 155). Washington D.C.: Smithsonian Institution.

Shell Middens, Excavation

A type of site in which shell is the most prominent component of the matrix visually (see Figure). The term *midden* infers that the shell was left behind when the meat was consumed for food. But food debris is not the only origin of shell deposits; the ethnographic record provides many examples of systemic uses for discarded shell and reasons for intentionally accumulating shells in one place. These reasons include industrial waste (eg., shell button, cameo, dye, porcelain, lime manufactures), architectural features (eg., bleachers, breakwaters, flooring, graves, mounds, retaining walls), and waste from fish-bait production. Several excavators have specified the ratio of shell to sediment or the density of shell per unit volume in a definition of shell midden, attempting to standardize the term. Several species of birds and terrestrial mammals are known to mound shells, such as the scrub fowl in Australia and the oyster catcher in eastern North America, and modern ocean-dredging operations have created shell-bearing sites in dredge-spoil areas. Until the archaeologist can determine the formation processes of individual shell accumulations, functionally neutral terms, such as *shell-bearing site* or *shell matrix site,* are preferred to *shell midden.*

History of Research

Large piles of shell on land were clearly in need of explanation, and early speculators attributed their creation to wind, water, and humans. John Lubbock devoted a chapter to the Danish *kjokkenmoddings,* (kitchen middens) in 1869, when voices were already calling for their preservation. These sites have attracted the attention of archaeologists for well more than 150 years and were the scene of some of the earliest biological studies in archaeology due to the chemical properties of calcium that act to protect bone from decay.

Archaeologists now know that humans accumulated notable quantities of marine shells as early as 70,000 years ago in rockshelters and open-air sites at Klasies River Mouth in South Africa. Shell-matrix sites date to 18,000 years ago in Cantabria, Spain. A dramatic increase in the quantity of shells amassed in South Africa and in Cantabria coincides with the Late Pleistocene and Early-to-Middle Holocene periods, and this site type is known for the first time ca. 9,000 years ago in Italy, Japan, Denmark, Argentina, and California.

The majority of shell-bearing sites worldwide appear sometime after 8,000 years ago, when sea-level rise slowed considerably and modern shorelines were established. Of particular interest to prehistorians, and as yet unexplained, is the co-occurrence of shell-matrix sites with the earliest evidence of horticulture in the Japanese Jomon culture and the Valdivia culture in Ecuador, and with the earliest pottery in Denmark, South America, North America, and Japan. In both North and South America, the shell-matrix sites with the earliest pottery are a peculiar ring shape. The oldest artificially constructed mounds in North America are composed of shells.

Theorists have posited that the increased harvesting of molluscs was triggered by population pressure—either restriction in territory or reduction in the quantities of foodstuffs, environmental changes, or technological developments. Mounds of shell and rings of shell suggest other hypotheses. Today, most

The shell-matrix site of Dogan Point, New York. Dogan Point, on the Hudson River, is composed of oyster shells deposited from 5,000 to 2,400 B.C. and again 500 to 200 B.C. Photograph by Cheryl Claassen.

archaeologists assume that widespread utilization of shellfish flesh and shells did not begin in the last 8,000 years but that thousands of earlier marine-shell-matrix sites are inundated or eroded, and riverine sites are buried by flood deposits.

Shell-bearing sites consist not only of marine shell, but also of freshwater shell. In western New South Wales, Australia, piles of freshwater shells date as early as 35,000 years ago. Accumulations of freshwater shells also mark the shores of the Nile and the Amazon, lakes and streams in California, Oregon, the Pyrenees, Provence, Libya, Greater Andaman Island, and Veracruz. In the interior eastern United States (Shell Mound Archaic tradition), mounds of riverine shells dating to 8,000–2,000 years ago were the loci of burials for hundreds of human skeletons.

Some of the earliest stratigraphic digging done in the United States was conducted in shell middens by Jeffries Wyman on the Atlantic coast and the St. John's River of Florida in 1875. Pacific coastal and U.S. freshwater-shell-matrix sites are typically marked by a large number of molluscan species. Seventy-one species of shells were recovered from the 9,600-year-old SLO-2 site in Diablo Canyon, California, and more than forty species from the 5,000-year-old Carlston Annis shell mound in Kentucky. Such tremendous variation in species often provides visual markers of dump episodes in those sites allowing for stratigraphic excavation. But on the Atlantic and Gulf of Mexico coasts, sites are often composed of only one or two species of shell, leading to the perception that stratigraphy is lacking in shell-matrix sites, with excavation often proceeding in arbitrary levels.

Site-Formation Processes

Formation processes play a crucial role in the appearance and contents of a shell-bearing site at the time it is excavated. A shell matrix is more porous than a dirt matrix and, consequently, one in which small objects, such as flakes and bones, travel downward much more readily. Because the deposit is porous, it is easy for earthworms, rodents, and tree roots to penetrate it, for sediments to fill in the interstices, and for snails to travel to the bottom to hibernate. It is very difficult to assume the contemporaneity of artifacts and ecofacts (floral, fauna) with the matrix from which they were recovered.

Shells are composed of ca. 40 percent calcium carbonate. As the shell degrades, the liberated calcium creates alkaline soil, which greatly facilitates the preservation of bones, plant parts, and shells. This same chemical alteration of shells impedes analytical procedures, however. Shell weight is decreased by acid deterioration; calcification (impregnation with calcium) renders shells and bones useless for growth-ring studies and can obscure cell structure, preventing speciation of wood and charcoal.

Natural forces other than decay operate on shell and bone to eliminate some of both materials. Wind and water can remove shells, and water can introduce shells, fish, or plants to a site. Burned shell fractures more easily than does unburned shell. There is an extensive literature on shell taphonomy that suggests ways to identify not only macrostratigraphy (large, obvious natural subdivisions of a site), but also microstratigraphy (thin, subtle subdivisions). Clusters of one species, shell orientation, fragmentation, and articulation tell archaeologists much about disturbance in shell-bearing sites and constitute microstratigraphy.

Cultural practices have severely impacted the archaeological record of shell-bearing sites, which have been mined for lime kilns and cottage lime production, for mortar, for poultry feed, and for road and parking-lot fill. Wave erosion of coastlines has resulted in the disappearance of countless sites.

Sampling and Excavation

Numerous authors have discussed how to sample a shell-bearing site. Some excavators argue that the component is the appropriate sampling universe, rather than the site, while others view occupational areas as the most appropriate sampling arena, and still others excavate in geological facies. It is unfortunate that occupational episodes and even components can be extremely elusive in many of these sites.

There are two fundamentally different perceptions of what is preserved in shell-matrix sites. On the one hand are excavators who believe that shell middens are in systemic context a deflated mass of multiple deposits,

the stew from millennia of activities. On the other hand are those excavators who hold the opposite perception, that shell middens are conflations of discrete deposits, each mixed with and separated by the shells deposited along with the other debris. The former attitude will most likely encourage excavation in arbitrary levels with small exposures and a shell-bearing-site typology based on excavated information; the latter attitude encourages excavation in natural levels, extensive exposures, and a systemic-based typology. Experimental work with shell deposits will help resolve this fundamental conflict. One cannot see what one previously has determined is not present, regardless of sampling strategy.

What type of excavation exposure to use—whether block, column, square, trench, or facies—was a question raised often in the 1980s. During the 1930s and 1940s in the United States, huge freshwater shell mounds were excavated as blocks of matrix. Column sampling became the favored way of testing shell-matrix sites in the 1970s and has both proponents and critics. Faunal analysts find column sampling well suited for subsistence studies. While column sampling is not designed to recover examples of rare species or isolated deposits, it is useful for sampling the matrix, particularly shell. Columns should not be employed as the exclusive excavation-unit type because of the highly restricted view of the component contents they provide. For the same reason, they should not be the only source of materials for the faunal analyst. When used as the exclusive source of material in refuse that may have accumulated as basket dumps, they must be employed at intervals that match the spatial scale of the activities that created the deposit, an impossible task. Other excavators have employed column samples specifically to quantify the strata visible in wall profiles and to provide shell-seasonality samples.

Some archaeologists have advocated sampling strategies that are flexible and include several different types of exposures, employed probabilistically and nonprobabilistically. Since knowledge of component extent and variability is learned as excavation progresses, yet is necessary in planning the sampling strategy, a flexible strategy is essential to the success of the sampling program. But a sampling strategy must be decided case by case, on the basis of the research objective, site stratification, variability in contents, distribution of features, origin of deposits, and so on. Shell that has been amassed for architectural purposes need not be sampled in the same fashion as food debris. Adequacy of sample is not achieved with absolute size but with the proportion of the universe sampled.

Research Questions

Because of a growing awareness of the complexity of dietary reconstruction for humans, many research questions that typified shell-midden excavations of the first half of the twentieth century are no longer pursued. The California school of shell-midden analysis attempted to determine the length of time represented in the shell accumulation, as well as the number of people consuming the molluscan flesh. To do so required tiers of assumptions about the role of the shells, daily caloric intake, daily shellfish consumption, diets of individuals in different sociological subsets, shellfish nutrition, shell fragmentation, shell preservation, and meat weights, assumptions that contemporary archaeologists are no longer willing to make. Even meat weights are rarely calculated because their purpose—dietary reconstruction—is plagued with insurmountable problems.

Archaeologists are also, in the 1990s, more sophisticated in their recognition of the role of site-formation processes. Numerous studies have found species-ratio changes from the bottom to the top of a deposit, typically in column samples. With the realization that shell-matrix sites are highly diverse in composition and origin, sampling strategies have moved toward greater horizontal exposure, with the result that shell, bone, stone, and plant contents and proportions are seen to vary horizontally. Before questions about changes in shell-species ratios vertically can be assessed, the excavator must understand the significance of species changes horizontally. Variability in shell composition is unlikely to be the result of a single factor, and it is the responsibility of the excavator to isolate the cultural and natural formation processes of the site under exploration, while avoiding the normative assumption that all shell debris is food debris, and to ensure that shells are gathered randomly from the site area.

Although research is still hampered by the lack of experimentation and ethnoarchae-ological observations of topics such as shell-fishing, shell use, shell symbolism, midden collapse, and plant colonization of shell deposits, small projects have begun making inroads into these areas. Research programs for shell-matrix sites in the 1990s have often aimed at elucidating site formation, seasonality of the various activities, paleoenvironment, and culture history. The analysis of shells and bones alone is insufficient for these tasks, which require the use of multidisciplinary teams of investigators who take and analyze marine-sediment cores, terrestrial-sediment (chemistry, texture) geomorphology, and samples of woods, pollen, accidental invertebrate inclusions, and the like.

Cheryl Claassen

See also ANIMAL REMAINS, IDENTIFICATION AND ANALYSIS: MOLLUSCS; ARCHAEOLOGICAL SITES, FORMATION PROCESSES; GROWTH-RING ANALYSIS AND SEASONALITY STUDIES

Further Readings

Campbel, S. (1981) The Duwamish No. 1 Site: A Lower Puget Sound Shell Midden. (Office of Public Archaeology Research Report 1). Seattle: University of Washington Press.

Stein, J. (1992) Deciphering a Shell Midden. Orlando: Academic.

Waselkov, G. (1987) Shellfish gathering and shell midden archaeology. In M.B. Schiffer (ed.): Advances in Archaeological Method and Theory, vol. 10, pp. 93–210. Orlando: Academic.

Shepard, Anna Osler (1903–1973)

American scientist and archaeologist. Born May 9, 1903, in Merchantville, New Jersey, Shepard began her degree in anthropology at the Teachers College of Southern California (later California State College, San Diego). After two years, she transferred to the University of Nebraska and received her bachelor's in anthropology in 1928. She did postgraduate work in anthropology at the University of New Mexico and supplemented her education through coursework in physics, chemistry, and geology at the Carnegie Geophysical Laboratory, the National Bureau of Standards, Massachusetts Institute of Technology, and various other universities until her retirement.

In addition to archaeological fieldwork in the Southwest, Shepard also conducted research in museums, taking museology coursework at the School of American Research in 1924, where she became a fellow in archaeology. In 1928, she began a museum career as curator of ethnography for the Museum of Man in San Diego, California, where she conducted a significant amount of fieldwork and laboratory analysis on Mimbres pottery. Her collaboration with the associate director of the museum, Wesley Bradfield, influenced the direction of Shepard's research toward technological and petrographic analysis of ceramics. From 1931 to 1937, she was a research associate in ceramics at the Laboratory of Anthropology in Santa Fe, New Mexico, where she began her research into the utility of petrographic analysis for technological studies of ancient ceramics. It was also during this period that she began her long collaboration with Alfred V. Kidder on analysis of Pueblo ceramics from Pecos and the Rio Grande Valley. During the 1930s, Shepard, together with her father, Henry Warren Shepard, a research chemist, conducted many experiments to reconstruct the firing of both contemporary and prehistoric Pueblo pottery. In 1937, she received a full-time appointment at the Division of Historical Research of the Carnegie Institution of Washington, allowing her to work on her Ceramic Technology Project, an ambitious and highly successful program of analytical studies of both Maya and Anasazi pottery. In that same year, she moved to Boulder, Colorado, and established an extensive laboratory in her home, where she conducted both petrographic and chemical analyses of ceramics for the remainder of her life. She retired from the Carnegie Institution of Washington in 1968 and died in Boulder, Colorado, on July 19, 1973.

Shepard was a pioneer in the scientific study of clays and pottery fabrics and in the applications of petrographic and spectroscopic analysis for the study of pottery from archaeological contexts. She was among the first to utilize the petrographic microscope for the study of thin sections of ceramics to determine the points of origin of the clays used in the manufacture of the pottery samples in question. Shepard used such methods in her study of pottery from the Pecos Pueblo in New Mexico, in which she identified several types of imports and pottery of local manufacture. She also conducted extensive analyses of ceramics from sites throughout the Southwest, as well as on pottery from Mexico, Guatemala and Belize (formerly British Honduras). Her *Ceramics for the Archaeologist,* which has been reprinted numerous times, became a standard work since its publication in 1956 for archaeologists wishing to apply scientific techniques to the study of pottery.

Joseph J. Basile

See also CLAYS AND CERAMICS, CHARACTERIZATION; PETROGRAPHY

Further Reading

Bishop, R.L., and Lange, F.W. (1991) The Ceramic Legacy of Anna O. Shepard. Niwot: University Press of Colorado.

Kidder, A.V. and Shepard, A.O. (1936) The Pottery of Pecos, vol. 2. (Papers of the Phillips Academy Southwestern Expedition 7.) New Haven, CT: Yale University Press.

Morris, E.A. (1974) Anna O. Shepard, 1903–1973. American Antiquity 39:448–451.

Shepard, A.O. (1942) Rio Grande Glaze Paint Ware: A Study Illustrating the Place of Ceramic Technological Analysis in Archaeological Research. (Contributions to American Anthropology and History 39, Publication 528.) Washington, D.C.: Carnegie Institution of Washington.

Shepard, A.O. (1948a) Plumbate: A Mesoamerican Tradeware. (Publication 473). Washington, D.C.: Carnegie Institution of Washington.

Shepard, A.O. (1948b) The Symmetry of Abstract Design with Special Reference to Ceramic Decoration. (Contributions to American Anthropology and History 47, Publication 574.) Washington, D.C.: Carnegie Institution of Washington.

Shepard, A.O. (1956) Ceramics for the Archaeologist. (Publication 609.) Washington, D.C.: Carnegie Institution of Washington. (12th printing, 1985.)

Shepard, A.O. (1964) Ceramic development of the Lowland and Highland Maya. In Actas y Memorias del XXXV Congreso Internacional de Americanistas (Mexico City, 1962), vol. 1, pp. 249–262. Mexico

S

City: Instituto Nacional de Antropologiá e Historia.

Shepard, A.O. (1965) Rio Grande glaze-paint pottery: A test of petrographic analysis. In F.R. Matson (ed.): Ceramics and Man, pp. 62–87. (Viking Fund Publications in Anthropology 41.) New York: Wenner-Gren Foundation for Anthropological Research.

Shepard, A.O. (1971) Ceramic analysis: The interrelations of method; the relations of analysts and archaeologists. In R.H. Brill (ed.): Science and Archaeology, pp. 55–63. Cambridge, MA: MIT Press.

Sieving

Method, also known as *screening* or *sifting,* used to recover quantifiable data from excavations. Prior to the New Archaeology of the 1960s, sieving was not widely practiced and usually was restricted to the use of coarse-mesh sieves for the recovery of small artifacts, such as coins and beads. Indeed, some archaeologists actively discouraged the use of sieves on the grounds that the exact original position of finds cannot usually be determined using sieves. Any attempt at quantification, however, required total, or near total, recovery from at least samples of a site. Extensive overuse of fine-mesh sieving in disturbed or mixed contexts is often of dubious value and wastes limited resources of archaeological time and money. Sieving should be concentrated on sealed and well-dated contexts.

The types of sieve or screen used and their mesh size will depend on the specific aim of the excavation. Early sites, such as Palaeolithic flint-working sites, are usually subjected to more, finer-mesh, sieving than, for example, postmedieval urban contexts. To recover a total sample of ceramic types (but not every potsherd), a 10-mm mesh is usually adequate. To recover fish and bird bones, a 1-mm mesh is required. The actual size, shape, and design of the sieve depends on the size of the excavation and the volume of soil to be sieved. For small samples, ready-made garden sieves are often adequate for artifact recovery, while small laboratory sieves are suitable for the recovery of small bones. For larger volumes, sieves are often specially made.

There are many designs of sieves for bulk sieving. The most important aspect of design is to enable workers to operate the equipment safely and efficiently. Sieves should, therefore, be designed so that workers do not have to hold the heavy weight of sieve and soil or bend their backs too much while operating the sieve. Also, the location of the sieving is important to prevent either the sievers or other site workers from breathing too much of the dust generated. The sieve frame may be from 50 cm^2 to 1 m or more. Small sieves may have four handles and be shaken by two workers. Larger sieves should be mounted on rollers or rockers or suspended with ropes from a frame or tree branch.

Dry sieving tends to damage fine lithic edges, often adding to the problems of microware analysis. It can also damage carbonized material, making identification difficult. To reduce the abrasive effects of dry sieving, the sieve can be immersed in a container of water. Such wet sieving is especially suitable for the recovery of fine lithics, while carbonized material is better recovered through flotation.

When publishing the results from excavations, it is important to indicate both what areas of the site were sieved and what mesh size was used. This will enable site comparisons to be made. Bone assemblages, for example, can be compared only when the same mesh sizes are employed. The absence of fish and bird bones in published reports may often be the result of too large a mesh size having been employed.

Peter L. Drewett

See also FLOTATION

Further Readings

Barker, P. (1993) Techniques of Archaeological Excavation, 3rd ed. London: Batsford.

Drewett, P.L. (1999) Field Archaeology: An Introduction. London: University College London Press.

Site Mapping

The production of site plans or maps as an essential part of any archaeological field project. Many surveying instruments are available for site mapping; some simple and cheap, others complex and expensive. Instruments selected for any particular survey will depend on an assessment of required accuracy and available resources. The principles of site mapping, however, remain the same whether undertaking a taped survey or using a *total station*.

Prior to any measurements being taken, the nature of the site to be mapped should be assessed. Its rough size and shape should be determined, together with its main features. On the basis of this information, surveying techniques and the required equipment can be selected.

A basic survey can be undertaken with limited equipment. This would consist of two 30-m plastic tapes, six ranging poles, surveyor's arrows or wooden pegs, and a prismatic compass for orienting the plan. If contours are required, then a level, a tripod, and a staff will be essential. Alternatively, a simple plan of a fairly level site can be produced using a plane table. Complex sites may require the use of a *theodolite, electronic distance measurement* (EDM), or a total station.

Any survey should start with the establishment of a framework of fixed survey points. For a small, simple site the framework could be a single straight line, known as a *base line*. For a more complex site, a network of triangles or squares, known as a grid, may be used.

To lay out a single straight line of short length, ranging poles can be sighted with considerable precision by eye. Ranging poles, made of wood, plastic, or metal, are 2 m long, ca. 2-3 cm in diameter, and painted in red and white units, usually of 50 cm. The poles are sighted into a line by one surveyor standing close to the first pole with one eye shut. The second surveyor moves the other poles until all are hidden behind the first pole. These poles must then all be in a straight line. Pegs or surveyor's arrows can be spaced at regular intervals, say 30 m, along this line. The line can also be established using a level or a theodolite.

Right-angle offsets can be laid out from the base line to fix points to be measured, such as the top and bottom of banks or the base of a wall. Alternatively, triangles could be laid out from the base line, with the apex of the triangle being the point to be measured (Figure 1).

For larger sites, the framework should surround the entire site, with all measurements coming in from the framework. Such measurements can, again, be by either offset or triangulation. Any measurements made with tapes should be taken horizontally, and points on the ground obtained by using a plumb bob from the tape. Alternatively, a theodolite could be used.

The plane table is now rarely used by professional land surveyors because of inherent sources of error. Archaeologists are also using total stations with increased frequency (Figure 2). However, the plane table is accurate enough for most archaeological purposes and has the advantage of being simple. As the plan is built up in the field, it has clear advantages when the archaeologist is attempting to interpret sites, especially earthworks.

The plane table consists of a flat drawing surface attached to a tripod. On this is placed a sighting device with a straight edge, known as an *alidade*. Other accessories

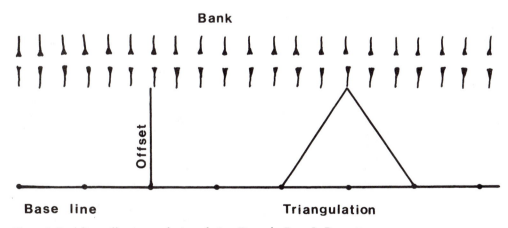

Figure 1. Base line, offsetting, and triangulation. Figure by Peter L. Drewett.

Figure 2. Surveying with a total station. Photograph by Peter L. Drewett.

required are a spirit level, a plumb bob, 30-m plastic tape, and a ranging pole. The plane table should be set up in a position where as much of the site as possible can be seen. The table is made level with the spirit level and the plumb bob used to set it above a fixed point marked by an arrow or wooden peg. The plane table should be covered with plastic drafting film sealed down around the edges.

The alidade is used to sight onto points to be recorded and temporarily marked by ranging poles. The distance from the plane table to the point is then measured, and, having been scaled down, is recorded on the plane table. To reduce inaccuracies that otherwise would be unrecognizable, each point should be recorded from two stations, a technique known as the *intersection method.*

After the plan is completed, whether by offsetting, triangulation, or using the plane table, it is essential that it be oriented in relation to north. This can be achieved using a prismatic compass. These vary in design, but all have some form of sighting mark, which is sighted onto a known point within the area planned. When one is viewing that point, a prism in the compass enables a reading from the compass card. This will be read as so

many degrees from magnetic north. It is often convenient to take such a reading along a base line or other line of the survey framework. True north can then be plotted by using a protractor.

Peter L. Drewett

See also BASE LINE; LEVELING; OFFSETTING; THEODOLITE

Further Readings

Bannister, A., and Raymond, S. (1985) Surveying, 5th ed. London: Pitman.

Bettress, F. (1992) Surveying for Archaeologists, 2nd ed. Durham: University of Durham.

Pugh, J.C. (1975) Surveying for Field Scientists. London: Methuen.

Social Archaeology

The study of past social units and structure on the basis of archaeological evidence and the explication of social change. Social archaeologists generally hold the view that social change is *the* most important component of human development. Unlike biology, with the gene, archaeology has no natural units of classification, and, thus, there are still major disagreements within the discipline on what is social and what is not. An increasing number of archaeologists take the broad view that a social component can be identified in all forms of evidence.

Early Concepts of Society

Attempts at past social classifications are closely related to the contemporary social context. In medieval Europe, a biblical model of society predominated, while the rise of colonialism in the Age of Enlightenment led to an ethnographic model of society, with a logical order of contemporary societies ranged from simple to complex. In the nineteenth-century phase of European nation-state formation, a nationalist model of society was developed, based on ethnic groups, such as Celts and Slavs, and including historical-linguistic entities, such as the Illyrians. It was not until the 1860s that the human groups producing archaeological material dubbed *Palaeolithic* and *Mesolithic* were compared to modern ethnographic societies in Gabriel de Mortillet's unilinear evolutionary scheme. A major opposition developed between the social evolutionary, or stadial, approach and the *Kulturkreise* model of Gustav Kossinna, in which diffusion and migrations were identified as major forces in social change.

Archaeological "Cultures"

Kossinna's model led to the development of the concept of the archaeological *culture,* which has been used ever since by the majority of archaeologists as the building blocks of further analysis, social and otherwise. The cultural model of human groups within bounded space was based partly on an ethnic model drawn from nineteenth-century ethnography and partly on the modern European nation-state. British archaeologists such as Grahame Clark used archaeological cultures as the basis for a reconstruction of social history.

Soviet archaeologists in the 1920s and 1930s strongly opposed Kossinna's *Kulturkreise* approach, which by then had become associated with the Nazi ideology, and developed a unilinear evolutionary model of preclass social change, based on Friedrich Engels, Karl Marx and, ultimately, Lewis Morgan. The important development was not so much the evolutionary position, but rather the attempt to understand how social systems worked in terms of their own internal dynamics and the contradictions of every social formation. These ideas influenced V. Gordon Childe, who synthesized Eurasian prehistory using a social interpretation of archaeological cultures that admitted both diffusion and internal development.

V. Gordon Childe

Childe was undoubtedly the most important social archaeologist in the first half of the twentieth century—the man who created order out of archaeological chaos. From an initial concern with the spread of Indo-European languages and cultural systematics, Childe shifted his focus to social evolution on a Eurasian scale. What began as an unilinear evolutionary model, indicating progress from savagery to barbarism to civilization, developed into a demonstration of the social and economic implications of the three-age system. On a broad level, Childe contrasted the relative self-sufficiency of Neolithic communities based on territorial mixed farming with European Bronze Age communities whose integration through trade enabled advances in industrial production and a real sense of European identity. These communities, in turn, differed markedly from the Asiatic states with their theocratic conservatism. Above all, Childe emphasized the social production and transmission of knowledge, arguing that social groups lived within their conceptual model of reality and stressing that economic and technological innovations could be resisted through religious and political factors. These Marxist influences led Childe to new ways of approaching archaeological cultures, the full range of whose material culture could be interpreted in social terms. In his *Social Evolution,* Childe defined twelve (relatively unstructured) classes of pertinent evidence: the rural economy, specialization of labor, the means of transport, the volume and extent of trade, warfare, population, the form of the family unit, descent, ownership by individuals, the existence of chiefs and administrators, slavery, and art. These fields have defined many of the principal arenas of interest in social archaeology ever since. However, lack of total excavations in most regions inhibited Childe in his aims of detailed community reconstruction using all of these fields of data.

S

Settlement Patterns and Society

In the 1950s, interpretational shifts in America led to a new departure in the relationship between spatial and social archaeology. In his Viru Valley, Peru, survey, Gordon R. Willey attempted a reconstruction of a total society, not just the elite segment, through his settlement-pattern analyses, which paid attention to the relationship between settlement hierarchies and social organization. Kwang-Chih Chang built on Willey's settlement research and his identification of basic household types to define three fundamental social units in settlement studies: the household, the community, and the aggregate. These developments led toward one strand of the New Archaeology of the 1960s.

Processual Approaches

The New Archaeology was instrumental in introducing new sampling strategies and excavation techniques to recover the data that Childe and his contemporaries had lacked, thus permitting the development of fresh problematics in social archaeology. However, the majority of New Archaeologists, including Lewis R. Binford, emphasized culture as an adaptive system and placed a low priority on the reconstruction of social systems. Explanations of cultural change were framed not so much in terms of internal sociocultural developments but rather as prime movers, such as population growth and environmental change.

However, other New Archaeologists took a more explicitly social view of causality. Both Colin Renfrew and Kent V. Flannery used a systemic perspective to examine the changes leading to the growth of social complexity and, eventually, the causes of state formation. Renfrew proposed that state-level organization was an organizational response to the problems of economic and social differentiation in the Aegean region. Flannery considered state formation as a series of hierarchical levels in an organizational system, which needed greater control with ever-increasing numbers of decisions. In both cases, the scale of political organization was emphasized over the nature of basic social units.

Another group of New Archaeologists studied site-level problems through the implications of artifact distributions. James J.F. Deetz and William A. Longacre based studies of intrasite pottery distributions on the assumption of certain kinship residential patterns, attempting to document matrifocal and matrilinear patterns of social organization from artifactual data. However innovative these studies, they were criticized for adopting a reflectionist position ("social order reflects spatial order") and for ignoring the impact of site-formation processes.

Social Networks

In much of the New Archaeological research on social processes, the Childean building blocks of the archaeological culture had hardly been challenged. It was the merit of David L. Clarke to propose an alternative term—*social networks*—that was free from the accumulated baggage of the term *culture*. The implications of networks were twofold: a more dynamic picture of social interaction and a greater importance for trade and exchange. Clarke developed both avenues at both an intrasite level (for Glastonbury, England) and for European prehistory, with his sophisticated studies of trade and industry.

Social Evolution

However, the most important social concomitant of the New Archaeology was its adoption of the social typology of Marshall Sahlins and Elman Service, in which four stadial organizational types—*bands, tribes, chiefdoms,* and *states*—were defined on the basis of recent ethnographic research. An outgrowth of an earlier evolutionary framework, this typology stimulated many archaeologists to identify criteria for a particular stage in any given social group. While evolutionary typologies had the effect of stimulating a much wider interest in social archaeology than was evident previously, the essentialist strategy of identifying social groups as chiefdoms or tribes had no pretensions for explaining changes in stages in general or why one group had reached a particular stage. Such Sahlinesque evolutionary typologies were the focus of many studies in mortuary archaeology.

The Sahlins-Service evolutionary scheme had another effect: the clustering of archaeological research into groups and individuals specializing in bands, tribes and chiefdoms, or states, leading to the generation of subdisciplinary theoretical fields studying hunter-gatherer social structure, the social structure of farmers, and the development of state-level institutional inequalities. More promising trends that stressed integration of the data were clearly defined by Renfrew (1984) in his clarion call for the subfield of social archaeology: a *new* subject, not merely the prehistoric counterpart of social anthropology.

Household Archaeology

The basic units of social analysis continue to be the subject of vigorous debate, nowhere moreso than in early hominid studies, in which taphonomic studies have cast doubt on the existence of open-air base camps (the alternative is long-term artifact distributions in the same locale), as well as cave base camps (alternatively, scavenger dens), hence bringing the model of the early hominid nuclear family into question. A strong component of American social archaeology has been the development of household archaeology, derived from Willey and Chang and attempting to define social households on the basis of structural remains of houses. This has enabled researchers such as Richard Wilk and Ruth Tringham to use much finer intrasite comparisons and develop a dynamic of changing household forms to explain wider sociocultural change. In her model of the Neolithic of southeast Europe, Tringham has defined an early farming phase with short-lived houses and small associated assemblages, a second phase when large, comfortable and well-provisioned houses were constructed, and a third phase with short-term settlement and emphasis on mortuary remains rather than houses. The two continuing problems in household archaeology remain the firmness of the association between houses and nuclear families and the primacy of social change given to changes in household structures rather than wider lineage or intercommunity transformations.

The Early State Module

In discussions of state formation, a critical step forward was the identification of primary-state modules, as distinct from the large number of secondary states that tend to appear soon after the initial transformation. Not surprisingly, this crucial distinction has had a major impact on discussions of core-periphery relations between complex societies (see below).

Increasing Complexity

The second theme of increases in organizational complexity concerns all levels of society. In the hunter-gatherer case, James Woodburn has defined two classes of foragers: immediate-return and delayed-return groups. It is logical to recognize in the second class, with its tendency for investment of many different resources, its different attitudes to time and labor, and its varied forms of food sharing and exchange, the potential for increased complexity. Kenneth Ames and Alain Testart have defined changes in the key variables of scheduling and food storage as important stimulants to forager complexity, while Barbara Bender has argued that increases in social and ritual activities promote increased productivity and, hence, greater cooperation and economic intensification. More recently, Marek Zvelebil has argued that complex foragers share many of the same social traits as initial farmers, indicating one route to the adoption of food production.

Epigenetic Transformations

A major model based on transformations of the basic social unit is Jonathan Friedman and Michael Rowlands' epigenetic model of social change. In this neo-Marxist formulation of social change in the Near East, the starting point is a group of interacting lineages, with circulation of marriage partners and bridewealth. Inequalities in exchange products lead to the emergence of a dominant lineage, whose increasingly skewed relations with other lineages presage the formation of, first, a conical clan and, later, a small-scale Asiatic state. The notion of cyclical change, in which conical clans are created and then fall within centuries, provides a dynamic for the archaeological context, helping explain such early supernovae as Jericho (Palestine) and Çatal Hüyük, in Turkey, as much as pristine states, such as Uruk and Warka, in Iraq.

The Prestige-Goods Model

The prestige-goods model has provided the stimulus for a major explanation of organizational change, namely, the increased production necessary for interelite exchange denoted by exotic symbols of power, which in turn legitimizes the elites in their dominant position. Susan Frankenstein and Rowlands apply such a model to the establishment of Early Iron Age polities north of the Alps, on the basis of variations in the balance between local production of surplus for exchange with the south and control of prestige goods brought by Greek traders to the north. The instability of the prestige-goods system is well illustrated by the replacement of the Heuneburg polity by the Hochdorf polity in successive decades of the sixth century B.C.

Capital Intensification

An alternative pathway toward organizational complexity has been taken by those who maintain that agricultural intensification and capital investment are more significant factors than the long-distance exchange of exotic goods. Archaeologists such as John Bintliff have identified a long-term cycle of intensification and deintensification in the Aegean sequence from the Neolithic to the medieval period. Here, social complexity developed in central places coeval with population expansion and arable extension, while less-hierarchical organization was correlated with dispersed settlements and population and agricultural contraction. A more materialist alternative is Antonio Gilman's identification in the European Bronze Age of numerous fixed-location facilities, such as the plough, irrigation, vineyards, and fruit trees, which provide the potential for intensification while tying owners and users to a particular locale and giving economic advantages to those elites controlling such capital facilities.

State-Level Settlement Hierarchies

Since the development of systems theory, the modeling of state formation has focused on the establishment of organizational hierarchies as much as on the determination of modes of exploitation of subjugated populations. Relying on Robert Adams and Hans Nissen's excellent data from the Uruk and Warka regions, Gregory Johnson used *central-place theory* and *rank-size modeling* to establish the scale of the settlement hierarchies, assuming a parallel field of social hierarchy. However, the theoretical deficiencies of these two models led Renfrew to develop an alternative model based on dominance of alternative central places, in which the largest center dominates the largest region, except for boundary zones of disputed territory. Ecologically, it is clear that the key zone to dominate is the irrigable zone, which in modern times produces 80 percent of the crop in the Fertile Crescent. This is the key to Michael Mann's social-cage model, which relies on population increase and settlement nucleation in the irrigable zone to such an extent that it is socially and economically impossible to relocate outside—hence, the

cage, which limits increasingly nucleated settlement to the main rivers and permits the development of increasingly complex hierarchies of control and domination. In each of these models for state formation, the archaeological criterion for organizational hierarchies has been settlement patterns produced by intensive, systematic survey. An alternative approach to state formation and maintenance is the origins of inequality (see below).

Mortuary Archaeology

A major field of social archaeological research has been the mortuary domain. An early insight was that the occasion of death presents an opportunity for the whole community to make a statement about, or indeed attempt to change, the existing social structure. Recent ethnoarchaeological insights have emphasized that only certain aspects of funerary behavior are preserved in the archaeological mortuary record. An example is John O'Shea's study of Bronze Age cemeteries in the Middle Danube Basin, where preservation of artifacts indicating the status or rank of individuals is far better than for artifacts signifying identities such as clan or lineage membership.

Processual research into the mortuary domain often adopted a reflectionist approach, in which the variety of grave goods, their quantity, or the energy required to produce them was regarded as a direct reflection of the world of the living. It is interesting to note that, long before, Childe had maintained that a peak of rich grave goods was often the sign of abrupt social change, while a shortage of grave goods tended to indicate social stability (see below, the Varna cemetery). These observations foreshadow the postprocessual critique of the reflectionist position.

Hunter-Gatherer Burials

In hunter-gatherer archaeology, the paucity of preserved burials makes every human remain an important find. The debate about the existence of genuine Neanderthal burials strikes at the heart of the cultural and social identity of *Homo sapiens sapiens*. Some argue that all claimed Neanderthal burials are the result of taphonomic or postdepositional processes rather than deliberate human action, privileging modern humans with the first symboling and spiritual behavior parallel to Upper Palaeolithic art. Others claim that the burials are genuine, reinforcing the potential of premodern hominids for this "advanced" behavior and suggesting a Mousterian origin for this cluster of cultural traits.

The Earliest Cemeteries

In late foraging groups, such as in Mesolithic Europe, the occurrence of so-called cemeteries, spatially distinct from domestic settlements, has been interpreted as evidence for increasing sedentism and cultural complexity. In fact, the majority of such cemeteries represent combinations of the domestic and the mortuary arena, in which domestic residues form the context for burials used to define a group identity through attachment to ancestral places. Examples include Ertebølle sites in Scandinavia and the Mesolithic sites of the Iron Gates Gorge of the Danube.

Cemeteries of Early Farming Communities

In early farming groups, the increasing creation of spatially separate cemeteries is an indication of the ideology of group formation and identity, one of the ways in which the lineage social structure is frequently reproduced. A good example of a cemetery interpreted in various ways is the Varna cemetery on the Black Sea coast of Bulgaria. Within more than 250 graves, this Copper Age cemetery has a cluster of seven rich graves containing the richest collection of pre-Bronze Age gold in the Old World, as well as many other finds in a wide variety of materials. Renfrew interprets Varna as the sign of a chiefdom on the basis of the existence of supernumerary grave goods. The excavator, Ivan Ivanov, attributes Varna to the workings of an ancient state, probably incorrectly. The richest graves also contain emblems from many parts of Bulgaria, suggesting that it is the cemetery of a supraregional polity whose component lineages compete with gold to provide the next paramount. There are also many symbolic artifacts, the meanings of which remain ambiguous but which are closely related to the domestic domain of tell settlements. Varna is a symbol of the potential of mortuary archaeology for new and varied social interpretations.

The Contribution of Physical Anthropology

A further advance in mortuary archaeology is the combination of physical anthropological, dietary, and archaeological information. In the search for status differentials, the biological hypothesis that elites had access to better diets could be tested through isotopic analysis of human bone. In her analysis of Hopewell populations in the Lower Illinois Valley, Jane E. Buikstra contrasted a higher mammalian meat protein content in the diet of males shown to be high ranking from grave-goods analysis with a vegetable-based diet for lower-status males. In her analysis of the diets of males and females in the Saura of Peru, Christine Hasdorf demonstrates a change from a similar diet in males and females in the pre-Inca period to higher consumption of high-status maize and meat by males than by the females under the Inca hegemony—a change interpreted as a greater male participation in the political life of gatherings, workforces, and rituals. Such biological studies shed complementary light on traditional artifact-based analyses and stimulate important social insights from the mortuary domain.

Exchange and Trade

Another cross-cutting theme is interaction, in terms of both exchange and trade. In its processual definition as "action at a distance," trade was used as a comparative indicator of the extent of social control and wealth. A hierarchy of forms of exchange and trade was developed paralleling the stages in social evolutionary theory: sharing for foragers, reciprocity for egalitarian groups, redistribution for chiefdoms, and market exchange for states. A whole battery of scientific characterization techniques was developed to source "exotic" artifacts, thus providing solid spatial data for exchange studies. This reflectionist scheme failed when it became clear that the exchange and social typologies did not correlate well; an example is Christopher Peebles and Susan Kus's finding that Hawaiian chiefdoms played no clear redistributional role in their political system. Subsequently, many exchange studies became more closely integrated with the sequence of production, especially in cases of craft specialization. The differentiation of attached and peripatetic craft specialists proved an important breakthrough, as did the refinement of the notion of *value* in exchanged artifacts.

World Systems Theory

A major theme in exchange studies since the late 1970s was the prospect of re-creating a precapitalist world system, in the manner of Immanuel Wallerstein's global model for the sixteenth century A.D. If a world system is defined as large-scale structural interdependence among economically complementary zones, it is hard to see such a system operating before the Bronze Age of the Near East or the Iron Age of Europe. Philip Kohl has developed a model of an Asiatic world system in the third millennium B.C., stretching from the eastern Mediterranean to Central Asia and the Indus Valley. However, with multiple centers, shared technologies, logistical constraints on overland trade, and military rather than trading tendencies, this is a different system from that of Wallerstein. The existence of exotic prestige goods alone is unlikely to define a world system, but rather a system of political gift alliances with few economic overtones, as is the preferred interpretation for prestige-goods exchange between royal elites in Celtic Europe.

The Social Construction of Landscape

More recently, an important theme for social investigations has been the consideration of the imprinting of social relationships on the landscape. Timothy Ingold has made a tripartite distinction among different forms of territory: one-dimensional (places as dots on a map), two-dimensional (paths across a landscape), and three-dimensional (fixed areas of land under tenure). In foraging and mobile farming groups, the first two forms of territoriality are common, with relatively few traces except for specific locales surviving in the landscape. The emphasis lies in cultural practices that stress cyclical time and returning to places already imbued with cultural memories. It is with the growth of the tenurial approach to land that there tends to be a proliferation of territorial divisions or boundaries, with the enclosure of land, settlements, or monuments. If initial enclosure is related to statements about group identity and social formations, continued land division is concerned with inheritance and lineage or family power. The construction of spectacularly large monuments, such as Silbury Hill in England or Moundsville in Alabama, is now considered to relate less to short-term peaks in exploitative powers of elite leadership—reflected, for processualists, by labor estimates—than to the creation of a long-term, multiperiod cultural landscape re-

plete with ancestral, as well as current, power.

The Archaeology of Capitalism

The increasing concentration of wealth in state-level landscapes indicates a high level of surplus production and consumption in magnificent monuments, which are especially elaborate early in the process of social transformations. Archaeological investigations of the landscapes characteristic of more recent times have revealed the ideological basis of capitalist societies, as Randall H. McGuire has shown for the development of late-nineteenth and twentieth-century Binghamton, New York; the townscape and its rural hinterland revealed its ideological roots in Social Darwinism, in which industrialists used the landscape as a tool in the negotiation of a new ideology of class and society.

Social Power

This example leads to the final cross-cutting theme of social power, authority and exploitation. The traditional archaeological approach to power is based on analyses of the power that accrues to institutions, as reflected in monumental art and architecture, such as the ziggurats, pyramids, and temple complexes featured in Childe's ten criteria for civilization. However, a multidimensional approach to social power has been developed by Mann, in his IEMP model, in which ideological, economic, military, and political power form coeval social networks in which the tensions of the four power formations are constantly played out. The origins of inequality can be located in any of these power networks and relate to asymmetrical divisions of resources between individuals and groups, whether by gender, class, or kinship group. Reinforcement of an initial asymmetry by ideological means, through controlling cultural norms and values, broadens the power differential and deepens the inequalities. The study of social power in prehistory is in its infancy, yet it possesses great potential for the explanation of hitherto unexplained social transformations.

In summary, social archaeology has progressed from a largely reflectionist methodology closely linked to Sahlinesque social typologies to a more varied research field in which social power, authority, and inequalities are analyzed in all facets of the material record—in the landscape, the monument, the settlement, and the grave.

John Chapman

See also CHILDE; VERE GORDON; ETHNOAR-CHAEOLOGY; EXPERIMENTAL ARCHAEOLOGY; GENDER ARCHAEOLOGY; MARXIST ARCHAE-OLOGY; NEW/PROCESSUAL ARCHAEOLOGY; POSTPROCESSUAL ARCHAEOLOGY; SETTLE-MENT ARCHAEOLOGY, THEORY

Further Readings

Chapman, R., Kinnes, I., and Randsbord, K., eds. (1971) The Archaeology of Death. Cambridge: Cambridge University Press.

Childe, V.G. (1944) Man Makes Himself. London: Watts.

Childe, V.G. (1951) Social Evolution. London: Watts.

Flannery, K.V., and Marcus, J. (1983) The Cloud People. London: Academic.

Frankenstein, S., and Rowlands, M. (1978) The internal structure and regional context of Early Iron Age society in southwestern Germany. University of London Institute of Archaeology Bulletin 15:74–112.

Friedman, J., and Rowlands, M., eds. (1975) The Evolution of Social Systems. London: Duckworth.

Mann, M. (1986) The Sources of Social Power, vol. 1: From the Beginnings to A.D. 1760. Cambridge: Cambridge University Press.

McGuire, R.H., and Paynter, R., eds. (1991) The Archaeology of Inequality. Oxford: Blackwell.

Renfrew, C. (1972) The Emergence of Civilisation. London: Methuen.

Renfrew, C. (1984) Approaches to Social Archaeology. Edinburgh: Edinburgh University Press.

Renfrew, C., and Shennan, S.J., eds. (1982) Ranking, Resources and Exchange. Cambridge: Cambridge University Press.

Service, E.R. (1971) Primitive Social Organization: An Evolutionary Perspective. New York: Random House.

Soil and Sediment Analysis

Analysis of the sedimentary and soil matrix where artifacts are found for information on the age, landscape, and environmental setting of human occupations and the cultural processes that formed the archaeological record. Most archaeological data are recovered from sedimentary deposits or associated soils. Without examining the sedimentary matrix and the chemical residues, one cannot reconstruct the wide range of cultural and natural processes of site formation.

Sediments accumulate either mechanically or chemically. Mechanical accumulation includes the deposition of fine sands and mud particles that have buried human occupations on floodplains. Artifacts in these sites also may be eroded, transported, and redeposited as sedimentary particles. Chemical accumulations, such as lime mud in lake basins, can cover and protect prehistoric sites once situated near the shoreline. After deposition, other natural and cultural processes often alter sediments. For example, later human activity can add chemical elements, such as phosphate, to sediments and soils.

After deposition, a variety of changes can occur within a sediment or archaeological layer. Such alterations are superimposed on the original makeup of the sediment and its constituents. These alterations reflect postdepositional and postoccupational environments and climatic settings. In some instances, the weathering cycle begins again. This time, the weathering leads to the development of soils and the production of secondary alterations and accumulations. While disruptive of primary relationships, secondary accumulations, such as carbonate crusts on artifacts, can provide minimum ages for the artifacts and evidence of changing environmental conditions.

The term *archaeological sediment* is used to distinguish deposits that form that part of the sedimentary record resulting directly from past human activities. The term also is used to refer to artifacts or archaeological features that are in primary context. Sometimes it is difficult to ascertain when artifacts are not in primary context. Sedimentary deposits can be composed of artifacts that have been so greatly disturbed by postoccupational processes that original patterns produced by human activities have been lost.

There are three main groups of sediments and sedimentary rocks: *clastic, chemical,* and *organic.* Sediments composed of fragments of other rocks and deposited by physical processes are termed clastics. Objects such as stone tools, pottery, and bones can be deposited as clastic sediments. Chemical and biogenic deposition results in the formation of carbonate, evaporate, and organic deposits. Materials introduced as byproducts of animal waste, such as phosphate, would be a chemical deposit. Organics include decomposed artifacts made from plants and animals used by humans.

Most artifacts (including lithics, metal, sherds, and beads) that are part of a sedimentary deposit are clastic particles. Clastic deposits are classified by geologists in terms of two basic attributes: mineral composition and the range of particle sizes. The latter is partly encompassed by the term *texture*. There are several scales used to differentiate particle sizes.

The second major category of sediments consists of minerals that have been deposited by precipitation from solution. The most widespread of these minerals is calcite (calcium carbonate). A wide range of chemical deposits can be utilized in evaluating paleoenvironmental settings of archaeological sites. Many, such as iron oxide, manganese oxide, sulfate, silica, and phosphate, also have been important resources for humans. Humans and human activity are important contributors of chemicals to sedimentary systems.

Decayed and decomposed plants and animals form the third critical component of the sedimentary system. Organic material is an important aspect of soil-forming processes and is a valuable indicator of past environmental conditions. Because it contains carbon, organic material is critical for radiocarbon dating. Organic matter in sediments can reach levels of nearly 100 percent in some Quaternary peatlike deposits. Sediments containing high amounts of organic matter are termed *carbonaceous*. Once deposited, organic matter may be reused by plants and animals, undergo biochemical decay, or be destroyed by oxidation.

The onset of cultivation and agriculture ushered in a more intensive use of the Earth's surface, and the importance of available soil types became vital to human affairs. An understanding of soils is equally vital to archaeology. A *soil horizon* is a layer of soil, approximately parallel to the soil surface, with characteristics produced by soil-forming processes. The upper part of a sedimentary deposit can contain pedogenic materials, which are weathering profiles developed within preexisting sediments. Soils are the result of horizontal sequences superimposed on sediments. These horizontal sequences are created by weathering, alteration, and accumulation in the top part of a deposit. Soil formation results in the development of a *soil profile* exhibiting a vertical series of horizons. Perhaps the single most important concept applicable to archaeological interpretations derived from the study of sedimentary processes is that artifact distributions can be influenced by the same sedimentological principles as other clastic particles. Artifacts and archaeological features are subject to the processes of weathering, transport, deposition, and alteration.

Description and analysis of sediments and soils from archaeological sites and the areas surrounding them provide a means to identify depositional processes and environments, as well as postdepositional alterations. Following is a presentation of some of the characteristics of soils and sediments, including color, cementation, texture, and composition, that are important in archaeological interpretation.

Color

One of the most obvious attributes of an archaeological deposit is color. The factors that most influence color are the source rocks, the conditions of weathering, the physical and chemical conditions at the site of deposition, and postdepositional changes. Sediment and soil color relate to a large number of phenomena. Color determination using a Munsell color chart can contribute to recognizing and interpreting the processes and conditions under which sediments and soils have formed. Darker colors often indicate the accumulation of organic matter in a deposit, but also can mean the presence of manganese oxide, or dark-colored rock or mineral fragments. Unfortunately, sediment color may be postdepositional as well as primary. Postdepositional alterations, including contributions from human activities, tend to darken sediments. In occupational deposits, dark colors may be the result of human activity depositing organics or forming charcoal in hearths. The effect of groundwater phenomena such as oxidation/reduction reactions can produce sharp-edged color patterns very confusing to archaeologists.

Cementation

Natural cementation transforms loose sediments into consolidated rock. There are practical reasons for understanding the nature of the cementation in archaeological deposits. The ability to excavate strata and recover artifacts and faunal material is influenced by the degree of cementation. While loose sediments may make maintaining profiles and retaining information on the location and orientation of artifacts difficult, well-cemented deposits tend to result in the preferential recovery of larger artifacts and bones and more fragmentation of the materials that are recovered. Calcite cement is commonly an indication of initial diagenesis and lithification of sedimentary deposits. Cementation and induration (i.e., hardening due to pressure or heat) of a sediment may imply that the deposit has once been saturated with water. Lithified materials may be natural substances, such as stone, used by humans in structural features, or they may be materials, such as mud brick, that are consolidated because of the activities of humans. Cementation of deposits overlying artifact-bearing deposits provides protection from weathering and erosion, thus helping preserve intact the surfaces of occupation.

Texture

The texture of sediments refers to the size, shape, sorting, and orientation of particles. From the perspective of artifacts as sedimentary particles, the principles used to characterize the texture of a deposit are applicable to archaeological components within sedimentary deposits. The particle-size frequency distribution in a sediment provides an indication of the transport and depositional systems that resulted in the accumulation of the sediments and artifacts. It is obviously important to know whether a site sedimentary matrix is *eolian* (wind deposited) or *fluvial* (river deposited). Fossils and artifacts are also sedimentary components that can be regarded as either unique particles in a depositional system or as inclusions.

Grain shape may be the result of transport processes or a relic of the source of the particles. The spatial orientation of particles (called the *petrofabric*) can reveal information on sediment history and artifact movement. The surface textures of quartz grains are related to the source and transport mechanisms. Characteristic fractures in quartz grains also can reveal severe burning of a soil. Soil structures are a guide not only to *pedogenesis* (soil formation), but also to environmental change. The development of a soil profile is gradual, and periods of landscape stability may be interrupted by periods of erosion or deposition. The key to site-setting analysis lies in the sedimentary record.

The shape and roundness of clastic particles depend in part on the medium and mode of transport. The edges of grains become more rounded and the grains become more spherical during transport. Postdepositional trampling also affects grain roundness. Soil-formation processes alter the fabric of the original deposit by translocation of materials.

The grain-size distributions of lithic debris reflect the lithic-manufacturing process, one size for material produced by flake reduction and another size for material detached during the flake-reduction process. Grain-size analysis is used frequently in archaeology to reconstruct the source of the site sedimentation matrix. This has been applied successfully to caves and rockshelters, tells, middens, and alluvial sites.

Composition

The composition of a deposit refers to the clastic, chemical, and organic constituents of a sediment or soil, as well as fossil and artifact inclusions. Those physical and chemical compositions should be determined that aid in the interpretation of the deposits. The relative amount of clastics compared to components formed after deposition can be used to distinguish different sedimentary environments. Clastic particles derived from an external source area are called *exogenic*. In contrast, *endogenic* materials are derived from material in solution or near the point of deposition.

The composition of the clay-sized fraction of soils and sediments is often studied in relation to prehistoric agriculture, pedological processes, site-formation processes, and diagenesis. Soil formation alters the chemical and mineral composition of the original deposit.

The types of minerals precipitated from solution can be used to infer environmental settings associated with archaeological accumulations. The principal endogenic phase is calcite. Pedogenic *calcrete* (a concrete-like layer of calcium carbonate created by regular soil-formation processes) can be formed by downward migration *(illuviation)*. Early stages of *caliche* formation can form powdery or indurated isolated nodules of carbonate. With time, these can become extensive horizons of carbonate. Various stages in this progression have been used as indicators of age and climate.

Phosphorus is the best chemical indicator of archaeological deposits and their complex evolution. It has been shown that the relative proportions of different kinds of phosphate could be related to past human land use. Very soluble phosphates were found to be associated with lands used for crop production, specifically for mixed vegetable cultivation. These lands contained low amounts of two other types of phosphate: (1) tightly bound iron and aluminum phosphate and (2) calcium phosphates. In land used as forests, there were low amounts of calcium phosphates but about equal proportions of easily soluble iron and aluminum phosphates. In abandoned residential land-use areas, the amounts of these three types of phosphates were about the same. These patterns indicate that some chemicals produce spatial patterns indicative of particular human uses of the landscape. Inorganic-phosphate analysis has proved successful in detecting abandoned settlement sites. Phosphorus and magnesium analyses have been used to differentiate rodent burrows from post molds.

The acidity (pH) can be used to distinguish archaeological strata, features from nonfeatures, and pedogenesis. Low pH (high acidity) increases the potential for pollen and phytolith preservation in soils and sediments but decreases the potential for preservation of bone and shell.

Most chemical nutrients required for all life on land are supplied from the soil. Nitrogen, oxygen, and carbon dioxide are supplied from the atmosphere, and water is taken from the hydrosphere. Human activities, even in nonfarming settlements, alter the levels of micro and macro plant nutrients. Macro nutrients are the chemical elements nitrogen (N), phosphorous (P), potassium (K), calcium (Ca), magnesium (Mg), and sulfur (S). Because these elements are used by all plants, the removal of vegetation by human activities depletes their concentration in soils and underlying sediments. Substantial amounts of nitrogen, phosphorus, and calcium are added to the soil by food wastes and human/animal wastes. Wood burning raises the amount of magnesium in the soil.

Organic content in carbonaceous deposits reflects the past presence of plants or other biota. Peats, composed chiefly of organic material, form in freshwater environments, although they can also develop in salt marshes or slightly brackish waters. *Sapropels,* consisting of dark organic-rich sediments, form under more diverse conditions of organic decomposition in lake basins. Plant and organic matter also are introduced into sedimentary contexts as part of the detrital component. This can complicate the use of basin sedimentary sequences for developing paleoecological and chronological interpretations. Pollen stratigraphies, for example, may represent regional watershed environmental conditions instead of the local, site-specific setting. In other instances, "dead" carbon can be washed in, making radiocarbon measurements produce dates that are too old.

Fossils and artifacts are also sedimentary components that can be regarded as either unique particles in a depositional system or as inclusions. Depending on whether they are in primary or secondary context, they can provide information about depositional contexts. The artifact or fossil taphonomy and sedimentology of these "inclusions" is a critical aspect of archaeological interpretation. Both fossils and artifacts can be used as biostratigraphic markers when due consideration is given to taphonomic agencies of redeposition.

Control Samples

To evaluate the relative contributions of natural versus cultural processes in the formation of archaeological deposits, it is necessary to collect comparative samples from one or more control areas off the site affected by human activity but nearby in similar geomorphical and soil regimes. Control samples form the basis for assessing soil genesis in site-formation processes, the nature of site depositional events, sediment sources, transport agents, site boundaries, and postdepositional (diagenetic) alterations.

Analytical Techniques

One of the most basic methods of sediment and soil analysis is grain-size analysis, which determines the frequency distribution of the sizes of clastic particles. (Grain-size analysis is covered in a separate entry.) Techniques of chemical analysis, both trace and macro, are far too numerous and so well documented that a review is not warranted here. The determination of pH is accomplished by pH tapes or pH meters, both readily available. Standard analytical techniques are described in other entries in this encyclopedia (e.g., X-ray diffraction and X-ray fluorescence analyses). Special techniques designed for archaeological contexts are included in the Further Readings.

One of the most underutilized techniques available to archaeologists is *petrography,* using a polarizing microscope to identify and study materials either as individual grains or in thin section. The polarizing microscope is the most important instrument for determining the optical properties of minerals. Information can be obtained easily and quickly. The polarizing microscope has two functions: to provide an enlarged image of an object placed on the microscope stage and to provide plane and crossed polarized light and convergent light. Minerals exhibit a host of distinguishing characteristics in plane and crossed polarized light and in convergent polarized light. As with other compound microscopes, polarizing microscopes contain a variety of other lenses and devices that can modify the transmission of light for specialized studies. Automated procedures are now available to evaluate the volumetric size distribution of grains from digital images of thin sections.

Microscopic techniques are used for grain morphology (e.g., roundness and sphericity) and identification when the particle size is greater than ca. 20 microns. The analysis of sand-size particles is most often determined by the microscopic point counting of grains. Many particles can be identified strictly on the basis of their morphology (e.g., volcanic shards and many fibers). The study of surface textures in silt and sand grains and the morphological characteristics of fine particles are best done with a scanning electron microscope (SEM). SEM provides a continuous range of magnification from 100x to ca. 60,000x. The chemical composition of individual grains can be determined using an electron microprobe or a SEM with energy dispersive X-ray spectrometry (EDS). The heavy-mineral fraction (i.e., minerals with a density greater than 2.9 gm/cm^3) can be separated by heavy-liquid

techniques for greater ease in identification. Heavy-mineral analysis is used in provenance and correlation studies.

The use of thin-section petrography in soil and sediment analyses is referred to as *micromorphology.* Petroleum-based products have been developed that can successfully impregnate and indurate soils and soft sediments. This technique allows observation of the microfabric (including pore features) and composition of the material. Other sedimentological techniques disaggregate the sample, losing all fabric and microcontextual information. Thin-sections also provide the opportunity to examine bedding, texture, and porosity through the use of *microradiography.* Micromorphology is the only technique that allows detailed study of small or micro features, such as floors, hearths, burning episodes, fecal residues, and many aspects of pedogenesis.

Although many techniques are available for the determination of organic carbon and carbonates, the one most commonly used is the *loss-on-ignition method,* which is reliable and cost effective. As with all analytical techniques, special problems, such as the percent of clay in the sample, must be understood before accurate determinations can be made (see Stein 1987). Determination of the percentage of clay in a sample is accomplished easily by settling-tube techniques in grain-size analysis. Accurate clay mineral identification requires the use of X-ray diffraction accompanied by special preparation procedures.

George R. Rapp, Jr.

See also ARCHAEOLOGICAL SITES, FORMATION PROCESSES; GRAIN-SIZE ANALYSIS; PETROGRAPHY; STRATIFICATION; STRATIGRAPHY; TAPHONOMY; X-RAY DIFFRACTION (XRD) ANALYSIS; X-RAY FLUORESCENCE (XRF) ANALYSIS

Further Readings

Butzer, K. (1981) Cave sediments, Upper Pleistocene stratigraphy, and Mousterian facies in Cantabrian Spain. Journal of Archaeological Science 8:133–183.

Courty, M., Goldberg, P., and Macphail, R. (1989) Soils and Micromorphology in Archaeology. Cambridge: Cambridge University Press.

Eidt, R. (1985) Theoretical and practical considerations in the analysis of anthrosols. In G. Rapp, Jr., and J. Gifford (eds.):

Archaeological Geology. New Haven, CT: Yale University Press.

Farrand, W. (1979) Chronology and paleoenvironment of Levantine prehistoric sites as seen from sediment studies. Journal of Archaeological Science 6:369–392.

Gifford, J., Rapp, G., and Moss, C. (1982) The sedimentary matrix. In G. Rapp, Jr., and J. Gifford (eds.): Troy: The Archaeological Geology. Princeton, NJ: Princeton University Press.

Hassan, F. (1978) Sediments in archaeology: Methods and implications for palaeoenvironmental and cultural analysis. Journal of Field Archaeology 5:197–213.

Rosen, A. (1986) Cities of Clay. Chicago: University of Chicago Press.

Shackley, M. (1981) Environmental Archaeology. London: Allen and Unwin.

Stein, J., (1987) Deposits for archaeologists. In M.B. Schiffer (ed.): Advances in Archaeological Method and Theory, vol. 11, pp. 337–395. San Diego: Academic.

Stein, J., and Farrand, W., eds. (1985) Archaeological Sediments in Context. Orono, ME: Center for the Study of Early Man, Institute for Quaternary Studies, University of Maine.

Sonar

A Second World War United States Navy acronym for "sound navigation and ranging." Originally developed in the early twentieth century for the acoustic detection of icebergs, what is now called *sonar* was soon used for detecting First World War submarines. Its potential for locating ancient shipwrecks, however, was not demonstrated until 1967. Earlier in the decade, near the town of Yalıkavak on the Turkish coast, spongers had netted two statues, but weeks of visual survey in 1965, using both towed television and a towed one-person capsule, could not locate the wreck that yielded them. In only one day in 1967, side-scan sonar located a wreck 85 m deep in the search area. Since then, sonar has played an increasingly important role in archaeology, for it is a powerful tool for locating submerged sites in areas where depth, visibility, and/or the size of the search area preclude visual search by divers, television-equipped remotely operated vehicles (ROVs), or research submarines. Two types of sonar are used for archaeological prospecting: *side-scan sonar,* for sites that protrude above the sea, lake, or river bed, and *sub-bottom profilers,* for sites that lie invisible beneath the bottom sediments of similar bodies of water.

Side-Scan Sonar

The sonar unit, commonly shaped like a small torpedo and sometimes called a *fish,* is towed by cable as close to the bottom as is practical behind a surface vessel. One or more transducers on the towed sonar emit narrow beams of high-frequency (20 kHz to 1 mHz) sound pulses downward and outward to either side. The pulses are reflected back toward the sonar by the seabed just as sound waves in air bounce off surfaces and return to their source as echoes. The strengths of the echoes are transmitted by coaxial cable to the surface vessel, where they are displayed on either a computer screen or chemically treated paper that moves continuously through a recorder. If the bottom is flat and featureless, the echoes will be very weak, but detectable, providing a flat-background signal on the recorder or computer screen. Any object protruding from the bottom, however, will provide a much stronger echo, which is translated by the sonar system into a darker image on the recorder paper; on the computer screen, stronger echoes are displayed in different colors. As the surface vessel and sonar are constantly moving forward, several pulses per second can record the shape of the object being sensed. Because at slower speeds the sonar can send more pulses to the seabed object while passing it, producing a picture with greater definition, the towing vessel usually travels at only two to four knots. The size of the target is of consequence. A small cluster of amphoras on the seabed, all that may be visible of a large cargo, can resemble a rock outcrop, whereas the War of 1812 schooner *Hamilton,* lying ca. 90 m deep in Lake Champlain, or the mid-nineteenth-century *Breadalbane,* found slightly deeper in Canada's Northwest Passage, appeared with almost photographic clarity when located, their standing masts clearly visible on the paper printouts.

More recent sonar systems have the advantage of feeding information from the sonar into a computer that can process the data. The data are initially stored in computer memory, from which any bottom feature on the screen can be pulled up into a window where it can be magnified or processed with averaging programs and filters to make the image easier to interpret; a wide selection of colors and intensities can be assigned to different signal strengths, producing acoustic maps that are more representative of the seabed than those printed on paper.

Although there have been serendipitous discoveries of ancient wrecks by sonar, as in the case of a Roman amphora carrier found during the search for a DC-9 airplane 1,100 m deep in the Tyrrhenian Sea, sonar surveys for otherwise unknown ancient wrecks usually follow chance discoveries of artifacts in fishermen's nets. In these cases, the search area may be only a few square kilometers, depending on the memory and reliability of the fisherman. Searches for historic wrecks, however, must in general be preceded by archival research to define the search area. In the case of the successful search for the *Hamilton,* and its sister ship *Scourge,* the survey area was 85 km²; the search area for the famed Civil War *Monitor* was a rectangle 10 × 25 km, or 250 km² of ocean floor; the *Titanic* was found 4,000 m deep by a U.S.-French expedition in a 390-km² zone; and the *S.S. Central America,* lost in 1857, was identified in 1987 after a forty-day survey of an astonishing 3,600 km² of ocean floor the previous year. In the case of the *Central America,* sunk in water nearly 2.5 km deep ca. 320 km off the coast of South Carolina, the search team first made a probability map based on contemporary accounts of the ship's last position, and modern estimates of winds and currents at the time, using a modification of a United States Coast Guard CASP (computer-assisted search-planning program).

Precise navigation is needed for efficient search patterns in the chosen survey area. The sonar is towed as much as possible in straight lines. If the search lanes are too close, bottom coverage will overlap needlessly, wasting time and money, whereas if they are too far apart, a crucial area may be missed. The widths of search swaths vary according to conditions. In some cases, they may be only 100 m wide. For the huge *Central America* search area, however, search swaths were 2,500 m on a side, covering a lane 5 km wide.

Precise navigation is also critical because, once targets are sighted, the survey ship must be able to return to them. For the first archaeological detection of an ancient wreck by sonar, near Yalıkavak, Turkey, in 1967, two land-based transit operators radioed directions to the fishing trawler that towed the sonar, while a third member of the expedition manually plotted the course on board, recording the transit bearings every two minutes. Sighting from these stations and plotting the data required three additional people in the team, but this simple method gave such precision that a year later, directed from the same transit stations, the survey team was able to return to the target and lower a television camera directly onto the amphora pile 85 m below. Later, electronic ranging systems became available, but they were expensive and still required base stations established on shore. By the 1990s, however, the new global positioning system (GPS) made all such methods obsolete.

The advent of GPS has made it possible to plot the towing vessel's position with extremely high accuracy by means of an inexpensive, hand-held receiver. Data from the GPS are fed electronically to the computer so that, for each sonar pulse, the instantaneous position of the research vessel is recorded. With this information, the computer program can calculate and display the coordinates of any anomaly that appears on the screen. It is important to note, however, that these positions relate to the research vessel itself and not to the sonar fish, which may be hundreds of meters behind it and perhaps off to one side; the distance between the navigation receiver and the sensor fish is called *layback.* To know the position of the fish, one can mount transducers on each side of the towing vessel's stern and compute the sonar's position.

For military reasons, the U.S. government has chosen to introduce random errors into GPS signals so that they no longer provide the high accuracy a tight search pattern requires. To counteract this, differential GPS units (DGPS) have been developed. These use an additional shore-based station to monitor the variations in the GPS satellite information and transmit these data to the research vessel, which adjusts its own "fix" accordingly.

When one or more likely targets have been recorded, they must be identified visually. In the case of the wreck off Yalıkavak, the target was identified from the two-person submarine *Asherah* as a first-century B.C. amphora mound and, later, with television simply dangled from a fishing boat, like the still cameras and television lowered onto the

Monitor when it was found in 1973 (ironically, not by side-scan sonar, but by a simpler acoustic depth finder being used by a team member who was fishing over the side of the survey vessel). Only two years later, in 1975, the *Hamilton* and the *Scourge* were inspected more efficiently by ROVs, which have become standard on most surveys, although the *Breadalbane* was examined in 1980 from a one-person submersible called a WASP, and remains of the *Titanic* were inspected both with an ROV and from the deep-diving submarine *Alvin*.

Sub-Bottom Profilers

Like the side-scan sonar, the sub-bottom profiler sends out acoustic pulses and listens for echoes, but the pulses are directed downward toward the seabed and have a much lower frequency, typically 3.5–5 kHz, that can actually penetrate sand to significant depths.

For distinguishing "rocks from wrecks" during sonar surveys, sub-bottom profiling is sometimes a viable alternative to deploying an ROV. Typically, a rock outcrop has the signature of a broad sub-bottom mountain with its peak sticking out of the sand around it. In contrast, a partly covered amphora mound will be seen to continue only a few meters below the bottom before the sand it is lying on becomes visible.

Some wrecks and other archaeological remains are completely imbedded in the seafloor and, thus, cannot be detected at all by side-scanning sonar. These can be detected by a sub-bottom profiler whose sound pulses penetrate sediment but are reflected off ballast, pottery, or other objects, including organic cargoes that have produced deposits of gaseous sludge, which is an excellent reflector.

Sub-bottom sonar, sending its sound pulses almost straight down, has an extremely narrow search swath and is useful only in very small areas, such as harbors. In an unsuccessful search of St. Ann's Bay, Jamaica, for two caravels abandoned by Columbus during his fourth voyage, six eighteenth-century British ships were found. As with targets found by side-scan sonar, actual identification of these targets was difficult, in each case requiring the removal of meters of sediment for visual inspection.

George F. Bass
Donald A. Frey

See also NAUTICAL ARCHAEOLOGY; REMOTELY OPERATED VEHICLES; UNDERWATER ARCHAEOLOGY

Further Readings

Bass, G.F., and Joline, L.T. (1968) Problems of deep wreck identification. Expedition 11(1):9–12.

Fish, J.P., and Carr, H.A. (1990) Sound Underwater Images. Orleans, MA: Lower Cape.

Stone, L.D. (1992) Search for the SS *Central America*: Mathematical treasure hunting. Interfaces 22(1):32–54.

Spatial Analysis

The study of the spatial distributions of archaeological objects. The scale of the study can vary from regional, in which the objects are archaeological sites or artifact types (*intersite analysis*), to the individual site, in which the objects are artifacts and/or ecofacts (*intrasite analysis*). The term does not include similar analyses at smaller scales (e.g., microscopic study of wear on flint or thin sections of pottery), which are normally called *image analysis*. Ian Hodder developed the subject as a coherent body of theory in the 1970s, working mainly at the intersite level and trying to provide a rigorous foundation for the common archaeological practice of studying distribution maps of sites and artifacts and drawing conclusions from them. He pointed out that, although the human eye is very good at seeing patterns that may exist in distribution maps or plots, it is also good at seeing patterns when they do not exist (e.g., in random data); archaeologists needed a more rigorous approach than the eyeball method. One major problem is the quality and consistency of data, particularly if they have been collected over a wide area by many people over a long period of time. For this reason, subsequent work (e.g., by Robert Whallon) tended to concentrate on the intrasite level, where it was easier to control the quality of the data. Recent trends have begun to incorporate spatial analysis into geographic information systems (GIS), but it remains a body of theory in its own right.

Intersite Analysis

The study of archaeological distribution maps has a long history, going back well into the nineteenth century. A theoretical impetus came from the Quantitative Revolution of geography in the 1960s, which provided models for the analysis of settlement patterns and of the regional distributions of artifacts and artifact types, as well as statistical techniques for studying such patterns. *Central-place theory* gave a model for the study of the way in which sites of different sizes in a region relate to each other, particularly emphasizing the way in which complex settlement patterns can develop out of simple ones. Statistical techniques can also elucidate relationships between settlement patterns and topographical factors. The study of artifact distributions at this scale can yield information on (1) the definition of cultural or stylistic areas within a region and (2) the mechanisms of the distribution of artifacts from a center of production. The aim of (1) is to detect groups of artifact types that tend to co-occur spatially within an area and not to co-occur with other types found in nearby areas. Archaeologists can interpret these spatial patterns according to the period of study and their own theoretical inclinations. The aim of (2) is to go beyond the simple observation that the proportion of artifacts of a certain type generally decreases as the distance from their center of production increases, to study *how* it decreases (*fall-off patterns*). Models of different mechanisms of distribution (e.g., down-the-line distribution, distribution through market centers) yield different theoretical distribution patterns; comparison with observed patterns can suggest appropriate mechanisms and highlight differences between models and data. Often such differences are more interesting than the actual model—for example, in a classic study of the distribution of pottery from a late Roman production center north of Oxford, England, discrepancies between the data and a simple model of uniform fall-off rates strongly suggested that the main means of distribution was by water rather than overland (Fulford and Hodder 1974).

Intrasite Analysis

Intrasite analysis grew up in the 1970s as a way of exploring patterns of activity on open sites, based on the premise that patterned activity should result in patterned distributions of artifact types. Initially, it borrowed many of its techniques from plant ecology, but it gradually developed methods that were more congruent to archaeological data. It passed rapidly through examination of the randomness or otherwise of the distributions of single artifact (or ecofact) types to the examination of the co-occurrence of two or more types, with a view to establishing toolkits (groups of types used together in some common task). Many problems arose, both theoretical (e.g., concerning the validity of the toolkit concept) and practical (especially concerning the definition of a site, since redefining the boundary of a site can greatly affect the outcome of an analysis). The approach today is generally more open ended and flexible, simply looking for and highlighting patterns of co-occurrence. Recent work (e.g., Blankholm 1991) takes into account the smearing effect on data of processes that disturb sites after the deposition of artifacts. Indeed, the study of site-formation processes through the distribution of artifacts, and, in particular, through the identification of *conjoins* (artifacts, such as flint flakes or pottery sherds, that join each other but are recovered from different parts of a site), has emerged as a subtopic in its own right. A second distinct subtopic is the study of the layout of cemeteries, with the aims of establishing the sequence of burials and the organization of the cemetery from the distributions of artifact types, skeletal traits, and aspects of burial rite, usually in the absence of stratigraphic information.

Techniques

There are two families of techniques: *point-pattern techniques* and *surface techniques*. The former examine the patterns of individual locations, whether of sites or artifacts in a region or artifacts on a site, while the latter take the locations as given and are concerned with the numbers or proportions of artifacts of different types at those locations. Techniques of point-pattern analysis include *quadrat methods, distance methods, second-order methods, cluster analysis* (including *unconstrained clustering*), *change-point analysis,* and *multiresponse permutation procedures.* The choice of technique depends partly on the questions being asked and partly on the nature of the data, a fundamental division being between data comprising the exact locations of objects and data comprising merely the counts of objects in predefined areas (usually, but not necessarily, grid squares). The latter are of lower quality than the former but are cheaper and easier to collect. The main surface techniques in archaeology are *regression analysis* and *trend surface analysis; spectral analysis* has been (rarely) used, and *kriging, natural-neighbor interpolation,* and *spatial autocorrelation* have potential.

Quadrat Methods

In quadrat methods, the data consist of the counts of objects of one or more types in the cells *(quadrats)* of a grid. The earliest and simplest technique is to examine the randomness of the distribution of a single object type, using the variance-to-mean (V/m) test. This creates the index of dispersion of a distribution pattern: values around one indicate random distributions; higher values indicate an *aggregated* pattern (the objects are more "bunched up" than in a random pattern); while lower values indicate a *uniform* pattern (the objects are more evenly spread than in a random pattern). This technique has two serious weaknesses: Both the scale of the grid and the definition of the edge of the site or region *(edge effects)* can crucially affect the outcome. Indeed, a pattern may be aggregated at one scale, random at another, and uniform at a third. It is, therefore, very important for archaeologists to know the scale of patterning they are seeking.

Whallon's *dimensional analysis of variance* is similar, but it attempts to define the scale at which patterning occurs, if any, by progressively grouping quadrats into large and larger blocks. It requires sites or areas to be square or double square in shape and, like V/m, can suffer badly from edge effects.

A common approach if there are two or more types of objects is to count the numbers of quadrats in which both, each separately, or neither of a pair of types occur, thus creating a small *contingency table.* Various statistics can show the strength and significance of the association between two types (i.e., the extent to which they co-occur). Once again, scale and edge effect can crucially affect the outcome.

Distance Methods

Methods based on the distances between objects are especially useful if there are very many objects, as they allow the possibility of sampling from them. The best-known method, *nearest-neighbor analysis,* uses as data the distances from each object to the one nearest to it of the same type (its nearest neighbor); variants look at second- or third-nearest neighbors. The ratio of the average nearest-neighbor distance to the theoretical average distance of a random pattern is a measure of the spatial randomness of a pattern. This statistic ranges from near zero (aggregated patterns) through one (random patterns) to just over two (perfectly uniform patterns). It can suffer very badly from edge effects, because, for objects near the edge of the study area (site or region), their real nearest neighbor may lie outside the area and be inaccessible; the apparent nearest-neighbor distance exaggerates the true figure. This approach can also deal with several types of object: For each object of each type, the archaeologist records the type to which its overall nearest neighbor belongs and presents the results as a contingency table. As for quadrat methods, there are statistics of the strength and significance of associations between pairs of types. This approach can detect association at a smaller scale than can quadrat methods.

Second-Order Methods

These techniques look at the second-order properties of spatial distributions, i.e., local and small-scale covariational patterns, in contrast to global, first-order properties such as mean densities. They are common in the mathematical literature; the only one that has made an impact on archaeology is Ian Johnson's *local-density analysis* (perhaps because it is the only one devised by an archaeologist and not by a mathematician). The basic idea is to calculate the density of objects of each type inside circles of a chosen radius around the objects of each other type. If this density is high for two types, it is evidence for association between them. The ensuing calculations cleverly eliminate edge effects, but the technique is open to the criticisms that (1) it tends to detect only circular patterns; (2) the choice of the radius is arbitrary; and (3) it is possible for one type to be more closely associated with another type than with itself. The last seems to be a psychological rather than a mathematical problem, while the second leads to the suggestion of repeated analyses at several different radii (as is done in the more mathematical methods), a comparison of which could yield useful information in its own right. The first led to the suggestion that cluster analysis should be used.

Cluster Analysis

Cluster analysis has a long history as a classificatory technique in multivariate analysis. Its suggested use in the two-dimensional world of spatial analysis is surprising, as its main advantage is its ability to reduce the dimensionality of a problem; two dimensions scarcely need reduction. The idea is that a spatial distribution of one type of object can be divided into zones or clusters, so that the density of the type "bunches up" in the centers of the clusters and "thins out" near the edges where the clusters abut. Certainly, if there are distinct clumps of a type, cluster analysis will find them, but so will visual inspection. Conversely, it will create clusters from purely random data and tempt the archaeologist to interpret them.

A more sophisticated approach is Whallon's unconstrained clustering (uc). This uses a surface method (trend surface analysis) to study point patterns of several types of object. It starts by taking the distribution of each type of object in turn and making a contour plot of its density (i.e., of the number of objects per unit area). This gives a figure for the density of any type at any point. The technique then takes each location of any object and calculates the densities at that location of every type, expressing the figures as percentages of the overall density of all types taken together. A cluster analysis then groups together in clusters all of the locations with similar sets of proportions and identifies them on the plan of the site. For example, all locations that have a relatively high density of a certain type and relatively low densities of all other types will belong to the same cluster and appear on the plot with the same symbol. Clusters do not have to be of any particular shape or even contiguous. It is then up to the archaeologist to interpret the resulting plot. Despite the acclaim that welcomed this technique, it appears to have serious defects: It complicates rather than simplifies (there are often more clusters than types), and it can easily create spurious clusters. A root problem seems to be the smoothing implicit in the creation of density contours, which blur the edges that the subsequent cluster analysis tries to create.

Change-Point Analysis

Change-point analysis takes an opposite approach to unconstrained clustering by assuming that there are edges to areas and setting out to find them. It examines series of data values from a *transect* taken across a site or region and looks for sudden changes in the value (e.g., of the density of an artifact type or the concentration of a soil chemical, such as phosphate). This is a promising technique that deserves to be better known.

Multiresponse Permutation Procedure (mrpp)

Unlike other methods, multiresponse permutation procedure makes no assumptions about the locations of the objects. Instead, it takes the locations as given but examines which types are present at which locations. This makes it particularly useful for studying cemeteries, since the spatial pattern of graves is usually more uniform than random. It calculates a test statistic based on the distances between objects of the same type and compares it to the average that would have been obtained by allocating the same number of objects randomly across all of the locations. If the test statistic is less than the hypothetical average, it is evidence of clustering; if more, it is evidence of a dispersed distribution. This approach can compare one type with another (to see if they "avoid" or "attract" each other) or one with all other types (to see if its distribution is clustered relative to the site or region as a whole).

Regression Analysis

Regression analysis belongs to the family of techniques that compare the number or, more commonly, the proportions of artifacts of a certain type at a number of sites or locations. It seeks to examine the way in which this proportion decreases with distance from some supposed center—usually the place of manufacture of an artifact type but possibly also a local center of distribution. Distance from the center, therefore, takes the role of the independent, or explanatory, variable, while the proportion becomes the dependent, or explained, variable. Statistical regression analysis then attempts to fit a mathematical equation (the *fall-off curve*) to the relationship between distance and proportion. Since it is easiest to fit straight lines, but the relationship is not usually in the form of a straight line, it is usually necessary to transform the data in some way before undertaking the analysis (e.g., by taking the logarithm of the proportion, the distance, or both). The archaeologist can compare the equations relating to different types of artifacts to come to conclusions about their relative worth and ease of transport.

An examination of the differences between the data and the equation fitted to them—known as the *residuals*—can often yield valuable further information. For example, they can reveal the presence of competing centers of production, unexpected obstacles to, or links in, the distribution of artifacts from their center of production.

Trend Surface Analysis

One criticism of regression analysis is that it assumes that the fall-off curve is the same in all directions from the center, and this may well not be the case. One solution is to fit a three-dimensional mathematical surface through the data, rather like contours on a map, with the contours representing the proportion rather than height. There are many techniques for doing this; they divide into global and local techniques. *Global techniques* seek to fit one mathematical equation to the whole data set (just as regression analysis does); differences between the outcome of this and of regression analysis can show directional effects, and, once again, the examination of residuals can be very useful. A serious failing of this approach is that its equations are often unrealistic and can lead to bizarre conclusions. *Local techniques* are more appropriate, as their use in unconstrained clustering shows. They are much more like conventional techniques for contouring maps. A crucial question is the extent to which one should smooth the data: Too little smoothing produces a "pimply" surface that obscures any deviations from the overall pattern, while too much smoothing produces a bland pattern that can have the same problems as global techniques.

Other Techniques

Ian Graham, drawing on his experience in astronomy, demonstrated the possibilities of spectral analysis, but the mathematical and conceptual difficulties of this approach have prevented its general use in archaeology. Techniques available in other disciplines (e.g., kriging, a surface method used in mining, and natural-neighbor interpolation, a mathematical

technique) have archaeological potential but lack evaluation. The study of spatial autocorrelation (the tendency for data values at nearby locations to be correlated with each other) is widespread in geography but relatively rare in archaeology.

Clive Orton

See also GEOGRAPHICAL INFORMATION SYSTEMS; SETTLEMENT ARCHAEOLOGY, THEORY; STATISTICAL METHODS IN ARCHAEOLOGY

Further Readings

Barnett, V., ed. (1981) Interpreting Multivariate Data. Chichester: Wiley.

Blankholm, H.P. (1991) Spatial Analysis in Theory and Practice. Aarhus: Aarhus University Press.

Buck, C.E., Cavanagh, W.G., and Litton, C.D. (1996) Bayesian Approach to Interpreting Archaeological Data. Chichester: John Wiley.

Cliff, A.D., and Ord, J.K. (1973) Spatial Autocorrelation. London: Pion.

Fulford, M.G. and Hodder, I. (1974) A regression analysis of some late Romano-British fine pottery: A case study. Oxoniensia 39:26–33.

Hietala, H., ed. (1984) Intrasite Spatial Analysis in Archaeology. Cambridge: Cambridge University Press.

Hodder, I.R., and Orton, C.R. (1976) Spatial Analysis in Archaeology. Cambridge: Cambridge University Press.

Ripley, B.D. (1977) Modelling spatial patterns. Journal of the Royal Statistical Society B39:172–212.

Whallon, R. (1973) Spatial analysis of occupation floors. I. Application of dimensional analysis of variance. American Antiquity 38:266–278.

Whallon, R. (1974) Spatial analysis of occupation floors. II. The application of nearest neighbor analysis. American Antiquity 39:16–34.

Spaulding, Albert Clanton (1914–1990)

American archaeologist and anthropologist. Born on August 13, 1914, in Choteau, Montana, Spaulding was educated at Montana State University, where he received his bachelor's in 1935; at the University of Michigan, where he received his master's in 1937; and at Columbia University, where he earned his doctorate in 1946. Spaulding began his career at the University of Kansas, where he was assistant professor of anthropology and assistant curator of the University Museum in 1946. He returned to Michigan a year later, eventually attaining the rank of full professor of anthropology and curator of the Lowie Museum of Anthropology. Spaulding served as professor of anthropology and department chair at the University of Oregon (1963–1966), then as professor of anthropology at the University of California at Santa Barbara, where he was also dean of the College of Letters and Sciences (1967–1971). A recipient of numerous awards and prizes, Spaulding was a Fellow of the American Anthropological Association and the Society for American Archaeology, of which he was also president (1964–1965).

A specialist in American archaeology and archaeological theory, Spaulding is most well known for his debates with James A. Ford in the professional journals during the 1950s and 1960s. Spaulding criticized Ford's approaches to material culture, particularly Ford's use of typologies and diffusionistic explanation of culture change. In his landmark "Statistical Techniques for the Discovery of Artifact Types," Spaulding used statistical analysis of material remains to advance his own theory that culture change occurred not in a regular manner, but rather in punctuated fashion of rapid jumps and periods of slow change; statistical clusterings represented discovered, not arbitrarily designated, types and would show the pattern of culture change and reveal past behavior in relation to cultural evolution. While the importance of this debate diminished as archaeology in America moved into its processual stage, Spaulding's definition of type—and scientific use of statistics—remain notable.

Joseph J. Basile

See also SERIATION; STATISTICAL METHODS IN ARCHAEOLOGY

Further Readings

Spaulding, A.C. (1953) Statistical techniques for the discovery of artifact types. American Antiquity 18:305–313.
Spaulding, A.C. (1960) The dimensions of archaeology. In G.E. Dole and R.L. Carneiro (eds.): Essays in the Science of Culture in Honor of Leslie A. White, pp. 437–456. New York: Crowell.
Spaulding, A.C. (1968) Explanation in archeology. In S.R. Binford and L.R. Binford (eds.): New Perspectives in Archeology, pp. 33–39. Chicago: Aldine.

St. Joseph, J. Kenneth S. (1912–1993)

A British aerial reconnaissance surveyor, St. Joseph was one of the most influential pioneers of aerial photography for archaeology, as well as a number of disciplines. He was educated at Bromsgrove School, then went to Selwyn College, Cambridge, to study geology. He founded the Cambridge University Committee for Air Photography, having been made the first curator of aerial photography in 1949. He was made professor of air photographic studies in 1973 and was awarded the OBE (1964) and the CBE (1979).

Having learned from the work of Osbert G.S. Crawford, he saw the potential of aerial photography for archaeology, geology, human geography, ecology, landscape history, and agriculture. Apart from his passionate interest in the study of Roman Britain, his work also helped the new studies of medieval and industrial archaeology. His publications include *The Uses of Air Photography, Monastic Sites from the Air* (with M.C. Knowles), *Medieval England: An Aerial Survey* (with M.W. Beresford), and *Roman Britain from the Air* (with S.S. Frere), as well as more than fifty papers in the journal *Antiquity* reporting the discoveries of recent reconnaissance. His approach was Europeanwide, and he undertook surveys in Britain, Ireland, Denmark, France, and the Netherlands. Although he retired in 1980, he continued his work on Roman Scotland and assisted in reconnaissance flights in Germany and Hungary.

Robert H. Bewley

See also AERIAL PHOTOGRAPHY IN ARCHAEOLOGY; CRAWFORD, OSBERT G.S.

Further Readings

Beresford, M.W. and St. Joseph, J.K.S. (1979) Medieval England: An Aerial Survey, 2nd ed. Cambridge, UK/New York: Cambridge University Press.
Frere, S.S. and St. Joseph, J.K.S. (1983) Roman Britain from the Air. Cambridge, UK/New York: Cambridge University Press.

Knowles, D. and St. Joseph, J.K.S. (1952) Monastic Sites from the Air. Cambridge, UK: Cambridge University Press.

Maxwell, G.S., ed. (1983) The Impact of Aerial Reconnaissance on Archaeology. (Research Report 49). London: Counsil for British Archaeology.

St. Joseph, J.K.S., ed. (1977) The Uses of Air Photography, rev. ed. London: J. Baker.

Statistical Methods in Archaeology

The application of scientific method, as distinct from scientific techniques, to archaeological questions. This sees archaeological research as the interplay between archaeological theory, represented by *hypotheses,* and the real world of archaeological objects (e.g., sites, artifacts, chemical and physical analyses), represented by *data.* The relationship is cyclic, proceeding from theory to data and back again, starting at either end and going round for any number of times. The chosen starting point depends on the predisposition of the archaeologist and the nature of the archaeological problem. It is possible to start from a hypothesis and to seek to collect data with which to test it (the *deductive* approach); it is equally possible to acquire data and seek to make sense of them (the *inductive* approach). These positions imply different statistical approaches—*confirmatory statistics* for the former and *exploratory statistics* for the latter.

Whichever the starting point, between theory and data sits a *model* (a simplified representation of a real-world situation), which enables the two to relate to each other. It is needed because archaeologists cannot directly observe their subject of interest—past human activity—but only its effects and must, therefore, model what the effect of hypothesized activity would be on material that they can observe and measure. The next step *(research design)* is to decide how many data, of what sorts, are needed to answer the question or test the hypothesis, how they should be collected, and how they should be analyzed. Once the archaeologists have collected their data (by fieldwork, from museums, or from the literature), the statistical analysis should be a formality, leading to provisional conclusions about the model. A final step, *archaeological interpretation,* leads back to the original hypothesis, which may be confirmed, rejected, or modified by the whole process. If archaeologists start from the data end of the cycle, the situation is more open ended, since they may use and contrast several exploratory techniques to gain insight into their data.

An important point that emerges from this is that statistics is not just the stage of formal analysis—it is the whole cycle. If the question has not been formulated properly, or the research has not been designed properly, or the data not collected properly, then no amount of sophisticated analysis can retrieve the situation. If statistical advice is to be sought, it should be at as early a stage as possible, and certainly not at the "here are my data, what do I do with them?" stage.

History

The earliest recognized statistical approach in archaeology was Sir William Flinders Petrie's analysis of grave groups from Naqada in Egypt, published in 1899, which gave rise to the technique of *seriation.* There was little input from statistics until the collaboration between George W. Brainerd and W.S. Robinson in 1951 initiated a series of theoretical and practical investigations into seriation that continue to this day. In the 1960s, interest focused on classification, usually of individual objects, partly as a result of new techniques drawn from numerical taxonomy, such as *cluster analysis,* and partly because of the potential of computers then becoming available. The latter also made possible the use of many techniques of *multivariate statistical analysis,* such as *principal-components analysis, factor analysis* and *correspondence analysis.* In the 1970s, techniques for the analysis of spatial data appeared, deriving mainly from geography and ecology. The spread of the *quantitative idiom* into many areas of archaeology in the 1970s and 1980s has led, in some cases, to the adoption of standard statistical techniques (ones developed for use in other disciplines) and, in others, to the development of specifically archaeological techniques. Examples of the latter are techniques for the analysis of cemeteries, such as Frank R. Hodson's *socistat* (social-status analysis), which he devised for use on the Hallstatt cemetery, Austria, and techniques for the statistical analysis of assemblages of broken objects (e.g., pottery, animal bone), such as the *pie-slice* package. In the mid-1990s, some archaeologists have used bayesian statistics as a way of combining data from disparate sources (e.g., stratigraphy and scientific dating determinations). This approach is based on the deceptively simple equation:

prior belief + data = posterior belief

and provides techniques needed to implement it. In this example, stratigraphy provides the prior belief (e.g., A is earlier than B) and scientific dating determinations provide the data; the two are combined to give a more precise estimate of date. The approach has been used, more experimentally, in classification and spatial analysis. It is in the spirit of the integrative wave noted in computer applications.

Techniques
Cluster Analysis
Cluster analysis is a collection of techniques that share the aim of dividing a collection of objects into groups (clusters) on the basis of the similarities among them. Ideally, they should create groups that consist of objects that are similar to one another but less similar to objects in other groups. The techniques differ in the ways in which they measure the similarities among objects (or its converse, the statistical distances between them), and in the ways in which they build clusters of objects. Archaeologists now use mostly either the *k-means method* or *Ward's method*. Ward's method is the most complex of a family of *hierarchical agglomerative procedures,* which also includes *single-linkage, average-linkage,* and *complete-linkage* methods. In such methods, all objects are initially treated as separate clusters, which are successively amalgamated to form fewer and fewer clusters, until in the end all objects form a single cluster. Hierarchical structures are not always appropriate, so the k-means method is sometimes preferred; this seeks to find the *best* grouping of objects into a chosen number (k) of clusters. Since it is not usually obvious what the value of k should be, several values are usually tried and compared (cf. Baxter 1994). The main criticisms of cluster analysis are that it creates clusters whether or not any exist in the data, and the choice of the number of clusters is often arbitrary.

Contingency Tables
A contingency table is a table that shows the number of objects that take certain values of two or more variables (e.g., the number of coins of different periods found on different sites—the objects here being coins and the variables period and site). The aim is to discover whether variables are associated (i.e., whether certain values of one occur more or less frequently with certain values of another than one would expect if there were no relationship between them). For example, do coins from a certain site concentrate in a certain period? The usual technique for analyzing such tables is the *chi*-square test; others are *loglinear analysis* and *correspondence analysis.*

Correspondence Analysis (CA)
Correspondence analysis is a technique of multivariate analysis similar to principal-components analysis, but for use on two-way tables of counts (i.e., contingency tables). It extracts from the data axes of maximum variability (called *inertia*), against which it plots the data. The usual output takes the form of a scattergram on which the values of both variables are plotted (e.g., both period and site in the above example), together with various diagnostic statistics to aid interpretation. Its main advantage over other techniques is the way in which it gives a simultaneous plot of both variables, thus making it much easier to interpret one in terms of the other (e.g., which periods are the most common on which sites).

Discriminant Analysis
Discriminant analysis is a technique of multivariate analysis that seeks to discover which variable(s) best distinguish, or discriminate, between groups of objects that an archaeologist or a technique such as cluster analysis has already defined. It can, for example, pinpoint the key variables in a typology, to simplify the assignment of new objects to types.

Goodness-of-Fit Test
A goodness-of-fit test measures how well a set of data fits a chosen model or statistical distribution. The usual approach is to test a hypothesis that the data do fit the model and to see to what extent this is supported by the data. The most common test is the *chi*-square test, which is appropriate for data that can take only certain values (e.g., counts); for continuous data, the *Kolmogorov-Smirnov test* is usually preferable. The latter tests for differences between continuous distributions, using as its test-statistic the greatest difference between their cumulative frequency distributions. When the comparison is between two or more sets of data, instead of one set and a

model, the problem usually becomes one of contingency tables.

Multidimensional Scaling (MDSCAL)

MDSCAL is a way of reducing the dimension of a multidimensional set of data. The number of dimensions is reduced one at a time from the original number (the number of variables used to describe a set of objects) to some chosen smaller number, usually two, which can then plot as a scattergram. The method is to preserve, as far as possible, the relationships between the relative distances between pairs of objects. For example, if the distance between object A and object B in the original data is greater than the distance between objects C and D, then the same should be true of the distances on the final scattergram. It is usually not possible to achieve this exactly; the measure of how much the result departs from the original relationships is the *strain,* which shows how well the pattern has been preserved. The technique is very demanding of computer time.

Principal-Components Analysis (PCA)

PCA seeks to represent a multivariate set of data as a scattergram, supported by diagnostic statistics. The principal components are combinations of the original variables and represent a rotation of the original space to show as much as possible of the pattern of the points in it. The first axis of the scattergram is the first principal component of the data (i.e., the axis that achieves the greatest possible dispersion of the points when they are plotted along it). The second axis is the one that achieves the greatest possible dispersion not already accounted for by the first. The data should be continuous variables and all measured on the same scale (e.g., all lengths in mm). If this is not the case, it is necessary to standardize the data (i.e., express each data value as so many standard deviations above or below the mean value of its variable) before using PCA.

Regression Analysis

Regression analysis is a family of techniques for examining the relationship between two or more continuous variables, each measured on the same set of objects (e.g., heights and capacities of a set of pottery vessels). *Linear regression* seeks the best straight-line relationship between two variables and enables the

archaeologist to examine the *residuals* (the differences between the actual and the ideal data). The extent to which the relationship can be described by a straight line is measured by the correlation coefficient. There is also *curvilinear regression,* which seeks a more complicated relationship between two variables, and *multiple regression,* which seeks a relationship between one *dependent* variable and several *independent* ones.

Social-Status Analysis

Social-status analysis starts from a table showing the presence or absence of a set of functional types of artifacts in each of the graves in a cemetery. It assigns a score to each type according to the average number of other types found with it in graves. Next, it orders the graves according to the total score of the types found in it (as an alternative, the archaeologist may choose to score each grave according to the score of the highest-scoring type found in it). This creates a ranking of the graves, from those with many different types through those with few types to those with one or none. The archaeologist must then interpret this ranking. The technique works best with large numbers of graves (100 or more), and it is often necessary to analyze male and female graves separately.

Uses

Many archaeologists use simple statistical techniques, both numerical and graphical, as everyday tools for analyzing and presenting data. The addition of statistical tests and chart-drawing facilities to the current generation of spreadsheets will encourage this trend. There are two main types of use: *description* and *comparison.* The former is useful for characterizing material and making data available in summarized form to other archaeologists, but it is really only a first step toward the latter. The heart of statistical analysis in archaeology is comparison. Archaeologists need to compare data at a wide range of scales—scientific analyses, individual artifacts, assemblages, sites—for many purposes, of which the two most common are *classification* (grouping entities) and *ordering* (putting entities into an order). Also, simple comparative techniques can help an archaeologist to decide whether two entities (e.g., assemblages of flints) are essentially the same, in the sense that the observed differences between them are no more than one would expect between two samples from the same population. Spatial statistics have their own techniques.

Classification

The success of numerical taxonomy in biology in the 1960s suggested to archaeologists that they could perhaps improve their classification of artifacts and their construction of typologies by using formal methods of classification, such as cluster analysis or multidimensional scaling. The idea was to describe each object in terms of a set of variables (e.g., dimensions, angles, presence or absence of certain features), which would define the axes of a multidimensional space. So, for example, the recording of six variables on each of a set of artifacts would define each as a separate point in a six-dimensional space. If *types* of such artifacts exist, they should correspond to clusters of points in the space, separated by zones with fewer points in them. Since one cannot envisage such spaces directly, formal techniques are needed to reduce their dimension, typically to two, while preserving as much as possible of the pattern of the points in the original space. The archaeologist can examine the outcome for apparent groupings that may represent types.

Attempts to create alternative groupings to those that archaeologists had devised subjectively tended to show little or no improvement. Probably more successful were attempts to study existing groupings, either ones already created by archaeologists or of replicated material (e.g., waste flint flakes) generated in archaeological experiments. In such cases, it was possible, using discriminant analysis, to determine which variables were responsible for the existing divisions into groups, thus giving an insight into the archaeologist's ideas of typology or into, for example, waste flakes produced under different knapping methods. Such studies also reinforced the point that there is no such thing as a single all-purpose typology for a given set of artifacts, but different typologies depending on the purpose to which an archaeologist wishes to put them (e.g., functional or stylistic typologies).

It could be argued that these approaches used classificatory techniques at the wrong level and that attempting to improve on such a central activity is perhaps futile. Greater success might be expected when archaeologists cannot actually see the objects being classified (e.g., the outcomes of scientific analyses, or assemblages rather than individual artifacts). This has turned out to be the case: Although still with problems, the classification of pottery fabrics by the study of their chemical composition has proved to be a fruitful area, as has the characterization of stone (e.g., marble) by stable-isotope analysis. In such cases, PCA and related techniques are particularly useful.

The classification of assemblages of artifacts from different parts of a site can provide useful information on possible differences in status or function of those parts. On a regional scale, such comparisons can help elucidate the distribution of artifact types from their centers of production. Chronological patterns are more likely to show themselves as ordering of points in the space (see below). If the data consist of counts of objects of different types in different assemblages, CA is a good technique for examining their structure. For ceramics (and other classes of object usually found broken and incomplete), the archaeologist must transform the data before analysis in this way; the necessary calculations form part of the pie-slice package for the comparison of ceramic assemblages.

Ordering

The idea of searching for an order in data goes back to Petrie's seriation of cemetery data. The usual interpretation is that, if an order exists, it represents a chronological trend; however, other interpretations are possible, such as the ranking by status or wealth that often forms part of an analysis of cemetery data. The differences between two such orderings of the same data lie in the choice of typology: A *stylistic* typology tends to produce a chronological order, while a *functional* typology tends to produce a status order. Some techniques, specifically designed for seriation, simply create an order, possibly accompanied by diagnostic statistics to show how appropriate the procedure was and how stable the order is. Other, more general, techniques such as PCA and CA, produce a plot of the data that the archaeologist can inspect for an order. Contrary to initial expectations, evidence for an order will show as a horseshoe-shaped curve on the plot, not as a straight line.

S

Other Uses. One area that requires special statistical techniques is the analysis and interpretation of scientific dating determinations, especially radiocarbon dating, which has peculiar difficulties because of the need to calibrate dates. Bayesian statistics are useful here in combining the determinations with other sources of evidence (e.g., stratigraphic relationships).

There will always be a need for specially designed ad hoc techniques to answer particular archaeological problems. In such cases, archaeologists will need to consult with a sympathetic statistician.

Clive Orton

See also COMPUTERS IN ARCHAEOLOGY; SPATIAL ANALYSIS

Further Readings

Aldenderfer, M.S., ed. (1987) Quantitative Research in Archaeology: Progress and Prospects. Newbury Park, CA: Sage.

Baxter, M.J. (1994) Exploratory Multivariate Analysis in Archaeology. Edinburgh: Edinburgh University Press.

Buck, C.E., Cavanagh, W.G. and Litton, C.D. (1996) Bayesian Approach to Interpreting Archaeological Data. Chichester: John Wiley.

Djindjian, F. (1991) Méthodes pour l'Archéologie. Paris: Armand Colin.

Doran, J.E., and Hodson, F.R. (1975) Mathematics and Computers in Archaeology. Edinburgh: Edinburgh University Press.

Hodson, F.R. (1977) Quantifying Hallstatt. American Antiquity 42:394–411.

Madsen, T. (1988) Multivariate Archaeology: Numerical Approaches in Scandinavian Archaeology. Aarhus: Jutland Archaeological Society.

Orton, C.R. (1980) Mathematics in Archaeology. London: Collins.

Orton, C.R., and Tyers, P.A. (1992) Counting broken objects: The statistics of ceramic assemblages. In A.M. Pollard (ed.): New Developments in Archaeological Science, pp. 163–184. Oxford: Oxford University Press.

Shennan, S. (1997) Quantifying Archaeology, 2nd ed. Edinburgh: Edinburgh University Press.

Thomas, D.H. (1978) The awful truth about statistics in archaeology. American Antiquity 43:231–244.

Step Trenching

Technique used to excavate deeply stratified sites in a series of steps. Large sites with a considerable depth of archaeological deposits, such as a Near Eastern tell, should ideally be excavated by open-area excavation. Such an excavation would produce maximum information and be very safe. This type of excavation would, however, be extremely expensive. An alternative would be to excavate trenches, which, although providing good vertical information, provide little horizontal information and, unless properly shored, can be extremely dangerous. A compromise strategy often employed is step trenching.

Step trenching involves opening a large area at the top of the site. This can be conducted as an open-area excavation to a safe depth, usually not more than 1 m. The area of the excavation is then reduced, perhaps by 1 m all round, and then the new area is excavated for another meter in depth. The excavation proceeds in this way, resulting in a series of steps. Naturally, the depth to which one can excavate will depend on the surface area opened up at the start of the excavation.

Peter L. Drewett

See also OPEN-AREA EXCAVATION

Further Readings

Barker, P. (1993) Techniques of Archaeological Excavation, 3rd ed. London: Batsford.

Drewett, P.L. (1999) Field Archaeology: An Introduction. London: University College London Press.

Stone, On-Site Conservation

Techniques for protection and treatment of stone artifacts during and immediately after excavation. The condition of a stone artifact upon excavation depends on the properties of the stone and its interaction with the burial environment. A basic knowledge of stone properties is essential for the excavator to assess the condition of an artifact, the method of excavation, and the necessary conservation treatment in the field.

Mechanisms of Deterioration of Stone

Most stone is brittle and, therefore, subject to fracture under stress. Flints and chert, while resistant to surface scratching, are particularly brittle and easily chipped by the slightest impact. Softer stones, such as limestone, sandstone, and volcanic tuff, are easily damaged by abrasion or scratching. Burial conditions may weaken stone by leaching out soluble components, leading to further fracture in excavation. The leaching of binding material from sandstone often results in a friable surface (individual particles breaking away from the stone matrix).

Stone exposed to weather for long periods prior to burial will exhibit some loss of surface due to erosion by water and windborne particles. Softened by groundwater during burial, many stones will be extremely susceptible to further erosion in postexcavation exposure to weather. Groundwaters may also include water-soluble salts, which, upon removal from burial environment and drying, crystallize within the pores or on the surface of the stone (efflorescence), causing dislocation of grains (powdering, crumbling, or friability) or thin sheets of stone (spalling and flaking). Similarly, water within the stone matrix may repeatedly freeze and thaw, resulting in spalling and, sometimes, fracture.

Stone exposed to bright sunlight will develop high temperatures at the surface while remaining cooler within; the slight expansion at the surface due to heating may develop stress between the interior and the exterior, resulting in fracture (thermal-stress cracking), even in hard stones such as basalt.

Groundwater may carry dissolved solids (usually carbonates or silicates) that are then deposited on the stone surfaces, frequently entraining surrounding soils, resulting in accretions. Deposition of accretions may be enhanced by the presence of roots, resulting distinctive root marks. In marine archaeology, heavy deposits of accretion from higher life forms may completely encase artifacts. In addition to accretions, the penetration of roots from trees may result in dislocation and breakage of large stones. Metal ions in groundwater may penetrate stone during burial, resulting in staining. Staining may be enhanced by biological activity or proximity to deteriorating metal artifacts, particularly iron and copper. Once exposed, deteriorated stone surfaces provide excellent environments for the growth of lichen, fungus, and/or moss, resulting in further disfigurement through accretion, staining, and etching.

Techniques for Initial Excavation

Ideally, no tool used in excavation should be harder than the surface of the artifact being excavated; however, tools commonly used by excavators, such as trowels, picks, and shovels, often strike stone artifacts with sufficient force to cause scratches and occasional breakage. Once a stone object has been located, damage during excavation can be mitigated by an immediate change to softer tools, such as wooden sticks and brushes. Removal of soil immediately surrounding stone artifacts should proceed slowly and only with soft brushes to avoid loss of paint traces (polychromy) that might remain on the surface.

Stone objects are often damaged when partly exposed artifacts are unprotected while other activities continue in the immediate vicinity. Artifacts in an active sector should be clearly identified and provided with physical protection to prevent accidental breakage and foot traffic on the object or structure. Protection may consist of simple flags, such as strips of cloth or colored plastic sheet tied or anchored near the object, or physical barriers, such as wooden frames or rope fencing.

Removal of Stone Objects from the Excavation Site

Whenever possible, artifacts that are removed during excavation should be lifted and transported to a workspace with a thin layer of soil left on the surface. A badly shattered, friable, or spalling object should be lifted as a block with the surrounding soil intact for microexcavation by a conservator in the laboratory. All loose fragments surrounding a fractured artifact must be retained for possible reintegration. Small, badly damaged artifacts may be lifted from an excavation using block-lifting techniques similar to those used for ceramics and other materials. These techniques usually require a rigid support around the object and the insertion of a flat board beneath it, bearing in mind that stone is considerably heavier than most other materials, and the supports must be able to bear the additional weight.

Careful assessment of the stability and weight of large stone objects is required prior to removal from an excavation. Lifting should be done with soft nylon straps or ropes and at no time should steel equipment, such as pry bars, picks, or cables, be allowed to touch the surface of a stone artifact without padding.

Large stone artifacts with cracks or other evidence of deterioration may require the construction of an exterior support or cradle prior to lifting. Consolidation or facing may be required prior to lifting and should be carried out in consultation with a conservator (see below). The removal of most large objects will require cooperation among the conservator, the excavator, and the architect or engineer.

Protection from Drying and Salt Efflorescence

Exposure of stone artifacts to air will almost always initiate drying. Some stones, notably shale, will contract upon drying, causing distortion and fracture, and so must be protected from rapid desiccation by temporary storage in plastic bags or covering with plastic sheets. Likewise, recrystallization of soluble salts will be initiated by drying once an artifact is exposed to air. Partially excavated objects are particularly susceptible to damage from salt efflorescence, as they are still in contact with the source of moisture and will act as a wick for salt solutions in groundwater. Large objects and those that will remain in situ must be protected from rapid drying during excavation, by shading and/or covering with plastic sheeting, and monitored on a daily basis for evidence of salt efflorescence. Shading is also an effective mitigation against thermal-stress cracking.

Protection from Freeze-Thaw Cycling

In temperate or cold climates, stone objects left partly excavated during cold seasons must also be protected from freeze-thaw cycling. Protection may consist of covering the object or structure with a separating material (such as a geotextile) and backfilling with a protective fill, such as clean sand or expanded clay or vermiculite. The choice of separators and fill materials should be made by a conservator and integrated into the general program for site preservation.

Treatment in the Field and Field Laboratory

The primary goal of conservation treatment of stone artifacts undertaken the field is to stabilize the object and prevent loss of evidence of the artifacts' method of manufacture, use, and original appearance. Field treatment may, at times, be extended to include simple analysis, cleaning, and small repairs. All treatment should be undertaken by, or under the supervision of, a trained conservator. In situations in which objects cannot immediately be treated or a conservator is unavailable, every effort should be made to store artifacts in an environment that closely resembles the burial conditions.

Salt Removal

If soluble salts are present, objects must be stored in an environment that will avoid fluctuations in relative humidity and drying until they can be treated. In situ treatment of stone for salt efflorescence will be effective only if the object is isolated from the source of the moisture and salt. Techniques for isolation from salt migration are similar to those for rising damp (water rising from the soil into the walls) in standing architectural remains.

Soluble salts may be removed from small to medium-size objects in the field by soaking in successive changes of salt-free water until the soaking water is relatively salt free. The progress of the treatment is monitored by measuring the salt content of the soaking solution, either with wet chemical tests or with a conductivity meter. Salts in larger objects and, in some cases, standing architectural and sculptural elements in situ may be removed by poultices consisting of paper pulp soaked in salt-free water, applied successively to the surface and allowed to dry between each application. Objects from a marine environment should be immediately immersed in fresh water to initiate desalinization.

Stabilization

Flaking, spalling, or crumbling stones require stabilization during excavation or prior to removal, frequently by application of a resin solution to the stone (consolidation). A layer of paper or cotton cloth may be applied to the surface of a stone artifact (a facing) in conjunction with consolidation to ensure alignment of the fragments. It is imperative that the application of consolidants in the field be made in consultation with a conservator. When inappropriately applied, salt and\or moisture buildup behind resin films can create sufficient pressure to cause accelerated spalling and flaking of the surface. In addition, the application of a consolidant to a surface that has not been cleaned may inhibit subsequent cleaning. Consolidants used by conservators in the field often consist of acrylic resin in organic solvents or aqueous emulsion.

Cleaning

The development of a system for cleaning stone objects at a particular site will depend on the type of stone and the nature of the environment in which it was buried. In sandy soils and in relatively dry environments, removal of soil is best accomplished with soft brushes and wooden sticks. In clay-containing soils and some wet environments, soils and accretions are more easily removed by washing while the objects are still damp from burial. Washing objects in water only or water with mild detergents (preferably anionic or nonionic), using soft or medium-hard bristle brushes (such as toothbrushes), and rinsing well with clear (salt-free) running water is safe for most dense stone surfaces that are in sound condition, such as granite and marble. Caution must be exercised when cleaning porous stones, such as sandstone and limestone, and harder stones that are crumbling or spalling. The application of aqueous cleaning solutions to porous stones may drive stains or soil into the stone, making cleaning impossible or result in uneven cleaning.

If polychromy is present, treatment should be undertaken only by a conservator as part of a broader program of treatment, usually involving consolidation of the paint layers. At no time should metal tools, such as picks, knives, or dental tools be used in the initial cleaning of artifacts, as they may leave modern tool marks on the stone surface that will confuse subsequent analysis of the method of manufacture and use of the artifact. Secondary cleaning of stone to remove insoluble accretions or stains, requires specialized skills and should be undertaken only in a well-equipped field or museum laboratory.

Repairs and Reconstruction

Field repairs should be made only to the minimum extent necessary for emergency retention of fragments of an artifact and only in consultation with a conservator. Adhesives and consolidants should be applied only to clean surfaces and should be chosen with due consideration to subsequent treatment the object is likely to receive. Small repairs may be made with adhesive alone, while larger repairs will require metal dowels in conjunction with an adhesive. All repairs should be easily reversible, using adhesives that are known to be stable. Acrylic resin in organic solvent is widely used as both an adhesive and a consolidant and is preferred for its stability and reversibility. Polyester and epoxy resins, while considerably stronger, should be used only in conjunction with an isolating layer of acrylic resin.

Molding

Molds or *squeezes* are often part of the documentation and study of stone objects, particularly inscriptions. The use of a rigid molding material, such as plaster of paris, is a highly specialized skill for three-dimensional objects. Flexible molding materials, such as latex or silicone rubber, are more commonly used but can be applied only after a careful assessment of the condition of the stone. Stone surfaces to be molded must be sufficiently stable to withstand the stress of mold removal or must be consolidated prior to molding. To prevent penetration of the molding materials into the pores in the stone and to ensure safe separation of the mold, molding materials are usually applied only after the application of a reversible coating and an appropriate release agent. The entire system of consolidants, release agents, and molding materials must be tested on a discrete area of the surface prior to broad application. Creation of a paper squeeze, by tamping wetted paper pulp onto an inscription with a stiff brush, requires the absence of soluble salts in the stone and a sufficiently strong surface to withstand the pounding with the brush.

Kent Severson

See also IN SITU CONSERVATION; ROCKS AND MINERALS, CHARACTERIZATION

Further Readings

Cronyn, J.N. (1990) The Elements of Archaeological Conservation. London and New York: Routledge.

Sease, C. (1994) A Conservation Manual for the Field Archaeologist, 3rd ed. Los Angeles: Institute of Archaeology, UCLA.

Stratification

The physical layout and basic characteristics of depositional layers, or strata, in archaeological sites. Stratification is most clearly observed by examining the side walls of excavated areas and constructing sections, which are detailed illustrations of depositional layers. To differentiate strata and construct sections, characteristics such as soil texture, color, and compactness are observed. In some situations, such as the excavation of shell middens, natural strata may not be clearly visible, and archaeologists artificially impose uniform layers. Whether clearly visible or imposed layers are excavated, the physical characteristics of strata are always meticulously recorded. Measurements of layers are kept, and the nature and the content of strata are investigated. Disturbance from cultural or natural factors is also considered. For instance, burials often disturb deposits from earlier periods, and burrowing rodents can move artifacts. Layers are labeled, mapped, and sometimes photographed so they can be associated with strata from other excavated areas. The analysis of the interrelationship of these depositional layers, called *stratigraphy*, is often the basis for constructing cultural chronologies at archaeological sites.

Edward Luby

See also NATURAL STRATIGRAPHY; STRATIGRAPHY

Further Readings

Barker, P. (1993) Techniques of Archaeological Excavation, 3rd ed. London: Batsford.

Joukowsky, M. (1980) A Complete Manual of Field Archaeology. Englewood Cliffs, NJ: Prentice-Hall.

Stratigraphy

The analysis and interpretation of depositional layers, or strata, in excavated areas. In archaeology, stratigraphy is distinguished from stratification, which is the actual physical layout of strata. Stratigraphy involves a careful consideration of the characteristics of individual soil layers in order to understand how these layers relate to one another. The layers may be clearly visible or artificially imposed by excavators in situations in which strata are difficult to see. A basic stratigraphic principle, borrowed from geology, is called

the *Law of Superposition:* With some exceptions, the earliest depositional layers at a site are situated at the bottom, while the latest layers are situated at the top. However, a variety of cultural and natural factors, such as disturbance by intrusive pits or rodent burrowing, must be considered during stratigraphic analysis. An important aim of stratigraphy is to impose order on a site. Once stratigraphic sequences and depositional histories have been elucidated, a relative chronology is often constructed. When combined with an analysis of the distribution of temporally sensitive artifacts throughout strata at a site, stratigraphy is a powerful tool for studying change and building cultural chronologies.

Edward Luby

See also METRICAL STRATIGRAPHY; NATURAL STRATIGRAPHY; STRATIFICATION

Further Readings

Barker, P. (1993) Techniques of Archaeological Excavation, 3rd ed. London: Batsford.

Joukowsky, M. (1980) A Complete Manual of Field Archaeology. Englewood Cliffs, NJ: Prentice-Hall.

Stripping

The removal, as efficiently as possible, of all deposits above those considered to be archaeologically important. In an urban context, this may involve removing the remains of a recently demolished concrete building. In the countryside, it may involve removing a recent ploughsoil from above in situ archaeological deposits. Archaeologists will rarely agree about what is actually archaeologically significant, so the decision about what to strip off an excavation area must be made on a site-by-site basis by the project director. Some archaeologists who consider themselves purists, by treating everything from the surface down as archaeology, simply waste archaeology's limited resources and make archaeologists appear silly in the eyes of the wider public.

After establishing how much overburden the site has, either by augering or digging test pits, area stripping can commence. In countries with cheap labor, this may be undertaken by gangs of laborers. An alternative is to use heavy machinery. There is a wide variety of machines available for hire in most countries. Bulldozers, which push soil off the site by driving over the cleared area, are not suitable. A machine that drags soil back away from the site is the best for archaeological work. A machine with a backhoe consisting of a hydraulic bucket is particularly suitable for clearing small sites. For larger sites, a machine with a scraping blade may be suitable. Digging machines are often used with dump trucks to speed up removal of soil. The presence of any machinery on archaeological sites presents a major safety problem that must be considered when establishing a work program.

Peter L. Drewett

See also OPEN-AREA EXCAVATION

Further Readings

Barker, P. (1993) Techniques of Archaeological Excavation, 3rd ed. London: Batsford.

Drewett, P.L. (1999) Field Archaeology: An Introduction. London: University College London Press.

Struever, Stuart McKee (1931–)

American anthropologist and archaeologist. Born on August 4, 1931, in Peru, Illinois, Struever received his bachelor's from Dartmouth College in 1953, master's from Northwestern University in 1960, and doctorate from the University of Chicago in 1968. After a year as instructor of anthropology at the University of Chicago (1964–1965), he returned to Northwestern, as instructor in anthropology (1965–1968), assistant professor (1968–1969), associate professor (1969–1972), and full professor (1972–). Struever was chair of the department (1975–1978) and director of the archaeology program and president of the Center for American Archaeology from 1964. He also served as chairman of the board of directors of the Foundation for Illinois Archaeology, director of the Illinois Archaeological Survey, and member of the board of archaeological consultants of the Tennessee Valley Authority. He was president of the Society for American Archaeology (1975–1976) and has been a grantee of the National Science Foundation, the National Geographic Society, the National Endowment for the Humanities, the National Park Service, the American Philosophical Society, and the Wenner-Gren Foundation for Anthropological Research. Struever was President of the Crow Canyon Archaeological Center in Cortez, Colorado, before his retirement in 1992. In 1995, he received the Distinguished Service Award from the Society for American Archaeology.

Struever is an important figure in the development of anthropological archaeology in the United States and a key proponent of the New Archaeology during the 1960s and 1970s. Using an ecosystem model, Struever outlined the development of Woodland-period cultures in the Illinois Valley in a paper that appeared in Lewis R. Binford's highly influential *New Perspectives in Archaeology* ("Woodland Subsistence Settlement Systems in the Lower Illinois Valley"). In it, Struever argued that food-procurement systems are so important to prehistoric societies that settlement patterns and even cultural traits can be predicted by a study of the environment. While this model was subsequently criticized, it served as an exciting example of the uses of the deductive approach in processual archaeology. He is also known for his excavations at the Koster site in Illinois and the Kampsville project, a model of scientific, interdisciplinary archaeology and a training ground for New World prehistorians. The story of the Kampsville project is told in *Koster: Americans in Search of Their Prehistoric Past* (with Felicia Antonelli Holton), a book that served as a popular introduction to the New Archaeology.

Joseph J. Basile

See also BINFORD, LEWIS R.; NEW/ PROCESSUAL ARCHAEOLOGY

Further Readings

Struever, S. (1968) Woodland subsistence settlement systems in the Lower Illinois Valley. In S.R. Binford and L.R. Binford (eds.): New Perspectives in Archaeology, pp. 285–312. Chicago: Aldine.

Struever, S. (1971) Prehistoric Agriculture. Garden City, N.Y.: Natural History Press.

Struever, S. and Holton, F.A. (1979) Koster: Americans in Search of their Prehistoric Past. Garden City, N.Y.: Anchor/Doubleday/New York: New American Library.

Suess, Hans Eduard (1909–1993)

Austrian-born American chemist. Born on December 6, 1909, in Vienna, Suess was educated at the University of Vienna, where he received his doctorate in 1935, and at the University of Hamburg, where he received a doctorate in chemistry in 1939. His career began in Europe at the University of Hamburg, where he was research associate (1937–1948) and associate professor of chemistry (1949–1950). He moved to the United States shortly after this eventually becoming a naturalized citizen. At first a geochemist with the United States Geological Survey, Suess was appointed professor of chemistry at the University of Chicago in 1955 and was named emeritus professor in 1977. In his long and distinguished career, Suess received numerous honors, including the Goldschmidt Medal of the Geochemical Society, a Guggenheim Award, the Humboldt Foundation Award, membership in the National Academy of Sciences, and an honorary degree from Queen's University, Belfast. In December 1993, three months after his death, he was awarded the Pomerance Medal for Scientific Contributions to Archaeology of the Archaeological Institute of America.

Suess is best known for his contributions to the development of the radiocarbon method of dating. Specifically, Suess was one of the first to examine critically the work of Willard F. Libby and suggest that there were flaws in the original research. In the 1960s, Suess discovered that the concentration ratio of radiocarbon, assumed by Libby to be relatively constant, in fact varied. These variations, now known as *Suess wiggles,* were considered slight by Libby but were significant enough to produce errors in dating that would increase dramatically with the antiquity of the sample being tested. The work of Suess and those who followed him to correct the flaws in the radiocarbon method eventually produced a recalibration of the process and a revision of the half-life of radiocarbon from 5,568 years to 5,730 years.

Joseph J. Basile

See also LIBBY, WILLARD FRANK; RADIOCARBON DATING

Further Reading

Houtermanns, J., Suess, H.E., and Oeschger, H. (1973) Reservoir models and production rate variations of natural radiocarbon. Journal of Geophysical Research 78:1897–1908.

Suess, H.E. (1965) Secular variations of the cosmic-ray-produced carbon 14 in the atmosphere and their interpretations. Journal of Geophysical Research 70:5937–5952.

Suess, H.E. (1970) Bristlecone-pine calibration of the radiocarbon time-scale 5200 B.C. to the present. In I.U. Olsson (ed.): Radiocarbon Variations and Absolute Chronology, pp. 303–309. Stockholm: Almqvist & Wiksell/New York: J. Wiley.

Suess, H.E. (1970) The three causes of the secular C-14 fluctuations, their amplitudes and time constants. In I.U. Olsson (ed.): Radiocarbon Variations and Absolute Chronology, pp. 595–604. Stockholm: Almqvist & Wiksell/New York: J. Wiley.

Suess, H.E. (1979) A calibration table for conventional radiocarbon dates. In R. Berger and H.E. Suess (eds.): Radiocarbon Dating: Proceeedings of the Ninth International Conference, pp. 777–784. Berkeley, CA: University of California Press.

Suess, H.E. (1979) The C-14 level during the fourth and second half of the fifth millennium B.C. and the C-14 calibration curve. In R. Berger and H.E. Suess (eds.): Radiocarbon Dating: Proceedings of the Ninth International Conference, pp. 538–544. Berkeley, CA: University of California Press.

Survey Design, Theory

Consideration of the interrelationships among the characteristics of archaeological phenomena, the data requirements of archaeological research problems, and the design of archaeological surveys.

Archaeological survey is an integral, some would argue fundamental, aspect of contemporary archaeological research. Historically, however, archaeological survey has not been so highly regarded. Before the 1970s, surveys were conducted (1) to find "typical" sites, (2) to document the distribution of particular site types (e.g., sites with kivas [i.e., ceremonial chambers]), or (3) most commonly, to locate potentially "productive" sites. Consequently, descriptions of the archaeological record were somewhat biased (i.e., only the more obtrusive or clustered portions of the archaeological record were recorded as "sites").

Today, however, survey is a major data-gathering method for archaeological research projects, especially cultural resource management (CRM) studies. To appreciate how sophisticated survey research has become, a theoretical foundation is provided that illustrates how the connections between archaeological phenomena and archaeological problems influence the design of archaeological surveys.

The surface archaeological record can be considered a "more or less continuous distribution of artifacts over the land surface with highly variable density characteristics" (Dunnell and Dancey 1983:272). This clinal notion should be extended, as Francis P. McManamon argued in 1984, to include all potentially informative phenomena, such as features, structures, organic and inorganic residues, and anthropic horizons—in short, any archaeological trace that might convey information about the cultural past.

Depending on the problem being investigated, the general strategy of survey archaeology is to enhance or maximize the "discovery probabilities of archaeological materials" (Schiffer et al. 1978:2). One useful way to conceptualize how archaeologists design surveys, therefore, is to view target archaeological phenomena as anomalies (i.e., as phenomena whose origins can be attributed ultimately, if not exclusively, to cultural behavior) that have probabilistic occurrences in natural landscapes. Hence, to identify relevant phenomena of interest (e.g., artifacts, features, anthrosols), archaeologists must first acquire relatively detailed knowledge of natural phenomena and processes in the area where a problem-oriented survey is planned. Archaeological survey, then, consists of theoretically warranted procedures for maximizing the probability of encountering the range of archaeological phenomena that pertains to a certain problem.

Archaeological Survey and Archaeological Problems

Compared to excavated data, survey data are equally as important although far less expensive to acquire. In fact, various initiatives and problems in archaeology entail phenomena that are acquired conventionally only by means of survey, as several contributions in *Surface Archaeology* (Sullivan 1998) attest. For example, in North American archaeology today, surveys are conducted routinely in areas that have been designated for alteration; in these cases, such as the construction of a reservoir or a highway, survey is statutorily required. In addition, often in conjunction with legislative mandates (e.g., the National Historic Preservation Act of 1966, as amended), surveys are designed to supplement the range of archaeological phenomena known from excavation alone; the Wupatki Archaeological Survey Project in northern Arizona is a good case in this regard (Anderson 1990). However, as exemplified by the work of John E. Cherry and colleagues on northwest Keos in the Cyclades Islands (1991), modern surveys often are designed and executed to solve problems, such as the emergence of, and change in, land-use patterns, that are developed independently of a legislative mandate and of the necessity to provide a regional context for site-specific excavation data.

As the scope of archaeological survey has evolved to embrace a wider range of phenomena, the theoretical consequences of conventional nomenclature have been rethought (Wandsnider 1998). For example, problems that examined organizational changes in resource-acquisition activities have eschewed the "site" as the principal descriptive taxon, using instead variation in the frequency, taxonomic diversity, and spatial distribution of individual artifacts; such an approach has been termed *distributional archaeology* by James I. Ebert. Regardless of how units of observation are designated, survey design invariably involves interpretation and judgments by the archaeologist. These decisions are informed, however, by considering the factors that affect the probability of encountering phenomena that are implicated by specific archaeological problems.

Archaeological Survey Design: Independent Variables

Anomalous phenomena in natural landscapes, such as variation in artifact density, disclose several properties that affect the design of archaeological surveys. These factors are considered independent variables (i.e., variables that the archaeologist is powerless to control but that determine, nonetheless, how archaeological surveys are designed and executed). They are also considered independent to the extent that variation in one of the variables does not affect variation in the others.

The five most common independent variables fall into two classes: *archaeological* and *contextual*. Information about the archaeological class of variables, which includes abundance, distribution, and obtrusiveness, is imperfect at best but intrinsically affects decision making in survey design. *Abundance* refers to the frequency of archaeological phenomena in the research area and is commonly measured in terms of the number of occurrences of a phenomenon calibrated by a standard unit of measurement, such as artifacts per square meter, masonry ruins per square kilometer, or subsurface anomalies per hectare. *Distribution* refers to how the phenomena of interest are arrayed spatially across the area of interest. In qualitative terms, archaeological phenomena may be randomly distributed (e.g., projectile-point fragments), evenly distributed (e.g., Roman forts in Iron Age Britain), or clustered (e.g., prehistoric cities, such as Teotihuacan, Mexico). *Obtrusiveness* refers to the degree to which archaeological phenomena contrast with their natural surroundings. Prehistoric earthen mounds and enclosures in the central Ohio Valley, for example, are highly obtrusive because they are positive topographic features situated on relatively flat (in many cases, glaciated) terrain. In contrast, Late Archaic/Early Ceramic-period occupation surfaces in the desert Southwest are relatively unobtrusive because they are often covered by several meters of alluvium.

Within the contextual class, visibility and accessibility have dramatic consequences for survey design. *Visibility* refers to the extent to which contemporary environmental factors affect the detection of archaeological phenomena independently of their abundance, distribution, and obtrusiveness. For example, abundant and obtrusive groups of so-called "house mounds" may be nearly invisible in the tropical forests of Central America, whereas similarly configured archaeological phenomena can often be seen on aerial photographs in the comparatively highly visible countryside of the American Southwest. *Accessibility* refers to contemporary constraints on the ability of surveyors to inspect the landscape. Accessibility is influenced by climate and its seasonal fluctuations (it is difficult to inspect the ground's surface when it is buried under snow), vegetation type and density (e.g., impenetrable thickets of catclaw or rhododendron), topography, road networks, and land-holding patterns (e.g., mosaics of public land and private land create jurisdictional obstacles in gaining access to areas to be surveyed [assuming the investigator already possesses the necessary permits to conduct archaeological research]).

Relationships among these factors affect the discovery probabilities of archaeological phenomena. If obtrusiveness, visibility, and accessibility are held constant, then the discovery probabilities of surface archaeological phenomena vary directly with abundance and inversely with clustering. However, if archaeological phenomena are abundant and nonclustered, and if obtrusiveness and visibility are unrestricted, then the rate (i.e., the number of archaeological phenomena encountered per person/day) at which they are encountered will vary directly with accessibility (low rates in areas of poor accessibility, high rates in areas of good accessibility).

Archaeological Survey Design: Direct Observation by Noninvasive Methods

The most common type of archaeological survey conducted in North America, which probably characterizes most other regions of the world as well, is the *single-pass sweep* of the countryside (i.e., the survey area, designated by either a problem or a construction project that will disturb the ground, is essentially reconnoitered only once). Multistage projects are the few exceptions that require revisiting a previously surveyed area.

For theoretical purposes, assume that (1) the survey area is accessible, (2) relevant background studies have been completed, and (3) the surveyors are equipped with small-scale, preferably color, aerial photographs. Assume, as well, that the surveyors have embryonic knowledge of target archaeological phenomena in terms of their abundance, distribution, and obtrusiveness. The objective of the survey is to determine the range of archaeological phenomena in the project area.

Under these conditions, the principal factor that affects the discovery probabilities of archaeological phenomena is *intensity*, which refers to the "degree of detail with which the ground surface of a given survey unit is inspected" (Plog et al. 1978:389). Intensity may be measured by the distance (or spacing interval) between surveyors and by the amount of time spent covering a given area.

Discovery probabilities of target archaeological phenomena can be enhanced by varying survey intensity in response to the five principal independent variables noted above. Although low-intensity (30 m or more between surveyors) and medium-intensity (15–30 m between surveyors) surveys have been conducted in areas of high visibility, good accessibility, and where archaeological phenomena are relatively obtrusive, they have become increasingly uncommon as archaeologists have adopted a regional perspective. The case studies in Suzanne K. Fish and Stephen A. Kowalewski's edited volume, *The Archaeology of Regions,* for example, convincingly demonstrate the interpretive value of large-scale, intensive surveys. Without question, high-intensity survey (preferably 10–15 m between surveyors) is now the preferred method; in fact, its effectiveness and indispensability are well illustrated in the controlled study reported by LuAnn Wandsnider and Eileen Camilli in 1992.

Survey unit shape has an effect on discovery probabilities and, hence, can be manipulated to the advantage of the archaeologist. For example, if survey-unit area is held constant, more phenomena are likely to be encountered along the margins of long, narrow transects than along the perimeters of large quadrats (the *edge effect* of Plog et al. 1978:399). In the interest of maximizing survey efficiency, it is preferable to situate survey units with respect to unmistakable landscape features, such as roads, drainages, and clearings, because they are easier to locate on aerial photos and maps and thus also in the field. Experience has shown that locating and marking the perimeters of randomly defined survey units wastes time and can produce imprecise locational data.

Archaeological Survey Design: Indirect Observation by Noninvasive Methods

Noninvasive visibility-enhancing discovery strategies were designed initially to detect geophysical anomalies in natural phenomena. In the case of archaeological survey, however, their principal focus is on differentiating anomalies that are attributable to cultural behavior from those that are not. Historically, the most commonly used techniques have been *magnetometry, resistivity,* and *ground-penetrating radar,* which are discussed exhaustively in *Archaeological Prospecting and*

Remote Sensing by Irwin Scollar and collaborators. Each of these techniques measures, generally by means of sophisticated electronic equipment, variation in the geophysical property. For example, *magnetometry* measures deviation in the Earth's magnetic field that originate in conjunction with human-related activities (e.g., walls, pits, burned structures or hearths). *Resistivity* measures deviations from a constant source of electrical current; abnormally high or low departures are then investigated to determine if human activity is responsible for the anomalies. *Ground-penetrating radar,* similarly, is designed to detect variations in the travel times of radar waves that encounter soil horizons, features, and other anomalies that differentially affect wave propagation and decay through subsurface contexts. Instrumental subsurface surveying, however, may be more impractical than coring for the discovery of archaeological phenomena because the requisite equipment is not always highly portable, often requires substantial setup time and calibration, and has narrowly defined use parameters (e.g., relatively flat and unobstructed [unvegetated] surface topography). Like coring, it may be useful for ascertaining the presence of buried features and anthropic soil horizons once larger-scale phenomena have been located by conventional surface-inspection strategies. Other noninvasive anomaly-detecting techniques, such as chemical testing (e.g., phosphorus assaying) and remote sensing (e.g., aerial photography and various imaging procedures), have applications that are limited by highly localized environmental conditions; interestingly, their results ultimately are dependent upon ground verification by pedestrian survey.

Archaeological Survey Design: Direct Observation by Invasive Methods

Survey strategies can be adjusted by means of artificial exposures to increase surface visibility where it is low (i.e., less than 20 percent per unit area). One of the most common invasive visibility-enhancing techniques is *shovel-testing,* which has a long history of application and refinement in the heavily vegetated U.S. Eastern Woodlands. Typically (Table 1), units 30-50 cm across are excavated up to 50 cm deep and the soil matrix is screened through 6.4 mm mesh to determine if archaeological material is present. The units are

TABLE 1.

Variation in Shovel Testing Methods Recommended by Various State Historic Preservation Offices (SHPO)

Agency	Shovel Test Exposure Size	Maximum Depth*	Matrix Disposition	Maximum Interval	Slope	Visibility
AL SHPO	30cm diam.	50cm	screen	30m	- - - -	- - - -
IN SHPO	30cm diam.	40cm	screen	15m	<20%	<25%
	30cm diam.	40cm	hand-sort	10m	<20%	<25%
KY SHPO	30cm diam.	- - - -	screen	20m	- - - -	"poor"
OH SHPO	.25m²	50cm	screen	15m	<20%	<20%
PA SHPO	.25m²	50cm	screen	30m	<15%	<20%
VA SHPO	30cm diam.	- - - -	screen	15m	<15%	<50%

*This depth or until subsoil is encountered, whichever comes first.

spaced initially 15-30 m from one another, depending partly on terrain; however, if a unit produces archaeological material, the interval may be decreased to provide a more fine-grained view of the material's spatial distribution. Another artificial exposure technique, *raking,* has been recommended for those areas, such as the Ponderosa Pine life zone of the American Southwest, where the ground's surface is obscured by duff (accumulated needles, cones, bark).

Soil cores (2-3 cm diameter cylinders) and auger cores (greater than 3-15 cm diameter cylinders) are also used to detect traces of buried archaeological phenomena. Cores obtained from comparatively homogeneous deposits, such as lacustrine sediments, have produced well-dated sequences of paleoenvironmental data that document changing land-use practices. Environmental factors (e.g., rocky or impenetrable calcareous horizons) and archaeological factors (e.g., frequency and obtrusiveness of target phenomena), however, may limit the extent and the effectiveness of coring applications.

Finally, archaeologists have discovered that systematically placed backhoe trenches efficiently reveal the depth and extent of buried horizons, features, and artifacts. However, simulation studies published by David A. Abbott in 1985 show that, unless the distance between parallel backhoe trenches is equal to or slightly less than the average diameter of certain feature classes, such as pithouse basins, estimates of the frequency of subsurface phenomena may be unreliable. Despite their somewhat destructive nature, which in general has been exaggerated, *backhoe*

trenching has become one of the most widely adopted means for discovering buried archaeological phenomena (Stafford 1995).

Archaeological Survey Design: Some Avoidable Complications

Even under the best circumstances (i.e., in areas of unobstructed visibility and high accessibility), archaeological survey, especially in areas with little previous work, is error prone. Hence, it is worth examining briefly three common, albeit avoidable, complications that affect the conduct and the results of archaeological survey.

First, beware of the tyranny of previous work. Designing survey strategies that are based on the results of so-called probabilistic sample surveys, unintensive surveys, or phenomenon-specific surveys will bias the discovery of previously unrecorded or unprecedented phenomena, such as the G.E. Mound near Evansville, Indiana, which was so large that veteran surveyors thought it was a natural landscape feature (Munson et al. 1995).

Second, exercise caution in the selection of units of observation. One common problem is the use of units that are based on interpretive conventions, such as when an artifact scatter is recorded as a "limited-activity site." Equally problematic is rigid adherence to previously established formulaic criteria, such as when a "site" is denoted by any cluster of artifacts that exceeds five per m². These practices tend, especially when combined with inexperience, to introduce inflexibility into the prosecution of archaeological survey designs, thereby reducing the probability of recording the full range of phenomena.

Third, and perhaps most serious, is the still common practice of disregarding how visibility affects the quality of survey data. Unless archaeologists design surveys that can accommodate variation in visibility, they are likely to skew the range of recorded phenomena toward large, abundant, and obtrusive remains, which produces a highly biased view of the contents of the archaeological record and, consequently, compromises its interpretive potential.

Alan P. Sullivan III

See also SCOLLAR, IRWIN; SURVEYS, MULTI-STAGE AND LARGE-SCALE

Further Readings

Abbott, D.A. (1985) Unbiased estimates of feature frequencies with computer simulation. American Archeology 5:4–11.

Anderson, B.A., ed. (1990) The Wupatki Archaeological Inventory Survey Project: Final Report. (Professional Paper 35). Santa Fe, NM: National Park Service, Southwest Cultural Resources Center, Division of Anthropology.

Cherry, J.F., Davis, J.L., and Mantzourani, E., eds. (1991) Landscape Archaeology as Long-Term History: Northern Keos in the Cycladic Islands from Earliest Settlement until Modern Times. Los Angeles: UCLA Institute of Archaeology.

Dunnell, R.C. and Dancey, W.S. (1983) The siteless survey: A regional scale data collection strategy. In M.B. Schiffer (ed.): Advances in Archaeological Method and Theory, vol. 6, pp. 267–287. New York: Academic.

Ebert, J.I. (1992) Distributional Archaeology. Albuquerque: University of New Mexico Press.

Fish, S.K. and Kowalewski, S.A., eds. (1990) The Archaeology of Regions: A Case for Full-Coverage Survey. Washington, D.C.: Smithsonian Institution Press.

McManamon, F.P. (1984) Discovering sites unseen. In M.B. Schiffer (ed.): Advances in Archaeological Method and Theory, vol. 7, pp. 223–292. New York: Academic.

McManamon, F.P. (1992) Managing America's archaeological resources. In L. Wandsnider (ed.): Quandaries and Quests: Vision's of Archaeology's Future, pp. 25–40. Carbondale, IL: Southern Illinois University Press.

Munson, C.A., Jones, M.M., and Fry, R.E. (1995) The GE Mound: An ARPA case study. American Antiquity 60:131–159.

Plog, S., Plog, F., and Wait, W. (1978) Decision making in modern surveys. In M.B. Schiffer (ed.): Advances in Archaeological Method and Theory, vol. 1, pp. 383–421. New York: Academic.

Schiffer, M.B., Sullivan, A.P., and Klinger, T.C. (1978) The design of archaeological surveys. World Archaeology 10:1–28.

Scollar, I., Tabbagh, A., Hesse, A. and Herzog, I. (1990) Archaeological Prospecting and Remote Sensing. Cambridge: Cambridge University Press.

Schott, M.J. (1992) Commerce or service: Models of practice in archaeology. In L. Wandsnider (ed.): Quandaries and Quests: Visions of Archaeology's Future, pp. 9–24. Carbondale, IL: Southern Illinois University Press.

Stafford, C.R. (1995) Geoarchaeological perspectives on paleolandscapes and regional subsurface archaeology. Journal of Archaeological Method and Theory 2:69–104.

Sullivan, A.P., III, ed. (1998) Surface Archaeology. Albuquerque: University of New Mexico Press.

Wandsnider, L. (1998) Regional scale processes and archaeological landscape units. In A.F. Ramenofsky and A. Steffen (eds.): Unit Issues in Archaeology, pp. 87–102. Salt Lake City: University of Utah Press.

Wandsnider, L., and E.L. Camilli (1992) The character of surface archaeological deposits and its influence on survey accurancy. Journal of Field Archaeology 19:169–188.

Waters, M.R. (1992) Principles of Geoarchaeology. Tucson: University of Arizona Press.

Surveying and Site Examination, Manual Methods

The discovery and examination of archaeological resources through manual subsurface investigation of soil deposits. Discovery investigations often are referred to as *archaeological surveys* and have as their goal the identification of all or a portion of the archaeological resources in a given study area. Examination investigations, also known as *site testing* or evaluation, focus on extracting information about the size, contents, and structure of an archaeological site, a portion of a site, a number of related sites, or, perhaps, the spatial distribution of archaeological remains within an area, such as all or part of a river valley, a canyon, or an embayment; this last kind of investigation and focus has been advocated by Robert C. Dunnell, William Dancey, James I. Ebert, and LuAnn Wandsnider, among others. This approach to examining the archaeological record is referred to as *distributional archaeology, nonsite archaeology,* and a *landscape approach* to archaeology (Rossignol and Wandsnider 1992).

Choosing the Technique(s)

Choice of appropriate technique for discovery or examination investigation will depend upon a variety of factors. First, one must consider the purpose of the investigation. Is the target one kind of site (e.g., a prehistoric mound or a site of a particular time period), or is the goal to find all kinds of sites within a given area, as typically is the case for cultural resources management and historic preservation studies? If a particular kind of site is the target, one can focus on a technique that detects the kinds of characteristics displayed by the particular type of site. If a wide range of sites are the target, one will want to choose a technique or techniques that will detect the characteristic(s) most commonly shared by all of the expected site types.

The archaeological record is composed of physical and chemical phenomena spatially distributed on the surface and within near-surface soil layers of the Earth. The constituents of archaeological resources that commonly are considered in making decisions about techniques for discovery and examination are: artifacts, features, and anthropic soil horizons. Anthropic soil horizons are relatively large deposits that result from concentrated human activity, often dumping of organic refuse or trash. Shell and trash middens are common examples of anthropic soil horizons. They typically are more extensive spatially and less clearly delimited than features and may contain artifacts among the accumulations of secondarily deposited refuse that constitute them. Additional site constituents exist in the form of human-generated anomalies of soil chemistry, resistivity, magnetism, and vegetation. These latter kinds of site constituents usually require nonmanual techniques, such as use of an instrument or a physical or chemical test, to detect them.

The abundance and the distribution of different kinds of constituents vary among sites, within given areas, and within site areas. In most cases, artifacts will be the site constituent most frequently found and most widely distributed within archaeological sites or spread across a larger area. Artifacts are made, used, and enter the archaeological context through a wider variety of human behaviors than any of the other constituents listed above. For example, features result from the construction, maintenance, and use of facilities, such as storage pits, hearths, and structures. Anthropic soil horizons result from various kinds of intensive or concentrated activity, such as shellfish processing or trash dumping. Each of these kinds of archaeological constituent frequently also includes artifacts as part of the feature or soil matrix. However, there are many archaeological deposits that contain artifacts but not features or anthropic soil horizons.

A further concept to consider when archaeological discovery and examination investigations are being designed is the *obtrusiveness* of the archaeological remains being sought. Obtrusiveness refers to the extent to which the archaeological remains contrast or stand out against their natural surroundings in or above the soil. Additional considerations of survey design are *visibility* (i.e., the extent to which modern natural or cultural components mask the archaeological remains) and *accessibility* (i.e., the extent to which, and ease with which, areas to be inspected or tested can be reached by field crews). Useful and sensible discussions of these general considerations can be found in two articles, both published in 1978: one by Stephen Plog and colleagues, the other by Michael B. Schiffer and colleagues.

Four kinds of manual techniques for discovery or examination are described below: *surface inspection, soil cores, soil augers,* and *shovel test pits.* Excavation units of various sizes and shapes also are an appropriate technique for site-examination investigations; however, the care needed in setting these up in the field and their relatively large size limit their use for discovery investigations. Other nonmanual techniques sometimes are used for discovery and examination investigations but are not described in this entry. Among these techniques are use of heavy digging equipment, chemical analysis, geophysical techniques, and remote sensing.

Surface Inspection

Historically, *archaeological survey* has implied surface inspection rather than any other site discovery technique. This has changed since the 1970s as investigations with the goal of discovering archaeological sites in environments in which they are not readily visible on the surface have become much more common. In arid parts of the world, such as the American Southwest, parts of Mexico and South America, and parts of the Middle East, surface inspection by teams of archaeologists walking systematically over an area, recording and/or collecting structures and artifacts, remains the standard means of site discovery. Systematic surface collection also is used in such environments as a means of site examination or to examine a larger area or a number of sites and make inferences about demography, economic relationships, and other aspects of human adaptation.

Surface inspection also has been used in parts of the world where vegetation or soil aggradation has covered archaeological materials. In such areas, such as agricultural portions of the eastern United States, surface inspections of plowed fields has had a long tradition as a primary discovery technique. There are some problems with the use of surface inspection, though. It requires that site constituents be visible on the surface or, when plowed fields are being inspected, within reach of the plow. It requires that artifacts, the site constituent that is almost always the target of surface inspection efforts, be abundant so that they are easily detected. In areas in which dense vegetation covers the surface, it will not work unless the sites of interest also contain remnants of structures that stand out and are detectable despite the vegetation.

Soil Cores

Soil cores are small diameter (2–4 cm) tubes pushed into soil and extracted with a column of soil held by friction within the coring instrument. This column is then inspected to detect the site constituent being tested for. Because they are small and can be extracted quickly, soil cores initially seem an ideal technique; however, investigators have found that, in practice, cores primarily detect dense an-

thropic soil horizons, such as shell and trash middens. Unfortunately, such dense deposits are relatively infrequent among archaeological sites and tend to be spatially concentrated rather than widespread within site areas. This limits the effectiveness of soil cores as a discovery technique. Some soil types also present technical difficulties to the use of cores. In sandy soils, the soil column may be too dry to be extracted intact. In very clayey or rocky soils, insertion of the soil core tube may be difficult or impossible. However, soil cores have proven to be a useful technique for site examination, particularly for exploring the spatial distribution and structure of deeply buried and intricately structured anthropic soil horizons. Julie Stein, in particular, has used soil coring to investigate and map the complex stratigraphy of anthropic soil horizons in shell middens in the Midwest and the Pacific Northwest of the United States.

Soil Augers

Like soil cores, augers extract a cylinder of soil; however, augers have wider diameters: ca. 10–15 cm. The contents of the auger fill can be inspected to detect artifacts, and the profile of the auger hole can be inspected to detect features and anthropic soil horizons. Inspection of the profile becomes more difficult with the depth of the auger, however, because the holes are quite narrow. Soil augers have been used in a variety of investigations in the eastern United States. Their effectiveness for site discovery seems to be related strongly to the intrasite distribution of artifacts. Augers can detect artifacts when they are abundantly and widely distributed within sites; however, augers are less likely to detect artifacts that are scarce, though widely distributed, or plentiful but highly aggregated. Although augers would seem to be capable of detecting features or anthropic soil horizons, none of the investigations reviewed reported the frequent or consistent discovery of these kinds of site constituents by soil augers. Sandy, clayey, and rocky soils present technical challenges to augers, making digging and effective extraction difficult. Soil augering can be an effective technique for site discovery. Because augers increase the volume of soil extracted and inspected, artifacts are more easily detected by them than by soil cores. However, experience suggests that augers do not effectively detect artifacts within site boundaries unless the distribution of artifacts is both abundant and widespread.

Shovel Test Pits

Shovel tests range in size and shape. They may be circular and from 25 to 75 cm in diameter or square with sides from 25 to 100 cm. Usually, they are excavated until culturally sterile soil is reached, but they cannot be dug effectively below 100 cm. Shovel tests can detect artifacts, features, and anthropic soil horizons. They excavate a much larger volume of soil than soil augers, which is an important factor in making shovel tests a more effective discovery technique. In a controlled experiment within known site areas at Cape Cod National Seashore (McManamon 1984), 78 percent of shovel tests detected artifacts, compared with only 45 percent of the soil augers excavated.

The volume of subsurface tests are also an important factor in determining the effectiveness of different techniques for site discovery. Consider the following abstract model of an archaeological site, or a portion of a site, 10 m² and 50 cm deep. Within this site area, artifacts are evenly distributed, an unlikely characteristic of a real site but necessary for examining the relationship between test volume and artifact discovery. Given this model, the probability that a test will discover an artifact, thereby discovering the archaeological site, is a function of the number of artifacts in the site matrix and the size of the subsurface tests. Table

1 shows the discovery probabilities of different volume tests and variations in the number of artifacts in the site area. This table shows, not unexpectedly, that the greater the number of artifacts and the larger the volume of the test, the more likely the intersection of an artifact by a subsurface test and, hence, the greater the likelihood of successful site discovery. It also shows that, as the number of artifacts decreases, the probability that smaller volume tests will intersect an artifact drops rapidly. The table provides some general advice about selection of an appropriate technique for site discovery investigations.

The drawback of using the larger volume tests, of course, is that they take more time to excavate. This means that fewer of them can be done in a given amount of time than the smaller probes. Larger tests require more time to dig, screen, and record. Screening of test soil is an important component of this technique. It has the advantages of detecting the most common site constituent, artifacts. It is preferable to simply inspecting the soil fill visually, which risks missing small artifacts even if carefully done. Screening also overcomes the problem of visibility posed by dirt adhering to artifacts or hiding them from view in another way.

The effectiveness of shovel tests as a discovery technique has been debated in the professional literature since the mid-1980s. A series of articles by Keith Kintigh, Kent Lightfoot, Jack Nance and Bruce Ball, and

TABLE 1.

Probabilities of Single Subsurface Probe Recovering an Artifact within a Site Area

Probe Diameter	Number of Possible Probes (per 10 m²)	Number of Artifacts Distributed Evenly in Area				
		10,000 (100/m²)	5,000 (50/m²)	1,000 (10/m²)	100 (1/m²)	10 (1/m²)
Auger (10 cm)	10,000	1.00	0.50	0.10	0.01	0.001
Auger (20 cm)	2,500	1.00	1.00	0.40	0.04	0.004
Shovel test (25 cm)	1,600	1.00	1.00	0.63	0.06	0.006
Shovel test (50 cm)	400	1.00	1.00	1.00	0.25	0.025
Shovel test (100 cm)	100	1.00	1.00	1.00	1.00	0.100

Assumptions of model: (1) dimensions of area being tested are 10 m × 10 m × 0.5 m; (2) depth of each probe is 50 cm; (3) the potential probe locations are packed evenly within the 10-m² area; (4) spaces between potential probe locations are devoid of artifacts; (5) probabilities are calculated as the number of artifacts divided by the number of probes per 10 × 10-m area. Table by Francis P. McManamon

Michael Shott present the various aspects of this debate. Shovel tests are an imperfect means of archaeological site investigation for discovery. However, for much of the world, where surface visibility of archaeological resources is poor or nonexistent, this technique is a reasonable one. It is an effective site discovery technique and more effective than other smaller volume subsurface probes at discovering artifacts, the most frequent and widespread constituent of archaeological sites. Yet, shovel testing also is time consuming. To reduce the costs of the technique, careful planning and skillful, diligent field execution of the investigation are necessary. The arguments in the articles cited above concerning the effectiveness of the technique provide potential users with various means of evaluating the utility of shovel testing for the investigation they are contemplating.

Shovel tests have been used for site examination investigations also. In large site areas or areas in which archaeological remains are being investigated using a nonsite approach, they can provide relatively quick views of the spread of artifacts and spatial variation in the density and occurrence of artifacts and other kinds of deposits. This kind of site examination application has been used by Francis P. McManamon and others (e.g., to describe and interpret the prehistoric and historic patterns of land use on the outer portion of Cape Cod, Massachusetts).

Sampling in Discovery and Examination

Almost all archaeological discovery and examination investigations involve some kind of sampling. If an investigation does not discover or examine all of the remains in a site or all of the archaeological resources in an area, it deals with a portion, or sample, of them. Archaeologists must always be concerned about how accurately the data they have collected reflects the actual archaeological record about which they are making inferences.

Sampling methods may be *judgmental* (i.e., is based upon past knowledge or present interpretations) or *probability based* (i.e., with sample units selected mathematically). Frequently, the most productive method for an investigation will be one that combines judgment with probability. A typical example of a combined method is the use of probability techniques to select sample units within sampling strata described based upon judg-

ment. The value of incorporating probability methods of sampling selection into archaeological sampling is that, if utilized appropriately, they provide a means of evaluating the precision of the quantitative results of the investigation. Appropriate application of probability methods requires careful consideration of the objects of interest, be they sites, artifacts, or some other archaeological phenomenon, and their relationship to the sample units (i.e., the units by which data are collected in the investigation). Other important considerations are the number of sample units, the size and shape of sample units, the extent to which sample units are completely checked for objects of interest, and the way in which sample units are selected for inspection.

There is no single best way to sample the archaeological record, but archaeologists almost always are engaged in some kind of sampling. It is important, therefore, for investigators to be aware of the bias that the kind of sampling they are engaged in has upon the results of their investigations. In reporting on investigations and making interpretations about the past, the effect of sampling upon the results of a discovery or examination investigation must be explicitly and carefully considered.

Francis P. McManamon

See also: AERIAL PHOTOGRAPHY FOR ARCHAEOLOGY; ARCHAEOLOGICAL PROSPECTING; CULTURAL RESOURCE MANAGEMENT (CRM); ELECTRICAL AND ELECTROMAGNETIC PROSPECTING; GEORADAR; MAGNETIC PROSPECTING; SEISMIC REFRACTION SURVEYING; SURVEY DESIGN, THEORY; SURVEYS, MULTISTAGE AND LARGE-SCALE

Further Readings

Cowgill, G.L. (1975) A selection of samplers: Comments on archaeo-statistics. In J.W. Mueller (ed.): Sampling in Archaeology, pp. 170–191. Tucson: University of Arizona Press.

Kintigh, K.W. (1988) The effectiveness of subsurface testing: A simulation approach. American Antiquity 53(4):686–707.

Lightfoot, K.G. (1986) Regional surveys in the eastern United States: The strengths and weaknesses of implementing subsurface testing programs. American Antiquity 51(3):484–504.

McManamon, F.P. (1984) Discovering sites unseen. In M. B. Schiffer (ed.): Advances in Archaeological Method and Theory, vol. 7, pp. 223–291. New York: Academic.

McManamon, F.P. (1994) Discovering and estimating the frequencies and distribution of archaeological sites in the northeast. In J.E. Kerber (ed.): Cultural Resource Management, pp. 99–114. Westport: Bergin and Garvey.

Nance, J.D., and Ball, B.F. (1989) A shot in the dark: Shott's comments on Nance and Ball. American Antiquity 54(2):405–412.

Plog, S. (1978) Sampling in archaeological surveys: A critique. American Antiquity 38(1):280–285.

Plog, S., Plog, F., and Wait, W. (1978) Decision making in modern surveys. In M.B. Schiffer (ed.): Advances in Archaeological Method and Theory, vol. 1, pp. 383–421. New York: Academic.

Redman, C.L. (1987) Surface collection, sampling, and research design: A retrospective. American Antiquity 52(2):249–265.

Rossignol, J., and Wandsnider, L. (1992) Space, Time, and Archaeological Landscapes. New York and London: Plenum.

Schiffer, M.B., Sullivan, A.P., and Klinger, T.C. (1978) The design of archaeological surveys. World Archaeology 10:1–28.

Shott, M.J. (1989) Shovel-test sampling in archaeological survey: Comments on Nance and Ball, and Lightfoot. American Antiquity 54(2):396–404.

Surveys, Multistage and Large-Scale

Respectively, surveys involving more than a single inspection of an area for archaeological phenomena, and surveys seeking to locate archaeological phenomena in areas that typically exceed 2.59 km^2 (note that pipeline and transmission-line corridors are excluded from this definition). Both survey types are designed to enhance the probability of obtaining reliable data regarding the range of archaeological phenomena that are pertinent to a research design. However, neither type of survey necessarily implies the other. Each has different purposes, depending on the problems being investigating.

Multistage Survey

In contrast to large-scale surveys (see below), multistage surveys have a relatively short history in archaeological research. Discussions of the usefulness of multistage research first appeared, principally in the New World literature, during the mid-1960s and were expanded during the 1970s and early 1980s. As described by Michael B. Schiffer and Susan J. Wells in their 1982 paper, "Archaeological Surveys: Past and Future," multistage-survey research essentially is a contingent strategy wherein the results of initial work determine the design of subsequent stages (hence, the term *multistage*). In their most elaborate form, multistage survey designs include probability sampling techniques.

One type of multistage survey, according to Schiffer and colleagues in their 1978 article, "The Design of Archaeological Surveys," varies design features, such as intensity, survey-unit size, and survey-unit shape, among stages. For example, the first survey stage may consist of randomly oriented narrow transects whose content variation determines the placement and proportional number of large blocks that are to be intensively inspected during the second stage. This type of multistage survey is premised on the proposition that it is inefficient to record both site-level and other phenomena simultaneously during a single inspection of the ground's surface. Instead, as argued by William H. Doelle in 1977, the first stage should focus on discovering and recording site-level phenomena using relatively low-intensity techniques (i.e., surveyors spaced more than 30 m apart). Then, in the second stage, a high-intensity survey, perhaps guided by probability-based sampling protocols, would endeavor to discover and record subsite or nonsite phenomena.

The second type of multistage survey is characterized by designs whose features do not vary among stages. The goal of this type is to obtain a complete inventory of archaeological phenomena by repeated intensive survey of the same area. This practice also allows archaeologists to assess the severity of the *Brigadoon Effect,* which refers to situations where archaeological phenomena seemingly appear and then disappear in response to seasonal fluctuations in rainfall and vegetative cover. Also, employing secondary or tertiary sampling designs of the same area enables archaeologists to increase the accuracy or quantity of surface survey data, with the objective of achieving "a continuous series of closer approximations" of the archaeological resource base (Dunnell and Dancey 1983:280).

Finally, in many parts of the world, the history of research has produced what might be called *de facto* multistage surveys. Archaeological survey in its various forms has become so common in Greece, for example, that some landscapes have been inspected dozens of times in the twentieth century. In their 1987 book, *Beyond the Acropolis: A Rural Greek Past,* Tjeerd H. Van Andel and Curtis N. Runnels note that in the Southern Argolid, as in much of Greece, the landscape already had been examined informally by archaeologists before modern surveys were undertaken. Then, in the early 1980s, initial systematic extensive surveys were followed by highly intensive surveys of a small part of the larger study area.

Multistage surveys were conceived in an optimistic era in archaeology (ca. 1964–1982), when it was thought that probabilistic sampling schemes would acquire high-quality data at relatively low cost. Subsequent tests revealed that, at least within cultural resource management (CRM) contexts, such optimism was unwarranted for two reasons: the highly unreliable statistical effects of extrapolating regional population parameters from nonnormally distributed sample statistics and the prohibitive costs associated with resurveying the same areas repeatedly. However, multistage surveys that have focused on reliability studies, such as those reported by Stephen Plog in 1986 that assess the effects of intercrew recording variation on survey data characteristics, have been instructive in pinpointing potential sources of error that can affect data quality. With the exception of those projects where detailed recording of select sites follows a large-scale intensive survey, however, multistage surveys are unlikely to be used as widely as once thought.

Large-Scale Survey

For many years, low-intensity, wide-ranging surveys were the principal means for documenting regional archaeological variability. Nowadays, however, large-scale systematic surveys are conducted routinely, as the case studies in *The Archaeology of Regions* (Fish and Kowalewski 1990) illustrate, because at least two advantages are associated with their intensive (i.e., 15 m or less between surveyors), inventory nature. First, large-scale surveys are more likely to encounter the full range of archaeological phenomena, which is especially important for those projects that investigate occupational processes associated with long-term land-use patterns; the interdisciplinary research described in *Sandy Pylos: An Archaeological History from Nestor to Navarino* (Davis 1998) exemplifies their usefulness. Second, as articulated especially well by Jack D. Nance in 1983, spatial analyses can be conducted without being compromised by the possibility that potentially significant, though perhaps rare, phenomena are not part of the database.

Factors Affecting Large-Scale and Multistage Survey

Despite the advantages of systematic large-scale surveys, several factors influence their productivity, which refers to the yield of problem-dependent information obtained per unit of effort (e.g., "sites" per person per day). First, the occupational history of a region affects how much terrain can be covered. If a region had been used heavily, for example, then such a profusion of material may have been discarded that little territory could be covered quickly, especially if discovery and recording occurred simultaneously. In the Mediterranean area, for instance, John Bintliff and Anthony Snodgrass's 1988 study shows that high artifact densities are the result of ca. 10,000 years of artifact production and discard coupled with geomorphological factors that are favorable to the preservation and concentration of surface material. Consequently, hundreds of ceramic types and dozens of stone-tool forms confront the field archaeologist. Moreover, because noncollection survey strategies largely have been abandoned in Greece, in contrast to many surveys conducted on federal lands in the western United States, the great quantity of surface artifacts there makes it difficult to study them *in situ*. Hence, most projects include specialists, often recruited from museum staffs, to determine the dates and functions of surface artifacts. In these kinds of situations, a multistage approach that incorporates high-intensity inspection followed by selective recording of problem-dependent phenomena would appear to be warranted.

Second, the kind of unit of observation affects survey productivity, depending on the

S

abundance and clustering of archaeological phenomena in a study area. As illustrated in James I. Ebert's *Distributional Archaeology*, for instance, the individual artifact as the unit of observation may be useful in those archaeological landscapes that exhibit low densities of artifacts with little or no clustering. In many parts of the Mediterranean and the American Southwest, in contrast, the nearly continuous distribution of surface artifacts has caused archaeologists to experiment with a variety of observational units, including isolates, features, and mapping units. Whatever the unit of observation, however, archaeologists have been challenged to formulate explanatory models for continuous artifact distributions, that may originate from overlapping activity areas, dispersed accumulations of refuse, or natural processes, as numerous studies in *Surface Archaeology* (Sullivan 1998) reveal.

Finally, attempts to synthesize the results of recent large-scale surveys have disclosed problems in data comparability. It is still relatively rare to find sufficiently explicit descriptions of field methods or discussions of the effects that environmental conditions or variation in abilities of surveyors may play in shaping the data sets assembled by a survey team. That such factors can profoundly influence our views of the cultural past is convincingly argued in *Landscape Archaeology as Long-Term History* (Cherry, Davis, and Mantzourani 1991).

In the future, archaeologists will need to focus increasingly more attention on developing interpretation-neutral units of observation and modes of analysis that will facilitate interproject data comparability. This is especially important as large-scale surveys, perhaps with multistage components, supplant excavation as the most cost-effective technique for acquiring information about the properties of the archaeological record.

Alan P. Sullivan III
Jack L. Davis

See also SURVEY DESIGN, THEORY

Further Readings

Bintliff, J., and Snodgrass, A. (1988) Off-site pottery distributions: A regional and interregional perspective. Current Anthropology 19:506–513.

Cherry, J.F., Davis, J.L., and Mantzourani, E., eds. (1991) Landscape Archaeology as Long-Term History: Northern Keos in the Cycladic Islands from Earliest Settlement until Modern Times. Los Angeles: UCLA Institute of Archaeology.

Davis, J.L., ed. (1998) Sandy Pylos: An Archaeological History from Nestor to Navarino. Austin: University of Texas Press.

Doelle, W.H. (1977) A multiple survey strategy for cultural resource management studies. In M.B. Schiffer and Gumerman, G.J. (eds.): Conservation Archaeology: A Guide for Cultural Resource Management Studies, pp. 201–209. New York: Academic.

Dunnell, R.C., and Dancey, W.S. (1983) The siteless survey: A regional scale data collection strategy. In M.B. Schiffer (ed.): Advances in Archaeological Method and Theory, vol. 6, pp. 267–287. New York: Academic.

Ebert, J.I. (1992) Distributional Archaeology. Albuquerque: University of New Mexico Press.

Fish, S.K. and Kowalewski, S.A., eds. (1990) The Archaeology of Regions: A Case for Full-Coverage Survey. Washington, D.C.: Smithsonian Institution Press.

Nance, J.D. (1983) Regional sampling in archaeological survey: The statistical perspective. In M.B. Schiffer (ed.): Advances in Archaeological Method and Theory, vol. 6, pp. 289–356. New York: Academic.

Plog, S. (1986) The survey strategy. In S. Plog (ed.): Spatial Organization and Change: Archaeological Survey on Northern Black Mesa, pp. 32–49. Carbondale, IL: Southern Illinois University Press.

Schiffer, M.B., Sullivan, A.P., and Klinger, T.C. (1978) The design of archaeological surveys. World Archaeology 10:1–28.

Schiffer, M.B. and Wells, S.J. (1982) Archaeological surveys: Past and future. In R.H. McGuire and Schiffer, M.B. (eds.): Hohokam and Patayan: Prehistory of Southwestern Arizona, pp. 345–383. New York: Academic.

Sullivan, A.P., III, ed. (1998) Surface Archaeology. Albuquerque: University of New Mexico Press.

Van Andel, T.H. and Runnels, C.N. (1987) Beyond the Acropolis: A Rural Greek Past. Stanford, CA: Stanford University Press.

Symbolic Archaeology

The study of material culture's past symbolic meanings, using structural, contextual, and cognitive analyses, often supplemented by ethnoarchaeology, ethnographic analogy, or the direct-historic approach. Authors rarely label themselves as symbolic archaeologists, but, broadly defined, the term describes many studies of visual imagery, art, symbolism, ideology, ritual, and religion in the past. The uniquely human ability to create and use symbols has fascinated archaeologists from the beginning of the discipline. Examples of symbolic archaeology cited here and in the Further Readings represent most of the recent theoretical approaches but only a small fraction of widely ranging subject matter, including Upper Palaeolithic cave paintings, Mayan glyphs, Pueblo architecture, and historic South African rock art.

Symbolic Meaning

A variety of studies with different concerns may be subsumed under symbolic archaeology. Some scholars reconstruct specific symbolic meanings of prehistoric iconography. Linda Schele examined detailed Mayan paintings and carvings depicting ritual activities, such as blood letting (autosacrifice), and translates Mayan writing accompanying such imagery. Together with ethnohistoric accounts, these data form an unusually secure basis for her reconstructions of the specific ways Mayan elites communicated with the supernatural and how the Maya understood time, space, and cosmology. The reconstructions are not ends in themselves but are key to understanding social and political processes in the Mayan world.

The work of artists who had no formal writing system is more difficult to understand in terms of content. In direct-historic studies, texts and oral traditions from the present or recent past are linked with prehistoric iconography presumed to come from the same culture area. For example, Robert Hall bases interpretations of prehistoric Adena and Hopewell iconography on ethnographic accounts of myth and religion from eastern United States tribes from the seventeenth century on. In a 1977 *American Antiquity* article entitled, "An Anthropocentric Perspective for Eastern United States Prehistory," Hall's interpretations of Hopewell spear throwers (atlatls) and pipes as staffs of office with life-giving powers, consecrated with tobacco, are linked to the documented uses of flat-stemmed ritual pipes in many historic tribes. His arguments rest on two assumptions, one cognitive and one historical. First, all humans share certain associative mental processes. Metaphor (a form of analogy) and synecdoche (substitution of a part for a whole) are some ways humans create social meanings from observations of natural processes, such as seasonal cycles, astronomical phenomena, life and death, and animal behavior. Second, basic associations underlying the religious practices of specific cultures are likely to persist for hundreds of generations. Not all symbolic archaeologists agree that Hall's assumptions are valid, however.

Studies that aim to reveal principles that structured past thought and behavior have a long and rich history. Three important examples of structuralist archaeology are Andre Leroi-Gourhan's studies of Franco-Cantabrian cave paintings dating to ca. 35,000–10,000 years ago, James J.F. Deetz's 1977 study of the artifacts of colonial New England, *In Small Things Forgotten;* and Henry Glassie's 1975 *Folk Housing of Middle Virginia.* All three authors study the relationships among objects more than the objects themselves in attempts to reveal generative principles or grammarlike rules in the minds of the makers.

Leroi-Gourhan's study was particularly innovative and ambitious because he had no historic documents or ethnographic information with which to support his argument that cave paintings were deliberately placed in relation to one another. He viewed them as a system of signs, organized according to structural rules or generative principles. Using quantitative methods, he demonstrated that images of various animals, humans, and geometric "signs" were not randomly placed. Certain kinds of images were consistently associated with each other in certain parts of caves. In one study, he identified some abstract signs as male and female, based on their general resemblance to genitalia. He suggested that images consistently associated with each of these signs were also classified as male and female, so that certain animal pairings and certain parts of the cave could be interpreted according to the male/female binary opposition.

Many structuralist analyses avoid addressing the cultural context of the production

S

and use of the art and do not address changes in form or meaning that may have taken place during prehistory. Leroi-Gourhan did not address the specific meanings of the various signs within the male and female categories; he treated art from a 25,000-year period as one data set; and human actions and intentions are absent from his interpretations. Yet, he was more interested in meaning than other researchers who conduct formal structuralist analyses of art styles. For example, using symmetry analysis, a formalist technique, to look for pottery-style boundaries between social groups is not symbolic archaeology unless the meanings of the boundaries and the role of decoration in producing and maintaining boundaries are addressed explicitly.

Structuralism continues to play an important role in symbolic archaeology, but it usually serves as a starting point, not an end in itself. Binary oppositions such as nature/culture, raw/cooked, inside/outside, and even male/female are seen as hypotheses rather than simple universals. Binary oppositions may change in form and emphasis over time, and their specific contents are culturally constituted. For instance, in many cultures, such as Hopi and Zuni Pueblos, snakes are symbolically important because they move between the Earth surface and the underworld. A petroglyph depicting a snake can be suggested to have something to do with this transition. Inferring the snake's other potential meanings, such as association with lightning, rain, and earthquakes, would be problematic without ethnographic information. In addition, human symbolic systems often focus on transformations, reversals, and mediation of oppositions. Weapons kill, thereby mediating life and death. In some contexts, however, weapons symbolize not death but protection, life, or even peace, as in Hall's proposed transformation of the spear thrower into the sacred pipe mentioned above.

Many studies investigate the roles or functions of art and religion. Rather than attempt to reconstruct specific meanings or structural organization of symbols, they ask how people used visual imagery for social and political purposes. John Fritz's 1978 study of eleventh-century sites in Chaco Canyon, New Mexico, drew on both structural analysis and historic Puebloan ethnography to explore the adaptive roles of ideational systems and how information is organized and transmitted through architecture. One of Margaret Conkey's earlier studies of the Upper Palaeolithic art of Europe linked intensification of artistic activities to increasing social pressures resulting from aggregating populations and consequent competition for resources. Conkey's recent work moves beyond the functions of art and religion to explore the very nature of gender categories and gender relations.

All of the above authors insist that interpretation of meaning is just as important as identification of the environment or analysis of economic systems for understanding past lifeways. As these examples show, concern with meaning predates the development of postprocessual archaeology in the 1980s, although postprocessualists have been the most vocal proponents of the study of meaning, cognition, and symbolic systems. Postprocessual archaeologists reject explicitly empiricist and positivist science and embrace ideas from Marxism, hermeneutics, and (to varying and contested degrees) postmodernism on the one hand and postpositivism on the other.

Contextual Archaeology

Explicitly postprocessual symbolic archaeology is primarily associated with the work of Ian Hodder and Daniel Miller in the mid-1980s in England. Hodder terms this approach *contextual archaeology*. Much of his work focuses on the Neolithic and Bronze Ages of Northern Europe. He examines the forms and spatial organizations of houses, tombs, and associated artifacts over time and space. He concludes that, at some times and places, tombs meant houses. These tombs were symbolic homes, too, for living members of dispersed and shifting farming communities. The tombs housed the ancestors and provided territorial foci for the living. Hodder links processes of plant and animal domestication and gender ideology to the development of ideas about houses, which he calls the idea of *domus* in contrast to ideas about *agrios,* outside or undomesticated spaces. The influence of French structuralism is apparent in Hodder's use of this binary opposition, but he also provides temporal and cultural context for the ideas of *domus* and *agrios.* Hodder shows how the meanings of houses changed between the Neolithic period and the Bronze Age. The symbolic anthropology of Victor Turner and Mary Douglas also has a strong influence on Hodder's approach.

Miller, using an ethnoarchaeological approach, examines the expression of ideas about social class and ideology in material culture. He shows that individuals and families, using material items to negotiate their social position, drive changes in the artifacts and in the very structure of the class system. Forms and functions of pottery and metal containers in India are specific to different castes. Miller shows how lower castes emulate higher classes, in part, by copying a higher class's vessel assemblage. Higher castes, in turn, adopt innovative forms in an attempt to retain their distinctiveness.

Contextual archaeology sees environment and ecology as constraining rather than directing change. As seen in Miller's study, change is located in the active social roles of individuals and things. In contrast, processual archaeology, at least through the 1970s, tended to view artifacts and art styles as passive reflections of social and political orders and minimized the roles of individual actions and class conflicts. Hodder writes: "Behind functioning and doing there is a structure and content which has partly to be understood in its own terms, with its own logic and structure. This applies as much to refuse distributions and 'the economy' as it does to burial, pot decoration and art" (Hodder 1982:4).

Contextual archaeologists define the relationship between mental and physical aspects of culture as recursive. Beliefs and symbolic meanings affect the form of objects and behavior. At the same time, objects and behavior affect the structure of the symbolic system. This perspective derives from Marxist approaches in French and British anthropology, dating to the 1960s: Anthony Giddens, Jürgen Habermas, and Pierre Bordieu are often cited as providing philosophical underpinnings.

Contextual archaeology also insists on a historical framework. Although the functions of ideological systems, as well as economic systems, can be examined cross-culturally, a relatively small proportion of social and cultural behavior is generalizable. Certainly, there is no reason to expect religious practice, iconography, art styles, or architectural patterns current at one time and place to extend to other societies except through specific historical events, such as colonization. The very structuring principles that assign cosmological, social structural, or gender meanings to objects, buildings, and spaces change over

time and vary from place to place. Hodder states that "the cultural framework within which we act, and which we reproduce in our actions, is historically derived" and "each culture is a particular historical product" (Hodder 1982:4). Hodder does not call for the rejection of generalization, predictive laws, and the cross-cultural method, which are very useful for understanding the mechanical, ecological, and cognitive constraints on human behavior. Nor does he call for return to historical particularism. Rather, Hodder seeks a recognition that, to move beyond functionalist explanations of patterns in the archaeological record, it is necessary to understand long-term culture history in each case study.

The archaeological record results from the cumulative behaviors of individuals. Hodder, therefore, insists that "adequate explanations of social systems and social change must involve the individual's assessments and aims" (Hodder 1982:4). It is not necessary to identify the work of specific individuals by their fingerprints, for example. Nor is it necessary to understand the emotional states of these individuals, although some of Hodder's earlier writing implies a concern with feelings and motivations. Rather, one must view past societies as made up of active individuals, possibly with diverse goals, not as unthinking, undifferentiated masses acting collectively and predictably.

Symbolic archaeologists generally, and contextual archaeologists in particular, intend to produce strong interpretations rather than the predictive models and covering laws characteristic of processual archaeology. As in processual archaeology, symbolic archaeologists evaluate competing interpretations against archaeological evidence. The directed search for new evidence is very much a part of the interpretive process. Most symbolic archaeologists take a broad, sometimes explicitly "postpositivist" or "realist," view of science. They reject materialism that rejects meaning and so reject the materialist/idealist dichotomy itself. Rather than simple falsification or hypothesis testing, the goal is inference to the best hypothesis. Many, including Hodder, characterize this interpretive process as a *hermeneutic spiral* (i.e., continually working back and forth between theory and data, adding knowledge and understanding with each turn).

Symbolic archaeology is also necessarily informed by *critical theory*. It is important to constantly guard against projecting present-day assumptions and political agendas into the past. This is a clear danger in the investigation of past symbolic and cognitive systems. It must be noted, however, that critical theory is important in other study domains as well: Projection of capitalist goals onto past foragers, for instance, is a common pitfall.

Cognitive Archaeology

Much work that can be called symbolic archaeology because of its concern with past symbols and meaning is part of a broader and explicitly scientific approach termed *cognitive archaeology*. Colin Renfrew defines cognitive archaeology as "the study of past ways of thought as inferred from material remains." Some practitioners identify with postprocessualism; others, such as Renfrew, do not. Renfrew explicitly seeks to move the study of meaning and cognition beyond the recent theoretical debates and "study the way in which cognitive processes operated in specific contexts, and to investigate the interrelationship between those processes and the social contexts which harbored and promoted them" (Renfrew and Zubrow 1994:5).

One branch of cognitive archaeology, primarily associated with archaeologists at the University of the Witwatersrand in South Africa, is grounded in universal psychoneurological processes. David Lewis-Williams used direct-historic evidence together with the study of human neuropsychological universals to show that much South African rock art depicts the visions and experiences of shamans in trance states. The paintings include *entoptic images* or *phosphenes*—simple geometric forms that all humans see in altered states of consciousness. These forms are produced in the brain and optic systems of all humans and can be found in the art of shamans virtually everywhere, as well as in drawings of visual disturbances suffered during migraines. The meanings assigned to these forms or to hallucinations that often follow are culturally constituted, however. Lewis-Williams showed how many depictions of animals in South African rock art served as metaphors for the shaman's experiences entering other worlds and contacting spirit helpers. This study provides the basis for a new interpretation of Upper Palaeolithic rock art of Europe, in

which the same geometric forms appear together with representational art that may have had similar metaphoric meanings. In the Great Basin of the western United States, David S. Whitley used a similar combination of direct-historic evidence for Numic shamanism, formal analysis of rock-art forms and contexts, and neuropsychological evidence to argue that rock art there was produced by shamans. Most important, he addresses the social context of shamanic practice and rock art and shows that shamanism preserved and mystified social asymmetries between men and women and between shamans and nonshamans.

New Synthesis

Symbolic archaeology today (i.e., 1998) might best be viewed as a new synthesis of processual and postprocessual approaches, breaking down and transcending this dichotomy, as well as those between science and humanism, materialism and idealism, nature and culture, and natural and social sciences. It does not purport to replace other approaches, and it is not a new paradigm as such. Rather, it is largely defined by its subject matter and the kinds of questions asked, by the suite of attitudes and techniques most appropriate to exploring imagery, belief, cognition, and religious practice in the past. Of the three major approaches discussed here—structural, contextual, and cognitive—two are actively pursued today; structural archaeology has been subsumed by the other two. Contextual archaeology most specifically aims to understand past symbolic systems through interpretation of meanings, but it requires especially rich data. For this reason and because interpretations cannot be extended from one case to others, contextual archaeology cannot be applied in all times and places. Cognitive archaeologists are more interested in the roles and development of symbolic systems than in specific meanings. Because it is grounded in neuropsychology and cognitive science, this approach holds great promise for broad applications. Cognitive archaeologists are joining with other disciplines to move away from vague psychological generalizations to neuropsychology, and from simple analogies between the structures of language and art styles to studies of the cognitive bases for both language and material expressions of meaning. In this sense, cognitive archaeology provides the unique long-term perspective to a larger, interdisciplinary enterprise.

Kelley Ann Hays-Gilpin

See also DEETZ, JAMES J. FANTO; ETHNOARCHAEOLOGY; HODDER, IAN; LEROI-GOURHAN, ANDRE; NEW/PROCESSUAL ARCHAEOLOGY; POSTPROCESSUAL ARCHAEOLOGY; RENFREW, ANDREW COLIN

Further Readings

Fritz, J. (1978) Paleopsychology today: Ideational systems and human adaptation in prehistory. In C.L. Redman (ed.): Social Archaeology: Beyond Subsistence and Dating, pp. 37–59. New York: Academic.

Hodder, I., ed. (1982) Symbolic and Structural Archaeology. Cambridge: Cambridge University Press.

Hodder, I., ed. (1987) The Archaeology of Contextual Meanings. Cambridge: Cambridge University Press.

Hodder, I., ed. (1989) The Meanings of Things: Material Culture and Symbolic Expression. London: Unwin Hyman.

Hodder, I. (1992) Theory and Practice in Archaeology. London: Routledge.

Inskeep, R., ed. (1994) Reading art. World Archaeology 24:287–396.

Leone, M. (1986) Symbolic, structural, and critical archaeology. In D. Meltzer, D. Fowler, and J. Sabloff (eds): American Archaeology Past and Future, pp. 415–438. Washington, D.C.: Smithsonian Institution Press.

Renfrew, C., and Zubrow, E. B., eds. (1994) The Ancient Mind: Elements of Cognitive Archaeology. Cambridge: Cambridge University Press.

Watson, P.J., and Fotiadis, M. (1990) The razor's edge: Symbolic-structuralist archeology and the expansion of archeological inference. American Anthropologist 92:613–629.

Whitley, D.S. (1992) Prehistory and postpositivist science: A prolegomenon to cognitive archaeology. In M. B. Schiffer (ed.): Archaeological Method and Theory, vol. 4, pp. 57–100. Tucson: University of Arizona Press.

S

T

Taphonomy

The study of the transition, in all its details, of animal and plant remains from the biosphere into the lithosphere (Efremov 1940). Taphonomy considers the relationship between organic remains and their environment and encompasses all changes that follow from death until collection and examination of the fossil.

This review focuses upon animal (including human) remains in the archaeological context. Living animals are composed of a variety of organic biomolecules, such as nucleic acids, carbohydrates, proteins, and lipids, as well as a range of inorganic components. The potential for survival of these biomolecules in archaeological context is generally low, but a variable proportion of them is usually preserved in some burial conditions. They survive in environments in which microbial decomposition is restricted. Such environments are characterized by desiccation, low temperatures, the presence of substances inhibitory to microbial growth, and close association with inorganic matrices.

There are recorded survivals of archaeological material from the first three extreme environments: the mummification of bones and soft tissue from human remains due to sun drying, the preservation of soft and hard tissue from both mammoths and frozen human corpses in permafrost regions, and the classic mummification processes of ancient Egypt, which preserved human tissue (both soft and hard) by the presence of waxes, oils, and plant extracts.

The majority of animal and plant remains, however, have not been subjected to such successful preservation environments. The most common component of human and animal origin to survive in the archaeological record are the hard tissue parts. In vertebrates, this is skeletal material (e.g., bones); in invertebrates, shell. It is the taphonomy of these matrices that is discussed below.

Bone Structure

The vertebrate body comprises a number of variously shaped and sized bones that disarticulate easily once the soft tissue that surrounds them has been lost. Bone is a highly specialized composite material that combines an organic phase (predominantly protein) with an inorganic phase (chiefly calcium hydroxyapatite). The organic phase of bone is composed of ca. 90 percent protein (type I collagen), with the remaining 10 percent being composed of the noncollagenous proteins (i.e., osteocalcin), lipids, and carbohydrates. Type I collagen is a triple-helical molecule of more than 3,000 amino-acid residues (ca. 1,000 amino acids make up each of the chains of the triple helix). Every third residue (33 percent) is glycine (the smallest amino acid), which means that the chains can be tightly coiled when the glycine residues are all aligned toward the center of the helix. The molecule also has a high proportion of proline and hydroxyproline (together making up 20 percent), which inhibit the action of many protein-degrading enzymes.

The inorganic phase of bone is predominantly the mineral calcium phosphate (hydroxyapatite, $Ca_{10}(PO_4)_6.2OH$). The phosphate (PO_4^{2-}) can be readily substituted by carbonate (CO_3^{2-}); Mg^+, Na^+ and K^+ can replace the Ca^+; and fluoride ions (F^-) can easily replace the hydroxide ions (OH^-). Therefore, hydroxyapatite is a variable mineral, and bone can, at best, be said to be poorly mineralized. Once the collagen has been laid down, the mineral is deposited around it, and the collagen is said to be mineralized.

The association between protein and mineral is intimate, and, although the exact alignment is still a matter of debate, the presence of the hydroxyapatite in such close association with the protein has a protective role. For the collagen-specific enzymes (collagenases) to act, the bone collagen must be demineralized.

Shell Structure

The structure of shell is not as ordered or as defined as that of bone. The proteins in shell are very difficult to extract in their entirety and, therefore, are problematical to characterize. As with bone, however, the association of mineral and protein can be intimate. Shell mineral is composed of either or both of the crystal forms of calcium carbonate: aragonite or calcite. The exact interaction of the organic matrix with the mineral is uncertain; treatment of the shell with bleach will remove most (but not all) of the protein, so that the majority of shell proteins are intercrystalline. The protein matrix is secreted into the extracellular space, and, following this secretion, mineral is deposited in close proximity to the newly synthesized organic phase. The organic matrix is composed of both acid-soluble and acid-insoluble components; the major component of the organic matrix is the acid-insoluble part, which contains macromolecular carbohydrates and proteins. The acid-soluble part contains a heterogeneous mixture of proteins, some of which are linked to polysaccharides through serine.

Taphonomic Aspects of Human and Animal Remains

To appreciate the importance of taphonomy, a definition of paleoecology is required. Paleoecology is concerned with the relationship between the paleoenvironment and once-living organisms; success in this field is dependent upon being able to allow for the changes occurring due to taphonomy. The aim of paleoecology is to reconstruct ancient communities, whereas taphonomy is concerned with postmortem processes. Taphonomic considerations are a prerequisite for paleoecological studies, and the neglect of these processes will lead, inevitably, to erroneous conclusions.

As can be seen from Figure 1, taphonomic processes affect the survival or loss of organic remains. Paleoecological interpretation of these remains, when paralleled against modern counterparts, will be affected. It is, therefore, essential to understand and quantify, to a degree, the taphonomic changes occurring within a population so that proper interpretation of that population in an archaeological context is possible.

The processes of taphonomic change can be assigned to three subdivisions (Figure 1): *death* (thanatic considerations), *biostratinomy* (the interaction of the organic remains with the environment until burial), and *diagenesis* (the chemical, biological, and mechanical alterations within the burial environment). Because of taphonomic processes, only a few, if any, members of each population will survive in the fossil record. These surviving populations are called *assemblages*. For this review, an assemblage is a group of organic remains found in association with one another and, therefore, deduced to be the residue of one population over one time period. The length of the time period may vary;

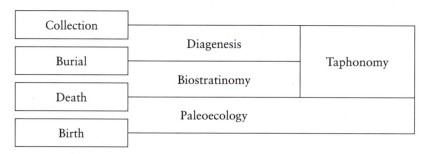

Subdivisions based upon the time interval in the history of the organisms under study. Modified from Lawrence 1968 by Angela Gernaey-Child

the population may be made up of several different species; the area over which the assemblage may spread may also vary.

Thanatic Factors

Thanatic factors are those associated with the death of an organism. The cause, location, and season of death are associated with the speed of burial of organic remains, as are the age, sex, and species, because an important thanatic factor is predation.

Cause of Death

Different causes of death will result in a fossil assemblage that may not reflect that of the living population. *Mass mortality* of the whole population caused by instant killing would produce an assemblage that exactly matched that of the living population. *Attritional mortality,* owing to a steady death rate throughout the year, would result in an assemblage that combined the effect of birth rate, growth rate, and death rate and would reflect the turnover of the population. *Seasonal mortality* is characterized by pronounced fluctuations in the attritional mortality.

To avoid confusion, it is necessary to distinguish among these three types of death assemblage. Assemblages influenced mainly by seasonal variations will yield information on ecology, but they are too variable to be of much use in studying the population as a whole.

Time of Death

The time of death will influence the probability of survival of organic remains, and several factors are involved. Animal availability is seasonal, and the habits of predators will also be seasonal, as will their selection of prey. The rates of weathering, exposure, and burial will also be seasonal but are better included as biostratinomic factors.

Location of Death

Various burial environments have different preservation potentials for organic residues; important variables are pH, oxygen concentration, and temperature of the environment. Generally, the greater part of the fossil record is composed of aquatic organisms. Members of this group are prone to more rapid burial than land organisms and, therefore, tend to survive better, since most land mammals die on dry land. The preservation potential of dry land is low because the possibility of rapid burial is slight. In times of drought, terrestrial animals may gather around waterholes, leading to a concentration of organic remains.

Biostratinomic Factors

Biostratinomic factors include the rate of decomposition, physical damage, and transportation of animals (including human) remains. These are readily affected by climate and length of exposure prior to burial. Biostratinomic changes are deleterious; therefore, the speed with which tissues are buried will affect their preservation potential.

Rate of Decomposition

The rate of decomposition of organic remains depends upon the external environmental conditions. Water is the most important agent of decay; it is required by microorganisms for their life processes, which are suppressed in dry conditions. Desiccation, therefore, promotes preservation. The water-soluble fractions of organic remains are lost in wet conditions through leaching.

Generally, the rate of chemical and biochemical reactions is nearly doubled by a 10°C rise in temperature; therefore, seasonal variations in temperature will affect rates of decomposition. Seasonal fluctuations also dictate floral and faunal activity. Various insects and microorganisms will attack the dead remains of flora and fauna.

The concentration of oxygen will control decomposition rates. Decomposition will proceed rapidly in environments that are high in oxygen *(oxic).* While decomposition will not stop in those environments low in oxygen *(anoxic),* the rate will slow drastically by comparison. Microorganisms (bacteria and fungi) affect the soft tissues of the corpse, rotting the flesh very quickly. The aerobic bacteria and fungi are faster than the anaerobic bacteria at degrading organic remains. This rate of degradation may be augmented by the presence of carrion feeders (insects). Some species will destroy unmineralized material, while others will only disturb it. The speed of burial dictates whether insect damage will be severe, but rapid burial does not exclude their activity. The eggs of carrion insects can be laid on the body very soon after death, and the depth of burial does not always exclude their activity. Active members of the species *Collembola* have been found at a depth of 2 m in graveyards. Insects can also change the gross physical appearance of bones; in one case, lesions thought to have been due to syphilis in life were shown conclusively to be due to the activities of a beetle after death.

Most species of land snails are scavengers and carrion feeders. As with insects, they have the ability to survive in the burial environment, so, following infestation of the organic material, they will damage the organic remains prior to and after burial. Some species are burrowers, and some species of the genus *Helix* will hibernate underground. The surface of hard tissues may be damaged by carnivorous snails, and this sometimes presents problems of differentiation for the paleopathologist.

Physical Damage

Both flora and fauna (micro- and macro-) may damage organic remains, either directly or indirectly. Direct attack takes the form of structural damage and immediate (over archaeological time spans) loss of organic material. Indirect attack is less easy to characterize but usually constitutes some form of disturbance that may result in either preservation or loss of organic remains.

Mammals, large and small, both burrowers and scavengers, may alter organic remains by disturbance; hard tissues are particularly susceptible to gnawing, splitting, and cracking. Mammals may also completely remove small bones and teeth, thereby changing the potential fossil assemblage. It is the corpse, not the skeleton, that is of most interest to the carrion feeders and scavengers, which explains why the skeleton is the most common material of animal origin to survive over archaeological time.

The physical damage to the corpse produced by the activities of humans cannot be excluded from this review. The ancient burial practices of human corpses include burning and burying, with and without additional animal sacrifice. Preservation procedures include pickling, smoking, and embalming; corpses may be exposed prior to burial or merely abandoned; they may be disarticulated prior to burial or buried in their entirety.

Humans have been responsible for some of the physical alteration seen in archaeological bone; bones have been used as the basis of a variety of artifacts. Some, such as bone needles, are easy to distinguish, but the differentiation between cracking of bone due to the behavior of animals, the effects of the elements, and that deliberately produced by the action of ancient humans is the subject of many publications.

Transportation

As defined earlier, an assemblage occupies a discrete space in time. Any disruption of this results in a loss of information. Remains may be relocated by scavengers, and wind and water are also involved in the transport of either whole or disarticulated sections of organic remains. Within an unburied assemblage, these movements may constitute a significant taphonomic alteration.

Humans may also be involved in this transport; the contribution to collections of materials, such as bones or shells, can usually be attributable to human dietary needs. The paleoecologist must, therefore, distinguish between real assemblages and taphonomic ones, the latter being influenced by both human activities and the elements.

Diagenetic Factors

Diagenesis occurs postburial, and the factors that control it are the environmental conditions of the sediment. For the purposes of this review, a *sediment* is the burial environment, whether subaquatic or subaerial. Sedimentary variables include the pH of the permeating water, oxygen concentration, flora and fauna, and temperature.

pH

Generally, acidic environments do not promote the survival of organic hard tissues. The mineral phase is removed by dissolution, revealing the organic phase, which is then susceptible to rapid decomposition.

Under certain acid bog conditions, however, some organic material will survive due to the presence of tannins. Peat marshes are well known to have a preserving effect for corpses; in Britain and Denmark, several have been recovered (e.g., Tollund Man in Denmark). The collagen in the skin and the bone is preserved by the presence of plant extracts that interact with the collagen molecules, causing cross-linking between collagen molecules, thus increasing resistance of the collagen to protein-degrading enzymes and collagenases. Bones from the more acidic peat bogs show a poorer state of preservation than others. The lower the pH, the more likely that collagen peptide bonds are broken, hydrolyzing the protein.

Under mildly acidic conditions, the mineral will first dissolve and then recrystallize. Recrystallization occurs because the mineral phase acts as a buffer, neutralizing the pH. Once acidic conditions have been negated, the mineral will reform. In shells, dissolved calcite recrystallizes as calcite, but dissolved aragonite will also recrystallize as calcite. In bone, the dissolved calcium phosphate recrystallizes variously as calcium hydroxyapatite, brushite, and amorphous calcium phosphate.

Oxygen Concentration
The oxygen concentration of the burial environment will be less than that of the exposed environment. Nonetheless, some aerobic microbial decomposition will proceed until the oxygen concentration drops, when anaerobic microbial decomposition starts. There are exceptions, but, generally, under anaerobic microbial decomposition, the end products of metabolism are CO_2, NO_2, H_2O and SO_2, with no appreciable reduction in pH; under anaerobic microbial decomposition, the end products of metabolism are a range of organic acids and amino acids, the identity of which depends upon the starting material. Anoxic conditions are required for the dissolution of the mineral in hard tissues; hence, preservation of entrapped proteins is likely to be enhanced if decomposition is solely aerobic.

Anaerobic decomposition has a potential to be self-propagating, leading to the loss of all of the organic fraction. As the rate of anaerobic degradation slows due to the lack of metabolites, oxygen will slowly diffuse into the system. Eventually, the rate of anaerobic digestion will be surpassed by the rate of oxygen diffusion, and the system will return to its aerobic state, when the rate of aerobic degradation will be determined by the concentration of bioavailable organic matter.

Temperature
The temperature of sediments is more stable than the temperature of the air. At a depth of 2 m, British (at Oxford) soil temperatures are constant at $10 \pm 2°C$, but in North America (at San Francisco) the average soil is $18 \pm 3°C$. The temperature of the sediment will dictate the types of organism that will be active in it, and the general rule of a doubling of activity for every $10°C$ rise in temperature still holds true. Generally then, the lower the sediment temperature, the more preservation is promoted, and the less diagenetic change will occur.

Flora and Fauna
As with thanatic and biostratinomic factors, these same groups of organisms are involved with the diagenetic loss of information from hard tissues; there are subtle differences between buried and unburied materials, however:

1. Burial will alter the types of microorganisms available to decompose hard tissues by reducing both the temperature and the oxygen concentration.
2. Burial will restrict many insects and other carrion feeders from ovulating on the organic material and will also inhibit the full development of many that may have already been deposited. Some will still develop, however.
3. Burial will restrict access by humans and other scavengers, though burrowing fauna will still affect hard tissues deposited in sediments.

Plant roots may grow over the surfaces of deposited hard and soft tissue; these roots sometimes etch the surfaces of bones, mimicking paleopathological change, and differentiation between these two is essential.

Physical Damage
Buried mineralized matrices are still subject to physical damage. This takes the form of crushing, warping, and splintering due to the weight of soil pressing on hard tissue. In the case of bone, the larger it is, the more it will be subject to physical damage. Groundwater levels will also affect hard tissue. Leaching of the mineral will reduce the likelihood that the matrix will survive. Groundwater has also been shown to carry ions into, as well as out of, bones.

Taphonomic Loss of Information
There are many examples that could be given of taphonomic losses of information. This entry is not intended to be an exhaustive review of them, and only a few examples are given here.

Inhumations
There have been a few studies on the taphonomic (diagenetic) loss of bones from the

human skeleton. Studies using inhumations from cemeteries have provided interesting results. In most cases, the bones that first disappear completely are the very small phalanges and other bones of similar size. Their disappearance from sites that are apparently free from disturbance has been associated with microbial decomposition.

Medium-size and large bones tend to remain, except the long bones (femur and humerus) if they have been splintered during burial. Generally, the spinal vertebrae and ribs high in the thoracic region remain, while those associated with the digestive tract (the lower ribs and, particularly, the lumber vertebrae) tend to be lost. This preferential bone loss associated with the abdomen indicates the severe microbial decomposition that proceeds during initial soft-tissue decomposition.

Bone Diagenesis

Exhumed archaeological bone contains tunnels in addition to those present during life. These tunnels (called *microscopical focal destruction,* or MFD) are assumed to be produced by fungi and bacteria growing through the bone and are much more prevalent in bones from well-drained terrestrial sites. Aquatic conditions suppress the formation of these tunnels, probably due to anoxic conditions that would suppress fungal activities. The MFD mostly have dimensions commensurate with fungi, and it is possible that these fungi tunnel using acids excreted at the tip of the hyphae. These acids would demineralize the bone and hydrolyze the protein. Whether these microorganisms diagenetically alter the remaining proteins is not known, but this must be assumed to be the case. Severely tunneled bone is not used for archaeometry.

Another feature of diagenesis in archaeological bone is the change in amino-acid content. When most of the collagen (98 percent) has been diagenetically removed, the amino acid content of the remainder changes, showing a reduction in glycine, proline, and hydroxyproline and an enrichment of aspartic and glutamic acids. These acidic amino acids interact strongly with calcium hydroxyapatite and are suggested to be either non collagenous proteins or the residues of decomposition of collagen.

Summary

Taphonomy is the study of all of the changes that occur within plant and animal remains following death until collection and examination. These changes occur in three stages: death (thanatic), preburial (biostratinomic), and postburial (diagenetic). Taphonomic changes in animal (including human) remains center on changes in the hard tissues (bones, teeth, and shells). Various factors control the changes, which may be macroscopic (i.e., the loss of whole bones), microscopic (tunnels produced by microorganisms), or chemical (loss of proteins from shell and bones). The ability to differentiate between damage during life, taphonomic change, and deliberate alteration is essential for correct interpretation of organic materials from archaeological sites.

Angela Gernaey-Child

See also BONE, CHARACTERIZATION; PALEOPATHOLOGY, HUMAN; ZOOARCHAEOLOGY

Further Readings

Allison, P.A., and Briggs, D.E.G., eds. (1991) Taphonomy. New York: Plenum.

Boddington, A., Garland, A.N., and Janaway, J.C. (1987) Death, Decay, and Reconstruction. Manchester: Manchester University Press.

Buchardt, B., and Weiner, S. (1981) Diagenesis of aragonite from Upper Cretaceous ammonites: A geochemical case-study. Sedimentology 28:423–438.

Child, A.M. (1995) Towards an understanding of the microbial decomposition of archaeological bone in the burial environment. Journal of Archaeological Science 22:165–174.

Donovan, S.K., ed. (1991) The Processes of Fossilisation. London: Belhaven.

Efremov, I.A. (1940) Taphonomy: A new branch of palaeontology. Pan-American Geologist 74:81–93.

Lawrence, D.R. (1968) Taphonomy and information losses in fossil communities. Geological Society of America Bulletin 79:1315–1330.

Noe-Nygaard, N. (1987) Taphonomy in archaeology, with special emphasis on man as a biasing factor. Journal of Danish Archaeology 6:7–62.

Tephrochronology

The use of volcanic ash and tuff deposits for relative dating of archaeological sites and for absolute age correlations when their ages can be determined using chronometric techniques, such as potassium-argon (K/Ar) dating. Over the last three million years, large regions of the world have witnessed extensive volcanic eruptions of the type that produce massive quantities of ash that may spread over tens or even hundreds of thousands of square kilometers. Perhaps the best-known application of dating volcanic tuff in archaeology comes from the volcanic rift zone in East Africa. Olduvai, Laetolil, Omo, Turkana, and Hadar are now nearly household words in the lexicon of hominid evolution. Without these volcanic deposits, interbedded with the surface sediments and soils on which the hominids lived, archaeologists would not be able to provide the relatively tight chronologial framework they have for hominid evolution.

Much nearer to the present, one of the major questions in eastern Mediterranean Bronze Age archaeology relates to the dating of the volcanic eruption on the Aegean island of Thera. Bronze Age Thera was the site of an extensive Minoan culture of sea traders. In the middle of the second millennium B.C., two-thirds of the island was blown away in a catastrophic eruption. The whole center of the island, once a mountain, became a great caldera open to the sea. A once-thriving Bronze Age seaport on the southern tip of the island was buried under volcanic ash. The ancient town situated on one of the remnant islands, now called Akrotiri from the name of the nearby village, is being excavated by the Greek Archaeological Service. This site and its fate have tremendous importance in their own right but have received worldwide attention because this cataclysmic eruption and attendant destruction might have been the source of the inspiration for Plato's legend of Atlantis.

Volcanic eruptions eject large quantities of fine particles and sulfur compounds into the upper-atmosphere circulation system. These materials return slowly to Earth in rain and snow. A significant increase in acidity from this sulfur is found in distinct layers in glacier ice cores. A Greenland ice core has a strong acidity peak at 1644 ± 20 B.C. This has been interpreted as recording the eruption of Thera. Artifacts from Akrotiri, linked to the Egyptian calendar, put the Thera eruption more than 100 years later. While this controversy remains open, the volcanic activity recorded in the Greenland ice core may be from nearby Iceland rather than from the eastern Mediterranean (this may be testable by comparing chemical signatures).

In addition to supplying datable material, volcanic ash or *tephra* (pyroclastic rock fragments that are ejected from a volcanic vent) provides marker horizons for correlation. The mineralogy of the separate volcanic eruptions is normally distinct enough that, with sufficient petrological study, ash horizons can be correlated over large regions, establishing a firm tephrostratigraphy. Although erosion strips large quantities of each ash/tephra mantle from exposed areas of the landscape, enough falls in protected niches and areas of active deposition to provide widespread preservation.

In western North America, three postglacial volcanic-ash deposits are useful marker beds for the Latest Pleistocene and Early Holocene. Glacier Peak Layers G and B (youngest) and Mount St. Helens J ashes date to the Late Pleistocene. The Glacier Peak ashes are from a volcano in north-central Washington and date to 11,200 B.P. The Mount St. Helens J ash comes from southern Washington and consists of ash layers erupted ca. 11,500–10,800 B.P. The most widespread ash in western North America, the Mazama ash, was derived from the volcano at Crater Lake in Oregon in an eruption dated at ca. 6845 B.P. The ages of these ashes have been determined primarily on the basis of radiocarbon dating.

Tephrochronology has been used to help date many archaeological contexts and stratigraphic sequences in western North America. The Clovis cache at the Wenatchee site in Washington was dated by eruptions from the Glacier Peak volcano. At this site, pumice-rich sediments derived from the Glacier Peak tephra were found directly underlying the Clovis artifacts. A nearby stratigraphic sequence contained the Mazama tephra. Glacier Peak Layer G ashfall was identified at the Indian Creek Site in western Montana. The ash was dated, using radiocarbon, to ca. 11,125 B.P. and underlies an assemblage of Folsom-related artifacts dated to ca. 10,980 B.P. The Mazama ash was also found within the Indian Creek sequence. Because these two ash deposits have been dated, all that is needed to use them as time markers is their identification. This can sometimes be done on the basis of thickness or color, but field identification needs to be checked using mineralogical or geochemical properties to characterize the volcanic ashes.

Tephrochronology is a young science, with most of the advances coming in the second half of the twentieth century. This research is carried out worldwide by geologists, sometimes in cooperation with archaeologists. For archaeologists, the first problem is to recognize tephra or ash when it occurs at a site. When these materials occur at archaeological sites, they are likely to be in a disturbed context. However, careful study of the site's archaeological and geological sediments will reveal the glass shards that are a significant component of ash and tephra.

George R. Rapp Jr.

Further Readings

Rapp, G., Jr., and Vondra, C., eds. (1981) Hominid Sites: Their Geologic Settings. Boulder, CO: Westview.

Rapp, G., Jr., Cooke, S., and Henrickson, E. (1973) Pumice from Thera (Santorini) identified from a Greek mainland archaeological excavation. Science 197:471–473.

Steen-McIntyre, V. (1977) A Manual for Tephrochronology: Collection, Preparation, Petrographic Description, and Approximate Dating of Tephra (Volcanic Ash). Golden: Colorado School of Mines Press.

Steen-McIntyre, V. (1985) Tephrochronology and its application to archaeology. In G. Rapp, Jr., and J. Gifford (eds.): Archaeological Geology. New Haven, CT: Yale University Press.

Sheets, P., ed. (1983) Archaeology and Volcanism in Central America: The Zapotitan Valley of El Salvador. Austin: University of Texas Press.

Wilcox, R. (1965) Volcanic Ash Chronology. In H. Wright, Jr., and D. Frey (eds.): The Quaternary of the United States. Princeton, NJ: Princeton University Press.

Theodolite

An optical instrument for measuring horizontal and vertical angles for mapping archaeological sites. The theodolite consists of a telescope that can be moved horizontally or vertically. Measurements are taken using graduated circles: one horizontal to measure horizontal angles, and the other vertical to measure vertical angles. The theodolite is mounted on a tripod and centered above the first station of a survey. It is made level by using the plate bubble.

There are a variety of different types of theodolite. Most can provide very accurate measurements by the direct reading of degrees, minutes, and seconds.

An electronic distance measurement (EDM) system can be mounted above a theodolite to provide automatic readout of horizontal and vertical distances. This is done by sending out a beam from a theodolite-mounted transmitter, which is bounced back from a reflector to the transmitter. When the theodolite and the EDM system are mounted in a single housing, the instrument is known as a *total station*. This instrument presents distances, vertical angles, and horizontal angles in digital form. Total stations are connected to automatic recording devices so the operator does not have to write anything down.

Peter L. Drewett

See also SITE MAPPING

Further Readings

Barker, P. (1993) Techniques of Archaeological Excavation, 3rd ed. London: Batsford.

Drewett, P.L. (1999) Field Archaeology: An Introduction. London: University College London Press.

Thermal Prospecting

An airborne method of archaeological-site discovery based on variation in ground-surface temperatures.

As may be observed during a period of melting snow or ice or in the varied appearance of hoarfrost, the temperature of the ground surface is not homogeneous, and its distribution may be the reflection of structures that are present under the surface. Nothing, therefore, opposes utilizing it in prospecting as in the use of magnetic or electric fields. However, the temperature of the ground varies relatively quickly during the course of a day, and, if one wishes to avoid elaborate corrections of these temporal variations in order to keep only the spatial ones, it is necessary to find a measuring technique that permits the readings to be taken rapidly over the whole area of interest. This is all the more important since the information given by the thermal prospecting must present advantages when compared with the group of methods based on electrical resistivity. One of these advantages lies in the radiometric measurement of temperature. Utilizing a photoconductive detector, the measurement of temperature at a point takes only a few nanoseconds. In addition, it can be done at a distance from an aircraft, and it is easy to conceive of scanning systems that permit coverage of a large area to be explored.

Paradoxically, thermal prospection, which in practice must be done very quickly, is poorly suited to ground-level surveying. It is an airborne method that complements other prospecting tools where electric or magnetic techniques are inadequate due to insufficient volume of the sought-after structures.

Radiometric Measurement of Temperature

All bodies emit electromagnetic radiation whose spectral distribution and intensity depend on their temperatures. This physical phenomenon is described by Planck's Law. At the usual soil-surface temperatures, this radiation is in the infrared zone. For a temperature of 17°C, 290 K, the wavelength (λ) corresponding to the maximum of radiance is equal to 10 μm. But the measurement of temperature at a distance is possible only for those wavelengths at which air is transparent. There are two atmospheric windows of this type, at 3–5 μm and 8–14 μm. The second, which corresponds to the maximum of the Planck curve at ambient temperatures and for which there is no reflected solar component, is used for the purposes of thermal prospection. A black body (which conforms perfectly to Planck's Law) will do. The radiance is reduced by a ratio, ε, called the *emissivity*. The emissivity depends on the chemical and mineralogical nature of the materials present at the surface, and it rises with the degree of surface roughness and moisture content. In the considered window, emissivity approaches 95 percent. Multispectral analysis, using several wavelengths simultaneously to detect spectral variations in ε, is a possible future path for prospection that has not been used up to now for archaeological applications. In general, one assumes that ε is constant and that the variations observed are due to temperature alone.

To cover the surface to be investigated, a radiometer is incorporated in a scanning system, as shown in Figure 1. A rotating faceted

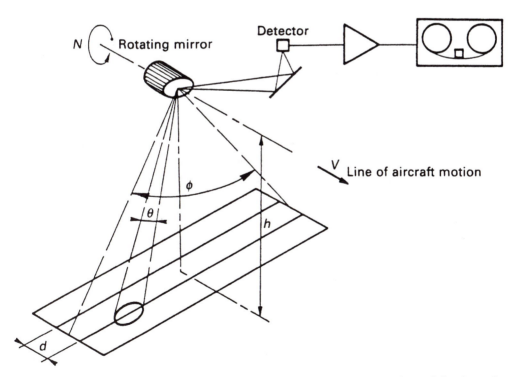

Figure 1. *Setup and direction of motion of an airborne scanning radiometer. Figure by Michel Dabas and Alain Tabbagh.*

mirror permits the scanning of a single line. The movement of the aircraft carries the scan from one line to the next. The recording of the values is carried out over an angle φ that is of the order of 90°. The instantaneous field of view θ is of the order of 0.002 radian. Because of the system of scanning, irregularities in the motion of the aircraft (roll, pitch, yaw) are translated into a deformation of the image, which must be corrected later using ground control points or control information recorded while in flight. Typical values of the parameters for a radiometer for archaeological prospecting are a ground resolution of 1 m per pixel, a scan swath of the order of 1 km, and the length of a scan of several kilometers. The surface surveyed is, therefore, from 3 to 5 km² and it is covered in ca. two minutes of flight. The sensitivity of the measurement of temperature is ca. 0.05°C and the anomalies vary between 0.1 and several degrees.

Energy Balance of the Soil Surface and Thermal Properties of Soil

The temperature of the ground surface translates the reaction of the soil to the heat flux that it has received and receives. This flux, Q, depends on the balance that is established among the different forms of gain or loss of energy: radiation, evaporation or condensation of water, air convection, and diffusion in the ground.

The thermal anomalies observed at the soil surface, therefore, may represent the local variations in one or the other of the terms of the heat-balance equation, including the variation of radiation in the case of relief, the variation of evaporation in the presence of water or vegetation, and the effects from wind.

Where the heat-balance terms are laterally uniform, anomalies are caused by the different reactions of the subsurface soil to the flux Q. They are, thus, the consequence of variations in the thermal properties of the subsoil.

The transfer of heat in soils is principally by conduction. When heat is applied to a homogeneous body, its temperature rises inversely to its thermal inertia, this being the inertia P. One may translate the variations of temperature into variations of apparent thermal inertia, this being the inertia of a homogeneous soil that gives the same temperature that obtains at a given point. The heterogeneities of the subsoil intervene as contrasts in thermal inertia with

the surrounding milieu. The thermal inertia principally depends on two parameters, the porosity and the granularity of the soil. Thus a nonconductive peat may have an inertia of 1200 S.I. (with 1 S.I. = $1 \, J \times K^{-1} m^{-2} s^{-1/2}$) where S.I. = International System units, J = Joule (energy = heat quantity), K = degrees Kelvin, m = meters, s = seconds. Whereas, a compact wet, sandy soil may attain 3,000 S.I. Generally, thermal inertias are greater on coarse soils and smaller on fine-grained soils.

Depth of Investigation and Most Favorable Times for Prospecting on Bare Soils

Temporal variations of temperature at the surface and of the flux are reduced as a function of depth. For a homogeneous soil and a sinusoidal flux variation, this reduction is exponential and is characterized by a *skin depth* (p), which depends on the period and the diffusivity. For diurnal variations, p is of the order of 15 cm; thus, it affects only the cultivated superficial surface zone. Reciprocally, structures located beneath this layer do not appear at the surface if only the diurnal variation is present. The depth of penetration of annual variation is ca. twenty times more important, but its exact effect is difficult to estimate, given the variation of the different properties of the milieu due to agriculture, fluctuation in moisture content, and the changes that take place in the vegetation cover. Variations correspond to the changing weather of several days and have a transient character. To characterize them, the prospector must follow the evolution of thermal flux in the ground and the predictions of the meteorologists. The simplest way to determine the flux in the ground is to use the repeated measurement of temperatures at different depths that are made by the meteorological stations. Usually, one is near enough to a station so that one does not have to install one's own temperature measuring system.

The conditions that are most favorable for carrying out thermal prospecting are the following:

1. The measurements must be made after a change in the weather that produces a marked change in flux lasting several days.
2. It is preferable to fly in the morning so that the anomalies connected with the hetero-

geneities present in the surface layer are not too strong and, therefore, do not mask the anomalies of deeper origin. It is important that these anomalies remain observable, since the material from deeper heterogeneities contaminate the surface layer and, therefore, appear.

3. It is also preferable to fly in clear skies to detect the anomalies due to microrelief. One might also add that the calmer the air and the more stable the aircraft, the better the recording and the fewer the corrections that have to be carried out afterward.

Temperature Anomalies Linked to Microrelief

An important number of archaeological remains remain in the form of microrelief (e.g., ditches, buildings). But the most important discovery due to thermal prospecting has been the abundance of information gained by the association of a warm anomaly on the side most exposed to direct solar radiation and a cold anomaly on the opposite side. These anomalies, in contrast with photographs made with oblique lighting, last several hours if the difference in radiation on the two sides is sufficiently strong. As the image of the French commune of Lion en Beauce (Figure 2) shows, the microrelief corresponds, in part, to the roads but, for the major part, to the limits of the fields perpendicular to the direction of plowing where the soil accumulates little by little with each passage of the plowshare. These data are largely confirmed by old cadastral maps, but it has the advantage of showing the real structures of old agricultural exploitation. The precise dating of these structures is difficult; most of them date to medieval and modern times, but some of them may date from protohistoric or Roman periods.

Temperature Anomalies Linked to Heterogeneities of the Subsoil

Anomalies of this type are abundant but are often difficult to identify among the many natural structures of dissolution and cryoturbation. When a geometric shape is sufficiently evident, identification is possible. When this is not the case, comparison of thermal anomalies with information obtained by other means, such as field walking, and by research in old archives permits identification of a site. The site of the

Figure 2. Mosaic of apparent temperature at Lion en Beauce in France, showing both microrelief anomalies and anomalies due to subsurface heterogeneities. Both types show ancient field limits and lanes. Precise dating is difficult. Some features are medieval or modern A.D. 900–1800; others date from Roman or protohistoric periods. Figure by Michel Dabas and Alain Tabbagh.

Figure 3. Apparent temperature at St. Vincent, l'hostellerie de Flée, France, showing complex cold anomalies corresponding to a medieval deserted village. Figure by Michel Dabas and Alain Tabbagh.

medieval deserted village of St. Vincent, l'hostellerie de Flée, Maine et Loire, France, constitutes an example of this type. The flight was carried out after a positive thermal flux of 10 W/m^2 that lasted seven days. The traces of construction are characterized by cold anomalies, but, as Figure 3 shows, these traces are complex, and it is the additional information gained from fourteenth-century texts that permitted identification of the site.

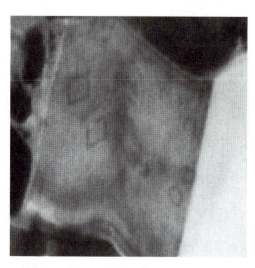

Figure 4. Protohistoric (Bronze Age and Iron Age) enclosures at Prépoux, Villeneuve la Guyard, Yonne, France revealed by the higher evapotranspiration rate of the wheat above the ditches. Figure by Michel Dabas and Alain Tabbagh.

Anomalies Tied to Vegetation Temperature

Evapotranspiration, the evaporation of water that plants use to limit the rise of temperature at their surfaces, is one of the major terms in the heat-balance equation. It may cause marked anomalies to appear if certain plants in the ground cover are in advance of or behind their immediate neighbors or if they experience difficulty in getting water out of the subsoil. Thus, the temperature of plants may indirectly reflect all of the heterogeneities in the composition of the subsoil. The anomalies obtained during the study of the site at Prépoux, Villeneuve la Guyard, Yonne, France, on winter wheat during the course of its growth are of the order of -1.5°C and show the complete remains of protohistoric enclosures, which were confirmed by later excavation (Figure 4).

One may, therefore, observe three types of temperature anomalies that are of importance to archaeology: microrelief, anomalies on bare soil directly related to heterogeneities of the subsoil, and anomalies in vegetation due to evapotranspiration.

The application of this method has been limited to temperate climatic areas in western Europe, but it could also be used in others climatic zones. It necessitates permission to fly, which is difficult to obtain in countries where military or political conflicts exist.

The depth of investigation of the method depends, on the one hand, on the duration and the intensity of the flux variation and, on the other hand, on the volume of the structures and on the thermal-inertia contrast with their surrounding medium. It can reach 1 m in the most favorable conditions. As a consequence, there does not exist a category of archaeological targets easy to detect using thermal prospecting, but linear features are easier to identify on the thermographs.

Michel Dabas
Alain Tabbagh

See also AERIAL PHOTOGRAPHY FOR ARCHAEOLOGY

Further Readings

Perisset, M.C., and Tabbagh, A. (1981) Interpretation of thermal prospection of bare soils. Archaeometry 23:169–187.

Scollar, I., ed. (1990) Archaeological Prospecting and Remote Sensing. Cambridge: Cambridge University Press.

Thermoluminescence Dating

A branch of *luminescence dating,* applicable to such materials as pottery and other forms of baked clay, burnt stone, burnt flint, volcanic products, stalagmitic calcite, and windblown and waterborne sediment. Taking pottery as an example: If a small ground-up portion of an ancient sherd is heated rapidly to 500°C, there is a weak emission of light, measurable by means of a sufficiently sensitive photomultiplier. This thermoluminescence (TL), emitted from ca. 250°C onward, is in addition to the red-hot glow (or incandescence, also referred to as *black body*) emitted when any substance is sufficiently hot; unlike this latter, though, the thermoluminescence is emitted only during the first heating of a sample. It comes from mineral grains in the pottery, principally quartz and feldspar, and it results from the cumulative effect of prolonged exposure to the weak flux of nuclear radiation emitted by radioactive impurities in the pottery and in the surrounding burial soil; there is also a contribution, usually small, from cosmic radiation. The impurities are potassium-40, rubidium-87, thorium, and uranium at concentrations of a few parts per million; the flux of radiation is constant over millions of years.

The thermoluminescence acquired by the minerals during geological times is drained when the raw clay is fired by the potter, thereby setting the *thermoluminescence clock* to zero. From cooling onward, the thermoluminescence begins to accumulate afresh, and, when measured today, it is indicative of the years that have elapsed since firing. The amount of thermoluminescence is also proportional to the energy absorbed from the radiation flux and to the sensitivity of the minerals in acquiring thermoluminescence. The rate of absorption of energy is referred to as the *dose rate* or the *annual dose* and is calculated from radioactive analysis of pottery and soil (or measured directly). The sensitivity is measured by exposing portions of the same sample to radiation from a calibrated radioisotope source. Then, in principle, the basic equation by which the age, in calendar years, is evaluated is:

$$\text{Age} = \frac{(\text{thermoluminescence})}{(\text{dose rate}) \times (\text{sensitivity})}$$

In practice, there are many complications, and at least a dozen measured quantities, rather than three, are involved in the evaluation. Also, for accurate results, it is necessary to make measurements on particular groups of grains separately (see below). One reason for complications is that the nuclear radiation consists of alpha and beta particles from the sample itself and gamma radiation from the soil, all three having different penetrating power; additionally, the sensitivity to alpha particles is substantially less than to the other two types of radiation.

Because of the way in which the measurements are made, it is convenient to utilize the concept of *paleodose* (P)—the dose of nuclear radiation (from laboratory radioisotope sources) needed in order for artificially induced luminescence to be equal to the "as-found" or "natural" thermoluminescence. The age equation then simplifies to:

$$\text{Age} = \frac{(\text{paleodose})}{(\text{dose rate})}$$

Alternative names used for paleodose are: *equivalent dose* (ED), *past radiation dose* (D_e), *total dose* (TD), *accrued dose, accumulated dose,* and *archaeological dose* (the three latter being denoted by AD). The unit of dose is the *gray* (Gy).

Heat is also the zeroing agency for burnt flint (by accidentally falling into the fire or through deliberate heat treatment), volcanic products, and other burnt materials. For stalagmitic calcite, the latent thermoluminescence is effectively zero at crystal formation. For unburnt sediment, the zeroing occurs through exposure to light during deposition, but, depending on circumstances, it is not always complete.

The thermoluminescence is carried in the form of *trapped electrons*. These are electrons that have been displaced by nuclear radiation from their usual locations in the crystal structure of the mineral concerned and held, metastably, at trapping sites in that structure. Elevation of temperature causes release of trapped electrons, and those of them that find luminescence centers give rise to thermoluminescence. Light can also cause release in some minerals (e.g., quartz, feldspar, and zircon).

Development and Scope

Although the phenomenon of thermoluminescence had been studied since the seventeenth century, it was not until the 1960s that development for dating began. Initially, this was in application to archaeological pottery, mineral grains being present by having been added as temper. Subsequently, it has been extended to types of samples that enable TL dating to reach back well beyond the limit of radiocarbon. Burnt flint, in particular, is useful in this context, extending to several hundred thousand years. An important application has been to flints associated with skeletons found in cave sites in western Asia in establishing the presence there of anatomically modern humans at ca. 100,000 years ago, a result adding weight to the view that these hominids developed in parallel with Neanderthals rather than being descendants, as had been accepted formerly. Stalagmitic calcite is also useful in dating the occupancy of Palaeolithic caves, reaching ca. 500,000 years, though the mass-spectrometric uranium-series technique is usually to be preferred for this material. During the late 1980s, the potential of unburnt sediment for TL dating was increasingly explored. Although of primary importance for Quaternary Earth-science studies, this application is useful, too, in paleoanthropology (e.g., in the dating of sand deposits in northern Australia in which artifacts indicative of human arrival there were found).

Because of its lesser precision than radiocarbon dating, the impact of thermoluminescence during more recent periods has not been so great. Nevertheless, the technique does have the strong advantage in dating pottery that it is directly linking to archaeological chronology, and uncertainties of association are avoided. From the late 1960s onward, the technique has had a dominant role in testing the authenticity of ceramics from historical periods, precision being of less importance since it is usually a matter of deciding between an age of less than a 100 years and one of several hundred years or more.

Sampling Requirements

Because part of the radiation dose rate is provided by gamma rays from the burial soil (or other surroundings) within ca. 0.3 m of the sample, in general it is possible to obtain an accurate date only when samples are extracted in the course of excavation or when the section from which they were obtained is still available. An exception is when there are plentiful zircon grains in the sample or when it is feasible to employ the *isochron technique* (the separate measurement of thermoluminescence on different mineral fractions within a single pottery sample provides a dating curve) but there are not many laboratories specializing in these. However, in testing for authenticity, the accuracy attainable without knowledge of the gamma-ray component is usually adequate.

Close collaboration between archaeologist and laboratory scientist is essential; ideally, the latter is on site at the time the samples are extracted or, at any rate, has visited the site. There are a number of ways in which the gamma-ray component may be assessed, and which of these is employed depends on sample type, laboratory facilities, and the feasibility of on-site measurements of radioactivity. The latter can be made by means of a portable gamma ray spectrometer of which the measurement head is inserted 0.3 m into the section by means of an auger hole. The head is positioned in as similar a situation as possible to the sample location. Alternatively, the measurement is by means of a highly sensitive thermoluminescence phosphor contained in a small capsule (ca. 30 mm long × 10 mm in diameter) that is likewise buried to a depth of 0.3 m. Whereas the spectrometer measurement can be completed in an hour or less, the capsule needs to be left in position for several

months, ideally a year. When on-site measurements are not feasible, the assessment can be made through radioactive analysis in the laboratory of a sample of the burial soil. Particularly in this case, it is important that the soil is uniform (in terms of radioactivity) to a distance of 0.3 m from the sample. This means that the sample needs to be at a depth of at least 0.3 m, but it is also important that it has been covered to at least that depth for the major part (say, two-thirds) of its burial time.

Another quantity that enters into the date calculation is an estimate of the average water content over the whole burial period, and various approaches are employed by different laboratories. Sites that have always been dry are advantageous. Knowledge of average water content is required, for both sample and soil, because the water absorbs part of the radiation that would otherwise reach the mineral grains.

For pottery dating, between six and twelve samples are required from each archaeological level; as far as possible, the size should be ca. 10 mm thick × 30 mm across. Requirements for other sample types are similar, except that, for sediment, it is convenient and advantageous to collect substantially more. The minimum thickness is dictated by the need to saw off, in dim red light in the laboratory, a 2-mm surface layer; this eliminates material in which the beta dose rate is poorly defined, being transitional between sample and soil, and, at the same time, avoids utilization of material in which reduction of the thermoluminescence through bleaching by light may have taken place. It is, nevertheless, prudent to avoid undue exposure of samples to light after extraction, and, in the case of unconsolidated sediment, special precautions should be taken to avoid any exposure at all. A critical question with burnt flint is whether the degree of heating was sufficient to set all previously acquired thermoluminescence to zero; a check on this is intrinsic to the measurement procedure: the so-called *plateau test* mentioned below.

Measurement of Paleodose

The plot of thermoluminescence emitted versus temperature is called a *glow curve,* and it is obtained by placing an aliquot of the sample on an electrically heated plate, which is rapidly raised to $500°C$, usually at a rate of ca. $10°C$ per second. To avoid the emission of parasitic (spurious) luminescence, the heating must be done in an oven flushed with high-purity nitrogen or other inert gas. Color filters are placed in front of the photomultiplier to avoid the signal being swamped by red-hot glow. The paleodose is determined by comparing the natural glow curve with glow curves obtained from portions to which known doses of artificial radiation have been administered. This can be done, say, every 10°C of the glow curves, and a plot is then made of paleodose *versus* temperature. For a dating to be valid, the paleodose should rise to a steady level somewhat above 300°C; samples that do not pass this *plateau test* are rejected.

The rationale of the test is as follows. Within a given mineral, there are traps of different depths, and it is only deep traps that stably retain electrons over a million years or more—as required for a sample that is a 100,000 years old. These deep traps do not release their captive electrons until the temperature rises to ca. 300°C or more; the deeper the trap, the higher the temperature needed for release. Luminescence observed below 300°C is liable to be associated with traps from which there has been leakage of electrons during burial; such leakage will not have had time to occur in the case of the artificially induced signal; hence, the ratio of the natural signal to the latter will be lower than in the region of stability. Once the temperature is high enough, the ratio, and, hence, the paleodose, reach a steady value.

There are various forms in which aliquots of the sample may be prepared (always in dim red light). After removal of the 2-mm surface layer and crushing, suspension in acetone allows deposition of polymineral fine grains (2–8 μm) onto aluminum or stainless steel discs, usually 10 mm in diameter. Alternatively, in the case of pottery and burnt stones, mineralogical techniques are used to obtain coarse-grain (upward of 100 μm) portions of quartz, zircon, potassium feldspar, or plagioclase feldspar; these, too, are carried on discs for measurement.

With either type of feldspar (and with polymineral fine grains, since the signal is usually dominated by feldspar luminescence), there is risk that even in the plateau region of the glow curve there will have been leakage of electrons during burial and, hence, that the age obtained is erroneously low. Such *anomalous fading* is present only in some samples and can be detected by experiments in which artificially irradiated portions are stored for long periods, several months or more. When anomalous fading is present, the sample must be rejected unless the characteristics of the fading for the sample in question are such that storage at elevated temperature (e.g., 100°C) prior to measurement is efficacious.

With unburnt sediment, special procedures are necessary to make allowance for incomplete setting to zero at deposition. Use of optical dating is advantageous in this respect.

Measurement of Dose Rate

Various techniques are employed: alpha counting, beta counting, gamma spectrometry, neutron activation analysis, X-ray fluorescence analysis, flame photometry, and thermoluminescence dosimetry. The possibility that there was significant escape of radon (a radioactive gas forming part of the uranium-decay chain) during burial is a source of uncertainty, as are other forms of radioactive disequilibria arising from geochemical leaching. High-resolution gamma spectrometry is advantageous in giving assessment of these possibilities. As mentioned earlier, the effective dose rate is influenced by the past water content of soil and sample; uncertainty about this is a more common limitation in the accuracy with which the dose rate may be determined—typically, ±5 percent at the 68 percent level of confidence.

Accuracy and Age Range

In general terms, the error limits (at the 68 percent level of confidence) on a date are in the range ± 5 percent to ± 10 percent of the age (i.e., the error limits on a date of 1000 B.C. are usually in the range ± 150 to ± 300 years). Although these do not rival the precision obtainable with radiocarbon, it should be stressed that thermoluminescence gives ages directly in calendar years. Hence, its real importance is in Palaeolithic archaeology beyond the range of radiocarbon calibration and, even more so, beyond the 50,000-year range at which meaningful radiocarbon determinations can normally be made.

Two effects limit the maximum age that can be reached: Saturation (i.e., all available traps have become full) and instability (i.e., there is significant leakage of trapped electrons during the time period involved).

Notably in quartz and flint, saturation is the limitation, and so the limiting age is greatest on sites of low radioactivity, where it can be as high as 500,000 years; but on sites of high radioactivity, saturation may set in before 1,000 years. Instability is the limitation with feldspar and calcite, the limiting age being ca. 500,000 years, but for polymineral fine grains, probably because of weathering effects, the limit is liable to be substantially lower.

At the other end of the age range, thermoluminescence can date pottery and bricks fired as recently as a few decades ago for clay of moderate radioactivity that carries constituent grains of high sensitivity. For other types of sample, the limit is usually a few thousand years.

Martin J. Aitken

See also LUMINESCENCE DATING; OPTICAL DATING

Further Readings

Aitken, M.J. (1985) Thermoluminescence Dating. London: Academic.

Aitken, M.J. (1990) Science-Based Dating in Archaeology. London and New York: Longman.

Aitken, M.J. (1998) Introduction to Optical Dating. Oxford: Oxford University Press.

Aitken M.J., and Valladas, H. (1992) Luminescence dating relevant to human origins. Philosophical Transactions of the Royal Society London B337:139–144.

Fleming, S.J. (1970) Thermoluminescent dating: Refinement of the quartz inclusion method. Archaeometry 12:133–147.

Fleming, S.J. (1979) Thermoluminescence Techniques in Archaeology. Oxford: Clarendon.

Roberts, R.G. (1997) Luminescence dating in archaeology: From origins to optical. Radiation Measurements 27:819–892.

Roberts, R.G., Bird, M., Olley, J., Galbraith, R., Lawson, E., Laslett, G., Jones, R., Fullagar, R., Jacobsen, G., and Hua, Q. (1998) Optical and radiocarbon dating at Jinmium rock shelter in northern Australia. Nature 393:358–363.

Zimmerman, D.W. (1967) Thermoluminescence from fine grains from pottery. Archaeometry 10: 26–28.

Thomas, David Hurst (1945–)

American anthropologist and archaeologist. Born on May 27, 1945, in Oakland, California, Thomas was educated at the University of California at Davis, where he received his bachelor's in 1967, his master's in 1968, and his doctorate in anthropology in 1972. He served as assistant curator at the American Museum of Natural History (1972–1977), associate curator (1977–1982), and since 1982 full curator of anthropology. A recipient of numerous awards, Thomas was a National Science Foundation grantee (1977–1978) and is a member of the Society for American Archaeology, the American Anthropological Association, and the American Association for the Advancement of Science.

Thomas is an important figure in analytical and anthropological archaeology and a specialist in the archaeology of the Southwestern United States, ethnoarchaeological methodology, and the analysis of lithic and faunal evidence. A pioneer in the use of advanced statistical methods to analyze cultural remains and create predictive models, Thomas was among the first to realize the important role computers would play in archaeological research, not merely for the storage of data, but as an aid in model building. Articles that Thomas wrote on quantitative methods and computerized statistical analyses have made archaeologists realize that, to use the author's own words, "archaeology can no longer apply the techniques of the 1950s to the problems of tomorrow."

Joseph J. Basile

See also COMPUTERS IN ARCHAEOLOGY; ETHNOARCHAEOLOGY; QUANTITATIVE METHODS IN ARCHAEOLOGY; STATISTICAL METHODS IN ARCHAEOLOGY

Further Readings

Thomas, D.H. (1972) The use and abuse of numerical taxonomy in archaeology. Archaeology and Physical Anthropology in Oceania 7:31–49.

Thomas, D.H. (1976) Figuring Anthropology: First Principles of Probability and Statistics. New York: Holt, Rinehart and Winston.

Thomas, D.H. (1978) The awful truth about statistics in archaeology. American Antiquity 43(2):231–244.

Thomas, D.H. (1986) Refiguring Anthropology: First Principles of Probability and

Statistics. Prospect Heights, IL: Waveland.

Thomsen, Christian Jürgensen (1788–1865)

Danish antiquarian and archaeologist. Born on December 29, 1788, in Copenhagen, Denmark, Thomsen was the son of a prosperous merchant. He was privately educated and became fascinated with numismatics and the antiquities of his native land. Thomsen excavated and collected extensively and became the curator of the National Museum of Denmark in Copenhagen in 1816. A firm believer that important collections of antiquities should be available to all, he was the first curator to open the museum to the public. He also founded Denmark's first ethnographic museum. Thomsen served as curator of the National Museum until his death on May 21, 1865.

Thomsen is credited as being the individual most responsible for the adoption of a tripartite system of chronology, dividing human antiquity into Stone, Bronze, and Iron Ages. He based these periods on the materials used to make tools and other implements. Thomsen used this system to help organize the collections at the National Museum, which originally were arranged in no particular order in a room at the library of Copenhagen University and reserved solely for the use of research scholars and the cognoscenti. His system passed into the popular consciousness when he opened the museum to the general public in 1819, and it first appeared in print in the guidebook to the museum entitled *Ledertraad til Nordisk Oldkyndighed,* published in 1836. The English translation, *A Guide to Northern Archaeology,* was prepared by Lord Ellesmere in 1848 and had a profound impact on the practice of archaeology in the English-speaking world.

It is important to note that the Three Age system had, in fact, been discussed by several European prehistorians as early as the first half of the eighteenth century. Antoine Yves Goguet published a theory in 1738 that clearly stated that tools of bronze preceded those of iron, and that, before bronze, stone was used for the manufacture of implements. Danish historian Peter F. Suhm adopted the Three Age system in his *History of Denmark, Norway, and Holstein,* published in 1776. It

was Thomsen, however, and his assistant, the Danish archaeologist Jens J.A. Worsaae, who applied the system in a concrete way to an existing collection of antiquities and then made it possible for people to see how this new ordering system affected the way the ancient world might be viewed. Thus, Thomsen can truly be called the "father of the Three Age system."

Joseph J. Basile

Further Readings

Ellesmere, F.E., ed. (1848) Guide to Northern Archaeology. London: J. Bain.

Petersen, N.M. and Thomsen, C.J. (1836) Ledertraad til Nordisk Oldkyndighed. Kjöbenhavn: S.L. Møllers.

Street-Jensen, J., ed. (1985) Christian Jürgensen Thomsen und Ludwig Lindenschmit: Eine Gelehrtenkorrespondenz aus der Frühzeit der Altertumskunde, 1853–1864: Beiträge zur Forschungsgeschichte. (Monographien 6). Mainz: Verlag des Römisch-Germanischen Zentralmuseums/Bonn: R. Habelt.

Trench Excavation

In a limited sense, excavation of a long, narrow portion of a site or, in practice, excavation of any area of a site. Increasingly, however, the term *trench* is used to refer to small or sample excavations as opposed to area excavations. Even a large-area excavation is only a sample of an archaeological landscape and so is really a large trench.

The *shovel test* is the smallest trench. This technique, used in North American archaeology but rarely in Europe, involves digging shovel-width holes, preferably in a grid pattern, across areas of archaeological potential. Such shovel testing is used simply to locate archaeological deposits and not to dig into them.

Having located an archaeological site, it may be sampled by digging trial trenches, test pits, or *sondages*. These are often 1-m-×-1-m squares dug in a regular or systematic grid across the site, but they could be of any size, depending on the size of the site involved. Alternative sampling designs may include *simple random, stratified random,* or *stratified systematic unaligned.* A simple random sample involves gridding the area to be sampled and numbering the two axes of the grid. Pairs of random coordinates are selected to establish the position of sondages. If, however, the site has any natural divisions (e.g., between areas of rock, alluvium, and sand), then the area can be divided into natural areas. Each area is then randomly sampled. This process, known as stratified random sampling, ensures a sample from each natural zone. Any area sampled using a random procedure runs the risk of clustering of samples. To avoid this, the trial trenches or test pits could be dug in a stratified, systematic, unaligned way. This involves gridding the area and then randomly locating a test pit in each grid square. This has the advantage of a regular grid, but with a random element. The purpose of such trial-trench sampling is essentially to provide horizontal information about the extent of archaeological deposits across a site. The trial trenches may be excavated only to the first archaeological deposit. At this stage, it may be decided to change the excavation strategy to, for example, area excavation.

Larger trenches, sometimes referred to as *transects,* are usually excavated to provide information about sequences of events (*stratigraphy*) rather than horizontal information about activity. Trenches were traditionally used on deeply stratified sites. Such trenches were often long, narrow, and deep. Unless carefully shored (shuttered), trenches can be extremely dangerous. Practically all fatalities on archaeological sites occur in deep, narrow trenches.

Trenches do, however, often provide a reasonably reliable sequence of events. It should be remembered that the sequence recorded may be only the sequence crossed by the trench and not the full sequence of the site. Trenches are especially useful for obtaining sequences of development through linear features, such as ramparts, banks, or field systems (e.g., lynchets). However, a five-phase reconstruction of a rampart at one point does not necessarily mean the total reconstruction of the whole rampart five times. Any trench excavated on a site is only a sample, which may, or may not, be representative of the whole site.

Peter L. Drewett

See also SAMPLING; STRATIGRAPHY; SURVEYING AND SITE EXAMINATION, MANUAL METHODS

Further Readings

Barker, P. (1993) Techniques of Archaeological Excavation, 3rd ed. London: Batsford.

Drewett, P.L. (1999) Field Archaeology: An Introduction. London: University College London Press.

Triangulation

A surveying method used in archaeological mapping to establish the precise horizontal location of points. Triangulation is based on the principle that, given any two points separated by a known distance, it is possible to locate a third point by measuring it from the first two points. When plotted on a scaled map, the intersection of these measurements forms a triangle that accurately depicts the location of the third point. The angles between the first two points and the third are sometimes measured as part of the process. In archaeological settings, successive triangulation can be used to map entire sites. A base line between two fixed points is established, and a series of third points are measured. Some of these latter points serve as temporary fixed points for mapping successive triangles across the site. During excavation, triangulation is sometimes used to plot the location of artifacts or features. Two corner stakes are designated as fixed points, and the third point is the artifact or feature to be mapped. Triangulation is an important method for providing precise locational information in mapping, an essential component of any archaeological investigation.

Edward Luby

See also SITE MAPPING

Further Readings

Barker, P. (1993) Techniques of Archaeological Excavation, 3rd ed. London: Batsford.
Drewett, P.L. (1999) Field Archaeology: An Introduction. London: University College London Press.

Trigger, Bruce Graham (1937–)

Canadian anthropologist and archaeologist. Born on June 18, 1937, in Cambridge (formerly Preston), Ontario, Canada, Trigger was educated at the University of Toronto, where he received his bachelor's in 1959, and at Yale University, where he received his doctorate in 1964. After taking his degrees, Trigger was appointed assistant professor of anthropology at McGill University (1964), associate professor (1967), and full professor of anthropology (1969). He served as chairman of the department (1970–1975). Trigger is the recipient of numerous awards and honors, including the Canada Silver Jubilee Medal, the Prix du Quebec, the James R. Wiseman Book Award of the Archaeological Institute of America, and honorary degrees from the University of New Brunswick and the University of Waterloo. He is a Fellow of the Royal Society of Canada and the Prehistoric Society.

A noted archaeologist, Trigger has worked in the New World on the Huron Indians of Canada *(The Huron: Farmers of the North)* and in the Old World on settlement patterns in Nubia and the Sudan *(History and Settlement in Lower Nubia; Nubia under the Pharaohs)*. He is most well known, however, as a historian of archaeology and as a critic of developing trends in archaeological thought. Beginning in 1978 with *Time and Traditions,* Trigger has sought to systematically examine and explain—not merely describe—the development of archaeology as a discipline, including the most recent advances in methodology stemming from systems theory and the New Archaeology. His *Gordon Childe: Revolutions in Archaeology* serves not only as the definitive biography of Childe but also as an examination of the theoretical importance of his work and its impact on the development of archaeology as a discipline. His *A History of Archaeological Thought* is probably the most useful work to date (i.e., 1998) on the evolution of archaeological methodology and the general history of archaeology. Modifying Gordon R. Willey and Sabloff's classic four-stage model (Speculative, Classificatory-Descriptive, Classificatory-Historical, Explanatory) for the development of New World theory as defined in their *A History of American Archaeology,* Trigger outlines the history of archaeological thought (including advances in Marxist/Soviet archaeology) and examines methodologies in a critical manner. He has expressed concerns over the unchecked expansion of archaeological inquiry into such areas as experimental archaeology, while contending that the diversification of archaeological theory is helping to break down disciplinary sectarianism and focus archaeologists on both the potential and the limitations of their field.

Joseph J. Basile

See also CHILDE, VERE GORDON; WILLEY, GORDON RANDOLPH

Further Readings

Trigger, B.G. (1965) History and Settlement in Lower Nubia. (Yale University Publications in Anthropology 69). New Haven, CT: Yale University Press.

Trigger, B.G. (1968) Beyond History: The Methods of Prehistory. New York: Holt, Rinehart and Winston.

Trigger, B.G. (1976) Nubia under the Pharaohs. London: Thames and Hudson/Boulder, CO: Westview.

Trigger, B.G. (1978) Time and Traditions: Essays in Archaeological Interpretation. Edinburgh: Edinburgh University Press/New York: Columbia University Press.

Trigger, B.G. (1980) Gordon Childe, Revolutions in Archaeology. New York: Columbia University Press.

Trigger, B.G. (1989) A History of Archaeological Thought. Cambridge, UK/New York: Cambridge University Press.

Trigger B.G. (1990) The Huron: Farmers of the North, 2nd ed. Fort Worth, TX: Holt, Rinehart and Winston.

Trigger B.G. (1998) Sociocultural Evolution: Calculation and Contingency. Oxford/Malden, MA: Blackwell.

Tylecote, Ronald Frank (1916–1990)

British scientist, metallurgist, historian, and archaeologist. Born on June 15, 1916, in Manchester, England, Tylecote was educated at Cambridge University. Originally a mechanical engineering student, he switched to metallurgy and the history of technology after a climbing accident in Wales left him with permanent injuries and made the practical side of mechanical engineering too strenuous. Widely considered to be the "father of archaeometallurgy"—the scientific study of metals recovered from archaeological contexts and ancient metal technology—Tylecote made archaeologists aware of the importance of metal artifacts, not merely as art objects and chronological indicators, but also as a means by which scholars might discover information concerning mining, smelting, and manufacturing of metals in ancient times. He led the way in the study of ancient metal technologies and forge sites and opened the door for later scientific study of ancient metals, for instance the processes currently used to determine places of origin of metal finds through compositional analysis. Tylecote, who worked with metal finds from ancient Britain, Israel, Spain, Nigeria, Cyprus, and the Sudan, was a student of historic as well a prehistoric metallurgy. He founded the Historical Metallurgy Society in 1962 to preserve the great blast furnaces of the Industrial Revolution, which at the time were being torn down all over Britain. The *Bulletin* of the Historical Metal Society eventually became the *Journal,* of which Tylecote was chief editor, and soon became the preeminent publication concerning archaeometallurgy. His *Prehistory of Metallurgy in the British Isles* and *A History of Metallurgy* have become the standard works of the historical and archaeological study of metals and metal technology.

Joseph J. Basile

See also METALLOGRAPHY; METALS, CHARACTERIZATION

Further Readings

Tylecote, R.F. (1962) Metallurgy in Archaeology: A Prehistory of Metallurgy in the British Isles. London: E. Arnold.

Tylecote, R.F. (1986) The Prehistory of Metallurgy in the British Isles. London: Institute of Metals.

Tylecote, R.F. (1987) The Early History of Metallurgy in Europe. London/New York: Longman.

Tylecote, R.F. (1992) A History of Metallurgy, 2nd ed. London: Institute of Materials.

Tylecote, R.F. and Gilmour, B.J.J. (1986) The Metallography of Early Ferrous Edge Tools and Edged Weapons. (BAR British Series 155). Oxford: British Archaeological Reports.

Type-Variety System

A hierarchic system of artifact classification developed by culture historians to measure time/space relations.

During the last quarter of the nineteenth century, the first systematic method proposed for artifact classification in North America focused on projectile points and used three dimensions of geometric shape to create a set of universally applicable classes. The authors,

Charles Rau and Thomas Wilson, made no special claims for the system, but even they were disappointed that the resulting classes did not seem to make temporal or spatial sense. Other archaeologists were even more critical, and, after the turn of the century, attempts at systematic archaeological classification in North America were abandoned for decades. Archaeologists followed their own personal whims in constructing classifications, the purpose of which is usually identified solely as the reduction of the volume of descriptive detail. Modern American artifact classification has its origins in the disarray that followed the failure of the Rau-Wilson classification. Workers such as Alfred L. Kroeber in the American Southwest and Henry B. Collins in the Southeast noticed that, if pottery were described in a certain way—a way that came to be called *stylistic* or *historical*—the objects belonging to a type displayed distributions that were contiguous in both time and space and monotonic (had a single frequency peak) in time. Kroeber and some of his students, such as Leslie Spier, quickly realized that this observation could be turned into a powerful, entirely archaeological, dating tool, *seriation.* By the middle 1930s, the success of seriation and the classification method upon which it depended were firmly established as what has since come to be called *culture history,* the first methodological consensus in American archaeology.

The late 1930s and early 1940s saw a number of exegeses of the method used to construct historical types, including important works by James A. Ford, Alex D. Krieger, and Irving Rouse. Because the culture historians did not attempt to explain why the use of stylistic characters resulted in the observed distributions, these accounts are strongly empiricist and focus on the practicalities of how to construct particular types rather than why they worked in the chronological role. This bias created a paradox. All culture historians realized, to one degree or another, that artifact types were archaeological constructions, not empirical discoveries; yet, because they had not attempted to explain why their generalizations about type distributions were true, the only means to rationalize the culture-historical type was to claim that it was "real" (i.e., discovered). Today, archaeologists understand stylistic attributes to be selectively neutral variants (i.e., traits that do not affect the fitness of the bearers) and that it is this property that accounts for their temporal and spatial distribution.

The basic approach is sometimes described as *Kriegerian* because of Krieger's (1944) detailed exposition and criticism of previous classification methods. In brief, Krieger describes putting together piles of "look-alikes," refining those piles by constructing objective definitions that cite specific attributes, and then testing their time/space contiguity using distributional data. Quite subtly, artifact classification had shifted from universal classes (on the model of the periodic table) to a universal method of defining classes (on the model of species). No definition that did not organize artifacts into contiguous time/space distributions, the test of historical significance, could be called a type. While the paradox is unresolved, Krieger exposed the trial-and-error way in which types were defined (i.e., how one determined what was stylistic), codified what has since come to be called the *test of historical significance,* and argued for its general applicability by extending the method to lithics.

Neither Krieger's account nor those of his contemporaries, however, addressed a crucial problem that arose in practice. A great many types that met the test of historical significance also differed greatly in scale. Some had extensive distributions in time and/or space, while others covered little, making it difficult to integrate studies using different Kriegerian classifications. The type-variety system addressed this failure, and, in doing so, culture-historical classification assumed the form that it still holds in American archaeology.

Krieger had railed against hierarchic classification because it entailed ranking criteria (i.e., some criteria were more important than others in defining kinds), and ranking assumed knowledge not in evidence. This led culture historians to reject biological classification, *taxonomy.* As Robert C. Dunnell (1971) showed, however, hierarchy can be introduced just by varying the number of criteria employed. Thus, the assumptive input necessary to introduce hierarchy can be reduced to little more than that required of all classifications, so long as the classification is dimensional (i.e., the criteria employed are arranged as mutually exclusive and exhaustive sets). This is precisely what the type-variety system does, even though its inventors, just like those of the original culture-historical method, were unaware of this at the time.

The first frank exposition of the type-variety method was made by Joe Wheat and colleagues (1958) using ceramic materials from the American Southwest. This was quickly followed by a series of papers that extended its application geographically and attempted to improve and rationalize the methodology. As is often the case, Wheat and colleagues had attempted to make as few waves as possible and preserved as much of the traditional pottery classification as was feasible; in doing so, they were compelled to use the term *type* in an ambiguous fashion, applying it to two different concepts at different levels. As a result, it was the terminology of Philip Phillips (1959), who was the first to apply the method outside the Southwest, that came to be fixed. In the original scheme of Wheat and colleagues, the *established type* and varieties were at the same level of inclusiveness, the established type having only formal or historical priority over varieties. Variety and the established type made up *ceramic clusters;* ceramic clusters were organized in *ceramic systems,* the most inclusive category. In Phillips's revision, the established type is replaced by the *established variety* and indicates only historical priority in naming; ceramic cluster is replaced by *type,* and it is types that are organized into ceramic clusters. Phillips also recognized that types could be organized in more than one set of higher categories. The term *ware,* for example, was already in use for groups of types that shared similar technological features. Phillips and later workers also tried to introduce Rouse's *mode* concept as the lowest level in the system. This did not work because modes were classes of attributes and, thus, differed in scale from the other units, whereas varieties and types were kinds of pot sherds (or pots) and, thus, differed from each other in level. In practice, larger units, such as ceramic system, likewise failed to find a role in culture-historical methodology and gradually were dropped. One of the inventors, James Gifford (1960), went on to attempt to rationalize the Wheat and colleagues formulation in ethnological terms. *Varieties,* for example, were to be understood as small group/individual variation and occurred over the smallest amounts of time and space; *types* occurred over larger amounts of time and space and represented larger interacting units. Since varieties were contained in types (i.e., a variety had all of the attributes for membership in a type *plus* additional attributes limited to the variety), the distributional properties that Gifford attributed to cultural processes were simply mechanical effects of hierarchic definitions. Fewer items meet the requirements for "red physics book" than meet the requirements of "book." Both varieties and types still must meet the test of historical significance (i.e., they must be distributed contiguously in time and in space). As such, they measure homologous similarities, and, to this extent, Gifford's rationales find justification.

Because the system, at least the two-tier variety and type units, has been in use since the 1960s in virtually every area of American research, it is rarely discussed or even noticed; it is just the way most artifact classification is done. In the 1930s, when Kriegerian classifications were first being established in many regions, proposed changes and additions to existing classifications were often vetted by regional associations of archaeologists (e.g., Pecos Conference in the American Southwest and the Southeastern Archaeological Conference in the American Southeast). By the time the type-variety system was being adopted, the influence of such organizations on the details of typology had waned. Additions and changes tend to be ad hoc and syntheses the product of individual scholars. The most comprehensive treatment of North American projectile points (Justice 1988), for example, is entirely within this model, even though the author does not make an issue of classification or the type-variety system. Phillips's Yazoo Basin monograph (1970) is perhaps the best exposition of the method in its modern form, as well as one of its more comprehensive and influential applications.

Robert C. Dunnell

See also DUNNELL, ROBERT C.; FORD, JAMES ALFRED; ROUSE, IRVING BENJAMIN

Further Readings

Dunnell, R.C. (1971) Systematics in Prehistory. New York: Free Press.

Dunnell, R.C. (1986) Methodological issues in artifact classification. In M.B. Schiffer (ed.): Advances in Archaeological Method and Theory, vol. 9 pp. 149–207. New York: Academic.

Gifford, J.C. (1960) The type-variety method. American Antiquity 25:341–347.

Justice, N.D. (1987) Spear and Arrowpoints of the Midcontinental and Eatern United States. Bloomington, IN: Indiana University Press.

Krieger, A.D. (1944) The typological concept. American Antiquity 9:271–288

Phillips, P. (1959) Application of the Wheat-Gifford-Wasley taxonomy to eastern ceramics. American Antiquity 24:117–125.

Phillips, P. (1970) Archaeological Survey in the Yazoo Basin, Mississippi, 1949–1955. (Papers of the Peabody Museum of Archaeology and Ethnology 25). Cambridge, MA: Peabody Museum of Archaeology and Ethnology, Harvard University.

Smith, R.E., Willey, G.R., and Gifford, J.C. (1960) The type-variety system as a basis for the analysis of Maya pottery. American Antiquity 25:330–340.

Wheat, J.B., Gifford, J.C., and Wasley, W.W. (1958) Ceramic variety, type cluster, and ceramic system in Southwest pottery analysis. American Antiquity 24:34–47.

U

Underwater Archaeology

The location and excavation of submerged sites. The term refers to any type of site that must be excavated under water and should be distinguished from nautical archaeology. Relevant field techniques fall into several main areas: *survey, excavation, mapping,* and *site stabilization.* Many techniques normally used on dry sites can be adapted directly or with minimal modification to underwater sites. Differences derive largely from restrictions placed on the excavator by the environment. One of the primary problems with underwater excavation is the limited site time available to the excavator. The deeper the site, the more limited that time is and the more efficient techniques must be. For example, at a depth of 3 m, a healthy diver can spend all day under water, but, at 50 m, total bottom time may be as little as thirty minutes per day, split between two dives. It is a hostile environment, which combines with the often bulky and restricting equipment divers must wear to limit their mental and physical abilities. Dives must be carefully planned if the safety of the archaeologist is to be maintained and maximum efficiency on the bottom is to be achieved. A final factor that often does not occur to terrestrial archaeologists is the difficulty of communicating under water. Messages can be written on slates, but the process is time consuming, so team or group tasks must be carefully worked out beforehand.

Survey

Underwater surveys normally follow one of two methodological approaches: the designated area is searched to reveal the number and type of sites present, or a specific site known from previous research (most commonly, archival identification of a specific shipwreck or group of wrecks) is sought. Both approaches rely on the same techniques, most of which are classified as *remote sensing,* because the bottom of the sea, lake, or river is not visually inspected until after evidence of a possible site is detected by nonvisual means. Many of the survey methods used in underwater archaeology were originally developed in other fields, such as petroleum geology and engineering, to search for geological, physical, and man-made features on the seafloor.

Remote-sensing methods usually involve towing a sensor or an array of sensors in a regular pattern over the bottom and correlating the sensor signal with position information. Different arrays are used in different conditions. If site remains project above an otherwise flat or smooth bottom, they can be detected by *side-scan sonar,* which sends out a series of horizontal sound pulses and records the reflected signal. The output from the processor appears as a series of acoustic surfaces and shadows very similar to a photograph, so that ships sitting upright on the bottom may be immediately recognizable. Even small, low features, such as scattered debris and potsherds, may be detectable by this means if the conditions are favorable. The swath covered in a single pass can be quite wide (100 m or more), so the method is relatively efficient if a large area must be searched. Side-scan sonar is less applicable where the bottom is uneven or rocky, as it can be difficult to distinguish an archaeological site from rock outcrops and other "noise." Another method used to locate sites projecting above the bottom sediment is *video scanning* with a towed camera or remotely operated vehicle (ROV). This method has the advantage that targets are immediately identifiable in most cases, but as visible light is rapidly absorbed in water, even if turbidity is low, the swath width is relatively small compared to sonar, and video is nearly useless as a survey tool if the water is not exceptionally clear. If the water is shallow, it is possible to use *aerial photography* to search for submerged sites.

If the site is buried under bottom sediment, it can still be located, usually either with *sub-bottom profiling sonar* or magnetometry. Sub-bottom profilers were originally developed as a geological survey tool for mapping deep sedimentary stratigraphy, but those with higher resolution can be used to locate archaeological sites. By sending a sonar pulse into the sediment and measuring the reflected signal, the unit can identify and locate layers or objects of different density or hardness. As shipwrecks often include components, such as stone ballast or cannon, that are acoustically distinct from soft mud or sand, they can be located by this method. Architectural features on submerged coastal sites can be located in the same way. Disadvantages of sub-bottom profiling include difficulties in getting a clear reflected signal if the bottom sediments contain gas pockets, such as those caused by decomposing organic matter, and the narrowness of the swath. The pulse goes straight down, so the resulting image is not a broad picture but a vertical section through the sediment. If the track of the array does not pass directly over the target, it will not register, and if the track crosses the target where structure is minimal or oriented oddly, an archaeological target may not be readily identifiable in the resulting image.

Magnetometry measures local variations in the strength of the Earth's magnetic field. This field is not everywhere constant and can be significantly distorted by concentrations of ferrous or other magnetic material, such as iron cannon or even large concentrations of fired archaeomagnetic clay. Normally, spot measurements are taken in a grid pattern, and the resulting data plotted as a magnetic contour map. The equipment is relatively easy to use, and the resulting data, once processed, can pinpoint potential sites quite accurately. Unfortunately, the resulting image gives no real clue as to the nature of the magnetic anomaly, and the site must be inspected by

other means; sewer pipes and cannon produce similar magnetic signatures.

All of these methods require accurate recording of the position of the sensor, so that potential sites can be relocated. Near shore, the traditional practice has been to establish ranges in parallel lines, down which the vessel towing the sensor "fish" travels. Its position along these ranges can be recorded by observers on shore or by noting bearings of landmarks from the vessel. With the availability of global positioning systems (GPS), it has become possible to simplify this part of the operation. GPS readings can be tied directly into the sensor data to produce maps in "real time."

A nonelectronic survey method that has been found to work well in areas where sites stand proud of the bottom, even if the bottom is rocky, is to interview local fishermen and divers. In the eastern Mediterranean, the well-developed sponge-fishing industry provided a natural survey force that effectively, if inadvertently, inspected large areas of the sea bottom within diving limits. By educating the divers about the appearance of ancient wrecks and paying a bounty for reported sites, archaeologists have been able to locate a large number of sites that would have been inaccessible with conventional remote-sensing equipment. Similar contacts with sport divers in other areas have yielded good results, but it needs to be stressed that, if sport divers believe that they will be excluded from sites "taken over" by archaeologists, they will not be very helpful in locating sites.

For detailed assessment of potential sites in a small area, divers can be used directly, either swimming over the bottom or towed behind a small boat. *Swim surveys* have the advantage that potential sites can be readily identified and their locations marked with small buoys towed or carried by the diver. The survey can be halted for assessment of particular sites, and the location determined with high accuracy before going on. Because of the limited time a diver can stay under water, swim surveys are not suited to large areas. Needless to say, good visibility increases the chances of success, but surveys have been carried out in "black water" largely by touch.

Once a potential site has been found or reported, it must be inspected visually by divers (or by an ROV carrying camera equipment) to confirm its existence and to determine its date, type, level of preservation, and so forth. This is most often accomplished by a simple swim survey. Buried potential sites may also be tested by conventional terrestrial techniques, such as *coring* or *test excavation,* and the extent of buried material determined through *probing.* Underwater probes range from the simple stick or iron bar to a length of small-diameter pipe through which compressed air or pressurized water is pumped to make it easier to force into stiff sediments.

Excavation

One of the few archaeological tasks that is easier under water is the removal of overburden. Rather than being shoveled into buckets and carried to screening dumps, it can be sucked up and transported off site mechanically. The primary tools for this task are the *airlift* and the *induction dredge.* The first is nothing more than a length of pipe suspended over the site, with the upper end directed down current and away from the excavation area. Compressed air is introduced into the mouth of the pipe, and, as it rises toward the upper end, it expands and accelerates, creating suction at the mouth. Bottom sediments are swept toward the mouth, either by hand fanning or brushing, sucked up the lift, and spewed out the upper, exhaust end to be carried down current or to fall back to the seabed. Sieves or screening apparatus can be attached to the exhaust end to retrieve small artifacts inadvertently collected by the airlift. It is considered bad practice to plunge the mouth of the airlift directly into the bottom unless removing sterile backfill, and there should be a control at the mouth to regulate how much compressed air is introduced into the tube.

The alternative to the airlift, which is most effective in depths of 10 m or more, is the induction dredge. In this device, water is pumped at relatively high speed to the dredge head, a metal or PVC pipe of moderate diameter, where it is directed into the pipe and back toward the exhaust end. The high-speed water, flowing out of the small supply hose into the larger dredge pipe and back, creates suction at the mouth. As with the airlift, the exhaust can be screened, and the diver should have a control to regulate the amount of water pumped into the dredge. Many excavators find that the

metal dredge head is too heavy or potentially damaging to the site, so they attach a length of flexible hose to the mouth. This works well as long as the hose is not too long, in which case it will cause a noticeable drop in suction. The exhaust must be staked down or otherwise fixed, or it will flap about. The ability to direct the exhaust does offer several advantages over the airlift: The spoil can be placed more conveniently; the dredge has less tendency to fill the water column with sediment; and it can be used more effectively for backfilling. Whether using the airlift or the dredge, care must be exercised not to destroy site stratigraphy. Even if the sediment is not stiff enough to permit the cutting of baulk profiles, stratigraphic layers can still be identified and recorded horizontally.

On some sites, corroding metal artifacts (especially those of iron) will cause the deposition of hard calcium carbonates (concretion) on the artifacts and surrounding material. Where there are large quantities of iron (e.g., cannon, anchors, nails, bolts) and the deposition of carbonates is rapid (notably on high-energy sites in tropical waters), the site may consist of extremely large masses of concretion containing hundreds of artifacts, ballast stones, and bottom sediment. In these conditions, it may be necessary to break the concretion into pieces small enough to raise and transport, then bring them to a laboratory where the individual artifacts can be removed by mechanical means. The process of breaking up the site concretion may involve hammers and chisels, pneumatic tools, and, in some cases, the controlled use of explosives. In the lab, the pieces can be X-rayed to identify and map the contents before cleaning.

Mapping

The process of establishing context can be one of the most time-consuming aspects of excavating an underwater site. Traditionally, the primary methods of mapping have involved tape measures and plumb bobs to establish horizontal location and a variety of methods to determine relative depths. Other methods, such as plane table and alidade (or string and protractor) have been tried, and such polar methods are still used on initial surveys for their speed. In shallow water near shore, a leveling rod on site and a transit on shore can be used to determine elevations, but the process is tedious and often requires the diver to travel back and forth between the bottom and the surface, which can be dangerous. Another method uses a bubble tube, a length of clear tubing into which an air bubble is introduced. The tube will then bow upward in the center, and the ends of the bubble will be at the same height. Relative depths can then be determined by placing the ends of the bubble at two points and noting the vertical distances to the bubble ends. Diving depth gauges have been used for rough estimation of relative depth but are generally not accurate enough for detailed mapping. A more accurate depth gauge, developed by the Dutch Archaeological Service, is effective, but extremely expensive (Botma and Maarleveld 1987).

The difficulties of using tape and plumb bob in the high-relief and complex interior spaces of the Tudor warship *Mary Rose* led, during the 1970s and early 1980s, to the development of a mapping method, now widely used in Europe, known as *direct survey measurement* (DSM), in which distances from artifacts are measured directly to four or more datum points (Rule 1989). The distances then become the arguments in three-dimensional trigonometric calculations similar to those used in geodesic mapping; the calculations can be done by hand or even worked out geometrically, but the process is slow, and a computer program is normally used. The result is a location expressed as three-dimensional cartesian coordinates. Because it is virtually impossible to get perfectly accurate measurements, and there seems to be an average incidence of blunders of 5 percent in underwater measurements, the computer software developed by Nicholas Rule to process these measurements also applies a best-fit algorithm to quantify the errors. If sufficient measurements are taken, it is possible not only to quantify the level of confidence in the final result, but also to identify bad measurements. A great advantage of this method is that it significantly reduces the time spent mapping under water, as both horizontal and vertical location are measured at the same time, and direct measurements are much easier than level plumbed measurements.

In the 1980s, tape measures were rendered potentially obsolete by the development of SHARPS (sonic high-accuracy ranging and positioning system) by Martin Wilcox. Sonic transceivers are fixed around the site, and a mobile unit is taken to points to be mapped. The mobile unit sends out a sonic pulse, and the time it takes to arrive at the fixed transceivers is measured. The distances thus determined are the arguments for geodesic calculations, and the output can be sent directly to a computer-aided drafting (CAD) program for plotting and display. Once the equipment is set up and calibrated, it is extremely fast, but there have been problems in practice with accuracy, especially on sites with high topographic relief creating false echoes of the sonic pulses. There is also the difficulty of setting up and maintaining the underwater electronics and cabling, so the system, once perfected, is better suited to large-scale excavations rather than surveys or test trenches.

Conventional terrestrial techniques of mapping have also been adapted under water, especially photographic mapping. *Stereophotogrammetry* has been in use since the 1970s; it provides a rapid method of developing a rough site plan, and it can be used to produce detailed maps of small areas. By combining photography with DSM or SHARPS and making sure that a number of mapped points or targets appear in each photograph, complex excavation units or layers can be mapped with acceptable accuracy quite rapidly. More sophisticated systems, involving the photography of graduated cubes placed on site, will greatly speed the mapping process and may even obviate the need for most direct measurement. There have also been experiments with developing site maps directly from video footage, using frame-capture technology and geodesic formulae.

Ship remains, a primary component of many underwater sites, are usually recorded by combining archaeological-mapping methods with hull-recording techniques used in naval architecture. Longitudinal and transverse sections of the remains will produce a record not only of the hull's shape, but also of the arrangement and location of major components. Details, such as joinery, fastenings, and tool marks, can be recorded by measured sketches, drawing frames (a string grid on two levels, so that, by aligning the upper and lower grids, parallax errors can be minimized), and photography. Other methods that have been used for hull recording under water include tracing surfaces full size onto clear plastic sheet with grease pencil and taking molds in polysulfide rubber. In general, it is best to begin with general data and work toward the finer detail.

Site Stabilization

Backfilling can be accomplished quite easily under water, especially with induction dredges, but it has been observed that it can be difficult in some sediments to create a stable, anaerobic environment. In loose sand especially, it has been noted that significant degradation of organic material may occur in just one year if the site is only lightly covered. In areas affected by currents, erosion may be a serious problem. If remains are being left in place, it is best to cover them with something more than loose sediment. Sandbags laid over the remains will stay in place and help to stabilize the sediment. They also provide an easily identifiable, sterile layer over the remains, so that, when excavation begins in the next season, the backfill can be removed quickly without fear of damaging the site below.

Frederick Hocker

See also NAUTICAL ARCHAEOLOGY; REMOTELY OPERATED VEHICLES; WOOD (WATERLOGGED), CONSERVATION

Further Readings

Arnold, J.B., III (1981) Remote sensing in underwater archaeology. International Journal of Nautical Archaeology 10:51–62.

Botma, H.C., and Maarleveld, T. J. (1987) Underwater heightmeter: A new hand-held precision instrument for elevation measuring in underwater surveying. International Journal of Nautical Archaeology 16:87–94.

Dean, M., Ferrari, B., Oxley, I., Redknap, M., and Watson, K., eds. (1992) Archaeology Underwater: The NAS Guide to Principles and Practice. London: Nautical Archaeology Society.

Green, J. (1990) Maritime Archaeology: A Technical Handbook. London: Academic.

Rule, N. (1989) The direct survey method (DSM) of underwater survey, and its application underwater. International Journal of Nautical Archaeology 18:157–162.

Unit-Level Method

A methodologically unsound excavation technique. Although still practiced by some field archaeologists in North America, it rarely even appears in textbooks elsewhere.

The unit-level method involves dividing the site into 1 m × 1 m units that are generally excavated in arbitrary 10 cm levels. One excavator is responsible for excavating one unit at a time. All arbitrary levels are excavated on horizontal planes established by reference to a previously established site datum. If applied rigorously, this technique cuts right across the natural and archaeological stratigraphy of a site. It creates particular problems on sloping sites. Understanding of the site is confused during excavation as each unit is excavated to different arbitrary levels at the same time. This technique generally makes simple sites complex and appears scientific when, in fact, it is absurd and should be abandoned by those few practitioners still using it.

Peter L. Drewett

Uranium-Series Dating

A family of dating techniques based on the measurement of disequilibria in the uranium-decay chains *(uranium series)*. There are two different uranium-decay chains: the ^{238}U and the ^{235}U decay chains, both of which are created by the radioactive decay of the parent isotope. The isotope ^{238}U decays in various intermediate steps to the isotope ^{206}Pb, and ^{235}U decays to ^{207}Pb (Figure 1). In old samples, these two decay chains are in equilibrium: The number of atoms of the parent isotope decaying in a given time interval (= *activity*) is equal to the number of atoms of each daughter isotope decaying in the same time interval. In other words, if in one hour ca. 10,000 atoms of ^{238}U decay, during the same hour ca. 10,000 atoms of ^{234}U, ^{230}Th, ^{226}Ra, and so on will also decay. The ratio of the activities of the daughter isotope over the parent is *unity* (= 1). If disequilibrium occurs, this activity ratio is not equal to one. If the daughter isotope is depleted relative to the parent, the activity ratio is smaller than one; if the daughter isotope is enriched, the activity ratio is greater than one. After the event that led to the disturbance of equilibrium, the activity ratio will change into the direction of equilibrium. The rate of change is controlled by the half-life of the daughter isotope.

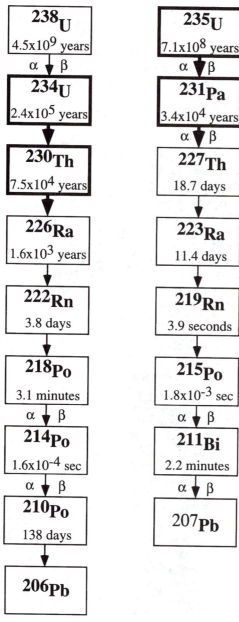

Figure 1. The ^{238}U and ^{235}U decay chains (alpha decays only), isotopes, and half-lives. The bold boxes show the isotope pairs that have been used for dating archaeological sites. α and β annotate a series of an alpha and one or two beta decays between the isotopes shown. Figure by Rainer Grün.

Dating Techniques

There are two daughter/parent isotope pairs used for U-series dating in archaeological contexts: ^{230}Th and ^{234}U, and ^{231}Pa and ^{235}U. The dating techniques based on these two

pairs are often called Th/U and Pa/U dating. Dating becomes possible because thorium (Th) and protactinium (Pa) have a geochemical behavior completely different from that of uranium (U). The latter is water soluble, whereas Th and Pa are water insoluble. Minerals precipitated from water, such as speleothems or shells, and organic matter, such as peat and bones, contain traces of uranium but are virtually free of thorium and protactinium. When the sample is formed, the $^{230}Th/^{234}U$ and the $^{231}Pa/^{235}U$ activity ratios (henceforth, Th/U and Pa/U ratios) are, therefore, zero. With time, some ^{234}U decays into ^{230}Th, and ^{235}U decays into ^{231}Pa, increasing the Th/U and Pa/U ratios. After one half-life of ^{230}Th (ca. 75,000 years), the Th/U ratio is 0.5; after two half-lives, the ratio is 0.75; after three half-lives, the ratio is 0.875, and so on. The changes of the Th/U and Pa/U ratios with time are shown in Figure 2. The U-series age estimates are calculated from the measurement of Th/U or Pa/U ratios and associated uncertainties. Although the errors in the activity ratios are symmetrical, the errors of the U-series age estimate are asymmetric. The error in the upper age limit is larger than that in the lower age limit, caused by the curvature of the activity-ratio plot (Figure 3B). Age estimates can be obtained only as long as the measured activity ratio is smaller than unity. If the equilibrium value is within the error range, the sample may be of infinite age. Because of the much shorter half-life of ^{231}Pa (32,500 years) compared to ^{230}Th, Th/U dating can be carried out over a much larger time range than Pa/U dating. Additionally, the natural ^{235}U activity is less than 5 percent of ^{238}U, which makes it more difficult to measure the isotopes of the ^{235}U decay chain. Therefore, most U-series age estimates are based on the Th/U method.

The change of the Th/U ratio is complicated by the observation that most samples show an excess of ^{234}U compared to ^{238}U. The curves shown in the upper diagram of Figure 2 are valid only for $^{234}U/^{238}U$ ratios of 1.0. For samples that show other initial $^{234}U/^{238}U$ ratios, usually ^{234}U excess, the temporal change of Th/U ratio is shown in the lower diagram of Figure 2. The mathematical treatment of the U-series age equations has been published in various reviews.

Until recently, the isotopes for U-series dating were measured by alpha spectrometry. The different elements are chemically separated and measured with an alpha counter. This technique has the disadvantage that only a very small portion of atoms can be registered, namely, those decaying during the measurement time. The vast quantity of atoms that do not decay (greater than 99.999 percent) cannot be measured. Similar to the advances in radiocarbon dating achieved by accelerator mass spectrometry (AMS), thermal ionization mass spectrometry (TIMS) has led to a breakthrough in U-series dating, particularly Th/U dating. Mass spectrometry measures the number of atoms present. Compared to alpha counting, TIMS allows the measurement of smaller samples (by a factor of 30 to 100) with greatly improved precision. These differences are shown in Figure 3A and B. In the age range of 125,000–130,000 years, typical alpha-spectromic (AS) and mass-spectrometric (MS) uncertainties (2σ) in the measurement of the Th/U ratios lie in the 2 percent and 0.35 percent range, respectively, which convert to age uncertainties of 5,200 and 1,300 years. These differences become more pronounced at older ages: Typical alpha-spectrometric uncertainties of 0.05 and exceptionally good ones of 0.02 limit the alpha-spectrometric Th/U method to 325,000 and 425,000 years. Therefore, a general upper dating limit of ca. 350,000 years has been proposed. TIMS, on the other hand, allows the measurement of the Th/U ratio that are distinctively different from unity for samples older than 500,000 years. At the lower end of the dating range, samples as old as 200 years have been measured with uncertainties of ca. 5 years, which is more precise than radiocarbon dating.

Th/U and Pa/U ratios can also be measured by gamma spectrometry. The advantages of this technique are that no pretreatment of the sample is required and it is completely nondestructive. The disadvantage lies in the much lower detection limits of high-resolution gamma counters compared with alpha or mass spectrometry, and, therefore, gamma spectrometry is associated with much larger errors (e.g., 5–15 percent in the 100,000-years range).

Applications and Limitations

A sample suited for U-series dating must satisfy the following criteria: (1) it must have been formed at a well-defined event; (2) it must contain measurable amounts of uranium; (3) no uranium can have leached from the sample or been accumulated by the sample (closed system); and (4) it must not contain any ^{230}Th or ^{231}Pa at the time of formation, or the amount of ^{230}Th or ^{231}Pa at the time of formation must be measurable. All ^{230}Th and ^{231}Pa atoms of samples complying with the above conditions have been formed by the decay of uranium rather than chemical alteration. Unfortunately, there are only a few materials found in common archaeological sites that are suitable for reliable U-series dating.

The main problems in dating secondary carbonates, such as speleothems, travertines, or marl, are high porosities and clay-mineral contents. Porosity is often an indication of recrystallization and solution of the material, leading to an alteration of the uranium and thorium concentrations in the sample. Clay minerals contain high concentrations not only of the isotope ^{232}Th, but also of ^{230}Th.

If a calcite sample contains variable amounts of clay-minerals, the condition that the initial ^{230}Th/^{234}U ratio is zero is violated. To overcome this problem, *isochron dating* can be carried out (Figure 4): Various portions of the sample are repeatedly measured, and the ^{230}Th/^{232}Th activity ratios are plotted against the ^{234}U/^{232}Th ratios. The data points are fitted with a straight line. The intersection with the Y-axis yields the amount of unsupported (= detrital) ^{230}Th (^{234}U = 0). The slope of the line (isochron) is the Th/U ratio and, therefore, gives the age of the sample.

Speleothems are secondary carbonates in caves (stalagmites, stalactites, flowstones) and are often associated with archaeological remains. Most samples seem well suited for Th/U dating, although some have uranium concentrations that are too low for measurement, and others are very porous and chemically altered. Sites dated by U-series include Caune de l'Arago, France; Grotta della Basura, Italy; Grotta Guattari, Italy; Klasies River Mouth Cave, South Africa; La Chaise de Vouthon, France; Pech de l'Aze II, France; Petralona, Greece; Pontnewydd Cave, Wales; and Zuttiyeh, Israel.

Travertines are layers or crusts of calcite precipitated around springs or barriers of slow-moving streams. In the Mediterranean, travertine deposits may reach thicknesses in the 100-m range. Most samples are not well suited for U-series dating because of very high porosity supporting chemical alteration and high clay contents. Archaeological sites that have been dated include Abric Romani, Spain; Bilzingsleben,

U

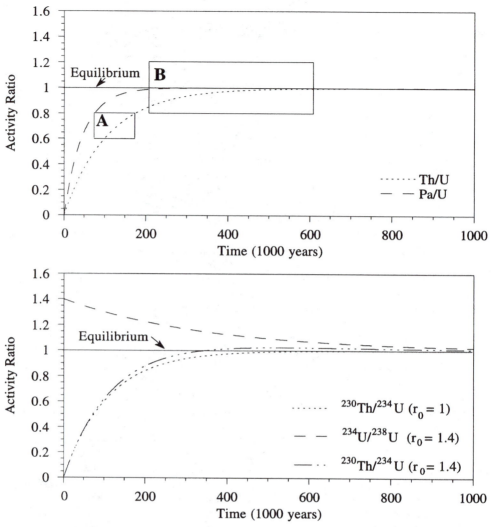

Figure 2. *(Upper diagram): Change of the Th/U and Pa/U activity ratios with time. Because of the shorter half-life of ^{231}Pa compared to ^{230}Th, the Pa/U ratio reaches unity much earlier than the Th/U ratio. Therefore, Pa/U dating covers only half the range of Th/U and is only rarely applied. The boxes A and B are shown in more detail in Figure 3. (Lower Diagram): Change of the Th/U ratio for different initial ^{234}U/^{238}U ratios, r_0. If r_0 is not equal to 1.0, the ^{234}U/^{238}U ratio influences the Th/U ratio. Instead of approaching unity, the Th/U ratio approximates the ^{234}U/^{238}U ratio. Equilibrium is reached after ca. 1.5 million years. Figure by Rainer Grün.*

Germany; Ehringsdorf, Germany; Nahal Agev, Israel; Nahal Mor, Israel; Vertesszöllös, Hungary; and Tata, Hungary.

Marl is a lake-deposited travertine. The material is usually not well suited for U-series dating because of high porosity and clay-mineral contents. Dated archaeological sites include Bir Tarfawi, Egypt, and Bañolas, Spain.

Biogenic carbonates, such as mollusc shells or gastropods, have been studied by nu-merous U-series analyses. Unfortunately, systematic investigations came to the conclusion that mollusc shells behave as open systems, showing strong chemical exchange of uranium, as well as thorium. U-series age estimates of such materials may, therefore, be unreliable.

Recent U-series studies of peat have overcome the problem of open-system behavior of peat layers. Although no archaeological sites in peat layers had been dated as of 1998, it

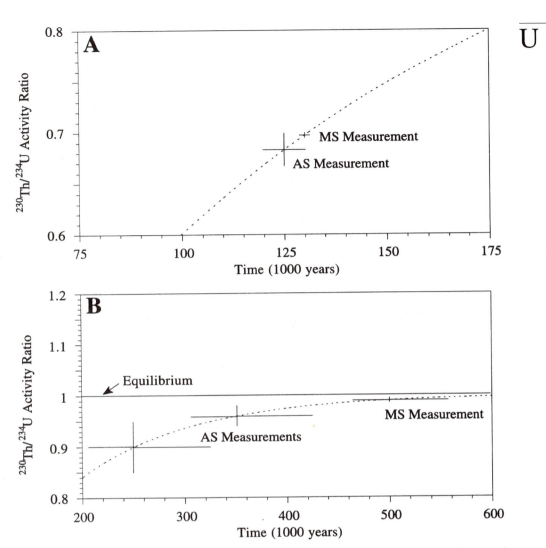

Figure 3. *Comparison of alpha-spectrometric (AS) and mass-spectrometric (MS) measurements. Because of the much higher precision of MS compared to AS, the MS age results are far more precise (Figure A), and MS allows the extension of the practical dating range to more than 500,000 years (Figure B). Figure by Rainer Grün.*

may be expected that this application will provide valuable chronological information for many archaeological sites.

The application of U-series dating on bones and teeth is still fraught with significant problems that require systematic work. At the present stage, all age estimates should be viewed with some caution. It has become clear that buried faunal remains experience uranium migration, mainly uptake. This diminishes the reliability of the age result. Researchers have reported the apparently successful application of U-series dating to bone (Rae and Ivanovich 1986). The dating model is based on the following assumptions: (1) the uranium concentration near to the surface of a bone reaches saturation within a short time compared to the age of the sample; (2) when uranium decays to thorium, the latter remains fixed in place; and (3) any later accumulated uranium passes though the saturated zone. If these assumptions are correct, the closed-system U-series age is a good approximation to the true age. Subsequent studies by the same authors cast doubt on the validity of this simple model, though.

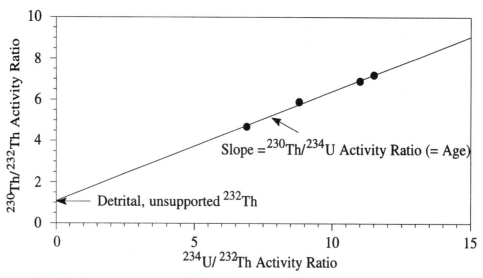

Figure 4. Isochron dating of contaminated samples. The sample is repeatedly analyzed, and the $^{230}Th/^{232}Th$ activity ratios are plotted against the $^{234}U/^{232}Th$ activity ratios. The data points are fitted with a straight line. The intersection with the Y-axis ($^{234}U = 0$) gives the amount of detrital ^{230}Th that is not supported by the ^{234}U present in the sample. The slope of the line (isochron) is the Th/U ratio and, therefore, gives the age of the sample. In this example, the slope of 0.5311 corresponds to an age of ca. 82,400 years ($r_0 = 1$). Without isochron analysis, the plotted data points would give uncorrected ages in the range of 125,000 to 158,000 years. Figure by Rainer Grün.

An extensive U-series study on bone, dentine, and enamel came to a similar conclusion that U-series dating was possible (McKinney 1991). Tooth enamel seemed to approximate more of a closed system for uranium than dentine or bone did; however, multiple analyses are necessary to ensure accuracy. Bone results were consistently younger than corresponding Carbon-14 (^{14}C) age estimates, implying continuing uranium accumulation. Th/U and Pa/U ratios have been measured on bone samples from Chinese Palaeolithic sites, and an open-system model was developed (Chen and Yuan 1988). Both ratios can be used to obtain independent age estimates. However, because of the significantly different half-lives of ^{230}Th and ^{231}Pa, they yield concordant results only if the uranium was accumulated within a short time interval and remained a closed system afterwards. If the age results differ, open-system ages can be calculated. It was found that of thirty-eight samples, twenty-three showed closed systems, eleven had signs of uranium accumulation, and four had signs of uranium leaching. In contrast, an intensive dating study has been carried out on samples from Tournal Cave in France and came to the conclusion that neither bone nor tooth enamel was consistent with stratigraphic position or independent ^{14}C control. This also applied to samples in which similar Th/U and Pa/U ages were obtained, implying a closed system and, therefore, supposedly reliable results.

Bone samples that have been measured with nondestructive high-resolution gamma spectrometry include hominid fossils from Caune de l'Arago, France, and Fate, Italy. The method can measure Th/U and Pa/U ratios simultaneously and these have been used to overcome the open system problem.

A combination of U-series and electron spin resonance (ESR) dating alleviates the uncertainty created by the unknown history of uranium uptake. Both methods are influenced by uranium accumulation but to a different extent. By measuring all parameters for both dating methods, it becomes possible to estimate the history of uranium uptake. This method has been applied to paleoanthroplogical sites in Israel, such as Tabun, Skhul and Qafzeh.

Rainer Grün

See also ELECTRON SPIN RESONANCE (ESR) DATING

Further Readings

Bischoff, J.L., Rosenbauer, R.J., Tavoso, A., and DeLumley, H. (1988) A test of uranium-series dating of fossil tooth enamel: Results from Tournal Cave, France. Applied Geochemistry 3:145–151.

Chen, T.M. and Yuan, S. (1988) Uranium-series dating of bones and teeth from Chinese Palaeolithic sites. Archaeometry 30: 59–76.

Edwards, R.L., Chen, J. H., and Wasserburg, G.J. (1987) ^{238}U–^{234}U–^{230}Th–^{232}Th systematics and the precise measurement of time over the past 500,000 years. Earth and Planetary Science Letters 81:175–192.

Heijnis, H., and van der Plicht, J. (1992) Uranium/thorium dating of Late Pleistocene peat deposits in NW Europe: Uranium/thorium isotope systematics and open system behavior of peat layers. Chemical Geology 94:161–171.

Ivanovich, M., and Harmon, R.S. (1992) Uranium Series Disequilibrium: Application to Environmental Problems in the Earth Sciences. Oxford: Oxford University Press.

Kaufman, A., Broecker, W. S., Ku, T. L., and Thurber, D. L. (1971) The status of U-series methods of mollusk dating. Geochimica Cosmochimica Acta 35:1155–1189.

McDermott, F., Grün, R., Stringer, C.B., and Hawkesworth, C.J. (1993) Mass-spectrometric U-series dates for Israeli Neanderthal/early modern hominid sites. Nature 363:252–255.

McKinney, C.R. (1991) The determination of the reliability of uranium series dating of enamel, dentine, and bone. (Unpublished PhD thesis). Dallas: Southern Methodist University.

Rae, A. M., and Ivanovich, M. (1986) Successful application of uranium series dating of fossil bone. Applied Geochemistry 1:419–426.

Schwarcz, H. P. (1989) Uranium series dating of Quaternary deposits. Quaternary International 1:7–17.

Yokoyama, Y. and Nguyen, H. V. (1981) Datation directe de l'homme de Tautavel par la spectrometrie gamma, non destructive, du crane humain fossile Arago XXI. Comptes Rendus des Seances de l'Academie des Sciences, Paris, Serie III 292:741–744.

U

Use-Wear Analysis

The study of damage accruing to stone tools as a result of their utilization. Four principal types of use-wear have been identified: *edge fracturing, edge rounding, polish,* and *striations*. The first of these obeys laws of fracture mechanics; the latter three, of surface abrasion.

Early Research

The analysis of prehistoric stone tools has traditionally proceeded from studies of typology and technology. Since the late nineteenth century, it has been recognized that the utilization of stone produces wear and that the interpretation of that wear might provide insight into the ways in which tools were manipulated prehistorically. The development of these ideas did not occur rapidly, however, and, by the 1930s, functional attention was focused on the obvious use-polish on sickles, but no compendium of other types of use-wear existed.

This situation changed drastically in 1957 with the publication, in Russian, of the first comprehensive treatment of wear on large numbers of stone implements, soon to be referred to as *lithic use-wear analysis*. This study was conducted by Sergei A. Semenov, the director of a large archaeological laboratory in Leningrad. Its translation into English under the title *Prehistoric Technology* in 1964 became so popular among lithic analysts that it was the most frequently referenced work in journals such as *American Antiquity* for at least a decade. The reason for this was that few other scholars were conducting research of this type, but everybody recognized its importance and felt compelled to refer to it.

The publication and translation of Semenov's book stimulated research on functional issues in America and in Europe. A major portion of this research was experimental, because analysis of use-wear on archaeological tools was perceived as proceeding from analogy to use-wear produced experimentally. Experimentation of this nature was conducted either by replicating specific tasks on implements, such as hoes, scraper planes, and end scrapers, or by reproducing reasonably comprehensive sets of tasks likely to have been performed by a group of prehistoric people.

Blind Tests and High-Magnification Analysis

By the mid-1970s, enough use-wear research had been performed in the West to warrant a conference for the purpose of ironing out terminological inconsistencies and forging new directions. Brian Hayden was able to include most of the major actors in such a conference in Vancouver, British Columbia, in 1977, resulting in a volume entitled *Lithic Use-Wear Analysis*—certainly the most influential series of articles ever published in this field. At this point, several directions were being pursued, and methodological heterogeneity, and enthusiasm, were high.

Other researchers remained skeptical of this new field, however. Among the skeptics was lithic technologist Mark Newcomer at the London Institute of Archaeology, who arranged to give a blind test to use-wear analyst Lawrence Keeley, then at Oxford University. The blind test was conducted by Newcomer, who made and used a series of stone tools that he then gave to Keeley for analysis of their use. Keeley was relatively successful at interpreting the location of use on the implement, tool motion, and types of materials contacted.

Keeley's success in the blind tests proved to be a boon to the specific technique and equipment he was using—a Wild M20 metallurgical microscope with incident-light attachment (i.e., light directed down through the lens) and capabilities of magnification to 400x. This equipment does not provide a stereoscopic image, but it is useful for distinguishing surface topography and specific types of use-polish on the surfaces of tools. The utility of this technique was immediately demonstrated through Keeley's dissertation on the functions of implements from the English Palaeolithic and through his interpretations of the Belgian Mesolithic habitation of Meer II. These studies stimulated a host of graduate students to produce intensive analyses of material from both the Old World and the New.

Use-wear techniques employing metallurgical microscopes were so new at this point that conventions had to be established and potential problems ironed out. Thus, considerable attention was paid to issues such as appropriate sampling and recording systems, artifact cleaning, and postdepositional surface modification (PDSM). Some of these issues continue to be debated.

Meanwhile, blind testing of analysts continued, as the profession sought to ascertain whether or not Keeley's results were spurious and whether other analysts could duplicate his success. At first, tests confirmed Keeley's results, but then events took an ugly turn. The original skeptic, Mark Newcomer, conducted another series of assays, this time involving several use-wear analysts and a lithic technologist with a hand lens. Ten implements apiece were employed in three series: first, evaluating functional parameters as usual; then, observing only tool surfaces to assess the claim that functional parameters could be correctly postdicted through polishes alone; and, finally, giving the analysts the information that five specific materials had been worked and that two tools were used in each activity. The results of all three series were substantially lower than Keeley's, throwing some doubt on the entire technique. More embarassing, perhaps, was the fact that the technologist had done just as well as the use-wear specialists. Comments on these experiments by interested parties expressed general agreement that the ten minutes apiece for which the tools had been used was not long enough for polish to have developed past the undifferentiated "generic" stage to a stage at which different polishes can be distinguished from one another.

About the same time, another blind test was conducted among four high-magnification use-wear analysts from different countries (Unrath et al. in Owen and Unrath 1986). In a difficult assay, the analysts achieved satisfactory success in assessing the used area of the piece but considerably less success in determining tool motion and worked material. Despite the happy face the analysts tried to put on these results, it was obvious that improvements could be made. Subsequently, greater success in blind tests has been achieved by at least one other researcher (Bamforth et al. 1990).

Low-Magnification Techniques

While techniques involving high-magnification binocular microscopes with incident lighting became dominant during the 1980s, other techniques continued to be practiced. Of these, the one with the most adherents has been called the *low-power* technique (Tringham et al. 1974; Kamminga 1982), referring to its use of stereoscopic microscopes employing reflective lighting (i.e., light from an external source directed at an angle toward the object) and relatively low magnification (usually to ca. 100x). The facility with which artifacts can be scanned at these magnifications enables observation to proceed much more quickly than at higher magnifications and allows considerably larger samples to be processed. The recognition of use location and distinct tool motions is comparable to that achieved at higher magnifications. On the other hand, although virtually all of the damage recognized at higher magnifications can also be seen at lower power, the reflective lighting does not enable surface polishes to be distinguished as well as with incident lighting. Therefore, in low-magnification analyses, worked materials are designated according to a relative-resistance scale, a scale that usually corresponds closely to known, specific substances.

The development of low-power analyses parallelled, to some degree, that of high-power analyses. Shortly after the appearance of Keeley and Newcomer's blind tests, George Odell and Frieda Odell-Vereecken (1980) conducted a comparable series in British Columbia basalt using low-magnification techniques. Success rates on the various parameters were somewhat lower than for the Keeley/Newcomer series but within an acceptable 60–80 percent range. Subsequently, John Shea and Thomas Richards have reported relatively high success rates using low-power techniques.

Some serious misunderstandings concerning the nature and capabilities of low-power analysis persisted throughout the 1980s, but these appear to have been cleared up subsequently. Since fracturing is an important element of edge wear visible at low magnifications, problems with low-power techniques include occasional difficulties in distinguishing wear fractures from intentional retouch and from extraneous damage produced by excavation equipment, trampling, and the like. Given the paucity of researchers engaged in developing this technique, resolution of these problems has proceeded slowly.

Scanning Electron Microscope

Another technique that has been employed for use-wear analysis involves the scanning electron microscope (SEM). This machine is not ideal for systematic observation of lithic collections because of several inherent problems, some of which are machine-specific, including the necessity to coat the outer surface of the stone with a thin metal compound and the use of small or broken pieces to fit into the vacuum chamber. The fact that some of these problems can be ameliorated through casts or acetate peels does not obviate the essential difficulty of using the SEM for basic observations of an assemblage.

However, the SEM has been effectively employed to study the genesis of wear formation in situations in which a specific process can be scrutinized in detail. For example, using this equipment, Daryl Fedje demonstrated the process of autostriation (i.e., pieces of an edge flaking off and scratching the surface of the same tool); Kjel Knutsson investigated the formation of wear on quartz at very high magnifications; and Patricia Anderson reported recognizing plant phytoliths, which she interpreted as "melting into" the surface of the flint, although Romana Unger-Hamilton's subsequent experiments suggested that they were more likely spicules or particles of the flint itself.

Ongoing Research Issues

The problems that have beset use-wear analysis since its inception remain incompletely resolved, though researchers have continued to chip away at individual aspects. For instance, the masking and confusion of use polishes through postdepositional surface modification have been identified, and some of the parameters of PDSM have been established. The practice of artifact preparation through washing with an acid and a base, questioned by Emily Moss, now appears less bothersome, as subsequent experiments using weaker (and perhaps more realistic) basic solutions have not produced the extreme surface modification of Moss's experiments. Edge damage caused by transportation, storage, screening, laboratory processing, and trampling by cows and humans has been described and compared to use-wear. In none of these situations does perfect discrimination between use and nonuse damage exist, but each study increases archaeologists' knowledge of the relevant ranges of variation.

Optimal discrimination of use traces will never occur until the genesis of wear is completely comprehended, a consideration that justifies considerable research effort.

The formation of polish may be produced mechanically, or chemically, or both, depending upon operative conditions. Some work has been done on the formation of use-striae, including the autostriating already mentioned, and it appears that some discrimination of use-striae will be possible, especially on obsidian. Use-fracturing follows laws of fracture mechanics, though most of it is probably caused by bending rather than Hertzian principles involving a cone of force, particularly on relatively acute edges. Many of these principles are now understood, though their application to specific functional situations needs substantially more work.

A problem that has plagued use-wear analysis from the beginning is that it remains an interpretive study, based on comparison to relatively comprehensive sets of functional experiments. For years, researchers have sought to objectify the process by instituting less interpretive measures once wear has been identified. For example, Keeley (1980) attempted to measure the intensity of use-polishes quantitatively by recording their average light-meter readings. Other attempts have been made at quantification of use-polishes, notably, interferometry and image processing, but nobody has yet succeeded in satisfactorily discriminating the various polishes from one another. In fact, one recent study reported no significant correlations between the fractal properties of digital flint images and the substances with which the flint came in contact (Rees et al. 1991).

The most successful attempt at use-wear quantification has been by John Tomenchuk who, employing a low-magnification microscope, measured several aspects of use-scars on unretouched edges. On this basis, he was able to discriminate different tool motions and worked materials from one another. This was the first, and only, time to date that satisfactory discrimination of discrete functional sets through objective measures has been attained with any use-wear technique. Tomenchuk's system possesses problems of its own, notably, length of recording time and nonapplication to retouched edges, but it demonstrates the correspondence of fracturing variables to use-wear formation.

As research has progressed into the 1990s, the low- and high-magnification use-wear camps, previously far apart in goals and types of research, have coalesced somewhat. Mutual acceptance appears to have been attained (though grudgingly in many cases), and there has been a call to practice both types of analysis as the situation warrants—a seemingly innovative notion if one disregards its expression at the Vancouver Conference back in 1977. In fact, Roger Grace (1989) has developed the use of *expert systems,* in which both types of microscopes are used and all information is input into computerized format. Grace has claimed considerable accuracy for the technique, though the analysis is time consuming, and his blind tests possessed the unconventional feature of combining the input of four analysts.

Issues other than accuracy of recognition are also beginning to receive attention. One of the most informative of these concerns the manner by which tools were held, or prehended, throughout prehistory. Utilized tools exhibit wear not only on that portion that contacts a worked substance, but often also on the part that is grasped in the hand or held in a haft. Most researchers have traditionally not recorded prehensile traces, although lately some interest in them has been expressed. The study of prehension is not just an academic nicety, because prehension is a behavioral response to socioeconomic demands that can produce insight into issues such as the development of sedentary societies and the organization of hunter-gatherer mobility (Odell, 1994).

In fact, the most pertinent criticism of use-wear analysis that can be made today is that its emphasis on small samples and small problems and its lack of attention to anthropological theory have diluted its impact within archaeology. If use-wear analysis is to have a positive effect on the future development of archaeology, then it is going to have to approach larger-scale questions than it has previously. For scholars who are used to taking one–two hours per artifact for their observations or who are not used to applying their research to theoretical concerns, this problem may be insurmountable.

George H. Odell

See also EXPERIMENTAL ARCHAEOLOGY; SEMENOV, SERGEI ARISTARKHOVICH

Further Readings

Bamforth, D.B., Burns, G.R., and Woodman, C. (1990) Ambiguous use traces and blind test results: New data. Journal of Archaeological Science 17:413–430.

Grace, R. (1989) Interpreting the Function of Stone Tools: The Quantification and Computerisation of Micro-Wear Analysis. (BAR International Series 474). Oxford: British Archaeological Reports.

Hayden, B., ed. (1979) Lithic Use-Wear Analysis. New York: Academic.

Kamminga, J. (1982) Over the Edge: Functional Analysis of Australian Stone Tools. (Occasional Papers in Anthropology 12). St. Lucia: University of Queensland.

Keeley, L.H., (1980) Experimental Determination of Stone Tool Uses: A Microwear Analysis. Chicago: University of Chicago Press.

Keeley, L.H. and Newcomer, M.H. (1977) Microwear analysis of experimental flint tools: A test case. Journal of Archaeological Science 4:29–62.

Newcomer, M.H., Grace, R., and Unger-Hamilton, R.(1986) Investigating microwear polishes with blind tests. Journal of Archaeological Science 13:207–217.

Odell, G.H. (1994) Prehistoric hafting and mobility in the North American midcontinent: Examples from Illinois. Journal of Anthropological Archaeology 13:51–73.

Odell, G.H., and Odell-Vereecken, F. (1980) Verifying the reliability of lithic use-wear assessments by "blind tests": The low-power approach. Journal of Field Archaeology 7:87–120.

Owen, L.R., and Unrath, G., ed. (1986) Technical aspects of microwear studies on stone tools, part I. Early Man News 9–11.

Rees, D., Wilkinson, G.G., Grace, R., and Orton, C.R. (1991) An investigation of the fractal properties of flint microwear. Journal of Archaelogical Science 18:629–640.

Semenov, S.A. (1964) Prehistoric Technology. Trans. by M.W. Thompson. Bath, U.K.: Adams and Dart.

Tringham, R., Cooper, G., Odell, G., Voytek, B., and Whitman, A. (1974) Experimentation in the formation of edge damage: A new approach to lithic analysis. Journal of Field Archaeology 1:171–196.

U

V

Varve Analysis

Rhythmic accumulations of sediments forming distinctive laminae that can be used in dating. When the laminations arise because of annual variations in supply and type of sediment, a common occurrence in the geologic record, they are called *varves*. The potential of annually laminated sediments as a means of dating was first exploited by the Swedish geologist Gerard de Geer in the late nineteenth century. The name *varve* comes from the Swedish word *varv*, meaning a periodic repetition. Varves provide absolute ages when only one varve date is known. For still-active lakes, the top layer belongs to last year, thereby anchoring the chronology. Varve counting then gives the elapsed time in years. Whether the period is annual or some other length, one needs to know only the period for any rhythmite to be useful as a measure of absolute time. Varves have also provided absolute calibration of the radiocarbon time scale and for pollen stratigraphies.

The varve dating technique is based on variation in sediment deposition during an annual cycle. Commonly, finer particles or chemical precipitates may be deposited during the winter months, while coarser particles are deposited during the summer. The two layers combined represent an annual cycle of deposition. In Scandinavia, varve sequences go as far back as 13,000 years. The technique was initially developed in the Baltic region by de Geer, while in North America the work of Ernst Antevs from the 1920s to the 1940s is representative of early efforts to use varve chronologies.

The Quaternary rhythmites most extensively studied are those deposited in the pro-glacial lakes (i.e., located in front of a glacier or ice sheet) of northern Europe and North America during the last deglaciation 10,000 B.P. Generally, each varve couplet is from a few millimeters to a few centimeters in thickness. Suspended sediment consisting chiefly of silt and clay entered the lakes from streams fed by melting glaciers that coursed the land during spring and summer. The silt settled rapidly, but the clay remained in suspension, settling only gradually during fall and winter after melting had ceased and the surface of the lakes became frozen. The resumption of melting in the spring brought new coarse sediment, which settled rapidly, producing a sharp boundary on top of the older couplet.

The resulting laminations are normally easy to distinguish because the light-colored summer sediment alternates with the much darker winter laminae. Unfortunately, bioturbation (the churning of a sediment by organisms) and other phenomena often disturb the laminations in all but the deepest lakes. Nevertheless, varve chronologies have long provided a calibration for Late Quaternary events. Ca. 10,000 laminations have been recorded in a 5-m core from Elk Lake, Minnesota, thus extending varve chronology back to the onset of the Holocene in central North America (10,000 B.P.).

Varves can also occur in more-temperate climates. Sediment load, biomass accumulation, and chemical precipitation all tend to vary seasonally. If the resulting sediments are not reworked by bioturbation or current action, annual layering will be recorded. In some lakes, the resulting laminations are visible. In others, they are apparent only through analytical and microscopic study. In limestone regions, light-colored summer layers of calcium carbonate alternate with dark winter layers rich in humus. Many lakes precipitate carbonate only in the summer, when photosynthesis keeps carbon dioxide levels low and pH high. When one of the layers is rich in organic material, radiocarbon dating by accelerator mass spectrometry (AMS) is feasible.

In contrast to the clastic sedimentation in most temperate-zone lakes, the present-day sedimentation in Lake Zurich, Switzerland, is mostly biogenic and chemical, because flood-control dams have almost stopped fluvial sediment input into the lake since the beginning of the twentieth century. The varved sediments laid down in this lake are a response to an annual chemical and biologic cycle.

Annually laminated lake sediments from nonglacial contexts have been discovered since the 1980s in increasing abundance. Seasonality of sediment supply can be controlled by geologic, biologic, or cultural processes. Laminations may be clastic, calcareous, biogenic, or ferrogenic. Annually laminated sediments can provide data on climatic change, vegetation history, erosion rates, and environmental pollution. It should be noted that special field and laboratory techniques are required to study many of the particular properties of these varved sediments.

In a fashion similar to tree-ring dating, under ideal conditions varve sequences can be correlated among regional lakes, allowing a longer time span than available from a single lake. This correlation is facilitated when microfossils are present, permitting the development of a firm biostratigraphy, or when sufficient pollen grains are present to provide the material for AMS dating.

George R. Rapp Jr.

See also RADIOCARBON DATING

Further Readings

O'Sullivan, P. (1983) Annually-laminated lake sediments and the study of Quaternary environmental changes: A Review. Quaternary Science Reviews 1:245–313.

Renberg, I. (1981) Improved methods for sampling, photographing, and varve-counting of varved lake sediments. Boreas 10:255–258.

Wall Paintings, Conservation

First-aid treatment for wall paintings found in situ; techniques for removal of paintings destined for laboratory conservation. The aims of on-site conservation are to minimize the deterioration of objects during excavation and to ensure that as much as possible of the evidence contained in the objects is available for study and analysis. First-aid measures are employed to prevent rapid changes taking place when wall paintings are first exposed; longer-term measures are used to preserve them temporarily or permanently in situ. When the site is to be destroyed, or the paintings are particularly vulnerable, they may be removed for treatment in a conservation laboratory.

The term *wall painting* covers a wide range of decoration applied to both interior and exterior walls and to ceilings. The paint or pigment may be applied to a variety of different substrates but, most commonly, to some form of plaster. Wall paintings can be found in any state, from small numbers of scattered fragments to whole decorative schemes still in place on the wall. The larger and the more complete the wall painting, the greater the conservation challenge.

The construction of a wall painting involves a support (wall), ground (plaster), and pigment or paint. The wall may be made of any building material (e.g., wood, stone, mud brick), and the role of the ground is to provide a surface to take the paint. The ground may be crude or carefully prepared and applied; it may be lime plaster (calcium carbonate), gypsum plaster (calcium sulfate), or mud plaster; and there may be additives, such as plant material (to minimize shrinkage) or marble powder (to create decorative effects). Earth

pigments, such as iron oxides, and green earths are normally found, but some synthetic and organic pigments also occur; they may be mixed with a medium such as oil or egg to form a paint that adheres to the ground *(tempera),* or they may be applied to fresh lime plaster, which, in setting, attaches the pigments firmly to the surface *(fresco).*

Wall paintings are of archaeological interest because they say something about the quality, and sometimes the role, of the building or room, and they provide stylistic and technological information. The whole decorative scheme, the raw materials (plasters, fillers, pigments), and the methods of execution are all significant.

Aims of On-Site Conservation

Conservation aims to preserve evidence. The practice of conservation rests on five central principles: preservation of the integrity of the object; use of the least-invasive treatments; use of reversible treatments (although there are known limits to reversibility); preventive care; and documentation of object and treatment.

Although significant sites may themselves be conserved, on-site conservation is normally first-aid treatment applied to excavated moveable objects, which is followed by full assessment and further treatment in the conservation laboratory. Conservation of wall paintings, therefore, presents special problems, since, by their nature, the paintings are not strictly moveable. The treatment of wall paintings is influenced by the long-term provision for the site itself, as well as for the paintings. There are two main options: to leave the painting in situ and provide appropriate long-term protection or to remove it for treatment and storage or display elsewhere. Variations on these options involve leaving the painting in situ temporarily until removal can be organized or removing the painting to be treated in the laboratory before being replaced in situ. Because paintings present particular problems, treatment is usually carried out by a specialist conservator.

Practical and Ethical Issues

A wall painting is part of the structure of the building, and its removal affects the integrity of the architectural whole. Preservation in situ is the least-invasive approach to conservation, but it has implications in terms of the long-term care of the building and the site. When the site is under threat, removal may be the only way to save a painting, but it is a major intervention that is time consuming and expensive—and the start of a long program of conservation and reconstruction. After removal of the painting, the conservator may be faced with large quantities of painted plaster; unlike artifacts, such as ceramics, which can be dealt with selectively, each fragment requires attention, since it is a unique part of a much larger whole.

Thus, it may be difficult or impossible for the conservator to preserve the integrity of an excavated wall painting, and the conservation options may be invasive, though every effort is made to change both plaster and pigment as little as possible. Documentation of the painting records its appearance as found and its relationship to building and site; documentation of the on-site conservation treatment provides a basis for future care of the painting. As far as possible, all treatments are followed by continuous and well-monitored preventive care to minimize any further change.

Factors Affecting Condition

The behavior of the painting during burial is affected by the way it was constructed, by the quality of the raw materials used, and by the way in which they were applied. Any one of the components may have failed: The wall may have collapsed, or the plaster may have separated from the wall, or the pigments may have deteriorated. A common problem is the failure or demolition of the wall resulting in partial or total disintegration of the painting, so that it is found as fragments within the building. Where parts of the walls still stand, some of the painting may remain attached.

The history of the site and the burial conditions are also important. In some cases, the walls may have remained standing and exposed for a time before final collapse or demolition, so the painting may have been weathered before burial. Both wall and ground material are normally porous, so water, salts, and staining materials can enter the structure and be deposited in or on the paintings. The presence of decoration may not always be apparent, since soil and salts may obscure the surface completely. Where burial is shallow, frost may cause damage, and plant roots may cause cracking and erosion. In damp or, worse, acid conditions the plaster can be significantly softened.

Uncovering material on an excavation inevitably exposes it to a new combination of environmental factors (e.g., light, heat, oxygen, wind). Although most pigments used in archaeological wall paintings are not affected by light, some may be damaged. There is a tendency for salts to crystallize and obscure the surface and for accretions of all kinds to become harder once the surface is exposed. This poses a conservation problem, since accretions can become harder than the underlying painted surface, and their removal puts the decoration at risk. A related problem is that the soil around wall painting fragments may harden to the extent that excavation of the fragments becomes very difficult.

Conservation Processes

An important first step must be to try to establish how much of the wall painting remains and what condition it is in. It can be difficult to estimate the extent of the material when it first appears; the conservator's initial assessment will be based on the position and the condition of the visible areas of wall painting, as well as the soil conditions. The second step is to protect the paintings as soon as they are even partly exposed. A temporary overhead shelter (roof) is the best approach, or backfilling with soil or clean sand. In cool climates, black polyethylene sheet can be used for very short-term protection.

Preservation in Situ

The way in which preservation in situ is approached depends on the future of the site. The first type of in situ conservation usually involves reburial. This may be necessary until a decision is reached on long-term conservation measures, or it may be a permanent measure in itself. The painting must be covered to protect from weather and human interference, using a method that allows it to be readily relocated and that does not prevent the free passage of water through the soil. A common mistake is to place polyethylene sheet as a barrier directly over the surface of the paintings or fragments before reburial, but this is potentially damaging because condensation can form between the sheet and the paintings. Clean sand or well-sifted soil should be used in conjunction with a permeable sheet, such as plastic mosquito screening or, better, a geotextile (a textile specifically designed for long-term use in soils).

If there are plans to preserve the site and open it to visitors, the painting may be left on the wall, but this is problematic, since it is difficult to conserve paintings effectively if they are exposed in this way. Both painting and wall may need some cleaning and consolidation (though the use of consolidants in this situation is the subject of research and debate). If the painting is in poor condition, it may be removed from the wall, treated in a laboratory, and repositioned in situ. Whatever treatment is used, some form of permanent overhead shelter will be needed to protect the wall and the painting from extremes of temperature and from wind and rain—which will inevitably change the appearance of the site. It is particularly important to prevent water in the form of groundwater, rain, or condensation from reaching the wall or the surface of the painting, and both shelter and other modifications, such as improved drainage, need to be properly designed. The painting must be protected from vandalism, and it must be regularly monitored, so that any change in condition is detected as soon as possible. Obviously, this form of on-site conservation will involve not just conservators, but also a team including archaeologist, architect or engineer, and site custodians.

Removal

If the decision is made to reconstruct the fragments of a painting, the first stage is to remove them from the ground. If a site is to be destroyed, it may be necessary to remove paintings that remain attached to a wall. Unless the amounts of painting are small, removal from the site is the beginning of a long-term project that may involve a team of conservators, working over a considerable time, and require large areas of storage and working space. Once the painting has been reconstructed, it may require display space, too. Thus, unless the painting will be destroyed if left in situ, it is important to consider carefully whether there are adequate resources available for effective and long-term conservation.

The first stage of any removal process is to record the relationship of the painting to the remains of the building. When dealing with fragments, the superimposed layers must be meticulously recorded. Plans of walls and fragments can be made at reduced scale (e.g., 1:10), and these can be augmented by 1:1 tracings of individual groups of fragments in the ground.

Conservation on site involves preventing hardening of soil and salt deposits or cracking of fragments and damage to the painted surface; at the same time, it involves retaining the relationship between individual fragments to aid future reconstruction. Sometimes, fragments are strong enough to be uncovered and removed from the soil in the normal way, but it is important to assess their condition as they are exposed. Where they are lying face down, it is difficult to estimate the condition of the painted surface, and it is often difficult to establish how much material lies below and how closely packed adjacent fragments are.

The plaster may be so soft and cracked that normal excavation techniques may be ruled out. In such cases, the conservator resorts to the various support or strengthening methods described in field-conservation textbooks. There are two main ways of providing strength: by providing external support and by applying a consolidant (normally, a diluted adhesive material). The first method is preferable to the second, since it does not involve introducing any material directly into the painting or plaster. External support is provided either by gently sliding a rigid sheet (e.g., metal or plywood) beneath the fragment, or by retaining as much soil as possible around each fragment and lifting it in a block of soil, or by exposing the fragment and applying a jacket of supporting material. Where fragments are closely packed with little soil between them, it may be difficult to use the rigid-sheet or the soil-support methods. A close-fitting jacket of plaster of paris may provide enough support to allow a fragment to be released safely from the mass of other fragments. If this method is used, a protective covering (e.g., aluminum foil) is applied to the fragment to prevent the plaster of paris adhering to the surface.

Cracked fragments may disintegrate on being moved. Provided the painted surface is in good condition, a fine cloth or paper facing can be firmly attached over the surface, using a reliable, reversible adhesive, and the whole fragment given the additional support of a rigid jacket to hold it together during movement. The facing is intended to provide just enough strength to prevent damage to the surface and should remain in place for as short a time as possible.

The conservator will use the facing method on a larger scale to remove sheets of painting attached to a wall and to keep them whole as far as possible. The technique is described in texts on conservation of wall paintings. The surface is held together by attaching paper or cloth facings, then either the painted surface alone or the paint and some of the ground is removed from the wall. This is a specialist's task and requires careful planning and proper provision for aftercare. The facing material must have the required strength and stability; the adhesive must be reliably reversible; and the paintings must be taken to a laboratory for further treatment (notably, removal of the facing) as soon as possible.

Some cautious partial cleaning (using soft brushes or swabs of selected solvents) may be undertaken on site to establish condition, but full investigative cleaning requires laboratory conditions and equipment, such as microscopes; any wall painting removed from site is taken to a laboratory for cleaning as soon as possible, particularly if there is any danger of drying and hardening of surface deposits. Full reconstruction is also a major laboratory project, but routine joining of groups of fragments may be undertaken on site simply to retain the relationship of small pieces or to repair inevitable minor breaks. The main requirement is a conservation-grade reversible adhesive with known stable properties.

In practice, it is difficult to identify fragments needed for analysis until a later stage, since the full range of plasters and pigments may not be evident, and the part each fragment plays in the reconstruction is not yet known.

Preventive Care

Fragments of wall painting are surprisingly heavy and may be cracked and weak, so they should be handled as little as possible and then only with great care. It is helpful to use a padded box or tray to support and carry fragments. Whole sheets of plaster removed from a wall need their own supporting padded boards or trays constructed for the purpose.

Sturdy, portable wooden or plastic crates are needed for packing, storage, and transport (some types of fruit crate are very suitable). Fragments are laid flat in the crates, with plenty of good-quality (preferably acid-free) paper padding, polyethylene foam, or bubble pack between each layer. All containers are clearly labeled to indicate the contents.

Excavated wall paintings present special problems, and options for treatment and reconstruction need to be carefully evaluated before selecting the most appropriate method for their long-term conservation.

Elizabeth Pye

Further Readings

Cronyn, J.M. (1990) The Elements of Archaeological Conservation. London: Routledge.

Hodges, H.W.M., ed. (1987) In Situ Archaeological Conservation. Mexico City: Instituto Nacional de Antropologia e Historia Century City, CA: J. Paul Getty Trust.

Sease, C. (1994) A Conservation Manual for the Field Archaeologist, 3rd ed. Los Angeles: Institute of Archaeology, UCLA.

Watkinson, D., Neal, V., and Swain, H. (1998) First Aid for Finds, 2nd ed. London: UKIC/Rescue/Museum of London.

Watson, Patty Jo (1932–)

American archaeologist and anthropologist. Born on April 26, 1932, in Superior, Nebraska, Watson received her master's from the University of Chicago in 1956 and her doctorate in anthropology from the same institution three years later. After taking her degrees, she moved west, teaching anthropology at the University of Southern California and Los Angeles State University. Watson returned to the University Chicago as an archaeologist and research associate at the Oriental Institute (1964–1970), then was appointed assistant professor of anthropology at Washington University in St. Louis. She was named associate professor soon after and full professor in 1973. Watson is currently the Edward Mallinckrodt Distinguished University Professor. A Fellow of the American Anthropological Association and the American Association for the Advancement of Science, Watson has been the recipient of numerous awards from the National Science Foundation, the National Endowment for the Humanities, and the National Geographic Society.

Watson is known for her work in both New and Old World prehistory, ethnoarchaeology, and the origins of agriculture. She has worked in Kentucky and the southeastern United States, at Halafian sites in Turkey, and in the Zagros Mountains of Iran for her studies of the Palaeolithic/Neolithic transition. She is probably most well known, however, for two collaborative works with Steven A. LeBlanc and Charles L. Redman: *Explanation in Archaeology: An Explicitly Scientific Approach* and *Archaeological Explanation: The Scientific Method in Archaeology*. These books, classics of the New Archaeology movement of the 1960s and 1970s, outline an explicitly scientific model for archaeology, stating that the rigorous frameworks used to govern the creation of laws and theories in the hard sciences could also be applied to social sciences such as anthropology and archaeology. *Explanation in Archaeology* became a rallying point for anthropological archaeologists and remains one of the most important methodological works to come out of the New Archaeology movement.

Joseph J. Basile

See also NEW/PROCESSUAL ARCHAEOLOGY; REDMAN, CHARLES L.

Further Readings

Cowan, C.W. and Watson, P.J. (1992) The Origins of Agriculture: An International Perspective. Washington, D.C.: Smithsonian Institution Press.

Watson, P.J. (1979) Archaeological Ethnography in Western Iran. Tucson, AZ: University of Arizona Press.

Watson, P.J., LeBlanc, S.A., and Redman, C.L. (1971) Explanation in Archeology: An Explicitly Scientific Approach. New York: Columbia University Press.

Watson, P.J., LeBlanc, S.A., and Redman, C.L. (1984) Archeological Explanation: The Scientific Method in Archeology. New York: Columbia University Press.

Wheeler, Sir Robert Eric Mortimer (1890–1976)

British archaeologist. Also known as Mortimer Wheeler, this well-known scholar was a military man first, and, like General Augustus Pitt-Rivers, used his training and discipline to bring new rigor to archaeological field methodology. A student of archaeology at University College London, Wheeler entered the Army and served as an artillery major in France during the First World War. Upon his return, he worked in Wales at the National Museum (1920–1926) and then in London as lecturer in British archaeology at University College and honorary director of the Institute of Archaeology, which he founded. He resumed his military career during the Second World War as a lieutenant-colonel, leading troops in North Africa and Italy. While involved with government missions to India and Pakistan, Wheeler became fascinated with the antiquities of these regions and was named director general of archaeology, India, in 1944. He soon returned to Britain, where he was made professor of the archaeology of the Roman provinces at the University of London in 1948; he was professor of ancient history to the Royal Academy from 1965 until his death on July 22, 1976. He was knighted in 1952. Wheeler's 1955 autobiography, *Still Digging* describes his colorful life of adventure and discovery.

Wheeler is well known for his contributions in the area of field methodology. At the University of Wales, he had the opportunity to work on Roman sites and Iron Age hill forts. Wheeler would later dig the hill fort at Maiden Castle in Dorset (1934–1937); this excavation was such a paragon of rigorous technique and explicit methodology that it would have a lasting impact on archaeology. *Maiden Castle,* published in 1943, quickly became a guide for what came to be known as the *Wheeler method,* his system of excavating regularized trenches with balks and mapping and recording all significant features. The Wheeler method gained popularity throughout the West, then passed into Asia in 1943 when he brought his system of excavating with him to India and Pakistan. While Sir

John Marshall had already made significant discoveries along the Indus Valley, most notably at Harappa and Mohenjo-daro, as early as 1924, Wheeler brought new life to Indian archaeology. He set up an archaeological administration, reorganized museums, safeguarded sites and antiquities, and trained a new generation of Indian archaeologists in his exacting field methods. He succeeded Marshall at Harappa and Mohenjo-daro, was the first to truly connect prehistory and the Bronze Age in India to later historic periods, and brought Indian archaeology to the attention of the West through publications such as *Civilizations of the Indus Valley and Beyond* and *Early India and Pakistan.* He again outlined the Wheeler method in the now-classic *Archaeology from the Earth,* which introduced later generations to the importance of rigorous field methodology.

Joseph J. Basile

Further Readings

Clark, J.G.D. (1979) Sir Mortimer and Indian Archaeology. New Delhi: Archaeological Survey of India.

Wheeler, R.E.M. (1943) Maiden Castle, Dorset. (Reports of the Research Committee of the Society of Antiquaries of London 12). Oxford: University Press.

Wheeler, R.E.M. (1955) Archaeology from the Earth. Oxford: Clarendon.

Wheeler, R.E.M. (1955) Still Digging. London: M. Joseph/New York: Dutton.

Wheeler, R.E.M. (1966) Civilizations of the Indus Valley and Beyond. London: Thames and Hudson/New York: McGraw Hill.

Wheeler, R.E.M. (1968) Early India and Pakistan: To Ashoka, revised ed. London: Thames and Hudson/New York: Praeger.

Wheeler, R.E.M. (1976) My Archaeological Mission to India and Pakistan. London: Thames and Hudson.

Willey, Gordon Randolph (1913–)

American archaeologist and anthropologist. Born on March 7, 1913, in Chariton, Iowa, Willey was educated at the University of Arizona, where he received his bachelor's in 1935 and master's in 1936, and at Columbia University, where he earned his doctorate in 1942. He was an anthropologist with the Bureau of American Ethnology (1943–1950) and a professor of archaeology at Harvard University (1950–1987). Currently Professor Emeritus, he is also on the staff of Harvard's Peabody Museum. In his long career, Willey has received numerous honors, including the Order of the Quetzal of Guatemala, the Viking Fund Medal, the Gold Medal of the Archaeological Institute of America, the Huxley Medal of the Royal Anthropological Association, and honorary degrees from the University of Arizona, Harvard University, Cambridge University, and the University of New Mexico. He is a Fellow of the American Anthropological Association, the National Academy of Science, the London Society of Antiquaries, the American Philosophical Society, and the Royal Anthropological Institute of Great Britain and Ireland.

Willey is one of the most significant figures in American archaeology of the twentieth century. He was among the first to formulate explicit methodological frameworks in the New World, and his work is similar to the efforts of V. Gordon Childe in that it attempts to systematize the past instead of merely describe it. The groundbreaking 1941 article "An Interpretation of the Prehistory of the Eastern United States," (coauthored with James A. Ford), collected material from all over Eastern North America created a synthesis and chronological sequence for that region for the very first time. Willey and Ford's five-part scheme—Archaic, Burial Mound I (Early Woodland), Burial Mound II (Middle Woodland), Temple Mound I (Early Mississippian), and Temple Mound II (Late Mississippian)—is still in use today. In *Method and Theory in American Archaeology* (coauthored with Philip Phillips), the authors created a diffusionist model that presented Native American cultures as having persistent traits, which modify slowly to form traditions and diffuse to create chronological stages that Willey and Phillips called *horizons.* This work also saw the appearance of another important five-part chronological scheme—Lithic, Archaic, Formative, Classic, and Postclassic—also still in use. Willey pioneered settlement archaeology in the New World, as seen in *Prehistoric Settlement Patterns in the Virú Valley, Peru,* and has been an important historian of archaeology in America. *A History of American Archaeology* (coauthored with Jeremy A. Sabloff) is a standard work in the field.

Joseph J. Basile

See also FORD, JAMES ALFRED; SETTLEMENT ARCHAEOLOGY, THEORY

Further Readings

Daniel, G. (1989) The Pastmasters. New York: Thames and Hudson.

Ford, J.A. and Willey, G.R. (1941) An interpretation of the prehistory of the Eastern United States. American Anthropologist 43:325–363.

Willey, G.R. (1953) Prehistoric Settlement Patterns in the Virú Valley, Peru. (United States Bureau of American Ethnology 155). Washington, D.C.: U.S. Government Printing Office.

Willey, G.R., ed. (1956) Prehistoric Settlement Patterns in the New World. (Viking Fund Publications in Anthropology 23). New York: Wenner-Gren Foundation for Anthropological Research.

Willey, G.R. (1988) Portraits in American Archaeology: Remembrances of Some Distinguished Americanists. Albuquerque: University of New Mexico Press.

Willey, G.R. (1990) New World Archaeology and Culture History: Collected Essays and Articles. Albuquerque: University of New Mexico Press.

Willey, G.R. and Phillips, P. (1958) Method and Theory in American Archaeology. Chicago: University of Chicago Press.

Willey, G.R. and Sabloff, J.A. (1993) A History of American Archaeology, 3rd ed. New York: W.H. Freeman.

Wood (Waterlogged), Conservation

The stabilization and conservation of archaeological wood from marine, freshwater, waterlogged, and frozen conditions. *Archaeological wood* was defined in 1990 by Roger Rowell and Jamie Barbour as any wood that gives information about human development and human culture. It may include wood from shipwrecks and from wet or frozen archaeological sites. The term *waterlogged* indicates burial in water-saturated and anaerobic conditions that have protected the wood against decay fungi. Wood, many thousands of years old, has been preserved thus. A wooden trackway, the Sweet Track in Britain, was dated at ca. 4,000 B.C. by John Coles and his colleagues (1990), and wooden material from the Bay West site in Florida is dated at 4,500 B.C. by Barbara Purdy (1991). Although dry wood

is occasionally found in archaeological deposits, archaeological wood (along with other organic materials) is usually preserved only in waterlogged conditions—hence, its importance for the archaeologist.

Conservation means stabilization of the size and shape, as well as the condition, of the wood. Conservation includes all measures taken to protect wood, whether it has been disturbed, undisturbed, treated with chemicals, and the like. Conservation treatment should be reversible (i.e., it should be possible to return the object to the waterlogged condition for retreatment) and should interfere with or modify the wood only minimally. English Heritage has accepted a code of practice in which professional responsibilities for conservation are divided among archaeologists, wood specialists, biological specialists, conservators, and curators.

Conservation has the following phases: (1) pre-excavation planning; (2) excavation and maintenance; (3) on-site recording; (4) removal from site; (5) environmental recording and sampling; (6) sample retention; (7) pretreatment (passive storage, recording, sampling, analysis); (8) conservation treatment (stabilization, impregnation, drying); (9) posttreatment (conditioning, restoration, recording, analysis); (10) disposal or reburial; (11) curation and storage; and (12) display.

Archaeological wood is usually degraded. The cellulose component (rather than the lignin) of the wood is subject to loss, sometimes total, by bacterial degradation. The simplest indicators of the condition of waterlogged wood are (1) the *conventional density,* which is the oven dry weight divided by the volume occupied in the waterlogged condition (Clifford Cook and David Grattan have developed a simple nondestructive weighing technique to measure this); (2) the *pin test,* in which gentle probing is used to determine soft degraded regions; and (3) the *squeeze test,* in which cracks are indicated by exuding water on application of gentle pressure.

Generally speaking, the archaeologist is well advised to obtain the assistance of a qualified archaeological conservator before attempting the conservation of waterlogged wood. If wet wood is discovered, excavation should be halted temporarily until advice or assistance becomes available. Newly exposed wood is at risk from drying out and, if not kept wet, may shrink and crack. If sufficiently degraded, drying wood irreversibly collapses from the effects of capillary-tension forces. Waterlogged wood is also at risk from accelerated fungal decay once it is reexposed to an aerobic environment.

One safety hazard is that waterlogged wood has very occasionally been found to be host to dangerous microorganisms. Highly toxic fruiting structures of fungi have been encountered occasionally. Rubber gloves and particulate-filtering masks are advisable precautions to take when dealing with waterlogged wood on a routine basis. Fungal deterioration is avoided by using cool conditions and keeping stabilizing treatments rapid. During the course of field operations, excavated wood should be kept wet and cool; direct sunlight should be avoided.

Effective biocides, such as the commonly used sodium pentachlorophenate and isothiazolones, as tested by Andras Morgos and colleagues, or quaternary ammonium salts, as used by Per Hoffmann, are sometimes necessary. However, biocides may be dangerous both to human health and sometimes to the wood itself and are best avoided, if possible. It is usually not necessary to apply biocides immediately when wood is discovered, and they should be employed only following the advice of a conservator or scientist.

Two general techniques of stabilization are used: *impregnation* to replace all or part of the water and *controlled drying* to minimize or counter drying stresses.

Impregnation is usually carried out by soaking wood in aqueous solutions, although a number of techniques employ other solvents. Polyethylene glycol, PEG (Carbowax®) is the most commonly used impregnant. PEG is a water-soluble resin available in a wide range of molecular weights: PEG 200, 400, and 600 are viscous liquids; PEG 540 blend is a paste; PEG 3350 and 6000 are waxy solids. PEG is employed in many different ways according to the circumstances. Staff of the National Museum of Denmark—notably, Kirsten Jespersen—have demonstrated how impenetrable oak can be freeze-dried after being impregnated in PEG 3350 in t-butanol solution. Large structures of impenetrable oak are treated by a two-step procedure, developed by Hoffmann, with aqueous solutions of PEG 200 and PEG 3350. A freeze-drying procedure, developed by Cook and Grattan, using mixed aqueous solutions of PEG 200 and

PEG 3350 can be adjusted to suit various species and conditions of wood. PEG-treated wood can have a waxy or soapy feel. It may sweat in humid conditions (over 80 percent relative humidity), and it may become very dark if impregnation solutions are heated. Other impregnation treatments have employed many other resins (e.g., rosin or dammar; melamine formaldehyde condensation resins, such as Lyofix DML; in situ polymerizing resins, such as styrene/polyester). Techniques using various sugars offer many advantages and are gaining popularity. In most impregnation treatments, wood is soaked in a gradually increasing concentration of the resin until equilibrium is achieved. Spray application has been employed for very large objects.

After impregnation (and sometimes without any impregnation), the wood must be dried. Solvent drying (especially for delicate objects) and slow drying (i.e., drying in controlled conditions at a slow rate—a process often used for large wooden structures) may be used, but freeze-drying is now most commonly employed, particularly with PEG-impregnated wood. After the drying, the wood is conditioned (i.e., kept at ambient, or slightly above, relative humidity until stable).

Restoration is carried out next. In this phase, the wood may be cleaned (i.e., excess impregnant removed) and reshaped if necessary; broken pieces reassembled with adhesives, such as PVA emulsion or epoxy resin; and lacunae filled with suitable gap-filling compounds. Then follows preparation for display, recording, or storage. Lastly, the conservator prepares suitable mounts and recommends conditions for future usage.

There is a rapidly growing body of literature on the subject of waterlogged wood— (particularly in the publications of the International Council of Museums (ICOM) Working Group on Waterlogged Organic Archaeological Materials)—and those interested in conducting treatments are strongly advised to consult the recent literature.

David W. Grattan

Further Readings

Christensen, B.B. (1970) The Conservation of Waterlogged Wood in the National Museum of Denmark (Studies in Museum Technology 1). Copenhagen: National Museum of Denmark.

Coles, J.M. (1984) The Archaeology of Wetlands. Edinburgh: Edinburgh University Press.

Coles, J.M., Coles, B.J., and Dobson, M.J. (1990) Waterlogged Wood: The Recording, Sampling, Conservation, and Curation of Structural Wood. London: WARP/English Heritage.

Cook, C., and Grattan, D.W. (1991) A method of calculating the concentration of PEG for freeze-drying waterlogged wood. In Per Hoffmann (ed.): Proceedings of the Fourth ICOM Wet Organic Archaeological Materials Working Group Conference, pp. 239–252. Bremerhaven, Germany: Wet Organic Archaeological Materials Working Group, International Council of Museums (ICOM).

Grattan, D.W. (1982) A practical comparative study of treatments for waterlogged wood, part 1. Studies in Conservation 27:126–136.

Grattan, D.W., and Clarke, R. (1986) Conservation of waterlogged wood. In Colin Pearson (ed.): Conservation of Marine Archaeological Objects, pp. 164–206. London: Butterworths.

Morgos, A., Strigazzi, G., and Preuss, H. (1993) Microbiocides in sugar conservation of waterlogged archaeological wooden finds: The use of isothiazolones. Proceedings of the Fifth ICOM Wet Organic Archaeological Materials Working Group Conference, pp. 463–484. Bremerhaven, Germany: Wet Organic Archaeological Materials Working Group, International Council of Museums (ICOM).

Purdy, B.A. (1991) The Art and Archaeology of Florida's Wetlands. Boca Raton, FL: CRC.

Rowell, R.M., and Barbour, R.J., eds. (1990) Archaeological Wood: Properties, Chemistry, and Preservation. (Advances in Chemistry Series 225). Washington, D.C.: American Chemistry Society.

WPA Archaeology

Archaeological research conducted in the United States as part of federal work-relief programs implemented during the Great Depression of the 1930s. Between 1929 and 1941, unemployment in the United States rose to nearly 24 percent of the labor force. In an effort to create jobs and increase the purchasing power of people on relief, the federal government established programs that put people to work in a variety of areas, from constructing buildings and roads to painting murals and performing in musical events. An administrator of one of these programs approached the Smithsonian Institution asking about the potential of using workers on relief for archaeological projects. This suggestion was taken up in the summer of 1933, when Frank M. Setzler of the Smithsonian Institution and James A. Ford directed a crew of more than 100 people from the Federal Civil Works Administration in the excavation and restoration of a large site with numerous mounds and earthworks near Marksville, Louisiana (the site is now a park in the city of Marksville). Setzler, in writing about this inaugural event, reported that the administrators of the relief programs were pleased that more than 90 percent of the costs of an archaeological project went to labor. The names of the federal work-relief programs changed every few years, and the Federal Civil Works Administration (FCWA) was followed by the Federal Emergency Relief Administration (FERA) and, finally, by the Works Progress Administration (WPA). The phrase *WPA archaeology* is commonly used to refer to any of the research conducted as part of this succession of federal work-relief programs.

Encouraged by the success at Marksville, the Bureau of American Ethnology (part of the Smithsonian Institution) launched another eleven projects in Florida, Georgia, North Carolina, Tennessee, and California by the end of 1933. Such programs continued for another eight years (1933–1941), mostly in the southeastern states, and included excavation and survey, as well as laboratory projects. The projects were not limited to American prehistory. George Quimby describes his first experience on a WPA laboratory project, fittingly housed in the building of a failed bank, that analyzed materials from excavations conducted by the University of Michigan in Iraq.

Excavation Management

Efficiency on WPA projects was gauged in terms of the ratio of supervisors to laborers, and this became one of the chief frustrations of WPA work. On the Marksville excavation project, two archaeologists supervised more than 100 untrained laborers. This ratio was fairly typical in succeeding projects, although at the Peachtree Mound and Village site in North Carolina, Jesse D. Jennings appears to have been the only "nonrelief" supervisor (i.e., the only professional archaeologist) in charge of a crew of 100 people. Many of the people in the Southeast were accustomed to working in coal mines, where each individual performed a specific task, and they carried this organization over into archaeology. Each crew provided by the relief agencies was led by a foreman and might also include timekeepers, clerks, and a rod man for assistance in mapping. The host of other workers, although untrained in archaeology, nonetheless rapidly became specialized in the use of a particular tool, such as shovel, mattock, wheelbarrow, or trowel. Quimby describes work on a typical WPA field project. The deposit was first loosened by workers wielding pickaxes and mattocks. These men then stood aside while the loosened dirt was shoveled into the wheelbarrows by a second crew, and, finally, the "barrow man" pushed the material to the dump. If an archeological feature was encountered, the archaeologist took over, along with yet another group of laborers with experience in the use of trowels and brushes. The objective was to employ large numbers of people, and it mattered little that perhaps as much as two-thirds of the crew might be standing around idle at any one time during the process of the excavation. Crew members were also put to a variety of other tasks, including building photo towers out of saplings held together by wire and nails and constructing a "field house" from scavenged logs and planks for the night watchman. Some field houses also included a clay fireplace.

This somewhat ungainly organization worked relatively well on excavation and laboratory projects but proved nearly impossible on surveys. Archaeological surveys were hampered by additional bureaucratic obstacles, as recounted by Robert Wauchope of his two field years (1938–1940) spent in surveying portions of northern Georgia. Since there were no resources for field camps, the field crew had to be transported each morning from town over dirt roads to the survey location. Wauchope was also obligated to employ a new crew every time he crossed over into a new county, which made it next to impossible to develop an experienced crew. Other archaeologists encountered this difficulty in a different form: in some areas, relief workers were organized in shifts of twenty each, and each shift worked two days a week, apparently to bring more unemployed people into the programs. Over the course of a week, the archaeologists might face as many as three different sets of workers.

Although WPA archaeology led to considerable advances in archaeology, the program was also beset with serious problems related to the supervision of untrained personnel (which was inadequate) and the lack of overall organization (which was nonexistent from an archaeological perspective). The ratio of one archaeologist to fifty untrained workers was more than ten times higher than that commonly used in non-WPA projects of the time. Wauchope complained that the system bred false values and protested that archaeologists "should not have to choose between two evils: either failing to employ the needy and, incidently, not getting archaeology done at all, or employing too many and getting it done in a slovenly way" (Wauchope 1966:vii). A related problem was that the government subsidy extended only to covering the cost of labor, and the "sponsor" was responsible for equipment, supplies, facilities and, more important, the preparation of the written reports. A large number of reports did get written, and with beneficial influence on the growth of the discipline, but, for a number of other projects, the field notes and artifact collections were simply turned over to the National Museum (part of the Smithsonian Institution) for curation with no provisions being made for reporting. In 1944, growing concern among archaeologists led the Society for American Archaeology to form a special planning committee to review the situation. The committee, and the discipline at large, recognized that the scientific success of large archaeology projects rested heavily on good management. It was against this background that several scientific societies joined in 1945 to form the Committee for the Recovery of Archaeological Remains, which was delegated to deal with the federal government in developing salvage archaeology programs following the end of the Second World War.

Contributions to Method, Theory, and Professional Training

The short decade of WPA archaeology contributed substantially to the growth of American archaeology, much of it deriving from the sheer volume of data that became available as the fieldwork commenced. For the first time, American archaeologists had the labor needed to excavate sites at a grand scale comparable in coverage to what had previously been obtained only in the Middle East and Mediterranean areas. Although written reports did not begin to appear until the next decade, Quimby reports that WPA archaeologists regularly exchanged data by letter, on visits to each other's sites, and at meetings of the newly formed Southeastern Archaeological Conference.

An important innovation in method and theory was Ford's combination of seriation and stratigraphic sequences as tools for constructing regional chronological sequences. Ford borrowed Leslie Spier's procedure, employed in the study of ruins in the American Southwest, of calculating relative frequencies of pottery types by stratigraphic levels. By comparing frequencies of sherd types, Ford was able to match long stratigraphic sequences from excavated sites to each other and to surface collections made at unexcavated sites. The stratigraphic relationships imbedded in the seriations provided an independent check of the chronological validity of the seriations. This remains an important archaeological method (and is one of the few methods that was developed largely by archaeologists rather than borrowed from another discipline) and was the only widely applicable procedure for formulating regional chronologies until the development of radiocarbon dating in the 1960s. An example of Ford's application of seriation is found in *Archaeological Survey in the Lower Mississippi Alluvial Valley, 1940–1947* (Phillips et al. 1951).

This advance in method, coupled with copious data from numerous sites, laid the ground for the first archaeological syntheses of the Southeast. James B. Griffin's work in standardizing the definitions of ceramic types for the eastern and midwestern states was also instrumental in this regard. Among the regional syntheses based on WPA archaeology were Ford and Gordon R. Willey's article "An Interpretation of the Prehistory of the Eastern United States" and Griffin's book *Cultural Change and Continuity in Eastern United States Archaeology*.

WPA archaeology was also the training ground for a number of young archaeologists who later gained prominence in the discipline. In addition to Ford, Griffin, Quimby, Wauchope, and Willey mentioned above, they included James R. Caldwell, Madeline D. Kneberg, Thomas M.N. Lewis, Alex D. Krieger, Albert Spaulding, and William S. Webb. Quimby provides a participant-observer description of WPA archaeology in his 1979 article, and, although he refers nostalgically to the WPA days as a Golden Era for archaeologists, the description is balanced by a consideration of the shortcomings and difficulties of WPA archaeology as well. The preface of Wauchope's *Archaeological Survey of Northern Georgia* includes a more negative, but nonetheless equally thoughtful, critique.

Glen Eugene Rice

See also CULTURAL RESOURCE MANAGEMENT (CRM); FORD, JAMES ALFRED; SALVAGE/RESCUE ARCHAEOLOGY; SERIATION; SPAULDING, ALBERT CLANTON; WILLEY, GORDON RANDOLPH

Further Readings

Ford, J.A. and Willey, G.R. (1941) An interpretation of the prehistory of the eastern United States. American Anthropologist 43:325–363.

Griffin, J.B. (1946) Cultural Change and Continuity in Eastern United States Archaeology. (Robert S. Peabody Foundation for Archaeology Papers 3:37). Andover, MA: Robert S. Peabody Foundation for Archaeology.

Phillips, P. Ford, J.A., and Griffin, J.B. (1951) Archaeological Survey in the Lower Mississippi Alluvial Valley, 1940–47. (Papers of the Peabody Museum of American Archaeology and Ethnology 25). Cambridge, MA: Peabody Museum of American Archaeology and Ethnology, Harvard University.

Quimby, G.I. (1979) A brief history of WPA archaeology. In W. Goldschmidt (ed.): The Uses of Anthropology, pp. 110–123. (Special Publication of the American Anthropological Association 11). Washington, D.C.: American Anthropological Association.

Stoltman, J.B. (1973) The southeastern United States. In J.E. Fitting (ed.): The Development of North American Archaeology, pp. 117–150. University Park: Pennsylvania State University Press.

Wauchope, R. (1966) Archaeological Survey of Northern Georgia. (Memoirs of the Society for American Archaeology 21). American Antiquity 31(5):part 2. Salt Lake City: Society for American Archaeology.

X-Ray Diffraction (XRD) Analysis

The primary method available for identifying the mineral and metal phases present in a material (i.e., the method identifies the chemical compounds present rather than determine the concentrations of the constituent elements).

The sample to be analyzed is bombarded with a beam of monochromatic X rays (i.e., X rays with a sharply defined wavelength). The X rays are diffracted from the successive layers of atoms in the crystal lattice, and diffraction peaks occur at those angles, given by Bragg's Law (see ELECTRON-PROBE MICROANALYSIS), at which the contributions from successive layers are in phase. Thus, a crystalline sample will produce a series of X-ray diffraction peaks at angles that are determined by the spacings between the crystal lattice layers of its constituent minerals or metals. This pattern of lattice spacings then provides the basis for identifying the mineral or metal phases present.

For the XRD analysis of archaeological materials, the *powder diffraction method* is normally employed, using either a diffraction camera or a diffractometer. With the *diffraction-camera method,* a pinhead-size sample is mounted on the axis of the cylindrical X-ray camera, around the inside of which is wrapped a photographic film. The beam of monochromatic X rays is diffracted from the sample as it is rotated on its axis, with each lattice spacing producing a pair of arcs on the film. From measurement of the distances between pairs of arcs, the associated lattice spacings can be calculated, and from appropriate tables of lattice spacings, the crystalline phases present in the sample can be identified. The degree of blackening

of the arcs depends on the intensity of the diffracted X rays; hence, it provides some indication of the concentrations of the associated mineral or metal phases.

With the *diffractometer method,* a powdered sample is either placed in a shallow tray or spread over the surface of a glass microscope slide. The beam of monochromatic X rays is diffracted from the surface of the sample as the tray or slide is rotated with respect to the X-ray beam. The diffracted X rays are detected with a proportional counter to provide a plot of X-ray intensity versus angle between the X-ray beam and the sample surface. The associated lattice spacings can then be calculated from these angles, and the crystalline phases present in the sample identified. The recorded peak heights again provide some indication of the concentrations of these phases. Although the diffractometer method requires significantly larger samples than the camera method, it is the preferred method for estimating the concentrations of the different crystalline phases present.

A particular feature of XRD analysis, especially in the camera mode, is that very small samples are required, so that the technique can be regarded as virtually nondestructive. The method has been used extensively in the identification of precious and semiprecious stones, including a major program for the identification of the wide range of minerals (hematite, quartz), rock types (greenstone, limestone), and synthetic materials (faience, ceramic) used for Near Eastern cylinder seals (Collon 1989; Sax 1991). It has also been used in combination with X-ray fluorescence (XRF) analysis and electron-probe microanalysis for the identification of mineral pigments on wall paintings and opacifiers in glasses and glazes (Rooksby 1962).

A further important application of XRD analysis has been in the investigation of the various types of surface decoration applied to metals, including the range of metal sulfides employed for the black inlaid niello used to decorate nonferrous metals (La Niece 1983) and the different methods employed for the tinning of the surfaces of bronzes (Meeks 1986). The method is also invaluable for identifying different metal corrosion products, which can provide information on both burial environments and conservation requirements.

XRD has only very limited application in the identification of the rock types used for stone artifacts, such as tools and weapons, since this depends critically on the shape, size, arrangement, and concentration of the different mineral phases, and the identification of the minerals present by itself is of limited value. Thus, for the identification of rock types, optical petrography is the preferred technique.

However, XRD does have an important role in the identification of the high-temperature phases (e.g., wollastonite, anorthite, diopside, mullite) formed during the firing of pottery, since these phases are normally too fine grained to be identified by optical petrography. On the basis of the high-temperature phases present, it is normally possible to estimate the firing temperatures employed in the production of the pottery (Maggetti 1982; Echallier and Mery 1992). The method is particularly powerful in the case of pottery made from calcareous clays.

Michael S. Tite

See also ELECTRON-PROBE MICROANALYSIS; X-RAY FLUORESCENCE (XRF) ANALYSIS

Further Readings

Collon, D. (1989) Materials and techniques of ancient Near Eastern cylinder seals. In T. Hackens and G. Moucharte (eds.): Technology and Analysis of Ancient Gemstones, pp. 11–19. (PACT 23). Strasbourg: Council of Europe.

Echallier, J.C., and Mery S. (1992) L'evolution mineralogique et physico-chimique des pates calcaires au cours de la cuisson: experimentation en laboratoire et application archeologique. In S. Mery (ed.): Sciences de la Terre et Ceramiques Archeologiques: Experimentations, Applications, pp. 87–120. (Documents et Travaux IGAL 16). Cergy-Pontoise: Centre Polytechnique Saint-Louis.

La Niece, S. (1983) Niello: An historical and technical survey. Antiquaries Journal 58:279–297.

Maggetti, M. (1982) Phase analysis and its significance for technology and origin. In J.S. Olin and A.D. Franklin (eds.): Archaeological Ceramics, pp. 121–133. Washington, D.C.: Smithsonian Institution Press.

Meeks, N.D. (1986) Tin-rich surfaces on bronze: Some experimental and archaeological considerations. Archaeometry 28:133–162.

Rooksby, H.P. (1962) Opacifiers in opal glasses through the ages. GEC Journal of Science and Technology 29:20–26.

Sax, M. (1991) The composition of the materials of first millennium B.C. cylinder seals from western Asia. In P. Budd, B. Chapman, C. Jackson, R. Janaway, and B. Ottaway (eds.): Archaeological Sciences 1989, pp. 104–114. (Oxbow Monograph 9). Oxford: Oxbow.

X-Ray Fluorescence (XRF) Analysis

A method available for the determination of the bulk elemental composition of inorganic materials. The sample to be analyzed is irradiated with primary X rays from a high-voltage X-ray tube. These primary X rays excite electrons from the inner energy levels of the constituent atoms, and, when these vacant energy levels are refilled by outer electrons, secondary, or fluorescent, X rays are emitted. The energies, or wavelengths, of these fluorescent X rays are characteristic of the elements excited and, hence, provide the basis for the identifying the elements present in the sample. Further, the intensity or number of the X rays at these energies provide a measure of the concentrations of the corresponding elements present in the sample.

One method of analysis is to detect the fluorescent X rays using a semiconductor crystal (energy dispersive spectrometer, or EDS), which simultaneously determines both energies and intensities of all of the X rays. Alternatively, the fluorescent X rays are separated into their constituent wavelengths by diffraction using a suitable crystal (wavelength dispersive spectrometer, or WDS) and are then sequentially detected, and their intensities determined, with a proportional counter. EDS analysis, is extremely rapid in operation and can be used for either qualitative or quantitative analysis, whereas WDS analysis is much slower in operation but can achieve higher accuracy and lower detection limits and is, therefore, normally used only for quantitative analysis. For quantitative analysis, the conversion from X-ray intensities to elemental concentrations is achieved through a combination of reference standards of known composition and theoretical calculation to take account of the sample-matrix effects rising from major differences in composition.

A major advantage of XRF analysis is its ability to provide direct nondestructive analysis of an archaeological artifact without the need for prior removal of a small sample. However, analysis in the nondestructive mode places a number of restrictions on the applicability of the method. Because of the short range of X rays, the analysis relates only to a thin surface layer (20–200 µm, depending on the composition of the material and the element being analyzed), which may not be representative of the bulk. Further, unless the artifact is small enough to be accommodated in a vacuum chamber, light elements, such as sodium, magnesium, aluminum, and silicon, cannot be detected because the associated X rays are absorbed by air, potassium (atomic number 19) normally being the lightest element detectable.

An alternative method of using XRF analysis is to remove, first, a small sample (typically 100 mg) from the artifact. This powdered sample is then mixed with a suitable flux, typically lithium tetraborate, and fused to form a homogeneous pellet. These pellets can be then be accommodated within a vacuum chamber so that, in conjunction with an automatic sample changer, a rapid throughput of fully quantitative analyses for all elements from sodium (atomic number 11) upward can be achieved.

In its nondestructive mode, XRF has been used extensively for the analysis of nonferrous metals (i.e., gold, silver, copper and its alloys), since, for these elements, measurement can be made in air. Thus, XRF provides the primary technique for the qualitative identification of the different nonferrous metals and alloys used in antiquity. The method has also been widely used for the quantitative analysis of gold and silver artifacts, such as Dark Age (i.e., post-Roman) jewelry (Hawkes et al. 1966) and Roman silver plate (Hughes and Hall 1979), and for the investigation of the debasement of coinage, including Celtic gold coins (Cowell 1992) and Roman silver coins (Walker 1980).

The principal problem associated with the method is that the analyses are not always fully representative of the bulk composition, both because of surface corrosion in the case of copper and silver alloys and because of surface enrichment in the case of gold. Therefore, for fully quantitative analyses, it is frequently necessary to remove a thin corroded or enriched surface layer. Typically, the surface of the coin or piece of jewelry is first cleaned, then analyzed; lightly abraded and reanalyzed; the sequence of abrasion and reanalysis continuing until consecutive analyses yield the same compositions. Such a procedure is no longer strictly nondestructive and is time consuming. Therefore, it is now frequently decided that the removal of a small drilling, which immediately provides an analysis of the core of the artifact, is preferable to abrasion of the surface. Although this drilling could be analyzed by XRF, analysis is normally undertaken using an electron microprobe.

XRF, in its nondestructive mode operating in air, is of limited use for the analysis of pottery or glass, since many of the light elements of interest (sodium, magnesium, aluminum, and silica) cannot be detected. However, the method can be used qualitatively to identify the colorants (e.g., copper, cobalt, manganese, iron) added to glasses and glazes and, as in the case of the cobalt blue used in Chinese porcelain (Young 1956) and in Egyptian glass (Kaczmarczyk 1986), to infer the form in which the colorant was added. Similarly, XRF can be used in combination with X-ray diffraction (XRD) analysis for the identification of the mineral pigments used, for example, on wall paintings (Cesareo et al. 1972) and stone sculpture.

If a sample can be removed from the object, the principle use of XRF has been for the analysis of pottery and stone artifacts in provenance studies in which the major-, minor- and trace-element concentration patterns provide "fingerprints" for distinguishing between pottery from different production centers (Picon et al. 1971) and stone from different geological sources. In the latter case, a recent application has been the investigation of the source and the mode of transport of the Stonehenge bluestones (Thorpe et al. 1991). In contrast, when samples are taken from metal artifacts, XRF is only rarely used. Instead, the samples are normally analyzed either directly on the drilling, using an electron microprobe, or after solution in acid, using, for example, inductively coupled plasma–atomic emission spectrometry or atomic absorption (AA) spectrometry.

Michael S. Tite

See also ATOMIC ABSORPTION (AA) SPECTROMETRY; INDUCTIVELY COUPLED PLASMA–ATOMIC EMISSION SPECTROMETRY; X-RAY DIFFRACTION (XRD) ANALYSIS

Further Readings

Cesareo, R., Frazzoli, F.V., Mancini, C., Sciuti, S., Marabelli, M., Mora, P., Rotondi, P., and Urbani, G. (1972) Nondestructive analysis of chemical elements in paintings and enamels. Archaeometry 14:65–78.

Cowell, M.R. (1992) An analytical survey of the British Celtic gold coinage. In M. Mays, (ed.): Celtic Coinage: Britain and Beyond, pp. 207–233. (BAR British Series 222). Oxford: British Archaeological Reports.

Hawkes, S.C., Merrick, J.M., and Metcalf, D.M. (1966) X-ray fluorescent analysis of some Dark Age coins and jewelry. Archaeometry 9:98–138.

Hughes, M.J., and Hall, J.A. (1979) XRF analysis of late Roman and Sassanian silver plate. Journal of Archaeological Science 6:321–344.

Kaczmarczyk, A. (1986) The source of cobalt in ancient Egyptian pigments. In J.S. Olin and M.J. Blackman (eds.): Proceedings of the Twenty-Fourth International Archaeometry Symposium, pp. 369–376. Washington, D.C.: Smithsonian Institution Press.

Picon, M., Vichy, M., and Meille, E. (1971) Composition of the Lezoux, Lyon, and Arezzo Samian ware. Archaeometry 13:191–208.

Thorpe, R.S., Williams-Thorpe, O., Jenkins, D.G., and Watson, J.S. (1991) The geological sources and transport of the bluestones of Stonehenge, Wiltshire, UK. Proceedings of the Prehistoric Society 57(2):103–157.

Walker, D.R. (1980) The silver contents of the Roman Republican coinage. In D.M. Metcalfe and W.A. Oddy (eds.): Metallurgy in Numismatics, vol. 1, pp. 55–72. (Royal Numismatic Society Special Publication 13). London: Royal Numismatic Society.

Young, S.A. (1956) An analysis of Chinese blue-and-white. Oriental Art 2:43–47.

Z

Zeuner, Frederick Everard (1905–1963)

German-born British geologist, paleontologist, and environmental archaeologist. Born on March 8, 1905, in Berlin, Zeuner was educated at the Universities of Berlin, Tübingen, and Breslau, where he received his doctorate in 1927. A pioneer in the application of geological and environmental sciences to the field of archaeology, Zeuner moved from Breslau to Freiburg, where he was a lecturer in geology and paleontology. After serving as a research associate in paleontology at the British Museum in 1934, Zeuner resolved to stay in Britain and was made a lecturer in geochronology at the Institute of Archaeology of the University of London. In 1946, he was named professor of environmental archaeology at the University of London, a post he held until his death in 1963. Zeuner was the recipient of numerous honors, including foreign memberships in Istituto Italiana di Paleontologia, Istituto Italiana di Preistoria, and the Anthropologische Gesellschaft (Vienna) and an honorary doctorate from the University of London. He died in London on November 5, 1963.

A geologist by training, Zeuner made contributions in the field of archaeological methodology in his utilization of advances in geochronology and environmental sciences for the study of faunal remains, ancient soils, and paleoclimates. He was among the first to recognize the importance of Willard F. Libby's radiocarbon discoveries and pioneered the use of the radiocarbon dating method on the carbonized remains of paleobotanical material recovered from prehistoric sites. Zeuner's *Dating the Past: An Introduction to Geochronology,* published in 1946, was one of the first syntheses describing the advances and applications of geochronological dating methods and introduced many archaeologists to the importance of these new developments. He was also an important figure in the field of paleoclimatology, analyzing ancient soils for the geological and palynological clues they contained, as archaeologists began to follow the lead of figures such as Grahame Clark in their attempts to reconstruct the ancient environment. His work with faunal remains from prehistoric sites led to his *A History of Domesticated Animals,* an important study detailing the uses of changes in bone morphology in following the development of domesticated animals in the archaeological record.

Joseph J. Basile

See also ZOOARCHAEOLOGY

Further Readings

Zeuner, F.E. (1956) Bones for the Archaeologist. London: Phoenix House.

Zeuner, F.E. (1958) Dating the Past: An Introduction to Geochronology, 4th ed. London: Methuen/New York: Hafner.

Zeuner, F.E. (1959) The Pleistocene Period: Its Climate, Chronology, and Faunal Successions. London: Hutchinson Scientific & Technical.

Zeuner, F.E. (1963) A History of Domesticated Animals. London: Hutchinson/New York: Harper & Row.

Zooarchaeology

The study and interpretation of nonhuman animal remains from archaeological sites. Other terms used are faunal analysis, archaeozoology, paleoethnozoology, and osteoarchaeology. *Faunal analysis* is the most general of these, designating the study of the vestiges of dead nonhuman animals from any past depositional environment no matter how old or how formed. Thus, those who study naturally deposited fossils (i.e., those who consider themselves to be doing *paleontology*), also carry out faunal analyses. *Archaeozoology*, largely synonymous with zooarchaeology, is a term widely employed outside of the United States, Canada, and Great Britain. Practitioners tend to come from zoology or veterinary medicine backgrounds rather than have their first training in archaeology, as is more usual with those who consider themselves to be zooarchaeologists. As a result, archaeozoological studies may emphasize biology-based and evolutionary-based interpretations more than the culturally oriented ones favored by zooarchaeologists. *Paleoethnozoology* refers to the study of how humans interacted with nonhuman animals in the past. Sources of information may be iconographic, textual, architectural, and artifactual, as well as faunal. Archaeozoologists and zooarchaeologists are increasingly employing such sources as aids to the interpretation of faunal remains. Most of these investigators would agree that they are concerned with the role that nonhuman animals played in human societies, although few actually use the term paleoethnozoology. Finally, *osteoarchaeology* comprises the study of bones and teeth from archaeological sites. As such, it includes parts of the domains of both zooarchaeology and *physical anthropology*, dealing as it does with all human and nonhuman animals with endoskeletons (i.e., vertebrates). In contrast, animals with exoskeletons (i.e., invertebrates, such as molluscs and insects) also form part of the domains of zooarchaeology, archaeozoology, faunal analysis, paleoethnozoology, and paleontology.

Zooarchaeology, Taphonomy, and Early Hominids

The practice of zooarchaeology and related fields involves a core series of procedures carried out within the context of particular problems or questions defined by the investigator. These procedures include the preparation, identification, characterization, and documentation of faunal remains and the presentation and interpretation of data so generated. Affecting the nature of the faunal corpus, but beyond the control of the faunal analyst, are taphonomic processes and often the character of the areas excavated and the types of recovery procedures used. Of these, *taphonomy*, (i.e., "the laws of burial" or what happens as organisms pass from the biosphere into the lithosphere) has become a subject of major concern in both paleontology and zooarchaeology. The basic question asked is: "How did the bones (or other faunal remains) get to be distributed and modified the way they are?" To the extent that an investigator is trying to reconstruct the nature of past animal populations and communities, it is necessary to strip away any taphonomic overprint, as well as other "biases" resulting from area excavated and from recovery. This is increasingly seen as a futile exercise, however, and the focus has turned to controlled comparisons of assemblages and to evaluating and explaining the similarities and differences between them, often using models based on observations of what are thought might be modern analogs. Furthermore, in the archaeological context, as taphonomic processes are often cultural in origin, they form important subjects for study in their own right.

Given the vast domain of study (i.e., hominid-nonhuman animal relations over three million or more years), zooarchaeologists tend to specialize in both a time period and an area of the world. One major focus of activity has been in sub-Saharan Africa, and in other areas with appropriately ancient remains, where investigators are concerned with how hominids from the end of the Pliocene to the last glacial maximum exploited various animal taxa. On a continuum from scavenging all animal resources to hunting all such resources, where did a particular hominid population fall? Are there changes through time, trends through space, or variability by season of the year or by exploited taxon in hominid utilization of scavenged as opposed to hunted animals? Were there significant changes in faunal-exploitation practices with the advent of anatomically modern humans? To what degree were various hominid populations reacting to opportunities presented as opposed to planning the food quest? And what does all of this say about human evolution in terms of changes in physical structure, behavior, and the interplay between the two?

Investigation of these and related questions has been stimulated by iconoclastic tracts from Lewis R. Binford, the quiet questioning by Charles K. Brain of Raymond A. Dart's concept of an *osteodontokeratic culture,* and an increasing concern with taphonomy and paleoecology in vertebrate paleontology as exemplified by the work of Anna K. Behrensmeyer and Nanna Noe-Nygaard. Discarding the often implicit assumption that an association of bones, stone tools, and sometimes hominid fossils indicates hunting—or even precise contemporaneity of one class of evidence with the others—has led not only to the detailed study (and restudy) of the bone remains from ancient hominid localities, but also to the documentation of modern bone accumulations and the means by which they form. Thus, researchers have examined the scavenging behaviors and signatures of hyenas, porcupines, and other bone accumulators, as well as the distributions of "natural" deaths and carnivore kills over the landscape. They have documented how exposed carcasses become skeletons, the sequence in which the different bones of the skeleton disarticulate, how these bones come to be scattered varying distances from their original location, and how bones might enter the archaeological record. Investigators have recorded variation in bone mass, density, and marrow content to try to account for differential fragmentation and preservation, and, for the same purpose, they have studied the effects of exposure and weathering on bones and teeth. They have examined scratches on ancient bones to determine if these were created by stone tools or by trampling under the hoofs of animals and tried to replicate such marks on fresh bone under controlled conditions. And they have studied the food acquisition, transport, preparation, and sharing behaviors of modern hunters, both human and nonhuman, in different parts of the world.

One intriguing aspect of this middle-range research—actualistic, experimental, and ethnoarchaeological—is that the resulting observations made in the present for the purpose of interpreting the past, along with the study and restudy of a few key archaeological assemblages, have generated a disproportionately large and frequently impassioned literature, with the relatively few investigators sometimes seeming to speak past one another to address their (mis)conceptions of what others have written and to advance their own often entrenched points of view. In spite of this, however, zooarchaeology has benefited greatly from the questioning of cherished and often implicit assumptions about site-formation processes and hominid behavior. This is true not only for the early periods of hominid existence, but for the later ones as well.

Zooarchaeology and the Study of Holocene Faunas

The domain of study of the vast majority of those who consider themselves zooarchaeologists begins with the end of the last glacial maximum when the world's faunas had become essentially "modern." As a result, collections of endo- and exoskeletons that have been assembled since the 19th century are essential to the field, serving as the basis for the comparative morphological studies that provide the foundation for analysis of Holocene (10,000 B.P. to the present) faunas. Much of the best comparative work has been accomplished by researchers in Europe, where there is a more than 100-year tradition of archaeozoological investigations beginning with analyses of the bone remains from "Swiss Lake Dwelling" sites that were published by Ludwig Rütimeyer (1825–1895) in the early 1860s. A traditional field of investigation, particularly there and in western Asia, centers on the exploitation of domestic animals, with the origins and course of animal domestication being a topic of abiding interest and continuing research. More recently, other parts of the world, including East Asia, South Asia, Africa, and highland South America, have begun to provide data that suggest independent domestication of specific animals in those areas as well.

Increasingly, faunal remains are being analyzed in conjunction with other archaeological materials to provide insight into a variety of cultural practices in both complex and less-complex societies. One topic of interest is seasonality in the use of resources and in the occupation of sites, the two not necessarily congruent. Some animals are available to be hunted or gathered only during certain parts of the year, obvious examples being certain species of birds, fish, and even mammals that are known to be migratory today. The presence of their remains in archaeological sites suggests occupation at least during those seasons. Some animals, however, may be available in an area year-round but be hunted only seasonally. Identification of patterned kill-off can provide clues to such activity as, for example, in those mammals in which age at death, especially for younger individuals, can be determined from the state of eruption and wear of teeth or from state of fusion of the long bones. If only certain age grades are represented and not others, then seasonal kill-off could be a factor. This line of reasoning was used by Tony Legge and Peter Rowley-Conwy in their analysis of gazelle remains from Epipaleolithic levels at the site of Abu Hureyra in Syria. They suggested that gazelles were exploited heavily during the birthing season in April and May, a hypothesis that has subsequently received support from studies of incremental structures in the cementum of gazelle teeth recovered from the site.

Bones, teeth, and exoskeletons are modified throughout the life of the animal through remodeling or through the apposition of new organic matter with embedded mineral (increments). The microstructure of these incrementally added hard parts often varies in its optical properties because of structural differences resulting from seasonal changes in quality and availability of food or in aspects of the environment that affect the metabolism of the animal. Based on comparison with known standards, characteristics of the last (outer) increment can sometimes tell the investigator at what season deposition of that "growth zone" was interrupted by death. Although reading incremental structures is not always straightforward and the necessary background research and preparation of samples is time consuming, this technique is being employed successfully for various species of mammals, fish, and molluscs. Furthermore, it can be used not only for determining season of death, but also for ascertaining age at death, a purpose for which it has been employed for many years in wildlife-management and fisheries research.

Age at death or kill-off can provide important information about the nature of animal exploitation. The presence of specific age classes may suggest particular hunting, gathering, or fishing practices. For example, some fish are estuarine at one stage of their life and live offshore during another. The presence of the remains of one without the other might be interpreted to indicate that one environmental zone was exploited while the other was not. Increasing numbers of remains from young hunted or gathered animals may signal the beginnings of overexploitation of that resource.

Hunting or gathering pressure will lead to animals no longer being able to live long enough to reach old age or, coincidentally, to attain the large size that, especially in fish and molluscs, can come with old age. For some investigators, increasingly high proportions of remains from young mammals is also an indicator of incipient animal domestication, the argument being that the keeping and breeding of domestic stock at the very least produces many expendable young males, even if all females are maintained alive to more advanced ages in order to increase the breeding population. As selective hunting could produce age and sex profiles that mimic this pattern, however, such demographic data need to be supplemented by other kinds of evidence, both faunal and otherwise.

Animal Domestication

Domesticating animals, particularly ungulates like sheep, goat, cattle, and pigs, involved human conceptual and behavioral shifts. Instead of hunting or scavenging for immediate return, people had to learn to keep individual animals alive in captivity and breed them to guarantee future returns, thus reducing risk and increasing security. The resulting restrictions on animal mobility and ability to forage at will led early domesticates to grow smaller in size than their wild relatives, while changed selection pressures led to increased variability in both size and morphology. These features can be documented from faunal remains by taking measurements and by noting changes in the shapes of particular skeletal parts, such as horncores in bovids and the skull in pigs. In addition, with domestication, there is often a change in the relative contributions of different taxa to faunal assemblages, with the bones of domestic animals coming to greatly outnumber those of nondomestic forms. For example, studies by a number of investigators have shown that, in parts of the Middle East, sheep and goats replaced gazelles as the dominant form in the faunal record; in parts of Europe, cattle and pigs replaced deer; and, in the Andes, camelids replaced cervids. Other characteristics of early domestic populations that can sometimes be identified by zooarchaeologists are a much higher incidence of skeletal pathology and of neonatal mortality than are normally found in wild populations. Thus, at the Pre-Pottery Neolithic B site of Ain Ghazal in Jordan, Ilse Köhler-Rollefson has recorded an exceptionally high number of diseased foot bones among the remains of what are probably early domestic goats, while, in highland Peru, Jane Wheeler proposed that the increased incidence of infant mortality among mid-Holocene camelids was due to a disease that attacked neonatal animals born in captivity. Effects such as these, along with size diminution, are likely to have resulted from the less than optimal nutritional and living conditions under which early domestic animals would have been kept.

With time, however, animal keepers learned to selectively breed their animals for secondary products, such as milk, hair, or wool, and traction or for an increased amount of a primary product—meat. The development of breeds is attested in the textual and iconographic records of ancient civilizations, as well as in the bones that begin to show that domestic animals were becoming increasingly differentiated in size and build on both a local and a regional basis. Other animals—secondary domesticates—also came to be bred in captivity in Eurasia, including the chicken, equids (horse, donkey, and hybrids), Bactrian and dromedary camels, and water buffalo, although the last may have been a primary domesticate in East Asia. In South America, two distinct forms of camelid (the guanaco and the vicuna) were transformed into four (add the llama and the alpaca) probably through selective breeding. Again, by analysis of kill-off patterns, by noting pathological conditions, by measuring specimens, and by studying morphological features, zooarchaeologists have been successful in documenting many of these elaborations of animal keeping that formed part of the economic foundation for increasingly complex societies.

The Zooarchaeology of Social Complexity
The development of highly differentiated social orders was not necessarily dependent on exploiting domestic animals, as evidence from much of the New World clearly shows. But, in concert with their colleagues working in the Andes, in the Old World, and on post-fifteenth-century A.D. materials from around the globe, zooarchaeologists studying archaeofaunas from prehistoric North America, Mesoamerica, and lowland South America are beginning to document differential access to animal products by different strata of society and by different ethnic and cultural groups. Careful attention is being paid to the archaeological contexts in which faunal materials are found, to the associated artifactual and structural remains, and to contemporary written documents when those are available. Although the picture is ambiguous in some cases, analyses of taxonomic and skeletal-part distributions in assemblages from different contexts have shown patterned variability that is attributed to differential access to sources of animal protein and, in some cases, to food taboos. It even happens that written historic records are found to be less than accurate in their rendering of what actually was taking place as far as consumption is concerned, instead reflecting what the writer thought should be happening or what the writer was told was going on.

Much of this analysis is based on features of animal anatomy. In vertebrates, flesh is not distributed evenly over the skeleton, there being meat-rich areas through the thoracic and lumbar regions of the animal (including the upper limbs in terrestrial animals) and meat-poor areas across the extremities (lower limbs, head and neck, and tail). Within each of these two broad categories, there are also differences in meat quality, and the relative values placed on these can vary by ethnic group. Also variable by group are perceptions about the desirability of different animals as food sources and the costs versus benefits of killing off individuals of different taxa at particular stages in their lives. In the choice of animal to slaughter, such cultural factors are weighed against animal availability and physical condition, which vary due to season of the year, mating behavior, condition of the animal's habitat, disease and parasites, and the effects of other predators. Thus, to interpret patterns in the faunal record, it is necessary for the zooarchaeologist to keep in mind a wide variety of factors, both cultural and noncultural in nature, including taphonomic processes. Nevertheless, by documenting relative frequencies of bones from meat-rich and meat-poor parts of the skeleton in different contexts, by examining patterns of age and sex at death, and by looking at variations in taxonomic representation, the analyst takes an important step toward understanding some of the complexities of animal exploitation and how these might relate to sociocultural parameters.

Z

Recovery Procedures

The kind of contextual analysis necessary for documenting social differentiation is largely dependent upon the cooperation of the archaeologist in supplying details about the excavation. Also dependent upon the archaeologist is recovery of the faunal assemblage. If only "grab samples" are taken and dry screening or wet sieving is not carried out, there is a high likelihood that a significant fraction of the archaeofaunal record will be missed in excavation. This problem is particularly acute for those analyzing the remains of small mammals, reptiles, amphibians, birds, fish, and insects, any and all of which can provide critically important information on ancient environments and faunal-exploitation practices. An example from Peru and another from Israel provide valuable lessons in this regard.

For years, some archaeologists believed that Preceramic societies of coastal Peru did not exploit the rich marine fisheries of the region to any great extent, but instead depended upon terrestrial resources, principally from the *lomas,* coastal ecological communities which derive moisture from seasonal fog banks. This picture was developed largely on field impressions of unsieved archaeological deposits. But fine-screened samples from Archaic-period middens at Paloma (5700-3000 B.C.) analyzed by Elizabeth Reitz produced thousands of tiny bones from anchovies and other fish, thereby laying to rest what, on the face of it, had been a highly unlikely reconstruction of coastal subsistence patterns. On the basis of her analysis, Reitz was also able to suggest that inshore fisheries were the ones most extensively used and that the environment of the Paloma region probably was similar then to what it is today.

In Israel, the careful recovery of rodent and bird bones from Late Epipaleolithic sites permitted Eitan Tchernov to identify high proportions of remains of commensal animals, most notably, the domestic house mouse and house sparrow. Because these animals require constant replenishment of their food supplies through proximity to human habitation, he was able to suggest that some Natufian sites were intensively occupied probably on a year-round basis. This conclusion about sedentism in the Natufian has been confirmed by analyses of cementum increments in gazelle teeth carried out by Daniel Lieberman that show year-round hunting of that animal. In another study by Tchernov, the nature of the rodent remains from Late Quaternary deposits at Qafzeh and Kebara Caves in Israel led him to propose that, based on patterns of faunal succession, the levels containing the remains of anatomically modern humans in the former should be earlier than those with Neanderthals in the latter. This sequence has subsequently been confirmed by thermoluminescence (TL) and electron spin resonance (ESR) dating.

While these examples show how important fine-scale recovery techniques can be, it is often not possible to fine-screen or water-sieve every cubic centimeter excavated from a site. Increasingly, archaeologists and zooarchaeologists are adopting sampling protocols that seem appropriate for the site being excavated. One approach is that, during excavation, the field supervisor determines the quality, integrity, and importance of individual deposits and, on the basis of this evaluation, decides on the type of recovery to use. Another approach is to err on the side of caution, screen everything through a standard mesh (2–6 mm^2), water-sieve or fine-screen a standard fraction of each excavation unit, and decide later on analytical priorities once the quality of each context can be evaluated. No matter what sampling strategy is used, however, they all require communication and understanding between excavator and analyst and, ideally, the participation of the zooarchaeologist in planning and executing the excavation program.

Zooarchaeological Procedures

Most zooarchaeologists today record a certain basic set of data, which is supplemented by more detailed observations appropriate to the site, time period, or problem being addressed. For each fragment, the first thing an investigator must try to determine and note down is what part of the body is represented. If it is not possible to identify the body part, it is generally not possible to unequivocally identify the taxon represented more specifically than to the level of taxonomic class (e.g., mammal, bird, fish). If the body part is identifiable by the analyst, then, depending upon the experience of the investigator, the nature of the comparative collection available, and how much comparative morphological study has been carried out, it will be possible to identify the specimen to order, family, genus, or species. Identification to the subspecific level is rarely possible based on objective morphological criteria, although there are exceptions to this general rule.

Other noncultural data usually recorded for identified elements include the following: symmetry (side of the body from which the specimen comes); portion (proximal, distal, cranial, caudial, medial, lateral, and so forth, as appropriate for the skeletal part); specimen weight; objective measures of age at death of the animal from which the specimen is derived (e.g., in mammals, bone fusion and tooth eruption and wear); objective indicators of sex; and the nature of any pathologies on the specimen. In addition, more and more analysts are measuring specimens to document animal size and proportion, to assist in differentiation of morphologically similar taxa, or to determine sex in dimorphic species. The basic protocol for measurement of mammal and bird bones was prepared by Angela von den Driesch and published in 1976. It is based on procedures developed by the Munich school of archaeozoology under Joachim Boessneck (1925–1991) but has roots going back to the 1920s to the work of J. Ulrich Duerst. By general agreement, if investigators take measurements different from, or additional to, those defined by von den Driesch, they should be carefully described and illustrated. Zooarchaeologists are in the process of developing similar protocols for fish and invertebrates.

In addition to the biological attributes of a specimen, most analysts are interested in noting cultural and taphonomic traits. The recording of these, however, is less standardized and depends, to a large extent, on the nature of the material being analyzed and the questions being addressed by the investigator. Attributes sometimes recorded include: size of fragment; condition of fragment; type(s) of break(s); location(s) of break(s); the presence, location, and nature of cut marks, burning, carnivore gnaw marks, and rodent chew marks; evidence for use as a raw material in craft activities; and modification for, and use as, a tool. In the past, signs of burning on a specimen were *de facto* evidence for cooking. In fact, all that burning indicates is exposure to fire, which can take place at any time from initial butchery to long after a specimen is deposited. For this reason and because of discolorations caused by diagenesis, investigations

of cooking practices using faunal remains have not been particularly successful. A notable exception is when whole or partial animals were routinely roasted over an open fire. Areas of bone that were covered with thicker layers of flesh show lesser degrees of burning than those more thinly covered.

Following recording of a faunal assemblage, the primary data so generated are abstracted by quantifying them in different ways and presenting the results in tables, charts, scatterplots, and prose. Caroline Grigson has drafted a blueprint for faunal reports that is increasingly followed by zooarchaeologists. Gone are the days when it was sufficient to present only a list of taxa represented at a site. The analysis of faunal remains can provide much more information than mere presence of particular species. Just how much more, however, depends on the site, the nature of the excavations, recovery procedures, the state of preservation of the faunal remains, analytical protocols, and the questions being asked by the zooarchaeologist. And as more assemblages are being analyzed and published in detail, it is becoming possible to delineate faunal-exploitation practices not only on a site-by-site basis, but on the regional level and beyond.

Richard H. Meadow

See also ANIMAL REMAINS, IDENTIFICATION AND ANALYSIS: FISH; ANIMAL REMAINS, IDENTIFICATION AND ANALYSIS: INSECTS; ANIMAL REMAINS, IDENTIFICATION AND ANALYSIS: MAMMALS; ANIMAL REMAINS, IDENTIFICATION AND ANALYSIS: MOLLUSCS; ANIMAL REMAINS, QUANTIFICATION; GROWTH-RING ANALYSIS AND SEASONALITY STUDIES; GROWTH STUDIES: FISH OTOLITHS; GROWTH STUDIES: MAMMAL TEETH

Further Readings

Clutton-Brock, J., ed. (1989) The Walking Larder. London: Unwin Hyman.

Clutton-Brock, J., and Grigson, C., eds. (1983–1984) Animals and Archaeology, 4 vols. (BAR International Series 163, 183, 202, 227). Oxford: British Archaeological Reports.

Davis, S.J.M. (1987) The Archaeology of Animals. New Haven, CT: Yale University Press.

Driesch, A. von den (1976) A Guide to the Measurement of Animal Bones from

Archaeological Sites. (Peabody Museum Bulletin 1).Cambridge, MA: Peabody Museum of American Archaeology and Ethnology, Harvard University.

Grigson, C. (1978) Towards a blueprint for animal bone reports in archaeology. In D.R. Brothwell, K.D. Thomas, and J. Clutton-Brock (eds.): Research Problems in Zooarchaeology, pp. 121–128. (Occasional Publication 3). London: Institute of Archaeology.

Klein, R.G., and Cruz-Uribe, K. (1984) The Analysis of Animal Bones from Archeological Sites. Chicago: University of Chicago Press.

Lieberman, D.E. (1993) The rise and fall of seasonal mobility among hunter-gatherers: The case of the southern Levant. Current Anthropology 14:599–631.

Lyman, R.L. (1994) Vertebrate Taphonomy. New York: Cambridge University Press.

Reitz, E.J. (1988) Faunal remains from Paloma, an Archaic site in Peru. American Anthropologist 90:310–322.

Tchernov, E. (1981) The biostratigraphy of the Middle East. In J. Cauvins and P. Sanlaville (eds.): Préhistoire du Levant, pp. 67–97. Paris: Editions du Centre national de la recherche scientifique.

Subject Index

A

Abandoned Shipwreck Act, 1–2, 392
Activation analysis, 401–402
Adaptation, 163–164, 190, 441
Advances in Archaeological Method and Theory
(journal), 542
Aerial photography for archaeology, 3–10, 544,
589
    aerial photographic libraries, 8
    aerial surveying, 7–9
    crop and soil marks, 5
    development of the discipline, 3–5, 544,
      137–138
    satellite imagery, 8–9
    shadow sites, 5
African American archaeology, 284
Age composition (human populations), 421
Agriculture
    agricultural soils, 239–240
    agriculture and plant medicines, 447
    crop identification, 489, 491
    cultivated plant foods, 435–436
    ecological interpretations, 162
    history of research, 98, 216, 279, 663
    use of insect remains, 23
    use of palynology, 450
    see also Domestication; Paleoethnobotany;
      Plants
Albumin, 433
Amber, characterization, 11–13, 81, 307, 400–401
American Antiquity (journal), 116
Amino acid racemization/epimerization dating,
    13–17, 67, 75–76, 145
Analogical reasoning, 397
    see also Ethnographic analogy
Ancient DNA, 79–82
Animal protein, residual, 130
Animal remains, identification and analysis
    fish, 17–21
      fish-catching methods, 19–20
      identification and comparative material,
        17–18
      processing of fish and trade, 20–21

      retrieval and sampling, 17
      seasonality, 20
      size reconstructions, 18
      species diversity, 19
      taphonomical processes, 18–19
    insects, 21–26
      agriculture and population movements,
        23–24
      human-induced paleoenvironmental changes,
        24–25
      landscape studies, 24
      paleoenvironmental reconstruction, 23
      parasitism, 23
      retrieval and identification, 22–23
      status of research, 25–26
    mammals, 26–29
      comparative material, 27–28
      identification of age at death, 28
      identification of sex, 28
      identification of species, 26–27
      identification of symmetry, 28
    molluscs, 29–31
      analysis, 30
      anatomy and reproduction, 29
      ecology, 30
      nutrition from molluscs, 31
      taphonomy, 31
    see also Zooarchaeology
Animal remains, quantification, 31–33
    general utility index (GUI), 33
    minimum number of animal units (MAU or
      MNU), 33
    minimum number of elements (MNE), 32–33
    minimum number of individuals (MNI), 32
    modified general utility index (MGUI), 33
    number of identified specimens per taxon
      (NISP), 32
Ankara machine, 217
Annales school, 353
    influence on postprocessual archaeology, 497
Anthropological archaeology, 73, 329, 518, 599,
    663
    see also New/processual archaeology

Anthropomorph, 527
Antibodies, 432–433, 434, 448
Antigens, 432–433, 442, 448
Antiquarianism, 373
Antiquities Act of 1906, 33–35, 63
Archaeobotanical record, 424
    formation processes, 426–427
Archaeobotany, 423
Archaeologia e Calcolatori (journal), 116
Archaeological context, 70
Archaeological geology, 237
Archaeological resource management, 138
    see also Cultural resource management (CRM)
Archaeological prospection, 35–39, 48, 330,
        543–544
    see also Prospection
Archaeological sites, formation processes, 39–44
    cultural formation processes: deposition
        abandonment, 41
        burial, 41
        caching, 40–41
        curate behavior, 41
        de facto refuse, 41
        discard, 40
        loss, 40
        primary refuse, 40
        secondary refuse, 40
    cultural formation processes: reclamation
        archaeological excavation, 42
        collecting, 41
        salvage, 42
        scavenging, 41
        treasure hunting, 41–42
    cultural formation processes: disturbance
        major construction projects, 42
        plowing, 42
        trampling, 42
    cultural formation processes: reuse
        conservation, 43
        lateral cycling, 42
        recycling, 42–43
        secondary use, 43
    environmental formation processes
        aeroturbation, 43
        argilliturbation, 43
        cryoturbation, 43
        faunalturbation, 43
        floralturbation, 43
        graviturbation, 43
        pedoturbation, 43
Archaeological sites, protection and conservation
    in situ conservation, 294–297
    legislative protection, 1–2, 33–35, 60–64
Archaeological theory, history of, 637
Archaeological Computing Newsletter, 116
Archaeological Method and Theory (journal),
        542
Archaeomagnetic dating, 44–47, 149
    archaeomagnetic field direction dating, 47
    archaeomagnetic field strength dating, 45–47
Archaeometry (journal), 10, 47, 173, 316

Archaeometry (discipline), 47–52
    materials science, 51
    prospecting, 48–50
    provenance studies, 50–51
Archaeoparasitology, 52–60, 445
    ectoparasites, 53
    endoparasites, 53
    human-parasite ecology, 56–59
    parasite, 52
    parasitic protozoa, 53
    role of parasites in archaeological interpretation
        animal domestication, 56
        diet, 54–55
        environmental reconstruction, 55
        health and disease, 55–56
        living conditions, 55
        sanitation, 55
        site-formation processes, 56
        transhumance, 55
Archaeoseismology, 241
Archaeozoology, 676
Archeological and Historic Preservation Act
        (AHPA), 60–62
Archeological Resources Protection Act (ARPA),
        35, 62–64, 141
Architecture (ancient)
    deterioration, 532
    documentation by photogrammetry, 467
    in situ conservation, 294–297
    materials of construction, 531
    photography, 476–477
Archives, use of, 8–9, 37
Art (prehistoric), 120, 233
    see also Cave art, interpretation; Rock art, in-
        terpretation; Rock-art sites, recording
        and analysis
Artifacts
    definition, 558
    indigenous, 279
    infiltrated, 279
    illustration, 289–294
    interpretation, 69–72, 283, 286, 301, 303, 304
    intrusive, 279
    residual, 279
Artificial intelligence, 119
Asphalt, identification, 400
Atomic absorption (AA) spectrometry, 83, 64–65,
        262, 366, 532
Australian Journal of Historical Archaeology, 280

B

Baked clay, dating, see Ceramics, dating; Heated
        materials, dating
Base line, 68
Bark cloth, on-site conservation, 207, 208
Basketry, on-site conservation, 207, 208, 210
Behavioral archaeology, 69–73, 542–543, 558
    applications to contemporary objects, 70, 543
    c-transforms, 71
    criticism of adaptationist theory, 72

cultural-system context, 70
four dimensions of artifact variability, 69–70, 71
garbologists, 70, 511–512
laws of human behavior, 70
life history of artifacts, 70, 71
New Behavioralists, 72
symbolic analysis, 72
theory and behavioral archaeology, 71–72
Bioarchaeology, state of research, 513, 514, 516–517
Biodeterioration
effects on paleoserological analyses, 449
of human remains, 449
see also Taphonomy
Blood and blood proteins
blood grouping, 448–449
human vs. animal blood, 433
immunochemical methods, 432–434
in cave art, 434
on tools, 433
speciation, 433, 434
survival, 432–434
Bog bodies, magnetic resonance imaging, 401
Bone
ancient DNA, 79–82
blood typing of, 448
characterization, 74–79
composition, 74, 82–85, 298, 307–310, 619–620
dating, 15–16, 74, 177, 218–225, 307, 649–650
evidence of aggression and war, 440
evidence of disease, 440–441
evidence of occupations, 440
evidence of social rank, 440
paleodiet studies, 307–311
photography, 483–484
taphonomy, 619–624
trace element analysis, 82–85
Botanical remains
analysis, 429, 435–436
identification, 429–430
interpretation, 430–431
preservation of, 427
quantification, 430
retrieval, 124, 125, 127, 216–218, 427–429
sampling, 427
sorting, 429
see also Paleoethnobotany; Palynology; Phytolith analysis; Plants; Pollen; Seeds
Brainerd and Robinson Index of Agreement (also known as Brainerd and Robinson Coefficient), 549
Brass, 361–362
see also Metals, characterization
Bricks, dating of fired, 214
British Museum, 102
Bronze, 358–359
provenance, 315–318
see also Metals, characterization

Building materials, 531
Burials and burial grounds, *see* Mortuary sites
Burnt flint, dating, *see* Heated materials, dating
Burnt stone, dating, *see* Heated materials, dating
Butchering experiments, 202
Butchering sites, interpretation, 286–287

C

C_3/C_4/CAM plants, 308, 309, 438
CAD, 117, 118, 289
Capitalism, archaeology of, 284, 576
Carbon-14, *see* Radiocarbon dating
Carbon isotopes, stable
paleodiet studies, 76–77, 307–311
provenance of marble, 340–344,
sourcing of elephant ivory, 314
uptake by C_3/C_4/CAM plants, 438, 76–77
Cathodoluminescence, 340–341
Cation-ratio (CR) dating, 524–525
Cave art
dating, 523–527
interpretation, 86, 120, 233, 331, 613
Caves
documentation, 93
excavation, 89–94, 330–331
paleoecology, 94
sedimentology, 90, 267
stratigraphic control, 91
Cementum, 273–275
Cemeteries, *see* Mortuary sites
Central-place theory, 574, 585
Ceramics
applications of materials science, 51
burnishing, 108
characterization, 105–110, 173, 298, 300, 402, 403, 404
computer applications, 119
dating, 110, 382, 630–634
definition, 106
deterioration, 95–96
ethnoarchaeological studies, 184, 333
firing temperatures, 380, 382
function, 201
history of research, 286, 566–568
illustration, 291–293
kiln atmosphere, 109, 381–382
manufacturing, 107–109
clay preparation, 107
firing, 109
object formation, 108
prefire decoration, 108
postfire treatment, 109
on-site conservation, 94–97
condition and deterioration, 95–96
excavation, 96
strengthening, 96–97
cleaning and removing salts, 97
preventive care, 97
packaging, 97, 420
petrography, 458–462

Paper, conservation, 207
Papyrus, conservation, 207
Parasitism, 23, 52–59, 124, 445
Parks Canada, 283, 302
Particle-induced X-ray emission (PIXE), 406
Peer polity interaction model, 136, 197
Periscope camera, 330
Petroglyphs, 523, 527
Petrography, 240, 243, 458–462, 530, 567
    applications to archaeology, 459–461
    issues in methodology and interpretation, 461–462
    microscopy, 459
    sample selection and preparation, 458
Petrology, 458
Phosphate analysis, 239, 580
Photogrammetric Engineering and Remote Sensing (journal), 467
Photogrammetry, 8, 48, 462–469
    basic principles, 462–463
    rectified photography, 463
    new tools, 463–464
    applications to archaeology, 464–468
Photography, archaeological, 469–485
    archaeological site photography, 469–477
    archaeological object photography, 477–485
    rock-art sites, 527–528
    see also Aerial photography for archaeology; Photogrammetry; Radiography in archaeology
Phytoliths, 425, 426
    analysis, 485–492
    applications in paleoecology
    applications of phytolith analysis, 489–491
    identification, 430, 487, 489
    quantification, 430, 489
    retrieval, 124, 125, 129, 239–240, 487–488
Pictographs, 523, 527
Piltdown Man forgery, 76, 148, 219
Pits, excavation, 277–278
Plane of collimation, 331–332
Plantation archaeology, 284
Plants
    and culture, 423–424, 436–437
    dietary vs. pharmaceutical, 447
    domestication, 435–437, 489–491
    macroremains, 424–425
    medicinal, 443–447
    microremains, 424, 425–426
    psychotropic, 444
    see also Botanical remains
Pollen
    agricultural studies, 451
    analysis, 455–456
    determining functions of structures, 451
    determining use of containers, 452
    determining use of mortars and grinding stones, 452
    embedded in building materials, 452
    from medicinal plants, 445–446

    from urban sites, 451
    in human coprolites, 452, 455
    in ritual contexts, 451
    in shipwrecks, 453
    on stone tools, 452
    retrieval, 124, 125, 128–129
    sampling, 94, 453–455
    see also Palynology
Polymerase chain reaction (PCR), 80
Population movements, 24, 55, 193, 205, 286, 448, 528, 533, 571
Postholes, excavation, 277–278
Post Medieval Archaeology (journal), 280
Postprocessual archaeology, 281, 285, 398–399, 494–499
    archaeological record as text, 494
    archaeology as long-term history, 497
    archaeology as a political practice, 498
    critical theory, 497
    criticisms of processual archaeology, 494–495
    diversity of people's pasts, 494
    empathetic understanding, 495
    First Peoples and their past, 498
    human subjects and objects of study, 495
    ideology, 496
    material record, 496
    phenomenology of the past, 498
    relativism, 495
    structures of meaning, 495–496
    time, space, and place, 497
Potassium/argon (K/Ar) dating, 145, 146, 147, 176
Pottery, *see* Ceramics
Prestige good theory, 196–197
Processual archaeology, 398
    see also New/processual archaeology
Prospection
    aerial photography for archaeology, 3–10, 589
    electrical and electromagnetic prospection, 165–170
    georadar, 251–258
    magnetic prospecting, 335–339, 642
    prospection for underwater sites, 641–643
    remotely operated vehicles (ROVs), 520–521
    thermal prospecting, 626–630
Prospezioni Archeologiche (journal), 330
Proteins
    methods of analysis, 178–181
    survival and identification, 432–435
    see also Blood and blood proteins
Proton activation analysis (PAA), 405–406
Public education in archaeology, 118, 205
Public interest in archaeology, 529
Public perception of history, 329

Q

Quantitative methods in archaeology, 501–502, 634
    animal remains, 31–33
    botanical remains, 430
    ceramic analysis, 461–462
    theoretical issues, 502

endogenic materials, 579
eolian, 579
exogenic materials, 579
fluvial, 579
illuviation, 580
loss-on-ignition method, 581
micromorphology, 581
organic content, 580
pedogenesis, 579
pedogenic calcrete, 579–580
petrofabric, 579
phosphate analysis, 239, 580
sapropels, 580
texture of sediments, 579
see also Grain size analysis
Solid modeling, 118
Sonar, 582–584
differential GPS (DGPS), 583
Global Positioning System, 583
side-scan sonar, 582–584, 641
sub-bottom profilers, 582, 584, 642
Sondages, 635
see also Test pits
Sonic high-accuracy ranging and positioning system (SHARPS), 644
Soviet archaeology, 323, 571, 637
Spatial analysis, 285, 501, 584–588
change-point analysis, 585, 587
cluster analysis, 585, 587, 591
contingency tables, 586, 591
distance methods, 585, 586
intersite analysis, 584–585
intrasite analysis, 585
kriging, 586, 588
local-density analysis, 586
multiresponse permutation procedures, 585, 587
natural-neighbor interpolation, 586, 588
nearest-neighbor analysis, 586
point-pattern techniques, 585
quadrat methods, 585, 586
regression analysis, 586, 587, 592
second-order methods, 585, 586
spatial autocorrelation, 586, 588
spectral analysis, 586, 588
surface techniques, 585–586
trend surface analysis, 586, 587
see also Statistical methods in archaeology
Spores, 450
see also Palynology
Statistical methods in archaeology, 101, 132, 329, 589, 590–594, 634
bayesian statistics, 594
chi-square test, 591
classification of artifacts, 592, 593
cluster analysis 585, 587, 591
confirmatory statistics, 590
contingency tables, 586, 591
correspondence analysis, 591
discriminant analysis, 591

exploratory statistics, 590
history of research, 590–591
k-means method, 591
Kolmogorov-Smirnov test, 591
log-linear analysis, 591
multidimensional scaling, 592
ordering, 592, 593
principal-components analysis, 592
regression analysis, 586, 587, 592
social-status analysis, 592
Ward's method, 591
see also Spatial analysis
Step trenching, 594
Steroid analysis, 130
Stone, 530
see also Lithics; Rocks and minerals
Stone, on-site conservation, 532, 594–597
cleaning, 597
deterioration, 532, 594–595
efflorescence, 595
excavation techniques, 595
molding, 597
protection from drying, 596
protection from freeze-thaw cycle, 596
protection from salt efflorescence, 596
repairs and reconstruction, 597
salt removal, 596
stabilization, 596–597
thermal-stress cracking, 595
Strata
natural, 278
upstanding, 278
Stratification, 597–598
Stratigraphic control, 91–92, 457, 493
Stratigraphic succession, 239, 278
Stratigraphy, 148, 267, 598, 636
Harris Matrix, 112, 278–279, 353
metrical, 370–371
natural, 278, 389
reverse, 523
see also Superposition
Striae of Retzius, 275–276
Stripping, 598–599
Strontium isotopes, 311, 313–315, 343
Strontium/calcium ratios, 83–84
Structural archaeology, 329, 331
Structural-functionalism, 395–396
Structural-Marxist theory, 347, 348
Substantivists, 195
Superposition, 145, 148, 278, 373, 538, 598
see also Stratigraphy
Survey design, theory, 600–605
avoidable complications, 604–605
direct observation
invasive methods, 603–604
noninvasive methods, 602–603
distributional archaeology, 601, 606
indirect observation by noninvasive methods, 603
survey design: independent variables, 601–602

Name Index

Abbot, David A., 604
Acsádi, György, 420
Adams, Robert McCormick, **3**, 574
Adorno, Theodore, 497
Aitken, Martin J., **10–11**, 49, 544
Alberti, Leon Battista, 69
Althusser, Louis, 347
Alva, Walter, 516
Ambrose, Walter, 411
Ames, Kenneth, 573
Anderson, Patricia, 653
Angel, J. Lawrence, 420, 421
Antevs, Ernst, 657
Araújo, Adauto, 53
Armelagos, George J., 422, 436, 441
Arriaza, Bernardo, 517
Ashworth, Alan, 25
Aufderheide, Arthur, 64

Bada, Jeffrey L., **67**
Baillie, Michael G. L., **68**
Ball, Robert, 200
Barbour, Jamie, 665
Barreda, Elias Mujica, 516
Barrett, John, 496, 497
Bass, George Fletcher, **68–69**, 391, 392, 393
Beaudry, Mary C., 283
Beck, Lane, 514
Bednarik, Robert, 524
Bellue, Michael, 216
Bender, Barbara, 135
Berryman, Hugh, 421
Binford, Lewis R., **73–74**, 86, 183, 186, 216, 266, 329, 353, 394, 522, 552, 559, 572, 677
Binford, Sally, 73, 394
Bintliff, John, 497, 574, 611
Blanton, Richard, 135, 554
Blegen, Carl, 103
Bocquet-Appel, Jean-Pierre, 422
Bodner, Connie, 218
Boessneck, Joachim, 28, 681
Bohrer, Vorsila, 436

Bordieu, Pierre, 615
Bordes, François, **85–86**
Boserup, Ester, 189, 420
Boucher de Perthes, Jacques, 188
Bowdler, Sandra, 512
Braidwood, Robert, 522
Brain, Charles K., 677
Brainerd, George, 549, 590
Braudel, Fernand, 497
Brenton, Berry, 439
Breuil, Henri, **86**
Brew, John O., 535
Brill, Robert, 315
Brown, Antoinette, 435
Brown, Francis, H., 173
Brumfiel, Elizabeth, 496
Bruton, Guy, 89
Bryant, Vaughn M., 125, 426, 451, 452
Buikstra, Jane E., 58, 420, 422, 446, 575
Butters, Luiz Jaime Castillo, 516
Butzer, Karl W., **87**

Caldwell, James R., 669
Callen, Eric, 125, 426
Cameron, Thomas, 426
Camilli, Eileen, 603
Carnot, Adolphe, 219
Caton-Thompson, Gertrude, **89**
Chamberlin, Thomas C., 237
Chang, Kwang-Chih, 556, 558, 573
Chapman, Carl, 60
Chapman, Robert, 514
Charles, James A., 173
Chase-Dunn, Christopher, 135–136
Cherry, John E., 601
Child, Angela Gernaey, 15–16
Childe, Vere Gordon, **98**, 133, 189, 226, 347, 498, 522, 571, 574, 576, 637
Chisholm, Brian S., 309
Clark, John Desmond, **99**
Clark, John Grahame Douglas, **99–100**, 522, 551, 552, 675

Clarke, David L., **100–101**, 394, 554, 572
Cohen, Mark, 436
Coles, John, 665
Collingwood, Robin, 495, 496
Collins, Henry B., 638
Condori, Mamami, 498
Conkey, Margaret Wright, **120**, 234, 614
Cook, Clifford, 665, 666
Coppens, Ives, 286
Cousteau, Jacques, 391
Cowgill, George L., 549
Crabtree, Don, 200, 201
Crawford, Osbert G. S., 3–4, 100, **137–138**, 589
Crumley, Carole, 136
Cutler, Hugh, 216

Damblon, François, 453
Dancey, William, 606
Daniel, Glyn, 237
Danielson, Dennis, 129
Dart, Raymond A., 677
Darwin, Charles, 190, 191
de Geer, Gerard, 657
de Mortillet, Gabriel, 571
de Rochebrune, Anthony T., 424
de Saint-Mathurin, Suzanne, 233
Deetz, James J. Fanto, **150**, 281, 333, 395, 572, 613
Deagan, Kathleen, 281
Dean, Glenna, 218
Desmond, Lawrence, 467
Doelle, William H., 610
Dinan, Elizabeth, 492
Dioscorides, 443
Donahue, James, 492
Donaldson, M., 436
Dorn, Ronald, 526
Dorpfeld, Wilhelm, 102
Douglas, Mary, 614
Ducomet, Georges, 167
Duerst, J. Ulrich, 681
Dunnell, Robert C., **155–156**, 397, 549, 550, 557, 558, 606

Ebert, James I., 601, 606, 612
Echo-Hawk, R.C., 514
Echo-Hawk, W.R., 514
Elias, Scott, 25
Engelhardt, Conrad, 390
Engels, Friedrich, 347, 571
Esper, Johann, 439
Evans, Sir Arthur, 103, 187
Evans, Sir John, **187–188**

Fagan, Brian Murray, **205–206**
Fairbanks, Charles, 281, 284
Fedje, Daryl, 653

Feinman, Gary, 135
Ferreira, Luiz, 53
Fewkes, Jesse W., 181
Fink, Michael, 436
Fish, Suzanne, 436
Flannery, Kent Vaughn, **215–216**, 396, 437, 552, 554, 572
Fletcher, Roland, 554
Ford, James Alfred, **226–227**, 549, 550, 589, 638, 664, 667, 669
Ford, Richard I., 423
Fowler, Don D., 138
Fox, Richard, A., 282
Frankenstein, Susan, 573
Freeman, Leslie, 286
Freestone, Ian C., 173
French, David, 217
Friedman, Irving, 409, 410
Friedman, Jonathan, 573
Frison, George C., 536
Fritz, John, 614
Fry, Gary, 438, 444

Gagnan, Emil, 391
Gale, Noel H., 313
Garrod, Dorothy, 86, **233**
Gasser, Robert, 436
Giddens, Anthony, 615
Gifford, James, 639, 640
Gilbert, Robert, 435
Gilman, Antonio, 574
Gilmore, Melvin R., 425, 430
Girling, Maureen, 25
Gish, Jan, 436
Glassie, Henry, 613
Glavimans, Cornelis, 390
Glob, Peter, 450
Goguet, Antoine Yves, 635
Goodman, Alan, 441
Gould, Richard Allan, 184, 186, **266**, 392
Grace, Roger, 654
Grant, Lauryn, 513
Graham, Ian, 588
Graham, Martha, 559
Grattan, David, 665, 666
Greig, James, 451
Griffin, James B., 371, 669
Grigson, Caroline, 681
Guthe, Carl, 425

Habermas, Jürgen, 497, 615
Hagedoorn, Johan G., 545
Hall, Robert, 613
Handsman, Russell, 498
Hanson, Julienne, 554
Harlan, Thomas P., 152
Harrington, Jean Carl, 280
Harris, Edward C., 278